DATE DUE

Neuropsychological Assessment
of Neuropsychiatric Disorders

Neuropsychological Assessment of Neuropsychiatric Disorders

SECOND EDITION

edited by

Igor Grant, M.D., F.R.C.P.(C)
Professor and Vice Chair, Department of Psychiatry
Director, HIV Neurobehavioral Research Center
University of California, San Diego
La Jolla, California
Chief of Ambulatory Care for Psychiatry
Veterans Affairs Medical Center
San Diego, California

Kenneth M. Adams, Ph.D., A.B.P.P.
Professor of Psychology
University of Michigan
Chief, Psychology Service
Veterans Affairs Medical Center
Ann Arbor, Michigan

New York   Oxford
OXFORD UNIVERSITY PRESS
1996

Oxford University Press

Oxford   New York
Athens   Auckland   Bangkok   Bombay
Calcutta   Cape Town   Dar es Salaam   Delhi
Florence   Hong Kong   Istanbul   Karachi
Kuala Lumpur   Madras   Madrid   Melbourne
Mexico City   Nairobi   Paris   Singapore
Taipei   Tokyo   Toronto
and associated companies in
Berlin   Ibadan

Copyright © 1996 by Oxford University Press, Inc.

Published by Oxford University Press, Inc.,
198 Madison Avenue, New York, New York 10016

Oxford is a registered trademark of Oxford University Press

Library of Congress Cataloging-in-Publication Data
Neuropsychological assessment of neuropsychiatric
disorders / edited by Igor Grant, Kenneth M. Adams. — 2nd ed.
p.   cm. Includes bibliographical references and index.
ISBN 0-19-509073-X
1. Mental illness—Diagnosis.
2. Nervous system—Diseases—Diagnosis.
3. Neuropsychological tests.
I. Grant, Igor, 1942–   .   II. Adams, Kenneth M., 1948–
[DNLM: 1. Central Nervous System Diseases—diagnosis.
2. Organic Mental Disorders—diagnosis.   3. Neuropsychological Tests.
4. Outcome Assessment (Health Care)   WM 141 N494 1996]
RC473.N48N47   1996
616.89′075—dc20
DNLM/DLC
for Library of Congress   95-49329

1 2 3 4 5 6 7 8 9

Printed in the United States of America
on acid-free paper

Dedicated to
JoAnn Nallinger Grant
and Carol Bracher Adams

PREFACE

It has been a decade since the first edition of *Neuropsychological Assessment of Neuropsychiatric Disorders* was published. At the time, we aimed to fulfill two major goals: first, to present in concise form some of the leading approaches to neuropsychological assessment in patients with neuropsychiatric diseases; second, to provide a comprehensive yet concise assessment of the state of our knowledge regarding the neuropsychology of some of the more important and problematic neuropsychiatric disorders.

The second edition follows broadly the organization of the first edition. Thus, we begin with a section on current approaches to assessment, and then proceed to the main body of the text that addresses major neuropsychiatric and medical disorders. Because of the growing interest in understanding the psychosocial moderators and "real-life consequences" of neuropsychological impairment, we have added a third part on outcomes to this edition. This section is briefer than the others, reflecting the relative infancy of this field of neuropsychological research. If there is a third edition, we hope that scholarly work on neuropsychological outcomes will have advanced to a point where this topic will receive much fuller treatment.

While we have retained the general structure from the first edition, this book is far more than an "update." Virtually the entire text has been rewritten not only to reflect the current state of knowledge but also to keep pace with changes in neuropsychological emphasis. For example, new topics in Part I include the Iowa-Benton approach to neuropsychological assessment and cognitive screening methods. The original chapter on the role of the computer has been replaced with a more specific discussion of computers and memory. The remaining chapters on neuropsychological methods have been fully updated.

Part II has been expanded and reorganized. We have added new chapters on Gilles de la Tourette syndrome, Huntington's disease, acute and chronic hypoxemia, HIV infection, and schizophrenia. The original chapter on Parkinson's disease (PD) has been replaced by a new, broader treatment of PD and other movement disorders. To make room for all these additions, we have integrated some material that was previously presented as separate chapters into more comprehensive combined chapters and we have deleted a few chapters. For example, the work on Wernicke-Korsakoff syndrome has been integrated into a completely revised chapter on the neuropsychology of alcoholism, reflecting the reality of the clinical problem.

We have mentioned already that a new section—Part III—has been added to provide an introduction to the psychosocial context of neuropsychological impairment and its impact on day-to-day functioning. This section deals with nonneuropsychological factors contributing to outcomes in head injury, life-quality outcome in head injury, and neuropsychological functioning and health-related quality of life in chronic obstructive pulmonary disease. These provide new data representing the type of information that will increasingly be sought to show that laboratory tests "matter," yet must be analyzed in a broader context of patients' lives.

In an effort to keep the treatment of old topics fresh, we have invited several new authors either to rewrite chapters from their own perspective or to work with the previous contributors in revising the chapters. Twenty-five new authors have contributed to this edition.

Thoughtful comments, both formal and informal, from many people have helped shape the second edition. We were fortunate that the response to the first edition was favorable. This meant that we had a solid framework upon which to build the current second edition. We hope that we have succeeded in retaining the best of the first edition while revising and expanding its content to keep pace with the rapid growth that neuropsychology has undergone in the past decade.

We wish to thank our publisher, Oxford University Press, and in particular Jeffrey House, for the strong encouragement we have received to create the second edition. As before, Mr. House has been a thoughtful, interested, and proactive partner in the process of creating this edition.

We wish to offer particular thanks and special acknowledgment to Mary Beth Hiller, working in Igor Grant's office, who contributed her formidable talents as editorial assistant in assuring the high quality and complete nature of the manuscripts. In particular, Mary Beth's attention to details of the textual material, identification of inadvertent errors, and focus on assuring that the references by all of our contributors were complete and up to date are gratefully acknowledged.

Finally, we wish to thank two people whose spiritual and moral support has been indispensable as we have tried to balance our editorial, academic, and family responsibilities. It is with a sense of deep affection and gratitude that we dedicate this second edition to JoAnn Grant and Carol Adams.

La Jolla, CA Igor Grant, M.D.
Ann Arbor, MI Kenneth M. Adams, Ph.D.
June 1995

CONTENTS

CONTRIBUTORS

KENNETH M. ADAMS, Ph.D.
Professor of Psychology
University of Michigan
Chief, Psychology Service
Veterans Affairs Medical Center
Ann Arbor, Michigan

BRADLEY N. AXELROD, Ph.D.
Staff Psychologist
Director of Neuropsychology
Veterans Affairs Medical Center
Detroit, Michigan

ANNE DULL BAIRD, Ph.D.
Senior Staff Psychologist
Division of Neuropsychology
Department of Psychiatry
Henry Ford Hospital
Detroit, Michigan

SIMON BARON-COHEN, B.A. (Oxon),
    M.Phil., Ph.D.
Departments of Experimental Psychology and
    Psychiatry
University of Cambridge
Cambridge, England

MARK W. BONDI, Ph.D.
Research Psychologist
San Diego Veterans Affairs Medical Center
Assistant Adjunct Professor of Psychiatry
University of California, San Diego
La Jolla, California

ROBERT A. BORNSTEIN, Ph.D.
Professor and Associate Chairman
Department of Psychiatry
Neuropsychology Program
Ohio State University
Columbus, Ohio

JASON BRANDT, Ph.D.
Professor of Psychiatry
Director, Division of Medical Psychology
Johns Hopkins University
School of Medicine
Baltimore, Maryland

GREGORY G. BROWN, Ph.D.
Associate Chief of Psychology
San Diego Veterans Affairs Medical Center
Associate Professor of Psychiatry
University of California, San Diego
La Jolla, California

NELSON BUTTERS, Ph.D.*
Psychology Service
San Diego Veterans Affairs Medical Center
Professor of Psychiatry
University of California, San Diego
La Jolla, California

ERIC D. CAINE, M.D.
Professor of Psychiatry and Neurology
Associate Chair, Department of Psychiatry
University of Rochester
School of Medicine
Rochester, New York

ALBERT S. CARLIN, Ph.D.
Associate Professor of Psychiatry and Behavioral
    Sciences
University of Washington
School of Medicine
Seattle, Washington

THOMAS H. CROOK, III, Ph.D.
President, Memory Assessment Clinics, Inc.
Scottsdale, Arizona

JEFFREY L. CUMMINGS, M.D.
Professor of Neurology and Psychiatry
University of California, Los Angeles
School of Medicine
Director, UCLA Alzheimer's Disease Center
Los Angeles, California

SUREYYA S. DIKMEN, Ph.D.
Professor of Rehabilitation Medicine
University of Washington
School of Medicine
Seattle, Washington

PAULA ALTMAN FULD, Ph.D.
Independent Practice
Granada Hills, California

*Deceased, 11/18/95

ROBERT S. GOLDMAN, Ph.D.
Chief, Neuropsychology Laboratory
Hillside Hospital
Division of Long Island Jewish Medical Center
Glen Oaks, New York

IGOR GRANT, M.D., F.R.C.P.(C)
Professor and Vice Chair, Department of
  Psychiatry
Director, HIV Neurobehavioral Research Center
University of California, San Diego
La Jolla, California
Chief, Ambulatory Care for Psychiatry
Veterans Affairs Medical Center
San Diego, California

ROBERT K. HEATON, Ph.D.
Professor of Psychiatry
University of California, San Diego
La Jolla, California

NANCY HEBBEN, Ph.D.
Chief Consultant in Neuropsychology
McLean Hospital
Belmont, Massachusetts
Clinical Instructor in Neuropsychology
Department of Psychiatry
Harvard Medical School
Boston, Massachusetts

EDITH KAPLAN, Ph.D.
Associate Professor of Psychiatry and Neurology
Boston University School of Medicine
Affiliate Professor, Department of Psychology
Clark University
Consulting Neuropsychologist
Department of Psychology
Baycrest Centre for Geriatric Care
North York, Canada

ALFRED W. KASZNIAK, Ph.D.
Professor of Psychology
The University of Arizona
College of Arts and Sciences
Tucson, Arizona

MARK D. KELLY, Ph.D.
Assistant Project Scientist
HIV Neurobehavioral Research Center
Department of Psychiatry
University of California, San Diego
La Jolla, California

DEBORAH A. KING, Ph.D.
Associate Professor of Psychiatry and Psychology
University of Rochester
School of Medicine and Dentistry
Rochester, New York

KAREN T. LABUHN, Ph.D., R.N.
School of Nursing
Wayne State University
Detroit, Michigan

GLENN J. LARRABEE, Ph.D.
Faculty Associate, Center for Neuropsychological
  Studies, and Independent Practice
University of Florida
Sarasota, Florida

TOR LØBERG, Ph.D.
Professor of Psychology
Department of Clinical Psychology
University of Bergen
Bergen, Norway

JOAN MACHAMER, M.A.
Department of Rehabilitation Medicine
University of Washington
School of Medicine
Seattle, Washington

THOMAS D. MARCOTTE, Ph.D.
Assistant Project Scientist
HIV Neurobehavioral Research Center
Department of Psychiatry
University of California, San Diego
La Jolla, California

CHARLES G. MATTHEWS, Ph.D.
Professor of Neurology
Director, Neuropsychology Laboratory
University of Wisconsin Center for Health
  Sciences
Madison, Wisconsin

PAT MCKENNA, Ph.D.
The National Hospital for Neurology and
  Neurosurgery
Queen Square
London, England

SUSAN MCPHERSON, Ph.D.
Assistant Clinical Professor of Psychiatry and
  Biobehavioral Sciences
University of California, Los Angeles
School of Medicine
Los Angeles, California

A. JOHN MCSWEENY, Ph.D.
Professor of Psychiatry and Neurology
Director, Neuropsychology Laboratory
Medical College of Ohio
Toledo, Ohio

WILLIAM P. MILBERG, Ph.D.
Director of Geriatric Neuropsychology
GRECC, Veterans Affairs Medical Center
West Roxbury, Massachusetts
Associate Professor of Psychology
Department of Psychiatry
Harvard Medical School
Boston, Massachusetts

SCOTT R. MILLIS, Ph.D.
Assistant Professor
Wayne State University
Rehabilitation Institute of Michigan
Detroit, Michigan

MAURA MITRUSHINA, Ph.D.
Associate Clinical Professor
University of California, Los Angeles
School of Medicine
Los Angeles, California
Associate Professor, California State University,
  Northridge, California.

STEPHANIE O'MALLEY, Ph.D.
Associate Professor of Psychiatry
Yale University
New Haven, Connecticut

STEVEN H. PUTNAM, Ph.D.
Assistant Professor
Wayne State University
Rehabilitation Institute of Michigan
Northville, Michigan

RALPH M. REITAN, Ph.D.
Reitan Neuropsychology Laboratory
South Tucson, Arizona

MARY M. ROBERTSON, M.B.Ch.B., M.D.,
  D.P.M., F.R.C.Psych
Reader in Neuropsychiatry
University College London Medical School
Consultant Neuropsychiatrist
The National Hospital, Queen Square
London, England

SEAN B. ROURKE, Ph.D.
Neuropsychology Research Fellow
Department of Psychiatry
University of California, San Diego
La Jolla, California
Assistant Professor of Psychiatry
University of Toronto
The Wellesley Hospital
Toronto, Ontario, Canada

LEE RYAN, Ph.D.
Assistant Research Scientist
Department of Psychiatry
University of California, San Diego
La Jolla, California

DAVID P. SALMON, Ph.D.
Associate Professor in Residence
Department of Neurosciences
University of California, San Diego
La Jolla, California

TAMMY M. SAVOIE, Ph.D.
Chief, Psychological Services
Maxwell Air Force Base
Alabama

MARK W. SHATZ, Ph.D.
Rehab Pathways Group, Inc.
Southfield, Michigan

ARTHUR P. SHIMAMURA, Ph.D.
Associate Professor of Psychology
University of California, Berkeley
Berkeley, California

LARRY R. SQUIRE, Ph.D.
Professor in Residence
Departments of Psychiatry and Neurosciences
University of California, San Diego
La Jolla, California
Career Research Scientist
Veterans Affairs Medical Center
San Diego, California

NANCY R. TEMKIN, Ph.D.
Associate Professor of Neurological Surgery and
  Biostatistics
University of Washington
School of Medicine
Seattle, Washington

STEPHAN F. TAYLOR, M.D.
Lecturer
Department of Psychiatry
University of Michigan
Ann Arbor, Michigan

PAMELA J. THOMPSON, C.Psychol. AFBPsS.
Head of Psychological Services
Chalfont Centre for Epilepsy
Gerrards Cross, Buckinghamshire, England

DANIEL TRANEL, Ph.D.
Professor of Neurology
University of Iowa College of Medicine
Benton Neuropsychology Laboratory, and
  Department of Psychology
University of Iowa
Iowa City, Iowa

MICHAEL R. TRIMBLE, F.R.C.P., F.R.C.Psych
Consultant Physician in Psychological Medicine
  and Professor of Behavioral Neurology
Institute of Neurology
University Department of Clinical Neurology
The National Hospital for Neurology and
  Neurosurgery
Queen Square
London, England

ELIZABETH K. WARRINGTON, Ph.D.,
  Sc.D., F.R.S.
Professor and Head, Department of
  Neuropsychology
The National Hospital for Neurology and
  Neurosurgery
Queen Square
London, England

DEBORAH WOLFSON, Ph.D.
Reitan Neuropsychology Laboratory
South Tucson, Arizona

Methods of Comprehensive Neuropsychological Assessment

1 Theoretical, Methodological, and Validational Bases of the Halstead-Reitan Neuropsychological Test Battery

RALPH M. REITAN and DEBORAH WOLFSON

Background and Development of the Halstead-Reitan Battery (HRB)

After earning a Ph.D. in physiological and comparative psychology at Northwestern University in 1935, Ward Halstead moved to the University of Chicago, established a working relationship with two neurosurgeons, Percival Bailey and Paul Bucy, and started the first full-time laboratory for the examination and evaluation of brain-behavior relationships in human beings.

Halstead's first step in evaluating brain-damaged patients was to observe them in their everyday living situations and attempt to discern which aspects of their behavior were different from the behavior of normal individuals. Fortunately, Halstead was relatively unencumbered by knowledge of the routine approach that existed in this era concerning the effects of brain damage. In fact, at this time and for quite a number of years previously, the principal approach of psychologists was to develop a single test that would diagnose brain damage.

Halstead's observations of persons with cerebral lesions made it apparent at the very beginning that brain-damaged individuals had a wide range of deficits and that a single test would not be able to adequately identify and evaluate the severity of their deficits. Some patients demonstrated motor and sensory-perceptual disorders, often involving one side of the body more than the other.

Some patients had specific language deficits representing dysphasia. Other individuals were confused in a more general yet pervasive way (even though in casual contact they often appeared to be quite intact).

As Halstead studied brain-damaged persons in their typical everyday living situations, he observed that most of them seemed to have difficulties in understanding the essential nature of complex problem-situations, in analyzing the circumstances that they had observed, and in reaching meaningful conclusions about the situations they faced in everyday life.

The initial orientation and approach to research and evaluation may have long-term implications. For example, Binet and Simon (1916) began developing intelligence tests using academic competence as the criterion. IQ tests, though used to assess cerebral damage, are probably still best known for their relationship to school success. It was important and fortuitous that Halstead decided to observe the adaptive processes and difficulties that brain-damaged persons demonstrated in everyday life. If he had focused only upon academic achievement or classroom activities, it is probable that he would have developed tests quite different from the ones he did produce. The tests that eventually have been included in the Halstead-Reitan Battery have emanated basically from a general consideration of neuropsychological impairment and, as a result, have much more relevance than IQ measures to practical aspects of rehabilitation and adaptive abilities.

Halstead devised and experimented with a great number of psychological testing procedures. The design of his instruments placed them more in the context of standardized experiments than conventional psychometric tests. Many of the procedures developed by Halstead contrasted sharply with psychometric testing procedures, inasmuch as they required the subject not only to solve the problem, but to observe the nature of the problem, analyze the essential elements, and after having defined the problem, proceed to solve it.

Halstead developed a series of 10 tests that ultimately formed the principal basis for his concept of biological intelligence. He described these tests in detail and presented his theory in his book, *Brain and Intelligence: A Quantitative Study of the Frontal Lobes* (Halstead, 1947). Only seven of the original 10 tests have withstood the rigors of both clinical and experimental evaluation. These seven tests constitute a substantial component of the Halstead-Reitan Battery and are the seven tests used to compute the Halstead Impairment Index.

It became apparent that Halstead's seven tests had to be supplemented with an extensive array of additional procedures in order for the battery to attain clinical usefulness. The General Neuropsychological Deficit Scale (GNDS), a measure that provides an overall characterization of an individual's neuropsychological abilities and has proved to be very useful clinically as a method of comparing areas of deficit, is based upon a total of 42 variables derived from measures in the Halstead-Reitan Battery (including the original seven tests developed by Halstead) (Reitan and Wolfson, 1988, 1993).

Another significant feature of the Halstead-Reitan Battery is that it was developed and validated not only by formal research, but also by evaluating thousands of patients with brain lesions as well as control subjects. This procedure involved administering the tests, evaluating the results, preparing a written report about their significance for brain functions, and only then turning to the independent data produced by complete and independent evaluations done by neurologists, neurological surgeons, and neuropathologists.

After the two sets of data had been collected, conferences were held to correlate the neuropsychological findings with the independently obtained history and neurological, neurosurgical, and neuropathological data (concerning location, type, duration, etc., of the lesion). In this way each subject served as an independent experiment. Using this procedure, Reitan studied a total of over 8,000 patients. The HRB served as a focus for research in the area of human brain-behavior relationships long before the area of clinical neuropsychology emerged as a discipline, and in this sense the Halstead-Reitan Battery has played a role in the actual development of the field of neuropsychology.

During the 1950s and early 1960s our published research stimulated much interest; however, it also generated a considerable degree of skepticism and criticism from psychologists as well as neurologists and neurological surgeons. There was a general reluctance toward accepting findings that proposed that the higher-level aspects of brain functions (which had been elusive for so many years) could actually be measured, quantified, and even used as a basis for predicting "blindly" the location and type of brain lesion (Reitan, 1964). The HRB was being used with increasing frequency in many hospitals and clinics in the United States and other countries, and the general validity of the findings among researchers and clinicians gradually overcame this kind of skepticism.

Hartlage and DeFilippis (1983) reported the results of a survey conducted in 1980 of all neuropsychologists in the National Academy of Neuropsychologists and all members of the Division of Clinical Neuropsychology of the American Psychological Association. The results indicated that 89% of the respondents used the Wechsler Scales in their neuropsychological assessments, 56% included portions of the Halstead-Reitan Battery, 49% used the Bender-Gestalt Test, 38% used the entire Halstead-Reitan Battery, 32% employed the Benton Visual Retention Test, and 31% used the Luria-Nebraska Battery.

Dean (1985) reviewed the Halstead-Reitan Neuropsychological Test Battery in the *Ninth Mental Measurements Yearbook*. In his review he indicated that, "neuropsychological assessment in North America has focused on the development of test batteries that would predict the presence of brain damage while offering a comprehensive view of a patient's individual functions. Numerous batteries have been offered as wide-band measures of the integrity and functioning of the brain. However, the HRB remains the most researched and widely utilized measure in the United States."

Meier (1985) also reviewed the Halstead-Reitan Neuropsychological Test Battery and had the following introductory comment:

This comprehensive neuropsychological test battery has a long and illustrious history of clinical research and application in American clinical neuropsychology. Following its inaugural presentation to the psychological community (Halstead, 1947), and the careful nurturance of concept and application by Reitan (1974), the battery has had perhaps the most widespread impact of any approach in clinical neuropsychology. It seems reasonable to state that in the first half of the period since World War II, during which neuropsychology expanded so remarkably, this approach was the primary force in stimulating clinical research and application in this country.

Practical Considerations in the Development of a Neuropsychological Test Battery

Relation to Specialized Neurological Diagnostic Procedures

The relationship between neuropsychological testing and the many excellent specialized medical diagnostic procedures (especially computed tomography [CT] and magnetic resonance imaging [MRI]) is important in validating neuropsychological tests. In addition, it has been a cause of concern regarding the independent value of neuropsychological testing to those psychologists and physicians who consider the principal purpose of neuropsychological examination to be diagnosis of brain damage rather than evaluation of brain-behavior relationships.

It is important to recognize that neuropsychological evaluation draws on a different domain of evidence, at least to a major extent, than the diagnostic methods used by neurologists and neurological surgeons. The Halstead-Reitan Battery focuses on higher-level aspects of brain functions (and more specifically on central processing), whereas the neurological diagnostic procedures relate principally to lower-level aspects of brain functioning, electrophysiological manifestations, or brain imaging procedures. Neuropsychological evaluation provides the *only* rigorous and objective method of assessing higher-level aspects of brain functions.

Computed tomography and MRI scans are highly accurate diagnostic techniques. Both of these procedures identify structural abnormalities in the brain, such as space-occupying lesions and the types of tissue abnormalities characteristic of diseases such as multiple sclerosis. However, in cases of closed head injury, in which small vascular lesions or shearing of neurons may occur on a widespread basis, CT and MRI scans are not infrequently within normal limits. Despite their sensitivity to structural lesions, CT and MRI are not able to identify deficits in higher-level aspects of brain functions. An important need, therefore, has arisen for detailed studies of the correlation between these imaging procedures and neuropsychological test results, because CT and MRI cannot evaluate an individual's general intelligence or other adaptive abilities. Even more useful neuropathological-neuropsychological correlates may eventually emerge in the study of positron-emission tomography (PET) and single-photon emission computed tomography (SPECT). (The usefulness of the clinical neurological examination and specialized neurological diagnostic procedures is discussed in detail in Reitan and Wolfson, 1992.)

The fact that results from the Halstead-Reitan Battery have been shown to correlate closely with the findings of the neurological examination validates the neuropsychological data as indicators of the biological condition of the brain. However, it is important to recognize that these various procedures complement rather than compete with each other in providing information about the patient. If an individual's higher-level aspects of brain functions need to be evaluated, a neuropsychological examination must be performed in order to obtain the relevant information.

"Fixed" versus "Flexible" Neuropsychological Testing Procedures

The comparative advantages of fixed (or standard) versus flexible (or composed to meet the immediate assessment needs) batteries has received a considerable amount of attention (Incagnoli et al., 1986).

The terms "fixed battery" and "flexible battery" are misleading, insofar as fixed may be taken to mean inflexible and not able to be supplemented with other tests. Flexible, on the other hand, may imply that adaptations are possible to meet the requirements of the individual situation without a loss of validity in evaluation. In practice, one could easily equate fixed batteries with a standard set of instruments that has been validated through extensive research with thousands of patients, with resulting consensus among thousands of psychologists around the world.

In contrast, flexible batteries are made up by the psychologist evaluating the patient, usually according to the history and complaints of each patient. To the degree that they differ from standard batteries, these individualized series of tests have never been evaluated as a battery in research studies or assessed by consensus of other psychologists.

Flexible batteries tend to deny the actual concept of a battery of tests that has been designed to assess human brain functions. In this sense, fixed batteries might be better labeled as "validated" batteries, and flexible batteries as "casually composed" batteries that have never been rigorously validated or, in most instances, used to diagnose a single pathological condition (such as traumatic brain injury, cerebrovascular disease, etc.).

To the extent that they are composed to assess specific referral complaints or the subjective complaints of the patient (Christensen, 1975), flexible batteries may be referred to as "symptom-oriented" batteries.

Supposed advantages of the flexible battery include the prerogative to select tests to evaluate specific areas of function that accord with the patient's complaints. Of course, such a procedure might be quite circular in nature if the end result were only to confirm through psychological testing the patient's own initial self-evaluation (self-diagnosis).

Further, if the patient's subjective complaints are not sufficiently comprehensive, or if the patient is not able to offer an adequate and complete self-diagnosis, the resulting test battery may fail to recognize and evaluate significant areas of cerebral dysfunction. In any case, the series of tests selected by the psychologist will demonstrate a range of scores. Consequently, using this approach, the tests with low scores are usually selected as indicators of cognitive impairment.

In contrast, the fixed battery approach uses a constant group of tests. In this sense, the Halstead-Reitan Battery might be thought of as a comprehensive battery, validated on thousands of patients in order to be certain that all relevant areas of brain functions are included in the assessment and providing a balanced representation of the various neuropsychological functions subserved by the brain.

Finally, each test in the Halstead-Reitan Battery has been subjected to rigorous research in order to be validated as a neuropsychological test. In addition, the tests in the HRB have been further validated for their complementary significance and interpretation for assessment of the individual.

Results obtained on the Halstead-Reitan Battery regularly demonstrate the advantage of using a standard and comprehensive battery of tests. As shown in formal studies (Reitan, 1964), it is often possible, using only the HRB test results, to determine that cerebral damage has been sustained, to identify the area or location of principal involvement, and to assess whether the injury is recent or the brain has had an opportunity to stabilize. Further, from the point of view of rehabilitation, it is imperative to have a balanced representation of the nature and degree of neuropsychological deficit.

Considering the importance of assessing all neuropsychological aspects of brain function in a balanced and comparative manner, the advantages of determining the complementary nature of results on various tests (and thus achieving a battery effect in which the sum is greater than the individual components), and the obvious facilitation of validational research, Halstead and Reitan decided at the beginning to develop a standardized battery rather than use a variable selection of individual tests.

Differing Approaches to Neuropsychological Interpretation

Neuropsychologists have developed differing attitudes toward neuropsychological testing and the use of supplemental information to obtain valid results. The problem appears to arise from an attempt to emulate the medical model or, more specifically, the procedures used in neurology. In the field of neurology, it is routinely recommended that the results of the EEG, CT, MRI, and other specialized diagnostic procedures be evaluated only in the context of the patient's clinical history. This approach represents a double-edged sword inasmuch as history information may influence the interpretation of the diagnostic procedure or the diagnostic procedure may be used to controvert the history information.

Some neuropsychologists contend that neuropsychological evaluation is of value only if the test results are interpreted with full knowledge of the patient and his or her usual behavior. In some instances, the neuropsychologist requires personal observation of the patient at considerable length and in various types of settings in order to obtain enough information to be able to interpret the test results. In other instances, the neuropsychologist requires the findings of other professionals, knowledge of the subject's de-

mographic and personal behavior characteristics, detailed academic and occupational histories, and interaction with family members and other persons in the environment as a basis for interpreting the neuropsychological test results. Psychologists who adopt this approach obviously feel that neuropsychological test data does not constitute a significant source of independent information and needs to be interpreted in the framework of complementary sources of information to achieve validity.

Other neuropsychologists believe that neuropsychological testing is of value, but that a score or index cannot adequately reflect a subject's performances. This contention derives historically from the insistence by Kurt Goldstein (1942a,b) that the procedures used by brain-damaged individuals to solve problems differ from the methods utilized by persons with normal brain functions, and that the principal value of the testing has been lost if the procedures used by the patient are not observed and recorded. Goldstein felt that a final score, representing the adequacy of the subject's performances, was entirely inadequate, and that the process by which the individual achieved the end result was of critical importance. This contention has been carried forward by a number of other investigators (most notably Edith Kaplan), who have differentiated performances on the same task in accordance with the types of errors made by the subject, and related such information to neuropsychological interpretations of brain functions.

A final approach to this problem, represented principally by Reitan and others, recommends that the neuropsychological examination evaluate brain functions generally for every subject, and that a "blind" interpretation of the test findings be prepared before referring to any history information, conclusions reached by other professionals, or the results of additional diagnostic procedures. If the psychologist administers the tests personally, it is inescapable that he/she will observe the subject's performances and will formulate opinions based on the process the subject used to perform a task rather than on the test scores alone. The important point in this procedure, however, is related to the *sequence* the neuropsychologist follows to evaluate the subject. We recommend the sequential steps described below.

First, the neuropsychological test data are evaluated, including notations about any deviations from standard testing procedures, and perhaps even the process the subject uses to reach a solution. This first step should be completed before referring to any additional information, such as the history, findings of other examinations, or conclusions of other professionals. This procedure allows the neuropsychologist to evaluate the relevance of the test data and determine the extent to which it can make an independent contribution to understanding the patient's brain functions and cognitive structure.

After interpreting the neuropsychological test data "blindly," all additional information should be evaluated, including the complete history, the results of examinations by other professionals, the findings of neurological diagnostic procedures, the individual's behavior in everyday living situations, his/her interaction with family members and other significant persons in the environment, and the academic, employment, military, and professional records. Wolfson (1992) has systematized our history-gathering procedures by preparing a formal guide that explores an extensive range of relevant areas. The reader will notice that our method differs from the other approaches mentioned above only in terms of the sequence in which information is reviewed. In our system, the final interpretation of the data depends (as it does in the other approaches) upon an integration and evaluation of the consistency of all available information relating to the patient.

We prefer to avoid the risk of prejudicing the interpretation of the neuropsychological test results with supplemental information. We therefore perform an initial "blind" interpretation of the test data, and then relate these findings to any other available information. It is important to recognize that much of the history information and personal observations of the patient's behavior are obtained under inadequately standardized and uncontrolled conditions, which certainly impair interjudge reliability and the potential for unprejudiced interpretation of the test data.

A number of neuropsychologists have emphasized the importance of supplementing the information provided by the quantitative testing with observations of qualitative behavior. Such qualitative observations can be useful, but it must be recognized that some psychologists are more adept than others in reaching valid conclusions on the basis of their behavioral observations. In fact, if conclusions are based on impressions of qualitative aspects of behavioral manifestations, a considerable degree of interjudge unreliability is likely to result. Many studies have shown that behavioral ratings among psychologists and/or psychiatrists tend to be quite variable, even when the judges are thoroughly experienced. However, these kinds of problems of reliability do not necessarily detract from the valid observations that may be made by some judges. In our own practice we have observed many subjects experiencing the stress involved with neuropsychological testing. The Tactual Performance Test, for example, is often more stressful for brain-damaged persons than individuals with normal brain functions. Thus, the difficulty level of the task and the subject's reactions during the testing almost certainly contribute information over and beyond the quantitative score for the test.

Halstead and Reitan, having observed the various approaches to problem solving utilized by normal and brain-damaged persons, were keenly aware of the potential implicit in assessing a subject's qualitative performances during neuropsychological testing. They were interested, nevertheless, in exploring the potential value of standardized procedures that produced quantitative scores as a basis for evaluating brain-behavior relationships. It is generally accepted that a standardized procedure that produces a quantitative score is more replicable and reproducible—and thus has greater reliability—than judgments about the qualitative aspects of behavior. In discussing the strategy that they wished to employ in neuropsychological examination, Halstead and Reitan felt that it would be desirable to differentiate and separate the quantitative scores (which more closely meet the hallmark in science of replicability) from the observations of the patient's behavior. This decision was not intended to either deny the potential value of behavioral observations or to rule out the use of behavioral observations to supplement and complement the quantitative data produced by neuropsychological testing. However, if neuropsychology was to be established as a science rather than an art, it was critical to define the standardized testing procedures which would produce quantitative scores separate from the clinician's insightful observations of the subject's behavior.

It is not surprising that many investigators continue to emphasize the importance of qualitative observations. In fact, it appears that neuropsychologists who depend upon these procedures have a clinical orientation and, through their training, have developed skills in understanding impaired brain functions through the subject's behavioral manifestations. Proponents of this approach may also include psychologists who have had a lesser degree of success in validating their conclusions based upon interpretation of quantitative scores.

The debate concerning the use of qualitative versus quantitative methods for assessment of the effects of cerebral damage has a long history. Qualitative observations and analyses of behavior necessarily precede translation of such observations into standardized and quantified neuropsychological tests, which is the precise procedure used by Halstead and Reitan in developing the tests included in the HRB. Kurt Goldstein (1942a,b) argued that *only* quantitative evaluations were valid, and that quantitative assessments only confused the issue because a brain-impaired and a normal subject might earn the same quantitative score but use different approaches to do so. Goldstein claimed that brain damage inevitably produced a "concrete" approach to problemsolving, whereas the person with normal brain functions was able to adopt an "ab-

stract" approach. According to Goldstein, it was imperative to observe the performances of brain-damaged subjects in order to determine whether the brain damage had imposed any limitations on the individual's cognitive functioning.

Luria (personal communication, 1967) had a very similar orientation towards this question. In a letter to one of us (R.M.R.), he stated quite explicitly that little, if anything, could be gained by translating neuropsychological deficits into quantitative values, and believed that it was necessary to observe the performance style of the brain-damaged individual in order to understand that person's limitations.

As we have noted, the use of a standardized and replicable procedure in neuropsychological examination in no way obviates or even interferes with the use of clinical observation by those neuropsychologists who feel that they are skilled in this respect. At the same time, clinical observation (as contrasted with quantitative measurement of performances) should not be proposed—as Goldstein and Luria have done—as the *only* method that can validly identify the deficits of brain-injured persons.

The Development and Incorporation of Multiple and Complementary Methods of Inferring Cerebral Damage into a Single Battery

The critical incident leading to the development of the HRB into a battery that describes the uniqueness of brain impairment of individual subjects occurred in 1945. One of us (R.M.R.) had examined an extremely competent physician who had sustained a depressed skull fracture and complained of various significant deficits following the injury. Despite his complaints, this physician consistently performed well above average on the tests he had been given. Although the examination demonstrated that he had excellent abilities, his complaints seemed clinically valid. If this physician was indeed impaired as compared to his premorbid status, we needed to find a way to assess his deficits. Thus, the challenge was set. The problem required a methodology that described the impairment in the individual subject, regardless of whether the subject's premorbid level of functioning was high or low.

We realized that it was necessary to design the battery in such a way that methods of inference other than level of performance contributed to the clinical conclusions. Four approaches could be used to evaluate a subject's performances: (1) level of performance (how well the subject performed compared to others), (2) pathognomonic signs (specific deficits that rarely occur without cerebral damage), (3) patterns and relationships among test results (identification of score patterns that reflected localized or lateralized damage as well as relationships that compared premorbid abilities with evidence of acquired impairment), and (4) comparisons of a subject's performances on the same test on each side of the body. A great deal of formal research and clinical evaluation was necessary to develop tests that met the above requirements and also were valid measurements of the biological integrity of the brain. It was necessary that the tests complemented each other in interpretation, were as economical as possible in the time required for administration, were consistently sensitive to cerebral damage or dysfunction across a broad range of neurological conditions, and reflected an individual's deficits in a balanced and equivalent manner.

Content of the Halstead-Reitan Battery and its Conceptual and Theoretical Bases

Theory-building requires basic facts on which to develop constructs, and the short lives of many of the molar theories of brain-behavior relationships can be directly attributed to their inconsistency with the facts (see Reitan and Wolfson, 1988, 1993 for a review of theories in clinical neuropsychology). Our method of developing a theory was rather different from the one customarily used. We tried at first to generate a fairly extensive body of facts that in turn could lead us to a broader conceptualization or generalization about relationships between the brain and

neuropsychological functions. Our approach was therefore "fact-driven" rather than "theory-driven." We tried initially to meet the methodological requirements noted above and to compose a set of tests (the HRB) that was consistently valid, in both research and clinical application, as a basis for describing the ways in which the brain relates to behavior. Our empirical approach, guided by validated research findings and clinical verification in the individual case, led to the development of the Reitan-Wolfson model of neuropsychological functioning. We believe that this procedure may have more objectivity than an approach that postulates a theory and then searches for facts to support it.

The brain-based functions an individual needs in order to be efficient in his or her everyday behavior fall in several categories. The Reitan-Wolfson model of neuropsychological functioning (Fig. 1-1) provides a conceptual framework for organizing the behav-

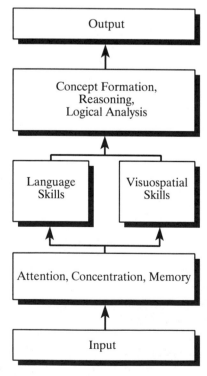

Figure 1-1. A graphic representation of the Reitan-Wolfson model of neuropsychological functioning.

ioral correlates of brain functions and describing the tests that measure these functions.

A neuropsychological response cycle first requires input to the brain from the external environment via one or more of the sensory avenues. Primary sensory areas are located in each cerebral hemisphere, indicating that this level of central processing is widely represented in the cerebral cortex and involves the temporal, parietal, and occipital areas particularly (see Reitan and Wolfson, 1993 for a description of the anatomical structures and systems for each of the elements of the Reitan-Wolfson model).

Once sensory information reaches the brain, the first step in central processing is the "registration phase" and represents alertness, attention, continued concentration, and the ability to screen incoming information in relation to prior experiences (immediate, intermediate, and remote memory). When evaluating this level of functioning, the neuropsychologist is concerned with answering questions such as, how well can this individual pay attention to a specified task? Can he or she utilize past experiences (memory) effectively and efficiently to reach a reasonable solution to a problem? Can the person understand and follow simple instructions?

If an individual's brain is not capable of registering incoming information, relating the new information to past experiences (memory), and establishing the relevance of the information, the subject is almost certainly seriously impaired in everyday behavior. A person who is not able to maintain alertness and a degree of concentration is likely to make very little progress as he or she attempts to solve a problem. Persons with such severe impairment have limited opportunity to utilize effectively any of the other higher level abilities that the brain subserves, and they tend to perform quite poorly on almost any task presented to them.

Because alertness and concentration are necessary for all aspects of problem-solving, a comprehensive neuropsychological test battery should include measures that evaluate the subject's attentiveness. Such tests should not be complicated and difficult, but should require the person to pay close attention over time to specific stimulus material. The Halstead-Reitan Battery evaluates this first level of central processing primarily with two measures: the Speech-Sounds Perception Test (SSPT) and the Rhythm Test.

The Speech-Sounds Perception Test consists of 60 spoken nonsense words that are variants of the "ee" sound. The stimuli are presented on a tape recording, and the subject responds to each stimulus by underlining one of four alternatives printed on an answer sheet. The SSPT requires the subject to maintain attention through the 60 items, perceive the spoken stimulus through hearing, and relate the perception through vision to the correct configuration of letters on the test form.

The Rhythm Test requires the subject to differentiate between 30 pairs of rhythmic beats. The stimuli are presented by a standardized tape recording. After listening to a pair of stimuli, the subject writes "S" on the answer sheet if he or she thinks the two stimuli sounded the same, and writes "D" if they sounded different.

The Rhythm Test requires alertness to nonverbal auditory stimuli, sustained attention to the task, and the ability to perceive and compare different rhythmic sequences. Although many psychologists have presumed that the Rhythm Test is dependent upon the integrity of the right cerebral hemisphere (because the content is nonverbal), the test is actually an indicator of generalized cerebral functions and has no lateralizing significance (Reitan and Wolfson, 1989).

After an initial registration of incoming material, the brain customarily proceeds to process verbal information in the left cerebral hemisphere and visual-spatial information in the right cerebral hemisphere. At this point the specialized functions of the two hemispheres become operational.

The left cerebral hemisphere is particularly involved in speech and language functions, or the use of language symbols for communication purposes. It is important to remember that deficits may involve quite simple kinds of speech and language skills or, conversely, may involve sophisticated higher-level aspects of verbal communication. It also must be recognized that language functions may be impaired in terms of expressive capabilities, receptive functions, or both (Reitan, 1984). Thus, the neuropsychological examination must assess an individual's ability to express language as a response, to understand language through both the auditory and visual avenues, and to complete the entire response cycle, which consists of perception of language information, central processing and understanding of its content, and the development of an effective response.

The Halstead-Reitan Battery measures both simple and complex verbal functions. The Reitan-Indiana Aphasia Screening Test (AST) is used to evaluate language functions such as naming common objects, spelling simple words, reading, writing, enunciating, identifying individual numbers and letters, and performing simple arithmetic computations.

The AST is organized so that performances are evaluated in terms of the particular sensory modalities through which the stimuli are perceived. Additionally, the receptive and expressive components of the test allow the neuropsychologist to judge whether the limiting deficit for a subject is principally receptive or expressive in character. The verbal subtests of the WAIS are also used to obtain information about verbal intelligence.

Right cerebral hemisphere functions are particularly involved with spatial abilities (mediated principally by vision but also by touch and auditory function) and spatial and manipulatory skills (Reitan, 1955a; Wheeler and Reitan, 1962). It is again important to remember that an individual may be impaired in the expressive aspects or the receptive aspects of visual-spatial functioning, or both. It must also be kept in mind that we live in a world of time and space as well as in a world of verbal communication. Persons with impairment of visual-spatial abilities are often severely handicapped in terms of efficiency of functioning in a practical, everyday sense.

The HRB assesses visual-spatial functions with simple as well as complex tasks. Particularly important are the drawings of the square, cross, and triangle of the Aphasia Screening Test, the WAIS Performance subtests, and to an extent, Parts A and B of the Trail Making Test.

In evaluating the drawings on the AST, the criterion of brain damage relates to specific distortions of the spatial configurations rather than to artistic skill. The square and triangle are relatively simple figures, and do not usually challenge an individual's appreciation and production of spatial configurations. The cross involves many turns and a number of directions, and can provide significant information about a subject's understanding of visual-spatial form.

Comparisons of performances on the two sides of the body, using both motor and sensory-perceptual tasks, provide information about the integrity of each cerebral hemisphere, and more specifically, about areas within each hemisphere. Both finger tapping and grip strength yield information about the posterior frontal (motor) areas of each cerebral hemisphere.

The Tactual Performance Test (TPT) requires complex problem-solving skills and can provide information about the adequacy of each cerebral hemisphere. The subject is blindfolded before the test begins and is not permitted to see the formboard or blocks at any time. The first task is to fit the blocks into their proper spaces on the board using only the preferred hand. After completing this task (and without having been given prior warning), the subject is asked to perform the same task using only the nonpreferred hand. Finally, and again without prior warning, the task is repeated a third time using both hands. The amount of time required to perform each of the three trials provides a comparison of the efficiency of performance of the two hands. The Total Time score of the test reflects the amount of time needed to complete all three trials.

After the subject has completed the third trial, the board and blocks are taken out of the testing area and the subject's blindfold is removed. The subject is then asked to draw a diagram of the board with the blocks in their proper spaces. The Memory score is the number of shapes correctly remembered; the Localization score is the number of blocks correctly identified by both shape and position on the board.

An important aspect of the Tactual Performance Test relates to the neurological model. The test's design and procedure allows the functional efficiency of the two cerebral hemispheres to be compared and provides information about the general efficiency of brain functions. During the first trial, data is being transmitted from the preferred hand to the contralateral cerebral hemisphere (usually from the right hand to the left cerebral hemisphere). Under normal circumstances, positive practice-effect results in a reduction of time of about one third from the first trial to the second trial. A similar reduction in time occurs between the second trial and the third trial.

The TPT is undoubtedly a complex task in terms of its motor and sensory requirements, and successful performance appears to be principally dependent on the middle part of the cerebral hemispheres. Ability to correctly place the variously shaped blocks on the board depends upon tactile form discrimination, kinesthesis, coordination of movement of the upper extremities, manual dexterity, and an appreciation of the relationship between the spatial configuration of the shapes and their location on the board. Obviously, the TPT is considerably more complex in its problem-solving requirements than either finger tapping or grip strength.

The tests for bilateral simultaneous sensory stimulation include tactile, auditory, and visual stimuli. Impaired perception of stimulation occurs on the side of the body contralateral to a damaged hemisphere.

The Tactile Form Recognition Test requires the subject to identify shapes through the sense of touch and yields information about the integrity of the contralateral parietal area. Finger localization and fingertip number writing perception also provide information about the parietal area of the contralateral cerebral hemisphere. Fingertip number writing requires considerably more alertness and concentration, or perhaps even

more general intelligence, than finger localization (L. C. Fitzhugh et al., 1962).

In the Reitan-Wolfson theory of neuropsychological functioning, the highest level of central processing is represented by abstraction, reasoning, concept formation, and logical analysis skills. Research evidence indicates that these abilities are generally represented throughout the cerebral cortex (Doehring and Reitan, 1962). The generality and importance of abstraction and reasoning skills may be suggested biologically by the fact that these skills are distributed throughout the cerebral cortex rather than being limited as a specialized function of one cerebral hemisphere or a particular area within a hemisphere. Generalized distribution of abstraction abilities throughout the cerebral cortex may also be significant in the interaction of abstraction with more specific abilities (such as language) that are represented more focally.

Impairment at the highest level of central processing has profound implications for the adequacy of neuropsychological functioning. Persons with deficits in abstraction and reasoning functions have lost a great deal of the ability to profit from experience in a meaningful, logical, and organized manner. However, since their deficits are general rather than specific in nature, such persons may appear to be relatively intact in casual contact. Because of the close relationship between organized behavior and memory, these subjects often complain of "memory" problems and are grossly inefficient in practical, everyday tasks. They are not able to organize their activities properly, and frequently direct a considerable amount of time and energy to elements of a situation that are not appropriate to the nature of the problem.

This nonappropriate activity, together with an eventual withdrawal from attempting to deal with problem situations, constitutes a major component of what is frequently (and imprecisely) referred to as "personality" change. Upon clinical inquiry, such changes are often found to consist of erratic and poorly planned behavior, deterioration of personal hygiene, a lack of concern and understanding for others, and so on. When examined neuropsychologically, it is often discovered that these behaviors are largely represented by cognitive changes at the highest level of central processing rather than emotional deterioration per se.

Finally, in the solution of problems or expression of intelligent behavior, the sequential element from input to output frequently involves an interaction of the various aspects of central processing. Visual-spatial skills, for example, are closely dependent upon registration and continued attention to incoming material of a visual-spatial nature, but analysis and understanding of the problem also involves the highest element of central processing, represented by concept formation, reasoning, and logical analysis. Exactly the same kind of arrangement between areas of functioning in the Reitan-Wolfson model would relate to adequacy in using verbal and language skills. In fact, the speed and facility with which an individual carries out such interactions within the content categories of central processing probably in itself represents a significant aspect of efficiency in brain functioning.

The HRB uses several measures to evaluate abstraction skills, including the Category Test, the Trail Making Test, and the overall efficiency of performance demonstrated on the Tactual Performance Test.

The Category Test has several characteristics that make it unique compared to many other tests. The Category Test is a relatively complex test of concept formation that requires ability (1) to note recurring similarities and differences in stimulus material, (2) to postulate reasonable hypotheses about these similarities and differences, (3) to test these hypotheses by receiving positive or negative information (bell or buzzer), and (4) to adapt hypotheses based on the information received after each response.

The Category Test is not particularly difficult for most normal subjects. Because the subject is required to postulate solutions in a structured (rather than permissive) context, the Category Test appears to require particular competence in abstraction ability. The test in effect presents each subject with a learning experiment in concept formation.

This is in contrast to the usual situation in psychological testing, which requires solution of an integral problem situation.

The primary purpose of the Category Test is to determine the subject's ability to use both negative and positive experiences as a basis for altering and adapting his or her performance (i.e., developing different hypotheses to determine the theme of each subtest). The precise pattern and sequence of positive and negative information (the bell or buzzer) in the Category Test is probably never exactly the same for any two subjects (or for the same subject upon repetition of the test). Because it can be presumed that every item in the test affects the subject's response to ensuing items, the usual approaches toward determination of reliability indices may be confounded. Nevertheless, the essential nature of the Category Test, as an experiment in concept formation, is clear.

The Category Test is probably the best measure in the HRB of abstraction, reasoning, and logical analysis abilities, which in turn are essential for organized planning. As noted above, subjects who perform especially poorly on the Category Test often complain of having "memory" problems. In fact, the Category Test requires organized memory (as contrasted with the simple reproduction of stimulus material required of most short-term memory tests), and is probably a more meaningful indication of memory in practical, complex, everyday situations than most so-called "memory" tests, especially considering that memory, in a purposeful behavioral context, necessarily depends on relating the various aspects of a situation to each other (see Reitan and Wolfson, 1988, 1993, for a discussion of this concept).

The Trail Making Test is composed of two parts, A and B. Part A consists of 25 circles printed on a sheet of paper. Each circle contains a number from 1 to 25. The subject's task is to connect the circles with a pencil line as quickly as possible, beginning with the number 1 and proceeding in numerical sequence. Part B consists of 25 circles numbered from 1 to 13 and lettered from A to L. The task in Part B is to connect the circles, in sequence, alternating between numbers and letters. The scores represent the number of seconds required to complete each part.

The Trail Making Test requires immediate recognition of the symbolic significance of numbers and letters, ability to scan the page continuously to identify the next number or letter in sequence, flexibility in integrating the numerical and alphabetical series, and completion of these requirements under the pressure of time. It is likely that the ability to deal with the numerical and language symbols (numbers and letters) is sustained by the left cerebral hemisphere, the visual scanning task necessary to perceive the spatial distribution of the stimulus material is represented by the right cerebral hemisphere, and speed and efficiency of performance may reflect the general adequacy of brain functions. It is therefore not surprising that the Trail Making Test, which requires simultaneous integration of these several abilities, is one of the best measures of general brain functions (Reitan, 1955c, 1958).

Validation of the Halstead-Reitan Neuropsychological Test Battery

As noted previously, Dean (1985) cited the HRB as the "most researched" neuropsychological battery in the United States. Of even greater significance is the fact that the clinical usefulness of the HRB has been demonstrated in thousands of settings around the world, in laboratories ranging from clinical offices to major medical centers and universities.

Reitan's own research efforts began with general issues relating to brain-behavior relationships and proceeded to increasingly specific questions. Investigations were ordered in such a way that serially forthcoming information would arrive in a context of prior data.

First, the general effects of heterogeneous brain lesions were investigated; second, the differential effects of lateralized cerebral lesions without regard to type were studied; third, regional localization effects were identified; fourth, differences in effects of various pathologies and duration of lesion were researched; fifth, the neuropsychological corre-

lates of brain lesions that were relatively chronic and static were compared with lesions that were acute and/or rapidly progressive; and sixth, the interaction among these variables and their relationship to the full range of cerebral damage, disease, and disorders was studied. Because our unit of value continually focused on the individual, the generality and specificity of application of the research results to individual subjects was routinely evaluated.

General Neuropsychological Effects of Cerebral Damage

Reitan's first study on the HRB compared results obtained with Halstead's ten tests in a group of 50 subjects with documented cerebral damage or dysfunction and a group of 50 control subjects who had no history of cerebral disease or dysfunction (Reitan, 1955b). A heterogeneous and diverse group of subjects with cerebral damage was included in order to ensure that an extensive range of conditions would be represented.

Persons with diverse medical conditions were deliberately included among the control subjects, and persons with brain damage were carefully excluded. Normally functioning individuals made up 24% of the control group, and the remaining 76% was composed of patients hospitalized for a variety of difficulties *not* involving impaired brain functions. The control group included a substantial proportion of paraplegic and neurotic patients in order to minimize the probability that any intergroup differences could be attributed to variables such as hospitalization, chronic illness, and affective disturbances.

The two groups were matched in pairs on the basis of race and gender, and as closely as possible for chronological age and years of formal education. The difference in mean age for the two groups was .06 years, and the difference in mean education was .02 years. The two groups were obviously very closely matched for age and education, and the standard deviations for age and education in the two groups were nearly identical.

Although the two groups should have produced essentially comparable results on the basis of the controlled variables alone, the presence of brain damage in one group was responsible for a striking difference in the test results. Seven of the measures devised and described by Halstead showed differences between the mean scores for the two groups with relation to variability estimates, which achieved striking significance from a statistical point of view. In fact, according to the most detailed tables we had been able to find, the probability estimates not only exceeded the .01 or .001 levels, but exceeded .000000000001. However, even these tables were inadequate to express the appropriate statistical probability level.

As noted above, statistical comparisons of the two groups reached extreme probability levels on seven of the ten measures contributing to the Halstead Impairment Index, and these seven tests have been retained in the Battery. The most striking intergroup differences were shown by the Category Test and the Halstead Impairment Index (even though three of the 10 measures contributing to the Impairment Index were not particularly sensitive to brain damage). Not one brain-damaged subject performed better than his matched control on the Impairment Index (although the Impairment Indices were equal in six of the 50 matched pairs).

The Category Test was the most sensitive of any single measure to the effects of cerebral damage. Three subjects with brain lesions performed better than their matched control, but in the remaining 47 pairs of subjects the control performed better than the brain-damaged subject.

These results indicated that Halstead demonstrated remarkable insight in developing tests that reflected the nature of neuropsychological impairment caused by brain damage. On three of the tests the results were not statistically impressive, but this may have been due to procedural problems in administration of these tests (Reitan and Wolfson, 1993). The remaining seven tests covered a broad range of adaptive abilities, involving such diverse performances as finger-tapping speed, attentional capabilities to verbal and nonverbal stimuli, psychomotor problem-solving capability, memory for stimulus material to which the subject previously had been exposed, and abstraction, reasoning, and logical analysis skills.

These results, demonstrating highly significant differences between groups with and without cerebral damage, were produced at a time when most investigations had shown relatively minimal differences. Hebb (1939, 1941) had recently reported case studies of persons who had obtained IQ values in the superior range despite having had as much as one third of their cerebral hemispheres surgically removed. A serious question existed, therefore, about why brain-damaged persons should perform so much more poorly than control subjects, especially considering the findings that had been reported by other researchers in earlier investigations.

At our current stage in the development of clinical neuropsychology, a retrospective review of this apparent conflict provides an explanation. Psychologists had been using measures devised to evaluate general intelligence, presuming that these tests would also be equivalently sensitive to impaired brain functions. However, as research has clearly demonstrated over the years since that time, tests developed to predict academic success are quite different from tests that are specifically sensitive to the biological condition of the brain. In fact, the IQ measures, which relate more closely to academic success, also appear to be heavily influenced by environmental and cultural advantages. On the other hand, tests developed specifically to evaluate impairment of brain functions seem to be fairer (unbiased) in terms of cultural and environmental experiences and advantages.

The basic reason for the striking differences in the results obtained using Halstead's tests and other measures appeared therefore to stem directly from the procedures used to develop the tests. As noted above, general intelligence measures were initially designed to predict academic success. Halstead ignored factors of this type almost entirely, and instead directly observed the daily living activities of persons with cerebral damage (having had these individuals identified for him by neurological surgeons who had operated on their brains). It is not surprising that Halstead's measures appear to relate much more closely to the biological adequacy of brain functions as well as to practical aspects of everyday life.

We continued to conduct additional studies of all of the measures that eventually have been included in the Halstead-Reitan Battery, comparing groups of patients who had documented cerebral damage with groups of subjects who had no history of cerebral disease. In one study the results indicated that the Trail Making Test was extremely sensitive to the biological condition of the brain (Reitan, 1958). Although Part A showed significant results, the results for Part B were even more striking.

Similar results were obtained with the Aphasia Screening Test (Wheeler and Reitan, 1962). Most persons with cerebral damage do not show any significant evidence of dysphasia, and essentially no individuals without past or present evidence of brain damage demonstrate such signs. However, when evidence of impairment is demonstrated on the AST, it almost invariably is associated with independent (medical) evidence of brain disease or injury. Minor deficits are sometimes exhibited by control subjects, but any significant evidence of dysphasia is a valid sign of cerebral damage, particularly involving the left cerebral hemisphere (Reitan, 1984).

The Halstead-Reitan Battery customarily includes the Wechsler Adult Intelligence Scale (WAIS). Certain of the Verbal subtests of the WAIS are usually within the normal range in persons with cerebral damage, provided that no evidence of aphasia has been elicited on the Aphasia Screening Test. In addition, control subjects usually show no evidence of frank dysphasic manifestations. Scores for the Wechsler subtests are usually somewhat lower for brain-damaged subjects than controls, except for the Digit Span subtest, which is often poorly performed by control subjects as well as brain-damaged subjects (Reitan, 1959).

Lateralization Effects

The highly significant results obtained in comparing non–brain-damaged control subjects and groups with heterogeneous cerebral damage laid the foundation for more detailed studies of human brain-behavior relationships using the Halstead-Reitan Battery. One of these studies compared groups of subjects with left and right cerebral lesions in order to obtain information about the differential or specialized functions of the two cerebral hemispheres.

The initial investigation involved the Wechsler-Bellevue Intelligence Scale (Reitan, 1955a) and was one of the first studies to lay the groundwork for the "left brain versus right brain" differentiation. The findings indicated that the Verbal IQ was consistently depressed in persons with destructive lesions of the left cerebral hemisphere, whereas Performance IQ was lowered in persons with right cerebral damage.

These results were confirmed in an extensive series of studies that used various criteria for implicating the left or right cerebral hemisphere. These lateralized criteria included EEG disturbances (Kløve, 1959), homonymous visual field defects (Doehring et al., 1961), and dysphasia versus constructional dyspraxia (Kløve and Reitan, 1958). Thus, a number of studies established the differential impairment of VIQ and PIQ to damage of the left and right cerebral hemispheres.

Throughout these investigations we continued to monitor the extent to which the generalizations applied to individual cases, and found that certain subjects did not fit the expected pattern, even though they had lateralized cerebral lesions. Other studies identified factors in addition to lateralization that influenced scores on neuropsychological tests. These factors included chronicity of the lesion, the developmental period during which the lesion occurred (childhood as compared with adulthood), the age of the adult subject when the lateralized brain damage was sustained, the education level, and even the type of cerebral damage.

For example, extrinsic tumors, which usually do not involve the brain tissue in a direct structural sense, demonstrated no evidence of differential impairment of verbal and performance intelligence, regardless of the side of the brain involved. Traumatic head injuries showed a statistically significant but rather mild effect, correlating with the diffuse or generalized involvement (as well as lateralized damage) from a blow to the head from the outside environment.

The set of conditions that demonstrated the most profound effect on verbal or performance intelligence as a result of lateralized cerebral damage included: (1) normal prior development into adulthood of brain-behavior relationships, (2) a recent lateralized insult to a previously normal brain, and (3) a lesion that represented definite cerebral tissue damage and also structurally involved only one cerebral hemisphere. Interestingly, these conditions tend to describe persons who were normal before the lateralized cerebral damage was sustained (in contrast to a number of subjects included in split-brain studies and in evaluation of surgical excisions for epilepsy), and therefore have generalization value for normal brain functions (as contrasted with impairment of the brain sustained before neuropsychological maturation) (Reitan and Wolfson, 1993).

In their review of the historical development of clinical neuropsychology, Reitan and Wolfson (1993) have identified two historical trends—one emanating from the areas of biopsychology and clinical psychology and the other developing from the medical field of neurology. Precedents in psychology have led largely to the development of tests and procedures rated on continuous distributions that generally follow the normal probability curve. Conversely, the rather simple procedures and tests derived from the field of behavioral neurology customarily produce dichotomous distributions, with results classified as either normal or abnormal.

The Halstead-Reitan Battery was deliberately composed to include procedures from each of these historical areas. The tradition of behavioral neurology is principally represented in the HRB by the Aphasia Screening Test and the Sensory-Perceptual Examination. Control subjects almost always earn normal scores on these simple tasks, and even persons with cerebral damage often do well (see Reitan and Wolfson, 1986, 1988, 1993, for detailed discussions of the limitations of the "sign" approach).

When abnormal performances are demonstrated on these relatively simple tasks, the results frequently have a fairly specific significance for implicating either the left or right cerebral hemisphere, and often identify impaired regional areas within each cerebral hemisphere. Deficits elicited by the sign approach, derived from procedures in behavioral neurology, therefore have special significance. However, considering the relatively simple nature of the tasks, normal performances are expected from non–brain-damaged subjects as well as a substantial number of persons with cerebral damage.

Using these procedures, we have compared the performances of control subjects with groups having left, right, and generalized cerebral damage (Doehring and Reitan, 1961a,b; Heimburger and Reitan, 1961; Wheeler and Reitan, 1962). In each of these studies the subjects met independent neurological criteria for the groups to which they were assigned. Subjects selected for inclusion in the study had had the advantage of normal physical growth and development without being influenced by cerebral damage early in life. The subjects for these groups permitted inferences about the organization of neuropsychological functions subserved by normal development rather than deviant neuropsychological organization influenced by the effects of early cerebral damage.

The results indicated that manifestations of dysphasia were consistently associated with left cerebral damage, whereas the presence of constructional dyspraxia (deficits in ability to deal effectively with simple spatial relationships) characterized subjects with right cerebral damage. Many deficits were nearly exclusively manifested in association with damage to either the left or right hemisphere.

For example, dysnomia occurred in 53% of subjects with left cerebral lesions, but did not appear at all among subjects with right cerebral damage. This type of deficit occurred in 1% of the controls and 17% of the subjects with diffuse cerebral involvement.

Similar results were obtained on measures included in the Sensory-Perceptual Examination. For example, finger agnosia involving the right hand occurred in 36% of subjects with left cerebral damage, but in less than 2% of subjects with right cerebral damage. Impairment on a sensory-perceptual task on one side of the body had adverse implications for the contralateral cerebral hemisphere.

Wheeler and Reitan (1962) compared 104 control subjects, 47 subjects with left cerebral lesions, 45 subjects with right cerebral lesions, and 54 subjects with bilateral or diffuse damage. Four simple rules were developed to classify any subject to one of the four groups. Applying these rules gave the following conditional probabilities of correct classifications: controls, 78%; left cerebral damage, 80%; right cerebral damage, 85%; and nonlateralized cerebral damage, 84%. These findings indicate that results from the HRB are quite accurate not only in identifying and differentiating subjects with and without cerebral damage, but also in identifying which hemisphere is involved.

Similar studies have been done using discriminant function analyses to produce a single weighted score for each subject and an optimum, least-squares type of separation. Wheeler et al. (1963) used a total of 24 scores for each subject (11 from the Wechsler Scales and 13 from the HRB) and analyzed them using groups of 61 control subjects, 25 subjects with left cerebral damage, 31 subjects with right cerebral damage, and 23 subjects with diffuse or bilateral involvement.

The bases for classifying subjects to these groups were derived entirely from independent neurological, neurosurgical, and neuropathological findings. Analysis of the tests results fell in the following categories of correct predictions: controls versus all categories of cerebral damage, 90.7%; controls versus left damage, 93.0%; controls versus right damage, 92.4%; controls versus diffuse damage, 98.8%; and right versus left damage, 92.9%.

A number of studies compared persons with acute versus chronic brain lesions. Clinical observations suggested that specific deficits tend to resolve, at least partially, as the patient progresses from an acute to chronic stage. In this context, Fitzhugh et al. (1961, 1962a,b, 1963) studied results from the Halstead-Reitan Battery, the Wechsler

Scale, and the Trail Making Test. The results generally indicated that persons who had chronic brain lesions (thus implying the possibility of some recovery of function over time) tended to perform somewhat better than subjects with recent, acutely destructive lesions.

Particularly striking were the results concerning the association between lateralized cerebral damage and differential impairment on the VIQ and PIQ. Persons with recent lateralized cerebral lesions showed consistent impairment of either VIQ or PIQ, depending upon the hemisphere involved. However, persons with chronic lateralized cerebral damage demonstrated much less consistent relationships between differential VIQ and PIQ scores and the side of the brain that was injured. These results supported our later finding that neuropsychological recovery occurs in the area of initial deficit (Reitan and Wolfson, 1988).

Clinical Inferences Regarding Individual Subjects

Finally, we have been interested in applying these various research results to interpretation of test protocols for individual subjects. In order to test the validity and accuracy of the HRB, we conducted a complex study in which both location and type of cerebral damage were carefully controlled (Reitan, 1964).

The first step in the procedure was to identify subjects with criterion-quality frontal, nonfrontal, or diffuse cerebral lesions. In order to provide a rigorous test of the generality of any conclusions relating to these various groups, we designed the study so that each group had the same number of subjects with various types of lesions. Each regional localization group was therefore composed of equal numbers of subjects with intrinsic tumors, extrinsic tumors, cerebral vascular lesions, and focal traumatic lesions.

Through a review of thousands of neurological protocols, we were able to identify four individual subjects with each of these types of lesions in each of the left anterior, left posterior, right anterior, and right posterior cerebral locations. We therefore had a total of 64 subjects. When subdivided into groups of 16 subjects with different locations of damage, each group contained equal representations of four different types of lesions. When subdivided into groups of 16 subjects according to type of lesion, each group had equal representations of the four different locations. Three additional groups were included in the study: 16 subjects with diffuse cerebral damage or dysfunction due to cerebrovascular disease, 16 subjects with closed head injuries, and 16 subjects with multiple sclerosis. The inclusion of these groups resulted in a total of 112 patients.

In the first study, a form was designed to record independent judgments based on the psychological test results for each subject. This form required three general decisions: first, a judgment was made from the neuropsychological test results alone about whether the lesion was focal or diffuse; second, a lesion category was selected; finally, more detailed judgments were made within certain lesion categories. For example, if the initial decision was that the lesion was focal rather than diffuse, the next judgment required selection of the right or left cerebral hemisphere, followed by selection of an anterior or posterior location within the hemisphere.

Next, a judgment was made about whether the lesion represented cerebral vascular disease, tumor, multiple sclerosis, or trauma. If the cerebral vascular disease category was selected, the lesion was further classified as a hemorrhage or vascular insufficiency. Additional forced judgments about the underlying basis for the evidence of cerebral vascular disease were made under each of these two categories.

If the tumor category was selected, the rater had to judge whether the lesion was intrinsic or extrinsic. If the intrinsic tumor category was selected, a further classification was made concerning whether the lesion was metastatic or a primary glioma.

Under the trauma category, the lesions were classified as an open or closed head injury. All of these ratings were based solely on the neuropsychological test results.

The rating form was sufficiently complete to permit classification of all subjects according to neurological criterion information. Because the classification of subjects to their respective groups had initially been based on neurological information, judgments made on the basis of neurological information represented the criterion. The purpose was to determine the degree of concurrence between neurological criterion information and ratings made on the basis of the psychological test results alone.

Each of the 112 subjects was assigned a number before the ratings were begun, and all information other than the psychological data was concealed in order to avoid any identifying clues when the ratings were made. There was no attempt to assign an appropriate number of subjects to any particular group. For example, no running record was kept to limit assignment of only 16 subjects to the multiple sclerosis group, etc. Every effort was made to classify the test results for each subject independently, and ratings were completed without using any type of running tally.

Using the neurological ratings as the criterion, there were 64 subjects with focal cerebral lesions. Of these subjects, 57 were classified correctly on the basis of psychological testing, and 7 were judged to have diffuse damage. In the group of 48 subjects with diffuse cerebral damage, 46 were classified correctly and 2 were judged to have focal lesions.

As mentioned above, there were 16 subjects in each regional localization group. The number of correct classifications on the basis of psychological test results for each of the locations was as follows: left anterior, 9; left posterior, 11; right anterior, 7; and right posterior, 15. Thus, 42 of the 64 patients were placed in their correct groups. Adding to this the correct classification of 46 of the 48 subjects with diffuse cerebral involvement, 88 of the 112 subjects were correctly classified.

With respect to the type of lesion, the 112 subjects fell in the following neurological diagnoses: intrinsic tumor, 16; extrinsic tumor, 16; cerebral vascular disease, 32 (16 focal, 16 diffuse); head injury, 32 (16 focal, 16 diffuse); and multiple sclerosis, 16.

The number of correct classifications on the basis of psychological inferences was as follows: intrinsic tumor, 13; extrinsic tumor, 8; cerebral vascular disease, 28; head injury, 30; and multiple sclerosis, 15. Thus, 94 of the 112 patients were correctly classified according to type of lesion.

Additionally, 13 of the 16 subjects with focal cerebral vascular disease were classified correctly, and 12 of these 13 were judged to have focal lesions. Of the 15 subjects with diffuse cerebral vascular disease who were correctly placed in this category, 14 were judged to have diffuse cerebral vascular disease. A total of 30 of the 32 head injury subjects had been placed in this category on the basis of their psychological test results, and 27 of these 30 had been correctly classified according to whether the lesion was focal or diffuse. It is particularly noteworthy that the HRB is differentially sensitive to traumatic brain injury, considering the frequency with which subjects in this category are involved in litigation. A review of the literature did not identify any other neuropsychological test or methods able to differentiate traumatic brain injury from other conditions of brain damage.

The degree of concurrence between the neurological criteria and the neuropsychological ratings indicated above could scarcely have happened by chance. The results confirmed that neuropsychological test results are differentially influenced by (1) focal and diffuse lesions, (2) which cerebral hemisphere sustained damage, (3) frontal and non-frontal lesions within the hemisphere involved, (4) type of lesion (intrinsic tumors, extrinsic tumors, cerebral vascular lesions, head injuries, and multiple sclerosis), (5) focal occlusion as compared with generalized insufficiency in cerebral vascular disease, and (6) focal as compared with diffuse damage from head injuries.

It is important to note that a study of this type serves a significant purpose in providing some insight into the degree to which psychological test results may be determined by brain lesions. Furthermore, this study indicates the complexity of the concept of "brain damage," and demonstrates that many neurological variables, which occur in varying combinations for individual subjects, are relevant in determining psychological measurements.

The validational studies of the Halstead-Reitan Battery leave no doubt that an individual's test results are closely dependent on his or her neurological status or diagnosis. The research findings reveal not only statistically significant intergroup differences, but also demonstrate the validity of the test results for specific neuropathological conditions.

The Halstead-Reitan Battery and Current Problems in Neuropsychology

A number of recent studies have used the HRB to investigate problems of current clinical significance in neuropsychology. While the human brain subserves a broad range of abilities ranging from sensory-perceptual functions, through complex aspects of central processing, to adaptive motor responses (see the Reitan-Wolfson model described previously), a need has existed both for clinical and research purposes for an overall indicator of general neuropsychological status. The Halstead Impairment Index (Halstead, 1947; Reitan, 1955b) and the Average Impairment Rating (Russell et al., 1970) have demonstrated validity and have served usefully, but these measures do not summarize fully the broad range of tests included in the HRB.

A Summary Index of Overall Performance on the HRB

Reitan and Wolfson (1988, 1993) addressed this deficiency by developing the General Neuropsychological Deficit Scale (GNDS), an instrument that produces a summary score based on 42 variables from the Halstead-Reitan Neuropsychological Test Battery for Adults. The field of clinical neuropsychology has identified major areas of neuropsychological functioning, and there is general recognition that a comprehensive evaluation requires assessment of these areas for clinical purposes as well as for planning a rehabilitation regimen.

The GNDS was developed for this purpose, and was devised in such a manner that four methods of evaluating data are represented. Of the 42 variables that contribute to the GNDS score, 19 are based on level of performance and reflect how well the subject performed on a broad range of neuropsychological functions. Nine variables representing motor and sensory-perceptual performances evaluate differences between the preferred and the nonpreferred sides of the body. This approach reflects the fact that brain damage often affects one side of the body more than the other side. Using the differential-score approach, two variables evaluate relationships among tests that differentiate brain-damaged subjects from control subjects. Finally, 12 variables representing dysphasia and constructional dyspraxia constitute the pathognomonic sign approach.

The GNDS was not designed to replace competent clinical interpretation of the test results (which involves characterization of the individual's deficits), but only as an overall indication of the degree of neuropsychological impairment. To achieve this purpose, each of the 42 variables contributing to the GNDS score is represented by four score ranges: 0 (a perfectly normal performance), 1 (a normal performance that is mildly deviant, but without clinical significance), 2 (a mildly to moderately impaired performance), and 3 (a severely impaired performance). These score ranges are useful when the clinician wants to assess a subject's degree of impairment on an individual test in the Halstead-Reitan Battery, and the cutoff score between 1 and 2 differentiates normal from brain-damaged subjects. Thus, in a general sense, the classifications represent normative data.

The GNDS score represents the sum of the scores for the 42 variables on which it is based. This procedure produces low GNDS scores for normal controls and high GNDS scores for persons with cerebral dysfunction. The normal range extends from 0 to 25; mild impairment from 26 to 40; moderate impairment from 41 to 67; and severe impair-

ment from 68 to the maximum possible score of 168 (Reitan and Wolfson, 1988, 1993). More detailed information about the GNDS as well as computerized scoring is published in Reitan and Wolfson (1993).

Using control groups and brain-damaged groups, Reitan and Wolfson (1988, 1993) presented the results of several validational studies indicating that the GNDS was adversely affected by (1) left, right, or generalized heterogeneous cerebral damage, (2) left, right, or generalized cerebral vascular damage, (3) left, right, or diffuse cerebral damage due to trauma, and (4) left or right cerebral damage when type of lesion was held comparable. All of the non–brain-damaged control groups had lower (better) mean GNDS scores than any of the brain-damaged groups. The following control groups were used: (1) a normal group with a mean Full Scale IQ of 129.26 (mean GNDS, 12.48), (2) a young group (mean GNDS, 15.90), (3) a heterogeneous group (mean GNDS, 17.20), and (4) an older group (mean GNDS, 24.82) (see Reitan and Wolfson, 1988, for additional details). A group of subjects who had sustained a cerebral concussion but had not demonstrated any objective evidence of brain damage, examined at the time of discharge from the hospital, had a mean GNDS score of 25.36, a score that was significantly poorer than the score earned by a heterogeneous control group.

The groups with definite brain damage consistently had mean GNDS scores ranging from 43.73 to 64.33 (subjects with traumatic brain injuries tended to score better than other groups, and subjects with left cerebral strokes tended to do most poorly). No significant differences were found within studies among subjects with left, right, or generalized cerebral damage, suggesting that the GNDS score, as intended, was a valid overall summary indicator. Males and females showed no significant differences on the GNDS when other variables were held constant. In a study comparing a group of subjects who had cerebral concussion with a group of traumatic brain-injured subjects who had documented tissue damage, the group with concussion had a significantly better mean GNDS score. Studies comparing older and younger control subjects demonstrated that the older groups performed more poorly.

Sherer and Adams (1993) published a cross-validation study of the GNDS and indices reported by Reitan and Wolfson (1988) to be differentially sensitive to damage of the left or right cerebral hemisphere, and concluded that their findings provided "limited support for the validity of these new scales with patients commonly seen in clinical practice" (p. 429). These investigators compared 73 brain-damaged subjects with 41 "pseudoneurologic" subjects. The pseudoneurologic group was composed of subjects who reported "neurologic" symptoms but had no biomedical evidence of brain damage and included "30 subjects who had received psychiatric diagnoses" (p. 429).

The results of Sherer and Adams agreed essentially with the findings reported by Reitan and Wolfson (1988), insofar as (1) the brain-damaged group was significantly more impaired on the GNDS than the pseudoneurologic group, (2) the subgroups with left, right, or generalized damage did not differ on the GNDS, (3) males and females showed no statistical difference, and (4) older subjects performed more poorly than younger subjects. The principal differences between results reported by Sherer and Adams (1993) and Reitan and Wolfson (1988) were that 53.6% of the pseudoneurologic group scored in the brain-damaged range as compared to only 10% of Reitan and Wolfson's controls. Sherer and Adams (1993) state that "the poor classification of our pseudoneurologic subjects may be due to a limitation with the use of pseudoneurologic control groups" (p. 434).

Wolfson and Reitan (1995) designed an additional study to further investigate the validity of the GNDS in differentiating between groups of subjects with and without evidence of cerebral damage, comparing 50 brain-damaged subjects with 50 control subjects that were similar in age and education.

The mean GNDS score for the brain-damaged group (55.02) was very similar to the mean of 53.22 reported by Reitan and Wolfson (1988) for 169 brain-damaged sub-

jects. The mean GNDS score for the control subjects (19.66) was slightly higher than the mean of 17.20 found for 41 controls (Reitan and Wolfson, 1988). In each case, the brain-damaged subjects performed more poorly than the controls at a highly significant level.

In Reitan and Wolfson's 1988 study, the best cutoff score was 25/26, which resulted in a 9% rate of misclassification. The 1995 study identified 28/29 as the best cutoff score, which misclassified 12% of the subjects. An inspection of the two distributions indicated that individual cases of GNDS scores differing by one or two points were responsible for the differences in the two distributions. In the 1995 study, 80% of the controls and 96% of the brain-damaged subjects were classified correctly using the original cutoff score of 25/26, again yielding a 12% rate of misclassification. Obviously, the "best" cutoff score depends upon whether one wishes to avoid false negatives or false positives, but the best clinical conclusion would identify the "gray" area (where the groups overlap) as falling between 26 and 29 points.

Sherer and Adams (1993) stated that the value of using pseudoneurologic controls was that such patients are frequently seen in clinical practice. However, their pseudoneurologic control group had a mean GNDS score of 26.56, a value considerably higher than the means reported by Reitan and Wolfson (17.20, Reitan and Wolfson, 1988; 19.66, 1995a). In order to obtain completely "clean" comparisons, we feel that the initial validation studies should compare groups of subjects who fall unequivocally into either a brain-damaged or non–brain-damaged group.

Following such a determination, other comparison groups, composed according to clinically relevant criteria, may be evaluated, and a pseudoneurologic comparison group would certainly be clinically relevant. The group with cerebral concussion reported by Reitan and Wolfson (1988) would be another such relevant group, and it might also qualify as a pseudoneurologic group since all members of the group had "neurologic" complaints but no biomedical evidence of brain damage (see Reitan and Wolfson, 1988, for a review of the debate concerning whether the symptoms of concussion should be considered "psychiatric" or "neurologic"). In Reitan and Wolfson's previous study, the group with cerebral concussion had a mean GNDS score of 25.36, a value very similar to the mean of 26.56 reported by Sherer and Adams for their pseudoneurologic group (Reitan and Wolfson, 1988).

In summary, it appears that the GNDS score is a valid general indicator of the presence or absence of cerebral damage.

Traumatic Brain Injury and the Halstead-Reitan Battery

Traumatic brain injury is another area in which there has been considerable research using the HRB as well as other tests.

Reitan and his associates conducted a broadly based longitudinal study of deficits resulting from traumatic head injury and the natural history of the recovery process over an 18-month period. The results of these investigations are described briefly elsewhere in this volume and reported in a number of publications, including Dikmen and Reitan (1976, 1977a,b), Dikmen et al. (1983), and Reitan and Wolfson (1988).

Examinations of individual subjects enrolled in the study followed a systematic schedule. Initial evaluations were performed soon after the head injury (at about the time the patient was ready for discharge from the hospital insofar as the head injury was concerned), and subsequent examinations were done 12 and 18 months after the first examination. In addition to comprehensive documentation of the neurological findings at the time of hospitalization, EEGs, neurological examinations, and extensive neuropsychological testing were done at each of the follow-up examinations.

This study was designed to investigate (1) the neuropsychological deficits accompanying head injury, (2) the recovery process in various areas of functioning as it relates to the initial degree of deficit, and (3) the ability to predict an individual's status at the 18-month examination from the data obtained

during the first three post-injury months. A series of analyses were performed to answer several clinical questions:

1. Did the head-injured subjects show spontaneous improvement in time as they recovered from their initial deficits? A trend analysis over the three evaluations indicated that a highly significant degree of improvement occurred, particularly in comparisons of the initial and 12-month examinations. The degree of improvement exceeded retest changes of control subjects, indicating that positive practice-effects were an unlikely explanation for the better scores.

2. Did a differential degree of improvement characterize the recovery pattern of persons with (A) mild initial deficits and (B) moderate to severe initial deficits? The neuropsychological performances of the normal control group were compared with the performances on three serial evaluations of the two traumatic brain injury groups. The results indicated greater recovery in those subjects with more severe initial deficits, although such patients continued to demonstrate greater neuropsychological deficits 18 months following the injury. The head injury group with mild initial deficits showed improved scores compared to the control group, but the final results still indicated that, in terms of absolute performance levels, the controls did best, the subjects with mild head injury were intermediate, and the subjects with moderate to severe head injury performed the poorest.

3. Is it possible to predict an individual's outcome 18 months post-trauma on the basis of data obtained soon after the injury occurred? Four main sources of information, obtained within the first 3 months after the head injury was sustained, were used to predict outcome: (1) the initial neuropsychological evaluation, (2) the 3-month neurological examination, (3) the initial and 3-month EEG recordings, and (4) the characteristics of head injury and associated neurological condition at the time of the injury. Three discriminant

analyses, using different sets of information, were performed to predict neuropsychological status at 18 months. Subjects were assigned to one of two outcome groups: normal or mildly dysfunctional individuals or definitely dysfunctional individuals.

Using the point of minimum overlap as a cutoff point, the first discriminant analysis based on nine variables derived from the information available on "characteristics of head injury and associated neurological condition" correctly classified 76% of the subjects. The second discriminant analysis utilizing ten variables derived from all four sources of information resulted in a 94% correct prediction rate. *Finally, a 91% correct prediction rate was obtained by the third analysis, which was based on 15 variables entirely derived from objective neuropsychological measures.*

These results suggest that the important clinical question of recovery potential may, upon cross-validation, have an accurate solution based on objective data. While many studies have used the Glasgow Coma Scale to assess the severity of the initial deficits and to predict outcome, the above results suggest that a comprehensive evaluation with the HRB would provide more useful information in this respect. However, administration of the HRB following head injury does require that the subject be sufficiently alert to be able to take the tests, and as noted above, our initial administration of the HRB usually was done just prior to discharge from the hospital.

4. Is the course of recovery consistently progressive for every individual who sustains a brain injury? Although recovery, in a general sense, appears to be the rule, clinical evaluation of individual cases indicated that between the 12- and the 18-month examinations some subjects showed an unexpected neuropsychological deterioration that was not explained by EEG or conventional neurological findings. This deterioration tended to occur principally in the areas of neuropsychological functioning that had been most impaired on initial examination and that had shown a substantial degree of recovery at the time of the 12-month examination.

The subjects who showed this late-term deterioration were usually persons in whom the initial evaluation had shown evidence of specific lesions (contusions and definite tissue damage) rather than subjects who had no initial evidence of focal cerebral damage. We postulate that in some patients there is a type of pathological tissue change (possibly gliosis) in the late recovery period that underlies the selective neuropsychological deterioration.

Based on our series of investigations (Dikmen and Reitan, 1976; Reitan and Wolfson, 1988), we concluded that:

1. Traumatic brain injured subjects demonstrate definite impairment of higher-level brain functions.
2. Recovery occurs with apparently greatest improvement in the first year.
3. Greater improvement occurs in subjects who demonstrate substantial as compared to mild initial impairment, although seriously impaired patients continue to show greater residual deficits 18 months after their head injury.
4. Recovery or reorganization of brain functions occurs as a natural phenomenon, even without specific rehabilitation (although cognitive retraining may facilitate, complement, and consolidate gains made through spontaneous recovery).
5. A high degree of predictive accuracy may be possible regarding neuropsychological status 18 months after the injury.
6. Following initial recovery, some traumatic brain injury patients demonstrate definite deterioration of neuropsychological functions in the late recovery period.

Mild Head Injury

Minor head injury has started a recent flurry of interest that has arisen from a number of reports of significant deficits occurring in such cases. Rimel et al. (1981) reported on the initial evaluations of 538 patients with mild head injury and follow-up evaluations performed 3 months later. They noted that at the follow-up evaluation these subjects had many complaints and a relatively low rate of employment. In addition, a subgroup of these patients was examined neuropsychologically, and was found to have difficulties with concentration, memory, and judgment.

Barth et al. (1983) examined neuropsychological functions in a sample of these patients, identified areas of cognitive impairment, and felt that there was a significant relationship between the presence of cognitive impairment and post-injury employment. Findings of this type led Guilmette (1991) to comment that there was much more disability resulting from mild head injury than had initially been thought, and led the National Head Injury Foundation to describe head injury as the "silent epidemic."

Alves and Jane (1985) added further emphasis to the category of mild brain injury with their chapter in *The Central Nervous System Trauma Status Report* (1985). Even though these authors believed that mild brain injury does not form a distinct class of injury, it does include a continuum ranging from very mild blows to the head to impacts that cause instant death. Obviously, if death is a possible outcome, mild brain injury may sometimes be more serious than the term "mild" would seem to imply.

Alves and Jane point out that mild brain injury often causes deficits that are more extensive than previously thought, and may include verbal and communicative problems, intermediate and short-term memory difficulties, deficits in information processing and reaction time, impairment of perceptual functions, and difficulties with concept formation and general reasoning abilities. They conclude that it is clear, as previously noted by Boll (1982), "that what may be relatively mild and perhaps clinically invisible decreases in cognitive capabilities may significantly alter a person's ability to perform tasks at a personally adequate level or in a fashion minimally acceptable to others" (p. 262).

These types of observations have led to the impression that a large number of individuals who sustain a mild head injury may experience subtle deficits that are often unrecognized but may have profound consequences.

Alves and Jane (1985) also reviewed reports concerned with social and economic outcome following head injury. These authors cite Rimel and her associates (1981, 1982), noting that in many cases mild brain injury leads to work morbidity. As expected, similar findings were reported among cases of moderate head injury (Rimel et al., 1982), which led Alves and Jane (1985) to state that "their findings are very important: more moderately injured patients experience the problems reported in their minor trauma series, suggesting that the same sorts of problems are experienced across a considerable range of injury severity. The work morbidity of previously employed patients was 69% for this series, or twice that of patients with minor injury" (p. 263).

The great concerns generated by these reports concerning the adverse effects of mild head injury prompted a number of investigations, although earlier studies, of course, had been done over the years (Aita et al., 1947a,b; Gronwall and Sampson, 1974; Gronwall and Wrightson, 1974; Gronwall, 1976, 1977; Levin et al., 1982). Rather than focus on head-injured subjects with clinical problems, these investigators, in the main, established criteria for mild head injury and enrolled subjects into their studies if they met these criteria, regardless of whether or not they had present or continuing clinical complaints.

The first of these studies used the HRB and was begun by Reitan in 1974, and as noted above, reported in a number of studies including Dikmen and Reitan (1976), Dikmen et al. (1983), and Reitan and Wolfson (1988). These investigators reported that a group with mild head injuries had a mean GNDS score of 25.36, not a great deal worse than the mean GNDS of 17.20 for the non–brain-damaged controls (although the means differed beyond the .02 level). The group with definite tissue damage of the brain, however, had a mean GNDS of 53.06, a score well within the brain-damaged range and quite comparable to other groups with documented brain damage (Reitan and Wolfson, 1988).

Additional studies of mild head injury (McLean et al., 1983; Dikmen et al., 1986; Gentilini et al., 1989; Gronwall, 1989; Levin et al., 1989; Ruff et al., 1989), although using various neuropsychological tests, differing criteria for mild head injury, and variable time schedules for follow-up testing (see Reitan and Wolfson, 1994a, for a more complete summary) reached essentially the following conclusions:

1. Mild neuropsychological impairment can be detected among persons who have sustained a mild head injury.
2. There is potential advantage in identifying persons with mild impairment so they can be assisted during the recovery period.
3. Recovery to a pre-injury status occurs within a few weeks to about 3 months.
4. There may be some persons who will not recover fully within 3 months and who will have continuing neuropsychological deficits and even frank neurological disorders.

These findings indicate that recovery occurs spontaneously, and although complaints may continue, such complaints are also endorsed by control subjects (Dikmen et al., 1986) and are not necessarily attributable to the mild head injury.

A number of researchers who have studied mild head injury have concluded that the neuropsychological deficits that characterize this condition are represented by measures of attention, verbal learning, and speed of information processing (Van Zomeren, 1981; Gentilini et al., 1989; Gronwall, 1989) and that "a general survey of neuropsychological abilities, as in test batteries aimed at examining different cognitive functions, may well be inefficient in isolating specific impairments" (Gentilini et al., 1989, p. 105). Curiously, however, these researchers have usually administered principally tests that fall in these functional areas, and considering the broad

range of neuropsychological functions subserved by the brain, do not have a strong basis for identifying selective impairment.

Providing a solution to this type of problem, in fact, represents one of the great advantages of the HRB inasmuch as the procedure by which it was developed focused on evaluation of the full range of brain-dependent abilities. The question of correlation of specific deficits with particular conditions can be answered only by having a sufficient range of measurements on each subject, and the HRB has provided this range of measurements not only for traumatic brain injury, but for many other conditions as well. The effects of mild brain injury, when present after a head blow, would be expected to be represented principally by neuronal shearing and petechial hemorrhages (Reitan and Wolfson, 1992), which are not focal but instead involve the brain generally. Considering the nature of the pathology, neuropsychological deficits would not be expected to fall into neat, specific categories. In fact, this question was studied with the HRB and the results indicated that general deficits, rather than specific and isolated deficits, were found (see below).

Up to this point, we have seen that most persons who sustain a mild head injury either suffer no significant neuropsychological impairment or, if initially impaired, recover in a week, a few weeks, or at most, 2 to 3 months. On this basis it would seem that minor head injury is not a very significant clinical problem. The significant problems experienced by the subjects studied by Rimel et al. (1981) must be considered. Do persons with mild head injury have residual symptoms and deficits or do they recover fully in short order? Ruff et al. (1993) state that a large proportion recover fully, but that a minority have persistent complaints even years after the head injury. It would appear that mild head injury can cause, in some instances, neuropsychological problems even though most subjects recover fully.

Most of the research studies have used a procedure—admission of consecutive subjects to the study regardless of complaints—

that has severely diluted the clinical significance of the investigations. As a clinician, whom are you likely to see and evaluate: mild head injured subjects who have no complaints (the majority) or mild head injured subjects who have residual deficits (the minority)? Obviously, if research is to have clinical value to the practitioner, it must deal with the subjects seen by the practitioner.

Realizing that no studies have been done on the relevant population of persons with mild head injuries, we pursued the question, performing comparisons among controls, cases of mild head injury routinely accessed into a research study, more seriously head injured subjects routinely accessed into a research study, a heterogeneous sample of persons with definite brain damage, and, finally, a group of subjects that met criteria for mild head injury but who failed to recover fully, had continuing problems including serious memory loss, mental slowing, posttraumatic epilepsy, and other sequelae. The basic question concerned the neuropsychological performances of this latter group compared to the other groups.

The results of this study, communicated more fully by Reitan and Wolfson (1994a), may be summarized.

The findings indicated (1) striking impairment of brain-damaged groups compared to control groups (regardless of whether the subjects were "research" or "clinical" cases), (2) that the "research" mild head injury group showed mild impairment (GNDS poorer than controls, $p<.02$), but tended to simulate the control groups, and (3) that the "clinical" mild head injury group showed definite impairment that tended to simulate the brain-damaged groups.

Thus, individuals who have sustained a mild head injury can be subdivided into two categories: (a) subjects who recover rapidly and have no residual problems (the majority of mild head injury subjects fall in this group), and (b) subjects who sustain brain impairment and often have significant neuropsychological deficits. The latter group requires careful and detailed neuropsychological evaluation and clinical care, and should not be presumed to be malingerers or suffering only from emotional problems. Instead, we must recognize that these subjects must be assessed with a comprehensive neuropsychological battery, considering that our evaluation of this group revealed the presence of diversified neuropsychological deficits that covered the full range of brain-related abilities.

The results of this study made it quite clear that we should not permit the results based on evaluation of "research" cases, routinely accessed into the study, to confuse the issue of significant impairment among mild head injured subjects who apparently sustain brain damage.

Frontal Lobe Deficits

The Halstead-Reitan Battery has also served to address the question of specific frontal lobe deficits. In a review of frontal lobe studies, Reitan and Wolfson (1994b) noted that there appears at present to be a great interest in the frontal lobes, expressed at a level that nearly matches that of the late 1930s and the 1940s. Even a brief perusal of the recent literature reveals the current emphasis being placed on the frontal lobes in neuropsychological functioning. A casual literature review identified 16 articles published within the past few years that reached conclusions about the frontal lobes. Eight articles reported empirical findings (Boone et al., 1990; Fiducia and O'Leary, 1990; Shute and Huertas, 1990; Gnys and Willis, 1991; Welsh et al., 1991; Axelrod et al., 1992; Grodzinsky and Diamond, 1992; Rybash and Colilla, 1994); in one article the authors reported a meta-analysis of tests for diffuse brain damage, and felt that it was useful to include a category of tests intimately related to the frontal lobes (Chouinard and Braun, 1993); and seven theoretical review articles were devoted to explicating frontal and prefrontal functions (Goldman-Rakic, 1993; Grafman et al., 1993; Hart and Jacobs, 1993; Lezak, 1993; Schwartz et al., 1993; Sohlberg et al., 1993; Varney and Menefee, 1993).

The topics of the empirical articles included the following:

1. The deterioration of frontal lobe functions among healthy older subjects (two articles);
2. The maturation of frontal lobe functions in children (two articles);
3. Establishing the test-retest reliability and construct validity of tests of executive functioning in young children;
4. Investigating the relationship of a Piagetian formal operational reasoning process to measures of frontal lobe dysfunction;
5. Determining the role of frontal lobe functions in boys with attention deficit–hyperactivity disorder;
6. The relationship of a special type of memory (source memory) to a particular dimension of frontal lobe functioning.

Except for the test-retest reliability study (in which the results were not fully supportive of the hypothesis), each of these investigations drew conclusions about the role of the frontal lobes in neuropsychological functioning. In fact, one study of normal aging effects (Axelrod et al., 1992) "revealed the sensitivity of the MMSE (Mini-Mental State Examination) to changes in frontal lobe functioning" (p. 70), essentially because performances on the MMSE, like the performances on three "frontal lobe" tests, deteriorated across the age span of 50 to 90 years. In addition, these authors found a correlation of 0.49 between the MMSE and a composite score based on the three frontal lobe tests, and viewed this finding as "noteworthy because the MMSE was intended as a measure of gross cognitive status rather than of frontal lobe functioning" (p. 68).

Although each of the studies noted above drew conclusions about the frontal lobes (except for the study that did not fully support its hypothesis), none of the investigations used any subjects who had documented evidence of frontal lobe involvement. In addition, none of the subjects in any of the studies were examined neurologically for independent evidence of frontal lobe damage. What, then, was the basis for such conclusions? The presumption that certain tests had previously been validated as frontal lobe tests, and any evidence of impairment on

these tests was, ipso facto, an indication of frontal lobe impairment. (In most cases the tests used with children had to be adapted or even changed substantially from the adult versions, and they had never been validated by investigations of children with frontal lobe lesions. However, this lack of validation was rarely considered to be a detriment to drawing conclusions about frontal lobe functioning.)

The pervasive belief in the specificity of certain tests to reflect frontal lobe functioning has persisted in spite of cautionary statements. Bigler (1988) stated that "clinical neuropsychology long has sought specific tests of frontal lobe damage but to date no such tests exist that are exclusively sensitive to frontal lobe function." He also noted that tests purported to evaluate frontal lobe function, such as the Wisconsin Card Sorting Test and the Category Test, are not specific to frontal lobe damage.

Wang (1987) also reviewed neuropsychological functions supposedly related to the frontal lobes, and concluded that there are no tests specifically sensitive to frontal lobe damage or dysfunction. Similarly, Costa (1988) concluded that although many tests are sensitive to cerebral dysfunction, few tests are uniquely sensitive to particular cortical areas. Concerning frontal lobe dysfunction specifically, he wrote that "it is easy to find tests that are sensitive to frontal lobe dysfunction and very difficult to find tests that are specific for it!" (p. 6).

The Category Test and Part B of the Trail Making Test are often identified as "frontal lobe tests" (Bigler, 1988; Butters et al., 1994; Farmer, 1994; Jarvis and Barth, 1994), and were used in two of the investigations cited above (Shute and Huertas, 1990; Grodzinsky and Diamond, 1992). Using these tests, Reitan and Wolfson (1995a) compared groups with frontal and nonfrontal cerebral lesions that were approximately equivalent for types of lesions and other variables. No intergroup differences were found on the Category Test and Part B of the Trail Making Test. These results, together with a literature review (Reitan and Wolfson 1994b), suggest that neuropsychologists should adopt a more critical attitude concerning so-called "frontal lobe deficits."

Differing Effects of Age and Education in Brain-Damaged Versus Non–Brain-Damaged Groups

Recent studies have shown that attribute variables of age and education relate differently to neuropsychological and intelligence tests scores in normal versus brain-damaged groups. Yet, common practice calls for age and education adjustments, based on normal subjects, to be applied to brain-damaged persons. This practice appears to be in error among tests sensitive to the condition of the brain because the effects of brain damage often tend to overrule or even obliterate the effects of age and education among persons with brain damage.

Reitan and Wolfson (1995b) studied this matter using 50 brain-damaged adult subjects and 50 control subjects, who had comparable distributions for age and education. The results indicated, as expected, that age and education had a significant effect on the General Neuropsychological Deficit Scale (GNDS) for the control group. However, age and education had relatively little effect, either in terms of level of performance or relationships between variables, on the GNDS scores of brain-damaged subjects. When the groups were subdivided at the median for age and education, the younger and better educated controls had significantly better GNDS scores than did the older and less well educated controls. When the same procedure was applied to the brain-damaged group, there were no significant differences. Apparently, brain damage had become the dominant determiner of the variance, and impaired GNDS scores emerged regardless of age or education. Being young or having a good education seemed to do little to protect against the impairment caused by brain damage.

Reitan and Wolfson (1995b) also investigated the effects of age and education on Verbal, Performance, and Full Scale IQs based on the WAIS. A more complex set of results emerged, apparently because of the lesser sensitivity of the IQ variables to brain damage (as compared with the GNDS) and greater sensitivity particularly to education. In general, the Verbal IQ showed more similar relationships to age and education among the controls and brain-damaged subjects than did the Performance IQ. While certain significant similarities occurred in VIQ, PIQ, and FSIQ measurements for brain-damaged and non–brain-damaged groups, differences were also present that would serve to caution against adjusting IQ values for brain-damaged subjects on the basis of normative data based on tests results for non–brain-damaged subjects.

Finally, Reitan and Wolfson (in press a) investigated the relationships of age and education to the results of individual WAIS subtests, which were selected as neuropsychological measures in preference to the WAIS-R subtests because of the greater availability of validity information. Data analyses were concerned with the effects of level of each attribute variable (each group subdivided at the median) on subtest scores and the correlations between attribute variables and subtest scores. The results revealed a number of differences in the two groups, with attribute variables having a weaker and less consistent relation to WAIS subtest scores in the brain-damaged than the control group. The results suggest that the relationships of attribute variables to psychological test scores is complex, and that adjustment or transformation of raw scores for brain-damaged subjects, according to tables based upon non–brain-damaged subjects, may produce erroneous data.

If additional research confirms these findings, what are the clinical implications, especially since neuropsychological evaluation is concerned mainly with clinical assessment of persons with known or suspected brain impairment and is involved much less often with the assessment of normal or non–brain-damaged persons? The diminished significance of age and education among brain-damaged subjects indicates that interpretation of neuropsychological data should depend on test results that are definite indicators of brain damage or impairment rather than rely on scores adjusted for attribute variables.

When significant brain damage occurs, neither young age nor higher education seems to protect the individual from neuropsychological impairment. Given this fact, it seems that the logical course in clinical evaluation would be to determine, first, whether brain damage is present. Then, if brain damage is not present, one should consider the subject's age and education to gain a complete understanding of the test scores.

For the total group of non–brain-damaged controls, age and education generated coefficients of correlation with the GNDS of 0.69 and −0.66, respectively. Although these coefficients are statistically significant, they account for only approximately 44% to 48% of the variance and should be used judiciously, even among non–brain-damaged subjects.

Development of a Dissimulation Index Using Variables From the Halstead-Reitan Battery and the Wechsler Scale

Malingering and/or failure to perform as well as the subject can constitutes a basis for serious concern regarding the validity of neuropsychological test results, particularly in situations where the subject has prospects of personal gain by producing poor or impaired scores. The *Diagnostic and Statistical Manual of Mental Disorders* (DSM-IV) (American Psychiatric Association, 1994) includes the recommendation that malingering should be strongly suspected in certain circumstances, such as when the subject is evaluated in a medicolegal context (e.g., the subject is involved in litigation and has been referred by an attorney for examination). In a review of psychological testing in cases of malingering following minor head trauma, Binder (1990) stated that malingering should be considered a possibility whenever the test results may be related to the opportunity for financial gain.

Spurred by the growing involvement of psychologists in evaluation of brain damage in personal injury cases (Doerr and Carlin, 1991), there has been a spate of books, chapters, and experimental studies on malingering, dissimulation, factitious disorders, and the invalidity of neuropsychological test results (Faust et al., 1988; Pankratz, 1988; Rogers, 1988; Schretlen, 1988; Franzen et al., 1990; Cullum et al., 1991; Schretlen et al., 1991; Lee et al., 1992; Binder, 1993).

Nies and Sweet (1994) reviewed various tests, methods, and procedures used to detect malingering. Many studies reported in the literature compared the test scores of groups of subjects with valid deficits to the test scores of subjects who were asked (or paid) to simulate impairment of a specific condition. This method of identifying malingering obviously depends on how accurately and convincingly an untrained, unimpaired person can simulate the symptoms of brain damage. Such an approach should prompt the reader to consider: Where would we be in our understanding of the effects of brain damage if our methods of assessment had been based on people merely pretending to be brain-damaged?

Individual tests have also been used to detect malingering. This approach often depends upon the subject producing performances that fall significantly below chance levels of correct responses. In this procedure, the examiner usually tells the subject that the test is quite difficult when it is in fact quite easy. If the subject "falls for the bait" (that is, believes the examiner) and performs below a chance level, the presumption is that the subject has malingered. The usefulness of this approach is seriously impeded by the fact that many brain-damaged persons score below a chance level on tests such as the Seashore Rhythm Test for a number of valid reasons, including near-total confusion.

Some other approaches to detect malingerers depend upon identifying disparate test scores that go beyond clinical expectations; however, given the limited availability of groups of subjects who are verified malingerers, these interest relationships are difficult to define precisely. Few subjects admit that they were malingering, and compelling independent evidence is rarely available.

Considering these difficulties in conducting research in the area of malingering and in identifying test results or patterns that characterize true malingerers, we elected to review neuropsychological test results of head-injured subjects who were involved in litigation and compare them to the test results of head-injured subjects who were not involved in litigation (Reitan and Wolfson, in press b).

Most of the psychometric approaches to detecting malingering have evaluated test scores based on a single examination in terms of adequacy of performance. This method has the disadvantage of battling the normal probability curve (obviously, 50% of the normal population falls below the average level of performance) as well as very poor scores from many legitimately severely impaired people. Thus, poor performances, even on an easy task, may fall in a score range that is not represented exclusively by malingerers.

Cullum et al. (1991) described three cases that employed "a previously unstudied method for detecting invalid test results" (p. 168). These authors compared performances on an extensive battery of tests on serial examinations and found highly variable performances that went beyond the range of normal subjects or neurologically stable patients. Cullum et al. suggested that "examination of performance reliability across testings may be a powerful means by which the neuropsychologist can detect patients who are not consistently putting forth adequate effort on the examination" (p. 168).

Recognizing the value in neuropsychological assessment of intraindividual comparisons (using the subject as his or her own control) and the problems implicit in interindividual evaluations (Reitan and Wolfson, 1993), we decided to compare test results obtained in two separate examinations of head-injured subjects involved in litigation versus head-injured subjects not involved in litigation. Our postulate was that head-injured subjects involved in litigation would perform more poorly on the second examination than on the first, whereas the head-injured subjects not in litigation would show improvement on the second examination (due to positive

practice effects as well as spontaneous recovery). In accordance with the principle demonstrated by Reitan and Wolfson (1988) in their study of spontaneous recovery after head injury, we expected the greatest degree of improvement to occur on tests that are most sensitive to brain damage.

Among the test studied, only those that achieved a probability level of .025 or less in comparing the two groups were used for computations leading to the Retest Consistency Index. Six tests reached the specified level of significance in differentiating the two groups: Comprehension, Picture Arrangement, Digit Symbol, the Category Test, Part B of the Trail Making Test, and TPT–Localization. Difference scores on these tests for the litigation and non-litigation groups combined were transformed using a 5-point scale to reflect the degree of inconsistency (a score of 5 indicated the greatest degree of inconsistency, a score of 1 reflected the least degree of inconsistency). Using t-tests, means, standard deviations, and comparisons of distributions were computed for the two groups as well as for the total of the scaled scores for the six most sensitive tests (the Retest Consistency Index).

The distributions, based on the 5-point scale, were compared for the litigation group and the non-litigation group, and a cutoff point that best differentiated the two groups was determined for the Retest Consistency Index.

The results clearly indicated that head-injured subjects involved in litigation tend to demonstrate much less consistent scores on retesting than head-injured subjects not in litigation. Using the best cutoff point, the Retest Consistency Index differentially classified 90% of the litigation subjects and 95% of the non-litigation subjects. Differentiation of the two groups was achieved at highly significant levels.

Reitan and Wolfson (in press c) performed another study using the same two groups of subjects (both head-injured but one group involved in litigation and the other group not so involved). The consistency of responses to individual items of the Wechsler Information, Comprehension, Arithmetic, Similarities, and Vocabulary subtests on two separate testings were compared. A scoring system was devised to reflect responses that were different on the second testing, and this raw score was converted to a scaled score. The Response Consistency Index was designed to represent the sum of the scaled scores for the five subtests. The Response Consistency Index scores showed that retest responses were less consistent in the litigation group than in the non-litigation group. The best cutoff point separated the groups with accuracies of 90% (litigation group) and 100% (non-litigation group).

The intergroup comparisons for each test yielded highly significant differences, with the litigation group demonstrating less consistency in responses between testing 1 and testing 2 in every instance. As would be expected considering the greater degree of stability that tends to characterize summary measures, comparisons based on the Response Consistency Index yielded the highest *t* ratio.

The Response Consistency Index scores for individual subjects ranged from 5 (most consistent) to 25 (least consistent). The best cutoff score for differentiating the two groups was 15/16, with 100% of the non-litigation group having scores of 15 or less and 90% of the litigation group earning scores of 16 or more.

The results of this study indicate that subjects involved in litigation were much less consistent between two testings in their responses to individual items on the Information, Comprehension, Arithmetic, Similarities, and Vocabulary subtests than were subjects not involved in litigation. A summary score that represented the sum of scaled scores for the individual subtests (the Response Consistency Index) correctly classified 100% of the non-litigants and 90% of the litigants. There seems to be little doubt that the groups differed strikingly.

The differences between the litigation group and the non-litigation group were derived from comparisons of performances on two testings (intraindividual comparisons that in effect used each subject as his or her own control) rather than from intergroup comparisons. Data analyses suggested that level of performance, as evaluated with relation to normative distributions, would have been far less productive of differences between the groups than the evaluation of intragroup changes (the procedure used in this study). In fact, both the Retest Consistency Index and the Response Consistency Index were based solely on intraindividual changes in performances on two testings and level of performance was not considered.

Realizing that the Retest Consistency Index and Response Consistency Index, although methodologically distinct, were complementary, Reitan and Wolfson (in press d) decided to combine them into a third scale called the Dissimulation Index. The same groups of head-injured subjects were used, one involved with litigation and the other not so involved. Both groups had been examined twice, about 12 to 14 months on the average between testings, and the mean interest intervals did not differ significantly. Because both the Retest Consistency Index and the Response Consistency Index were represented by a 5-point standard score scale for each of the 11 tests involved, addition of the two scores yielded a possible range for the Dissimulation Index of 11 to 55 points.

The mean Dissimulation Index for the litigation group was 42.05 (SD = 6.14) and 23.50 (SD = 3.00) for the non-litigation group, indicating that the subjects in litigation were far more likely than the group not in litigation to show inconsistencies between the first and second testing. In fact, the Dissimulation Indexes ranged from 33 to 55 for the litigation group, but extended from 18 to 29 for the non-litigation group. There was no overlap between the distributions, and in fact, a 4-point gap between them.

The method described above appears to derive its strength from using the subject as his or her own control. The value of this method has been demonstrated both in neurological (DeMyer, 1994) and neuropsychological evaluation (Reitan and Wolfson, 1993). While it has frequently been used clinically to compare the same performances on the two sides of the body, many subjects, particularly those in litigation, are tested two or more times before the case comes to trial or is settled.

Our hypothesis was that there would be a great advantage in comparing the subject's test results with his or her test results at an earlier testing, rather than comparing the subject's performances with the rest of the population. If the subject was performing to the best of his or her ability on both examinations, one would presume that the scores would be at least comparable or possibly better (because of practice effects) on the second testing. If the subject was not putting forth his or her best effort, the scores on the two testings would be more variable, and perhaps even worse on the second testing, because of the need to "prove" one's impairment as the time for a judgment came closer.

We should note that neuropsychologists have devised a number of ingenious techniques and approaches that, in some cases, are very helpful in detecting invalid test results. As noted above, tests have been devised that actually are very easy but are presented to the subject as being very difficult (Lee et al., 1992; Binder, 1993). Some subjects appear to "fall for the bait," perform well below a chance level, and thereby produce results that suggest that they have not made an honest effort. Clinical observations of some severely brain-damaged persons, however, suggest that performances below chance levels can also be caused by significant neuropsychological impairment.

Reitan and Wolfson (1992), as well as others, have indicated that subjects involved in litigation sometimes perform exceedingly poorly on some tests and very well on others, presenting combinations of scores that rarely if ever occur clinically. Pankratz (1988) and his associates have developed a method called "symptom validity testing," applicable for evaluation of sensory and memory complaints. This technique used a forced-choice paradigm in which a 50% rate of correct responses represents a chance performance. The chance probability of scoring below the 50% level may readily be calculated, indicat-

ing the likelihood that any particular poor level of performance would occur by chance.

Each of these approaches may yield strong presumptive evidence of malingering in the case of certain subjects, depending on their scores. There is no assurance, however, that all instances of invalid test results are detected, and they are all based on results obtained during a single examination. It would appear that comparisons of the consistency of results produced in separate examinations provides an additional powerful method of detecting invalid test results among persons suing for recovery of damages represented by neuropsychological impairment in cases of head injury.

REHABIT: A Structured Program for Retraining Neuropsychological Abilities Based on the Halstead-Reitan Battery

The final step in the neuropsychological sequence involves remediation. After the deficits have been identified, what can be done to remediate them? The neuropsychologist must (1) identify neuropsychological deficits, (2) conclude validly that these deficits are due to brain damage rather than other possible causes, and (3) define and select training procedures that are pertinent to the needs of the individual. If a remediation program is to be of value, the behavioral deficits must be evaluated in terms of their comparative severity for the individual, and rehabilitation must be appropriate to the subject's ability level and needs. These requirements presume that the neuropsychological evaluation has assessed the full range of brain-related functions. Evidence indicates that results on the HRB provide this kind of information by identifying an individual's neuropsychological impairment in the framework of a comprehensive model of brain-behavior relationships. Thus, evaluation with the HRB provides a diagnosis that serves as the basis for developing a rehabilitation program capable of remediating an individual's particular deficits.

Training of both children and adults is viewed within this same framework. Differences in neuropsychological evaluation of children and adults must be recognized, largely because of the fact that children are in a developmental phase of achieving brain-related abilities. However, children and adults who sustain impairment in a particular area may demonstrate many of the same types of neuropsychological deficits. The training program materials for children and adults are essentially similar, except that in many instances the training begins at a more simple level for the child.

As noted above, verbal and language functions are customarily related to the integrity of the left cerebral hemisphere, and visual-spatial and manipulatory skills are dependent on the status of the right cerebral hemisphere. Recent investigations have emphasized the specialization of brain functions in association with the cerebral hemisphere involved; however, the nonspecialized types of abilities, which are dependent upon the brain *generally*, have been relatively neglected. Because the abilities that characterize generalized brain functions involve all cerebral tissue rather than representing specialized capabilities, it might be reasonable to postulate that these abilities are of special significance in a cognitive retraining program.

Our research has shown that the broad range of abstraction abilities represents cerebral cortical functioning generally and may be more fundamental than the specialized skills. A cognitive retraining program that emphasizes abstraction and reasoning abilities would seem to provide the most appropriate basis for rehabilitation, especially considering both the research and clinical findings that demonstrate the pervasive and limiting effects of impairment in this area.

REHABIT (Reitan Evaluation of Hemispheric Abilities and Brain Improvement Training) was developed by Reitan in 1979 to provide tasks that reflected the specific as well as the generalized functions of the brain. The REHABIT training program does not use a "shotgun" approach to brain retraining; instead, it has specifically been organized to remediate an individual's neuropsychological deficits, as determined by an evaluation with the Halstead-Reitan Battery.

Considering the importance of abstraction abilities and their central role in brain training, five tracks of training materials have been established in REHABIT:

1. *Track A* contains equipment and procedures specifically designed for developing expressive and receptive language and verbal skills and related academic abilities.
2. *Track B* also specializes in language and verbal materials, but deliberately includes an element of abstraction reasoning, logical analysis, and organization.
3. *Track C* includes various tasks that do not depend upon particular content as much as reasoning, organization, planning, and abstraction skills.
4. *Track D* also emphasizes abstraction, but its content focuses on material that requires the subject to use visual-spatial, sequential, and manipulatory skills.
5. *Track E* specializes in tasks and materials that require the subject to exercise fundamental aspects of visual-spatial, sequential, and manipulatory skills.

Regardless of the content of the training materials being used for the individual subject, every effort is made to emphasize the basic neuropsychological functions of attention, concentration, and memory.

With many children and adults it is necessary to provide training in each of the five tracks. In some instances, one area should be emphasized more than the other areas. The decision for prescribing training should be based upon the results of testing with the HRB. The REHABIT program, which includes over 600 items, provides extensive training in all areas of neuropsychological functioning.

Formal research regarding the effectiveness of REHABIT has been developing slowly, but this is to be expected, considering the difficulties inherent in evaluating a procedure which, for each individual subject, is extended over a substantial period of time. The first study was possible only through the occurrence of fortuitous circumstances that resulted in collaboration by Reitan and Sena (1983). Sena had collected neuropsychological test results on subjects before and after 12 months' training with REHABIT. In order to study the effects of practice and spontaneous recovery, it was necessary to compose two control groups: (1) normal subjects who had been tested initially and retested 12 months later (to evaluate positive practice effects), and (2) brain-injured subjects who had been tested initially and retested 12 months later but had not received any training with REHABIT or any other cognitive rehabilitation program (to study spontaneous recovery of neuropsychological functions). Fortunately, one of us (RMR) did have data on such groups, and a preliminary study was devised (Reitan and Sena, 1983).

The findings indicated that the subjects who had been trained with REHABIT demonstrated substantial improvement on neuropsychological tests compared with the other two groups. The results reached levels of statistical significance on a number of variables (even considering the small number of subjects). This investigation suggested that cognitive brain retraining using REHABIT was a definite advantage in terms of facilitating the recovery process.

Sena and his associates have continued investigating the efficacy of REHABIT. One study conducted by Sena (1985) evaluated a group of 12 subjects who had sustained brain injury an average of 18.4 months before the initial evaluation. Spontaneous recovery should have been largely completed before the subjects were enrolled in the study. In addition, retesting 12 months after the initial examination may well have represented a long enough interval to minimize positive practice effects.

The retest results indicated that statistically significant improvement occurred on 31 of 39 measures, covering a broad range of neuropsychological functions. However, additional evaluation was necessary to make direct comparisons of persons who had undergone treatment with REHABIT as compared with those who had not received such treatment.

Sena and Sena (1986) retrained 13 subjects with two to three sessions of REHABIT per week for at least one year and compared their initial and retest results with a group of eight subjects who had similar brain injuries but had received no cognitive retraining. The initial testing indicated that the neuropsychological functions of the two groups were essentially similar before training with REHABIT was begun. The subjects were also similar with respect to age, education, and gender distribution, and the only known difference between the groups related to cognitive training.

Neuropsychological retesting was done for both groups 12 months after the initial examination. The group that had received no treatment showed little change in their test results, earning scores essentially similar to those that were obtained initially. However, the group receiving training with REHABIT demonstrated significant improvement on 18 of 30 measures.

These studies also included six subjects who had continued cognitive rehabilitation over a second year. Improvement in neuropsychological test scores from year one to year two continued on 42% of the measures, yielding evidence of statistically significant improvement on 90% of the tests in the Battery used for assessment over the 2-year period.

Sena et al. (1986a) administered an extensive range of neuropsychological tests to family members of the brain-injured sample in order to assess changes at a 12-month interval. They found that the family members who had not sustained brain damage or disease showed minimal changes on the test results obtained 12 months later. Another study by Sena et al. (1986b) compared test results of brain-injured subjects and those of the family members, and found that the brain-injured subjects who had received cognitive retraining showed substantially more improvement than their family members.

Alfano and Meyerink (1986) and Meyerink et al. (1985) have also reported a great degree of improvement of neuropsychological functions in brain-injured persons who received training oriented toward remediation of deficits as compared with a match control group, most of whom had received only traditional rehabilitation therapies such as speech therapy, occupational therapy, or physical therapy. Excellent reviews of this subject have also been published by Alfano and Finlayson (1987) and Finlayson et al. (1987). In summary, this series of studies supports a conclusion that cognitive retraining is of value in facilitating the recovery process in persons with brain injury.

Summary

We have presented a brief description of the Halstead-Reitan Neuropsychological Test Battery, including information that relates the test results to the biological condition of the brain, as well as the implications and uses of the test results for retraining neuropsychological deficits.

This chapter reviewed the roots from which Halstead began his investigations, the significance of his original collaboration with neurological surgeons, and the long-term implications of his practical approach of observing the problems and limitations in everyday living experienced by brain-damaged patients. This practical approach resulted in the development of neuropsychological tests that represent standardized experiments in adaptive behavior as contrasted with more conventional psychometric instruments.

The HRB was gradually developed by adding tests, organized in accordance with complementary inferential procedures, until a battery had been developed that covered the full range of neuropsychological dysfunction as determined by evaluation of thousands of patients with brain disease and damage. The sensitivity of the HRB to neuropsychological deficit has been demonstrated by the differential relationship of the test results to a broad range of neurological variables including location, type, and status of brain lesion. Recent research has demonstrated the value of results of the HRB with relation to a number of current clinical problems, ranging from deficits in mild head injury, the relation of attribute variables to neuropsychological test results, the possibility of specific frontal lobe deficits, to the development of an index for dissimulation or possible malingering. This comprehensive development of a set of

measures sensitive to cerebral damage has laid the groundwork for a cognitive retraining program that incorporates neuropsychological evaluation (identification of the subject's neuropsychological needs) and cognitive retraining, using an approach that can be designed to restore the individual's functional ability structure (as contrasted with approaches oriented only toward a general, nonspecific notion of "brain damage").

References

Aita, J. A., Armitage, S. G., Reitan, R. M., and Rabinovitz, A. (1947a). The use of certain psychological tests in the evaluation of brain injury. *Journal of General Psychology, 37,* 25–44.

Aita, J. A., Reitan, R. M., and Ruth, J. M. (1947b). Rorschach's Test as a diagnostic aid in brain injury. *American Journal of Psychiatry, 103,* 70–79.

Alfano, A. M., and Meyerink, L. H. (1986). Cognitive retraining with brain-injured adults. *VA Practitioner, 12,* 13.

Alfano, D. P., and Finlayson, M.A.J. (1987). Clinical neuropsychology in rehabilitation. *The Clinical Neuropsychologist, 1,* 105–123.

Alves, W. M., and Jane, J. A. (1985). Mild brain injury: Damage and outcome. In D. P. Becker and J. T. Povlishock, eds., *Central Nervous System Trauma Research Status Report.* Bethesda, MD: National Institute of Neurological and Communicative Disorders and Stroke, National Institutes of Health, pp. 255–270.

American Psychiatric Association. (1994). *Diagnostic and Statistical Manual of Mental Disorders (DSM-IV)* (4th Ed.). Washington, D.C.: American Psychiatric Press.

Axelrod, B. N., Goldman, R. S., and Henry, R. R. (1992). Sensitivity of the Mini-Mental State Examination to frontal lobe dysfunction in normal aging. *Journal of Clinical Psychology, 48,* 68–71.

Barth, J. R., Macciocchi, S. N., Giordani, B., Rimel, R., Jane, J. A., and Boll, T. J. (1983). Neuropsychological sequelae of minor head injury. *Neurosurgery, 13,* 529–533.

Bigler, E. D. (1988). Frontal lobe damage and neuropsychological assessment. *Archives of Clinical Neuropsychology, 3,* 279–297.

Binder, L. M. (1990). Malingering following minor head trauma. *The Clinical Neuropsychologist, 4,* 25–36.

Binder, L. M. (1993). Assessment of malingering

after mild head trauma with the Portland Digit Recognition Test. *Journal of Clinical and Experimental Neuropsychology*, 15, 170–182. [Published erratum appears in *Journal of Clinical and Experimental Neuropsychology*, 15, 852.]

Binet, A., and Simon, T. (1916). *The Development of Intelligence in Children*. Baltimore: Williams and Wilkins.

Boll, T. J. (1982). Behavioral sequelae of head injury. In P. R. Cooper, ed., *Head Injury*. Baltimore: Williams and Wilkins, pp. 363–375.

Boone, K. B., Miller, B. L., Lesser, I. M., Hill, E., and D'Elia, L. (1990). Performance on frontal lobe tests in healthy, older individuals. *Developmental Neuropsychology*, 6, 215–223.

Butters, M. A., Kaszniak, A. W., Glisky, E. L., Eslinger, P. J., and Schacter, D. L. (1994). Recency discrimination deficits in frontal lobe patients. *Neuropsychology*, 8, 343–353.

Chouinard, M. J., and Braun, C.M.J. (1993). A meta-analysis of the relative sensitivity of neuropsychological screening tests. *Journal of Clinical and Experimental Neuropsychology*, 15, 591–607.

Christensen, A. (1975). *Luria's Neuropsychological Investigation*. New York: Spectrum.

Costa, L. (1988). Clinical neuropsychology: Prospects and problems. *The Clinical Neuropsychologist*, 2, 3–11.

Cullum, C., Heaton, R. K., and Grant, I. (1991). Psychogenic factors influencing neuropsychological performance: Somatoform disorders, factitious disorders, and malingering. In H. O. Doerr and A. S. Carlin, eds., *Forensic Neuropsychology: Legal and Scientific Bases*. New York: Guilford Press, pp. 141–171.

Dean, R. S. (1985). Review of Halstead-Reitan Neuropsychological Test Battery. In J. V. Mitchell, ed., *The Ninth Mental Measurements Yearbook*. Highland Park, NJ: The Gryphon Press, pp. 642–646.

DeMyer, W. E. (1994). *Technique of the Neurologic Examination. A Programmed Text*. (4th Ed.). New York: McGraw-Hill.

Dikmen, S., McLean, A., and Temkin, N. (1986). Neuropsychological and psychosocial consequences of minor head injury. *Journal of Neurology, Neurosurgery, and Psychiatry*, 49, 1227–1232.

Dikmen, S., and Reitan, R. M. (1976). Psychological deficits and recovery of functions after head injury. *Transactions of the American Neurological Association*, 101, 72–77.

Dikmen, S., and Reitan, R. M. (1977a). Emotional sequelae of head injury. *Annals of Neurology*, 2, 492–494.

Dikmen, S., and Reitan, R. M. (1977b). MMPI correlates of adaptive ability deficits in patients with brain lesions. *Journal of Nervous and Mental Disease*, 165, 247–254.

Dikmen, S., Reitan, R. M., and Temkin, N. R. (1983). Neuropsychological recovery in head injury. *Archives of Neurology*, 40, 333–338.

Doehring, D. G., and Reitan, R. M. (1961a). Behavioral consequences of brain damage associated with homonymous field visual defects. *Journal of Comparative and Physiological Psychology*, 54, 489–492.

Doehring, D. G., and Reitan, R. M. (1961b). Certain language and non-language disorders in brain-damaged patients with homonymous visual field defects. *Archives of Neurology and Psychiatry*, 5, 294–299.

Doehring, D. G., and Reitan, R. M. (1962). Concept attainment of human adults with lateralized cerebral lesions. *Perceptual and Motor Skills*, 14, 27–33.

Doehring, D. G., Reitan, R. M., and Kløve, H. (1961). Changes in patterns of intelligence test performances associated with homonymous visual field defects. *Journal of Nervous and Mental Disease*, 132, 227–233.

Doerr, H. O., and Carlin, A. S. (1991). *Forensic Neuropsychology: Legal and Scientific Bases*. New York: Guilford Press.

Farmer, M. E. (1994). Cognitive deficits related to major organ failure. The potential role of neuropsychological testing. *Neuropsychology Review*, 4, 117–160.

Faust, D., Hart, K., and Guilmette, T. J. (1988). Pediatric malingering: The capacity of children to fake believable deficits on neuropsychological testing. *Journal of Consulting and Clinical Psychology*, 56, 578–582.

Fiducia, D., and O'Leary, D. S. (1990). Development of a behavior attributed to the frontal lobes and the relationship to other cognitive functions. *Developmental Neuropsychology*, 6, 85–94.

Finlayson, M.A.J., Alfano, D. P., and Sullivan, J. F. (1987). A neuropsychological approach to cognitive remediation: Microcomputer applications. *Canadian Psychology*, 28, 180–190.

Fitzhugh, K. B., Fitzhugh, L. C., and Reitan, R. M. (1961). Psychological deficits in relation to acuteness of brain dysfunction. *Journal of Consulting Psychology*, 25, 61–66.

Fitzhugh, K. B., Fitzhugh, L. C., and Reitan, R. M. (1962a). The relationship of acuteness of organic brain dysfunction to Trail Making Test performances. *Perceptual and Motor Skills, 15,* 399–403.

Fitzhugh, K. B., Fitzhugh, L. C., and Reitan, R. M. (1962b). Wechsler-Bellevue comparisons in groups with "chronic" and "current" lateralized and diffuse brain lesions. *Journal of Consulting Psychology, 26,* 306–310.

Fitzhugh, K. B., Fitzhugh, L. C., and Reitan, R. M. (1963). Effects of "chronic" and "current" lateralized and non-lateralized cerebral lesions upon Trail Making Test performances. *Journal of Nervous and Mental Disease, 137,* 82–87.

Fitzhugh, L. C., Fitzhugh, K. B., and Reitan, R. M. (1962). Sensorimotor deficits of brain-damaged subjects in relation to intellectual level. *Perceptual and Motor Skills, 15,* 603–608.

Franzen, M. D., Iverson, G. L., and McCracken, L. M. (1990). The detection of malingering in neuropsychological assessment. *Neuropsychology Review, 1,* 247–279.

Gentilini, M., Nichelli, P., and Schoenhuber, R. (1989). Assessment of attention in mild head injury. In H. S. Levin, H. M. Eisenberg, and A. L. Benton, eds., *Mild Head Injury.* New York: Oxford University Press, pp. 163–175.

Guys, J. A., and Willis, W. G. (1991). Validation of executive function tasks with young children. *Developmental Neuropsychology, 7,* 487–501.

Goldman-Rakic, P. S. (1993). Specification of higher cortical functions. *Journal of Head Trauma Rehabilitation, 8,* 13–23.

Goldstein, K. (1942a). *Aftereffects of Brain Injuries in War.* New York: Grune and Stratton.

Goldstein, K. (1942b). The two ways of adjustment of the organism to cerebral defects. *Journal of Mt. Sinai Hospital, 9,* 504–513.

Grafman, J., Sirigu, A., Spector, L., and Hendler, J. (1993). Damage to the prefrontal cortex leads to decomposition of structured event complexes. *Journal of Head Trauma Rehabilitation, 8,* 73–87.

Grodzinsky, G. M., and Diamond, R. (1992). Frontal lobe functioning in boys with attention-deficit hyperactivity disorder. *Developmental Neuropsychology, 8,* 427–445.

Gronwall, D. (1976). Performance changes during recovery from closed head injury. *Proceedings of the Australian Association of Neurology, 13,* 143–147.

Gronwall, D. (1977). Paced auditory serial addition task: A measure of recovery from concussion. *Perceptual and Motor Skills, 44,* 367–373.

Gronwall, D. (1989). Cumulative and persisting effects of concussion on attention and cognition. In H. S. Levin, H. M. Eisenberg, and A. L. Benton, eds., *Mild Head Injury.* New York: Oxford University Press, pp. 153–162.

Gronwall, D., and Sampson, H. (1974). *The Psychological Effects of Concussion.* Auckland, NZ: Auckland University Press.

Gronwall, D., and Wrightson, P. (1974). Delayed recovery after minor head injury. *Lancet, 2,* 605–609.

Guilmette, T. J. (1991). Cognitive and behavioral symptoms of mild head injury: Considerations for brain damage litigation. *Rhode Island Bar Journal, 39,* 91–96.

Halstead, W. C. (1947). *Brain and Intelligence: A Quantitative Study of the Frontal Lobes.* Chicago: University of Chicago Press.

Hart, T., and Jacobs, H. E. (1993). Rehabilitation and management of behavioral disturbances following frontal lobe injury. *Journal of Head Trauma Rehabilitation, 8,* 1–12.

Hartlage, L. C., and DeFilippis, N. A. (1983). History of neuropsychological assessment. In C. J. Golden and P. J. Vicente, eds., *Foundations of Clinical Neuropsychology.* New York: Plenum Press, pp. 1–23.

Hebb, D. O. (1939). Intelligence in man after large removals of cerebral tissue: Report of four left frontal lobe cases. *Journal of General Psychology, 21,* 73–87.

Hebb, D. O. (1941). Human intelligence after removal of cerebral tissue from the right frontal lobe. *Journal of General Psychology, 25,* 257–265.

Heimburger, R. F., and Reitan, R. M. (1961). Easily administered written test for lateralizing brain lesions. *Journal of Neurosurgery, 18,* 301–312.

Incagnoli, T., Goldstein, G., and Golden, C. J. (1986). *Clinical Application of Neuropsychological Test Batteries.* New York: Plenum Press.

Jarvis, P. E., and Barth, J. T. (1994). *The Halstead-Reitan Neuropsychological Battery: A Guide to Interpretation and Clinical Applications.* Odessa, FL: Psychological Assessment Resources.

Kløve, H. (1959). Relationship of differential electroencephalographic patterns of distribution of Wechsler-Bellevue scores. *Neurology, 9,* 871–876.

Kløve, H., and Reitan, R. M. (1958). The effect of dysphasia and spatial distortion on Wechsler-Bellevue results. *Archives of Neurology and Psychiatry, 80,* 708–713.

Lee, G. P., Loring, D. W., and Martin, R. C. (1992). Rey's 15-Item Visual Memory Test for the detection of malingering: Normative observations on patients with neurological disorders. *Psychological Assessment, 4,* 43–46.

Levin, H. S., Benton, A. L., and Grossman, R. G. (1982). *Neurobehavioral Consequences of Closed Head Injury.* New York: Oxford University Press.

Levin, H. S., Eisenberg, H. M., and Benton, A. L. (1989). *Mild Head Injury.* New York: Oxford University Press.

Lezak, M. D. (1993). Newer contributions to the neuropsychological assessment of executive functions. *Journal of Head Trauma Rehabilitation, 8,* 24–31.

McLean, A., Temkin, N. R., Dikmen, S., and Wyler, A. R. (1983). The behavioral sequelae of head injury. *Journal of Clinical Neuropsychology, 5,* 361–376.

Meier, M. J. (1985). Review of Halstead-Reitan Neuropsychological Test Battery. In J. V. Mitchell, ed., *The Ninth Mental Measurements Yearbook.* Highland Park, NJ: The Gryphon Press, pp. 646–649.

Meyerink, L. H., Pendleton, M. G., Hughes, R. G., and Thompson, L. L. (1985). Effectiveness of cognitive retraining with brain-impaired adults. *Archives of Physical Medicine and Rehabilitation, 66,* 555.

Nies, K. J., and Sweet, J. J. (1994). Neuropsychological assessment and malingering: A critical review of past and present strategies. *Archives of Clinical Neuropsychology, 9,* 501–552.

Pankratz, L. (1988). Malingering on intellectual and neuropsychological measures. In R. Rogers, ed., *Clinical Assessment of Malingering and Deception.* New York: Guilford Press, pp. 169–192.

Reitan, R. M. (1955a). Certain differential effects of left and right cerebral lesions in human adults. *Journal of Comparative and Physiological Psychology, 48,* 474–477.

Reitan, R. M. (1955b). An investigation of the validity of Halstead's measures of biological intelligence. *Archives of Neurology and Psychiatry, 73,* 28–35.

Reitan, R. M. (1955c). The relation of the Trail Making Test to organic brain damage. *Journal of Consulting Psychology, 19,* 393–394.

Reitan, R. M. (1958). The validity of the Trail Making Test as an indicator of organic brain damage. *Perceptual and Motor Skills, 8,* 271–276.

Reitan, R. M. (1959). The comparative effects of brain damage on the Halstead Impairment Index and the Wechsler-Bellevue Scale. *Journal of Clinical Psychology, 15,* 281–285.

Reitan, R. M. (1964). Psychological deficits resulting from cerebral lesions in man. In J. M. Warren and K. A. Akert, eds., *The Frontal Granular Cortex and Behavior.* New York: McGraw-Hill, pp. 295–312.

Reitan, R. M. (1974). Methodological problems in clinical neuropsychology. In R. M. Reitan and L. A. Davison, eds., *Clinical Neuropsychology: Current Status and Applications.* Washington, D.C.: Hemisphere Publishing Corporation, pp. 19–46.

Reitan, R. M. (1984). *Aphasia and Sensory-Perceptual Deficits in Adults.* Tucson, AZ: Neuropsychology Press.

Reitan, R. M., and Sena, D. A. (1983). The efficacy of the REHABIT technique in remediation of brain-injured people. Paper presented at the meeting of the American Psychological Association, Anaheim, CA.

Reitan, R. M., and Wolfson, D. (1986). *Traumatic Brain Injury. Vol. I. Pathophysiology and Neuropsychological Evaluation.* Tucson, AZ: Neuropsychology Press.

Reitan, R. M., and Wolfson, D. (1988). *Traumatic Brain Injury. Vol. II. Recovery and Rehabilitation.* Tucson, AZ: Neuropsychology Press.

Reitan, R. M., and Wolfson, D. (1989). The Seashore Rhythm Test and brain functions. *The Clinical Neuropsychologist, 3,* 70–78.

Reitan, R. M., and Wolfson, D. (1992). *Neuroanatomy and Neuropathology: A Clinical Guide for Neuropsychologists* (2nd ed.). Tucson, AZ: Neuropsychology Press.

Reitan, R. M., and Wolfson, D. (1993). *The Halstead-Reitan Neuropsychological Test Battery: Theory and Clinical Interpretation* (2nd ed). Tucson, AZ: Neuropsychology Press.

Reitan, R. M., and Wolfson, D. (1994a). Practical approaches to puzzling problems in interpretation using the Halstead-Reitan Battery. Workshop presented at the annual meeting of the National Academy of Neuropsychology, Orlando, FL.

Reitan, R. M., and Wolfson, D. (1994b). A selective and critical review of neuropsychological deficits and the frontal lobes. *Neuropsychology Review, 4,* 161–198.

Reitan, R. M., and Wolfson, D. (1995a). *Neuropsychological Evaluation of Young Children.* Tucson, AZ: Neuropsychology Press.

Reitan, R. M., and Wolfson, D. (1995b). The influence of age and education on neuropsychological test results. *The Clinical Neuropsychologist, 9,* 151–158.

Reitan, R. M., and Wolfson, D. (in press, a). Relationships of age and education on Wechsler Adult Intelligence Scale IQ values in brain-damaged and non-brain-damaged groups. *The Clinical Neuropsychologist.*

Reitan, R. M., and Wolfson, D. (in press, b). Consistency of neuropsychological test scores of head-injured subjects involved in litigation compared with head-injured subjects not involved in litigation: Development of the Retest Consistency Index. *The Clinical Neuropsychologist.*

Reitan, R. M., and Wolfson, D. (in press, c). Consistency of responses on retesting among head-injured subjects in litigation versus head-injured subjects not in litigation. *Applied Neuropsychology.*

Reitan, R. M., and Wolfson, D. (in press, d). The question of validity of neuropsychological test scores among head-injured litigants: Development of a Dissimulation Index. *Archives of Clinical Neuropsychology.*

Rimel, R. W., Giordani, B., Barth, J. T., Boll, T. J., and Jane, J. A. (1981). Disability caused by minor head injury. *Neurosurgery, 9,* 221–228.

Rimel, R. W., Giordani, B., Barth, J. T., and Jane, J. A. (1982). Moderate head injury: Completing the clinical spectrum of brain trauma. *Neurosurgery, 11,* 344–351.

Rogers, R. (1988). *Clinical Assessment of Malingering and Deception.* New York: Guilford Press.

Ruff, R. M., Levin, H. S., Mattis, S., High, W. M., Marshall, L. F., Eisenberg, H. M., and Tabaddor, K. (1989). Recovery of memory after mild head injury: A three-center study. In H. S. Levin, H. M. Eisenberg, and A. L. Benton, eds., *Mild Head Injury.* New York: Oxford University Press, pp. 176–188.

Ruff, R. M., Wylie, T., and Tennant, W. (1993). Malingering and malingering-like aspects of mild closed head injury. *Journal of Head Trauma Rehabilitation, 8,* 60–73.

Russell, E. W., Neuringer, C., and Goldstein, G. (1970). *Assessment of Brain Damage: A Neuropsychological Key Approach.* New York: Wiley.

Rybash, J. M., and Colilla, J. L. (1994). Source memory deficits and frontal lobe functioning in children. *Developmental Neuropsychology, 10,* 67–73.

Schretlen, D. J. (1988). The use of psychological tests to identify malingered symptoms of mental disorder. *Clinical Psychology Review, 8,* 451–476.

Schretlen, D., Brandt, J., Krafft, L., and Van Gorp, W. (1991). Some caveats in using the Rey 15-Item Memory Test to detect malingered amnesia. *Psychological Assessment, 3,* 667–672.

Schwartz, M. F., Mayer, N. H., FitzpatrickDeSalme, E. J., and Montgomery, M. W. (1993). Cognitive theory and the study of everyday action disorders after brain damage. *Journal of Head Trauma Rehabilitation, 8,* 59–72.

Sena, D. A. (1985). The effectiveness of cognitive retraining for brain-impaired individuals. *The International Journal of Clinical Neuropsychology, 7,* 62.

Sena, D. A., Sena, H. M., and Sunde, R. R. (1986a). Changes in cognitive functioning on non-impaired family members. *Archives of Clinical Neuropsychology, 1,* 263.

Sena, D. A., Sena, H. M., and Sunde, R. R. (1986b). Comparison of changes in cognitive functioning of non-impaired family members and brain-impaired patients. *Archives of Clinical Neuropsychology, 1,* 262.

Sena, H. M., and Sena, D. A. (1986). A quantitative validation of the effectiveness of cognitive retraining. *Archives of Clinical Neuropsychology, 1,* 74.

Sherer, M., and Adams, R. L. (1993). Cross-validation of Reitan and Wolfson's Neuropsychological Deficit Scales. *Archives of Clinical Neuropsychology, 8,* 429–435.

Shute, G. E., and Huertas, V. (1990). Developmental variability in frontal lobe function. *Developmental Neuropsychology, 6,* 1–11.

Sohlberg, M. M., Mateer, C. A., and Stuss, D. T. (1993). Contemporary approaches to the management of executive control dysfunction. *Journal of Head Trauma Rehabilitation, 8,* 45–58.

Van Zomeren, A. H. (1981). *Reaction Time and Attention After Closed Head Injury.* Lisse: Swets and Zeitlinger.

Varney, N. R., and Menefee, L. (1993). Psychosocial and executive deficits following closed head injury: Implications for orbital frontal cortex. *Journal of Head Trauma Rehabilitation, 8,* 32–44.

Wang, P. L. (1987). Concept formation and frontal lobe function: The search for a clinical frontal lobe test. In E. Perecman, ed., *The Frontal Lobes Revisited.* New York: The IRBN Press, pp. 189–205.

Welsh, M. C., Pennington, B. F., and Groisser, D. B. (1991). A normative-developmental study of executive function: A window on prefrontal function in children. *Developmental Neuropsychology, 7,* 131–149.

Wheeler, L., Burke, C. J., and Reitan, R. M. (1963). An application of discriminant functions to the problem of predicting brain damage using behavioral variables. *Perceptual and Motor Skills [Monograph suppl.], 16,* 417–440.

Wheeler, L., and Reitan, R. M. (1962). The presence and laterality of brain damage predicted from responses to a short Aphasia Screening Test. *Perceptual and Motor Skills, 15,* 783–799.

Wolfson, D. (1992). *The Neuropsychological History Questionnaire.* Tucson, AZ: Neuropsychology Press.

Wolfson, D., and Reitan, R. M. (1995). Cross-validation of the General Neuropsychological Deficit Scale (GNDS). *Archives of Clinical Neuropsychology, 10,* 125–131.

2 The Analytical Approach to Neuropsychological Assessment

PAT McKENNA and ELIZABETH K. WARRINGTON

The major advances in neurology at the turn of the century were followed by a developmental period that lasted until the late 1950s, when clinicians no longer felt forced to concede that the brain was characterized by homogeneity of function. Remnants of equipotentialist thinking can still be found, but they are confined to minor aspects of organization such as the controversy over whether or not rudimentary language can be coaxed from the nondominant hemisphere in patients who have sustained near-total damage to the dominant hemisphere. Other areas of investigation, which still give a certain degree of credence to this idea, are those of functional organization in left-handed subjects and patients who have sustained early brain damage. For the most part, however, clinicians and neuroscientists agree about the broad functional specialization and localization along the dimensions of language, perception, memory, and movement.

Beyond this point, however, any further investigation encounters diverse schools of thought, a proliferation of documented syndromes of cognitive disorders, and an unwieldy empirical literature without, more often than not, any clear theoretical basis, and certainly not one that is shared throughout the field. This state of the science clearly limits the contribution of neuropsychologists to the diagnosis, assessment, and treatment of patients because the efficiency of clinical tools must ultimately depend on the progress of research. Indeed, Yates (1954) and Piercy (1959) very clearly described the frustration of being a clinician at this stage of development and could lament the lack of an adequate theory of brain function and the concomitant limitations of clinical tests.

The present climate is far more optimistic—developments in neuropsychological research are accelerating, and we are now attempting to incorporate the new levels of understanding into an expanding battery of more efficient and specific tests of brain function. These developments have resulted from a method that combines traditional neurological observation with the modern empiricism of cognitive psychology, which we claim overcomes the very real barrier posed by notions of equipotentiality.

Until recently, clinical tests fell into one of two categories. First, experimental psychologists provided formal tests based on global facets of cognitive behavior along gross dimensions such as aptitudes and intelligence. These tests were really measures of behavioral skills—the final orchestrated result of many different cognitive functions. They were originally intended for, and far better suited to, group studies within the normal population. Second, a "hunch" led the more innovative clinicians to improvise test stimuli to collect samples of behavior that indicated more skill-specific difficulties in particular patients. This latter approach underlies the anecdotal evidence of neurologists who, though providing new insights, could not progress without formal tests to validate and replicate results. Our method is a synthesis of both the empirical and intuitive styles and is one that started to evolve in the late 1950s and still continues to do so. In this chapter we attempt to describe how this methodology has affected the theoretical orientation, research techniques, and clinical tests of our department and finally their application to the assessment of neurological and neuropsychiatric patients.

Theoretical Orientation

Evidence is rapidly accumulating to show that the organization of cognitive functions is more complex than has hitherto been supposed. Beyond the first sensory levels of analysis, the cumulative evidence for higher stages of information processing has not revealed any parallel processing between the hemispheres but instead increasingly points to their independent organization and specialization. This appears to be particularly applicable to the temporal and parietal lobes, those areas subserving functions with which we have made most progress. The focus of this research has been memory (short-term, semantic, and event), perception, and reading and writing, and how these skills interrelate. The benefits of a commitment to the theory of cerebral specialization are already evident in the analysis of complex neurological syndromes. For example, constructional apraxia, most commonly observed in a patient's inability to draw, is often described as arising from either left or right hemisphere damage. It now seems clear that such deficits arising as a result of right hemisphere damage are secondary to impaired space perception, which precludes the ability to draw, whereas left hemisphere lesions give rise to the primary praxis deficit, the inability to carry out purposive voluntary movements (Warrington, 1969; McCarthy and Warrington, 1990).

Some of the most persuasive evidence for hemisphere specialization comes from the relationship between perception and meaning. We have found that the post-Rolandic regions of the right hemisphere appear to be critical for visuo-spatial and perceptual analysis, whereas the post-Rolandic regions of the left hemisphere are implicated in the semantic analysis of perceptual input. Furthermore, if one accepts this differentiation of modalities in semantic analysis, certain controversies are resolved. For example, word comprehension is generally acknowledged to be a predominantly left hemisphere function, but the visual equivalent, visual object agnosia, is often denied (Riddoch et al., 1988), ignored (Caramazza and Hillis, 1990), or implicitly attributed to the right hemisphere (Farah, 1990). This state of affairs provides enormous scope for clinicians and researchers alike to communicate at cross purposes and, like the apraxia example above, it illustrates the conceptual and terminological confusion that often serves to fuel and perpetuate controversies in the literature.

The degree and complexity of specialization of brain functioning are even more striking when one investigates a particular cognitive system. The following sections outline some of the evidence for delineation of complex behaviors into systems and their subsystems and illustrates that the deficits witnessed in patients with cerebral pathology can be analyzed in terms of a greater degree of functional specialization than had hitherto been supposed.

A major consequence of this theoretical orientation has been a reappraisal of the role of traditional neurological syndromes—which tend to be clusters of commonly occurring symptoms in neurological patients—as a basis for research. This basis of classification may reflect no more than the facts of anatomy, such as the distribution of the arterial system, and may contribute little to the understanding of the cerebral organization of the components of complex skills. The commonly adopted strategy of comparing Broca and Wernicke aphasics is a clear example. The traditional syndromes of language breakdown are now seen to fractionate. For example, we have found conduction aphasia to be a double deficit of at least two partially unrelated functions—articulation and short-term memory (Shallice and Warrington, 1977a). The already quoted example of constructional apraxia is a further example of the multicomponent nature of a traditional neurological syndrome and while it is understandable how neurologists came to give the same label to such fundamentally different deficits, there is little justification for neuropsychologists to perpetuate the confusion. A syndrome should now be function-based rather than symptom-based and should serve to elucidate the nature of a neurobehavioral system or one of its subsystems.

In summary, it is our experience that cognitive functions can best be studied and understood by an information-processing approach to the analysis of a complex skill into its functional components and subcomponents. This approach has resulted in a commitment to a theory of differentiation and localization between and within cognitive functions that overrides notions of equipotentiality.

Research Methods and Testing Materials

The three stages in our research are, first, the use of a single case study to observe and document properties of a neurological syndrome or cognitive deficit; second, the validation of significant findings in appropriate clinical groups to test their pragmatic strength in terms of frequency of occurrence, detectability, and their localization value; and third, the harnessing of results of these validation studies to new tests that have greater specificity and sensitivity for diagnosis and assessment, our ultimate aim being to provide an exhaustive battery of function-specific and subfunction-specific tests.

Shallice (1979, 1988) has provided a full discussion of the single case study approach, but for the purpose of this chapter suffice it to say that given a patient with an observed deficit that appears to be selective (to a system or subsystem) and is consistent and quantifiably significant, then a series of exhaustive experiments can be prepared and repeated to specify the nature and extent of the deficit. One important aspect of single case study methodology is the notion of dissociation. For example, given a patient who has a specific difficulty in reading abstract

words as opposed to concrete ones (Shallice and Warrington, 1975), the conclusion that concrete and abstract words are organized separately requires a prediction that it is equally possible to observe the reverse deficit such that a patient cannot read concrete words but can read abstract words (Warrington, 1981a). Thus, for any particular hypothesis of functional organization, it is possible to draw up a table of predictions of double or even triple dissociations. Without the use of single case studies, it would be impossible, or extremely difficult, to progress in mapping out the organization of cognitive skills.

The second, or intermediate, stage in our research is, when appropriate, to prepare a series of tests based on the results of a single case study for a group study to provide information on lateralization, localization, and frequency of the observation in the clinical population. For example, having discovered single incidents of material-specific deficits of perception (Whiteley and Warrington, 1977), a consecutive series of patients with right hemisphere lesions were tested using the same stimulus materials to determine the frequency of these dissociations (Warrington, 1982a).

The third stage aims to standardize tests that have been successfully validated in order to provide more appropriate tools for clinical use in the diagnosis and assessment of cognitive deficits. We are now attempting to standardize tests of literacy, memory, perception, naming, and reasoning, all of which have evolved from our more analytical research investigations.

Clinical Testing of Cognitive Functions

Intelligence and General Factors

Despite our increasing awareness of and sensitivity to the individual variation in strengths and weaknesses of different cognitive skills, it is undoubtedly the case that patients can still usefully be screened according to general level of intellectual ability. Though age affects many skills to their detriment, an individual's intelligence level remains constant in relation to his age group.

Furthermore, in any given individual, levels of performance on different aspects of cognitive behavior will tend to be more similar than not. In common with most clinicians in Britain and the United States we use the concept of IQ as measured by the Wechsler Adult Intelligence Scale–Revised (WAIS-R) for a preliminary overview of the patient (Wechsler, 1955, 1981). Though it is an example of subtests that are sampling patterns of skills rather than specific functions, it is able to give a rough guide to some of the more commonly occurring syndromes. The Progressive Matrices—a test of abstract problem solving using nonverbal stimulus materials—is also useful in this regard (Raven, 1960). We have recently standardized and validated a test of inductive reasoning that has parallel verbal and spatial forms (Langdon and Warrington, 1995).

At this general level of clinical assessment, the overriding and growing problem is to detect an incipient decline in intellectual powers over and above the aging process and often in the presence of depression. Our efforts to provide some indication of premorbid level of functioning have resulted in a formula based originally on the Schonell reading test, which can predict optimal level of functioning up to IQ 115, and in the National Adult Reading Test (NART), which has a higher ceiling of IQ 131 (Nelson and McKenna, 1975; Nelson, 1992). These tests were made viable in the first instance on the findings that reading vocabulary is IQ-related (reinforcing the point made above that performances on different tests tend to be correlated) and that reading is one of the most resistant skills in any process of intellectual decline (Paque and Warrington, 1995). The NART resulted from research on dyslexic syndromes that showed word knowledge to be essential for reading irregularly spelled words.

Visual Perception

We are often so preoccupied with the complexity of meaning that it renders us insensitive to our remarkable (and probably more perfected) skill in organizing our visual world. This is in spite of there being a comparable, if not greater, area of brain subserving visual function. Our evidence indicates that the perceptual systems are capable of equating diverse percepts of a single stimulus-object and of categorizing certain visual stimuli *before*, and independently of, any investment of meaning in the percept. Should this appear paradoxical, it is only because of a commonsense bias toward semantics as the essential criterion of intelligent behavior. Our evidence points to two distinct stages of visual perception prior to semantic analysis, and individual case studies show dissociations between and within all three stages.

Before implicating a deficit at the level of categorical perception, it is necessary to establish that visual analysis is intact. It is known that lesions of the primary and secondary visual cortex give rise to, in the first place, impaired brightness and acuity discrimination and in the second, deficits of color, contour, and location. Visual disorientation, sufficiently marked to be a handicap in everyday life, is invariably associated with bilateral lesions. However, more detailed investigation has revealed unilateral visual disorientation in both the right or left half field of vision in patients with a lesion in the contralateral hemisphere (Cole et al., 1962). This also appears to be the case for color imperception (Albert et al., 1975). The inference from such observations is that the functions of the secondary visual cortex, as is the case for the primary visual cortex, maintain a retinotopic organization. Thus, there appears to be no lateralization at this stage of visual analysis, and the identification of such deficits with "free" vision indicates bilateral dysfunction.

The more complex processes of the second stage of perceptual analysis appear to be functions lateralized to the right hemisphere. Two major systems have been identified—that subserving space perception and that subserving form perception. The overriding conclusion from research to date is that these two classes of deficit are dissociated. Furthermore, recent findings suggest that each of these may fractionate into subcomponents.

SPACE PERCEPTION. The concept of space perception implies more than the location of a single point in space; it implies the integration of successive or simultaneous stimuli in a spatial schema. The essential principle guiding our methods of testing for spatial disorders is that the involvement of other cognitive skills be minimized, in particular, praxis skills, including drawing. The test we have evolved, the Visual Object and Space Perception Battery (VOSP, Warrington and James, 1991) has incorporated three such tests ranging in level of difficulty from counting scattered dots to fine position discrimination (the subject is merely required to say which figure has the dot *exactly* in the center). The ability to perform such tests has been shown to be selectively impaired in patients with right parietal lesions (Taylor and Warrington, 1973). Further observations suggest there may be two components of this syndrome—the ability to discriminate position and a dissociable defect in the more abstract facility of spatial imaging. In this regard, we are exploring the use of the Stanford-Binet cube analysis tests also included in the battery.

FORM PERCEPTION. This stage of visual perceptual analysis—postsensory but presemantic—is difficult to conceptualize and is best introduced by the research findings that led to it being postulated. First, we have shown that although some patients were able to identify and name prototypical views of common objects, they were significantly impaired in identifying the same object from an unfamiliar orientation or less typical view (Warrington and Taylor, 1973). In a further experiment, it was shown that when a prototypical view was paired with a less usual view, patients with a right parietal lesion were unable to judge whether the two had the same *physical* identity (Warrington and Taylor, 1978). It was on the basis of these studies that an unusual-view photograph test was devised. Furthermore, it has been shown in both individual case and group studies that patients with unilateral lesions of the left hemisphere resulting in impaired semantic processing can do these tests rela-

tively normally (e.g., Warrington, 1975; Warrington and Taylor, 1978) though they may not know what the object is. A final set of tests that manipulate the angle of view of silhouettes of objects was derived from these earlier stages and is also incorporated in the VOSP.

Further tests, based on similar principles of departure from the prototype, use other visual stimuli such as letters and faces. In addition to providing a more comprehensive measure of form perception, discrepancies in performance of some individuals alerted us to the possibility of further fractionation of this perceptual function, namely, the material selectivity of perceptual categorization. Comparing perception of objects, faces, letters, and buildings in 50 patients with right hemisphere lesions, we have observed nine of the possible 12 single dissociations and three of the possible six double dissociations (Warrington, 1982a). Again, these deficits are all held to be at a postsensory presemantic perceptual processing lateralized to the right hemisphere.

The Semantic System

The function of the semantic system is to process percepts in order to achieve meaning. It is not a reasoning system, but a store of concepts, perhaps analogous to a thesaurus or encyclopedia. In the domain of nonverbal knowledge systems in man, the visual modality is by far the most important. Extensive knowledge of the visual world is a very early acquisition and almost certainly precedes verbal knowledge. However, language, par excellence, illustrates a system subserving meaning. Our approach to investigating and assessing the verbal semantic system has been to focus on single word comprehension, thus mirroring an early manifestation of language acquisition.

Our evidence to date suggests that there can be a double dissociation between deficits of visual and verbal knowledge, indicating that the semantic system fractionates into at least two independent modality-specific systems and that they are both associated with damage to the posterior dominant hemisphere (for a review see McKenna and Warrington, 1993). This conclusion is based on evidence from (1) patients with intact recognition of the visual representation of a concept but not its verbal representation (verbal agnosia); (2) patients with the mirror image deficit—the recognition of the verbal representation of a concept but not its visual representation (visual agnosia); and (3) studies of patients in whom both verbal and visual representations of a concept are intact but a disconnection between the two systems (optic aphasia) can be demonstrated (e.g., Lhermitte and Beauvois, 1973; Manning and Campbell, 1992).

Within these two domains, the predominant recurrent findings are category specificity and a hierarchical organization. These findings derive from two lines of investigation. The first draws on evidence of the pattern of loss of conceptual knowledge in patients with agnosic deficits. It has been shown that supraordinate information is often relatively preserved. The order of loss of conceptual knowledge appears to be constant going from the particular to the general. Thus, a canary can be identified as living, animal, and a bird but not as yellow, small, and a pet. These effects have been demonstrated for visual as well as verbal knowledge and for comprehension of the written as well as the spoken word (Warrington and Shallice, 1979). Secondly, our investigations suggest that the selective impairment of particular semantic categories in naming and comprehension tasks occur much more commonly than has hitherto been supposed. It has long been accepted in the neurological literature that selective anomias for objects, symbols, colors, and body parts can occur, and our own growing evidence from individual case studies would add proper names (with further subdivision of people and place names), animate, inanimate, concrete, and abstract dimensions (Warrington, 1981b; Warrington and Shallice, 1984; Warrington and McCarthy, 1987). We would interpret these data in terms of the categorical organization of the semantic knowledge systems. Evidence for further subdivisions within these categories is available, and ongoing group studies on

patients with left hemisphere pathology have provided feedback on the incidence in our clinical population of category-specific impairment (McKenna and Parry, 1994a).

We have studied the organization of semantic memory for the most part as observed in agnosic, dysphasic, and dyslexic patients, but there is every reason to suppose that our formulations apply to other classes of conceptual knowledge. For example, we have observed a patient with a highly specific acalculia whereby the arithmetical facts of addition, subtraction, division, and multiplication were no longer accessible to him though he continued to display a superior facility with mathematical reasoning. It was argued that arithmetical facts are a further independent category of our knowledge systems (Warrington, 1982b).

In summary, it is held that there are modality-specific semantic systems that are hierarchically and categorically organized (Warrington and McCarthy, 1987). Our understanding of these systems is too incomplete as yet to do other than speculate on the range of modality-specific subsystems and categories and on their interaction with episodic memory, reasoning, and linguistics. However, the disproportionate difficulty in later life of learning new "facts" and skills compared with the recall of ongoing "events" would possibly be explained in maturational terms by the capacity of the semantic system reaching its asymptote by the time adulthood is reached.

The clinical relevance of our findings is twofold. First, at a conceptual level it has enabled us to differentiate and delineate a deficit of semantic processing, as opposed to sensory or perceptual processing, which can confidently be diagnosed as having pathology in the posterior dominant hemisphere. Secondly, new tests have been developed based on our findings. A test of arithmetical facts has been finalized for clinical use following the discovery of selective impairment of this ability in the patient described above (Jackson and Warrington, 1986), and a single word comprehension task has been validated in patients with unilateral cerebral lesions (Coughlan and Warrington, 1978). The emergence of patients with specific category loss restricted to one modality has further strengthened the argument for multiple representations of concepts in separate modality stores. One such example is the selective loss of the verbal representation of living things (McCarthy and Warrington, 1988). The Graded Naming Test (McKenna and Warrington, 1983) is now accompanied by a new category naming and comprehension test that can differentiate both category and modality effects (McKenna and Parry, 1994b). Although a formal clinical battery of visual semantic tests is not available, the Pyramids and Palm Trees Test can be used to compare visual and verbal semantics (Howard and Patterson, 1992). The differentiation of a deficit at the level of perceptual processing and semantic processing entirely within the visual domain can be tested by comparing the patient's ability to match photographs of objects by physical and functional identity (Warrington and Taylor, 1978) and by the Object Decision Test of the VOSP, a test that requires the viewer to recognize which black shape is actually a real object. This combination of standardized clinical tests and research techniques can thus provide an extensive array of methods with which to explore semantic deficits.

Literacy

Neurologists have long since identified two major syndromes of reading disorders: dyslexia with dysgraphia and dyslexia without dysgraphia. The value of this distinction was to acknowledge some independence of the reading and writing skills, but they did not succeed in developing this taxonomy further. More recently, there has been a renewed interest in this area. Patients with unique reading and writing difficulties have been investigated using experimental methods, and a detailed analysis of their deficits is yielding a coherent perspective of the organization of these skills.

With regard to reading, it has been suggested that acquired dyslexia can arise from "peripheral" or "central" deficits. Peripheral dyslexias share the property of failing to achieve a visual word-form (the integrity of the pattern or gestalt provided by the written word, or part thereof) at a purely visual level of analysis. These include (1) neglect dyslexia, characterized by letter substitutions at one end of a word, usually the beginning (Kinsbourne and Warrington, 1962; Warrington, 1991), (2) attentional dyslexia, when a single letter can be read but not if accompanied by other letters in the visual field (Shallice and Warrington, 1977b; Warrington et al., 1993), and (3) word-form or spelling dyslexia, characterized by letter-by-letter reading resulting in a greater difficulty reading words written in script than in print (Warrington and Shallice, 1980; Warrington and Langdon, 1994). On balance it is considered these difficulties do not reflect general properties of the perceptual system but are specific to the reading system.

Central dyslexias describe an inability to derive meaning from the written word given intact visual analysis of it. There is little disagreement in the present literature that there appear to be two main reading routes—the phonological and the semantic. These are the inevitable inferences from characteristics of two classes of acquired dyslexias. In the first type, there is a complete, or near complete, dependence on the use of phonology for reading. Thus, the patient can read regular words (those that use commonly occurring grapheme-phoneme correspondences) but is unable to read irregular words: the greater the deviation from the regular phoneme-grapheme correspondence the greater the difficulty in reading. In these patients, in whom the direct semantic route is inoperative, the characteristics of the phonological route are open to inspection. Though some patients in this category can apply only the most regular, grapheme-phoneme rules, others show a much more versatile facility, which leads us to believe that the properties of the phonological processing are more extensive than at first thought, such patients being able to use irregular rules to some extent (Shallice et al., 1983; McCarthy and Warrington, 1986).

In the second type of acquired dyslexia, there is an inability to use phonology and words are recognized as units analogous to pictures. Patients are able to read real words but cannot begin to read nonsense words. In the extreme case, they are unable to sound single letters or pronounce two-letter combinations. This type of dyslexic has a relatively (sometimes completely) intact semantic route, such that the visual word-form has direct access to verbal semantic systems. The properties and characteristics of the semantic route can be investigated in patients in whom the phonological route is inoperative and there has been partial damage to the semantic route. For example, category specificity has been observed (Warrington, 1981a) or indeed may be commonly the case (McKenna and Parry, 1994a). Furthermore, this class of dyslexic patient has been further subdivided into those having an "access" deficit or a "storage" deficit (Shallice and Warrington, 1980).

Following these advances in research on dyslexia, data have emerged from investigations on dysgraphic patients that show a similar organization for writing (Baxter and Warrington, 1987). A single case study of a patient who could not write irregular words but could write phonologically regular words, whether real or nonsense words, has been reported (Beauvois and Derouesne, 1979). Evidence for a double dissociation between the inferred phonological and direct routes to writing has now been found. Shallice (1981) has reported a patient who could write real words and letter names but could write neither nonsense syllables nor letter sounds.

A graded-difficulty irregular-word reading test is already available for clinical purposes, as described earlier, and a comparable graded-difficulty irregular spelling test is now available (Baxter and Warrington, 1994). The assessment of nonsense-word reading and writing together with these two standard tests is sufficient to identify the majority of acquired central dyslexic syndromes in the neurological population.

Language

For theoretical purposes, experimental psychologists have found it profitable to differentiate syntax and semantics in research on language. Certainly our own experience would lend support to the notion that these are dissociable aspects of language. Syntax, however, is the area we have least explored because our efforts to date have been concentrated on single word comprehension. However, for diagnosis and assessment, our strategy is very similar to our assessment of other cognitive skills. Because most of the available tests of dysphasia are insufficiently sensitive to detect minor degrees of deficit in the general neurological population, our aim has been to develop a battery of graded-difficulty language tests.

A series of tests based on a group study of patients with unilateral lesions has provided a preliminary test battery of selected language skills. To some extent, this battery illustrates our methodological approach in that it attempts to test various unitary functions that it seems reasonable to assume are implicated in word comprehension and usage. This approach represents a departure from the traditional taxonomic basis of language batteries that are tuned to the symptomatology of the classic neurological syndromes such as Broca's and Wernicke's. Thus the battery includes tests for word perception, word comprehension, word retrieval, and word articulation.

Though some of these tests are modified versions of existing ones, such as the Peabody and Token tests, most of them are new. The hard-core tests, and indeed the ones we have found most useful, attempt to distinguish between visual and verbal presentation and between word comprehension and word retrieval. From the point of view of localization, it has been demonstrated that certain of these tests (word retrieval and comprehension) have localizing value—temporal lobe structures are implicated—whereas others have merely lateralizing value.

The usefulness of these tests motivated the development of a graded-difficulty naming test. Like the reading and spelling tests described above, it has the added advantage of taking into account a person's general intellectual level in clinical assessment (McKenna and Warrington, 1983).

Our preliminary research findings suggest

that word frequency and word length are important variables for speech production and that the degree of meaningfulness and transitional probabilities are the crucial parameters for verbal repetition. From detailed investigation of patients with conduction aphasia we have developed new graded-difficulty tests of speech production and verbal repetition (the two components of the syndrome) (McCarthy and Warrington, 1984).

As yet our range of standardized and graded-difficulty tests is far from comprehensive. The most obvious shortcoming is that we have limited our analysis of language skills to single words—which, of course, we appreciate would hardly be accepted as an adequate assessment of language functions. However, the Test for the Reception of Grammar (TROG), a test of comprehension of grammar, overcame, to some extent, these limitations (Bishop, 1982).

Event Memory

Psychologists and laypeople alike often use the concepts of knowing and remembering interchangeably. A further area of confusion is provided by the phenomenon of repeating, which is also implicated in commonsense ideas of "being able to remember." Among psychologists, both experimental and clinical, short-term memory is now generally acknowledged to be an independent and dissociable system that can be conceptualized as a limited-capacity system that "holds" auditory verbal information in an acoustic store for very short time durations. More controversial is the relationship between "knowing" and "remembering." Indeed, many psychologists argue that the difference is one of degree and that the same cognitive systems subserve, for example, "knowing" a word and "remembering" who telephoned yesterday. However, the evidence now supports the view that memory for facts and memory for events are independent systems that can be selectively impaired. The amnesic syndrome is characterized by an almost total inability to recall or recognize autobiographical events either before or since the onset of their illness, yet amnesics' memory for other classes of knowledge can be on a par with normal

subjects and they can score normally on tests of intelligence. The complementary syndrome, the impairment of semantic systems, or of memory for facts, has been observed in patients in whom memory for past and present events is relatively well preserved. We have now documented triple dissociations between these three systems: short-term memory, memory for facts (semantics), and memory for events. In this section we discuss only the investigation and assessment of event memory.

Event memory appears to be an independent system with unique properties for mapping ongoing experiences on to an individual schema of events. Contrary to the commonly held assumption that memory for remote events is less vulnerable compared to memory for recent events, Warrington and Sanders (1971) showed that although memory for events (tested either by recall or recognition) declined with age in normal subjects, there was no greater vulnerability of memory for recent as compared to remote events in any age group. Similarly, no sparing of remote memories could be demonstrated in amnesic patients (Sanders and Warrington, 1971). Furthermore, after closed head injuries the severity of the anterograde deficit roughly correlates with the severity of the retrograde deficit (Schacter and Crovitz, 1977). We would interpret this evidence as indicating that a unitary memory system subserves both recent and remote events, and consequently the assessment of new learning and retention over short recall intervals is appropriate and sufficient to document event memory impairment. This strategy has the additional advantage that artifacts such as differences in the salience of past experiences, interference during recall intervals, and differences in rehearsal activity can be avoided. The subjective ease with which well-worn memories from the distant past are continuously evoked in older individuals may indicate that they have attained the status of semantic concepts. This fact-like recall is well illustrated in a patient with global amnesia who would repeat a skeletal account of the main life events such as number of children, education, date of marriage, etc., in almost identical sentence structures whenever asked

(Warrington and McCarthy, 1988). The same patient displayed intact semantic knowledge of famous public figures in the sense that he could designate a famous face in an anonymous group and he could complete the name given a prompt but had no idea of the public events that individual was famous for, nor have any subjective recognition of the person. Finally, he had also retained semantic concepts (e.g., AIDS, the shuttle) that he had acquired during the long period for which he had lost autobiographical knowledge.

Numerous investigations have established the occurrence of modality-specific memory deficits. Since the classic studies of Milner (1966) it is widely accepted that verbal memory deficits are associated with unilateral lesions of the left hemisphere and nonverbal memory deficits with the right hemisphere. Our aim was to develop a test for specific investigation of event memory that would incorporate the verbal/nonverbal dichotomy. A recognition paradigm was chosen in preference to recall because the former task appears to be much less influenced by affective disorders and by the normal aging process; in addition, identical procedures can be used for the separate assessment of verbal and nonverbal material. Consequently, a forced two-choice recognition memory test for 50 common words and 50 unknown faces (previously described by Warrington [1974] in the context of the analysis of the amnesic syndrome) has been standardized. The normalized scores provide a quantitative measure of performance that can be compared directly with other measures of cognitive skills. Validation studies have been successful insofar as a right hemisphere group was shown to be impaired on the face recognition memory test but not on the word recognition test. By contrast the left hemisphere group, although mildly impaired on the face recognition, had a clear-cut deficit on the word recognition test. Perhaps of greater relevance for the majority of assessment problems was the fact that the test was sufficiently sensitive to detect memory deficits in patients with only a mild degree of atrophy. Thus, the findings of a number of investiga-

tions have led to the development of a test with the discriminative power to detect minor degrees of modality-specific memory deficits (Warrington, 1984). An easy version of each of these tests is now available for the assessment of older subjects (Clegg and Warrington, 1994).

Further characteristics of the event memory system have emerged from investigations of the "pure amnesic syndrome"—a very severe yet circumscribed memory impairment. It has become increasingly apparent that the amnesic memory deficit is not so absolute nor so dense as either clinical impressions or conventional memory test results would suggest. For example, strikingly different results are obtained when retention is tested by cueing recall and prompting learning; retention scores can be normal or near normal and learning can occur albeit more slowly than for the normal subject (Warrington and Weiskrantz, 1968, 1970). These observations have led to the development of two memory tests to attempt to differentiate cortical and subcortical memory deficits. First, retention of words tested by a yes/no recognition procedure is compared with retention tested by cueing recall with the first three letters of the word. A discrepancy in the level of performance on these two tasks (cued recall superior to recognition memory) we interpret to indicate a subcortical amnesia and validation studies (in progress) should indicate the generality and robustness of this pattern of test scores. Second, perceptual learning is tested by giving repeated trials to identify fragmented visual stimuli. Two versions of this test, incomplete word learning and incomplete picture learning, have been adapted from the original technique used to investigate retention in amnesic patients. Our aim in validating these memory tests is to achieve a test that would be useful not only in assessment, but also for differential diagnosis. Preliminary results suggest that there are three patterns of response to this task, indicating cortical impairment, subcortical impairment, and nonorganic impairment.

Our approach to the assessment of memory deficits illustrates the three stages of investigation we initially outlined. Analytic research studies led to group studies that in turn have led to the development of standardized tests that can be used in a much broader population of neurological and neuropsychiatric patients.

Reasoning and Behavior

We cannot claim to have made any progress in furthering the understanding of reasoning processes, which neuropsychologists find the most baffling and elusive phenomena to study. It is not unusual for a patient recovering from frontal lobe treatment to be sent home with no discernible deficit only to be readmitted a few weeks later with a history of job incompetence or other atypical behavior. Again, performance on formal structured tests of cognitive function can be normal. Even more frustrating is for the clinician to assess the patient's behavior subjectively as somewhat "odd" but be unable to be more specific. Blanket terms such as "inappropriate," "apathetic," "impulsive," or even "disinhibited" behavior give no clue to what psychological process is implicated. Nevertheless, it is clear that the frontal lobes play a major, if little understood, part in the planning, orchestration and adaptation of our cognitive systems in our ongoing behavior (and systems subserving affect, though this is beyond the scope of the present chapter).

At a theoretical level, neuropsychological research has clarified to some extent which cognitive operations can be eliminated from the reasoning process. For example, our investigations of a patient with acalculia suggest that the core deficit was accessing the "facts" of arithmetic; that is, given that the sum 3 + 2 is comprehended, the solution 5 can be accessed directly, computation being unnecessary (though this presumably need not be the case during acquisition). Indeed, the generally accepted finding that frontal patients can perform relatively well on intelligence tests that follow the format of the WAIS-R may well be due to its loading on stable, well-practiced cognitive skills, which it seems clear are subserved by post-Rolandic regions of the cerebral hemispheres. We

concur with the generally held view that impairment of reasoning abilities in such patients may only emerge with tests, such as the Progressive Matrices, that require relatively novel cognitive strategies.

Following this principle of novel manipulations in problem-solving behavior, the Cognitive Estimates test was developed (Shallice and Evans, 1978), which requires the subject to manipulate data and deduce an approximation to an answer he does not actually know. For instance, the example given to the patient for demonstration purposes is "what is the height of a double decker bus?" We have found this test to be very useful in diagnosing frontal pathology. Sometimes even a single answer can give a definitive diagnosis, as when a patient produces a ridiculous answer (e.g., 1000 feet as the height of a double decker bus) and with encouragement will modify it only slightly.

However, at this stage of our understanding, our battery is composed of pragmatically validated materials—for example, Weigl Sorting Test (Weigl, 1941), Wisconsin Card Sorting Test (Berg, 1948), Stroop Test (Stroop, 1935)—for localization purposes and cannot as yet provide a functional breakdown of the processes that make up reasoning. Further research into different aspects of "novel" manipulation in problem solving is being done using the methodology of group studies. It is hoped that the more analytical focus of these frontal lobe research studies will result in a battery of tests that will have greater clinical application than any now available.

Differential Diagnosis

Most, but not all, of our research efforts are concentrated on the neurological patient population, which has provided a most beneficial, if oblique, approach to differential diagnosis in the neuropsychiatric patient group. The fundamental problem posed by this group is to distinguish between impairment of an organic nature and impairment of a functional nature. The most obvious indication is a mismatch between subjective complaints and objective performance. A further indication lies in the recurrent theme in all areas of our research, that cognitive systems not only fractionate but they do so along dimensions that do not necessarily follow commonsense ideas of what constitutes a function. Unless a patient is aware of the "rules" of breakdown, he cannot produce the correct pattern of disability other than on an organic basis. Thus it becomes more and more possible, with our increasing understanding of cognitive organization, to differentiate between organic and functional elements of a symptom.

Most referrals that touch on this problem request a differential diagnosis between depression and dementia, organic or functional memory loss, and investigation of general complaints of intellectual inefficiency. One test of memory described earlier has proved particularly useful and illustrates the mismatch of common sense and the "rules" of cognitive breakdown, namely perceptual learning. This task makes small demands on memory resources for it has been shown that patients with dementia and patients with the amnesic syndrome are able to learn and to retain over relatively long time delays. A gross impairment on this learning task can be accepted as a strong indication of nonorganic factors. Similarly, intact performance on this test effectively eliminates a memory disorder. A further example from the amnesic syndrome that has very direct application to this differential diagnosis is the generally accepted "rule" that the degree of anterograde amnesia is highly correlated with the degree of retrograde amnesia. Thus patients who present with a severe anterograde amnesia but no retrograde amnesia do not conform to any known organic pattern (Pratt, 1977). However, recent case reports suggest that this formula may be too simplistic (e.g., Hodges and McCarthy, 1993).

An occasionally observed mismatch is the patient who is alert and able to perform relatively normally in a day-to-day situation but obtains test scores compatible with a gross degree of intellectual failure. More commonly, the mismatch is the reverse; namely, patients and their relatives complain of failing intellectual and memory skills, which even after exhaustive testing cannot be demonstrated objectively. In the area of word retrieval skills, a failure to show the very robust frequency effects of either accuracy or latency would be very strong indication for nonorganic factors.

Sometimes the reverse situation occurs, when our knowledge of a cognitive system confirms that an apparently bizarre or noncommonsense symptom could indeed have an organic basis. For example, individual case studies suggest that infrequently there may be a treble dissociation in the deficits associated with the secondary visual cortices, namely visual analysis of contour, color, and location. Visual disorientation, the inability to locate in space, is a particularly handicapping syndrome that together with normal acuity may suggest a mismatch when in fact none exists.

Summary

We have outlined an approach to neuropsychological assessment that has been developing since the 1950s, when an impasse had been reached in the understanding and measurement of cognitive impairment. In 1954, Yates claimed that "a purely empirical approach is unlikely to yield satisfactory results, nor is an approach based on a theory which has not been adequately tested experimentally." Our strategy attempts to use the findings of analytical research either from single case or group studies in a clinical situation by devising more specific tests of cognitive function. Thus we are committed in the first instance to research aimed at furthering the understanding of cognitive functions (albeit still at an embryonic stage of development) and second, to improved clinical tests based on this knowledge. We have cited investigations that, for the most part, have originated at the National Hospital, Queen Square, to illustrate our approach. A full account of the work emanating from this department is now published (McCarthy and Warrington, 1990). However, the procedures that we have developed and are developing still in no way override our use of other tools and techniques available; they are merely intended to supplement them. Indeed, we are of the opinion that a flexible and eclectic approach is essential for the assessment of the neuropsychological and neuropsychiatric patient.

Acknowledgments

We are most grateful to Dr. P. C. Gautier Smith for his advice in the preparation of this manuscript.

References

Albert, M. L., Reches, A., and Silverberg, R. (1975). Hemianopic colour blindness. *Journal of Neurology, Neurosurgery and Psychiatry*, *38*, 546–549.

Baxter, D. M., and Warrington, E. K. (1987). Transcoding sound to spelling: Single or multiple sound unit correspondence? *Cortex*, *23*, 11–28.

Baxter, D. M., and Warrington, E. K. (1994). Measuring dysgraphia: A graded-difficulty spelling test (GDST). *Behavioural Neurology*, *7*, 107–116.

Beauvois, M. F., and Derouesne, J. (1979). Phonological alexia: Three dissociations. *Journal of Neurology, Neurosurgery and Psychiatry*, *42*, 1115–1124.

Berg, E. A. (1948). A simple objective technique for measuring flexibility in thinking. *Journal of General Psychology*, *39*, 15–22.

Bishop, D. (1982). *Test for the Reception of Grammar*. Abingdon: Thomas Leach.

Caramazza, A., and Hillis, A. E. (1990). Where do semantic errors come from? *Cortex*, *26*, 95–122.

Clegg, F., and Warrington, E. K. (1994). Four easy memory tests for older adults. *Memory*, *2*, 167–182.

Cole, M., Schutta, H. S., and Warrington, E. K. (1962). Visual disorientation in homonymous half-fields. *Neurology*, *12*, 257–263.

Coughlan, A. K., and Warrington, E. K. (1978). Word-comprehension and word retrieval in patients with localized cerebral lesions. *Brain*, *101*, 163–185.

Farah, M. J. (1990). *Visual Agnosia: Disorders of Object Recognition and What They Tell Us About Normal Vision*. London: MIT Press.

Hodges, J. R., and McCarthy, R. A. (1993). Autobiographical amnesia resulting from bilateral paramedian thalamic infarction: A case study in cognitive neurobiology. *Brain*, *116*, 921–940.

Howard, D., and Patterson, K. E. (1992). *Pyramids and Palm Trees*. Bury St. Edmunds: Thames Valley Test Company.

Jackson, M., and Warrington, E. K. (1986). Arithmetic skills in patients with unilateral cerebral lesions. *Cortex*, *22*, 610–620.

Kinsbourne, M., and Warrington, E. K. (1962). A variety of reading disabilities associated with right hemisphere lesions. *Journal of Neurology, Neurosurgery and Psychiatry*, *25*, 339–344.

Langdon, D. W., and Warrington, E. K. (1995). *VESPAR: A Verbal and Spatial Reasoning Test*. Hove, Sussex: Lawrence Erlbaum.

Lhermitte, F., and Beauvois, M. F. (1973). A visual-speech disconnection syndrome: Report of a case with optic aphasia, agnosia, alexia and color agnosia. *Brain*, *96*, 695–714.

Manning, L., and Campbell, R. (1992). Optic aphasia with spared action naming: A description and possible loci of impairment. *Neuropsychologia*, *30*, 587–592.

McCarthy, R. A., and Warrington, E. K. (1984). A two-route model of speech production: Evidence from aphasia. *Brain*, *107*, 463–485.

McCarthy, R. A., and Warrington, E. K. (1986). Phonological reading: Phenomena and paradoxes. *Cortex*, *22*, 359–380.

McCarthy, R. A., and Warrington, E. K. (1988). Evidence from modality-specificity meaning systems in the brain. *Nature*, *334*, 428–430.

McCarthy, R. A., and Warrington, E. K. (1990). *Cognitive Neuropsychology: A Clinical Introduction*. London: Academic Press.

McKenna, P., and Parry, R. (1994a). Category specificity in the naming of natural and manmade objects: Normative data from adults and children. *Neuropsychological Rehabilitation*, *4*, 255–281.

McKenna, P., and Parry, R. (1994b). Category and modality deficits of semantic memory in patients with left hemisphere pathology. *Neuropsychological Rehabilitation*, *4*, 283–305.

McKenna, P., and Warrington, E. K. (1983). *Graded Naming Test Manual*. Windsor, England: NFER-Nelson Publishing Company Limited.

McKenna, P., and Warrington, E. K. (1993). The neuropsychology of semantic memory. In F. Boller and J. Grafsman, eds., *Handbook of Neuropsychology/VIII*. Amsterdam: Elsevier Science Publishers, pp. 193–213.

Milner, B. (1966). Amnesia following operation on the temporal lobes. In C.W.M. Whitty and O. L. Zangwill, eds., *Amnesia*. London: Butterworths, pp. 109–133.

Nelson, H. E. (1992). *The National Adult Reading*

Test Manual/II. Windsor, England: NFER-Nelson Publishing Company Limited.

Nelson, H. E., and McKenna, P. (1975). The use of current reading ability in the assessment of dementia. *British Journal of Social and Clinical Psychology, 14,* 259–267.

Paque, L., and Warrington, E. K. (1995). A longitudinal study of reading ability in patients suffering from dementia. *Journal of the International Neuropsychological Society, 1,* 517–524.

Piercy, M. (1959). Testing for intellectual impairment—some comments on the tests and testers. *Journal of Mental Science, 105,* 489–495.

Pratt, R.T.C. (1977). Psychogenic loss of memory. In C.W.M. Whitty and O. L. Zangwill, eds., *Amnesia.* London: Butterworths, pp. 224–232.

Raven, J. C. (1960). *Guide to the Standard Progressive Matrices.* London: H. K. Lewis.

Riddoch, M. J., Humphreys, G. W., Coltheart, M., and Funnell, E. (1988). Semantic system or systems? Neuropsychological evidence re-examined. *Cognitive Neuropsychology, 5,* 3–25.

Sanders, H. I., and Warrington, E. K. (1971). Memory for remote events in amnesic patients. *Brain, 94,* 616–668.

Schacter, D. L., and Crovitz, H. F. (1977). Memory function after closed head injury: A review of the quantitative research. *Cortex, 13,* 150–176.

Shallice, T. (1979). Case study approach in neuropsychological research. *Journal of Clinical Neuropsychology, 1,* 183–211.

Shallice, T. (1981). Phonological agraphia and the lexical route in writing. *Brain, 104,* 413–429.

Shallice, T. (1988). *From Neuropsychology to Mental Structure.* Cambridge: Cambridge University Press.

Shallice, T., and Evans, M. E. (1978). The involvement of the frontal lobes in cognitive estimation. *Cortex, 14,* 294–303.

Shallice, T., and Warrington, E. K. (1975). Word recognition in a phonemic dyslexic patient. *Quarterly Journal of Experimental Psychology A, 27,* 187–199.

Shallice, T., and Warrington, E. K. (1977a). Auditory-verbal short-term memory impairment and conduction aphasia. *Brain and Language, 4,* 479–491.

Shallice, T., and Warrington, E. K. (1977b). The possible role of selective attention in acquired dyslexia. *Neuropsychologia, 15,* 31–41.

Shallice, T., and Warrington, E. K. (1980). Single and multiple component central dyslexic syndromes. In M. Coltheart, K. E. Patterson, and J. C. Marshall, eds., *Deep Dyslexia.* London: Routledge and Kegan Paul, pp. 119–145.

Shallice, T., Warrington, E. K., and McCarthy, R. A. (1983). Reading without semantics. *Quarterly Journal of Experimental Psychology A, 35,* 111–138.

Stroop, J. R. (1935). Studies of interference in serial verbal reactions. *Journal of Experimental Psychology, 18,* 643–662.

Taylor, A. M., and Warrington, E. K. (1973). Visual discrimination in patients with localized cerebral lesions. *Cortex, 9,* 82–93.

Warrington, E. K. (1969). Constructional apraxia. In P. J. Vinkin and G. W. Bruyn, eds., *Handbook of Clinical Neurology/IV.* Amsterdam: Elsevier Science Publishers, pp. 67–83.

Warrington, E. K. (1974). Deficient recognition memory in organic amnesia. *Cortex, 10,* 289–291.

Warrington, E. K. (1975). The selective impairment of semantic memory. *Quarterly Journal of Experimental Psychology A, 27,* 635–657.

Warrington, E. K. (1981a). Concrete word dyslexia. *British Journal of Psychology, 72,* 175–196.

Warrington, E. K. (1981b). Neuropsychological studies of verbal semantic systems. *Philosophical Transactions of the Royal Society of London (B), 295,* 411–423.

Warrington, E. K. (1982a). Neuropsychological studies of object recognition. *Philosophical Transactions of the Royal Society of London (B), 298,* 15–33.

Warrington, E. K. (1982b). The fractionation of arithmetical skills. A single case study. *Quarterly Journal of Experimental Psychology A, 34,* 31–51.

Warrington, E. K. (1984). *Manual for Recognition Memory Tests.* Windsor, England: NFER-Nelson Publishing Company Limited.

Warrington, E. K. (1991). Right neglect dyslexia: A single case study. *Cognitive Neuropsychology, 8,* 193–212.

Warrington, E. K., Cipolotti, L., and McNeil, J. (1993). Attentional dyslexia: A single case study. *Neuropsychologia, 31,* 871–885.

Warrington, E. K., and James, M. (1991). *The Visual Object and Space Perception Battery.* Bury St. Edmunds: Thames Valley Test Company.

Warrington, E. K., and Langdon, D. (1994). Spelling dyslexia: A deficit of the visual word-form. *Journal of Neurology, Neurosurgery and Psychiatry, 57,* 211–216.

Warrington, E. K., and McCarthy, R. A. (1987).

Categories of knowledge: Further fractionations and an attempted interpretation. *Brain, 110,* 1273–1296.

Warrington, E. K., and McCarthy, R. A. (1988). The fractionation of retrograde amnesia. *Brain and Cognition, 7,* 184–200.

Warrington, E. K., and Sanders, H. I. (1971). The fate of old memories. *Quarterly Journal of Experimental Psychology A, 23,* 432–442.

Warrington, E. K., and Shallice, T. (1979). Semantic access dyslexia. *Brain, 102,* 43–63.

Warrington, E. K., and Shallice, T. (1980). Word-form dyslexia. *Brain, 103,* 99–112.

Warrington, E. K., and Shallice, T. (1984). Category specific semantic impairments. *Brain, 107,* 829–853.

Warrington, E. K., and Taylor, A. M. (1973). The contribution of the right parietal lobe to object recognition. *Cortex, 9,* 152–164.

Warrington, E. K., and Taylor, A. M. (1978). Two categorical stages of object recognition. *Perception, 7,* 695–705.

Warrington, E. K., and Weiskrantz, L. (1968). New method of testing long-term retention with special reference to amnesic patients. *Nature, 217,* 972–974.

Warrington, E. K., and Weiskrantz, L. (1970). Amnesic syndrome: Consolidation or retrieval? *Nature, 228,* 628–630.

Wechsler, D. (1955). *The Wechsler Adult Intelligence Scale: Manual.* New York: Psychological Corporation.

Wechsler, D. (1981). *WAIS-R Manual: The Wechsler Adult Intelligence Scale-Revised.* New York: Harcourt, Brace, Jovanovich.

Weigl, E. (1941). On the psychology of so-called processes of abstraction. *Journal of Abnormal and Social Psychology, 36,* 3–33.

Whiteley, A. M., and Warrington, E. K. (1977). Prosopagnosia: A clinical, psychological and anatomical study of three patients. *Journal of Neurology, Neurosurgery and Psychiatry, 40,* 395–403.

Yates, A. (1954). The validity of some psychological tests of brain damage. *Psychological Bulletin, 51,* 4.

3 The Boston Process Approach to Neuropsychological Assessment

WILLIAM P. MILBERG, NANCY HEBBEN, and EDITH KAPLAN

The Boston Process Approach is based on a desire to understand the qualitative nature of behavior assessed by clinical psychometric instruments, a desire to reconcile descriptive richness with reliability and quantitative evidence of validity, and a desire to relate the behavior assessed to the conceptual framework of experimental neuropsychology and cognitive neuroscience (see Delis et al., 1990).

In the past twenty years, the practice of clinical neuropsychology has progressed rapidly. Initially, neuropsychological assessment techniques were known only to a few self-trained clinicians or consisted of test batteries designed with the modest goal of determining the presence of the clinical diagnosis of "organicity." These formerly esoteric practices have grown into a widely respected specialty of clinical assessment based on a growing body of research (Lezak, 1995). To its credit, the American tradition of clinical neuropsychology is supported by a bulwark of empirical clinical research directly relating test scores to central nervous system (CNS) damage. It is now possible for an experienced clinician to use a series of test scores to reliably determine the presence or absence of brain damage in nonpsychiatric patients and somewhat less reliably to localize and establish the etiology of this damage.

Unfortunately, most of the assessment techniques used in clinical neuropsychology evolved with little attention to advances in experimental, cognitive, and developmental psychology, experimental neuropsychology, and the clinical science of behavioral neurology. The historical separateness of clinical and experimental psychological science has been lamented by many (e.g., Cronbach, 1957), but it could be argued that in no discipline is this separateness more obvious than in the practice of clinical neuropsychology. For example, many of the assessment techniques require the clinician to use norms (Reitan and Davison, 1974), keys (Russell et al., 1970), and patterns of scores (Golden, 1981), while little emphasis is given to the cognitive functions that underlie these scores, the way the patient attained these scores, the preserved functions the scores reflect, or the way in which these scores relate to the patient's daily life and rehabilitation program.

Development of the Boston Process Approach

The Boston Process Approach had its origins in the efforts of one of the authors (Kaplan, 1983) to apply Heinz Werner's distinction between "process and achievement" in development (Werner, 1937) to understanding the dissolution of function in patients with brain damage. The early studies focused on apraxia. It was observed that the loss of voluntary movement to a command was not a unitary phenomenon, in that the clinical subtypes of motor, ideomotor, and ideational apraxia were understood best when one actually observed the incorrect attempts of patients to follow simple commands (Goodglass and Kaplan, 1963).

The quality of the patients' responses differed depending on the size and location of their lesion. Some patients would be unresponsive to certain commands; others attempted to follow the command with a primitive, undifferentiated version of the response, such as using a body part as the object; and still others used well-differentiated but irrelevant responses, such as brushing their teeth when they were asked to comb their hair (paramimia). These early observations permitted precise description of the clinical phenomena and provided important data for understanding the development of gestural behavior (Kaplan, 1968), and the disruption of such behavior in relationship to the locus of the lesion (Geschwind, 1975).

A similar strategy was then applied to analyzing the process by which patients pass or fail various Wechsler Adult Intelligence Scale (WAIS) (Wechsler, 1955) and Wechsler Adult Intelligence Scale–Revised (WAIS-R) (Wechsler, 1981) subtests. This led to the development of the WAIS-R as a Neuropsychological Instrument (WAIS-R NI) (Kaplan et al., 1991). The focus on process also led to modifications in administration and scoring of the Wechsler Memory Scale (WMS) (Wechsler, 1945) subtests, as well as a number of other commonly employed clinical measures.

Another test developed with the process approach in mind, the Boston Diagnostic Aphasia Examination (Goodglass and Kaplan, 1972), allows the precise characterization of the breakdown of language function in patients with aphasia using a series of finely grained quantitative scales. As the Boston group and other investigators developed new and better tests to measure brain function, they were adapted and integrated into the collection of core and satellite tests used clinically as part of the Boston Process Approach.

If one were to examine the literature from the past 10 to 20 years in clinical psychology

journals, one would find that many of the tests originally intended as tests of personality (e.g., Rorschach Test: Rorschach, 1942), cognitive development (e.g., Bender-Gestalt Test: Bender, 1938), and cognitive function (e.g., Wechsler Memory Scale: Wechsler, 1945; Standard Progressive Matrices: Raven, 1960; Seguin-Goddard Formboard or Halstead Tactual Performance Test: Halstead, 1947) were also sensitive to brain damage in both adults and children. Recently, Perry et al. (in press) found that a neuropsychological process approach to the analysis of Rorschach responses was sensitive to the types of perseverative and linguistic errors characteristic of the deficits seen in patients with dementia of the Alzheimer type.

A number of principles have been formulated to account for tests that appear to differentiate patients with dysfunction from those without brain dysfunction (Russell, 1981). These include the principles of "complexity" and "fluidity." Complex functions are those composed of a number of simpler subelements; fluid functions are those requiring the native intellectual ability of an individual. Fluid intellectual functions are distinguished from crystallized intellectual functions, the latter being well-learned abilities that are dependent on training and cultural experience (Horn and Cattell, 1967). The tests most sensitive to brain damage are those that measure complex and fluid functions. Unfortunately, although tests of complex functions can be used to measure specific cognitive domains (e.g., abstraction), most are not sufficiently differentiated to allow the clinician to specify what component of intellectual competence is impaired or what cognitive strategies the patient used to solve specific problems. A new sorting test has recently been developed by Delis et al. (1992) that does permit a componential analysis of abstract problem solving ability.

Modern experimental psychology has demonstrated that each general category of human cognitive function is made up of many subcomponents (Neisser, 1967), and that as information is processed it appears to pass through numerous, distinct subroutines. These subroutines are not necessarily used rigidly by every individual in the same way, and there is variation that naturally occurs in the selection and sequencing of these sub-components. Subjects vary in their use of the underlying cognitive components, and thus they may be said to differ in their cognitive style (Hunt, 1983), skill (Neisser et al., 1963), or general level of intellect (Sternberg, 1980; Hunt, 1983).

Unfortunately, many of the paradigms of experimental psychology have had limited utility in the clinical setting. The major difficulty has been the relative insensitivity of many experimental procedures to the effects of brain lesions. Although some of the experimental techniques might not be useful on their own, the Boston group believed that they held promise in enhancing existing clinical neuropsychological procedures. With this in mind, they gradually combined tests that had been proven valid in the clinical discrimination of patients with and without brain damage with tests that purported to measure narrow specifiable cognitive functions. They also performed careful systematic observations of the problem-solving strategies used by patients (i.e., the way they successfully solved or failed to solve each problem presented to them). The resulting method allowed both a quantitative assessment of a patient's performance and a dynamic serial "picture" of the information processing style that each patient used (Kaplan, 1988, 1990).

Description of the Process Approach

General Procedures

Although the Boston Process Approach uses a core set of tests for most patients, it cannot accurately be characterized as a "battery approach" because the technique can be used to assess the pattern of preserved and impaired functions no matter which particular tests are used. In addition to the core tests, several "satellite tests" are used to clarify particular problem areas and to confirm the clinical hypotheses developed from early observations of the patient. The satellite tests may consist of standardized tests or a set of

tasks specifically designed for each patient. The only limits to the procedures that are employed (beyond the patient's tolerance and limitations) are the examiner's knowledge of available tests of cognitive function and his or her ingenuity in creating new measures for particular-deficit areas (e.g., Milberg et al., 1979; Delis et al., 1982). Of the patients seen clinically during the last 5 years of Dr. Kaplan's tenure at the Veterans Administration Medical Center in Boston (1983–1987), approximately 90% were given a selection from the basic core set of tests shown in Table 3-1.

It has been necessary to modify many original test measures to facilitate the collection of data about individual cognitive strategies. In most cases, however, an attempt was made to make modifications that did not interfere with the standard administration of the tests. Thus, one could still obtain reliable and generalizable test scores referable to available normative data because most of the modifications involved techniques of data collection and analyses rather than changes in the test procedures themselves. For example, we keep a verbatim account of a patient's answers in verbal tasks and a detailed account of a patient's performance on visuospatial tasks.

We also emphasize "testing the limits" whenever possible. Patients with neuropsychological disorders can meet the criterion for discontinuing a subtest and still be able to answer the more difficult items not yet administered. This may occur for a variety of reasons—for example, because of fluctuations in attention, or because brain damage often does not cleanly disrupt a function. Thus, patients may be forced to use new, less efficient strategies that produce an inconsistent performance. Information can be preserved, but not be reliably accessible (Milberg and Blumstein, 1981). This can be tested only by asking patients to respond to questions beyond the established point of failure and by simplifying response demands.

In addition, certain forms of damage may produce a loss of the ability to initiate a response rather than a loss of the actual function tested. In these instances it is criti-

Table 3-1. A Representative Sample of the Tests Used in the Boston Process Approach to Neuropsychological Assessment

Name of Test	Reference
Intellectual and Conceptual Functions	
Wechsler Adult Intelligence Scale–Revised	Wechsler, 1981
Wechsler Adult Intelligence Scale–Revised as a Neuropsychological Instrument	Kaplan et al., 1991
Standard Progressive Matrices	Raven, 1960
Shipley Institute of Living Scale	Shipley, 1940
Wisconsin Card Sorting Test	Grant and Berg, 1948
Proverbs Test	Gorham, 1956
Visual Verbal Test	Feldman and Drasgow, 1960
Memory Functions	
Wechsler Memory Scale	Wechsler, 1945
Wechsler Memory Scale–Revised	Wechsler, 1987
California Verbal Learning Test	Delis et al., 1987
Rey-Osterreith Complex Figure	Osterreith and Rey, 1944
Benton Visual Recognition Test (Multiple Choice Form)	Benton, 1950
Consonant Trigrams Test	Butters and Grady, 1977
Cowboy Story Reading Memory Test	Talland, 1965
Spatial Span	Kaplan et al., 1991
Language Functions	
Narrative Writing Sample	Goodglass and Kaplan, 1972
Boston Naming Test	Kaplan et al., 1983
Tests of Verbal Fluency (Word List Generation)	Thurstone, 1938
Visuoperceptual Functions	
Cow and Circle Experimental Puzzles	WAIS-R NI, Kaplan et al., 1991
Automobile Puzzle	WAIS-R NI, Kaplan et al., 1991
Spatial Quantitative Battery	Goodglass and Kaplan, 1972
Hooper Visual Organization Test	Hooper, 1958
Judgment of Line Orientation	Benton et al., 1983
Academic Skills	
Wide Range Achievement Test	Jastak and Jastak, 1984
Executive-Control and Motor Functions	
Porteus Maze Test	Porteus, 1965
Stroop Color-Word Interference Test	Stroop, 1935
Luria Three-Step Motor Program	Christiansen, 1975
Finger Tapping	Halstead, 1947
Grooved Peg Board	Kløve, 1963
The California Proverb Test	Delis et al., 1984
Boston Evaluation of Executive Functions	Levine et al., 1993
Screening Instruments	
Boston/Rochester Neuropsychological Screening Test	Kaplan et al., 1981
Geriatric Evaluation of Mental Status	Milberg et al., 1992
MicroCog	Powell et al., 1993

cal to push beyond consistent "I don't know" responses, and minimal responses of one-or-two-word elliptical phrases. Test questions may have to be repeated and patients encouraged to try again or try harder. Testing the limits and special encouragement are critical when it appears that a patient's premorbid level of functioning should have produced a better performance. When done at the end of a subtest this encouragement can occur without substantially affecting the reliability of a test score.

Another procedural modification involves time limits. In most cases, when a patient is near a solution as the time limit approaches, he or she is allowed additional time to complete the problem at hand. Response slowing often accompanies brain damage, and its effects on test performance need to be examined separately from the actual loss of information-processing ability. A patient who consistently fails because of inertia in the initiation of a response or because he or she works too slowly must be distinguished from a patient who cannot complete problems no matter how much time is given. Allowing more time may also identify patients who actually perform more poorly if allowed additional time after their initial response. A record of response latencies is critical so that performance on timed tests can be compared to performance on untimed tasks. This comparison allows one to distinguish general slowing from slowness related to the specific demands of a particular test.

Specific Test Modifications

Other procedural modifications involve adding new components to published tests so that the functions of interest are measured more comprehensively. These additions will be described here but, because of space limitations, only two of the most commonly used tests, the Wechsler Adult Intelligence Scale–Revised (WAIS-R) (Wechsler, 1981) and the Wechsler Memory Scale (WMS) (Wechsler, 1945, 1987) are described. Following a description of our revised test procedures we will give examples of the variety of data that can be collected with these techniques, and

how these data can be used to answer clinical neuropsychological questions. It should be kept in mind that, though its description is limited here to two tests, the method can be used on all neuropsychological tests.

The WAIS-R as a Neuropsychological Instrument (WAIS-R NI)

The WAIS-R NI (Kaplan et al., 1991) is largely based on the Boston Modification of the WAIS-R (Kaplan and Morris, 1985). In general, fewer modifications have been made to the administration of the verbal subtests than to the administration of the performance subtests. This is so because it is difficult to engineer modifications that make the covert processes underlying verbal problem-solving accessible within the context of standard test administration.

Overall, the verbal subtests represent an opportunity to analyze the form and content of a patient's speech. On any verbal test it is important to look for basic speech and language difficulties such as dysarthria, dysprosody, agrammatism, press of speech, perseveration, and word-finding problems as evidenced in paraphasias, as well as tendencies to be circumlocutory, circumstantial or tangential. In addition, the verbal subtests require a patient to comprehend orally presented information and then to produce an oral response.

Both the verbal and performance subtests can be examined for scatter because the items within most of the subtests are ordered in levels of increasing difficulty. Patients from different clinical populations can have the same total subtest score, but differing amounts of scatter within their protocol require different interpretations of performance. We turn now to the specific Wechsler Intelligence Scale subtests.

INFORMATION. The information subtest samples knowledge gained as part of a standard elementary and high school education. A pattern of failure on easy items and success on more difficult items on this subtest may suggest retrieval difficulties. Poor performance that is not due to difficulties in language production usually stems from difficulty retrieving information from long-term memory. Retrieval difficulties may arise because the information was never learned, because over-learned information was not available, or because of a deficit recalling information from one of the specific content areas represented (e.g., numerical information, geography, science, literature, and civics). The latter difficulty may be observed in some patients with functional rather than brain-related dysfunction. Some conditions that characteristically manifest fluctuations in attention, such as attention deficit disorder and temporal lobe epilepsy, may account for the presence of significant scatter and result in a specific impairment of this subtest (Milberg et al., 1980). In contrast, a poor score may be the result of a preponderance of "don't know" responses. Patients who have sustained a head injury, or who are clinically depressed, show a marked tendency to be "minimal responders." These individuals may perform considerably better when the information items are presented in a multiple-choice format, thus reducing demands for active retrieval processes. Further, the visual presentation may minimize the effects of inattention and auditory acuity or comprehension problems. Reducing the task to one of recognition provides a better assessment of the fund of information an individual still has in remote memory. Joy et al. (1992) demonstrated the efficacy of using the WAIS-R NI Information Multiple-choice subtest in a population of healthy community-dwelling elderly adults (see Table 3-2).

COMPREHENSION. This WAIS-R subtest addresses a patient's ability to interpret orally presented information. A patient's answers can reveal thinking disorders such as con-

creteness, perseveration, and disturbed associations. This subtest also can show specific deficits in a patient's knowledge of the various areas represented: personal and social behavior, general knowledge, and social obligations. A number of the questions are rather lengthy and so a patient's performance may be compromised by reduced span of apprehension or inattention. To address this issue all questions may be visually presented and for those patients who were unable to generate interpretations for the proverbs, a multiple-choice version is available. The foils for this task as well as for all the multiple-choice subtests of the WAIS-R NI were carefully selected to provide rich information regarding the underlying cognitive problems a patient may have.

ARITHMETIC. This subtest measures the patient's ability to perform computations mentally, and thus a variety of factors that may impair performance should be controlled. Patients with a short attention span, for example, on the completion of the subtest, are given a visual presentation of the auditorially presented verbal problems that they failed. In this way deficits in the ability to organize the problem and solve it can be separated from short-term memory problems. If a patient still cannot adequately execute the problems mentally, paper and pencil are provided to assess the patient's ability to transform the verbal problem into a mathematical representation and to evaluate his or her more fundamental computational skills. In addition, by examining the patient's written formulation, errors due to misalignment can be distinguished from those secondary to impairment in arithmetic functions per se and from difficulties in ordering the series of operations.

Incorrect answers in this subtest are ana-

Table 3-2. The WAIS-R NI Information Subtest Among Healthy Older Adults by Age Group

	50–59 yrs (n = 40)		60–69 yrs. (n = 51)		70–79 yrs. (n = 52)		80–89 yrs. (n = 34)	
	Mean	SD	Mean	SD	Mean	SD	Mean	SD
Information Standard	22.12	4.65	20.24	3.34	19.94	4.96	18.65	5.21
Information Multiple choice	22.20	3.37	21.67	2.85	22.15	3.69	21.06	2.92

lyzed to learn how a specific answer was derived. A typical error includes the use of numbers without consideration of the content of the problem. This error occurs when a patient is impulsive or becomes stimulus-bound and attempts to simplify a multi-step problem, or when he or she is distracted by the numbers themselves at the expense of the computation required. To isolate primary computation problems, the WAIS-R NI computational form of the arithmetic problems is available in a response booklet form.

SIMILARITIES. This test requires the patient to form a superordinate category relating pairs of words. The kind of errors a patient makes will vary. His or her answers might be concrete or he or she might only be able to provide definitions for each word but not be able to integrate the pairs. He or she might provide an answer related to only one word in a pair or describe differences between the words, while ignoring the task of finding similarities. For patients who have difficulty establishing the set to identify similarities, or who have difficulty articulating or elaborating a response, or who tend to say "I don't know," the foils in the multiple-choice format for this subtest help to clarify the nature of the underlying cognitive problems.

DIGIT SPAN. In this subtest we consider it especially important to record the patient's response verbatim. Although we discontinue the subtest after failure of both trials of any series, if a patient is able to recall all of the digits, although in the wrong order, we administer the next series. Because the patient's "span of apprehension," or the number of digits recalled, is separate from the process of making errors in the order of recall, two different scores for both forward and backward recall are available for this subtest: the patient's span with correct order of recall and the patient's span regardless of order. We also note if the patient "chunked" digits by repeating them in sets of 2 or 3 digits or multiple unit integers. In addition, the record indicates impulsive performances, such as patients beginning a series before the examiner is finished or repeating the digits at a very rapid rate.

Although the WAIS-R manual gives equal weight to the number of series successfully repeated forward and backward in computing the digit span scaled score, we have found that there is a dissociation between the capacity to repeat digits forward and backward in patients with brain dysfunction (Lezak, 1995). Repeating digits forward seems to require only the capacity to briefly hold several bits of simple information in short-term memory. The elementary nature of this process is underscored by the fact that patients with severe amnesia can have normal or even above normal digit spans (Butters and Cermak, 1980). Repeating digits backward makes far greater demands on working memory and requires some cognitive processing of the information. This may be achieved by rehearsing the series of digits again and again, or by transforming the auditorially presented information to a "visual" representation, and then successively "reading" the digits backwards. The former strategy is heavily reliant on repetition and is susceptible to interference and perseveration within and between series. The latter requires flexible movement between modalities. In either event, digit span backward is more sensitive to brain dysfunction than digit span forward. In general, digit span forward is usually equal to, or better than, digit span backward. With some patients, however, it is not uncommon to find their backward span to be longer than their forward span because they perceive that the former is a more demanding task and thus requires a mobilization of energy and active engagement in the task. This finding is frequently noted in patients with depression.

An analysis of the nature of errors such as omissions, additions, substitutions of digits, and whether they occur at the beginning or the end of the series, may suggest problems that relate to vulnerability to interference effects (proactive and retroactive).

SPATIAL SPAN. The WAIS-R NI introduced a 10-cube spatial-span test to provide a visual analog to Digit Span. It is scored in the same way as Digit Span is scored. In addition to the error types noted above, evidence of errors in the left visual field versus errors in the right visual field provide lateralizing information.

VOCABULARY. This subtest, like Information and Comprehension, taps a patient's established fund of knowledge and is highly related to educational, socioeconomic, and occupational experience. It is generally considered the best single measure of "general intelligence" and is least affected by CNS insult except for lesions directly involving the cortical and subcortical language zones. The standard administration of this test calls for the examiner to point to each word listed on a card while saying each word aloud. Because of the many visual and attentional disorders in patients with CNS dysfunction, we also have available a printed version with enlarged words to help focus patients who become distracted when a word is embedded in a list of other words.

Numerous types of errors can occur in this subtest. One is defining a word with its polar opposite. This is frequently seen in patients with a history of developmental learning disabilities.

Patients may also be distracted by the phonetic or perceptual properties of words and provide associative responses. A tendency to perseverate may be seen in the presence of the same introduction to each response by a patient. In addition, although a patient can be credited with one of the two score points for responses that use examples to define the word, such responses can reveal CNS dysfunction when they reflect an inability to pull away from the stimulus.

The multiple-choice version of this subtest allows us to determine whether or not a patient still knows the meaning of the word even though he or she is now unable to retrieve the words to adequately express his or her knowledge of the word. Thus, the WAIS-R NI multiple-choice format for the Vocabulary subtest can effectively provide the best estimate of an individual's premorbid level of intelligence.

DIGIT SYMBOL. Adequate performance on this multifactorial subtest is dependent on a number of abilities; for example, motor speed, incidental learning of the digit-symbol pairs, and scanning ability (rapidly moving one's gaze to and from the reference key). To understand the nature of the underlying difficulty a patient may have on this task, we have introduced the following procedural modifications. To begin with, we administer this subtest in the usual manner, except that as the patient proceeds with the task, the examiner places marks on the WAIS-R NI record form every 30 seconds to indicate the patient's progress. This allows an analysis of changes over time in the rate of transcription, changes that can signal fatigue or practice effects. After the 90-second time limit expires, the examiner allows the patient to continue until he or she has completed at least three full lines of the form. This equalizes patient experience with the symbols used in the subtest. If the patient is proficient enough, however, to complete more than three lines of the form within 90 seconds, then he or she is stopped at 90 seconds. At the end of three complete lines, the patient is provided only the last row and, in the absence of the reference key, the patient is required to write the symbol for each of the digits. After this, the patient is instructed to write in any order all the symbols he or she can remember. The measurement of paired and free recall of the symbols permits examination of the amount of incidental learning which has taken place during the subtest.

We find it important to examine the actual symbols produced by the patient. Are they rotated, flipped upside down, or transformed into perceptually similar letters? Are the characters produced by the patient micro- or macrographic? Does the patient use the box as part of the symbol, that is, is the patient "pulled" to the stimulus box? Does the patient consistently make incorrect substitutions, or skip spaces or lines of the task? All these attributes help define the patient's cognitive difficulties and may aid in localizing pathology. For example, we have observed that the systematic inversion of symbols to form alphabetic characters (e.g., V for   or T for   may be associated with pathology of the dorsolateral surface of the right frontal lobe, whereas a patient is more likely to become "stimulus bound" with bilateral frontal lobe pathology.

One major change in the Digit Symbol subtest is an addition called Symbol Copy, which is administered later in the evaluation. This version is like the original except that there is no key. The patient copies each symbol in the space directly below the symbol, and 30-second intervals are marked for a total of 90 seconds. This version allows the dissociation of motor speed in the patient's performance from the process of learning the symbols. This is especially important with older patients because motor slowing can confound interpretation of the test score. Joy et al. (1992) found that healthy, community-dwelling elderly between the ages of 50 and 89 showed motor slowing on the symbol copy condition (70% of the variance was attributable to motor slowing), and that there was a dissociation between paired digit/symbol recall and free recall of just symbols. There was a marked reduction in paired incidental learning with increasing age, while the number of symbols freely recalled was not affected by age (see Table 3-3).

PICTURE COMPLETION. This is a subtest that requires visual discrimination and verbal labeling of, or discrete pointing to, the essential missing component in meaningful visual stimuli. Failures on specific items can be related to any number of factors. A patient's perception of the stimulus item may be impaired due to primary visual problems, or visual or secondary visuo-organizational problems. Complete misidentification of the stimulus may occur in patients with visual agnosia. A patient may have difficulty identifying missing embedded features but no difficulty when the important feature belongs to the contour. A patient may have difficulty with items requiring inferences about symmetry, inferences based on the knowledge of the object, or inferences based on knowledge of natural events. Finally, he or she may have difficulty making a hierarchy of the missing details. Errors may also be analyzed with regard to whether the missing part is on the left or right side of the picture.

BLOCK DESIGN. Valuable information can be gained by observing the strategy the patient uses in his or her constructions on this subtest, so we keep a flow chart—we record the exact process a patient goes through in completing a design. We note (1) the quadrant in which the patient began his or her construction; (2) whether the patient worked in the normally favored directions for a right-hander (left to right and top to bottom); (3) whether the patient rotated the blocks in place or in space; (4) whether the patient broke the 2 × 2 or 3 × 3 matrix configurations on the way to solution; (5) whether the patient produced a mirror image or an up-down reversal of the actual design as his final product; (6) whether the patient perseverated a design across items; and (7) the side of the design the patient made more errors on. Later in this chapter the strategy of "breaking the configuration" (see point 4 above) will be addressed in more detail.

For further modifications in both administration and scoring, see the WAIS-R NI manual (Kaplan et al., 1991).

PICTURE ARRANGEMENT. Visual perception, integration, memory of details, and serial ordering are all important for success in this

Table 3-3. The WAIS-R NI Digit Symbol Subtest Among Healthy Older Adults by Age Group

	50–59 yrs. (n = 40)		60–69 yrs. (n = 51)		70–79 yrs. (n = 52)		80–89 yrs. (n = 34)	
	Mean	SD	Mean	SD	Mean	SD	Mean	SD
Digit Symbol	50.39	8.94	47.84	10.44	37.98	8.73	28.52	9.04
Time to End	123.34	25.81	133.86	31.31	166.86	40.40	235.27	72.23
Copying Time	59.12	15.55	69.10	15.56	75.08	12.09	98.91	26.08
Incidental learning	5.41	2.69	5.20	2.32	4.62	2.33	3.76	2.74
Symbol free recall	7.41	1.41	7.16	1.34	6.96	1.34	6.39	1.52

subtest. As with the Picture Completion subtest, the examiner must be sensitive to visual field and visuospatial neglect deficits. The cards may have to be placed in a vertical column in front of the patient to minimize such effects.

After the subtest is completed, we ask the patient to tell the story for each sequence as he or she sees it. Several consequences may result: (1) the patient may provide the appropriate story to a correctly sequenced series; (2) he or she may provide the correct story for a disordered arrangement; or (3) he or she may provide neither the correct story nor the correct sequence of cards. The verbal account following each arrangement permits a closer analysis of the underlying problems in all incorrect arrangements. For some patients giving a verbal account will bring into focus illogical elements in their arrangements and may guide them to a correct rearrangement. The verbal account may also reveal misperceptions of detail, lack of appreciation of spatial relationships, or overattention to details, which results in the inability to perceive similarities across pictures.

By allowing a patient to work past the specified time limits on this subtest, his or her capacity to comprehend and complete the task in spite of motor slowing or scanning deficits can be evaluated. Again, we observe the process by which a patient arranges the cards. Some patients may study the cards and preplan their arrangement. Other patients may arrange them impulsively, and still other patients may require the visual feedback of their productions as they arrange the cards, study them, and then rearrange them.

Errors may occur for a variety of reasons. A patient may not move cards from their original location because of a poor strategy or because of attentional deficits. The former suggests a strategy characterized by inertia, which is often seen in patients with frontal lobe dysfunction; the latter suggests a strategy more often seen in posterior damage. A patient may fail because of inattention to detail, or focus on irrelevant details. A patient may misunderstand the task and attempt to align the visual elements within the cards, or he may separate the cards into subgroups based on similar features.

SENTENCE ARRANGEMENT. This task was designed to be a verbal analogue to Picture Arrangement so that sequencing ability for verbal material could be contrasted with sequencing for pictorial material. Patients with prefrontal damage have difficulty manipulating information in a flexible manner, and have difficulty shifting from one meaning of a word to another. In addition, these patients are "captured" (Shallice, 1982; Stuss and Benson, 1986) by high-probability, familiar word sequences and become stimulus bound.

OBJECT ASSEMBLY. Three additional puzzles have been added to the four standard puzzles in this subtest in order to elucidate the effect of certain stimulus parameters such as the presence or absence of internal detail on solutions. As in the Block Design subtest, the actual process employed by the patient to solve each puzzle is recorded. The Automobile puzzle from the Wechsler Intelligence Scale for Children (WISC-III) (Wechsler, 1991) has been added because it is rich in internal detail and permits a comparison between the puzzles that rely heavily on edge alignment information (i.e., Hand and Elephant) for solution.

Two other experimental puzzles, the Circle and the Cow (Palmer and Kaplan, 1985), have been added to demonstrate a patient's reliance on one of these two strategies to the exclusion of the other. The Circle can only be solved by using contour information whereas the Cow, constructed so that each juncture is an identical arc, cannot be solved by using contour information and demands, instead, a piece-by-piece analysis. Patients who rely too heavily on contour information will fail to solve the Cow, and patients who are unable to appreciate the relationship between pieces will fail to solve the Circle. Many of the test modifications described above have been incorporated into the WAIS-R NI (Kaplan et al., 1991). Table 3-4 presents a sample of some of the modifications contained within the WAIS-R NI.

Boston Revision of the Wechsler Memory Scale (WMS)

Many of the changes recommended for the WMS have been obviated by the publication of the Wechsler Memory Scale–Revised (WMS-R) (Wechsler, 1987). Because not all of the recommended changes for the WMS were incorporated in the WMS-R, we will describe the additional subtests and procedural modifications we had introduced to make the WMS a more complete assessment of a patient's ability to learn and recall new verbal and visuospatial information.

GENERAL INFORMATION AND ORIENTATION. A number of items based on autobiographical information have been added to these two subtests so that recall of personal, current, and old information can be assessed more fully.

MENTAL CONTROL. Two items that have been found to be useful in the characterization and localization of retrieval deficits (Coltheart et al., 1975) have been added to this subtest. After reciting the alphabet, patients are asked to name all the letters of the alphabet that rhyme with the word "key" and then to name all the letters of the alphabet that contain a curve when printed as capital letters. These two items provide specific information about a patient's ability to retrieve information from memory, based on specific auditory or visual physical characteristics.

LOGICAL MEMORY. A number of additions have been made to this subtest. First, following the standard immediate recall condition, a cued recall condition is administered. Here specific questions about the details in the passage serve as prompts. For example, if, for the first story, the patient had not spontaneously said the woman's name or where she was from, the examiner queries, "What was the woman's name? Where was she from?" These kinds of direct prompts are helpful in identifying whether the information had indeed registered despite the impoverished account the patient had given spontaneously.

Table 3-4. A Sampler of WAIS-R Modifications Included in the WAIS-R NI

Subtest	Modification
Information	Discontinue rule not followed; multiple choice version administered later.
Picture Completion	Time limit is not observed; discontinue rule is not followed.
Digit Span	Discontinue rule is not followed.
Picture Arrangement	Time limit is not observed; discontinue rule need not be followed. Examinee is asked to tell a story for each of his or her arrangements.
Vocabulary	Vocabulary multiple choice version; discontinue rule need not be followed.
Block Design	Extra blocks provided; discontinue rule not followed. Examinee asked to judge correctness of his or her constructions.
Arithmetic	Time limit is not observed; discontinue rules need not be followed. Examinee is presented with printed version of failed items; for items then failed, paper and pencil are provided; for items still failed, computational form is presented.
Object Assembly	Examinee is asked to identify the object as soon as he or she recognizes it; time limit is not observed.
Comprehension	Multiple choice version for proverbs. Examinee is presented printed version.
Digit Symbol	Examinee is asked to complete third row if he or she has not completed it in 90 secs.; paired and unpaired recall of symbols is requested; symbol copy condition presented.
Similarities	Discontinue rule need not be followed; multiple-choice version is administered later.

Source: Based on Kaplan et al. (1991), p. 5.

Then, following the 20-minute delayed recall, a multiple-choice condition is presented. With these modifications it is then possible to determine whether the information had been registered, and what the fate of the information was over time. Patients with adequate attentional and rote memory may do well when they initially recall the information, but may show severe deficits on delayed recall and may not even benefit from a recognition task (multiple-choice). On the other hand, a patient (depressed or hypoactive) may have had a minimal account initially, but given the structure of the prompts may perform significantly better after a delay. Impairment after a delay may be due to inadequate retrieval strategies or defective storage abilities.

In addition to the two auditorially presented paragraphs, a third paragraph (viz., the Cowboy Story; Talland, 1965), which is read aloud by the patient, thus assuring registration, is then tested for recall immediately and after a 20-minute delay. This additional paragraph allows examination of complaints from patients about an inability to retain information that has been read, as well as testing for selective modality of input differences.

Beyond quantifying how much information is learned and recalled, we also take note of qualitative features of the responses, such as impoverishment, confabulation, disorganization, and confusion of details across stories.

ASSOCIATIVE LEARNING. Three major modifications have been made to this subtest. First, immediately after the third standard trial, "backward retrieval" is measured. The order of each pair of words is reversed, and the patient is presented with the second word of the pair and asked to recall the first. Second, 20 minutes later, free, uncued recall of the pairs is assessed. Third, following this, the first word of each pair is provided as a cue and paired recall is measured once again. Patients who are able to perform better on the third trial than on the reversed trial have been found to perform less well on delayed recall (Guila Glosser, personal communication). Presumably, these patients demonstrate a more shallow level of information processing (phonemic), whereas patients who do not do more poorly on the reversed condition have a higher level of information processing (semantic). As in the Logical Memory

subtest, these recall conditions allow deficits in immediate recall to be examined separately from those in delayed recall. Patient responses on this task may reflect internal and external intrusions, perseveration, or a simple inability to learn new information.

VISUAL REPRODUCTION. It cannot be assumed that the difficulty a patient has reproducing a geometric design that has been exposed for a brief period is an indication of poor visual memory. It may be that the patient had difficulty perceiving the design, or had difficulty at the visuomotor execution level. The following conditions serve to clarify the source of the patient's problem: After the designs have been drawn (immediate reproduction), a multiple-choice task is presented (immediate recognition), followed by a copy condition, a 20-minute delayed recall, and, finally, a matching condition is presented if any question of a visuoperceptual problem remains. The copy condition provides an opportunity to assess a patient's visuoperceptual analysis of the designs. The delayed recall condition assesses changes in recall following an added exposure to the designs. The recognition and matching conditions remove the possible contamination a visuomotor problem might contribute. For all drawings we use a flow chart—that is, we record the manner in which the patient produces each design. Such analysis can provide information about brain dysfunction, as will be discussed in greater detail later in this chapter. In addition, we note the type of errors a patient makes. Recall can be characterized by impoverishment, simplification and distortion of details, disorganization, and confusion between designs.

The revision of the WMS (WMS-R) contains delayed recall conditions for Logical Memory, Verbal Paired Associates, Visual Reproductions and for a new subtest called the Visual Paired Associates Test.

Screening Instruments

In the past few years a number of screening instruments have emerged that attempt to capture some of the features of the procedures used in the Boston Process Approach. Examples of these instruments include the Boston/Rochester Neuropsychological Screening Test (Kaplan et al., 1981), the Geriatric Evaluation of Mental Status (the GEMS) (Milberg et al., 1992), and Micro-Cog, a computerized assessment of cognitive status (Powell et al., 1993).

The Boston/Rochester, which was the first screening battery designed to allow for the analysis of cognitive processes, includes mental status questions and measures of repetition, praxis, reading comprehension immediate and delayed verbal and design memory, and a number of other tasks that lend themselves to a detailed analysis of patients' cognitive strategies and abilities. The Boston/Rochester takes 1 to 2 hours to administer.

The GEMS, developed more recently, was designed to be extremely brief (15–20 minutes) and easily administered to elderly patients. It contains a number of tasks to assess visual and verbal memory, language and executive functions. A number of these tasks were designed specifically for the GEMS, and contain features that allow the examiner to make inferences about the details of a patient's cognitive abilities. The GEMS is currently undergoing formal validation (Hamann et al., 1993), but has already been shown to be considerably more sensitive than the Mini-Mental State Examination (Folstein et al., 1975) in detecting general cognitive impairment (Berger, 1993). It recently has been shown to accurately classify 96% of a sample of 100 inpatient geriatric patients and age-matched controls with extremely low (7%) false-positive rates (Sachs et al., 1995).

MicroCog is a well-standardized instrument that samples a broad spectrum of cognitive functions on line. It provides indices for attention/mental control, memory, reasoning/calculation, spatial processing, and reaction time. In addition it separates out information-processing speed from information-processing accuracy. The Standard Form contains 18 subtests and takes about an hour; the Short Form has 12 subtests and can be completed in half an hour.

Using the Process Approach to Localize Lesions

The modifications of testing and data-recording procedures specific to the Boston Process Approach that allow the clinician to obtain a dynamic record of a patient's problem-solving strategy were described above. In this section, we will show how the specific strategic information that can be collected with the process approach can be useful in the analysis of brain and behavior relationships and in the prediction of behavior outside the clinical laboratory. For purposes of this discussion we will concentrate on several broad categories of cognitive strategies that can be observed across many different measures.

Featural Versus Contextual Priority

Most tasks that are useful in assessing brain damage consist of a series of elements or basic stimuli arranged together within a spatial, temporal, or conceptual framework. One important strategic variable, therefore, is the extent to which patients give priority to processing low-level detail or "featural" information versus higher-level configural or contextual information (see Schmeck and Grove, 1979, for related literature from experimental and educational psychology). Recently, a number of studies have appeared that support the observation of part/whole processing differences among patients with unilateral cortical lesions (e.g., Delis et al., 1986; Robertson and Delis, 1986).

This dichotomy of information, featural on one hand and contextual on the other, can be used to characterize both verbal and visuospatial information within each of the sensory modalities. For example, words and their basic phrase structure within a sentence can be thought of as the basic elements or features important in linguistic analysis. Phrases are put together into sentences, and sentences are put together into a conceptually focused paragraph to create a higher-level context or organization. Aside from simple phonemes and acoustic energy transitions, the word or phrase seems to represent the first major point at which the basic units of language can be isolated from their use in expressing organized thought. Similarly, a photograph of a street scene can be broken down into low-level categorical units of perception, such as cars, people, or litter, and then organized into relational information placing these disparate elements into a larger conceptual or spatial unit.

To successfully interpret most test material requires the use and integration of both featural and contextual information. Brain damage produces a lawful fractionation of a patient's ability to use both types of information simultaneously. Furthermore, the type of information processing given priority is related to the laterality and location of a patient's lesion. Specifically, patients with damage to the left hemisphere are more likely to use a strategy favoring contextual information, whereas patients with damage to the right hemisphere are more likely to give priority to featural information.

We can infer the type of informational strategy favored by a patient from many of the tasks described earlier. For example, a patient may in the course of assembling a block design shaped like a diagonal rectangle within a square (see Fig. 3-1) align pairs of solid blocks to form a diagonal rectangle without regard for the 3 × 3 matrix in which it is placed (Fig. 3-1a).

This is an example of a patient giving attentional priority to the internal features of the design without regard for the configuration. Another patient may assemble the same design by retaining the 3 × 3 shape but drastically simplifying the diagonal rectangle into a line of three solid red blocks (Fig. 3-1b). In this case the patient is giving attentional priority to the configuration with little regard for the accuracy of the internal features. Similar performance strategies have been found in analyses of block design performance in normal subjects (Royer, 1967; Haeberle, 1982) though not with the rigidity or consistency found in patients with pathology of the CNS. Normal performance is typically characterized by the integration of featural

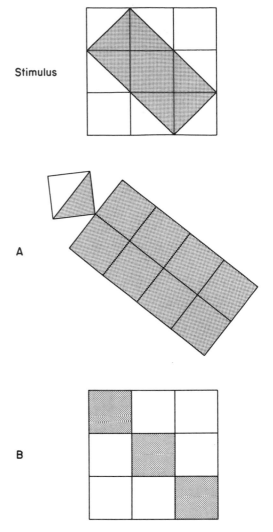

Figure 3-1. Two examples of informational strategies pursued by patients in solving complex tasks.

and configural information, whereas pathological performance is characterized by their dissociation. Thus, normal subjects will rarely neglect one source of information completely while using the other.

Using featural information to the exclusion of contextual information can also be seen on the Rey-Osterreith Complex Figure (Osterreith and Rey, 1944). By keeping a flow chart of the patient's method of copying or recalling the Rey Figure (Rey, 1964) (see Fig. 3-2), evidence about the strategy used by a patient can be obtained. The Rey-

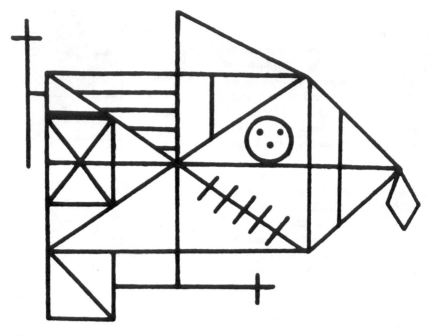

Figure 3-2. The Rey-Osterreith Complex Figure (Osterreith and Rey, 1944).

Osterreith Figure includes smaller rectangles, squares, and other details placed within and around it.

A normal strategy for copying this complex design makes use of the obvious organizational features, such as the large rectangle and the large diagonals, to organize and guide performance. Some patients will copy the design as if they were using a random scan path, adding small line segments until their final design resembles the original. Such a painstaking performance can be taken as evidence of a featural priority strategy in the perceptual organization of the design.

Other patients may approach the task of copying the design by producing the entire extreme outline but omitting smaller features. This approach is evidence of a strategy of contextual priority. Additional evidence for the emphasis of one or the other of these strategies can often be seen in the patient's recall of the design after a delay. A patient who is overly dependent on featural information may show a performance like that seen in the left column of Figure 3-3, whereas a patient who directs his attention primarily to configural information may show a produc-

tion like that seen in the right column of Figure 3-3.

Occasionally, patients will actually retrieve featural information independently of the spatial context in which it originally appeared. For example, a patient may recall one of the designs from the Visual Reproduction subtest of the WMS when asked to recall the Rey-Osterreith Complex Figure, or he or she may recombine features from two different designs into one. Stern et al. (1994) have developed a comprehensive qualitative scoring system that provides scoring criteria for configural elements, clusters, details, fragmentation, planning, size (reduction and expansion), rotation, perseveration, confabulation, neatness, and asymmetry. Shorr et al. (1992) have developed a scoring system to analyze perceptual clustering. They found that for a population of neuropsychiatric patients, configural or perceptual clustering on copy was a better predictor of memory performance than was copy accuracy.

Similar deficits in a balance between featural and contextual priorities can be seen in verbal tasks. A patient may show evidence of featural priority when recalling the Logical

Memory stories from the WMS. He or she may recall many of the correct items from the original stories but in an incorrect order along with additional irrelevant information based on his or her own associations to the stories or to other stories presented in the course of testing.

For example, when recalling the second story from the WMS (Form 1), a patient with a lesion in the right frontal lobe may respond: "15 passengers were rescued and the purser was on board." In this case, the patient has recombined elements from the two stories into one. Anna Thompson, a character in the first story, was robbed of 15 dollars, and a purse was made up to compensate her for her loss. This patient has borrowed the elements of 15 and purse from that story and added them to the second story. A patient

may also show evidence of configural or contextual priority when recalling the stories. In that case he or she would be able to explain the general theme of the story, but he or she would rely too heavily on paraphrases and he or she would be unable to recall specific details.

The dimension of featural versus configural priority is useful in predicting behavior outside the clinical laboratory. For example, patients who show an inability to process contextual information despite a preserved ability to process featural information are often found to be handicapped in situations that require an ability to spontaneously organize and direct one's own behavior. This inability to organize personal behavior along with an impaired ability to detect organization and to interpret complex arrays of infor-

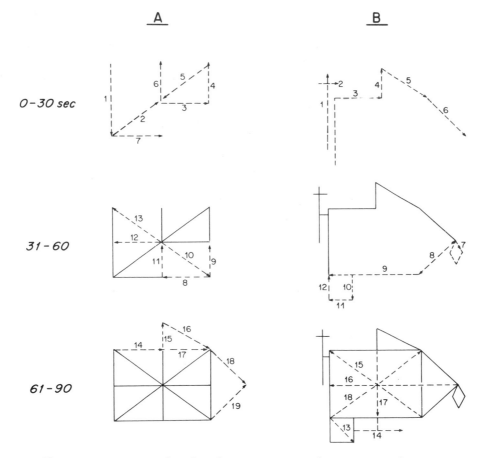

Figure 3-3. Two examples of performance strategies by patients on the Rey-Osterreith Complex Figure.

mation greatly diminishes large-scale goal-directed behavior. These deficits are subtle, but often manifest in tasks that require responsibility and self-direction.

Thus, the business executive who favors a strategy of "featural" priority after a head injury may begin to experience difficulty in his or her job because he or she is unable to make long-range decisions, give consistent orders, and complete complex assignments. Despite this, he or she may still have an intimate knowledge of the workings of his or her business, he or she may still be able to function in a minor advisory capacity, and he or she may still be able to perform more circumscribed tasks requiring less long-term planning. It is not unusual for this loss of sensitivity to the overall organization and cohesion of information to have a profound negative effect on social and personal adjustment.

In contrast, patients who have retained their ability to process configural or contextual information but who suffer from a diminished ability to process the "fine details" of their world, may be inefficient and even forgetful, but in many cases will still be able to make accurate long-range decisions, and to relate to others in a consistent appropriate fashion. Patients who have recovered from aphasia often show this latter pattern of deficits.

Professionals who have sustained a head injury that resulted in aphasia may often return to work even though they still have difficulty processing featural information. These patients will be less efficient and need more time to accomplish tasks that they once accomplished easily. Of course, their deficits are likely to be most pronounced in areas requiring verbal competence. Thus, the analysis of strategy can be useful in developing rehabilitation programs.

Hemispatial Priority

Though not strictly a cognitive strategy, the direction in which patients deploy attention in analyzing and solving spatial problems, and the accuracy with which they are able to use information presented visually to the left and right side of space, is an important source of data concerning the integrity of the brain.

It is well known that visual system lesions posterior to the optic chiasm and in the occipital lobe result in visual field losses contralateral to the side of the lesion (Carpenter, 1972). In addition, lesions that occur in the anterior dorsolateral portion of the occipital lobe or in the parietal cortex may result in neglect of, or inattention to, the side of space contralateral to the lesion (Heilman, 1979). Subtle manifestations of "neglect" or "inattention" may be observed in a patient's attempt to solve various spatial problems, even though the full-blown clinical syndrome is not present.

For example, right-handed adults tend to begin scanning spatial problems on the left side of space, although over the course of many problems they may shift from beginning on one side of the stimulus to beginning on the other. In contrast, patients with lesions of the right hemisphere will characteristically scan from right to left on spatial problems, whereas patients with lesions of the left hemisphere will often use a stereotyped left-to-right strategy.

The latter case can be distinguished from a strong normal tendency to scan from left to right because in addition to using an inflexible left-to-right scanning approach to problems a patient with a lesion in the left hemisphere will tend to make more errors and to be slower processing information in the field contralateral to his or her lesion. Hence, patients with lesions in the left hemisphere will often have difficulty completing the right side of a design or they will omit details from the right side of a design. Adults without brain lesions may show a strong preference for working from left to right on spatial problems but will not tend to make more errors in one particular field.

Other Specific Strategies

The observation of the informational and spatial priorities that a patient uses can be made across materials, modalities, and functions. These are only two of the many possible process variables that have been isolated. They were presented here because of their pervasiveness and ease of observation. Specific cognitive functions, such as memory, praxis, and language, have special sets of process variables related to each of them and this information has been detailed in Butters and Cermak (1975) and Goodglass and Kaplan (1972).

Strengths of the Process Approach

This method of qualitative analysis affords several advantages over other approaches to the assessment of the neuropsychological sequelae of brain damage. For the purposes of diagnosis, it is as valid for the detection and localization of cortical lesions as other widely used methods (i.e., Halstead-Reitan: Reitan and Davison, 1974; Luria-Nebraska: Golden, 1981). Trained neuropsychologists using the procedures described herein report agreement with radiological evidence in at least 90% of their cases. In some instances, the qualitative data are inconsistent with the quantitative data (i.e., test scores). For example, a patient who works quickly may be able to overcome his use of pathological, haphazard strategies and achieve a normal test score, so his test score will not reflect impairment. In cases like this, the hit rate using the qualitative analysis method is superior to the hit rate from methods that do not take qualitative information into account. A similar conclusion was reached by Heaton et al. (1981) when they demonstrated that clinicians who rated Halstead-Reitan results had better success in correctly classifying brain-damaged cases than did a psychometric formula approach rooted heavily in level of performance. Heaton et al. (1981) believed that the clinicians' superiority was related to their ability to supplement test scores with consideration of the qualitative and configural features of their data.

Clinical Relevance

The greatest strength of this method may be its usefulness in treatment planning and its relevance to patients' daily lives. Qualitative analysis provides the most precise delineation of function available, and allows the relative strengths and weaknesses of each patient to become obvious in a "face valid" manner.

Resistance to Practice Effect

This method also shares with other methods the advantages of repeatability and comparability across testing intervals (Glosser et al., 1982). Although strategic variables are to some extent more difficult to quantify, they are less susceptible to the practice and repetition effects that can confound interpretation of test scores. This makes qualitative data more useful than test scores alone in the assessment of recovery. Using both qualitative and quantitative data assures the reliable estimate of change that can be evaluated normatively from test scores combined with an estimate of the effects of change independent of the effects of practice.

Effects of Aging

Aging systematically alters neuropsychological test performance. Aging also affects strategic variables, changes that have been discussed in detail by Albert and Kaplan (1980). In brief, it appears that normal aging produces strategic changes akin to those observed among some patients with frontal system disorder, including cognitive slowing and loss of ability to process configural information (Hochanadel and Kaplan, 1984; Hochanadel, 1991).

The process approach permits relatively easy differentiation of aging from specific asymmetric neuropathologies, such as left frontal or right frontal disease. It is less effective in sorting out aging from mild generalized cerebral disorder, as occurs in very early dementia. In common with other approaches, we base our differentiation partly on estimates of premorbid functioning by considering demographic indices (Wilson et al., 1979; Karzmark, 1984) and performance on tests relatively resistant to the effects of brain damage. We also pay attention to memory impairment that exceeds that to be expected with the benign senescent forgetfulness of normal aging, and to strategic pathologies reflecting frontal lobe dysfunction that are more severe than one ordinarily encounters in the elderly. Regrettably, our normative work is not yet sufficiently advanced to propose specific rules or norms to aid in this important distinction.

Effects of Education

In terms of qualitative information, people who are 50 to 60 years old and who have completed at least ninth grade show little difference in strategy from individuals who have completed high school and college on most tasks involving visuospatial information. Amount of education does not appear to produce strategic differences in scanning, stimulus selectivity, and contextual or featural sensitivity. Verbal skills, naturally, are more sensitive to the effects of education.

Nonetheless, through the combined use of qualitative and quantitative information, the effects of education can be differentiated from changes in cognitive function due to brain disease. Likewise, culture and bilingualism also have an effect on various verbal skills, but the effects of these factors on test performance can also be distinguished from those of acquired brain injury through the combined use of qualitative and quantitative data.

Sensory Motor Handicaps

Our method emphasizes separating strategic differences from generalized slowing. Being slow must be distinguished from being slowed-up by the difficulty of the task (Welford, 1977). Peripheral handicaps often make it difficult to work quickly, but by observing the strategy used by a disabled patient on verbal and visuospatial tasks one can distinguish the defects caused by peripheral injury from those caused by cognitive dysfunction.

Psychopathology

Differentiating severe psychopathology from dysfunction related to neurologic processes is one of the most difficult tasks for the neuropsychologist. Patients with severe psychopathology sometimes perform on neuropsychological tests like patients with confirmed lesions of the CNS.

Chronic schizophrenics often have naming problems (Barr et al., 1989), difficulties analyzing details in visuospatial tasks, and difficulty maintaining attention, deficits that we associate with left hemisphere pathology. Patients with severe depression resemble patients with subcortical depression (Massman et al., 1992) and may also be similar to patients with known right hemisphere pathology and, in particular, right frontal lobe dysfunction. These patients can have difficulty analyzing contextual information relative to a preserved ability to use details. In addition, they can have difficulty with visuospatial memory, although their memory for verbal materials is relatively intact in terms of recalling details.

Summary

The Boston Process Approach has, over the years, developed a systematic method for assessing qualitative neuropsychological information, which, taken in concert with more traditional test performance data, adds sensitivity and meaning to neuropsychological assessment. We have discussed two strategic elements—featural versus contextual priority and hemispatial priority—to illustrate the possibilities of our approach. As the method we have described is refined both in our laboratory and by other investigators, we foresee that it will help move neuropsychological assessment beyond a reliable cataloging of deficits toward an understanding of the underlying processes. With such an understanding, neuropsychology will be in a better position to assist in the more important task of treatment planning and rehabilitation.

Acknowledgments

The work was supported in part by VA Merit Review 097–44–3765–001 to William Milberg at the West Roxbury VA Medical Center and

NINDS Program Project Grant NS 26985 to Boston University School of Medicine.

References

Albert, M. S., and Kaplan, E. (1980). Organic implications of neuropsychological deficits in the elderly. In L. W. Poon, J. L. Fozard, L. S. Cermak, D. Arenberg, and L. W. Thompson, eds., *New Directions in Memory and Aging*. Hillsdale, NJ: Lawrence Erlbaum Associates, Inc., pp. 403–432.

Barr, W. B., Bilder, R. M., Goldberg, E., and Kaplan, E. (1989). The neuropsychology of schizophrenic speech. *Journal of Communication Disorders, 22*, 327–349.

Bender, L. A. (1938). A visual motor gestalt test and its clinical use. *American Orthopsychiatric Association Research Monographs*, No. 3.

Benton, A. L. (1950). A multiple choice type of visual retention test. *Archives of Neurology and Psychiatry, 64*, 699–707.

Benton, A. L., Hamsher, K. deS., Varney, N. R., and Spreen, O. (1983). *Judgment of Line Orientation*. New York: Oxford University Press.

Berger, M. (1993). *Sensitivity of Neuropsychological Instruments*. Unpublished doctoral dissertation. S.U.N.Y., Albany, NY.

Butters, N., and Cermak, L. S. (1975). Some analyses of amnesia syndrome in brain damaged patients. In K. Pribram, and R. Isaacson, eds., *The Hippocampus*. New York: Plenum Press, pp. 377–409.

Butters, N., and Cermak, L. S. (1980). *The Alcoholic Korsakoff's Syndrome. An Information Processing Approach to Amnesia*. New York: Academic Press.

Butters, N., and Grady, M. (1977). Effects of predistractor delays on the short-term memory performance of patients with Korsakoff's and Huntington's Disease. *Neuropsychologia, 13*, 701–705.

Carpenter, M. B. (1972). *Core Text of Neuroanatomy*. Baltimore: Williams and Wilkins.

Christiansen, A. L. (1975). *Luria's Neuropsychological Investigation: Text, Manual, and Test Cards*. New York: Spectrum.

Coltheart, M., Hull, E., and Slater, D. (1975). Sex differences in imagery and reading. *Nature, 253*, 438–440.

Cronbach, L. J. (1957). The two disciplines of scientific psychology. *American Psychologist, 12*, 671–684.

Delis, D. C., Direnfeld, L., Alexander, M. P., and Kaplan, E. (1982). Cognitive fluctuations associated with the on-off phenomenon in Parkinson's disease. *Neurology, 32*, 1049–1052.

Delis, D. C., Kramer, J. H., Fridland, A. J., and Kaplan, E. (1990). A cognitive science approach to neuropsychological assessment. In P. McReynolds, J. C. Rosen, and G. Chelune, eds., *Advances in Psychological Assessment* (vol. 7). New York: Plenum Press, pp. 101–132.

Delis, D. C., Kramer, J. H., and Kaplan, E. (1984). *The California Proverbs Test*. Boston: Boston Neuropsychological Foundation.

Delis, D. C., Kramer, J. H., Kaplan, E., and Ober, B. A. (1987). *The California Verbal Learning Test. Manual*. San Antonio, TX: The Psychological Corporation.

Delis, D. C., Robertson, L. C., and Efron, R. (1986). Hemisphere specialization of memory for visual hierarchical organization. *Neuropsychologia, 24*, 205–214.

Delis, D. C., Squire, L. R., Bihrle, A., and Massman, P. J. (1992). Componential analysis of problem-solving ability: Performance of patients with frontal lobe damage and amnesic patients on a new sorting test. *Neuropsychologia, 30*, 683–697.

Feldman, M. J., and Drasgow, J. (1960). *The Visual-Verbal Test. Manual*. Beverly Hills, CA: Western Psychological Services.

Folstein, M. F., Folstein, S. E., and McHugh, P. R. (1975). "Mini-mental State." A practical method for grading the cognitive state of patients for the clinician. *Journal of Psychiatric Research, 12*, 189–198.

Geschwind, N. (1975). The apraxias: Neural mechanisms of disorders of learned movement. *American Scientist, 63*, 188–195.

Glosser, G., Kaplan, E., and LoVerme, S. (1982). Longitudinal neuropsychological report of aphasia following left subcortical hemorrhage. *Brain and Language, 15*, 95–116.

Golden, C. J. (1981). A standardized version of Luria's neuropsychological tests. In S. J. Filskov and T. J. Boll, eds., *Handbook of Clinical Neuropsychology*. New York: John Wiley and Sons, pp. 608–642.

Goodglass, H., and Kaplan, E. (1963). Disturbance of gesture and pantomime in aphasia. *Brain, 86*, 708–720.

Goodglass, H., and Kaplan, E. (1972). *The Assessment of Aphasia and Related Disorders*. Philadelphia: Lea and Febiger.

Gorham, D. R. (1956). *Proverbs Test*. Missoula: Psychological Test Specialists.

Grant, D. A., and Berg, E. A. (1948). A behavioral analysis of degree of reinforcement and ease of shifting to new responses in a Weigl-type card sorting program. *Journal of Experimental Psychology, 38,* 404–411.

Haeberle, K. C. (1982). Multidimensional scaling of block design patterns. Paper presented at the annual meeting of the Eastern Psychological Association, Baltimore, Maryland.

Halstead, W. C. (1947). *Brain and Intelligence: Quantitative Study of the Frontal Lobes.* Chicago: University of Chicago Press.

Hamann, C. McGlinchey-Berroth, R., Minaker, K., and Milberg, W. (1993). *Validation of a Neuropsychological Screening Instrument of Older Adults.* Geriatric Research Training Center, Project 7 (Core 2), Harvard Division on Aging.

Heaton, R. K., Grant, I., Anthony, W. Z., and Lehman, R. A. W. (1981). A comparison of clinical and automated interpretation of the Halstead-Reitan Battery. *Journal of Clinical Neuropsychology, 3,* 121–141.

Heilman, K. M. (1979). Neglect and related disorders. In K. M. Heilman and C. Valenstein, eds., *Clinical Neuropsychology.* New York: Oxford University Press, pp. 268–307.

Hochanadel, G. (1991). *Neuropsychological Changes in Aging: A Process Oriented Error Analysis.* Unpublished doctoral dissertation. Clark University, Worcester, MA.

Hochanadel, G., and Kaplan, E. (1984). Neuropsychology of normal aging. In M. L. Albert, ed., *Clinical Neurology of Aging.* New York: Oxford University Press, pp. 231–244.

Hooper, H. E. (1958). *The Hooper Visual Organization Test Manual.* Los Angeles: Western Psychological Services.

Horn, J. L., and Cattell, R. B. (1967). Age differences in fluid and crystallized intelligence. *Acta Psychologica, 26,* 107–129.

Hunt, E. (1983). On the nature of intelligence. *Science, 219,* 141–146.

Jastak, J. F., and Jastak, S. R. (1984). *The Wide Range Achievement Test Manual (Revised).* Los Angeles: Western Psychological Services.

Joy, S., Kaplan, E., and Fein, D. (1992). The Information Test of the WAIS-R as a Neuropsychological Instrument among healthy older adults. Paper presented at the 14th European Conference of the International Neuropsychological Society, Durham, England.

Joy, S. Kaplan, E., and Fein, D. (1992). Factors affecting Digit Symbol performance in aging. Paper presented at the 100th Annual Convention, American Psychological Association, Washington, D.C.

Kaplan, E. (1968). *Gestural Representation of Implement Usage: An Organismic-Developmental Study.* Unpublished doctoral dissertation. Clark University, Worcester, MA.

Kaplan, E. (1983). Process and achievement revisited. In S. Wapner and B. Kaplan, eds., *Toward a Holistic Developmental Psychology.* Hillsdale, NJ: Lawrence Erlbaum Associates, Inc., pp. 143–156.

Kaplan, E. (1988). A process approach to neuropsychological assessment. In T. Boll and B. K. Bryant, eds., *Clinical Neuropsychology and Brain Function: Research, Measurement, and Practice.* Washington, D.C.: American Psychological Association, pp. 125–167,

Kaplan, E. (1990). The process approach to neuropsychological assessment of psychiatric patients. *Journal of Neuropsychiatry and Clinical Neurosciences, 2,* 72–87.

Kaplan, E., Caine, E., and Morse, P. (1981). *Boston/Rochester Neuropsychological Screening Test.* Unpublished Test.

Kaplan, E., Fein, D., Morris, R., and Delis, D. C. (1991). *WAIS-R as a Neuropsychological Instrument. Manual.* San Antonio, TX: The Psychological Corporation.

Kaplan, E., Goodglass, H., and Weintraub, S. (1983). *The Boston Naming Test* (2nd ed.). Philadelphia: Lea and Febiger.

Kaplan, E., and Morris, R. (1985). *Boston Modification of the WAIS-R.* Unpublished Test.

Karzmark, P., Heaton, R. K., Grant, I., and Mathews, C. G. (1984). Use of demographic variables to predict full scale IQ and level of performance on the Halstead-Reitan Battery. *Journal of Consulting and Clinical Psychology, 52,* 663–665.

Kløve, H. (1963). *Grooved Pegboard.* Lafayette, IN: Lafayette Instruments.

Levine, B., Milberg, W., and Stuss, D. (1993). *Boston Evaluation of Executive Functions.* Unpublished Test.

Lezak, M. D. (1995). *Neuropsychological Assessment* (3rd ed.). New York: Oxford University Press.

Massman, P. J., Delis, D. C., Butters, N., Dupont, R. M., and Gillin, J. C. (1992). The subcortical dysfunction hypothesis of memory deficits in depression: Neuropsychological validation in a subgroup of patients. *Journal of Clinical and Experimental Neuropsychology, 5,* 687–706.

Milberg, W., and Blumstein, S. E. (1981). Lexical decision and aphasia: Evidence for semantic processing. *Brain and Language, 14,* 371–385.

Milberg, W., Cummings, J., Goodglass, H., and Kaplan, E. (1979). Case report: A global sequential processing disorder following head injury: A possible role for the right hemisphere in serial order behavior. *Journal of Clinical Neuropsychology, 1*, 213–225.

Milberg, W., Greiffenstein, M., Lewis, R., and Rourke, D. (1980). Differentiation of temporal lobe and generalized seizure patients with the WAIS. *Journal of Consulting and Clinical Psychology, 48*, 39–42.

Milberg, W., MacDonald, R., Odenheimer, G., McGlinchey-Berroth, R., Hamann, C., Weitzen, S., and Minaker, K. (1992). *Geriatric Evaluation of Mental Status.* Unpublished Test, Brockton/West Roxbury Geriatric Research, Education, Clinical Center.

Neisser, U. (1967). *Cognitive Psychology.* New York: Appleton, Century, Crofts.

Neisser, U., Novick, R., and Lager, R. (1963). Searching for ten targets simultaneously. *Perceptual and Motor Skills, 17*, 955–961.

Osterreith, P., and Rey, A. (1944). Le test de copie d'une figure complexe. *Archives de Psychologie, 30*, 206–356.

Palmer, P., and Kaplan, E. (1985). *The Cow and Circle Experimental Object Assemblies.* (New Object Assembly components of the WAIS-R NI. San Antonio, TX: The Psychological Corporation.)

Perry, W., Potterat, E., Auslander, L., Kaplan, E., and Jeste, D. (in press). A neuropsychological approach to the Rorschach in patients with dementias of the Alzheimer type. *Assessment.*

Porteus, S. D. (1965). *Porteus Maze Test.* Palo Alto: Pacific Books.

Powell, D. H., Kaplan, E., Whitla, D., Weintraub, S., Catlin, R., and Funkenstein, H. H. (1993). *MicroCog Assessment of Cognitive Functioning. Manual.* San Antonio, TX: The Psychological Corporation.

Raven, J. C. (1960). *Guide to the Standard Progressive Matrices.* London: H. K. Lewis.

Reitan, R. M., and Davison, L. A. (1974). *Clinical Neuropsychology: Current Status and Applications.* New York: Winston/Wiley.

Rey, A. (1964). *L'Examen Clinique en Psychologie.* Paris: Presses Universitaires de France.

Robertson, L. C., and Delis, D. C. (1986). 'Part-whole' processing in unilateral brain-damaged patients: Dysfunction of hierarchical organization. *Neuropsychologia, 24*, 363–370.

Rorschach, H. (1942). *Psychodiagnostics: A Diagnostic Test Based on Perception* (P. Lemkau and B. Kronenberg, translators). Berne: Huber; U.S. Distributor: Grune and Stratton.

Royer, F. L. (1967). Information processing in the Block Design task. *Intelligence, 1*, 23–50.

Russell, E. W. (1981). Some principles of psycho-metric neuropsychology and the Halstead-Reitan Battery. *Perspectives in V. A. Neuropsychology Rehabilitation: Proceedings of the Mental Health and Behavioral Sciences Service Conference.* Salt Lake City, Utah.

Russell, E. W., Neuringer, C., and Goldstein, G. (1970). *Assessment of Brain Damage: A Neuropsychological Key Approach.* New York: John Wiley and Sons.

Sachs, W., Milberg, W., and McGlinchey-Berroth, R. (1995). The detection of cognitive impairment in elderly inpatients using the Geriatric Evaluation of Mental Status. Manuscript in preparation.

Schmeck, R. R., and Grove, E. (1979). Academic achievement and individual differences in learning processes. *Applied Psychological Measurement, 3*, 43–49.

Shallice, T. (1982). Specific impairment in planning. In D. E. Broadbent and L. Weiskrantz, eds., *The Neuropsychology of Cognitive Function.* London: The Royal Society, pp. 199–209.

Shipley, W. C. (1940). A self-administering scale for measuring intellectual impairment and deterioration. *Journal of Psychology, 9*, 371–377.

Shorr, J. S., Delis, D. C., and Massman, P. J. (1992). Memory for the Rey-Osterreith figure: Perceptual clustering, encoding, and storage. *Neuropsychology, 6*, 43–50.

Stern, R., Singer, E. A., Duke, L. M., Singer, N. G., Morey, C. E., Daughtrey, E. W., and Kaplan, E. (1994). The Boston Qualitative Scoring System for the Rey-Osterreith Complex Figure: Description and interrater reliability. *The Clinical Neuropsychologist, 8*, 309–322.

Sternberg, R. J. (1980). Sketch of a componential subtheory of human intelligence. *Behavioral Brain Science, 3*, 573–614.

Stroop, J. R. (1935). Studies of interference in serial verbal reactions. *Journal of Experimental Psychology, 18*, 643–662.

Stuss, D. T., and Benson, D. F. (1986). *The Frontal Lobes.* New York: Raven Press.

Talland, G. A. (1965). *Deranged Memory.* New York: Academic Press.

Thurstone, L. L. (1938). *Primary Mental Abilities.* Chicago: University of Chicago Press.

Wechsler, D. A. (1945). A standardized memory scale for clinical use. *Journal of Psychology, 19*, 87–95.

Wechsler, D. A. (1955). *Wechsler Adult Intelligence Scale.* New York: The Psychological Corporation.

Wechsler, D. A. (1981). *Wechsler Adult Intelligence Scale-Revised.* New York: The Psychological Corporation.

Wechsler, D. A. (1987). *Wechsler Memory Scale-Revised.* San Antonio, TX: The Psychological Corporation.

Wechsler, D. A. (1991). *Wechsler Intelligence Scale for Children-III.* San Antonio, TX: The Psychological Corporation.

Welford, A. T. (1977). Causes of slowing of performance with age. *Interdisciplinary Topics in Gerontology, 11,* 43–45.

Werner, H. (1937). Process and achievement: A basic problem of education and developmental psychology. *Harvard Educational Review, 7,* 353–368.

Wilson, R. S., Rosenbaum, G., Brown, G., and Grisell, J. (1979). An index of premorbid intelligence. *Journal of Consulting and Clinical Psychology, 46,* 1554–1555.

4 The Iowa-Benton School of Neuropsychological Assessment

DANIEL TRANEL

Historical Introduction

Early Developments

The Iowa-Benton (I-B) school of neuropsychological assessment dates back more than four decades. In 1950, Arthur Benton set up a small neuropsychology unit at the invitation of Dr. Adolph Sahs, who was the Head of the Department of Neurology at the University of Iowa Hospitals and Clinics (UIHC). Benton's service was placed in the Department of Neurology, where it has remained until the current day, and this close affiliation with neurology has been an important influence in the development of the Iowa approach. In the initial arrangement, Benton agreed to evaluate patients referred by either Dr. Sahs or Dr. Russell Meyers, who was the Chair of the Division of Neurosurgery at UIHC. In return, Benton and his students were permitted to use case material from neurology and neurosurgery for research purposes.

In the early days, the Neuropsychology Clinic was a very modest operation. Since Benton was a full-time member of the Department of Psychology and the director of its graduate program in clinical psychology, these roles occupied almost all of his time. He typically would spend two afternoons and a Saturday morning each week in the Neuropsychology Clinic. The operation gradually grew in scope, however, helped by the labor provided by a succession of graduate students. By 1952, a number of graduate students had begun to receive practicum training in neuropsychological assessment, with their training in neuropsychology supplemented by attendance at the Saturday morning staff conferences of the neurology and neurosurgery staffs. In 1953, thesis and dissertation research in neuropsychology was instituted; some of Benton's first students included Heilbrun (1954), Wahler (1954), Swanson (1954, 1955), and Blackburn (1955, 1957). In 1956, Benton started a seminar in neuropsychology, aimed at residents in neurology and neurosurgery and also open to graduate students.

During the first few years of this operation, Benton's research focused on *development and disturbances of body schema* (Benton and Abramson, 1952; Benton, 1955a,b; Benton and Cohen, 1955; Swanson and Benton, 1955; Benton and Menefee, 1957; Swanson, 1957). Another early theme was *hemispheric differences in neuropsychological performance patterns* (Heilbrun, 1956, 1959). *Reaction time* was another early research interest (Blackburn and Benton, 1955; Blackburn, 1958), as were *qualitative features of performance* (Wahler, 1956). In addition, Benton wrote several papers on *historical aspects* of the development of neuropsychology (Benton, 1956), including one in which he discussed the Gerstmann syndrome (Benton and Meyers, 1956; for an interesting historical comparison, see Benton, 1992).

Neuropsychology Expands

Benton accepted a joint appointment as Professor of Neurology and Psychology in 1958, and moved his main office to the University Hospitals. Thereafter, the neuropsychology unit expanded considerably, becoming what would be known as the "Neuropsychology Laboratory." A technician and full-time secretary were engaged. In 1961, Otfried Spreen joined the Laboratory as a second professional staff member, and the Laboratory became a major center for practicum training and thesis/dissertation research. Between the years of 1959 and 1978, the Neuropsychology Laboratory sponsored 25 Ph.D. dissertations and 17 M.A. theses. The research program was highly productive, and the influence of the Laboratory permeated the cognate specialties of behavioral neurology and neuropsychiatry, as well as the field of neuropsychology. During the 1960s and 1970s, the Laboratory produced about 170 scientific and scholarly publications on diverse topics in neuropsychology, many of which are recognized still as standards in the field (cf. Costa and Spreen, 1985; Hamsher, 1985).

Although he achieved emeritus status in 1978, Benton remained active as a scholar, mentor, and leader in the field of neuropsychology. At that point, the Neuropsychology Laboratory became a core facility in the Division of Behavioral Neurology, established in the late 1970s by Drs. Antonio Damasio and Hanna Damasio. Under the leadership of Paul Eslinger, Ph.D., the Laboratory played a key role in the development of the ambitious research program in cognitive neuroscience instituted by the Damasios in the early 1980s. In 1986, direction of the Laboratory was taken over by Daniel Tranel, Ph.D. Tranel made a distinction between the Neuropsychology Laboratory (which had been officially designated as the Benton Neuropsychology Laboratory), which was responsible for all neuropsychological operations in the Department of Neurology (including research, training, and clinical practice), and the Neuropsychology Clinic, which, comprised as a subunit of the Benton Laboratory, focused specifically on delivery of clinical neuropsychological services.

A Philosophy of Assessment

Virtually all of Benton's professional career was spent in medical facilities, where he had the opportunity of watching skilled neurologists and psychiatrists such as Spafford Ackerly, Macdonald Critchley, Raymond Garcin, and Phyllis Greenacre evaluate patients. Having conducted a brief "mental status" examination, these clinicians would probe the diagnostic possibilities by diverse questions and maneuvers, the reasons for which were not always apparent to the audience at grand rounds. Their evaluations were extremely variable in length. Some were completed in 15 minutes and others took more than an hour, after which the "chief" would discuss the significance of the findings generated by the questions and procedures in relation to the diagnosis. What forcibly impressed Benton was the flexibility in choice of procedures and the continuous hypothesis testing that these astute examiners engaged in as they explored the diagnostic possibilities.

Benton was also struck by the essential identity in the approaches of an "organic" neurologist (Critchley) and a psychoanalytically oriented psychiatrist (Greenacre). Both adopted flexible procedures as they pursued one or another lead that might disclose the basic neuropathology or psychopathology underlying a patient's overt disabilities. Benton concluded that neuropsychological assessment should follow the model exemplified by the diagnostic strategy of these eminent physicians. Even though neuropsychological assessment involved the use of standardized objective tests, it could be flexible. It need not consist of the administration of a standard battery of tests measuring a predetermined set of performances in every patient. It was a clinical examination, not a laboratory procedure. On one occasion, Benton wrote that "neuropsychological assessment is essentially a refinement of clinical neurological observation and not a 'laboratory procedure' in the same class as serology, radiology, or electroencephalography. . . . Neuropsychological testing assesses the same behavior that the neurologist observes clinically. It serves the function of enhancing clinical observation. . . . neuropsychological assessment is very closely allied to clinical neurological evaluation and in fact can be considered to be a special form of it" (Benton, 1975, p. 68). Subsequently, he restated his position in these words:

The fact is that none of the batteries that are widely used today adequately meet the need for a well focused analysis of the cognitive status of patients with actual or suspected brain disease. Such a battery should provide reliable assessments of a number of learning and memory performances and of at least the semantic aspects of language function as well as of visuoperceptive and visuospatial functions. But even a fairly comprehensive battery of tests cannot be regarded as necessarily being the endpoint of assessment since it cannot possibly answer (or attempt to answer) all the questions that may be raised about different patients. Moreover, the administration of such a battery tends to be wasteful of time and expense.

Instead it may be useful to think in terms of a core battery of modest length, perhaps five or six carefully selected tests that would take not more than 30 minutes to give. Then, depending upon both the specific referral question *and* the patient's pattern of performance on the core battery, exploration of specific possibilities may be indicated, e.g., an aphasic disorder, a visuoconstructive disability, a visuospatial disorder, or specific impairment in abstract reasoning. For this purpose we should have available a large inventory of well-standardized tests from which a selection can be made in an attempt to answer the diagnostic questions. Administration of the core battery may suffice to answer the referral question in some cases. In other cases, 20 tests may have to be given and even then the answer to the question may not be forthcoming. In short, I think that we should regard neuropsychological assessment in the same way as we view the physical or neurological examination, i.e., as a logical sequential decision-making process rather than as simply the administration of a fixed battery of tests. (Benton, 1985; p. 15)

More recently, he wrote:

Neuropsychological assessment consists essentially of a set of clinical examination procedures and hence does not differ in kind from conventional clinical observation. Both neuropsychological assessment and clinical observation deal with the same basic data, namely, the behavior of the patient. Neuropsychological assessment may be viewed as a refinement and extension of clinical observation—a refinement in that it describes a patient's performances more precisely and reliably, and an extension in that, through instrumentation and special test procedures, it elicits types of performance that are not accessible to the clinical observer. (Benton, 1991; p. 507)

This conception of the nature of neuropsychological assessment was reflected in his Neuropsychology unit at the University Hospitals. In the 1960s the core battery for a nonaphasic patient would consist typically of three WAIS subtests (Information, Comprehension, Arithmetic) from the Verbal Scale and three (Block Design, Picture Arrangement, Picture Completion) from the Performance Scale. Then, depending on the referral question and the characteristics of the patient's performance on the core battery, additional tests (which might include some or all of the remaining WAIS subtests) would be given to explore the diagnostic possibilities. This core battery was gradually modified over the years so that, for example, in the late 1970s, only the Arithmetic and Block Designs subtests of the WAIS were given while other tests such as Temporal Orientation, the Token Test, and the Visual Retention Test found a place in it. It was in the context of giving additional tests to answer specific questions that the need for different types of tests emerged. This provided the impetus for the development of the diverse test methods associated with the Iowa laboratory, e.g., facial recognition (Benton and Van Allen, 1968), controlled oral word association (Bechtoldt et al., 1962; Fogel, 1962), three-dimensional constructional praxis (Benton and Fogel, 1962), motor impersistence (Joynt et al., 1962), and judgment of line orientation (Benton et al., 1978).

Current Practice

The Iowa-Benton School of Neuropsychology

The philosophy of neuropsychological assessment in the current Iowa-Benton (I-B) school has remained essentially unchanged from that developed by Benton over the past several decades. The principal objective is *to obtain quantitative measurements of key domains of cognition and behavior, in a time-efficient manner, in sufficient breadth and depth that the referral question can be answered.* The amount of testing required to meet this objective varies considerably across different patients, situations, and referral questions, ranging from a lower figure of 15 to 30 minutes to a high of 7 hours or even longer. The I-B approach is *flexible* and *hypothesis-driven.* The selection of tests is guided by a number of factors including the nature of the patient's complaint, the questions raised by the referring agent (physician, family, social agency, etc.), the impressions gained from the initial interview, and above all, by the diagnostic possibilities raised by the patient's performances during the course of the examination. In brief, the procedure involves the administration of relevant tests selected from the rich armamentarium available to neuropsychologists. The results of the tests are interpreted in the context of other contextual and diagnostic information, which typically includes the history, neurological findings, and neuroimaging (computed tomography [CT], magnetic resonance [MR] imaging) and electroencephalographic (EEG) results. The interpretation strategy used in the I-B school is integrative and hypothesis-focused, in a manner similar to the neuropsychological testing procedure.

The amount of testing is *not* predetermined, although we typically begin with a core set of procedures (as described below). Instead, the test protocol is formulated anew for each patient, according to the particular exigencies of the situation, and the examina-tion is pursued to the extent necessary to achieve the main objective. The following two examples illustrate opposite ends of the I-B assessment continuum.

CASE WB. Patient WB, a 68-year-old, right-handed woman from a town in central Iowa, was referred to the Neuropsychology Clinic for evaluation. WB had been a resident in a state-supported care facility for several years, and was under the care of the unit's resident physician. She had an 8-year history of declining mental status, and problems managing her everyday affairs had prompted the initial placement in the care facility. Now, she was being considered for admission to a special unit of the facility, in which residents with severe dementia receive intensive care and supervision. Admission to this unit, however, required an expert opinion as to the condition of the applicant's mental status. It was for this reason that WB was referred to us. Specifically, the referral question was, "What is the severity of this patient's dementia?"

Upon arrival at the Neurology Outpatient Clinic at the University of Iowa Hospitals and Clinics, WB was quite restless and agitated. She paced around the waiting room and repeatedly made requests to leave. She was brought to an examining room in the Neuropsychology Clinic, where the neuropsychologist conducted a brief interview. It was apparent that WB would not be amenable to extensive formal assessment. She would not stay in her chair and was unable to attend to the examiner for more than several minutes at a time. She made frequent attempts to leave the room. The neuropsychologist assigned the following tests for administration: (1) Temporal Orientation; (2) Benton Visual Retention Test (BVRT); (3) Controlled Oral Word Association (COWA); and (4) the Information and Block Design subtests from the WAIS-R.

The results of the examination are presented in Table 4-1. WB's age-corrected scaled score of 9 on the WAIS-R Information subtest, given her background of high school education and long-time employment as a secretary, was interpreted as within expecta-

Table 4-1. Neuropsychological Test Results of Patient WB

Test/Function	Score/Result
Temporal Orientation	−95
WAIS-R Information subtest	ACSS = 9 (raw = 16)
WAIS-R Block Design subtest	ACSS = 3 (raw = 1)
Benton Visual Retention Test	1 correct, 13 errors (items 1–6 only)
Controlled Oral Word Association	Score = 7 (0th %ile)

tions. All other performances were severely impaired. She obtained a raw score of 1 on Block Design—she finished the first design on a second attempt and was unable to complete the second design or any thereafter. She produced a total of only seven words on COWA. On the BVRT, she was correct only on the first design, and thereafter made numerous errors, particularly omissions and distortions (the test was discontinued after item 6). She had little notion as to the current date or time, providing an inaccurate guess about the year and wildly incorrect answers about other aspects of temporal orientation.

The multi-domain cognitive impairment disclosed by the neuropsychological examination, considered in conjunction with the patient's history, was interpreted as indicating an advanced demential syndrome. The findings suggested some preservation of retrograde declarative memory, but severe inability to acquire and maintain accurate on-line information. A recommendation was made to have WB admitted to the intensive care unit of the referring facility, as the severity of her mental decline clearly warranted such a level of supervision. The neuropsychological examination, including the interview by the neuropsychologist, was completed in 25 minutes.

CASE HR. HR is a 32-year-old, right-handed man who was referred to the Neuropsychology Clinic by an attorney who was defending an insurance company. The company was the target of a lawsuit filed by HR, who was claiming a post-concussive syndrome from injuries sustained in a motor vehicle accident 3 years ago. HR's complaints included headaches, dizziness, concentration and memory impairment, loss of intellectual abilities, and depression.

HR had been evaluated 2 years previously by a clinical psychologist, at the request of HR's attorney. The psychologist found a severe "organic brain syndrome" and "organic affective disorder," conditions that were interpreted to be related to closed cranial trauma suffered in the car accident. The psychologist stated in his report that HR suffered severe, permanent amnesia, and would be 100-percent disabled for the remainder of his life.

The defense attorney took the deposition of HR. During the course of this, several important observations surfaced. HR appeared to have detailed recall of the events surrounding the accident, including particulars of the accident scene and events immediately subsequent (the ride to the hospital, examination in the emergency room). Also, it turned out that HR had returned to full-time work as an instructor at a community college shortly after his accident. In previous head injury cases, this defense attorney had learned that post-traumatic amnesia was a common sequela in closed cranial trauma, and the detailed recall of HR seemed at odds with this. Also, the attorney was surprised to learn that HR had been able to return to work, because the report of the clinical psychologist indicated severe cognitive impairment that would not appear compatible with such employment. Hence, the defense attorney requested from us an independent neuropsychological evaluation.

On arrival at our clinic, HR was interviewed by the neuropsychologist. HR was seemingly straightforward in manner, providing reasonable answers to questions and cooperating with the procedures. He reported to us that he had sustained a significant blow to the head in the car accident three years ago, stating that he had struck his head on the dashboard and was momentarily "dazed" and "out of it." The neuropsychologist selected a comprehensive set of tests and assigned the case to a technician. The performances of HR are listed in Table 4-2. The neuropsychologist reviewed the initial

Table 4-2. Neuropsychological Test Results of Patient HR: Basic Data

Test/Function	Score/Result	Test/Function	Score/Result
Orientation		*Speech/Language*	
Temporal	−4 (3rd %ile)	Fluency	Normal
Personal information	3/4	Paraphasias	Occasional
Place	2/2	Articulation and prosody	Normal
		Boston Naming Test	45/60
Intellect		MAE Token Test	41/44
(WAIS-R ACSS)		Chapman Reading Test	8 correct
Information	6		(in 120 sec.)
Digit Span	6		
Arithmetic	7	*Visuoperception/Visuoconstruction*	
Comprehension	6	Facial Discrimination Test	37/54
Similarities	7	Judgment of Line Orientation	18/30
Picture Completion	5	Complex Figure Copy	35/36
Picture Arrangement	7	Grooved Pegboard Test	
Block Design	10	Right hand	95 sec., 0 drops
Object Assembly	5	Left hand	182 sec., 2 drops
Digit Symbol	4		
		"Executive" Functions	
Academic Achievement		Wisconsin Card Sorting Test	
(WRAT-R Standard Scores)		# Categories	6
Reading	80	# Perseverations	13
Spelling	90	# Perseverative errors	10
		Trail Making Test	
Memory		Part A	57 sec., 0 errors
AVLT		Part B	115 sec., 1 error
Trials 1–5	4, 6, 6, 4, 6	Controlled Oral Word Association	28 words
30-min delayed recall	3		
30-min delayed recognition	19/30	*Personality*	
Wechsler Memory Scale–Revised		MMPI (T-scores)	
Logical Memory	Raw score = 19/50	Validity Scales	L = 45, F = 90,
Verbal Paired Associates	2/8, 2/8, 3/8		K = 57
VRT	6 correct, 7 errors	Clinical Scales	1 = 90, 2 = 101,
Complex Figure Recall	13/36		3 = 94, 4 = 73,
Recognition Memory Test			5 = 63, 6 = 80,
Words	26/50		7 = 95, 8 = 113,
Faces	29/50		9 = 70, 0 = 90
		Beck Depression Inventory	Score = 25
		Beck Anxiety Inventory	Score = 13

set of test data with the technician, and noted several oddities about HR's performances. For example, on the Information subtest of the WAIS-R, HR had missed item 5 (saying the sun came up "in the sky") and several other of the easier items, while answering correctly a number of more difficult items. On the AVLT, HR never obtained more than six words correct on a trial, and there was no indication of a recency effect. On several other tests, there were examples of HR missing easy items and performing accurately on more difficult ones. In addition, on the

MMPI, HR produced an F-K index of +15, as well as a "floating" clinical profile (T-scores on nine of 10 clinical scales were at or above 70). These observations raised to the neuropsychologist the question of malingering. In order to explore this hypothesis, several additional tests were administered. The tests and HR's scores are listed in Table 4-3.

The additional tests corroborated the neuropsychologist's tentative hypothesis that HR was malingering. On the 15-item learning test, for example, HR's scores were severely impaired on the first three trials, and by the

Table 4-3. Neuropsychological Test Results of Patient HR: Supplemental Data

Test/Procedure[a]	Score/Result
15-item Learning Test (# correct/15, Trials 1–5)	6, 6, 6, 12, 12
Dichotomous Forced Choice Procedures	
AVLT 6-hour delayed recognition (2AFC)	10/30 (below chance at .05 level)
Red-green judgments	33/100 (below chance at .01 level)
Finger counting judgments	29/100 (below chance at .01 level)
Dot Counting Procedure	
Random dot placements	Inconsistent response times
Grouped dot placements	Inconsistent response times

[a]References for tests and procedures cited in this table include Lezak (1995), Rogers (1988), and Binder (1993).

fifth trial, he only managed 12 of 15 correct responses. On dichotomous forced-choice tests, his performances were consistently below chance. The final diagnosis was that HR more than likely did not suffer organic brain damage or post-concussive syndrome related to the motor vehicle accident, given that (1) there was minimal evidence of trauma, as indicated by the facts of the accident; (2) HR had returned to work successfully; and (3) his performance pattern on the neuropsychological tests was consistent with the hypothesis that he was malingering. The entire examination, including the interview, initial comprehensive testing, and additional tests aimed at detection of malingering, lasted 7 hours.

These examples illustrate our strategy of testing patients until we can support in a reasonably compelling fashion a particular hypothesis about what is wrong with the patient and what caused it. Most of our cases fall somewhere in between the two examples described above; in fact, the typical examination time in our clinic is in the vicinity of 2 hours. As noted above, our approach is *hypothesis-driven* and *flexible*. If we can support a particular hypothesis with 15 minutes of testing (and, if need be, rule out alternative ones), the exam will be terminated at

that point; by contrast, it may require many hours of testing to arrive at a firm conclusion, and the testing will go on until such a conclusion is reached (obviously there are some cases in which an unequivocal resolution is simply not possible).

A CORE BATTERY. It was noted earlier that Benton developed a core battery of tests, which evolved over the years. This tradition continues in the current I-B school. In fact, Benton has pointed out that one risk of a "flexible" method is that it can become too flexible, so that no two examinations are the same, and neuropsychologists begin using idiosyncratic sets of tests that have little or no overlap with those used by other practitioners. To avoid this problem, and to provide a structured set of tests that serves as a starting point for neuropsychological assessment, we utilize a Core Battery in the I-B school. The Core Battery is enumerated in Table 4-4 (the tests are listed in order of administration).

All examinations begin with an interview of the patient by the neuropsychologist. The interview is an indispensable and crucial source of information. It provides clues about

Table 4-4. The Iowa-Benton Core Battery[a]
Interview

1. Orientation to time, personal information, and place
2. Recall of recent presidents
3. Information subtest (WAIS-R)
4. Complex Figure Test (copy and delayed recall)
5. Auditory Verbal Learning Test (with delayed recall)
6. Draw a clock
7. Arithmetic subtest (WAIS-R)
8. Block Design subtest (WAIS-R)
9. Digit Span subtest (WAIS-R)
10. Similarities (WAIS-R)
11. Trail Making Test
12. Digit Symbol subtest (WAIS-R)
13. Controlled Oral Word Association
14. Benton Visual Retention Test
15. Benton Facial Discrimination Test
16. Picture Arrangement subtest (WAIS-R)

[a]References for tests in the Core Battery are Wechsler (1981), Benton et al. (1983), Lezak (1995), Spreen and Strauss (1991), and Benton Neuropsychological Laboratory (1993).

the nature and cause of the patient's presenting complaints, the patient's capacity and motivation to cooperate with the testing procedures, and the extent to which the patient is aware of his or her situation. Typically, the neuropsychologist will formulate a working hypothesis about the case during the initial interview. In keeping with the I-B philosophy, the interview varies considerably in length, depending on how rapidly and to what degree of certainty the neuropsychologist can formulate a testable hypothesis about the case. During the interview, the neuropsychologist oftentimes administers a few tests to the patient. The examination then proceeds with the collection of formal test data by a technician.

The Core Battery has evolved over the years to satisfy mutual objectives of *comprehensiveness* and *efficiency*. Thus, we aim to probe all major domains of cognition, including intellectual function, memory, speech and language, visual perception, "executive" functions, and attention and orientation. Sampling of these higher brain functions usually suffices to reveal patterns of performance that can be related to particular diagnoses and etiologies, and in many cases, the Core Battery will provide all the testing that is needed. In some instances, as illustrated by Case WB summarized earlier, the examination will not even include the entire Core Battery, and more selective assessment will be implemented.

Whenever necessary, and depending on a multitude of factors including the referral question, the patient's stamina, time considerations, and, in particular, the evolving performance profile of the patient, the Core Battery is supplemented with various follow-up procedures. For example, consider a case in which evaluation of a patient referred for "dementia workup" disclosed severe language disturbance, to the point where the technician was uncertain that the patient could produce valid performances on language-dependent tests (e.g., verbal subtests of the WAIS-R, verbal memory tests). The course of the patient's problems had been slowly progressive, and the neuropsychologist posited that the patient may have

a condition known as primary progressive aphasia (Mesulam, 1982; Tranel, 1992a). To explore this hypothesis, the neuropsychologist chose to add a number of tests from the Multilingual Aphasia Examination and the Boston Diagnostic Aphasia Examination. Other tests, such as the AVLT, were omitted entirely, because the validity of such procedures would be questionable in a patient with substantial language disturbance.

The most frequent procedures utilized for in-depth follow-up are presented in Table 4-5, grouped according to domain of function. The tests are drawn from various sources throughout the field of neuropsychology, and many come from other test batteries and sources such as the WAIS-R (Matarrazo, 1972) and the Halstead-Reitan (Reitan and Wolfson, 1985). (Incidentally, these procedures constitute not only the armamentarium available for in-depth follow-ups in the Neuropsychology Clinic, but also the core protocol utilized for neuropsychological characterization of subjects studied under the aegis of the Damasios' research program.)

It should be mentioned that although the I-B assessment approach is flexible in its clinical implementation, there are a number of research-related applications in which fixed sets of tests are utilized, to satisfy experimental demands for uniform data collection. Examples include: (1) early detection of incipient dementia in elderly persons (Eslinger et al., 1985); (2) cognitive changes associated with normal pressure hydrocephalus (Graff-Radford et al., 1989); (3) measurement of HIV-related cognitive changes (Jones and Tranel, 1991); (4) discrimination of dementia from "pseudodementia" (Jones et al., 1992); and (5) investigation of neuropsychological correlates of traumatic brain injury (Godersky et al., 1990; Rizzo and Tranel, 1996). Such research efforts are implemented separately from clinical service activities, although in many cases, neuropsychological data collected in connection with a research protocol can be utilized as well to inform the clinician about the patient's condition.

Normative data for the procedures utilized in the Benton Neuropsychology Laboratory

Table 4-5. Follow-Up Neuropsychological Tests[a]

A. Intellectual Function and Academic Achievement	10. Finger Localization and Recognition
1. Complete Wechsler Scales (WAIS, WAIS-R, WAIS-RNI, WISC-R)	11. Gestural Praxis
2. Raven's Progressive Matrices	12. Seashore Measures of Musical Talents
3. Shipley-Hartford Scales	13. Assessment of Writing
4. National Adult Reading Test–Revised	
5. Wide Range Achievement Test–Revised	**D. Visuoperceptual/Visuospatial/Visuoconstructional**
	1. Judgment of Line Orientation Test
B. Memory	2. Hooper Visual Organization Test
1. Wechsler Memory Scale (original and 1987 revision)	3. Mooney Face Closure Test
2. Recognition Memory Test	4. Extended Drawing Assessment
3. Route Learning Test	5. 3-dimensional Block Construction
4. Stanford-Binet IV Subtests	6. Grooved Pegboard Test
5. Boston Remote Memory Battery	7. Line Cancellation Test
6. Iowa Autobiographical Memory Questionnaire	
7. Iowa Famous Faces Test	**E. "Executive" Functions**
8. Rotor Pursuit Learning	1. Wisconsin Card Sorting Test
9. Mirror Tracing Test	2. Stroop Color and Word Test
	3. Category Test
C. Speech, Language, and Related Functions	4. Proverbs Test
1. Multilingual Aphasia Examination	5. Design Fluency
2. Boston Diagnostic Aphasia Examination	
3. Boston Naming Test	**F. Personality and Awareness**
4. Auditory Recognition and Naming	1. Minnesota Multiphasic Personality Inventory (I and II)
5. Tactile Recognition and Naming	2. Beck Depression Inventory
6. Philadelphia Comprehension Battery for Aphasia	3. Beck Anxiety Inventory
7. Dichotic Listening Test	4. Anderson Awareness Questionnaire
8. Chapman Reading Test	5. Rorschach Inkblot Test
9. Right-left Discrimination	6. Thematic Apperception Test

[a]References for tests in the Follow-up Battery are Wechsler (1981), Benton et al. (1983), Lezak (1995), Kaplan et al. (1991), Spreen and Strauss (1991), and Benton Neuropsychological Laboratory (1993).

are derived from three primary sources: (1) tables provided in connection with the particular test (e.g., WAIS-R, BVRT, WMS-R); (2) the compendiums of Lezak (1995) and Spreen and Strauss (1991), both of which contain many useful sets of normative observations; and (3) specific norms that have been collected in the Benton Neuropsychology Laboratory. Regarding the latter source, we have found over the years that there are a number of valuable procedures that do not have satisfactory norms, either because such norms do not exist, or because the populations on which norms were established are too different from the rural midwestern population from which most of our patients come. Hence, we have conducted a number of our own norming studies. Our usual approach in these studies has been to obtain 20 subjects at each of three levels of age (20–39, 40–59, 60+), divided by gender (10

males, 10 females), as a starting point (e.g., Barrash et al., 1993).

It may be noticed that the I-B school places relatively little emphasis on the assessment of basic motor and sensory functions. This may be curious, because such testing has received rather extensive emphasis in other neuropsychological assessment philosophies, especially some of the fixed-battery methods (e.g., HRNB). There is certainly nothing wrong with testing of grip strength, finger tapping, pitch discrimination, and so on; however, we have found that such tests provide relatively little information for the time investment. This is especially true in the age of modern neuroimaging, which has reduced substantially the extent to which neuropsychology is needed for "lesion localization" (see section below). For example, there is little point in spending an hour or two determining that the patient suffers "left hemisphere dysfunction" based on deficient motor and sensory performances with the right hand, when a neuroimaging study (e.g., CT scan) has revealed clearly that the patient has a left frontal tumor. Of course, neuropsychological testing may reveal signs of hemispheric dysfunction in cases in which neuroimaging is negative, an outcome not uncommon in the early stages of multiple sclerosis, progressive demential syndromes (e.g., SDAT, Pick's), HIV-related dementia, or mild head injury. However, we have found that most basic motor and sensory tests are less helpful in this regard than tests aimed at higher-order cognitive capacities.

THE IMPORTANCE OF NEUROANATOMY. As indicated in the Historical Introduction, the I-B school derives from a strong tradition of neuropsychology practiced in a medical setting. Benton practiced within the medical complex, working closely with Sahs, Van Allen, the Damasios, and other physicians. Tranel has continued that tradition. Influenced by this association and, in recent years, by a close affiliation with the far-reaching cognitive neuroscience research program of the Damasios, the Benton Neuropsychology Laboratory has remained decidedly committed to a close connection between neuropsychological assessment and neuroanatomy.

In the I-B school, the interpretation of neuropsychological data is informed, to as large an extent as possible, by knowledge of the neuroanatomical findings in a patient. Neuroanatomical information on patients is typically available in our facility. Nearly all patients come to the clinic with a neuroimaging study (CT, MR), and we usually have access to both the interpretation of the study (as provided by the radiologist), and to the "raw data" (the CT or MR film). Taking advantage of on-site expertise (viz., H. Damasio and her methodology; see Damasio and Damasio, 1989; Damasio and Frank, 1992; Damasio, 1995), our neuropsychologists frequently can avail themselves of first-hand readings of neuroimaging data, and this information is incorporated directly into the neuropsychological examination, both as a means of guiding test selection and as infor-

mation to be factored into the impressions and conclusions.

Another factor that has been important in influencing the strong anatomical tradition of the I-B school has been the location of the neuropsychological operation in the Department of Neurology, within the University Hospitals. The Neuropsychology Clinic is situated within the outpatient and inpatient units of Neurology, and the neuropsychologists and technicians have direct access to neurological patients. The neuropsychologists have the opportunity to be involved in the acute management of neurological patients, and are frequently requested to perform examinations at bedside in patients who are only a few hours or days out of a cerebrovascular accident, anoxic/ischemic event, head injury, or other cerebral trauma.

In keeping with the anatomical tradition of the I-B school, one overriding principle in our approach to assessment is to furnish information that will allow the development of hypotheses regarding the status of various neural systems in a particular patient's brain. Such information may come into play in several different ways.

1. Detecting a lesion not indicated by acute neuroimaging studies. In some cases, neuropsychological findings may indicate the presence of a lesion that has not been detected by early neuroimaging studies. For example, a patient presents with a severe aphasia, with marked defects in both comprehension and speech production; however, the patient has no motor or sensory defect. No lesion is evident on an acute CT conducted the day of onset. Neuropsychological examination the following day indicates that the patient has a severe global aphasia, with marked defects in all aspects of speech and language. The pattern indicates pronounced dysfunction of the perisylvian region, including both Broca's area and Wernicke's area; however, the absence of a right-sided motor defect (hemiparesis) is unusual, and suggests that the lesion is *not* of the typical middle cerebral artery pattern (i.e., extensive destruction of posterior frontal,

inferior parietal, posterior temporal, and subcortical regions). The neuropsychologist concludes that the findings suggest the condition of *global aphasia without hemiparesis*, which typically involves two separate, noncontiguous lesions affecting Broca's area and Wernicke's area, but sparing primary motor cortices; such a pattern has been linked to an embolic etiology (Van Horne and Hawes, 1982; Tranel et al., 1987a). An MR conducted on the sixth day post onset confirms this precise pattern of lesion locus (Fig. 4-1). Note that the negative acute CT, a rather common finding in older-generation CT scanners, represents a phenomenon known as "isodensity" (Damasio and Damasio, 1989).

2. Corroboration of other findings. Neuropsychological data may corroborate impressions gained from other findings. For instance, consider a patient in whom the neuroimaging data have indicated a lesion in the left posterior superior temporal

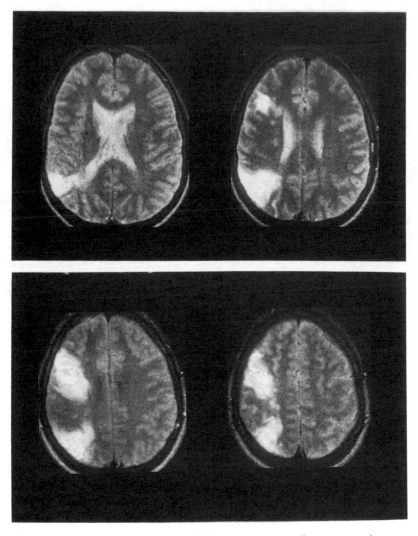

Figure 4-1. Magnetic resonance (MR) imaging scan of a patient who presented with global aphasia without hemiparesis. Note the two discrete areas of increased signal in the left hemisphere; the anterior lesion involves the frontal operculum (Broca's area), and the posterior lesion involves the inferior parietal lobule and posterior superior temporal gyrus (Wernicke's area).

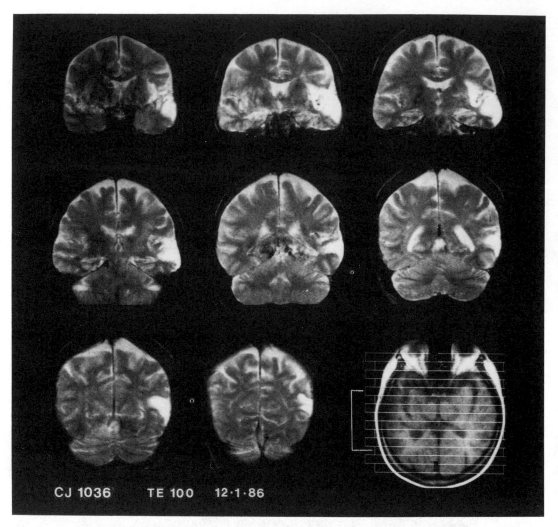

Figure 4-2. Magnetic resonance (MR) imaging scan of a patient who developed Wernicke's aphasia following a left middle cerebral artery infarction (note that the left hemisphere is on the right in these coronal sections). The lesion (area of increased signal) is centered in Wernicke's area, including the posterior superior temporal gyrus and part of the inferior parietal lobule.

gyrus and inferior parietal region (Fig. 4-2). The neuropsychological examination conducted on the second day following lesion onset confirms that the patient has a fluent, Wernicke-type aphasia, in the setting of normal visuospatial capacities. This pattern indicates dysfunction in the left temporoparietal region, especially posterior area 22 and the supramarginal gyrus (area 40).

3. Noncontributory results from other diagnostic methods. The neuropsychological

findings may indicate dysfunction in certain neural systems, even when other diagnostic procedures (neurological exam, neuroimaging, electroencephalography) have not revealed specific regions of impairment. Consider the scenario in which a patient involved in a motor vehicle accident sustained a brain injury caused by sudden deceleration forces, without actual cranial trauma. Neuroimaging studies (CT and MR) obtained in both the acute and chronic epochs did not indicate structural abnormality. The neurological exam was normal, and EEG indicated nonfocal abnormalities of uncertain diagnostic significance. Neuropsychological examination, however, generated evidence of significant impairment of "executive functions," with deficits on verbal associative fluency, the Wisconsin Card Sorting Test, and the Trail Making Test. Moreover, the patient has a clear post-morbid change in personality. The data are interpreted as reflecting dysfunction in the ventromedial frontal region, including orbital and lower mesial frontal cortices, caused by the tearing of brain tissues in this region produced by movement of the ventral part of the frontal lobes across bony protrusions from the inferior surface of the cranium (Damasio and Anderson, 1993; Tranel, 1994a; Tranel et al., 1994).

Examples such as these indicate that neuropsychological data can furnish important information regarding dysfunction of particular neural systems, even in cases in which neuroimaging studies are negative. However, it should be noted that the use of neuropsychological procedures to localize lesions has declined sharply following the advent of modern neuroimaging techniques, particularly CT in the mid-1970s and MR in the mid-1980s (e.g., Benton, 1989; Boller et al., 1991; Tranel, 1992b,c). These methods have tremendous power to detect even minimal structural abnormalities, and this power can be enhanced by special applications such as the three-dimensional reconstruction method (Brainvox) developed by Damasio and Frank (1992; Damasio, 1995).

INDICATIONS FOR NEUROPSYCHOLOGICAL ASSESSMENT. As noted above, the availability of fine-grained information on structural abnormalities has changed dramatically the need to use neuropsychological data for lesion localization. Thus, in most cases neuropsychological assessment will play a more important role as a source of information on the cognitive strengths and weaknesses of a patient than as a means of localizing a brain lesion. Some of the more frequent uses to

which neuropsychological assessment is directed in the Benton Laboratory are enumerated below.

1. Characterization of cognitive capacities in brain-injured patients to determine rehabilitation needs, placement, return to work. In patients who have suffered brain injury due to stroke, head trauma, infection, anoxia/ischemia, and so forth, neuropsychological assessment provides detailed information regarding the cognitive strengths and weaknesses of the patients, which is useful in planning for placement, rehabilitation, and return to work. In most instances, assessment is performed as early in the recovery epoch as possible, provided the patient is awake and alert enough to cooperate with the procedures. This evaluation, termed the *acute epoch assessment*, provides a baseline to which further recovery can be compared, and initiates contact with the neuropsychologist and related professionals who will figure prominently in the long-term management of the patient. *Chronic epoch assessments* (i.e., assessments conducted 3 or more months following onset of brain injury) assist in monitoring recovery, determining the effects of therapy, and making long-range decisions regarding educational and vocational rehabilitation.

2. Monitoring the neuropsychological status of patients who have undergone medical or surgical intervention. Serial neuropsychological assessment is used to track the course of patients who are undergoing medical or surgical treatment for neurological disease. Typical examples include drug therapy for patients with Parkinson's disease or seizure disorders (especially complex partial seizures), and surgical intervention in patients with normal pressure hydrocephalus or brain tumors. Neuropsychological assessment provides a baseline profile of cognition and behavior, to which changes can be compared, and it provides a sensitive means of monitoring changes that occur in relationship to particular treatment regimens.

3. Distinguishing "organic" from psychiatric

disease. Neuropsychological assessment provides crucial evidence to distinguish conditions that are primarily or exclusively "organic" from those that are primarily or exclusively "psychiatric." For example, a common diagnostic dilemma faced by both neurologists and psychiatrists is distinguishing between "true dementia" (e.g., cognitive impairment caused by Alzheimer's disease) and "pseudodementia" (e.g., cognitive impairment associated with depression). Neuropsychological assessment frequently yields the evidence needed to make this distinction (e.g., Jones et al., 1992).

4. Medicolegal situations. There has been a proliferation recently of cases in which "brain injury" and "cognitive impairment" are claimed as damages by plaintiffs who allegedly have sustained minor head injury or have been exposed to toxic chemicals. In particular, there are many cases in which "hard" or "objective" signs of brain dysfunction (e.g., weakness, sensory loss, impaired balance) are absent, neuroimaging and EEG results are normal, and the entire case rests on self-reported claims of cognitive deficiencies. Neuropsychological assessment in such cases is crucial to evaluate claims of cognitive impairment.

5. Developmental disorders. Neuropsychological assessment can assist in identifying developmental learning disorders that may influence the cognitive and behavioral presentation of a patient, such as dyslexia, attention deficit disorder, and nonverbal learning disability (Tranel et al., 1987b; Rourke, 1988).

6. Conditions in which known or suspected neurological disease is not detected by standard neurodiagnostic procedures. As noted earlier, there are some situations in which the findings of standard neurodiagnostic procedures, including neurological examination, neuroimaging, and EEG, are equivocal, even though the history indicates that a brain injury or brain disease is likely. Mild closed head trauma, the early stages of degenerative demential syndromes (e.g., Alzheimer's disease or

Pick's disease), and early HIV-related dementia, are examples. Neuropsychological assessment in such cases frequently provides the most sensitive means of evaluating the patient's brain function.

7. Monitoring changes in cognitive function across time. A situation that warrants special mention is the evolution of cognitive and behavioral changes across time. In the degenerative dementias in particular, it is not uncommon to have equivocal findings in the initial diagnostic workup. In such cases, follow-up neuropsychological evaluations can provide important confirming or disconfirming evidence regarding the patient's status.

8. Cognitive rehabilitation. Another common application of serial neuropsychological assessment is in cases in which a patient undergoes cognitive rehabilitation. Here, neuropsychological data collected at the initial assessment epoch can help determine how to orient the rehabilitation effort. Subsequent examinations can be used to measure progress during the course of therapy (Anderson, 1996).

INTERPRETATION. The results of the neuropsychological examination are interpreted in the context of other pertinent information. The primary sources of such information are the neurological examination, neuroimaging procedures, EEG studies, and the history. In keeping with the basic philosophy of the I-B school, the interpretation strategy is flexible and hypothesis-focused, and varied degrees of effort are expended to obtain and factor in other information, depending on the particulars of the case. For example, if the premorbid caliber of the patient is equivocal or difficult to estimate, we typically request the patient's grade transcripts from high school and college (if relevant). Other helpful sources of information are patient "collaterals"—spouses, children, and other individuals who know the patient well and who can provide details about the patient's typical behavior in the day-to-day environment (in fact, there are cases in which we devote more time interviewing collateral sources than we do testing the patient). It is also important to mention that interpretation of neuropsychological data takes into account the nature and pattern of the patient's performances, in addition to the actual scores and outcomes.

TRAINING MODEL. The training required for neuropsychologists who wish to practice according to the I-B school follows in general the outline provided in recent INS/Division 40 task force guidelines (INS Div. 40 Task Force, 1987). We emphasize in particular the Generic Psychology Core, the Generic Clinical Core, and training in Basic Neurosciences (Table 4-6). Our philosophy is that solid graduate student training in these areas is a necessary foundation for postgraduate specialization in neuropsychology. A second important feature is an emphasis on basic

Table 4-6. Core Graduate Training in Preparation for Clinical Neuropsychology[a]

A. *Generic Psychology Core*

1. Statistics and Methodology
2. Learning, Cognition, and Perception
3. Social Psychology
4. Personality Theory
5. Physiological Psychology
6. Developmental Psychology
7. History

B. *Generic Clinical Core*

1. Psychopathology
2. Psychometric Theory
3. Interview and Assessment Techniques
   i. Interviewing
   ii. Intelligence Assessment
   iii. Personality Assessment
4. Intervention Techniques
   i. Counseling and Psychotherapy
   ii. Behavior Therapy
5. Professional Ethics

C. *Neurosciences Core*

1. Basic Neurosciences
2. Advanced Physiological Psychology and Pharmacology
3. Neuropsychology of Perceptual, Cognitive, and Executive Processes
4. Neuroanatomy
5. Neuroimaging Techniques

[a]Adapted from the Report of the INS–Division 40 Task Force on Education, Accreditation, and Credentialing (INS–Division 40 Task Force, 1987)

research training. The I-B method rests squarely on the scientific principles of hypothesis testing, probabilistic reasoning, and inferential conclusion drawing, and practitioners must be solidly trained in basic research methodology.

All four of the current staff neuropsychologists in the Benton Neuropsychology Laboratory were trained in clinical psychology. For several reasons, this training background is considered in our view to be essential for the practice of clinical neuropsychology. First, basic graduate training in psychopathology incorporating issues of theory, assessment, and treatment is of indispensable value. Knowledge about psychopathology becomes essential in neuropsychological practice on several accounts: (1) Many patients bring to the neuropsychological examination some degree of psychopathology, whether that be of an incapacitating degree or simply the distress that often characterizes persons who have sustained cerebral insult. This has an inevitable influence on the manner in which the patient approaches and deals with the neuropsychological assessment situation. Understanding this influence is critical for accurate interpretation of the performances of patients on tests, not to mention the collection of reliable and valid data. (2) The presence of significant psychopathology is often a salient component of the reason for referral. The neuropsychologist is frequently called upon to document such presence, to determine its relationship to other aspects of the patient's cognition and behavior, and finally, to offer impressions about its cause. (3) Typically, referrals to neuropsychologists are from neurologists and psychiatrists. There is considerable overlap in the populations of patients that originate in these two specialty areas, and in the types of signs and symptoms that such patients present. Having the capability of factoring in accurately the contributions of psychopathology to the presentations of such patients is extremely important.

A final rationale for coming to neuropsychology from a clinical psychology background is that such a background furnishes basic training in psychological appraisal, which underlies the standardized nature of clinical neuropsychological assessment. Knowledge about test development and construction, reliability, and validity is crucial when employing standardized psychological tests to measure cognition and behavior.

Other Considerations

PERSONNEL. The Benton Neuropsychology Laboratory is staffed currently by four clinical neuropsychologists and a postdoctoral fellow. Tranel is the chief of the operation, and Steven Anderson, Ph.D., provides executive assistance and also directs a Cognitive Rehabilitation Laboratory within the Benton Laboratory (discussed below). Dr. Benton acts as senior consultant. There are several neuropsychology technicians and support staff.

USE OF NEUROPSYCHOLOGY TECHNICIANS. The I-B method has utilized neuropsychology technicians since its inception. Technicians are charged with the responsibility for most of the hands-on test administration. They collect pertinent background information, record presenting complaints, and administer the series of tests prescribed by the supervising neuropsychologist. The technicians are specifically trained in the I-B method, and are encouraged to facilitate the flexible, hypothesis-driven approach. This requires that they maintain an awareness of the patient's ongoing performance profile, so that on-line adaptations in the testing procedure can be made. The technicians do *not* administer a rigid set of tests to a patient if it is obvious that the data being collected are of questionable reliability or validity, or, equally importantly, if the data appear to be uninformative vis-à-vis the referral question. Final decisions regarding changes in testing, e.g., pursuing a particular hypothesis and dropping others, rest with the supervising neuropsychologist; nevertheless, the technicians have the prerogative to raise questions about alternative hypotheses during the course of test administration.

We are very much aware that the I-B method places significant demands on the neuropsychology technicians. The method

requires a certain degree of decision making, creativity, and vigilance on the part of the technicians; by contrast, administering a prescribed set of tests in adherence with a fixed-battery philosophy is probably simpler and more straightforward. Accordingly, training technicians in the I-B school requires a significant initial investment; however, we have found that once technicians are comfortable with our basic philosophy and the various procedures, they tend to engage the assessment process at a deeper level than might be the case when their charge is simply to collect a specified set of test data.

Technicians are "recalibrated" annually. Neuropsychologists observe the technicians, with attention to the manner in which the technicians conform to specified instructions for administration of the tests. Departures from standard procedure are discussed and rectified as appropriate. This typically involves a reminder to the technician about the standard method of administration. At times, however, a technician may have developed a procedure that proves to be superior to the standard method, and this may ultimately be incorporated as a revision in the basic method. Making a permanent revision is a sensitive issue, as one must be extremely careful not to create a situation in which the normative information for the test becomes uninformative or misleading because of a different method of administration. We are, however, quite open to the possibility of revising our procedures, and over the years, the insightful observations of highly experienced technicians have proved invaluable in making decisions about improving the effectiveness of a variety of assessment procedures. We also encourage "testing the limits"—that is, finding out whether a patient can perform a particular task under conditions that are less demanding than those called for by the formal test protocol. This process often furnishes information about patient capabilities that is not reflected in test scores per se, but that has important value for diagnostic purposes and especially for designing rehabilitation programs (cf. Kaplan, 1985; Milberg et al., Chapter 3).

The use of technicians offers a distinct

advantage in permitting "blind" hypothesis testing in the neuropsychological assessment procedure. The technician has relatively little at stake in the outcome of the procedure; by contrast, the neuropsychologist may have any number of prevailing presuppositions about how the patient might perform, due to forensic issues, research considerations, and so on. Hence, the technician is probably in a better position than the neuropsychologist to collect and record objective findings and to avoid problems related to "experimenter bias."

We find that it is cost- and time-efficient to utilize technicians. The standard I-B procedure can be performed twice and sometimes three times daily by a technician. Given the current personnel, we can accommodate between 10 and 20 patients per day, and the annual throughput of the Benton Neuropsychology Laboratory is approximately 2000 examinations.

REPORT WRITING. Reports from our Neuropsychology Clinic comprise three main sections: (1) identification and background; (2) data reporting; (3) impressions and recommendations. The scope of the report varies according to the nature of the situation, but most consultation reports generated for referrals from within the University of Iowa Hospitals are relatively brief, on the order of 250 to 500 words. In more complicated cases, our reports are typically somewhat longer, in the range of 500 to 750 words. We typically produce longer reports for outside referral agencies; for example, when more detailed questions regarding long-term management of the patient are raised, or in forensic referrals. Such reports may extend up to 1000 or more words.

We have a policy of *not* including scores and other "raw" data in our reports. The primary reason for this is because of the potential misuse of such information by persons not trained in neuropsychology or psychological appraisal. Psychological data, particularly IQ scores, memory quotients, and scores reported as "percentiles," are quite vulnerable to misinterpretation, because nonexperts frequently fail to appreciate the

importance of factors such as the estimated premorbid level of functioning of the patient, the quality of normative information, and the type of population on which the test was standardized. Because reports are usually placed in hospital charts or other sources that can be accessed fairly easily by nonexperts, it seems prudent to omit raw data from such reports. Rather than scores, we emphasize the reporting of *interpretations* of patient performances—whether the patient performed normally or abnormally, the degree of abnormality, and so forth.

Two additional comments are in order here. First, with regard to IQ scores, the reporting of such scores is not only unwise for the reasons mentioned above, but the use of such scores per se in neuropsychological assessment has been seriously questioned (Lezak, 1988). Second, the recently revised Ethical Principles of the American Psychological Association (APA, 1992) have outlined a clear position *against* the release of "raw" data to nonexperts (see Tranel, 1994b). Hence, inclusion of data (numbers, scores) in reports that are likely to end up in the hands of nonexperts is hazardous from an ethical point of view as well. There are different views on this issue (e.g., see Freides, 1993), but we have found that refraining from using scores in reports in no way diminishes the quality or usefulness of the reports, and in many cases, actually encourages the authors (neuropsychologists) to provide a higher level of interpretation of the data, which ought to be an objective of a good report.

Cognitive Rehabilitation Laboratory

A Cognitive Rehabilitation Laboratory, developed and directed by neuropsychologist Steven Anderson (Anderson, 1996), has recently been added to the Benton Neuropsychology Laboratory. This service provides on-site rehabilitation programs for brain-injured patients. The approach to cognitive rehabilitation follows the same philosophical approach as the Iowa-Benton assessment method. Interventions are tailored to individual patients to meet circumscribed goals in a time-efficient manner. Specific interventions are selected from an inventory of empirically supported procedures, with the selection process guided by the findings of the neuropsychological evaluation and by the complaints and goals expressed by the patient and family. Emphasis is placed on education of the patient and family regarding the patient's neuropsychological condition, and on compensatory strategies designed to minimize the consequences of the acquired cognitive impairments. Interventions range from a single session or once-per-year consultation (e.g., for the family of a patient with Alzheimer's disease), to daily sessions over several weeks (e.g., for a patient with attention and language impairments from a left hemisphere stroke). Among the services provided are training in the use of compensatory devices (e.g., memory books) and strategies (e.g., use of American Sign Language by severely aphasic patients), computer-assisted attentional training, psychotherapeutic interventions for depression, anxiety, and behavioral control, and awareness training for anosognosia.

Typically, patients are referred to Anderson's rehabilitation program after an initial examination in the Neuropsychology Clinic, when the conclusion has been reached that the patient needs and would probably benefit from cognitive rehabilitation. Thereafter, the Neuropsychology Clinic provides periodic reexaminations, to track the course of the patient's recovery.

Summary

The Iowa-Benton school of neuropsychological assessment takes a flexible, hypothesis-driven approach to standardized measurement of higher brain functions in brain-damaged patients. The objective is to obtain quantitative measurements of key domains of cognition and behavior, in a time-efficient manner, in sufficient breadth and depth that the referral question can be answered. Starting from a Core Battery, we are guided in the selection of tests by a multitude of factors including the nature of the patient's complaint, the questions raised by the referring

agent, the impressions gained from the initial interview, and above all, the diagnostic possibilities raised by the patient's performances during the course of the examination. A close link to neuroanatomy is maintained, and the neuropsychological data both inform and are informed by neuroanatomical findings derived from CT, MR and other procedures. Whenever possible, the neuropsychological findings are used to infer the integrity or lack thereof of various neural systems in the patient's brain. Interpretation of neuropsychological data is conducted in the context of pertinent historical and diagnostic information regarding the patient.

Acknowledgments

This work is supported by Program Project Grant NS19632. I am indebted to Steven Anderson for providing helpful comments on an earlier draft, and to Kerry Hamsher for details about the development of the research program. Arthur Benton provided information about the early history of the Laboratory. I would also like to acknowledge Dr. Benton's steady encouragement and guidance of my endeavors in the further development of neuropsychology at Iowa.

References

American Psychological Association. (1992). Ethical principles of psychologists and code of conduct. *American Psychologist, 47,* 1597–1611.

Anderson, S. W. (1996). Cognitive rehabilitation in closed head injury. In M. Rizzo and D. Tranel, eds., *Head Injury and Post-Concussive Syndrome.* New York: Churchill Livingstone, pp. 457–468.

Barrash, J., Tranel, D., and Damasio, H. (1993). Standardization and validation of a route learning test. *Journal of Clinical and Experimental Neuropsychology, 15,* 66 (Abst).

Bechtoldt, H. P., Benton, A. L., and Fogel, M. L. (1962). An application of factor analysis in neuropsychology. *Psychological Record, 12,* 147–156.

Benton, A. L. (1955a). Development of finger localization capacity in school children. *Child Development, 26,* 225–230.

Benton, A. L. (1955b). Right-left discrimination and finger localization in defective children. *Archives of Neurology and Psychiatry, 74,* 383–389.

Benton, A. L. (1956). Jacques Loeb and the method of double stimulation. *Journal of the History of Medicine and Allied Sciences, 11*, 47–53.

Benton, A. L. (1975). Neuropsychological assessment. In D. B. Tower, eds., *The Nervous System*, Vol. 2 *(The Clinical Neurosciences)*. New York: Raven Press, pp. 67–74.

Benton, A. L. (1985). Some problems associated with neuropsychological assessment. *Bulletin of Clinical Neurosciences, 50*, 11–15.

Benton, A. L. (1989). Neuropsychology: Past, present and future. In F. Boller and J. Grafman, eds., *Handbook of Neuropsychology*, Vol. 1. Amsterdam: Elsevier, pp. 1–27.

Benton, A. L. (1991). Basic approaches to neuropsychological assessment. In S. R. Steinhauer, J. H. Gruzelier, and J. Zubin, eds., *Handbook of Schizophrenia*, Vol. 5. Amsterdam: Elsevier, pp. 505–523.

Benton, A. L. (1992). Gerstmann's syndrome. *Archives of Neurology, 49*, 445–447.

Benton, A. L., and Abramson, L. S. (1952). Gerstmann symptoms following electroshock therapy. *Archives of Neurology and Psychiatry, 68*, 248–257.

Benton, A. L., and Cohen, B. D. (1955). Right-left discrimination and finger localization in normal and brain-injured subjects. *Proceedings of the Iowa Academy of Science, 62*, 447–451.

Benton, A. L., and Fogel, M. L. (1962). Three-dimensional constructional praxis: A clinical test. *Archives of Neurology, 7*, 347–354.

Benton, A. L., Hamsher, K., Varney, N. R., and Spreen, O. (1983). *Contributions to Neuropsychological Assessment*. New York: Oxford University Press.

Benton, A. L., and Menefee, F. L. (1957). Handedness and right-left discrimination. *Child Development, 28*, 237–242.

Benton, A. L., and Meyers, R. (1956). An early description of the Gerstmann syndrome. *Neurology, 6*, 838–842.

Benton, A. L., and Van Allen, M. W. (1968). Impairment in facial recognition in patients with unilateral cerebral disease. *Cortex, 4*, 344–358.

Benton, A. L., Varney, N. R., and Hamsher, K. (1978). Visuospatial judgment: A clinical test. *Archives of Neurology, 35*, 364–367.

Benton Neuropsychology Laboratory. (1993). *Manual of Operations*. Department of Neurology, University of Iowa Hospitals and Clinics, Iowa City, Iowa.

Binder, L. M. (1993). Assessment of malingering after mild head trauma with the Portland Digit Recognition Test. *Journal of Clinical and Experimental Neuropsychology, 15*, 170–182.

Blackburn, H. L. (1958). Effects of motivating instructions on reaction time in cerebral disease. *Journal of Abnormal and Social Psychology, 56*, 359–366.

Blackburn, H. L., and Benton, A. L. (1955). Simple and choice reaction time in cerebral disease. *Confinia Neurologica, 15*, 327–338.

Boller, F., Swihart, A. A., Forbes, M. M., and Denes, G. (1991). Neuropsychology in its daily practice: Past and present. In F. Boller and J. Grafman, eds., *Handbook of Neuropsychology*, Vol. 5. Amsterdam: Elsevier, pp. 379–388.

Costa, L., and Spreen, O. (1985). *Studies in Neuropsychology: Selected Papers of Arthur Benton*. New York: Oxford University Press.

Damasio, A. R., and Anderson, S. W. (1993). The frontal lobes. In K. M. Heilman and E. Valenstein, eds., *Clinical Neuropsychology* (3rd ed.). New York: Oxford University Press, pp. 409–460.

Damasio, H. (1995). *Human Brain Anatomy in Computerized Images*. New York: Oxford University Press.

Damasio, H., and Damasio, A. R. (1989). *Lesion Analysis in Neuropsychology*. New York: Oxford University Press.

Damasio, H., and Frank, R. (1992). Three-dimensional *in vivo* mapping of brain lesions in humans. *Archives of Neurology, 49*, 137–143.

Eslinger, P. J., Damasio, A. R., Benton, A. L., and Van Allen, M. (1985). Neuropsychologic detection of abnormal mental decline in older persons. *Journal of the American Medical Association, 253*, 670–674.

Freides, D. (1993). Proposed standard of professional practice: Neuropsychological reports display all quantitative data. *The Clinical Neuropsychologist, 7*, 234–235.

Fogel, M. L. (1962). The Gerstmann syndrome and the parietal symptom-complex. *Psychological Record, 12*, 85–99.

Godersky, J. C., Gentry, L. R., Tranel, D., Dyste, G. N., and Danks, K. R. (1990). Magnetic resonance imaging and neurobehavioral outcome in traumatic brain injury. *Acta Neurochirurgica, 51* (Suppl.), 311–314.

Graff-Radford, N., Godersky, J., Tranel, D., Eslinger, P. J., and Jones, M. P. (1989). Neuropsychological testing in normal pressure hydrocephalus. In J. T. Hoff and A. L. Betz, eds., *Intracranial Pressure* (7th ed.). Berlin: Springer-Verlag, pp. 422–424.

Hamsher, K. (1985). The Iowa group. *International Journal of Neuroscience, 25*, 295–305.

Heilbrun, A. B., Jr. (1956). Psychological test performance as a function of lateral localization of cerebral lesion. *Journal of Comparative and Physiological Psychology, 49,* 10–14.

Heilbrun, A. B., Jr. (1959). Lateralization of cerebral lesion and performance on spatial-temporal tasks. *Archives of Neurology, 1,* 282–287.

INS–Division 40 Task Force. (1987). Reports of the INS-Division 40 Task Force on Education, Accreditation, and Credentialing. *The Clinical Neuropsychologist, 1,* 29–34.

Jones, R. D., and Tranel, D. (1991). Development of a screening battery for the detection of HIV-related cognitive deficits. *Archives of Clinical Neuropsychology, 6,* 198.

Jones, R. D., Tranel, D., Benton, A. L., and Paulsen, J. (1992). Differentiating dementia from "pseudodementia" early in the clinical course: Utility of neuropsychological tests. *Neuropsychology, 6,* 13–21.

Joynt, R. J., Benton, A. L., and Fogel, M. L. (1962). Behavioral and pathological correlates of motor impersistence. *Neurology, 12,* 876–881.

Kaplan, E. (1985). A process approach to neuropsychological assessment. In T. Boll and B. K. Bryant, eds., *Clinical Neuropsychology and Brain Function: Research, Measurement, and Practice.* Washington: American Psychological Association, pp. 125–167.

Kaplan, E., Fein, D., Morris, R., and Delis, D. C. (1991). *The Wechsler Adult Intelligence Scale-Revised as a Neuropsychological Instrument.* San Antonio, TX: The Psychological Corporation.

Lezak, M. D. (1988). IQ: R.I.P. *Journal of Clinical and Experimental Neuropsychology, 10,* 351–361.

Lezak, M. D. (1995). *Neuropsychological Assessment* (3rd ed.). New York: Oxford University Press.

Matarazzo, J. D. (1972). *Wechsler's Measurement and Appraisal of Adult Intelligence* (5th ed.). New York: Oxford University Press.

Mesulam, M.-M. (1982). Slowly progressive aphasia without generalized dementia. *Annals of Neurology, 11,* 592–598.

Milberg, W. P., Hebben, N., and Kaplan, E. (1996). The Boston process approach to neuropsychological assessment. In I. Grant and K. M. Adams, eds., *Neuropsychological Assessment of Neuropsychiatric Disorders* (2nd ed.). New York: Oxford University Press

Reitan, R. M., and Wolfson, D. (1985). *The Halstead-Reitan Neuropsychological Test Battery: Theory and Clinical Interpretation.* Tucson, AZ: Neuropsychology Press.

Rizzo, M., and Tranel, D., eds. (1996). *Head Injury and Post-Concussive Syndrome.* New York: Churchill Livingstone.

Rogers, R., ed. (1988). *Clinical Assessment of Malingering and Deception.* New York: Guilford Press.

Rourke, B. P. (1988). The syndrome of nonverbal learning disabilities: Developmental manifestations in neurological disease, disorder, and dysfunction. *The Clinical Neuropsychologist, 2,* 293–330.

Spreen, O., and Strauss, E. (1991). *A Compendium of Neuropsychological Tests: Administration, Norms, and Commentary.* New York: Oxford University Press.

Swanson, R. A. (1957). Perception of simultaneous tactual stimulation in defective and normal children. *American Journal of Mental Deficiency, 61,* 743–752.

Swanson, R. A., and Benton, A. L. (1955). Some aspects of the genetic development or right-left discrimination. *Child Development, 26,* 123–133.

Tranel, D. (1992a). Neurology of language. *Current Opinion in Neurology and Neurosurgery, 5,* 77–82.

Tranel, D. (1992b). Neuropsychological assessment. *Psychiatric Clinics of North America, 15,* 283–299.

Tranel, D. (1992c). The role of neuropsychology in the diagnosis and management of cerebrovascular disease. In H. P. Adams, ed., *Handbook of Cerebrovascular Diseases.* New York: Marcel Dekker, pp. 613–636.

Tranel, D. (1994a). "Acquired sociopathy": The development of sociopathic behavior following focal brain damage. *Progress in Experimental Personality and Psychopathology Research, 17,* 285–311.

Tranel, D. (1994b). The release of psychological data to non-experts: Ethical and legal considerations. *Professional Psychology: Research and Practice, 25,* 33–38.

Tranel, D., Anderson, S. W., and Benton, A. L. (1994). Development of the concept of "executive function" and its relationship to the frontal lobes. In F. Boller and J. Grafman, eds., *Handbook of Neuropsychology,* Vol. 9. Amsterdam: Elsevier, pp. 125–148.

Tranel, D., Biller, J., Damasio, H., Adams, H. P., Jr., and Cornell, S. H. (1987a). Global aphasia without hemiparesis. *Archives of Neurology, 44,* 304–308.

Tranel, D., Hall, L. E., Olson, S., and Tranel, N. N. (1987b). Evidence for a right-hemisphere developmental learning disability. *Developmental Neuropsychology, 3*, 113–127.

Van Horn, G., and Hawes, A. (1982). Global aphasia without hemiparesis: A sign of embolic encephalopathy. *Neurology, 32*, 403–406.

Wahler, H. J. (1956). A comparison of reproduction errors made by brain-damaged and control patients on a memory-for-designs test. *Journal of Abnormal and Social Psychology, 52*, 251–255.

Wechsler, D. (1981). *Manual for the Wechsler Adult Intelligence Scale-Revised.* New York: Psychological Corporation.

5 Computers and Memory

GLENN J. LARRABEE and THOMAS H. CROOK, III

This chapter explores the use of computers in the neuropsychological evaluation and rehabilitation of memory disorders. We first consider general issues related to the use of computers in neuropsychology and then briefly discuss issues relevant specifically to memory assessment. Next we review various applications of computerized memory testing. Finally, we discuss the use of computers in memory rehabilitation and include specific examples.

General Issues Concerning Use of Computers in Neuropsychology

The use of computers in neuropsychology has been increasing in recent years. In general, computers have been used for data storage, data analysis, scoring of neuropsychological tests, analysis of test profiles for diagnosis or classification, test administration, and rehabilitation (Adams, 1986; Adams and Brown, 1986; Gianutsos, 1986).

The advantages of computer-administered neuropsychological tests include increased reliability of measurement, enhanced capacity for generating complex stimuli, greater facility in measuring response accuracy and latency, standardization of stimulus presentation across test sites, and ease of administration, which reduces the need for highly skilled personnel (Adams and Brown, 1986; Branconnier, 1986; Wright et al., 1987; Kapur, 1988; Maulucci and Eckhouse, 1988).

In the field of cognitive rehabilitation, computers have been used as specific learning tools, for cognitive exercise mediation, for performance feedback, and as prosthetic devices (Gianutsos, 1986; Chute et al., 1988).

Although there are advantages to computerized cognitive assessment and rehabilitation, there are also limitations. Adapting existing neuropsychological tests to computerized administration changes the nature of the tests. This in turn can influence the nature of the patient's perception of the test, which can affect his or her motivation and response style (Adams and Brown, 1986). Kapur (1988) cautions that most computerized measures have significant visuoperceptual demands, which can cause difficulty for patients with reduced visual acuity or neglect. Additionally, most computerized test batteries require the patient to utilize manipulanda that may be unfamiliar, such as a joystick or computer keyboard. This may pose particular difficulty for severely impaired patients, especially the elderly (Larrabee and Crook, 1991).

Finally, it is important that psychologists utilizing computers for evaluation or rehabilitation adhere to professional standards regarding such instruments (Division 40 Task Force Report on Computer-Assisted Neuropsychological Evaluation, 1987; Matthews et al., 1991). Computerized neuropsychological evaluation in general, and memory testing in particular, should be conducted in line with

APA guidelines for test instruments concerning reliability and validity, and user qualifications.

General Considerations in the Evaluation of Memory Function

The examination of memory is of central importance in neuropsychological evaluation because memory disturbance is a cardinal feature of several different neurological and neuropsychiatric disorders (Kapur, 1988; Lezak, 1995). A variety of material-specific (i.e., for verbal or visual material) as well as generalized memory disturbances can be seen following vascular lesions, hypoxia, trauma, and neoplasms (Kapur, 1988). In early-stage Alzheimer-type dementia, memory disturbance is usually the initial presenting symptom (Albert and Moss, 1992; Cummings and Benson, 1992). Persons surviving severe closed head trauma may suffer profound memory deficits that persist for several years after the original trauma (Levin et al., 1982).

Much progress has been made in developing memory test procedures over the past 10 years (Larrabee and Crook, 1995). This progress has been influenced by theory and research in cognitive and experimental psychology as well as by psychometric research. Information-processing models have focused on both the structure (primary, secondary, and tertiary memory; cf. Kaszniak et al., 1986) and function of memory processes (e.g., levels of processing and release from proactive inhibition; cf. Wickens, 1970; Craik and Lockhart, 1972). Influential experimental paradigms include selective reminding (Buschke, 1973), which has been used extensively in head trauma and dementia research (Levin et al., 1982; Larrabee et al., 1985b, 1988); signal detection methodology (Hannay, 1986), which has been employed in visual recognition memory testing (Hannay et al., 1979; Trahan and Larrabee, 1988); and the delayed nonmatching-to-sample paradigm (Mishkin, 1978), which has been used to evaluate memory in Alzheimer's disease (Albert and Moss, 1992).

Factor-analytic research has led to an increased understanding of the various dimensions underlying performance on memory tests and batteries (Larrabee et al., 1983, 1985a; Larrabee and Levin, 1986; Larrabee and Curtiss, 1995). It is noteworthy that this research, demonstrating factors of immediate memory/attention and concentration/information processing, recent verbal and visual memory, and remote memory, matches structural information-processing categories of primary, secondary, and tertiary memory (Kaszniak et al., 1986). Although the research suggests that measures of each of these three dimensions should be incorporated into any omnibus memory examination, the most important dimensions having the greatest sensitivity (i.e., to incipient dementia; subacute stages of recovery from severe head trauma) are measures of primary memory/information processing and secondary memory (Larrabee and Crook, 1988a, 1991).

Other factors relevant to memory testing procedures include face or "ecologic" validity (cf. Cunningham, 1986; West, 1986; Wilson et al., 1989) and the availability of alternate forms (Larrabee and Crook, 1988a). Standard memory tests, such as the Wechsler Memory Scale–Revised (WMS-R; Wechsler, 1987) have been criticized because of their lack of relevance to everyday memory tasks (Cunningham, 1986). Availability of alternate forms is important for monitoring recovery from traumatic brain injury or deterioration in degenerative conditions (Larrabee and Crook, 1988a, 1991).

Computerized Memory Assessment

Two basic approaches have been employed in computerized memory assessment. The first, exemplified by the Unified Tri-Service Cognitive Performance Assessment Battery (UTC-PAB; Englund et al., 1987; Perez et al., 1987), the Sbordone-Hall Memory Battery (Sbordone et al., 1985), the Alzheimer's Disease Assessment Battery (ADAB; Branconnier, 1986), the Microcomputer-based Tested System (Foree et al., 1984), Micro-Cog (Powell et al., 1993), CogScreen-AE (Kay, 1995), and the Nonverbal Selective Reminding Test (Kane and Perrine, 1988) adapts standard memory tasks and stimuli to computerized administration and scoring. The second approach, exemplified by the battery developed by Memory Assessment Clinics, Inc. (Crook et al., 1986b; Larrabee and Crook, 1988a,b), makes use of computer imaging technology to simulate memory tasks of everyday life.

The UTC-PAB, Tester's Workbench, and ANAM

The UTC-PAB (Englund et al., 1987; Perez et al., 1987) was designed for the assessment of cognitive performance in a multiple-level drug evaluation program. The UTC-PAB measures a variety of language, reasoning, and perceptual tasks as well as tasks related to memory and efficiency of information processing. Drawing heavily from experimental psychology, the memory and related information-processing tasks include continuous recall of digits (in serium); four-choice serial reaction time; vigilance; a modified Sternberg memory search task; short term spatial memory (similarity of histogram patterns; similarity of matrix patterns; recognition memory for dot patterns); recognition memory for sequences of consonants; a variant of the WAIS Coding subtest (the subject must recall digit and symbol paired associates); dual task processing (memory search combined with a motor response task); and dichotic listening.

Currently, data are being collected on the reliability and validity of the UTC-PAB. Data on the reliability and validity of the various tasks are discussed (Perez et al., 1987); however, these figures are related to values reported for similar tasks in the experimental literature, upon which the UTC-PAB was based. To date, there are no published data on the reliability or validity of this particular instrument. These normative limitations suggest current use of these procedures in research applications, pending more extensive psychometric development.

The reader wishing more extensive information concerning the UTC-PAB is referred to Kane and Kay (1992). The newest modification of the UTC-PAB is known as the Test-

ers WorkBench (TWB), and the clinical adaptation of the TWB is known as the Automated Neuropsychological Assessment Metrics (ANAM) system (Kane, 1995).

A number of publications have recently appeared on ANAM. Bleiberg et al. (1993) utilized ANAM to evaluate the effects of dexedrine on the performance consistency of a 55-year-old attorney who had sustained a moderately severe closed head injury. ANAM, which was designed with the specific goal of examining the effects of battlefield chemical warfare antidotes on cognitive performance, is available in multiple parallel forms. These are designed to be administered repeatedly until practice effects reach asymptote and a stable baseline is achieved. Bleiberg et al. demonstrated improvements in both level and variability of performance for their head-injured subject on dexedrine versus placebo and versus lorazepam. ANAM is employed in a number of ongoing investigations of closed head injury, normal pressure hydrocephalus, and coronary artery bypass graft surgery (Spector et al., 1993). Normative data are limited at present; however, the battery was specifically designed for utilization in subject-as-own-control investigations. Levinson and Reeves (1994a) present preliminary normative data on 22 subjects with mild to moderate closed head injury and on 40 healthy control subjects (Levinson and Reeves, 1994b). Of particular interest, Levinson and Reeves (1994a) found that efficiency or throughput (number of correct responses per unit time) was the most sensitive discriminating variable relative to head trauma severity.

Sbordone-Hall Memory Battery

The Sbordone-Hall Memory Battery (SHMB; Sbordone et al., 1985; Putnam, 1987) was designed for use with the Apple II line of personal computers. The SHMB includes seven subtests (Putnam, 1987): (1) free recall of alphanumeric stimuli; (2) recognition of alphanumeric stimuli; (3) immediate recognition of familiar words; (4) delayed recognition of pictures; (5) recognition of single geometric figures; (6) delayed recognition of familiar words; and (7) recognition of multiple geometric figures. There is a separate data analysis and display package that provides a short (1½ pages) or full (12 pages) analysis of each patient's performances. Initial validity and reliability data are reported (Sbordone et al., 1985). The normative groups included 93 patients (20 female, 73 male) with previously diagnosed cases of organic brain dysfunction, 23 patients previously diagnosed as having psychiatric disorders without brain damage (8 female, 15 male), and 20 female and 29 male college students with no history of psychiatric or neurologic disorders. Validity data are reported in terms of construct validity (factor analysis) and a discriminant function analysis performed on the scores of the brain-damaged subjects, psychiatric patients, and normal control college students. The factor analysis yielded four factors, accounting for 52% of the variance, which were interpreted by the authors as measuring General Verbal Memory, Visual Recognition Deficit, Verbal Memory Deficit, and Deficit in Verbal Discrimination Memory. The discrimination of college students from patients with organic brain damage was reliable; however, the discrimination of psychiatric patients from organic patients was not reliable. Test-retest reliabilities (n = 31) ranged from .02 (d' value, picture recognition) to .91 (alphanumeric free recall—maximum stimuli).

These initial data are of interest. The normative database needs expanding, to cover different ranges of education other than college, and to cover the full adult age range. Consequently, current use of this procedure should be confined to research settings, pending more complete normative data.

Alzheimer's Disease Assessment Battery

The Alzheimer's Disease Assessment Battery (ADAB; Branconnier, 1986) was designed for use on an Apple II+ computer with a 4-MHz, Z80 CPU with 48K of RAM. The operator (test administrator) uses a Sanyo 12-inch green screen monitor with 24 × 80 character resolution, an Apple dual-drive floppy disk subsystem and CP/M disk op-

erating system, and an Epson MX-80 dot matrix printer for hard-copy output. The patient uses a separate station consisting of a 15-inch Sanyo terminal, an RCA VP 3301 alphanumeric keyboard, and a Nutone Intercom for communication of verbal responses. Four measures make up the ADAB: (1) assessment of intellectual deterioration based on comparing the National Adult Reading Test (NART; Nelson and McKenna, 1975) with a Verbal IQ prorated on the basis of WAIS Information, Similarities and Vocabulary; (2) a 10-word, five-trial Verbal Selective Reminding Test; (3) the FAS Word Fluency subtest of the Neurosensory Center Comprehensive Examination for Aphasia (Spreen and Benton, 1977); and (4) a computerized version of the Standardized Road Map Test of Direction Sense (Money et al., 1965).

Branconnier (1986) reported on the ADAB's discriminant validity in a study contrasting the performance of 32 patients with Alzheimer's disease and 20 normal elderly control subjects. All ADAB performance measures discriminated the two groups significantly, with the greatest proportion of variance accounted for by a d' statistic based on the Verbal Selective Reminding Test. These initial data are promising. Normative expansion is needed, however, as well as data on alternate forms. Lastly, several areas of memory-related functions (e.g., attention, psychomotor speed) and visual memory are not assessed.

The Microcomputer-based Testing System

The Microcomputer-based Testing System (MTS; Foree et al., 1984; Eckerman et al., 1985) was originally developed in cooperation with the U.S. Environmental Protection Agency to be used as a tool to assess toxic effects of environmental pollutants. The MTS contains a variety of measures of perception, reaction time, and reasoning, in addition to memory tasks. It is noteworthy that the MTS combines both traditional memory (continuous recognition of words as well as a Sternberg paradigm) and "everyday" stimuli (digit supraspan learning administered via touch telephone; object location recall for six items in one of six locations in and around a house). Preliminary results demonstrate the sensitivity of the MTS reaction-time measures to alcohol level and carbon monoxide level (Eckerman et al., 1985). At present, normative data are limited.

The Nonverbal Selective Reminding Test

Kane and Perrine (1988) have developed a nonverbal analogue to the Selective Reminding Test. This consists of 21 abstract designs, seven used as target stimuli, 14 as distractors, administered in a recognition format with selective reminding prior to each recognition attempt. Factor analysis of the Nonverbal Selective Reminding Test (NSRT), in the context of other measures of verbal and nonverbal memory and intellectual functions, provided initial support for the construct validity of the NSRT as a measure of visual memory. At present, the NSRT has been employed in research projects including the relationship of head injury to marital aggression, and the effects of Aspartame on cognitive functions (Kane and Kay, 1992). Kane and Perrine (1988) have also developed a computerized version of the Verbal Selective Reminding Test. Normative data are limited at present but undergoing expansion. The Verbal and Nonverbal Selective Reminding Tests can be administered independently or in conjunction with Cog-Screen—AE (Kay, 1995) to enhance that battery's assessment of memory (Kane and Kay, 1992).

MicroCog

MicroCog was developed out of initial efforts to identify cognitive status changes in physicians and other professionals that might interfere with occupational performance (Powell et al., 1993; Kane, 1995). The test has subsequently been developed as a general neuropsychological screening instrument.

Five primary neurobehavioral domains are assessed, including Attention/Mental Control, Memory, Reasoning/Calculation, Spatial Processing and Reaction time. The Attention/Mental Control Domain includes span tasks (numbers forward and reversed), a continuous performance task (Alphabet subtest) requiring identification of letters of the alphabet as they appear in sequence within a series of random letters, and a supraspan word list test (Wordlists subtest) presented in continuous performance format, with subsequent assessment of incidental learning. Memory is assessed for immediate and delayed recognition of the content of two stories and delayed recognition of an address, assessed in a multiple-choice format. Reaction time assesses visual and auditory simple reaction time. The Spatial Processing domain also includes a visual working memory subtest, in which the subject must reproduce, following a 1-second presentation, a grid pattern in a 3×3 matrix, in which either three, four, or five of the spaces are colored.

MicroCog can be administered in the 18-subtest standard form in one hour, or as a 12-subtest short form in 30 minutes. Scores are provided for accuracy, speed, and proficiency (a combination of speed and accuracy). Measures of general cognitive function and proficiency are also computed.

A particular strength of MicroCog is the normative database of 810 adults (45 females and 45 males in each of nine age groups: 18–24, 25–34, 35–44, 45–54, 55–64, 65–69, 70–74, 75–79, 80–89). Test data are also presented for a variety of clinical groups including dementia, lobectomy patients, depression, and schizophrenia. Data are provided for percentage correct classification, sensitivity, and specificity for each clinical group. Additionally, mean levels of performance for the five neurobehavioral domain index scores, processing speed, processing accuracy, general cognitive function, and proficiency are provided for each clinical group.

Factor analytic data are provided that demonstrate two factors: information-processing accuracy and information-processing speed. Concurrent validity data are provided relative to the correlation of various MicroCog scales with external test criteria (e.g., the MicroCog Attention/Mental Control Index correlates .57 with the WMS-R Attention/Concentration Index; the MicroCog Memory Index correlates .44 with the WMS-R General Memory Index). Data relevant to construct validity are provided by Ledbetter and Hurley (1994). In a combined MicroCog WMS-R factor analysis, MicroCog Alphabet, Word List, and Numbers Forward and Reversed loaded on the same attention factor as WMS-R Digit Span and Visual Memory Span, whereas MicroCog immediate recognition/recall of two stories loaded on a memory factor with WMS-R Logical Memory I.

Kane (1995) has recently reviewed Micro-Cog, including a technical consideration of the MicroCog proficiency measures relative to Department of Defense (DOD) measures of response latency and throughput (with throughput computed as the number of correct responses per unit of time). Kane noted the strengths of MicroCog included the computerization of a number of traditional neuropsychological measures, the addition of proficiency scores, the provision of detailed information on standard error of measurement for subtests and general performance indices, and sizable age- and education-based norms. Weaknesses were noted to be the use of a multiple key interface and lack of motor and divided attention tasks.

CogScreen–AE

CogScreen–AE (Kay, 1995) was developed in response to the Federal Aviation Administration's (FAA) need for an instrument that could detect subtle changes in cognitive function relative to poor pilot judgment or slow reaction time in critical flight situations. As such, CogScreen was intended to measure the underlying perceptual, cognitive, and information-processing abilities associated with flying.

In general, the CogScreen–AE is heavily biased toward measures of attention, concentration, information processing, immediate memory span, and working memory, as would be expected given the origin of the battery as a measure of cognitive functions related to piloting skills. CogScreen includes Backward Digit Span; Mathematical Reasoning; a Visual Sequence Comparision Task in which the subject must identify two simulta-

neously presented alphanumeric strings as same or different; a Symbol Digit Coding Task (analogous to WAIS-R Digit Symbol), which also includes immediate and delayed incidental learning trials; a Matching-to-Sample Task involving presentation of a 4 × 4 grid of filled and empty cells followed by a brief delay and presentation of two new matrices, one of which is identical to the original (requiring visuoperceptual speed, spatial processing, and visual working memory); the Manikin subtest presents a male human figure at different orientations holding a flag that the subject must identify as being in the left or right hand; a Divided Attention Task combining visual monitoring and visual sequencing; Auditory Sequence Comparision requiring identification of two tonal sequences as the same or different (analogous to the Seashore Rhythm Test); a Pathfinder Test similar to the Trail Making Test; a Shifting Attention Test requiring subjects to alter their responses dependent on changing rules (involving attribute identification, mental flexibility, sustained attention, deductive reasoning, response interference, and a variety of other cognitive skills); and Dual Task, which presents two tasks (visual-motor tracking and a visual memory span task for numbers) independently, then simultaneously. Tests are available in 12 alternate forms.

CogScreen–AE requires about 30 minutes for administration, and all subject responses are input with a light pen except for the tracking component of the Dual Task, which requires the subject to use the keyboard's ctrl and alt keys (Kane and Kay, 1992). Scoring is provided for response speed, accuracy, throughput (number of correct responses per minute), and, on certain tasks, process measures (e.g., impulsivity; perseverative errors). CogScreen also provides for entry of important demographic and performance-related variables (e.g., age, education, flight status, total flight hours logged, and nature of referral such as alcohol-related or head injury). Norm-based reports are provided. The CogScreen–AE U.S. aviator normative base includes 584 U.S. pilots, screened for health status and alcohol and substance abuse. The CogScreen manual includes analysis of age effects, gender, education, and IQ on performance. Gender and education had minimal effects, whereas age and IQ reflected modest degrees of association with CogScreen performance (maximum age effect 12.3% of the variance with any one measure; maximum IQ effect of 9% of variance).

Validity data are provided in terms of concurrent validity (correlation of CogScreen measures with related WAIS-R tasks, and correlations of CogScreen measures with specialized neuropsychological tasks such as the Wisconsin Card Sorting Test, PASAT, and Trail Making Test). Additionally, data are provided on the perceived aviation relevance of the CogScreen tasks as rated by 320 pilots. Factor analyses of CogScreen scores are provided. Additional data are provided contrasting CogScreen performance of pilots selected from the normative base and matched on age and education with non-pilot controls and with patients with mild brain dysfunction. There were no significant differences between pilots and nonpilot controls; however, both groups performed at a superior level compared to the patient group. Additional data are provided on pilot groups with suspicion of alcohol abuse, pilots with questionable proficiency, pilots referred for evaluation of the impact of psychiatric disturbance on cognitive function, and pilots with both suspected and confirmed neurologic disorders.

To date, independent reviews of Cog-Screen–AE have not been published. The test development, normative, and validity data would certainly support using the test in the evaluation of pilots who are suspected to have undergone decline in the cognitive functions related to piloting skill. The tasks also would appear to be relevant to the information-processing difficulties secondary to diffuse neurological conditions such as closed head trauma, neurotoxic exposure, or multiple sclerosis. As noted earlier, the test is biased toward assessment of attention, concentration, information processing, immediate memory, and working memory, although additional memory assessment can be conducted with the Kane and Perrine Verbal and Nonverbal Selective Reminding procedures (Kane and Kay, 1992). Again, this bias is a direct result of the original purpose of the test as a measure of cognitive functions relative to piloting. By contrast, MicroCog provides a broader coverage of various neurobehavioral areas, at the expense of less intensive focus on information-processing skills.

Other Computerized Batteries Employing Traditional Memory Stimuli

In their extensive review of computerized neuropsychological assessment, Kane and Kay (1992) discuss other performance assessment batteries that include memory tasks. Several of these batteries have been developed by national or international government agencies (FAA; NATO) or by the U.S. military, including the Walter Reed Performance Assessment Battery, Naval Medical Research Institute Performance Assessment Battery, and NES 2. The batteries reviewed by Kane and Kay contain a variety of measures of attention/working memory (e.g., continuous performance task; Sternberg search/scan paradigm) and learning and memory (e.g., list recall; associate learning). Kane and Kay (1992) have actually reviewed earlier versions of MicroCog and CogScreen (the reader should note that the earlier version of Micro-Cog is reviewed as the Assessment of Cognitive Skills or ACS).

MAC Computer-Simulated Everyday Memory Battery

The preceding batteries all share the feature of evaluating memory using traditional psychometric stimuli. The Memory Assessment Clinics (MAC) Computer-Simulated Everyday Memory Battery is unique in that stimuli are employed that are more relevant to everyday memory tasks.

The MAC Computer-Simulated Everyday Memory Battery represents a second-generation version of earlier work by Crook and colleagues (1979, 1980; Ferris et al., 1980). The original second-generation version (Crook et al., 1986b; Crook and Larrabee, 1988a; Larrabee and Crook, 1988b) employed an AT&T 6300 computer equipped with a 20 megabyte hard-disk drive and customized computer graphics hardware; a Pioneer LDV-6010 laser disk player; a Sony 19-inch PVM 1910 color monitor with a personal touch touchscreen; and various customized peripheral hardware including a touch-tone telephone. The most recent version substitutes CD-ROM for the laser disk player.

Tests were designed in multiple alternative forms, using computer-imaging technology to simulate demands of everyday life. This heightened everyday realism was combined with current memory measurement paradigms such as selective reminding, signal detection, delayed nonmatch to sample, and associate learning.

Procedures include *Name-Face Association* (Crook and West, 1990) in which live video recordings of persons introducing themselves are presented (via laser disk or CD-ROM) for span memory (two, four, six name-face pairs, single presentation); supraspan learning (the same 14 name-face pairs presented over three trials); and 40-minute delayed recall of the 14 name-face pairs. On each span or supraspan test trial, the person to-be-remembered states the city he is from as a potential recall cue. These city "cues" also provide the stimuli for the *Incidental Memory* test, which assesses the subject's recall of the cities each person in *Name-Face Association* is from, following the 40-minute delayed Name-Face trial (Crook et al., 1993a). A different type of associate learning is evaluated with the *First-Last Names* test, which measures associate learning of six paired first and last names over five trials (the subject must recall the first name associated with each last name; Youngjohn et al., 1991). *Narrative Recall* measures the subject's ability to answer 25 factual, multiple-choice questions about a 6-minute television news broadcast (Crook et al., 1990b). *Selective Reminding* uses the paradigm devised by Buschke (1973) to evaluate learning and retention of 15 grocery items over five trials with a 30-minute delayed recall (Youngjohn et al., 1991).

Misplaced Objects is a visual-verbal asso-ciative task in which the subject "places" (by touching the touch-sensitive screen) 20 common objects (e.g., shoes, eyeglasses) in a 12-room house; 40 minutes later the subject is given a first and a second chance at object location recall (Crook et al., 1990c).

Two measures are employed for facial recognition memory assessment (Crook and Larrabee, 1992). The first, *Recognition of Faces–Signal Detection*, employs signal detection procedures for evaluation of recognition memory employing 156 facial photographs, with scores based on acquisition, as well as on 40-minute delayed recognition memory. The second, *Recognition of Faces–Delayed Non-Matching to Sample*, employs a delayed nonmatch to sample paradigm (Mishkin, 1978) in which the subject must identify the new facial photograph on each of 24 successive trials (starting with one face, the task increments by a new face each trial).

Attentional functions and primary memory are evaluated with the *Telephone Dialing Test* and *Reaction Time*. *Telephone Dialing* (West and Crook, 1990) requires the subject to dial 7- or 10-digit numbers after seeing these displayed on the video monitor. The test can also be administered with an interference format, in which the subject, after dialing, will hear either a ring or a busy signal; if the busy signal is heard, the subject must hang up, and then redial the telephone.

Reaction Time (Crook et al., 1993b) can be administered in one of two formats. First, reaction time can be measured under the single-task condition in which the subject must lift his or her finger off a computer-simulated (on the touchscreen) image of a gas pedal or brake pedal in response to a red or green traffic light. Both lift and travel (from gas to brake pedal or vice versa) reaction times are computed. Second, this task can be administered under the simultaneous processing task (divided attention) condition where the subject must perform the gas pedal/brake pedal maneuvers while listening to a radio broadcast of road and weather conditions. In this administration, both lift and travel reaction times are computed, as well as the subject's recall of the radio broadcast information.

The MAC Computer-Simulated Everyday Memory Battery has undergone extensive standardization and psychometric analysis. Crook and Larrabee (1988a) factor analyzed a variety of scores from the battery and demonstrated factors of general memory, attentional vigilence, psychomotor speed, and basic attention. The factor structure did not vary as a function of age, suggesting that although level of performance changed with age, the interrelationships of the tests did not. Hence, one can be assured that the tests are measuring the same constructs, irrespective of the adult subject's age.

In a second study, Larrabee and Crook (1989a) demonstrated a more varied factor structure, when First-Last Names and Selective Reminding were added to the battery. In this study, both verbal and visual factors emerged, in addition to an attentional factor and psychomotor speed factor. Concurrent validity was established by a combined factor analysis of the MAC Computer-Simulated Everyday Battery, WAIS Vocabulary, Wechsler Memory Scale (WMS) Logical Memory and Paired Associates Learning, and the Benton Visual Retention Test (see Table 5-1).

Further evidence on validity is provided by four recent papers. Larrabee and Crook (1989b) reported cluster analyses that yielded a variety of everyday memory subtypes. Larrabee et al. (1991) demonstrated a significant canonical correlation of .528 between memory self-ratings (MAC-S; Crook and Larrabee, 1990) and factor scores from the MAC Computer-Simulated Everyday Memory Battery. Youngjohn et al. (1992a) reported a discriminant function analysis that correctly distinguished 88.39% of subjects with Alzheimer's disease from subjects with Age-Associated Memory Impairment (cf. Crook et al., 1986a; Crook and Larrabee, 1988b). Finally, Ivnik et al. (1993) demonstrated that the Reaction Time, Name-Face Association, and Incidental Memory procedures were sensitive to the cognitive effects of dominant temporal lobectomy.

Crook et al. (1992) analyzed the equivalency of alternate forms of the various tests. Six equivalent forms were found for Telephone Dialing, Name-Face Association, First-Last Name Memory and Selective Reminding. Eight equivalent forms were found for Misplaced Objects and Recognition of Faces–Delayed Non-Matching-to-Sample.

Youngjohn et al. (1992b) analyzed test-retest correlations when form A was administered twice (21-day test-retest interval).

Table 5-1. Varimax-Rotated Principal Components Analysis—Everyday and Standard Memory Tests[a]

Variable	\multicolumn{6}{c}{Factors}
	1	2	3	4	5	6
Name-Face Association, six faces	.45			.38	.36	
Name-Face Association, sum	.75				.34	
Recognition of Faces–Delayed Non-Matching-to-Sample					.75	
Recognition of Faces—Signal Detection					.55	
Reaction Time, lift component			.75			
Reaction Time, travel component			.76			
Telephone Dialing, 7 digits				.83		
Telephone Dialing, 10 digits				.68		
Incidental Memory for Radio Broadcast		.60				
First-Last Names	.75					
Selective Reminding, total consistent long-term retrieval	.69					
WMS Logical Memory		.84				
WMS Easy Paired Associates						.82
WMS Hard Paired Associates	.65					.42
Benton Visual Retention Test, errors				.50	−.53	
WAIS Vocabulary		.82				

From Larrabee and Crook (1989a). Copyright 1989 by the American Psychological Association. Reprinted with permission.

[a] Loadings of .30 or greater are reported. N = 110; WMS = Wechsler Memory Scale; WAIS = Wechsler Adult Intelligence Scale.

Correlations ranged from a low of .18 (for Recognition of Faces, Signal Detection–Delayed) to a high of .83 (for total acquisition over the three learning trials for Name-Face Memory). Typically, the less attentionally demanding measures had the highest test-retest correlations (e.g., Selective Reminding Total Recall over acquisition, r = .74; Misplaced Objects Total Found, r = .77).

At present, American normative data for adults ages 18 to 90 range from 488 (TV News) to 2,204 (Name-Face Memory), with sample sizes in the 1,300 to 1,900 range for most measures (Crook et al., 1990a; West et al., 1992; Larrabee and Crook, 1994). Additional data are collected on over 200 persons with Alzheimer's disease and over 2,000 persons with age-associated memory impairment. The tests are available in several languages including English, a British (Anglicized) version, French, Italian, Swedish, Finnish, Danish, German, and Spanish.

The principal current use of the MAC Computer-Simulated Everyday Memory Battery is for evaluation of treatment effects in clinical trials of pharmacologic compounds with potential benefit for ameliorating age-related memory disorders. To date, the battery has been utilized in several clinical trials in both the United States and Europe. Recently, Crook et al. (1991) reported significant improvement on the computerized everyday memory tasks in a group of persons with age-associated memory impairment (AAMI; Crook et al., 1986a) who were taking the drug phosphatidylserine. Additional collaborative research is being conducted among subjects with AIDS dementia and subjects undergoing rehabilitation following severe closed head trauma, and as part of an investigation of post–cardiac surgery cognitive deficits. The Italian version of the battery comprises a mobile memory laboratory that has been utilized to randomly assess memory in over 1,800 Italian adults, in a project jointly sponsored by the NIMH, the Italian National Research Council, and Fidia Pharmaceutical Corporation (Lebowitz and Zappala, 1990).

General Considerations in Computerized Memory Rehabilitation

The recently published Division 40 Guidelines for Computer-Assisted Neuropsychological Rehabilitation and Cognitive Remediation (Matthews et al., 1991) highlight several important issues pertaining to computer-assisted training in general and memory rehabilitation in particular. Indeed, the area of memory therapy provides a focal point for these guidelines.

Matthews et al. (1991) emphasize that the computer is only a tool, yet this "tool" is confused with treatment itself. They cite Ben-Yishay and Prigatano (1990), who note that cognitive remediation is meaningful only if it is integrated with other neuropsychological rehabilitation efforts. Consequently, resolution 1.2 of these Division 40 guidelines requires that a clear distinction be made between software properly viewed as a component in an organized treatment program in contrast to software improperly viewed as treatment itself.

In reviewing empirical evidence in the area of memory rehabilitation, this task force considered research in restoration of memory processes, reduction of negative impact through mnemonic strategies, use of the computer as a memory "prosthesis" (cf. Chute et al., 1988), and training in domain-specific knowledge and skills (cf. Glisky and Schacter, 1987). Overall, the Task Force concluded that research did not support use of memory drills to restore function. Some support was noted for training in mnemonic strategies (although inconsistent use and generalizability were problems). Initial results on "prosthetic" use were promising, as was research on acquiring domain-specific knowledge and skills.

In their review of other cognitive domains, Matthews et al. (1991) noted support for efficacy of interventions in rehabilitation of attentional deficits. In this respect, if effective memory functioning is viewed from an information-processing perspective, one might expect some indirect improvement in memory function through remediation of attentional deficits (Sohlberg and Mateer, 1989).

The reader is referred to the Division 40 Guidelines for Computer-Assisted Neuropsychological Rehabilitation and Cognitive Remediation (Matthews et al., 1991) for further information pertaining to the professional and ethical use of computer-assisted rehabilitation. In the following section, we discuss examples of computer applications in rehabilitation of memory.

Computer Applications in Memory Rehabilitation

Gianutsos (1981) employed a microcomputer to both assess as well as train the short (STS) and long-term (LTS) verbal recall of an amnestic, post-encephalitic college professor. Using a multiple baseline design, Gianutsos demonstrated improvement of STS after span training. This did not generalize to LTS, which did not improve until mnemonic elaboration training was initiated. Mnemonic elaboration involved asking the patient to relate a mnemonic image or story that would foster longer-term retention. Anecdotal reports concerning the patient's improved orientation and memory in everyday life suggested generalization of the training; however, Gianutsos cautioned that there was no way of confirming any association between the study and these improvements.

Skilbeck (1984) reported on using a microcomputer to train a severely head-injured 11-year-old girl, who had memory dysfunction secondary to hemorrhagic injury to the left frontal lobe, in use of the "Peg" system. She had poor spontaneous verbal recall but good visual memory. Skilbeck utilized the computer to capitalize on her good visual memory. This was successfully conducted despite the fact that computer graphics were not employed; that is, she had to visualize (relying on her own visual imagery) the association of the pegs ("one is a bun") with the to-be-remembered item, in this case, "tea" (she imagined a "bun" floating on a cup of "tea"). Skilbeck noted that for patients with visual imagery difficulties, microcomputers with advanced graphics could be employed. In-

deed, this was the approach taken by West and Crook (1992) in a recent investigation of imagery training in mature, healthy adults.

The West and Crook investigation utilized the computer-simulated everyday memory battery described in the earlier section of this chapter on computerized memory assessment (Crook et al., 1986b; Crook and Larrabee, 1988a; Larrabee and Crook, 1988b). As West and Crook observed, one limitation of traditional visual imagery training techniques is that they may not be used outside the laboratory. These authors utilized the graphic image capacity of the computer to construct a videotape with imagery training for recall of names and faces, grocery list learning, and object location recall. Employing a wait list control group, West and Crook demonstrated improved performance on relevant tasks in the computer-simulated everyday memory battery when the videotape was used by patients outside the laboratory in self-administered training sessions using their personal VCRs. It should be emphasized that these positive results were obtained on normal elderly, most of whom met the criteria for age-associated memory impairment (AAMI; Crook et al., 1986a). Additionally, no investigation was made of the generalization of training to actual daily application of the techniques. Nonetheless, these initial results are promising.

Generalization of these results to neurological populations requires additional study. Because the AAMI subjects performed in the -1 to -2 SD range compared with 20- to 30-year-old young adults, targeting young brain-injured patients performing in this range may yield generalizable findings, particularly if only one domain (i.e., name-face or grocery list or object location recall) was trained at a time.

Lastly, Glisky and colleagues (1986a,b; Glisky and Schacter, 1987) have conducted particularly intriguing research on acquisition of domain-specific knowledge using the method of vanishing cues to train densely amnestic patients in the use of a microcomputer. In their initial study, Glisky et al. (1986a) observed that several investigators had suggested that a personal computer had potential to serve as a compensatory device (memory prosthesis) for memory-impaired individuals. Consequently, Glisky et al. explored whether amnestic patients could acquire the knowledge necessary to operate and interact with a microcomputer. In their first investigation, Glisky et al. (1986a) demonstrated that organic amnestic patients could learn a small vocabulary of computer-related terms, through multiple learning trials using the method of vanishing cues. In a subsequent study, Glisky et al. (1986b) demonstrated that the method of vanishing cues could be extended to learning basic computer operations. Finally, Glisky and Schacter (1987) demonstrated that this type of training could be generalized to the work setting; they were able to train a densely amnestic patient to work effectively at a computer data-entry job in a real-world work environment, as quickly and accurately as experienced data-entry employees.

Summary

The studies reviewed in this chapter demonstrate the many advantages of computer-assisted memory evaluation and rehabilitation, but it is important to exercise caution in the application of computers in clinical settings. Despite the technological sophistication of several available computerized memory tests, they do not all meet APA criteria for test instruments concerning reliability, validity and normative data. Indeed, several of the procedures reviewed here, although appropriate for research, cannot yet be recommended for actual clinical application, due to limited data on normative samples and psychometric properties. An even more cautious approach is advisable in computerized memory rehabilitation.

Nonetheless, significant progress has been made in the application of computers to memory evaluation and remediation in recent years. Continued growth can be expected in this area. There is a certain "technological seduction" concerning computerized assessment and remediation, but current as well as future applications of computers with memory-disordered patients should be carefully considered in relation to the Division 40 guidelines for use of computers in evaluation and rehabilitation (Division 40 Task Force Report on Computer-Assisted Neuropsychological Evaluation, 1987; Matthews et al., 1991).

References

Adams, K. M. (1986). Concepts and methods in the design of automata for neuropsychological test interpretation. In S. B. Filskov and T. J. Boll, eds., *Handbook of Clinical Neuropsychology* (vol. 2). New York: Wiley, pp. 561–576.

Adams, K. M., and Brown, G. C. (1986). The role of the computer in neuropsychological assessment. In I. Grant and K. M. Adams, eds., *Neuropsychological Assessment of Neuropsychiatric Disorders*. New York: Oxford, pp. 87–89.

Albert, M., and Moss, M. (1992). The assessment of memory disorders in patients with Alzheimer's disease. In L. R. Squire and N. Butters, eds., *The Neuropsychology of Memory* (2nd ed.). New York: Guilford Press, pp. 211–219.

Ben-Yishay, Y., and Prigatano, G. P. (1990). Cognitive remediation. In M. Rosenthal, E. R. Griffith, M. R. Bond, and J. D. Miller, eds., *Rehabilitation of the Adult and Child with Traumatic Brain Injury*. Philadelphia: F. A. Davis, pp. 393–409.

Bleiberg, J., Garmoe, W., Cederquist, J., Reeves, D., and Lux, W. (1993). Effects of dexedrine on performance consistency following brain injury. A double-blind placebo cross-over case study. *Neuropsychiatry, Neuropsychology and Behavioral Neurology*, 6, 245–248.

Branconnier, R. J. (1986). A computerized battery for behavioral assessment in Alzheimer's disease. In L. W. Poon, T. Crook, K. L. Davis, C. Eisdorfer, B. J. Gurland, A. W. Kaszniak, and L. W. Thompson, eds., *Handbook for Clinical Memory Assessment of Older Adults*. Washington, D.C.: American Psychological Association, pp. 189–196.

Buschke, H. (1973). Selective reminding for analysis of memory and learning. *Journal of Verbal Learning and Verbal Behavior*, 12, 543–549.

Chute, D. L., Conn, G., DiPasquale, M. C., and Hoag, M. (1988). ProsthesisWare: A new class of software supporting the activities of daily living. *Neuropsychology*, 2, 41–57.

Craik, F. I. M., and Lockhart, R. S. (1972). Levels of processing: A framework for memory research. *Journal of Verbal Learning and Verbal Behavior, 11*, 671–684.

Crook, T. Bartus, R. T., Ferris, S. H., Whitehouse, P., Cohen, G. D., and Gershon, S. (1986a). Age-Associated Memory Impairment: Proposed diagnostic criteria and measures of clinical change—Report of a National Institute of Mental Health work group. *Developmental Neuropsychology, 2*, 261–276.

Crook, T. H., Ferris, S., and McCarthy, M. (1979). The Misplaced-Objects Task: A brief test for memory dysfunction in the aged. *Journal of the American Geriatrics Society, 27*, 284–287.

Crook, T. H., Ferris, S. H., McCarthy, M., and Rae, D. (1980). Utility of digit recall tasks for assessing memory in the aged. *Journal of Consulting and Clinical Psychology, 48*, 228–233.

Crook, T. H., and Larrabee, G. J. (1988a). Interrelationships among everyday memory tests: Stability of factor structure with age. *Neuropsychology, 2*, 1–12.

Crook, T., and Larrabee, G. J. (1988b). Age-Associated Memory Impairment: Diagnostic criteria and treatment strategies. *Psychopharmacology Bulletin, 24*, 504–514.

Crook, T. H., and Larrabee, G. J. (1990). A self-rating scale for evaluating memory in everyday life. *Psychology and Aging, 5*, 48–57.

Crook, T. H., and Larrabee, G. J. (1992). Changes in facial recognition memory across the adult life span. *Journal of Gerontology, 47*, P138–141.

Crook, T. H., Larrabee, G. J. and Youngjohn, J. R. (1990a). Diagnosis and assessment of Age-Associated Memory Impairment. *Clinical Neuropharmacology, 13* (Suppl. 3), S81–S91.

Crook, T. H., Larrabee, G. J., and Youngjohn, J. R. (1993a). Age and incidental recall for a simulated everyday memory task. *Journal of Gerontology, 48*, P45–47.

Crook, T. H., Salama, M., and Gobert, J. (1986b). A computerized test battery for detecting and assessing memory disorders. In A. Bes, J. Cahn, S. Hoyer, J. P. Marc-Vergenes, and H. M. Wisniewski, eds., *Senile Dementias: Early Detection.* London-Paris: John Libbey Eurotext, pp. 79–85.

Crook, T. H., Tinklenberg, J., Yesavage, J., Petrie, W., Nunzi, M. G., and Massari, D. C. (1991). Effects of phosphatidylserine in Age-Associated Memory Impairment. *Neurology, 41*, 644–649.

Crook, T. H., and West, R. L. (1990). Name recall performance across the adult life span. *British Journal of Psychology, 81*, 335–349.

Crook, T. H., West, R. L., and Larrabee, G. J. (1993b). The Driving-Reaction Time Test: Assessing age declines in dual-task performance. *Developmental Neuropsychology, 9*, 31–39.

Crook, T. H., Youngjohn, J. R., and Larrabee, G. J. (1990b). The TV News Test: A new measure of everyday memory for prose. *Neuropsychology, 4*, 135–145.

Crook, T. H., Youngjohn, J. R., and Larrabee, G. J. (1990c). The Misplaced Objects Test: A measure of everyday visual memory. *Journal of Clinical and Experimental Neuropsychology, 12*, 819–833.

Crook, T. H., Youngjohn, J. R., and Larrabee, G. J. (1992). Multiple equivalent test forms in a computerized everyday memory battery. *Archives of Clinical Neuropsychology, 7*, 221–232.

Cummings, J. L., and Benson, D. F. (1992). *Dementia. A Clinical Approach* (2nd ed.). Boston: Butterworth-Heinemann.

Cunningham, W. R. (1986). Psychometric perspectives: Validity and reliability. In L. W. Poon, T. H. Crook, K. L. Davis, C. Eisdorfer, B. J. Gurland, A. W. Kazniak, and L. W. Thompson, eds., *Handbook for Clinical Memory Assessment of Older Adults*. Washington, D.C.: American Psychological Association, pp. 27–31.

Division 40 Task Force Report on Computer-Assisted Neuropsychological Evaluation. (1987). *The Clinical Neuropsychologist, 2*, 161–184.

Eckerman, D. A., Carroll, J. B., Foree, D., Gullion, C. M., Lansman, M., Long, E. R., Waller, M. B., and Wallsten, T. S. (1985). An approach to brief field testing for neurotoxicity. *Neurobehavioral Toxicology and Teratology, 7*, 387–393.

Englund, C. E., Reeves, D. L., Shingledecker, C. A., Thorne, D. R., Wilson, K. P., and Hegge, F. W. (1987). *Unified Tri-Service Cognitive Performance Assessment Battery (UTC-PAB). Design and Specification of the Battery.* Bethesda, MD: Naval Medical Research and Development Command.

Ferris, S. H., Crook, T. H., Clark, E., McCarthy, M., and Rae, D. (1980). Facial recognition memory deficits in normal aging and senile dementia. *Journal of Gerontology, 35*, 707–714.

Foree, D. D., Eckerman, D. A., and Elliott, S. L. (1984). M.T.S.: An adaptable microcomputer-based testing system. *Behavior Research Methods, Instruments, and Computers, 16*, 223–229.

Gianutsos, R. (1981). Training the short- and long-term verbal recall of a post-encephalitic amnesic. *Journal of Clinical Neuropsychology, 3,* 143–153.

Gianutsos, R. (1986). The state of the art and science of computer augmentation in cognitive rehabilitation. Presented at the annual meeting of the American Psychological Association, Washington, D.C..

Glisky, E., and Schacter, D. (1987). Acquisition of domain specific knowledge in organic amnesia: Training for computer-related work. *Neuropsychologia, 25,* 893–906.

Glisky, E. L., Schacter, D. L., and Tulving, E. (1986a). Learning and retention of computer-related vocabulary in memory-impaired patients: Method of vanishing cues. *Journal of Clinical and Experimental Neuropsychology, 8,* 292–312.

Glisky, E. L., Schacter, D. L., and Tulving, E. (1986b). Computer learning by memory-impaired patients: Acquisition and retention of complex knowledge. *Neuropsychologia, 24,* 313–328.

Hannay, H. J. (1986). Psychophysical measurement techniques and their application to neuropsychology. In H. J. Hannay, ed., *Experimental Techniques in Human Neuropsychology.* New York: Oxford University Press, pp. 45–94.

Hannay, H. J., Levin, H. S., and Grossman, R. G. (1979). Impaired recognition memory after head injury. *Cortex, 15,* 269–283.

Ivnik, R. J., Malec, J. F., Sharbrough, F. W., Cascino, G. D., Hirschorn, K. A., Crook, T. H., and Larrabee, G. J. (1993). Traditional and computerized assessment procedures applied to the evaluation of memory change after temporal lobectomy. *Archives of Clinical Neuropsychology, 8,* 69–81.

Kane, R. L. (1995). MicroCog: A review. *Bulletin of the National Academy of Neuropsychology, 11,* 13–16.

Kane, R. L., and Kay, G. G. (1992). Computerized assessment in neuropsychology: A review of tests and test batteries. *Neuropsychology Review, 3,* 1–117.

Kane, R. L., and Perrine, K. R. (1988). Construct validity on a nonverbal analogue to the selective reminding verbal learning test. Presented at the annual meeting of the International Neuropsychological Society, New Orleans, Louisiana.

Kapur, N. (1988). *Memory Disorders in Clinical Practice.* London: Butterworths.

Kaszniak, A. W., Poon, L. W., and Riege, W. (1986). Assessing memory deficits: An information-processing approach. In L. W.

Poon, T. H. Crook, K. L. Davis, C. Eisdorfer, B. J. Gurland, A. W. Kaszniak, and L. W. Thompson, eds., *Handbook for Clinical Memory Assessment of Older Adults.* Washington, D.C.: American Psychological Association, pp. 168–188.

Kay, G. G. (1995). *CogScreen-Aeromedical Edition. Professional Manual.* Odessa, FL: Psychological Assessment Resources.

Larrabee, G. J., and Crook, T. H. (1988a). Assessment of drug effects in age-related memory disorders: Clinical, theoretical and psychometric considerations. *Psychopharmacology Bulletin, 24,* 515–522.

Larrabee, G. J., and Crook, T. H. (1988b). A computerized everyday memory battery for assessing treatment effects. *Psychopharmacology Bulletin, 24,* 695–697.

Larrabee, G. J., and Crook, T. H. (1989a). Dimensions of everyday memory in Age-Associated Memory Impairment. *Psychological Assessment, 1,* 92–97.

Larrabee, G. J., and Crook, T. H. (1989b). Performance subtypes of everyday memory function. *Developmental Neuropsychology, 5,* 267–283.

Larrabee, G. J., and Crook, T. H. (1991). Computerized memory testing in clinical trials. In E. Mohr and P. Brouwers, eds., *Handbook of Clinical Trials: The Neurobehavioral Approach.* Amsterdam: Swets and Zeitlinger, B. V., pp. 293–306.

Larrabee, G. J., and Crook, T. H. (1994). Estimated prevalence of Age-Associated Memory Impairment derived from standardized tests of memory function. *International Psychogeriatrics, 6,* 95–104.

Larrabee, G. J., and Crook, T. H. (1995). Assessment of learning and memory. In R. L. Mapou and J. Spector, eds., *Clinical Neuropsychological Assessment, A Cognitive Approach.* New York: Plenum Press, pp. 185–213.

Larrabee, G. J., and Curtiss, G. (1995). Construct validity of various measures of verbal and visual memory. *Journal of Clinical and Experimental Neuropsychology, 17,* 536–547.

Larrabee, G. J., Kane, R. L., and Schuck, J. R. (1983). Factor analysis of the WAIS and Wechsler Memory Scale: An analysis of the construct validity of the Wechsler Memory Scale. *Journal of Clinical Neuropsychology, 5,* 159–168.

Larrabee, G. J., Kane, R. L., Schuck, J. R., and Francis, D. E. (1985a). Construct validity of various memory testing procedures. *Journal of Clinical and Experimental Neuropsychology, 7,* 239–250.

Larrabee, G. J., Largen, J. W., and Levin, H. S. (1985b). Sensitivity of age-decline resistant ("Hold") WAIS subtests to Alzheimer's disease. *Journal of Clinical and Experimental Neuropsychology, 7,* 497–504.

Larrabee, G. J., and Levin, H. S. (1986). Memory self-ratings and objective performance in a normal elderly sample. *Journal of Clinical and Experimental Neuropsychology, 8,* 275–284.

Larrabee, G. J., Trahan, D. E., Curtiss, G., and Levin, H. S. (1988). Normative data for the Verbal Selective Reminding Test. *Neuropsychology, 2,* 173–182.

Larrabee, G. J., West, R. L., and Crook, T. H. (1991). The association of memory complaint with computer-simulated everyday memory performance. *Journal of Clinical and Experimental Neuropsychology, 13,* 466–478.

Lebowitz, B., and Zappala, G. (1990). Progetto Memoria: Preliminary results of a normative study of memory in the Italian population. Symposium, 43rd Annual Meeting of the Gerontological Society of America, Boston, Massachusetts.

Ledbetter, M., and Hurley, S. (1994). A construct validation study of the attention and memory domains on the Assessment of Cognitive Functioning Test. *Archives of Clinical Neuropsychology, 9,* 154.

Levin, H. S., Benton, A. L., and Grossman, R. G. (1982). *Neurobehavioral Consequences of Closed Head Injury.* New York: Oxford University Press.

Levinson, D. M., and Reeves, D. L. (1994a). *Automated Neuropsychological Assessment Metrics (ANAM). ANAM V1.0 TBI Norms.* Irvine, CA: National Cognitive Recovery Foundation.

Levinson, D. M., and Reeves, D. L. (1994b). *Automated Neuropsychological Assessment Metrics (ANAM). ANAM V1.0 Normative Data.* Irvine, CA: National Cognitive Recovery Foundation.

Lezak, M. D. (1995). *Neuropsychological Assessment* (3rd. ed.). New York: Oxford University Press.

Matthews, C. G., Harley, J. P., and Malec, J. F. (1991). Guidelines for computer-assisted neuropsychological rehabilitation and cognitive remediation. *The Clinical Neuropsychologist, 5,* 3–19.

Maulucci, R. A., and Eckhouse, R. H., Jr. (1988). The use of computers in the assessment and treatment of cognitive disabilities in the elderly: A survey. *Psychopharmacology Bulletin, 24,* 557–564.

Mishkin, M. (1978). Memory in monkeys severely impaired by combined but not by separate removal of amygdala and hippocampus. *Nature, 273,* 297–298.

Money, J., Alexander, D., and Walker, H. T. (1965). *Manual for a Standardized Road Map Test of Direction Sense.* Baltimore, MD: Johns Hopkins University Press.

Nelson, H. E., and McKenna, P. (1975). The use of current reading ability in the assessment of dementia. *British Journal of Social and Clinical Psychology, 14,* 259–267.

Perez, W. A., Masline, P. J., Ramsey, E. G., and Urban, K. E. (1987). *Unified Tri-Services Cognitive Performance Assessment Battery: Review and Methodology.* Alexandria, VA: Defense Technical Information Center.

Powell, D. H., Kaplan, E. F., Whitla, D., Weintraub, S., Catlin, R., and Funkenstein, H. H. (1993). *MicroCog. Assessment of Cognitive Functioning. Manual.* Orlando, FL: The Psychological Corporation.

Putnam, S. H. (1987). Software for cognitive rehabilitation. *The Clinical Neuropsychologist, 1,* 191–196.

Sbordone, R. J., Hall, S. B., Towner, L. W., Cripe, L., Gerner, R., and White, M. (1985). The validity and reliability of the Sbordone-Hall Memory Battery. Presented at the annual meeting of the International Neuropsychological Society, San Diego, California.

Skilbeck, C. (1984). Computer assistance in the management of memory and cognitive impairment. In B. A. Wilson and N. Moffat, eds., *Clinical Management of Memory Problems.* Rockville, MD: Aspen Publications, pp. 112–131.

Sohlberg, M. M., and Mateer, C. A. (1989). *Introduction to Cognitive Rehabilitation.* New York: Guilford Press.

Spector, J. D., Reeves, D., and Lewandoski, A. (1993). Automated neuropsychological assessment: DOD contributions. Paper presented at the 1993 AMEDD Clinical Psychology Short Course, Walter Reed Army Medical Center, Washington, D.C.

Spreen, O. F., and Benton, A. L. (1977). *Manual of Instructions for the Neurosensory Center Comprehensive Examination for Aphasia.* Victoria, British Columbia, Canada: University of Victoria.

Trahan, D. E., and Larrabee, G. J. (1988). *Professional Manual: Continuous Visual Memory Test.* Odessa, FL: Psychological Assessment Resources.

Wechsler, D. A. (1987). *Wechsler Memory Scale-*

Revised: Manual. San Antonio: The Psychological Corporation.

West, R. L. (1986). Everyday memory and aging. *Developmental Neuropsychology, 2,* 323–344.

West, R. L., and Crook, T. H. (1990). Age differences in everyday memory: Laboratory analogues of telephone number recall. *Psychology and Aging, 5,* 520–529.

West, R. L., Crook, T. H. (1992). Video training of imagery for mature adults. *Applied Cognitive Psychology, 6,* 307–320.

West, R. L., Crook, T. H., and Barron, K. L. (1992). Everyday memory performance across the life span: The effects of age and noncognitive individual difference factors. *Psychology and Aging, 7,* 72–82.

Wickens, D. D. (1970). Encoding categories of words: An empirical approach to meaning. *Psychological Review, 77,* 1–15.

Wilson, B. A., Cockburn, J., Baddeley, A., and Hiorns, R. (1989). The development and validation of a test battery for detecting and monitoring everyday memory problems. *Journal of Clinical and Experimental Neuropsychology, 11,* 855–870.

Wright, G. M., Van der Cammen, T. J. M., and Scott, L. C. (1987). Memory clinics aid diagnosis, help improve patient management. *Geriatric Medicine, 17,* 17–20.

Youngjohn, J. R., Larrabee, G. J., and Crook, T. H. (1991). First-Last Names and the Grocery List Selective Reminding Tests: Two computerized measures of everyday verbal learning. *Archives of Clinical Neuropsychology, 6,* 287–300.

Youngjohn, J. R., Larrabee, G. J., and Crook, T. H. (1992a). Discriminating Age-Associated Memory Impairment from Alzheimer's disease. *Psychological Assessment, 4,* 54–59.

Youngjohn, J. R., Larrabee, G. J., and Crook, T. H. (1992b). Test-retest reliability of computerized, everyday memory measures and traditional memory tests. *The Clinical Neuropsychologist, 6,* 276–286.

6 Cognitive Screening Methods

MAURA MITRUSHINA and PAULA ALTMAN FULD

Assessment of mental status has been essential to psychiatric evaluation since the inception of psychiatry as a field of medicine. However, methods used to evaluate the patient's condition and to record clinical findings have undergone dramatic changes, largely because different approaches to the mental status evaluation have been determined by the theoretical view of human behavior prevailing at different periods. Psychodynamic and humanistic approaches emphasized the subjectivity and uniqueness of an individual's behavior and therefore relied on narrative and highly subjective methods of clinical evaluation, including the recording of observations without any attempt at organization. With the rapid growth of the natural sciences and advances in biological taxonomy, psychiatrists were prompted to seek structure and organization for their methodology and thus to make the evaluation process more objective, improve the communication of findings between clinicians, and bring the field of psychiatry up to the standards of contemporary science.

The first structured mental status examination was introduced in 1918 by Adolf Meyer in "Outlines of Examinations" (Meyer, 1918; Winters, 1951). This work was a milestone in developing a scientific approach to psychiatry because it provided a uniform method of evaluation and recording. But it still required extensive narrative descriptions of the patient's behavior, and thus retained some subjectivity in recording the results of evalua-

tion. Subsequently, a number of structured systems of mental status examination were proposed which preserved the basic format of Meyer's approach but attempted to improve it by utilizing more objective and precise methods of evaluation and recording (Wittenborn, 1950; Rowell, 1951).

Continuing efforts to structure the mental status examination have resulted in the adoption of a quantitative approach to measuring important aspects of mental functioning. This approach allows the conversion of subjective clinical impressions into numbers, which facilitates comparison of the patient's status to some expected level of functioning and allows the clinician to monitor changes in the patient's mental state over time. The earlier developments in this methodology are represented in a variety of "clinical tests of sensorium" (Shapiro et al., 1956; Hinton and Withers, 1971; Withers and Hinton, 1971). The quantitative approach to the evaluation of mental status has proven to be successful from the perspective of both utility in diagnostic decision making and prediction of treatment outcome. It is therefore widely used by clinicians in different medical disciplines today.

Cognitive Assessment With Brief Structured Examinations for Medical Patients

The definition of mental status encompasses all aspects of an individual's behavior, including level of consciousness, cognitive functioning, process and content of thought, and emotional state. Whereas complete mental status evaluation is of primary concern to psychiatrists, clinicians of non-psychiatric disciplines are frequently more concerned with assessment of the cognitive component of mental status, because of the high incidence of impaired cognition in medical patients. Impaired cognition is frequently caused by metabolic or structural brain damage as well as homeostatic change in the organism resulting from physical disorders. In addition, adverse effect on cognitive functioning of some medications that are given to control physical symptoms is well documented in the literature (Abramowicz, 1986).

Mental status disorders resulting from medical conditions were classified in the third edition of the American Psychiatric Association's *Diagnostic and Statistical Manual* (DSM-III-R: APA, 1987) in the category of Organic Mental Disorders. The 1994 revision of DSM (DSM-IV: APA, 1994) abandons the term "organic" in favor of "Delirium, Dementia, and Other Cognitive Disorders." The most frequent of these are delirium and dementia. Whereas the distinction between these two conditions is based on the presence or absence of disturbed consciousness, they both involve marked global deterioration of cognitive and severe interference in occupational or social functioning. DSM-IV also introduces a new category, at present tentative, mild neurocognitive disorder (MND). MND differs from delirium or dementia in severity of cognitive impairment (milder) and impact on day to day functioning (less profound). A similar concept exists in the 10th revision of the *International Classification of Diseases* (ICD-10) (WHO, 1992; see also review of mild neurocognitive disorder in Gutierrez et al., 1993).

Timely detection of cognitive impairment in medical patients may provide a clue to the course and prognosis of the underlying physical disorder and, consequently, may determine a choice of treatment or medication adjustment. Prompt, effective intervention in many cases would result in the reversal of cognitive changes and would facilitate physical recovery (Grant, 1996).

A precise estimate of the functional level within different cognitive domains is unnecessary for most medical patients; the question of the presence versus absence of global cognitive impairment is of main concern to the physician. This task can be accomplished through the use of brief bedside screening measures, which in a limited amount of time allow the examiner to tap important aspects of cognitive abilities. By definition, *screening* refers to the assessment of a population of medical patients in order to identify individuals with a high probability of global cognitive impairment, assuming that the likelihood of such identification based solely on the clinical observations of the medical staff would be low.

Many investigators agree that screening is medically, economically, and socially justified under the following conditions: (1) when dealing with a high-risk population; (2) when treatment for the disturbance is available and early detection would improve prognosis; (3) when an available screening test is simple, acceptable to a patient, convenient in administration, reliable, and cost-effective (Sackett and Holland, 1975; Grant, 1982; Larson, 1986).

The use of brief structured mental status examinations as screening tools for the detection of cognitive impairment meets the above conditions and is well justified in medical settings. The clinical value of these examinations is enhanced by their many *strengths*:

1. Such measures are brief and nondemanding for the patient, and they can be easily administered at the bedside.
2. They show little practice effect.
3. They can be administered by appropriately trained paraprofessionals and do not require much formal training for their interpretation.
4. They originate from traditional clinical evaluation of mental status, are convenient, and deal with constructs familiar to physicians.
5. They utilize a structured-interview for-

mat, which provides uniformity in administration and scoring.

6. They provide quantified presentation of results, which facilitates decision processes and allows comparison across time and among different clinicians.

In spite of these assets of mental status examinations, test results in each individual case should be interpreted with caution because of their following *limitations:*

1. They produce high false-negative rates because most of the questions making up mental status examinations can be answered by a majority of patients, even if they have mild cognitive impairment. Focal brain dysfunctions, especially related to the nondominant cerebral hemisphere, are likely to be missed because mental status measures tend to be constructed mainly of verbal items. In addition, habitual reliance on a global estimate of cognitive functioning makes the detection of isolated deficits less likely. Another source of false-negative identifications is high premorbid intelligence and education of the patient.

2. False-positive errors arise primarily from confounding effects of age and ethnic background, low premorbid intelligence, low education and socioeconomic status, and poor knowledge of English (Pfeiffer, 1975; Anthony et al., 1982; Holzer et al., 1983; Escobar et al., 1986). Several investigators have attempted to control for these factors, but reliable normative data that correct for the effects of demographic characteristics are generally unavailable. Another source of false-positive errors is limited cooperation and motivation.

3. Mental status instruments are unable to differentiate between organic and functional disturbances, because in many patients these two conditions blend and reinforce each other. For example, organic pathology frequently produces symptoms of depression and anxiety, whereas affective disturbance might cause attentional and memory deficits.

4. Similarly, such tests do not distinguish

between acute and chronic organic problems.

5. Organic Mental Disorders, particularly delirium, may have a waxing and waning course, which results in fluctuations in the cognitive status of the patient. Any one evaluation would not provide sufficient information on the course of cognitive changes, and serial evaluations might be warranted.

In addition to these empirically defined properties of mental status examinations, extensive research has been done to document their accuracy and utility statistically.

Description of Different Mental Status Examinations

A variety of brief mental status examinations have been introduced in an effort to condense lengthy test batteries into short tests that would be acceptable to elderly and other groups of examinees. These abbreviated versions of the tests included items that demonstrated the best discriminative power. An example of such examinations is a 10-question *Abbreviated Mental Test (AMT)* (Hodkinson, 1972), which was derived from the Roth-Hopkins test (Roth and Hopkins, 1953). The use of another abbreviated four-item mental status examination in the assessment of surgical patients under intensive care was reported by Katz et al. (1972). In addition to abbreviations of longer batteries, a number of examinations derived directly from clinical practice were introduced. The most commonly used as well as the most recent examinations for different age and diagnostic groups are outlined in Table 6-1. The results of reliability and validity studies for these examinations are presented in Table 6-2.

One of the oldest examinations that is currently widely used is the *Mental Status Questionnaire (MSQ)* (Kahn et al., 1960). The original test contained 31 items, from which the authors extracted and extensively validated a 10-item version, containing the most discriminating items.

The *Short Portable Mental Status Ques-*

Table 6-1. Description of Structured Mental Status Examinations

Test/Authors	Functions Assessed	Primary Use	Test Properties
Mental Status Questionnaire Kahn et al. (1960)	Orientation, general and personal information	Detection of cognitive impairment in geriatric patients	Score—sum of errors; 10 items derived from 31-item version; maximum score—10; 5–10 min.
Short Portable Mental Status Questionnaire Pfeiffer (1975)	Orientation, general and personal information, serial 3's	Detection of cognitive impairment in geriatric patients	Score—sum of errors with correction for race and education; 10 items; 5–10 min.
Mini-Mental Status Examination Folstein et al. (1975)	Orientation, concentration, serial 7's, immediate and delayed verbal memory, language, 3-step praxis, copy of geometric design	Detection of cognitive impairment in patients of different ages with a broad range of medical and psychiatric diagnoses	Score—sum of the correct responses; maximum score—30 on 11 items; 5–10 min.
Cognitive Capacity Screening Exam Jacobs et al. (1977)	Orientation, concentration, serial 7's, immediate and delayed verbal memory, language, verbal concept formation, digit span, arithmetic	Detection of diffuse organic mental syndrome/delirium in medical patients	Score—sum of the correct responses; maximum score—30 on 30 items; 5–15 min.; cutoff <20 correct
Blessed Information-Memory Concentration Test (Fuld's modif.) Fuld (1978)	Orientation, concentration, immediate and delayed memory, and unique items	Detection of cognitive impairment in geriatric patients	Score—sum of errors; maximum score—33 on 28 items; 10–20 min.; cutoff >7 errors
(Short form) Katzman et al. (1983)	Orientation, concentration, immediate and delayed memory	Detection of cognitive impairment in geriatric patients	Score—sum of errors; maximum score—28 on 6 items; 3–6 min.; cutoff >10 errors
Neurobehavioral Cognitive Status Examination Kiernan et al. (1987)	Orientation, attention, comprehension, repetition, naming, construction, memory, calculation, similarities, judgment	Detection of organic mental syndrome in medical patients	Uses screen and metric approach; allows to plot a profile for 10 domains; requires 5–30 min.

tionnaire (SPMSQ) (Pfeiffer, 1975) is another test using 10 items. There is a considerable overlap between MSQ and SPMSQ items, although scoring on some items differs. SPMSQ scoring system provides corrections for education and race. According to Pfeiffer's scoring system (1975), the patient's score places him or her into one of the four groups: intact, mildly, moderately, and severely impaired. However, in his original validation study, Pfeiffer used a two-group classification: intact/mildly impaired and moderately/severely impaired. Smyer et al. (1979) explored validity of SPMSQ under four- versus three- versus two-group classifi-

cation systems and reported a preference for a three-group classification.

Another commonly used instrument in the assessment of mental status is the *Mini-Mental State Exam (MMSE)* (Folstein et al., 1975). This test comprises 11 items that are derived from the traditional mental status examination proposed by Meyer (1918). It was originally designed for use with psychiatric patients, but later was validated on a broad range of diagnoses. The cutoff criterion varies among different studies. Anthony et al. (1982) suggested a cutoff adjustment for education and age. Other authors have also suggested the importance of demographics

Table 6-2. Summary of Selected Validation Studies of Structured Mental Status Examinations

Authors	Subjects	Validation Criteria	Results
Mental Status Questionnaire			
Kahn et al. (1960)	1077 institutionalized psychogeriatric patients	Psychiatric diagnosis of organic mental disorder, management problems	High relationship of number of errors with diagnosis and management problems
Zarit et al. (1978)	153 geriatric patients	Tests of cognition	High relationship with performance on tests of cognition
Brink et al. (1978)	112 geriatric patients—extended care facility, 40 community-residing elderly	Staff rating of confusion	High agreement with staff rating; effect of education, immigrant status, presence of delusions
Fillenbaum (1980)	83 community-residing elderly	Psychiatric diagnosis of organic mental disorder	96% true negative, 55% true positive, with a two-error cutoff; regression analysis on individual items
Cresswell and Lanyon (1981)	61 psychogeriatric inpatients	Psychiatric rating on four variables, multiple regression analysis	Inter-rater reliabilities on four variables ($p < .001$); correlation with criterion measures ($p < .001$): organicity ($r = -.87$), depression ($r = .58$), negative prognosis ($r = -.69$), global psychopathology ($r = -.59$); multiple regression–MSQ is better predictor of the degree of organic impairment than demographic variables and incontinence
Pfeffer et al. (1981)	195 geriatric patients and normal elderly	Neurological diagnosis	Detection of dementia: sensitivity—36%, specificity—100%, differences in scores among diagnostic groups
Davous et al. (1987)	133 neurological patients and 23 patients with functional disorder	Neurological diagnosis	Sensitivity—72%, specificity—97%, false positive—5%, false negative—12%, with cutoff 8 errors
Short Portable Mental Status Questionnaire			
Pfeiffer (1975)	997 community-residing elderly, 243 geriatric patients	Psychiatric evaluation of cognitive impairment	Differences in scores among diagnostic groups; cutoff four errors; validity indices for two-group classification: Study 1: (N = 133) true positive—92%, true negative—82%; Study 2: (N = 80) true positive—88%, true negative—72%; test-retest reliability (4-weeks) $r = .82$

Table 6-2. *(Continued)*

Authors	Subjects	Validation Criteria	Results
Haglund and Schuckit (1976)	279 male geriatric medical and surgical patients	Clinical diagnosis of organic brain syndrome, stepwise multiple regression	Correlation with diagnosis ($r = .63$, $p < .00001$); correlation with 31-item MSQ ($r = .85$); SPMSQ is the best predictor of diagnosis
Smyer et al. (1979)	181 institutionalized and community-residing elderly	Clinical rating, self-care capacity, discriminant function analysis	Validity indices vary as a function of four versus three versus two group classification of SPMSQ errors; self-maintenance and socioeconomic variables are the best predictors
Fillenbaum (1980)	83 community-residing elderly	Psychiatric diagnosis of organic mental disorder	True positive—55%, true negative—98% with a two-error cutoff; regression analysis on individual items
Winograd (1984)	56 nursing home residents	Self-care capacity	Correlation with Self-Care Scale ($r = .37$, $p < .05$), and Mental Competence Scale ($r = .58$, $p < .0001$)
Wolber et al. (1984)	95 psychogeriatric inpatients	Psychiatric diagnosis of organic mental disorder, tests of cognition	Differences in scores among diagnostic groups; high correlations: with Bender .60, Digits Forward .49, Digits Backward .63, Digit Span .66, and Basic Living Skills Assessment .57
Foreman (1987)	66 elderly medical-surgical patients	DSM-III diagnosis	Correlation with diagnosis (Spearman $r = .71$), sensitivity—73%, specificity—91%, positive predictive value—89%, negative predictive value—77%, internal consistency reliability-coefficient alpha = .90, convergent validity-correlation with Dementia Rating Scale $p < .001$, discriminant validity-correlation with Visual Analogue Scale for Depression was low
Erkinjuntti et al. (1987)	118 community-residing elderly, 262 medical geriatric inpatients	Clinical diagnosis of dementia or delirium	Sensitivity and specificity vary as a function of a cutoff (four, three, or two errors)
Davis et al. (1990)	116 normal elderly and patients with SDAT of different severity	SDAT diagnosis, CDR rating	Kendall Tau correlation coefficient with CDR ($r = .79$)
Albert et al. (1991)	467 community-residing elderly	Neurological and neuropsychological evaluation	Sensitivity—34.4%; specificity—94.3%; positive predictive value—50.3%; negative predictive value—91.0%

(continued)

Table 6-2. Summary of Selected Validation Studies of Structured Mental Status Examinations *(Cont.)*

Authors	Subjects	Validation Criteria	Results
Roccaforte et al. (1994)	100 geriatric outpatients	Clinical diagnosis of dementia given by consensus of a gero-psychiatrist and geriatrician, CDR rating	Correlations between face-to-face and telephone versions of SPMSQ was .83. Test-retest reliability over 8.7 days was more than .45 for almost all items. Correlations of SPMSQ with MMSE were .81 and .73 for face-to-face and telephone versions, respectively. Sensitivity and specificity were .74 and .79 for the telephone version, .74 and .91 for the face-to-face version, respectively.

Mini-Mental Status Form

Authors	Subjects	Validation Criteria	Results
Folstein et al. (1975)	69 psychogeriatric inpatients, 137 psychogeriatric outpatients, 63 normal controls	Psychiatric diagnosis, response to treatment, tests of cognition	Correlation ($p < .001$) with diagnosis; scores of depressed patients improved with treatment; cutoff <24; correlation ($p < .001$) with WAIS Verbal IQ ($r = .78$), and Performance IQ ($r = .66$) on 26 patients; test-retest reliability for 22 depressed (24-hour) $r = .89$, for 23 clinically stable geriatric patients (28 days) $r = .99$; inter-rater reliability for 19 depressed (24-hour) $r = .83$.
Knights and Folstein (1977)	57 medical patients	Clinical judgment	Cutoff <22; MMSE is more efficient in detection of cognitive impairment than resident's judgment
DePaulo and Folstein (1978)	126 neurological patients	Neurological diagnosis	Significant group differences between the patients with peripheral versus cerebral lesions (Chi-square = 16.54, $p < .0005$); cutoff <24
Tsai and Tsuang (1979)	63 neurological patients	Results of CT scan	Difference between the patients with and without atrophy at $p < .01$
DePaulo et al. (1980)	197 neurological patients	Neurological diagnosis, CT scan, tests of cognition	Correlation with WMS MQ ($r = .58$, $p < .001$), WAIS PIQ ($r = .56$, $p < .001$), VIQ ($r = .40$, $p < .05$) for 35 patients; with CT scan ($r = .35$, $p < .001$) for 85 patients
Pfeffer et al. (1981)	195 geriatric patients and normal elderly	Neurological diagnosis, discriminant function analysis	Detection of dementia: sensitivity—30%, specificity—100%; differences in scores among diagnostic groups; good predictor of diagnosis of dementia

Table 6-2. *(Continued)*

Authors	Subjects	Validation Criteria	Results
Anthony et al. (1982)	97 medical patients of different age, race, education	Diagnosis of delirium or dementia	Sensitivity—87%, specificity—82%, false positive—39.4% (elderly, less than 9 years of education), false negative—4.7% with cutoff <24 (in addition, cutoff was adjusted for education and age); test-retest reliability (24 hours) $r = .85$ for 58 patients without diagnosis, $r = .90$ for 12 demented patients, $r = .56$ for 7 delirious patients
Cavanaugh (1983)	335 medical inpatients of different age, race, SES and education	Score on BDI, multiple regression on demographic variables	Correlation with BDI ($r = -.14$, $p < .015$), main effect of race, SES, and age
Dick et al. (1984)	126 neurological and neurosurgical patients, 17 patients with cognitive impairment	Neurological diagnosis aided with CT scan, lab findings, tests of cognition	True positive—76%, false positive—4.3%, with cutoff <24; moderate correlation with WAIS VIQ ($r = .55$, $p < .01$), PIQ ($r = .56$, $p < .02$), FSIQ ($r = .52$, $p < .02$) for 37 patients; test-retest reliability (24 hours for 30 pts. and 7–70 days for 14 pts.) $r = .95$; interrater reliability (24 hours) $r = .92$; test is insensitive to focal damage
Klein et al. (1985)	72 demented and 144 nondemented medical patients	Clinical diagnosis of dementia, multivariate discriminant equation for items	Accuracy of diagnosis of dementia depends on decision rule
Foreman (1987)	66 elderly medical-surgical patients	DSM-III diagnosis	Correlation with diagnosis (Spearman $r = .78$), sensitivity—82%, specificity—80%, positive predictive value—80%, negative predictive value—82%, internal consistency reliability-coefficient alpha = .96, convergent validity–correlation with Dementia Rating Scale $p < .001$, discriminant validity–correlation with Visual Analogue Scale for Depression was low; scores were sums of errors
Horton et al. (1987)	12 neurological patients	Tests of cognition	Correlation with WAIS-R VIQ ($r = .17$, $n = 8$), PIQ ($r = -.15$, $n = 6$), FSIQ ($r = .27$, $n = 6$), WMS MQ ($r = .64$)

(continued)

Table 6-2. Summary of Selected Validation Studies of Structured Mental Status Examinations *(Cont.)*

Authors	Subjects	Validation Criteria	Results
Teng et al. (1987)	141 DAT patients	Diagnosis of DAT, duration of illness	Correlation with duration of illness ($r = -.50$, $p < .001$)
Fillenbaum et al. (1987)	36 SDAT patients, 24 retested	Diagnosis of SDAT supported by radiological, EEG, and neuropsychological findings, factor analysis	Correlation with OMCT ($r = -.83$), test-retest reliability (1 month) ($r = .89$), factorial structure—two factors
Davous et al. (1987)	133 neurological patients and 23 patients with functional disorder	Neurological diagnosis	Sensitivity—81%, specificity—97%, false positive—5%, false negative—8%, with cutoff 21
Schwamm et al. (1987)	30 neurosurgical patients	Neurological diagnosis aided with CT scan, MRI, biopsy	False negative—47%
Burch and Andrews (1987)	36 medical inpatients, 23 cognitively intact control patients	Psychiatric consultation, score on ADAS-COG	Correlation with Alzheimer's Disease Assessment Scale–Cognitive ($r = -.90$, $p < .01$); effect of education
Strain et al. (1988)	97 medical-surgical patients	Clinical rating of Organic Mental Disorder	Sensitivity—52%, specificity—76%, positive predictive value—74%
Iliffe et al. (1990)	1170 outpatients over age 75	Referred by general practitioners	Prevalence of cognitive impairment (score <25) was 12.8%; no gender or SES differences in the proportion of low scorers
Galasko et al. (1990)	74 Alzheimer's patients, 74 elderly controls	Neurological diagnosis based on an extensive workup	High sensitivity and specificity of individual items and abbreviated form of MMSE based on logistic regression
Ward et al. (1990)	116 elderly outpatients	Psychiatric evaluation	Evaluation in patient's residence yielded higher scores than retest in the clinic
Ashford et al. (1992)	112 outpatients and 45 nursing home residents with dementia	Neurological diagnosis	High correlation among scores on extended MMSE, GAD, and ADL tests for the probable Alzheimer's disease group

Cognitive Capacity Screening Exam

Jacobs et al. (1977)	24 medical patients, 25 psychiatric inpatients, 61 medical patients, 25 normals	Psychiatric diagnosis, lab data and EEG	High correlations with lab data; differences in scores among diagnostic groups; inter-rater reliability ($r = 1.00$)
Kaufman et al. (1979)	59 neurological inpatients	Neurological evaluation	True positive—43%, true negative—30%, false positive—3%, false negative—15%, questionably negative—10%

Table 6-2. *(Continued)*

Authors	Subjects	Validation Criteria	Results
Gehi et al. (1980)	106 medical patients	Diagnosis, lab data, EEG, discharge disposition	Association with diffuse EEG slowing ($p < .0001$); effect of education and age; consistency in scores at admission and discharge
Omer et al. (1983)	65 hospitalized patients and 60 matched community-dwelling elderly	Diagnosis of organic mental syndrome	Differences in scores among diagnostic groups
Webster et al. (1984)	62 patients referred for a neuropsychological consultation	Neurological evaluation including review of medical records, lab data, EEG, and CT scan	Sensitivity—49%, specificity—90%
Foreman (1987)	66 elderly medical-surgical patients	DSM-III diagnosis	Correlation with diagnosis (Spearman $r = .87$), sensitivity—1.00%, specificity—1.00%, positive predictive value—1.00%, negative predictive value—1.00%; internal consistency reliability-coefficient alpha = .97, convergent validity—correlation with Dementia Rating Scale $p < .001$, discriminant validity—correlation with Visual Analogue Scale for Depression was low; scores were sums of errors
Schwamm et al. (1987)	30 neurosurgical patients	Neurological diagnosis aided with CT scan, MRI, biopsy	False negative—57%
Strain et al. (1988)	97 medical-surgical patients	Clinical rating of Organic Mental Disorder	Sensitivity—54%, specificity—85%, positive predictive value—83%
Blessed Information-Memory-Concentration Test			
Katzman et al. (1986)	350 residents of a skilled nursing facility	Neuropathological findings	Correlations at $p < .001$ with total cortical plaque count ($r = .73$) and with hippocampal level of enzyme choline acetyltransferase ($r = .69$)
Katzman et al. (1989)	488 community-residing normal elderly	Diagnosis of Alzheimers disease at follow-up	High concordance with the diagnosis of Alzheimer's disease at 2- and 5-year follow-up
Parmelee et al. (1989)	708 residents of a home for the aged	Clinical diagnosis of dementia or depression	Detection of cognitive impairment: true positive—87.2% for the cutoff <10 errors
Davis et al. (1990)	116 normal elderly and patients with SDAT of different severity	SDAT diagnosis, CDR rating	Kendall Tau correlation coefficient with CDR ($r = .81$)

(continued)

Table 6-2. Summary of Selected Validation Studies of Structured Mental Status Examinations (*Cont.*)

Authors	Subjects	Validation Criteria	Results
Katzman et al. (1983)	321 and 170 nursing home residents, 52 community-residing elderly	Neuropathological findings	Short form: correlation with 26-item Blessed Mental Status (r = .94); correlation with plaque count (r = .54, $p < .001$)
Davous et al. (1987)	133 neurological patients and 23 patients with functional disorder	Neurological diagnosis, tests of cognition	Short form: sensitivity—88%, specificity—94%, false positive—11%, false negative—5%, with cutoff < 10; for N = 21 SDAT patients correlation with WMS MQ (r = −.56, $p < .01$), and with reaction time (r = .46, $p < .05$); test-retest reliability (1 month) for 18 SDAT patients (r = .83, $p < .001$)
Fillenbaum et al. (1987)	36 SDAT patients, 24 retested	Diagnosis of SDAT supported by radiological, EEG, and neuropsychological findings	Short form: Correlation with MMSE (r = −.83), test-retest reliability (1 month) (r = .77)
Davis et al. (1990)	116 normal elderly and patients with SDAT of varying severity	SDAT diagnosis, CDR rating	Short form: Kendall Tau correlation coefficient with CDR (r = .79)

Neurobehavioral Cognitive Status Examination

Authors	Subjects	Validation Criteria	Results
Kiernan et al. (1987)	119 healthy adults, 30 neurosurgical patients	Neurosurgical diagnosis of brain lesion	Differences in scores among diagnostic groups
Schwamm et al. (1987)	30 neurosurgical patients	Neurological diagnosis aided with CT scan, MRI, biopsy	False negative—7%
Cammermeyer and Evans (1988)	11 neurosurgical patients	Neurological diagnosis of brain tumor, SDH, and hydrocephalus	Correspondence between test-retest NCSE changes and medical indications of postsurgical condition
Meek et al. (1989)	34 inpatients treated for substance abuse	Documented history of alcohol and/or illicit substance abuse	Several cognitive areas are compromised; retest scores improved as a function of treatment
Mysiw et al. (1989)	38 stroke patients	Physical exam and CT scan	NCSE is more sensitive than MMSE and Albert's test; attention, calculation and judgment are the best predictors of rehabilitation outcome
Kewman et al. (1991)	73 musculoskeletal pain patients	Severity of pain rated using McGill Pain Questionnaire	NCSE performance is related to level of pain, disability and psychological distress
Osmon et al. (1992)	24 unilateral stroke patients and 12 orthopedic controls	Clinical and radiologic criteria for CVA	Differences between clinical and control groups; differences in profiles as a function of lateralization of CVA; intercorrelations between the scales were explored

Table 6-2. *(Continued)*

Authors	Subjects	Validation Criteria	Results
Fields et al. (1992)	Geriatric inpatients	Psychiatric determination of cognitive impairment	NCSE and MMSE were compared using discordant pair analysis; NCSE sensitivity—100%, specificity—11%, positive predictive value—43%, negative predictive value—100%
Logue et al. (1993)	866 psychiatric inpatients	DSM-III-R diagnosis	Decrement in mean performance as a function of age across all scales was observed. Intercorrelations between NCSE subtests ranged from .22 to .48.
Lamarre and Patten (1994)	72 psychiatric inpatients	Psychiatric diagnosis of organic mental disorder	Sensitivity—83%, specificity—47%, positive predictive value—24%, negative predictive value—93%, test-retest reliability (within 1 week) r = .69, inter-rater reliability r = .57

in performance on the MMSE (Crum et al., 1993). A telephone version of MMSE for use with geriatric patients was developed by Roccaforte et al. (1992). A comprehensive review of the literature accumulated in the past 3 decades on the properties and utility of MMSE as a screening tool for dementia is offered by Tombaugh and McIntyre (1992).

Mayeux et al. (1981) introduced a modified version of MMSE, which included Digit Span (forward and backward), recall of general information, confrontation naming of 10 items from the Boston Naming Test, an additional sentence for repetition, and copying of two designs. The maximum score is 57 and the cutoff is below 25. Administration of this version requires 30 to 45 minutes, but the inclusion of additional items improves the validity of the test.

Another modification of MMSE was proposed by Teng and Chui (1987). Their version *(3MS)* incorporates four added items, more graded scoring—which leads to an extended range of scores, 0–100—and other minor changes. It retains the brevity, but, according to the authors of the test, it improves the sensitivity of certain items.

The *Cognitive Capacity Screening Exam*

(CCSE) (Jacobs et al., 1977) was designed specifically for the detection of diffuse brain pathology in medical patients. Although it assesses only verbal skills (in contrast to MMSE, which includes visual-motor tasks), its statistics are almost identical to those of the MMSE.

The *Blessed Information-Memory-Concentration Test (BIMC)*, modified by Fuld (Fuld, 1978; Katzman et al., 1983) represents a six-item version of the Blessed Mental Status Test. The most discriminating items were extracted from Fuld's (1978) version of the test using stepwise discriminant analysis technique. The resulting short form has proven to correlate with senile plaque count almost as well as the original-length test (Katzman et al., 1983).

The *Neurobehavioral Cognitive Status Examination (NCSE)* (Kiernan et al., 1987) has the advantage over other screening instruments of providing a profile of cognitive status across 10 domains (see Mueller, 1988). Each section except for Memory and Orientation begins with a screening item that is rather demanding (it produces about 20% failure rate in the normal population). If the examinee passes the screen, the particular skill represented by this item is considered to be intact and examiner proceeds to assess another skill. If the screening item is failed, questions of graded difficulty are administered to assess the level of competence in this particular skill. Performance within each domain is scored independently, placing the score on one of the following levels: intact, mildly, moderately, and severely impaired. The results are presented in the form of a graph. Administration time varies between 5 minutes for cognitively intact individuals to 30 minutes for patients with cognitive impairments. Statistical properties of this test with medical and psychiatric populations are described in a number of articles.

Other mental status evaluations are available, but the instruments described above are most frequently used in screening medical and neuropsychiatric patients. These tests were extensively researched and the most confirming information about their clinical utility is available. For detailed review of the reliability and validity of these and other mental status examinations see also Cohen et al. (1984) and Nelson et al. (1986). It should be noted that this list does not include tests intended to rate the severity of cognitive impairment. For this purpose more comprehensive tests are usually used.

The measures reviewed in this chapter do not include tests specifically designed as screening or staging instruments for dementia because a large number of comprehensive reviews on this topic are available in the literature (Engedal et al., 1988; Ritchie, 1988; Baker, 1989; Davis et al., 1990; McDougall, 1990; Yazdanfar, 1990; Alexopoulos and Mattis, 1991; Kluger and Ferris, 1991; Zec et al., 1992).

The mental status examinations discussed above are frequently supplemented with other tests to improve the validity of the assessment. Because these examinations tend to be primarily verbal, they are often administered concurrently with measures of visual-motor functioning, motor coordination, and sensory-perceptual tests, such as Memory for Designs (Haglund and Schuckit, 1976; Webster et al., 1984), the Symbol Digit Modalities Test (Pfeffer et al., 1981), and the

Face-Hand Test (Kahn et al., 1960; Haglund and Schuckit, 1976).

A number of new screening tests have been introduced in recent years. Among these are the following: the High Sensitivity Cognitive Screen (Faust and Fogel, 1989); the Cortical Function Assessment Test (Herst et al., 1990); the BNI Screen for Higher Cerebral Functions (Prigatano, 1991); the Cognitive Status Examination (Gillen et al., 1991); and the Executive Interview (Royall et al., 1992). These measures are brief (up to 30 minutes of administration time) and impose minimal demands on the patients. Validation studies for these tests are currently in progress.

Assessment of Reliability and Validity of Mental Status Measures

Many validation studies on various mental status examinations have been reported. They differ in design, scoring, and presentation of research findings. In order to facilitate the reader's understanding of the results of different studies summarized in Table 6-2, we include a brief review of the basic statistical measures that were used by different authors in assessing the reliability and validity of the tests. To exemplify the use of each statistic, we provide reference to the relevant validation studies tabulated in Table 6-2.

Reliability

Many investigators have focused on three types of reliability that are relevant to the estimation of accuracy and consistency of Mental Status Examinations. It is not appropriate to compare reliability coefficients obtained by different methods.

Test-retest reliability estimates the stability of the test scores over time. It is presented as a correlation between test scores at different times (Folstein et al., 1975; Pfeiffer, 1975; Anthony et al., 1982; Dick et al., 1984; Fillenbaum et al., 1987).

Inter-rater reliability refers to a rate of agreement (correlation) in test scores, or in ratings on individual items, when obtained by different examiners (Folstein et al., 1975;

Jacobs et al., 1977; Cresswell and Lanyon, 1981; Dick et al., 1984).

Internal consistency reliability reflects the degree of relationship between different test items. It is commonly measured with coefficient alpha, which in case of dichotomous scores is known as Kuder-Richardson Formula 20 (Foreman, 1987). Some studies explored internal consistency reliability using factor analysis of the individual items (Fillenbaum et al., 1987).

Validity

Several aspects of the validity, or usefulness, of mental status examinations have been studied:

Content Validity

Content validity refers to the extent to which the content of the questions adequately taps different aspects of mental status. It is inferred in many studies from clinical relevance of the test, from high internal consistency of the test items, and from high correlations with other mental status examinations (Haglund and Schuckit, 1976; Katzman et al., 1983; Fillenbaum et al., 1987; Foreman, 1987).

Criterion-Related Validity

This aspect of validity reflects the relationship between scores on the test and a reference criterion that is assumed to represent a "true state" of a patient. Criteria vary among different studies and include discharge disposition, staff ratings, management problems, self-care capacity, response to treatment, duration of illness, and radiological, EEG, neuropathological, and lab findings. However, most studies use clinical diagnosis by a psychiatrist or neurologist as a criterion.

COMPARISON OF GROUP MEANS. Many studies derive information on the validity of certain tests from comparison of mean test scores for different criterion groups, e.g., patients with and without clinically identifiable delirium (Pfeiffer, 1975; Jacobs et al., 1977; DePaulo and Folstein, 1978; Tsai and Tsuang, 1979; Pfeffer et al., 1981; Wolber et al., 1984; Kiernan et al., 1987).

Whereas information on the efficiency of the test in discriminating between different criterion groups is important for a researcher, it is of little help to a clinician, who is concerned with the probability of correct classifications afforded by a test (see Meehl and Rosen, 1955; Webster et al., 1984).

CORRELATION BETWEEN TEST AND CRITERION. Several studies report the relationship between test scores and a criterion as measured by a correlation coefficient (Folstein et al., 1975; Haglund and Schuckit, 1976; Jacobs et al., 1977; Gehi et al., 1980; Cresswell and Lanyon, 1981; Katzman et al., 1983; Foreman, 1987).

However, the use of correlation coefficients in this situation yields relatively low values, because it measures the degree of *exact* concordance between two sets of scores. In contrast, the definition of the screening test assumes a *probabilistic* nature of prediction, which lends itself better to the decision theory approach.

DECISION THEORY. The decision theory approach is the most relevant for estimating the probability of correct identification of cognitive impairment afforded by different screening tests. According to this approach, all patients are classified into cognitively intact (negative) or impaired (positive) groups, based on their test scores. Similar distinction is made according to the criterion (clinical diagnosis). Comparison between these two classifications provides information on the number of correctly identified and misidentified patients on the basis of their test scores. The relative number of cases in each cell representing true (T) or false (F), and negative (N) or positive (P) outcomes (i.e., TP, TN, FP, FN) yields several indices of test validity.

Sensitivity refers to the ability of a test to correctly identify individuals who have cognitive impairment—the ratio of "true positives" to all impaired patients (true positives/[true positives + false negatives]). *Specificity* indicates the ability of the test to correctly identify absence of cognitive impairment—the ratio of "true negatives" to all intact patients (true negatives/[true negatives + false positives]). These characteristics of the test vary, depending on the "cutoff" points for classification into negative and positive groups, which have been selected by an investigator on the basis of experience.

Manipulation of the cutoffs affects the balance between sensitivity and specificity and, therefore, produces different cost-benefit ratios. For example, if the cutoff is set so that only patients making a very large number of errors are considered impaired, only those patients with pronounced cognitive impairment would be identified. This would result in high specificity and a small number of "false positives." However, many mild cases would be missed, resulting in low sensitivity and a high number of "false negatives." Failure to detect cognitive impairment prevents timely therapeutic intervention that otherwise might allow stabilization or reversal of cognitive symptoms, and such delay may even result in further deterioration of the patient's condition.

Fixing the cutoff at a small number of errors allows the clinician to correctly identify a majority of individuals with even mild signs of cognitive impairment, which ensures high sensitivity of the test and reduces the number of "false negatives." However this strategy increases the proportion of intact individuals who are identified as "positives," thus lowering the specificity of the test and providing a high number of "false positives." Costs of such an outcome include inappropriate treatment and psychological distress, as well as adverse social and economic consequences on the part of intact individuals who are mistakenly identified as cognitively impaired.

Therefore, the cutoff should often be set at values that ensure a reasonable balance between sensitivity and specificity, so that only "borderline" patients will be likely to be incorrectly classified. Under certain circumstances, however, one would prefer to maximize sensitivity even at the expense of specificity and vice versa.

Another index of validity is especially useful for the clinician who is concerned with the identification of cognitive impairment accurately in each individual case. This is the *predictive value* (PV) of a positive test, which represents the probability that the patient is indeed cognitively impaired, given positive test results—true positives/true positives + false positives. Similarly, the PV of a negative test reflects the probability that the patient is cognitively intact given negative test results—true negatives/true negatives + false negatives. Because predictive value is a probabilistic construct, relating the number of correctly classified individuals to the total number of individuals falling into a corresponding classification category, it is affected by the prevalence of the disturbance in the population (for more information see Sackett and Holland, 1975; Grant, 1982; Hoeper et al., 1984; Robins, 1985; Goldberg, 1986; Larson, 1986; Foreman, 1987; Strain et al., 1988). Many studies outlined in Table 6-2 used Decision Theory approach (Kaufman et al., 1979; Pfeffer et al., 1981; Anthony et al., 1982; Webster et al., 1984; Davous et al., 1987; Erkinjuntti et al., 1987; Foreman, 1987; Strain et al., 1988).

ITEM ANALYSIS. Several studies employed item analysis to explore the relationship between individual test items and a certain criterion. Validity indices derived from such item analyses in some studies were cross-validated on an independent sample (Klein et al., 1985).

MULTIPLE REGRESSION. A number of researchers explored the efficiency of test batteries or individual items in predicting a criterion measure of cognitive impairment by entering scores on different tests or items into a multiple regression analysis. Obtained regression coefficients estimated the contribution of each variable into total predictive accuracy (Haglund and Schuckit, 1976; Fillenbaum, 1980; Cresswell and Lanyon, 1981).

DISCRIMINANT FUNCTION ANALYSIS. Another multivariate technique used by several researchers was Discriminant Function Analysis, which identifies the optimal combination of tests or items and assesses predictive accuracy of the test batteries in classification of patients into positive and negative criterion groups (Smyer et al., 1979; Pfeffer et al., 1981; Klein et al., 1985).

Construct Validity

The accuracy of the assumption that mental status examinations actually measure the underlying hypothetical construct of the cognitive component of mental status is established by documenting high correlations of particular Mental Status examination with other tests presumably measuring the same construct *(convergent validity)* versus low correlations with tests that are expected to measure different constructs—for example, affective state *(discriminant validity)*. In addition to product-moment correlation, some studies used rank-order correlations, such as Spearman rank or Kendall Tau to explore agreement in scores on two measures (Fuld, 1978).

Tests used by many researchers to establish convergent validity included WAIS and WAIS-R Verbal, Performance and Full Scale IQ, WMS MQ, Bender Gestalt, Dementia Rating Scale, Alzheimer's Disease Assessment Scale–Cognitive component. In addition, convergent validity was assessed with intercorrelations among several mental status examinations. Discriminant validity was assessed with the Visual Analogue Scale for Depression and the Beck Depression inventory (Folstein et al., 1975; Haglund and Schuckit, 1976; DePaulo et al., 1980; Cavanaugh, 1983; Katzman et al., 1983; Dick et al., 1984; Wolber et al., 1984; Burch and Andrews, 1987; Fillenbaum et al., 1987; Foreman, 1987; Horton et al., 1987; Davis et al., 1990).

Summary

Clinical practice suggests that many physical conditions adversely affect cognitive functioning. Therefore, routine evaluation of mental status in medical patients is of utmost importance for timely detection of cognitive impairment and choice of appropriate treatment, which in many cases may result in reversal of cognitive changes. However, diminished attention and high fatigability of medical patients should be taken into consideration in the selection of assessment instruments.

The use of brief structured mental status examinations as screening tools for the detection of cognitive impairment is well justified by their ease in administration, familiarity to the clinician, convenience for the patient, structured format allowing uniformity in administration and scoring, and quantified presentation of the results. An increase in diagnostic accuracy through the use of screening mental status examinations, suggesting their high incremental validity, is well documented in the literature.

Review of validation studies on selected screening mental status examinations suggests that they have adequate reliability, discriminate well between different criterion groups, are good predictors and correlate well with diagnostic criteria, demonstrate high convergent validity against standard neuropsychological tests as well as high discriminant validity against tests assessing noncognitive functioning.

However, a major drawback of the mental status examinations is their high rate of false-negative identifications (sometimes exceeding 50%). Screening examinations are the least sensitive to mild global impairment and to deficits produced by localized brain dysfunction. High false-negative rates are of considerable concern to a clinician, because reliance on the results of the mental status examination in diagnostic and treatment decisions might deprive the patient of treatment that otherwise would facilitate his recovery.

The rate of false-positive errors is generally low, which suggests that screening examinations are relatively accurate in ruling out cognitive impairment in cognitively intact patients. However, the rate of false-positive errors is of lesser concern to the clinician from a diagnostic perspective, because the assumption of cognitive impairment can be ruled out in the course of subsequent workup. Both types of errors in identification of cognitive impairment are influenced by sociodemographic variables.

How accurate are the estimates of validity that are reported in the reviewed studies in the form of misclassification rates? Such estimates of validity are generally evaluated against a criterion such as psychiatric or neurological diagnosis. In spite of the extensive clinical workup that underlies diagnoses made for research purposes, there have been many reports that such diagnoses, themselves, have low reliability. Therefore, it would seem preferable to use a body of data, such as that which is included in the clinical workup, or in a neuropsychological evaluation, or in any quantified sample of behavioral and other relevant data as the criterion against which to evaluate validity estimates, rather than depending on a clinical judgment that may, itself, be relatively unreliable.

Thus, estimates of the validity of mental status examinations from different studies summarized in Table 6-2 are somewhat biased. The actual number of correct identifications and errors in the same sample of patients might vary, depending on the criterion chosen. This manipulation would not affect correct identifications of intact versus moderately or severely impaired patients; however, it would have an impact on the classification of "borderline" intact or mildly impaired patients. Classification of these patients would also be influenced by varying a cutoff score. For this reason, several authors have suggested three-group classification—for example, severe, questionable, and asymptomatic (Smyer et al., 1979; Robins, 1985)—to identify patients who need to be assessed further. However, such classification has not been well validated to date.

What are the implications of the above discussion for the individual clinician? Although it is clear that the mental status screening examination should be a part of routine evaluation in any clinical setting, the choice of the instrument used would depend on the patient population and the clinician's familiarity with the instrument. Because the predictive value of the instrument depends on the prevalence of the disturbance in a given population, norms should be collected locally (within each clinic using the test), using patients likely to obtain scores "typical" for this particular population. This would also allow the clinician to adjust the cutoff scores to ascertain a reasonable balance between sensitivity and specificity and, therefore, to equalize the likelihood of false-negative and false-positive errors. The distribution of scores on the screening examination should be validated against the patients' performance on neuropsychological tests or against other reliable criteria. Separate sets of norms should be developed with respect to different age, education, race, and socioeconomic status groups that would allow one to adjust the cutoff for cognitive impairment correspondingly.

The clinician might modify a standard screening examination to make it relevant for each individual patient. He might also design his own set of items, which would be the most relevant for a particular patient population. In addition, a clinician might supplement a standard screening examination with additional measures, particularly with tests tapping nonverbal abilities. In view of possible fluctuations in the patient's cognitive status, planned readministration of the examination at standard time intervals would be warranted—with appropriate normative studies to indicate the likelihood that a change in score represents a change in the patient, rather than a measurement error.

Because of the relatively high rates of misclassification, final diagnostic decisions, especially for patients falling within the "borderline" or "uncertain" category, should take into account the patient's behavior, history, and other available data.

References

Abramowicz, M. (1986). Drugs that cause psychiatric symptoms. *The Medical Letter on Drugs and Therapeutics, 28,* 81–86.

Albert, M., Smith, L. A., Scherr, P. A., Taylor, J. O., Evans, D., and Funkenstein, H. H. (1991). Use of brief cognitive tests to identify individuals in the community with clinically diagnosed Alzheimer's disease. *International Journal of Neuroscience, 57,* 167–178.

Alexopoulos, G. S., and Mattis, S. (1991). Diagnosing cognitive dysfunction in the elderly: Primary screening tests. *Geriatrics, 46,* 33–44.

American Psychiatric Association (APA). (1987). *Diagnostic and Statistical Manual of Mental Disorders (DSM-III-R)* (3rd rev. ed.). Washington, D.C.: American Psychiatric Association Press.

American Psychiatric Association (APA). (1994). *Diagnostic and Statistical Manual of Mental Disorders (DSM-IV)* (4th ed.). Washington, D.C.: American Psychiatric Association Press.

Anthony, J. C., LeResche, L., Niaz, U., von Korff, M. R., and Folstein, M. F. (1982). Limits of the 'Mini-Mental State' as a screening test for dementia and delirium among hospital patients. *Psychological Medicine, 12,* 397–408.

Ashford, J. W., Kumar, V., Barringer, M., Becker, M., Bice, J., Ryan, N., and Vicari, S. (1992). Assessing Alzheimer severity with a global clinical scale. *International Psychogeriatrics, 4,* 55–74.

Baker, F. M. (1989). Screening tests for cognitive impairment. *Hospital and Community Psychiatry, 40,* 339–340.

Brink, T. L., Capri, D., de Neeve, V., Janakes, C., and Oliveira, C. (1978). Senile confusion: Limitations of assessment by the Face-Hand Test, Mental Status Questionnaire, and staff ratings. *Journal of the American Geriatrics Society, 26,* 380–382.

Burch, E. A., and Andrews, S. R. (1987). Cognitive dysfunction in psychiatric consultation subgroups: Use of two screening tests. *Southern Medical Journal, 80,* 1079–1082.

Cammermeyer, M., and Evans, J. E. (1988). A brief neurobehavioral exam useful for early detection of postoperative complications in neurosurgical patients. *Journal of Neuroscience Nursing, 20,* 314–323.

Cavanaugh, S. (1983). The prevalence of emotional and cognitive dysfunction in general medical population: Using the MMSE, GHQ, and BDI. *General Hospital Psychiatry, 5,* 15–24.

Cohen, D., Eisdorfer, C., and Holm, C. L. (1984). Mental status examinations in aging. In M. L. Albert, ed., *Clinical Neurology of Aging.* New York: Oxford University Press, pp. 219–230.

Cresswell, D. L., and Lanyon, R. I. (1981). Validation of a screening battery for psychogeriatric assessment. *Journal of Gerontology, 36,* 435–440.

Davis, P. B., Morris, J. C., and Grant, E. (1990).

Brief screening tests versus clinical staging in senile dementia of the Alzheimer type. *Journal of the American Geriatrics Society, 38,* 129–135.

Davous, P., Lamour, Y., Debrand, E., and Rondot, P. (1987). A comparative evaluation of the short orientation memory concentration test of cognitive impairment. *Journal of Neurology, Neurosurgery and Psychiatry, 50,* 1312–1317.

DePaulo, J. R., and Folstein, M. F. (1978). Psychiatric disturbances in neurological patients: Detection, recognition, and hospital course. *Annals of Neurology, 4,* 225–228.

DePaulo, J. R., Folstein, M. F., and Gordon, B. (1980). Psychiatric screening on a neurological ward. *Psychological Medicine, 10,* 125–132.

Dick, J.P.R., Guiloff, R. J., Stewart, A., Blackstock, J., Bielawska, C., Paul, E. A., and Marsden, C. D. (1984). Mini-Mental State Examination in neurological patients. *Journal of Neurology, Neurosurgery and Psychiatry, 47,* 496–499.

Engedal, K., Haugen, P., Gilje, K., and Laake, P. (1988). Efficacy of short mental tests in the detection of mental impairment in old age. *Comprehensive Gerontology. Section A, Clinical and Laboratory Sciences, 2,* 87–93.

Erkinjuntti, T., Sulkava, R., Wikstrom, J., and Autio, L. (1987). Short Portable Mental Status Questionnaire as a screening test for dementia and delirium among the elderly. *Journal of the American Geriatrics Society, 35,* 412–416.

Escobar, J. I., Burnam, A., Karno, M., Forsythe, A., Landsverk, J., and Golding, J. M. (1986). Use of the Mini-Mental State Examination (MMSE) in a community population of mixed ethnicity. Cultural and linguistic artifacts. *The Journal of Nervous and Mental Disease, 174,* 607–614.

Faust, D., and Fogel, B. S. (1989). The development and initial validation of a sensitive bedside cognitive screening test. *Journal of Nervous and Mental Disease, 177,* 25–31.

Fields, S. D., Fulop, G., Sachs, C. J., Strain, J., and Fillit, H. (1992). Usefulness of the Neurobehavioral Cognitive Status Examination in the hospitalized elderly. *International Psychogeriatrics, 4,* 93–102.

Fillenbaum, G. G. (1980). Comparison of two brief tests of organic brain impairment, the MSQ and the short portable MSQ. *Journal of the American Geriatrics Society, 28,* 381–384.

Fillenbaum, G. G., Heyman, A., Wilkinson, W. E., and Haynes, C. S. (1987). Comparison of two screening tests in Alzheimer's disease. The correlation and reliability of the Mini-Mental

State Examination and the modified Blessed test. *Archives of Neurology, 44,* 924–927.

Folstein, M. F., Folstein, S. E., and McHugh, P. R. (1975). Mini-Mental State. A practical method for grading the cognitive state of patients for the clinician. *Journal of Psychiatric Research, 12,* 189–198.

Foreman, M. D. (1987). Reliability and validity of mental status questionnaires in elderly hospitalized patients. *Nursing Research, 36,* 216–220.

Fuld, P. A. (1978). Psychological testing in the differential diagnosis of the dementias. In R. Katzman, R. D. Terry, and K. L. Bock, eds., *Alzheimer's Disease: Senile Dementia and Related Disorders* (Vol. 7). New York: Raven Press, pp. 185–193.

Galasko, D., Klauber, M. R., Hofstetter, C. R., Salmon, D. P., Lasker, B., and Thal, L. J. (1990). The Mini-Mental State Examination in the early diagnosis of Alzheimer's disease. *Archives of Neurology, 47,* 49–52.

Gehi, M., Strain, J. J., Weltz, N., and Jacobs, J. (1980). Is there a need for admission and discharge cognitive screening for the medically ill? *General Hospital Psychiatry, 2,* 186–191.

Gillen, R. W., Kranzler, H. R., Kadden, R. M., Weidenman, M. A. (1991). Utility of a brief cognitive screening instrument in substance abuse patients: Initial investigation. *Journal of Substance Abuse Treatment, 8,* 247–251.

Goldberg, D. (1986). The usefulness of screening for mental illness. In M. Shepherd, G. Wilkinsen, and P. Williams, eds., *Mental Illness in Primary Care Setting.* London: Tavistock, pp. 72–77.

Grant, I. (1996). Mild neurocognitive disorder. In *Monograph Proceedings of the CINP Regional Conference.* Basel, Switzerland: S. Karger AG.

Grant, I.W.B. (1982). Screening for lung cancer. *British Medical Journal Clinical Research Ed., 284,* 1209–1210.

Gutierrez, R., Atkinson, J. H., and Grant, I. (1993). Mild neurocognitive disorder: Needed addition to the nosology of cognitive impairment (organic mental) disorders. *Journal of Neuropsychiatry and Clinical Neurosciences, 5,* 161–177.

Haglund, R.M.J., and Schuckit, M. A. (1976). A clinical comparison of tests of organicity in elderly patients. *Journal of Gerontology, 31,* 654–659.

Herst, L. D., Voss, C. B., and Waldman, J. (1990). Cortical function assessment in the elderly. *Journal of Neuropsychiatry and Clinical Neurosciences, 2,* 385–390.

Hinton, J., and Withers, E. (1971). The usefulness of the clinical tests of the sensorium. *British Journal of Psychiatry, 119,* 9–18.

Hodkinson, H. M. (1972). Evaluation of a mental test score for assessment of mental impairment in the elderly. *Age and Ageing, 1,* 233–238.

Hoeper, E. W., Nycz, G., Kessler, L. G., Burke, J. D., and Pierce, W. E. (1984). The usefulness of screening for mental illness. *Lancet, 1,* 33–35.

Holzer, C. E., Tischler, G. L., Leaf, P. J., and Myers, J. K. (1983). An epidemiologic assessment of cognitive impairment in a community population. *Research in Community and Mental Health, 4,* 3–32.

Horton, A. M., Jr., Slone, D. G., and Shapiro, S. (1987). Neuropsychometric correlates of the Mini-Mental State Examination: Preliminary data. *Perceptual and Motor Skills, 65,* 64–66.

Iliffe, S., Booroff, A., Gallivan, S., Goldenberg, E., Morgan, P, and Haines, A. (1990). Screening for cognitive impairment in the elderly using the Mini-Mental State Examination. *British Journal of General Practice, 40,* 277–279.

Jacobs, J. W., Bernhard, M. R., Delgado, A., and Strain, J. J. (1977). Screening for organic mental syndromes in the medically ill. *Annals of Internal Medicine, 86,* 40–46.

Kahn, R. L., Goldfarb, A. I., Pollack, M., and Peck, A. (1960). Brief objective measures for the determination of mental status in the aged. *American Journal of Psychiatry, 117,* 326–328.

Katz, N. M., Agle, D. P., DePalma, R. G., and DeCosse, J. J. (1972). Delirium in surgical patients under intensive care. *Archives of Surgery, 104,* 310–313.

Katzman, R., Aronson, M., Fuld, P., Kawas, C., Brown, T., Morgenstern, H., Frishman, W., Gidez, L., Eder, H., and Ooi, W. L. (1989). Development of dementing illnesses in an 80-year-old volunteer cohort. *Annals of Neurology, 25,* 317–324.

Katzman, R., Brown, T., Fuld, P., Peck, A., Schechter, R., and Schimmel, H. (1983). Validation of a short Orientation-Memory-Concentration Test of cognitive impairment. *American Journal of Psychiatry, 140,* 734–739.

Katzman, R., Brown, T., Fuld, P., Thal, L., Davies, P., and Terry, R. (1986). Significance of neurotransmitter abnormalities in Alzheimer's Disease. In J. B. Martin and J. D. Barchas, eds., *Neuropeptides in Neurologic and Psychiatric Disease.* New York: Raven Press, pp. 279–286.

Kaufman, D. M., Weinberger, M., Strain, J. J., and Jacobs, J. W. (1979). Detection of cognitive deficits by a brief mental status examination: The Cognitive Capacity Screening Examination, a reappraisal and a review. *General Hospital Psychiatry, 1,* 247–255.

Kewman, D. G., Vaishampayan, N., Zald, D., and Han, B. (1991). Cognitive impairment in musculoskeletal pain patients. *International Journal of Psychiatry in Medicine, 21,* 253–262.

Kiernan, R. J., Mueller, J., Langston, J. W., and Van Dyke, C. (1987). The Neurobehavioral Cognitive Status Examination: A brief but differentiated approach to cognitive assessment. *Annals of Internal Medicine, 107,* 481–485.

Klein, L. E., Roca, R. P., McArthur, J., Vogelsang, G., Klein, G. B., Kirby, S. M., and Folstein, M. (1985). Diagnosing dementia. Univariate and multivariate analyses of the mental status examination. *Journal of the American Geriatrics Society, 33,* 483–488.

Kluger, A., and Ferris, S. H. (1991). Scales for the assessment of Alzheimer's disease. *Psychiatric Clinics of North America, 14,* 309–326.

Knights, E. B., and Folstein, M. F. (1977). Unsuspected emotional and cognitive disturbance in medical patients. *Annals of Internal Medicine, 87,* 723–724.

Lamarre, C. J., and Patten, S. B. (1994). A clinical evaluation of the Neurobehavioral Cognitive Status Examination in a general psychiatric inpatient population. *Journal of Psychiatry and Neuroscience, 19,* 103–108.

Larson, E. (1986). Evaluating validity of screening tests. *Nursing Research, 35,* 186–188.

Logue, P. E., Tupler, L. A., D'Amico, C., and Schmitt, F. A. (1993). The Neurobehavioral Cognitive Status Examination: Psychometric properties in use with psychiatric inpatients. *Journal of Clinical Psychology, 49,* 80–89.

Mayeux, R., Stern, Y., Rosen, J., and Leventhal, J. (1981). Depression, intellectual impairment, and Parkinson disease. *Neurology, 31,* 645–650.

McDougall, G. J. (1990). A review of screening instruments for assessing cognition and mental status in older adults. *Nurse Practitioner, 15,* 18–28.

Meehl, P. E., and Rosen, A. (1955). Antecedent probability and efficiency of psychometric signs, patterns, or cutting scores. *Psychology Bulletin, 52,* 194–216.

Meek, P. S., Clark, H. W., and Solana, V. L. (1989). Neurocognitive impairment: The unrecognized component of dual diagnosis in substance abuse treatment. *Journal of Psychoactive Drugs, 21,* 153–160.

Meyer, A. (1918). *Outlines of Examinations.* New York: Bloomingdale Hospital Press.

Mueller, J. (1988). A new test for dementia syndromes. *Diagnosis, 10,* 33–40.

Mysiw, W. J., Beegan, J. G., and Gatens, P. F. (1989). Prospective cognitive assessment of stroke patients before inpatient rehabilitation. The relationship of the Neurobehavioral Cognitive Status Examination to functional improvement. *American Journal of Physical Medicine and Rehabilitation, 68,* 168–171.

Nelson, A., Fogel, B. S., and Faust, D. (1986). Bedside cognitive screening instruments. A critical assessment. *Journal of Nervous and Mental Disease, 174,* 73–83.

Omer, H., Foldes, J., Toby, M., and Menczel, J. (1983). Screening for cognitive deficits in a sample of hospitalized geriatric patients: A reevaluation of a brief mental status questionnaire. *Journal of the American Geriatrics Society, 31,* 266–268.

Osmon, D. C., Smet, I., Winegarden, B., and Gandhavadi, B. (1992). Neurobehavioral Cognitive Status Examination: Its use with unilateral stroke patients in a rehabilitation setting. *Archives of Physical Medicine and Rehabilitation, 73,* 414–418.

Parmelee, P. A., Katz, I. R., and Lawton, M. P. (1989). Depression among institutionalized aged: Assessment and prevalence estimation. *Journal of Gerontology, 44,* M22–29.

Pfeiffer, E. (1975). A short portable mental status questionnaire for the assessment of organic brain deficit in elderly patients. *Journal of the American Geriatrics Society, 23,* 433–441.

Pfeffer, R. I., Kurosaki, T. T., Harrah, C. H., Jr., Chance, J. M., Bates, D., Detels, R., Filos, S., and Butzke, C. (1981). A survey diagnostic tool for senile dementia. *American Journal of Epidemiology, 114,* 515–527.

Prigatano, G. P. (1991). BNI Screen for Higher Cerebral Functions: Rationale and initial validation. *BNI Quarterly, 7,* 2–9.

Ritchie, K. (1988). The screening of cognitive impairment in the elderly: A critical review of current methods. *Journal of Clinical Epidemiology, 41,* 635–643.

Robins, L. N. (1985). Epidemiology: Reflections on testing the validity of psychiatric interviews. *Archives of General Psychiatry, 42,* 918–924.

Roccaforte, W. H., Burke, W. J., Bayer, B. L., and Wengel, S. (1992). Validation of a telephone version of the Mini-Mental State Examination. *Journal of the American Geriatrics Society, 40,* 697–702.

Roccaforte, W. H., Burke, W. J., Bayer, B. L., and Wengel, S. P. (1994). Reliability and validity of the Short Portable Mental Status Questionnaire administered by telephone. *Journal of Geriatric Psychiatry and Neurology, 7*, 33–38.

Roth, M., and Hopkins, B. (1953). Psychological test performance in patients over 60. *Journal of Mental Science, 99*, 439–450.

Rowell, J. T. (1951). An objective method of evaluating mental status. *Journal of Clinical Psychology, 7*, 255–259.

Royall, D. R., Mahurin, R. K., and Gray, K. F. (1992). Bedside assessment of executive cognitive impairment: The executive interview. *Journal of the American Geriatrics Society, 40*, 1221–1226.

Sackett, D. L., and Holland, W. W. (1975). Controversy in the detection of disease. *Lancet, 2*, 357–359.

Schwamm, L. H., Van Dyke, C., Kiernan, R. J., Merrin, E. L., and Mueller, J. (1987). The Neurobehavioral Cognitive Status Examination: Comparison with the Cognitive Capacity Screening Examination and the Mini-Mental State Examination in a neurosurgical population. *Annals of Internal Medicine, 107*, 486–491.

Shapiro, M. B., Post, F., Lofving, B., and Ingles, J. (1956). "Memory functions" in psychiatric patients over sixty, some methodological and diagnostic implications. *Journal of Mental Science, 102*, 233–246.

Smyer, M., Hofland, B., and Jonas, E. (1979). Validity study of the short portable mental status questionnaire for the elderly. *Journal of the American Geriatrics Society, 27*, 263–269.

Strain, J. J., Fulop, G., Lebovits, A., Ginsberg, B., Robinson, M., Stern, A., Charap, P., and Gany, F. (1988). Screening devices for diminished cognitive capacity. *General Hospital Psychiatry, 10*, 16–23.

Teng, E. L., and Chui, H. C. (1987). The modified Mini-Mental State (3MS) examination. *Journal of Clinical Psychiatry, 48*, 314–318.

Teng, E. L., Chui, H. C., Schneider, L. S., and Metzger, L. E. (1987). Alzheimer's dementia: Performance on the Mini-Mental State Examination. *Journal of Consulting and Clinical Psychology, 55*, 96–100.

Tombaugh, T. N., and McIntyre, N. J. (1992). The Mini-Mental State Examination: A comprehensive review. *Journal of the American Geriatrics Society, 40*, 922–935.

Tsai, L., and Tsuang, M. T. (1979). The Mini-Mental State Test and computerized tomography. *American Journal of Psychiatry, 136*, 436–438.

Ward, H. W., Ramsdell, J. W., Jackson, J. E., Renvall, M., Swart, J. A., and Rockwell, E. (1990). Cognitive function testing in comprehensive geriatric assessment. A comparison of cognitive test performance in residential and clinic settings. *Journal of the American Geriatrics Society, 38*, 1088–1092.

Webster, J. S., Scott, R. R., Nunn, B., McNeer, M. F., and Varnell, N. (1984). A brief neuropsychological screening procedure that assesses left and right hemispheric function. *Journal of Clinical Psychology, 40*, 237–240.

Winograd, C. H. (1984). Mental status tests and the capacity for self-care. *Journal of the American Geriatrics Society, 32*, 49–55.

Winters, E. E. (1951). *The Collected Papers of Adolf Meyer* (Vol. 3). Baltimore: Johns Hopkins Press.

Withers, E., and Hinton, J. (1971). Three forms of the clinical tests of the sensorium and their reliability. *British Journal of Psychiatry, 119*, 1–8.

Wittenborn, J. R. (1950). A new procedure for evaluating mental patients. *Journal of Consulting Psychology, 14*, 500–501.

Wolber, G., Romaniuk, M., Eastman, E., and Robinson, C. (1984). Validity of the Short Portable Mental Status Questionnaire with elderly psychiatric patients. *Journal of Consulting and Clinical Psychology, 52*, 712–713.

World Health Organization. (1992). *The ICD-10 Classification of Mental and Behavioural Disorders: Clinical Descriptions and Diagnostic Guidelines.* Geneva, Switzerland: World Health Organization, pp. 64–65.

Yazdanfar, D. J. (1990). Assessing the mental status of the cognitively impaired elderly. *Journal of Gerontological Nursing, 16*, 32–36.

Zarit, S. H., Miller, N. E., and Kahn, R. L. (1978). Brain function, intellectual impairment and education in the aged. *Journal of the American Geriatrics Society, 26*, 58–67.

Zec, R. F., Landreth, E. S., Vicari, S. K., Feldman, E., Belman, J., Andrise, A., Robbs, R., Kumar, V., and Becker, R. (1992). Alzheimer Disease Assessment Scale: Useful for both early detection and staging of dementia of the Alzheimer type. *Alzheimer Disease and Associated Disorders, 6*, 89–102.

II | Neuropsychiatric Disorders

7 Demographic Influences on Neuropsychological Test Performance

ROBERT K. HEATON, LEE RYAN, IGOR GRANT, and CHARLES G. MATTHEWS

A primary goal of clinical neuropsychological assessment is to determine whether a given set of test results suggests brain pathology. This is done by comparing a person's performance to available normative standards, which for most tests are based on the results of a "typical" North American sample of neurologically normal adults. Unfortunately, most neuropsychological tests have only a single set of norms that do not include adjustment for the demographic characteristics of the individual being considered. This state of affairs is, quite clearly, a major impediment to adequate clinical assessment of many patients. Consider, for example, a 60-year-old woman with a grade school education, whose first language was Spanish and who began learning English at age 15. It would be quite inappropriate to compare this patient's performances on most neurobehavioral tests with those of the average adult in North America.

In the first edition of this book, our chapter focused on a study assessing the differences in neuropsychological test performance associated with age, education, and sex (Heaton et al., 1986). The results of the study highlighted the pressing need for more complete normative data that take multiple demographic variables into account. Since the publication of that chapter, a substantial amount of work has been done in this area. For this edition we have expanded and updated the previous presentation by reviewing new studies on the effects of demographic variables and by providing information on several recently available sets of demographically corrected norms for widely used neuropsychological tests. We have added a discussion of the information available on two groups that are served particularly poorly by most available normative data: the very elderly and ethnic minorities. We begin with a review of general issues related to the use of normative data in neuropsychological assessment.

"Normality" and Adequate Normative Data

The debate over what constitutes "normal" is clearly a central issue for neuropsychologists. In determining whether an individual's test performance is the result of brain disorder, it is essential to distinguish that performance from normal variations in cognitive ability. Neuropsychological assessment's most straightforward task is to identify a complete *loss of function* secondary to brain damage. The resulting behavior falls well outside the range of ability for the entire normal population and thus is relatively simple to detect. Examples of a loss of function include visual agnosia (the inability to identify common objects visually despite intact visual functioning) and facial apraxia (the loss of motor programs for facial expression). More often, however, neuropsychologists are asked to determine whether an *impairment in function* has occurred; that is, whether test performance constitutes a change in normal functioning *for the individual*. Such a judgment should not be taken lightly as it may have a major impact on an individual's medical evaluation and treatment, self-esteem, family functioning, independence, and access to future opportunities and resources. These judgments are based primarily on tests developed by researchers of a particular cultural, educational, and socioeconomic stratum. An individual's test performance is judged, perforce, in comparison to some standard that the clinician chooses. We espouse a relativistic approach to normality (and hence, abnormality), where normal is defined as the range of behaviors and abilities within a group of like individuals who share social, educational, cultural, and generational backgrounds. Western Caucasian middle- to upper-class clinicians cannot assume that their own demographically defined group may be used as a definitive standard.

The purpose of normative data is to provide information on the range of an ability within a specifically defined population. The clinical utility of norms will depend on several factors, including the representativeness of the normative sample, the goodness-of-fit between the individual and the normative sample, and the degree to which the norms consider demographic variables that account for variations in test performance. Each of these factors will be discussed below.

First, an adequate normative sample must be representative of the general population; that is, the scores included in the data set are assumed to be an unbiased sample of the population of interest. Often, normative standards are derived from small sample sizes that result in poor classification rates when applied to larger samples. For example, the Russell et al. (1970) norms for the Halstead-Reitan Battery continue to be widely used by clinicians and researchers, despite the fact that they were originally based on a combination of clinical judgment and the test results of a sample of 26 neurologically normal subjects. Large sample size alone, however, does not ensure representa-

tiveness. Methods of recruitment, sampling techniques, inclusion criteria, and compliance rates are all critical factors in assessing possible sources of bias in a sample (for discussion, see Anastasi, 1988). Erickson et al. (1992) have pointed out that sampling procedures in normative studies are quite often opportunistic, making use of a population at hand rather than being expressly designed to create an unbiased sample. The effect of this practice may be biases in the sample that are difficult to detect. Publications of standardization samples should thus provide a description of the sampling procedures and subject recruitment procedures employed in the study, as well as rates of subject compliance, so that clinicians may make informed judgments regarding the generalizability of published norms.

Secondly, assessing whether norms are appropriate for an individual requires sufficient knowledge of the characteristics of the subject sample. The description of the criteria for subject inclusion will define the population from which the sample was drawn, and will essentially constitute the researchers' definition of normality. Important characteristics may include (1) the numbers of subjects in various strata of demographic variables such as age, education, socioeconomic status, and ethnic group; (2) whether the subjects were living independently in the community; (3) current or past histories of factors that might influence cognitive performance, including chronic illness, significant medical history (including head trauma), drug and alcohol use, prescription drug use, and psychiatric diagnoses, and (4) whether there was any independent screening (e.g., mental status exam) to rule out serious cognitive disturbance.

Finally, the utility of norms will depend on whether demographic variables that have a significant impact on test performance have been adequately considered. Performance on most neuropsychological tests are significantly related to the subject's age, education, ethnicity, and, for a few tests, sex (Parsons and Prigatano, 1978; Heaton et al., 1991). The influence of demographic factors is apparent for neurologically normal individuals as well as for those who have cerebral disorders (Reitan, 1955; Finlayson et al., 1977). Unfortunately, as Lezak (1987) notes, despite decades of awareness of the effects of demographic variables, the vast majority of psychological and neuropsychological tests in common use today do not stratify their samples on these variables. Even for test norms that stratify subject groups on age or education, information concerning the effects of such factors in combination is lacking. Equally important is the issue of how recently norms were collected. Demographic and cultural factors cannot be assumed to be comparable for groups of subjects who were tested decades apart. For example, cross-sectional studies may overestimate age effects by confounding these with educational, nutritional, or occupational differences among groups of subjects from different generations (Anastasi, 1988). Successive generations may differ in language patterns and problem-solving styles (Albert, 1981), or perhaps along dimensions that have not yet been identified (Flynn, 1984, 1987). Thus, norms collected 20 years ago, even if they take into account age and education, may contain systematic errors in current use.

While gathering normative data is a time-consuming and labor-intensive enterprise, the importance of such research cannot be overemphasized. Standardization samples that provide adequate descriptions of sampling methods, subject characteristics, and that are stratified on important demographic variables, are critical to clinical neuropsychology. Expanded and updated norms will continue to be needed as society evolves over time.

Demographic Influences on Test Performance: Age, Education, Sex

Age

Of the instruments considered in this chapter, by far the most well-known and widely used are the Wechsler Adult Intelligence Scale (WAIS; Wechsler, 1955) and its 1981 revision, the Wechsler Adult Intelligence Scale–Revised (WAIS-R; Wechsler, 1981).

Findings with both the WAIS and WAIS-R standardization samples reflect lower average performances for each successive age group tested after their mid-thirties. Age differences are more pronounced for nonverbal than for verbal subtests, reflecting the fact that different abilities change at different rates; in the "classic pattern," verbal skills and well-learned information hold up best over time while perceptual-integrative and psychomotor skills decline the most with advancing age (Botwinick, 1967; Leckliter and Matarazzo, 1989).

Performances on most of the individual tests in the Halstead-Reitan Battery (HRB) also show a significant negative relationship with age (Reitan, 1955, 1957; Vega and Parsons, 1967). Reitan warned that after age 45 many normals score in Halstead's brain-damaged range on the Impairment Index. As an illustration, Price et al. (1980) studied a group of 49 retired, healthy schoolteachers (mean age, 72 years) and found that 56% of the subjects scored in the impaired range according to the standard norms on the HRB. Considerable variability was seen in the number of subjects misclassified as brain-damaged by the different subtests in the battery (ranging from 18% to 90%). Thus, impaired performance on the HRB appears to occur with most but not all normal elderly subjects, and age-related deficits are more pronounced on some tests than on others. In their review of the literature, Reitan and Wolfson (1986) concluded that age effects on the HRB are found primarily in complex, novel tasks that require reasoning, abstraction, and logical analysis, while tests related to prior learning, past experience, and language ability are generally spared.

Interestingly, Yeudall et al. (1987) did not find a strong association between age and HRB performance with subjects below the age of 40. In a sample of 225 community recruited males and females between the ages of 15 and 40 years, correlation coefficients were reported ranging from .00 to .27 on various subtests. The evidence suggests that, as with the Wechsler scales, age becomes an increasingly important factor in the fourth decade and beyond. It should be noted, however, that decreased performance in later years may not be solely attributable to age, but may also be due to generational differences in education, health services, access to media information, and many other factors. Because the majority of studies in this area are cross-sectional rather than longitudinal, the presence of mediating factors other than age cannot be ruled out.

Education

Performance on the Wechsler Intelligence Scales is even more closely correlated with educational achievement than with age, hardly a surprising finding given that the original purpose of intelligence tests was to predict academic success (Anastasi, 1988). Matarazzo (1972) reported a Pearson correlation of .70 between highest grade completed and WAIS IQ; Matarazzo and Herman (1984) reported a correlation of .54 for the WAIS-R standardization sample of 16- to 74-year-olds. The latter correlation appeared to be spuriously lowered because of the inclusion of 16- to 24-year-olds, many of whom had not yet completed their education. When this age group was excluded, the correlation between IQ and years of education increased to .62. Kaufman et al. (1988) also observed that education effects were less prominent in the youngest age group (16 to 19 years), suggesting that education effects are attenuated among individuals who are still actively participating in the educational system. Examining the WAIS-R standardization sample, Reynolds et al. (1987) reported significant differences across education groups for Verbal, Performance, and Full Scale mean IQs. IQ scores varied from 26 to 33 points between the lowest education group (less than 8 years) and the highest (16 years or more). In contrast to age effects, Kaufman et al. (1988) found that education had more of an impact on verbal than nonverbal tests.

The relationship between education and HRB performance is less well documented. For example, Finlayson et al. (1977) tested normal individuals with grade school (less than 10 years), high school (grade 12, without college experience) and university level (at least 3 years college experience) education. They found significant differences between the groups on the Category Test, the Seashore Rhythm Test, Speech-Sounds Perception Test, and Trail Making A and B. No effect of education was evident on the Tactual Performance Test or Finger Tapping. With three similar groups of brain-damaged individuals, education effects were less pronounced, and were significant only on the Seashore Rhythm Test and Speech-Sounds Perception Test. Finlayson et al. (1977) suggested that the effects of brain damage may produce sufficient decreases in performance to "wash out" the effects of education.

Vega and Parsons (1967) reported Pearson correlations between years of education and HRB subtest performance as high as −.58 for Speech-Sounds Perception Test, .58 for the Seashore Rhythm Test, and −.45 for errors on the Category Test. When the effects of education were partialled out, the correlations between the HRB subtests and age weakened, but remained significant, suggesting two independent sources of performance variability. In reviewing the extant literature, Leckliter and Matarazzo (1989) concluded that although correlation coefficients were generally lower between years of education and HRB performance compared to age and HRB performance, highly educated individuals consistently performed better than those individuals with fewer years of education.

The Rate of Age-related Decline

A question addressed in several previous studies is whether the rate of age-related cognitive decline is related to subjects' initial level of functioning or socioeconomic status (education, occupation). In reviewing this literature, Botwinick (1967) noted that cross-sectional studies have provided some inconsistent evidence that subjects with lower initial ability and lower occupational status show greater age-related impairment on some tests. The available longitudinal studies do not support this hypothesis. However, these studies are limited by the use of a restricted range of tests over relatively brief age ranges, and by the selective attrition of initially less able subjects. Birren and Morrison (1961) found no significant age-by-education interaction effects using data from the WAIS standardization sample. A similar pattern is apparent for the WAIS-R standardization sample (Reynolds et al., 1987), but no statistical analyses were done to assess the interactions between age and education. The possibility of interactions between age and education on the HRB had not been investigated prior to our exploration of the issue for the first edition of this book (see below).

Gender

Research on gender differences in ability has found males and females to be equivalent in general intelligence. Reynolds et al. (1987) did not find that the sexes differed significantly on any of the three summary scores on the WAIS-R. Sex differences on the WAIS and WAIS-R do not normally appear, because questions that produced clear-cut sex differences were excluded or counterbalanced during the developmental stages of the tests (Matarazzo, 1972; Matarazzo et al., 1986). Nevertheless, on tests of specific ability areas, some sex differences are found. Males tend to do better on tests that involve manipulating spatial relationships, quantitative skills, physical strength, and simple motor speed, whereas females show advantages on tests of certain verbal abilities (for review, see Buffery and Gray, 1972; Maccoby and Jacklin, 1974). For example, on the HRB, Fromm-Auch and Yeudall (1983) found that women were slower on Finger Tapping than men, and men had stronger grip strength on the Dynamometer than women for both dominant and nondominant hands.

Halstead-Reitan Normative Data Pool

In the first edition of this book, we presented a study that highlighted the importance of demographic variables for performance on the WAIS and an extended version of the Halstead-Reitan Battery. The main points of the study will be discussed here; the reader

is referred to the original chapter for more details (Heaton et al., 1986). The goal of the study was to address the issue of how performance on the various neuropsychological tests relates to age and education when high and low values of these demographic factors were adequately represented in the subject sample. Which tests are more sensitive to age effects and which appear to be more related to educational attainment? Are there significant age-by-education interaction effects on tests in the battery and, if so, are they consistent with the hypothesis that better-educated groups show less age-related decline in neuropsychological functioning? How well or how poorly does a previously published set of HRB norms work for groups of normal subjects at different age and education levels? Finally, which tests in the battery show significant sex differences, and are these differences large enough to necessitate developing separate norms for males and females?

Subjects and Methods

Subjects consisted of all normal controls (356 males and 197 females) for whom there were complete WAIS and HRB data available at the neuropsychology laboratories of the University of Colorado (N = 207), University of California at San Diego (N = 181), and the University of Wisconsin (N = 165) Medical Schools. None of the subjects had any history of neurological illness, significant head trauma, or substance abuse. Forty subjects (7.2%) were left-handed and 513 were right-handed. Their ages ranged from 15 to 81 years, with a mean of 39.3 (SD = 17.5 years). Years of education ranged from zero (no formal education) to 20 (doctoral degree), with a mean of 13.3 (SD = 3.4) years. For analyses designed to assess age-by-education interaction effects, subjects were divided into three age categories (< 40 years, 40–59 years, and ≥ 60 years) and three education categories (< 12 years, 12–15 years, and ≥ 16 years). Respectively, the total numbers of subjects in the three age categories were 319, 134, and 100, and in the three education categories, 132, 249, and 172. All nine age/education subgroups included over 25 subjects except for the high age/high education category (n = 17).

In order to assess sex differences in neuropsychological test performance, males and females were individually matched within 5 years in age and within 2 years in education. This resulted in 177 matched pairs, well matched on mean age (36.6 for males, 36.7 for females) and education (13.2 for males, 13.1 for females).

All subjects were tested by trained technicians, and all were rated as having put forth adequate effort on their evaluations. The 11 subtests of the WAIS and an expanded HRB were administered. The latter battery has been described elsewhere (Reitan and Wolfson, 1986) and included the Category Test, Tactual Performance Test (Time, Memory, and Location components), Seashore Rhythm Test, Speech-Sounds Perception Test, Aphasia Screening Exam, Trail Making Test, Spatial Relations Assessment, Sensory-Perceptual Exam, Tactile Form Recognition Test, Finger Tapping Test, Hand Dynamometer, and Grooved Pegboard Test.

Scores for the WAIS subtests were regular scaled scores (not age-corrected). The Russell et al. (1970) scoring system was used for the Aphasia Screening Exam, Spatial Relations, Sensory-Perceptual Exam, and Average Impairment Rating. In addition, the cutoff scores provided in the Russell et al. (1970) book were used to determine how many

subjects in the different age and education categories were correctly classified as normal by the Average Impairment Rating and each of its component test measures.

Results

AGE EFFECTS. Figure 7-1 shows the percent of variance accounted for by age (R squared) on each test measure. All the correlations between test measures and age were significant ($p < .05$), with the exception of Vocabulary and Hand Dynamometer, and consistently indicated poorer performance associated with older age. Among the Wechsler subtests, substantial age effects were apparent on Digit Symbol and Picture Arrangement, whereas age showed minimal relationship with performance on Vocabulary, Information, and Comprehension. Performance on several of the HRB tests was strongly related to age, particularly for measures of psychomotor speed, conceptual ability, flexibility of thought, and incidental memory. In contrast, scores on HRB tests of language skills and simple sensory and motor abilities showed relatively weak associations with age.

EDUCATION EFFECTS. Education significantly correlated with all WAIS and HRB measures, indicating better performance with higher education levels. Figure 7-2 shows the percent variance in each test ac-

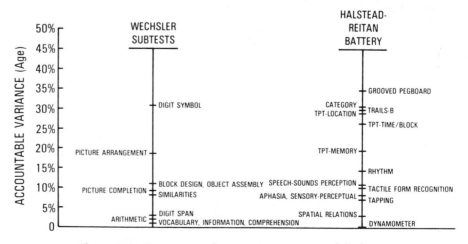

Figure 7-1. Percentage of test variance accounted for by age.

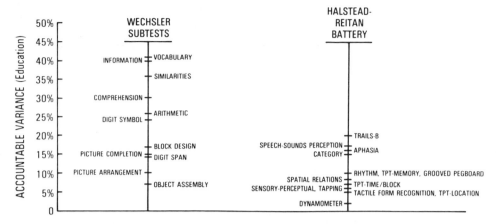

Figure 7-2. Percentage of test variance accounted for by education.

counted for by education (R squared). Even for measures of simple motor and sensory functions, better test performance was associated with higher previous educational attainment. In contrast to the results shown previously for age, education level was most strongly related to scores on the WAIS Verbal subtests, and somewhat less related to scores on the HRB. Consistent with this,

within the HRB, correlations were highest with tests of language skills, conceptual ability, and cognitive flexibility.

TESTS SHOWING RELATIVELY GREATER AGE OR EDUCATION SENSITIVITY. Figure 7-3 shows for each test measure the difference between the amount of variance accounted for by age versus education. In general,

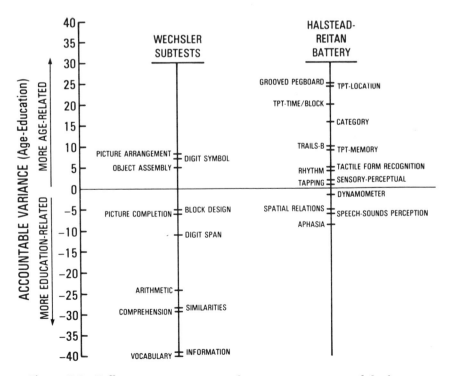

Figure 7-3. Difference in percentage of test variance accounted for by age versus education (i.e., age variance minus education variance).

WAIS subtests tend to be more education-related, and the HRB subtests tend to be more age-related. Not surprisingly, within both batteries tests of verbal skills and past accumulated knowledge are more education-related, whereas nonverbal tests of psycho-motor speed and/or new problem solving are more age-related.

THE INTERACTION BETWEEN AGE AND EDUCATION. The 3 x 3 analyses of variance (ANOVAs) performed on all test measures produced age and education main effects that were in agreement with the results of the correlational analysis. That is, tests previously found to be more age-related or more education-related were similarly classified by these analyses. In addition, significant age-by-education interaction effects were obtained on WAIS Comprehension, Picture Completion, Block Design, Picture Arrangement, as well as on the HRB Impairment Index, Average Impairment Rating, Category Test (errors), Trail Making–B, TPT Memory and Location, and Speech-Sounds Perception.

Three possible patterns of age-by-education interaction might be expected: (1) subjects with the most education show less age-related impairment; (2) subjects in the lowest education group show more age-related impairment; and (3) a regression toward the mean occurs, with less effect of education between older groups than between younger groups. These three patterns are not necessarily mutually exclusive. A test may be consistent with pattern (1) or (2) across the first two age levels, but fit pattern (3) between the second and third age levels.

To explore the possible patterns of interaction effects, mean test scores of subgroups at each education level were plotted across the three age levels. While it is tempting to consider this type of graph to be a longitudinal view of how groups at each education level may change with advancing age, it must be recognized that the curves do not reflect *change* in any direct sense, as each point on the graph reflects the performance of a separate subject group that was tested only once.

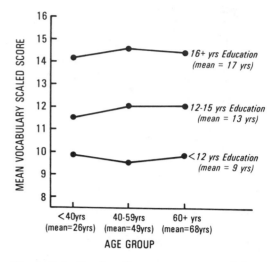

Figure 7-4. Results of groups in nine age/education categories on WAIS Vocabulary test.

Several of these graphs are presented here. Figure 7-4 summarizes the data on Vocabulary, a test that is known to show little change in older age groups. The curves for each education level indicated no significant age-related decrease in test performance. Furthermore, the comparability of the three age subgroups within education levels suggests that the subgroups were fairly well matched in terms of previously learned information.

In contrast, consider the graphs for two WAIS subtests that have significant age-by-education interaction effects (see Figs. 7-5 and 7-6). On Picture Arrangement, the results across the first two age levels suggested more age-related impairment for the least educated subgroup, consistent with pattern (2) above. On Block Design, the curves across the first two age levels were more consistent with pattern (1), suggesting less age-related impairment for the subgroup with 16+ years of education. On both of these subtests, however, the curves from the second to the third age level fit pattern (3), that is, there was less difference between education subgroups at the older age level. Other tests, including Trail Making–B and the Category Test showed patterns similar to Picture Arrangement; that is, they showed pattern (2) between the first two age levels

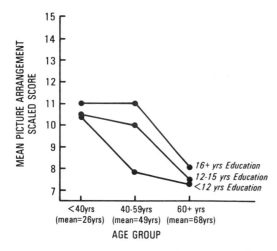

Figure 7-5. Results of groups in nine age/education categories on WAIS Picture Arrangement.

and pattern (3) between the second and third age levels.

The final graph (Fig. 7-7) shows the percentage of subjects classified as normal by the Average Impairment Rating. This pattern was apparent for most standard cutoff scores for the test measures in the HRB. The results indicate that the cutoff scores are adequate for all education subgroups at the first age level. At the second age level the cutoffs misclassify only a few more normal subjects in the two higher education subgroups, but misclassify the majority of the subjects in the lower education subgroup. Finally, although a significant minority of subjects in the oldest subgroup still perform at a level that would be considered normal for a young adult, the vast majority of the subjects in this age group are misclassified as "brain-damaged." It is apparent that the standard cutoffs are not appropriate as norms for most subjects over the age of 60 or, equally important, for most subjects with less than a high school education, regardless of their age.

SEX EFFECTS. T-tests for paired samples were used to compare results of our matched male and female groups on all WAIS and HRB measures. There was virtually no difference between these groups on any WAIS IQ value or HRB summary score. Thus, the males and females were comparable with respect to general intelligence and overall neuropsychological functioning. On individual tests, as expected, males did much better ($p < .001$) with each hand on tests of motor speed (Finger Tapping Test) and grip strength (Hand Dynamometer). Differences were also obtained on the Tactual Performance Test and the Aphasia Screening Exam that were not expected, but are consistent with the general psychological literature on sex differences in normals. Males did significantly better ($p < .05$) on the TPT Total Time score (13.5 minutes vs. 15.6 minutes for

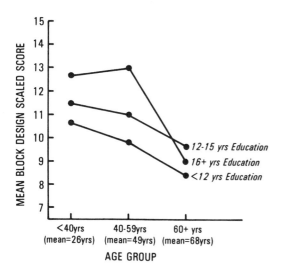

Figure 7-6. Results of groups in nine age/education categories on WAIS Block Design.

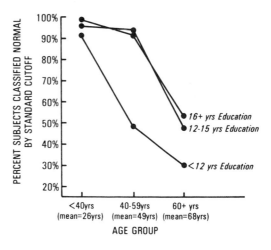

Figure 7-7. Results of groups in age/education categories: percentage classified as normal by Average Impairment Rating.

females). However, the females showed an advantage ($p < .001$) on the Aphasia Screening Exam, obtaining a mean error score of 2.7 versus 4.0 for males. Finally, there was a statistically significant ($p < .05$) but clinically trivial difference on the WAIS Comprehension subtest (mean scores of 12.7 for females and 12.1 for males).

WAIS VERSUS WAIS-R PATTERNS. Since 1981, the WAIS has been replaced in clinical practice by the WAIS-R. Albert and Heaton (1988) reported findings similar to those described above on the WAIS-R subtests. They compared the results of the WAIS-R standardization sample with results of 543 adults who were given the WAIS. Similar relationships were obtained between test performance and both age and education on the two versions of the Wechsler Adult Intelligence Scales. The relationship of scores to education was the inverse of that to age, education correlating more highly with Verbal measures than with Performance measures. Once again, the effect of sex on test performances appeared too small to be of clinical significance.

SPECIFICITY VERSUS SENSITIVITY. A separate, but extremely important, issue in developing normative data is knowing the usefulness of a test in distinguishing groups with known brain dysfunction from the normative sample group. That is, in addition to knowing the likelihood of correctly classifying normal individuals, the neuropsychologist needs to know the sensitivity of the norms, or the true positive classification rate for people with various cerebral disorders. In the pres-

ent study, correct classification rates for the normal group (described earlier) were compared with those of the 382 brain-damaged subjects. All subjects in the patient group were clinical referrals for neuropsychological testing, and all had structural brain abnormalities that were verified with appropriate neuroradiological procedures (primarily computerized tomographic scans and magnetic resonance image scans). They had a mean age of 43.7 years (SD = 1.0) and a mean of 12.9 years (SD = 3.1) of formal education; 249 (65.2% of the sample) were males. The most frequent diagnoses were closed head injury (n = 73), cerebrovascular accident (n = 65), intrinsic tumor (n = 49), Alzheimer's disease (n = 48), extrinsic tumor (n = 30), hydrocephalus (n = 23), infectious or toxic encephalopathies (n = 22), penetrating head injury (n = 18), multiple sclerosis (n = 9), and cerebral anoxia (n = 8); other etiologies included vascular malformations, epilepsy with structural abnormalities, other dementias, and depressed skull fractures (n = 37).

Table 7-1 lists the percentages of the normal and brain-damaged subjects in six age and education subgroups who were correctly classified on the HRB Average Impairment Rating using the Russell et al. (1970) normative criteria. Within the normal group, the percentage of subjects correctly classified as normal decreases with age, but increases with education. In contrast, the *opposite* pattern is evident for the brain-damaged group. Generally, the standard Average Impairment Rating cutoff is relatively poor at identifying brain-damaged individuals who are young and/or well educated. In the older samples, more brain-damaged subjects are correctly

Table 7-1. Percentage of Subjects (553 Normal Control Subjects and 382 Brain-damaged Subjects) in Six Age and Education Subgroups Who Were Correctly Classified as Normal or Brain-Damaged by the Russell et al. (1970) Criteria on the Average Impairment Rating from the Halstead-Reitan Battery

	Age (in years)			Education (in years)		
	< 40	40–59	60+	< 12	12–15	16+
Normal Control Subjects	97% (n = 319)	84% (n = 134)	39% (n = 100)	58% (n = 132)	90% (n = 249)	93% (n = 172)
Brain-Damaged Subjects	55% (n = 167)	83% (n = 138)	94% (n = 77)	87% (n = 99)	71% (n = 191)	60% (n = 92)

classified (from 55% at < 40 years to 94% at 60 + years of age), while as education increases, fewer subjects are correctly classified as brain-damaged (from 87% at < 12 years to 60% at 16 + years of education).

This comparison highlights the need for validation of normative data and classification cut points on known brain-damaged groups, as well as on normal controls at different levels of age and education. The Russell et al. (1970) norms obtain fairly good (and balanced) sensitivity and specificity at middle levels of age and education, but at the extremes of these demographic variables, result in unacceptable percentages of false positive or false negative errors.

Implications

The results of our study accord well with Cattell's (1963) distinction between "fluid" and "crystallized" intelligence. Crystallized intelligence is measured by tests of knowledge and skills that were acquired in previous learning experiences. Crystallized intelligence develops rapidly during the first 20 years of life and then levels off, remaining relatively stable over the ensuing decades. Thus, performance on tests such as Information or Vocabulary from the WAIS does not decline with age, although it is clearly related to level of education. By contrast, fluid intelligence is considered most dependent upon biological factors such as the normal development and continued integrity of the central nervous system. This form of intelligence is measured by tasks requiring learning, conceptual, and problem-solving operations within the context of novel situations. Speed of responding and spatial "visualization" skills may be required in certain tests of fluid intelligence, but are not integral parts of this ability factor. Rather, these might be considered as separate ability factors under the rubric of "information processing efficiency" (Shallice, 1988). Horn and Cattell (1966) presented data to suggest that fluid intelligence develops as the result of biological maturation and reaches its peak in the late teens or early twenties. This form of

intelligence is expected to deteriorate at a rate that is dependent upon various accumulating insults to the CNS that occur during the life span of the individual. Thus, decline in performance on tests such as the Category Test, Block Design, or Picture Arrangement is not attributable to age per se, but to the prevalence of accumulated CNS insults in older groups. Hence, it is possible for healthy older individuals to show very little decline in cognitive functioning.

The results of the study suggest that different patterns of age-related decline in fluid intelligence occur for groups with different educational levels. Groups at the lowest education level showed greatest cognitive decline between the young and middle-age periods. However, the better-educated group tended to "catch up" by the later age period. At older ages, the level of functioning was not much different between the three education levels. Once again, these age-by-education interaction effects occurred only on certain test measures, mostly those of the fluid intelligence variety.

There are several possible explanations why such age-by-education interaction effects might occur. First, subjects with lower education and lower socioeconomic status may tend to have less optimal health care, resulting in a higher prevalence during middle age of health problems that compromise brain function (e.g., high blood pressure). It might also be that people in the higher education groups tend to have better functioning central nervous systems to begin with, and as a consequence are more resilient to absolute losses in CNS integrity. A third possibility is that subjects in the lower education subgroups tend to have less intellectually stimulating jobs and general life styles, so that fluid intelligence declines faster due to "disuse" during the middle-age years; better educated subjects might then catch up due to increasing disuse during their retirement years. The latter hypothesis is attractive because it suggests that intellectually stimulating activities may sustain fluid intelligence in old age. We note once again that these data derive from a cross-sectional design. As such, they demonstrate age-related differences in abilities, but not age-related changes in ability. Longitudinal studies are needed to establish that changes have occurred.

Age- and Education-Corrected Norms

Clearly, demographic variables such as age, education, and sex should be considered together when evaluating neuropsychological test performance. In recent years, norms have been published that present data corrected for both age and education for several widely used tests. The data from the Halstead-Reitan normative data pool described above have been developed into a set of norms for an extended version of the HRB (Heaton et al., 1991). Norms are presented separately for males and females, for 10 age groups (ages 20–34, then in increments of 5 years to age 80), crossed with education level (6–8, 9–11, 12, 13–15, 16–17, and 18+ years).

Heaton (1992) also has developed age, education, and gender corrections for the WAIS-R subtests using the data from the WAIS-R standardization sample (Wechsler, 1981). The norms are presented separately for males and females, with age groups in increments of 3 years, ranging from 18 through 74, crossed with education levels ranging from 0 to 7 years to 16-plus years. In a validation sample of 420 subjects, less than 1% of the variance of the resultant demographically corrected T-scores could be predicted by the demographic variables in question. Thus, the T-scores were found to be essentially free of any linear relationship with age, education, or gender, and did not result in interactions of age-by-education on any WAIS-R variable. A recent study showed that, while raw scores from the WAIS and WAIS-R resulted in appreciable differences between two groups of demographically matched normal subjects, the corrected T-scores showed no differences for the two versions of the test (Thompson et al., 1989).

Age and education corrected norms have been published for two summary scores of the Benton Visual Retention Test (BVRT; Youngjohn et al., 1993), namely, number correct and total number of errors. Subjects included 1,128 healthy individuals, ranging in age from 17 to 84 years. Unfortunately, subjects with less than a high school education were not included in the study; data are presented for three categories of education, 12 to 14 years, 15 to 17 years, and 18-plus years. Sex was not considered in the norms since it did not significantly add to performance prediction in a multiple regression analysis. The BVRT has good discriminant validity for the purposes of differentiating dementia from the effects of normal aging (Youngjohn et al., 1992).

The Mini-Mental Status Examination (MMSE; Folstein et al., 1975) is a brief, standardized screening procedure for cognitive impairment that is widely used in both research and clinical settings. A recently published population-based normative study for the MMSE highlights the importance of both age and education in performance on the MMSE (Crum et al., 1993). The study included 18,571 adult participants tested between 1980 and 1984 in five centers across the United States. The age, education, and race distributions of the sample matched those of the 1980 U.S. census. Norms are provided for age groups in increments of 5 years from 18 years to over 85 years, and are stratified by years of education (0–4, 5–8, 9–12, and college experience or higher degree). The total score on the MMSE varied appreciably between educational groups and age groups, ranging from a median score of 19 (out of a possible 30 points) among individuals 85 years and older with 0 to 4 years of education to a median score of 29 for the youngest group with more than a high school diploma. Scores were also found to be more variable among subjects with fewer years of education. While the authors suggest several explanations, the larger variance may simply be due to the fact that fewer subjects were included in the 0 to 4 year education category (with n's as small as 17 and 23) than in the high school graduate category (with most cells containing 200 or more subjects). Although the subject sample was selected to reflect the racial distribution of the 1980 census, the study does not present separate data for racial groups, or even describe the percentages of the sample that come from varied ethnic backgrounds. It should be emphasized that these are population-based norms; the survey procedures did not screen out individuals with prior head injury, developmental disorder, or current cognitive dysfunction. Thus, at least some differences in the scores, particularly in the lowest education group and the oldest age group, may be due to the inclusion of these subjects. For example, lower MMSE scores at later ages may partially be attributable to the inclusion of elderly persons who are experiencing dementing diseases. Nevertheless, it is clear that both age and level of education should be considered in interpretation of the MMSE score.

Finally, Spreen and Strauss (1991) have compiled a manual of norms for many other widely used neuropsychological tests. Their purpose was to describe each test, present the best normative data available at the time of publication, and comment on issues such as the validity and reliability of the test. An effort was made to combine normative samples from several sources into one table, thereby increasing the numbers of subjects in each age group. In some cases, the authors have made extrapolations or estimations of other ages and educational groups from extant data, although it is unclear how this was accomplished. Most welcome is the addition, where available, of norms for children. While these efforts are laudatory, they cannot make up for the basic deficiencies in the field. It remains the case that most tests are sorely lacking in adequate normative data and in information regarding the reliability and discriminant validity of the tests. Nevertheless, the Spreen and Strauss (1991) compendium is a useful source of the most recent references on standardization samples and literature for currently used tests. The clinician employing a particular test is advised to refer to the cited sources if in doubt about the appropriateness of the norms.

Norms for the Very Elderly

Cognitive change is a typical, if not inevitable, consequence of aging. Visual spatial ability, some aspects of memory, speed of processing, and verbal fluency tend to decline with increasing years, particularly over the age of 70 (Labouvie-Vief, 1985; Poon, 1985). Generally, ability on tasks involving basic skills and overlearned information remains stable into very late decades, whereas earlier decline is evident on tasks that involve manipulation of novel situations or materials (Leckliter and Matarazzo, 1989). Generalized slowing of response is the most ubiquitous finding across all cognitive tasks, although the removal of time limits does not improve the performances of older persons to the level of younger adults (Lezak, 1983).

The growing number of the elderly in our society has increased the demand for specialized geriatric medical and psychological services in health care settings. More and more elderly are being seen in clinics for the assessment of dementing diseases such as Alzheimer's, or for assessment of their ability to continue to function independently in the community. Surprisingly, even for the most thoroughly developed and comprehensively normed neuropsychological instruments, virtually none includes norms for the very elderly. Lezak (1987) notes that "the dearth of . . . adequate age-graded norms becomes even more astonishing in light of the hundreds of published studies on age-related changes for the full range of discrete to complex cognitive functions, sensory capacities, and motor responses" (p. 2). Normative studies that do exist for a given test often obtain disconcertingly different results. For example, D'Elia et al. (1989) compared studies with normative data for the Wechsler Memory Scale (WMS) that include elderly subjects between the ages of 55 and 89 years (including, among others, Hulicka, 1966; Klonoff and Kennedy, 1966; Haaland et al., 1983). They found wide discrepancies between the obtained means and standard deviations in these studies, most likely due to the influence of other important variables, such as education (Bak and Greene, 1981), that were not considered. The Duke University study (McCarty et al., 1982) has identified sex and race as other important variables on the WMS.

An issue of particular importance to consider when employing norms for the elderly is the health status of the participants in normative studies. Given the frequency of chronic illness in adults over the age of 65, excluding elderly subjects on the basis of current chronic illness such as diabetes or hypertension would likely result in a sample that is not representative of the general elderly population. This poses a dilemma for the researcher gathering normative data. Albert (1981) argues that, on the one hand, the clinician may be concerned with differentiating between the cognitive changes related to chronic illness and those related to aging. Systemic disease such as hypertension or metabolic dysfunction can have an adverse impact on cognitive functions that, in some cases, ameliorates with treatment. Conversely, norms that are based upon data from only healthy older individuals may be setting standards that are unrealistically high for elderly patients. Several projects have dealt with the issue differently. A recent normative project at the Mayo Clinic (Ivnik, 1992b, described below), for example, included in their sample subjects with chronic illness such as hypertension and diabetes, but whose cognitive capacity and daily functioning were not considered to be adversely affected by their illness. Alternatively, Birren et al. (1963) categorized subjects into those who were "optimally healthy" or those "with systemic disease."

The Spreen and Strauss (1991) test manual is, once again, worth mentioning as a source of information on normative data for the elderly. As well, a bibliography of articles containing norms for older persons on a number of neuropsychological instruments is available (Erickson et al., 1992). This bibliography is the result of an extensive search for articles and publications that include norms for persons over 60 years of age. Studies with small sample sizes were not included when comparable larger samples were available.

The studies are tabulated under six categories: Mental Status Questionnaires, Intellectual Abilities, Neuropsychological Batteries, Memory Functions, Perceptual Speed and Coordination, and Executive Functions.

As a result of their survey, Erickson et al. (1992) make several observations regarding the state of affairs in the area of norms for the elderly. The authors come to the sobering conclusion that, at the present time, most of the available norms constitute little more than "rules of thumb," particularly for persons over the age of 75, or for those individuals who do not fit the description of the average North American; namely, White, educated at or beyond the high school level, and middle-class. Too few studies, in their opinion, are concerned with comparing the ability of various instruments to discriminate between individuals with other demographic characteristics who are normal versus those who have acute neurological conditions or dementing diseases. Even fewer studies provide information on *how* people succeed or fail at a task as well as *what* they achieve and how quickly. Age-related changes in individual cognitive processes may be important diagnostic factors that are not reflected adequately in total scores on complex tests that require the efficient coordination of multiple abilities.

The Mayo Older Americans Normative Studies Project (MOANS)

A major research project that has made a considerable contribution to the area of norms for the elderly has been undertaken at the Mayo Clinic in Rochester, Minnesota. The goal of the project is to provide normative data from a large subject sample that is representative of the elderly in the community. The MOANS project has already produced excellent age- and education-corrected norms for the WAIS-R, as well as age-corrected norms for the Wechsler Memory Scale–Revised and Rey's Auditory Verbal Learning Test (Ivnik et al., 1992a–c; Malec et al., 1992). The project is worth describing in some detail, not only because of the welcome contribution it makes to the field, but because of the excellence of the design and the care the authors have taken in characterizing the normative sample.

The initial MOANS subject sample included 530 subjects between the ages of 54 and 74. Subjects were recruited from the community by random solicitation, with a 34% compliance rate. All the subjects were cognitively capable of independent living, although they had a variety of medical conditions common to the elderly (see Malec et al., 1993). Subjects considered themselves normal and were considered normal by their primary care physician. The authors' criteria for normality included no active central nervous system or psychiatric conditions, no complaint of cognitive difficulty, no findings on physical examination suggesting a disorder with potential to affect cognition, and no psychoactive medication in amounts that would be expected to compromise cognition. Prior history of disorders potentially affecting cognition (e.g., head injury, substance abuse) or current chronic medical illness (e.g., diabetes, hypertension, cardiac problems) did not automatically exclude a subject from the study, as long as the condition was not reported by his or her physician to compromise cognition. A major caveat is that the subject sample was almost exclusively Caucasian with low average to superior intellectual functioning, residing in a predominantly suburban setting with good access to health care facilities. The use of these norms for an individual with little education, or whose ethnic or socioeconomic background differs markedly from the normative sample, is questionable.

One major goal of the MOANS project was to provide an extension of the existing normative data for WAIS-R IQ scores (Wechsler, 1981) for subjects beyond age 74. The WAIS-R was administered to 222 subjects over the age of 74 (range 75 to 97) and to 290 subjects between the ages of 56 and 74. The resultant MOANS norms were derived from age groups defined by overlapping, midpoint age ranges (Pauker, 1988) that maximize the amount of information obtained from the normative sample. Despite relatively small sample sizes for each 5-year in-

terval, the normative data are presented for age ranges with midpoints every 3 years from age 61 to age 88, with a 10-year range in each group. Thus, an individual can be compared to the distribution that most closely fits his or her age, and the subject sample included in each distribution is large enough to provide percentile information for the individual. The MOANS scaled scores and resultant IQs can be further corrected on a set of tables for educational level. Consistent with the research described earlier, the authors show that correction for education level is most necessary at the extremes. In fact, corrections for education for high school graduates or those with up to a few years of college results in little change in scaled scores, and are thus unnecessary.

A second major contribution of the MOANS project has been in the area of memory assessment. Memory decline is typically associated with normal aging (as defined above), but is also an important early manifestation of neurocognitive disorders, such as Alzheimer's disease (Poon, 1985). Difficulty with memory is one of the most common complaints among the elderly on referral for neuropsychological testing, and its evaluation is a critical component of a neuropsychological assessment. The MOANS project has published norms for ages 55 to 97 on two widely used memory assessment instruments, the Wechsler Memory Scale–Revised (WMS-R; Wechsler, 1987), and the Rey Auditory Verbal Learning Test (AVLT; Rey, 1964). The instructions give precise information for test administration, scoring, and computation of the subtest scores. Clinicians should familiarize themselves with the instructions in order to use the norms, since several important changes in test administration of the WMS-R were incorporated, so that the delayed recall index of the WMS-R can be computed taking into account the initial level of learning (Cullum et al., 1990). The concordances between the MOANS WMS-R indices and the original WMS-R indices (Wechsler, 1987) were within five points (plus or minus) for 96.4% of the sample on the verbal index, 90.5% on the visual index, 85.8% on the general memory index, and 93.8% on the attention/concentration index. Norms for several summary indices of the AVLT are also published (Ivnik et al., 1992c). These are an expanded version of the norms previously published by this group (Ivnik et al., 1990).

Ethnicity in Neuropsychological Test Performance

Finally, we turn to a discussion of the issue of ethnicity as a variable in neuropsychological test performance. The discussion is by no means exhaustive; our goal is to highlight the pressing need for research in this area and the development of culture-specific normative standards for use in neuropsychological clinical practice. The reader is referred to other sources for a more complete discussion, including Triandis and Berry (1980), Olmedo (1981), Reynolds and Brown (1984), Anastasi (1988), and Geisinger (1992). We should note that our work, and most published observations by others, emanate from experience in the United States. The point of view, and the examples provided, therefore, reflect the North American context. While broader generalizations might not be appropriate from some of the specific data, the general principles should be applicable to other multi-ethnic and multicultural settings.

At issue, when assessing a patient whose heritage differs from one's own, is whether adequate consideration has been given to the contribution of ethnic and cultural factors to test design and performance. A culturally sensitive assessment has been described as one that balances the application of general population norms with culture-specific norms (Lopez et al., 1989). Unfortunately, not only are normative data nonexistent for most ethnic groups on most tests, in many cases we do not even know on which tests ethnicity is or is not an important variable to consider. On the other hand, sufficient evidence exists to establish that it is a clinical myth that ethnicity is only an important variable on language- or knowledge-based tests. Ethnic background is sometimes, but not always, an important variable even on tests that are supposedly "culture free." For exam-

ple, Japanese subjects do better than American subjects on the Porteus Mazes and other spatial tests (Porteus, 1959; Lee et al., 1991). In contrast, American and Italian children perform virtually the same on the Judgment of Line Orientation Test (Riva and Benton, 1993).

Whether or not a low test performance is in part due to cultural influences may depend not only on ethnic background, but on the patient's level of "acculturation," referring to the degree to which an individual engages in a particular culture's customs, values, beliefs, social practices, and language (Arnold and Orozco, 1989). Integration into the North American cultural setting will depend on numerous factors, some of which include the age at which the person immigrated, the language of origin, the age at which English was learned, and years of education in the American school system. Education and language fluency alone, however, are insufficient to gauge acculturation (for example, see Orozco et al., 1993). Some individuals and some ethnic groups continue to participate fully in the traditions and social milieu of their culture, often continuing to speak their own language at home and in social settings.

The importance of "acculturation" in comparison to "ethnicity" is highlighted by recent research with Mexican-Americans. For example, in a study by Arnold et al. (1994) three groups of subjects were identified who differed in their level of North American acculturation; Anglo-Americans, Mexican-Americans, and Mexicans. Acculturation was assessed using an instrument developed by Cuellar et al. (1980; Acculturation Rating Scale for Mexican-Americans, ARSMA) that considers such elements as oral language usage, historical familial identification, contact with Mexico, ease with reading and writing Spanish, and generalized perceptions of identification with the Mexican culture (Orozco et al., 1993). The Mexican group was tested using a Spanish translation of the HRB. The authors found considerable differences among these three groups on the Halstead-Reitan Battery. On the aggregate T score index, the Anglo-American group scored significantly higher than the Mexican-

Americans, who in turn scored significantly higher than the Mexican group. However, this was clearly not the case for all tests in the battery. On several tests, including the Trail Making Test, Location and Memory components of the Tactual Performance Test, and Finger Tapping, similar performances were observed across the groups. In contrast, the Mexican group was significantly slower than either comparison group on Tactual Performance Test, even when age, gender, and SES were controlled for statistically. On the Categories Test, Anglo-Americans scored higher than both Mexican-Americans and Mexicans, while on the Seashore Rhythm Test, it was the Mexican-American group that scored significantly higher than either Mexicans or Anglo-Americans. The authors suggest this latter finding may be due to an increased sensitivity to auditorily processed materials in bilingual individuals.

Clearly, level of acculturation is a significant factor in neuropsychological test performance, and, importantly, not always in the direction of "more Anglo-American is better." However, few objective instruments exist for reliably measuring acculturation among members of different ethnic groups. The general paucity of research in this area means that we simply do not know what factors override ethnic differences. Thus, the best advice remains to use caution when interpreting the test scores of an individual from an ethnic background other than White Anglo-American.

African-Americans and Tests of Intelligence

Reynolds et al. (1987) used the WAIS-R standardization sample to investigate the effect of race and its interactions with education on Verbal, Performance, and Full Scale IQs (VIQ, PIQ, and FSIQ, respectively). The data from 1,664 Whites and 192 African-Americans were broken into four education categories; 0 to 8 years, 9 to 11 years, 12 years, and 13 to 16 years. Not surprisingly, the FSIQs of individuals with a college education were two standard deviations higher than those with minimal formal schooling. Across all levels of education, a difference of about one standard deviation in favor of Whites over African-Americans was found. The pattern of results was similar for VIQ and PIQ measures. The overall difference of one standard deviation in IQ scores is consistent with previous research (for review, see Reynolds and Brown, 1984). The increases in IQ for African-Americans across educational levels were substantial, but tended to be smaller than corresponding differences for Whites, although this interaction was not statistically significant. African-Americans with at least 1 year of college scored 15 to 16.5 IQ points higher than those with 0 to 8 years of education; for Whites, the IQ differences were between 18.5 to 24 IQ points. Similar effects were reported by Kaufman et al. (1988) on the individual subtests of the WAIS-R. All subtests produced significant differences in favor of Whites, although the differences were most prominent on Block Design and Vocabulary. One common Wechsler short form that is used for clinical screening is the Vocabulary–Block Design dyad (Sattler, 1982). Examiners should recognize that the use of that dyad as a short form will be particularly penalizing to African-Americans.

The differences in IQ scores between African-Americans and Whites exist even when scores are corrected for age, education, and sex. When Heaton's (1992) age, sex, and education corrected T scores are computed for the WAIS-R standardization sample, the differences among ethnic/racial groups are smaller than those described by Kaufman's group, but remain appreciable (see Table 7-2).

The source of these differences has been the subject of intense and often bitter debate. Recent evidence supports the notion that ethnic differences on intellectual testing are a barometer of educational, economic, and environmental opportunity. For example, Vincent (1991) has shown that IQ differences between African-American and White children in U.S. schools is shrinking. He reviewed pre-1980 and post-1980 studies comparing the performance of African-Americans and Whites on various tests of intellectual functioning. Studies with adults

Table 7-2. WAIS-R Mean Verbal IQ (VIQ), Performance IQ (PIQ), and Full Scale IQ (FSIQ) Expressed as T scores, for Adult (age 20+) Standardization Sample Subjects in Four Ethnic Groups, Computed Using the Heaton (1992) Age-, Education-, and Sex-Corrected Norms

	Total Sample (n = 1680)	White (n = 1461)	Black (n = 166)	Hispanic (n = 34)	Other (n = 19)
VIQ	50.0	50.7	44.6	45.9	45.5
PIQ	50.0	50.8	43.8	47.4	46.2
FSIQ	50.1	51.0	43.8	45.8	45.6

included such tests as the WAIS, WAIS-R, and Raven's Progressive Matrices; studies with children employed the WISC-R, Raven's Colored Progressive Matrices, the Kaufman-ABC, and the Stanford-Binet. African-American *adults* consistently obtained mean test scores that were approximately one standard deviation below the U.S. general population mean in studies carried out both before and after 1980. In contrast, although African-American *children* tested prior to 1980 also scored one standard deviation below the U.S. mean, studies conducted after 1980 obtained group differences that were, on average, less than half as large. In one study (Krohn and Lamp, 1989), no differences were found between African-American and White children on the Kaufman-ABC and the Stanford-Binet when socioeconomic factors were controlled. Vincent (1991) suggests that the most obvious explanation for these findings is that the shrinking difference in intellectual test scores mirrors the increased integration of African-American children into the mainstream American cultural milieu.

Norms for Spanish-speaking Adults

The United States has the fifth largest Spanish-speaking population in the world, numbering some 20 million. The population is composed primarily of Latin-American immigrant families from Mexico, Puerto Rico, Cuba, and Colombia. For first-generation immigrants, limited English language skills may preclude the use of many tests, regardless of whether or not culture-specific norms exist. In these cases, several Spanish translations of neuropsychological instruments are

available that were standardized with Spanish-speaking populations. The most widely used of these tests is the Spanish translation of the WAIS, the Escala de Inteligencia Wechsler para Adultos (EIWA; Wechsler, 1968), standardized on a large sample of Spanish-speaking adults from Puerto Rico. Lopez and Romero (1988) examined the comparability of the EIWA and the WAIS (Wechsler, 1955). They found that in the conversion of raw scores to scale scores, performance on a given subtest can result in a scale score difference of up to 5 points, depending on whether one applies the WAIS or EIWA norms. For instance, a raw score of 16 on the Object Assembly, a subtest that is identical on the WAIS and EIWA, translates into a scaled score of 5 for the WAIS and 10 for the EIWA. Lopez and Romero (1988) conclude that for some Spanish-speaking adults, particularly for those with low educational levels, low occupational status, and rural backgrounds, the EIWA may be most appropriate, because this was the combined background of most of the EIWA standardization sample subjects. In interpreting EIWA scores, however, it is important to note that they reflect adequacy of performance with reference to a particular subject sample that differs considerably from the general American population *and* the general Hispanic population within the United States. Thus, if Spanish-speaking is the only criterion for deciding to use the norms, persons with higher educational and occupational backgrounds than the EIWA standardization sample will produce overestimates of actual versus expected intellectual functioning using this instrument.

One recent contribution to the area of

language assessment for Spanish-speaking adults is the compilation of Rosselli et al. (1990) of normative data for the Boston Diagnostic Aphasia Examination (BDAE) Spanish version (Garcia-Albea et al., 1986). A sample of 180 native Spanish speakers was obtained in Bogota, Colombia, and stratified according to sex, age (16–30, 31–50, and 51–65) and education (0–5, 6–12, and 13 years or more). The results are consistent with the data from U.S. White/Anglophone subject samples (such as Borod et al., 1980) showing that the BDAE is most markedly sensitive to education differences but is affected by age as well. The authors provide means and standard deviations for age and education subgroups, together with cutoff scores for normal performance on each subtest of the BDAE by years of education. The norms may be particularly useful for assessing predominantly Spanish-speaking subjects whose language functioning is in question. Although these norms were collected in Colombia, they are arguably the most applicable norms currently available for Spanish speakers in the United States.

Summary

The adequate assessment of an individual's cognitive functioning entails a knowledge of the demographic variables that have an effect on neuropsychological test performance. Many of the assumptions that clinicians and researchers sometimes make, such as that Finger Tapping is not affected by education, that "nonverbal" or "performance" tests are culture-free, that matching on age and education level is sufficient to equate performance on tests between people of different ethnic backgrounds, are not warranted. Whenever a subject differs in important characteristics from the "average" person in a set of published norms, caution is the best advice. For a 60-year-old woman with a grade school education, whose first language was Spanish and who began learning English at age 15, the most that neuropsychological tests will tell us for sure is whether and how much she differs from the average American. They will not tell us whether she has experi-

enced a decline in functioning, in what area this decline has occurred, or, if decline has occurred, what impact it will have on her ability to care for herself and her family in the community. In this case, it is particularly important to consider the test results within the context of a detailed and comprehensive history from her family about how she copes with the demands of her daily life, and the changes, if any, that have occurred in recent days, weeks, or years. Also, the interpretation of initial neuropsychological results will necessarily rely more on consideration of *pattern* features (e.g., right-left differences on sensory-perceptual, motor, and psychomotor tests) than on *level* of performance, because the expected values for the latter are uncertain. On the other hand, interpreting major changes across successive neuropsychological evaluations is less dependent on baseline norms and can contribute to more secure diagnostic inferences.

Regardless of whether an individual does or does not match the demographic characteristics of the normative samples, the interpretation of neuropsychological test scores will ultimately depend on multiple factors, including one's definition of normal and abnormal, the goal and context of the assessment, the relationship of current test performance and daily functioning to prior levels of functioning, together with a consideration of the likely impact of the results on diagnostic and treatment decisions. As with all clinical information, judgment is required to weigh the importance of a false-positive or false-negative error.

Perhaps the most critical piece of information that is lacking in the research literature is the ecological validity of the tests we administer. Limited information exists regarding how test performance relates to everyday functioning, despite the fact that the focus for neuropsychological evaluation is quite regularly the ability of an individual to provide adequately for his or her daily needs (Heaton and Pendleton, 1981). Price et al. (1980) tested independent, socially active, elderly persons without evidence of neuropathology, yet found that as many as 90% of the subjects scored within the impaired range on the HRB Tactual Performance Test and the Trail Making Test. In a functional assessment, the goal of the neuropsychological evaluation is not to know how a person performs on a test, but how a test score correlates with coping skills in daily life situations (Albert, 1981). Nevertheless, clinical practice cannot be anything but enhanced by the addition of thorough and comprehensive norms for standard neuropsychological tests. Without these, the interpretation of test scores will continue to rely more on educated guesswork than on science.

References

Albert, M. S. (1981). Geriatric neuropsychology. *Journal of Consulting and Clinical Psychology, 49,* 835–850.

Albert, M. S., and Heaton, R. K. (1988). Intelligence testing. In M. S. Albert and M. B. Moss, eds., *Geriatric Neuropsychology.* New York: Guilford Press, pp. 13–32.

Anastasi, A. (1988). *Psychological Testing,* 6th ed. New York: Macmillan.

Arnold, B. R., Montgomery, G. T., Castaneda, I., and Longoria, R. (1994). Acculturation and performance of Hispanics on selected Halstead-Reitan neuropsychological tests. *Assessment, 1,* 239–248.

Arnold, B. R., and Orozco, S. (1989). Physical disability, acculturation, and family interaction among Mexican Americans. *Journal of Applied Rehabilitation Counseling, 20,* 28–32.

Bak, J. S., and Greene, R. L. (1981). A review of the performance of aged adults on various Wechsler Memory Scale subtests. *Journal of Clinical Psychology, 37,* 186–188.

Birren, J. E., Butler, R. N., Greenhouse, S. W., Sokoloff, L., and Yarrow, M. R. (1963). *Human Aging: A Biological and Behavioral Study.* Washington, D.C.: U.S. Government Printing Office.

Birren, J. E., and Morrison, D. F. (1961). Analysis of WAIS subtests in relation to age and education. *Journal of Gerontology, 16,* 363–369.

Borod, J. C., Goodglass, H., and Kaplan, E. (1980). Normative data on the Boston Diagnostic Aphasia Examination and the Boston Naming Test. *Journal of Clinical Neuropsychology, 2,* 209–215.

Botwinick, J. (1967). *Cognitive Processes in Maturity and Old Age.* New York: Springer.

Buffery, A. W., and Gray, J. A. (1972). Sex differences in the development of spatial and linguistic skills. In C. Ounsted and D. C. Taylor, eds., *Gender Differences: Their Ontogeny and Significance.* Baltimore: Williams and Wilkins, pp. 123–157.

Cattell, R. B. (1963). Theory of fluid and crystallized intelligence: A critical experiment. *Journal of Educational Psychology, 54,* 1–22.

Crum, R. M., Anthony, J. C., Bassett, S. S., and Folstein, M. F. (1993). Population-based norms for the Mini-Mental State Examination by age and educational level. *Journal of the American Medical Association, 269,* 2386–2391.

Cuellar, I., Harris, L. C., and Jasso, R. (1980). An acculturation scale for Mexican American normal and clinical populations. *Hispanic Journal of Behavioral Sciences, 2,* 199–217.

Cullum, C. M., Butters, N., Troster, A. I., and Salmon, D. P. (1990). Normal aging and forgetting rates on the Wechsler Memory Scale-Revised. *Archives of Clinical Neuropsychology, 5,* 23–30.

D'Elia, L., Satz, P., and Schretlen, D. (1989). Wechsler Memory Scale: A critical appraisal of the normative studies. *Journal of Clinical and Experimental Neuropsychology, 11,* 551–568.

Erickson, R. C., Eimon, P., and Hebben, N. (1992). A bibliography of normative articles on cognition tests for older adults. *The Clinical Neuropsychologist, 6,* 98–102.

Finlayson, M. A., Johnson, K. A., and Reitan, R. M. (1977). Relationship of level of education to neuropsychological measures in brain-damaged and non-brain-damaged adults. *Journal of Consulting and Clinical Psychology, 45,* 536–542.

Flynn, J. R. (1984). The mean IQ of Americans: Massive gains 1932 to 1978. *Psychological Bulletin, 95,* 29–51.

Flynn, J. R. (1987). Massive IQ gains in 14 nations: What IQ tests really measure. *Psychological Bulletin, 101,* 171–191.

Folstein, M. F., Folstein, S. E., and McHugh, P. R. (1975). Mini-Mental State: A practical method for grading the cognitive state of patients for the clinician. *Journal of Psychiatric Research, 12,* 189–198.

Fromm-Auch, D., and Yeudall, L. T. (1983). Normative data for the Halstead-Reitan Neuropsychological Tests. *Journal of Clinical Neuropsychology, 5,* 221–238.

Garcia-Albea, J. E., Sanchez-Bernardos, M. L., and del Viso-Pabon, S. (1986). Test de Boston para el diagnostico de la afasia: Adaptacion Espanola. In H. Goodglass and E. Kaplan, eds.,

La Evaluacion de la Afasia y de Transtornos Relacionados (2nd ed.) (translated by Carlos Wernicke). Madrid: Editorial Medica Panamericana, pp. 129–198.

Geisinger, K. F. (1992). *Psychological Testing of Hispanics*. Washington, D.C.: American Psychological Association.

Haaland, K. Y., Linn, R. T., Hunt, W. C., and Goodwin, J. S. (1983). A normative study of Russell's variant of the Wechsler Memory Scale in a healthy elderly population. *Journal of Consulting and Clinical Psychology, 51*, 878–881.

Heaton, R. K. (1992). *Comprehensive Norms for an Expanded Halstead-Reitan Battery: A Supplement for the WAIS-R*. Odessa, FL: Psychological Assessment Resources.

Heaton, R. K., Grant, I., and Matthews, C. G. (1986). Differences in neuropsychological test performance associated with age, education, and sex. In I. Grant and K. M. Adams, eds. *Neuropsychological Assessment of Neuropsychiatric Disorders*. New York: Oxford University Press, pp. 100–120.

Heaton, R. K., Grant, I., and Matthews, C. G. (1991). *Comprehensive Norms for an Expanded Halstead-Reitan Battery: Demographic Corrections, Research Findings, and Clinical Applications*. Odessa, FL: Psychological Assessment Resources.

Heaton, R. K., and Pendleton, M. G. (1981). Use of neuropsychological tests to predict adult patients' everyday functioning. *Journal of Consulting and Clinical Psychology, 49*, 807–821.

Horn, J. L., and Cattell, R. B. (1966). Age differences in primary mental ability factors. *Journal of Gerontology, 21*, 210–220.

Hulicka, I. M. (1966). Age differences in Wechsler Memory Scale scores. *Journal of Genetic Psychology, 109*, 135–145.

Ivnik, R. J., Malec, J. F., Smith, G. E., Tangalos, E. G., Petersen, R. C., Kokmen, E., and Kurland, L. T. (1992a). Mayo's older Americans normative studies: WAIS-R norms for ages 56 to 97. *The Clinical Neuropsychologist, 6* (suppl.), 1–30.

Ivnik, R. J., Malec, J. F., Smith, G. E., Tangalos, E. G., Petersen, R. C., Kokmen, E., and Kurland, L. T. (1992b). Mayo's older Americans normative studies: WMS-R norms for ages 56 to 94. *The Clinical Neuropsychologist, 6* (suppl.), 49–82.

Ivnik, R. J., Malec, J. F., Smith, G. E., Tangalos, E. G., Petersen, R. C., Kokmen, E., and Kurland, L. T. (1992c). Mayo's older Americans normative studies: Updated AVLT norms for ages 56 to 97. *The Clinical Neuropsychologist, 6* (suppl.), 83–104.

Ivnik, R. J., Malec, J. F., Tangalos, E. G., Petersen, R. C., Kokmen, E., and Kurland, L. T. (1990). The Auditory-Verbal Learning Test (AVLT): Norms for ages 55 and older. *Psychological Assessment, 2*, 304–312.

Kaufman, A. S., McLean, J. E., and Reynolds, C. R. (1988). Sex, race, residence, region, and education differences on the 11 WAIS-R subtests. *Journal of Clinical Psychology, 44*, 231–248.

Klonoff, H., and Kennedy, M. (1966). A comparative study of cognitive functioning in old age. *Journal of Gerontology, 21*, 239–243.

Krohn, E. J., and Lamp, R. E. (1989). Concurrent validity of the Stanford-Binet Fourth Edition and K-ABC for Head Start children. *Journal of School Psychology, 27*, 59–67.

Labouvie-Vief, G. (1985). Intelligence and cognition. In J. E. Birren and K. W. Schaie, eds., *Handbook of the Psychology of Aging* (2nd ed.). New York: Van Nostrand Reinhold Company, pp. 500–530.

Leckliter, I. N., and Matarazzo, J. D. (1989). The influence of age, education, IQ, gender, and alcohol abuse on Halstead-Reitan Neuropsychological Test Battery performance. *Journal of Clinical Psychology, 45*, 484–512.

Lee, G. P., Sasanuma, S., Hamsher, K. D., and Benton, A. L. (1991). Constructional praxis performance of Japanese and American, normal and brain-damaged patients. *Archives of Clinical Neuropsychology, 6*, 15–25.

Lezak, M. D. (1983). *Neuropsychological Assessment* (2nd ed). New York: Oxford University Press.

Lezak, M. D. (1987). Norms for growing older. *Developmental Neuropsychology, 3*, 1–12.

Lopez, S. R., Grover, K. P., Holland, D., Johnson, M. J., Kain, C. D., Kanel, K., Mellins, C. A., and Rhyne, M. C. (1989). Development of culturally sensitive psychotherapists. *Professional Psychology: Research and Practice, 20*, 369–376.

Lopez, S., and Romero, A. (1988). Assessing the intellectual functioning of Spanish-speaking adults: Comparison of the EIWA and the WAIS. *Professional Psychology: Research and Practice, 19*, 263–270.

Maccoby, E. E., and Jacklin, C. N. (1974). *The Psychology of Sex Differences*. Stanford CA: Stanford University Press.

Malec, J. F., Ivnik, R. J., and Smith, G. E. (1993). Neuropsychology and normal aging: Clinician's perspective. In R. W. Parks, R. F. Zec, and R. S. Wilson, eds., *Neuropsychology of Alzheimer's Disease and Other Dementias*. New York: Oxford University Press, pp. 81–111.

Malec, J. F., Ivnik, R. J., Smith, G. E., Tangalos, E. G., Petersen, R. C., Kokmen, E., and Kurland, L. T. (1992). Mayo's older Americans normative studies: Utility of corrections for age and education for the WAIS-R. *The Clinical Neuropsychologist, 6* (suppl.), 31–47.

Matarazzo, J. D. (1972). *Wechsler's Measurement and Appraisal of Adult Intelligence*. Baltimore: Williams and Wilkins.

Matarazzo, J. D., Bornstein, R. A., McDermott, P. A., and Noonan, J. V. (1986). Verbal IQ vs. performance IQ difference scores in males and females from the WAIS-R standardization sample. *Journal of Clinical Psychology, 42*, 965–974.

Matarazzo, J. D., and Herman, D. O. (1984). Relationship of education and IQ in the WAIS-R standardization sample. *Journal of Consulting and Clinical Psychology, 52*, 631–634.

McCarty, S. M., Siegler, I. C., and Logue, P. E. (1982). Cross-sectional and longitudinal patterns of three Wechsler Memory Scale subtests. *Journal of Gerontology, 37*, 169–175.

Olmedo, E. L. (1981). Testing linguistic minorities. *American Psychologist, 36*, 1078–1085.

Orozco, S., Thompson, B., Kapes, J., and Montgomery, G. T. (1993). Measuring the acculturation of Mexican Americans: A covariance structure analysis. *Measurement and Evaluation in Counseling and Development, 25*, 149–155.

Parsons, O. A., and Prigatano, G. P. (1978). Methodological considerations in clinical neuropsychological research. *Journal of Consulting and Clinical Psychology, 46*, 608–619.

Pauker, J. D. (1988). Constructing overlapping cell tables to maximize the clinical usefulness of normative test data: Rationale and an example from neuropsychology. *Journal of Clinical Psychology, 44*, 930–933.

Poon, L. W. (1985). Difference in human memory with aging: Nature, causes, and clinical implications. In J. E. Birren and K. W. Schaie, eds., *Handbook of the Psychology of Aging* (2nd ed.). New York: Van Nostrand Reinhold Company, pp. 427–462.

Porteus, S. D. (1959). *The Maze Test and Clinical Psychology*. Palo Alto: Pacific Books.

Price, L. J., Fein, G., and Feinberg, L. (1980). Neuropsychological assessment of cognitive functioning in the elderly. In L. W. Poon, ed., *Aging in the 1980s: Psychological Issues*.

Washington, D.C.: American Psychological Association, pp. 78–85.

Reitan, R. M. (1955). The distribution according to age of a psychological measure dependent upon organic brain functions. *Journal of Gerontology, 10*, 338–340.

Reitan, R. M. (1957). Differential reaction of various psychological tests to age. In *Fourth Congress of the International Association of Gerontology*. Fidenza: Tito Mattioli, pp. 158–165.

Reitan, R. M. and Wolfson, D. (1986). The Halstead-Reitan Neuropsychological Test Battery and aging. In T. L. Brink, ed., *Clinical Gerontology: A Guide to Assessment and Intervention*. New York: Haworth Press, pp. 39–61.

Rey, A. (1964). *L'examen Clinique en Psychologie*. Paris: Presses Universitaires de France.

Reynolds, C. R., and Brown, R. T. (1984). *Perspectives on Bias in Mental Testing*. New York: Plenum Press.

Reynolds, C. R., Chastain, R. L., Kaufman, A. S., and McLean, J. E. (1987). Demographic characteristics and IQ among adults: Analysis of the WAIS-R standardization sample as a function of the stratification variables. *Journal of School Psychology, 25*, 323–342.

Riva, D., and Benton, A. (1993). Visuospatial judgment: A crossnational comparison. *Cortex, 29*, 141–143.

Rosselli, M., Ardila, A., Florez, A., and Castro, C. (1990). Normative data on the Boston Diagnostic Aphasia Examination in a Spanish-speaking population. *Journal of Clinical and Experimental Neuropsychology, 12*, 313–322.

Russell, E. W., Neuringer, C., and Goldstein, G. (1970). *Assessment of Brain Damage: A Neuropsychological Key Approach*. New York: Wiley-Interscience.

Sattler, J. M. (1982). *Assessment of Children's Intelligence and Special Abilities* (2nd ed.). Boston: Allyn and Bacon.

Shallice, T. (1988). *From Neuropsychology to Mental Structure*. Cambridge: Cambridge University Press.

Spreen, O., and Strauss, E. (1991). *A Compendium of Neuropsychological Tests: Administration, Norms, and Commentary*. New York: Oxford University Press.

Thompson, L. L., Heaton, R. K., Grant, I., and Matthews, C. G. (1989). A comparison of the WAIS and WAIS-R using T-score conversions that correct for age, education, and sex. *Journal of Clinical and Experimental Neuropsychology, 11*, 478–488.

Triandis, H. C., and Berry, J. W. (1980). *Handbook of *Cross-cultural Psychology* (vols. 1 and 2). Boston: Allyn and Bacon.

Vega, A., Jr., and Parsons, O. A. (1967). Cross-validation of the Halstead-Reitan tests for brain damage. *Journal of Consulting Psychology, 31,* 619–625.

Vincent, K. R. (1991). Black/White IQ differences: Does age make the difference? *Journal of Clinical Psychology, 47,* 266–270.

Wechsler, D. (1955). *Manual for the Wechsler Adult Intelligence Scale.* New York: Psychological Corporation.

Wechsler, D. (1968). *Escala de Inteligencia Wechsler para Adultos.* New York: Psychological Corporation.

Wechsler, D. (1981). *WAIS-R Manual: Wechsler Adult Intelligence Scale-Revised.* New York: Psychological Corporation.

Wechsler, D. (1987). *Wechsler Memory Scale-Revised. Manual.* New York: Psychological Corporation.

Yeudall, L. T., Reddon, J. R., Gill, D. M., and Stefanyk, W. O. (1987). Normative data for the Halstead-Reitan neuropsychological tests stratified by age and sex. *Journal of Clinical Psychology, 43,* 346–367.

Youngjohn, J. R., Larrabee, G. J., and Crook, T. H. (1992). Discriminating age-associated memory impairment from Alzheimer's disease. *Psychological Assessment, 4,* 54–59.

Youngjohn, J. R., Larrabee, G. J., and Crook, T. H. (1993). New adult age- and education-correction norms for the Benton Visual Retention Test. *The Clinical Neuropsychologist, 7,* 155–160.

8 The Neuropsychology of Dementia

MARK W. BONDI, DAVID P. SALMON, and ALFRED W. KASZNIAK

As increasing numbers of individuals are surviving into older age in most developed countries (Myers, 1990), the prevalence of dementing illness has risen (Manton, 1990). Accordingly, clinical and research efforts in the neuropsychology of dementia have also expanded, particularly over the past two decades (La Rue, 1992; Poon et al., 1992). From a clinical perspective, neuropsychological assessment has come to play a critical role in identifying the presence of dementia and in contributing to the differential diagnosis of its myriad causes. Clinical neuropsychological assessment of the person with known or suspected dementia may be performed to address any or all of the following aims (see Bayles and Kaszniak, 1987; Albert and Moss, 1988; La Rue, 1992; Zec, 1993; Lezak, 1995): (1) to identify the presence of cognitive impairment and contribute to diagnosis, particularly where the degree of impairment is mild, where the patient is of high premorbid intellectual ability, or where there is an unusual combination of cognitive impairments; (2) to provide information to patients, family members, and health care providers about the specific nature of strengths and weaknesses in the patient's cognitive functioning; (3) to contribute to recommendations for treatment and management of cognitive and behavior problems; and (4) to provide a baseline measurement against which treatment effects or disease progression can be judged.

Research efforts in the neuropsychology of dementia have focused on identifying the pattern, progression and neuropathological correlates of the cognitive deficits associated with various dementing disorders. These efforts have led to increased knowledge about the particular neuropsychological deficits that occur in the earliest stages of a dementing disorder such as Alzheimer's disease (AD), and have recently provided information on cognitive changes that appear to presage the development of dementia. In addition, research has shown that dementia is not a unitary disorder, but that different patterns of relatively preserved and impaired cognitive abilities can be identified among dementing diseases that have different etiologies and sites of neuropathology.

These recent advances in research on the neuropsychology of dementia, and their clinical implications, will be discussed in further detail in the present chapter. Before embarking on such a discussion, however, it will be useful to describe the dementia syndrome and to briefly review its clinical and epidemiological features. Our discussion will also be facilitated by a brief review of the clinical, etiological and neuropathological features of a number of the most common dementing disorders.

The Syndrome of Dementia: Description, Prevalence, and Risk Factors

Dementia refers to a syndrome of acquired intellectual impairment of sufficient severity to interfere with social or occupational functioning that is caused by brain dysfunction. According to most definitions (e.g., Bayles and Kaszniak, 1987; Cummings and Benson, 1992; American Psychiatric Association, 1994), the syndrome of dementia involves deterioration in two or more of the following domains of psychological functioning: memory, language, visuospatial skills, judgment or abstract thinking, and emotion or personality. In some diagnostic schemes (DSM-IV; American Psychiatric Association, 1994), memory impairment and at least one other cognitive deficit must be present and severe enough to significantly interfere with social or occupational functioning. Furthermore, the cognitive impairment must represent a significant decline from a previous level of functioning, and it must not occur exclusively during the course of delirium.

Estimates of the prevalence of dementia vary widely due to differences in dementia definitions, sampling techniques, and sensitivity of instruments used to identify cases. In studies of dementia in various countries, prevalence rates have ranged from 2.5% to 24.6% for persons over the age of 65 (see Ineichen, 1987). Cummings and Benson (1992), calculating the average of prevalence estimates across studies, suggest that approximately 6% of persons over the age of 65 have severe dementia, with an additional 10% to 15% having mild to moderate dementia. The prevalence of the syndrome of dementia is age-related, doubling approximately every 5 years after age 65 (Jorm et al., 1987). Not surprisingly, the prevalence of dementia is higher among hospital and nursing home residents than among those living within the community (for reviews, see Kramer, 1986; Smyer, 1988).

Significant advances in our understanding of the epidemiology of dementia have occurred during the past decade. Katzman and Kawas (1994) summarize a number of clear-cut findings that have emerged. First, by all accounts, age is the single most important risk factor for dementia. Community (population) studies in many different countries have confirmed that the prevalence of the most common causes of dementia—AD and vascular disease—rises in an approximately exponential fashion between the ages of 65 and 85. Importantly, however, data on individuals greater than age 85, who represent the fastest growing segment of our population, are insufficient to determine whether this apparently exponential relationship remains in this advanced age group or whether it asymptotes beyond age 85.

Second, gender may be a significant risk factor for dementia. A large-scale epidemiological survey in Shanghai identified female gender, along with age and education, as an independent predictor of dementia (Zhang et al., 1990). A number of other studies suggest that women have a slightly greater risk for AD than men (although men may be at somewhat greater risk for vascular dementia). The results of these studies must be considered carefully, however, because the increased prevalence of AD in women may be attributable to differential survival after the onset of dementia as a result of their longer life expectancy. Although a 2.8 to 1 (female to male) ratio of AD was observed in the Framingham prevalence study (Bachman et al., 1992), no gender difference in the incidence of either dementia or AD was found in this cohort (Bachman et al., 1993).

Third, lack of education has been associated with an increased risk of dementia. An uneducated individual over age 75 is at about twice the risk for dementia as is someone who has completed at least a grade school education (Mortimer, 1988; Zhang et al., 1990; Katzman, 1993; Katzman and Kawas, 1994). Stern and colleagues (1994) recently demonstrated a similar relationship between risk of dementia and lifetime occupational attainment; they also found that the combination of both low education and low lifetime occupational attainment yielded a greater relative risk (i.e., close to a threefold increase in risk) than either one alone.

With regard to Alzheimer's disease, both Katzman (1993) and Stern et al. (1994) suggest that a decrease in risk of dementia with increasing level of educational or lifetime occupational attainment might be observed if these variables are a surrogate for a brain or cognitive reserve that helps to delay the onset of the usual clinical manifestations of the disease. To address this issue, Stern et al. (1992) reasoned that if advanced education imparts a brain or cognitive reserve, then more severe pathological changes would be present in patients with high education than in those with low education at a time when the groups were matched for overall severity of dementia. Consistent with their prediction, these investigators observed a significantly greater parietotemporal blood flow deficit in high-education probable AD patients than in equally demented low-education patients.

Fourth, the risk of developing dementia is increased approximately fourfold by a family history of AD in a first-degree relative (i.e., mother, father, brother, or sister; van Duijn et al., 1991). Given some of the recent findings of specific point mutations on the amyloid precursor protein gene of chromosome 21 and linkage studies identifying gene loci on chromosomes 14 and 19, there is now little question that this familial association is genetically based. Furthermore, the $\epsilon 4$ allele of the apolipoprotein E gene located on chromosome 19 has recently been identified as another major risk factor for dementia because of its overrepresentation in patients with AD (Corder et al., 1993; Saunders et al., 1993; Strittmatter et al., 1993). Although this striking association between the $\epsilon 4$ allele and AD has been repeatedly confirmed (Mayeux et al., 1993; Poirier et al., 1993; van Duijn et al., 1994; see also Katzman, 1994, for review), Frisoni et al. (1995) recently reported on data suggesting that disease duration might be longer in $\epsilon 4$ carriers and that this might at least partly account for the cross-sectional association between the $\epsilon 4$ allele and late-onset AD.

Finally, head injury has been identified as a risk factor for the development of dementia (Mortimer et al., 1991). Dementia pugilistica may occur in individuals who have suffered repeated blows to the head while boxing (Corsellis et al., 1973), and the risk of developing AD is doubled for individuals with a history of a single head injury that led to loss of consciousness or hospitalization (Mortimer et al., 1991). This latter finding, however, may be restricted to those persons who have a genetic susceptibility to AD (Mayeux et al., 1995). Mayeux and colleagues (1995) recently examined the interaction between the apolipoprotein $\epsilon 4$ allele and head injury and found a 10-fold increase in the risk of AD in people with both risk factors, compared to a twofold increase in risk conferred by the apolipoprotein $\epsilon 4$ allele alone. Head injury in the absence of an apolipoprotein $\epsilon 4$ allele did not significantly increase the risk of AD.

The epidemiological evidence to date suggests that as the population ages dementia will increasingly become the dominant disorder in late life. However, recent advances in identifying risk factors may, in the short-term, improve our ability to detect dementia in its earliest stages when palliative treatments may be most effective, and may, in the long term, lead to the discovery of specific biological mechanisms that cause the disease. Knowledge of the risk factors for dementia, and particularly AD, is growing rapidly. If one assumes that the various risk factors are simply additive at the population level, then the attributable risk of developing AD from these known factors appears to be between 40% and 50% (and probably more given the recent addition of apolipoprotein $\epsilon 4$ associated risk). By way of comparison, as Katzman and Kawas (1994) point out, the attributable risk of heart attacks from obesity, high cholesterol, lack of exercise, and diabetes together is about 40%.

Specific Dementing Illnesses: Clinical and Neuropathological Features

Dementia can be associated with more than 50 different causes of brain dysfunction (Haase, 1977; Katzman, 1986). Alzheimer's disease (AD) has typically been found to be the most common cause of dementia, accounting for about 50% of all cases (for review, see Cummings and Benson, 1992). Multi-infarct dementia (MID), or vascular dementia, is usually regarded as the second most common cause; however, in some community surveys (particularly, although not exclusively, those in Japan and China), MID has been found to be more prevalent than AD (Folstein et al., 1985; Rorsman et al., 1986; Shibayama et al., 1986; Li et al., 1989). It is not clear whether such differences in relative prevalence estimates reflect actual regional disparities or, rather, methodological variation across studies. Other, less prevalent, degenerative neurological diseases (e.g., Huntington's disease, Parkinson's disease, progressive supranuclear palsy) may also produce dementia, and have recently been the focus of neuropsychological research. The neuropathological and clinical features of some of the more common dementing disorders are briefly presented below. A more detailed discussion of these and other less common causes of dementia are available elsewhere (see Heston and Mastri, 1982; Cummings 1990; Cummings and Benson, 1992; Huber and Cummings, 1992; Parks et al., 1993; Grant and Martin, 1994; Terry et al., 1994).

Alzheimer's Disease

Alzheimer's disease is a progressive degenerative brain disorder that is characterized by neocortical atrophy, neuron and synapse loss (Terry et al., 1981, 1991), and the presence of senile plaques and neurofibrillary tangles (Alzheimer, 1907; Terry and Katzman, 1983). The neuropathological changes of AD occur primarily in the hippocampus and entorhinal cortex, and in the association cortices of the frontal, temporal and parietal lobes (Terry and Katzman, 1983; Hyman et al., 1984). Although the temporal progression of the neuropathological changes of AD are not fully known, recent studies suggest that the hippocampus and entorhinal cortex are involved in the earliest stage of the disease, and that frontal, temporal and parietal association cortices become increasingly involved as the disease progresses (Hyman et

al., 1984; Pearson et al., 1985; Braak and Braak, 1991; Arriagada et al., 1992; Bancher et al., 1993; De Lacoste and White, 1993). In addition to these cortical changes, subcortical neuron loss occurs in the nucleus basalis of Meynert and in the locus coeruleus, resulting in a decrement in neocortical levels of cholinergic and noradrenergic markers, respectively (Bondareff et al., 1982; Whitehouse et al., 1982; Mann et al., 1984).

Although the cause of AD remains unknown, it was recently discovered that the $\epsilon 4$ allele of apolipoprotein E, a low-density lipoprotein (LDL) cholesterol carrier, is overrepresented in patients with AD (Corder et al., 1993). Thus, there now appears to be a major genetic susceptibility factor for the disease. The APOE $\epsilon 4$ allele has been found to be present in 50% to 60% of AD patients (compared to 20% to 25% of healthy older adults), regardless of whether or not they have a family history of dementia, and it is now considered the most common known risk factor for AD (for review, see Katzman, 1994; Katzman and Kawas, 1994).

Studies suggest that there is remarkable variability in the frequency of the APOE $\epsilon 4$ allele in different racial and ethnic groups (Hallman et al., 1991; Gerdes et al., 1992; Mayeux et al., 1993). The frequency of the $\epsilon 4$ allele has been reported to be as high as 0.244 in the Finnish population, 0.291 in the Sudanese, and 0.25 in Inuit Eskimos, and as low as 0.08 to 0.09 in the Chinese and Japanese populations (see Katzman, 1994). The frequency in the populations of Western countries is approximately 0.15. Although the frequency of the $\epsilon 4$ allele in the Finnish population is almost twice that of other Western populations, it should be noted that there is not a corresponding doubling of AD prevalence in that population (Katzman, 1994).

In a preliminary study, Mayeux and colleagues (1993) found APOE $\epsilon 4$ allele frequencies to be approximately the same in African-American (0.36), White (0.35), and Hispanic (0.35) AD patients in a multiracial region of Manhattan. However, while these frequencies reflect an overrepresentation in both the Hispanic and White groups, the $\epsilon 4$ allele frequency in AD patients and nondemented subjects was roughly the same in the small sample of African-American subjects. This preliminary finding raises the possibility that the APOE $\epsilon 4$ risk factor may be less important for this subgroup of patients. Hendrie and colleagues (1995), however, demonstrated that the $\epsilon 4$ allele frequency was strongly associated with AD in a population of 85 African-American individuals age 65 and over. The $\epsilon 4$ allele frequency in the 31 AD patients was over 40% compared with 14% in the 54 nondemented control subjects, and approximately 23% of the AD patients were homozygous for the $\epsilon 4$ allele compared with less than 4% of the control subjects. Thus, in contrast to the findings of Mayeux et al. (1993), Hendrie et al. (1995) suggest that the strong association between the APOE $\epsilon 4$ allele and AD is observed in elderly African-American individuals as well.

The primary clinical manifestation of Alzheimer's disease is a profound global dementia characterized by severe amnesia with additional deficits in language, "executive" functions, attention, and visuospatial and constructional abilities (Bayles and Kaszniak, 1987; Cummings and Benson, 1992; Bondi et al., 1994b). Because there are no known peripheral markers for the disease, AD can only be diagnosed clinically by documenting the presence of dementia and excluding all other potential causes. To aid in this process, and to standardize the diagnosis to some degree, criteria for the clinical diagnosis of *probable* and *possible* AD were developed by the Work Group on the Diagnosis of Alzheimer's Disease established by the National Institute of Neurological and Communicative Disorders and Stroke and the Alzheimer's Disease and Related Disorders Association (NINCDS-ADRDA; McKhann et al., 1984). These NINCDS-ADRDA clinical criteria have been tested against autopsy verified diagnoses and found to be quite effective (Kawas, 1990; Galasko et al., 1994). Very similar criteria defined by previous editions of the Diagnostic and Statistical Manual of Mental Disorders (e.g., DSM-III-R, and more recently, DSM-IV; American Psychiat-

ric Association, 1994) have also been employed and have shown both acceptable interclinician reliability (Kukull et al., 1990a) and reasonable sensitivity and specificity, when compared to neuropathologic and long-term follow-up criteria (Kukull et al., 1990b). It should be kept in mind, however, that AD can be definitively diagnosed only by histopathological criteria (Khachaturian, 1985).

Vascular Dementia

Vascular dementia refers to a cumulative decline in cognitive functioning secondary to multiple or strategically placed infarctions, ischemic injury, or hemorrhagic lesions. Criteria for vascular dementia outlined in DSM-IV require that multiple cognitive deficits be present, that there be significant impairment and decline in either social or occupational functioning, and that the deficits not occur exclusively during the course of a delirium. Furthermore, there must be focal neurological signs and symptoms, or laboratory (e.g., CT or MRI scan) evidence indicative of cerebrovascular disease, that are thought to be etiologically related to the cognitive impairment.

A relationship between dementia and cerebrovascular disease is often indicated if the onset of dementia occurs within several months of a recognized stroke, there is an abrupt deterioration in cognitive functioning, or the course of cognitive deterioration is fluctuating or stepwise. Vascular dementia will also sometimes be accompanied by gait disturbances and a history of unsteadiness and frequent falls, urinary disturbances not related to urologic disease, pseudobulbar palsy, and mood and personality changes (e.g., depression, emotional incontinence) (Cummings and Benson, 1992).

In order to differentiate some forms of vascular dementia from primary degenerative dementia (e.g., Alzheimer's disease), Hachinski and colleagues (1974, 1975) developed an ischemia scale based on the distinguishing characteristics and risk factors for multi-infarct dementia (see Rosen et al.,

1980, for a modification of this scale). Using their scale, these investigators found that 24 patients with comparable levels of dementia fell cleanly into two non-overlapping groups. Patients who scored 4 or less on the scale best fit the profile for dementia of the Alzheimer type, and patients scoring 7 or higher on the scale were considered to have multi-infarct dementia. Subsequent studies with pathological or radiological verification demonstrated that the ischemia scale score correctly classified more than 70% of patients with MID and almost 90% of patients with AD (Rosen et al., 1980; Loeb and Gandolfo, 1983; Molsa et al., 1985).

Because the Hachinski ischemia scale was primarily directed toward vascular dementia arising from one cause (i.e., medium or large vessel cortical infarcts), specific research criteria for the diagnosis of broadly defined vascular dementia were recently proposed by an international workgroup supported by the Neuroepidemiology Branch of the National Institute of Neurological Disorders and Stroke (NINDS) and the Association Internationale pour la Recherche et l'Enseignement en Neurosciences (AIREN) (Roman et al., 1993; see Chui et al., 1992, for similar diagnostic criteria). These criteria are intended to encompass dementia resulting from all vascular causes, including infarction, ischemia and hemorrhagic brain lesions. The NINDS-AIREN criteria include diagnoses of probable, possible, and definite vascular dementia, as well as a subcategorization of the specific types of vascular lesions (as determined by clinical, radiologic, and neuropathologic features). As with the NINCDS-ADRDA criteria for AD, the diagnosis of definite vascular dementia requires histopathologic evidence of cerebrovascular disease. In addition, this evidence must occur in the absence of neurofibrillary tangles and neuritic plaques exceeding those expected for age, and without clinical evidence of any other disorder capable of producing dementia (e.g., Pick's disease, diffuse Lewy bodies, etc.). It should also be noted that the NINDS-AIREN criteria specify that the term "AD with cerebrovascular disease" should be used to classify patients who meet the NINCDS-ADRDA criteria for possible AD, and who also show clinical and/or brain imaging evidence of relevant cerebrovascular disease.

Huntington's Disease

Huntington's disease (HD) is an inherited, autosomal dominant neurodegenerative disorder that results in movement disturbances and dementia. Neuropathologically, HD is characterized primarily by a progressive deterioration of the neostriatum (caudate nucleus and putamen), with a selective loss of the spiny neurons and a relative sparing of the aspiny interneurons (Bruyn et al., 1979; Vonsattel et al., 1985). The onset of HD usually occurs in the fourth or fifth decade of life (Bruyn, 1968; Folstein, 1989), although a juvenile form of the disease with onset before the age of 20 has been described (Hayden, 1981).

The primary clinical manifestations of HD include choreiform movements, a progressive dementia, and emotional or personality changes (Folstein et al., 1990). Often, the earliest behavioral features of HD are insidious changes in behavior and personality (e.g., depression, irritability, and anxiety), as well as complaints of incoordination, clumsiness, and fidgeting. As the disease progresses, most patients develop severe chorea and dysarthria and may also develop gait and oculomotor dysfunction. As discussed in the chapter by Brandt and Butters in the present volume (Chapter 14), the cognitive disturbances associated with HD early in its course include deficits in memory retrieval, executive functions and verbal fluency with relatively preserved general intellect.

Markers for the Huntington's disease gene have recently been identified (MacDonald et al., 1993) and genetic testing is currently available for determining whether an at-risk individual is likely to develop the disease. Such testing provides the opportunity to track individuals who will definitely develop the disease in an effort to identify behavioral and cognitive changes that may precede the usual clinical diagnosis (Brandt et al., 1989; see also Brandt and Butters, Chapter 14). Although genetic testing for HD is becoming widely available, it must be done with caution given the high prevalence of suicide in the face of this devastating disease (Folstein et al., 1983). As the DSM-IV guidelines suggest, such testing might be best conducted by centers with experience in counseling and adequate mechanisms for treatment and follow-up of affected individuals.

Parkinson's Disease

Idiopathic Parkinson's disease (PD) is a neurodegenerative disorder characterized neuropathologically by a loss of pigmented cells in the compact zone of the substantia nigra and the presence of Lewy bodies (abnormal intracytoplasmic eosinophilic neuronal inclusion bodies) in the substantia nigra, locus ceruleus, dorsal motor nucleus of the vagus and the substantia innominata (Jellinger, 1987; Hansen and Galasko, 1992; see also the chapter by McPherson and Cummings [Chapter 13]). The neurodegeneration that occurs in Parkinson's disease also results in a major depletion of dopamine in the brains of affected individuals.

Parkinson's disease is identified clinically by the classic motor-symptom triad of resting tremor, rigidity, and bradykinesia (Jankovic, 1987). A number of other motor symptoms, such as postural stooping and gait disturbances (shuffling gait), may also be present. Associated clinical features of the disease may include masked facies, micrographia, hypophonia, dysarthria, and poor prosody (monotoned speech). The onset of the disorder usually occurs between the ages of 40 and 70, with a peak onset in the sixth decade. Approximately 1 in 100 people over the age of 60 are affected by the disease (Duvoisin, 1984; see also McPherson and Cummings [Chapter 13]).

Although not included in James Parkinson's original description of the disease, there is a higher prevalence of dementia in patients with PD than in the general population of the same age. Estimates of the prevalence of dementia in PD vary tremendously (from 4% to 93%; see Cummings, 1988), but Cummings (1988) recently calculated the average prevalence across studies as approximately 40% (an estimated prevalence of 25% was suggested by Brown and Marsden, 1984).

The source of the dementia in PD also remains controversial and may be due to the direct effects of subcortical degenerative changes (i.e., dopaminergic depletion of striatal structures secondary to cell losses in the substantia nigra), superimposed Alzheimer type degenerative changes, or a combination of these two factors (Freedman, 1990; see also McPherson and Cummings [Chapter 13]). Furthermore, a number of recent studies have shown that all, or very nearly all (i.e., 96%), brains of patients with PD have Lewy bodies in the neocortex (Perry et al., 1991; Schmidt et al., 1991; Hughes et al., 1992).

Lewy Body Variant of Alzheimer's Disease

A number of investigators have recently described a neuropathologic condition in demented patients that is characterized by the typical cortical distribution of senile plaques and neurofibrillary tangles of Alzheimer's disease; the typical subcortical changes in the substantia nigra, locus ceruleus, and dorsal vagal nucleus of Parkinson's disease; and, in addition, Lewy bodies that are diffusely distributed throughout the neocortex (Kosaka et al., 1984; Dickson et al., 1987; Gibb et al., 1987; Lennox et al., 1989; Hansen et al., 1990; Perry et al., 1990). Although only recently identified, this neuropathologic condition is not rare and may occur in approximately 25% of all demented patients (Gibb et al., 1987; Joachim et al., 1988; Bergeron and Pollanen, 1989; Galasko et al., 1994).

The clinical manifestation of this disorder, which is sometimes known as the Lewy body variant (LBV) of Alzheimer's disease (Hansen et al., 1990), is similar to that of AD in many respects and these patients are often diagnosed with probable or possible AD during life. However, retrospective studies indicate that LBV may be clinically distinguishable from "pure" AD. While both disorders are associated with a severe and progressive dementia, a number of investigators have reported an increased prevalence of mild extrapyramidal motor findings (e.g., bradykinesia, rigidity, masked facies) (Hansen et al., 1990; Perry et al., 1990; Galasko et al., in press) and hallucinations (Dickson et al., 1987; Perry et al., 1990) in patients with LBV, as well as a more rapid course (Armstrong et al., 1991).

Neuropsychological Assessment

The neuropsychologist has available a variety of standardized tests that have known reliability and sensitivity for the detection of cognitive deficits associated with either focal or diffuse cerebral damage (Kolb and Whishaw, 1990; Heaton et al., 1991; Spreen and Strauss, 1991; Lezak, 1995; see also Chapters 1 through 4 in the present volume). These tests have been designed to assess specific aspects of a wide range of cognitive functioning, including general intellectual ability, orientation and attention, language functions, spatial cognition and perceptual functions, visuomotor and constructional ability, memory functions, abstract and conceptual reasoning, and so-called "executive" functions (i.e., goal formulation, planning, and the execution of goal-directed plans). Because neuropsychological tests generally meet psychometric criteria of acceptable reliability and construct validity, they provide accurate procedures for describing the cognitive strengths and weaknesses of an individual. Such accurate description, as reviewed within the present chapter, is of considerable importance in detecting the presence of (particularly mild) dementia, and in determining whether the pattern of relatively impaired and preserved cognitive functions is consistent with that expected in some particular dementia etiology. Neuropsychological assessment can also help patients and their caregivers (personal and professional) to understand the patient's psychological status, and thereby reduce anxiety and confusion, and suggest possible treatment or management strategies (see Lezak, 1995).

General Considerations in the Neuropsychological Assessment of Older Adults

Given the age-associated prevalence of most dementing illnesses, the majority of persons referred for neuropsychological assessment because of suspected or known dementia will be older adults. The competent neuropsychological evaluation of older persons requires knowledge of those aspects of aging that impact upon the conduct and interpretation of psychological testing. The most important of these aging-related factors have been reviewed in detail previously (Bayles and Kaszniak, 1987; La Rue, 1992; Storandt, 1994) and will only be summarized here.

The first aspect of aging to be considered, influencing both selection of test materials and their interpretation, concerns sensory changes characteristic of normal aging and age-related sensory disorders. Changes in auditory (Corso, 1985; Fozard, 1990; Schieber, 1992) and visual (Johnson and Choy, 1987; Kosnik et al., 1988) acuity with age have been well documented. Decreased auditory acuity for high frequencies (termed presbycusis), and more severe hearing loss (estimated to occur in up to 50% of individuals over the age of 75; Plomp, 1978), can affect speech comprehension and oral communication (Pickett et al., 1979; Plomp and Mimpen, 1979) and may compromise the results of verbal tests of cognitive status, leading to inaccurate interpretations of test performance (e.g., Weinstein and Amsel, 1986; Peters et al., 1988; Roccaforte et al., 1992). Similarly, visual capability declines with age (about half of all individuals over the age of 65 have visual acuity of 20/70 or less) and blindness or other serious visual problems affect more than 7% of the population between 65 and 75 years of age and 16% of those over age 75 (Owsley and Sloane, 1990; Schieber, 1992). Reduced visual capacity may contribute to apparent disorientation and behavioral deterioration in older adults (O'Neil and Calhoun, 1975) and may adversely affect any cognitive test that requires processing of visual information.

Normal aging also leads to an increased

likelihood of other physical disabilities, such as neuromuscular disorders or severe arthritis, that may negatively affect an individual's performance on neuropsychological tests. Such an effect has been demonstrated on mental status examinations, which are less effective in discriminating demented individuals from nondemented individuals with some physical disability than from those without a disability (Jagger et al., 1992). The influence of physical disability on neuropsychological test performance is of particular concern when evaluating the oldest old, as it has been estimated that 29% of all persons over age 85 suffer from severe disability (Kunkel and Applebaum, 1992).

General slowing of cognitive and motor performance occurs with age and has been objectively demonstrated with both simple and choice reaction time tests (Wilkinson and Allison, 1989; Lima et al., 1991). This slowing may result in a slight underestimation of a subject's ability (Storandt, 1977) on neuropsychological tests that award bonus points for speeded performance, such as the Arithmetic and Block Design subtests of the Wechsler Adult Intelligence Scale–Revised (WAIS-R; Wechsler, 1981). To obtain a truer picture of a person's cognitive strengths and weaknesses, some investigators suggest that the older individual be allowed to continue working on a task after standard cutoff times have elapsed (Kaplan, 1988; see also chapter by Milberg et al. [Chapter 3]). The general slowing that occurs with age also indicates that older adults will take longer to complete various neuropsychological testing procedures than younger adults (Storandt, 1994) and, if ill or frail, they may require more frequent rest breaks to combat fatigue (Cunningham et al., 1978).

Because performance on many neuropsychological tests is negatively correlated with adult age (Kaszniak et al., 1979; Vannieuwkirk and Galbraith, 1985; Heaton et al., 1986; Reitan and Wolfsen, 1986; Albert, 1988; Albert et al., 1988; Mittenberg et al., 1989; Moehle and Long, 1989; Kaszniak, 1990; La Rue, 1992; Petersen et al., 1992; Elias et al., 1993) or educational background (e.g., Kaszniak et al., 1979; Barona et al., 1984;

Heaton et al., 1986), these factors must be taken into account when interpreting test results. This is usually accomplished through a comparison with age and education appropriate normative data (see the chapter by Heaton et al. [Chapter 7]). In the past, adequate normative data for the oldest old (i.e., those over age 85) were lacking (Albert, 1981; Kaszniak, 1987; Zec, 1990; Erickson et al., 1992), but recent studies provide normative data for up to age 90 on some of the more commonly employed neuropsychological tests (Van Gorp et al., 1986; Ivnik et al., 1992a,b,c; Malec et al., 1992; also see Erickson et al., 1994). The consideration of educational level is especially important in the assessment of dementia in the elderly because low education may be an independent risk factor for the disorder (Berkman, 1986; Katzman, 1993).

The validity of neuropsychological testing can also be influenced by non–age-associated factors that must be considered in the dementia assessment. For example, testing a person in a language other than his primary one has been shown to produce poorer than normal performance on a brief mental status examination, the Mini-Mental State Exam (MMSE; Folstein et al., 1975) (Loewenstein et al., 1993), although this language-related decrement was not noted on an assessment of instrumental activities of daily living, nor on certain other neuropsychological tests that constituted a more comprehensive neuropsychological evaluation (Loewenstein et al., 1992). Other cultural and socioeconomic factors may also influence neuropsychological test performance in the potentially demented patient and should be taken into account when interpreting test results (for review, see Tombaugh and McIntyre, 1992).

Depression can have a major impact on neuropsychological test performance and may produce results in the elderly that are similar to those of patients with a progressive dementing illness. Indeed, a review of current studies indicates that between 1% and 31% of patients diagnosed as having a progressive dementing illness may actually be depressed (Katzman et al., 1988b). These findings have led to the term "dementia syndrome of depression" (La Rue et al., 1986) to describe these cases. The identification of patients with depression that is masking as dementia is extremely important because the condition may be treatable and the cognitive deficits reversible. While neuropsychological assessment may play an important role in differentiating between dementia and depression in older adults (see the chapter by King and Caine [Chapter 9]; Kaszniak and Christenson, 1994), an interdisciplinary effort with physicians and other health-care providers is required (Cummings and Benson, 1992; Depression Guideline Panel, 1993).

Finally, although brief mental status tests have been shown to be quite effective in screening for dementia in large-scale community-based studies, they cannot substitute for a comprehensive neuropsychological assessment, particularly when attempting to detect the disease early in its course when no evidence of cognitive deficit is noticed on commonly employed mental status screening tests (Storandt and Hill, 1989; Bondi et al., 1993a, 1994b; Petersen et al., 1994; Bondi et al., 1995; see also the chapter by Mitrushina and Fuld [Chapter 6]), when the subject is highly (Nelson et al., 1986; O'Connor et al., 1989) or poorly (Anthony et al., 1982; Murden et al., 1991) educated, or when attempting to identify a pattern of cognitive deficits that may be indicative of a specific dementia etiology (Naugle et al., 1990).

Neuropsychological Detection of Dementia

As noted in the beginning of this chapter, neuropsychological research concerning AD and other dementing illnesses has increased dramatically over the past few decades. Much of this research has focused on understanding the nature of cognitive dysfunction in Alzheimer's disease (for review, see Nebes, 1992), determining the utility of neuropsychological testing for differentiating between early dementia and normal aging, and for distinguishing among the different causes of dementia (for review, see La Rue, 1992; La Rue et al., 1992c; Parks et al., 1993; Bondi et al., 1994b). Many of the studies on

the diagnostic utility of neuropsychological tests have employed patients with clinically diagnosed probable AD (of mild to moderate dementia severity) and have compared their performance on a battery of tests to that of carefully screened healthy older adults (e.g., Storandt et al., 1984; Eslinger et al., 1985; Kaszniak et al., 1986; Huff et al., 1987; Bayles et al., 1989). The results of these studies have consistently shown that AD patients are impaired in a wide variety of cognitive functions, and that the most effective neuropsychological measures for distinguishing between these subjects and healthy elderly individuals are those that assess the ability to learn new information and retain it over time.

Welsh and colleagues (1991), for example, compared the effectiveness of measures of learning, retention, confrontation naming, verbal fluency and constructional ability for differentiating between very mildly demented patients with probable AD and normal elderly individuals. These investigators found that the highest diagnostic accuracy (90%) was achieved with a delayed free recall measure on a verbal memory task. Similar results demonstrating the effectiveness of memory measures have been obtained in other studies (Knopman and Ryberg, 1989; Flicker et al., 1991; Morris et al., 1991), and in one study (Morris et al., 1991) the results were confirmed by subsequent postmortem histopathologic evidence of AD in all of those psychometrically classified as mildly impaired and in none of those classified as normal elderly.

Although measures of learning and retention are the most effective neuropsychological indices for differentiating between mildly demented and normal elderly individuals, measures of language, "executive" functions, and constructional abilities also have some diagnostic value (Salmon et al., in press). For example, Monsch and colleagues (1992) compared the performances of mildly demented patients with probable AD and normal elderly control subjects on several types of verbal fluency tasks and found that the semantic category fluency task had greater than 90% sensitivity and specificity for the diagnosis of dementia. Similarly high sensitivity (94%) and specificity (87%) for the diagnosis of dementia was demonstrated for the number of categories achieved on a modified version of the Wisconsin Card Sorting Task (Nelson, 1976) in a study that compared the performances of mildly demented probable AD patients and normal elderly subjects (Bondi et al., 1993b).

In addition to detecting subtle cognitive impairment in the early stages of a dementing illness, neuropsychological testing is important for tracking the progression of cognitive decline throughout the course of the disease. Several studies have shown that brief, standardized mental status examinations can effectively document general cognitive decline (Katzman et al., 1988a; Thal et al., 1988; Ortof and Crystal, 1989; Salmon et al., 1990). For example, a two to five point annual decline on the MMSE has been reported for patients with probable AD (Teri et al., 1990; Salmon et al., 1990). Salmon and colleagues (1990) compared the rate of decline of probable AD patients on the MMSE and two other widely used mental status tests, the information-memory-concentration (IMC) test (Blessed et al., 1968) and the Mattis (1976) Dementia Rating Scale (DRS). These investigators found that all three mental status examinations were effective in tracking decline through the early and middle stages of the disease, but that the DRS was superior to the other two scales in the more advanced stages because of its inclusion of a wider range of items that varied in degree of difficulty (also see, Tombaugh and McIntyre, 1992). On average, the annual rate of decline of AD patients on the MMSE in this study was approximately 3 ± 4 (SD) points, on the IMC was 3 ± 3 points, and on the DRS was 11 ± 11 points.

In addition, Terry and colleagues (1991) have examined the relationship between neuropathological indices of AD and patients' global cognitive status prior to death. Quantitative measures of synaptic loss, senile plaques (SP) and neurofibrillary tangles (NFT) in cortical association areas of 15 patients with autopsy-proven AD were correlated with these patients' performance on several standardized mental status examinations (administered within a median of 12 months prior to death). Quantification of synapses was performed by microdensitometry of tissue sections reacted with anti-synaptophysin in mid-frontal, inferior parietal, and superior temporal brain regions. Prior to death these patients had been assessed neuropsychologically with the IMC test, the MMSE, and the DRS. Of the neuropathological variables, mid-frontal synaptic density demonstrated the greatest degree of correlation with the three measures of global cognitive impairment: IMC (r = −.76), MMSE (r = .73) and DRS (r = .67) (see Fig. 8-1). Similarly, mid-frontal synaptic density accounted for the greatest amount of variance in mental status scores in stepwise multiple regression analyses that included all the neuropathological variables. A smaller, but still significant, degree of variance in test scores was contributed by inferior parietal and mid-frontal plaques, and by inferior parietal synaptic density. The results of this study suggest that the loss of synapses may be the primary determinant of cognitive loss in AD.

Despite the effectiveness of mental status examinations for assessing general cognitive decline, comprehensive neuropsychological testing is often required to track the progres-

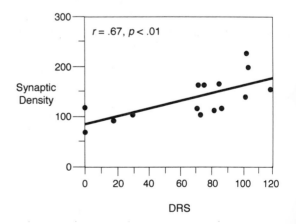

Figure 8-1. Linear correlation between corrected optical density of the mid-frontal antisynaptophysin reaction (i.e., synapse density) and the total score of the Mattis Dementia Rating Scale (DRS). Reprinted from Terry et al. (1991), with permission of the American Neurological Association.

sion of dementia, particularly when it is necessary to detect changes in specific cognitive domains, or to evaluate the efficacy of a potential treatment (Flicker, 1988; Berg et al., 1992). A number of studies have shown that tests of memory and other neuropsychological functions are sensitive to the cognitive decline that occurs between the mild and moderate stages of dementia severity (Hill et al., 1992; Welsh et al., 1992). However, these studies have also shown that neuropsychological measures other than memory are most effective in this regard. Because even mildly demented patients often have severe memory deficits that result in near floor performance on tests of free recall, measures of recognition memory, verbal fluency, confrontation naming, and praxis may be better suited for staging dementia severity or tracking its progression (Kaszniak et al., 1986; Welsh et al., 1992).

The diagnosis of dementia requires that an individual has declined from his or her premorbid level of cognitive functioning. However, in most cases the results from previous neuropsychological testing are not available at the time of the initial dementia evaluation. In such cases, the clinician must rely on a history of progressive cognitive deterioration provided by an informant. Several studies have shown that informants (usually a close relative of the patient) are able to provide valid reports of progressive deterioration in dementia patients (McGlone et al., 1990; Bayles and Tomoeda, 1991; La Rue et al., 1992b).

McGlone et al. (1990), for example, had relatives rate memory decline in elderly people with memory complaints who subsequently showed, or failed to show, progressive dementia as determined by follow-up neuropsychological assessment. Patients who did not become demented were correctly rated by their relatives as not showing abnormal cognitive decline, whereas the patients who became demented were accurately rated by their relatives as having become significantly worse. Furthermore, the relatives' assessments of patients' memory deficits were significantly correlated with objective memory test scores. A similar significant correla-tion between informant (caregiver) reports of memory and linguistic communication symptoms and patients' performance on corresponding items from a linguistic-communication test battery have also been reported (Bayles and Tomoeda, 1991).

Although such results encourage the use of caregiver reports for ascertaining the presence of cognitive decline, these reports may be influenced by the nature of the relationship between the caregiver and the patient. La Rue and colleagues (1992b) found that spouses of memory-impaired patients reported lower levels of impairment than did younger relatives. Thus, the accuracy of the reports of cognitive decline may be enhanced by questioning more than one family informant or by seeking a family consensus. Clinically useful formats for obtaining (from a relative or other informant) a cognitive, psychosocial, emotional/psychiatric, and medical history, relevant to suspected dementia, is provided by Strub and Black (1988, pp. 143–145), and by Williams and colleagues (Williams et al., 1986; Williams, 1987).

Neuropsychological Detection of Preclinical (Incipient) Dementia

A recent development in the neuropsychology of dementia centers on research that attempts to identify cognitive markers of incipient AD. These attempts arise from the view that AD is a chronic disease, much like cancer, in which an individual is predisposed by genetic factors, traumatic events, or other unknown factors toward entering a malignant phase that is characterized by intracellular events that lead to neuritic degeneration, the formation of neurofibrillary tangles, and neuron and synapse loss (Katzman and Kawas, 1994) (see Fig. 8-2). Over a period of time, the neural degeneration gradually reaches a level that initiates the clinical symptoms of the dementia syndrome. This framework for understanding the development of AD suggests that cognitive deficits associated with the disease also appear gradually and might be identified before the degree of neural degeneration reaches a level necessary to produce clinically diagnosable

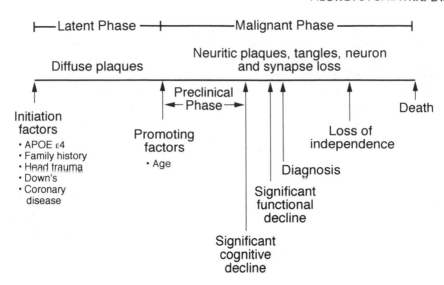

Figure 8-2. Chronic disease model of Alzheimer's disease. Adapted from Katzman and Kawas (1994), with permission of Raven Press.

dementia (i.e., when both cognitive and functional impairments are evident).

Although the precise length of this preclinical phase of AD is not known and may vary considerably among affected individuals, a growing body of evidence demonstrates that subtle cognitive impairments can be detected several years prior to the clinical diagnosis of dementia (Bayles and Kaszniak, 1987; Fuld et al., 1990; La Rue et al., 1992a; Bondi et al., 1994a; Masur et al., 1994; Linn et al., 1995; Bondi et al., 1995). Some of the earliest evidence for this possibility was provided by La Rue and Jarvik (1987, 1980), who longitudinally studied aging twins. These investigators found that poor performance by nondemented subjects on three subtests of the Wechsler Adult Intelligence Scale (WAIS; Vocabulary, Similarities, and Digit Symbol) was associated with the development of dementia some 20 years later.

Although the study by La Rue and Jarvik has important theoretical significance, the results were based on a relatively small number of subjects and the investigators did not differentiate between different dementia etiologies (Linn et al., 1995). Katzman and colleagues (1989) avoided these limitations in a longitudinal investigation from the Bronx Aging Study in which 434 community-

dwelling older adults were evaluated for dementia over a 5-year period. When enrolled in the study, all subjects were ambulatory, nondemented, functionally independent, and between the ages of 75 and 85 years. The results demonstrated that the 59% of the cohort who made zero to two errors (out of 33 possible errors) on the IMC test (Blessed et al., 1968) during the initial evaluation had a less than 0.6% per year chance of developing probable or possible AD, whereas the 16% of the cohort with five to eight errors on this test (but who were not clinically demented) developed probable or possible AD at a rate of over 12% per year. Thus, difficulty on this brief cognitive screening measure predated the subsequent clinical diagnosis of AD by 2 to 5 years. In contrast to the results of La Rue and Jarvik (1980), initial WAIS Vocabulary and Similarities subtest scores did not predict the subsequent development of dementia in this cohort.

Because the earliest neuropathological changes of AD are thought to occur in the hippocampus and entorhinal cortex, some investigators have postulated that memory deficits may be an early, preclinical manifestation of the disease (Fuld et al., 1990; Masur et al., 1990). In support of this notion, Fuld and colleagues (1990) found that correct recall of six or fewer of the 10 items on the Fuld Object Memory Test (Fuld, 1977) at an initial evaluation identified 32 of the 56 subjects (57% sensitivity) who subsequently became demented over the next 5 years in the Bronx Aging Study. In a related investigation from the Bronx Aging Study, Masur and colleagues (1990) found that poor performance on measures of recall from the Selective Reminding Test (Buschke and Fuld, 1974) correctly predicted subsequent dementia in approximately 45% of the subjects who became demented 1 to 2 years later.

In an effort to improve the sensitivity and specificity of neuropsychological predictors of incipient dementia, and to better understand the cognitive features of the preclinical phase of the disorder, several recent studies have used a variety of neuropsychological tests to retrospectively examine the performance of nondemented elderly subjects who subsequently became demented (Masur et al., 1994; Linn et al., 1995). Masur et al. (1994), for example, tracked, over an 11-year period, 317 nondemented elderly individuals from the Bronx Aging Study who had received comprehensive neuropsychological testing during their initial assessment. Sixty-four subjects developed dementia at least 6 months or more following their initial evaluation and 253 subjects remained nondemented over at least 4 years of follow-up. A logistic regression model predicting dementia outcome indicated that initial performance on the delayed recall measure from the Selective Reminding test, a recall measure from the Fuld Object Memory Test, the Digit Symbol Substitution Subtest from the WAIS, and a measure of verbal fluency were all significant predictors of the subsequent development of dementia. The model provided excellent specificity for identifying subjects who remained free of dementia (238/253; 94%); however, the sensitivity of the model for correctly identifying subjects who later developed dementia was, at best, moderate (32/64; 50%).

In a similar study, Linn and colleagues (1995) prospectively examined the initial neuropsychological test performance of 1,045 nondemented elderly individuals who partic-

ipated in the Framingham study. Of these subjects, 55 developed probable AD at some point during their 13-year participation in the study. The subsequent development of AD was predicted by the subject's initial performance on measures of delayed recall (WMS Logical Memory percent retained) and immediate auditory attention span (WAIS Digit Span). Interestingly, subjects who later developed AD performed better on the Digit Span Test at initial screening than those who did not. It is also interesting to note that the recall and digit span measures predicted the subsequent development of dementia even when the initial screening examination preceded the clinical onset of dementia by 7 years or more. This study, in conjunction with the study by Masur et al. (1994), suggests that the identification of incipient dementia can be enhanced by considering memory and additional neuropsychological measures.

Recently, investigators have attempted to improve the possibility of detecting incipient dementia with neuropsychological test measures by targeting groups of elderly subjects who have an increased risk of developing the disorder (La Rue et al., 1992a; Smalley et al., 1992; Bondi et al., 1994a; Feskens et al., 1994; Hom et al., 1994; Bondi et al., 1995). Several studies have focused on tracking the cognitive status of nondemented elderly who have a positive family history for AD and/or a genotype with the $\epsilon 4$ allele of apolipoprotein E.

A number of studies employing nondemented elderly subjects with a positive family history (FH+) of AD have demonstrated that a subgroup of subjects perform poorly on tests of learning and memory. In one of these studies, La Rue and colleagues (1992a) examined the cognitive performance of 32 elderly individuals with a positive family history (FH+) of AD (i.e., siblings and children of patients with AD) at two time points separated by approximately 4 years. Although the average scores on all neuropsychological test measures at both time points were within normal limits, relatives of patients with early-onset dementia (≤ 67 years) were more likely to show a decline in performance from the first to the second testing than relatives of patients with late-onset dementia. In another study, Smalley and colleagues (1992) found that a subgroup of 106 nondemented offspring (mean age 40.6 years) of 54 AD patients performed well below levels expected for their age and education on the Benton Visual Retention Test, the Paired Associate Learning Test, and the Fuld Object Memory Evaluation.

It has also been demonstrated that nondemented FH+ elderly subjects perform worse than nondemented, family history negative (FH−) subjects on tests of learning and memory. Hom and colleagues (1994) compared the neuropsychological test performance of 20 nondemented FH+ elderly individuals with that of an age- and education-matched control group of 20 nondemented FH− older adults. Although the average performances of both groups were within normal limits, the FH+ subjects performed significantly worse than the FH− subjects on tests of verbal intelligence and verbal learning and memory.

The results of the studies reviewed above suggest that measures of learning and memory may be useful for detecting incipient dementia of the Alzheimer type, particularly when the family history risk factor is taken into account. In a direct test of this notion, Bondi and colleagues (1994a) longitudinally assessed nondemented FH+ and FH− subjects with quantitative and qualitative indices derived from the *California Verbal Learning Test* (CVLT; Delis et al., 1987). Although the groups were carefully matched in terms of demographic variables and performance on standardized mental status examinations, the FH+ subjects recalled significantly fewer items than the FH− subjects during learning and delayed recall in the initial evaluation, and produced more intrusion errors and demonstrated a greater recency effect. Five of the nondemented subjects in this study initially performed on the CVLT in a manner qualitatively similar to that of a group of mild AD patients and were subsequently diagnosed with AD 1 to 2 years following their initial evaluation. Four of these five

subjects were FH+ and one had an uninformative family history because no first-degree relative lived long enough to express AD.

The identification of a specific genetic risk factor for AD, the APOE ϵ4 allele, has allowed researchers to extend and refine the search for cognitive markers of incipient AD. Two recent studies have focused on episodic memory changes in nondemented elderly subjects who possess this risk factor. In the first study, Reed and colleagues (1994) found that nondemented elderly men with the ϵ4 allele exhibited poorer mean performance on a test of visual memory than their dizygotic twin who did not have the ϵ4 allele. In the second study, Bondi et al. (1995) demonstrated that the verbal learning and memory performance of nondemented subjects with the APOE ϵ4 allele was qualitatively (though not quantitatively) similar to that of early stage AD patients. Furthermore, the nondemented subjects with the APOE ϵ4 allele recalled fewer items during the learning trials and over delay intervals, and utilized a less effective organizational strategy for learning, than carefully matched nondemented subjects without the APOE ϵ4 allele (see Fig. 8-3). Follow-up examinations of some of the subjects in this study revealed that six of 14 subjects with the ϵ4 allele subsequently developed either probable AD or questionable AD (i.e., cognitive decline without evidence of significant functional impairment), whereas none of 26 subjects without an ϵ4 allele demonstrated any cognitive decline.

Another recent population-based study completed by Feskens et al. (1994) determined whether the ϵ4 allele predicted cognitive deterioration in the general population. They longitudinally assessed cognitive function with the MMSE in 538 Dutch men aged 70–89 and found the largest decline in MMSE scores for ϵ4/ϵ4 homozygotes (mean decline of 2.4 points), intermediate decline in those heterozygous for ϵ4 (mean decline of 0.7 points), and little or no decline in men without an ϵ4 allele (mean decline of 0.1 points). Thus, Feskens et al. (1994) found that the ϵ4 allele represented a predisposi-

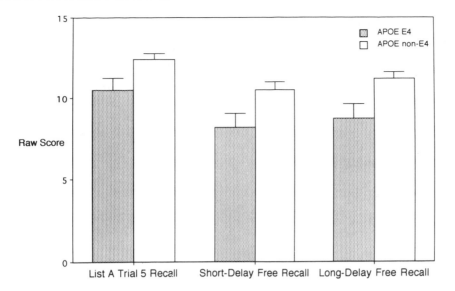

Figure 8-3. California Verbal Learning Test raw scores of demographically matched groups of nondemented older adults with the apolipoprotein ε4 allele (n = 17) compared to those lacking an ε4 allele (n = 35). Each of the three group comparisons depicted represent a significant difference at the p <.05 level. Adapted from Bondi et al. (1995).

tion for cognitive decline in a general population of older adult men.

In summary, a growing number of investigations provide converging evidence that a preclinical phase of detectable cognitive decline, particularly in memory abilities, can precede the clinical diagnosis of dementia by several years. Furthermore, these studies suggest that the detection of incipient AD may be enhanced if risk factors such as a positive family history or the presence of the APOE ε4 allele are considered in conjunction with cognitive findings. It should be emphasized, however, that the combination of various genetic risk factors can provide only an estimate of an individual's risk of eventually developing AD. Therefore, regardless of the APOE genotype or the family history of an older adult, sensitive neuropsychological indices appear to provide the most salient markers of preclinical Alzheimer's disease. Although considerable progress has been made, additional studies are necessary to enhance our ability to detect AD clinically in its earliest stages when neuroprotective

agents designed to impede the progression of the disease might be most effective.

Neuropsychological Differentiation of Dementia Etiologies

Over the past several decades it has become increasingly clear that etiologically and neuropathologically distinct dementing diseases are associated with different patterns of relatively preserved and impaired cognitive abilities. One distinction that has generated considerable research interest has been drawn between the dementia syndromes associated with neurodegenerative diseases that primarily involve regions of the cerebral cortex (e.g., Alzheimer's disease, Pick's disease) and those that have their primary locus in subcortical brain structures (e.g., Huntington's disease, Parkinson's disease, progressive supranuclear palsy; Albert et al., 1974; McHugh and Folstein, 1975; Cummings, 1990).

The dementia associated with AD, a prototypical "cortical" dementia syndrome, is broadly characterized by prominent amnesia

with additional deficits in language and semantic knowledge (i.e., aphasia), abstract
reasoning, other "executive" functions, and
constructional and visuospatial abilities (see
Bayles and Kaszniak, 1987; Parks et al.,
1993). In contrast, the dementia associated
with Huntington's disease, a prototypical
"subcortical" dementia syndrome, includes
only a moderate memory disturbance, attentional dysfunction, problem-solving deficits,
visuoperceptual and constructional deficits,
and a deficiency in performing arithmetic
(Butters et al., 1978; see also the chapter by
Brandt and Butters (Chapter 14)). Huntington's disease results in little or no aphasia,
although patients may be dysarthric as the
result of the motor dysfunction inherent in
the disease.

EPISODIC AND SEMANTIC MEMORY. A number of recent studies utilizing the concepts
and experimental procedures of cognitive
psychology have shown that AD and HD
patients can be further differentiated by the
nature and pattern of their respective memory deficits. Patients with AD exhibit a severe episodic memory deficit that appears
to result from ineffective consolidation (i.e.,
storage) of new information (see the chapter
by Squire and Shimamura [Chapter 11]). Evidence for a consolidation deficit in AD patients includes their showing little improvement in acquiring information over repeated
learning trials (Buschke and Fuld, 1974; Wilson et al., 1983; Moss et al., 1986; Masur et
al., 1989), a tendency to recall only the most
recently presented information (i.e., a
heightened recency effect) in free recall tasks
(Miller, 1971; Pepin and Eslinger, 1989;
Delis et al., 1991; Massman et al., 1993), an
inability to benefit normally from effortful or
elaborative encoding at the time of acquisition (Knopman and Ryberg, 1989), and a
failure to demonstrate a normal improvement in performance when memory is tested
with a recognition rather than a free recall
format (Miller, 1971; Wilson et al., 1983;
Delis et al., 1991). In addition, a consolidation deficit is suggested by AD patients' rapid
forgetting of information over time (Moss et
al., 1986; Butters et al., 1988; Welsh et al.,

1991; Tröster et al., 1993). As mentioned
earlier, this feature of the memory impairment of AD patients has important clinical
implications because delayed recall and savings score (i.e., percent retained over a period of time) measures that reflect rapid forgetting have been proposed as important
neuropsychological markers for the early diagnosis of AD.

In contrast to the consolidation deficit of
AD patients, the memory disorder of patients with HD is thought to result from a
general difficulty in initiating a systematic
retrieval strategy when recalling information
from either episodic or semantic memory.
Although these patients, like AD patients,
have difficulty in learning and recalling information in a free recall task, they exhibit a
marked improvement in performance when
memory is tested with a recognition format
(Moss et al., 1986; Delis et al., 1991; however, see also Brandt et al., 1992). In addition, HD patients are able to retain information over a delay in near normal fashion
(Moss et al., 1986; Delis et al., 1991).

Given these differences in the nature and
pattern of the memory impairment exhibited
by patients with AD and HD, Delis and
colleagues (1991) reasoned that these patient
groups might be differentiated by their performances on a widely used clinical memory
test that assesses these memory processes.
The CVLT (Delis et al., 1987) is a standardized memory test that assesses rate of learning, retention after short- and long-delay
intervals, semantic encoding ability, recognition memory (i.e., discriminability), intrusion and perseverative errors, and response
biases. In the test, individuals are verbally
presented five presentation/free recall trials
of a list of 16 shopping items (four items in
each of four categories) and are then administered a single trial using a second, different
list of 16 items. Immediately after this final
trial, individuals are administered first a free-
recall and then a cued-recall test for the
items on the first shopping list. Twenty minutes later, the free-recall and cued-recall
tests are repeated, followed by a yes-no recognition test consisting of the 16 items on
the first shopping list and 28 distractor items.

Delis and colleagues found that despite comparable immediate and delayed free- and cued-recall deficits in the AD and HD patients, these patient groups could be differentiated by several CVLT measures (see Fig. 8-4). A discriminant function equation was developed using two measures derived from the CVLT: (1) the percent cued recall intrusions, and (2) the difference between recognition memory performance and recall on trial 5 of the initial learning trials. The first measure was chosen to reflect the previously demonstrated greater susceptibility of AD patients than HD patients to proactive interference in memory tasks (Fuld et al., 1982; Tröster et al., 1989; Jacobs et al., 1990). The second measure was chosen because recognition occurs after a delay and therefore both retention over time and any potential benefit of a recognition format over free recall were assessed. With this discriminant function equation, 17 out of 20 AD patients and 16 out of 19 HD patients were correctly classified.

In a related study, Massman and colleagues (1992) subjected the CVLT scores of depressed patients to a similar discriminant function equation and found that 49% of these patients were classified as normal, 22.4% were not well classified, 28.6% were classified as HD-like, and none were classified as AD-like. These results suggest that

when affective disorders produce deficits in memory, the pattern is similar to that of patients with a "subcortical" dementia syndrome.

Patients with cortical and subcortical dementia syndromes can also be differentiated by their performances on tests of remote memory. Patients with AD have a severe retrograde amnesia (i.e., loss of memory for information acquired prior to the onset of their disease) affecting all decades of their lives (Wilson et al., 1981; Beatty et al., 1988; Sagar et al., 1988; Kopelman, 1989; Hodges et al., 1993). Several studies indicate that in the early stages of AD, remote memory loss is temporally graded, with memories from the more distant past (i.e., childhood and early adulthood) better remembered than memories from the more recent past (i.e. mid and late adulthood) (Beatty et al., 1988; Beatty and Salmon, 1991; Hodges et al., 1993).

In contrast, patients with HD (Albert et al., 1981; Beatty et al., 1988) or PD (Freedman et al., 1984) suffer only a mild degree of retrograde amnesia that is equally severe across all decades of their lives. These results suggest that the remote memory deficit of patients with subcortical dementia is another reflection of a general retrieval deficit that equally affects recollection of information

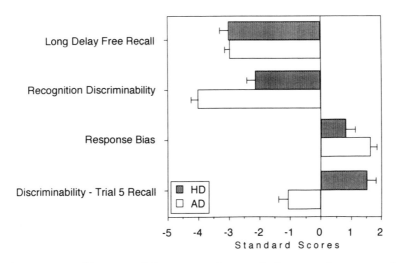

Figure 8-4. California Verbal Learning Test standard scores of patients with Alzheimer's disease (AD) and Huntington's disease (HD). Adapted from Delis et al. (1991), with permission of the American Psychological Association.

from any decade of their lives, whereas the temporally graded remote memory loss of AD patients is indicative of a failure to adequately consolidate information through repeated processing, rehearsal or re-exposure (see Zola-Morgan and Squire, 1990 for a discussion of the role of consolidation in temporally graded retrograde amnesia; see also the chapter by Squire and Shimamura [Chapter 11]).

One of the major distinctions between cortical and subcortical dementia syndromes is the presence of severe language and semantic knowledge deficits in many of the cortical dementias with little or no impairment in these abilities in most subcortical dementias. Patients with AD, for example, are noted for mild anomia and word-finding difficulties in spontaneous speech, as well as for a decline in their general fund of knowledge concerning common facts of history, geography, arithmetic, and science. Patients with Huntington's disease, in contrast, generally retain these abilities, although their performance on some language tasks (such as verbal fluency) may be adversely affected by their general retrieval deficit.

Recent neuropsychological research suggests that patients with AD may suffer a loss of semantic knowledge and a breakdown in the organization of semantic memory (for reviews, see Hodges et al., 1991; Salmon and Chan, 1994). Consistent with this view, patients with AD are disproportionately impaired on verbal fluency tasks when they must generate exemplars from a semantic category compared to when they must generate words that begin with a particular letter (Butters et al., 1987; Monsch et al., 1992); they perform poorly on tests of confrontation naming and tend to produce semantic errors (Bayles and Tomoeda, 1983; Huff et al., 1986; Smith et al., 1989; Hodges et al., 1991); and they consistently miss the same item across language tests that use different methods and modes of access (Chertkow and Bub, 1990; Hodges et al., 1992).

In contrast to the performance of patients with AD, HD patients perform at near normal levels on tests of confrontation naming and the errors they produce are often visuoperceptually based rather than semantically

based (Hodges et al., 1991). Furthermore, patients with HD perform poorly on tests of verbal fluency, but are equally impaired regardless of the semantic demands of the task (Butters et al., 1987; Monsch et al., 1994). This finding suggests that their poor fluency performance may be related to their general deficiency in initiating an effective retrieval strategy.

Investigators have recently begun to examine the language and knowledge deficits associated with dementia within the framework of current cognitive psychological models of semantic memory (e.g., Collins and Loftus, 1975) that propose that our representations of knowledge are organized as a network of interrelated categories, concepts, and attributes (for review, see Salmon and Chan, 1994). In several recent studies, Chan and colleagues (1993a,b; 1995a,b) attempted to model the organization of semantic memory in AD and HD patients using clustering and multidimensional scaling techniques (Romney et al., 1972; Shepard et al., 1972; Tversky and Hutchinson, 1986). Multidimensional scaling provides a method for generating a spatial representation of the degree of association between concepts in semantic memory. The spatial representation, or cognitive map, generated in this manner clusters concepts along one or more dimensions according to their proximity, or degree of relatedness, in the patient's semantic network. The distance between concepts in the cognitive map reflects the strength of their association.

One study in this series compared the cognitive maps of AD, HD, and age-matched normal control (NC) subjects. The strength of association between concepts, or their proximity, was estimated using a triadic comparison task in which subjects chose, from among three concepts (i.e., among three animals), the two that are most alike. Every possible combination of three animals, from a total sample of 12 animals, was presented. This procedure produced a proximity score reflecting strength of association for each pair of animals in relation to all other animal names; that is, how often those two animals were chosen as most alike.

The proximity data derived in this manner

for the three subject groups were subjected to multidimensional scaling analysis. Although the semantic networks of both the AD and elderly NC subjects generated in this analysis were best represented by three dimensions (domesticity, predation, and size), they differed significantly in a number of ways. First, AD patients focused primarily on concrete perceptual information (i.e., size) in categorizing animals, whereas control subjects stressed abstract conceptual knowledge (i.e., domesticity). Second, a number of animals that were highly associated and clustered together for control subjects were not strongly associated for patients with AD. Third, AD patients were less consistent than NC subjects in utilizing the various attributes of animals in categorization.

In contrast to the AD patients, the semantic networks of HD patients and their age-matched control subjects were best represented by two dimensions (domesticity and size). The cognitive maps of these two groups were virtually identical, and for both groups, domesticity was the most salient dimension for categorizing animals. Furthermore, HD patients and their controls did not differ in the importance applied to the various dimensions or in their reliance on a particular dimension for categorization.

The results from these multidimensional scaling studies are consistent with the notion that AD patients suffer a breakdown in the structure and organization of semantic memory. Because of this semantic deterioration, AD patients tend to rely heavily on a concrete perceptual dimension (i.e., size) in categorizing animals rather than the more semantically demanding abstract conceptual dimension (i.e., domesticity) used by NC subjects and patients with HD (see Fig. 8-5).

It is important to note that AD patients' deficits in semantic memory can affect their performances in other cognitive domains. This was recently demonstrated in a study by Rouleau and colleagues (1992) that examined the visuoconstructive deficits exhibited by AD and HD patients when drawing and copying clocks. In the command condition of this task, subjects are asked to "draw a clock, put in all the numbers, and set the hands to 10 past 11." In the copy condition, subjects

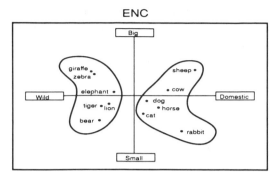

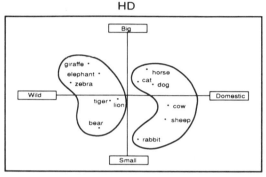

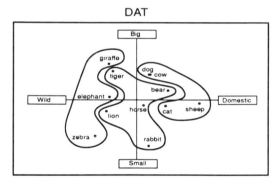

Figure 8-5. The cognitive map of elderly normal control (ENC), Huntington's disease (HD), and Alzheimer's disease (DAT) patients obtained from a two-dimensional multidimensional scaling (MDS) and ADDTREE clustering analysis of a verbal fluency task. The position of each animal is determined by MDS; animals in the same cluster, according to ADDTREE, are encircled together. Adapted from Chan et al. (1993a), with permission of the MIT Press.

are asked to copy a drawing of a clock. Both the AD and HD patients were impaired on this task relative to control subjects, but a qualitative analysis of the types of errors produced revealed a dissociation in their performances. Whereas the HD patients made graphic, visuospatial, and planning errors in both the command and copy conditions, the AD patients often made conceptual errors (e.g., misrepresenting the clock by drawing a face without numbers or with an incorrect use of numbers; misrepresenting the time by failing to include the hands; incorrectly using the hands; or writing the time in the clock face) in the command condition but not in the copy condition. Thus, the AD patients' performance seems to reflect a loss or deficit in accessing knowledge of the attributes, features, and meaning of a clock (see Fig. 8-6; see also Freedman et al., 1994, for detailed discussion of error types in AD as well as in other neurological patient groups).

In a subsequent study, Rouleau et al. (in press) found that these conceptual errors in the command condition of the Clock Drawing Test occurred early in the course of AD and increased over time. Furthermore, the presence of conceptual errors at the initial evaluation of an AD patient was associated with a steeper decline on the DRS over the subsequent 2 years than when these errors were not present on the initial evaluation. Based on the results of this study, Rouleau et al. suggested that the degree of conceptual or semantic knowledge loss in AD might predict the disease's rate of progression. A direct test of this notion was provided in a

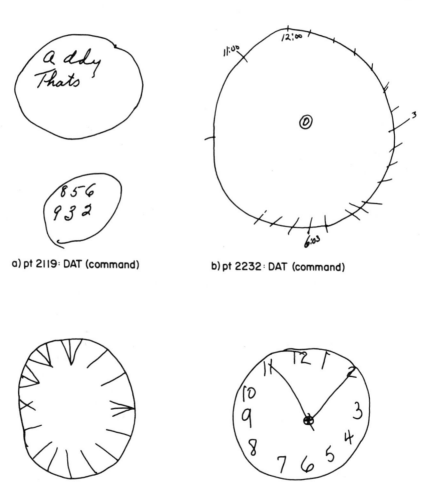

a) pt 2119: DAT (command)

b) pt 2232: DAT (command)

c) pt 2179: DAT (command)

d) pt 2179: DAT (copy)

Figure 8-6. Examples of conceptual errors in the clock drawings of Alzheimer's disease (DAT) patients. Examples (c) and (d) represent a single DAT patient's (pt. 2179) attempts to draw the clock to command (c) and to copy (d). Reprinted from Rouleau et al. (1992), with permission of Academic Press.

longitudinal study by Chan and colleagues (1995a) that examined the relationship between rate of cognitive decline and the integrity of semantic knowledge in AD. Results from this study demonstrated that an index of the abnormality of the semantic network obtained from a multivariate scaling analysis (i.e., the triadic comparison task) accurately predicted the subsequent rate of global cognitive decline, as measured by the DRS, in patients with AD.

Although neurodegenerative disorders are often classified as producing a "cortical" or "subcortical" dementia (Albert, 1978; Cummings, 1990), some disorders do not neatly fit into either heuristic category. The Lewy body variant (LBV) of AD (Hansen et al., 1990), for example, is characterized by a combination of cortical and subcortical neuropathological changes, and this overlap is reflected in the neuropsychological manifestation of the disorder.

Hansen and colleagues (1990) found that patients with LBV and with "pure" AD exhibit equivalent deficits in cognitive abilities usually affected by AD (e.g., memory, confrontation naming), but that the LBV patients displayed disproportionately severe deficits in attention, fluency, and visuospatial processing. Thus, the LBV patients exhibited a combination of both cortical and subcortical neuropsychological impairment.

IMPLICIT MEMORY. Recent investigations also indicate that patients with cortical and subcortical dementia syndromes can be differentiated by their performances on various implicit memory tasks (for reviews, see Bondi et al., 1994b; Butters et al., 1994). Implicit memory refers to the unconscious recollection of knowledge that is expressed indirectly through the performance of the specific operations comprising a task. Classical conditioning, lexical and semantic priming, motor skill learning, and perceptual learning are all considered forms of implicit memory (Squire, 1987). In all of these instances, an individual's performance is facilitated "unconsciously" simply by prior exposure to stimulus material. Implicit memory has been described as a distinct memory "system" independent from the conscious, episodic memory system (Schacter, 1987; Squire, 1987; Schacter and Tulving, 1994). Neuropsychological and neurobiological evidence for this distinction is provided by numerous studies over the past decade that have demonstrated preserved implicit memory in patients with severe amnesia arising from damage to the hippocampal formation or to diencephalic brain regions (for review, see Squire et al., 1993).

Patients with AD have been found to be significantly impaired on lexical (Shimamura et al., 1987; Bondi and Kaszniak, 1991), semantic (Salmon et al., 1988) and pictorial (Heindel et al., 1990) priming tests, whereas HD patients have demonstrated normal verbal (Salmon et al., 1988) and pictorial priming ability (Heindel et al., 1990). For example, Shimamura and colleagues (1987; Salmon et al., 1988) compared the lexical priming performance of patients with AD, HD, or alcoholic Korsakoff syndrome (i.e., circumscribed amnesia) on the word stem completion priming task previously used by Graf and colleagues (1984). In this task, subjects were first exposed to a list of 10 target words (e.g., motel, abstain) and asked to rate each word in terms of "likeability." Following two presentations and ratings of the entire list, the subjects were shown three-letter stems (e.g., mot, abs) of words that were and were not on the presentation list, and were asked to complete the stems with the "first word that comes to mind." Half of the stems could be completed with previously presented words, while the other half were used to assess baseline guessing rates. Priming is indicated by an increased propensity to complete stems with the previously presented words even though the previous words are not consciously remembered. The subjects' ability at free recall and recognition (i.e., explicit memory) were assessed with other lists of words.

Although all three patient groups were severely and equally impaired on free recall and recognition of the presented words, the Korsakoff and HD patients exhibited intact stem completion priming. In contrast, the AD patients showed little or no tendency to complete the stems with the previously presented words and demonstrated significantly less priming than normal control subjects and the HD and Korsakoff patients. The results of this and other studies of priming in demented patients suggests that this form of implicit memory may be dependent on the association cortices that are damaged in AD but relatively intact in HD and Korsakoff syndrome.

In contrast to the priming results, HD patients are impaired on motor skill learning (Heindel et al., 1988, 1989), prism adaptation (Paulsen et al., 1993), and weight biasing (Heindel et al., 1992) tasks that are performed normally by AD patients. All of these tasks involve the generation and refinement (i.e., learning) of motor programs to guide behavior. For example, in one motor skill learning task, rotary pursuit, subjects must learn over repeated trials to maintain contact between a stylus held in the preferred hand and a small metallic disk on a rotating turntable. Heindel and colleagues (1988) tested AD, HD, and amnesic patients on this task over six blocks of trials, with each block consisting of four 20-second trials. The total time on target for each trial was recorded.

The results of this study showed that AD and amnesic patients, as well as normal control subjects, all demonstrated systematic and equivalent improvement across blocks of trials. In contrast, the HD patients were severely impaired in the acquisition of the pursuit rotor motor skill, showing only slight improvement over the blocks of trials. This motor skill learning deficit in HD patients was not correlated with their general motor impairment (i.e., chorea) and was confirmed with other tasks that have little, if any, motor component (e.g., weight biasing, prism adaptation). These results suggest that motor skill acquisition is dependent on the integrity of the basal ganglia structures damaged in HD and independent of the cortical, hippocampal and diencephalic brain regions affected in AD and circumscribed amnesia.

The double dissociation between AD and HD patients on these various implicit memory tasks suggests that different forms of implicit memory, all of which are intact in patients with amnesic syndromes, are not mediated by a single neurological substrate. Rather, it appears that there are at least two psychologically and neurologically distinct implicit memory systems. Verbal and pictorial priming may both involve the temporary activation of stored representations in semantic memory, and may be dependent on the functional integrity of the neocortical association areas damaged in Alzheimer's disease. Motor skill learning, prism adaptation, and the biasing of weight perception, on the other hand, may all involve the modification of programmed movement parameters that are likely mediated by a corticostriatal and basal ganglia system that is severely compromised in HD.

Summary

The syndrome of dementia represents one of the most important and challenging public health problems for the coming decades, particularly because it primarily affects one of the fastest growing segments of our population—persons over the age of 65. The most common cause of dementia, Alzheimer's disease, for example, is thought to currently afflict approximately 4 million people in the United States and is projected to afflict nearly 14 million people within 50 years (Khachaturian et al., 1994). This growing prevalence of dementia will result in a tremendous rise in the emotional and social burden to patients, families, and caregivers, as well as a major increase in the financial costs in dealing with this debilitating disorder.

Although the causes of many of the diseases that produce dementia remain unknown, recent research has uncovered etiologic factors that may prove to be useful in eventually preventing or treating some of these disorders. The gene mutation that produces Huntington's disease, for example, was recently identified (MacDonald et al., 1993), and a major genetic risk factor for Alzheimer's disease (APOE ε4 allele) was recently discovered (Corder et al., 1993; Strittmatter et al., 1993; Saunders et al., 1993). Furthermore, significant neurobiological advances have been made in identifying mechanisms of cellular dysfunction in some of these diseases (see Terry et al., 1994, for review). These advances may one day lead to the development of interventions (e.g., molecular genetic or pharmacologic) that can correct the extracellular and intracellular deficits that may lead to synapse loss and neuron death, or alternatively lead to the development of treatments that maintain synaptic stability and that ensure the survival of neurons before the cascade of neuropathologic events lead to significant cognitive and functional decline (see Khachaturian et al., 1994, for discussion).

Until the causes and methods of prevention of neurodegenerative diseases like Alzheimer's disease and Huntington's disease are discovered, neuropsychology will continue to play an important role in the early detection of dementia, in tracking dementia progression, in assessing the efficacy of potential therapeutic drugs, and in differentiating among dementia syndromes associated with specific neurologic disorders. As the review in this chapter attests, neuropsychological research over the past several decades has already made important contributions to developing and refining our abilities in each of these areas, and it will continue to do so in the future.

Acknowledgments

This research was supported by NIH grants AG12674, AG05131, AG12963, and MH48819 to the University of California and by funds from the Medical Research Service of the Department of Veterans Affairs. The authors wish to thank their many collaborators at the UCSD Alzheimer's Disease Research Center.

References

Albert, M. L. (1978). Subcortical dementia. In R. Katzman, R. D. Terry, and K. L. Bick, eds., *Alzheimer's Disease: Senile Dementia and Related Disorders*. New York: Raven Press, pp. 173–179.

Albert, M. L., Feldman, R. G., and Willis, A. L. (1974). The "subcortical dementia" of progressive supranuclear palsy. *Journal of Neurology, Neurosurgery, and Psychiatry, 37*, 121–130.

Albert, M. S. (1981). Geriatric neuropsychology. *Journal of Consulting and Clinical Psychology, 49*, 835–850.

Albert, M. S. (1988). Assessment of cognitive function. In M. S. Albert and M. B. Moss, eds., *Geriatric Neuropsychology*. New York: Guilford Press, pp. 57–81.

Albert, M. S., Butters, N., and Brandt, J. (1981). Development of remote memory loss in patients with Huntington's disease. *Journal of Clinical and Experimental Neuropsychology, 3*, 1–12.

Albert, M. S., Heller, H. S., and Milberg, W. (1988). Changes in naming ability with age. *Psychology and Aging, 3*, 173–178.

Albert, M. S., and Moss, M. B. (1988). *Geriatric Neuropsychology*. New York: Guilford Press.

Alzheimer, A. (1907). Über eine eigenartige Erkrankung der Hirnrinde. *Allgemeines Zeitschrift für Psychiatrie, 64*, 146–148.

American Psychiatric Association. (1994). *Diagnostic and Statistical Manual of Mental Disorders* (4th ed.). Washington, DC: American Psychiatric Association Press.

Anthony, J. C., LaResche, L., Niaz, U., Von Koroff, M. R., and Folstein, M. F. (1982). Limits of the 'Mini-Mental State' as a screening test for dementia and delirium among hospital patients. *Psychological Medicine, 12*, 397–408.

Armstrong, T., Hansen, L., Salmon, D. P., Masliah, E., Pay, M., Kunin, I., and Katzman, R. (1991). Rapidly progressive dementia in a patient with the Lewy body variant of Alzheimer's disease. *Neurology, 41*, 1178–1180.

Arriagada, P. V., Growdon, J. H., Hedley-Whyte, E. T., and Hyman, B. T. (1992). Neurofibrillary tangles but not senile plaques parallel duration and severity of Alzheimer's disease. *Neurology, 42*, 631–639.

Bachman, D. L., Wolf, P. A., Linn, R., Knoefel, J. E., Cobb, J. L., Belanger, A. J., D'Agostino, R. B., and White, L. R. (1992). Prevalence of dementia and probable senile dementia of the Alzheimer type in the Framingham Study. *Neurology, 42*, 115–119.

Bachman, D. L., Wolf, P. A., Linn, R., Knoefel, J. E., Cobb, J. L., Belanger, A. J., White, L. R., and D'Agostino, R. B. (1993). Incidence of dementia and probable Alzheimer's disease in a general population: The Framingham Study. *Neurology, 43*, 515–519.

Bancher, C., Braak, H., Fischer, P., and Jellinger, K. A. (1993). Neuropathological staging of Alzheimer lesions and intellectual status in Alzheimer's and Parkinson's disease patients. *Neuroscience Letters, 162*, 179–182.

Barona, A., Reynolds, C. R., and Chastain, R. (1984). A demographically based index of premorbid intelligence for the WAIS-R. *Journal of Consulting and Clinical Psychology, 52,* 885–887.

Bayles, K. A., Boone, D. R., Tomoeda, C. K., Slauson, T. J., and Kaszniak, A. W. (1989). Differentiating Alzheimer's patients from the normal elderly and stroke patients with aphasia. *Journal of Speech and Hearing Disorders, 54,* 74–87.

Bayles, K. A., and Kaszniak, A. W. (1987). *Communication and Cognition in Normal Aging and Dementia.* Boston: College-Hill/Little, Brown and Company.

Bayles, K. A., and Tomoeda, C. K. (1983). Confrontation naming impairment in dementia. *Brain and Language, 19,* 98–114.

Bayles, K. A., and Tomoeda, C. K. (1991). Caregiver report of prevalence and appearance order of linguistic symptoms in Alzheimer's patients. *Gerontologist, 31,* 210–216.

Beatty, W. W., and Salmon, D. P. (1991). Remote memory for visuospatial information in patients with Alzheimer's disease. *Journal of Geriatric Psychiatry and Neurology, 4,* 14–17.

Beatty, W. W., Salmon, D. P., Butters, N., Heindel, W. C., and Granholm, E. L. (1988). Retrograde amnesia in patients with Alzheimer's disease or Huntington's disease. *Neurobiology of Aging, 9,* 181–186.

Berg, L., Miller, J. P., Baty, J., Rubin, E. H., Morris, J. C., and Figiel, G. (1992). Mild senile dementia of the Alzheimer type. 4. Evaluation of intervention. *Annals of Neurology, 31,* 242–249.

Bergeron, C., and Pollanen, M. (1989). Lewy bodies in Alzheimer disease—one or two diseases? *Alzheimer's Disease and Associated Disorders, 3,* 197–204.

Berkman, L. F. (1986). The association between educational attainment and mental status examinations: Of etiologic significance for senile dementia or not? *Journal of Chronic Disease, 39,* 171–174.

Blessed, G., Tomlinson, B. E., and Roth, M. (1968). The association between quantitative measures of dementia and of senile change in the cerebral grey matter of elderly subjects. *British Journal of Psychiatry, 114,* 797–811.

Bondareff, W., Mountjoy, C. Q., and Roth, M. (1982). Loss of neurons of origin of the adrenergic projection to cerebral cortex (nucleus locus ceruleus) in senile dementia. *Neurology, 32,* 164–167.

Bondi, M. W., and Kaszniak, A. W. (1991). Implicit and explicit memory in Alzheimer's disease and Parkinson's disease. *Journal of Clinical and Experimental Neuropsychology, 13,* 339–358.

Bondi, M. W., Kaszniak, A. W., Bayles, K. A., and Vance, K. T. (1993a). Contributions of frontal system dysfunction to memory and perceptual abilities in Parkinson's disease. *Neuropsychology, 7,* 89–102.

Bondi, M. W., Monsch, A. U., Butters, N., Salmon, D. P., and Paulsen, J. S. (1993b). Utility of a modified version of the Wisconsin Card Sorting Test in the detection of dementia of the Alzheimer type. *The Clinical Neuropsychologist, 7,* 161–170.

Bondi, M. W., Monsch, A. U., Galasko, D., Butters, N., Salmon, D. P., and Delis, D. C. (1994a). Preclinical cognitive markers of dementia of the Alzheimer type. *Neuropsychology, 8,* 374–384.

Bondi, M. W., Salmon, D. P., and Butters, N. (1994b). Neuropsychological features of memory disorders in Alzheimer disease. In R. D. Terry, R. Katzman, and K. L. Bick, eds., *Alzheimer Disease.* New York: Raven Press, pp. 41–63.

Bondi, M. W., Salmon, D. P., Monsch, A. U., Galasko, D., Butters, N., Klauber, M. R., Thal, L. J., and Saitoh, T. (1995). Episodic memory changes are associated with the ApoE-ε4 allele in nondemented older adults. *Neurology, 45,* 2203–2206.

Braak, H., and Braak, E. (1991). Neuropathological staging of Alzheimer-related changes. *Acta Neuropathologica, 82,* 239–259.

Brandt, J., Corwin, J., and Krafft, L. (1992). Is verbal recognition memory really different in Huntington's and Alzheimer's disease? *Journal of Clinical and Experimental Neuropsychology, 14,* 773–784.

Brandt, J., Quaid, K. A., Folstein, S. E., Garber, P., Maestri, N. E., Abbott, M. H., Slavney, P. R., Franz, M. L., Kasch, L., and Kazazian, H. H., Jr. (1989). Presymptomatic diagnosis of delayed-onset disease with linked DNA markers: The experience in Huntington's disease. *Journal of the American Medical Association, 261,* 3108–3114.

Brown, R. G., and Marsden, C. D. (1984). How common is dementia in Parkinson's disease? *Lancet, 2,* 1262–1265.

Bruyn, G. W. (1968). Huntington's chorea: Historical, clinical and laboratory synopsis. In P. J. Vinken and G. W. Bruyn, eds., *Handbook* of *Clinical Neurology: Diseases of the Basal Ganglia* (vol. 6). New York: Raven Press, pp. 83–94.

Bruyn, G. W., Bots, G., and Dom, R. (1979). Huntington's chorea: Current neuropathological status. In T. Chase, N. Wexler, and A. Barbeau, eds., *Advances in Neurology: Huntington's Disease* (vol. 23). New York: Raven Press, pp. 83–94.

Buschke, H., and Fuld, P. A. (1974). Evaluating storage, retention, and retrieval in disordered memory and learning. *Neurology, 24,* 1019–1025.

Butters, M. A., Salmon, D. P., and Butters, N. (1994). Neuropsychological assessment of dementia. In M. Storandt and G. R. VandenBos, eds., *Neuropsychological Assessment of Dementia and Depression in Older Adults: A Clinician's Guide.* Washington, D.C.: American Psychological Association, pp. 33–59.

Butters, N., Granholm, E., Salmon, D. P., Grant, I., and Wolfe, J. (1987). Episodic and semantic memory: A comparison of amnesic and demented patients. *Journal of Clinical and Experimental Neuropsychology, 9,* 479–497.

Butters, N., Salmon, D. P., Cullum, C. M., Cairns, P., Tröster, A. I., Jacobs, D., Moss, M. B., and Cermak, L. S. (1988). Differentiation of amnesic and demented patients with the Wechsler Memory Scale-Revised. *The Clinical Neuropsychologist, 2,* 133–148.

Butters, N., Sax, D. S., Montgomery, K., and Tarlow, S. (1978). Comparison of the neuropsychological deficits associated with early and advanced Huntington's disease. *Archives of Neurology, 35,* 585–589.

Chan, A. S., Butters, N., Paulsen, J. S., Salmon, D. P., Swenson, M. R., and Maloney, L. T. (1993a). An assessment of the semantic network in patients with Alzheimer's disease. *Journal of Cognitive Neuroscience, 5,* 254–261.

Chan, A. S., Butters, N., Salmon, D. P., and Johnson, S. A. (1995a). Semantic network abnormality predicts rate of cognitive decline in patients with probable Alzheimer's disease. *Journal of the International Neuropsychological Society, 1,* 297–303.

Chan, A. S., Butters, N., Salmon, D. P., Johnson, S. A., Paulsen, J. S., and Swenson, M. R. (1995b). Comparison of the semantic networks in patients with dementia and amnesia. *Neuropsychology, 9,* 177–186.

Chan, A. S., Butters, N., Salmon, D. P., and McGuire, K. A. (1993b). Dimensionality and clustering in the semantic network of patients

with Alzheimer's disease. *Psychology and Aging, 8,* 411–419.

Chertkow, H., and Bub, D. (1990). Semantic memory loss in dementia of Alzheimer's type. What do various measures measure? *Brain, 113,* 397–417.

Chui, H. C., Victoroff, J. I., Margolin, D., Jagust, W., Shankle, R., and Katzman, R. (1992). Criteria for the diagnosis of ischemic vascular dementia proposed by the State of California Alzheimer's Disease Diagnostic and Treatment Centers. *Neurology, 42,* 473–480.

Collins, A. M., and Loftus, E. F. (1975). A spreading activation theory of semantic processing. *Psychological Review, 82,* 407–428.

Corder, E. H., Saunders, A. M., Strittmatter, W. J., Schmechel, D. E., Gaskell, P. C., Small, G. W., Roses, A. D., Haines, J. L., and Pericak-Vance, M. A. (1993). Gene dose of apolipoprotein E type 4 allele and the risk of Alzheimer's disease in late onset families. *Science, 261,* 921–923.

Corsellis, J.A.N., Bruton, C. J., and Freeman-Browne, D. (1973). The aftermath of boxing. *Psychological Medicine, 3,* 270–303.

Corso, J. F. (1985). Communication, presbycusis, and technological aids. In H. K. Ulatowska, ed., *The Aging Brain: Communication in the Elderly.* San Diego: College-Hill Press, pp. 33–51.

Cummings, J. L. (1988). Intellectual impairment in Parkinson's disease: Clinical, pathologic and biochemical correlates. *Journal of Geriatric Psychiatry and Neurology, 1,* 24–36.

Cummings, J. L. (1990). *Subcortical Dementia.* New York: Oxford University Press.

Cummings, J. L., and Benson, D. F. (1992). *Dementia: A Clinical Approach* (2nd ed.). Boston: Butterworth-Heinemann.

Cunningham, W. R., Sepkoski, C. M., and Opel, M. R. (1978). Fatigue effects on intelligence test performance in the elderly. *Journal of Gerontology, 33,* 541–545.

De Lacoste, M. C., and White, C. L., 3rd. (1993). The role of cortical connectivity in Alzheimer's disease pathogenesis: A review and model system. *Neurobiology of Aging, 14,* 1–16.

Delis, D. C., Kramer, J. H., Kaplan, E., and Ober, B. A. (1987). *The California Verbal Learning Test.* New York: Psychological Corporation.

Delis, D. C., Massman, P. J., Butters, N., Salmon, D. P., Kramer, J. H., and Cermak, L. (1991). Profiles of demented and amnesic patients on the California Verbal Learning Test:

Implications for the assessment of memory disorders. *Psychological Assessment, 3*, 19–26.

Depression Guideline Panel. (1993). *Depression in Primary Care: Volume 1. Detection and Diagnosis. Clinical Practice Guideline, Number 5.* Rockville, MD: U.S. PHS, Department of Health and Human Services.

Dickson, D. W., Davies, P., Mayeux, R., Crystal, H., Horoupian, D. S., Thompson, A., and Goldman, J. E. (1987). Diffuse Lewy body disease: Neuropathological and biochemical studies of six patients. *Acta Neuropathologica, 75,* 8–15.

Duvoisin, R. C. (1984). *Parkinson's Disease: A Guide for Patient and Family.* New York: Raven Press.

Elias, M. F., Robbins, M. A., Walter, L. J., and Schultz, N. R., Jr. (1993). The influence of gender and age on Halstead-Reitan Neuropsychological Test performance. *Journal of Gerontology, 48,* P278–P281.

Erickson, R. C., Eimon, P., and Hebben, N. (1992). A bibliography of normative articles on cognitive tests for older adults. *The Clinical Neuropsychologist, 6,* 98–102.

Erickson, R. C., Eimon, P., and Hebben, N. (1994). A listing of references to cognitive test norms for older adults. In M. Storandt and G. R. VandenBos, eds., *Neuropsychological Assessment of Dementia and Depression in Older Adults: A Clinician's Guide.* Washington, D.C.: American Psychological Association, pp. 183–197.

Eslinger, P. J., Damasio, A. R., Benton, A. L., and Van Allen, M. (1985). Neuropsychologic detection of abnormal mental decline in older persons. *Journal of the American Medical Association, 253,* 670–674.

Feskens, E. J., Havekes, L. M., Kalmijn, S., de Knijff, P., Launer, L. J., and Kromhout, D. (1994). Apolipoprotein e4 allele and cognitive decline in elderly men. *British Medical Journal, 309,* 1202–1206.

Flicker, C. (1988). Neuropsychological evaluation of treatment effects in the elderly: A critique of tests in current use. *Psychopharmacology Bulletin, 24,* 535–556.

Flicker, C., Ferris, S. H., and Reisberg, B. (1991). Mild cognitive impairment in the elderly: Predictors of dementia. *Neurology, 41,* 1006–1009.

Folstein, M. F., Anthony, J. C., Parhad, I., Duffy, B., and Gruenberg, E. M. (1985). The meaning of cognitive impairment in the elderly. *Journal of the American Geriatrics Society, 33,* 228–235.

Folstein, M. F., Folstein, S. E., and McHugh, P. R. (1975). "Mini-Mental State": A practical method for grading the cognitive state of patients for the clinician. *Journal of Psychiatric Research, 12,* 189–198.

Folstein, S. E. (1989). *Huntington's Disease: A Disorder of Families.* Baltimore, MD: Johns Hopkins University Press.

Folstein, S. E., Abbott, M. H., Chase, G. A., Jensen, B. A., and Folstein, M. F. (1983). The association of affective disorder with Huntington disease in a case series and in families. *Psychological Medicine, 13,* 537–542.

Folstein, S. E., Brandt, J., and Folstein, M. F. (1990). Huntington's disease. In J. L. Cummings, ed., *Subcortical Dementia.* New York: Oxford University Press, pp. 87–107.

Fozard, J. L. (1990). Vision and hearing in aging. In J. E. Birren and K. W. Schaie, eds., *Handbook of the Psychology of Aging* (3rd ed.). New York: Van Nostrand Reinhold, pp. 150–170.

Freedman, M. (1990). Parkinson's disease. In J. L. Cummings, ed., *Subcortical Dementia.* New York: Oxford University Press, pp. 108–122.

Freedman, M., Leach, L., Kaplan, E., Winocur, G., Shulman, K. I., and Delis, D. C. (1994). *Clock Drawing: A Neuropsychological Analysis.* New York: Oxford University Press.

Freedman, M., Rivoira, P., Butters, N., Sax, D. S., and Feldman, R. G. (1984). Retrograde amnesia in Parkinson's disease. *Canadian Journal of Neurological Sciences, 11,* 297–301.

Frisoni, G. B., Govoni, S., Geroldi, C., Bianchetti, A., Calabresi, L., Franceschini, G., and Trabucchi, M. (1995). Gene dose of the ε4 allele of apolipoprotein E and disease progression in sporadic late-onset Alzheimer's disease. *Annals of Neurology, 37,* 596–604.

Fuld, P. A. (1977). *Fuld Object-Memory Evaluation.* Woodale, IL: Stoelting Company.

Fuld, P. A., Katzman, R., Davies, P., and Terry, R. D. (1982). Intrusions as a sign of Alzheimer dementia: Chemical and pathological verification. *Annals of Neurology, 11,* 155–159.

Fuld, P. A., Masur, D. M., Blau, A. D., Crystal, H., and Aronson, M. K. (1990). Object-memory evaluation for prospective detection of dementia in normal functioning elderly: Predictive and normative data. *Journal of Clinical and Experimental Neuropsychology, 12,* 520–528.

Galasko, D., Hansen, L. A., Katzman, R., Wiederholt, W., Masliah, E., Terry, R. D., Hill, L. R., Lessin, P., and Thal, L. J. (1994). Clinical-neuropathological correlations in Alzheimer's disease and related disorders. *Archives of Neurology, 51*, 888–895.

Galasko, D., Katzman, R., Salmon, D. P., Thal, L. J., and Hansen, L. A. (in press). Clinical and neuropathological findings in Lewy body dementias. *Brain and Cognition.*

Gerdes, L. U., Klausen, I. C., Sihm, I., and Faergeman, O. (1992). Apolipoprotein E polymorphism in a Danish population compared to findings in 45 other study populations around the world. *Genetic Epidemiology, 9*, 155–167.

Gibb, W.R.G., Esiri, M. M., and Lees, A. J. (1987). Clinical and pathological features of diffuse cortical Lewy body disease (Lewy body dementia). *Brain, 110*, 1131–1153.

Graf, P., Squire, L. R., and Mandler, G. (1984). The information that amnesics do not forget. *Journal of Experimental Psychology, Learning, Memory, and Cognition, 10*, 164–178.

Grant, I., and Martin, A. (1994). *The Neuropsychology of HIV Infection.* New York: Oxford University Press.

Haase, G. R. (1977). Diseases presenting as dementia. In C. E. Wells, ed., *Dementia* (2nd ed.). Philadelphia: F. A. Davis, pp. 27–67.

Hachinski, V. C., Iliff, L. D., Zilhka, E., Du Boulay, G. H., McAllister, V. L., Marshall, J., Russell, R. W., and Symon, L. (1975). Cerebral blood flow in dementia. *Archives of Neurology, 32*, 632–637.

Hachinski, V. C., Lassen, N. A., and Marshall, J. (1974). Multi-infarct dementia. A cause of mental deterioration in the elderly. *Lancet, 2*, 207–210.

Hallman, D. M., Boerwinkle, E., Saha, N., Sandholzer, C., Menzel, H. J., Csazar, A., and Utermann, G. (1991). The apolipoprotein E polymorphism: A comparison of allele frequencies and effects in nine populations. *American Journal of Human Genetics, 49*, 338–349.

Hansen, L. A., and Galasko, D. (1992). Lewy body disease. *Current Opinion in Neurology and Neurosurgery, 5*, 889–894.

Hansen, L., Salmon, D. P., Galasko, D., Masliah, E., Katzman, R., DeTeresa, R., Thal, L. J., Pay, M. M., Hofstetter, R., Klauber, M. R., Rice, V., Butters, N., and Alford, M. (1990). The Lewy body variant of Alzheimer's disease: A clinical and pathologic entity. *Neurology, 40*, 1–8.

Hayden, M. R. (1981). *Huntington's Chorea.* Berlin: Springer-Verlag.

Heaton, R. K., Grant, I., and Matthews, C. G. (1986). Differences in neuropsychological test performance associated with age, education, and sex. In I. Grant and K. M. Adams, eds., *Neuropsychological Assessment of Neuropsychiatric Disorders.* New York: Oxford University Press, pp. 100–120.

Heaton, R. K., Grant, I., and Matthews, C. G. (1991). *Comprehensive Norms for an Expanded Halstead-Reitan Battery: Demographic Corrections, Research Findings, and Clinical Applications.* Odessa, FL: Psychological Assessment Resources.

Heindel, W. C., Butters, N., and Salmon, D. P. (1988). Impaired learning of a motor skill in patients with Huntington's disease. *Behavioral Neuroscience, 102*, 141–147.

Heindel, W. C., Salmon, D. P., and Butters, N. (1990). Pictorial priming and cued recall in Alzheimer's and Huntington's disease. *Brain and Cognition, 13*, 282–295.

Heindel, W. C., Salmon, D. P., and Butters, N. (1992). The biasing of weight judgments in Alzheimer's and Huntington's disease: A priming or programming phenomenon? *Journal of Clinical and Experimental Neuropsychology, 13*, 189–203.

Heindel, W. C., Salmon, D. P., Shults, C., Walicke, P., and Butters, N. (1989). Neuropsychological evidence for multiple implicit memory systems: A comparison of Alzheimer's, Huntington's and Parkinson's disease patients. *Journal of Neuroscience, 9*, 582–587.

Hendrie, H. C., Hall, K. S., Hui, S., Unverzagt, F. W., Yu, C. E., Lahiri, D. K., Sahota, A., Farlow, M., Musick, B., Class, C. A., Brashear, A., Burdine, V. E., Osuntokun, B. O., Ogunniyi, A. O., Gureje, O., Baiyewu, O., and Schellenberg, G. D. (1995). Apolipoprotein E genotypes and Alzheimer's disease in a community study of elderly African Americans. *Annals of Neurology, 37*, 118–120.

Heston, L. L., and Mastri, A. R. (1982). Age at onset of Pick's and Alzheimer's dementia: Implications for diagnosis and research. *Journal of Gerontology, 37*, 422–424.

Hill, R. D., Storandt, M., and LaBarge, E. (1992). Psychometric discrimination of moderate senile dementia of the Alzheimer type. *Archives of Neurology, 49*, 377–380.

Hodges, J. R., Salmon, D. P., and Butters, N. (1991). The nature of the naming deficit in Alzheimer's and Huntington's disease. *Brain, 114*, 1547–1558.

Hodges, J. R., Salmon, D. P., and Butters, N. (1992). Semantic memory impairment in Alzheimer's disease: Failure of access or degraded knowledge? *Neuropsychologia, 30*, 301–314.

Hodges, J. R., Salmon, D. P., and Butters, N. (1993). Recognition and naming of famous faces in Alzheimer's disease: A cognitive analysis. *Neuropsychologia, 31,* 775–788.

Hom, J., Turner, M. B., Risser, R., Bonte, F. J., and Tintner, R. (1994). Cognitive deficits in asymptomatic first-degree relatives of Alzheimer's disease patients. *Journal of Clinical and Experimental Neuropsychology, 16,* 568–576.

Huber, S. J., and Cummings, J. L. (1992). *Parkinson's Disease: Neurobehavioral Aspects.* New York: Oxford University Press.

Huff, F. J., Becker, J. T., Belle, S. H., Nebes, R. D., Holland, A. L., and Boller, F. (1987). Cognitive deficits and clinical diagnosis of Alzheimer's disease. *Neurology, 37,* 1119–1124.

Huff, F. J., Corkin, S., and Growdon, J. H. (1986). Semantic impairment and anomia in Alzheimer's disease. *Brain and Language, 28,* 235–249.

Hughes, A. J., Daniel, S. E., Kilford, L., and Lees, A. J. (1992). Accuracy of clinical diagnosis of idiopathic Parkinson's disease: A clinicopathological study of 100 cases. *Journal of Neurology, Neurosurgery, and Psychiatry, 55,* 181–184.

Hyman, B. T., Van Horsen, G. W., Damasio, A. R., and Barnes, C. L. (1984). Alzheimer's disease: Cell-specific pathology isolates the hippocampal formation. *Science, 225,* 1168–1170.

Ineichen, B. (1987). Measuring the rising tide. How many dementia cases will there be by 2001? *British Journal of Psychiatry, 150,* 193–200.

Ivnik, R. J., Malec, J. F., Smith, G. E., Tangalos, E. G., Petersen, R. C., Kokmen, E., and Kurland, L. T. (1992a). Mayo's Older Americans Normative Studies: WAIS-R norms for ages 56 to 97. *The Clinical Neuropsychologist, 6* (suppl.), 1–30.

Ivnik, R. J., Malec, J. F., Smith, G. E., Tangalos, E. G., Petersen, R. C., Kokmen, E., and Kurland, L. T. (1992b). Mayo's Older Americans Normative Studies: WMS-R norms for ages 56 to 94. *The Clinical Neuropsychologist, 6* (suppl.), 49–82.

Ivnik, R. J., Malec, J. F., Smith, G. E., Tangalos, E. G., Petersen, R. C., Kokmen, E., and Kurland, L. T. (1992c). Mayo's Older Americans Normative Studies: Updated AVLT norms for ages 56 to 97. *The Clinical Neuropsychologist, 6* (suppl.), 83–104.

Jacobs, D., Salmon, D. P., Tröster, A. I., and Butters, N. (1990). Intrusion errors in the figural memory of patients with Alzheimer's and Huntington's disease. *Archives of Clinical Neuropsychology, 5,* 49–57.

Jagger, C., Clarke, M., and Anderson, J. (1992). Screening for dementia: A comparison of two tests using receiver operating characteristics (ROC) analysis. *International Journal of Geriatric Psychiatry, 7,* 659–665.

Jankovic, J. (1987). Pathophysiology and clinical assessment of motor symptoms in Parkinson's disease. In W. C. Koller, ed., *Handbook of Parkinson's Disease.* New York: Marcel Dekker, pp. 99–126.

Jellinger, K. (1987). The pathology of parkinsonism. In C. D. Marsden and S. Fahn, eds., *Movement Disorders 2: Neurology* (vol. 7). London: Butterworths, pp. 124–165.

Joachim, C. L., Morris, J. H., and Selkoe, D. J. (1988). Clinically diagnosed Alzheimer's disease: Autopsy results in 150 cases. *Annals of Neurology, 24,* 50–56.

Johnson, M. A., and Choy, D. (1987). On the definition of age-related norms for visual function testing. *Applied Optics, 26,* 1449–1454.

Jorm, A. F., Korten, A. E., and Henderson, A. S. (1987). The prevalence of dementia: A quantitative integration of the literature. *Acta Psychiatrica Scandinavica, 76,* 465–479.

Kaplan, E. (1988). A process approach to neuropsychological assessment. In T. Boll and B. K. Bryant, eds., *Clinical Neuropsychology and Brain Function: Research, Measurement, and Practice* (vol. 7). Washington, D.C.: American Psychological Association, pp. 127–167.

Kaszniak, A. W. (1987). Neuropsychological consultation to geriatricians: Issues in the assessment of memory complaints. *The Clinical Neuropsychologist, 1,* 35–46.

Kaszniak, A. W. (1990). Psychological assessment of the aging individual. In J. E. Birren and K. W. Schaie, eds., *Handbook of the Psychology of Aging* (3rd. ed.). San Diego: Academic Press, pp. 427–445.

Kaszniak, A. W., and Christenson, G. D. (1994). Differential diagnosis of dementia and depression. In M. Storandt, and G. R. VandenBos, eds., *Neuropsychological Assessment of Dementia and Depression in Older Adults: A Clinician's Guide.* Washington, D.C.: American Psychological Association, pp. 81–117.

Kaszniak, A. W., Garron, D. C., Fox, J. H., Bergen, D., and Huckman, M. (1979). Cerebral atrophy, EEG slowing, age, education, and cognitive functioning in suspected dementia. *Neurology, 29,* 1273–1279.

Kaszniak, A. W., Wilson, R. S., Fox, J. H., and Stebbins, G. T. (1986). Cognitive assessment in Alzheimer's disease: Cross-sectional and longitudinal perspectives. *Canadian Journal of Neurological Sciences, 13,* 420–423.

Katzman, R. (1986). Alzheimer's disease. *New England Journal of Medicine, 314,* 964–973.

Katzman, R. (1993). Education and the prevalence of dementia and Alzheimer's disease. *Neurology, 43,* 13–20.

Katzman, R. (1994). Apolipoprotein E and Alzheimer's disease. *Current Opinion in Neurobiology, 4,* 703–707.

Katzman, R., Aronson, M., Fuld, P., Kawas, C., Brown, T., Morgenstern, H., Frishman, W., Gidez, L., Eder, H., and Ooi, W. L. (1989). Development of dementing illness in an 80-year-old volunteer cohort. *Annals of Neurology, 25,* 317–324.

Katzman, R., Brown, T., Thal, L. J., Fuld, P. A., Aronson, M., Butters, N., Klauber, M. R., Wiederholt, W., Pay, M., Renbing, X., Ooi, W. L., Hofstetter, R., and Terry, R. D. (1988a). Comparison of rate of annual change of mental status score in four independent studies of patients with Alzheimer's disease. *Annals of Neurology, 24,* 384–389.

Katzman, R., and Kawas, C. (1994). The epidemiology of dementia and Alzheimer disease. In R. D. Terry, R. Katzman, and K. L. Bick, eds., *Alzheimer Disease.* New York: Raven Press, pp. 105–122.

Katzman, R., Lasker, B., and Bernstein, N. (1988b). Advances in the diagnosis of dementia: Accuracy of diagnosis and consequences of misdiagnosis of disorders causing dementia. In R. D. Terry, ed., *Aging and the Brain.* New York: Raven Press, pp. 17–62.

Kawas, C. H. (1990). Early clinical diagnosis: Status of NINCDS-ADRDA criteria. In R. E. Becker and E. Giacobini, eds., *Alzheimer Disease: Current Research in Early Diagnosis.* New York: Taylor and Francis, pp. 9–18.

Khachaturian, Z. S. (1985). Diagnosis of Alzheimer's disease. *Archives of Neurology, 42,* 1097–1105.

Khachaturian, Z. S., Phelps, C. H., and Buckholtz, N. S. (1994). The prospect of developing treatments for Alzheimer disease. In R. D. Terry, R. Katzman, and K. L. Bick, eds., *Alzheimer Disease.* New York: Raven Press, pp. 445–454.

Knopman, D. S., and Ryberg, S. (1989). A verbal memory test with high predictive accuracy for dementia of the Alzheimer type. *Archives of Neurology, 46,* 141–145.

Kolb, B., and Whishaw, I. Q. (1990). *Fundamentals of Human Neuropsychology.* New York: W. H. Freeman and Company.

Kopelman, M. D. (1989). Remote and autobiographical memory, temporal context memory and frontal atrophy in Korsakoff and Alzheimer patients. *Neuropsychologia, 27,* 437–460.

Kosaka, K., Yoshimura, M., Ikeda, K., and Budka, H. (1984). Diffuse type of Lewy body disease: Progressive dementia with abundant cortical Lewy bodies and senile changes of varying degree—A new disease? *Clinical Neuropathology, 3,* 185–192.

Kosnik, W., Winslow, L., Kline, D., Rasinski, K., and Sekuler, R. (1988). Visual changes in daily life throughout adulthood. *Journal of Gerontology, 43,* P63–P70.

Kramer, M. (1986). Trends of institutionalization and prevalence of mental disorders in nursing homes. In M. S. Harper and B. D. Lebowitz, eds., *Mental Illness in Nursing Homes: Agenda for Research.* Rockville, MD: National Institute of Mental Health, pp. 7–26.

Kukull, W. A., Larson, E. B., Reifler, B. V., Lampe, T. H., Yerby, M. S., and Hughes, J. P. (1990a). Interrater reliability of Alzheimer's disease diagnosis. *Neurology, 40,* 257–260.

Kukull, W. A., Larson, E. B., Reifler, B. V., Lampe, T. H., Yerby, M. S., and Hughes, J. P. (1990b). The validity of 3 clinical diagnostic criteria for Alzheimer's disease. *Neurology, 40,* 1364–1369.

Kunkel, S. R., and Applebaum, R. A. (1992). Estimating the prevalence of long-term disability for an aging society. *Journal of Gerontology, 47,* S253–S260.

La Rue, A. (1992). *Aging and Neuropsychological Assessment.* New York: Plenum Press.

La Rue, A., D'Elia, L. F., Clark, E. O., Spar, J. E., and Jarvik, L. F. (1986). Clinical tests of memory in dementia, depression, and healthy aging. *Psychology and Aging, 1,* 69–77.

La Rue, A., and Jarvik, L. F. (1980). Reflections of biological changes in the psychological performance of the aged. *Age, 3,* 29–32.

La Rue, A., and Jarvik, L. F. (1987). Cognitive function and prediction of dementia in old age. *International Journal of Aging and Human Development, 25,* 79–89.

La Rue, A., Matsuyama, S. S., McPherson, S., Sherman, J., and Jarvik, L. F. (1992a). Cognitive performance in relatives of patients with probable Alzheimer disease: An age at onset effect? *Journal of Clinical and Experimental Neuropsychology, 14,* 533–538.

La Rue, A., Watson, J., and Plotkin, D. A. (1992b). Retrospective accounts of dementia symptoms: Are they reliable? *Gerontologist, 32,* 240–245.

La Rue, A., Yang, J., and Osato, S. (1992c).

Neuropsychological assessment. In J. E. Birren, R. B. Sloane, and G. D. Cohen, eds., *Handbook of Mental Health and Aging* (2nd ed.). San Diego: Academic Press, pp. 643–670.

Lennox, G., Lowe, J., Landon, M., Byrne, E. J., Mayer, R. J., and Godwin-Austen, R. B. (1989). Diffuse Lewy body disease: Correlative neuropathology using anti-ubiquitin immunocytochemistry. *Journal of Neurology, Neurosurgery, and Psychiatry, 52*, 1236–1247.

Lezak, M. D. (1995). *Neuropsychological Assessment* (3rd ed.). New York: Oxford University Press.

Li, G., Shen, Y. C., Chen, C. H., Zhao, Y. W., and Li, S. R. (1989). An epidemiological survey of age-related dementia in an urban area of Beijing. *Acta Psychiatrica Scandinavica, 79*, 557–563.

Lima, S. D., Hale, S., and Myerson, J. (1991). How general is general slowing? Evidence from the lexical domain. *Psychology and Aging, 6*, 416–425.

Linn, R. T., Wolf, P. A., Bachman, D. L., Knoefel, J. E., Cobb, J. L., Belanger, A. J., Kaplan, E. F., and D'Agostino, R. B. (1995). The 'preclinical phase' of probable Alzheimer's disease: A 13-year prospective study of the Framingham cohort. *Archives of Neurology, 52*, 485–490.

Loeb, C., and Gandolfo, C. (1983). Diagnostic evaluation of degenerative and vascular dementia. *Stroke, 14*, 399–401.

Loewenstein, D. A., Ardila, A., Rosselli, M., Hayden, S., Duara, R., Berkowitz, N., Linn-Fuentes, P., Mintzer, J., Norville, M., and Eisdorfer, C. (1992). A comparative analysis of functional status among Spanish- and English-speaking patients with dementia. *Journal of Gerontology, 47*, P389–P394.

Loewenstein, D. A., Arguelles, T., Barker, W. W., and Duara, R. (1993). A comparative analysis of neuropsychological test performance of Spanish-speaking and English-speaking patients with Alzheimer's disease. *Journal of Gerontology, 48*, P142–P149.

MacDonald, M. E., Ambrose, C. M., Duyao, M. P., Myers, R. H., Lin, C., Srinidhi, L., Barnes, G., Taylor, S. A., James, M., Groot, N., MacFarlane, H., Jenkins, B., Anderson, M. A., Wexler, N. S., and Gusella, J. F. [The Huntington's Disease Collaborative Research Group]. (1993). A novel gene containing a trinucleotide repeat that is expanded and unstable on Huntington's disease chromosomes. *Cell, 72*, 971–983.

Malec, J. F., Ivnik, R. J., Smith, G. E., Tangalos, E. G., Petersen, R. C., Kokmen, E., and Kurland, L. T. (1992). Mayo's Older Americans Normative Studies: Utility of corrections for age and education for the WAIS-R. *The Clinical Neuropsychologist, 6* (suppl.), 31–47.

Mann, D.M.A., Yates, P. O., and Marcyniuk, B. (1984). A comparison of changes in the nucleus basalis and locus ceruleus in Alzheimer's disease. *Journal of Neurology, Neurosurgery, and Psychiatry, 47*, 201–203.

Manton, K. G. (1990). Mortality and morbidity. In R. H. Binstock and L. K. George, eds., *Handbook of Aging and the Social Sciences* (3rd ed.). San Diego: Academic Press, pp. 64–90.

Massman, P. J., Delis, D. C., and Butters, N. (1993). Does impaired primacy recall equal impaired long-term storage? Serial position effects in Huntington's disease and Alzheimer's disease. *Developmental Neuropsychology, 9*, 1–15.

Massman, P. J., Delis, D. C., Butters, N., Dupont, R. M., and Gillin, J. C. (1992). The subcortical dysfunction hypothesis of memory deficits in depression: Neuropsychological validation in a subgroup of patients. *Journal of Clinical and Experimental Neuropsychology, 14*, 687–706.

Masur, D. M., Fuld, P. A., Blau, A. D., Crystal, H., and Aronson, M. K. (1990). Predicting development of dementia in the elderly with the Selective Reminding Test. *Journal of Clinical and Experimental Neuropsychology, 12*, 529–538.

Masur, D. M., Fuld, P. A., Blau, A. D., Thal, L. J., Levin, H. S., and Aronson, M. K. (1989). Distinguishing normal and demented elderly with the Selective Reminding Test. *Journal of Clinical and Experimental Neuropsychology, 11*, 615–630.

Masur, D. M., Sliwinski, M., Lipton, R. B., Blau, A. D., and Crystal, H. A. (1994). Neuropsychological prediction of dementia and the absence of dementia in healthy elderly persons. *Neurology, 44*, 1427–1432.

Mattis, S. (1976). Mental status examination for organic mental syndrome in the elderly patient. In L. Bellack and T. B. Karasu, eds., *Geriatrics Psychiatry: A Handbook for Psychiatrists and Primary Care Physicians*. New York: Grune and Stratton, pp. 77–121.

Mayeux, R., Ottman, R., Maestre, G., Ngai, C., Tang, M.-X., Ginsberg, H., Chun, M., Tycko, B., and Shelanski, M. (1995). Synergistic effects of traumatic head injury and apolipoprotein $\epsilon4$

in patients with Alzheimer's disease. *Neurology, 45*, 555–557.

Mayeux, R., Stern, Y., Ottman, R., Tatemichi, T. K., Tang, M. X., Maestre, G., Ngai, C., Tycko, B., and Ginsberg, H. (1993). The apolipoprotein epsilon 4 allele in patients with Alzheimer's disease. *Annals of Neurology, 34*, 752–754.

McGlone, J., Gupta, S., Humphrey, D., Oppenheimer, S., Mirsen, T., and Evans, D. R. (1990). Screening for early dementia using memory complaints from patients and relatives. *Archives of Neurology, 47*, 1189–1193.

McHugh, P. R., and Folstein, M. F. (1975). Psychiatric symptoms of Huntington's chorea: A clinical and phenomenologic study. In D. F. Benson and D. Blumer, eds., *Psychiatric Aspects of Neurological Disease*. New York: Raven Press, pp. 267–285.

McKhann, G., Drachman, D., Folstein, M., Katzman, R., Price, D., and Stadlan, E. M. (1984). Clinical diagnosis of Alzheimer's disease: Report of the NINCDS-ADRDA Work Group under the auspices of the Department of Health and Human Services Task Force on Alzheimer's Disease. *Neurology, 34*, 939–944.

Miller, E. (1971). On the nature of memory disorder in presenile dementia. *Neuropsychologia, 9*, 75–81.

Mittenberg, W., Seidenberg, M., O'Leary, D. S., and DiGiulio, D. V. (1989). Changes in cerebral functioning associated with normal aging. *Journal of Clinical and Experimental Neuropsychology, 11*, 918–932.

Mochle, K. A., and Long, C. J. (1989). Models of aging and neuropsychological test performance decline with aging. *Journal of Gerontology, 44*, P176–P177.

Molsa, P. K., Paljarvi, L., Rinne, J. O., Rinne, U. K., and Sako, E. (1985). Validity of clinical diagnosis in dementia: A prospective clinicopathological study. *Journal of Neurology, Neurosurgery, and Psychiatry, 48*, 1085–1090.

Monsch, A. U., Bondi, M. W., Butters, N., Salmon, D. P., Katzman, R., and Thal, L. J. (1992). Comparisons of verbal fluency tasks in the detection of dementia of the Alzheimer type. *Archives of Neurology, 49*, 1253–1258.

Monsch, A. U., Bondi, M. W., Salmon, D. P., Paulsen, J. S., Butters, N., Brugger, P., and Swenson, M. (1994). A comparison of category and letter fluency in Alzheimer's disease and Huntington's disease. *Neuropsychology, 8*, 25–30.

Morris, J. C., McKeel, D. W., Jr., Storandt, M., Rubin, E. H., Price, J. L., Grant, E. A., Ball, M. J., and Berg, L. (1991). Very mild Alzheimer's disease: Informant-based clinical, psychometric, and pathologic distinction from normal aging. *Neurology, 41*, 469–478.

Mortimer, J. A. (1988). Do psychosocial risk factors contribute to Alzheimer's disease? In A. S. Henderson and J. H. Henderson, eds., *Etiology of Dementia of the Alzheimer's Type*. New York: John Wiley and Sons, pp. 39–52.

Mortimer, J. A., van Duijn, C. M., Chandra, V., Fratiglioni, L., Graves, A. B., Heyman, A., Jorm, A. F., Kokmen, E., Kondo, K., Rocca, W. A., Shalat, S. L., Soininen, H., and Hofman, A. (1991). Head trauma as a risk factor for Alzheimer's disease: A collaborative re-analysis of case-control studies. *International Journal of Epidemiology, 20* (suppl. 2), S28–35.

Moss, M. B., Albert, M. S., Butters, N., and Payne, M. (1986). Differential patterns of memory loss among patients with Alzheimer's disease, Huntington's disease and alcoholic Korsakoff's syndrome. *Archives of Neurology, 43*, 239–246.

Murden, R. A., McRae, T. D., Kaner, S., and Bucknam, N. E. (1991). Mini-Mental State Exam scores vary with education in blacks and whites. *Journal of the American Geriatrics Society, 39*, 149–155.

Myers, G. C. (1990). Demography of aging. In R. H. Binstock and L. K. George, eds., *Handbook of Aging and the Social Sciences* (3rd ed.). San Diego: Academic Press, pp. 19–44.

Naugle, R. I., Cullum, C. M., and Bigler, E. D. (1990). Evaluation of intellectual and memory function among dementia patients who were intellectually superior. *The Clinical Neuropsychologist, 4*, 355–374.

Nebes, R. D. (1992). Cognitive dysfunction in Alzheimer's disease. In F.I.M. Craik and T. A. Salthouse, eds., *The Handbook of Aging and Cognition*. Hillsdale, NJ: Lawrence Erlbaum Associates, pp. 373–446.

Nelson, A., Fogel, B. S., and Faust, D. (1986). Bedside cognitive screening instruments: A critical assessment. *Journal of Nervous and Mental Disease, 174*, 73–83.

Nelson, H. E. (1976). A modified card sorting test sensitive to frontal lobe defects. *Cortex, 12*, 313–324.

O'Connor, D. W., Pollitt, P. A., Hyde, J. B., Fellowes, J. L., Miller, N. D., Brook, C. P., and Reiss, B. B. (1989). The reliability and validity of the Mini-Mental State in a British community survey. *Journal of Psychiatric Research, 23*, 87–96.

O'Neil, P. M., and Calhoun, K. S. (1975). Sensory

deficits and behavioral deterioration in senescence. *Journal of Abnormal Psychology, 84,* 579–582.

Ortof, E., and Crystal, H. A. (1989). Rate of progression of Alzheimer's disease. *Journal of the American Geriatrics Society, 37,* 511–514.

Owsley, C., and Sloane, M. E. (1990). Vision and aging. In F. Boller and J. Grafman, eds., *Handbook of Neuropsychology* (vol. 4). Amsterdam: Elsevier, pp. 229–249.

Paulsen, J. S., Butters, N., Salmon, D. P., Heindel, W. C., and Swenson, M. R. (1993). Prism adaptation in Alzheimer's and Huntington's disease. *Neuropsychology, 7,* 73–81.

Parks, R. W., Zec, R. F., and Wilson, R. S. (1993). *Neuropsychology of Alzheimer's Disease and Other Dementias.* New York: Oxford University Press.

Pearson, R.C.A., Esiri, M. M., Hiorns, R. W., Wilcock, G. K., and Powell, T.P.S. (1985). Anatomical correlates of the distribution of the pathological changes in the neocortex in Alzheimer disease. *Proceedings of the National Academy of Sciences USA, 82,* 4531–4534.

Pepin, E. P., and Eslinger, P. J. (1989). Verbal memory decline in Alzheimer's disease: A multiple-processes deficit. *Neurology, 39,* 1477–1482.

Perry, E. K., McKeith, I., Thompson, P., Marshall, E., Kerwin, J., Jabeen, S., Edwardson, J. A., Ince, P., Blessed, G., Irving, D., and Perry, R. H. (1991). Topography, extent, and clinical relevance of neurochemical deficits in dementia of Lewy body type, Parkinson's disease, and Alzheimer's disease. *Annals of the New York Academy of Sciences, 640,* 197–202.

Perry, R. H., Irving, D., Blessed, G., Fairbairn, A., and Perry, E. K. (1990). Senile dementia of the Lewy body type: A clinically and neuropathologically distinct form of Lewy body dementia in the elderly. *Journal of the Neurological Sciences, 95,* 119–139.

Peters, C. A., Potter, J. F., and Scholer, S. G. (1988). Hearing impairment as a predictor of cognitive decline in dementia. *Journal of the American Geriatrics Society, 36,* 981–986.

Petersen, R. C., Smith, G. E., Ivnik, R. J., Kokmen, E., and Tangalos, E. G. (1994). Memory function in very early Alzheimer's disease. *Neurology, 44,* 867–872.

Petersen, R. C., Smith, G., Kokmen, E., Ivnik, R. J., and Tangalos, E. G. (1992). Memory function in normal aging. *Neurology, 42,* 396–401.

Pickett, J. M., Bergman, M., and Levitt, M.

(1979). Aging and speech understanding. In J. M. Ordy and K. Brizzee, eds., *Aging: Speech Systems and Communication in the Elderly* (vol. 10). New York: Raven Press, pp. 167–186.

Plomp, R. (1978). Auditory handicap of hearing impairment and the limited benefit of hearing aids. *Journal of the Acoustical Society of America, 63,* 533–549.

Plomp, R., and Mimpen, A. M. (1979). Speech reception threshold for sentences as a function of age and noise level. *Journal of the Acoustical Society of America, 66,* 1333–1342.

Poirier, J. Davignon, J., Bouthillier, D., Kogan, S., Bertrand, P., and Gauthier, S. (1993). Apolipoprotein E polymorphism and Alzheimer's disease. *Lancet, 342,* 697–699.

Poon, L. W., Kaszniak, A. W., and Dudley, W. N. (1992). Approaches in the experimental neuropsychology of dementia: A methodological and model review. In M. Bergner, K. Hasegawa, S. Finkel, and T. Nishimura, eds., *Aging and Mental Disorders: International Perspectives.* New York: Springer, pp. 150–173.

Reed, T., Carmelli, D., Swan, G. E., Breitner, J. C., Welsh, K. A., Jarvik, G. P., Deeb, S., and Auwerx, J. (1994). Lower cognitive performance in normal older adult male twins carrying the apolipoprotein E ϵ4 allele. *Archives of Neurology, 51,* 1189–1192.

Reitan, R. M., and Wolfson, D. (1986). The Halstead-Reitan Neuropsychological Test Battery and aging. *Clinical Gerontologist, 5,* 39–61.

Roccaforte, W. H., Burke, W. J., Bayer, B. L., and Wengel, S. P. (1992). Validation of a telephone version of the Mini-Mental State Examination. *Journal of the American Geriatrics Society, 40,* 697–702.

Roman, G. C., Tatemichi, T. K., Erkinjuntti, T., Cummings, J. L., Masdeu, J. C., Garcia, J. H., Amaducci, L., Orgogozo, J. M., Brun, A., Hofman, A., Moody, D. M., O'Brien, M. D., Yamaguchi, T., Grafman, J., Drayer, B. P., Bennett, D. A., Fisher, M., Ogata, J., Kokmen, E., Bermejo, F., Wolf, P. A., Gorelick, P. B., Bick, K. L., Pajeau, A. K., Bell, M. A., DeCarli, C., Culebras, A., Korczyn, A. D., Bogousslavsky, J., Hartmann, A., and Scheinberg, P. (1993). Vascular dementia: Diagnostic criteria for research studies. Report of the NINDS-AIREN International Workshop. *Neurology, 43,* 250–260.

Romney, A. K., Shepard, R. N., and Nerlove, S. B. (1972). *Multidimensional Scaling: Theory and Applications in the Behavioral Sciences* (vol. 2). New York: Seminar Press.

Rorsman, B., Hagnell, O., and Lanke, J. (1986). Prevalence and incidence of senile and multi-infarct dementia in the Lundby Study: A comparison between the time periods 1947–1957 and 1957–1972. *Neuropsychobiology, 15,* 122–129.

Rosen, W. G., Terry, R. D., Fuld, P. A., Katzman, R., and Peck, A. (1980). Pathologic verification of ischemic score in differentiation of dementias. *Annals of Neurology, 7,* 486–488.

Rouleau, I., Salmon, D. P., and Butters, N. (in press). Longitudinal analysis of clock drawing in Alzheimer's disease patients. *Brain and Cognition.*

Rouleau, I., Salmon, D. P., Butters, N., Kennedy, C., and McGuire, K. (1992). Quantitative and qualitative analyses of clock drawings in Alzheimer's and Huntington's disease. *Brain and Cognition, 18,* 70–87.

Sagar, H. J., Cohen, N. J., Sullivan, E. V., Corkin, S., and Growdon, J. H. (1988). Remote memory function in Alzheimer's disease and Parkinson's disease. *Brain, 111,* 185–206.

Salmon, D. P., Butters, N., Thal, L. J., and Jeste, D. V. (in press). Alzheimer's disease: Analysis for the DSM-IV task force. In T. A. Widiger, A. Frances, and H. Pincus, eds., *DSM-IV Sourcebook* (vol. 4). Washington, D.C.: American Psychiatric Association.

Salmon, D. P., and Chan, A. S. (1994). Semantic memory deficits associated with Alzheimer's disease. In L. S. Cermak, ed., *Neuropsychological Explorations of Memory and Cognition: Essays in Honor of Nelson Butters.* New York: Plenum Press, pp. 61–76.

Salmon, D. P., Shimamura, A., Butters, N., and Smith, S. (1988). Lexical and semantic priming deficits in patients with Alzheimer's disease. *Journal of Clinical and Experimental Neuropsychology, 10,* 477–494.

Salmon, D. P., Thal, L. J., Butters, N., and Heindel, W. C. (1990). Longitudinal evaluation of dementia of the Alzheimer type: A comparison of 3 standardized mental status examinations. *Neurology, 40,* 1225–1230.

Saunders, A. M., Strittmatter, W. J., Schmechel, D., St. George-Hyslop, P. H., Pericak-Vance, M. A., Joo, S. H., Rosi, B. L., Gusella, J. F., Crapper-MacLachlan, D. R., Alberts, M. J., Hulette, C., Crain, B., Goldgaber, D., and Roses, A. D. (1993). Association of apolipoprotein E allele ε4 with late-onset familial and sporadic Alzheimer's disease. *Neurology, 43,* 1467–1472.

Schacter, D. L. (1987). Implicit memory: History and current status. *Journal of Experimental Psychology. Learning, Memory, and Cognition, 13,* 501–518.

Schacter, D. L., and Tulving, E. (1994). *Memory Systems 1994.* Cambridge, MA: MIT Press.

Schieber, F. (1992). Aging and the senses. In J. E. Birren, R. B. Sloane, and G. D. Cohen, eds., *Handbook of Mental Health and Aging.* San Diego: Academic Press, pp. 251–306.

Schmidt, M. L., Murray, J., Lee, V.M.-Y., Hill, W. D., Wertkin, A., and Trojanowski, J. Q. (1991). Epitote map of neurofilament protein domains in cortical and peripheral nervous system Lewy bodies. *American Journal of Pathology, 139,* 53–65.

Shepard, R. N., Romney, A. K., and Nerlove, S. B. (1972). *Multidimensional Scaling: Theory and Applications in the Behavioral Sciences* (vol. 1). New York: Seminar Press.

Shibayama, H., Kasahara, Y., and Kobayashi, H. (1986). Prevalence of dementia in a Japanese elderly population. *Acta Psychiatrica Scandinavica, 74,* 144–151.

Shimamura, A. P., Salmon, D. P., Squire, L. R., and Butters, N. (1987). Memory dysfunction and word priming in dementia and amnesia. *Behavioral Neuroscience, 101,* 347–351.

Smalley, S. L., Wolkenstein, B. H., La Rue, A., Woodward, J. A., Jarvik, L. F., and Matsuyama, S. S. (1992). Commingling analysis of memory performance in offspring of Alzheimer patients. *Genetic Epidemiology, 9,* 333–345.

Smith, S. R., Murdoch, B. E., and Chenery, H. J. (1989). Semantic abilities in dementia of the Alzheimer type: 1. Lexical semantics. *Brain and Language, 36,* 314–324.

Smyer, M. A. (1988). The nursing home community. In M. A. Smyer, M. D. Cohn, and D. Brannon, eds., *Mental Health Consultation in Nursing Homes.* New York: New York University Press, pp. 1–23.

Spreen, O., and Strauss, E. (1991). *A Compendium of Neuropsychological Tests: Administration, Norms, and Commentary.* New York: Oxford University Press.

Squire, L. R., Knowlton, B., and Musen, G. (1993). The structure and organization of memory. *Annual Review of Psychology, 44,* 453–495.

Squire, L. R. (1987). *Memory and Brain.* New York: Oxford University Press.

Stern, Y., Alexander, G. E., Prohovnik, I., and Mayeux, R. (1992). Inverse relationship between education and parietotemporal perfusion deficit in Alzheimer's disease. *Annals of Neurology, 32,* 371–375.

Stern, Y., Gurland, B., Tatemichi, T. K., Tang,

M. X., Wilder, D., and Mayeux, R. (1994). Influence of education and occupation on the incidence of Alzheimer's disease. *Journal of the American Medical Association, 271,* 1004–1010.

Storandt, M. (1977). Age, ability level, and method of administering and scoring the WAIS. *Journal of Gerontology, 32,* 175–178.

Storandt, M. (1994). General principles of assessment of older adults. In M. Storandt and G. R. VandenBos, eds., *Neuropsychological Assessment of Dementia and Depression in Older Adults: A Clinician's Guide.* Washington, D.C.: American Psychological Association, pp. 7–32.

Storandt, M., Botwinick, J., Danziger, W. L., Berg, L., and Hughes, C. P. (1984). Psychometric differentiation of mild senile dementia of the Alzheimer type. *Archives of Neurology, 41,* 497–499.

Storandt, M., and Hill, R. D. (1989). Very mild senile dementia of the Alzheimer type. II. Psychometric test performance. *Archives of Neurology, 46,* 383–386.

Strittmatter, W. J., Saunders, A. M., Schmechel, D., Pericak-Vance, M., Enghild, J., Salvesen, G. S., and Roses, A. D. (1993). Apolipoprotein-E—High-avidity binding to β-amyloid and increased frequency of type 4 allele in late-onset familial Alzheimer disease. *Proceedings of the National Academy of Sciences USA, 90,* 1977–1981.

Strub, R. L., and Black, F. W. (1988). *Neurobehavioral Disorders: A Clinical Approach.* Philadelphia: F. A. Davis Company.

Teri, L., Hughes, J. P., and Larson, E. B. (1990). Cognitive deterioration in Alzheimer's disease: Behavioral and health factors. *Journal of Gerontology, 45,* P58–63.

Terry, R. D., and Katzman, R. (1983). Senile dementia of the Alzheimer type. *Annals of Neurology, 14,* 497–506.

Terry, R. D., Katzman, R., and Bick, K. L. (1994). *Alzheimer Disease.* New York: Raven Press.

Terry, R. D., Masliah, E., Salmon, D. P., Butters, N., DeTeresa, R., Hill, R., Hansen, L. A., and Katzman, R. (1991). Physical basis of cognitive alterations in Alzheimer's disease: Synapse loss is the major correlate of cognitive impairment. *Annals of Neurology, 30,* 572–580.

Terry, R. D., Peck, A., DeTeresa, R., Schechter, R., and Horoupian, D. S. (1981). Some morphometric aspects of the brain in senile dementia of the Alzheimer type. *Annals of Neurology, 10,* 184–192.

Thal, L. J., Grundman, M., and Klauber, M. R.

(1988). Dementia: Characteristics of a referral population and factors associated with progression. *Neurology, 38,* 1083–1090.

Tombaugh, T. N., and McIntyre, N. J. (1992). The Mini-Mental State Examination: A comprehensive review. *Journal of the American Geriatrics Society, 40,* 922–935.

Tröster, A. I., Butters, N., Salmon, D. P., Cullum, C. M., Jacobs, D., Brandt, J., and White, R. F. (1993). The diagnostic utility of savings scores: Differentiating Alzheimer's and Huntington's diseases with the logical memory and visual reproduction tests. *Journal of Clinical and Experimental Neuropsychology, 15,* 773–788.

Tröster, A. I., Jacobs, D., Butters, N., Cullum, C. M., and Salmon, D. P. (1989). Differentiating Alzheimer's disease from Huntington's disease with the Wechsler Memory Scale-Revised. *Clinics in Geriatric Medicine, 5,* 611–632.

Tversky, A., and Hutchinson, J. W. (1986). Nearest neighbor analysis of psychological spaces. *Psychological Review, 93,* 3–22.

van Duijn, C. M., de Knijff, P., Cruts, M., Wehnert, A., Havekes, L. M., Hofman, A., and Van Broeckhoven, C. (1994). Apolipoprotein E4 allele in a population-based study of early-onset Alzheimer's disease. *Nature Genetics, 7,* 74–78.

van Duijn, C. M., Hofman, A., and Kay, D. W., Eds. (1991). Risk factors for Alzheimer's disease: A collaborative re-analysis of case-control studies. *International Journal of Epidemiology, 20,* No. 2 (Suppl. 2).

Van Gorp, W. G., Satz, P., Kiersch, M. E., and Henry, R. (1986). Normative data on the Boston Naming Test for a group of normal older adults. *Journal of Clinical and Experimental Neuropsychology, 8,* 702–705.

Vannieuwkirk, R. R., and Galbraith, G. G. (1985). The relationship of age to performance on the Luria-Nebraska Neuropsychological Battery. *Journal of Clinical Psychology, 41,* 527–532.

Vonsattel, J.-P., Myers, R. H., Stevens, T. J., Ferrante, R. J., Bird, E. D., and Richardson, E. P., Jr. (1985). Neuropathological classification of Huntington's disease. *Journal of Neuropathology and Experimental Neurology, 44,* 559–577.

Wechsler, D. (1981). *Manual for the Wechsler Adult Intelligence Scale-Revised.* New York: Psychological Corporation.

Weinstein, B. E., and Amsel, L. (1986). Hearing loss and senile dementia in the institutionalized elderly. *Clinical Gerontologist, 4,* 3–15.

Welsh, K., Butters, N., Hughes, J., Mohs, R., and Heyman, A. (1991). Detection of abnormal memory decline in mild cases of Alzheimer's disease using CERAD neuropsychological measures. *Archives of Neurology, 48,* 278–281.

Welsh, K., Butters, N., Hughes, J., Mohs, R., and Heyman, A. (1992). Detection and staging of dementia in Alzheimer's disease: Use of the neuropsychological measures developed for the Consortium to Establish a Registry for Alzheimer's Disease. *Archives of Neurology, 49,* 448–452.

Whitehouse, P. J., Price, D. L., Struble, R. G., Clark, A. W., Coyle, J. T., and DeLong, M. R. (1982). Alzheimer's disease and senile dementia: Loss of neurons in the basal forebrain. *Science, 215,* 1237–1239.

Wilkinson, R. T., and Allison, S. (1989). Age and simple reaction time: Decade differences for 5,325 subjects. *Journal of Gerontology, 44,* P29–P35.

Williams, J. M. (1987). *Cognitive Behavior Rating Scales: Manual, Research Edition.* Odessa, FL: Psychological Assessment Resources.

Williams, J. M., Klein, K., Little, M., and Haban, G. (1986). Family observations of everyday cognitive impairment in dementia. *Archives of Clinical Neuropsychology, 1,* 103–109.

Wilson, R. S., Bacon, L. D., Fox, J. H., and

Kaszniak, A. W. (1983). Primary memory and secondary memory in dementia of the Alzheimer type. *Journal of Clinical Neuropsychology, 5,* 337–344.

Wilson, R. S., Kaszniak, A. W., and Fox, J. H. (1981). Remote memory in senile dementia. *Cortex, 17,* 41–48.

Zec, R. F. (1990). Neuropsychology: Normal aging versus early AD. In R. E. Becker and E. Giacobini, eds., *Alzheimer Disease: Current Research in Early Diagnosis.* New York: Taylor and Francis, pp. 105–117.

Zec, R. F. (1993). Neuropsychological functioning in Alzheimer's disease. In R. W. Parks, R. F. Zec, and R. S. Wilson, eds., *Neuropsychology of Alzheimer's Disease and Other Dementias.* New York: Oxford University Press, pp. 3–80.

Zhang, M. Y., Katzman, R., Salmon, D. P., Jin, H., Cai, G. J., Wang, Z. Y., Qu, G. Y., Grant, I., Yu, E., Levy, P., Kauber, M., and Liu, W. T. (1990). The prevalence of dementia and Alzheimer's disease (AD) in Shanghai, China: Impact on age, gender and education. *Annals of Neurology, 27,* 428–437.

Zola-Morgan, S., and Squire, L. R. (1990). The primate hippocampal formation: Evidence for a time-limited role in memory storage. *Science, 250,* 288–290.

9 Cognitive Impairment and Major Depression: Beyond the Pseudodementia Syndrome

DEBORAH A. KING and ERIC D. CAINE

When the first edition of this text was published 10 years ago, "pseudodementia" was a major concern. Clinicians, and a few researchers, sought to define specific features that would separate progressive neurodegenerative diseases (so-called "organic" conditions) from psychiatric ("functional") syndromes that would respond to treatment. We do not use the term "pseudodementia" anymore.

During the early and mid-1980s, there had been few controlled studies of the cognitive deficits associated with major mood disturbances. Since then, there has been what seems like a yearly exponential increase. Investigators have focused primarily on qualitative and quantitative characterization of neuropsychological abnormalities, especially among subjects with major depression, using both standardized procedures and experimental methods, comparing psychiatric subjects to healthy controls and to groups of patients with defined neurodegenerative diseases. For some researchers, there is no question that major depression, especially in older persons, is often associated with significant, reproducible intellectual deficits that are indicative of disordered brain function. We are in that camp. For others, however, that confident assertion rings hollow. We will consider their views as well.

When authors began to consider nearly two decades ago the quantitative (Folstein et al., 1975) and the qualitative (Caine, 1981)

features of neuropsychological dysfunction associated with depression, they represented a distinct minority view, one that pointed to clinically and pathobiologically meaningful changes in cognitive processes as a central component of major mood disturbance. Considering the shifts that have taken place since then, it now appears that most investigators accept the general notion that depression is associated with cognitive abnormalities, but there are many unresolved questions and controversies about their extent (severity), quality (pattern), or permanence; their association with age and medical comorbidity; and how commonly they occur across the range of depressive conditions, from subsyndromal (minor) depression, to dysthymia and major depression, to melancholia and psychotic depression. As well, investigators are now identifying physiological states (or are they traits?) and morphological differences between depressives and healthy controls using in vivo brain imaging techniques. Are these also associated with neuropsychological alterations? The necessary studies have yet to be done.

A major factor contributing to the abundant controversy about the effects of depression on neuropsychological functioning has been the failure of many investigators to clearly define who they were studying and for what purpose. As investigators have begun to focus more on elderly depressed patients, they have been confronted with the increased cognitive and medical heterogeneity inherent to the aging process (Nelson and Dannefer, 1992; Caine et al., 1993; Rediess and Caine, 1993). Only when we understand the interface between the cognitive effects of depression and the cognitive effects of aging will we be able to sort out the variability of findings in the field (Jorm, 1986).

This chapter develops a framework for organizing and approaching the expanding literature on the neuropsychology of depression. It is not our aim, however, to exhaustively review all of the studies that have emerged in this area; rather we provide a view of the variety of approaches that have been used to investigate the neuropsychology of clinically significant depressive disorders.

At least four distinct approaches have guided these investigations to date. Each has carried its own set of assumptions about the possible relationship between depression and intellectual function, as well as a particular emphasis on a population or populations for study. The early work on "pseudodementia" consisted largely of uncontrolled *clinical/anecdotal studies* that aimed to discriminate reversible depression from progressive brain disease. *Descriptive and comparative neuropsychological studies* have continued to differentiate categorical depression from other neurologic and psychiatric illnesses, along with normal control groups, operating from the assumption that there are distinguishable cognitive boundaries between illnesses and, naturally, focusing on patients with demonstrable neuro- or psychopathology. Another approach has used neuropsychological and neuropsychiatric methods to investigate possible neural substrates of depressive illness. Although we refer to this tradition as the *experimental neuropsychological approach,* the phrase is used in a broad sense to include some of the neuropsychiatric methodologies (e.g., imaging techniques) that have helped to elucidate behavior-brain relationships in depression. Finally, *cognitive psychological investigations* have had the primary aim of testing theoretical models of information processing, rather than focusing on a particular pathology and seeking to define its features.

Originally, this approach involved the study of nonclinical populations in order to define a template of how "normal" processing occurs. More recently, the cognitive psychological approach has been applied to clinically depressed individuals. We will review representative cognitive models that have demonstrated direct applicability to depression and to the aging process.

Throughout this chapter we will focus on investigations of patients with unipolar major depression (DSM-III-R), unless otherwise specified. As we review these studies from the four major "traditions," we will also consider conceptual and methodological issues pertinent to future research.

Clinical/Anecdotal Studies

In the first edition this chapter reviewed a series of studies conducted largely from the 1960s through the early 1980s by psychiatrists and neurologists who had the practical aim of distinguishing treatable patients from those with irreversible disease. Subjects were drawn from patient populations flowing through clinical services. Working from a practical vantage point, these investigators assumed that "reversibility" was a cornerstone concept in defining the so-called pseudodementia syndrome when they described poorly defined or heterogenous groups of psychiatric patients (e.g., Kiloh, 1961; Wells, 1979; Caine, 1981). These studies were useful in raising clinicians' index of suspicion about the dangers of misdiagnosing psychiatric patients as being demented, particularly those suffering from affective disorders. As well, they began to point to the complexity of attempting to define a distinct boundary between the so-called functional psychiatric disorders and the "organic" disorders. However, they were uncontrolled, descriptive series that oftentimes failed to define adequately the characteristics of their subjects. Most importantly, these types of studies generally accepted the untested assumption that the cognitive dysfunction associated with depression was reversible, in contrast to dementing disorders, despite indications that the intellectual deficits in question persisted in some study participants (Caine, 1981). These assumptions have not always held up well in relation to the severely depressed or to depressed elders, as seen in later studies. While this approach to research has largely disappeared, it proved valuable for stimulating more carefully controlled investigations of the neuropsychology of major depression. Some assumptions may have been proven incorrect, or at least partially so; others (e.g., regarding a subcortical pattern of intellectual impairment) have yet to be addressed fully, but have stimulated potentially productive lines of more carefully conceived research.

Descriptive and Comparative Neuropsychological Methods

Since the early 1980s, investigators increasingly have used quantitative neuropsychological methods to describe more fully the characteristics of strictly defined samples of patients suffering from major depression. Most work has excluded individuals with comorbid diseases, although recently researchers have turned their attention to characterizing cognitive deficits in subjects with bipolar disorder or primary neurological diseases. (We will not review the latter types of studies here.) We focus on controlled studies of various aspects or stages of memory processing in young and elderly subjects. As well, we selectively review "nonspecific" studies that compared depressives with patient groups on a range of neuropsychological functions.

Descriptive researchers often have studied memory exclusively, perhaps because of the high frequency of memory complaints among depressives (e.g., Zarit et al., 1981; Popkin et al., 1982). Investigations of stages of memory processing generally have attempted to discriminate retrieval deficits from encoding or retention deficits; one relatively crude method of making the differentiation has involved comparison of prompted recall (e.g., recognition memory) versus spontaneous or uncued testing of recall. It must be noted, however, that impairment on recognition testing may be the result of deficient encoding, as well as impaired retrieval processes.

Early clinical anecdotal observations suggested that depressives would have deficits primarily on spontaneous tasks because they involved more active or effortful retrieval from the memory store (Caine, 1981; Cummings and Benson, 1983). The suggestion that recognition memory was unaffected among subjects with major depression was supported by some investigations that studied, for the most part, outpatient samples that were mildly to moderately depressed and varied as to diagnostic subtype (Miller and Lewis, 1977; Niederehe and Camp, 1985). These studies also reported that depressives, in comparison to age- and education-matched controls, were characterized by a conservative style of responding rather than true memory impairment. Neither of these widely cited studies controlled for intellectual level, and the study by Miller and Lewis was not controlled for education, perhaps introducing variance that obscured important differences between groups. Another, more carefully controlled investigation by Dunbar and Lishman (1984) found no difference in recognition memory between young (mean age = 41.7 years) inpatient depressives and well-matched controls, although the depressed group was selected more broadly for "depressive illness" (Feighner criteria) rather than for major depression.

More recently, there have been several controlled studies with more severely depressed patients that have challenged the contention that recognition memory is unimpaired in these subjects. Watts and colleagues (1987) reported deficient recognition of words (presented once in 20-word lists) in a group of 36 young depressives (mean age = 37 years) compared to 24 age- and education-matched controls, even when intellectual level was controlled. Although the study must be interpreted with caution because patients were selected on the basis of a questionnaire (known to be highly correlated with DSM major depression), all patients had depression as a primary diagnosis and 75% were classified as having an endogenous pattern depression. Wolfe and colleagues (1987) found deficits in both immediate recall and recognition performance on the Rey Auditory Verbal Learning Test (RAVLT) in 20 young to middle-aged (mean age = 45.7 years) unipolar depressed inpatients compared with 20 age- and education-matched normal controls, although the depressives' deficits were less severe than those of patients with Huntington's disease or bipolar depression. As well, these authors reported that the depressed group had a significantly more liberal response style (i.e., a higher rate of "false alarms") than controls, indicating that their deficits could not be attributed to a conservative strategy, as suggested by earlier studies. Similarly, using a modification of the RAVLT, Brand and colleagues (1992) reported that a group of 24 young to middle-aged depressives (mean age = 41.9 years; most of whom were hospitalized) was deficient on immediate and delayed recall, and on recognition testing when the initial stimulus word list was presented for only one learning trial. However, only immediate recall was impaired when three learning trials were presented instead. Although intellectual level was not controlled in these two more recent studies, their findings with relatively young patients suggested that both encoding and retrieval deficits were present among the type of severely depressed patients who are admitted for hospital treatment. The results of Brand et al. suggested that one may need to constrain study conditions in these younger subjects (i.e., one learning trial versus three) in order to demonstrate clear results.

Several studies have investigated memory in older depressives compared to patients with progressive brain disease. Hart and colleagues (1987a) used a selective reminding procedure to compare 14 elderly depressed outpatients (mean age = 70.1 years) with 15 age- and education-matched patients with mild Alzheimer's disease (AD) and 16 controls. The depressives were impaired relative to controls on total recall and proportion of items retained from one trial to the next without reminding; as well, they were significantly different from controls in terms of their failure to benefit from imagery in retaining items. The depressives did not differ from controls on a test of delayed recogni-

tion, although ceiling effects made this result difficult to interpret. The depressives' memory performance was significantly superior to that of AD patients in all respects except for their failure to benefit from imagery. La Rue (1989) compared the performance of 41 elderly depressed inpatients (mean age not given by group) and 19 age- and education-matched AD patients using a different selective reminding task, the Fuld Object Memory Evaluation. As in the previous study, AD patients' overall performance was more severely impaired than that of depressives. However, the two groups could not be distinguished in terms of qualitative patterns of performance and both groups were impaired on a measure of delayed recognition. The depressives scored significantly below normative levels on all measures derived from initial learning and recall trials, as well as on the delayed recognition measure. Several methodologic differences between these studies might have accounted for the more pervasive deficits revealed by the latter study, including the fact that La Rue studied more severely depressed inpatients. However, both studies must be interpreted with caution because of a failure to control for intellectual level.

Hart and colleagues (1987b) also compared mild AD patients with elderly depressives (mean age = 70.1 years) in terms of rate of forgetting line drawings in a recognition memory paradigm. Although both depressed and AD patients demonstrated difficulty in learning the drawings, only the AD group had difficulty remembering the items 10 minutes after learning them to criterion. The authors concluded that the depressives had difficulty in the acquisition phase of learning, but not in consolidation or retention of learned information. This study found that depressed and AD patients were similar on intellectual testing, but significantly lower than controls. Therefore, the reported differences between the depressed and control subjects must be interpreted cautiously.

Niederehe (1986) provided a thoughtful review of the literature on memory function in depressed elderly and presented the results of a series of episodic, semantic, and constructive memory experiments performed by 24 mildly to moderately depressed elderly (mean age = 64.9 years) and 24 young (mean age = 30.8 years) outpatients with major or minor depression who were screened to exclude those with "evidence of diagnosable brain dysfunction" on a brief nonmemory testing battery. The depressives were compared to 48 age- and education-matched controls, although the older groups obtained higher scores on the Peabody Picture Vocabulary Test. The studies revealed significant effects of age on a variety of memory measures, but few effects of depression and a lack of depression-by-age interactions. As with other studies of less severely depressed outpatients, the depressives demonstrated conservative response styles and greater perceptions of memory difficulties.

What can one conclude about memory and depression from these various descriptive studies? First, as pointed out previously by Niederehe (1986) and by Weingartner (1986), there are dramatic differences in findings depending on the characteristics of the depressed sample. Severity of depression and/or hospitalization status seem to be critical methodological variables that consistently distinguish studies with positive findings from those with negative findings. Mildly to moderately depressed outpatients have fewer memory difficulties, although they are likely to be cautious in response strategy and concerned about their memory abilities. The more severe the disorder, or the greater the number of hospitalized patients in the sample, the greater the probability of finding significant memory deficits (i.e., both acquisition and retrieval processes when compared to controls). Some of the findings, especially those with younger patients, suggest that recognition memory is more likely to be deficient in depression when fewer learning trials are presented. That is, the depressed patient is less efficient in encoding information, but can perform adequately when given sufficient opportunity to compensate for or overcome their inefficiency. There is less evidence for a true retention deficit in major depression. It is important to note that we do not know whether the

critical variable differentiating studies is simply severity of the depressive illness (reflected by inpatient versus outpatient status), or whether there are other variables associated with hospitalization that influence cognitive functioning (Rohling and Scogin, 1993).

This review of comparative memory studies in depression has revealed considerable discrepancy across investigators as to what is considered adequate and appropriate control of potentially confounding variables. Most control for the effects of psychotropic medications, age, sex, and educational level on cognition, but relatively few control or test for effects of general intelligence. Obviously, matching on IQ is problematic in comparisons involving patients with primary dementia, but it is important for investigations to account for this variable when interpreting cognitive differences between depressed and nondepressed groups. As well, there is a surprising lack of control for nondepressive psychopathology in these and other neuropsychological studies; it is presently unclear whether the deficits reviewed here are specific to major depression or related to psychiatric illness in general.

Caine's (1981) early anecdotal survey of young and middle-aged depressed inpatients suggested that their inattention, slowed mental processing, and decreased verbal elaboration fit a "subcortical" pattern that could be clearly distinguished from the pattern of "higher cortical" dysfunction demonstrated by patients with primary degenerative dementia (Cummings and Benson, 1984). We reviewed previously studies that supported this point of view with regard to young and middle-aged depressives (King and Caine, 1990). Similarly, Weingartner (1986) posited that depressives' selective dysfunction in effort-demanding processing (see "Cognitive Psychological Approaches" below) involves a subcortically mediated system that regulates arousal and activation (and is possibly related to noradrenergic and dopaminergic systems). More recently, Massman and colleagues (1992) conducted a unique investigation of the subcortical hypothesis using indices from the California Verbal Learning

Test (CVLT) that were known to distinguish the memory performance of Huntington's disease (HD) patients, AD patients, and controls. Their study included 40 moderately depressed patients (mean age = 46.1 years), 20 HD patients, 20 AD patients, 9 bipolar patients, and 40 normal controls. Age and education were controlled except that the AD group was significantly older. To control for age and sex differences across groups, standardized CVLT scores stratified for age and sex were used. A discriminant function analysis (DFA) that included measures of immediate recall, intrusions (nontarget items), and the difference between recognition discriminability and free recall on the final learning trial (an index of the ability to benefit from cuing) successfully differentiated the HD, AD, and control groups. Application of the same DFA to the unipolar depressives resulted in classification of 12 of the depressives as "HDs" (DEP–HD) and 28 as "normals" (DEP–NC), revealing the significant heterogeneity of memory performance in the depressed group. Like the HD patients, the DEP–HDs were characterized by significant recall deficits, inefficient learning across trials, and reduced use of learning strategies. Although their performance improved on recognition testing, they remained mildly impaired, suggesting the existence of mild encoding deficits along with more severe retrieval problems. Among the deficits on other neuropsychological tasks, the DEP–HD group was mildly deficient on a confrontation naming task until phonemic cues were presented to aid retrieval. Although a significant proportion of the depressives were diagnosed with alcoholism, neither this factor nor most other clinical variables were related to classification of patients in the HD group or to performance on the neuropsychological variables. There was, however, a trend for DEP–HD patients to have an earlier age of onset than DEP–NC patients.

This study reinforced the observations by others (Cassens et al., 1990; King and Caine, 1990) of marked heterogeneity in subjects' cognitive function that characterized research subjects with categorically diagnosed depression. Although it was unclear whether

intelligence was controlled or whether the depressives were inpatients or outpatients, the study also provided important tentative evidence that a subset of young to middle-aged depressives exhibited a pattern of cognitive deficits similar to that of patients with prototypical "subcortical" disease.

Yet one must be extremely careful when interpreting such findings. Two cautioning points are apparent. The designations "subcortical" and "cortical" dementia are pseudo-anatomical descriptions of clinical conditions; they are meant to describe patterns or arrays of signs and symptoms, based upon presumptive pathological anatomies. Early in the course of many disease processes, clinicians may detect differences in the gestalt or holistic presentations of their patients, but these conditions evolve and one must be sensitive to the substantial overlap of these clinical pictures. Distinction on the basis of one domain of cognitive processing (i.e., explicit verbal memory), however central to overall intellectual functioning, falls short of the broad patterns described by these clinical terms. Many investigators doubt whether dementing disorders can be separated qualitatively and quantitatively (Brown and Marsden, 1988), and while we see clinical utility in the terms, it is clear to us that meaningful separation should cut across or include multiple cognitive measures. Second, neuroanatomical and neuropathological studies during the past two decades have underscored the multitude of reciprocal cerebral cortical-subcortical neural pathways. Were one to avoid pseudoanatomical terms and try to convey the intended clinical patterns of these disorders at the same time, terms such as "modulatory" dementia and "linguistic-gnostic-practic" dementia might be more effectively descriptive (Caine, 1986). Major depression, like HD, might be a candidate for the former. However, the cognitive picture remains muddled, as further illustrated by other important studies.

Speedie and colleagues (1990) investigated memory and naming performance in elderly depressed inpatients (DSM-III major depression), dementia patients, and controls who were classified according to scores on the Mini-Mental State Exam (MMSE; Folstein et al., 1975) before and after treatment. Twenty-one elderly depressives with "normal cognition" (MMSE ≥24, mean age = 69.9 years), 18 patients with "dementia of depression" (MMSE <24 pretreatment and ≥24 after treatment, mean age = 72 years), 22 patients with idiopathic irreversible dementia—presumed Alzheimer's disease (not depressed, MMSE <24)—and 17 controls were matched for age and education, but not for intelligence. Depressed patients who had been classified as cognitively normal performed worse than controls on a delayed verbal recognition task, but not on a confrontation naming task. Patients with dementia of depression performed worse than controls (and the other depressed group) on all verbal memory measures and *on confrontation naming,* but not on a visual recognition memory task. Dementia patients performed worse than the other groups on all measures, except that their performance on confrontation naming could not be distinguished from the cognitively impaired depressed group.

King and colleagues (1991a) attempted to distinguish the neuropsychological performance of 23 elderly depressed inpatients (mean age = 70.8 years) from 20 mildly to moderately advanced AD patients and 23 healthy controls. All groups were matched for age, sex, and education, but not for intellectual level. The depressives were less impaired than AD patients on language, memory, and copying tasks. Nevertheless, when compared with controls, the depressives were deficient on word generation tasks, immediate and delayed recall of a 10-word list, delayed list recognition, and delayed recall of geometric shapes. Moreover, there was a greater negative effect of age on depressives' performance of confrontation naming and immediate recall of geometric shapes.

Like the findings from studies of the stages of memory processing, these general descriptive studies must be interpreted cautiously because of failure to control for intelligence or nondepressive psychopathology. Nevertheless, the results obtained with older patients challenged contentions based upon earlier clinical/anecdotal reports (Caine, 1981; Cummings and Benson, 1983) that the cognitive effects of depression were circumscribed and associated primarily with attention-demanding tasks. The present work also pointed to a more complex array of cognitive deficits. With regard to naming, other controlled studies have failed to find a significant effect of depression. One such report used unspecified methods to screen out depressed patients with cognitive impairment thought to reflect "pseudodementia" (Emery and Breslau, 1989). Another carefully controlled study included only treatment responders and failed to find significant naming deficits in an elderly depressed inpatient sample (Hill et al., 1992).

In a pilot study of 15 of the elderly depressed patients described earlier, King et al. (1991b) reported that lower scores on pretreatment confrontation naming predicted more severe depression at 6-month follow-up. Moreover, there was not a significant change in naming performance after treatment, despite significant improvement in the level of depression in the group as a whole. Contrary to the assumption of many studies conducted from the clinical/anecdotal or descriptive neuropsychological perspectives, this initial pilot study found that some of the cognitive deficits associated with late-life depression did not change following effective treatment of the disordered mood state, and suggested that they may have been markers of subtle brain dysfunction that influenced the onset or course of the depressive illness. Viewed from another perspective, these findings also raised the question of whether some degree of impairment reflected a fundamental or lasting "trait," one that did not vary solely depending on the level of mood disturbance. It was unlikely that these patients had an undiagnosed progressive dementia; clinical follow-up of nearly all the patients for at least 2 years failed to detect cognitive decline or functional deficits consistent with a widespread dementing disease process. At this time, the question of dysnomia among elderly major depressives remains unresolved.

The Experimental Neuropsychological Approach

During the past decade, investigators have begun to search for the neurobiological substrates of major depression by defining specific correlates of its cognitive features. It is uncertain how widely applicable this method will be, given the variability of findings that we have described, but this line of work promises to provide insights about the pathobiological brain substrates of mood disturbances in many subjects.

Consistent with the subcortical model of depressive deficits, several investigators have reported physiological abnormalities of the basal ganglia using positron-emission tomography (PET; Baxter et al., 1985) and morphological differences revealed by magnetic resonance imaging (MRI; Coffey et al., 1989; Rabins et al., 1991; Krishnan et al., 1992). However, some of these studies also have reported cortical abnormalities related to depression (Coffey et al., 1989; Rabins et al., 1991).

More specific cognitive–brain correlative findings are especially intriguing. In a controlled computed tomographic (CT) study of 28 elderly depressed inpatients, compared with 13 AD patients and 31 controls (all groups matched for age, sex, and education), Pearlson and colleagues (1989) reported an association of greater ventricular brain ratio to decreased performance on immediate verbal recall (from the RAVLT) in the AD group and in a subgroup of the depressives selected for reversible deficit on the MMSE. Dolan et al. (1992) compared 10 elderly RDC diagnosed major depressives with cognitive impairment (MMSE ≤25) with 10 who had MMSE ≥29 using measures of regional cerebral blood flow derived from PET. The former had decreased blood flow in the left anterior medial prefrontal cortex and increased blood flow in the cerebellar vermis.

There is significant neuropsychological, electrophysiological, and cognitive experimental research that suggests lateralized cerebral deficits in depression (see Silberman and Weingartner, 1986; Cassens et al., 1990,

for reviews). Early neuropsychological studies reporting selective deficits of the nondominant hemisphere were difficult to interpret because of methodological problems, such as failure to include control groups or failure to control for educational level or intelligence. As discussed by Kluger and Goldberg (1990), many of these investigations also failed to control for different time constraints or levels of difficulty across purported right and left hemisphere tasks. More recent studies have eliminated or tested for these potential confounds. Deptula and colleagues (1991) reported an asymmetry in recall performance of 28 young (mean age = 34.2 years) hospitalized major depressives (eight of whom were bipolar) compared to a well-matched group of 14 controls; their verbal recall was superior to nonverbal recall. In a well-controlled study of 100 patients (mean age = 55.5 years) in an episode of endogenous major depression (SADS criteria), Sackheim and colleagues (1992) demonstrated that the depressives' deficit in performance IQ relative to verbal IQ could not be solely attributed to time constraints (34 patients were retested without time constraints and still demonstrated this pattern). Additionally, 33 patients who were retested 2 months after their last ECT treatment still demonstrated a superiority of verbal functions. The authors suggested that the verbal–performance IQ discrepancy of major depressives is a state-independent or trait phenomenon that may be due to bilateral or right-sided cerebral dysfunction.

Some investigators have begun to correlate neuropsychological performance in depression with indices of disorders in neurochemical systems. For example, Rubinow and colleagues (1984) reported that dysregulation of the hypothalamic-pituitary-adrenal (HPA) axis, as detected by increased mean 24-hour free cortisol excretion, was associated with errors on the Halstead-Reitan Category Test in a mixed group of unipolar and bipolar major depressives. Siegel's group (1989) reported an association of greater cognitive deterioration (on the Global Deterioration Scale) with post-dexamethasone cortisol levels in an uncontrolled study of elderly (mean age = 68 years) inpatients with major depression. Wolkowitz and coworkers (1990) found that depressed patients who did not suppress cortisol after dexamethasone made more errors of commission on a verbal recognition memory task compared to depressed suppressors and well-matched normal controls. Although other investigators have failed to find a relationship between HPA dysregulation and cognitive impairment in depression (Caine et al., 1984; Georgotas et al., 1986), these results have led investigators to suggest that HPA activity might be associated with the ability to selectively attend to information (i.e., to distinguish relevant from irrelevant information), perhaps through the effects of cortisol on the hippocampus.

Taken together, one may speculate from these studies that the purportedly subcortical type of cognitive deficits noted in young and middle-aged depressives may be associated with changes in the basal ganglia, whereas the deficits of depressed elderly may be associated with more widespread patterns of brain change. However, this conclusion remains highly tentative in the absence of more carefully controlled investigations that combine neuropsychological and brain imaging methods. Moreover, there is little evidence to date to tie specific types of neuropsychological dysfunction to focal brain regions. Indeed, this type of finding may not prove feasible, when considering that major mood disturbances (like both Huntington's disease and Alzheimer's disease) are likely the result(s) of disordered neurochemical systems rather than any focal or discrete abnormality. Thus one would need a methodology sensitive to potentially widespread neurobiological defects. Morphological abnormalities such as smaller caudate size may be a trait marker, or risk factor, but alone are insufficient to account for a disorder that typically has its onset in adulthood, waxes and wanes, and responds acutely to physiologically active pharmacotherapy. Future studies will likely require the combined application of morphological indices together with repeated measures using physiologically and neurochemically sensitive tools.

The Cognitive Psychological Approach

Cognitive psychological studies have focused on memory, for the most part, but have moved beyond the older question of *whether* memory fails, an issue fundamental to earlier clinical/anecdotal and descriptive/comparative approaches, to investigations of *how* memory fails. Our focus here is on models that have been demonstrated to be useful with both depressed and elderly subjects. Caine (1986) previously described the early work of Weingartner and colleagues that demonstrated the failure of young to middle-aged inpatient major depressives (both unipolar and bipolar) to spontaneously use learning strategies, although their performance improved significantly when processing cues were made inherent to the task at hand. The same group of investigators had found that verbal memory performance was highly correlated with the ability to sustain motor effort (Cohen et al., 1982).

These investigations, as well as the work by Hasher and Zacks (1979) that defined the distinction between "automatic" and "effortful" processing, triggered a flurry of interest in the hypothesis that depressives were selectively deficient in effortful (i.e., attention-demanding) processing (e.g., Roy-Byrne et al., 1986; Calev et al., 1989; Golinkoff and Sweeney, 1989; Tancer et al., 1989). Investigators operationalized the degree of "effortful" processing using concepts as varied as task difficulty, intentionality of processing, degree of structure inherent in the learning task, or specificity of retrieval demands. Despite this methodologic variability, most of the research supported the notion of greater memory deficit in depressives compared to healthy controls on tasks purported to be more effortful (Weingartner, 1986; Calev et al., 1989; Tancer et al., 1989; Danion et al., 1991). Unfortunately, many of the studies in this area were marred by methodologic or conceptual limitations, such as poorly defined or heterogeneous groups of depressives; failure to adequately control for important variables such as age, sex, or intelligence; failure to test the specificity of this concept to depression (as opposed to other psychiatric groups); or failure to adequately and consistently define the distinction between automatic and effortful processing on an a priori basis. These studies also used depressed samples whose average age was in the third, fourth, or fifth decades; the effects of older age were not addressed adequately.

The distinction between effortful and automatic processing posited by Hasher and Zacks (1979) is consistent with dual-process models of memory that distinguished between an intentional, conceptually driven, elaboration process and an automatic, data-driven, activation process (Jacoby, 1983; Graf and Mandler, 1984; Roediger, 1990; Tulving and Schacter, 1990). The former type of memory, known as explicit memory, includes direct tests of recall and recognition in which the subject is conscious of what is being tested. This type of memory requires conceptual processing, in that the event to be retrieved (e.g., a word) must be related to the context in which it occurred (e.g., the presentation of the word in a list). All of the research we have reviewed thus far from the clinical/anecdotal, descriptive neuropsychological, and experimental psychological approaches have involved tests of explicit memory. In contrast, implicit memory tasks do not necessarily involve the subject's awareness, but instead are based on unconscious activation of an item (e.g., a word) in the subject's lexicon that subsequently makes the item more accessible to consciousness. For example, subjects are more likely to succeed on tasks such as making words out of three-letter stems when they have had some recent exposure to the words (i.e., the repetition priming effect). Dissociation between explicit and implicit memory has been demonstrated in the elderly and in amnesic individuals (Light and Singh, 1987; Graf, 1990; Roediger, 1990; Howard, 1991; Tulving et al., 1991).

Studies of implicit memory and depression have typically asked subjects to rate lists of words on a dimension, such as whether they liked the word or whether the word applied to them, followed by a word completion task that tested priming effects. Subsequently,

free recall testing is conducted as a test of explicit memory. Danion and colleagues (1991) reported that 18 inpatients with unipolar major depression (mean age = 49 years) were impaired relative to 18 healthy controls matched for age, sex, and education on the explicit measure, but not the implicit measure. Similarly, Denny and Hunt (1992) found that 16 inpatient women with unipolar depression (mean age = 29 years) were impaired relative to age-matched controls on a free recall task (particularly recall for positive words) but demonstrated a similar priming effect.

In contrast to the findings of other investigators, Elliot and Greene (1992) demonstrated impaired explicit and implicit memory in a group of 10 major depressives (mean age = 31.5; six of 10 were inpatients) relative to 10 age-, sex-, and education-matched controls. Like the other investigations, this study used carefully diagnosed moderately to severely depressed patients and measured implicit memory by measuring the effects of priming on a word completion task. However, this investigation was unique in that subjects were only required to listen to presentation of words in the priming or exposure phase of the study. Danion et al. (1991) had instructed subjects to remember words prior to their immediate presentation in a list, then asked subjects to rate each word according to whether they liked or disliked it, and only then administered the word completion task. Denny and Hunt (1992) had not informed subjects of the need to remember words prior to the priming task, but they did require subjects to rate each word on the list according to "how well the word describes you or is consistent with what is happening in your life right now." Thus, subjects in these two studies were required to make conscious judgments of the words in the priming list prior to the implicit task, whereas subjects in the Elliot and Greene (1992) study were allowed to remain more passive in relation to the priming words. It is possible that the depressed subjects in this latter design did not listen to the words in the priming list, instead, for example, remaining focused on depressive ruminations extraneous to the experiment. Although the dual theory posits that conscious processing is not necessary for the demonstration of implicit memory, some degree of sensory processing of the list would seem necessary for activation effects to take place.

Despite the usefulness of the dual-process approach for further defining aspects of memory failure (i.e., explicit, elaborative processes) and preservation (i.e., implicit, automatic processes) in both depression and aging, we are not aware of studies that have examined directly the combined effects of mood disorder and age with respect to these cognitive operations. It remains to be seen whether individuals who are both very old and very depressed will show the same level of preservation of implicit memory as younger depressed individuals.

Another theory, one related to the distinction between automatic and effortful processing, is the contention that there is a fixed capacity or pool of resources available for attention-demanding (i.e., explicit) processing (Kahneman, 1973). It has been hypothesized that depressives have fewer resources available for conscious memory processing because of competition from depressive ruminations or a depression-related inability to filter out irrelevant aspects of a processing task (Ellis and Ashbrook, 1988; Channon et al., 1993). This approach has assumed that the learning of unstructured or poorly organized material demands more cognitive resources than the learning of material that has been organized (e.g., by clustering words in a list according to semantic properties). When applied to studies of memory and aging (Light and Anderson, 1985; Hasher and Zacks, 1988), or to mixed groups of bipolar and unipolar depressives (Weingartner et al., 1981; Silberman et al., 1983, Experiment 3), results have generally supported the proposition that depressives fail to use more effective learning strategies spontaneously, although they have the capacity to benefit from structure (e.g., semantic clustering) that is provided. Although several investigations of resource allocation and depression have been conducted using experimentally induced mood states (e.g., Leight

and Ellis, 1981; Hertel and Hardin, 1990), the generalizability of these studies to clinically depressed patients is questionable.

In a variation of this limited resource theme, several researchers have questioned whether the central deficit critical to depressives' poor performance on explicit memory tasks is reduced capacity (the ability to carry out attention-demanding tasks) or simply reduced initiation of processing strategies. Consistent with the original resource theory, the reduced initiative hypothesis predicts that depressives will not be impaired on highly structured tasks. In contrast to earlier resource accounts, however, the reduced initiative hypothesis predicts that depressives will show the greatest degree of deficit when attempting to learn material with a medium level of structure (where the spontaneous use of strategies would afford some benefit), rather than material with the least amount of inherent structure (where the use of strategies would not be beneficial). As predicted by this hypothesis, Channon and colleagues (1993) demonstrated that a group of 24 outpatients (mean age = 39 years) with unipolar major depression were impaired relative to nondepressed controls matched for age, sex, and intelligence on recall of material containing a medium degree of structure (i.e., semantically related words in randomized order), but not on recall of the most highly structured material (i.e., semantically related and clustered words) or unstructured material (i.e., semantically unrelated words). Providing further evidence that depressives have the capacity for intentional learning under more structured conditions, Hertel and Rude (1991) demonstrated that the deficits in verbal learning of a young (mean age = 41 years) group of depressed outpatients (22 with major depression, two with probable major depression, two with minor depression) resolved when the focus of attention was constrained by the requirements of the task.

Hasher and Zacks (1988) have proposed an age-related disturbance of inhibitory mechanisms that purportedly control the contents of working memory and help prevent task-irrelevant processing. Hertel and Rude

(1991) have proposed that this refinement of resource theory also accounts for the poorer performance of depressives on explicit, effortful memory tasks.

Another major area of cognitive psychological investigation is that of mood-congruent memory. Considerable evidence suggests that depressed mood is associated with enhanced memory for negatively toned material (see Blaney, 1986, for a review) and that this "bias" pertains exclusively to explicit memory processes in clinical depression (Denny and Hunt, 1992; Watkins et al., 1992). Although this line of research is promising in terms of its potential application for better understanding memory in major depression, much of the work conducted to date has involved induced mood states in nonclinical samples or heterogeneous groups of patients with varied forms of affective disorder.

Cognitive psychological approaches potentially have offered powerful theoretical and investigative tools to the overall study of the neuropsychology of depression. We anticipate that future research, perhaps under the broad umbrella of cognitive neuroscience (Lister and Weingartner, 1991) will combine these methods with approaches such as dynamic neuroimaging (e.g., PET), topographic mapping of average evoked responses, or study of the brain's magnetic fields to further reveal the brain bases of information processing in subjects with major depression.

Contrasting Views

Two recent reviews and commentaries have arrived at seemingly different conclusions than those presented here. Bieliauskas (1993) maintained that "depressive-like" symptoms in the elderly have little if any effect on cognitive abilities and that the case for "emotional influence" on these abilities has been greatly overstated. His conclusion is not surprising given that his report pertained, for the most part, to studies of elderly medical outpatients evaluated for depression using continuous measures of depressive symptoms, such as the Hamilton Depression Scale. As noted by previous investigators (Bornstein et al., 1991), this method is inadequate in that it does not select specifically for syndromically defined (DSM-III-R) major depression. Instead, it may include subjects with other clinically significant psychiatric syndromes, while failing to select for subjects with the type of severe categorical depression most likely to be associated with cognitive symptoms.

Based on a review of previous literature and new data from his own research group, Poon (1992) concluded that the effect of depression on older patients' cognitive abilities was not great. Again, as noted by Poon himself, characteristics of the depressed samples greatly influenced the findings. In his own study, the depressives and controls were screened to exclude those with "validated memory complaints." In the review of literature, studies were generally considered questionable if they did not use a cognitive screening measure to exclude patients who may have had a dementia. While we agree that cognitive screening measures may be useful for determining subgroups of depressed patients with and without cognitive symptoms, we believe that the exclusion of subjects based on cognitive test findings constitutes a confounding of independent and dependent variables.

Summary

We have presented a number of well-controlled investigations that clearly demonstrated depressives' deficits, especially in explicit verbal memory. Moreover, recent research has begun to point to both psychological and neurobiological mechanisms that may account for depression-associated cognitive dysfunction. Methodological differences across studies have contributed to confusion in the literature; most notably, the severity and/or inpatient status of the depressed sample and whether the sample was screened for cognitive impairment. Elsewhere, we have expressed our view that current methods of selecting samples of depressed patients for study has been overly restrictive; they minimize the variability of the effect being studied (Caine et al., 1993). This criticism applies as well to neuropsychological studies of depression that have attempted to first exclude dementing disorders principally by depending upon neuropsychological screening measures. Although it is critically important to make careful clinical judgments about potential subjects' diagnoses based on history and available information regarding medical, neurological, and functional status, it becomes a circular, potentially confounding process to use cognitive measures to define a group that will be studied neuropsychologically. At the same time, a less restrictive method might result in the inclusion of patients with undetected progressive neurodegenerative disease. For this reason it is imperative that subjects be followed longitudinally to ascertain whether theirs is a deteriorating course characteristic of Alzheimer's disease or multi-infarct dementia. While such an approach is time consuming, ultimately it enhances both validity (because of greater diagnostic certainty) and generalizability (because of the inclusion of a wider, more naturalistic range of subjects).

Although we have reported major progress in this area since the first edition of this book, few of the studies (especially those from the experimental and cognitive psychological perspectives) have grappled with Jorm's (1986) challenge to define the nature of the relationships between depression, aging, and cognition. First steps have been made that suggest that depressives may be more vulnerable to age effects on some tasks (Raskin, 1986; King et al., 1993), although recent studies of less severely depressed outpatients have failed to reveal interactive effects of depression and age (Boone et al., 1994; Lyness et al., 1994). These findings must be interpreted cautiously because of the use of a limited range of tests, failure to adequately match groups on important variables such as intelligence (King et al., 1993), or failure to examine the effects of age as a continuous variable or a nonlinear variable (Raskin, 1986; Boone et al., 1994; Lyness et al., 1994). While age itself is linear, aging as a neurobiological or psychological process may not have linear effects exclu-

sively; age effects may begin at different points in time for different cognitive tasks (Albert et al., 1987; King et al., 1993, 1995). Thus, we need to explore more fully aging and aging-related heterogeneity (Nelson and Dannefer, 1992; Caine et al., 1993; Rediess and Caine, 1993), using nonlinear statistical models that can help to discern multiple subgroups.

Another major methodological challenge is to control for the effects of antidepressant or other psychoactive medications. Most studies reviewed here tested patients prior to antidepressant treatment or made some attempt to account for this potential confound; it is unlikely that medication effects could explain the substantial deficits reported in many studies. However, control of medication status is becoming more difficult in today's climate of shifting healthcare priorities, aggressive outpatient treatment of mood disorders, and shortened lengths of hospital stays. Nonetheless, it remains important for future studies to assess the possible impact of psychotropic medications on depressives' intellectual functioning, especially as carefully designed studies of test performance before, during, and after standardized treatments may inform us as to the nature (and extent) of cognitive recovery, and its association to changes in mood state.

Perhaps the greatest challenge for future descriptive neuropsychological investigations of depression is to better define the cognitive heterogeneity of the disorder. Current research has not adequately addressed the relationship of depressives' cognitive functioning to factors such as comorbid medical illness or the age of onset of mood disturbance. Moreover, we do not know the relationship between neuropsychological function and subtypes of depression (major versus minor; melancholic versus nonmelancholic), whether the neuropsychological deficits presented here are specific to major depression as opposed to other psychiatric syndromes (see Johnson and Magaro, 1987 for a discussion), or whether depression-related cognitive impairment is a state or trait phenomenon. The neuropsychology of major depression remains poorly understood, if we define neuropsychology as encompassing the brain substrates of cognitive function.

As we noted at the outset of this chapter, we no longer use the term pseudodementia. For us, its utility has passed. All patients coming to our clinical services are scrutinized closely; we know that there are few final common symptomatic pathways for manifesting disordered brain functioning (Caine and Joynt, 1986). Disturbed mood may be a harbinger of Alzheimer's disease, just as cognitive impairment may be fully reversible with antidepressant pharmacotherapy. Phenomenology does not always predetermine clinical course. At the same time, we recognize that the concept inherent in "pseudodementia" remains poorly understood; while it is now clear to many investigators and clinicians that individuals suffering major depression manifest neuropsychological abnormalities consistent with altered cerebral functioning, and not merely an epiphenomenon of disordered mood or distracting ruminations, interested researchers remain both uncertain about the fundamental processes that cause these disturbances and ignorant regarding factors that lead to their marked variation among persons suffering the same categorically defined disorder. Perhaps the borders have been defined more clearly, but the interior landscape remains largely unexplored.

In this chapter we have considered the extent of progress over the past decade in studying the neuropsychology of depression. Major efforts ahead must include the careful correlation of descriptive and experimental psychological findings in precisely defined groups with thoughtfully conceived neuroimaging and neurochemical studies. State and trait should be separated, using longitudinal study methods whenever feasible. Depressive disorders are not static, nor should our approaches to research attempt to freeze these dynamic conditions in single, cross-sectional study designs. In the end, our success will depend on understanding both the heterogeneity and the variability of these common conditions. Perhaps then we will be able to resolve with greater certainty the contradictions and controversies that characterize the field at this time.

Acknowledgment

This work was supported in part by a grant from the NIMH (MH40381).

References

Albert, M., Duffy, F. H., and Naeser, M. (1987). Nonlinear changes in cognition with age and their neuropsychologic correlates. *Canadian Journal of Psychology, 41*, 141–157.

Baxter, L. R., Jr., Phelps, M. E., Mazziotta, J. C., Schwartz, J. M., Gerner, R. H., Selin, C. E., and Sumida, R. M. (1985). Cerebral metabolic rates for glucose in mood disorders. *Archives of General Psychiatry, 42*, 441–447.

Bieliauskas, L. A. (1993). Depressed or not depressed? That is the question. *Journal of Clinical and Experimental Neuropsychology, 15*, 119–134.

Blaney, P. H. (1986). Affect and memory: A review. *Psychological Bulletin, 99*, 229–246.

Boone, K. B., Lesser, I., Miller, B., Wohl, M., Berman, N., Lee, A., and Palmer, B. (1994). Cognitive functioning in a mildly to moderately depressed geriatric sample: Relationship to chronological age. *Journal of Neuropsychiatry and Clinical Neurosciences, 6*, 267–272.

Bornstein, R. A., Baker, G. B., and Douglass, A. B. (1991). Depression and memory in major depressive disorder. *Journal of Neuropsychiatry and Clinical Neurosciences, 3*, 78–80.

Brand, A. N., Jolles, J., and Gispen-deWied, C. (1992). Recall and recognition memory deficits in depression. *Journal of Affective Disorders, 25*, 77–86.

Brown, R. G., and Marsden, C. D. (1988). "Subcortical dementia": The neuropsychological evidence. *Neuroscience, 25*, 363–387.

Caine, E. D. (1981). Pseudodementia. Current concepts and future directions. *Archives of General Psychiatry, 38*, 1359–1364.

Caine, E. D. (1986). The neuropsychology of depression: The pseudodementia syndrome. In I. Grant and K. Adams, eds., *Neuropsychological Assessment of Neuropsychiatric Disorders*. New York: Oxford University Press, pp. 221–243.

Caine, E. D., and Joynt, R. J. (1986). Neuropsychiatry . . . again. *Archives of Neurology, 43*, 325–327.

Caine, E. D., Lyness, J. M., and King, D. A. (1993). Reconsidering depression in the elderly. *American Journal of Geriatric Psychiatry, 1*, 4–20.

Caine, E. D., Yerevanian, B. I., and Bamford, K. A. (1984). Cognitive function and the dexamethasone suppression test in depression. *American Journal of Psychiatry, 141,* 116–118.

Calev, A., Nigal, D., and Chazan, S. (1989). Retrieval from semantic memory using meaningful and meaningless constructs by depressed, stable bipolar and manic patients. *British Journal of Clinical Psychology, 28,* 67–73.

Cassens, G., Wolfe, L., and Zola, M. (1990). The neuropsychology of depressions. *Journal of Neuropsychiatry and Clinical Neurosciences, 2,* 202–213.

Channon, S., Baker, J. E., and Robertson, M. M. (1993). Effects of structure and clustering on recall and recognition memory in clinical depression. *Journal of Abnormal Psychology, 102,* 323–326.

Coffey, C. E., Figiel, G. S., Djang, W. T., Saunders, W. B., and Weiner, R. D. (1989). White matter hyperintensity on magnetic resonance imaging: Clinical and neuroanatomic correlates in the depressed elderly. *Journal of Neuropsychiatry and Clinical Neurosciences, 1,* 135–144.

Cohen, R. M., Weingartner, H., Smallberg, S. A., Pickar, D., and Murphy, D. L. (1982). Effort and cognition in depression. *Archives of General Psychiatry, 39,* 593–597.

Cummings, J. L., and Benson, D. F. (1983). *Dementia: A Clinical Approach.* Boston: Butterworth.

Cummings, J. L., and Benson, D. F. (1984). Subcortical dementia. Review of an emerging concept. *Archives of Neurology, 41,* 874–879.

Danion, J. M., Willard-Schroeder, D., Zimmermann, M. A., Grange, D., Schlienger, J. L., and Singer, L. (1991). Explicit memory and repetition priming in depression. Preliminary findings. *Archives of General Psychiatry, 48,* 707–711.

Denny, E. B., and Hunt, R. R. (1992). Affective valence and memory in depression: Dissociation of recall and fragment completion. *Journal of Abnormal Psychology, 101,* 575–580.

Deptula, D., Manevitz, A., and Yozawitz, A. (1991). Asymmetry of recall in depression. *Journal of Clinical and Experimental Neuropsychology, 13,* 854–870.

Dolan, R. J., Bench, C. J., Brown, R. G., Scott, L. C., Friston, K. J., and Frackowiak, R.S.J. (1992). Regional cerebral blood flow abnormalities in depressed patients with cognitive impairment. *Journal of Neurology, Neurosurgery and Psychiatry, 55,* 768–773.

Dunbar, G. C., and Lishman, W. A. (1984). Depression, recognition-memory, and hedonic tone: A signal detection analysis. *British Journal of Psychiatry, 144,* 376–382.

Elliott, C., and Greene, R. L. (1992). Clinical depression and implicit memory. *Journal of Abnormal Psychology, 101,* 572–574.

Ellis, H. C., and Ashbrook, P. W. (1988). Resource-allocation model of the effect of depressed mood states on memory. In K. Fiedler and J. Forgas, eds., *Affect, Cognition, and Social Behavior.* Gottingen: Hogrefe, pp. 25–43.

Emery, O. B., and Breslau, L. D. (1989). Language deficits in depression: Comparisons with SDAT and normal aging. *Journal of Gerontology, 44,* M85–92.

Folstein, M. F., Folstein, S. E., and McHugh, P. R. (1975). "Mini-Mental State." A practical method for grading the cognitive state of patients for the clinician. *Journal of Psychiatric Research, 12,* 189–198.

Georgotas, A., McCue, R. E., Kim, O. M., Hapworth, W. E., Reisberg, B., Stoll, P. M., Sinaiko, E., Fanelli, C., and Stokes, P. E. (1986). Dexamethasone suppression in dementia, depression, and normal aging. *American Journal of Psychiatry, 143,* 452–456.

Golinkoff, M., and Sweeney, J. A. (1989). Cognitive impairments in depression. *Journal of Affective Disorders, 17,* 105–112.

Graf, P. (1990). Life-span changes in implicit and explicit memory. *Bulletin of the Psychonomic Society, 28,* 353–358.

Graf, P., and Mandler, G. (1984). Activation makes words more accessible, but not necessarily more retrievable. *Journal of Verbal Learning and Verbal Behavior, 23,* 553–568.

Hart, R. P., Kwentus, J. A., Hamer, R. M., and Taylor, J. R. (1987a). Selective reminding procedure in depression and dementia. *Psychology and Aging, 2,* 111–115.

Hart, R. P., Kwentus, J. A., Taylor, J. R., and Harkins, S. W. (1987b). Rate of forgetting in dementia and depression. *Journal of Consulting and Clinical Psychology, 55,* 101–105.

Hasher, L., and Zacks, R. T. (1979). Automatic and effortful processes in memory. *Journal of Experimental Psychology: General, 108,* 356–388.

Hasher, L., and Zacks, R. T. (1988). Working memory, comprehension, and aging: A review and new view. In G. Bower, ed., *The Psychology of Learning and Motivation.* San Diego: Academic Press, pp. 193–225.

Hertel, P. T., and Hardin, T. S. (1990). Remembering with and without awareness in a depressed mood: Evidence of deficits in initiative. *Journal of Experimental Psychology: General, 119*, 45–59.

Hertel, P. T., and Rude, S. S. (1991). Depressive deficits in memory: Focusing attention improves subsequent recall. *Journal of Experimental Psychology: General, 120*, 301–309.

Hill, C. D., Stoudemire, A., Morris, R., Martino-Saltzman, D., Markwalter, H. R., and Lewison, B. J. (1992). Dysnomia in the differential diagnosis of major depression, depression-related cognitive dysfunction, and dementia. *Journal of Neuropsychiatry and Clinical Neurosciences, 4*, 64–69.

Howard, D. (1991). Implicit memory: An expanding picture of cognitive aging. In K. W. Schaie and M. P. Lawton, eds., *Annual Review of Gerontology and Geriatrics* (Vol. 11). New York: Springer, pp. 1–22.

Jacoby, L. L. (1983). Perceptual enhancement: Persistent effects of an experience. *Journal of Experimental Psychology, Learning, Memory, and Cognition, 9*, 21–38.

Johnson, M. H., and Magaro, P. A. (1987). Effects of mood and severity on memory processes in depression and mania. *Psychological Bulletin, 101*, 28–40.

Jorm, A. F. (1986). Cognitive deficit in the depressed elderly: A review of some basic unresolved issues. *Australian and New Zealand Journal of Psychiatry, 20*, 11–22.

Kahneman, D. (1973). *Attention and Effort*. Englewood Cliffs, New Jersey: Prentice Hall.

Kiloh, L. G. (1961). Pseudo-dementia. *Acta Psychiatrica Scandinavica, 37*, 336–351.

King, D. A., and Caine, E. D. (1990). Depression. In J. L. Cummings, ed., *Subcortical Dementia*. New York: Oxford University Press, pp. 218–230.

King, D. A., Caine, E. D., Conwell, Y., and Cox, C. (1991a). The neuropsychology of depression in the elderly: A comparative study with normal aging and Alzheimer's disease. *Journal of Neuropsychiatry and Clinical Neurosciences, 3*, 163–168.

King, D. A., Caine, E. D., Conwell, Y., and Cox, C. (1991b). Predicting severity of depression in the elderly at six-month follow-up: A neuropsychological study. *Journal of Neuropsychiatry and Clinical Neurosciences, 3*, 64–66.

King, D. A., Caine, E. D., and Cox, C. (1993). Influence of depression and age on selected cognitive functions. *Clinical Neuropsychologist, 7*, 443–453.

King, D.A., Cox, C., Lyness, J.M., and Caine, E.D. (1995). Neuropsychological effects of depression and age in an elderly sample: A confirmatory study. *Neuropsychology, 9*, 399–408.

Kluger, A., and Goldberg, E. (1990). IQ patterns in affective disorder, lateralized and diffuse brain damage. *Journal of Clinical and Experimental Neuropsychology, 12*, 182–194.

Krishnan, K.R.R., McDonald, W. M., Escalona, P. R., Doraiswamy, P. M., Na, C., Husain, M. M., Figiel, G. S., Boyko, O. B., Ellinwood, E. H., and Nemeroff, C. B. (1992). Magnetic resonance imaging of the caudate nuclei in depression. Preliminary observations. *Archives of General Psychiatry, 49*, 553–557.

La Rue, A. (1989). Patterns of performance in the Fuld Object Memory Evaluation in elderly inpatients with depression or dementia. *Journal of Clinical and Experimental Neuropsychology, 11*, 409–422.

Leight, K. A., and Ellis, H. C. (1981). Emotional mood states, strategies, and state dependency in memory. *Journal of Verbal Learning and Verbal Behavior, 20*, 251–266.

Light, L. L., and Anderson, P. A. (1985). Working memory capacity, age and memory for discourse. *Journal of Gerontology, 40*, 737–747.

Light, L. L., and Singh, A. (1987). Implicit and explicit memory in young and older adults. *Journal of Experimental Psychology, Learning, Memory, and Cognition, 13*, 531–541.

Lister, R. G., and Weingartner, H. J. (1991). *Perspectives on Cognitive Neuroscience*. New York: Oxford University Press.

Lyness, S. A., Eaton, E. M., and Schneider, L. S. (1994). Cognitive performance in older and middle-aged depressed outpatients and controls. *Journal of Gerontology: Psychological Sciences, 49*, P129–P136.

Massman, P. J., Delis, D. C., Butters, N., Dupont, R. M., and Gillin, J. C. (1992). The subcortical dysfunction hypothesis of memory deficits in depression: Neuropsychological validation in a subgroup of patients. *Journal of Clinical and Experimental Neuropsychology, 14*, 687–706.

Miller, E., and Lewis, P. (1977). Recognition memory in elderly patients with depression and dementia: A signal detection analysis. *Journal of Abnormal Psychology, 86*, 84–86.

Nelson, E. A., and Dannefer, D. (1992). Aged heterogeneity: Fact or fiction? The fate of diversity in gerontological research. *Gerontologist, 32*, 17–23.

Niederehe, G. (1986). Depression and memory

impairment in the aged. In L. W. Poon, ed., *Clinical Memory Assessment of Older Adults.* Washington, D.C.: American Psychological Association, pp. 226–237.

Niederehe, G., and Camp, C. J. (1985). Signal detection analysis of recognition memory in depressed elderly. *Experimental Aging Research, 11,* 207–213.

Pearlson, G. D., Rabins, P. V., Kim, W. S., Speedie, L. J., Moberg, P. J., Burns, A., and Bascom, M. J. (1989). Structural brain CT changes and cognitive deficits in elderly depressives with and without reversible dementia ('pseudodementia'). *Psychological Medicine, 19,* 573–584.

Poon, L. W. (1992). Toward an understanding of cognitive functioning in geriatric depression. *International Psychogeriatrics, 4* (Suppl. 2), 241–266.

Popkin, S., Gallagher, D., Thompson, L. W., and Moore, M. (1982). Memory complaint and performance in normal and depressed older adults. *Experimental Aging Research, 8,* 141–145.

Rabins, P. V., Pearlson, G. D., Aylward, E., Kumar, A. J., and Dowell, K. (1991). Cortical magnetic resonance imaging changes in elderly inpatients with major depression. *American Journal of Psychiatry, 148,* 617–620.

Raskin, A. (1986). Partialling out the effects of depression and age on cognitive functions: Experimental data and methodologic issues. In L. W. Poon, ed., *Clinical Memory Assessment of Older Adults.* Washington, D.C.: American Psychological Association, pp. 244–256.

Rediess, S., and Caine, E. D. (1993). Aging associated cognitive changes: How do they relate to the diagnosis of dementia? *Current Opinion in Psychiatry, 6,* 531–535.

Roediger, H. L., III. (1990). Implicit memory: Retention without remembering. *American Psychologist, 45,* 1043–1056.

Rohling, M. L., and Scogin, F. (1993). Automatic and effortful memory processes in depressed persons. *Journal of Gerontology: Psychological Sciences, 48,* P87–P95.

Roy-Byrne, P. P., Weingartner, H., Bierer, L. M., Thompson, K., and Post, R. M. (1986). Effortful and automatic cognitive processes in depression. *Archives of General Psychiatry, 43,* 265–267.

Rubinow, D. R., Post, R. M., Savard, R., and Gold, P. W. (1984). Cortisol hypersecretion and cognitive impairment in depression. *Archives of General Psychiatry, 41,* 279–283.

Sackheim, H. A., Freeman, J., McElhiney, M., Coleman, E., Prudic, J., and Devanand, D. P. (1992). Effects of major depression on estimates of intelligence. *Journal of Clinical and Experimental Neuropsychology, 14,* 268–288.

Siegel, B., Gurevich, D., and Oxenkrug, G. F. (1989). Cognitive impairment and cortisol resistance to dexamethasone suppression in elderly depression. *Biological Psychiatry, 25,* 229–234.

Silberman, E. K., and Weingartner, H. (1986). Hemispheric lateralization of functions related to emotion. *Brain and Cognition, 5,* 322–353.

Silberman, E. K., Weingartner, H., and Post, R. M. (1983). Thinking disorder in depression. *Archives of General Psychiatry, 40,* 775–780.

Speedie, L. J., Rabins, P. V., and Pearlson, G. D. (1990). Confrontation naming deficit in dementia of depression. *Journal of Neuropsychiatry and Clinical Neurosciences, 2,* 59–63.

Tancer, M. E., Brown, T. M., Evans, D. L., Ekstrom, D., Haggerty, J. J., Pedersen, C., and Golden, R. N. (1989). Impaired effortful cognition in depression. *Psychiatry Research, 31,* 161–168.

Tulving, E., Hayman, C.A.G., and Macdonald, C. (1991). Long-lasting perceptual priming and semantic learning in amnesia: A case experiment. *Journal of Experimental Psychology, Learning, Memory, and Cognition, 17,* 595–617.

Tulving, E., and Schacter, D. L. (1990). Priming and human memory systems. *Science, 247,* 301–306.

Watkins, P. C., Mathews, A., Williamson, D. A., and Fuller, R. D. (1992). Mood-congruent memory in depression: Emotional priming or elaboration? *Journal of Abnormal Psychology, 101,* 581–586.

Watts, F. N., Morris, L., and MacLeod, A. K. (1987). Recognition memory in depression. *Journal of Abnormal Psychology, 96,* 273–275.

Weingartner, H. (1986). Automatic and effort-demanding cognitive processes in depression. In L. W. Poon, ed., *Clinical Memory Assessment of Older Adults.* Washington, D.C.: American Psychological Association, pp. 218–225.

Weingartner, H., Cohen, R. M., Murphy, D. L., Martello, J., and Gerdt, C. (1981). Cognitive processes in depression. *Archives of General Psychiatry, 38,* 42–47.

Wells, C. E. (1979). Pseudodementia. *American Journal of Psychiatry, 136,* 895–900.

Wolfe, J., Granholm, E., Butters, N., Saunders,

E., and Janowsky, D. (1987). Verbal memory deficits associated with major affective disorders: A comparison of unipolar and bipolar patients. *Journal of Affective Disorders, 13*, 83–92.

Wolkowitz, O. M., Reus, V. I., Weingartner, H., Thompson, K., Breier, A., Doran, A., Rubinow, D., and Pickar, D. (1990). Cognitive effects of corticosteroids. *American Journal of Psychiatry, 147*, 1297–1303.

Zarit, S. H., Cole, K. D., and Guider, R. L. (1981). Memory training strategies and subjective complaints of memory in the aged. *Gerontologist, 21*, 158–164.

10 The Neuropsychiatry and Neuropsychology of Gilles de la Tourette Syndrome

MARY M. ROBERTSON and SIMON BARON-COHEN

In this chapter we review the neuropsychiatric and neuropsychological literatures on Gilles de la Tourette Syndrome (GTS). Whereas the former is quite extensive, the latter is still fairly undeveloped and, in our opinion, represents an important area for future research.

The diagnostic criteria for GTS include the presence of multiple motor tics and one or more vocal tics, both of which must exceed a year's duration (ICD-10, World Health Organization, 1992, 4th edition, *Diagnostic and Statistical Manual of Mental Disorders* [DSM-IV], American Psychiatric Association, 1994). The anatomical location, number, frequency, complexity and severity of the tics characteristically change over time. Although the exact prevalence of GTS is unknown, a currently accepted figure is 0.5 per thousand (approximately 110,000 patients in the United States and 25,000 in the United Kingdom) (Bruun, 1984), but even this may now prove to be an underestimate (Robertson, 1944).

The first clear medical description of GTS was made in 1825, when Itard reported the case of a French noblewoman, the Marquise de Dampierre (Itard, 1825), whose case was then redocumented by Georges Gilles de la Tourette in 1885 when he described nine cases of GTS, emphasizing the triad of multiple tics, coprolalia (unprovoked, inappropriate swearing), and echolalia (imitating the speech of others) (Gilles de la Tourette, 1885). Of note is that the Marquise also manifested symptoms of obsessive-compulsive disorder (OCD) in addition to a tic disorder. We will return to discuss the association between GTS and OCD later.

A convincing case has been made (McHenry, 1967; Murray, 1979) that Dr. Samuel Johnson suffered from GTS with multiple motor tics and a variety of vocal tics including "ejaculations of the Lord's prayer," sounds like the clucking of a hen and a whale exhaling (Boswell, 1867; McHenry, 1967; Murray, 1979). He also exhibited echolalia, mild self-injurious behavior, and it has been suggested that Dr. Johnson suffered from severe OCD in addition to his motor and vocal tics. He felt impelled to measure his footsteps, perform complex gestures when he crossed a threshold, and involuntarily touch specific objects (Murray, 1979).

Neuropsychiatry

Clinical Characteristics

The clinical characteristics of individuals with GTS appear to be independent of culture, as they occur with some degree of uniformity irrespective of the country of origin. The age of onset of GTS symptoms ranges from 2 to 15 years, with a mean of 7 years being commonly reported. The most frequent initial symptoms are tics involving the eyes (such as eye blinking), head nodding, and facial grimacing. GTS is often referred to as a tic disorder, but patients with the syndrome usually exhibit a wide variety of complex movements including touching, hitting, jumping, smelling of the hands or objects, spitting, kicking, stamping, squatting, and a variety of abnormalities of gait (Robertson, 1989, 1994).

The onset of vocal tics is usually later than that of the motor tics, with a mean age of 11 years. The usual utterances include grunting, coughing, throat-clearing, barking, yelping, snorting, explosive utterances, screaming, humming, hissing, clicking, colloquial emotional exclamations, and inarticulate sounds. Coprolalia (the uttering of obscenities) is reported in approximately one third of patients and usually has a mean age of onset of 14 years. Copropraxia (the making of obscene gestures) is reported in 3% to 21% of GTS patients. Echophenomena (the imitation of sounds, words, or actions of others) occur in 11% to 44% of patients. Tics and vocalizations are characteristically aggravated by anxiety, stress, boredom, fatigue, and excitement; sleep, alcohol, orgasm, fever, relaxation, and concentration lead to temporary disappearance of symptoms (Robertson, 1989, 1994). The significance of these factors for a causal model of GTS remains unclear.

There have been no substantial long-term follow-up studies to document the exact course of GTS. However, from the literature of case reports and from clinical experience, it is clear that it is a lifelong illness for the majority of patients, although a fortunate third of affected individuals can show spontaneous remission (Golden, 1984). Recent studies also suggest that many cases of GTS are mild, do not come to medical attention, and do not require pharmacological treatment (Kurlan et al., 1987; Caine et al., 1988; Robertson and Gourdie, 1990).

The majority of studies agree that GTS occurs three to four times more commonly in males than in females and that it is found in all social classes, although Asam (1982) and Robertson et al. (1988) reported respectively that over 60% of their GTS cohorts failed to attain their parental social class. This suggests that patients with GTS may well underachieve (Robertson, 1989).

Associated Psychopathology

Gilles de la Tourette (1899), acknowledging the writings of Guinon (1886), suggested that "tiqueurs" nearly always had associated psychiatric disorders, especially multiple phobias, arithmomania and agoraphobia, habits disorders, hypochondriasis, and enuresis. Grasset (1890) also referred to the obsessions and phobias of patients. To him these were an accompaniment of the tic disorder, representing "psychical" tics. Robertson and Reinstein (1991) translated, for the first time, these writings of Gilles de la Tourette, Guinon, and Grasset, illustrating the early documentation of psychopathology, with special reference to OCD. Subsequent work has confirmed a range of disturbances in patients with GTS (Corbett et al., 1969; Morphew and Sim, 1969). These include OCD, attention deficit disorder (ADD), hyperactivity (Robertson and Eapen, 1992), and learning difficulties, and these are often the symptoms for which the patient is referred to a physician (Robertson, 1989). In addition, antisocial behavior, inappropriate sexual activity, exhibitionism, aggressive behavior, discipline problems, sleep disturbances, and self-injurious behavior are found in a substantial percentage of clinic GTS populations (Robertson et al., 1988, 1989; Robertson, 1989). However, relatively few individuals with GTS in the community exhibit antisocial behaviors.

Depression and GTS

Depression has also been found in association with GTS (Montgomery et al., 1982). Comings and Comings (1987a), using a modified Beck questionnaire, confirmed significantly more depression in GTS patients than in controls, and a high "mania" score, as evidenced by feelings of being high or excited, spending sprees, hypersensitivity, talking too fast to be understood, inability to sleep, distractability, and feeling in possession of special powers. Depression also seems to be related to the duration of the GTS (Robertson et al., 1988). This finding is not surprising, given the fact that people with GTS have a chronic, socially disabling, and stigmatizing disease. However, a genetic predisposition to depressive illness should not be discounted. Robertson et al. (1993) found GTS patients to be significantly more depressed and anxious than a normal control group, and to have a different psychopathological profile from a depressed group. (This is discussed in more detail later.)

It is generally accepted that there is no association between psychosis and GTS apart from a few isolated case reports (Caine et al., 1978; Burd and Kerbeshian, 1984; Reid, 1984; Bleich et al., 1985; Takeuchi et al., 1986). Before leaving this section on associated psychopathology, it is worth saying a little more about the association between GTS and OCD, as this appears to have possible etiological significance.

Obsessive-Compulsive Disorder (OCD) in GTS

Kinnear-Wilson, a neurologist, like Gilles de la Tourette himself, acknowledged a relationship between tics and OCD: "no feature is more prominent in tics than its irresistibility . . . The element of compulsion links the condition intimately to the vast group of obsessions and fixed ideas." (Wilson, 1927).

The modern literature confirms that OCD and GTS are intimately related, although the percentage of patients with GTS who also show OCD varies from as low as 11% in some reports (Kelman, 1965) to as high as 80% in others (Yaryura-Tobias et al., 1981). Montgomery et al. (1982) further suggest that the OC symptoms increase in frequency with the duration of GTS. Of interest, Robertson et al. (1988) found that coprolalia and echophenomena were significantly associated with OC phenomena. In contrast to Montgomery et al. (1982), no relationships between age or duration of GTS and OC phenomena were found. Robertson et al. (1993)

compared GTS patients to depressed patients and normal controls, and showed that both patient groups scored significantly more on scores of obsessionality, depression, and anxiety than controls. The GTS subjects had similar scores on measures of obsessionality to those of the depressed subjects, but significantly lower scores on measures of depression and anxiety: this suggests that obsessionality is a prominent feature of GTS, and the psychopathological profile differs from that of patients with major depressive disorder.

Several controlled studies have demonstrated that GTS patients have significantly more OC behaviors than normal subjects and equal to OCD patients (Frankel et al., 1986; Green and Pitman, 1986; Comings and Comings, 1987a). The precise phenomenology of the OC thoughts and behaviors in patients with GTS has not been widely reported, but studies suggest that arithmomania (counting rituals or obsessions with numbers) and "evening up" or a concern with symmetry, checking, and arranging are common (Frankel et al., 1986; Pitman et al., 1987). Recently, George et al. (1993) documented that GTS patients with comorbid OCD had significantly more violent, sexual, and symmetrical obsessions, and more touching, blinking, counting, and self-damaging compulsions than a pure OCD group, who had more obsessions concerning dirt or germs and more cleaning compulsions. The patients with GTS and OCD reported that their compulsions arose spontaneously or de novo, whereas those with OCD alone reported that their compulsions were frequently preceded by cognitions. Robertson et al. (1988) also report a significant statistical association between OC phenomena in GTS and coprolalia, and found, like George et al. (1993), that thoughts and rituals in GTS are, by and large, not dominated by dirt, germs, and fear of contamination. One study (Frankel et al., 1986) documented that the items endorsed by GTS patients changed with age. Thus, younger patients endorsed more items relating to impulse control, whereas older GTS subjects were more concerned with checking, arranging, and fear of contamination.

Yaryura-Tobias and Neziroglu (1983) have proposed that GTS is actually a subtype of OCD, and suggest that it may be a hyposerotonergic condition. Cummings and Frankel (1985) comment on similarities between GTS and OCD, including age of onset; lifelong course; waxing and waning of symptoms; involuntary, intrusive, ego-alien behavior and experiences; occurrence in the same families; and worsening with depression and anxiety.

The clear association between GTS and OCD is strengthened by recent findings that many relatives of GTS patients also describe OC thoughts and actions in the absence of tics or vocalizations (Kurlan et al., 1986; Pauls et al., 1986a,b; Comings and Comings, 1987b; Robertson and Gourdie, 1990; Robertson and Trimble, 1991). All of these authors conclude that GTS and OCD may therefore be etiologically related (see below). It is of added interest that in the GTS twin study of Jenkins and Ashby (1983), both twins were described as "obsessional." It would appear, therefore, that OCD is an integral part of GTS (Robertson, 1995). Robertson (1989) and others have proposed that there is a genetic basis to GTS, and they report evidence showing that the phenotype may be expressed on a spectrum with or without OCD. The evidence for the genetic basis of GTS relies in part on family studies, and these are reviewed next.

Family Psychopathology

Gilles de la Tourette (1899) noted that the family history of patients with GTS was almost invariably "loaded for nervous disorder." Samuel Johnson's father also appeared to suffer from depression, "a general sensation of gloomy wretchedness," and it is thought to be from him that Dr. Johnson "inherited . . . a vile melancholy" (Boswell, 1867).

Montgomery et al. (1982) found that 70% of 30 first-degree relatives of 15 patients with GTS satisfied Feighner criteria for psychiatric illness, the most common diagnoses being unipolar depression, OC illness, and panic disorder. More recently, both Green and Pitman (1986), Pauls et al. (1986a,b), and

Robertson and Gourdie (1990) found the rate of OCD significantly higher among relatives of patients with GTS than in control populations. Robertson et al. (1988) reported that 48% of 90 probands had a positive family history of psychiatric illness, of which the most common disorders were depression, schizophrenia, and OCD. While it is acknowledged that these studies are not controlled, it would appear that there is increased psychiatric morbidity in the relatives of patients with GTS, and that OCD is the most common disorder found in these relatives. As suggested earlier, this implicates a common genetic basis to these disorders.

Neurology

In the group of patients with GTS examined by Shapiro et al. (1978), subtle neurological deficits were found in 57%, and 20% were left-handed or ambidextrous. Most (78%) had minor motor asymmetry, and 20% had chorea or choreoathetoid movements. Other abnormalities included posturing, poor coordination, nystagmus, reflex asymmetry, and unilateral Babinski reflexes. In contrast, Lees et al. (1984), using a standardized handedness questionnaire (Annett, 1970), found 87% of their sample of 53 patients to be right-handed, and other investigators have found minor nonspecific neurological abnormalities only in a few patients (Lees et al., 1984; Regeur et al., 1986; Erenberg et al., 1986; Caine et al., 1988; Robertson et al., 1988). Abnormalities have included chorea, dystonia, torticollis, dysphonia, dysdiadochokinesia, postural abnormalities, reflex asymmetry, and motor incoordination.

Electrophysiology and Neuroimaging

Shapiro et al. (1978) reviewed the literature on EEG findings in GTS in 11 studies. This revealed 66% of patients as showing abnormal EEGs. In their own cohort 47% had EEG abnormalities, this being more common in children (71%) than in adults (25%). Other studies have reported lower rates, with nonspecific abnormalities being found (Krumholz et al., 1983; Robertson et al.,

1988). It has been suggested that in patients with GTS who are more psychologically impaired and who have more learning disabilities, there are more dysrhythmias on the EEG (Lucas and Rodin, 1973). Visual evoked potentials in patients with GTS do not reveal any consistent abnormalities (Obeso et al., 1982; Krumholz et al., 1983). In contrast, auditory evoked potentials suggest that components in the range of 90 to 280 ms are affected (Van de Wetering et al., 1985).

Investigations of the structure of the brain using computed tomography (CT) scans (Robertson et al., 1988; Robertson, 1989) and magnetic resonance imaging (MRI) scans (Chase et al., 1986; Robertson and Trimble, 1991) have essentially not revealed any abnormalities, until recently, when two independent studies showed reduced basal ganglia volume with MRI (Peterson et al., 1993; Singer et al., 1993). Two MRI studies (Peterson et al., 1993; Singer et al., 1993) have also demonstrated loss of normal left-greater-than-right asymmetry in the basal ganglia. More recently, Hyde et al. (1995) demonstrated that on MRI, right caudate volume was slightly, but significantly, reduced in more severely affected GTS twins as compared to less affected twins: the mean volume of the left lateral ventricle was 16% smaller in the more severely affected twins. Finally, the normal asymmetry of the lateral ventricles (left greater than right) was not present in the more severely affected twins (Hyde et al., 1995). These recent MRI studies suggest subtle structural changes in the brain in GTS with particular reference to a loss of normal left-greater-than-right asymmetry and basal ganglia abnormalities. Studies investigating function (using positron-emission tomography, or PET) showed abnormalities in patients with GTS in the frontal cingulate and possibly insular cortex and in the inferior corpus striatum (Chase et al., 1984, 1986). Studies using single photon emission computed tomography (SPECT) initially found a wide range of perfusion deficits in GTS patients, in the frontal, parietal, and temporal cortex (Hall et al., 1990). Later, more controlled studies (George et al., 1992; Mori-

arty et al., 1995) demonstrated that as a group GTS patients showed frontal abnormalites compared with controls. Clearly more investigations are needed to clarify the relationship between the frontal and basal ganglia findings and GTS symptoms.

Neuropsychiatry: Preliminary Conclusions

It seems that associated psychopathology is common in people with GTS. In particular, they are more prone to depression, and the severity of this increases with the duration of GTS. This may the result of having a stigmatizing disorder. OCD, on the other hand, which is also more common in people with GTS, appears to be an integral part of the syndrome. Our recent complex segregation analyses of a large kindred (Curtis et al., 1992) and a consecutive UK cohort (Eapen et al., 1993) support the view that GTS is transmitted by an autosomal dominant gene, and that obsessive-compulsive behavior is a phenotype of the putative GTS gene(s). Neurological and electrophysiological examinations show minor nonspecific abnormalities; neuroimaging techniques, an avenue that deserves further study, demonstrate clear functional (but not structural) changes.

Neuropsychology

We turn now to the neuropsychology of GTS. In our review of this, we restrict our discussion to *cognition* in these patients. This term is both broad enough to include the major psychological processes (e.g., attention, learning, memory, intelligence, perception, and language), and yet focused enough to exclude such psychological systems as emotion. While we do not wish to claim that emotion is independent of cognition, emotion is discussed separately above (see *Associated Psychopathology*). As will become evident, the neuropsychology of GTS has hardly begun. We suggest that a scientific theory of this disorder must ultimately aim to give a thorough account of how cognition and emotion link with biology and behavior in patients with this condition.

Intelligence

More intelligence testing has been carried out in GTS than almost any other kind of cognitive investigation. A range of IQ tests have been used, a key one being the Wechsler Scales (e.g., Shapiro et al., 1974; Incagnoli and Kane, 1981). These studies show a relatively consistent set of findings: patients with GTS, as a group, have IQ scores in the normal range (Corbett et al., 1969), although GTS and mental handicap can of course coexist (Golden and Greenhill, 1981). In a proportion of the patients with overall IQs in the normal range, statistically significant discrepancies between verbal and performance IQ on the Wechsler Scales have been found (50% in the Shapiro et al. [1974] study). For most patients, performance IQ is significantly worse than verbal IQ, but significant discrepancies in the opposite direction are also sometimes found.

Within the subtests, Coding, written Arithmetic, and copying tasks (as measured, for example, in the Aphasia Screening Test of the Halstead-Reitan Battery), seem to cluster as a set of severe deficits. Incagnoli and Kane (1981) suggest this may represent dysfunction of "nonconstructional visuopractic abilities" (p. 168), although the relationship between this postulated cognitive deficit in visuographic skills and the symptomatology of the disorder remains to be fully explored. Furthermore, although Incagnoli and Kane stress specifically *non*-constructional visuopractic deficits, deficits have also been found in some constructional abilities, such as those measured by the Block Design or Object Assembly subtests of the Wechsler Scales (Shapiro et al., 1974; Bornstein et al., 1983). These differences may reflect developmental changes, since Shapiro et al. (1974) found deficits on the Block Design subtest in adults with GTS, but not in children. The exact nature of the postulated visuospatial difficulties in this disorder needs further investigation. It is important to note that a recent study that aimed to test if there was a "right hemisphere dysfunction" in GTS (on the basis of visuospatial tests such as the Bender Visual Motor Gestalt Test, and a Drawing Test) showed that the children with GTS were not impaired on these tasks (Lanser et al., 1993).

Language

Vocal tics are, of course, a major diagnostic symptom of GTS. Not all vocal tics are clearly *linguistic* however. Some vocal tics, for example, are nonverbal (e.g., throat-clearing, barking, or snorting). However, clear verbal tics make up some 35% of vocal tics (Ludlow et al., 1982), and these include coprolalia (unprovoked swearing), palilalia (frequent reiteration of syllables), jargon (production of strings of meaningless syllables), word-tics (interjection of words that are meaningful but are not part of speech), and echolalia (repetition of heard speech). Lees et al. (1984) estimate that coprolalia and echolalia occur in about 40% to 50% of patients with GTS. Most of these language abnormalities have simply been described, but not systematically studied. Apart from this set of symptoms, some studies also report a history of speech and language problems, even prior to the onset of GTS (O'Quinn and Thompson, 1980), though again, the precise nature of these early language problems remains unspecified.

Given the centrality of language abnormalities in these patients, it is somewhat surprising how few *psycholinguistic* studies of GTS have been carried out. Perhaps the best of the few that do exist is that reported by Ludlow et al. (1982). They studied 54 patients and 54 normal controls. Ten minutes of conversation and picture description was recorded from each subject. These authors found that, from the recordings of spontaneous speech, the majority of tics were produced at the beginning or end of speech clause production. Tics thus do not seem to interfere *randomly* with speech but are produced in synchrony with overall speech rhythms, mostly at speech boundaries. Motor tics, on the other hand, do not respect word boundaries (Frank, 1978). Second, Ludlow et al. (1982) used a range of language tests on the same patients, all part of the Neurosensory Center Comprehensive Examination of Aphasia (NCCEA), a standardized instrument. These tests included assessments of Visual Naming, Description of Use, Word Fluency, Sentence Construction, Sentence Repetition, Reading, Writing, and Copying. Significant differences between the groups appeared only on language expression, writing (expressive and dictation), and copying. These latter findings are consistent with the visuographic deficits revealed using intelligence tests, reviewed earlier.

In the Ludlow et al. (1982) study, reading was also poorer than normal, but this just failed to reach statistical significance. Although the studies of intelligence reviewed earlier suggested that arithmetic skills are more impaired in GTS than either reading or spelling skills (Bornstein et al., 1983), there are nevertheless a number of other studies reporting high levels of reading problems. Comings and Comings (1987a), for example, found severe reading difficulties (dyslexia) in 26.8% of their sample, in contrast to only 4.2% of their control group.

Sutherland et al. (1982) report that performance was low on a Word Fluency Test (naming as many objects, and then animals, as possible in one minute, and then alternating between giving color and bird names as often as possible in one minute). This was not explained by any gross anomaly such as abnormal speech lateralization, as a dichotic listening task confirmed a normal left hemisphere dominance for words. It is reasonable to surmise that the difficulties on the Word Fluency Test might be related to impairments in "frontal systems," rather than to purely linguistic factors, given the difficulties that patients with nonfocal frontal lesions have on such tests (Shallice, 1988). Frontal system factors are reviewed later in the chapter.

Attention

As mentioned earlier there is now little doubt that GTS is associated strongly with attentional difficulties. Thus, in a large study

by Comings and Comings (1987a), 62% of subjects with GTS were diagnosed as also having ADD (attention deficit disorder), compared with only 6.3% of randomly selected controls. In most cases, the ADD (or ADDH—with hyperactivity) started a few years *before* the motor and vocal tics. Such evidence gives a clue that attentional difficulties may play a causal role in the disorder, or at least may represent a *precursor* to the later pathology. These hypotheses also remain to be explored. There have also been suggestions that male GTS patients are more likely to have ADDH, and others that ADDH symptoms are more pronounced in those with more severe GTS symptomatology (Robertson and Eapen, 1992). There are those who suggest, however, that this high prevalence of ADDH in GTS patients is due to an ascertainment bias; that is, a patient with GTS and ADDH would be more severely disturbed and thus more likely to come to medical attention (Robertson and Eapen, 1992). However, this may be argued against, as an epidemiological study (Caine et al., 1998) reported 27% (11 of 41 GTS individuals) to have ADDH which is way in excess of the figures for the general population.

A similar or even higher rate of ADD has been reported in other studies of GTS (Mathews, 1988; Sverd et al., 1988). Most studies that have looked at this overlap have suggested that the attentional deficits may be a key reason for the ensuing school and learning difficulties that are reported in a proportion of patients, although this explanation is not by itself sufficient to account for the pattern of *specific* deficits (e.g., in visuospatial abilities), unless one posits attentional deficits that are specific to, for example, the visual modality. Some evidence that this may be the case comes from a study by Bornstein et al. (1983), which reported that their patients with GTS scored in the normal range on a test of auditory attention span (from the Wechsler Scales, mean scaled score = 9.6), but in the below average range on a test of visual attention span (using the Knox Cube Test). This pattern once again confirms the dysfunction in the visuospatial and visuomotor systems reviewed earlier.

Further research is needed in order to tease apart exactly where the deficit in this area lies. A recent attempt at this by Channon et al. (1992) showed, for example, that mild deficits were found using "complex" tests of attention, such as serial addition, block sequence span (forwards), the trail-making test, and a letter cancellation vigilance task. Given the very high proportion of GTS patients who show ADD, and given that attention is one of the most well-studied processes in experimental psychology, with a range of paradigms readily available (e.g., Allport, 1987), there is a clear need for more controlled experiments in this area. Important questions that remain to be considered include specifying how attention deficits in patients with GTS differ or compare to those in children without GTS but with ADD (Taylor, 1985); and whether the behavioral problems that are common in GTS are directly related to attentional deficits, or (as Wilson et al., 1982, found) to other factors such as severity of tics and level of IQ, or to both.

Memory

Ludlow et al. (1982) report that patients with GTS score in the normal range on tests of auditory memory (Sentence Repetition, Digit Repetition Forwards, and Digit Repetition Backwards). This intact auditory memory system (at least as regards short-term memory) contrasts with Sutherland et al.'s (1982) report that copying and drawing from memory is impaired in GTS, as is delayed recall of visual material (the Wechsler Memory Figures), relative to both mentally handicapped and schizophrenic controls groups.

Whether the memory deficits that have been identified represent *pure* memory problems, or are secondary to the attentional deficits reviewed above, remains to be established. For example, Sutherland et al. (1982) speculate that because of the urge many patients report to *repeat* what they hear, which must distract them from the *meaning* of the text being read, poor recall of stories may simply reflect distraction.

Perception

Although vision, audition, touch, and smell all appear normal in this disorder, some perceptual abnormalities have nevertheless been reported. Thus, visual scanning (as measured by the Trail Making Test) was abnormal in four of seven patients of Bornstein et al. (1983), and Cohen et al. (1982) reported deficits in perception of figure-ground discrimination in up to 30% of their patients with GTS. Given the visuospatial, visual memory, and attentional deficits reported earlier, it is clear that more studies of perception are needed. One likely hypothesis that is as yet untested is that any perceptual deficits that are found in this condition simply reflect the more fundamental attentional abnormalities.

Motor Skills

Motor tics are, of course, another pathognomonic symptom of this disorder. The range of motor tics is very wide, from mild blinking to conspicuous flailing of limbs. Perhaps more unusual, though, are motor phenomena that have specific *content*. Echopraxia is a clear example of this, where a patient involuntarily repeats ("echoes") the actions of another person immediately after observing them. Lees et al. (1984) report that echopraxia occurs in 21% of patients with GTS. Here is Gilles de la Tourette's own description of this extraordinary phenomenon:

S. is in the courtyard of the Salpêtrière in his usual way. He is moving about, making a few contortions and a few strange sounds, all of which is his ordinary practice. Another patient approaches him and decides to imitate one of his stranger movements, which consists of lifting the right arm and leg and stomping with the left foot, a peculiar position that one can clearly see is apt to cause a loss of balance. At the same time, he mimics one of our patient's more bizarre and characteristic utterances. Soon S., who has been rather calm, starts to imitate the screams and strange mannerisms of his fellow patient, and does it so vigorously that he falls, fortunately not hurting himself. Hospital guards have to stop this game, which could become dangerous. This incident, sadly, has become the source of many cruel episodes where other patients take sadistic advantage of S.'s irresistable imitative compulsion. (Gilles de la Tourette, in Goetz and Klawans [1982], p. 7–8.)

The notion of an "imitative compulsion" dramatically conveys how these movements might be triggered simply by the sight of another person's movements, the resulting imitation being entirely automatic and involuntary. Copropraxia (the gestural equivalent of coprolalia), like echopraxia, is another motor tic with content, and again suggests a single neurological or cognitive deficit may underlie symptoms at both levels, despite earlier arguments against this claim. Copropraxia remains to be studied in more detail.

Surprisingly, motor skills have not been examined experimentally in many studies, one exception being Bornstein et al.'s (1983) report of more general motor deficits as measured by the Grooved Pegboard Test (an index of visuomotor coordination). Golden (1984) reports that half of his patients actually showed superior motor skills, whereas the others showed impaired performance. Such super- and subnormal motor performance remains to be replicated. The question of whether the motor tics in this condition reflect abnormalities in the *planning* of action, or in the control of action, is currently unknown. Answers to these questions will contribute significantly to a better understanding of the syndrome.

Frontal Systems and the Intention Editor

Given that the symptoms of GTS seem to involve those systems that are central to the control of action, it is relevant to enquire about the functioning of the so-called frontal systems that are held to control action (and to be impaired in patients with nonfocal frontal lesions). In cognitive psychology the main mechanism that has been described in the Supervisory Attentional System (or the SAS:

Shallice, 1988). To understand the SAS, we must first mention what Shallice calls the Contention Scheduling System (CSS), which responds to external stimuli and repeats relevant, routine actions. The SAS oversees the CSS, by activating or inhibiting alternative schemata. The primary function of the SAS is to respond to novelty. Shallice (1988) has proposed that the SAS is impaired in patients with frontal lobe syndrome, resulting in disinhibition of actions.

There is little direct evidence of how patients with GTS perform on tests that tap the SAS as yet, although we are currently investigating this (see Baron-Cohen et al., 1994b). Tests that are held to tap the SAS include the Tower of Hanoi (a test of planning ability) and the Wisconsin Card Sorting Test (a test of the ability to shift flexibly between categories). The hypothesis we are testing is that patients with GTS will not be *generally* impaired in the SAS. Evidence for this is that, unlike frontal lobe patients, those with GTS appear to be able to switch to new actions in an action sequence, are not simply stimulus-driven in their actions, and do not report planning difficulties in their everyday lives.

In comparison, our recent work has shown that children with GTS are impaired in what we call "intention editing." This process is required whenever two or more intentions are activated simultaneously, only one of which can be executed into action. In the tasks we used, for example, we asked the children to simultaneously open one hand while closing the other, and then switch to doing this in the opposite pattern, carrying on this simultaneous alternation for 10 trials (this is Luria's Hand Alternation Task). A second task we used involved playing the Yes and No Game, in which the children could answer a question in any way they liked, so long as they did not answer with the words "Yes" or "No." On both tasks, children with GTS were severely impaired, relative to normal control groups (Baron-Cohen et al., 1994a). These deficits suggest the existence of a mechanism in the normal case (which we call the Intention Editor) that has failed to develop normally in children with GTS. Whether the Intention Editor is a specific subsystem of the SAS is a question we are currently investigating (see Baron-Cohen and Moriarty, 1995; Baron-Cohen and Robertson, 1995).

Neuropsychology: Preliminary Conclusions

The neuropsychology of GTS is currently very incomplete, in part because there have been insufficient experimental studies of key psychological systems, and in part because the studies that have been carried out have tended to include a wide mix of subjects, which may mask important neuropsychological differences that may exist between subgroups. For example, some studies have lumped together both old and young patients, or those with coprolalia and those without, those with an early and a late onset of GTS, and even those who are receiving medication and those who are not. This variation, in our opinion, prevents a careful comparison of homogenous subgroups within the disorder. It is hoped that future research in this area will adopt a more rigorous experimental approach, drawing on methods available in experimental psychology, and define patient groups more tightly, so that if subgroups do exist, these can be better understood. Why should some patients with GTS manifest coprolalia, for example, and others not? Neuropsychological factors accounting for these differences need to be identified.

Despite these reservations, some preliminary conclusions may be drawn. First, attentional deficits appear to be present from very early on in the condition. This needs clarification, because of its importance in understanding the ontogenesis of GTS. Second, our initial studies on frontal systems in GTS suggest that a specific mechanism, the Intention Editor, may be impaired during development, and this is postulated to underlie the production of tics in the range of output systems (speech, motor activity, etc.). This deficit might be expected to have a frontal lobe basis, with connections to basal ganglia systems, given what is known about these brain regions in the control of action (Shallice, 1988). An important question concerns

the relationship between the Intention Editing deficits and the attentional deficits.

Finally, reports that one third of patients have a spontaneous remission of their motor and vocal tics (Golden, 1984) raise the question as to whether, in this subgroup, cognitive deficits *also* remit, or whether these persist even in the absence of manifest tics. Such data is needed in order to answer the question of how cognitive deficits relate to symptoms.

Etiology

As suggested earlier, a genetic basis to GTS has been suggested and at present the evidence is mostly in support of a single autosomal dominant gene with varying penetrance (see Robertson, 1989). The neurochemical basis for GTS is, as yet, not known. In a good review, Caine (1985) examines the evidence for biochemical abnormalities; the main hypothesis is of an imbalance of central nervous system neurotransmitter agents. Dopamine has received most support, but this is based mainly on the fact that haloperidol reduces the symptoms in a large number of patients, whereas stimulants such as pemoline and methylphenidate exacerbate the symptoms (Robertson, 1989). Friedhoff (1986) addressed the possible role of D1 and D2 receptors in GTS, highlighting a distinction between the two, and it seems generally accepted that D2 blockers such as haloperidol and sulpiride (Robertson et al., 1990) are of particular use in treating GTS.

Summary

In this chapter we have reviewed neuropsychiatric and neuropsychological studies of GTS. The major finding in the former field is that there is a high rate of OCD in GTS; this is unlikely to be a consequence of the disorder and instead appears to be an integral part of it, perhaps etiologically/genetically related. Studies of the brain reveal functional abnormalities in the cingulate and basal ganglia, and many cases of GTS respond to dopamine-blocking agents such as haloperidol and sulpiride. Structural abnormalities have not been convincingly demonstrated as yet.

The major neuropsychological abnormalities that have been found are in Intention Editing and in attention. Exactly how these relate to each other and to the key symptoms in language and motor skills constitute promising avenues for future research. The findings from neuropsychiatry and neuropsychology suggest that GTS can no longer be thought of simply as a motor disorder. This change of perspective brings us closer to Georges Gilles de la Tourette's original view of this disorder.

Acknowledgments

Gratitude is expressed to the UK and US Tourette Syndrome Associations for their continuing financial support and encouragement.

References

Allport, A. (1987). Selection for action: Some behavioral and neurophysiological considerations of attention and action. In H. Heurer and A. Sanders, eds., *Perspectives on Perception and Action* (chap. 15). Hillsdale, N.J.: Lawrence Erlbaum, pp. 395–419.

American Psychiatric Association. (1994). *Diagnostic and Statistical Manual of Mental Disorders IV* (DSM-IV). Washington, D.C.: American Psychiatric Association.

Annett, M. (1970). A classification of hand preferences by association analysis. *British Journal of Psychology, 61,* 303–321.

Asam, U. (1982). A follow-up study of Tourette syndrome. In A. J. Friedhoff and T. N. Chase, eds., *Gilles de la Tourette Syndrome, Advances in Neurology, vol. 35.* New York: Raven Press, pp. 285–286.

Baron-Cohen, S., Cross, P., Crowson, M., and Robertson, M. (1994a). Can children with Gilles de la Tourette syndrome edit their intentions? *Psychological Medicine, 24,* 29–40.

Baron-Cohen, S., and Moriarty, J. (1995). Developmental dysexecutive syndrome: Does it exist? A neuropsychological perspective. In M. Robertson and V. Eapen, eds., *Movement and Allied Disorders in Childhood.* New York: John Wiley and Sons, Ltd., pp. 305-316.

Baron-Cohen, S., and Robertson, M. (1995). Children with either autism, Gilles de la Tourette syndrome, or both: Mapping cognition to specific syndromes. *Neurocase, 1,* 101-104.

Baron-Cohen, S., Robertson, M., and Moriarty, J. (1994b). The development of the will: A neuropsychological analysis of Gilles de la Tourette Syndrome. In D. Cicchetti and S. Toth, eds., *Rochester Symposium on Developmental Psychopathology: Disorders and Dysfunctions of the Self, vol. 5.* Rochester, NY: University of Rochester Press, pp. 57–77.

Bleich, A., Bernout, E., Apter, A., and Tyano, S. (1985). Gilles de la Tourette syndrome and mania in an adolescent. *British Journal of Psychiatry, 146,* 664–665.

Bornstein, R., King, G., and Carrol, A. (1983). Neuropsychological abnormalities in Gilles de la Tourette's syndrome. *Journal of Nervous and Mental Diseases, 171,* 497–502.

Boswell, J. (1867). *The Life of Samuel Johnson LLD.* London: George Routledge and Sons.

Bruun, R. D. (1984). Gilles de la Tourette's syndrome: An overview of clinical experience. *Journal of the American Academy of Child Psychiatry, 23,* 126–133.

Burd, L., and Kerbeshian, J. (1984). Gilles de la Tourette's syndrome and bipolar disorder. *Archives of Neurology, 41,* 1236.

Caine, E. D. (1985). Gilles de la Tourette's syndrome: A review of clinical and research studies and consideration of future directions for investigation. *Archives of Neurology, 42,* 393–397.

Caine, E. D., Margolin, D. I., Brown, G. L., and Ebert, M. H. (1978). Gilles de la Tourette's syndrome, tardive dyskinesia and psychosis in an adolescent. *American Journal of Psychiatry, 135,* 241–243.

Caine, E. D., McBride, M. C., Chiverton, P., Bamford, K. A., Rediess, S., and Shiao, J. (1988). Tourette syndrome in Monroe county school children. *Neurology, 38,* 472–475.

Channon, S., Flynn, D., and Robertson, M. (1992). Attentional deficits in Gilles de la Tourette syndrome. *Neuropsychiatry, Neurology, and Behavioral Neurology, 5,* 170–177.

Chase, T. N., Foster, N. L., Fedio, P., Brooks, R., Mansi, L., Kessler, R., and DiChiro, G. (1984). Gilles de la Tourette syndrome: Studies with the fluorine-18-labelled fluorodeoxyglucose positron emission tomographic method. *Annals of Neurology, 15* (Suppl.), S175.

Chase, T. N., Geoffrey, V., Gillespie, M., and Burrows, G. H. (1986). Structural and functional studies of Gilles de la Tourette syndrome. *Revue Neurologique* (Paris), *142,* 851–855.

Cohen, D. J., Detlor, J., Shaywitz, B., and Leckman, J. (1982). Interaction of biological and psychological factors in the natural history of Tourette's syndrome: A paradigm for childhood neuropsychiatric disorders. In A. Friedhoff and T. Chase, eds., *Gilles de la Tourette's Syndrome, Advances in Neurology, vol. 35.* New York: Raven Press, pp. 31–40.

Comings, D. E., and Comings, B. G. (1987a). A controlled study of Tourette's syndrome. 1. Attention-deficit disorder, learning disorders, and school problems. *American Journal of Human Genetics, 41,* 701–741.

Comings, D. E., and Comings, B. G. (1987b). Hereditary agoraphobia and obsessive compulsive behavior in relatives of patients with Gilles de la Tourette's syndrome. *British Journal of Psychiatry, 151,* 195–199.

Corbett, J., Mathews, A., Connell, P., and Shapiro, D. (1969). Tics and Gilles de la Tourette's syndrome: A follow-up study and critical review. *British Journal of Psychiatry, 115,* 1229–1241.

Cummings, J. L., and Frankel, M. (1985). Gilles de la Tourette syndrome and the neurological basis of obsessions and compulsions. *Biological Psychiatry, 20,* 1117–1126.

Curtis, D., Robertson, M., and Gurling, H. (1992) Autosomal dominant gene transmission in a large kindred with Gilles de la Tourette syndrome. *British Journal of Psychiatry, 160,* 845–849.

Eapen, V., Pauls, D., and Robertson, M. (1993). Evidence for autosomal dominant transmission in Tourette's syndrome. *British Journal of Psychiatry, 163,* 593–596.

Erenberg, G., Cruse, R. P., and Rothner, A. D. (1986). Tourette syndrome: An analysis of 200 pediatric and adolescent cases. *Cleveland Clinic Quarterly, 53,* 127–131.

Frank, S. (1978). Psycholinguistic findings in Gilles de la Tourette's syndrome. *Journal of Communication Disorders, 11,* 349–363.

Frankel, M., Cummings, J. L., Robertson, M. M., Trimble, M. R., Hill, M. A., and Benson, D. F. (1986). Obsessions and compulsions in Gilles de la Tourette's syndrome. *Neurology, 36,* 378–382.

Friedhoff, A. J. (1986). Insights into the pathophysiology and pathogenesis of Gilles de la Tourette syndrome. *Revue Neurologique* (Paris), *142,* 860–864.

George, M. S., Trimble, M. R., Costa, D. C., Robertson, M. M., Ring, H. A., and Ell, P. J. (1992). Elevated frontal cerebral blood flow in Gilles de la Tourette Syndrome: A 99Tcm-HMPAO SPECT study. *Psychiatry Research: Neuroimaging, 45,* 143–151.

George, M. S., Trimble, M. R., Ring, H. A., Sallee, F. R., and Robertson, M. M. (1993).

Obsessions in obsessive compulsive disorder with and without Gilles de la Tourette syndrome. *American Journal of Psychiatry, 150,* 93–97.

Gilles de la Tourette, G. (1885). Etude sur une affection nerveuse caracterisee par de l'incoordination motrice accompagnee d'echolalie et de copralalie. *Archives of Neurology, 9,* 19–42; 158–200.

Gilles de la Tourette, G. (1899). La maladie des tics convulsifs. *La Semaine Medicale, 19,* 153–156.

Goetz, C., and Klawans, H. (1982). Gilles de la Tourette's syndrome. In A. Friedhoff and T. Chase, eds., *Gilles de la Tourette's Syndrome, Advances in Neurology, vol. 35.* New York: Raven Press, pp. 1–16.

Golden, G., and Greenhill, L. (1981). Tourette syndrome in mentally retarded children. *Mental Retardation, 19,* 17–19.

Golden, G. S. (1984). Psychologic and neuropsychologic aspects of Tourette's syndrome. *Neurologic Clinics, 21,* 91–102.

Grasset, J. (1890). Lecons sur un cas de maladie des tics et un cas de tremblement singulier de la tete et des membres gauches. *Archives of Neurology, 20,* 27–45; 187–211.

Green, R. C., and Pitman, R. K. (1986). Tourette syndrome and obsessive-compulsive disorder. In M. A. Jenike, L. Baer, W. O. Minichiello, eds., *Obsessive-Compulsive Disorders: Theory and Management.* Littleton, MA: PSG Publishing Company, pp. 147–164.

Guinon, G. (1886). Sur la maladie des tics convulsifs. *Revue de Medicine, 6,* 50–80.

Hall, M., Costa, D., Shields, J., Heavens, J., Robertson, M. M., and Ell, P. J. (1990). Brain perfusion patterns with 99TcM-HMPAO/SPET in patients with Gilles de la Tourette syndrome: Short Report. *Nuclear Medicine, 27* (Suppl.), 243–245.

Hyde, T.M., Staley, M.E., Coppola, R., Handel, S.F., Rickler, K.C., and Weinberger, D.R. (1995). Cerebral morphometric abnormalities in Tourette's syndrome: A quantitative MRI study of monozygotic twins. *Neurology, 45,* 1176-1182.

Incagnoli, T., and Kane, R. (1981). Neuropsychoylogical functioning in Gilles de la Tourette's syndrome. *Journal of Clinical Neuropsychology, 3,* 165–169.

Itard, J.M.G. (1825). Memoire sur quelques fonctions involuntaires des appareils de la locomotion de la prehension et de la voix. *Archives of General Medicine, 8,* 385–407.

Jenkins, R. L., and Ashby, H. B. (1983). Gilles

de la Tourette syndrome in identical twins. *Archives of Neurology, 40,* 249–251.

Kelman, D. H. (1965). Gilles de la Tourette's disease in children: A review of the literature. *Journal of Child Psychology and Psychiatry, 6,* 219–226.

Krumholz, A., Singer, H. S., Niedermeyer, E., Burnite, R., and Harris, K. (1983). Electrophysiological studies in Tourette's syndrome. *Annals of Neurology, 14,* 638–641.

Kurlan, R., Behr, J., Medved, L., Shoulson, I., Pauls, D., Kidd, J. R., and Kidd, K. K. (1986). Familial Tourette's syndrome: Report of a large pedigree and potential for linkage analysis. *Neurology, 36,* 772–776.

Kurlan, R., Behr, J., Medved, L., Shoulson, I., Pauls, D., and Kidd, K. K. (1987). Severity of Tourette's syndrome in one large kindred: Implication for determination of disease prevalence rate. *Neurology, 44,* 268–269.

Lanser, J., Van Santen, H., Jennekens-Schinkel, A., and Roos, R. (1993). Tourette's syndrome and right hemisphere dysfunction. *British Journal of Psychiatry, 163,* 116–118.

Lees, A., Robertson, M., Trimble, M., and Murray, N. (1984). A clinical study of Gilles de la Tourette's syndrome in the United Kingdom. *Journal of Neurology, Neurosurgery, and Psychiatry, 47,* 1–8.

Lucas, A. R., and Rodin, E. A. (1973). Electroencephalogram in Gilles de la Tourette's disease. *Diseases of the Nervous System, 34,* 85–89.

Ludlow, C., Polinsky, R., Caine, E., Bassich, C., and Ebert, M. (1982). Language and speech abnormalities in Tourette's syndrome. In A. Friedhoff and T. Chase, eds., *Gilles de la Tourette's Syndrome, Advances in Neurology, vol. 35.* New York: Raven Press, pp. 351–362.

Mathews, W. (1988). Attention deficits and learning difficulties in children with Tourette's syndrome. *Psychiatric Annals, 18,* 414–416.

McHenry, L. C., Jr. (1967). Samuel Johnson's tics and gesticulations. *Journal of the History of Medicine, 22,* 152–168.

Montgomery, M. A., Clayton, P. J., and Friedhoff, A. J. (1982). Psychiatric illness in Tourette syndrome patients and first-degree relatives. In A. J. Friedhoff and T. N. Chase, eds., *Gilles de la Tourette Syndrome, Advances in Neurology, vol. 35.* New York: Raven Press, pp. 335–340.

Moriarty, J., Campos, C. D., Schmitz, B., Trimble, M. R., Ell, P. J., and Robertson, M. M. 1995. Brain perfusion abnormalities in Gilles de la Tourette's syndrome. *British Journal of Psychiatry, 167,* 249–254.

Morphew, J. A., and Sim, M. (1969). Gilles de la Tourette's syndrome: A clinical and psychopathological study. *British Journal of Medical Psychology, 42,* 293–301.

Murray, T. J. (1979). Dr. Samuel Johnson's movement disorders. *British Medical Journal, 1,* 1610–1614.

O'Quinn, A., and Thompson, R. (1980). Tourette's syndrome: An expanded review. *Pediatrics, 66,* 420–424.

Obeso, A., Rothwell, J. C., and Marsden, C. D. (1982). The neurophysiology of Tourette syndrome. In A. J. Friedhoff and T. N. Chase, eds., *Gilles de la Tourette Syndrome, Advances in Neurology, vol. 35.* New York: Raven Press, pp. 105–114.

Pauls, D. L., Leckman, J., Towbin, K. E., Zahner, G. E., and Cohen, D. J. (1986a). A possible genetic relationship exists between Tourette's syndrome and obsessive-compulsive disorder. *Psychopharmacology Bulletin, 22,* 730–733.

Pauls, D. L., Towbin, K. E., Leckman, J. F., Zahner, G. E., and Cohen, D. J. (1986b). Gilles de la Tourette's syndrome and obsessive compulsive disorder. *Archives of General Psychiatry, 43,* 1180–1182.

Peterson, B., Riddle, M., and Cohen, D. (1993). Reduced basal ganglia volumes in Tourette's syndrome using 3D reconstruction techniques from MRI. *Neurology, 43,* 941–949.

Pitman, R. K., Green, R. C., Jenike, M. A., and Mesulam, M. M. (1987). Clinical comparison of Tourette's disorder and obsessive-compulsive disorder. *American Journal of Psychiatry, 144,* 1166–1171.

Regeur, L., Pakkenberg, B., Fog, R., and Pakkenberg, H. (1986). Clinical features and long term treatment with pimozide in 65 patients with Gilles de la Tourette's syndrome. *Journal of Neurology, Neurosurgery and Psychiatry, 49,* 791–795.

Reid, A. H. (1984). Gilles de la Tourette syndrome in mental handicap. *Journal of Medical Deficiency Research, 28,* 81–83.

Robertson, M. M. (1989). The Gilles de la Tourette syndrome: The current status. *British Journal of Psychiatry, 154,* 147–169.

Robertson, M.M. (1994) Annotation: Gilles de la Tourette syndrome—an update. *Journal of Child Psychology and Psychiatry and Allied Disciplines, 35,* 597-611.

Robertson, M.M. (1995). The relationship between Gilles de la Tourette's syndrome and obsessive compulsive disorder. *Journal of Serotonin Research, Suppl. 1,* 49-62.

Robertson, M. M., Channon, S., Baker, J., and Flynn, D. (1993). The psychopathology of Gilles de la Tourette syndrome: A controlled study. *British Journal of Psychiatry, 162,* 114–117.

Robertson, M. M., and Eapen, V. (1992). Pharmacologic controversy of CNS stimulants in Gilles de la Tourette's syndrome. *Clinical Neuropharmacology, 15,* 408–425.

Robertson, M. M., and Gourdie, A. (1990). Familial Tourette's syndrome in a large British pedigree: Associated psychopathology, severity of Tourette's and potential for linkage analysis. *British Journal of Psychiatry, 156,* 515–521.

Robertson, M. M., and Reinstein, D. Z. (1991), Convulsive tic disorder. Georges Gilles de la Tourette, Guinon, and Grasset on the phenomenology and psychopathology of Gilles de la Tourette syndrome. *Behavioral Neurology, 4,* 29–56.

Robertson, M. M., Schneiden, V., and Lees, A. J. (1990). Management of Gilles de la Tourette syndrome using sulpiride. *Clinical Neuropharmacology, 13,* 229–235

Robertson, M. M., and Trimble, M. R. (1991). Gilles de la Tourette syndrome in the Middle East: An Arab cohort and pedigree. *British Journal of Psychiatry, 158,* 416–419.

Robertson, M. M., Trimble, M. R., and Lees, A. J. (1988). The psychopathology of the Gilles de la Tourette syndrome: A phenomenological analysis. *British Journal of Psychiatry, 152,* 383–390.

Robertson, M. M., Trimble, M. R., Lees, A. J. (1989). Self-injurious behavior and the Gilles de la Tourette syndrome. A clinical study and review of the literature. *Psychological Medicine, 19,* 611–625.

Shallice, T. (1988). *From Neuropsychology to Neural Structure.* Cambridge: Cambridge University Press.

Shapiro, A., Shapiro, E., and Clarkin, J. (1974). Clinical psychological testing in Tourette's syndrome. *Journal of Personality Assessment, 38,* 464–478.

Shapiro, A. K., Shapiro, E. S., Bruun, R. D., and Sweet, R. D. (1978). *Gilles de la Tourette Syndrome.* New York: Raven Press.

Singer, H., Reiss, A., Brown, J., Aylward, E. H., Shih, B., Chee, E., Harris, E. L., Reader, M. J., Chase, G. A., Bryan, R. N., and Denckla, M. B. (1993). Volumetric MRI changes in basal ganglia of children with Tourette's syndrome. *Neurology, 43,* 950–956.

Sutherland, R., Kolb, B., Schoel, W., Whishaw,

I., and Davies, D. (1982). Neuropsychological assessment of children and adults with Tourette's syndrome: A comparison with learning difficulties and schizophrenia. In A. Friedhoff and T. Chase, eds., *Gilles de la Tourette's Syndrome, Advances in Neurology, vol. 35.* New York: Raven Press, pp. 311–322.

Sverd, J., Curley, A., Jandorf, L., and Volkersz, L. (1988). Behavioral disorder and attention deficits in boys with Tourette's syndrome. *Journal of the American Academy of Child and Adolescent Psychiatry, 27,* 413–417.

Takeuchi, K., Yamashita, M., Morikiyo, M., Takeda, N., Morita, K., Tamura, T., and Kaiya, H. (1986). Gilles de la Tourette's syndrome and schizophrenia. *The Journal of Nervous and Mental Disease, 174,* 247–248.

Taylor, E. (1985). Syndromes of overactivity and attention deficit. In M. Rutter and L. Hersov, eds., *Child and Adolescent Psychiatry: Modern Approaches/II.* Oxford/Boston: Blackwells Scientific Publications, pp. 424–443.

Van de Wetering, B.J.M., Martens, C.M.C., Fortgens, C., Slaets, J. P., and van Woerkom, T. C. (1985). Late components of the auditory evoked potentials in Gilles de la Tourette syndrome. *Clinics in Neurology and Neurosurgery, 87,* 181–186.

Wilson, S.A.K. (1927). Tics and child conditions. *Journal of Neurology and Psychopathology, 8,* 93–109.

Wilson, R. S., Garron, D. C., Tanner, C. M., and Klawans, H. L. (1982). Behavior disturbance in children with Tourette syndrome. In A. J. Friedhoff and T. N. Chase, eds., *Gilles de la Tourette's Syndrome, Advances in Neurology, vol. 35.* New York: Raven Press, pp. 329–334.

World Health Organization. (1992). *International Classification of Diseases and Health-Related Problems/X.* Geneva: World Health Organization.

Yaryura-Tobias, J. A., Neziroglu, F., Howard, S., and Fuller, B. (1981). Clinical aspects of Gilles de la Tourette syndrome. *Journal of Orthomolecular Psychiatry, 10,* 263–268.

Yaryura-Tobias, J. A., and Neziroglu, F. (1983). Complex obsessive-compulsive disorders. In H. M. van Praag, M. H. Lader, S. Gershon, M. Lipton, and A. J. Prange, Jr., eds., *Obsessive-Compulsive Disorders, Pathogenesis-Diagnosis-Treatment, Experimental and Clinical Psychiatry Series, vol. 8, chap. 9.* New York: Marcel Dekker, pp. 81–103.

11 The Neuropsychology of Memory Dysfunction and Its Assessment

LARRY R. SQUIRE and ARTHUR SHIMAMURA

Memory disorders merit separate attention in a volume on clinical neuropsychology because complaints about memory are very common, particularly among neurological and psychiatric patients. Among neurological patients with organic illness, memory problems are considered to be the most common initial complaint (Strub and Black, 1977). Among psychiatric patients, memory problems are often reported in association with affective disorder (Sternberg and Jarvik, 1976; Stromgren, 1977) and schizophrenia (Chapman, 1966). Memory functions are also of special interest in cases of psychogenic amnesia (Nemiah, 1980), and in considerations of the side effects of treatments such as psychotropic drugs and electroconvulsive therapy (ECT) (Squire, 1986).

When memory disorders are evaluated with quantitative methods, it becomes possible to identify the various disorders that can occur, to understand the similarities and differences between them, and to follow their course reliably in individual patients. Several books and articles have appeared in recent years that consider the subject of memory disorders and memory testing (Squire, 1987; Mayes, 1988; Shimamura and Gershberg, 1992; Squire and Butters, 1992; Butters et al., 1995). The purpose of this chapter is to identify the neuropsychological tools of memory testing and to develop a rationale grounded in basic research for the neuropsychological evaluation of memory functions.

Of the higher cortical functions (e.g., perception, attention, language, memory, and action), memory is among the most studied and the best understood. Although understanding is still very incomplete, memory will probably be among the first of the higher brain functions to be explained—both at the cellular level, in terms of cellular events and synaptic change, and at the systems (or neuropsychological) level, in terms of brain systems and brain organization. Accordingly, when one turns to the topic of memory disorders from the perspective of clinical neuropsychology, one can bring to the subject a good deal of relevant information from cognitive psychology and neuroscience about normal memory and how it is organized in the brain. Readers may wish to consult any of several recent reviews and monographs that address these issues (McGaugh, 1989; Squire and Zola-Morgan, 1991; Kandel and Hawkins, 1992; Thompson, 1992; Lavond et al., 1993; Schacter et al., 1993; Squire, 1994).

Memory dysfunction most often occurs in association with other disorders of intellectual function, as in depression or dementia. If attention is impaired, acquisition of memory will be deficient. If language is impaired, it may be difficult to remember words or to use them with the usual facility. If intellectual functions are impaired, memory impairment is just one of a broad spectrum of disorders. In this sense, it might seem unfruitful, or even misleading, to speak about memory and memory disorders in isolation from other cognitive functions. However, there is an important reason for considering memory as a distinct neurological function. Disorders of memory can sometimes occur as a relatively pure entity. By studying them, one can learn to recognize and understand memory disorders, even when they occur in a web of other disorders.

Functional Amnesia

Disorders of memory have many causes and can take many forms. A first step in their classification is to distinguish disorders of functional or psychogenic origin from disorders that result from a direct perturbation of brain function; that is, neurological injury or disease. Functional amnesias may be the best known, having been the subject of frequent treatment in films and literature. They are not nearly as common, however, as the so-called "organic" or neurological amnesias, and these two general types of memory impairment are rather easy to distinguish.

A published case of functional amnesia is particularly instructive (Schacter et al., 1982). A 21-year-old man approached a policeman in downtown Toronto complaining of back pain. When brought to hospital, it was discovered that he did not know his own name or anything about his past, except for an isolated period 1 to 2 years earlier when he had worked for a courier service. He also gave a nickname, Lumberjack (this was the pseudonym used in the published report to protect the patient's identity), but did not know how he had come by that name. During 4 days of testing in the hospital, he exhibited a good capacity for learning new material and in informal conversation he also demonstrated a continuing awareness of what had occurred since his admission.

On a formal test of remote memory using photographs of famous persons who had come into the news at different times in the past, he obtained a normal score. In contrast, his performance on a test of past autobiographical memory was quite abnormal. This test asked for recall of past personal events in response to cue words (Crovitz and Schiff-

man, 1974). For example, he was given the word "box" and asked to recall a specific episode from his past that involved a box. Only 14% of his recalled episodes were dated by him as having occurred more than 4 days earlier, prior to hospitalization. By contrast, 91% of the episodes recalled by a control subject came from more than 4 days earlier. In addition, when the patient's amnesia subsequently cleared, he was given a second form of the test and now dated 92% of his episodes from the period prior to hospitalization. Thus, during his period of amnesia, his past was nearly barren of personal memories; yet his store of general information about past public events was good.

On the fourth day in the hospital, while watching a climactic funeral scene in the television version of *Shogun*, his personal past began to return to him. The recent death of a favorite grandfather had provoked his memory loss. Lumberjack had been a nickname given him during his time at the courier service, which had been a particularly happy time of his life. In the end his past memory fully recovered, except for a 12-hour period preceding his hospital admission. This case illustrates the essential features of functional disorders of memory. There is often loss of personal identity. Anterograde amnesia (loss of new learning capacity) does not usually occur. Retrograde amnesia (loss of memory for events that occurred before the onset of amnesia) is extensive; it can include the loss of personal identity; and it can be limited to autobiographical memory.

Amnesia Due to Neurological Injury or Disease

The "organic" amnesias have quite a different character. Distinguishing between the "organic" and the functional amnesias is a rather simple matter, because in the "organic" amnesias anterograde amnesia is severe, but loss of personal identity does not occur. The opposite is true in functional amnesia. Moreover, in "organic" amnesia retrograde amnesia is usually temporally graded, and public-event memory and autobiographical memory are similarly affected. In functional amnesia, retrograde memory function is determined more by memory content than by when the information was acquired.

"Organic" amnesia can occur for a number of reasons (e.g., temporal lobe surgery, chronic alcohol abuse, head injury, anoxia or ischemia, encephalitis, epilepsy, tumor, or vascular accident). In addition, memory dysfunction is typically a prominent and early sign of dementia, including Alzheimer's disease. Patients with memory dysfunction due to neurological injury or disease can appear normal to casual observation, even when the deficit is severe. These patients can have normal intelligence, as measured by conventional IQ tests, and normal ability to hold information in immediate memory, as measured by digit span tests (Cave and Squire, 1992). In conversation, they can exhibit appropriate social skills, have insight into their condition, and exhibit normal language ability.

Medial Temporal Lobe Amnesia

H.M., the best-known case of medial temporal lobe amnesia, sustained a bilateral medial temporal lobe resection in 1953 in an effort to relieve severe epilepsy (Scoville and Milner, 1957). The surgery presumably damaged much of the hippocampal formation, the amygdala, and adjacent medial cortex. Following surgery, H.M.'s seizure activity was attenuated, but he was unable to retain memory for events and information encountered after his surgery. That is, he exhibited profound anterograde amnesia. He also had several years of retrograde amnesia (i.e., memory impairment) for events that occurred prior to the onset of his amnesia (Corkin, 1984). In addition to his above-average IQ and intact immediate memory, H.M. was able to detect various kinds of linguistic ambiguity (e.g., "Racing cars can be dangerous"; "Charging tigers should be avoided" [Lackner, 1974]). H.M. was also capable of recalling some well-formed autobiographical episodes from his adolescence. In an often quoted passage, H.M. expresses his own experience of his memory disorder.

Right now, I'm wondering. Have I done or said anything amiss? You see, at this moment everything looks clear to me, but what happened just before? That's what worries me. It's like waking from a dream; I just don't remember. (Milner, 1970, p. 37)

Another patient has provided additional information about the role of the hippocampus itself in memory (Zola-Morgan et al., 1986). Patient R.B. became amnesic in 1978 at the age of 52 after an episode of global ischemia that occurred as a complication of open-heart surgery. Extensive neuropsychological assessment during the next 5 years revealed significant memory impairment in the absence of other cognitive dysfunction. Upon R.B.'s death in 1983, histological examination revealed a discrete bilateral lesion involving the full rostro-caudal extent of the CA1 field of the hippocampus. R.B.'s was the first reported case of human amnesia following a lesion restricted to the hippocampus in which extensive neuropsychological and neuropathological analyses were carried out. Thus, the hippocampus itself appears to be a critical structure for memory, and damage limited to the hippocampus is sufficient to produce an easily detectable and clinically significant memory impairment. This idea was later supported by an additional case in which memory dysfunction was associated with a bilateral hippocampal lesion (Victor and Agamanolis, 1990). It is important to note, however, that neither of these two patients was as severely amnesic as patient H.M. Accordingly, other regions within the medial temporal lobe, in addition to the hippocampus itself, must be important for memory functions. This supposition has recently been confirmed in studies based on an animal model of human amnesia in the monkey (Squire and Zola-Morgan, 1991). The important structures in addition to the hippocampal region itself (including the hippocampus proper, the dentate gyrus, and the subiculum) are the entorhinal, parahippocampal, and perirhinal cortices. The amygdala is not a component of this memory system.

Diencephalic Amnesia

Damage to the midline of the diencephalon can also produce severe amnesia. The most widely studied example of diencephalic amnesia is Korsakoff's syndrome (Victor et al., 1989). Korsakoff's syndrome can develop after many years of chronic alcohol abuse and nutritional deficiency. Neuropathological studies reveal bilateral damage along the diencephalic midline, especially involving the dorsomedial thalamic nuclei and mammillary nuclei (Mair et al., 1979; Mayes et al., 1988). These and other studies, involving both humans and experimental animals, point to the importance for memory function of the medial thalamus, including the mediodorsal nucleus, the anterior nucleus, and the connections and structures within the internal medullary lamina (Markowitsch, 1988; Zola-Morgan and Squire, 1993).

Transient Global Amnesia

Amnesia is not always permanent. Transient global amnesia (TGA) describes a disorder that is quite similar to the neurological amnesias just discussed. TGA generally occurs in persons over age 50, with an incidence per year of 23.5 per 100,000 for persons older than 50 (Kritchevsky, 1989). Patients who have had an episode of TGA do not have an increased risk of developing permanent memory dysfunction or of having a subsequent stroke. Episodes of TGA usually begin suddenly and last for several hours. The memory impairment is characterized by severe anterograde amnesia and a retrograde amnesia that is temporally graded and extends across as much as 20 years prior to the onset of amnesia. After the episode, there is full recovery of memory functions. However, patients are left with a gap in their memory: (1) memory for events that occurred during the period of anterograde amnesia does not recover, presumably because usable long-term memory was not being formed during

TGA; (2) there is recovery from most of the retrograde amnesia, but permanent retrograde amnesia can remain for events that occurred from a few hours to a day or two just prior to the episode.

Electroconvulsive Therapy

Transient amnesia also occurs after electroconvulsive therapy (ECT) (Squire, 1986), which is sometimes prescribed for severe depressive illness (Fig. 11-1). Anterograde amnesia can be quite severe, particularly in patients who receive bilateral ECT (Fig. 11-2). Retrograde amnesia is temporally graded such that the most recent memories are the most affected. By several months after ECT, there is extensive recovery of new learning capacity, and formal testing has not detected persisting memory impairment after this time. This is true even though the tests used

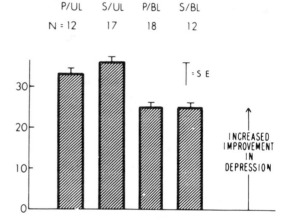

Figure 11-1. The acute effects of electroconvulsive therapy (ECT) on the severity of depression. Depressed patients were randomly assigned to receive either bidirectional-pulse (P) or sine-wave stimuli (S), using either unilateral nondominant (UL) or bilateral (BL) electrode placement. The values shown are the differences between depression scores obtained prior to ECT and again 2 to 3 days after the completion of ECT. The number of ECT treatments, seizure duration, and the number of missed seizures did not differ across groups. In this sample, unilateral ECT led to a somewhat greater therapeutic response than bilateral ECT. (From Weiner et al., 1984.)

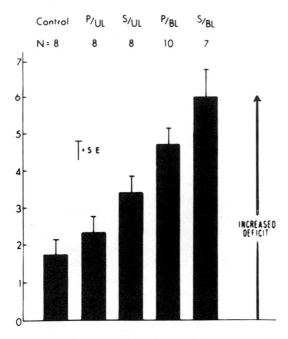

Figure 11-2. The acute effects of electroconvulsive therapy (ECT) on autobiographical memory function. For each group (see Fig. 11-1 caption), the fraction of questions are shown (0 to 0.7) that were answered prior to ECT but were not answered 2 to 3 days after the completion of ECT. Bilateral ECT produced more amnesia than unilateral ECT ($p < .01$) and sine-wave current produced somewhat more amnesia than pulse stimuli ($p = .08$). Abbreviations are the same as in Figure 11-1. (From Weiner et al., 1984.)

to assess memory are sensitive enough to detect changes in memory function during normal aging. Specifically, the tests can detect differences in memory function from decade to decade between groups of healthy normal subjects in their forties, fifties, and sixties. Retrograde amnesia also resolves by 6 to 9 months after ECT, except for memory for events that occurred during the weeks preceding ECT. Some spotty memory loss may remain for even earlier time periods. Although the biological basis of ECT-associated memory impairment is not known with certainty, it is likely to be due to transient electrophysiological abnormalities in the temporal lobe associated with the course of ECT (Abrams and Essman, 1982; Lerer et al., 1984; Malitz and Sackeim, 1986).

Head Injury

Memory dysfunction is also a common finding following traumatic head injury. In most circumstances, memory loss occurs in a constellation of other disorders. The neuropsychology of head injury has been reviewed previously (Levin et al., 1982; Newcombe, 1983). Though memory dysfunction may be the most ubiquitous sign of closed head injury, it commonly occurs together with a reduction in general intellectual capacity, disorders of language and visual perception, apraxias, impairment of attention, and personality change. These multiple disorders are consistent with the variable and widespread pattern of cerebral damage that can result from severe head injury.

One of the largest studies of memory impairment associated with head injury is the classic work of Russell and Nathan (1946). Their study of 1,031 consecutive cases makes several points about the relationship between anterograde and retrograde amnesia. First, based on 972 of these cases where information was available about memory loss, retrograde amnesia was typically brief, covering a period of less than 30 minutes in 90% of the cases. Second, the longer the anterograde amnesia, the longer the retrograde amnesia (Fig. 11-3). Third, retrograde amnesia was more severe in closed (concussive) head injury than in gunshot wounds or other cases of penetrating brain injury. Fourth, during the period of amnesia, neither the anterograde or retrograde component of memory loss could be influenced significantly by hypnosis or barbiturate drugs.

Whereas the great majority of patients admitted to hospitals with a head injury eventually make a good recovery, Newcombe (1983) notes that perhaps 1% have persisting signs of impairment. This impairment is now recognized in most cases to have a neurological basis, not a functional basis (e.g., compensation neurosis) as once believed. The neuropsychologist must address questions about the severity and nature of the deficit, the predicted rate of recovery, as well as ques-

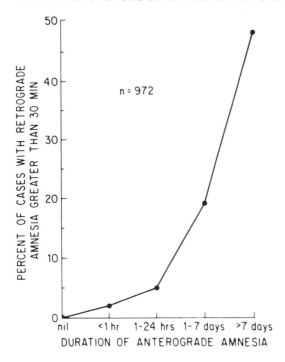

Figure 11-3. The relationship between antero-grade and retrograde amnesia in a large series of head-injury patients. (Reconstructed from Russell and Nathan, 1946.)

tions about possible rehabilitation. The memory deficits themselves have been care-fully reviewed by Schacter and Crovitz (1977).

The duration of post-traumatic amnesia is the best available index of severity of injury and is a good predictor of recovery (Jennett, 1976). Tests of immediate and delayed prose recall, considered below, correlate better with judgments by relatives of a patient's memory abilities than do other formal labora-tory tests of memory (Baddeley et al., 1982).

In general, techniques that improve mem-ory function in normal subjects improve memory functions in head injury patients (and other amnesic patients as well). Accord-ingly, the techniques most often mentioned in the context of rehabilitation or retraining are elaborate note-keeping, imagery, and re-hearsal. Imagery may be of special value in working with patients with memory impair-ment caused by left hemispheric dysfunction (Patten, 1972). However, for a balanced per-

spective on the difficulties of making simple generalizations about rehabilitation, see Newcombe (1983).

Dementia

Dementia is estimated to affect 5% to 15% of the population aged 65 to 85. Alzheimer's disease, the most common form of dementia, accounts for at least 50% of the cases (Katz-man, 1976; Moss and Albert, 1988; Boller and Grafman, 1991). Memory problems are perhaps the most common and often the earliest sign of the disease, but disorders of language (especially anomia) and visuospatial disorders can also occur early in the disease's course. The disease is progressive, eventu-ally involving most intellectual functions and typically develops over a period of 5 to 10 years. Although the diagnosis of Alzheimer's disease cannot be made definitively without neuropathological data, neuropsychological data together with a good medical history can reach a diagnosis that approaches 90% ac-curacy.

In many respects, the memory loss exhib-ited by patients diagnosed as having Alzhei-mer's disease can seem to resemble the memory loss exhibited by patients with more circumscribed amnesia. This conclusion is consistent with the finding that neuropatho-logical changes in Alzheimer's disease are prominent in the medial temporal lobe re-gion (Hyman et al., 1984; Van Hoesen et al., 1991). However, three features of memory dysfunction in Alzheimer's disease have been identified that are not observed in the cir-cumscribed amnesias. First, patients with even mild Alzheimer's disease have impaired digit span scores, whereas amnesic patients are usually normal at digit span tasks. Sec-ond, patients with Alzheimer's disease ex-hibit impaired priming of lexical information (Shimamura et al., 1987; Salmon et al., 1988). Third, patients with Alzheimer's dis-ease can exhibit extensive deficits in remote memory without any sign of a temporal gradi-ent (Wilson et al., 1981). With additional work, it should be possible to determine the typical sequence of the disease, what brain regions become affected at particular times, and to what extent good memory testing can succeed at making early diagnoses.

Neuroimaging

Recent advances in neuroimaging techniques, including magnetic resonance (MR) imaging and positron-emission tomography (PET), have permitted direct visualization of some of the brain structures damaged in amnesic patients. For example, analysis of MR scans of patients with Korsakoff's syndrome (Squire et al., 1990) extended earlier computed tomographic (CT) findings (Shimamura et al., 1988) by demonstrating reduced volume of the mammillary nuclei bilaterally. In addition, high-resolution protocols for imaging the hippocampus with MR now permit visualization of the hippocampal formation in considerable detail (resolution = 0.625 mm). Using this technique, which images the hippocampus directly perpendicular to its long axis, the hippocampal formation was found to be reduced in size (57% of the normal area) in four (non-Korsakoff) patients with amnesia. The temporal lobes were of normal size.

The development of high-resolution protocols for imaging the hippocampal formation and the diencephalon makes it possible to obtain unambiguous anatomical information in living patients (Squire et al., 1990). Such information is helping with the fundamental issue of patient classification and provides a foundation for exploring quantitative and qualitative differences between patients. Although study of amnesic patients using PET is just beginning (Fazio et al., 1992), this method provides a way to evaluate physiological and metabolic dysfunction associated with memory impairment.

Similarities and Differences Among the Amnesias: A First Approximation

Prior to the 1980s, patients with Korsakoff's syndrome were often taken as typical of amnesia in general, perhaps because this type of amnesia was the most available for study. However, Korsakoff's syndrome differs in several ways from other types of amnesia. Thus, Talland (1965), one of the first serious students of Korsakoff's syndrome, wrote that the memory disorder in patients with Korsakoff's syndrome "does not present simply a derangement in memory" (p. 108), and Zangwill (1977) suggested that "other and more extensive psychological dysfunction must coexist with amnesia for the classic picture of Korsakoff's syndrome to emerge" (p. 113). Some of these other deficits derive from frontal lobe dysfunction. Neuropsychological signs of frontal lobe impairment are commonly present in these patients and can influence neuropsychological test performance (Moscovitch, 1982; Squire, 1982b; Schacter, 1987; Shimamura et al., 1991).

It is also worth noting that the confabulation sometimes exhibited by patients with Korsakoff's syndrome is by no means a common feature of either amnesia in general or of Korsakoff's syndrome itself. Confabulation is the misstatement of fact, often in an amusing, bizarre, and self-contradictory way, which occurs as short-latency responses to questions (Mercer et al., 1977). Confabulation is seen most often in the acute phase of the disease, particularly in association with denial of illness, and is seen much less often in the chronic phase. Neuropsychological examination of patients with memory dysfunction must take into account this idea that etiologically distinct forms of amnesia may present with particular deficits superimposed on amnesia.

Putting aside the fact that many of the differences between types of amnesia are a result of frontal lobe pathology, the question remains whether memory impairment is similar or different following damage to the medial temporal lobe or diencephalon. Earlier studies raised the possibility that differences might exist in the rate of forgetting within long-term memory, but a more recent evaluation of this idea in patients with radiologically confirmed lesions indicated that forgetting occurs at an equivalent rate for patients with diencephalic or medial temporal lobe amnesia (McKee and Squire, 1992). It is worth emphasizing that this finding is entirely compatible with the well-known observation that in amnesia information is rapidly lost as one moves from short-term to long-term memory. In this sense, all the "organic" amnesias are syndromes of rapid forgetting. However, the point under discussion here is that the rate of forgetting within long-term memory is similar in the two major types of amnesia.

At present, there is no compelling basis for separating medial temporal lobe and diencephalic amnesia according to behavioral findings. Certainly, it is reasonable to suppose that the medial temporal lobe and the diencephalic midline should make different contributions to normal memory. However, each region may also be an essential component in a larger functional system, such that similar amnesia results from damage to any component. The question whether differences in the pattern of memory impairment can be detected remains a topic for study.

Neuropsychological Assessment of Memory Dysfunction

Formal neuropsychological testing permits one to compare objectively the scores of a given patient to a known group average. This protects us from the natural tendency to rationalize, minimize, or forget observations when they do not conform to expectation. These tendencies are, of course, not confined to clinical observers. In his autobiography, Charles Darwin (1892) wrote:

I had also, during many years, followed a golden rule, namely, that whenever a published fact, a new observation or thought came across me, which was opposed to my general results, to make a memorandum of it without fail and at once; for I had found by experience that such facts and thoughts were far more likely to escape from the memory than favorable ones. (p. 42)

It is also true that we have been so influenced by literature and film to look for psychological explanations of behavior that, in the absence of formal neuropsychological testing, we often tend to develop psychological explanations for "organic" memory disorders. Some years ago, one of us received a letter from a woman telling of her son's mem-

ory problems, which had resulted from a traumatic head injury sustained in an auto accident. Noting that his memory problems seemed greater sometimes than others, she had said to him, "You only remember what you want to." Whereupon, he had replied, "Don't we all?" Her son was probably right. Persons with memory dysfunction, so long as it is not so severe as to be absolute, have the same tendencies that we all have to remember more reliably things that seem important, compared to things that seem trivial, and in general to exercise the same denial, suppression, and selection that we all are heir to while learning or remembering. In amnesia these normal selective factors operate on an overall reduced retentive capacity.

The next sections describe the important elements of memory testing, where the objective is to assess new learning capacity. Then, specific tests and test batteries are considered.

Exceeding Immediate Memory Capacity

The critical feature of memory tasks that accounts for their sensitivity to amnesia is that the information presented to the patient must exceed the immediate memory capacity. Even severely amnesic patients can have a normal digit span and a normal ability to report back the relatively small amount of information that can be maintained in "conscious awareness." William James (1890) termed this capacity "primary memory":

an object in primary memory . . . was never lost; its date was never cut off in consciousness from that of the immediately present moment. In fact it comes to us as belonging to the rearward portion of the present space of time, and not to the genuine past . . . Secondary memory, as it might be styled, is the knowledge of a former state of mind after it had already once dropped from consciousness . . . It is brought back, recalled, fished up, so to speak, from a reservoir in which, with countless other objects, it lay buried and lost from view. (pp. 646–648)

This concept of primary memory remains quite useful in understanding the nature of the memory impairment in amnesia. An interesting study of five amnesic patients, including the noted surgical case H.M. (Drachman and Arbit, 1966), illustrates this point in a formal way. Patients and control subjects were given digit strings of increasing length until an error occurred. A string of digits of the same length was given repeatedly until it was reproduced correctly, or until 25 repetitions of the same digit string had been given. Each time a correct response was given, a new string of digits was presented that was one digit longer than the preceding string. With this procedure, normal subjects were able to increase their digit span to at least 20 digits. Amnesic patients, however, had great difficulty once their digit span capacity had been reached; that is, at the digit string length when their first error occurred. H.M. was unable, even after 25 repetitions of the same digit string, to increase his digit span by one digit beyond his premorbid level of six digits.

Thus for amnesic patients, performance on tests involving immediate recall depends on whether the amount of information to be remembered exceeds a finite processing capacity, termed "primary memory" or "immediate memory capacity." It is also true that memory performance will be poor, even when the amount of information to be remembered is within the limits of that capacity, whenever a delay filled with distraction is interposed between learning and retention testing in order to prevent active rehearsal. If the delay is very long (e.g., an hour or more), the natural distraction of ongoing activity is sufficient to prevent rehearsal and to reveal a deficit, if one is present. If the delay is short (e.g., seconds or minutes), a formal distraction procedure is needed to prevent rehearsal. The following observation of case H.M. makes this point.

Forgetting occurred the instant his focus of attention shifted, but in the absence of distraction his capacity for sustained attention was remarkable. Thus he was able to retain the number 584 for at least 15 minutes, by continuously working out mnemonic schemes. When asked how he had been able to retain the number for so long, he replied: "It's easy. You just remember 8. You see, 5, 8, and 4, add to 17. You remember 8, subtract it from 17 and it leaves 9. Divide 9 in half and you get 5 and 4, and there you are: 584. Easy." (Milner, 1970, p. 37)

The Importance of Delayed Recall Measures

With these considerations in mind, it is easy to understand that the hallmark of the "organic" amnesias is considered to be impaired performance on tests of delayed recall (with interpolated distraction). These tests form the cornerstone of any thorough neuropsychological assessment of memory functions. Tests of delayed recall are simply formal versions of the familiar bedside examination used by neurologists. Typically, the names of three objects are presented to the patient with the instruction to repeat them in order to demonstrate comprehension and attention (e.g., apple, tree, elephant). Then after a delay of several minutes, which is filled with the continuing mental status examination, the patient is asked to recall the words. This informal method can be expanded to yield more information by presenting word pairs instead of single words (e.g., green apple, tall tree, pink elephant), by asking patients at the time of recall how many items they had been asked to remember, by cueing them with synonyms or rhymes for any items that could not be produced in unaided recall, and finally by offering several words to patients and asking them to pick out the ones that had been presented earlier. Failure to recognize words as having been previously presented is a more reliable sign of memory disorder than failure to recall, and recognition failure denotes a more severe disorder as well. The use of recall and recognition tests together makes it possible to detect mild forms of impairment.

Because in many medical settings, patients are tested repeatedly by different physicians and students, it would be useful if the number of words given for memorization were sometimes four, not always three, and of course the words themselves should be different on each test session. Patients with memory problems, like the rest of us, may forget unique events but still retain information about events that are repeated. This sometimes enables them to defeat the purpose of mental status examinations by rehearsing the answers. A colleague tells the story of encountering a neurological patient one day in the hospital outside a room where the patient was about to be presented at Rounds. As the colleague passed by, the patient approached him, asking anxiously. "Say, doc, who's the president of the United States?"

DELAYED RECALL OF PROSE MATERIAL. There are several formal neuropsychological tests of delayed recall that can be used to good advantage. One useful test of this kind uses connected prose, such as the logical memory subtest of the Wechsler Memory Scale, and asks patients to repeat back the story immediately after hearing it and then again after some delay (Milner, 1958). Figure 11-4 shows the performance of 15 patients prescribed bilateral ECT on a test of this type (not the Wechsler Memory Scale), using a delay of 24 hours. Both immediate and

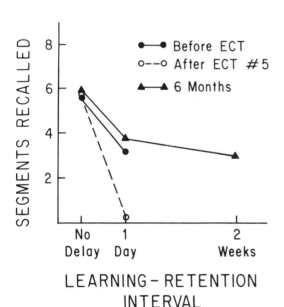

Figure 11-4. Delayed recall of a short prose passage by 15 patients administered bilateral electroconvulsive therapy (ECT). Testing occurred before treatment, 6 to 10 hours after the fifth treatment, and—for a different group of 16 patients—6 to 9 months after bilateral treatment.

delayed recall were assessed before ECT and then again, with an alternate form, 6 to 10 hours after the fifth treatment of the series. ECT had no effect on immediate recall of the prose passage, and by this measure one might have supposed memory functions to be very good. Indeed, by 6 to 10 hours after the fifth treatment, patients can score normally on tests of verbal IQ, show no signs of confusion or disorientation, and can carry on conversations in a normal and appropriate way. It is not uncommon at this time to hear comments from hospital staff not familiar with ECT that the patient's memory is all right or that the patient can remember what he/she wants to. Yet, delayed recall tests show that memory functions are not normal at this time. Whereas patients tested before their prescribed series of ECT showed considerable retention 24 hours after hearing the prose passage, only two of 15 patients could recall any part of the prose passage after ECT, and some could not remember having heard any passage or having seen the experimenter previously. Figure 11-4 also shows the performance of another group of subjects tested 6 to 9 months after the completion of treatment. The ability to learn and retain prose material has recovered by this time after treatment.

This pattern of deficit—impaired recall at a delayed test but not at an immediate test—helps to distinguish the so-called "organic" memory disorders from memory disorders caused by depression. Indeed, delayed recall tests are sensitive measures of neurological dysfunction and can detect early signs of progressive impairment. By contrast, depression affects immediate memory, presumably because patients are preoccupied or inattentive, but does not affect delayed recall beyond what would be expected from the level of recall achieved at immediate testing (Cronholm and Ottosson, 1961; Sternberg and Jarvik, 1976).

DELAYED RECALL OF NONVERBAL MATERIAL. Of the tests that have been used to assess delayed recall of nonverbal material, perhaps the best known is the Rey-Osterrieth figure (Fig. 11-5). The subject is

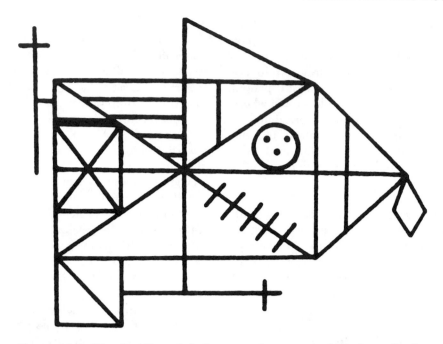

Figure 11-5. The Rey-Osterrieth figure used to assess delayed recall of nonverbal material. (From Osterrieth, 1944; also see Milner and Teuber, 1968.)

asked to copy the figure and then after a delay is asked to reconstruct it from memory without forewarning. An immediate test of reconstruction can be used as well. Milner and her colleagues have developed an alternate form for this figure and a standardized 36-point scoring system for both figures (Milner and Teuber, 1968). When patients have constructive deficits or other problems that preclude using memory tests that involve drawing, then other tests can be used—for example, recognition after a delay of previously presented faces (Milner, 1968b), recollection of the position of a dot on an 8-inch horizontal line (Milner, 1974; Cave and Squire, 1992), or recognition of wire shapes by touch or recognition of other objects that are not easily remembered by verbal labels (Milner and Teuber, 1968).

PAIRED ASSOCIATE LEARNING. Among tests specialized for the detection and quantification of memory dysfunction, perhaps the most sensitive is paired associate learning. Figure 11-6 shows the performance of three kinds of patients with memory problems who

attempted to learn 10 noun-noun word pairs (e.g., army-table, door-sky). In this case, three consecutive presentations of the word pairs were given, and after each presentation subjects were asked to try to produce the second word of the pair upon hearing the first. Patients with alcoholic Korsakoff's syndrome and other amnesic patients all performed poorly on this test, obtaining an average score of less than four correct responses across all 30 learning trials. Patients with frontal lobe lesions and control subjects performed much better. In this same test, case H.M. was unable to produce any correct responses after three trials, even when he was instructed in the use of imagery techniques for associating the words in each pair (Jones, 1974). The sensitivity of this test is due to the fact that the material to be remembered is too extensive to be retained within immediate memory. In addition, tests of recall are almost always more sensitive than tests of recognition (Haist et al., 1992).

Though paired associate learning is a sensitive technique for detecting memory impairment, it is limited by the fact that poor

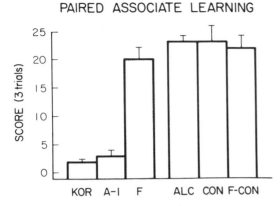

PAIRED ASSOCIATE LEARNING

Figure 11-6. Performance of amnesic patients, patients with frontal lobe lesions, and control subjects on a test of paired-associates learning. Key: KOR = seven patients with Korsakoff's syndrome; A-I = five other patients with anoxic or ischemic amnesia; F = seven patients with frontal lobe lesions; ALC = six alcoholic control subjects matched to the other amnesic patients; F-CON = 11 control subjects matched to the patients with frontal lobe lesions. Brackets show standard errors of the means. (From Janowsky et al., 1989.)

performance could result from factors other than circumscribed memory loss (e.g., depression, inattention, or dementia). Accordingly, perhaps the greatest value of the test is to rule out memory impairment in persons who perform well. If performance is poor, then further tests are needed to interpret the poor score.

FREE RECALL AND REMINDING TECHNIQUES. Two other useful single tests, which can generate useful information for individual subjects, involve assessing free recall of words across a series of five learning trials (Rey, 1964) or using a method of selective reminding or restricted reminding (Buschke and Fuld, 1974). For the first test, 15 unrelated words are presented five times in succession with an opportunity to recall the list after each presentation. Scores for this test as well as a related test of recognition memory are available from several groups of patients (Squire and Shimamura, 1986; Janowsky et al., 1989). For the second test (Buschke and Fuld, 1974), 10 words from a single category (e.g., animal names) are

presented, and subjects are asked to recall as many of them as possible after each of several presentations. In selective reminding, each successive presentation of the list includes only words not recalled on the preceding trial. Trials continue until the subject succeeds in recalling all of the words on a single trial. In restricted reminding, each successive presentation of the list includes only words that have not been recalled on any trial. Trials continue until the subject has succeeded in recalling each word once. These techniques can yield useful data from single subjects regarding both the ability to acquire new information and the consistency of performance.

THE WECHSLER MEMORY SCALE (WMS) AND THE WECHSLER MEMORY SCALE–REVISED (WMS-R). The most frequently used neuropsychological batteries provide for only limited testing of memory functions (Reitan and Davison, 1974; Golden et al., 1980). For many years, the best known memory battery was the Wechsler Memory Scale (WMS) (Wechsler, 1945). The original test battery had seven subtests including general orientation, short-term memory, verbal memory, and nonverbal memory. Based on the performance scores, a memory quotient (MQ) could be calculated (mean = 100 in the normal population, standard deviation = 15). To evaluate the severity of memory dysfunction, it became popular to compare performance on the WMS with performance on an IQ test, such as the Wechsler Adult Intelligence Scale (WAIS). Thus, in both clinical and experimental analyses of memory dysfunction, a large IQ-MQ difference (usually a difference greater than 15 or 20 points) suggested a significant and selective amnesic disorder.

In its original form, however, the WMS was inadequate to the task of characterizing memory disorders. The scale was limited because (1) scores were combined into one general MQ score, (2) there was a preponderance of verbal memory tests, (3) there were no measures of delayed memory retention (see Erickson and Scott, 1977; Herman, 1988), and (4) some subtests measured functions not typically affected in amnesia (e.g., digit-span memory and general orientation).

In 1987, the Wechsler Memory Scale–Revised (WMS-R) was introduced with the intention of overcoming some of the limitations of the original test battery (Wechsler, 1987). The WMS-R consists of 13 subtests that are combined to produce five indices: Attention/Concentration, General Memory, Verbal Memory, Visual Memory, and Delayed Recall. Each index is normalized to yield a mean score of 100 for normal subjects and a standard deviation of 15. Moreover, for each verbal subtest (e.g., digit span, prose recall, verbal paired-associates learning), there is a corresponding nonverbal subtest (e.g., visual memory span, visual reproduction, visual paired-associates learning). Several verbal and nonverbal tests are administered after a delay of about 30 minutes.

The WMS-R has significant advantages over its predecessor and, among readily available test instruments, the WMS-R provides perhaps the best general assessment of memory dysfunction. In the WMS-R, performance scores for subtests that do not depend on the kind of memory that is impaired in amnesia (digit span, visuo-spatial span, and mental control) are incorporated into a separate Attention/Concentration index. Amnesic patients exhibit normal scores on the Attention/Concentration index, despite severe impairment on the memory indices (Janowsky et al., 1989). In contrast, patients with frontal lobe lesions exhibit low scores on the Attention/Concentration index but normal scores on memory indices (Janowsky et al., 1989). One shortcoming of the WMS-R is that it does not provide numerical scores for subjects who score below 50. Because many amnesic patients obtain scores below 50, especially on the Delayed Recall Index, the WMS-R is not advantageous for discriminating among patients with severe memory impairment.

The WMS-R has also been useful in characterizing dementia. Patients with Alzheimer's disease or Huntington's disease exhibited significant impairment on the Attention/Concentration index as well as on the memory indices, whereas patients with amnesic

disorders (e.g., patients with Korsakoff's syndrome, hypoxia, or herpes encephalitis) exhibited significant impairment only on the memory indices (Butters et al., 1988). Finally, Chelune and Bornstein (1988) used the WMS-R to assess material-specific memory disorders in patients with unilateral brain lesions. In that study, significant interactions were observed between lesion site (left versus right) and stimulus type (verbal versus nonverbal). Thus, patients with left unilateral lesions exhibited more impairment on the verbal memory index than on the visual memory index, whereas the reverse was true for patients with right unilateral lesions.

RECOGNITION MEMORY TEST. The Recognition Memory Test (RMT) developed by Warrington (1984) consists of two forced-choice recognition tests—one for words and one for faces. Memory for words and faces are tested separately. For each test, 50 stimuli are presented sequentially. Immediately following the study phase, each stimulus is paired with a new one, and subjects are asked to indicate which of the two was presented earlier. The score is the number correct out of 50 for both words and faces. Whereas the WMS-R is useful in discriminating normal memory from abnormal memory, the RMT is useful for assessing different levels of severity among memory-impaired patients. An even more sensitive assessment can be obtained by administering the memory test one day after the study phase, instead of immediately afterwards (Squire and Shimamura, 1986).

CALIFORNIA VERBAL LEARNING TEST. The California Verbal Learning Test (CVLT) developed by Delis et al. (1987) provides several measures of word learning. Subjects are presented study-test trials of word lists to assess free recall of categorized word lists. The advantage of the CVLT is that multiple measures of memory are taken, and a pattern of memory performance can be obtained for a single subject. Several different indices are derived from the test, which provide information about the strategy used during learning, the rate at which information is acquired, the nature of the serial position effect, the ability to identify correct responses and reject incorrect responses, and susceptibility to proactive interference during learning. These indices were identified originally in a factor-analysis of performance scores, and test construction was motivated by ideas about learning and memory developed in cognitive psychology and neuroscience.

Performance profiles have been published for amnesic patients with Korsakoff's syndrome, patients with Alzheimer's disease, and patients with Huntington's disease (Delis et al., 1991). Performance on the CVLT is strongly correlated with performance on the WMS-R (Delis et al., 1988).

RIVERMEAD BEHAVIORAL MEMORY TEST. The Rivermead Behavioral Memory Test (RBMT) assesses a variety of everyday tasks of memory (Wilson et al., 1989). Subjects are asked to perform tasks, such as associating a name to a face, remembering the location of a hidden object, recalling a spatial route, and distinguishing previously presented faces from new ones. In addition, tasks involving remembering to remember are given, such as remembering to ask a certain question when an alarm sounds. The test battery stands in contrast to other clinical tests of memory in that it emphasizes the memory demands that are associated with everyday functioning. As such, it has the advantage of being strongly correlated with clinical prognosis of rehabilitation (Wilson, 1987). Three forms of the test battery have been constructed so that individuals can be assessed at different times after brain injury or disease. Thus, the RBMT provides a useful kind of clinical assessment. This test battery, however, may be less well suited for neuropsychological studies of memory function because task performance appears to be sensitive to attentional abilities and mnemonic strategies. Thus, performance can be significantly affected by attentional deficits or by deficits in general intellectual abilities. Nevertheless, as a way to predict progress during rehabilitation, the RBMT appears quite useful.

Material-Specific Memory Dysfunction and Its Assessment

In addition to addressing the issue of severity, neuropsychological testing of memory must also address the fact that memory dysfunction can be different, depending on whether the neurological injury or disease is bilateral, or whether the affected structures are left or right unilateral. The effect on memory follows from the asymmetry of hemispheric function with respect to language: verbal impairment from left-sided damage, nonverbal impairment from right-sided damage, "global" impairment from bilateral damage. This point has been best demonstrated in the thorough work of Brenda Milner on temporal lobe function (Milner, 1958, 1971). Patients with left medial temporal lobe resections complain, for example, that they cannot remember what they have read and they do poorly on verbal memory tests. Delayed recall tests of short prose passages, described above, are useful in bringing out this deficit. Patients who have sustained right medial temporal lobe resections complain, for example, that they do not remember where they have put things, and they do poorly on tests of memory for faces, spatial relationships, and other things that are not ordinarily encoded in words.

These disorders of memory, which arise from unilateral brain injury or disease, were termed material-specific disorders (Milner, 1968a) to signify that the side of the brain that is affected determines the kind of material that is difficult to learn and remember. The sensory modality through which material is learned (e.g., auditory, visual, or tactile) is ordinarily not important. For example, in the case of left medial temporal lobe injury, a short prose passage will be difficult to remember regardless whether the patient reads the story or hears it read. These material-specific effects have been demonstrated for left or right temporal lobe surgical lesions (Milner, 1971); epileptic foci of the left or right temporal lobe (Delaney et al., 1980); left or right unilateral ECT (in which the two electrodes are applied to the same side of the head, in contrast to bilateral ECT, in which one electrode is applied to each temple) (Cohen et al., 1968); unilateral diencephalic lesions (Teuber et al., 1968; Michel et al., 1982; Speedie and Heilman, 1982); and unilateral diencephalic brain stimulation (Ojemann, 1971).

Time-Line Measurements of Anterograde and Retrograde Amnesia

Because many patients have insight into their conditions, one useful way to obtain information about memory loss is to construct a time line of the deficit with the patient's assistance. This technique was used to good advantage by Barbizet (1970) as a way of identifying what past time periods were affected (Fig. 11-7). The method revealed in an approximate way the duration of both anterograde and retrograde amnesia, and showed how the deficit changed with the passage of time. In the case of Barbizet's patient, who had suffered a severe closed head injury, anterograde amnesia remained fixed at about 2 ½ months, even after mem-

ory capacities had largely recovered. This presumably occurred because the anterograde amnesia reflected a time when memories could not be formed in the normal way. Accordingly, even though the capacity to form new memories eventually recovered, memories did not return for those events that had occurred during the period of anterograde amnesia. Retrograde amnesia was initially severe and extensive, but gradually shrank to 2 weeks. Oldest memories recovered first.

A similar relationship between anterograde and retrograde amnesia holds for psychiatric patients undergoing a prescribed course of bilateral ECT (Fig. 11-8). Thirty-one patients were interviewed before, 7 months after, and 3 years after ECT. Before treatment, patients on average reported having difficulty remembering the 5 months prior to ECT, presumably because of their depressive illness. Seven months later, patients reported difficulty remembering events that occurred during the 3 months after treatment and during the 2 years preceding. Three years later, retrograde amne-

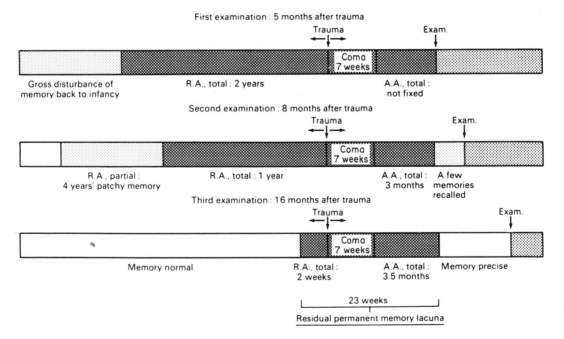

Figure 11-7. An illustration of time periods that were difficult to remember at three different intervals after a severe head injury. (From Barbizet, 1970.)

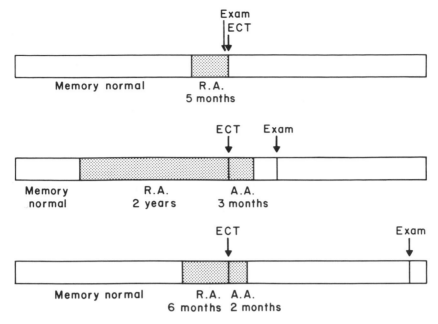

Figure 11-8. Estimates of time periods that were difficult to remember before (top bar), 7 months after (middle bar), and 3 years after (bottom bar) bilateral electroconvulsive therapy (ECT) (N = 31). Shaded areas represent the median time period perceived as affected both from the period before ECT (i.e., R.A., retrograde amnesia) and after ECT (i.e., A.A., anterograde amnesia). Because the first time estimate was obtained just prior to ECT (top bar), the 5 preceding months perceived as affected at that time presumably reflected memory problems associated with depressive illness. (From Squire and Slater, 1983.)

sia had shrunk to about the pre-ECT level, and anterograde amnesia remained fixed at 2 months (Squire and Slater, 1983).

Self-Ratings of Memory Performance

Self-reports of memory function are often useful in conjunction with formal testing. Of course, self-reports of memory function can be misleading. For example, in depressed elderly patients memory complaints were related more to depression than to performance on memory tests (Kahn et al., 1975). Conversely, patients receiving ECT who were clinically improved often denied memory impairment despite the fact that memory impairment could be documented by formal tests (Cronholm and Ottosson, 1961). Nevertheless, correlations between memory self-ratings and objective measures of perfor-

mance can be demonstrated (Zelinski et al., 1980; Baddeley et al., 1982).

Table 11-1 shows an 18-item self-rating scale that has been used with patients receiving ECT and with amnesic patients (Squire et al., 1979; Squire and Zouzounis, 1988). This scale takes advantage of the fact that memory problems caused by depression are different from memory problems caused by amnesia (Cronholm and Ottosson, 1961). The former impairs immediate recall but has no special effect on delayed recall. The latter impairs delayed recall, but has little or no effect on immediate recall—especially if the amount of material to be remembered is small and can be held in immediate memory (see earlier discussion of delayed recall of prose material). The scale was designed with the idea that patients might reflect this difference in their own assessments of their memory abilities. Patients given the scale were

Table 11-1. Self-rating Scale of Memory Functions

1. My ability to search through my mind and recall names I know are there is	11
2. I think my relatives and acquaintances now judge my memory to be	13
3. My ability to hold in my memory things that I have learned is	8
4. My ability to recall things when I really try is	4
5. The tendency for a past memory to be "on the tip of my tongue" but not available to me is	13.5
6. My ability to remember the names and faces of people I meet is	5
7. My ability to know when the things I am paying attention to are going to stick in my memory is	2.5
8. My ability to remember things that have happened more than a year ago is	12
9. My ability now to remember what I read and what I watch on television is	6.5
10. My ability to make sense out of what people explain to me is	17.5
11. My ability to remember what I was doing after I have taken my mind off it for a few minutes is	2.5
12. My ability to pay attention to what goes on around me is	10
13. If I were asked about it a month from now, my ability to remember facts about this form I am filling out would be	6.5
14. My ability to recall things that happened a long time ago is	17.5
15. My ability to reach back in my memory and recall what happened a few minutes ago is	9
16. My ability to follow what people are saying is	13.5
17. My general alertness to things happening around me is	15
18. My ability to recall things that happened during my childhood is	16

For each item subjects were asked to judge their ability as it seemed now compared to an earlier, specified time period. Subjects used a 9-point scale, ranging from −4 (worse than ever before), through 0 (same as before), to +4 (better than ever before). The items are ordered here according to the score obtained 1 week after ECT (see Fig. 11-9A and B). Item 1 produced the lowest score (mean = 2.5), and item 18 the highest score (mean = 0.6). The column of numbers to the right shows how the items would have appeared if the ordering had been done according to the responses of the amnesic patients (see Fig. 11.9C and D).

asked to rate each item from −4 (worse than ever before) through zero (same as before) to +4 (better than ever before).

Figure 11-9 (left panels) shows the findings for 35 patients prescribed bilateral ECT who were tested before and 1 week after treatment (mean = 11.1 treatments, range = 5–21). To display the data, the test items (1 through 18) were ordered according to the self-ratings obtained after ECT. Thus, item 1 (to the far left in Fig. 11-9) yielded the lowest score, and item 18 yielded the highest score. Before ECT, memory self-ratings were below the zero level and roughly similar across items. Thus depression itself, for which ECT had been prescribed, impaired self-ratings of memory to a measurable degree. One week after ECT, overall self-ratings were worse than before ECT, and in addition some items were now rated worse than others. That is, the profile of self-ratings obtained before and after ECT was different, indicating that ECT changed the patients' own experience of memory functions. Whereas reports of poor memory before ECT can probably be attributed to depression, reports of poor memory after ECT are probably influenced largely by the amnesic effects of the treatment.

Figure 11-9 (right panels) shows the results on the same self-rating scale for three other groups of patients: a group of depressed patients not prescribed ECT, amnesic patients with Korsakoff's syndrome, and non-Korsakoff amnesic patients. The amnesic patients were tested twice on two different occasions separated by about 2 months. The order of the items is the same as in the left panels. The memory self-ratings reported by the non-Korsakoff patients were similar to the self-ratings reported by patients after ECT, supporting the idea that memory complaints after ECT reflect primarily the experience of amnesia. The patients with Korsakoff's syndrome, who were as severely amnesic as the other patients as measured by formal tests, underestimated their memory impairment. The findings for Korsakoff's syndrome are probably due to the frontal lobe pathology associated with this patient group.

Self-rating scales could be useful in a variety of clinical settings where there is interest in understanding memory complaints and relating them to objective test performance. For example, such scales might be useful in characterizing patients with significant pa-

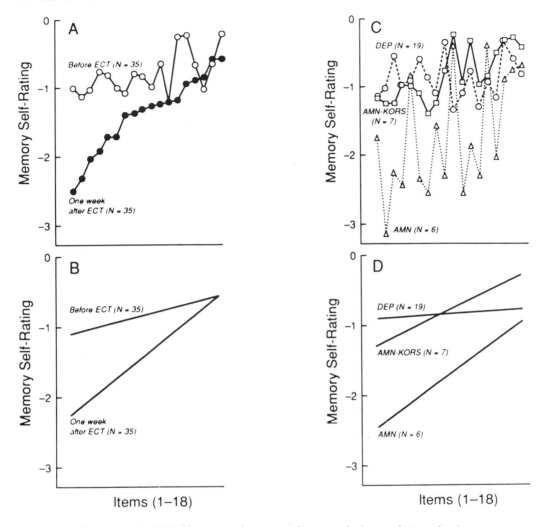

Figure 11-9. (A) Self-ratings of memory functions before and 1 week after bilateral ECT, as assessed by an 18-item test. (B) The same data are represented as best-fitting lines across the scores for all 18 test items. (C) Self-ratings of memory functions on the 18-item test, as reported by depressed patients (DEP), amnesic patients with Korsakoff's syndrome (AMN-KORS), and a group of non-Korsakoff amnesic patients (AMN). (D) The same data are represented as best-fitting lines across the scores for all 18 test items. For each panel, the order of the items from left to right is the same and is given in Table 11-1. (From Squire and Zouzounis, 1988.)

thology in neocortex, such as patients with Alzheimer's disease. These patients do not report accurate self-ratings of memory function (McGlynn and Kaszniak, 1991). Also, self-ratings might be useful in distinguishing depression in the elderly from incipient brain disease. Finally, they could be of use in assessing patients with memory disorders who are given pharmacological treatments to improve their memory functions. Some of

these treatments might work in part by improving mood, rather than by affecting memory directly, and such effects might be teased apart by self-rating scales.

Assessment of Remote Memory

One of the striking features of amnesia is that it commonly involves some loss of information for events that occurred before the onset of amnesia. Before considering the ret-rograde aspect of memory dysfunction, it is important to note that in memory disorders that have a gradual onset the distinction be-tween anterograde and retrograde amnesia is always blurred. In these cases, it becomes difficult to determine if information is un-available because it was not acquired in the first place (anterograde amnesia) or because it was acquired initially and then later lost as the result of the onset of amnesia (retrograde amnesia). Several instruments have been de-veloped to assess memory for remote events in a formal, quantitative way. When amnesia has a very recent onset, or a precise time of onset, one can know which test questions assess retrograde amnesia. Of the tests avail-able for clinical neuropsychological testing, most ask for information about public events that occurred at specified times in the past. This ensures that the information is verifiable and potentially accessible to all subjects.

TESTS OF PUBLIC (SEMANTIC) KNOWLEDGE. The first remote memory tests to explore the nature of memory disorders in amnesic patients consisted of questions about persons or events that had been in the news in Great Britain, or faces of famous people who had been prominent in Great Britain at different times in the past (Sanders and Warrington, 1971). By asking questions that covered the past several decades, it was possible to obtain a sampling of an individual's knowledge of past events. Subsequently, similar tests based on public events or famous faces were developed for use in the United States (Selt-zer and Benson, 1974; Squire, 1974; Albert et al., 1979) (Fig. 11-10, 11-11).

Another remote memory test that has found useful application in the study of mem-ory disorders is a test of former one-season television programs (Squire and Slater, 1975; Squire, 1989). It was designed to overcome an important limitation of other available re-mote memory tests—the difficulty of com-paring scores across different past time peri-ods. To make valid comparisons across time periods, the items selected must satisfy the criterion of equivalence; that is, they must sample past time periods in an equivalent

way so that the events from different time periods are likely to have been learned about to the same extent and then forgotten at similar rates. The television test appears to satisfy this criterion (Squire, 1989).

Remote memory tests cannot be assumed to satisfy the criterion of equivalence just because normal subjects obtain the same score (e.g., 75% correct) across all time peri-ods sampled by the test. As discussed in detail elsewhere (Squire and Cohen, 1982), the events selected from more remote time periods may initially have been more salient and more widely known than the events se-lected from more recent time periods. In addition, the events from more remote peri-ods could have been forgotten more slowly. Accordingly, it is not possible with such tests to compare performance across time periods.

These issues notwithstanding, all the re-mote memory tests have some useful applica-tion to the quantitative examination of mem-ory disorders. As with any measuring instrument, the appropriateness of the test depends on the particular question being asked. Thus, the television test, though ad-vantageous in some respects, is limited by the relatively short time span that it can reliably cover (about 20 years), and by the fact that it yields variable results when used clinically to explore the retrograde memory capacity of a single patient. Tests of remote memory for past public events and famous faces tests have also found useful application with amnesic patients who became impaired on a known calendar day (Squire et al., 1989). The findings were (1) extensive, temporally graded retrograde amnesia covering more than a decade occurs in patients with medial temporal lobe amnesia as well as in patients with diencephalic amnesia; (2) the impair-ment reflects a loss of usable knowledge, not a simple difficulty in retrieving an intact memory store that can be overcome given sufficient opportunities for retrieval; (3) very remote memory for factual information can be intact in amnesia, even when the tests are made so difficult that normal subjects can answer only 20% of the questions.

Prospective studies with experimental ani-mals have been needed to reveal the precise

Figure 11-10. Items from the Famous Faces Test of the Boston Retrograde Amnesia Battery (Albert et al., 1979). Top row, from left to right: John L. Lewis (1930s), Fulton Sheen (1940s), Joe McCarthy (1950s). Bottom row: Jimmy Hoffa (1960s), H. R. Haldeman (1970s), Tom Selleck (1980s). Items for the 1980s are available for the Battery, but the test has also been updated independently in San Diego. The 1980s item (above) is from the San Diego version.

shape of the temporal gradient of retrograde amnesia. The results have been that information acquired remote from surgery is remembered significantly better than information acquired recently (Winocur, 1990; Zola-Morgan and Squire, 1990; Kim and Fanselow, 1992; Cho et al., 1993). These results show that information that initially depends on the integrity of medial temporal lobe/diencephalic brain structures can eventually become independent of these structures. Initially these structures are needed for the storage and retrieval of memory. As time passes after learning, a process of con-solidation or reorganization occurs such that a more permanent memory is established that is independent of these structures (Squire and Alvarez, 1995). These studies with experimental animals have thus provided strong confirmation for the reality of temporal gradients of retrograde amnesia, an idea with a history of more than 100 years (Ribot, 1881).

TESTS OF AUTOBIOGRAPHICAL (EPISODIC) KNOWLEDGE. The remote memory tests just described share the advantage of being based on verifiable and publicly accessible information. Autobiographical memory tests do not

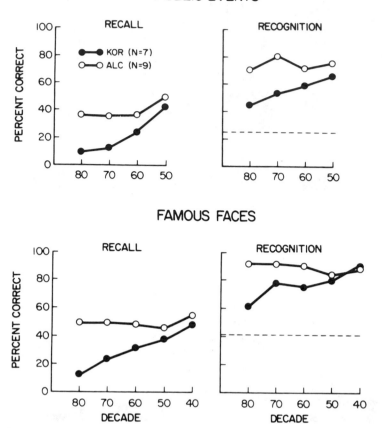

Figure 11-11. Performance of amnesic patients (Korsakoff) and alcoholic control subjects on a remote memory test for public events (recall and recognition) and on a remote memory test for famous faces (recall and recognition). The items came into the news in the decade shown. Dashed lines indicate chance performance levels (public events = 25%; famous faces = 41.5%). (From Squire et al., 1989.)

have this feature, but nevertheless can be of considerable value in the neuropsychological assessment of memory disorders. One such test derives from early quantitative studies by Galton (1879), and was modified and applied to the study of memory by Crovitz (Crovitz and Schiffman, 1974). The test is designed to obtain autobiographical remote memories about specific past episodes of a patient's life. Patients are given standard cue words (e.g., window, tree, ticket, bird) and are asked in each case to recall a specific memory from the past that involves the word. After recalling a memory for a given cue word, subjects are asked to date the memory as best they can. The responses can

be scored on the basis of the quality and quantity of recalled information, and provides useful information as well about the time periods from which recall is possible.

Even amnesic patients who obtain normal scores for recall may draw their memories from different time periods than normal subjects. This was true in the case of the patient with functional amnesia, described above, who atypically drew most of his memories from the immediately preceding 4 days—after the onset of his amnesic disturbance (Schacter et al., 1982). Patients with alcoholic Korsakoff syndrome, though they could obtain normal or near normal scores on the recall test, drew their memories from 10 years earlier than their alcoholic control subjects (Zola-Morgan et al., 1983). Similarly, patients who become amnesic as the result of anoxia or ischemia, and who had presumed or confirmed bilateral damage to the hippocampal formation, drew fewer memories from the 1980s than control subjects (testing conducted in 1988; MacKinnon and Squire, 1989). Under some conditions, the amnesic patients were able to recollect fully formed autobiographical episodes from their earlier life that could not be distinguished qualitatively or quantitatively from the recollections of normal subjects.

The material obtained in an autobiographical test, of course, is not easily corroborated. In some cases, a spouse or relative may be able to verify reported events and dates. Another way to check against outright fabrication is to ask subjects a second time, some time after initial testing, to date the memories they had recalled (Schacter et al., 1982). This procedure typically yields close agreement between the dates produced in the two sessions.

Assessment of Nondeclarative Memory

Recent work emphasizes that amnesia is a narrower deficit than once believed. Memory is not a single mental faculty that can be globally disrupted by amnesia. Rather, memory is composed of multiple separate systems (Squire, 1982a; Mishkin and Petri, 1984; Tulving, 1985; Schacter, 1987; Weiskrantz, 1990; Shimamura, 1993; Squire, 1994). One system provides the basis for conscious recollection of recently encountered facts and events and is selectively impaired in amnesia. This kind of memory has been termed declarative (or explicit) memory and is the main subject matter of this chapter. In contrast, nondeclarative (or implicit) memory is a heterogeneous collection of abilities, which result from experience but are not accessible to conscious recollection. Nondeclarative memory is preserved in amnesia and includes the capacity for skill and habit learning, simple forms of classical conditioning, and the phenomenon of priming (Fig. 11-12). In these cases, behavior cumulates in behavioral change independently of memory for particular prior encounters and without requiring conscious access to any memory content. Finally, whereas declarative memory depends on the integrity of the medial temporal lobe and diencephalic brain structures damaged in amnesia (and interactions between these structures and neocortex), nondeclarative forms of memory depend on other brain structures including the neostriatum, the amygdala, the cerebellum, and neocortex.

The relevance of these taxonomic considerations to the clinical evaluation of memory

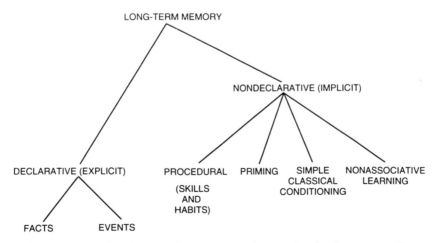

Figure 11-12. Classification of memory. Declarative (explicit) memory refers to conscious recollections of facts and events. Nondeclarative (implicit) memory refers to a heterogeneous collection of abilities whereby experience alters behavior nonconsciously without providing access to any memory content. (From Squire and Zola-Morgan, 1991.)

is that tests of nondeclarative memory can provide useful additional information to what is obtained with conventional memory tests. First, such tests can demonstrate the selectivity of memory impairment in the case of patients with circumscribed impairments of declarative memory. Second, such tests can indicate the involvement of other brain systems, as with patients having early-stage Alzheimer's disease. In addition to impaired declarative memory, these patients exhibit impaired performance on some tests of nondeclarative memory (Shimamura et al., 1987). Third, such tests can be useful with patient groups, such as patients with Huntington's disease, where a primary deficit may be present in nondeclarative forms of memory (Butters et al., 1990; Heindel et al., 1989, 1991; Saint-Cyr and Taylor, 1992).

For assessment purposes, the tests of most interest are those that have been used to demonstrate intact or near-intact performance in amnesic patients. These include tasks involving perceptuomotor skills such as mirror drawing and motor-pursuit, perceptual skills like reading mirror-reversed words, cognitive skills, adaptation-level effects, probabilistic classification learning, artificial grammar learning, prototype learning, and several kinds of priming (for review, see Squire et al., 1993).

Studies with speeded reading tasks, among other methods, indicate that nondeclarative learning can involve very specific information about the items that were encountered. The learning can also be based on novel material (Fig. 11-13). Learning of simple conditioned responses has also been demonstrated in amnesic patients. Patients exhibit progressive learning and 24-hour retention of a conditioned eye blink response, but they cannot describe the apparatus or what it had been used for (Weiskrantz and Warrington, 1979; Daum et al., 1989).

Priming refers to an improved facility for detecting or identifying stimuli based on recent experience with the stimuli (Shimamura, 1986; Tulving and Schacter, 1990). One widely used method for demonstrating priming is word-stem completion (Graf et al., 1984). In this task, words are presented to the subject (e.g., MOTEL). Later, three-

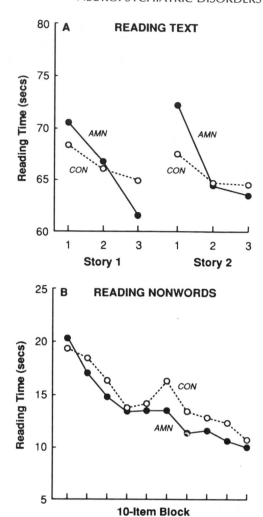

Figure 11-13. Intact learning by amnesic patients as measured by improved reading times. (A) Text-specific reading skill. Subjects read aloud a story three times in succession, followed immediately by three readings of a second story. (B) Acquisition of a reading skill for novel material. Subjects read aloud a 100-item list consisting of five nonwords repeated 20 times each. Amnesic patients improved their reading speed at the same rate as normal subjects. Key: AMN, amnesic patients; CON, control subjects. (From Musen et al., 1990; Musen and Squire, 1991.)

letter word stems (e.g., MOT) are presented, and subjects are asked to say the first word that comes to mind that completes each word stem. For both amnesic patients and control subjects, the probability of producing previously presented words was increased from about 10% (baseline word-stem completion) to about 50%. Words appear to "pop" into mind, and amnesic patients exhibit this effect as strongly as control subjects. In contrast, when subjects were asked to use the word stems as cues to recollect words from the study session, the control subjects performed better than amnesic patients.

Another task involves associative priming (Shimamura and Squire, 1984). Subjects are presented words (e.g., BABY) and later asked to "free associate," i.e., to say the first word that comes to mind when they hear other words (e.g., CHILD). Amnesic patients and control subjects exhibited a similar bias for using recently presented words in this word-association task. Other studies show that priming can occur for novel material (e.g., nonwords) as well as for familiar material (e.g., words), and priming occurs for such material in amnesic patients as strongly as in normal subjects (Fig. 11-14A). Under some conditions, priming can also be

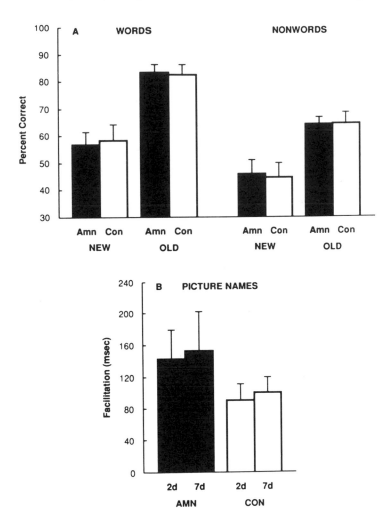

Figure 11-14. Intact repetition priming in amnesic patients. (A) Percent identification of briefly presented words and nonwords. Old items were presented once prior to the perceptual identification test. The advantage of identifying old items over new items indicates priming. (B) Facilitation of picture naming at 2 and 7 days after a single presentation. Priming was measured in each case by subtracting the time needed to name 50 new pictures from the time needed to name 50 old pictures. Brackets show standard errors of the mean. Key: AMN, amnesic patients; CON, control subjects. (From Haist et al., 1991; Cave and Squire, 1992.)

long-lasting, even after single presentations of study items (Fig. 11-14B).

Recommendations for Memory Testing

The preceding sections considered the issues involved in undertaking a clinical neuropsychological evaluation of memory functions. Specialized tests are available for assessing memory dysfunction, including tests of new learning capacity, remote memory, and nondeclarative memory. Of the readily available tests, the WMS-R provides a useful, general-purpose assessment of new learning ability. The RMT provides a discriminating assessment of the severity of impairment in patients. The CVLT is useful for obtaining a profile of performance from single patients.

For assessing retrograde memory function, tests of remote memory for public events provide a good objective instrument, but more subjective methods are also useful based on (1) questions about autobiographical knowledge; (2) the construction of time lines; and (3) self-rating scales. Table 11-2 lists a selection of tests that should serve most clinical needs. More than one test of each type can be used if the findings in any one area are ambiguous; and additional tests can be used as needed, once the clinician becomes familiar with the status of the patient's memory functions.

Neuropsychological testing of memory is most informative when memory tests are supplemented with tests of other cognitive functions. Table 11-3 lists a selection of readily available memory tests, together with tests that are useful for obtaining supplemental information. Additional tests establish valuable reference points that help in interpreting memory test scores. They can also identify or rule out other kinds of cognitive impairment, which if present could influence memory test scores. The WAIS-R IQ test is helpful, because it can identify the general test-taking ability of the patient (Wechsler, 1981). The Mattis Dementia Rating Scale is also useful in evaluating a wide range of abilities (Mattis, 1976).

Tests that assess language comprehension, confrontational naming, verbal fluency, constructional ability, and executive functions (i.e., frontal lobe functions) can also be valuable (Goodglass and Kaplan, 1972; Lezak, 1983; Kaplan et al., 1983; Delis et al., 1992; Monsch et al., 1992). For example, patients with anomia will perform poorly on some memory tests (e.g., recall tests of remote memory). Anomia is not always detectable by casual bedside examination, and a formal quantitative method that includes many low-frequency object names (protractor, trellis, paddle [Kaplan et al., 1983]) can reveal impairment that is missed by a more casual exam. Tests of frontal lobe function are also useful, because frontal lobe dysfunction can influence scores on many memory tests (Moscovitch, 1982; Shimamura et al., 1990).

Table 11-2. A Recommended Selection of Tests for the Neuropsychological Assessment of Memory

1. Construction of Time-line (Barbizet, 1970; Squire and Slater, 1983)
2. Immediate recall of prose passage (Milner, 1958)
3. Copy of Rey-Osterrieth figure (Milner and Teuber, 1968)
4. Paired associate learning (Jones, 1974)
5. Delayed recall of prose passage
6. Delayed reconstruction of Rey-Osterrieth figure
7. Remote memory for public events (Squire et al., 1989)
8. Cued recall of autobiographical memory (Crovitz and Schiffman, 1974)
9. Self-rating scale (Squire and Zouzounis, 1988)
10. Rey Auditory Verbal Learning Test (Recall and Recognition) (Rey, 1964; Squire and Shimamura, 1986)

Table 11-3. A Selection of Readily Available Memory Tests and Supplementary (Nonmemory) Tests

1. Wechsler Memory Scale–Revised (Wechsler, 1987)
2. Recognition Memory Test (Warrington, 1984)
3. California Verbal Learning Test (Delis et al., 1987)
4. Dementia Rating Scale (Mattis, 1976)
5. Boston Naming Test (Kaplan et al., 1983)
6. Wechsler Adult Intelligence Scale–Revised (Wechsler, 1981)

Summary

Having considered the available methods for testing memory, and identified various clinical settings where these methods can be usefully applied, it is worth noting that improvement in neuropsychological testing methods has depended importantly on basic research in cognitive psychology and neuroscience. An enormous amount has been learned in recent years about how the brain accomplishes memory storage, and an inventory of memory tests has been one of the fruits of this enterprise. The neuropsychological, brain-systems study of memory is part of a broader program of research aimed at understanding the biology of memory at all levels of analysis—from cellular and synaptic events to the whole behavior of complex animals including humans. A broad, basic research approach to problems of memory and the brain should continue to inform us about mechanism and organization, and at the same time yield improved methods for the assessment of patients with memory dysfunction. Ultimately, perhaps, these same research efforts may result in methods for the treatment of memory dysfunction.

References

Abrams, R., and Essman, W. B. (1982). *Electroconvulsive Therapy: Biological Foundations and Clinical Applications.* New York: Spectrum Publications, Inc.

Albert, M. S., Butters, N., and Levin, J. (1979). Temporal gradients in the retrograde amnesia of patients with alcoholic Korsakoff's disease. *Archives of Neurology, 36,* 211–216.

Baddeley, A., Sunderland, A., and Harris, J. (1982). How well do laboratory-based psychological tests predict patients' performance outside the laboratory? In S. Corkin, K. I. Davis, J. H. Growden, E. Usdin, and R. J. Wurtman, eds. *Alzheimer's Disease: A Report of Progress in Research.* New York: Raven Press, pp. 141–148.

Barbizet, J. (1970). *Human Memory and Its Pathology.* San Francisco: W. H. Freeman and Company.

Boller, F., and Grafman, J. (1991). *Handbook of Neuropsychology.* New York: Elsevier.

Buschke, H., and Fuld, P. A. (1974). Evaluating storage, retention, and retrieval in disordered memory and learning. *Neurology, 24,* 1019–1025.

Butters, N., Delis, D. C., and Lucas, J. A. (1995). Clinical assessment of memory disorders in amnesia. *Annual Review of Psychology, 46,* 493–523.

Butters, N., Heindel, W. C., and Salmon, D. P. (1990). Dissociation of implicit memory in dementia: Neurological implications. *Bulletin of the Psychological Society, 28,* 359–366.

Butters, N., Salmon, D. P., Cullum, C. M., Cairns, P., Tröster, A. I., Jacobs, D., Moss, M., and Cermak, L. S. (1988). Differentiation of amnesic and demented patients with the Wechsler Memory Scale-Revised. *The Clinical Neuropsychologist, 2,* 133–148.

Cave, C., and Squire, L. R. (1992). Intact and long-lasting repetition priming in amnesia. *Journal of Experimental Psychology, Learning, Memory and Cognition, 18,* 509–520.

Chapman, J. (1966). The early symptoms of schizophrenia. *British Journal of Psychiatry, 112,* 225–251.

Chelune, G. J., and Bornstein, R. A. (1988). WMS-R patterns among patients with unilateral brain lesions. *Clinical Neuropsychology, 2,* 121–132.

Cho, Y. H., Beracochea, D., and Jaffard, R. (1993). Extended temporal gradient for the retrograde and anterograde amnesia produced by ibotenate entorhinal cortex lesions in mice. *Journal of Neuroscience, 13,* 1759–1766.

Cohen, B. D., Noblin, C. D., Silverman, A. J., and Penick, S. B. (1968). Functional asymmetry of the human brain. *Science, 162,* 475–477.

Corkin, S. (1984). Lasting consequences of bilateral medial temporal lobectomy: Clinical course and experimental findings in H. M. *Seminars in Neurology, 4,* 249–259.

Cronholm, B., and Ottosson, J. O. (1961). Memory functions in endogenous depression. *Archives of General Psychiatry, 5,* 101–107.

Crovitz, H. F., and Schiffman, H. (1974). Frequency of episodic memories as a function of their age. *Bulletin of the Psychonomic Society, 4,* 517–518.

Darwin, F. (1892). *Life of Charles Darwin.* London: John Murray.

Daum, I., Channon, S., and Canavan, A. (1989). Classical conditioning in patients with severe memory problems. *Journal of Neurology, Neurosurgery and Psychiatry, 52,* 47–51.

Delaney, R. C., Rosen, A. J., Mattson, R. H.,

and Novelly, R. A. (1980). Memory function in focal epilepsy: A comparison of non-surgical, unilateral temporal lobe and frontal lobe samples. *Cortex, 16,* 103–117.

Delis, D. C., Cullum, C. M., Butters, N., and Cairns, P. (1988). Wechsler Memory Scale-Revised and California Verbal Learning Test: Convergence and divergence. *The Clinical Psychologist, 2,* 188–196.

Delis, D. C., Kramer, J. H., Kaplan, E., and Ober, B. A. (1987). *The California Verbal Learning Test.* New York: Psychological Corporation.

Delis, D. C., Massman, P. J., Butters, N., Salmon, D. P., Cermak, L. S., and Kramer, J. H. (1991). Profiles of demented and amnesic patients on the California Verbal Learning Test: Implications for the assessment of memory disorders. *Psychological Assessment, 3,* 19–26.

Delis, D. C., Squire, L. R., Bihrle, A., and Massman, P. (1992). Componential analysis of problem-solving ability: Performance of patients with frontal lobe damage and amnesic patients on a new sorting test. *Neuropsychologia, 30,* 683–697.

Drachman, D. A., and Arbit, J. (1966). Memory and the hippocampal complex. II. Is memory a multiple process? *Archives of Neurology, 15,* 52–61.

Erickson, R. C., and Scott, M. L. (1977). Clinical memory testing: A review. *Psychological Bulletin, 84,* 1130–1149.

Fazio, F., Perani, D., Gilardi, M. C., Colombo, F., Cappa, S. F., Vallar, G., Bettinardi, V., Paulesu, E., Alberoni, M., Bressi, S., Franceschi, M., and Lenzi, G. L. (1992). Metabolic impairment in human amnesia: A PET study of memory networks. *Journal of Cerebral Blood Flow and Metabolism, 12,* 353–358.

Galton, F. (1879). Psychometric experiments. *Brain, 2,* 149–162.

Golden, C. J., Hammeke, T. A., and Purisch, A. D. (1980). *The Luria-Nebraska Neuropsychological Battery: Manual.* Los Angeles: Western Psychological Services.

Goodglass, H., and Kaplan, E. (1972). *The Assessment of Aphasia and Related Disorders.* London: Henry Kimpton.

Graf, P., Squire, L. R., and Mandler, G. (1984). The information that amnesic patients do not forget. *Journal of Experimental Psychology. Learning, Memory and Cognition, 10,* 164–178.

Haist, F., Musen, G., and Squire, L. (1991). Intact priming of words and nonwords in amnesia. *Psychobiology, 19,* 275–285.

Haist, F., Shimamura, A. P., and Squire, L. R.

(1992). On the relationship between recall and recognition memory. *Journal of Experimental Psychology. Learning, Memory and Cognition, 18,* 691–702.

Heindel, W. C., Salmon, D. P., and Butters, N. (1991). The biasing of weight judgments in Alzheimer's and Huntington's disease: A priming or programming phenomenon? *Journal of Clinical and Experimental Neuropsychology, 13,* 189–203.

Heindel, W. C., Salmon, D. P., Shultz, C. W., Walicke, P. A., and Butters, N. (1989). Neuropsychological evidence for multiple implicit memory systems: A comparison of Alzheimer's, Huntington's, and Parkinson's disease patients. *Journal of Neuroscience, 9,* 582–587.

Herman, D. O. (1988). Development of the Wechsler Memory Scale-Revised. *Clinical Neuropsychology, 2,* 102–106.

Hyman, B. T., Van Hoesen, G. W., Damasio, A. R., and Barnes, C. L. (1984). Alzheimer's disease: Cell specific pathology isolates the hippocampal formation. *Science, 225,* 1168–1170.

James, W. (1890). *Principles of Psychology.* New York: Holt.

Janowsky, J. S., Shimamura, A. P., Kritchevsky, M., and Squire, L. R. (1989). Cognitive impairment following frontal lobe damage and its relevance to human amnesia. *Behavioral Neuroscience, 103,* 548–560.

Jennett, B. (1976). Assessment of the severity of head injury. *Journal of Neurology, Neurosurgery and Psychiatry, 39,* 647–655.

Jones, M. K. (1974). Imagery as a mnemonic aid after left temporal lobectomy: Contrast between material-specific and generalized memory disorders. *Neuropsychologia, 12,* 21–30.

Kahn, R. L., Zarit, S. H., Hilbert, N. M., and Niederehe, G. (1975). Memory complaints and impairment in the aged. The effect of depression and altered brain function. *Archives of General Psychiatry, 32,* 1569–1573.

Kandel, E. R., and Hawkins, R. D. (1992). The biological basis of learning and individuality. *Scientific American, 267,* 78–86.

Kaplan, E. F., Goodglass, H., and Weintraub, S. (1983). *The Boston Naming Test.* Philadelphia: Lea and Febiger.

Katzman, R. (1976). Editorial: The prevalence and malignancy of Alzheimer's disease. *Archives of Neurology, 33,* 217–218.

Kim, J. J., and Fanselow, M. S. (1992). Modality-specific retrograde amnesia of fear. *Science, 256,* 675–677.

Kritchevsky, M. (1989). Transient global amnesia. In F. Boller and J. Grafman, eds., *Handbook of Neuropsychology/III.* New York: Elsevier, pp. 167–182.

Lackner, J. R. (1974). Observations on the speech processing capabilities of an amnesic patient: Several aspects of H.M.'s language function. *Neuropsychologia, 12,* 199–207.

Lavond, D. G., Kim, J. J., and Thompson, R. F. (1993). Mammalian brain substrates of aversive classical conditioning. *Annual Review of Psychology, 44,* 317–342.

Lerer, B., Weiner, R. D., and Belmaker, R. H. (1984). *ECT: Basic Mechanisms.* London: John Libbey.

Levin, H. S., Benton, A. L., and Grossman, R. G. (1982). *Neurobehavioral Consequences of Closed Head Injury.* New York: Oxford University Press.

Lezak, M. (1983). *Neuropsychological Assessment.* New York: Oxford University Press.

MacKinnon, D., and Squire, L. R. (1989). Autobiographical memory in amnesia. *Psychobiology, 17,* 247–256.

Mair, W.G.P., Warrington, E. K., and Weiskrantz, L. (1979). Memory disorder in Korsakoff's psychosis: A neuropathological and neuropsychological investigation of two cases. *Brain, 102,* 749–783.

Malitz, S., and Sackeim, H. A. (1986). *Electroconvulsive Therapy: Clinical and Basic Research Issues.* New York: The New York Academy of Sciences.

Markowitsch, H. (1988). Diencephalic amnesia: A reorientation towards tracts? *Brain Research Reviews, 13,* 351–370.

Mattis, S. (1976). Dementia rating scale. In R. Bellack and B. Keraso, eds., *Geriatric Psychiatry.* New York: Grune and Stratton, pp. 77–121.

Mayes, A. (1988). *Human Organic Memory Disorders.* New York: Oxford University Press.

McGaugh, J. L. (1989). Involvement of hormonal and neuromodulatory systems in the regulation of memory storage. *Annual Review of Neuroscience, 12,* 255–287.

McGlynn, S. M., and Kaszniak, A. W. (1991). When metacognition fails: Impaired awareness of deficit in Alzheimer's disease. *Journal of Cognitive Neuroscience, 3,* 183–198.

McKee, R. D., and Squire, L. R. (1992). Equivalent forgetting rates in long-term memory for diencephalic and medial temporal lobe amnesia. *Journal of Neuroscience, 12,* 3765–3772.

Mercer, B., Wapner, W., Gardner, H., and Benson, F. (1977). A study of confabulation. *Archives of Neurology, 34,* 429–433.

Michel, D., Laurent, B., Foyatier, N., Blanc, A.,

and Portafaix, M. (1982). Infarctus thalamique paramedian gauche. *Revue Neurologique, 138,* 533–550.

Milner, B. (1958). Psychological defects produced by temporal lobe excision. *Research Publications Association for Research in Nervous and Mental Disease, 36,* 244–257.

Milner, B. (1968a). Disorders of memory after brain lesions in man. Preface: Material-specific and generalized memory loss. *Neuropsychologia, 6,* 175–179.

Milner, B. (1968b). Visual recognition and recall after right temporal lobe excision in man. *Neuropsychologia, 6,* 191–209.

Milner, B. (1970). Memory and the medial temporal regions of the brain. In K. H. Pribram and D. E. Broadbent, eds., *Biology of Memory.* New York: Academic Press, pp. 29–50.

Milner, B. (1971). Interhemispheric differences in the localization of psychological processes in man. *British Medical Bulletin, 27,* 272–277.

Milner, B. (1974). Hemispheric specialization: Scope and limits. In F. O. Schmitt and F. G. Worden, eds., *The Neurosciences: Third Study Program.* Cambridge: MIT Press, pp. 75–89.

Milner, B., and Teuber, H. L. (1968). Alteration of perception and memory in man: Reflection on methods. In L. Weiskrantz, ed., *Analysis of Behavioral Change.* New York: Harper and Row, pp. 268–375.

Mishkin, M., and Petri, H. L. (1984). Memories and habits: Some implications for the analysis of learning and retention. In L. R. Squire and N. Butters, eds., *Neuropsychology of Memory.* New York: The Guilford Press, pp. 287–296.

Monsch, A. U., Bondi, M. W., Butters, N., Salmon, D. P., Katzman, R., and Thal, L. J. (1992). Comparisons of verbal fluency tasks in the detection of dementia of the Alzheimer type. *Archives of Neurology, 49,* 1253–1258.

Moscovitch, M. (1982). Multiple dissociations of function in amnesia. In L. Cermak, ed., *Human Memory and Amnesia.* Hillsdale, NJ: Lawrence Erlbaum, pp. 337–370.

Moss, M. B., and Albert, M. S. (1988). Alzheimer's disease and other dementing disorders. In M. S. Albert and M. B. Moss, eds., *Geriatric Neuropsychology.* New York: Guilford Press, pp. 293–304.

Musen, G., Shimamura, A. P., and Squire, L. R. (1990). Intact text-specific reading skill in amnesia. *Journal of Experimental Psychology. Learning, Memory and Cognition, 16,* 1068–1076.

Musen, G., and Squire, L. R. (1991). Normal acquisition of novel verbal information in amnesia. *Journal of Experimental Psychology. Learn-*

ing, *Memory and Cognition, 17,* 1095–1104.

Nemiah, J. C. (1980). Dissociative disorders. In H. Kaplan, A. Freedman, and B. Sadock, eds., *Comprehensive Textbook of Psychiatry/III.* Baltimore: Williams and Wilkins, pp. 1544–1561.

Newcombe, F. (1983). The psychological consequences of closed head injury: Assessment and rehabilitation. *Injury, 14,* 111–136.

Ojemann, G. A. (1971). Alteration in nonverbal short term memory with stimulation in the region of the mammillothalamic tract in man. *Neuropsychologia, 9,* 195–201.

Osterrieth, P. A. (1944). Le test de copie d'une figure complexe [The test of copying a complex figure]. *Archives de Psychologie, 30,* 206–356.

Patten, B. M. (1972). The ancient art of memory. Usefulness in treatment. *Archives of Neurology, 26,* 25–31.

Reitan, R. M., and Davison, L. A. (1974). *Clinical Neuropsychology: Current Status and Applications.* Washington, D.C.: V. A. Winston.

Rey, A. (1964). *L'examen Clinique Psychologie.* Paris: Presses Universitaires de France.

Ribot, T. (1881). *Les Maladies de la Memoire* [English translation: *Diseases of Memory.* New York: Appleton-Century-Crofts.

Russell, W. R., and Nathan, P. W. (1946). Traumatic amnesia. *Brain, 69,* 280–300.

Saint-Cyr, J. A., and Taylor, A. E. (1992). The mobilization of procedural learning: The "key signature" of the basal ganglia. In L. R. Squire and N. Butters, eds., *Neuropsychology of Memory/II.* New York: Guilford Press, pp. 188–202.

Salmon, D. P., Shimamura, A. P., Butters, N., and Smith, S. (1988). Lexical and semantic priming deficits in patients with Alzheimer's disease. *Journal of Clinical and Experimental Neuropsychology, 10,* 477–494.

Sanders, H. I., and Warrington, D. K. (1971). Memory for remote events in amnesic patients. *Brain, 94,* 661–668.

Schacter, D., and Crovitz, H. F. (1977). Memory function after closed head injury: A review of the quantitative research. *Cortex, 13,* 150–176.

Schacter, D., Wang, P. L., Tulving, E., and Freedman, P. C. (1982). Functional retrograde amnesia: A quantitative case study. *Neuropsychologia, 20,* 523–532.

Schacter, D. L. (1987). Implicit memory: History and current status. *Journal of Experimental Psychology. Learning, Memory and Cognition, 13,* 501–518.

Schacter, D. L., Chiu, C. Y., and Ochsner, K. N. (1993). Implicit memory: A selective review. *Annual Review of Neuroscience, 16,* 159–182.

Scoville, W. B., and Milner, B. (1957). Loss of recent memory after bilateral hippocampal lesions. *Journal of Neurology, Neurosurgery and Psychiatry, 20,* 11–21.

Seltzer, B., and Benson, D. F. (1974). The temporal pattern of retrograde amnesia in Korsakoff's disease. *Neurology, 24,* 527–530.

Shimamura, A. P. (1986). Priming effects in amnesia: Evidence for a dissociable memory function. *Quarterly Journal of Experimental Psychology. A. Human Experimental Psychology, 38,* 619–644.

Shimamura, A. P. (1993). Neuropsychological analyses of implicit memory: Recent progress and theoretical interpretations. In P. Graf and M. E. Masson, eds., *Implicit Memory: New Directions in Cognition, Development, and Neuropsychology.* Hillsdale, NJ: Lawrence Erlbaum, pp. 265–285.

Shimamura, A. P., and Gershberg, F. B. (1992). Neuropsychiatric aspects of memory and amnesia. In S. C. Yudofsky and R. E. Hales, eds., *Textbook of Neuropsychiatry.* Washington, D.C.: American Psychiatric Press, pp. 345–362.

Shimamura, A. P., Janowsky, J. S., and Squire, L. R. (1990). Memory for the temporal order of events in patients with frontal lobe lesions and amnesic patients. *Neuropsychologia, 28,* 803–814.

Shimamura, A. P., Janowsky, J. S., and Squire, L. R. (1991). What is the role of frontal lobe damage in memory disorders? In H. D. Levin, H. M. Eisenberg and A. L. Benton, eds., *Frontal Lobe Function and Dysfunction.* New York: Oxford University Press, pp. 173–195.

Shimamura, A. P., Jernigan, T. L., and Squire, L. R. (1988). Korsakoff's syndrome: Radiological (CT) findings and neuropsychological correlates. *Journal of Neuroscience, 8,* 4400–4410.

Shimamura, A. P., Salmon, D. P., Squire, L. R., and Butters, N. (1987). Memory dysfunction and word priming in dementia and amnesia. *Behavioral Neuroscience, 101,* 347–351.

Shimamura, A. P., and Squire, L. R. (1984). Paired-associate learning and priming effects in amnesia: A neuropsychological analysis. *Journal of Experimental Psychology: General, 113,* 556–570.

Speedie, L. J., and Heilman, K. M. (1982). Amnestic disturbance following infarction of the left dorsomedial nucleus of the thalamus. *Neuropsychologia, 20,* 597–604.

Squire, L. R. (1974). Remote memory as affected by aging. *Neuropsychologia, 12,* 429–435.

Squire, L. R. (1982a). The neuropsychology of human memory. *Annual Review of Neuroscience, 5,* 241–273.

Squire, L. R. (1982b). Comparisons between forms of amnesia: Some deficits are unique to Korsakoff's syndrome. *Journal of Experimental Psychology. Learning, Memory and Cognition, 8,* 560–571.

Squire, L. R. (1986). Mechanisms of memory. *Science, 232,* 1612–1619.

Squire, L. R. (1987). *Memory and Brain.* New York: Oxford University Press.

Squire, L. R. (1989). On the course of forgetting in very long-term memory. *Journal of Experimental Psychology. Learning, Memory and Cognition, 15,* 241–245.

Squire, L. R. (1994). Declarative and nondeclarative memory: Multiple brain systems support learning and memory. In D. Schacter and E. Tulving, eds., *Advances in the Study of Memory and Memory Systems.* Cambridge: MIT Press, pp. 203–231.

Squire, L. R., and Alvarez, P. (1995). Retrograde amnesia and memory consolidation: A neurobiological perspective. *Current Opinion in Neurobiology, 5,* 169–177.

Squire, L. R., Amaral, D. G., and Press, G. A. (1990). Magnetic resonance imaging of hippocampal formation and mammillary nuclei distinguish medial temporal lobe and diencephalic amnesia. *Journal of Neuroscience, 10,* 3106–3117.

Squire, L. R., and Butters, N. (1992). *The Neuropsychology of Memory/II.* New York: Guilford Press.

Squire, L. R., and Cohen, N. J. (1982). Remote memory, retrograde amnesia, and the neuropsychology of memory. In L. Cermak, ed., *Human Memory and Amnesia.* Hillsdale, N.J.: Lawrence Erlbaum, pp. 275–303.

Squire, L. R., Haist, F., and Shimamura, A. P. (1989). The neurology of memory: Quantitative assessment of retrograde amnesia in two groups of amnesic patients. *Journal of Neuroscience, 9,* 828–839.

Squire, L. R., Knowlton, B., and Musen, G. (1993). The structure and organization of memory. *Annual Review of Psychology, 44,* 453–495.

Squire, L. R., and Shimamura, A. P. (1986). Characterizing amnesic patients for neurobehavioral study. *Behavioral Neuroscience, 100,* 866–877.

Squire, L. R., and Slater, P. C. (1975). Forgetting in very long-term memory as assessed by an improved questionnaire technique. *Journal of Experimental Psychology. Human Learning and Memory, 104,* 50–54.

Squire, L. R., and Slater, P. C. (1983). Electroconvulsive therapy and complaints of memory dysfunction: A prospective three-year follow-up study. *British Journal of Psychiatry, 142,* 1–8.

Squire, L. R., Wetzel, C. D., and Slater, P. C. (1979). Memory complaint after electroconvulsive therapy: Assessment with a new self-rating instrument. *Biological Psychiatry, 14,* 791–801.

Squire, L. R., and Zola-Morgan, S. (1991). The medial temporal lobe memory system. *Science, 253,* 1380–1386.

Squire, L. R., and Zouzounis, J. A. (1988). Self-ratings of memory dysfunction: Different findings in depression and amnesia. *Journal of Clinical and Experimental Neuropsychology, 10,* 727–738.

Sternberg, D. E., and Jarvik, M. E. (1976). Memory functions in depression. *Archives of General Psychiatry, 33,* 219–224.

Stromgren, L. S. (1977). The influence of depression on memory. *Acta Psychiatrica Scandinavica, 56,* 109–128.

Strub, R. L., and Black, F. W. (1977). *The Mental Status Examination in Neurology.* Philadelphia: F. A. Davis.

Talland, G. A. (1965). *Deranged Memory.* New York: Academic Press.

Teuber, H.-L., Milner, B., and Vaughan, H. (1968). Persistent anterograde amnesia after stab wound of the basal brain. *Neuropsychologia, 6,* 267–272.

Thompson, R. F. (1992). Memory. *Current Opinion in Neurobiology, 2,* 203–208.

Tulving, E. (1985). Memory and consciousness. *Canadian Psychologist, 26,* 1–12.

Tulving, E., and Schacter, D. L. (1990). Priming and human memory systems. *Science, 247,* 301–306.

Van Hoesen, G. W., Hyman, B. T., and Damasio, A. R. (1991). Entorhinal cortex pathology in Alzheimer's disease. *Hippocampus, 1,* 1–8.

Victor, M., Adams, R. D., and Collins, C. (1989). *The Wernicke-Korsakoff Syndrome and Related Neurologic Disorders Due to Alcoholism and Malnutrition.* Philadelphia: F. A. Davis.

Victor, M., and Agamanolis, J. (1990). Amnesia due to lesions confined to the hippocampus: A clinical-pathological study. *Journal of Cognitive Neuroscience, 2,* 246–257.

Warrington, E. K. (1984). *Recognition Memory*

Test. Windsor, England: NFER-Nelson Publishing Company Limited.

Wechsler, D. (1945). A standardized memory scale for clinical use. *Journal of Psychology, 19,* 87–95.

Wechsler, D. (1981). *Wechsler Adult Intelligence Scale-Revised*. New York: Psychological Corporation.

Wechsler, D. (1987). *Wechsler Memory Scale-Revised*. New York: Psychological Corporation.

Weiner, R. D., Rogers, H. J., Welch, C. A., Davidson, J.R.T., Miller, R. D., Weir, D., Cahill, J. F., and Squire, L. R. (1984). ECT stimulus parameters and electrode placement: Relevance to therapeutic and adverse effects. In B. Lerer, R. D. Weiner, and R. H. Bellmaker, eds., *ECT: Basic Mechanisms*. London: John Libbey and Company, pp. 139–147.

Weiskrantz, L. (1990). Some contributions of neuropsychology of vision and memory to the problem of consciousness. In A. Marcel and E. Bisiach, eds., *Consciousness and Contemporary Science*. New York: Oxford University Press, pp. 183–199.

Weiskrantz, L., and Warrington, E. K. (1979). Conditioning in amnesic patients. *Neuropsychologia, 17,* 187–194.

Wilson, B. A. (1987). *Rehabilitation of Memory*. New York: Guilford Press.

Wilson, B. A., Cockburn, J., Baddeley, A. D., and Hiorns, R. (1989). How do old dogs learn new tricks?: Teaching a technological skill to brain injured people. *Cortex, 27,* 115–119.

Wilson, R. S., Kaszniak, A. W., and Fox, J. H. (1981). Remote memory in senile dementia. *Cortex, 17,* 41–48.

Winocur, G. (1990). Anterograde and retrograde amnesia in rats with dorsal hippocampal or dorsomedial thalamic lesions. *Behavioural Brain Research, 38,* 145–154.

Zangwill, O. L. (1977). The amnesic syndrome. In C.W.M. Whitty and O. L. Zangwill, eds., *Amnesia: Clinical, Psychological, and Medicolegal Aspects/II*. London/Boston: Butterworths, pp. 104–117.

Zelinski, E. M., Gilewski, M. K., and Thompson, L. W. (1980). Do laboratory tests relate to self-assessment of memory ability in the young and old? In L. W. Poon, J. L. Fozard, L. S. Cermak, D. Arenberg, and L. W. Thompson, eds., *New Directions in Memory and Aging*. Hillsdale, NJ: Lawrence Erlbaum, pp. 519–544.

Zola-Morgan, S., Cohen, N. J., and Squire, L. R. (1983). Recall of remote episodic memory in amnesia. *Neuropsychologia, 21,* 487–500.

Zola-Morgan, S., and Squire, L. R. (1990). The primate hippocampal formation: Evidence for a time-limited role in memory storage. *Science, 250,* 288–290.

Zola-Morgan, S., and Squire, L. R. (1993). Neuroanatomy of memory. *Annual Review of Neuroscience, 16,* 547–563.

Zola-Morgan, S., Squire, L. R., and Amaral, D. G. (1986). Human amnesia and the medial temporal region: Enduring memory impairment following a bilateral lesion limited to field CA1 of the hippocampus. *Journal of Neuroscience, 6,* 2950–2967.

12 Neuropsychological Aspects of Epilepsy

PAMELA J. THOMPSON and MICHAEL R. TRIMBLE

Epilepsy is a clinical definition of a group of central nervous system disorders that have as their common symptom, seizures. The latter arise from disturbed electrical activity in the brain and take a variety of forms including episodes of disturbed movement, sensation, perception, and behavior, which are usually, but not inevitably, accompanied by alterations of the level of consciousness. Epilepsy is a relatively common disorder with a reported incidence of about 50 per 100,000 persons per year. The prevalence of active epilepsy is about 50 per 1000 persons, and it is estimated that between 2% and 5% of the general population will suffer at least one nonfebrile seizure during their lives (Sander and Shorvon, 1987). Epilepsy is a heterogeneous condition varying considerably with regard to severity, prognosis, and etiology. In about 60% to 70% of patients the condition remits. The remainder will continue to have seizures, although seizure frequency and severity will vary markedly among patients.

Classification of epilepsy is complicated, not least because it is a chronic condition with variable etiology, and a symptom pattern that may change over time. At present it is somewhat easier to classify seizure type based on the clinical description and underlying neurophysiological abnormalities associated with the episodes. An abbreviated version of the classification recommended by the International League Against Epilepsy is shown in Table 12-1 (Commission, 1981).

Partial seizures are those of focal origin that either remain focal or become generalized. Their symptomatology is described as simple or complex, the latter referring to the interference with higher level cerebral activity in which disturbance of consciousness occurs. Such patients present with a variety of experiences including hallucinations, affective disturbances, and thought disorder, and they usually have electroencephalographic, radiological, and neuropsychological evidence of temporal or frontal lobe disturbance.

Generalized seizures are due to bilateral disturbances that are usually symmetrical from the onset. There is always loss of consciousness. Classic tonic-clonic seizures have a sudden onset with loss of consciousness, tonic muscular contractions followed by clonic ones, after which the patient is unarousable for a short period of time. Absence attacks are sudden transient lapses of consciousness, which may be so slight as to be scarcely perceptible to an onlooker. Myoclonic and atonic seizures are also associated with momentary lapses of consciousness and in addition brief bilateral clonic jerking of the face, limbs, and/or trunk or a sudden loss of postural tone.

The term "status epilepticus" is used whenever a seizure persists for a sufficient

Table 12-1. Classification of Epileptic Seizures

1. Partial (focal, local) seizures
   1.1. Simple partial seizures:
      - With motor signs
      - With somatosensory symptoms
      - With autonomic symptoms
      - With psychic symptoms
   1.2. Complex partial seizures:
      - Simple partial onset followed by impairment of consciousness
      - Impairment of consciousness at outset
   1.3. Partial seizures evolving to secondary generalized seizures
2. Generalized seizures
   2.1. Absence seizures
      - Atypical absence
   2.2. Myoclonic seizures
   2.3. Clonic seizures
   2.4. Tonic seizures
   2.5. Tonic-clonic seizures
   2.6. Atonic seizures
3. Unclassified epileptic seizures

length of time, or is repeated frequently enough that recovery between attacks does not occur. Status epilepticus may be divided into partial status or generalized status (e.g., absence status or tonic-clonic status).

Epilepsy is more a group of syndromes than a specific disease. "The epilepsies" or epileptic syndromes have a classification separate from that of seizures that emphasizes the heterogeneity of the symptom complexes. An epileptic syndrome is defined as a disorder characterized by a cluster of signs and symptoms customarily occurring together (see Table 12-2; Commission, 1989). The most important division of the epilepsies is between epilepsy with a recognizable cause (symptomatic epilepsy) and epilepsy without a recognizable cause (idiopathic epilepsy).

The treatment of epilepsy is directed first toward removing any possible cause or precipitating factor, after which the prime aim is to control the main symptoms, namely the seizures. Pharmacological agents have become the standard form of treatment (Richens and Perucca, 1993). Table 12-3 displays some of the antiepileptic drugs currently available.

In a small proportion of patients, seizure control is achieved following surgery. Thus,

if epilepsy originates in a clearly demonstrable area of the brain that is accessible and whose removal will not produce significant neuropsychological and physical problems, surgery may be indicated, particularly if seizure control by medication has failed. The majority of operations for seizure control are undertaken on the temporal lobes with a smaller number on the frontal lobes. Corpus callosotomy, hemispherectomy, and multiple subpial resections are operations less frequently undertaken (Polkey and Binnie, 1993).

Neuropsychology

Alterations of cognitive functioning in epilepsy have been noted for centuries. In his 17th century Oxford lecture, for example, Willis stated, "It often happens that epileptic patients during their paroxysm and after-

Table 12-2. Classification of Epilepsies and Epileptic Syndromes (Abbreviated)

1. Localization-related (focal, local, partial)
   1.1. Idiopathic (with age-related onset)
      - Benign childhood epilepsy with centrotemporal spikes
      - Childhood epilepsy with occipital paroxysms
      - Primary reading epilepsy
   1.2. Symptomatic
      - Temporal lobe epilepsies
      - Frontal lobe epilepsies
      - Parietal lobe epilepsies
      - Occipital lobe epilepsies
   1.3. Cryptogenic epilepsy
2. Generalized epilepsies and syndromes
   2.1. Idiopathic (with age-related onset)
      - Benign neonatal familial convulsions
      - Benign neonatal convulsions
      - Juvenile absence epilepsy
      - Juvenile myoclonic epilepsy
   2.2. Symptomatic (in order of age)
      - West syndrome
      - Lennox-Gastaut syndrome
      - Epilepsy with myoclonic astatic seizures
3. Epilepsies and syndromes undetermined whether focal or generalized
      - Neonatal seizures
      - Epilepsy with continuous spike-waves during slow wave sleep
      - Acquired epileptic aphasia
4. Special syndromes
      - Febrile convulsions
      - Isolated seizures/status epilepticus

Table 12-3. Antiepileptic Drugs

Generic Name	Comments
Acetazolomide	Used as adjunctive therapy for intractable cases.
Carbamazepine	First choice medication for partial seizures, used also in generalized seizures.
Clobazam	Adjunctive therapy. A benzodiazepine.
Clonazepam	Adjunctive therapy. A benzodiazepine.
Diazepam	Used rarely as adjunctive therapy. A benzodiazepine.
Ethosuximide	Used only for primary generalized absence seizures.
Gabapentin	Newly introduced for adjunctive therapy.
Lamotrigine	Newly introduced for adjunctive therapy.
Phenobarbitone	Used less and less now because of side effects.
Phenytoin	Standard drug for partial and generalized seizures.
Primidone	Breaks down to phenobarbitone.
Sodium valproate	Standard drug, especially for generalized seizures.
Vigabatrin	Newly introduced, given as adjunctive therapy.

wards suffer a severe loss of memory, intellect and fantasy . . ." (Dewhurst, 1980). This aspect of epilepsy received prominent attention during the 19th century. Ideas of degeneracy introduced by Morrell and others implied that intellectual and moral deterioration was an inevitable part of the epileptic process. Since that time, especially since the 1950s, there has been fairly extensive discussion of the neuropsychological changes in epilepsy, and there is increasing awareness that a range of neuropsychological deficits can be observed (Bennett, 1992). These include transient cognitive disturbances that are related to the seizures (ictally related) and also more static deficits that are evident between seizures. These two categories will be discussed in turn.

Ictal Deficits

Seizure activity can be represented by a range of cognitive deficits of varying severity. Toward one end of the spectrum are brief epileptic seizures that to an onlooker have no obvious behavioral correlate and yet can be shown to underlie subtle short-lived impairments of cognition; the so-called phenomena of subclinical seizures (Binnie, 1991). Toward the other end of the spectrum there are episodes of status, notably partial, frontal, temporal, or absence, which can masquerade as a dementing syndrome or other prolonged cognitive impairments (Stores, 1990).

SUBCLINICAL SEIZURES. Awareness that fleeting disturbances of cognition may arise in association with subclinical EEG discharges has increased over the last decade, largely due to technological developments that allow the synchronization of EEG changes with neuropsychological test performance (Binnie, 1991; Rugland et al., 1991).

Rugland and colleagues (1991) over a number of years have developed computerized neuropsychological tests, specifically to look at the impact of subclinical epileptic activity. It is clear from their studies considerable individual variation exists as to whether impairment occurs and on which specific test deficits arise. The length of the discharge and type of task influence whether cognitive impairments are observed in association with subclinical discharges. Those tasks requiring continuous attention seem to be particularly sensitive. In one study, during testing epileptogenic activity decreased in 45% and increased in 16% of the patients compared with a relaxed baseline period (Rugland, 1990; Rugland et al., 1991). Significant impairments of performance during discharges were seen in 61% of the patients on either a simple reaction time test, a choice reaction time test or both. In patients with generalized discharges, 67% showed impaired performance compared to only 33% of patients with focal or marked asymmetrical discharges.

Aarts et al. (1984) described a study in which computer-based verbal and nonverbal memory tasks were performed over extended periods (30 to 60 minutes) with simultaneous EEG and video monitoring. They observed an impairment on both tasks during spike or spike-wave discharges. There was a significant association between locus of discharges and impairment on verbal and nonverbal tasks. Discharges during the stimulus presentation but not during the response phase were most disruptive of performance. Shewmon and Irwin (1988) have also reported a relationship between the locus of the epileptogenic activity and the nature of the cognitive deficits observed.

Some controversy exists as to whether subclinical discharges have relevance to everyday life. A number of investigations have suggested that children's learning ability and behavior may be adversely influenced by such discharges (Kasteleijn-Nolst et al., 1988; Siebelink et al., 1988; Rugland et al., 1991). The latter investigators comment, "There is no reason to conclude that impairment of memory and concentration caused by subclinical EEG discharges in the laboratory is any different from similar disturbance in school." Transient cognitive impairment (TCI), however, does not seem frequent in unselected samples. Aldenkamp et al. (1992) report no cases of TCI secondary to subclinical seizures in a sample of 88 patients referred for simultaneous EEG recording and neuropsychological assessment because of "inconsistent behaviour, fluctuating or other symptoms suggestive of a relationship between epileptic activity and behaviour."

Some investigators have proposed that seizure discharges from temporal lobe structures may underlie reported interictal cognitive deficits, particularly memory disturbance in people with epilepsy. Such phenomena, which are only revealed by depth recordings in patients undergoing presurgical electroencephalographic monitoring, are construed by some as subclinical hippocampal seizures (Bridgman, 1989). This may indeed be a possible explanation in some patients, particularly those cases who in addition to having a unilateral focal ictal discharge are shown during depth recordings to have interictal spiking in the contralateral temporal lobe (Halgren et al., 1991).

CLINICAL SEIZURES. Theoretically, any cognitive deficit could be the manifestation of an ictal discharge. Language disturbance in-

cluding speech arrest and dysphasic difficulties can occur with partial seizures arising from the frontal and dominant temporal lobes. Reports of ictal amnesia are also to be found in the literature defined as recurrent paroxysmal memory loss with no alteration in consciousness (Rowan and Rosenbaum, 1991). During an attack the person would appear normal and continue activities, including speaking, and personal identity would be retained. Such episodes, however, are often reported retrospectively and may be difficult to distinguish from transient global amnesia.

NONCONVULSIVE STATUS. Episodes of nonconvulsive status can severely disrupt cognitive processing. However, despite the severity of the symptoms that may present, it is surprising this cause of cognitive disturbance gets little acknowledgment in reviews of neuropsychological aspects of epilepsy. It is likely that many cases may go undiagnosed for considerable periods of time (Shorvon, 1994).

During absence status a range of disturbances have been reported. Roget and colleagues (1974) proposed a classification based on the severity of the symptoms, ranging from slight clouding to lethargy. With slight clouding, neuropsychological deficits may not be evident without resource to formal testing. Patients themselves may at most report a general lack of efficiency. Neuropsychological assessments during such episodes may reveal significant problems, particularly on tests of attention and sequential and organizational skills. Amnesia is uncommon and verbal skills are usually preserved. In cases of moderate clouding, impairments are more evident and amnesia is common. Such cases, if prolonged, may masquerade as dementia.

In reports of partial status, language disturbances are often predominant. In addition, cases of spatial disorientation, dysgraphia and perceptual deficits ranging in severity up to cortical blindness have been reported. Complex partial status has been associated with a range of deficits; Shorvon (1994) recently proposed that as many as 15% of intractable cases will have a history of one or more episodes of complex partial status, many of which have passed unrecognized. During complex partial status patients may appear confused, and it is common for them to experience language difficulties, mental slowness, and amnesia.

Electrical status epilepticus is a condition occurring during slow wave sleep (ESES) that may carry a poor prognosis for cognitive development. Morikawa et al. (1985) measured intelligence quotients of children, before, during, and after documented episodes of ESES and recorded falls in IQ of as much as 56 points. Language functions may be particularly affected and some argue that ESES and the Landau-Kleffner syndrome, a syndrome of acquired aphasia with seizures, are different facets of a similar underlying cerebral dysfunction (Roulet et al., 1991).

POSTICTAL DEFICITS. Recovery from seizures can be variable and for some individuals neuropsychological assessment, undertaken in close proximity to complex partial seizures and generalized attacks, may underestimate an individual's potential. Halgren et al. (1991) described cases who showed marked fluctuations in their competency on memory tests in relation to the proximity of the testing to a seizure. Patients assessed as much as two days following a bout of complex partial seizures performed significantly less well on tests of learning and memory than 2 weeks following the episode.

SEIZURE PRECIPITANTS. There are a number of case reports in the literature of specific neuropsychological processes inducing seizures. Seizure precipitants reported include reading, writing, arithmetic, memorizing, and chess and card playing (Antebi and Bird, 1992; Helmstaedter et al., 1992). Some cases suggest very specific seizure precipitants. Kartsounis (1988) described a case of primary reading epilepsy. Reading per se, however, was not a sufficient trigger. For example, reading nonsense words or other verbal material devoid of meaning (words in isolation) did not induce seizures. In contrast, reading meaningful material over a relatively short period of time consistently produced sei-

zures. It was found the greater the complexity of the text, the higher the frequency of the seizures. The author concluded there was little doubt comprehension associated with reading was the necessary and sufficient factor to induce seizures. Anderson and Wallis (1986) report the case of a 34-year-old accountant whose seizures appeared to be activated by difficult mental arithmetic. Written calculation, visualizing numbers, counting, digit span, and other activities involving numerical manipulation had no such effect. Yamamoto and colleagues (1991) describe cases of reflex epilepsy induced by using a soroban, a traditional Japanese calculator that resembles an abacus.

Interictal Deficits

There is no one cognitive deficit or profile of cognitive functions that is characteristic of people with epilepsy.

INTELLIGENCE. Considerable attention has been directed toward intellectual capacity in epilepsy. Toward the latter half of the 19th and early part of the 20th century, it was generally accepted that the majority of people with epilepsy had limited intellectual abilities and were likely, over the course of time, to deteriorate further. Reynolds (1861) noted that 61% of his patients had some degree of deterioration in mental function. Slightly higher figures were given by Turner (1907) who estimated 86% of patients at the Chalfont Colony had abnormalities, some 30% showing a pronounced degree of dementia. These early reports and many others that could be quoted clearly came from highly selected groups of patients and used purely clinical impressions to estimate intellectual capacity. Some later studies employed psychological tests of intelligence but reports seemed to support the early clinical impressions of subnormal intelligence (Reed, 1951). However, the samples under study were not representative, the majority being drawn from institutionalized populations.

From the 1950s onward a more enlightened view of intelligence in epilepsy began to emerge. Lennox and Lennox (1960) provided data on 1,105 patients and came to the conclusion that two thirds were mentally normal and only one seventh were indisputably subnormal. In a study of private patients, one quarter were found to have IQs greater than 120. More recent evidence supports the view that people with epilepsy encompass a range of intellectual abilities. A small, although significant proportion do deteriorate intellectually, and this is related to a variety of factors to be discussed below (Lesser et al., 1986; Thompson et al., 1986).

EDUCATIONAL ACHIEVEMENT. The number of children with epilepsy experiencing academic difficulties varies between studies, but it has been reported as being as high as 70% (Thompson, 1987). In a recent investigation, 40% of a sample of children with epilepsy were found to have repeated a grade at least once before their sixth grade (Huberty et al., 1992). Children with epilepsy have been found to underachieve in the areas of reading, spelling, and often more markedly in arithmetic (Seidenberg et al., 1986; Aldenkamp, 1987) and to do less well in terms of academic and vocational qualifications (Thompson, 1987). Mitchell and colleagues (1991) compared children designated as making satisfactory academic progress with those classified as making unsatisfactory progress. Results indicated that poor performance was related to specific cognitive deficiencies rather than low IQ. The unsuccessful children scored significantly lower on tests of language and attentional skills. No differences between the groups were noted in terms of visuospatial and gross motor ability.

MEMORY. Memory deficits have received most attention in the literature, and this probably reflects the prominence of complaints by patients themselves. Rowan and Rosenbaum (1991) noted, "Memory loss is one of the most frequently encountered complaints in the office of the epileptologist. Usually patients speak of increasing forgetfulness involving commonplace items such as appointments and what they were about to say." In a large survey of everyday memory failures of 760 people with epilepsy, just

over half complained of moderate to severe memory problems that they felt significantly interfered with functioning in daily life (Corcoran and Thompson, 1992; Thompson and Corcoran, 1992).

Research evidence has accumulated that gives some support for memory disturbance in epilepsy (Thompson, 1991). Studies report patients perform less well on memory tests than control subjects without epilepsy, that patients with temporal lobe seizures perform less well on memory tests than those with other seizure types, and those with temporal lobe seizures display material-specific memory disorders relating to the side of cerebral disturbance. Namely, those with left-sided seizure foci show impairments on measures of verbal memory, and those with right-sided seizure foci show impairments on nonverbal learning and memory. Not all studies, however, have found such clear-cut results.

The memory tests employed contribute to inconsistent findings in the literature, particularly measures of nonverbal memory. Many of the existing tests that purport to tap nonverbal memory are open to verbal mediation. More able individuals may therefore employ such strategies and mask the extent of their nonverbal memory impairments. Sample bias is another factor. For instance, many of the studies of temporal lobe cases are undertaken on individuals at the most severe end of the seizure disorder spectrum. Unfortunately, it is only with cases undergoing extensive neuropsychological and neuroradiological investigations, including invasive procedures, that clear data regarding side of seizure onset can be obtained. Studies involving less severe cases may not yield significant material-specific findings because better controlled cases do not have memory problems or, more likely, that lateralization data that has to be based on a few scalp interictal recordings may be less reliable.

Even for presurgical temporal cases who are perhaps most at risk for memory problems, there is variability in the extent to which deficits are found. Table 12-4 provides the results of surgical candidates with temporal lobe epilepsy on standardized measures of memory. All patients were seen at the

Table 12-4. Presurgical Memory Test Performance of Patients with Left or Right Seizure Foci

	Left sided (N = 14)		Right sided (N = 20)	
	Mean	SD	Mean	SD
Verbal IQ	96.9	(13.5)	97.1	(12.5)
Performance IQ	106.3	(13.8)	103.9	(18.1)
Verbal Memory				
List Learning Trials 1–5	43.2	(7.2)	42.4	(10.6)
Trial 6	9.1	(2.4)	7.5	(2.1)
List B	4.8	(1.7)	5.2	(1.4)
Story Recall: Immediate	34.5	(13.2)	38.3	(16.8)
Delayed	30.5	(16.4)	35.3	(16.7)
% Retained	83.0	(23.3)	92.3	(21.7)
Word Recognition	44.8	(5.1)	43.4	(4.9)
Nonverbal Memory				
Design Learning Trials 1–5	35.3	(7.5)	29.3	(8.6)
Trial 6	7.4	(1.9)	7.0	(2.7)
Design B	4.0	(2.2)	4.8	(2.0)
Complex Figure: Immediate	74.3	(25.2)	62.5	(19.2)
Delayed	70.4	(27.2)	54.9	(23.3)
% Retained	89.0	(19.7)	85.5	(16.2)
Face Recognition	44.8	(5.1)	43.4	(4.9)

National Hospital for Neurology and Neurosurgery in London. The patients have been grouped according to the side of seizure onset. Measures of verbal memory included the immediate and delayed recall of a short story, a list learning test where the patient had five trials to learn a 15-word list and a 50-item forced-choice word recognition test. Measures of nonverbal memory included a design learning test where the patient had five trials to learn a geometric design, immediate and delayed recall of a complex figure and a 50-item forced-choice face recognition test. All patients underwent the sodium amytal procedure and were left-hemisphere dominant for language. No significant differences in memory test performance were noted related to laterality, although the most consistent trend was impairment on measures of nonverbal memory in right-sided cases. Less clear-cut trends were observed for left temporal cases on measures of verbal memory and, as can be seen, on some verbal measures the left-sided cases performed better than the right-sided group.

Some studies suggest that memory disturbance in temporal lobe cases is related to the nature, extent, and location of underlying pathology in the temporal lobes. Miller et al. (1993) reported a delayed verbal recall deficit in patients with left hippocampal sclerosis but not in left temporal cases with other pathologies. Sass and colleagues examined the relationship between presurgical memory performance and hippocampal neuronal densities measured after surgery. Significant correlations were found between cell densities in one hippocampal subfield, specifically CA3, and the presurgical performance on the Logical Memory subtest of the Wechsler Memory Scale (WMS) and scores on a verbal learning test in patients with left hippocampal sclerosis (Sass et al., 1990a,b; 1992a). No relationship was found with measures of verbal intelligence or language (Sass et al., 1992b). The same investigators more recently have demonstrated correlations between left hippocampal magnetic resonance imaging (MRI) measures and percentage retention of the WMS logical memory index (Lencz et al., 1992). Barr and colleagues (1990) reported reduced hippocampal volumes on the side of the epileptic focus and showed that these measures significantly correlated with performance on material-specific memory tasks. Thus, a range of competency on memory tests may be evident in temporal cases.

Many patients with epilepsy complain bitterly about their memory but do not undergo such detailed neurophysiological, neuropsychological, and neuroradiological investigations as surgical candidates. We have undertaken a study that aimed to increase our understanding of the major causes of memory complaints in epilepsy (Corcoran and Thompson, 1992).

Neuropsychological test performance, patients' self-reports of memory failures and the use of memory support strategies were compared in two groups of 30 patients differing in their level of memory complaints. Those reporting significant memory difficulties performed more poorly on two measures of memory, namely, story recall and design learning. On other measures of memory including list learning and recognition memory tests for words and faces, the complainers performed at a comparable level to the noncomplainers. The story recall test has been found by other investigators to be a sensitive indicator of patients' complaints in daily life, and our findings would support this view (Goldstein and Polkey, 1992). The patients complaining of memory problems were found to be significantly more depressed and anxious and also to rely more on memory support strategies. It is not clear what effect the role of negative mood has. While having a poor or deteriorating memory must contribute to negative emotions, it seems likely that depression itself is contributing to or exaggerating the memory problems.

LANGUAGE FUNCTIONING. Language functioning in chronic epilepsy has been the subject of relatively little research. Verbal stickiness, confabulation, and verbal circumlocution have been described clinically. Mayeux et al. (1980) describe a study stimulated by their own clinical experience. Twenty-nine patients, 14 with left temporal lobe foci, seven with right, and eight with generalized epileptic disturbance participated in the study. Neuropsychological assessment included word fluency and naming tests. Marked differences between the left tempo-

ral lobe and the other groups were noted on naming tests. The authors go on to speculate that frequently when patients complain of memory difficulties they are in fact referring to subtle language deficits.

Mungas and colleagues (1985) also postulated linguistic processing plays a role in the memory disturbance of patients with complex partial seizures. In addition, Hermann et al. (1988) provide further evidence for this proposal. These investigators found that language functioning in general and measures of verbal comprehension, naming, and associative fluency emerged as the most robust predictors of verbal learning and memory performance in 25 patients with complex partial seizures of dominant temporal lobe origin.

A number of authors have commented upon the tendency of some patients with temporal lobe epilepsy to be overly talkative when describing personal feelings, ideas, and experiences. Early reports have been largely anecdotal. Hoepner et al. (1987) report a study in which speech of patients with various types of epilepsy and various foci were compared to the speech of control individuals. The participants in their study were requested to describe a complex picture. Dysfluencies, word repetitions, revisions, incomplete phrases, broken words and prolonged sounds were noted, as were the number of words given. Only four of the 29 patients were classified as verbose. All four had complex partial seizures originating in the left hemisphere. However, other patients with left-sided abnormalities did not show verbosity. The four verbose patients tended to be older than the others, with longer seizure and medication histories but were not different from the rest on levels of intelligence and verbal memory. Their verbosity was marked by reference to nonessential details. The number of words uttered by these patients ranged from 236 to 320, and this compared to 30 to 106 for the other left complex partial group. This led the author to suggest that verbosity may be an all-or-none phenomenon rather than a graded phenomenon.

The written equivalent of verbosity has

attracted much more attention, namely, hypergraphia. Such interest stems from reports made by Waxman and Geschwind in 1974. Hypergraphia was perceived by these authors as an unusual tendency for patients to write extensively, typically in a meticulous manner, and this characteristic was seen as part of an interictal personality change observed by these authors in patients with temporal lobe epilepsy. In their paper, the authors present detailed case histories of seven patients. All cases showed a preoccupation with minute detail, with words defined and redefined several times. Roberts and colleagues (1982) reported similar cases.

Sachdev and Waxman (1981) sent a letter to 63 previous inpatients with epilepsy. In the letter the patients were asked to "describe to the best of your ability your present state of health, understanding of the disease (seizure disorder) and the changes in your life resulting from it." Only 17 patients replied (27%). The authors reported patients with temporal lobe epilepsy were more likely to respond and show, in terms of length and content, characteristics of hypergraphia in contrast to patients with nontemporal lobe epilepsy. Hermann and colleagues (1983) also sent a letter to patients with epilepsy in which an open-ended question was asked about their general condition. Response rate, mean number of words per letter, the presence or absence of reference to philosophical, ethical, or religious themes were used as a measure for hypergraphia. Twenty-four percent of patients with temporal lobe epilepsy (19/80) responded, in contrast to 10% of the nontemporal lobe epilepsy group (2/31). Mean word length was actually reported to be greater in the nontemporal lobe group, 370 words in contrast to an average of 296 in the temporal lobe group. The two longest letters, however, were found in the temporal lobe group, with 1,176 and 1,229 words, respectively.

In a recent study of language functioning in patients with intractable seizures, Davey and Thompson (1991) reported a high level of difficulties. Sixty consecutive admissions to a special assessment facility for epilepsy were recruited. The Illinois Test of Psycholinguistic Ability (ITPA; Kirk et al., 1968) and the Brain Metabolism Unit Scale (BMU; Thompson, 1983) were employed. The former has been widely used following its introduction in the 1960s. It provides a detailed profile of an individual's performance across a range of language functions. It was designed for use with children but has been found clinically useful and acceptable by the population under consideration. The BMU was a newer measure, which consists of 32 tests of language, memory, orientation, praxis, and nonverbal intelligence. Many areas of functioning were observed to be impaired, but most widespread difficulties seemed to occur in the area of expressive language functioning and less so in receptive functions and in symbolic areas such as reading, the latter being relatively well preserved. It is important to note that no patient had recently received speech therapy input or evaluation and only two had done so in the very distant past. Thus, the language difficulties uncovered were hidden difficulties previously overlooked.

LANGUAGE DOMINANCE. In the general population most individuals, both right (97%) and left (80%) handers, are left-hemisphere dominant for language. In patients with epilepsy there is an increased incidence of crossed and mixed dominance. Dominance is best established using the intracarotid sodium amytal test (Dinner, 1991) (see below). Using this procedure, Rey and colleagues (1988) reported that 17 of 73 cases showed right hemisphere language dominance and a further 11 had language functions represented bilaterally. Such a shift in language dominance is more common where there is evidence of early brain damage or early onset of recurrent seizures (Rausch and Walsh, 1984). Some authors have proposed that the price paid for shifting language dominance is impaired development of other "right hemisphere" functions—the competitive crowding hypothesis (Strauss et al., 1990, 1992). Others have failed to find evidence to support this and report that on the contrary, right hemisphere language dominant patients with left seizure foci can show little cognitive impairment, the earlier shift seeming to extend to other cognitive functions including memory (Rausch et al., 1991).

Contributory Factors to Interictal Deficits

Seizure History

ETIOLOGY. Epilepsy can arise from a wide range of brain pathologies including head trauma, tuberous sclerosis, central nervous system infections and poisoning, brain tumors, vascular disease, and chronic alcoholism, to name the more frequent causes. Where there is significant underlying brain damage, then the expected incidence of cognitive difficulties is high (Holmes, 1991). This seems more likely the case with children, and Wallace (1993) writes, "Underlying aetiological determinants for epilepsy are the most important factors in the intellectual abilities of the child with epilepsy."

However, the difference in functioning between cases with and without brain damage has not been marked. For instance, Kløve and Matthews (1966) administered the Reitan Neuropsychological Battery to groups of patients with epilepsy of known and unknown etiology. The former group did a little more poorly but only on a small portion of the variables did this achieve statistical significance. Bourgeois et al. (1983) found the mean IQ of patients with symptomatic epilepsy to be average (102.5) and patients with idiopathic epilepsy to be low average (89.1), although significant overlap existed between the groups. Ellenberg et al. (1984, 1986) found preexisting neurological impairment to be a significant predictor of poor cognitive development.

With more advanced neuroradiological techniques it seems likely that to distinguish groups in terms of known versus unknown etiology will be too crude. There are now a number of etiologies, particularly those of neurodevelopmental origin such as cortical dysgenesis, that may not be expected to be associated with major cognitive deficits as a consequence of early reorganization of functions.

AGE OF ONSET. The trend in the literature suggests early age of onset is related to greater cognitive deficits, although the effect is not great (Lesser et al., 1986). It is obviously difficult to assess the role of this variable independently from etiology and seizure type. Corbett (1993) reported that convulsions, infantile spasms and severe myoclonic seizures in early infancy carry a particularly poor prognosis. He writes, "In many of these situations it is difficult to distinguish between the effects of the underlying neuropathology on intellectual development and the damaging effect of subsequent seizures, particularly if these are frequent and prolonged."

Dodrill (1993) looked at data from a sample of just over 500 adults with epilepsy. He reported a significant relationship between age of onset and level of test performance when grouped according to age bands and also a highly significant correlation between age of onset and intellectual ability, poorer scores being associated with earlier seizure onsets. Interpretation of analyses such as this is not clear-cut because of an interplay of potentially contaminating factors with the variable of interest. Those with early age of onset will also have more prolonged medication intake and will have increased exposure to psychosocial factors such as parental and teacher's expectations.

DURATION OF THE DISORDER. A long duration of epilepsy has been associated with poorer neuropsychological test performance. This variable, however, is weaker than many others, no doubt due to the influence of the degree of seizure control, which can fluctuate substantially from one person to the next (Lesser et al., 1986). A better variable is duration of active epilepsy and, indeed, Farwell et al. (1985) found a stronger relationship between this and mental abilities than duration of the disorder.

SEIZURE FREQUENCY. Those with frequent seizures have an increased risk of cognitive difficulties and deterioration (Dodrill and Troupin, 1976; Dikman and Matthews, 1977). Longitudinal studies show those with increased seizure frequency do less well on tests of intelligence and cognition at subsequent assessments (Seidenberg et al., 1981; Meinardi et al., 1991). Many studies, however, only consider recent seizure history. This is probably not long enough to appreciate losses in abilities that may accumulate over time.

Dodrill (1986) reports a study in which individuals with a history of status or more than one hundred convulsive attacks were more impaired neuropsychologically than other groups with less frequent seizures. Seizure severity in addition to frequency is a variable that also must be considered. Seizures of temporal origin can vary in clinical features and neurophysiological correlates. Patients with more extensive spread of epileptic discharges with more prolonged postictal slowing on the EEG may display more pronounced cognitive difficulties.

SEIZURE TYPE. There is poor prognisis with certain seizure types, especially infantile spasms, early myoclonus, and the Lennox-Gastaut syndrome. Children with partial epilepsies, particularly when symptomatic of brain damage, do less well cognitively when compared with children with generalized seizures, especially absences (Farwell et al., 1985). For adults whose cognitive functions have developed, partial seizures may have less of an impact than in the developing brain. In our own studies in adults with generalized seizures, atonic/tonic attacks had the poorest prognosis (Thompson et al., 1986; Mader et al., 1989). Evidence that more than one seizure type is associated with cognitive difficulties was reported by Rodin and colleagues (Rodin et al., 1976).

Psychosocial Factors

Much less attention has been devoted to the role of psychological and social factors in contrast to neurological and treatment related variables. This is somewhat disappointing as such factors may be more amenable to remediation, particularly if tackled early. For example, research evidence on children with epilepsy suggests parental and teacher's expectations regarding academic goals are low and may contribute to poor attainment in some people (Stores, 1990).

Depressed mood and elevated levels of anxiety have been reported in patients with epilepsy. There is increasing evidence from other psychological research that negative moods can influence neuropsychological test performance. Our own studies, as indicated earlier, found elevated levels of depression to be strongly predictive of poor memory test performance, particularly measures of verbal recall (Corcoran and Thompson, 1992).

Treatment

Medication

The majority of patients with epilepsy will be maintained for a number of years on antiepileptic medication. In recent years there has been much research on the effects of these drugs on cognitive abilities, an area that has occasioned controversy. Further, there are several new anticonvulsant drugs that have been introduced, or will be introduced, in various countries. These include designer drugs such as vigabatrin, a GABA transaminase inhibitor that reliably increases CNS GABA, and others with as yet unknown mechanisms of action such as lamotrigine, GABApentin, and felbamate.

For most of the anticonvulsants, favorable reports, based mainly on subjective impressions, are reported soon after their introduction. With more widespread use, and with careful testing, adverse effects are usually detected. In fact, detrimental effects on cognitive function have been reported for most of the anticonvulsants, although the profile of the behavioral toxicity probably differs between them. This is to be expected because they all have different structures, and hence different effects on CNS neurophysiology and neurochemistry. The extent, or the clinical significance, of the effects is sometimes questioned, but they are generally sufficient to be expected to reduce peak efficiency at school, at work, or during demanding daily activities.

The paper by Dodrill (1975) proved of

importance in stimulating research in this area. Data were presented from 70 adults, stabilized on phenytoin monotherapy, who performed a variety of cognitive tasks. Patients with higher mean serum levels of drug (mean 43 mg/l) performed significantly worse than those with lower levels (mean 17 mg/l). The cognitive tests used were from the complete Halstead-Reitan Battery, the WAIS, the Trail Making Test, and several motor tasks. Significant differences were noted at higher levels on a number of subtest scores, largely confined to those related to motor function. These data led Dodrill to conclude that ".... effects on motor related tasks are considerably more prominent than those related to higher mental functions."

In 1989, Dodrill published a further analysis of these data, essentially confirming his earlier conclusions (Dodrill and Temkin, 1989). Using his original data, he covaried his individual test scores for the effect of "the most simple measure of motor speed," namely, finger tapping. When this was done, all of his statistically significant differences disappeared. One interpretation of these data is that the influence of phenytoin on cognitive function may be a reflection of simple motor speed.

There are, however, several other studies where the influence of phenytoin on different aspects of cognitive function has been assessed, and in some a comparison with other anticonvulsants can be made. These are summarized in Table 12-5.

VOLUNTEER STUDIES. Although volunteer studies are often criticized for lack of relevance to the clinical situation, they are important for two main reasons. First, by having different ethical constraints, they allow for well-balanced experimental designs. Thus, it is possible to compare active drug against placebo, and to do double-blind procedures. Second, in the interpretation of the results, the confounding epilepsy variables noted above do not have to be taken into account. Matching for such variables in clinical studies is very difficult, the more so because quantification of even such apparently obvious events as seizures is problematic.

The most appropriate design for clinical studies is a within-patient investigation, testing longitudinally, the patient being his own control. Even this has design difficulties, notably the problem of practice effects of the tests, and changes in disease variables with time such as seizure frequency. Results from volunteer studies provide validity for clinical data if there is correspondence of results.

The only volunteer studies carried out with anticonvulsants where they have been given for more than a few days, and where comparisons between drugs can be made,

Table 12-5. Studies Comparing Different Anticonvulsant Drugs on Tests of Cognitive Function

Study	Subjects and Treatment Parameters	Drugs	Design	Preferred Drug
Thompson et al., 1981	Vol	PH, V, CBZ	DB, C, P	CBZ > V > PH
Thompson and Trimble, 1982	M	PH, V, CBZ	B, L	CBZ > V = PH
Andrewes et al., 1986	M	PH, CBZ	C	CBZ > PH
Brodie et al., 1987	M	CBZ, PH, VPA, POLY	C	No difference
Smith et al., 1987	M	CBZ, PH, PB	DB, L, C	CBZ > PH = PB
Gallassi et al., 1988, 1990	M, W	CBZ, PH, V	C, L	CBZ > PH
Meador et al., 1990	M	CBZ, PB, PH	B, L	No difference
Gillham et al., 1990	M	CBZ, PH, V	B, C	CBZ > PH (memory)
Duncan et al., 1990	P, W	CBZ, PH, V		CBZ > PH
Meador et al., 1991	Vol	CBZ, PH	DB, L, C	CBZ > PH (motor) PH > CBZ (Stroop)
Aldenkamp et al., 1993	P, W	CBZ, PH	L, C	CBZ > PH

M = Monotherapy; P = Polytherapy; W = Withdrawal; Vol = Volunteer; PH = Phenytoin; CBZ = Carbamazepine; PB = Phenobarbitone; V = Valproate; C = Control group; L = Longitudinal; B = Blind; DB = Double-blind.

are those of Thompson and colleagues (1981; Thompson and Trimble, 1981; Trimble and Thompson, 1983) and Meador et al. (1991). The cognitive battery used by Thompson and colleagues was designed specifically for the assessment of the effects of drugs on cognitive function, and incorporated the following features: (1) Tests had been shown in other studies to be of value in psychopharmacological investigations of cognitive toxicity. (2) Tests were given, where practicable, as parallel versions with repeated testing. (3) Tests were selected that seemed on repeated testing to be free of practice effects. (4) Automation of both presentation of stimulus and measurement of response times was considered important to minimize error and variability, which occur with manually presented tasks. (5) The cognitive domains chosen were thought to be relevant to patient complaints. The final battery included tests of attention, retention of new information, speed and accuracy of perceptual registration, decision making, and manual speed.

Volunteers were given either an active compound or placebo, each for a 2-week period, in a double-blind crossover design. Doses of anticonvulsants were: phenytoin, 100 mg three times daily; sodium valproate, 1000 mg/day; carbamazepine, 200 mg three times daily; clobazam, 20 mg nightly. The results of these studies may be summarized as follows: Phenytoin was the drug that impaired cognitive functions the most. Impairments were noted for several tasks that had minimal or no motor components (Table 12-6). Such tasks were chosen, in part, to test the hypothesis Dodrill had suggested.

Meador et al. (1991) used a different design, converting serum levels to percentages of standard therapeutic ranges, which were used in the covariance analysis. Carbamazepine and phenytoin were given to volunteers in a crossover design. Tests given included the Symbol Digit Modalities Test, the Selective Reminding Test, Complex Figures, the PASAT, Stroop, Finger Tapping, the Grooved Pegboard, and a Choice Reaction Time Task. No placebo comparisons were made and there were very few changes with

Table 12-6. Tests Showing Nonmotor Impairments of Anticonvulsants

Study	Tests
Thompson et al., 1981	Stroop (PH, CBZ), visual and auditory scan (V), perceptual
Thompson and Trimble, 1981	Speed (PH), decision making (PH, V), picture recall (PH)
Thompson et al., 1982	Picture recall (PH, V), visual scan (V)—with auditory distraction (PH, V), auditory detection (PH, V)
Andrewes et al., 1986	Accuracy on Sternberg, delayed cued recall, prose recall (all PH)
Smith et al., 1987	Tasks of concentration and attention (PH)
Gallassi et al., 1988	Digit span, verbal learning (PH)
Gillham et al., 1990	Digit span, paired associate learning, visual span (PH)
Duncan et al., 1990	Digit cancellation (PH)
Meador et al., 1991	Stroop (CBZ)
Aldenkamp et al., 1993	Visual searching (PH)

PH = Phenytoin; V = Valproate; CBZ = Carbamazepine

the serum (phenytoin). Significant differences were noted in favor of carbamazepine for the Grooved Pegboard, and for phenytoin for the Stroop Test.

An important test of drug effects in psychopharmacological research is to seek pharmacokinetic/pharmacodynamic interrelationships. In the studies of Thompson and colleagues, significant correlations were observed between the serum levels and the extent of the decline in performance between placebo and phenytoin conditions on several of the nonmotor tasks. Such interactions were not found for sodium valproate or carbamazepine.

PATIENT STUDIES—WITHDRAWAL. Two differing designs have been used in studies of patients withdrawing from medication. In the first, patients on polytherapy have one of their drugs systematically removed. In the second, patients on monotherapy have their only medication stopped.

In a study of the effects of withdrawal of a

single medication in patients on polytherapy, Duncan and colleagues (1990) carried out a series of investigations in a double-blind design before withdrawal, following withdrawal, and at 4 weeks' follow-up.

They used a simple, clinically applicable test battery consisting of measures of mental speed, attention, and concentration; performance of a learned skill; short-term memory and concentration; and a simple manual motor task. Patients were withdrawn from either phenytoin (N = 23), sodium valproate (N = 24), or carbamazepine (N = 25), and placebo was substituted. In addition, a control group (N = 25) not undergoing medication changes was tested at the same time intervals. Simple motor tasks improved on withdrawal of all three drugs and continued to improve over the subsequent 4 weeks. Performance on a measure of attention and concentration, a four-letter cancellation task, improved only on withdrawal of phenytoin.

Gallassi et al. (1988) have compared phenytoin, carbamazepine, and sodium valproate in a series of studies of patients on monotherapy. All patients were free of seizures for 2 years, and had elected to come off medications. In the first study, patients on either carbamazepine (N = 13) or phenytoin (N = 12), matched for demographic, clinical, and EEG features, were compared with 26 normal control subjects. Withdrawal was carried out over a 12-month period in a systematic fashion, such that neuropsychological assessment was carried out after reduction at half dose, at 3 months and 1 year after complete suspension of therapy. No patients had a baseline serum level above the therapeutic range. The psychological tests included Raven's Progressive Matrices, Simple and Complex Auditory Reaction Times, a Manual Tapping Task, the Trail Making Test, and tests of immediate memory and learning.

No differences between the drugs were noted for complex reaction times and the results for finger tapping were equivalent. Tests that distinguished the drugs were verbal digit span and a global performance score. For the latter, a significant correlation with duration of phenytoin therapy was noted. In these studies, at 1 year, no differences between the drugs and controls were recorded, indicating a reversibility of effect.

In a further study, the same design was used to study the effects of valproate (N = 20). Patients were initially impaired on the Complex Reaction Time Task, the Trail Making Task, and the Global Score, however, changes from controls disappeared at the 12-month follow-up. The impairments cleared more quickly than with phenytoin, but were more widespread than the changes associated with carbamazepine (Gallassi et al., 1990).

A Scandinavian group has recently reported a withdrawal study in children with epilepsy (Aldenkamp et al., 1993). One hundred children, seizure free for more than a year, and on monotherapy, were withdrawn from medication. Each child was matched to a healthy nonepileptic classmate for control. Patients were reassessed 3 to 4 months after withdrawal, but were excluded if they had a return of seizures. The battery of tests used included tasks of both psychomotor and higher cognitive function. This was by the FePsy, a computerized battery, which delivered tests of speed, information processing and attention, and memory. Differences between phenytoin and carbamazepine, favoring the latter, were suggested across a range of tests, significant for a visual searching task.

PATIENT STUDIES—MONOTHERAPY. Thompson and Trimble (1982), using the same test battery as outlined above, tested patients on monotherapy with either phenytoin (N = 9), sodium valproate (N = 8), or carbamazepine (N = 8), at two serum levels. The design was a within-patient study and patients were seen on two occasions with a 3-month interval between tests. After the first test session, approximately half the patients had their dose of medication increased, and half decreased. They were all, therefore, tested at both a high and a low serum level, the investigator being blind to the status of the patient at testing. The mean serum levels at the low level testing was about half that at the high levels, and all were within the quoted therapeutic ranges for the drug.

All impairments were for higher levels when performances at the two levels were compared, most differences being seen with phenytoin (P) and sodium valproate (V). Tests affected were: immediate recall of pictures (P,V) visual scanning (V), visual scanning with an auditory scanning task (P,V), auditory detection (P,V), decision-making task for category (P,V), motor speed (P). The only tasks affected by the higher levels of carbamazepine were the Stroop Test and a motor tapping task.

Brodie and colleagues (1987) have carried out a series of studies comparing patients on monotherapy and have especially examined the effects of carbamazepine. Their battery of tests included the Critical Flicker Fusion threshold (CFF), a Choice Reaction Time task (CRT), a memory task, finger tapping rate, and a card sorting task. Patients were allowed run-in sessions to acclimatize to the testing situation, and were tested on a single occasion.

Untreated patients did less well than control nonepileptic subjects on CRT, the memory task, and card sorting. However, on the same tasks they did better than treated patients. No difference was noted between four groups, namely, on carbamazepine, phenytoin, sodium valproate, or polypharmacy. No relationship to serum levels was found.

In further studies (MacPhee et al., 1986), the effects of carbamazepine at higher levels were tested, an additional dose of 400 mg being given to patients on monotherapy in a double-blind comparison with placebo. Impairments of CRT, card sorting, and a sedation score were noted, but no other tasks were impaired.

In an extended analysis of data, Gillham et al. (1990) used a larger test battery on patients on monotherapy with carbamazepine (N = 35), sodium valproate (N = 30), or phenytoin (N = 19), and compared their data with untreated epileptic patients (N = 26) and nonepileptic controls (N = 24). No individual test discriminated between the groups, but following z transformation, scores were summated to distinguish psychomotor performance (decision time, CRT, finger tapping, threshold detection, and movement detection) and memory (forward and backward digit span, paired associate learning, visual span). Patients on carbamazepine had lower psychomotor scores than patients on sodium valproate; those on phenytoin had poorer memory scores than those on sodium valproate.

In an investigation of similar design, namely, a single test session in patients on monotherapy, Andrewes et al. (1986) tested patients on carbamazepine (N = 21) and phenytoin (N = 63). Twenty-one untreated patients were also included in the study. Patients were not randomized, but there were no significant differences between the groups with regard to seizure type. The tests included the Sternberg Short Term Scanning Task, word list learning, memory for prose, decision making that included reaction time, and a tracking task.

Significant differences in favor of carbamazepine were noted for: the Sternberg Task, either when presentation of the digit series was 1, 3, and 5 combined, or on the 5-digit task (the difference was not for speed of response, but for accuracy); prose recall, on the delayed cued recall test (here number of items recalled was tested); and the list learning task, notably by the sixth trial on a measure of relearning. They also recorded some relationships between serum levels of the anticonvulsant and performance, high levels of phenytoin correlating with high scores on the tracking task, high carbamazepine levels showing a negative correlation.

Meador et al. (1990) have recently published a randomized and blinded crossover investigation of 15 patients given phenytoin, carbamazepine, or phenobarbitone for 3 months. There were no washout treatments, and subjects were on medication before incorporation into the study, preexisting drugs being tapered. Cognitive tests included: forward and backward digit span, a measure of verbal learning, Digit Symbol, Finger Tapping, LaFayette Grooved Pegboard, Choice Reaction Time, and a P3 evoked potential.

Patients were tested at the end of each 3-month treatment phase. The only significant difference was the poorer performance on the Digit Symbol for the phenobarbitone phase.

THE VA STUDY. The most comprehensive study to date, taking into account in its design many of the problems that some of the above studies have, is the multicenter VA study (Mattson et al., 1985). This was double-blind, with randomization for seizure type, and patients were new-onset cases prescribed carbamazepine, phenytoin, phenobarbitone, and primidone. They were given a battery of psychological tests before therapy, and observed at 1, 3, 6, and 12 months. Compliance was monitored by pill counts.

The battery, which was also given to a control nonseizure population on two occasions separated by 30 days, included the following tests: the WAIS, Digit Symbol, Digit Span, CFF, Discriminative Reaction Time, Word Finding, Finger Tapping, the LaFayette Pegboard, and Color Naming.

Differences between the drugs could be shown (Smith et al., 1987). Thus, a total behavioral toxicity score was derived by combining individual subtest scores transformed into weighted ordinal units based on published norms. Carbamazepine patients showed the least deterioration, patients on phenytoin or phenobarbitone showing significant deterioration at 1 and 3 months. Overall, the carbamazepine group showed the highest number of "best scores" (derived by counting the number of times the group scored better than two or more other treatment groups with a confidence level of >0.05) on measures of concentration and attention.

The results of the above studies, summarized in Table 12-5, suggest a consistent pattern of effects of these anticonvulsant drugs on cognitive function, at least in adults. Carbamazepine emerges as having a better profile, whether in volunteer or patient studies. In some patient studies it is equivalent to valproate (Brodie et al., 1987; Duncan et al., 1990), and in one study it is equivalent to phenytoin (Meador et al., 1991). In view of the discussions as to the relative effect of the drugs on different components of the cognitive profile, it is important to consider the tests employed and the design of the investigations. There is a problem with randomization in the investigations of Andrewes et al. (1986), Brodie et al. (1987), and Gallassi et al. (1988, 1990), although all groups have attempted to control for intergroup differences by demonstrating lack of statistical differences on key variables between groups. Numbers of patients in groups tested are not large in some studies (Thompson and Trimble, 1982; Meador et al., 1990; Gallassi et al., 1990), and blinding of testers is an issue in the investigations of Gallassi et al. (1990), Brodie and colleagues (1987), and Aldenkamp et al. (1993). The investigations with the most appropriate design are those on volunteers (Thompson et al., 1981; Meador et al., 1991), and the double-blind and/or placebo investigations of Duncan et al. (1990) and the VA study, all adopting a longitudinal design. The VA study is by far the largest of the studies, and in terms of design is the most appropriate of the patient studies.

Although most studies note differences between drugs, some do not, and reasons for this should be sought. It may be that there are no differences, but the investigations disproving this hypothesis by far outweigh those in favor. The main one is the study of Brodie and colleagues (1987) using a test battery composed largely of motor tasks. When this was expanded to include other tasks, differences did emerge, and motor effects were distinguished from memory impairments. The latter were worse with phenytoin.

In terms of differences between individual drugs, the only study reviewed that does not, on some tasks, distinguish carbamazepine from phenytoin, apart from that of Brodie and colleagues, is that of Meador et al. (1990). These patients all received monotherapy in a longitudinal design. There were no washout periods between treatments, which may have influenced the results as prolonged effects of drugs (up to at least 3 months) have been noted in some withdrawal studies (Thompson and Trimble, 1982; Gallassi et al., 1988, 1990). Furthermore, there are no data given in respect of any change of seizure frequency.

The studies and tests that suggest there are differences between phenytoin and the other drugs tested where there are minimal or no obvious simple motor elements to the tasks are shown in Table 12-6. These include, in particular, memory tasks, scanning and sensory detection tasks, and some accuracy measures, as opposed to response times.

Similar conclusions with regard to the relative effect of these anticonvulsant drugs on cognitive function, especially with regard to the comparisons of phenytoin and carbamazepine, are reached by other reviewers, including Hirtz and Nelson (1985), Smith (1991), and Bennett (1992).

NEW ANTIEPILEPTIC DRUGS. Of the newer drugs that are available, or about to become available for the treatment of epilepsy, only the 1,5 benzodiazepine clobazam and vigabatrin have been tested in any systematic way. Clobazam has a good cognitive profile and produces less impairment than clonazepam (Cull and Trimble, 1985).

Vigabatrin has, to date, not been shown to provoke effects on either motor (McGuire et al., 1992) or nonmotor tests (Dijkstra et al., 1992). Cognitive testing of the other new drugs is urgently required.

ANTICONVULSANT DRUGS AND COGNITION IN CHILDREN. In contrast to the large number of studies carried out in adults, studies in children are much more limited, and it is even more difficult to reach conclusions. The study of Aldenkamp et al. (1993) is quoted above.

In a longitudinal study of the IQ in 72 children with epilepsy over periods up to 6 years, Bourgeois et al. (1983) found eight children with a persisting decrease of their levels. These were found to have a significantly higher incidence of drug levels in the toxic range at some point in the study.

Phenobarbitone has been shown to impair performance in the very young (Camfield et al., 1979), and to be associated with deterioration of the IQ, an effect that continued

beyond prescription of the drug (Farwell et al., 1990). Nolte et al. (1980) have shown impairments at higher levels of phenytoin.

Carbamazepine has been the subject of several studies. In a comparison with phenytoin and sodium valproate, it was shown to provoke more impairment on memory tasks, in a dose-dependent way (Forsythe et al., 1991). Others have noted an improvement on some aspects of cognition with higher serum levels, especially on speed-related tasks and motor activity (Aman et al., 1990; Mitchell et al., 1993). This may be achieved at the expense of accuracy on some performance tasks.

Surgical Treatment

TEMPORAL LOBE SURGERY. Patients with medically intractable seizures documented to originate from the temporal lobe may be considered for unilateral temporal lobe surgery. In carefully selected cases this surgery has proven highly effective in controlling seizure activity (Polkey and Binnie, 1993). If unilateral resection of mesial temporal lobe structures is undertaken in a patient whose contralateral temporal lobe cannot maintain global memory functioning, a severe amnesic syndrome will occur. Penfield and Mathieson (1974) report a patient who underwent two surgeries on the left temporal lobe with an amnesic syndrome appearing after the second surgery. The first surgery involved excision of only the anterior 4 cm of the lateral temporal lobe. The second surgery leading to the amnesic syndrome removed the mesial structures including the amygdala and hippocampus. An autopsy was performed on the patient years later and revealed marked neuronal loss within the hippocampus of the unresected right temporal lobe. Warrington and Duchen (1992) report a similar case of an individual who underwent a unilateral temporal lobectomy and was left profoundly amnesic. Examination of the resected temporal lobe revealed no pathological changes. When the case later came to autopsy it was found that the contralateral hemisphere showed medial temporal sclerosis.

To avoid amnesic syndromes developing

in patients undergoing unilateral temporal lobe surgery, Milner and colleagues (1962) introduced the use of the sodium amytal procedure for memory testing. This has been adopted by most epilepsy surgery programs. Generally it involves the injection of sodium amobarbital into the internal carotid artery of the proposed surgical hemisphere. This results in a temporary 2- to 3-minute inactivation of the hemisphere. During this time, a brief assessment of language and memory competence of the contralateral hemisphere is made. There are, however, concerns about the validity and the reliability of this technique, and it is the subject of continued research (Loring et al., 1992).

Unilateral temporal lobe resections in the presence of an intact contralateral hemisphere are reported to result in material-specific memory losses. The most consistent finding is a decline in verbal memory following surgery on the hemisphere associated with speech (Novelly et al., 1984; Hermann and Wyler, 1988; Ivnik et al., 1988; Oxbury and Oxbury, 1989; Saykin et al., 1989; Chelune et al., 1991). Other researchers have reported nonverbal memory changes following temporal lobe surgery on the nondominant temporal lobe. Their studies indicate extensive mesial temporal lobe resections elicit deficits in nonverbal memory such as recall of a complex design or design learning (Jones-Gotman, 1986). Other centers report less consistent findings following nondominant temporal lobe resections.

While overall test scores reveal a decline in memory following temporal lobe resections, such figures mask considerable interpatient variability. One problem facing the neuropsychologist is the ability to predict which patients may be at risk for memory decline postoperatively. In general, there is an increasing agreement that the risk of memory loss is greatest for persons with the most intact memory preoperatively (Ojeman and Dodrill, 1987; Ivnik et al., 1988; Oxbury and Oxbury, 1989; Chelune et al., 1991). Intact memory may imply a reasonably unimpaired hippocampus and also a basically sound lateral cortex. Conversely, if these structures are dysfunctional, their removal

should be accompanied by fewer adverse changes.

The extent of resection is routinely cited as a factor relevant to memory loss, with larger resections associated with greater impairment postoperatively (Frisk and Milner, 1991; Grote et al., 1991; Jones-Gotman, 1991). Some centers undertake selective operations that spare much of the lateral cortex in an attempt to preserve memory functions (Wieser and Yasargil, 1982). In a recent study, Goldstein and Polkey (1993) compared the outcome for memory in 42 patients having either a temporal lobectomy or a selective amygdalohippocampectomy. On measures of verbal recall there was limited evidence of different outcome for right-sided operations. More radical operations resulted in a fall in immediate recall scores, whereas a selective operation led to an improvement. Verbal learning impairments were greater following left-sided resections, being most marked in cases undergoing lobectomies. In contrast, verbal learning impairments were greater following standard right-sided lobectomies than the right-sided selective operations. Recall of a complex figure did not distinguish between the operations. Overall, these findings provide limited evidence in support of the protective effect for memory of selective operations.

After dominant temporal lobectomy marked persisting aphasias are rare but declines in naming have been reported. Saykin et al. (1992) measured confrontation naming, phonemic and semantic fluency, repetition, comprehension, and reading recognition before and following surgery. For dominant hemisphere resections a relative decline in naming relative to other language skills was noted, and this occurred in those patients with a later onset of seizures and underlying pathology. This finding supports the view that an early age of onset, which may result in a degree of cerebral reorganization, can be a positive factor regarding deficits following surgery.

There is increasing consensus that decrements in intellectual ability following temporal lobe surgery are minimal and more likely to occur if testing occurs in the early months following surgery. Generally, no marked changes are documented in assessments undertaken a year or more postoperatively. Indeed, many patients show substantial gains, particularly in those cases who become seizure free. Some have reported improvements most likely in those cognitive functions served by the nonresected hemisphere (Naugle, 1991).

CORPUS CALLOSOTOMY. The early neuropsychological evaluation of these cases revealed no significant psychological sequelae (Akelaitis, 1944). A number of studies undertaken in the 1970s on the so-called split brain patients did elicit some cognitive processing abnormalities, but these generally required specialized investigative techniques such as tachistoscopic presentation. Furthermore, these detailed studies were not undertaken on the subjects preoperatively, and it is likely that a number of these patients had abnormal cerebral organization prior to surgery given the severity of their seizures and early ages of onset (Gazzaniga, 1970). Standard neuropsychological assessments have generally shown little or no negative effect when compared with premorbid level (Reeves, 1991). The outcome relates to the nature of the operation undertaken, operative complications, and success of the procedures in terms of seizure control (Oepen et al., 1985; Provinciali, 1990; Sass et al., 1992c).

The classic split brain syndrome follows complete callosotomy, which is generally not undertaken. In general, the syndrome is more likely to be evident on manual tasks where competition is observed between the right and left hands representing the two halves of the brain. It generally resolves in a few days as the patient uses external cues, although it may still be present on novel tasks requiring bimanual cooperation. A few cases are documented of persisting deficits.

Anterior sections may be accompanied by transient mutism in the first few days postoperatively, although there are a few cases of persisting language difficulties. These seem to be more prevalent in individuals who have been shown to have abnormal language lateralization (Sass et al., 1990a). Memory dysfunction has been noted in a minority of patients following partial and complete callosotomy. It is proposed that in these cases it may result from the disconnection of damaged but interdependent hippocampal formations by severing the hippocampal commissure.

HEMISPHERECTOMY. Generally, this surgical procedure is undertaken on patients who have an infantile hemiplegia and drug-resistant seizures (Polkey and Binnie, 1993). Many cases, in addition, have severe learning difficulties and behavior problems. Beardsworth and Adams (1988) present a follow-up study of 10 cases. Significant improvements in intellectual function, language, and behavior are documented.

Summary

In the decade that has elapsed since the publication of the first edition of this book, there has been considerable interest in, and research on, neuropsychological aspects of epilepsy. There is no "profile" of changes "typical" for epilepsy, although it seems that patients with seizure disorders may show deficits, compared with age- and sex-matched controls, before treatment.

Several seizure and nonseizure-related variables have been shown to impair cognitive function in patients with epilepsy; and in treatment there is sometimes a fine balance between the improvements that may accrue from extinguishing seizures and any impairments that arise from anticonvulsant drugs. The importance of subclinical discharges is now being recognized and has raised important conceptual issues, even the challenge: What is a seizure? How should it be defined?

There is considerable interest in the neuropsychological effects of treatments, including surgery, for epilepsy, but more work is urgently needed on the psychosocial impact of epilepsy and the way these variables may contribute to impaired vocational and educational status. Remedial treatments for neurocognitive deficits, especially in the domain of memory and attention, are urgently required, as are nontoxic, nonsedating new anticonvulsant drugs.

References

Aarts, J.H.P., Binnie, C. D., Smith, A. M., and Wilkins, A. J. (1984). Selective cognitive impairment during focal and generalized epileptiform activity. *Brain, 107,* 293–308.

Akelaitis, A.J.E. (1944). A study of gnosis, praxis and language following section of the corpus callosum and anterior commissure. *Journal of Neurosurgery, 1,* 94–102.

Aldenkamp, A. P., Alpherts, W. C., Blennow, G., Elmqvist, D., Heijbel, J., Nilsson, H. L., Sandstedt, P., Tonnby, B., Wahlander, L., and Wosse, E. (1993). Withdrawal of antiepileptic medication in children—effects on cognitive function: The Multicenter Holmfrid Study. *Neurology, 43,* 41–50.

Aldenkamp, A. P., Alpherts, W.C.J., Meinardi, H., and Stores, G. (1987). *Education and Epilepsy.* Amsterdam: Swets and Zeitlinger.

Aldenkamp, A. P., Gutter, T., and Beun, A. M. (1992). The effect of seizure activity and paroxysmal electroencephalographic discharges on cognition. *Acta Neurologica Scandinavica, 86* (suppl. 140), 111–121.

Aman, M. G., Werry, J. S., Paxton, J. W., Turbott, S. H., and Stewart, A. W. (1990). The effects of carbamazepine on psychomotor performance as a function of drug concentration, seizure, type, and time of medication. *Epilepsia, 31,* 51–60.

Anderson, N. E., and Wallis, W. T. (1986). Activation of epileptiform activity by mental arithmetic. *Archives of Neurology, 43,* 624–626.

Andrewes, D. G., Bullen, J. G., Tomlinson, L., Elwes, R.D.C., and Reynolds, E. H. (1986). A comparative study of the cognitive effects of phenytoin and carbamazepine in new referrals with epilepsy. *Epilepsia, 27,* 128–134.

Antebi, D., and Bird, J. (1992). The facilitation and evocation of seizures. *British Journal of Psychiatry, 160,* 154–164.

Barr, W. B., Ashtari, M., Schaul, N., and Bogerts, B. (1990). Relations between hippocampal volume and memory in patients with intractable seizures. *Journal of Clinical and Experimental Psychology, 12,* 86 (Abst.).

Beardsworth, E. D., and Adams, C.B.T. (1988). Modified hemispherectomy for epilepsy: Early results in 10 cases. *British Journal of Neurosurgery, 2,* 73–84.

Bennett, T. L. (1992). *The Neuropsychology of Epilepsy.* New York: Plenum Press.

Binnie, C. D. (1991). Methods of detecting transient cognitive impairment during epileptiform discharges. In W. E. Dodson, M. Kinsbourne, and B. Hiltbrunner, eds., *The Assessment of Cognitive Functions in Epilepsy.* New York: Remos Publications, pp. 127–138.

Bourgeois, B.F.D., Prensky, A. L., Palkes, H. S., Talent, B. K., and Busch, S. G. (1983). Intelligence in epilepsy: A prospective study in children. *Annals of Neurology, 14,* 438–444.

Bridgman, P. A., Malamut, M. A., Sperling, M. R., Saykin, A. J., and O'Connor, M. J. (1989). Memory during subclinical hippocampal seizures. *Neurology, 39,* 853–856.

Brodie, M. J., McPhail, E., MacPhee, G.L.A., Larkin, J. G., and Gray, J.M.B. (1987). Psychomotor impairment and anticonvulsant therapy in adult epileptic patients. *European Journal of Clinical Pharmacology, 31,* 655–660.

Camfield, C. S., Chaplin, S., Doyle, A. B., Shapiro, S. H., Cummings, C., and Camfield, P. R. (1979). Side effects of phenobarbital in toddlers: Behavioral and cognitive aspects. *Journal of Pediatrics, 95,* 361–365.

Chelune, G. J., Naugle, R., Luders, H., and Awad, I. A. (1991). Prediction of cognitive change as a function of preoperative ability states among temporal lobectomy patients. *Neurology, 41,* 477–485.

Commission on Classification and Terminology of the International League Against Epilepsy. (1981). Proposal for revised clinical and electroencephalographic classification of epilepsy seizures. *Epilepsia, 22,* 489–501.

Commission on Classification and Terminology of the International League Against Epilepsy. (1989). Proposal for revised classification of epilepsies and epileptic syndromes. *Epilepsia, 30,* 389–399.

Corbett, J. A. (1993). Epilepsy and mental handicap. In J. Laidlaw, A. Richens, and D. Chadwick, eds., *A Textbook of Epilepsy.* Edinburgh: Churchill Livingstone, pp. 631–636.

Corcoran, R., and Thompson, P. J. (1992). Epilepsy and poor memory: Who complains and what do they mean? *British Journal of Clinical Psychology, 32* (pt. 2), 199–208.

Cull, C. A., and Trimble, M. R. (1985). Anticonvulsant benzodiazepines and performance. In I. Hindmarch, P. D. Stonier, and M. R. Trimble, eds., *Clobazam. Human Psychopharmacology and Clinical Applications.* London: Royal Society of Medicine, pp. 121–128.

Davey, D., and Thompson, P. (1991). Interictal language functioning in chronic epilepsy. *Journal of Neurolinguistics, 4,* 381–399.

Dewhurst, K. (1980). *Thomas Willis' Oxford Lectures*. Oxford: Sanford.

Dijkstra, J. B., McGuire, A. M., and Trimble, M. R. (1992). The effect of vigabatrin on cognitive function and mood. *Human Psychopharmacology, 7*, 319–323.

Dikman, S., and Matthews, C. G. (1977). Effect of major motor seizure frequency upon cognitive intellectual functions in adults. *Epilepsia, 18*, 21–19.

Dinner, D. S. (1991). Intracarotid amobarbital test to define language lateralization. In H. Luders, ed., *Epilepsy Surgery*. New York: Raven Press, pp. 503–514.

Dodrill, C. B. (1975). Diphenylhydantoin serum levels, toxicity, and neuropsychological performance in patients with epilepsy. *Epilepsia, 16*, 593–600.

Dodrill, C. B. (1986). Correlates of generalized tonic-clonic seizures with intellectual, neuropsychological, emotional, and social function in patients with epilepsy. *Epilepsia, 27*, 399–411.

Dodrill, C. B. (1993). Neuropsychology. In J. Laidlaw, A. Richens, and D. Chadwick, eds., *A Textbook of Epilepsy* (4th ed.). Edinburgh: Churchill Livingstone, pp. 459–475.

Dodrill, C. B., and Temkin, N. R. (1989). Motor speed is a contaminating factor in evaluating the "cognitive" effects of phenytoin. *Epilepsia, 30*, 453–457.

Dodrill, C. B., and Troupin, A. S. (1976). Seizures and adaptive abilities. *Archives of Neurology, 33*, 604–607.

Duncan, J., Shorvon, S. D., and Trimble, M. R. (1990). Effects of removal of phenytoin, carbamazepine and valproate on cognitive function. *Epilepsia, 31*, 584–591.

Ellenberg, J. H., Hirtz, D. G., and Nelson, K. B. (1984). Age at onset of seizure in young children. *Annals of Neurology, 15*, 127–134.

Ellenberg, J. H., Hirtz, D. G., and Nelson, K. B. (1986). Do seizures in children cause intellectual deterioration? *New England Journal of Medicine, 314*, 1085–1088.

Farwell, J. R., Dodrill, C. B., and Batzel, L. W. (1985). Neuropsychological abilities of children with epilepsy. *Epilepsia, 26*, 395–400.

Farwell, J. R., Lee, Y. J., Hirtz, D. G., Sulzbacher, S. I., Ellenberg, J. H., and Nelson, K. B. (1990). Phenobarbital for febrile seizures—effects on intelligence and on seizure recurrence. *New England Journal of Medicine, 322*, 364–369.

Forsythe, I., Butler, R., Berg, I., and McGuire, R. (1991). Cognitive impairment in new cases of epilepsy randomly assigned to carbamazepine, phenytoin and sodium valproate. *Developmental Medicine and Child Neurology, 33*, 524–534.

Frisk, V., and Milner, B. (1991). Does left temporal lobectomy adversely affect the rate at which verbal memory can be processed? *Neuropsychologia, 20*, 113–123.

Gallassi, R., Morreale, A., Lorusso, S., Procaccianti, G., Lugaresi, E., and Baruzzi, A. (1988). Carbamazepine and phenytoin: Comparison of cognitive effects in epileptic patients during monotherapy and withdrawal. *Archives of Neurology, 45*, 892–894.

Gallassi, R., Morreale, A., Lorusso, S., Procaccianti, G., Lugaresi, E., and Baruzzi, A. (1990). Cognitive effects of valproate. *Epilepsy Research, 5*, 160–164.

Gazzaniga, M. S. (1970). *The Bisected Brain*. New York: Appleton-Century-Crofts.

Gillham, R. A., Williams, N., Wiedmann, K. D., Butler, E., Larkin, J. D., and Brodie, M. J. (1990). Cognitive function in adult epileptic patients established on anticonvulsant therapy. *Epilepsy Research, 7*, 219–225.

Goldstein, L. H., and Polkey, C. E. (1992). Everyday memory after unilateral temporal lobectomy or amygdalohippocampectomy. *Cortex, 28*, 189–201.

Goldstein, L. H., and Polkey, C. E. (1993). Short-term cognitive changes after unilateral temporal lobectomy or unilateral amygdalohippocampectomy for the relief of temporal lobe epilepsy. *Journal of Neurology, Neurosurgery and Psychiatry, 56*, 135–140.

Grote, C. L., Morrell, F., and Whisler, W. W. (1991). Verbal memory following dominant hippocampal resections: A comparison of two approaches. *Epilepsia, 32* (suppl. 3), 87.

Halgren, E., Stapleton, J., Domalski, P., Swartz, B. E., Delgado-Escueta, A. V., Walsh, G. O., Mandelkern, M., Blahd, W., and Ropchan, J. (1991). In D. Smith, D. Treiman, and M. Trimble, eds., *Advances in Neurology* (vol. 55). New York: Raven Press, pp. 385–410.

Helmstaedter, C., Hufnagel, A., and Elger, C. E. (1992). Seizures during cognitive testing in patients with temporal lobe epilepsy: Possibility of seizure induction by cognitive activation. *Epilepsia, 33*, 892–897.

Hermann, B. P., Whitman, S., and Arnston, P. (1983). Hypergraphia in epilepsy: Is there a specificity to temporal lobe epilepsy? *Journal of Neurology, Neurosurgery and Psychiatry, 46*, 848–853.

Hermann, B. P., and Wyler, A. R. (1988). Neuropsychological outcome of anterior temporal lobectomy. *Journal of Epilepsy, 1*, 35–45.

Hermann, B. P., Wyler, A. R., Steerman, H., and Richey, E. T. (1988). The inter-relationship between language function and verbal learning and memory performance in patients with complex partial seizures. *Cortex, 24*, 245–253.

Hirtz, D. G., and Nelson, K. B. (1985). Cognitive effects of antiepileptic drugs. In T. A. Pedley, and B. S. Meldrum, eds., *Recent Advances in Epilepsy* (No. 2). Edinburgh: Churchill Livingstone, pp. 161–182.

Hoeppner, J. B., Garron, D. C., Wilson, R. S., and Koch-Weser, M. P. (1987). Epilepsy and verbosity. *Epilepsia, 28*, 35–40.

Holmes, G. L. (1991). The long-term effects of seizures in the developing brain: Clinical and laboratory issues. *Brain and Development, 13*, 393–409.

Huberty, T. J., Austin, J. K., Resinger, M. W., and McNelis, A. M. (1992). Relationship of selected seizure variables in children with epilepsy to performance on school administered achievement tests. *Journal of Epilepsy, 5*, 10–16.

Ivnik, R. J., Sharborough, F. W., and Laws, E. R. (1988). Anterior temporal lobectomy for the control of partial complex seizures and information for counseling patients. *Mayo Clinic Proceedings, 63*, 783–793.

Jones-Gotman, M. (1986). Memory for designs: The hippocampal contribution. *Neuropsychologia, 24*, 193–203.

Jones-Gotman, M. (1991). Localization of lesions by neuropsychological testing. *Epilepsia, 82* (suppl. 5), S41–S52.

Kartsounis, L. D. (1988). Comprehension as the effective trigger in a case of primary reading epilepsy. *Journal of Neurology, Neurosurgery and Psychiatry, 51*, 128–130.

Kasteleijn-Nolst Trenite, D.G.A., Bakker, D. J., Binnie, C. D., Buerman, A., and Van Raaij, M. (1988). Psychological effects of subclinical epileptiform EEG discharges. I. Scholastic skills. *Epilepsy Research, 2*, 111–116.

Kirk, S. A., McCarthy, J. J., and Kirk, W. D. (1968). *Illinois Test of Psycholinguistic Abilities* (Rev. ed.). Urbana, IL: University of Illinois Press.

Kløve, H., and Matthews, C. G. (1966). Psychometric and adaptive abilities in epilepsy with different etiologies. *Epilepsia, 7*, 330–338.

Lencz, T., McCarthy, G., Bronen, R. A., Scott, T. M., Inserni, J. A., Sass, K. J., Novelly, R. A., Tim, J. H., and Spencer, D. D. (1992).

Quantitative magnetic resonance imaging in temporal lobe epilepsy: Relationship to neuropathology and neuropsychological function. *Annals of Neurology, 31*, 626–637.

Lennox, W. G., and Lennox, M. A. (1960). *Epilepsy and Related Disorders*. Boston: Little, Brown and Co.

Lesser, R. P., Luders, H., Wyllie, E., Dinner, D. S., and Morris, H. H. (1986). Mental deterioration in epilepsy. *Epilepsia, 27* (suppl. 2), S105–S123.

Loring, D. W., Meador, K. J., and Lee, G. P. (1992). Criteria and validity issues in Wada assessment. In T. L. Bennett, ed., *The Neuropsychology of Epilepsy*. New York: Plenum Press, pp. 233–245.

MacPhee, G.J.A., McPhail, E. M., Butler, E., and Brodie, M. J. (1986). Controlled evaluation of a supplementary dose of carbamazepine on psychomotor function in epileptic patients. *European Journal of Clinical Pharmacology, 31*, 195–199.

Mader, M. J., Thompson, P. J., and Sander, J.W.A.S. (1989). Intellectual decline and patterns of cognitive deficit in chronic epilepsy. Paper presented at the 18th International Epilepsy Congress, New Delhi.

Mattson, R. H., Cramer, J. A., Collins, J. F., and the VA Cooperative Study Group. (1985). Comparison of carbamazepine, phenobarbital, phenytoin, and primidone in partial and secondarily generalized tonic-clonic seizures. *New England Journal of Medicine, 313*, 145–151.

Mayeux, R., Brandt, J., Rosen, J., and Benson, D. F. (1980). Interictal memory and language impairment in temporal lobe epilepsy. *Neurology, 30*, 120–125.

McGuire, A. M., Duncan, J. S., and Trimble, M. R. (1992). Effects of vigabatrin on cognitive function and mood when used as add-on therapy in patients with intractable epilepsy. *Epilepsia, 33*, 128–143.

Meador, K. J., Loring, D. W., Allen, M. E., Zamrini, E. Y., Moore, E. E., Abney, O. L., and King, D. W. (1991). Comparative effects of carbamazepine and phenytoin in healthy adults. *Neurology, 41*, 1537–1540.

Meador, K. J., Loring, D. W., Huh, K., Gallagher, B. B., and King, D. W. (1990). Comparative cognitive effects of anticonvulsants. *Neurology, 40*, 391–394.

Meinardi, H., Aldenkamp, A. P., Beun, A. M., Nunes, B., Engelsman, M., and Forceville, E. (1991). Mental deterioration in a population of intractable epilepsy. In F. Pisani, E. Perucca,

G. Avanzini, and A. Richens, eds., *New Antiepileptic Drugs*. New York: Elsevier Science Publishing, pp. 6–15.

Miller, L. A., Munoz, D. G., and Finmore, M. (1993). Hippocampal sclerosis and human memory. *Archives of Neurology, 50,* 391–394.

Milner, B., Branch, C., and Rasmussen, T. (1962). Study of short-term memory after intracarotid injection of sodium amytal. *Transactions of the American Neurological Association, 87,* 224–226.

Mitchell, W. G., Chavez, J. M., Lee, H., and Guzman, B. L. (1991). Academic underachievement in children with epilepsy. *Journal of Child Neurology, 6,* 65–72.

Mitchell, W. G., Zhou, Y., Chavez, J. M., and Guzman, B. L. (1993). Effects of antiepileptic drugs on reaction time, attention and impulsivity in children. *Pediatrics, 91,* 101–105.

Morikawa, T., Seino, M., Ojawa, T., and Yagi, K. (1985). Five children with continuous spikewave discharges during sleep. In J. Roget, C. Dravet, M. Bureau, F. E. Dreifuss, and P. Wolf, eds., *Epileptic Syndromes in Infancy, Childhood and Adolescence*. London: John Libbey, pp. 205–212.

Mungas, D., Ehlers, C., Walton, N., and McCutchen, B. (1985). Verbal learning differences in epileptic patients with left and right temporal lobe foci. *Epilepsia, 26,* 340–345.

Naugle, R. I. (1991). Neuropsychological effects of surgery of epilepsy. In H. Luders, ed., *Epilepsy Surgery*. New York: Raven Press, pp. 637–645.

Nolte, R., Wetzel, B., Brugmann, G., and Brintzinger, I. (1980). Effects of phenytoin and primidone monotherapy on mental performance in children. In S. I. Johannessen, P. L. Morselli, C. E. Pippenger, A. Richens, D. Schmidt, and H. Meinardi, eds. *Antiepileptic Therapy, Advances in Drug Monitoring*. New York: Raven Press, pp. 81–88.

Novelly, R. A., Augustine, E. A., Mattson, R. H., Glaser, G. H., Williamson, P. D., Spencer, D. D., and Spencer, S. S. (1984). Selective memory improvement and impairment in temporal lobectomy for epilepsy. *Annals of Neurology, 15,* 64–67.

Oepen, G., Schultz-Welling, R., Zimmerman, P., Straesser, S., and Gitsbach, J. (1985). Long-term effects of partial callosal lesions. *Acta Neurochirurgica, 77,* 22–28.

Ojeman, G. A., and Dodrill, C. B. (1987). Intraoperative techniques for reducing language and memory deficits with left temporal lobectomy.

In P. Wolf, M. Dam, D. Janz, and F. E. Dreifuss, eds., *Advances in Epileptology: The 16th Epilepsy International Symposium*. New York: Raven Press, pp. 327–330.

Oxbury, J. M., and Oxbury, S. M. (1989). Neuropsychology, memory and hippocampal pathology. In E. H. Reynolds, and M. R. Trimble, eds., *The Bridge Between Neurology and Psychiatry*. London: Churchill Livingstone, pp. 135–150.

Penfield, W., and Mathieson, G. (1974). Memory: Autopsy findings and comments on the role of the hippocampus in experiential recall. *Archives of Neurology, 31,* 145–154.

Polkey, C. E., and Binnie, C. D. (1993). Neurosurgical treatment of epilepsy. In J. Laidlaw, A. Richens, and D. Chadwick, eds., *A Textbook of Epilepsy*. Edinburgh: Churchill Livingstone, pp. 561–612.

Provinciali, L., Del Pesce, M., Censori, B., Quattrini, A., Paggi, A., Ortenzi, A., Mancini, S., Papo, I., and Rychlicki, F. (1990). Evolution of neuropsychological changes after partial callosotomy in intractable epilepsy. *Epilepsy Research, 6,* 155–165.

Rausch, R., Boone, K., and Ary, C. M. (1991). Right hemisphere language dominance in temporal lobe epilepsy: Clinical and neuropsychological correlates. *Journal of Clinical and Experimental Neuropsychology, 13,* 217–231.

Rausch, R., and Walsh, G. O. (1984). Right hemisphere language dominance in righthanded epileptic patients. *Archives of Neurology, 41,* 1077–1080.

Reed, H. B. (1951). The intelligence of epileptics. *Journal of Genetic Psychology, 78,* 145–152.

Reeves, A. S. (1991). Behavioral changes following corpus callosotomy. In D. Smith, D. Treiman, and M. Trimble, eds., *Advances in Neurology* (vol. 55). New York: Raven Press, pp. 293–300.

Rey, M., Dellatolas, G., Bancand, J., and Talairach, J. (1988). Hemispheric lateralization of motor and speech functions after early brain lesions: Study of 73 epileptic patients with intracarotid amytal test. *Neuropsychologica, 26,* 167–172.

Reynolds, J. R. (1861). *Epilepsy: Its Symptoms, Treatment and Relation to Other Chronic Convulsive Diseases*. London: J. Churchill.

Richens, A., and Perucca, E. (1993). Clinical pharmacology and medical treatment. In J. Laidlaw, A. Richens, and D. Chadwick, eds., *A Textbook of Epilepsy*. Edinburgh: Churchill Livingstone, pp. 495–560.

Roberts, K. A., Robertson, M. M., and Trimble,

M. R. (1982). The lateralizing significance of hypergraphia in temporal lobe epilepsy. *Journal of Neurology, Neurosurgery and Psychiatry, 45,* 131–138.

Rodin, E. A., Katz, M., and Lennox, K. (1976). Differences between patients with temporal lobe seizures and those with other forms of epileptic attacks. *Epilepsia, 17,* 313–320.

Roget, J., Lob, H., and Tassinari, C. A. (1974). Status epilepticus. In P. J. Vinken and G. W. Bruyn, eds., *Handbook of Clinical Neurology* (vol. 15). Amsterdam: North-Holland Publishing Company, pp. 145–188.

Roulet, E., Deonna, T., Gaillard, F., Peter-Favre, C., and Despland, P. A. (1991). Acquired aphasia, dementia and behavior disorder with epilepsy and continuous spike and waves during sleep in a child. *Epilepsia, 32,* 495–503.

Rowan, A. J., and Rosenbaum, D. H. (1991). Ictal amnesia and fugue states. In D. Smith, D. Treiman, and M. Trimble, eds., *Advances in Neurology* (vol. 55). New York: Raven Press, pp. 357–367.

Rugland, A. L. (1990). Neuropsychological assessment of cognitive functioning in children with epilepsy. *Epilepsia, 31* (suppl. 4), 42–44.

Rugland, A. L., Henrikson, O., and Bjornaes, H. (1991). Computer-assisted neuropsychological assessment in patients with epilepsy. In W. E. Dodson, M. Kinsbourne, and B. Hiltbrunner, eds., *The Assessment of Cognitive Function in Epilepsy.* New York: Demos Publications, pp. 109–126.

Sachdev, H. S., and Waxman, S. G. (1981). Frequency of hypergraphia in temporal lobe epilepsy: An index of interictal behavior syndrome. *Journal of Neurology, Neurosurgery and Psychiatry, 44,* 358–360.

Sander, J.W.A.S., and Shorvon, S. D. (1987). Incidence and prevalence studies in epilepsy and their methodological limitations: A review. *Journal of Neurology, Neurosurgery and Psychiatry, 50,* 829–839.

Sass, K. J., Novelly, R. A., Spencer, D. D., and Spencer, S. S. (1990a). Postcallosotomy language impairments in patients with crossed cerebral dominance. *Journal of Neurosurgery, 72,* 85–90.

Sass, K. J., Spencer, D. D., Kim, J. H., Westerveld, M., Novelly, R. A., and Lencz, T. (1990b). Verbal memory impairment correlates with hippocampal pyramidal cell density. *Neurology, 40,* 1694–1697.

Sass, K. J., Sass, A., Westerveld, M., Lencz, T., Rosewater, K. M., Novelly, R. A., Kim, J. H.,

and Spencer, D. D. (1992a). Russell's adaptation of the Wechsler Memory Scale as an index of hippocampal pathology. *Journal of Epilepsy, 5,* 24–30.

Sass, K. J., Sass, A., Westerveld, M., Lencz, T., Novelly, R. A., Kim, J. H., and Spencer, D. D. (1992b). Specificity in the correlations of verbal memory and hippocampal neuron loss: Dissociation of memory, language and verbal intellectual ability. *Journal of Clinical and Experimental Neuropsychology, 14,* 662–672.

Sass, K. J., Spencer, S. S., Westerveld, M., and Spencer, D. D. (1992c). The neuropsychology of corpus callosotomy for epilepsy. In T. L. Bennett, ed., *The Neuropsychology of Epilepsy.* New York: Plenum Press, pp. 291–308.

Saykin, A. J., Gur, R. C., Sussman, N. M., O'Connor, M. J., and Gur, R. E. (1989). Memory deficits before and after temporal lobectomy: Effects of laterality and age of onset. *Brain and Cognition, 9,* 191–200.

Saykin, A. J., Robinson, L. J., Stefiniak, P., Kester, D. B., Gur, R. C., O'Connor, M. J., and Sperling, M. R. (1992). Neuropsychological changes after anterior temporal lobectomy: Acute effects on memory, language, and music. In T. L. Bennett, ed., *The Neuropsychology of Epilepsy.* New York: Plenum Press, pp. 263–290.

Seidenberg, M., Beck, N., Geisser, M., Giordani, B., Sackellares, J. C., Berent, S., Dreifuss, F. E., and Boll, T. J. (1986). Academic achievement in children with epilepsy. *Epilepsia, 27,* 753–759.

Seidenberg, M., O'Leary, D. S., Giordani, B., Berent, S., and Boll, T. J. (1981). Test-retest changes of epilepsy patients: Assessing the influence of practice effects. *Journal of Clinical Neuropsychology, 3,* 237–255.

Shewmon, D. A., and Erwin, R. J. (1988). The effect of focal interictal spikes on perception and reaction time. II. Neuroanatomic specificity. *Electroencephalography and Clinical Neurophysiology, 69,* 338–352.

Shorvon, S. D. (1994). *Status Epilepticus. Its Causes and Treatment in Children and Adults.* Cambridge: Cambridge University Press.

Siebelink, B. M., Bakker, D. J., Binnie, C. D., and Kasteleijn-Nolst Trenite, D. G. (1988). Psychological effects of subclinical epileptiform EEG discharges in children. II. General intelligence tests. *Epilepsy Research, 2,* 117–121.

Smith, D. B. (1991). Cognitive effects of antiepileptic drugs. In D. B. Smith, D. M. Treiman, and M. R. Trimble, eds., *Advances in Neuro-*

surgery. *Neurobehavioral Problems in Epilepsy* (vol. 55). New York: Raven Press, pp. 197–212.

Smith, D. B., Mattson, R. H., Cramer, J. A., Collins, J. F., Novelly, R. A., Craft, B., and the VA Cooperative Study Group. (1987). Results of a nationwide Veterans Administration cooperative study comparing the efficacy and toxicity of carbamazepine, phenobarbital, phenytoin and primidone. *Epilepsia, 28* (suppl. 3), S50–S58.

Stores, G. (1990). Electroencephalographic parameters in assessing the cognitive function of children with epilepsy. *Epilepsia, 31* (suppl. 4), S45–S49.

Strauss, E., Satz, P., and Wada, J. (1990). An examination of the crowding hypothesis in epileptic patients who have undergone the carotid amytal test. *Neuropsychologica, 28,* 1221–1227.

Strauss, E., Wada, J., and Hunter, M. (1992). Sex-related differences in cognitive consequences of early left hemisphere lesions. *Journal of Clinical and Experimental Neuropsychology, 14,* 738–748.

Thompson, I. (1983). Brain metabolism unit language scales. *Bulletin of College of Speech Therapists,* 1–3.

Thompson, P. J. (1987). Educational attainment in children and young people with epilepsy. In J. Oxley and G. Stores, eds., *Epilepsy and Education.* London: Medical Tribune Group, pp. 15–24.

Thompson, P. J. (1991). Memory function in patients with epilepsy. In D. B. Smith, D. M. Treiman, and M. R. Trimble, eds., *Advances in Neurology* (vol. 55). New York: Raven Press, pp. 369–384.

Thompson, P. J., and Corcoran, R. C. (1992). Everyday memory failures in people with epilepsy. *Epilepsia, 33* (suppl. 6), S18–S20.

Thompson, P. J., Huppert, F. A., and Trimble, M. R. (1981). Phenytoin and cognitive functions: Effects on normal volunteers. *British Journal of Social and Clinical Psychology, 20,* 155–162.

Thompson, P. J., Oxley, J. R., and Sander, J.W.A.S. (1986). Intellectual deterioration in severe epilepsy. In P. Wolf, M. Dam, D. Janz, and F. E. Dreifuss, eds., *Advances in Epileptology* (vol. 16). New York: Raven Press, pp. 611–614.

Thompson, P. J., and Trimble, M. R. (1981). Sodium valproate and cognitive functioning in normal volunteers. *British Journal of Clinical Psychology, 12,* 819–824.

Thompson, P. J., and Trimble, M. R. (1982). Comparative effects of anticonvulsant drugs on cognitive functioning. *British Journal of Clinical Practice, 18,* 154–159.

Trimble, M. R., and Thompson, P. J. (1983). Anticonvulsant drugs, cognitive function, and behavior. *Epilepsia, 24* (suppl. 1), S55–S63.

Turner, W. A. (1907). *Epilepsy.* London: MacMillan Press.

Wallace, S. J. (1993). Seizures in children. In J. Laidlaw, A. Richens, and D. Chadwick, eds., *A Textbook of Epilepsy* (4th ed.). Edinburgh: Churchill Livingstone, pp. 77–164.

Warrington, E. K., and Duchen, L. W. (1992). A reappraisal of a case of persistent lobal amnesia following a right temporal lobectomy: A clinicopathological study. *Neuropsychologia, 30,* 437–450.

Waxman, S. G., and Geschwind, N. (1974). Hypergraphia in temporal lobe epilepsy. *Neurology, 24,* 629–636.

Wieser, H. G., and Yasargil, M. D. (1982). Selective amygdalohippocampectomy as a surgical treatment of mesiobasal limbic epilepsy. *Surgical Neurology, 17,* 445–457.

Yamamoto, J., Egawa, I., Yamamoto, S., and Shimizu, A. (1991). Reflex epilepsy induced by calculation using a "soroban," a Japanese traditional calculator. *Epilepsia, 32,* 39–43.

13 Neuropsychological Aspects of Parkinson's Disease and Parkinsonism

SUSAN McPHERSON and JEFFREY L. CUMMINGS

Parkinson's disease (PD) is one of the most common neurological illnesses among elderly patients, affecting approximately 100 per 100,000 individuals over age 65. The prevalence of Parkinson's disease rises with age from approximately 50 per 100,000 at age 60 to as high as 130 per 100,000 at age 75. Behavioral and neuropsychological disorders are common in PD and other parkinsonian syndromes. Patients with PD may also have dementia, depression, anxiety, apathy, and a variety of drug-induced behavioral alterations.

Significant advances have been made in understanding the pathophysiology of PD. Although depletion of dopamine in the substantia nigra and basal ganglia has been recognized as responsible for the motor disturbances of the disease, recent evidence suggests that changes in the basal ganglia and frontal-subcortical circuits also play a role in the associated cognitive abnormalities (Taylor and Saint-Cyr, 1992).

The purpose of this chapter is to provide an overview of parkinsonian syndromes, including Parkinson's disease, progressive supranuclear palsy (PSP), and multiple-system atrophies (MSA). The clinical characteristics, pathology, treatment, and neuropsychological deficits associated with each disorder will be described.

Definitions and Classification

Parkinson's disease must be distinguished from the less specific clinical syndrome of parkinsonism. *Parkinsonism* refers to a cluster of motor symptoms consisting of slowness of movement (bradykinesia), difficulty initiating movement (akinesia), masked facies, muscular rigidity, a shuffling or unsteady gait, abnormal posture, and disturbances in equilibrium. Tremor may or may not be present. Parkinson's disease is a neurodegenerative disorder consisting of the symptoms of parkinsonism plus a pill-rolling type of resting tremor. Parkinson's disease typically improves with dopaminergic treatment. An absence or paucity of tremor and poor treatment response help differentiate non-PD parkinsonian syndromes from PD (Stacy and Jankovic, 1992).

Classification of Parkinsonism

Parkinsonism can be divided into four subgroups: primary, secondary, multiple system degeneration, and other neurodegenerative conditions (Table 13-1). Primary or idiopathic PD accounts for the majority of cases of parkinsonism and, although onset is rare before age 30, there is a juvenile form of the disease with onset before age 21. Secondary parkinsonism may occur in a variety of conditions including infections (encephalitis, slow virus), exposure to toxins, drugs (particularly antipsychotic medications), or trauma (pugilistic encephalopathy). There also exists a vascular form of the disease, usually caused by lacunar infarctions of the basal ganglia and characterized by markedly impaired gait with relatively spared upper body motor function-

Table 13-1. Classification of Parkinsonism

Primary (idiopathic) parkinsonism
  Parkinson's disease
  Juvenile Parkinson's disease
Secondary Parkinsonism (acquired)
  Drug-induced (antipsychotic agents, antiemetics)
  Infections (postencephalitic, slow virus, human
    immunodeficiency virus)
  Vascular (lacunar state)
  Toxins (MPTP,[a] manganese, carbon monoxide)
  Metabolic (parathyroid, hypothyroidism)
  Trauma (pugilistic encephalopathy)
  Tumor, normal-pressure hydrocephalus
Multiple-system degenerations (Parkinsonian-plus
    syndromes)
  Shy–Drager syndrome
  Olivopontocerebellar atrophy
  Striatonigral degeneration
Other neurodegenerative disorders
  Progressive supranuclear palsy
  Diffuse Lewy body disease
  Wilson's disease
  Rigid Huntington's disease
  Parkinsonian-ALS dementia complex
  Idiopathic basal ganglia calcification

[a] 1-methyl-4-phenyl-1, 2, 3, 6-tetrahydropyridine (MPTP)

ing (Fitzgerald and Jankovic, 1989). Multiple system degenerations account for the second largest number of parkinsonian plus disorders and include Shy-Drager syndrome, striatonigral degeneration, and olivopontocerebellar atrophy. Other degenerative causes of parkinsonism include conditions such as progressive supranuclear palsy (PSP), diffuse Lewy body disease, the rigid form of Huntington's disease, Wilson's disease, and idiopathic basal ganglia calcification.

Parkinson's Disease

Parkinson's disease is ranked among the most common chronic neurological disorders. Estimates of worldwide prevalence of PD vary widely, from as low as 31 per 100,000 (Ashok et al., 1986) to as high as 187 per 100,000 (Kurland, 1958). The estimated annual incidence rates (number of new cases per year) similarly vary from as low as 4.5 per 100,000 (Ashok et al., 1986), to as high as 20 per 100,000 (Kurland, 1958). Juvenile PD is rare and the incidence of PD rises with increasing age from 4.1 per 100,000 between ages 30

and 54, to 209 per 100,000 between ages 75 and 84 (Rajput et al., 1984). Although variations in prevalence and incidence might be accounted for by methodological differences among studies, factors such as genetic influences on susceptibility to the disease and differences in exposure to causative or protective factors might also contribute (Tanner, 1992). Mean age at onset is between 58 and 62 years of age and 75% to 80% of PD patients are between ages 60 and 79 (Marttila, 1987). Recent epidemiological surveys suggest that the disease affects men and women about equally (Rajput, et al., 1984; Marttila, 1987).

Community-based studies of PD indicate that the highest rates of the disease are observed in Europe and North America, with markedly lower rates in Japan, China, and Africa (Tanner, 1992). Although PD appears to occur at a lower prevalence rate in Japanese and Chinese as compared with Whites, no studies have been conducted comparing Asians and Whites sharing the same environment. One study found similar prevalence rates of PD in African-Americans and Whites over 40 years of age residing in the same geographic area (Schoenberg et al, 1985).

Clinical Characteristics

Movement disturbance is the hallmark of PD and the primary motor symptoms include akinesia, bradykinesia, rigidity, loss of associated movements, tremor, and neuroophthalmic abnormalities. Tremor is probably the best-recognized clinical feature in PD, but other motor disturbances may present as the initial sign. The primary symptom of PD, bradykinesia or hypokinesia, accounts for many of the characteristic features of the disease including difficulty with initiation of movement, expressionless face (*masked facies*), loss of associated movements, and micrographia. Muscular rigidity involves the upper and lower limbs, producing a lead-pipe rigidity to passive manipulation. The combination of tremor and rigidity bestows a ratchet or cogwheel character to the rigidity. The increase in rigidity also results in the postural changes seen in PD characterized by slight flexion of ankles, knees, hips, elbows, back, and neck (McDowell et al., 1978). Although hypokinesia is frequently associated with rigidity, the two can be dissociated and the psychomotor retardation of PD is not a result of rigidity (Selby, 1968). The characteristic tremor of the disease is a pill-rolling alternating contraction of opposing muscles, usually with a frequency of 4 to 6 cycles per second. The tremor typically develops in one upper extremity and may spread to all four limbs, face, and tongue (Cummings and Benson, 1992). This tremor is most apparent when the patient is in alert repose, is absent or minimal when the patient is relaxed or asleep, and is exacerbated by stress. In addition to the resting tremor, a minority of PD patients may exhibit an action tremor of 6 to 12 cps (McDowell et al., 1978).

Neuroophthalmologic changes and autonomic disturbances also occur in PD. Volitional upgaze and convergence are impaired. Rapid volitional eye movements tend to be fragmented into multiple saccades and pursuit movements are broken into a series of small saccadic steps (cogwheel eye movements) (Cummings and Benson, 1992). Autonomic disturbances often associated with PD include prominent gastrointestinal symptoms (Korczyn, 1990), orthostatic hypotension, constipation, impotence, and esophageal spasm (Langston and Forno, 1978; McDowell et al., 1978).

Pathology

Characteristic neuropathological changes in PD include neuron loss in the substantia nigra and other brain-stem nuclei (locus ceruleus, dorsal vagal nucleus, and sympathetic ganglia) and the presence of Lewy bodies in the remaining neurons of the involved nuclei (Den Hartog Jager and Bethlem, 1960). Lewy bodies are intracellular structures made up of protein and sphingomyelin (Turner, 1968; Alvord, 1971) and consist of loosely packed filaments in an outer zone surrounding a granular core. Although found in highest concentrations in the substantia nigra and locus ceruleus, they also occur in the nucleus basalis, dorsal vagal nucleus,

autonomic ganglia, and hypothalamus (Gibb, 1989).

Parkinson's disease is characterized neurochemically by the loss of dopamine in the basal ganglia and associated brain regions (Sourkes, 1976; McDowell et al, 1978). Dopamine content is markedly diminished in the caudal putamen (Kish et al., 1988b). Dopamine is also depleted in the caudate, frontal lobe cortex, and medial temporal lobes. Other neurotransmitters and modulators are decreased in PD; they include norepinephrine, glutamate decarboxylase, GABA, methionine-enkephalin, cholestokinin, and serotonin and its metabolite 5-hydroxyindoleacetic acid, albeit none to the extent of dopamine (Cummings and Benson, 1992). Dopamine receptor densities are unaffected (Pierot et al., 1988).

Treatment

Treatment of PD includes agents used to slow progression and preserve neurons and drugs used to relieve symptoms. The current mainstay of PD therapy is levodopa, a precursor to dopamine that readily crosses the blood-brain barrier and, once in the substantia nigra, is converted into dopamine. Levodopa is typically administered in conjunction with the dopa-decarboxylase inhibitor carbidopa, to minimize peripheral side effects. Levodopa has been found to be effective in alleviating the motor symptoms of PD in at least 60% of patients for a period of 1 to 4 years (McDowell et al., 1978). Unfortunately, levodopa produces many adverse effects including nausea, choreoathetotic dyskinesias, postural hypotension, and palpitations (Bianchine, 1976; McDowell et al, 1978). Psychiatric side effects such as sleep disturbances, hallucinations, delusions, anxiety, delirium, and hypomania are not uncommon (Cummings and Benson, 1992). Pergolide and bromocriptine are dopamine receptor agonists that also relieve parkinsonian symptoms and have side effects similar to levodopa. It is common to use a receptor agonist in conjunction with levodopa to minimize late-occurring on-off symptoms.

Anticholinergic agents were the primary

treatments of PD until therapy was revolutionized by the discovery of a central dopamine deficiency. Anticholinergic agents appear to alleviate rigidity and tremor but are only moderately effective for the relief of other symptoms (Gancher, 1992). Moreover, anticholinergic agents tend to produce poorly tolerated side effects including dry mouth, blurred vision, constipation, urinary retention, delirium, and memory loss and are generally used sparingly if at all (Gancher, 1992).

Selegiline is a monoamine oxidase (MAO) B inhibitor that reduces the generation of hydroxyl radicals. Free radicals interfere with maintenance of cell membranes and lead to cellular death; reduction of radical presence prevents cell death and may allow partially injured neurons to recover. Thus, administration of selegiline mitigates cell death and slows disease progression.

Neuropsychological Aspects of Parkinson's Disease

Patients with PD commonly exhibit deficits in cognitive abilities; in many cases, these deficits are confined to specific functions such as loss of cognitive flexibility, reduced ability for learning and recall of information, and psychomotor slowing. The following section presents the pattern of neuropsychologic deficits exhibited by PD patients without overt dementia.

ATTENTION. Simple attentional skills, as assessed by a patient's ability to repeat a series of digits or register a short list of words, is generally unimpaired in patients with PD, even in patients with severe motor dysfunction (Pillon et al., 1986; Huber et al., 1989).

MEMORY. There is considerable agreement in the literature documenting memory dysfunction in patients with PD (Table 13-2). Nondemented patients with PD often exhibit deficits in the areas of paired associates (Pirozzolo et al., 1982; Huber et al., 1986; El-Awar et al., 1987), verbal list learning (Villardita et al., 1982; Taylor et al., 1986a; Beatty et al., 1989), recall of brief prose

Table 13-2. Performance of Nondemented Parkinson's Disease Patients on Memory Tasks

Task	Free Recall	Recognition
Explicit Verbal Memory		
List learning	Impaired	Intact
Paired associate learning	Impaired	Intact
Paragraph recall	Impaired	Intact
Explicit Nonverbal Memory		
Reproduction of geometric designs from memory	Impaired	Intact
Implicit Memory		
Priming	Intact	
Pursuit rotor learning	Intact	
Remote Memory	Intact	

passages (Pirozzolo et al., 1982; Taylor et al., 1986a), and recall measures involving reproduction of complex designs (Bowen, 1976; Riklan et al., 1976). Patients are sensitive to the effects of proactive interference (Pillon et al., 1986; Taylor et al., 1986a; Beatty et al., 1989; Massman et al., 1990). While free recall of newly learned information is impaired, memory for remote information has been found to be unimpaired (Freedman et al., 1984), and recognition memory is also usually unaffected (Flowers et al., 1984; Breen, 1993). These results suggest that a specific profile of memory deficits exists in PD patients without overt dementia, as opposed to a more pervasive decline in memory function in patients with overt dementia.

LANGUAGE. Compared with other areas of cognitive functioning, language skills are relatively spared in PD, particularly vocabulary (Matison et al., 1982; Pirozzolo et al., 1982; Huber et al., 1986). There is somewhat greater controversy in the literature concerning confrontation naming and verbal fluency. Whereas some investigators have found no evidence of impaired performance on the Boston Naming Test (Freedman et al., 1984; Levin et al., 1989), other studies have found mildly diminished (Globus et al., 1985) to moderately impaired performance on the same measure (Matison et al., 1982).

The literature concerning performance of PD patients on tasks of verbal fluency, as assessed by asking the patient to generate a list of words according to some predetermined criteria (e.g., letters or semantic categories), also contains inconsistent findings. Although Lees and Smith (1983) found diminished verbal fluency for words beginning with the letter "M," they found normal output for words beginning with "D" or "B." Neither Miller (1985) or Levin and colleagues (1989) found diminished verbal fluency for PD patients as compared with controls on the Controlled Oral Word Association task (FAS). However, Levin and coworkers (1989) noted decreased categorical fluency (names of foods) among patients with early PD. Poor performance on tasks of verbal fluency are as likely to be secondary to deficits in executive function as to language dysfunction per se.

Studies of syntax and semantic knowledge in PD patients have found variable impairment in comprehension of complex commands (Cummings et al., 1988) and decreased syntactic complexity in spontaneous speech (Illes et al., 1988).

VISUOSPATIAL SKILLS. Assessment of visuospatial skills is difficult in patients with profound motor impairment. Even when the effects of motor slowing are taken into account, visuospatial and visuoconstructive skills are among the most frequently reported cognitive disturbances associated with PD (Pirozzolo et al., 1982; Boller et al., 1984; Brown and Marsden, 1984). Studies of visuospatial functions have found that PD patients exhibit deficits in visual analysis and synthesis (as assessed by performance on embedded figures tasks), visual discrimination and matching, and pattern completion (Pirozzolo et al., 1982; Villardita et al., 1982; Huber et al., 1986; Taylor et al., 1986a). Patients with PD exhibited impaired performance on tasks of constructional praxis (Goldenberg et al., 1986; Asso, 1969), even after the speed component has been eliminated to minimize motor demands (Levin et al., 1989). Patients with PD have been found

to perform poorly on tests of postural and vertical tilt (Proctor et al., 1964), line orientation tests (Girotti et al., 1988; Beatty et al., 1989), and spatial orientation tests (Hovestadt et al., 1987).

Not all aspects of visuospatial functioning are impaired in PD. Studies by Brown and Marsden (1984), and Taylor and coworkers (1986a) revealed that PD patients were as accurate as control subjects in making right/left judgments even when the task required mental rotation. Della Sala and colleagues (1986) found no differences between PD patients and control subjects in forecasting trajectories from partial line segments.

Somewhat variable findings have been reported on graphomotor visuoconstructive tasks, such as design copying, with some investigators reporting impairment (Villardita et al., 1982; Ransmayr et al., 1987) and others finding no differences between PD patients and controls on either simple or complex design copying (Stern et al., 1984; Caltagirone et al., 1985).

EXECUTIVE FUNCTIONS. The term executive function refers to a group of cognitive skills involved in the initiation, planning, and monitoring of goal-directed behaviors (Levin et al., 1992). Executive functions include the ability to establish and maintain set; shift from one set to another; form concepts and reason abstractly; use feedback to monitor behavior; program sequential motor activities; develop strategies to learn and copy complex figures; and exert emotional self-control and maintain socially appropriate behavior.

Impaired performance on tasks of executive functions are among the earliest cognitive deficits observed in patients with PD. Patients without overt dementia have been found to exhibit deficits on both card-sorting and odd-man-out techniques requiring the patient to shift from one identification or sorting criterion to another (Lees and Smith, 1983; Cools et al., 1984; Flowers and Robertson, 1985; Taylor et al., 1986a). Researchers have found consistently poor performance by PD patients, as compared with matched controls, on the Wisconsin Card Sorting Test (WCST), a task of concept formation and set shifting ability. Although most studies report that PD patients achieve significantly fewer categories (Bowen et al., 1975; Lees and Smith, 1983; Taylor et al., 1986a; Richards et al., 1993), there is disagreement among researchers on the frequency and type of errors. For example, two studies reported that PD patients make more perseverative errors (Milner; 1963; Levin et al., 1989), and another (Taylor et al., 1986a) found no difference in rate of both perseverative and nonperseverative errors in nondemented PD patients.

Verbal fluency or controlled oral word association tasks, in which the patient is asked to generate words according to specific rules, are also tests of executive function. As stated above, the literature on verbal fluency has produced somewhat inconsistent results with poorer performance on categorical retrieval and somewhat better performance on letter fluency tasks (e.g., FAS; see *Language* above). Lees and Smith (1983) found that early in the course of their disease, PD patients performed significantly more poorly on only the third letter of a verbal fluency task, secondary to perseverative intrusions from previous trials.

Frontal systems tests such as execution of serial hand sequences, production of alternating programs, initiation of nonrepresentational hand sequences, cancellation, and trail making are also compromised in PD patients as compared with age-matched controls (Piccirilli et al., 1981; Flowers, 1982; Matison et al., 1982; Pirozzolo et al., 1982; Lees and Smith, 1983; Sharpe et al., 1983; Cools et al., 1984; Goldenberg et al., 1986; Taylor et al., 1986a). Several authors have suggested that disturbances in frontal systems abilities and set aptitude may be the underlying mechanism accounting for the difficulties manifested by PD patients in the areas of memory, visuospatial skills, language, and perception (Bowen et al., 1976; Brown and Marsden, 1984; Stern et al., 1984; Della Sala et al., 1986; Frith et al., 1986; Levin et al., 1992).

Issues in the Neuropsychology of Parkinson's Disease

Although it is evident from the studies cited above that patients with PD may exhibit changes in cognitive abilities very early in the course of the disease, additional factors occurring in the course of the illness are likely to further impair the cognitive abilities of the PD patient. The following section will consider several of these factors: disease severity, the effect of "on-off" periods on cognitive functions, and the interaction of depression and anxiety with intellectual function.

EARLY VERSUS LATE PARKINSON'S DISEASE. Assessment of patients who have not yet begun treatment with anti-parkinsonian medications provides a clearer understanding of the specific impact of the disease on cognitive functioning. At least three studies have assessed recently diagnosed PD patients before treatment was begun with anti-parkinsonian medications (Lees and Smith, 1983; Weingartner et al., 1984; Hietanen and Teravainen, 1986). Results of these studies indicated that deficits in early PD are likely to be confined to the three areas of psychomotor slowing, loss of cognitive flexibility, and mildly reduced learning and recall (La Rue, 1992).

In contrast, patients with moderate to severe PD who have been under treatment for long periods of time often exhibit more marked neuropsychological impairments. A study by Pirozzolo and colleagues (1982) compared neuropsychological test results of 60 PD patients, with an average length of illness of 9 years, to an equal number of matched controls. These investigators found essentially no group differences on scores on the Digit Span, Vocabulary, and Information subscales of the WAIS-R (Wechsler, 1981), nor were significant differences noted in confrontation naming or a test of apraxia. Significant group differences ($p < .001$) were found on tests of psychomotor speed, visuospatial ability, and both verbal and nonverbal learning and recall.

COGNITIVE CHANGES ASSOCIATED WITH "ON-OFF" PERIODS. The "on-off" phenomenon refers to abrupt fluctuations between relatively mild motor disability or chorea ("on") and relatively severe motor disability ("off") that occur after chronic levodopa therapy and includes end-of-dose deterioration as well as unpredictable shifts between mobile or dyskinetic "on" states and akinetic "off" states unrelated to medication schedules. A modest amount of literature exists on the fluctuation of cognition coinciding with "on-off" periods. In a review of the literature, Delis and Massman (1992) compared results of studies of patients in "on" versus "off" phases, and results of studies of patients in the "on" phase versus normal controls. Comparison of neuropsychological performance of "on versus off" patients only revealed no significant differences in the areas of attention, simple reaction time, verbal fluency, visuospatial abilities, executive functions, immediate recall for short stories and paired associates, immediate and delayed recall of nonverbal memory, and delayed recall and recognition on a list learning task. However, significant differences were noted between on/off patients on tests of supraspan list learning, delayed recall of short stories and paired associates, and choice reaction time. In addition, Delis and Massman note that delayed recall was optimal when dopaminergic status was congruent during learning and later retrieval, indicating a state-dependent memory effect.

No consistent significant differences were found between normal control subjects and patients in the "on" phase on tasks of digit span, simple and choice reaction time, or verbal fluency. However, significant differences were noted on symbol cancellation, immediate and delayed recall of short stories, and card sorting. The fact that studies have found differences between normal elderly and "on" patients on tasks of memory and card sorting, offers additional support for, at the least, subtle cognitive deficits in PD.

DEPRESSION AND PARKINSON'S DISEASE. Depression ranks as one of most common psychiatric complications of PD and has been estimated to occur in approximately 40% of patients. In a systematic review of the available literature on PD and depression, Cummings (1992) found no consistent relationships between depressive symptoms and patient's current age, age at onset of PD, or duration of PD. At least two studies have identified a past history of depression as a risk factor for a major mood disorder after the onset of PD (Mayeux et al., 1981; Starkstein et al., 1989a). However, these same investigators did not find family history of psychiatric illness, or more specifically family history of mood disorder, to be a risk factor (Mayeux et al., 1981; Starkstein et al., 1989a). There is no consistently identified relationship between depression and patient gender (Gotham et al., 1986; Brown and MacCarthy, 1990; Ehmann et al., 1990; Huber et al., 1990).

The profile of symptoms of depression in PD differs from that in patients with idiopathic depression; depressed PD patients complain of feelings of sadness, but without the feelings of guilt or self-reproach characteristic of idiopathic depression (Taylor et al., 1986b; Brown et al., 1988; Levin et al., 1988; Huber et al., 1990). Other features that serve to distinguish the depression associated with PD from idiopathic depression include prominent anxiety (Gotham et al., 1986; Schiffer et al., 1988), a lack of delusions and hallucinations (Brown and MacCarthy, 1990), and a low suicide rate despite a high frequency of suicidal ideation.

Studies focusing on cognitive changes associated with depression and PD have found that depressed PD patients exhibit more neuropsychological deficits than nondepressed PD patients. Depressed PD patients perform more poorly on standard mental status examinations (Mayeux et al., 1981; Starkstein et al., 1992), tasks mediated by frontal systems such as set shifting and word list generation (Taylor et al., 1986b; Starkstein et al., 1989a,b; Wertman et al., 1993), memory functioning (Wertman et al., 1993), and reaction time (Rogers et al., 1987).

Additional research has explored the interaction of depression and severity of PD symptoms on cognitive functions. Starkstein and coworkers (1989a) compared performance of depressed and nondepressed PD patients with mild, moderate, and severe levels of PD. Patients with severe PD exhibited the poorest neuropsychological performance in general, and patients with severe deficits and depression exhibited significantly greater cognitive deficits, particularly on tasks of executive functions. These investigators speculate that pathological changes occurring in the later stages of the disease, particularly a critical level of frontocortical deafferentation, may be necessary to produce both mood disorder and cognitive changes.

ANXIETY IN PARKINSON'S DISEASE. Anxiety after initiation of levodopa treatment has been reported, with patients experiencing apprehension, nervousness, irritability, feelings of impending disaster, palpitations, hyperventilation and insomnia (Celesia and Barr, 1970). At least one investigator has reported finding symptoms of anxiety in PD patients prior to treatment with levodopa, with an exacerbation of symptoms following initiation of treatment (Rondot et al., 1984). Several investigators have observed an unusually high frequency of symptoms of anxiety in patients treated with pergolide (Lang et al., 1982; Markham and Diamond, 1986; Olanow and Alberts, 1986) and when selegiline was added to levodopa therapy (Yahr et al., 1983). Although preliminary in nature, these reports suggest that pergolide and selegiline may be more likely to induce anxiety than other parkinsonian agents (Cummings, 1991).

In contrast to the above findings, a few studies have reported that anxiety in PD is not related to duration of treatment or levodopa level (Stein et al., 1990), and may be related to coexistence of depression (Schiffer et al., 1988; Henderson et al., 1992). Stein and colleagues (1990) found a high incidence (38%) of anxiety in patients with PD, as assessed by a semistructured diagnostic interview. These investigators further compared PD patients with (n = 9) and without (n = 15) symptoms of anxiety and reported finding no differences in duration of levodopa exposure, current levodopa dose, or degree of motor disability. Henderson and colleagues (1992) reported the coexistence of depression and anxiety in 38% of PD patients as compared to only 8% of controls. Furthermore, these investigators reported that 66% of the PD group stated that onset of anxiety followed the onset of PD, with 44% reporting onset of anxiety before initiation of levodopa treatment. Given the high frequency of depression in PD patients in general, it has been hypothesized that the presence of anxiety in PD patients is a concomitant of depression, and may not be related to pathophysiologic changes associated with PD. Based upon this hypothesis Schiffer and coworkers (1988) investigated the presence of anxiety in depressed PD patients as compared with depressed multiple sclerosis (MS) patients. They found that 12 of 16 PD patients presented with coexisting depression and anxiety, as compared with only two of 20 MS patients. The findings suggested that the presence of depression alone cannot account for the concomitant anxiety associated with PD.

Dementia Syndromes of Parkinson's Disease

Considerable controversy exists regarding the frequency with which PD is accompanied by cognitive decline as well as the exact form of cognitive impairment associated with PD. Whereas some investigators have found the prevalence of dementia in PD patients to approach 70% (Pirozzolo et al., 1982), other studies report the frequency of dementia in PD patients to be as low as 15% (Celesia and Wanamaker, 1972; Lieberman et al., 1979; Brown and Marsden, 1984). In a review of the literature, Cummings (1988b) found that studies that used nonstandardized clinical examinations reported the lowest prevalence rates of dementia in PD patients (30.2%). Use of a structured examination, such as the Mini-Mental State Exam (Folstein et al., 1975) modestly increased the reported prevalence to 40.5%, and utilization of standardized psychological tests produced the highest documented prevalence rates of dementia (69.9%). Despite the controversy surrounding the frequency of dementia in PD, there is substantial agreement that PD patients experience some form of cognitive decline over the course of the illness. The widely varying estimates of the prevalence of dementia in PD differ according to the population studied, the sensitivity of assessment techniques, and the definition of dementia used by the investigators.

Several sets of diagnostic criteria for dementia exist. Dementia has been defined as an acquired and persistent impairment of intellectual functioning affecting at least three of the following domains: (1) memory, (2) language, (3) visuospatial skills, (4) complex cognition (abstraction, judgment, executive functions) and (5) emotion or personality (Cummings and Benson, 1992). Another commonly used set of criteria for dementia are provided in the fourth edition of the *Diagnostic and Statistical Manual of Mental Disorders* (DSM-IV; American Psychiatric Association, 1994). These guidelines require that the patient exhibit deficits in memory (short- or long-term), in addition to abnormalities in at least one additional area (abstract reasoning, language, visuospatial skills, or personality). The abnormalities must be of sufficient severity to interfere with work, social activities, or interpersonal relationships, and must not occur exclusively during the course of a delirium. Finally, the DSM-IV criteria require evidence of an "organic etiology" or evidence that the changes in intellectual functioning cannot be attributed to a reversible condition, such as depression. Patients such as those with PD and relatively mild cognitive deficits might fit the Cummings and Benson (1992) definition of dementia but not the DSM-IV definition.

Although dementia is often mistakenly considered a global disorder, there is no dementing illness that involves all areas of the brain equally or affects performance on all neuropsychological tasks to the same degree. Two basic patterns of neuropsychological impairment have been distinguished within the dementia syndrome and have been labeled according to involvement of neuroanatomic structures (Cummings and Benson, 1992). The first pattern, identified as the *cortical* dementias, involves conditions that affect primarily cerebral cortex, particularly Alzheimer's disease (AD). The second pattern includes *subcortical* dementias such as the extrapyramidal syndrome, white matter diseases, subcortical vascular disorders, and hydrocephalus that produce dysfunction in the basal ganglia, thalamus, and brain stem. Despite much controversy surrounding the cortical-subcortical dichotomy (Cummings and Benson, 1984; Whitehouse, 1986), the distinction between the two patterns is becoming increasingly accepted and aids clinicians in establishing an etiologic diagnosis and implementing appropriate management.

The clinical characteristics of the cortical and subcortical dementias are summarized in Table 13-3. The neuropsychological changes associated with the cortical dementias include naming difficulties and impaired comprehension, memory disturbances including deficits in both recall and recognition, agnosia (inability to recognize objects), and apraxia (loss of ability to perform skilled motor tasks). Visuospatial and constructional abilities are generally impaired as are judgment and the ability to perform mathematical calculations. Speech remains normal in volume and articulation and the motor system is spared until late in the course (Cummings and Benson, 1992). Personality may be relatively preserved but disinterest is common (Cummings, 1982; Cummings and Benson, 1986). In contrast to the clinical characteristics of the cortical dementias, neuropsychological deficits associated with subcortical dementing processes include slowing of cognition, memory disturbances characterized by poor recall with preservation of recognition abilities, executive dysfunction, and alterations in mood (Albert et al., 1974; Folstein et al., 1975; Cummings and Benson, 1984). Disturbances of mood are often associated with subcortical dementias, with depression as the most commonly described disorder, although apathy is also frequent. Motor disturbances are evident in the subcortical dementias and are marked by stooped or extended posture, increased muscle tone, tremor, choreas, dystonias, and

Table 13-3. Clinical Characteristics of Cortical and Subcortical Dementia

Characteristic	Cortical	Subcortical
Cognition		
Calculation	Acalculia	Slowed, dilapidated
Abstraction	Poor abstraction	Impaired
Judgment	Impaired judgment	Poor planning
Visuospatial	Impaired	Impaired
Memory		
	Storage deficit	Retrieval deficit
	Poor recall	Poor recall
	Poor recognition	Intact recognition
Verbal		
Language	Aphasic	Normal
Speech	Normal	Hypophonic, dysarthric, mute
Affect/mood		
	Disinhibited, unconcerned	Apathy, depression
Motor		
Posture	Normal[a]	Stooped or extended
Gait	Normal[a]	Abnormal
Tone	Normal[a]	Increased
Movements	Normal[a]	Tremor, chorea, dystonia

[a] Motor abnormalities appear late in the course of Alzheimer's disease.

asterixis, and dysarthric speech output (Cummings and Benson, 1992). Alzheimer's disease is categorized as a cortical dementia; the common pattern of intellectual change associated with PD, and most parkinsonian syndromes, is classified as subcortical dementia. Some patients with PD and dementia have AD and manifest both cortical and subcortical dysfunction.

The most frequent type of dementia in PD is characterized by a failure to initiate activities spontaneously, an inability to develop successful problem-solving strategies, impaired and slowed memory, impaired visuospatial skills, poor concept formation and word list generation, impaired set shifting ability, and a reduced rate of information processing (Cummings and Benson, 1992). The most apparent deficits of dementia in PD include slowness of response, impaired word list generation, abnormal constructions, deterioration in abstraction and concept formation, and poor performance on complex mathematical word problems. Cortical features such as aphasia, agnosia and severe amnesia are uncommon in PD dementia (Cummings and Benson, 1992). When the dementia of PD is severe and marked memory and language deficits are present, AD may simultaneously be present.

Neurobiology of Dementia in Parkinson's Disease

There may be several different types of dementia syndromes in PD reflecting a variety of cellular and biological changes (Cummings, 1988b). The neurobiological alterations associated with dementia in PD include: (1) a deficit of dopamine; (2) deficits of dopamine and acetylcholine; and (3) coexistence of an Alzheimer-type dementia.

SUBCORTICAL CHANGES WITH DOPAMINERGIC DEFICIT. Dopamine is markedly reduced in PD, particularly in the putamen and caudate nuclei where the reduction of dopamine is as high as 78% to 92% (Fahn et al., 1971; Hornykiewicz, 1973). Other areas of dopamine reduction include the substantia nigra, nucleus accumbens, lateral hypothalamus, ventral tegmental area, frontal lobe, cingulate gyrus, entorhinal cortex, and hippocampus (Hornykiewicz, 1973; Price et al., 1978; Javoy-Agid and Agid, 1980; Scatton et al., 1982, 1983). Several lines of evidence indicate that the subcortical dementia syndrome of PD may be attributable to the effects of the dopamine deficit on intellectual functioning (Cummings, 1988b). First, correlations between dopamine loss and akinesia, and between akinesia and severity of dementia, suggest that both dementia and akinesia are related to dopamine deficiency (Mortimer et al., 1982; Piccirilli et al., 1984; Portin et al., 1984). Second, the dementia syndrome improves mildly for the first 1 to 2 years following levodopa replacement therapy, particularly on tasks of memory, planning, set maintenance and shifting, frontal systems tasks, and general intellectual ability (Guthrie et al., 1970; Meier and Martin, 1970; Beardsley and Puletti, 1971; Marsh et al., 1971; Donnelly and Chase, 1973; Bowen et al., 1975; Morel-Maroger, 1977). Finally, subcortical dementia has been associated with other hypodopaminergic states including PSP- and MPTP-induced parkinsonism (Kish et al., 1985; Ruberg et al., 1985; Stern and Langston, 1985).

CHOLINERGIC DEFICIT. Investigations of cholinergic system markers such as choline acetyltransferase (CAT) in the dementia of PD have been stimulated by interest in the relationship between AD and PD-related dementia. Perry and colleagues (1985) found a reduction of CAT in the cortex of PD patients with overt dementia, and normal CAT levels in PD patients without overt dementia. Additional investigations have shown that CAT is usually decreased in patients with overt dementia and that CAT alterations are independent of any cortical histopathologic changes indicative of AD (Dubois et al., 1983; Ruberg et al., 1985). At least one study has reported normal CAT levels in one patient with overt dementia demonstrating that intellectual deterioration may occur without concomitant cholinergic system abnormali-

ties (Ruberg et al., 1985). Although based on a limited number of patient studies, most investigations (most of which depended on retrospective identification of dementia without benefit of neuropsychological assessment) have found cholinergic deficits in PD patients with overt dementia.

ALZHEIMER'S DISEASE. Several investigators have reported that neuropathological changes associated with AD, namely senile plaques and neurofibrillary tangles, are commonly present in the brains of demented PD patients (Boller et al., 1980; Perry et al., 1983, 1985; Gaspar and Grey, 1984; Jellinger and Riederer, 1984); others have failed to replicate this finding (Heston, 1980, 1981; Mann and Yates, 1983; Ball, 1984). Although dementia may occur in PD patients without the histopathologic changes characteristic of AD, the available studies indicate that, when present, AD pathology is more likely to be identified in PD patients with more severe dementia syndromes (Cummings, 1988b).

Studies using positron-emission tomography (PET) to assess cerebral glucose metabolism in PD with dementia have shown globally reduced metabolic activity or a disproportionate involvement of the temporoparieto-occipital junction regions. Although the latter pattern is characteristic of AD, not all PD-dementia patients with this finding have had AD-type pathology at postmortem. Thus, glucose-PET cannot distinguish among the different causes of dementia in PD with certainty (Peppard et al., 1992; Snow, 1992).

Several neuropsychological differences exist between patients with PD and patients with AD. First, although PD is marked by dysarthric and hypophonic speech, language skills are intact; in AD there are more pervasive deficits in naming, spontaneous verbalization, and language comprehension (La Rue, 1992; Levin et al., 1992). Memory is impaired in patients with both PD and AD, although the impairment in AD is more pronounced, with AD patients performing much more poorly on tasks of delayed recall and recognition. Most PD patients have largely preserved memory recognition skills. Visuospatial deficits are exhibited by both PD and AD patients, even when tasks do not involve motor speed or manual dexterity (Levin et al., 1992). PD and AD patients alike exhibit poor performance on tasks of cognitive flexibility. However, in PD poor performance on these tests (e.g., Wisconsin Card Sort) is oftentimes the sole or most striking deficit, as compared with AD, where memory is the most prominent deficit (La Rue, 1992). Finally, depression is common in PD with major affective episodes occurring in 40% to 60% of patients, whereas major depressive episodes are uncommon in AD (Cummings, 1988a). Thus, a PD patient with AD would present with intellectual deficits characteristic of both disorders including prominent disturbance in recall and recognition memory, deficits in language skills including naming and comprehension, dysarthria and hypophonic speech, and poor performance on tasks of cognitive flexibility.

DIFFUSE LEWY BODY DISEASE. Some patients with a parkinsonian syndrome and dementia have Lewy bodies throughout the cortex as well as in the brain stem structures typical of PD when they are studied at autopsy. Some patients have an excessive number of neuritic plaques typical of AD. Clinically, the patients manifest more marked dementia than is typical of PD and more extrapyramidal abnormalities than usually seen in AD. Depression and psychosis are common early in the disease course, and fluctuation of cognitive deficits is also characteristic (Byrne et al., 1989, 1990). It is currently unclear if diffuse Lewy body disease is a form of PD, a form of AD, or an entirely separate disease.

Parkinsonian Syndromes

There are several hypokinetic neurodegenerative disorders that share clinical similarities with PD. However, patients with these disorders typically exhibit additional neurological abnormalities and thus these syndromes are referred to as multiple-system atrophies or *parkinson-plus syndromes.*

Progressive Supranuclear Palsy

This unique PD-like extrapyramidal syndrome was first described by Steele and colleagues (1964). Age at onset is typically in the sixth or seventh decade and progresses to death in 5 to 10 years. The disease is sporadic and occurs more commonly in males than females (Steele et al., 1964; Steele, 1972). Progressive supranuclear palsy is an uncommon disease with a prevalence rate of 1.4 per 100,000 (Golbe et al., 1988).

CLINICAL CHARACTERISTICS. The four principal clinical characteristics of PSP are pseudobulbar palsy, axial rigidity, supranuclear paresis of gaze, and dementia. Pseudobulbar palsy is marked by a mask-like facies, increased jaw and facial jerks, dysarthria, dysphagia, and drooling (Cummings and Benson, 1992). Patients with PSP tend to have an astonished or worried facial expression secondary to rigidity and hypertonicity of the facial muscles (Jankovic, 1984). Speech in PSP is characterized by a monotonous, hypernasal, low-pitched, spastic dysarthria (Stacy and Jankovic, 1992), and patients may progress to total anarthria or mutism in late stages (Cummings and Benson, 1992).

Rigidity in the PSP patient is more evident in the midline structures such as the neck and trunk, as opposed to the limbs (e.g., axial rigidity). In contrast to the stooped posture, short and shuffling steps, narrow base, and flexed knees seen in patients with PD, patients with PSP assume an erect or hypererect posture and have a stiff and broad-based gait (Cummings and Benson, 1992; Stacy and Jankovic, 1992). Patients with PSP develop a profound bradykinesia during the course of the illness that resembles PD. Both resting and action tremor are unusual (Steele et al., 1964; Steele, 1972).

The neuroophthalmologic abnormalities of PSP vary according to the stage of the disease. Loss of volitional downward gaze is one of the most important distinguishing features of PSP and is oftentimes one of the earliest manifestations of the disease (Steele et al., 1964; Steele, 1972). Oculocephalic reflexes remain intact: the patient's eyes deviate upward when the head is tilted forward. Upward gaze is progressively impaired and volitional horizontal gaze is also lost as the disease progresses (David et al., 1968).

Although dementia is one of the clinical characteristics of PSP, intellectual deterioration is usually mild until the late stages of the illness. Vague changes in personality, including apathy and slowness, may be among the first features of PSP. The specific neuropsychological manifestations of the disease are discussed below.

PATHOLOGY. The motor, neuroophthalmic, and neurobehavioral changes that characterize PSP are reflections of the marked neuronal degeneration in the basal nucleus of Meynert, subthalamic nucleus, superior colliculi, mesencephalic tegmentum, substantia nigra, locus ceruleus, red nucleus, reticular formation, vestibular nuclei, cerebellum, and spinal cord (Steele, 1972; Zweig et al., 1987). The thalamus, globus pallidus, and putamen are involved only to a limited extent and the hypothalamus is not routinely affected. Most investigators report no changes in cortex (Steele et al., 1964). Neurofibrillary tangles, granulovacuolar degeneration, and gliosis are among the most striking histologic changes associated with PSP (Steele et al., 1964; Steele, 1972). However, unlike the twisted tangles associated with AD, the neurofibrillary tangles in PSP are composed of straight tubules that are smaller in diameter (150 nm vs. 20 to 24 nm) (Tellez-Nagel and Wisniewski, 1973; Powell et al., 1974; Roy et al., 1974; Tomonga, 1977).

The most striking neurochemical alteration in PSP is the marked reduction of nigrostriatal dopamine and a moderate decrease of CAT (Kish et al., 1985; Ruberg et al., 1985). There is an increase of glutamic acid, taurine, and GABA in subcortical structures (Perry et al., 1988), and a decrease in cortical concentrations of corticotropin-releasing factors (Whitehouse et al., 1988). Neurochemical alterations in PSP also feature a loss of nicotinic cholinergic receptors in the basal forebrain (Young, 1985), and a reduction of subcortical D2-type dopamine receptors

(Bokobza et al., 1984; Pierot et al., 1988; Whitehouse et al., 1988).

TREATMENT. Progressive supranuclear palsy is a relentlessly progressive disease for which there is no cure. However, several studies to date have investigated the use of a variety of pharmacological agents for control of the symptoms associated with the disease. Although most studies have found no response of PSP patients to levodopa (Gilbert and Feldman, 1969; Gross, 1969; Jenkins, 1969; Donaldson, 1973), other reports have been somewhat more optimistic. Akinesia, rigidity, and extraocular movements have been shown to improve with the use of levodopa in a few patients; cognitive functions did not improve (Dehaene and Bogaerts, 1970; Mendell et al., 1970; Klawans and Ringel, 1971; Donaldson, 1973; Mastaglia et al., 1973; Neophytides et al., 1982). Disturbances of gait and speech abnormalities have been partially remediated with benzotropine mesylate (Haldeman et al., 1981) and methysergide has been helpful in some patients with severe dysphagia (Rafal and Grimm, 1981).

Neuropsychological Aspects

There have been relatively few studies addressing the neuropsychological deficits associated with PSP. The existing research indicates that patients with PSP tend to exhibit difficulty on tests sensitive to executive dysfunction.

ATTENTION. Patients with PSP exhibit impaired performance on tasks of attention when compared to normal elderly and to patients with AD or PD (Maher et al., 1985; Pillon et al., 1986, 1991).

MEMORY. Studies of memory function in PSP have produced somewhat mixed results. Pillon and colleagues (1986) found that while patients with PSP performed significantly more poorly than control patients on all tests of memory, they performed better than patients with AD on tasks of paragraph recall and a verbal paired associate learning task.

Table 13-4. Differential Diagnosis of Progressive Supranuclear Palsy (PSP) and Parkinson's Disease

Characteristic	PSP	Parkinson's Disease
Clinical characteristics		
Rigidity	Axial > limb	Limb > axial
Posture	Extended	Stooped, bowed
Speech changes	Dysarthric, strangled	Hypophonic
	Mutism common late	Mutism uncommon
Tremor	Uncommon	Common
Gaze paresis	Downgaze lost first	Upgaze and convergence lost first
Response to levodopa	Little improvement	Substantial improvement
Neuropathology		
Location	Subthalamic nucleus, red nucleus, substantia nigra, dentate nucleus	Substantia nigra, locus ceruleus, ventral tegmental area
Type of change	Neurofibrillary tangles, granulovacuolar degeneration, cell loss, gliosis	Lewy bodies, gliosis, cell loss

Litvan and colleagues (1989) found that PSP patients performed significantly worse than control subjects on a 15-item list learning task and tasks of paragraph recall. These same investigators found that PSP patients also performed significantly below controls on a task of visual memory. A study by Grafman and colleagues (1990) provided similar results, with PSP patients achieving significantly lower Memory Quotient scores on the Wechsler Memory Scale (Wechsler, 1945) compared with controls. Other studies, however, have found intact memory functioning in PSP patients. For example, in a study by Milberg and Albert (1989), PSP patients did not differ significantly from normal subjects on tasks of both verbal and nonverbal memory.

LANGUAGE. Studies of confrontation naming have found impaired performance by PSP patients (Milberg and Albert, 1989; Grafman et al., 1990; Pillon et al., 1991); however, they performed slightly better than AD patients (Milberg and Albert, 1989).

Studies that have explored the performance of PSP patients on tasks of fluency have found poor performance on tasks of both letter (e.g., FAS; Milberg and Albert, 1989; Grafman et al., 1990) and lexical (e.g., "animals") fluency (Pillon et al., 1986; Litvan et al., 1989; Grafman et al., 1990). In the study by Milberg and Albert (1989), the decrease in fluency could not be attributed to the effects of psychomotor slowing.

VISUOSPATIAL FUNCTIONING. In general, most investigations of neuropsychological deficits in PSP patients have not emphasized performance on tests of visuospatial skills. This may be due, in part, to the fact that PSP patients present with deficits in motor function and volitional gaze (see above) that would clearly impact performance on tests of visuospatial ability, particularly timed tests. Nonetheless, most studies assessing visuospatial skills have found impaired performance (Maher et al., 1985; Pillon et al., 1986). Studies that compared the performance of PSP patients with patients with AD, PD, or Huntington's disease found no differences (Pillon et al., 1986; Milberg and Albert, 1989).

EXECUTIVE FUNCTIONING. Patients with PSP perform most poorly on tests that evaluate executive function (Albert et al., 1974; Maher et al., 1985; Pillon et al., 1986; Grafman et al., 1990). In a study by Grafman and colleagues (1990), PSP patients performed significantly more poorly than control subjects on tests of concept formation, reasoning, set shifting ability, lexical and letter fluency, and freedom from distraction. Furthermore, PSP patients were found to be particularly impaired when tasks required sequential movements, reasoning, conceptual shifting, and rapid retrieval of verbal information; all of which have been associated with dysfunction of prefrontal-subcortical circuits.

DIFFERENTIAL DIAGNOSIS. The most common disorder from which PSP must be distinguished is PD. Although both disorders are akinetic rigid states with dementia and abnormal extraocular movements, several distinguishing features characterize the two conditions (Table 13-4). Progressive supranuclear palsy is characterized by axial rigidity, extended posture, lack of tremor, and impairment in downgaze as the first neuroophthalmic disturbance. Conversely, PD is characterized by limb rigidity, stooped posture, early impairment in upgaze and convergence, and prominent tremor. Whereas patients with PD often exhibit substantial improvement when treated with levodopa, patients with PSP show little response.

Other Parkinsonian Syndromes

Olivopontocerebellar Atrophy (OPCA)

First coined in 1900 by Dejerine and Thomas, the term olivopontocerebellar atrophy (OPCA) is applied to disorders characterized clinically by ataxic gait, hypotonia, action tremor, limb unsteadiness, and dysarthria (Brown, 1971). The presence of ophthalmoplegia and pyramidal tract signs is used clinically to distinguish OPCA from pure cerebellar atrophy. Onset of OPCA is usually between ages 30 and 50 years and may be sporadic or inherited in an autosomal dominant pattern. The disease is slowly progressive and may have a 25-year course. Routine laboratory tests, EEG, and computed tomography (CT) scans are generally not helpful diagnostically. Computed tomography and magnetic resonance imaging (MRI) typically show cerebellar and brain stem atrophy, enlarged fourth ventricle and cerebellopontine angle cisterns, and demyelination

of transverse pontine fibers on T_2-weighted MRI (Berciano, 1988). Recent investigations using positron-emission tomography (PET) have found correlations between reduced cerebellar and brain stem glucose metabolic rates and severity of ataxia and dysarthria (Kluin et al., 1988; Rosenthal et al., 1988).

The dementia syndrome associated with OPCA is marked by slowly progressive intellectual degeneration with subcortical-type characteristics (Locke and Foley; 1960; Plaitakis et al, 1980; Naito and Oyanagi, 1982). The most prominent neuropsychological deficits include poor memory, slowing of cognition, frontal system disturbances, and apathy (Cummings and Benson, 1992) with an absence of cognitive disturbances characteristic of cortical dysfunction, such as aphasia and agnosia (Kish et al., 1988a).

Shy-Drager Syndrome

Shy-Drager syndrome (SDS) is associated with abnormalities of function of the autonomic nervous system including impotence, orthostatic hypotension, and urinary incontinence early in the clinical course. Other symptoms may include anhidrosis, pupillary changes, and decreased tearing. An akinetic, rigid parkinsonian syndrome develops several years after the onset of the autonomic dysfunction. Some patients may present with associated cerebellar, upper motor neuron, and/or lower motor neuron findings. The disease is more common in men and symptoms first begin in the sixth decade of life. Dementia rarely occurs in SDS. Pathological changes include cell loss and gliosis in the pigmented brain stem nuclei, striatum, pontine structures, and the intermediolateral cell column of the spinal cord (Shy and Drager, 1960; Thomas and Schirger, 1970; Bannister and Oppenheimer, 1972; Khurana et al., 1980).

Striatonigral Degeneration

Striatonigral degeneration and PD are clinically similar, and patients with striatonigral degeneration are often first diagnosed with

PD. However, tremor is uncommon in striatonigral degeneration and dementia is not a prominent feature. Except for parkinsonian symptoms, no other abnormalities exist and the main clinical feature is lack of responsiveness to levodopa (Koller, 1987). As a result, patients who initially present with symptoms of PD but show little response to high dosages of levodopa are generally labeled as having striatonigral degeneration. Diagnosis is confirmed only upon postmortem examination, which is significant for neuronal loss in the putamen and caudate nucleus (O'Brien et al., 1990). Lewy bodies and neurofibrillary tangles are not common.

Idiopathic Calcification of the Basal Ganglia (ICBG)

Idiopathic calcification of the basal ganglia (ICBG) is a progressive extrapyramidal syndrome manifesting dementia, parkinsonism, and extensive calcification of the basal ganglia, thalamus, and subcortical white matter (Cummings and Benson, 1992). The disease is familial with both autosomal dominant and autosomal recessive modes of inheritance (Moskowitz et al., 1971). There is an early- and late-onset clinical pattern associated with the disease. In the early-onset pattern, onset occurs between ages 20 and 40 and the disease initially manifests as a schizophrenia-type psychosis. The late-onset variety presents between ages 40 and 60 and is marked by dementia and a movement disorder (Francis, 1979; Cummings et al., 1983). The dementia associated with ICBG has characteristic subcortical features including poor attention and concentration, impaired calculation and abstraction, and poor recent memory. Although palilalia and dysarthria are common, aphasia does not occur (Boller et al., 1973). Pathological examination reveals extensive calcium deposits in the globus pallidus, putamen, thalamus, corona radiata, dentate nuclei, and cerebellar white matter (Friede et al., 1961; Kalambonkis and Molling, 1962; Neumann, 1963; Bruyn et al., 1964; Pilleri, 1966; Adachi et al., 1968). Differential diagnosis of ICBG includes a variety of disorders that present with impaired intellect and basal ganglia calcification, the most frequent of which is hypoparathyroidism (Eraut, 1974; Slyter, 1979).

Summary

Parkinson's disease is among the most common neurological illnesses affecting the elderly. It is characterized by motor symptoms including slowness of movement and difficulty initiating movement, masked facies, muscular rigidity, shuffling or unsteady gait, stooped posture, disturbances in equilibrium, and tremor. The use of levodopa continues to be the mainstay of treatment for PD. Other pharmacological therapies include the use of selegiline and dopamine receptor agonists. Although considerable controversy exists regarding the nature and frequency of dementia in PD, neuropsychologic deficits in nondemented PD patients include moderate impairment in verbal and nonverbal memory for both immediate and delayed recall, with generally good performance on tasks of recognition. Language functions are generally spared. Visuospatial and visuoconstructive skills are among the most frequently cited deficits in PD, even when the effects of motor slowing are taken into account. Executive functions are the earliest and most consistently impaired abilities. Depression is the most common psychiatric syndrome in PD and anxiety and apathy are also frequently observed.

Neurodegenerative disorders that share clinical similarities with PD include PSP, olivopontocerebellar atrophy, Shy-Drager syndrome, striatonigral degeneration, and idiopathic calcification of the basal ganglia.

Disorders that affect the head of the caudate nucleus or thalamus produce the syndrome of subcortical dementia with executive function abnormalities, memory loss, slowed cognition and mood and personality changes. The caudate nucleus, globus pallidus, and thalamus are member structures of frontal-subcortical circuits that link these subcortical nuclei with specific regions of the frontal lobe. Disruption of the circuits results in behavioral abnormalities and cognitive deficits similar to those occurring with frontal lobe dysfunction (Cummings, 1993). Many of the intellectual disturbances documented in PD and other basal ganglia syndromes can be ascribed to interruption of frontal-subcortical circuit function.

The high frequency of cognitive deficits, mood changes, anxiety, and personality changes among patients with PD and other movement disorders indicate that the basal ganglia play critical roles in human intellectual and emotional function.

Acknowledgment

Supported in part by the Department of Veterans Affairs and National Institute on Aging grants 1P30 AG10123 and AG11325-02.

References

Adachi, M., Wellman, K. F., and Volk, B. W. (1968). Histochemical studies on the pathogenesis of "idiopathic non-arteriosclerotic cerebral calcification." *Journal of Neuropathology and Experimental Neurology, 27,* 153–154.

Albert, M. L., Feldman, R. G., and Willis, A. L. (1974). The 'subcortical dementia' of progressive supranuclear palsy. *Journal of Neurology, Neurosurgery, and Psychiatry, 37,* 121–130.

Alvord, E. C. Jr (1971). The pathology of Parkinsonism. Part II: An interpretation with special reference to other changes in the aging brain. In F. H. McDowell and C. H. Markham, eds., *Recent Advances in Parkinson's Disease.* Philadelphia: F. H. Davis, pp. 131–161.

American Psychiatric Association (1994). *Diagnostic and Statistical Manual of Mental Disorders/ IV. (DSM-IV).* Washington D.C.: APA Press.

Ashok, P. P., Radhakrishan, K., Sridharan, R., and Mousa, M. E. (1986). Epidemiology of Parkinson's disease in Benghazi, North-East Libya. *Clinical Neurology and Neurosurgery, 88,* 109–113.

Asso, D. (1969). WAIS scores in a group of Parkinson's patients. *British Journal of Psychiatry, 115,* 555–556.

Ball, M. J. (1984). The morphological basis of dementia in Parkinson's disease. *Canadian Journal of Neurological Science, 11* (Suppl. 1), 180–184.

Bannister, R., and Oppenheimer, D. R. (1972). Degenerative diseases of the nervous system associated with autonomic failure. *Brain, 95,* 457–474.

Beatty, W. W., Staton, R. D., Weir, W. S., Monson, N., and Whitaker, H. A. (1989). Cognitive disturbances in Parkinson's disease. *Journal of Geriatric Psychiatry and Neurology, 2,* 22–33.

Beardsley, J. V., and Puletti, F. (1971). Personality (MMPI) and cognitive (WAIS) changes after levodopa treatment. *Archives of Neurology, 25,* 145–150.

Berciano, J. (1988). Olivopontocerebellar atrophy. In J. Jankovic and E. Tolosa, eds., *Parkinson's Disease and Movement Disorders.* Baltimore: Williams and Wilkins, pp. 131–152.

Bianchine, J. R. (1976). Drug therapy of parkinsonism. *New England Journal of Medicine, 295,* 814–818.

Bokobza, B., Ruberg, M., Scatton, B., Javoy-Agid, F., and Agid, Y. (1984). [3H]Spiperone binding, dopamine, and HVA concentrations in Parkinson's disease and supranuclear palsy. *European Journal of Pharmacology, 99,* 167–175.

Boller, F., Boller, M., Denes, G., Timberlake, W. H., Zieper, I., and Albert, M. L. (1973). Familial palilalia. *Neurology, 23,* 1117–1125.

Boller, F., Mizutani, T., Roessmann, V., and Gambetti, P. (1980). Parkinson's disease, dementia, and Alzheimer disease: Clinicopathological correlations. *Annals of Neurology, 7,* 329–335.

Boller, F., Passafiume, D., Keefe, N. C., Rogers, K., Morrow, L., and Kim, Y. (1984). Visuospatial impairment in Parkinson's disease. Role of perceptual and motor factors. *Archives of Neurology, 41,* 485–490.

Bowen, F. P. (1976). Behavioral alterations in patients with basal ganglia lesions. In M. D. Yahr, ed., *The Basal Ganglia.* New York: Raven Press, pp. 169–184.

Bowen, F. P., Burns, M. M., Brady, E., and Yahr, M. D. (1976). A note on alterations of personal orientation in Parkinsonism. *Neuropsychologia, 14,* 425–429.

Bowen, F. P., Kamienny, R. S., Burns, M. M., and Yahr, M. D. (1975). Parkinsonism: Effects of levodopa treatment on concept formation. *Neurology, 25,* 701–704.

Breen, E. K. (1993). Recall and recognition memory in Parkinson's Disease. *Cortex, 29,* 91–102.

Brown, D. G. (1971). Diseases of the cerebellum. In A. B. Baker and L. H. Baker, eds., *Clinical Neurology.* New York: Harper and Row, pp. 1–38.

Brown, R. G., and MacCarthy, B. (1990). Psychiatric morbidity in patients with Parkinson's disease. *Psychological Medicine, 20*, 77–87.

Brown, R. G., MacCarthy, B., Gotham, A. M., Der, G. J., and Marsden, C. D. (1988). Depression and disability in Parkinson's disease: A follow-up study of 132 cases. *Psychological Medicine, 18*, 49–55.

Brown, R. G., and Marsden, C. D. (1984). How common is dementia in Parkinson's disease? *Lancet, 2*, 1262–1265.

Bruyn, G. W., Bots, G., and Staal, A. (1964). Familial bilateral vascular calcifications in the central nervous system. *Psychiatria, Neurologia, and Neurochirurgia, 67*, 342–376.

Byrne, E. J., Lennox, G., Lowe, J., and Godwin-Austen, R. B. (1989). Diffuse Lewy body disease: Clinical features in 15 cases. *Journal of Neurology, Neurosurgery, and Psychiatry, 52*, 709–717.

Byrne, E. J., Lennox, G., Lowe, J., and Reynolds, G. (1990). Diffuse Lewy body disease: The clinical features. *Advances in Neurology, 53*, 283–286.

Caltagirone, C., Masullo, C., Benedetti, N., and Gainotti, G. (1985). Dementia in Parkinson's disease: Possible specific involvement of the frontal lobes. *International Journal of Neuroscience, 26*, 15–26.

Celesia, G. G., and Barr, A. N. (1970). Psychosis and other psychiatric manifestations of levodopa therapy. *Archives of Neurology, 23*, 193–200.

Celesia, G. G., and Wanamaker, W. M. (1972). Psychiatric disturbances in Parkinson's disease. *Diseases of the Nervous System, 33*, 577–583.

Cools, A. R., van den Bercken, J.H.L., Horstink, M.W.I., van Spaendonck, K.P.M., and Berger, H.J.C. (1984). Cognitive and motor shifting aptitude disorder in Parkinson's disease. *Journal of Neurology, Neurosurgery, and Psychiatry, 47*, 443–453.

Cummings, J. L. (1982). Cortical dementias. In D. F. Benson and D. Blumer, eds., *Psychiatric Aspects of Neurologic Disease/II*. New York: Grune and Stratton, pp. 93–120.

Cummings, J. L. (1988a). Intellectual impairment in Parkinson's disease: Clinical, pathologic, and biochemical correlates. *Journal of Geriatric Psychiatry and Neurology, 1*, 24–36.

Cummings, J. L. (1988b). The dementia of Parkinson's disease: Prevalence, characteristics, neurobiology, and comparison with dementia of the Alzheimer type. *European Neurology, 28* (Suppl. 1), 15–23.

Cummings, J. L. (1991). Behavioral complications of drug treatment of Parkinson's disease. *Journal of the American Geriatrics Society, 39*, 708–716.

Cummings, J. L. (1992). Depression and Parkinson's disease: A review. *American Journal of Psychiatry, 149*, 443–454.

Cummings, J. L. (1993). Frontal subcortical circuits and human behavior. *Archives of Neurology, 50*, 873–880.

Cummings, J. L., and Benson, D. F. (1984). Subcortical dementia. Review of an emerging concept. *Archives of Neurology, 41*, 874–879.

Cummings, J. L., and Benson, D. F. (1986). Dementia of the Alzheimer type: An inventory of diagnostic clinical features. *Journal of the American Geriatrics Society, 34*, 12–19.

Cummings, J. L., and Benson, D. F. (1992). *Dementia: A Clinical Approach*/II. Boston: Butterworth-Heinemann.

Cummings, J. L., Darkins, A., Mendez, M., Hill, M. A., and Benson, D. F. (1988). Alzheimer's disease and Parkinson's disease: Comparison of speech and language alterations. *Neurology, 38*, 680–684.

Cummings, J. L., Gosenfeld, L., Houlihan, J., and McCaffrey, T. (1983). Neuropsychiatric disturbances associated with idiopathic calcification of the basal ganglia. *Biological Psychiatry, 18*, 591–601.

David, N. J., Mackey, E. A., and Smith, J. L. (1968). Further observations in progressive supranuclear palsy. *Neurology, 18*, 349–356.

Dehaene, I., and Bogaerts, M. (1970). L-dopa in progressive supranuclear palsy. *Lancet, 2*, 470.

Delis, D. C., and Massman, P. J. (1992). The effects of dopamine fluctuation on cognition and affect. In S. J. Huber and J. L. Cummings, eds., *Parkinson's Disease: Neurobehavioral Aspects*. New York: Oxford University Press, pp. 288–302.

Della Sala, S., Di Lorenzo, G., Giordano, A., and Spinnler, H. (1986). Is there a specific visuospatial impairment in Parkinsonians? *Journal of Neurology, Neurosurgery, and Psychiatry, 49*, 1258–1265.

Den Hartog Jager, W. A., and Bethlem, J. (1960). The distribution of Lewy bodies in the central and autonomic nervous systems in idiopathic paralysis agitans. *Journal of Neurology, Neurosurgery, and Psychiatry, 23*, 283–290.

Donaldson, I. M. (1973). The treatment of progressive supranuclear palsy with L-dopa. *Australian and New Zealand Journal of Medicine, 3*, 413–416.

Donnelly, E. F., and Chase, T. N. (1973). Intellectual and memory function in parkinsonian and non-parkinsonian patients treated with L-dopa. *Diseases of the Nervous System, 34,* 119–123.

Dubois, B., Ruberg, M., Javoy-Agid, F., Ploska, A., and Agid, Y. (1983). A subcortico-cortical cholinergic system is affected in Parkinson's disease. *Brain Research, 288,* 213–218.

Ehmann, T. S., Beninger, R. J., Gawel, M. J., and Riopelle, R. J. (1990). Depressive symptoms in Parkinson's disease: A comparison with disabled control subjects. *Journal of Geriatric Psychiatry and Neurology, 3,* 3–9.

El-Awar, M., Becker, J. T., Hammond, K. M., Nebes, R. D., and Boller, F. (1987). Learning deficit in Parkinson's disease. Comparison with Alzheimer's disease and normal aging. *Archives of Neurology, 44,* 180–184.

Eraut, D. (1974). Idiopathic hypoparathyriodism presenting as dementia. *British Medical Journal, 1,* 429–430.

Fahn, S., Libsch, L. R., and Cutler, R. W. (1971). Monoamines in the human neostriatum: Topographic distribution in normals and in Parkinson's disease and their role in akinesia, rigidity, chorea, and tremor. *Journal of the Neurological Sciences, 14,* 427–455.

Fitzgerald, P. M., and Jankovic, J. (1989). Lower body parkinsonism: Evidence for vascular etiology. *Movement Disorders, 4,* 249–260.

Flowers, K. A. (1982). Frontal lobe signs as a component of Parkinsonism. *Behavioural Brain Research, 5,* 100–101.

Flowers, K. A., Pearce, I., and Pearce, J.M.S. (1984). Recognition memory in Parkinson's disease. *Journal of Neurology, Neurosurgery, and Psychiatry, 47,* 1174–1181.

Flowers, K. A., and Robertson, C. (1985). The effect of Parkinson's disease on the ability to maintain a mental set. *Journal of Neurology, Neurosurgery, and Psychiatry, 48,* 517–529.

Folstein, M. F., Folstein, S. E., and McHugh, P. R. (1975). "Mini-mental state": A practical method for grading the cognitive state of patients for the clinician. *Journal of Psychiatric Research, 12,* 189–198.

Francis, A. F. (1979). Familial basal ganglia calcification and schizophreniform psychosis. *British Journal of Psychiatry, 135,* 360–362.

Freedman, M., Rivoira, P., Butters, N., Sax, D. S., and Feldman, R. G. (1984). Retrograde amnesia in Parkinson's disease. *Canadian Journal of Neurological Sciences, 11,* 297–301.

Friede, R. L., Magee, K. R., and Mack, E. W. (1961). Idiopathic nonarteriosclerotic calcification of the cerebral vessels. *Archives of Neurology, 5,* 279–286.

Frith, C. D., Bloxham, C. A., and Carpenter, K. N. (1986). Impairments in the learning and performance of a new manual skill in patients with Parkinson's disease. *Journal of Neurology, Neurosurgery, and Psychiatry, 49,* 661–668.

Gancher, S. T. (1992). Pharmacology of Parkinson's disease. In S. J. Huber and J. L. Cummings, eds., *Parkinson's Disease: Neurobehavioral Aspects.* New York: Oxford University Press, pp. 273–287.

Gaspar, P., and Grey, E. (1984). Dementia in idiopathic Parkinson's disease. *Acta Neuropathologica, 64,* 43–52.

Gibb, W.R.G. (1989). Dementia and Parkinson's disease. *British Journal of Psychiatry, 154,* 596–614.

Gilbert, J. J., and Feldman, R. G. (1969). L-dopa for progressive supranuclear palsy. *Lancet, 2,* 494.

Girotti, F., Soliveri, P., Carella, F., Piccolo, I., Caffarra, P., Musicco, M., and Caraceni, T. (1988). Dementia and cognitive impairment in Parkinson's disease. *Journal of Neurology, Neurosurgery, and Psychiatry, 51,* 1498–1502.

Globus, M., Mildworf, B., and Melamed, E. (1985). Cerebral blood flow and cognitive impairment in Parkinson's disease. *Neurology, 35,* 1135–1139.

Golbe, L. I., Davis, P. H., Schoenberg, B. S., and Duvoisin, R. C. (1988). Prevalence and natural history of progressive supranuclear palsy. *Neurology, 38,* 1031–1034.

Goldenberg, G., Wimmer, A., Auff, E., and Schnaberth, G. (1986). Impairment of motor planning in patients with Parkinson's disease: Evidence from ideomotor apraxia testing. *Journal of Neurology, Neurosurgery, and Psychiatry, 49,* 1266–1272.

Gotham, A. M., Brown, R. G., and Marsden, C. D. (1986). Depression in Parkinson's disease: A quantitative and qualitative analysis. *Journal of Neurology, Neurosurgery, and Psychiatry, 49,* 381–389.

Grafman, J., Litvan, I., Gomez, C., and Chase, T. N. (1990). Frontal lobe function in progressive supranuclear palsy. *Archives of Neurology, 47,* 553–558.

Gross, M. (1969). L-dopa for progressive supranuclear palsy. *Lancet, 2,* 1359–1360.

Guthrie, T. C., Dunbar, H. S., and Weider, A. (1970). L-Dopa: Effect on highest integrative functions in Parkinsonism. *Transactions of the American Neurological Association, 95,* 250–252.

Haldeman, S., Goldman, J. W., Hyde, J., and Pribram, H.F.W. (1981). Progressive supranuclear palsy, computed tomography, and response to antiparkinsonian drugs. *Neurology, 31,* 442–445.

Henderson, R., Kurlan, R., Kersun, J. M., and Como, P. (1992). Preliminary examination of the comorbidity of anxiety and depression in Parkinson's disease. *Journal of Neuropsychiatry and Clinical Neurosciences, 4,* 257–264.

Heston, L. L. (1980). Dementia associated with Parkinson's disease: A genetic study. *Journal of Neurology, Neurosurgery, and Psychiatry, 43,* 846–848.

Heston, L. L. (1981). Genetic studies of dementia with emphasis on Parkinson's disease and Alzheimer's neuropathology. In J. A. Mortimer and L. M. Schuman, eds., *The Epidemiology of Dementia.* New York: Oxford University Press, pp. 101–114.

Hietanen, M., and Teravainen, H. (1986). The effect of age of disease onset on neuropsychological performance in Parkinson's disease. *Journal of Neurology, Neurosurgery, and Psychiatry, 51,* 244–249.

Hornykiewicz, O. (1973). Parkinson's disease: From brain homogenate to treatment. *Federation Proceedings, 32,* 183–190.

Hovestadt, A., de Jong, G. J., and Meerwaldt, J. D. (1987). Spatial disorientation as an early symptom of Parkinson's disease. *Neurology, 37,* 485–487.

Huber, S. J., Freidenberg, D. L., Shuttleworth, E. C., Paulson, G. W., and Christy, J. A. (1989). Neuropsychological impairments associated with severity of Parkinson's disease. *Journal of Neuropsychiatry and Clinical Neurosciences, 1,* 155–159.

Huber, S. J., Freidenberg, D. L., Paulson, G. W., Shuttleworth, E. C., and Christy, J. A. (1990). The pattern of depressive symptoms varies with progression of Parkinson's disease. *Journal of Neurology, Neurosurgery, and Psychiatry, 53,* 275–278.

Huber, S. J., Shuttleworth, E. C., Paulson, G. W., Bellchambers, M.G.J., and Clapp, L. E. (1986). Cortical vs. subcortical dementia. Neuropsychological differences. *Archives of Neurology, 43,* 392–394.

Illes, J., Metter, E. J., Hanson, W. R., and Iritani, S. (1988). Language production in Parkinson's disease: Acoustic and linguistic considerations. *Brain and Language, 33,* 146–160.

Jankovic, J. (1984). Progressive supranuclear palsy: Clinical and pharmacologic update. *Neurologic Clinics, 2,* 473–486.

Javoy-Agid, F., and Agid, Y. (1980). Is the mesocortical dopaminergic system involved in Parkinson disease? *Neurology, 30,* 1326–1330.

Jellinger, K., and Riederer, P. (1984). Dementia in Parkinson's disease and (pre)-senile dementia of Alzheimer type: Morphological aspects and changes in the intracerebral MAO activity. *Advances in Neurology, 40,* 199–210.

Jenkins, R. B. (1969). L-dopa for progressive supranuclear palsy. *Lancet, 2,* 742.

Kalambonkis, Z., and Molling, P. (1962). Symmetrical calcification of the brain in the predominance in the basal ganglia and cerebellum. *Journal of Neuropathology and Experimental Neurology, 21,* 364–371.

Khurana, R. K., Nelson, G., Azzarelli, B., and Garcia, J. H. (1980). Shy-Drager syndrome: Diagnosis and treatment of cholinergic dysfunction. *Neurology, 30,* 805–809.

Kish, S. J., Chang, L. J., Mirchandani, L., Shannak, K., and Hornykiewicz, O. (1985). Progressive supranuclear palsy: Relationship between extrapyramidal disturbances, dementia, and brain neurotransmitter markers. *Annals of Neurology, 18,* 530–536.

Kish, S. J., el-Awar, M., Schut, L., Leach, L., Oscar-Berman, M., and Freedman, M. (1988a). Cognitive deficits in olivopontocerebellar atrophy: Implications for the cholinergic hypothesis of Alzheimer's dementia. *Annals of Neurology, 24,* 200–206.

Kish, S. J., Shannak, K., and Hornykiewicz, O. (1988b). Elevated serotonin and reduced dopamine in subregionally divided Huntington's disease striatum. *Annals of Neurology, 22,* 386–389.

Klawans, H. L., Jr., and Ringel, S.D.P. (1971). Observations on the efficacy of L-dopa in progressive supranuclear palsy. *European Neurology, 5,* 115–129.

Kluin, K. J., Gilman, S., Markel, D. S., Koeppe, R. A., Rosenthal, G., and Junck, L. (1988). Speech disorders in olivopontocerebellar atrophy correlate with positron emission tomography findings. *Annals of Neurology, 23,* 547–554.

Koller, W. C. (1987). Classification of Parkinsonism. In W. C. Koller, ed., *Handbook of Parkinson's Disease.* New York: Marcel Dekker, pp. 51–80.

Korczyn, A. D. (1990). Autonomic nervous system disturbances in Parkinson's disease. *Advances in Neurology, 53,* 463–468.

Kurland, L. T. (1958). Epidemiology: Incidence, geographic distribution, and genetic considerations. In W. J. Field, ed., *Pathogenesis and*

Treatment of Parkinsonism. Springfield: Charles C. Thomas, pp. 5–43.

Lang, A. E., Quinn, N., Brincat, S., Marsden, C. D., and Parkes, J. D. (1982). Pergolide in late-stage Parkinson's disease. *Annals of Neurology, 12,* 243–247.

Langston, J. W., and Forno, L. S. (1978). The hypothalamus in Parkinson's disease. *Annals of Neurology, 3,* 129–133.

La Rue, A. (1992). *Aging and Neuropsychological Assessment.* New York: Plenum.

Lees, A. J., and Smith, E. (1983). Cognitive deficits in the early stages of Parkinson's disease. *Brain, 106,* 257–270.

Levin, B. E., Llabre, M. M., and Weiner, W. J. (1988). Parkinson's disease and depression: Psychometric properties of the Beck Depression Inventory. *Journal of Neurology, Neurosurgery, and Psychiatry, 51,* 1401–1404.

Levin, B. E., Llabre, M. M., and Weiner, W. J. (1989). Cognitive impairments associated with early Parkinson's disease. *Neurology, 39,* 557–561.

Levin, B. E., Tomer, R., and Rey, G. J. (1992). Cognitive impairments in Parkinson's disease. *Neurologic Clinics, 10,* 471–485.

Lieberman, A., Dziatolowski, M., Kupersmith, M., Serby, M., Goodgold, A., Korein, J., and Goldstein, M. (1979). Dementia in Parkinson's disease. *Annals of Neurology, 6,* 355–359.

Litvan, I., Grafman, J., Gomez, C., and Chase, T. N. (1989). Memory impairment in patients with progressive supranuclear palsy. *Archives of Neurology, 46,* 765–767.

Locke, S., and Foley, J. M. (1960). A case of cerebellar ataxia with a discussion of classification. *Archives of Neurology, 3,* 279–289.

Maher, E. R., Smith, E. M., and Lees, A. J. (1985). Cognitive deficits in the Steele-Richardson-Olszewski syndrome (progressive supranuclear palsy). *Journal of Neurology, Neurosurgery, and Psychiatry, 48,* 1234–1239.

Mann, D.M.A., and Yates, P. O. (1983). Pathological basis for neurotransmitter changes in Parkinson's disease. *Neuropathology and Applied Neurobiology, 9,* 3–19.

Markham, C. H., and Diamond, S. G. (1986). Pergolide: A double-blind trial as adjunct therapy in Parkinson's disease. In S. Fahn, C. D. Marsden, P. Jenner, and P. Teychenne, eds., *Recent Developments in Parkinson's Disease.* New York: Raven Press, pp. 331–337.

Marsh, G. G., Markham, C. M., and Ansel, R. (1971). Levodopa's awakening effect on patients with Parkinsonism. *Journal of Neurology, Neurosurgery, and Psychiatry, 34,* 209–218.

Marttila, R. J. (1987). Epidemiology. In W. C. Koller, ed., *Handbook of Parkinson's Disease.* New York: Marcel Dekker, pp. 35–50.

Massman, P. J., Delis, D. C., Butters, N., Levin, B. E., and Salmon, D. P. (1990). Are all subcortical dementias alike?: Verbal learning and memory in Parkinson's and Huntington's disease patients. *Journal of Clinical and Experimental Neuropsychology, 12,* 729–744.

Mastaglia, F. L., Grainger, K.M.R., Kee, F., Sadka, M., and Lefroy, R. (1973). Progressive supranuclear palsy (the Steele-Richardson-Olszewski syndrome) clinical and electrophysiological observations in eleven cases. *Proceedings of the Australian Association of Neurologists, 10,* 35–44.

Matison, R., Mayeux, R., Rosen, J., and Fahn, S. (1982). "Tip-of-the-tongue" phenomenon in Parkinson's disease. *Neurology, 32,* 567–570.

Mayeux, R., Stern, Y., Rosen, J., and Leventhal, J. (1981). Depression, intellectual impairment and Parkinson's disease. *Neurology, 31,* 645–650.

McDowell, F. H., Lee, J. E., and Sweet, R. D. (1978). Extrapyramidal disorders. In A. B. Baker and L. H. Baker, eds., *Clinical Neurology.* New York: Harper and Row, pp. 1–67.

Meier, M. J., and Martin, W. E. (1970). Intellectual changes associated with levodopa therapy. *Journal of the American Medical Association, 213,* 465–466.

Mendell, J. R., Chase, T. N., and Engle, W. K. (1970). Modification by L-dopa of a case of progressive supranuclear palsy. With evidence of defective cerebral dopamine metabolism. *Lancet, 1,* 593–594.

Milberg, W., and Albert, M. (1989). Cognitive differences between patients with progressive supranuclear palsy and Alzheimer's disease. *Journal of Clinical and Experimental Neuropsychology, 11,* 605–614.

Miller, E. (1985). Possible frontal impairments in Parkinson's disease: A test using a measure of verbal fluency. *British Journal of Clinical Psychology, 24,* 211–212.

Milner, B. (1963). Effects of different brain lesions on card sorting: The role of frontal lobes. *Archives of Neurology, 9,* 90–100.

Morel-Maroger, A. (1977). Effects of levodopa on "frontal" signs in parkinsonism. *British Medical Journal, 2,* 1543–1544.

Mortimer, J. A., Pirozzolo, F. J., Hansch, E. C., and Webster, D. D. (1982). Relationship of motor symptoms to intellectual deficits in Parkinson disease. *Neurology, 32,* 133–137.

Moskowitz, M. A., Winickoff, R. N., and Heinz,

E. R. (1971). Familial calcification of the basal ganglions: A metabolic and genetic study. *New England Journal of Medicine, 285,* 72–77.

Naito, H., and Oyanagi, S. (1982). Familial myoclonus epilepsy and choreoathetosis: Hereditary dentatorubral-pallidoluysian atrophy. *Neurology, 32,* 798–807.

Neophytides, A., Lieberman, A. N., Goldstein, M., Gopinathan, G., Liebowitz, M., Bock, J., and Walker, R. (1982). The use of lisuride, a potent dopamine and serotonin agonist, in the treatment of progressive supranuclear palsy. *Journal of Neurology, Neurosurgery, and Psychiatry, 45,* 261–263.

Neumann, M. A. (1963). Iron and calcium dysmetabolism in the brain. *Journal of Neuropathology and Experimental Neurology, 19,* 370–382.

O'Brien, C., Sung, J. H., McGeachie, R. E., and Lee, M. C. (1990). Striatonigral degeneration: Clinical, MRI, and pathologic correlation. *Neurology, 40,* 710–711.

Olanow, C. W., and Alberts, M. J. (1986). Double-blind controlled study of pergolide mesylate in the treatment of Parkinson's disease. In S. Fahn, C. D. Marsden, P. Jenner, and P. Teychenne, eds., *Recent Developments in Parkinson's Disease.* New York: Raven Press, pp. 315–321.

Peppard, R. F., Martin, W.R.W, Carr, G. D., Grochowski, E., Schulzer, M., Guttman, M., McGeer, P. L., Phillips, A. G., Tsui, J.K.C., and Calne, D. B. (1992). Cerebral glucose metabolism in Parkinson's disease with and without dementia. *Archives of Neurology, 49,* 1262–1268.

Perry, E. K., Curtis, M., Dick, D. J., Candy, J. M., Atack, J. R., Bloxham, C. A., Blessed, G., Fairburn, A., Thomlinson, B. E., and Perry, R. H. (1985). Cholinergic correlates of cognitive impairment in Parkinson's disease: Comparisons with Alzheimer's disease. *Journal of Neurology, Neurosurgery, and Psychiatry, 48,* 413–421.

Perry, R. H., Tomlinson, B. E., Candy, J. M., Blessed, G., Foster, J. F., Bloxham, C. A., and Perry, E. R. (1983). Cortical cholinergic deficit in mentally impaired Parkinsonian patients. *Lancet, 2,* 789–790.

Perry, T. L., Hansen, S., and Jones, K. (1988). Brain amino acids and glutathione in progressive supranuclear palsy. *Neurology, 38,* 943–946.

Piccirilli, M., Piccinin, G. L., and Agostini, L. (1981). Neuropsychological analysis of the frontal lobe functions in subjects with idiopathic

Parkinson's disease. *Pharmacology, 22,* 82–83.

Piccirilli, M., Piccinin, G. L., and Agostini, L. (1984). Characteristic clinical aspects of Parkinson patients with intellectual impairment. *European Neurology, 23,* 44–50.

Pierot, L., Desnos, C., Blin, J., Raisman, R., Scherman, D., Javoy-Agid, F., Ruberg, M., and Agid, Y. (1988). D_1 and D_2-type dopamine receptors in patients with Parkinson's disease and progressive supranuclear palsy. *Journal of the Neurological Sciences, 86,* 291–306.

Pilleri, G. (1966). A case of Morbus Fahr (nonarteriosclerotic, idiopathic intracerebral calcification of the blood vessels) in three generations. A clinico-anatomical contribution. *Psychiatria et Neurologia, 152,* 43–58.

Pillon, B., Dubois, B., Lhermitte, F., and Agid, Y. (1986). Heterogeneity of cognitive impairment in progressive supranuclear palsy, Parkinson's disease, and Alzheimer's disease. *Neurology, 36,* 1179–1185.

Pillon, B., Dubois, B., Ploska, A., and Agid, Y. (1991). Severity and specificity of cognitive impairment in Alzheimer's, Huntington's, and Parkinson's diseases and progressive supranuclear palsy. *Neurology, 41,* 634–643.

Pirozzolo, F. J., Hansch, E. C., Mortimer, J. A., Webster, D. D., and Kuskowski, A. (1982). Dementia in Parkinson's disease: A neuropsychological analysis. *Brain and Cognition, 1,* 71–83.

Plaitakis, A., Nicklas, W. J., and Desnick, R. J. (1980). Glutamate dehydrogenase deficiency in three patients with spinocerebellar syndrome. *Annals of Neurology, 7,* 297–303.

Portin, R., Raininko, A., and Rinne, U. K. (1984). Neuropsychological disturbances and cerebral atrophy determined by computerized tomography in parkinsonian patients with long-term levodopa treatment. *Advances in Neurology, 40,* 219–227.

Powell, H. C., London, G. W., and Lampert, P. W. (1974). Neurofibrillary tangles in progressive supranuclear palsy. Electron microscopic observations. *Journal of Neuropathology and Experimental Neurology, 33,* 98–106.

Price, K. S., Farley, I., and Hornykiewicz, O. (1978). Neurochemistry of Parkinson's disease: Relation between striatal and limbic dopamine. *Advances in Biochemical Psychopharmacology, 19,* 293–300.

Proctor, F., Riklan, M., Cooper, I., and Teuber, H. (1964). Judgment of visual and postural vertical tilt by parkinsonian patients. *Neurology, 14,* 287–293.

Rafal, R. D., and Grimm, R. J. (1981). Progressive

supranuclear palsy: Functional analysis of the response to methysergide and antiparkinsonian agents. *Neurology, 31,* 1507–1518.

Rajput, A. H., Offord, K. P., Beard, C. M., and Kurland, L. T. (1984). A case-control study of smoking habits, dementia, and other illnesses in idiopathic Parkinson's disease. *Neurology, 37,* 226–232.

Ransmayr, G., Poewe, W., Ploerer, S., Birbamer, G., and Gerstenbrand, F. (1987). Psychometric findings in clinical subtypes of Parkinson's disease. *Advances in Neurology, 45,* 409–411.

Richards, M., Cote, L. J., and Stern, Y. (1993). Executive function in Parkinson's disease: Set shifting or set maintenance? *Journal of Clinical and Experimental Neuropsychology, 15,* 266–279.

Riklan, M., Whelihan, W., and Cullinan, T. (1976). Levodopa and psychometric test performance in parkinsonism: Five years later. *Neurology, 26,* 173–179.

Rogers, D., Lees, A. J., Smith, E., Trimble, M., and Stern, G. M. (1987). Bradyphrenia in Parkinson's disease and psychomotor retardation in depressive illness. *Brain, 110,* 761–766.

Rondot, P., de Recondo, J., Coignet, A., and Ziegler, M. (1984). Mental disorders in Parkinson's disease after treatment with L-dopa. *Advances in Neurology, 40,* 259–269.

Rosenthal, G., Gilman, S., Koeppe, R. A., Kluin, K. J., Markel, D. S., Junck, L., and Gebarski, S. S. (1988). Motor dysfunction in olivopontocerebellar atrophy is related to cerebral metabolic rate studied with positron emission tomography. *Annals of Neurology, 24,* 414–419.

Roy, S., Datta, C. K., Hirano, A., Ghatak, N. R., and Zimmerman, H. M. (1974). Electron microscopic study of neurofibrillary tangles in Steele-Richardson-Olszewski syndrome. *Acta Neuropathologica, 29,* 175–179.

Ruberg, R. M., Javoy-Agid, F., Hirsch, E., Scatton, B., LHeureux, R., Hauw, J.-J., Duyckaerts, C., Gray, F., Morel-Maroger, A., Rascol, A., Serdaru, M., and Agid, Y. (1985). Dopaminergic and cholinergic lesions in progressive supranuclear palsy. *Annals of Neurology, 18,* 523–529.

Scatton, B., Javoy-Agid, F., Rouquier, L., Dubois, B., and Agid, Y. (1983). Reduction of cortical dopamine, noradrenaline, serotonin and their metabolites in Parkinson's disease. *Brain Research, 275,* 321–328.

Scatton, B., Rouquier, L., Javoy-Agid, F., and Agid, Y. (1982). Dopamine deficiency in the cerebral cortex in Parkinson's disease. *Neurology, 32,* 1039–1040.

Schiffer, R. B., Kurlan, R., Rubin, A., and Boer, S. (1988). Evidence for atypical depression in Parkinson's disease. *American Journal of Psychiatry, 145,* 1020–1022.

Schoenberg, B. S., Anderson, D. W., and Haerer, A. F. (1985). Prevalence of Parkinson's disease in the biracial population of Copiah County, Mississippi. *Neurology, 35,* 841–845.

Selby, G. (1968). Parkinson's disease. In P. J. Vinken and G. W. Bruyn, eds., *Diseases of the Basal Ganglia/VI, Handbook of Clinical Neurology.* New York: American Elsevier, pp. 173–211.

Sharpe, M. H., Cermak, S. A., and Sax, D. S. (1983). Motor planning in Parkinson's patients. *Neuropsychologia, 21,* 455–462.

Shy, G. M., and Drager, G. A. (1960). A neurological syndrome associated with orthostatic hypotension. *Archives of Neurology, 2,* 511–527.

Slyter, H. (1979). Idiopathic hypoparathyroidism presenting as dementia. *Neurology, 29,* 393–394.

Snow, B. J. (1992). Positron emission tomography in Parkinson's disease. *The Canadian Journal of Neurological Sciences, 19* (Suppl. 1), 138–141.

Sourkes, T. L. (1976). Parkinson's disease and other disorders of the basal ganglia. In G. J. Siegel, R. W. Albers, R. Katzman, and B. W. Agranoff, eds., *Basic Neurochemistry/II.* Boston: Little, Brown, pp. 668–684.

Stacy, M., and Jankovic, J. (1992). Differential diagnosis of Parkinson's disease and the parkinsonian plus syndromes. *Neurologic Clinics, 10,* 341–359.

Starkstein, S. E., Bolduc, P. L., Preziosi, T. J., and Robinson, R. G. (1989a). Cognitive impairments in different stages of Parkinson's disease. *Journal of Neuropsychiatry and Clinical Neurosciences, 1,* 243–248.

Starkstein, S. E., Mayberg, H. S., Leiguarda, R., Preziosi, T. J., and Robinson, R. G. (1992). A prospective longitudinal study of depression, cognitive decline, and physical impairments in patients with Parkinson's disease. *Journal of Neurology, Neurosurgery, and Psychiatry, 55,* 377–382.

Starkstein, S. E., Rabins, P. J., Berthier, M. L., Cohen, B. J., Folstein, M. F., and Robinson, R. G. (1989b). Dementia of depression among patients with neurological disorders and functional depression. *Journal of Neuropsychiatry and Clinical Neurosciences, 1,* 263–268.

Steele, J. C. (1972). Progressive supranuclear palsy. *Brain, 95,* 693–704.

Steele, J. C., Richardson, J. C., and Olszewski,

J. (1964). Progressive supranuclear palsy. *Archives of Neurology, 10,* 333–359.

Stein, M. B., Heuser, I. J., Juncos, J. L., and Uhde, T. W. (1990). Anxiety disorders in patients with Parkinson's disease. *American Journal of Psychiatry, 147,* 217–220.

Stern, Y., and Langston, J. W. (1985). Intellectual changes in patients with MPTP-induced parkinsonism. *Neurology, 35,* 1506–1509.

Stern, Y., Mayeux, R., and Rosen, J. (1984). Contribution of perceptual motor dysfunction to construction and tracing disturbances in Parkinson's disease. *Journal of Neurology, Neurosurgery, and Psychiatry, 47,* 983–989.

Tanner, C. M. (1992). Epidemiology of Parkinson's disease. *Neurologic Clinics, 10,* 317–329.

Taylor, A. E., and Saint-Cyr, J. A. (1992). Executive function. In S. J. Huber and J. L. Cummings, eds., *Parkinson's Disease: Neurobehavioral Aspects.* New York: Oxford University Press, pp. 74–85.

Taylor, A. E., Saint-Cyr, J. A., and Lang, A. E. (1986a). Frontal lobe dysfunction in Parkinson's disease. The cortical focus of neostriatal outflow. *Brain, 109,* 845–883.

Taylor, A. E., Saint-Cyr, J. A., Lang, A. E., and Kenny, F. T. (1986b). Parkinson's disease and depression: A critical re-evaluation. *Brain, 109,* 279–292.

Tellez-Nagel, I., and Wisniewski, H. M. (1973). Ultrastructure of neurofibrillary tangles in Steele-Richardson-Olszewski syndrome. *Archives of Neurology, 29,* 324–327.

Thomas, J. E., and Schirger, A. (1970). Idiopathic orthostatic hypotension: A study of its natural history in 57 neurologically affected patients. *Archives of Neurology, 22,* 289–293.

Tomonga, M. (1977). Ultrastructure of neurofibrillary tangles in progressive supranuclear palsy. *Acta Neuropathologica, 37,* 177–181.

Turner, B. (1968). Pathology of paralysis agitans. In P. J. Vinken and G. W. Bruyn, eds., *Diseases of the Basal Ganglia/VI, Handbook of Clinical Neurology.* New York: American Elsevier, pp. 211–217.

Villardita, C., Smirni, P., le Pira, F., Zappala, G., and Nicoletti, F. (1982). Mental deterioration, visuoperceptive disabilities and constructional apraxia in Parkinson's disease. *Acta Neurologica Scandanavica, 66,* 112–120.

Wechsler, D. (1945). A standardized memory scale for clinical use. *Journal of Psychology, 19,* 87–95.

Wechsler, D. (1981). *Wechsler Adult Intelligence Scale-Revised.* New York: Psychological Corporation.

Weingartner, H., Burns, S., Diebel, R., and LeWitt, P. A. (1984). Cognitive impairments in Parkinson's disease: Distinguishing between effort-demanding and automatic cognitive processes. *Psychiatry Research, 11,* 223–235.

Wertman, E., Speedie, L., Shemesh, Z., Gilon, D., Raphael, M., and Stessman, J. (1993). Cognitive disturbances in parkinsonian patients with depression. *Neuropsychiatry, Neuropsychology, and Behavioral Neurology, 6,* 31–37.

Whitehouse, P. J. (1986). The concept of subcortical and cortical dementia: Another look. *Annals of Neurology, 19,* 1–6.

Whitehouse, P. J., Martino, A. M., Marcus, K. A., Zweig, R. M., Singer, H. S., Price, D. L., and Kellar, K. J. (1988). Reductions in acetylcholine and nicotine binding in several degenerative diseases. *Archives of Neurology, 45,* 722–724.

Yahr, M. D., Mendoza, M. R., Moros, D., and Bergmann, K. J. (1983). Treatment of Parkinson's disease in early and late phases. Use of pharmacological agents with special reference to deprenyl (selegiline). *Acta Neurologica Scandinavica, 95* (Suppl.), 95–102.

Young, A. (1985). Progressive supranuclear palsy: Postmortem chemical analysis. *Annals of Neurology, 18,* 521–522.

Zweig, R. M., Whitehouse, P. J., Casanova, M. F., Walker, L. C., Jankel, W. R., and Price, D. L. (1987). Loss of pedunculopontine neurons in progressive supranuclear palsy. *Annals of Neurology, 22,* 18–25.

14 Neuropsychological Characteristics of Huntington's Disease

JASON BRANDT and NELSON BUTTERS

Huntington's disease (HD) is a progressive disease of the brain that causes movement abnormalities (especially chorea and dystonia), cognitive deterioration, and affective disturbances. Symptoms typically begin around age 40, with wide variation (Bell, 1934; Heathfield and McKenzie, 1971; Folstein et al., 1987). As in many other neurodegenerative disorders, early onset of HD is associated with more severe disease and a more rapid course. Onset of the disease in childhood is marked by akinesia, rigidity, severe intellectual impairment, and shorter survival (Merritt et al., 1969; Conneally, 1984; Bryois, 1989). Late-onset disease usually presents with severe chorea but milder cognitive impairment, and has a more gradual decline (Myers et al., 1985, 1991). Symptoms of HD progress relentlessly, with patients becoming severely demented, motorically dilapidated, unable to care for themselves, and eventually bedridden. There is no cure for the illness, and the only treatments currently available are either purely palliative or purely experimental. Death occurs an average of 15 to 17 years after disease onset (Folstein, 1989). Huntington's disease causes untold suffering for those afflicted and their loved ones.

Epidemiology and Genetics

Huntington's disease is a genetic condition, inherited as an autosomal dominant trait with complete lifetime penetrance. Each son or daughter of an affected person has a 50% chance of inheriting the gene, and all gene carriers will develop the illness if they live long enough. Estimates of the disease's prevalence range from approximately 5 to 8 per 100,000. If restricted to the population between the ages of 40 and 55, the prevalence rises to 12 per 100,000 (Folstein, 1989; Harper, 1991). It is found all over the world, and no racial or geographic group is exempt (Harper, 1991). There are, however, particular "hot spots" of HD around the world, presumed to be due to founding ancestors and lack of emigration (Penney et al., 1990; Harper, 1991). There also appears to be some phenotypic variation among racial groups (Folstein et al., 1987).

In 1983, the genetic locus for HD was localized to the short arm of chromosome 4 by linkage analysis of a restriction fragment length polymorphism (Gusella et al., 1983). Ten years later, the Huntington's Disease Collaborative Research Group (1993) identified the actual DNA mutation responsible for HD. This mutation consists of the expansion of a region in which there is a sequence of the three nucleotides *cytosine, adenine,* and *guanine* (CAG) that normally repeats between 11 and 34 times. On HD chromosomes, this region expands to more than 37 CAG repeats. The degree of expansion from parent to offspring is variable, but it appears to be greater with paternal than maternal transmission. A greatly expanded gene is associated with early onset of illness (Duyao et al., 1993), as well as more rapid progression (Brandt et al., 1996).

Neuroanatomy, Neurochemistry, and Neuropathology

On postmortem examination of the HD brain, the most obvious neuropathological feature is atrophy of the head of the caudate nucleus and, to a somewhat lesser extent, the putamen (e.g., Dom et al., 1976; Vonsattel et al., 1985). Microscopic analysis in the earliest stages of disease reveals loss of small, spiny neurons in the dorsomedial aspects of the head of the caudate nucleus. As the disease progresses, the entire caudate and putamen become involved (Vonsattel et al., 1985).

Although the major neuropathological changes in HD occur in the striatum, there is also evidence of cortical abnormalities. A significant thinning of the cerebral cortex has been reported by several teams of scientists (Forno and Jose, 1973; de la Monte et al., 1988). When two research groups counted cells in the dorsolateral prefrontal cortex in autopsied brains of HD patients and neurologically normal control subjects, they found a significant loss of neurons in layers III, V, and VI (Hedreen et al., 1991; Sotrel et al., 1991). Thus, the microscopic neuroanatomy of frontal lobes is clearly abnormal in HD and may be significant for understanding of the full clinical syndrome. Whether loss of cortical cells is a primary neuropathological feature of the disease, or is a reaction to loss of striatal neurons that project to the cortex, remains unknown.

A likely explanation for the pathogenesis of HD is provided by the "excitotoxin hypothesis." This hypothesis posits a defect in the N-methyl-D-aspartate (NMDA) subtype of glutamate receptors on striatal neurons (Coyle and Schwarz, 1976; McGeer and McGeer, 1976; Young et al., 1988). Glutamate and aspartate are the primary excitatory neurotransmitters in the brain and are abundant in striatum. Animal research has shown that injections of quinolinic, ibotenic, or kainic acid (analogues of glutamate) result in a pattern of striatal pathology that closely mimics that observed in autopsied HD patients

(Coyle and Schwarz, 1976; McGeer and McGeer, 1976; Hantraye et al., 1990). It is believed that glutamate and its analogues have their toxic effect by prolonged excessive excitation of neurons, which ultimately results in cell death (Albin et al., 1990).

Clinical Descriptions of the Dementia Syndrome

Coincident with the onset of motor signs of HD, features of an incipient dementia syndrome are present (Butters et al., 1978; Fisher et al., 1983; Josiassen et al., 1983; Brandt et al., 1984). Most vulnerable early in the disease are aspects of attention and memory (especially procedural memory), visuomotor and visuographic skill, and executive functions (planning, programming and monitoring of activities, set shifting, and mental flexibility) (Brandt and Butters, 1986; Brandt, 1991a; Brandt and Bylsma, 1993). Less vulnerable, though by no means completely spared, are primary sensory and perceptual abilities, most aspects of language, nonmotor spatial cognition, and recognition memory.

Screening tests for dementia, such as the Mini-Mental State Exam (MMSE) (Folstein et al., 1975), may not be sufficiently sensitive to detect the presence of disabling cognitive impairment in HD patients. Brandt et al. (1996; J. Brandt, F. W. Bylsma, and R. Gross, unpublished data) recently compared the neuropsychological performance of a group of HD patients who performed normally on the MMSE to a small group of people who were at genetic risk for the illness but who were shown by DNA analysis (discussed later) not to have the mutated gene. There were large differences between groups on most measures, with the greatest deficits in the HD group seen on attention-demanding tasks (Table 14-1).

The relationship between the cognitive disorder and the movement disorder of HD has been the subject of several investigators. Brandt et al. (1984) showed that the severity of memory disorder is predicted more accurately by the severity of voluntary motor impairment (and, to a lesser extent, by the

Table 14-1. Cognitive Performance of HD Patients Who Obtained Scores of 30 on the Mini-Mental State Exam and Persons at Risk for HD Who Were Shown by Genetic Analyses Not to Have the Mutated Form of the HD Gene

	Huntington's Disease	Mutation-Negative	p
N	10	11	
Age (yrs.)	47.20	43.09	.404
Education (yrs.)	16.10	14.64	.195
Duration of Illness (yrs.)	4.80	—	N/A
Mini-Mental State Exam	30.00	29.36	N/A
WAIS-R Vocabulary	10.80	11.18	.662
WAIS-R Block Design	8.70	12.45	.011
Brief Test of Attention	12.60	18.18	<.001
Controlled Oral Word Association Test	31.30	38.91	.281
Developmental Test of Visual-Motor			
Integration	37.00	44.18	.047
Hopkins Verbal Learning Test			
Total Recall	21.90	29.91	.001
Recognition Discrimination	10.00	11.64	.012
Stroop Color-Word Test			
Color	29.70	48.18	.001
Word	36.80	49.09	.007
Color-Word	35.30	52.00	<.001
Interference	50.60	53.45	.319
Trail Making Test			
Part A	48.30	25.73	.011
Part B	112.90	56.64	.041
Wisconsin Card Sorting Test			
Sorts	4.90	5.55	.431
Cards/Sort	32.79	22.94	.554
Perseverative Errors	5.40	1.54	.248

Source: From J. Brandt, F. W. Bylsma, and R. Gross (unpublished data; cited in Brandt, 1994).

severity of chorea) than by duration of illness. Girotti et al. (1988) reported that the cognitive performance of HD patients is correlated with their voluntary motor skills (reaction time, movement time, and praxis), but uncorrelated with the severity of involuntary movements (what they called "hyperkinesia"). Heindel and coworkers (Heindel et al., 1988, 1989) found that difficulty acquiring a limb motor skill (pursuit rotor task) correlated significantly with severity of dementia in HD, but not with ratings of chorea and motor disability. Thus, although chorea is a distinguishing feature of HD, it is likely caused by brain mechanisms quite separate from those responsible for the dementia syndrome. This is consistent with the observations of DeLong and associates from electrophysiological and anatomical studies of monkeys that there are distinct corticostriatal circuits subserving motor and cognitive functions (Alexander et al., 1986).

In many (perhaps most) cases of HD, the progressive cognitive impairment, rather than the progressive movement disorder, is the source of impaired daily functioning and disability. Shoulson and Fahn (1979) developed an index of total functional capacity (TFC), based on ratings of dependence in such daily activities as eating, dressing, engagement in occupation, and managing finances. Mayeux et al. (1986) found that cognitive impairment and depression contributed significantly to TFC scores, while duration of illness, degree of motor disability, and age of onset of illness did not. Bamford et al. (1989) also found that cognitive impairment (especially executive dysfunction) contributed more to disability in HD than did the movement disorder.

Unlike the TFC Scale, the HD Activities of Daily Living (HD-ADL) Scale (Folstein, 1989) developed at the Baltimore Huntington's Disease Center is sensitive to disease duration. It also correlates with scores on the Quantified Neurological Exam (QNE) (Brandt et al., 1984; Bylsma et al., 1993). Bylsma et al. (1993) recently reported that the HD-ADL scale is highly correlated with TFC scores ($r = 0.89$) and is more dependent on impaired voluntary movement and cognitive impairment (measured by the MMSE) than severity of chorea. Rothlind et al. (1993b) assessed the cognitive predictors of disability in HD by examining which neuropsychological tests were most highly correlated with HD-ADL score in a large sample of patients ($N = 80$). Performances on the Stroop Color-Word Test, Trail Making Test, and Benton Visual Retention Test (as well as the MMSE) all predicted HD-ADL score, even when the influence of motor impairment was controlled statistically. Interestingly, in this study, the severity of chorea had the lowest correlation of all the variables examined with the functional ability measure.

Comparison of Huntington's Disease With Other Dementia Syndromes

Huntington's disease and Alzheimer's disease (AD) were the first disorders characterized as "subcortical" and "cortical" dementias, respectively (McHugh and Folstein, 1973; Albert et al., 1974; Cummings, 1990). Whereas many of the cognitive impairments seen in HD appear to reflect an inability to initiate cognitive processes (e.g., retrieval of information from long-term memory), the deficits of AD patients represent true amnesias, aphasias, agnosias, and apraxias. To validate this distinction between cortical and subcortical dementias, Brandt et al. (1988) studied large samples of AD patients ($N = 145$) and HD patients ($N = 84$), stratified by overall level of cognitive functioning on the MMSE. Distinctly different cognitive profiles that were independent of severity of dementia were observed in each group.

Specifically, the AD patients had more severe deficits in orientation and short-term memory (recalling three words after a brief intervening task), whereas the HD patients were more impaired on attention-demanding mental arithmetic. The profile differences were sufficiently robust to classify patients as having AD or HD with 84% accuracy using discriminant function analyses. In a small cross-validation sample of 18 AD and 13 HD patients, correct classification was again 84%. Applying the discriminant equation to patients with Parkinson's disease (traditionally described as a subcortical dementia) and Pick's disease (classified as a cortical dementia) resulted in the Parkinson's patients being classified with the HD patients and the Pick's patients being classified with the AD patients. These results suggest that the qualitative differences in cognitive functioning seen in AD and HD might be typical of the cortical and subcortical dementias more generally. Salmon et al. (1989) subsequently reported results similar to Brandt et al. (1988) using the Dementia Rating Scale (DRS) (Mattis, 1988). They studied 23 HD patients and 23 AD patients, matched for years of education and total score on the DRS. Of the five DRS subscales, the groups differed most on Initiation/Perseveration (with the HD patients lower) and Memory (with the AD patients lower). A discriminant function analysis correctly classified 87% of the total sample.

Longitudinal Studies of Dementia in Huntington's Disease

Given that HD causes a progressive dementia, it is surprising that longitudinal studies of cognition in this disorder are so few in number. Folstein (1989) noted great variability in the rate of change on the MMSE in a series of patients followed longitudinally in the Baltimore HD Center Clinic. She reported that education and duration of illness were the strongest predictors of MMSE scores at any given point in time.

Brandt et al. (1993; cited in Brandt, 1994) examined the baseline and 1-year follow-up performance of 52 HD patients on the neuro-psychological test battery listed in Table 14-1. Given the frequent clinical observation that early-onset patients decline more rapidly than later-onset patients, the cohort was divided into two groups at the median age-of-onset (40 years). The 28 early-onset cases did not differ significantly from the 24 later-onset cases in education, duration of illness, or MMSE scores at visit 1. Interestingly, the only test for which there was a main effect of visit (i.e., worse performance after 1 year) was the MMSE. However, there were significant age-of-onset by visit interactions for the Brief Test of Attention (Schretlen and Bobholz, 1992) and the Hopkins Verbal Learning Test (Brandt, 1991b). On both of these measures, which are extremely sensitive to the presence of HD (see Table 14-1), early-onset patients declined; later-onset patients actually improved slightly when tested one year later. New verbal learning and divided attention may be particularly vulnerable to the neostriatal degeneration that takes place in this disease, and does so more rapidly (for reasons yet unknown) in early-onset cases.

Hodges et al. (1990) studied the decline of HD patients on tests of episodic and semantic memory over a 1-year period. The HD group was compared to a group of AD patients, matched for overall dementia severity. Unlike the AD group, the HD group displayed no decline on the Boston Naming Test, the Similarities subtest of the WAIS-R and a Number Information Test (tests of semantic memory) over the 12 months. Conversely, the HD group declined significantly on a letter fluency task but not on the category fluency task; the opposite pattern was observed in the AD group. The significance of differences in verbal fluency performance is addressed more thoroughly later in this chapter.

Specific Cognitive Functions

Attention and Concentration

Attention-demanding cognitive operations are among the first to deteriorate in HD.

Although there are few, if any, psychometric tests that assess aspects of attention in isolation, attentional difficulties can be inferred from poor performance on traditional tests. It has consistently been demonstrated, for example, that HD patients perform most poorly on subtests of the WAIS and WAIS-R that comprise the concentration or "freedom from distraction" factor (Arithmetic, Digit Span, and Digit Symbol) (Boll et al., 1974; Butters et al., 1978; Fedio et al., 1979; Josiassen et al., 1983; Brandt et al., 1984; Strauss and Brandt, 1986). Several research teams have commented on the severe difficulty HD patients have on tests of mental arithmetic (Caine et al., 1986; Brandt et al., 1988), a finding that may implicate attentional dysregulation. It also appears that complex attentional tasks, such as the Stroop Color-Word Test and the Brief Test of Attention are among the most sensitive tasks in early HD (see Table 14-1), and show the most decline over time.

Language

Despite the progressive nature of the dementia of HD, clinically significant aphasia is rarely seen. This stands in marked contrast to the dementia of AD, and may serve as a distinguishing feature of the cortical and subcortical dementias more generally (Cummings, 1990; Folstein et al., 1990). Nevertheless, motor speech impairments are typical of this illness. Dysarthria and dysprosodia are most common, affecting approximately 50% of early-stage patients. These speech disorders become more pronounced as the disease progresses, often precluding intelligible communication late in the disease (Gordon and Illes, 1987; Ludlow et al., 1987; Podoll et al., 1988; Wallesch and Fehrenbach, 1988; Illes, 1989). HD patients are also impaired in the comprehension of both affective and propositional prosody (Speedie et al., 1990).

Although HD patients do not typically have classical aphasia syndromes, they do develop specific abnormalities in the use of language. Caine et al. (1986) compared patients with HD to those with multiple sclerosis, another neurological disease in which subcortical lesions predominate. The HD group was found to be more impaired than the MS group in visual confrontation naming, repetition, and narrative language. Like patients with frontal lobe lesions (Alexander et al., 1989), HD patients initiate verbal communication less often, and participate little in ongoing conversations. They tend to have long response latencies to questions and pronounced intervals between phrases, resulting in conversation that is interspersed with long gaps of silence. Syntactic complexity of both spoken and written sentences becomes reduced, and phrase length is progressively restricted (Podoll et al., 1988). In advanced HD, spoken language consists of single words or short phrases that often do not constitute complete sentences. In contrast with the marked reduction in complexity, syntactic structure remains correct and speech content is usually appropriate until very advanced illness (Gordon and Illes, 1987; Podoll et al., 1988; Illes, 1989).

Early in the course of HD, reduced language generativity is evident on tasks such as the Controlled Oral Word Association Test ("FAS") (Borkowski et al., 1967) and category fluency tasks (e.g., naming of animals, fruits, and vegetables) (Butters et al., 1978, 1986, 1987). When HD and AD patients matched for overall level of dementia are compared on word list generation tasks, significant differences have often been found (Butters et al., 1987; Monsch et al., 1994). Patients with HD are impaired equally on letter and category fluency tasks, whereas AD patients are more impaired on category than on letter fluency (cf. Barr and Brandt, 1993). Indices of sensitivity and specificity have shown that letter and category fluency have equivalent psychometric value in differentiating HD patients from normal individuals. However, for early- and middle-stage AD patients, category fluency is far superior to letter fluency in distinguishing patients from healthy elderly individuals (Monsch et al., 1994). A likely explanation for these group differences on fluency tasks involves the disruption of retrieval processes and the deterioration of the structure of semantic knowledge in HD

and AD. Because HD patients have marked deficits in retrieval and little, if any, breakdown in semantic knowledge, they encounter as much difficulty retrieving and generating exemplars of "animals" as "words beginning with the letter *F*." AD patients, on the other hand, appear to suffer a bottom-up breakdown in the structure of semantic knowledge (Martin and Fedio, 1983). Thus, they have difficulty with fluency tasks that require some knowledge of the hierarchically organized semantic associations underlying such concepts as *animals, fruits,* and *vegetables.*

Further evidence in support of this explanation has been reported by Randolph et al. (1993). They compared HD and AD patients on a standard (uncued) category fluency task and a version of the task where patients were cued every 15 seconds with subcategories (e.g., "fruits and vegetables," "meat and seafood," "things people drink," and "household cleaning products" for the category *items found in a supermarket*). Although both HD and AD patients were severely impaired on the standard uncued version, the HD, but not the AD, patients' performance improved markedly when subcategory cues were provided. Also, the AD, but not the HD, patients' fluency scores correlated significantly with their scores on a confrontation naming test. Randolph and coworkers concluded that the HD patients' failures on category fluency are the result of retrieval deficits, whereas the AD patients' poor fluency scores reflect degraded knowledge of concepts and semantic categories.

In addition to the total number of correct words generated on fluency tests, the words produced by HD patients are often qualitatively different from those generated by other brain-disordered patients. Butters et al. (1986, 1987) showed that HD patients make many fewer perseverative responses than do AD patients or patients with alcoholic Korsakoff's syndrome (KS). In addition, intrusion errors, which permeate the performance of AD patients on verbal fluency tests (Fuld et al., 1982), are rarer in HD patients (Butters et al., 1987).

On semantic fluency tasks, mildly demented HD patients, like healthy subjects, tend to report category exemplars (e.g., "veal, beef, pork"), whereas AD patients tend to produce higher-order category labels (e.g., "meats, vegetables, fruits"). This suggests that AD patients, but not HD patients, lose the ability to make fine discriminations within broad semantic classes (Martin and Fedio, 1983). Similarly, Randolph (1991) has shown that the word associations of HD patients remain similar to those of healthy subjects, whereas equivalently demented AD patients give responses that are lower in associative frequency (i.e., more idiosyncratic responses). However, Tröster et al. (1989) reported that in more advanced HD patients, the ratio of items reported to categories sampled can be as low as that of AD patients. These data are among the first to suggest some disruption in the semantic system of HD patients. Smith et al. (1988) reached a similar conclusion about lexical semantics in HD based on the WAIS-R Vocabulary subtest and the Boston Naming Test (BNT) (Kaplan et al., 1978), and tests of associative fluency and semantic priming. Thus, in the later stages of HD, some mild deterioration in the structure of semantic knowledge may occur. However, this breakdown is not nearly as severe as that seen in AD.

Contrary to early reports (e.g., Butters et al., 1978), confrontation naming is clearly affected in HD (Caine et al., 1986; Smith et al., 1988). Performance on the BNT and similar tests becomes poorer as the disease progresses, but patients' errors are rarely paraphasic in nature until the advanced stages. More often, patients misperceive the stimulus drawings or give responses based on only a portion of the stimuli (Butters et al., 1978; Bayles and Tomoeda, 1983; Podoll et al., 1988; Hodges et al., 1991). Although frank visual agnosia is not a cardinal symptom of the cortical dementias, HD patients do demonstrate visuoperceptual deficiencies sufficient to affect their performance on confrontation naming. Hodges et al. (1991) compared the performance of 16 HD patients, 52 AD patients, and 52 healthy control subjects on the BNT. In addition to recording the number of errors made by each individual, Hodges and colleagues classified errors as visual, semantic-superordinate, semantic-associative, or phonemic. A double dissociation was found between patient group and error type. AD patients made more semantic-superordinate errors (e.g., calling a *harmonica* a "musical instrument") and semantic-associative errors (e.g., responding with "ice" when shown a picture of an *igloo*), whereas HD patients made more visual errors (e.g., calling a *stethoscope* a "tie"). This dissociation was apparent even when the two patient groups were equated for total number of errors. In an earlier investigation, Podoll et al. (1988) found that 65% of all visual confrontation errors made by HD patients suggested impaired visual recognition rather than impaired lexical selection. That is, the errors made by HD patients were due primarily to perceptual rather than linguistic impairments.

Praxis

Shelton and Knopman (1991) attempted to estimate the prevalence of ideomotor apraxia (impaired selection and sequencing of previously learned movements) in HD. Using very conservative criteria for the presence of apraxia, and taking great care to differentiate it from chorea, dystonia, ataxia, and motor impersistence, these investigators found three of nine HD patients but only one out of six AD patients they studied intensively to have unambiguous apraxia. Shelton and Knopman concluded that apraxia is common in HD and is likely caused by a disruption in one or more of the frontal cortex-to-neostriatum loops described by Alexander et al. (1986).

Spatial Cognition

Deficits in visuomotor performance are evident in even mild HD patients, although true constructional apraxia is rarely noted. As shown in Table 14-1, the ability to copy even simple geometric designs (i.e., the Developmental Test of Visual-Motor Integration) is impaired in early-stage HD. Patients early in the disease also take significantly longer than age- and education-matched controls to copy the Rey-Osterrieth Complex Figure and typically produce less-than-adequate renditions (Brouwers et al., 1984). Deficits are also noted on the Block Design and Object Assembly subtests of the WAIS-R, which assess spatial analysis and visuoconstructional abilities.

Visuospatial difficulties in HD are not fully attributable to chorea, as they often appear prior to clinically significant movement disorders (Josiassen et al., 1983). Deficits are also observed on visuospatial tests that do not require speed or motor responses. Using the untimed, motor-free Mosaic Comparisons Test, for example, Fedio and coworkers (1979) found HD patients to be less efficient than normal controls in identifying differences between checkerboard-like grids. In addition, as mentioned earlier, many of the visual confrontation errors of HD patients reflect perceptual misidentifications.

Mohr and associates (1991) administered a battery of six spatial tasks, plus the WAIS-R Performance subtests, to 20 mildly demented HD patients and healthy control subjects. The spatial test battery was reduced by principal components analysis to three factors, together accounting for 70% of the variance. The HD and normal control groups differed significantly on Factor 1 (general visuospatial processing) and Factor 3 (mental rotation and manipulation). They did not differ on Factor 2 (consistency of spatial judgment). Factor 1 was significantly correlated with performance on the Dementia Rating Scale, attesting to its status as a general factor. Only Factor 3, requiring the imagined movement of objects, was correlated with duration of illness.

A major visuospatial defect in HD involves the mental manipulation of personal, or egocentric, space (Brouwers et al., 1984). This was demonstrated vividly in an early experiment by Potegal (1971). Patients with HD and healthy control subjects viewed a visual target on a table; they were then blindfolded and instructed to point to the target. The patients were as accurate as the control subjects in localizing the target when standing

in front of it. Unlike the normal subjects, however, the HD patients were significantly less accurate after moving one step to the left or right. Potegal interpreted this finding as indicating that the caudate pathology of HD interferes with the adjustment of cognitive representation of position in space after self-initiated movements.

Patients with HD are also impaired on tasks where adjustments must be made for imagined alterations in their body positions in space. For example, they perform more poorly on the Standardized Road Map Test of Directional Sense (Money, 1976) than do either normal control subjects or AD patients matched for education and IQ (Fedio et al., 1979; Brouwers et al., 1984). Most significantly, HD patients display their greatest deficits on the "toward" portion of the Road Map test, where greater mental rotation is required (Brouwers et al., 1984).

Bylsma et al. (1992) replicated the finding of impaired Road Map Test performance in HD; although patients made no more errors than control subjects, they required significantly more time to complete the task. Bylsma and coworkers also found early- to mid-stage HD patients to be impaired on a version of the Semmes Route-Walking Task. Patients and control subjects were handed maps depicting routes to be walked in a 9-location grid (3×3) marked on the floor. The routes varied in the number of moves required (from 6 to 11). On half the trials, subjects were required to always orient their bodies forward while traversing the routes (No-Turn condition); on the other half, they were required to turn their bodies in the direction they were traveling (Turn condition). The HD patients were especially impaired on the Turn condition. Because the Turn condition requires the subject to mentally rotate the map to its original position to select the next move, these results support the interpretation of a defect in egocentric, or personal, orientation in HD.

Oscar-Berman and her colleagues have modified tasks typically used in research with nonhuman primates for the study of spatial cognition in HD. One of their first studies found that HD patients who have significant impairments on a visual pattern-reversal learning task perform normally on a spatial-reversal learning task (respond to the left stimulus until it is no longer reinforced, then respond to the right stimulus, and so on) (Oscar-Berman and Zola-Morgan, 1980). The authors were surprised by this finding and suggested that the spatial reversal task might have not have tapped sufficiently the egocentric spatial ability mediated by the caudate nucleus. In a second study, Oscar-Berman and colleagues (1982) found that HD patients who performed normally on a delayed response task were significantly impaired on a delayed spatial alternation task, suggesting that the role of the caudate in memory is most pronounced when there is a spatial component.

Memory

Memory disturbances are a very prominent and early-appearing cognitive feature of HD (Caine et al., 1977, 1986; Butters et al., 1978; Moses et al., 1981). Deficits are displayed in the learning and retention of new information (Caine et al., 1977; Weingartner et al., 1979; Moses et al., 1981), as well as in the retrieval of previously acquired information (Albert, et al., 1981a,b; Brandt, 1985; Beatty et al., 1988). In addition to these problems with explicit memory, there is now considerable evidence that specific forms of implicit memory are also impaired in HD (for review, see Butters et al., 1990a,b).

ANTEROGRADE MEMORY DEFICITS. Early studies of new learning in HD patients found poor recall of verbal material after short delays (Caine et al., 1977; Wilson et al., 1987). HD patients were found to use inadequate elaboration strategies during encoding, resulting in poor storage and subsequent recall of new information (Weingartner et al., 1979). However, later research demonstrated that the encoding deficits of HD patients are not as significant as those of KS or AD patients. Of these three groups, only HD patients benefit from being supplied verbal mediation strategies for enhancing memory

(Butters et al., 1983; Granholm and Butters, 1988). On the other hand, only KS (not HD or AD) patients benefit from longer rehearsal times and restricting the amount of interference during the learning-recall interval (Butters, 1984). These data indicate that the memory deficits experienced by HD patients are not entirely, or even primarily, attributable to encoding difficulties (see also Wilson et al., 1987).

Recent research has suggested relatively preserved recognition of recently presented material, despite marked deficits in recall. Investigators using various paradigms (e.g., free recall of word lists, selective reminding tasks, paired-associate learning) have reported that on-demand recall of new material is often as impaired in HD as in KS or AD (Caine et al., 1977; Butters et al., 1978; Moss et al., 1986; Granholm and Butters, 1988). However, HD patients demonstrate significantly better memory for the same information, often approaching that of healthy controls, when recognition paradigms are used (Caine et al., 1978; Butters et al., 1985, 1986; Moss et al., 1986; but cf. Brandt et al., 1992). These demonstrations of near-normal recognition of material that cannot be recalled explicitly has led to the hypothesis that inefficient retrieval is the major source of poor memory performance in HD (Butters et al., 1978, 1990b; Caine et al., 1978; Butters, 1984).

Three studies using the California Verbal Learning Test (CVLT) (Delis et al., 1987), a standardized verbal list-learning task, have reported similar dissociations between recall and recognition performance in HD (Kramer et al., 1988, 1989; Delis et al., 1991). Although HD patients perform as poorly as do AD and amnesic patients on the five recall trials of the 16-word list, their scores on the 44-item recognition test (16 targets and 28 distractors) are superior to those of the AD and amnesic patients (Delis et al., 1991). It is not certain, however, whether this difference between recognition and recall performance in HD is evident throughout the disease's progression. Kramer et al. (1988) reported that this superiority of recognition memory may be limited to mildly demented HD patients, whereas Brandt et al. (1992) raised the possibility that the phenomenon may be test-specific. The latter investigators found that well-matched groups of AD and HD patients did not differ in recognition accuracy on the Hopkins Verbal Learning Test.

Brandt (1985) used reaction time measures and metamemory judgments in addition to recall and recognition measures in a study of the ability of HD patients to search their long-term memories. Fourteen mildly-to-moderately demented HD patients and normal control subjects attempted to recall items of general information, then made "feeling of knowing" judgments about unrecalled items, and finally attempted to recognize correct answers. The HD patients had impaired recall, but they were as able as healthy subjects to recognize what they could not recall. In addition, they were as accurate as control subjects in predicting whether they could recognize unrecalled information. Unlike normal subjects, however, the HD patients did not spend more time searching for material they believed they were likely to recall than material they believed they were unlikely to recall. These results suggest that the dementia of HD includes a defect in the metamemorial control processes that orchestrate retrieval efforts. Such processes are often considered "executive" in nature, and are thought to be dependent on the integrity of the prefrontal cortex and its striatal connections.

Few studies, aside from those of Oscar-Berman and colleagues described earlier, have examined visuospatial memory in HD. Moss and coworkers (1986) assessed visual recognition of spatial positions, colors, patterns, faces, and words in normal controls and in HD, AD, and KS patients. The HD patients performed significantly worse than normal subjects for all types of memoranda except words, again reinforcing the relative preservation of verbal recognition in HD. Jacobs and colleagues (Jacobs et al., 1990a,b) found immediate visual memory to be only mildly affected in early HD patients. On the Visual Reproductions subtest of the WMS-

R, HD patients recalled and reproduced as many line drawings as control subjects, and significantly more than AD patients matched for level of dementia.

Two other features of HD patients' anterograde memory deficits are of some clinical importance. In comparison to AD and amnesic patients, HD patients make few intrusion errors on recall tasks and manifest relatively intact retention over a 30-minute delay period. On a test of memory for short passages (Butters et al., 1987), on the CVLT (Delis et al., 1991), and on the Visual Reproduction subtest (Jacobs et al., 1990a,b), AD patients produce more intrusion errors than do HD patients. Similarly, studies assessing patients' retention of verbal and figural materials over a 25- to 30-minute delay have found that HD patients forget significantly less information than AD and amnesic patients (Butters et al., 1988; Delis et al., 1991). Massman et al. (1990) reported that when indices of intrusion errors and forgetting rate are combined with the previously noted differences between recall and recognition performance in a discriminant function analysis, HD and AD patients can be differentiated with better than 80% accuracy.

RETROGRADE AMNESIA. Memory for past events in HD is qualitatively different from that in several other memory-disordered populations. For example, KS patients display a marked temporal gradient of retrograde amnesia, with events from the recent past more severely affected than events from the distant past (Albert et al., 1979; Kopelman, 1989). Patients with HD, even early in the course of the disease, are equally impaired in remembering public events from all periods of time (Albert et al., 1981a,b).

Beatty et al. (1988) compared mildly demented HD and AD patients on an updated version of the Boston Remote Memory Battery and essentially replicated the results of Albert et al. (1981a) for HD. These patients produced a "flat" retrograde amnesia profile, whereas the AD patients' retrograde amnesia had a steep temporal gradient. Like the results of verbal recognition studies, these

findings support the hypothesis that a retrieval deficit underlies HD patients' memory impairments. If hampered by a general
inability to retrieve adequately stored information, HD patients would be expected to
have equivalent deficits for all periods of
their lives (Butters and Albert, 1982).

IMPLICIT MEMORY. Implicit memory refers
to a class of performances that indicate the
influence of prior learning episodes but
which, unlike recall and recognition, do not
require the explicit, conscious recollection
of those episodes (Schacter, 1987). Classical
conditioning, lexical and semantic priming,
motor skill acquisition and perceptual learning have each been considered examples of
implicit memory. In each of these cases,
there is a facilitation of performance that
is traceable to prior exposure to stimulus
materials and that does not require the patient's awareness or allocation of attentional
resources. The importance of implicit memory for neuropsychology and neurological
models of memory stems from the frequent
observation that amnesic patients who are
consistently impaired on all traditional (explicit) indices of memory often perform like
healthy subjects when tested with implicit
memory paradigms. Thus, both hippocampal
and diencephalic amnesics who cannot recall
short lists of words after a brief delay can
display normal skill learning and repetition
priming (Milner, 1962; Corkin, 1968; Cohen
and Squire, 1980; Graf et al., 1984;
Schacter, 1987).

With the realization that implicit memory
is not dependent on the integrity of the
limbic/diencephalic memory system, there
has been increasing interest in identifying
the neural substrate for this type of learning.
Toward this end, several studies have compared the performances of AD and HD patients and amnesics on both priming and skill
learning tasks. In general, these studies have
found that although HD patients are unimpaired on most forms of lexical, semantic,
and pictorial priming (Heindel et al., 1989;
Bylsma et al., 1991), they encounter great
difficulty in acquiring motor, visuomotor,
perceptual, and cognitive skills. These obser-

vations have led to the hypothesis that the
neostriatum and its cortical connections are
critical for the acquisition of most forms of
skill-based (i.e., procedural) knowledge.

Martone and collaborators (1984) first reported that HD patients are impaired in the
acquisition of a perceptual skill. Patients with
HD and alcoholic KS patients were administered a task in which mirror-reflected word
triads were shown multiple times on each of
three successive days. The time required to
read each triad served as the measure of skill
acquisition. Following the third day of word
reading, a word recognition test was administered. The results revealed a double dissociation between the two patient groups in skill
learning and recognition. The amnesic KS
patients evidenced unimpaired skill learning
(i.e., their rate of improvement in mirror
reading was normal), but severely impaired
recognition of verbal stimuli. The HD patients, on the other hand, showed normal
recognition performance despite a significant
retardation in rate of skill acquisition.

Heindel and his colleagues (Heindel et al.,
1988, 1989) evaluated HD, AD, and amnesic
patients on a pursuit rotor task. The subjects
were told to try to maintain contact between
a stylus held in the preferred hand and a
small metallic disk on a rotating turntable.
The turntable speed was adjusted so that
subjects' initial performances ranged from
20% to 30% time on target. All subjects were
tested over three test sessions of eight 20-
second trials each. The results showed that
the HD patients were severely impaired in
the acquisition of this motor skill. Although
the AD patients, amnesic patients, and
healthy control subjects showed equivalent
improvement (about 25%) over the three test
sessions, the HD patients demonstrated only
slight increments (about 8%) in performance
(see Fig. 14-1). Furthermore, the HD patients' performance on the pursuit rotor tasks
was not correlated with their levels of functional disability (Heindel et al., 1988) or their
degree of chorea and other extrapyramidal
motor signs (Heindel et al., 1989). Because
only severity of dementia was significantly
correlated ($r = .58$) with the HD patients'
impairments on this task, Heindel et al.

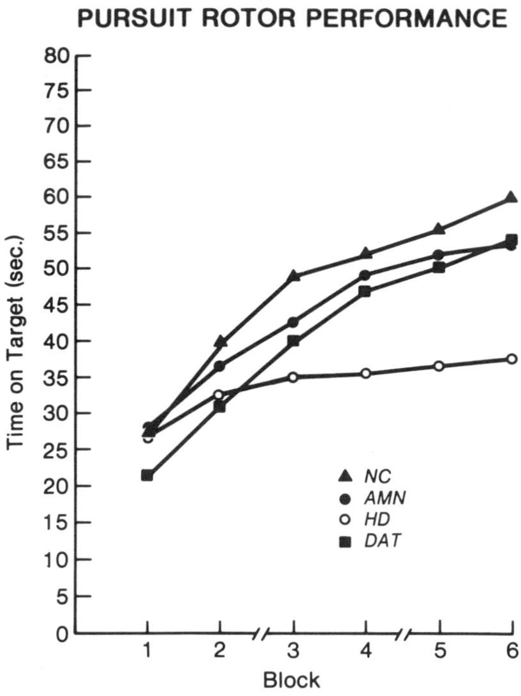

PURSUIT ROTOR PERFORMANCE

Figure 14-1. Performance of Alzheimer's disease (AD), Huntington's disease (HD), and amnesic (AMN) patients and normal control (NC) subjects on the pursuit rotor task. (Modified from Heindel et al., 1988.)

(1989) concluded that their deficiency in skill learning was a feature of their cognitive loss and not a consequence of primary motor disability.

To assess more directly whether HD patients suffer from an inability to initiate or modify central motor programs, Heindel et al. (1991) administered a weight-biasing task to HD patients, AD patients, and healthy control subjects. Because weight judgments are believed to involve motor programs and expectancies, and do not require complex movements for their execution, this task seemed ideal for use with HD patients, whose performance on motor skill learning tasks can easily be confounded by their profound extrapyramidal motor impairments. In this investigation, subjects were first exposed to either a relatively heavy or relatively light set of weights to bias their subsequent weight judgments (see Fig. 14-2). They were later asked to rate the heaviness of a standard set

of 10 weights using a 9-point scale. Both healthy control subjects and patients with AD perceived the standard set of weights as heavier following the light bias trials, despite the AD patients' poor recognition memory for the initial biasing session. In contrast, the weight judgments of the HD group were not influenced significantly by prior exposure to relatively heavy or light weights. As with the pursuit rotor task, the HD patients' weight-biasing performance was correlated with the severity of their dementia (see Fig. 14-3). Heindel et al. (1991) concluded that the HD patients' impaired biasing performance, like their problems in motor skill learning, reflects a deficit in the development of central motor programs.

Paulsen and her colleagues (1993) have reported additional evidence of the dependence of central motor programs on basal ganglia structures. Patients with HD, patients with AD, and normal controls were compared on a perceptual adaptation task involving laterally displaced vision. All subjects were asked to point to a target while wearing distorting prisms that shifted the perceived location of objects 20° to the right or left. Quantitative indices of pointing accuracy at *baseline* (without prisms and no visual feedback as to accuracy), *preadaptation* (with prisms and no visual feedback), *adaptation* (with prisms *and* visual feedback as to accuracy), *postadaptation* (with prisms and no feedback), and *aftereffects* (without prisms and no visual feedback) were obtained. It is generally believed that adaptation to such lateral spatial distortion is mediated by modification of central motor programs following visual feedback on the accuracy of intended movements. Paulsen et al. (1993) found that AD patients exhibited normal adaptation to prisms after visual feedback and normal negative aftereffects when the prisms were removed, whereas HD patients failed to demonstrate either phenomenon. Further, the amount of adaptation achieved by HD patients was negatively correlated with the severity of their dementia ($r = -.63$); no such significant correlation was noted for the AD patients ($r = .13$).

When these results for prism adaptation

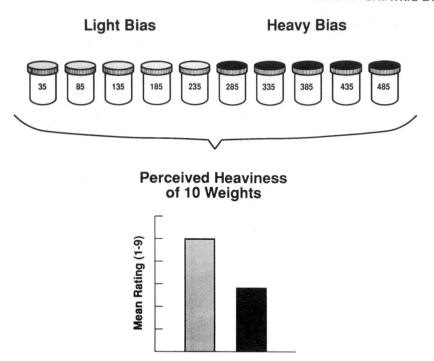

Figure 14-2. Schematic diagram illustrating the weight biasing effect. Subjects tend to perceive the 10 standard weights as relatively heavier when they are initially exposed to the five lightest weights (light shading), and as relatively lighter when they are initially exposed to the five heaviest weights (dark shading). (From Heindel et al., 1991.)

are considered in conjunction with those for the pursuit rotor and weight-biasing tasks, several conclusions emerge. First, HD patients' deficits likely reflect an inability to generate the central motor programs (or expectancies) that underlie skill learning, prism adaptation and some aspects of weight perception. Second, given the significant correlations between HD patients' impairments and the severity of their dementia, it is unlikely that their poor performances can be attributed to elementary motor dysfunction. Deficiencies in the production of motor programs seem to be a central feature of HD patients' cognitive losses. Third, the basal ganglia, especially the caudate nucleus and corticostriatal tracts, may be critical for the generation and retention of these motor programs.

Other studies of implicit memory in HD patients have reported impairments in the acquisition of "cognitive" skill-based knowl-

edge. Both Butters et al. (1985) and Saint-Cyr et al. (1988) found that HD patients are impaired in learning the cognitive skills necessary to solve the Tower of Hanoi puzzle. This task requires subjects to move four or five blocks stacked according to size from the first of three pegs to the third. The subjects' moves are restricted by a set of prescribed rules. For instance, subjects are permitted to move only one block at a time, and can never place a larger block on top of a smaller one. To solve the puzzle, subjects must shuttle the blocks back and forth among all three pegs. The optimal solution for the four-block puzzle can be accomplished in a minimum of 15 moves; for the five-block problem a minimum of 31 moves is necessary. Healthy subjects, some amnesics, and patients in the early stages of HD require fewer moves to solve the puzzle over successive trials. However, patients in the middle and advanced stages of HD showed little improvement on the puzzle over sessions. Although these findings are consistent with other reports of impaired skill learning in moderately demented HD patients (Heindel et al., 1989), it is difficult to ascertain whether the patients' impairments on the Tower puzzle are indicative of an implicit memory deficit, a problem-solving impairment, or a generalized deficit.

Bylsma et al. (1990) investigated implicit learning in HD with another type of problem-solving task. In their study, 15 HD patients and 15 intact control subjects were evaluated on a computerized maze-learning task. Three aspects of procedural memory were examined: (a) the learning of specific routes (i.e., improvement over repeated trials of the same maze), (b) the acquisition of the maze skill itself (i.e., facilitation across different mazes), and (c) the effects of route predictability on performance (i.e., the advantage of patterned over unpatterned routes). The HD patients learned individual maze routes at a normal rate, but were deficient in generalizing the cognitive skill across mazes. In addition, they failed to demonstrate superior performance on a maze with a predictable route (e.g., right, up, right, down, right, up, etc.) relative to mazes with unpredictable routes. Besides supporting the hypothesis that the neostriatum is important in the acquisition of skill-based procedural knowledge, these results suggest that the basal ganglia are crucial for generalizing across stimulus situations and for making use of the regularity, patterning, and organization of to-be-acted-upon stimuli. These can all be construed as aspects of central motor programming.

Knopman and Nissen have evaluated both AD patients (Knopman and Nissen, 1987) and HD patients (Knopman and Nissen, 1991) on a serial visual reaction time task with an embedded repeating sequence. When an asterisk appeared in one of four positions spaced horizontally across a computer screen, subjects were required to push a corresponding button on a response board as quickly as possible. Five blocks of 100 trials each were administered to all subjects.

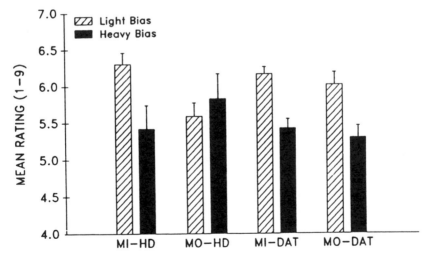

Figure 14-3. Mean heaviness ratings (1 = extremely light; 9 = extremely heavy) for the 10 test weights in the Light Bias and Heavy Bias conditions for the mildly demented (MI-HD) and moderately demented (MO-HD) HD patients, and for mildly demented (MI-DAT) and moderately demented (MO-DAT) Alzheimer (DAT) patients. Note that only the MO-DAT patients failed to show the expected weight biasing. (Modified from Heindel et al., 1991.)

For the first four blocks of 100 responses each, a 10-trial sequence of light positions was repeated 10 times. The beginnings and ends of the sequence were not noted, and the subjects were provided with no information concerning the repeated sequence. On the fifth block of 100 trials, the sequence of stimulus lights was random. Implicit learning was demonstrated by increased speed over the first four blocks of trials (repeated sequence) and slower responses on the fifth block (random sequence). The results showed that both AD patients and normal control subjects evidenced sequence-specific learning, despite little or no conscious awareness that a fixed sequence had been repeated over the first four blocks of trials. In contrast, the HD group was impaired in sequence-specific learning, and five of 13 HD patients demonstrated no learning when reaction times for the fourth and fifth blocks were compared. No specific index of cognitive function or motor disability was found to correlate with HD patients' performances on this reaction time task. Knopman and Nissen (1991) concluded that their data are consistent with the proposal that HD patients are impaired on implicit memory tasks involving the learning of skill-based knowledge.

Brandt and Bylsma (1993; reported in Brandt, 1994) performed a similar experiment, but found that HD patients, as a group, improved over blocks of repeated sequences at the same rate as healthy control subjects. These investigators reported that both sequence-specific learning and general skill acquisition were comparable in the two groups. However, in both the Knopman and Nissen (1991) and Brandt and Bylsma (1993) studies, the HD and normal control groups differed in their Block-1 reaction times, and the normal subjects' reaction times tended to asymptote before the last block. These limitations make interpretation of the implicit learning curves somewhat problematic.

Executive Functioning

The pattern of neuropsychological impairment in HD is similar in many ways to that seen in individuals with prefrontal cortical lesions. These parallels are not entirely unexpected, given the reciprocal connections between the frontal cortex and the basal ganglia. At least five functionally specific, anatomically discrete pathways connecting the frontal lobes to the striatum have been described; three of them involve the caudate nucleus (Alexander et al., 1986).

Many early-stage HD patients describe difficulties with planning, organizing, and scheduling day-to-day activities. Spouses and family members report that patients become less adaptable and behaviorally rigid; they tend to get "stuck" on an idea or task. In early HD, impairment of daily functioning is more likely to result from these cognitive deficits than from motor impairment (Bamford et al., 1989; Rothlind et al., 1993b). Similarities between HD and frontal lobe pathology are also reflected on neuropsychological tests. Both types of patients display impaired attention, decreased verbal fluency, poor motor programming, difficulty compensating for postural adjustments, inability to switch cognitive sets, and difficulties with abstraction (Potegal, 1971; Butters et al., 1978; Fedio et al., 1979; Josiassen et al., 1983; Alexander et al., 1989).

Noncognitive Psychological Features

In addition to their dementia and movement disorder, patients with HD often have prominent affective disturbances (Folstein et al., 1983a). Severe depression was recognized by George Huntington in his 1872 description of the syndrome. It recently has been argued that dyskinesia, dementia, and depression cosegregate in all the diseases of the basal ganglia, forming a "subcortical triad" (McHugh, 1989; Sano, 1991; Folstein et al., 1991).

The depression observed in HD frequently meets criteria for major affective disorder, and there are several lines of evidence to indicate that it is not simply an understandable reaction to the diagnosis of this incurable, degenerative disease. First, affective disturbances often precede the onset of cognitive or motor symptoms of HD. Second, approximately 10% of HD patients have manic phases, which are hard to reconcile with a reactive depression. Third, depression in HD appears to run true in families. That is, there are some families with prominent affective symptoms and others with only very mild affective symptoms. Affective disorder tends to be rare in African-American families with HD, for example (Folstein et al., 1987). Finally, the depression of HD is often accompanied by delusional beliefs and changes in self-attitude, symptoms that are again difficult to reconcile with a reactive depression.

Mindham and colleagues (1985) found that major affective disorder is more prominent in HD than it is in AD. These investigators studied 27 consecutive outpatients with HD and 27 consecutive outpatients with AD with the Diagnostic Interview Schedule. Even though the AD patients were older (and therefore had greater opportunity to develop affective disorder), only six of the AD patients (22%) had one or more episodes of major affective disorder, whereas 12 of the HD patients (44%) were so affected. Using data from the National Huntington's Disease Research Roster, Farrer (1986) found that 5.7% of the deaths of HD patients result from suicide, a figure almost four times greater than in the general population. Almost 28% of patients reported having attempted suicide at least once.

Irritability, aggression, and apathy are frequently reported to be prominent features of HD, but there have been few attempts to operationalize and quantify these phenomena. Burns et al. (1990) studied 31 AD patients and 26 HD patients using new scales to measure apathy and irritability. A modification of the Yudofsky Aggression Scale (Yudofsky et al., 1986) was used to assess aggression. Although a similar prevalence of apathy and irritability was found in the two patient groups, the HD patients were more aggressive than the AD patients. In subsamples of the two groups matched for degree of cognitive impairment, the HD patients were found to be more apathetic than the AD patients.

Other psychiatric disorders, including sexual disturbance, conduct disorders, substance abuse, and schizophreniform thought disorder, are also observed in HD, but less frequently (Dewhurst et al., 1970; McHugh and Folstein, 1975; Folstein et al., 1983b, 1990; Shoulson, 1990).

Is the Dementia of Huntington's Disease Due to Cortical or Striatal Pathology?

Several lines of evidence suggest that the disorders of complex cognition seen in HD result directly from degeneration of the caudate nucleus, rather than from either primary neuropathology of the prefrontal cortex or its secondary degeneration. First, patients with circumscribed lesions of the caudate nucleus display cognitive deficits strikingly similar to those noted in HD, namely, difficulty with planning, sequencing, and attention, impaired verbal recall with relatively better recognition, and language abnormalities (Mendez et al., 1989; Caplan et al., 1990). Second, measures of caudate atrophy on CT and MRI scans correlate strongly with many cognitive measures, including several subtests of the WAIS and WMS (Sax et al., 1983) and "complex psychomotor" tasks, including the Trail Making Test and the Stroop Color-Word Test (Bamford et al., 1989). Starkstein et al. (1988) found significant correlations between the bicaudate ratio on CT scans (a measure of caudate atrophy) and performance on the Symbol Digit Modalities Test, and parts A and B of the Trail Making Test. More recently, Starkstein et al. (1992), using MRI scans, found that the bicaudate ratio and a direct measurement of caudate area each correlated highly with a memory and speed-of-processing cognitive test factor. Impairment in everyday functioning, as indexed by the total functional capacity (TFC) score and the HD-ADL scale, is also related to caudate atrophy (Shoulson et al., 1982; Sax et al., 1983; Starkstein et al., 1988).

The third line of research implicating the caudate nucleus in the dementia of HD comes from functional brain imaging studies. PET and SPECT studies of HD patients indicate abnormalities in blood flow (Reid et al., 1988) and glucose metabolism (Hayden et al., 1987; Mazziotta et al., 1987; Berent et al., 1988) in the caudate, but not in the frontal cortex. These abnormalities of caudate glucose metabolism are highly correlated with clinical severity (Kuhl et al., 1982, 1984; Hayden et al., 1987; Young et al., 1986, 1987) and verbal memory (Berent et al., 1988). Weinberger and colleagues (1988) found that blood flow to the prefrontal cortex is normal in HD, even though these patients performed poorly on a computerized version of the Wisconsin Card Sorting Test. This suggests that the disorders of complex cognition seen in HD are not attributable to intrinsic cortical pathology, but are more likely reflections of the primary neostriatal degeneration.

Brandt et al. (1990) imaged D_2 dopamine receptors in the striatum of 21 HD patients and eight at-risk individuals using PET. A significant reduction in relative binding of ^{11}C-labeled 3-N-methylspiperone to the D_2 receptor was found in both the caudate and putamen of HD patients. Binding in the caudate was correlated with performance on Part B of the Trail Making Test and the oral form of the Symbol-Digit Modalities Test, whereas binding in the putamen was correlated only with duration of illness. The findings support the extensive neuroscience literature demonstrating that atrophic changes in the striatum are accompanied by dopamine (and probably many other) receptor alterations. They also support the previous work in both monkey and man indicating a larger role for the caudate nucleus in cognition than in motor functions.

A recent in vitro study supports the hypothesis that striatal pathology, rather than cortical abnormalities, underlie the cognitive deficits in HD. Reynolds et al. (1990) measured the activity of choline acetyltransferase (ChAT), as well as the neurotransmitter amino acids GABA and glutamate in postmortem brain tissue from severely demented and "nondemented" HD patients and neuropsychiatrically normal control brains. Although ChAT activity was reduced in the hippocampus and, to a lesser extent, in the frontal cortex of the HD brains, there was no greater reduction in the severely demented cases. In addition, the reductions in ChAT

activity were much smaller than those seen in AD or Parkinson's disease. GABA and glutamate were both reduced in the caudate, putamen, hippocampus, and frontal cortex of the HD brains. Only in the caudate nucleus, however, were levels of these neurotransmitters related to severity of dementia. Although the categorization of cases as severely demented and nondemented was very crude and retrospective in this study, this report is among the first to provide direct neurochemical evidence linking the caudate nucleus to dementia.

Not all studies find that abnormalities of the cerebral cortex contribute minimally to the clinical syndrome of HD. As discussed earlier, clear abnormalities of the cytoarchitecture have been found in HD prefrontal cortex (Hedreen et al., 1991). In living patients, atrophy of the frontal cortex, and reduced blood flow to it, have been found in HD (Sax et al., 1983; Tanahashi et al., 1985; Starkstein et al., 1988). Using MRI, Starkstein et al. (1992) found that cognitive tests requiring memory and rapid information processing were significantly correlated with indices of bifrontal and left temporal lobe atrophy, as well as caudate (but not putamen or thalamic) atrophy. In a recent SPECT study of early-stage HD patients, Harris and associates (unpublished data) found cerebral perfusion to be slightly reduced in a number of cortical areas, particularly the peri-rolandic sensory-motor area and the visual association cortex, in addition to the caudate and putamen. These cortical regions are precisely the areas that Lange (1981) found most markedly reduced in volume on postmortem examination.

Martin et al. (1992) reported that regional cerebral metabolic rate for glucose on PET scans was reduced by an average of 15% in the frontal and inferior parietal lobe among 23 patients who had been symptomatic for fewer than 5 years. No cognitive correlates of this cerebral metabolic abnormality were reported. Kuwert and associates (1990) examined glucose utilization in a number of cortical and subcortical structures in 23 patients with moderate to severe HD and 21 normal control subjects. Consistent with earlier reports, they found the most marked abnormalities to be in the caudate and putamen. Unlike other reports, however, they also found cortical hypometabolism in the HD patients, most marked in the frontal cortex. This study also found that severity of dementia and severity of disability were most strongly related to the degree of cortical, rather than striatal, abnormality. This study clearly challenges the notion that the dementia of HD is purely of subcortical origin.

Treatment and Management of Huntington's Disease

There is currently no treatment to arrest or slow the progression of HD. There have been several experimental trials of putative therapeutic agents, but none has demonstrated a significant effect. An early strategy was to replace striatal GABA, a neurotransmitter that is progressively depleted as striatal neurons die, with agonists. No therapeutic effects were noted (Shoulson et al., 1978; Foster et al., 1983). An alternate approach was to reduce levels of brain dopamine, as increased levels of striatal dopamine are noted at autopsy (Sanberg and Coyle, 1984). Dopamine antagonists tend to reduce involuntary motor symptoms, but have no effect on disease progression (Folstein, 1989). More recent trials have attempted to prevent or slow striatal cell death. Because administration of the excitatory neurotransmitter glutamate (or its agonists) results in striatal pathology that mimics that noted in autopsied brains of HD patients (Coyle and Schwarcz, 1976; McGeer and McGeer, 1976), Shoulson and colleagues (1989) administered Baclofen, a glutamate antagonist, to HD patients in a 3-year, double-blind, placebo-controlled trial. Equivalent rates of progression were found in the Baclofen-treated and placebo-treated groups. Despite these findings, compounds with more specific effects on the glutamate system are being studied in hopes of finding an effective therapy.

Although it is not currently possible to slow the progression of HD, many of the disease's symptoms are responsive to thera-peutic intervention, particularly early in the course of the illness. Chorea, but not the voluntary motor disorder, is often reduced by low doses of neuroleptic medications, such as haloperidol and fluphenazine. The emotional disturbance and psychiatric symptoms are also responsive to pharmacologic treatments: irritability is reduced by neuroleptics, anxiety by benzodiazapines, depression by tricyclic and SSRI antidepressants, and hallucinations and delusions by neuroleptics. Very often, environmental and behavioral interventions can reduce symptoms and improve adaptation. Reducing complexity and increasing consistency in the patient's environment and daily routine, as well as removing potential irritants and anxiety-inducing stimuli, often lessen agitation and anxiety.

A major component of any treatment program for HD is genetic counseling. Persons afflicted with HD need to appreciate that each child they have has a 50% chance of inheriting the illness. Those who already have children often need assistance in deciding when and how to convey this information to their children. The development of a reliable presymptomatic genetic test for HD (Meissen et al., 1988; Brandt et al., 1989) allowed individuals at risk to determine whether they carry the DNA marker that segregates with the disease in their family. The recent discovery of the actual gene mutation responsible for HD now allows for a technically simpler and even more definitive presymptomatic test. Knowing whether one will develop HD allows the at-risk person to make more informed decisions about marriage, childbearing, careers, and future care needs prior to the onset of symptoms. On the other hand, there is obviously great potential for psychological morbidity upon gaining this genetic knowledge.

Studies of Persons at Risk

Because HD is caused by a single, dominant gene, with onset typically in midlife, it affords neuropsychologists the unique challenge of determining whether a gene that creates disease only (so far as we can tell) in the brain has any preclinical manifestations. Past attempts at presymptomatic identification have examined physiological parameters (EMG and EEG) and the response to biochemical challenges (Petejan et al., 1979; Klawans et al., 1980). However, these measures have been found to be inadequately sensitive and/or specific as predictive tests.

Psychological characteristics have also been evaluated as potential presymptomatic "markers" of HD. Folstein et al. (1983b) found that conduct disorder and depression were common among the offspring of HD patients (i.e., youngsters at risk for HD). The former appears to be associated with family disorganization, and the latter with the presence of affective disorder in the parent with HD. This suggests that depression in an at-risk person may, in some cases, be predictive of the HD gene.

Several studies have examined whether performance on cognitive tests is abnormal in at-risk persons who will later go on to develop the disease (Baro, 1973; Fedio et al., 1979; Wexler, 1979; Josiassen et al., 1983). Some of these studies have found that at-risk persons, as a group, perform more poorly than not-at-risk persons, a finding that could certainly be due to the anxiety associated with being at risk for an incurable dementing illness. However, very little research has found that poor neuropsychological test performance predicts the later development of HD. In retrospective studies, Lyle and associates (Lyle and Quast, 1976; Lyle and Gottesman, 1977, 1979) found that low scores on the Bender-Gestalt test and the abstraction portion of the Shipley-Hartford scale were predictive of which at-risk subjects would be clinically affected 10 to 20 years later.

The WAIS profiles of patients with HD have been reported to differ from those of normal individuals, independent of overall IQ level. Strauss and Brandt (1986) performed discriminant function and hierarchical cluster analyses to explore the utility of WAIS patterns (not level of performance) information for the preclinical identification of HD. A discriminant function analysis using WAIS subtest scores adjusted for overall level correctly identified 79% of HD patients

and normal controls. When the discriminant equation was applied to a sample of 38 at-risk subjects, it classified 45% of them with the HD group and 55% with the normal control group. However, there were no clinical differences between the at-risk persons classified with the HD patients and those classified with the normal controls. Furthermore, those classified with affected patients were no more likely to become affected themselves within a 3-year follow-up period than those classified with normals. Cluster analysis failed to isolate distinct patient, at-risk, and control groups. Thus, although performance patterns on the WAIS clearly change very early in HD, they appear to be of limited value for the preclinical identification of the disease.

Some researchers have reported that ^{18}F-2-deoxyglucose PET scans reveal glucose hypometabolism in the caudate nucleus significantly prior to the development of structural changes on CT. Investigators at UCLA (Kuhl et al., 1982; Mazziotta et al., 1987) have reported that such metabolic findings are present months to years before symptom onset in some at-risk individuals. Grafton et al. (1990, 1992) reported that metabolic abnormalities in the caudate nucleus discerned by PET was superior to neurological examinations or CT scan measurements in distinguishing 20 at-risk individuals with high and low probability of developing HD (determined by genetic testing or by later becoming symptomatic). A sensitivity of 75% and a specificity of 88% was achieved when the 95% confidence interval for normal caudate-to-hemisphere ratio for glucose metabolic rate was the criterion. Other research teams (e.g., Young et al., 1987) maintain that caudate hypometabolism in HD occurs only coincident with clinical symptoms. These contrasting findings may be due partly to differences in definition of asymptomatic at-risk status among research centers.

Lanto et al. (1990) reported that 13 of 51 at-risk persons performed outside the 99.5% confidence interval of non-at-risk subjects on a word recognition memory test, due largely to an excess of false-positive errors. On PET scans, these subjects had lower glucose metabolism in the insula bilaterally, the left frontal cortex, and the right caudate nucleus than the 38 at-risk subjects with normal recognition memory performance. The authors suggest that certain tests of cognition and decision-making may be useful for the detection of HD among those at risk.

Presymptomatic Genetic Testing

Huntington's Disease is the first neuropsychiatric disorder for which a highly accurate presymptomatic test has been developed. In 1983, Gusella and coworkers discovered a DNA polymorphism (i.e., a site where variation among individuals is seen) on the short arm of chromosome 4 that is linked to the HD phenotype (Gusella et al., 1983). Subsequent linkage studies of many large HD kindreds have all confirmed this linkage (Folstein et al., 1985; Haines et al., 1986; Zweig et al., 1989), and it is now virtually certain that there is only one chromosomal locus for HD. The D4S10 marker discovered by Gusella is estimated to be approximately 4 to 5 centimorgans (recombination units) from the HD gene. Several additional markers have since been discovered, some of which are much closer to the HD gene than is D4S10. This makes any predictive test with these probes much more informative, with accuracy of 99% or better.

Hayden et al. (1987) combined DNA polymorphism studies with glucose PET studies for presymptomatic diagnosis. In their series, eight at-risk subjects had the HD marker and had a 90% or greater chance of having inherited the HD gene. Three of the eight had abnormally low rates of caudate glucose metabolism. One individual with a low risk of developing HD from his DNA marker study had abnormally low glucose utilization in the caudate nucleus. Hayden et al. suggested that this indicated a recombination between the linked marker and the HD gene in this individual. They commented that such studies combining DNA marker analysis and PET could not only confirm results of the DNA marker in some individuals, but could also detect when DNA results are incorrect due to recombination.

Thus far, there have been few studies of the neuropsychological characteristics of asymptomatic at-risk individuals who have tested either "marker-positive" (very high probability of HD) or "marker-negative" (very low probability of HD). In a study with a very small sample, Canadian researchers compared seven marker-positive subjects to three marker-negative subjects on 41 neuropsychological variables (Jason et al., 1988). Although only four of the 41 t-tests were significant at the .05 alpha level, the authors concluded that there were cognitive neuropsychological differences between presymptomatic marker-positive and marker-negative individuals. Similarly, Diamond et al. (1992), from the New England Huntington's Disease Center, reported that their five marker-positive subjects scored higher than their seven marker-negative subjects on 28 of the 37 neuropsychological test measures. However, only one of these statistical tests reached even the .05 level of significance. Strauss and Brandt (1990) administered a large battery of cognitive tests sensitive to HD (Symbol-Digit Modalities Test, subtests of the WAIS-R, Hopkins Verbal Learning Test, Standardized Road Map Test of Directional Sense, Wisconsin Card Sorting Test, Stroop Color-Word Test, a visual vigilance task, and a choice reaction-time task) and mood scales to 12 marker-positive and 15 marker-negative at-risk subjects and 15 non-at-risk control subjects. No differences between marker-positive and marker-negative individuals could be detected. In contrast to the finding of Lanto et al. (1990), Rothlind et al. (1993a) recently found that neither recall nor recognition parameters from the Hopkins Verbal Learning Test could distinguish marker-positive and marker-negative groups. They also found that tests of complex oculomotor function, which are extremely sensitive to the presence of early HD (Tian et al., 1991; Curie et al., 1992), failed to discriminate marker-positive and marker-negative groups.

Noncognitive psychological characteristics have also been examined for possible presymptomatic manifestations of the HD gene. Brandt et al. (1989) studied 42 at-risk persons before receiving genetic test results with the QNE, standardized psychiatric interviews (SADS-L), and extensive psychological testing of personality, coping style, psychological symptoms and mood states. There were no reliable differences between marker-positive and marker-negative groups in their social or psychiatric histories. Similarly, the psychological tests and questionnaires failed to discriminate those who subsequently tested positive from those who would test negative (Brandt et al., 1989; Brandt, 1993). Although larger samples are needed, this result suggests that the gene for HD may not have any measurable manifestations in clinically healthy, at-risk individuals. Recently, Baxter et al. (1992) and Diamond et al. (1992) replicated the finding that marker-positive and marker-negative at-risk subjects do not differ in their current or lifetime psychiatric histories, as assessed with the SADS-L. However, Baxter et al. (1992) did find that the at-risk subjects who were likely to develop HD (defined either by genetic testing or abnormal glucose PET scans) had higher scores on the anger/hostility scale of the Profile of Mood States (POMS).

Although there have been several descriptions of HD testing programs (Lam et al., 1988; Brock et al., 1989; Morris et al., 1989), there have been few published accounts of the consequences of disclosure of presymptomatic test results in HD. Meissen et al. (1988) reported that of 16 DNA tests performed, four were positive, seven were negative and five were uninformative. The authors report that the probable gene carriers were "surprised or shocked" by their test results; and half of them (i.e., two people) had periods of severe depression and the others had periods of moderate depression by 3-month follow-up. Wiggins et al. (1992), from the Canadian Collaborative Study of Predictive Testing, reported that even subjects who received "bad news" (i.e., that they were at high risk) had lower depression scores and higher well-being scores on follow-up than at baseline. They interpreted this finding as due to the beneficial effect of resolution of uncertainty.

At the Johns Hopkins Huntington's Disease Presymptomatic Testing Project, all participants are reevaluated at standard intervals after disclosure of DNA test results. Initial

reactions have ranged from extreme joy and relief to disappointment, sadness, and demoralization. Results to date suggest that there is no overall increased incidence of psychiatric disorder or social morbidity associated with testing positive for the HD marker (Brandt et al., 1989; Brandt, 1993; Codori and Brandt, 1994). However, a small number of marker-positive individuals have had significant marital and occupational difficulty after receiving their test results. This sample continues to be followed at regular intervals, which will allow us to address a large number of important issues, including: (a) determining with greater confidence whether the HD gene has neuropsychological manifestations prior to onset of diagnosable disease, (b) determining the baseline cognitive and emotional characteristics of those who cope well and those who cope poorly with news of their genetic status, and (c) determining the very earliest manifestations of striatal cell death as the disease begins its relentless course.

Acknowledgments

This research was supported by NIH grants NS16375 and MH46034 to the Johns Hopkins University and by funds from the Medical Research Service of the Department of Veterans Affairs. The authors thank their many collaborators, especially Drs. Frederick Bylsma, Ann Marie Codori, Marshal Folstein, Susan Folstein, Johannes Rothlind, and Milton Strauss. Dr. Jill Rich made helpful comments on the manuscript.

References

Albert, M. L., Feldman, R. G., and Willis, A. L. (1974). The 'subcortical dementia' of progressive supranuclear palsy. *Journal of Neurology, Neurosurgery and Psychiatry, 37,* 121–130.

Albert, M. S., Butters, N., and Brandt, J. (1981a). Patterns of remote memory in amnesic and demented patients. *Archives of Neurology, 38,* 495–500.

Albert, M. S., Butters, N., and Brandt, J. (1981b). Development of remote memory loss in patients with Huntington's disease. *Journal of Clinical Neuropsychology, 3,* 1–12.

Albert, M. S., Butters, N., and Levin, J. (1979). Temporal gradients in the retrograde amnesia of patients with alcoholic Korsakoff's disease. *Archives of Neurology, 36,* 211–216.

Albin, R. L., Young, A. B., Penney, J. B., Handelin, B., Balfour, R., Anderson, K. D., Markel, D. S., Tourtellotte, W. W., and Reiner, A. (1990). Abnormalities of striatal projection neurons and N-methyl-D-aspartate receptors in presymptomatic Huntington's disease. *New England Journal of Medicine, 322,* 1293–1298.

Alexander, G. E., DeLong, M. R., and Strick, P. L. (1986). Parallel organization of functionally segregated circuits linking basal ganglia and cortex. *Annual Review of Neuroscience, 9,* 357–381.

Alexander, M. P., Benson, D. F., and Stuss, D. T. (1989). Frontal lobes and language. *Brain and Language, 37,* 656–691.

Bamford, K. A., Caine, E. D., Kido, D. K., Plassche, W. M., and Shoulson, I. (1989). Clinical-pathologic correlation in Huntington's disease: A neuropsychological and computed tomography study. *Neurology, 39,* 796–801.

Baro, F. (1973). A neuropsychological approach to early detection of Huntington's chorea. In A. Barbeau, T. N. Chase, and G. W. Paulson, eds., *Advances in Neurology, Vol. 1: Huntington's Chorea, 1872–1972.* New York: Raven Press, pp. 329–338.

Barr, A. E., and Brandt, J. (1993). Verbal fluency deficits in dementia. *Journal of Clinical and Experimental Neuropsychology, 15,* 27 (Abst.).

Baxter, L. R., Jr., Mazziotta, J. C., Pahl, J. J., Grafton, S. T., St. George-Hyslop, P., Haines, J. L. Gusella, J. F., Szuba, M. P., Selin, C. E., Guze, B. H., and Phelps, M. E. (1992). Psychiatric, genetic, and positron emission tomographic evaluation of persons at risk for Huntington's disease. *Archives of General Psychiatry, 49,* 148–154.

Bayles, K. A., and Tomoeda, C. K. (1983). Confrontation naming impairment in dementia. *Brain and Language, 19,* 98–114.

Beatty, W. W., Salmon, D. P., Butters, N., Heindel, W. C., and Granholm, E. L. (1988). Retrograde amnesia in patients with Alzheimer's disease or Huntington's disease. *Neurobiology of Aging, 9,* 181–186.

Bell, J. (1934). Huntington's chorea. In R. A. Fisher, ed., *The Treasury of Human Genetics, Vol. 4.* London: Cambridge University Press, pp. 1–29.

Berent, S., Giordani, B., Lehtinen, S., Markel, D., Penney, J. B., Buchtel, H. A., Starosta-Rubenstein, S., Hichwa, R., and Young, A. B. (1988). Positron emission tomographic scan investigations of Huntington's disease: Cerebral metabolic correlates of cognitive function. *Annals of Neurology, 23,* 541–546.

Boll, T. J., Heaton, R., and Reitan, R. (1974). Neuropsychological and emotional correlates of Huntington's chorea. *Journal of Mental and Nervous Disorders, 158,* 61–69.

Borkowski, J. G., Benton, A. L., and Spreen, O. (1967). Word fluency and brain damage. *Neuropsychologia, 5,* 135–140.

Brandt, J. (1985). Access to knowledge in the dementia of Huntington's disease. *Developmental Neuropsychology, 1,* 335–348.

Brandt, J. (1991a). Cognitive impairments in Huntington's disease: Insights into the neuropsychology of the striatum. In F. Boller and J. Grafman, eds., *Handbook of Neuropsychology, Vol. 5.* Amsterdam: Elsevier Scientific Publisher, pp. 241–264.

Brandt, J. (1991b). The Hopkins Verbal Learning Test: Development of a new memory test with six equivalent forms. *The Clinical Neuropsychologist, 5,* 125–142.

Brandt, J. (1993). Ethical considerations in genetic testing, with examples from presymptomatic diagnosis of Huntington's disease. In K.W.M. Fulford, J. Soskice, and G. Gillett, eds., *Medicine and Moral Reasoning.* Cambridge: Cambridge University Press, pp. 41–59.

Brandt, J. (1994). Cognitive investigations in Huntington's disease. In L. Cermak, ed., *Neuropsychological Explorations of Memory and Cognition: Essays in Honor of Nelson Butters.* New York: Plenum Press, pp. 135–146.

Brandt, J., and Butters, N. (1986). The neuropsychology of Huntington's disease. *Trends in Neurosciences, 9,* 118–120.

Brandt, J., and Bylsma, F. W. (1993). The dementia of Huntington's disease. In R. W. Parks, R. F. Zec, and R. S. Wilson, eds., *Neuropsychology of Alzheimer's Disease and Other Dementias.* New York: Oxford University Press, pp. 265–282.

Brandt, J., Bylsma, F. W., Gross, R., Stine, O. C., Ranen, N., and Ross, C. (1996). Trinucleotide repeat length and clinical progression in Huntington's disease. *Neurology, 46,* 527–531.

Brandt, J., Corwin, J., and Krafft, L. (1992). Is verbal recognition memory really different in Huntington's and Alzheimer's disease? *Journal of Clinical and Experimental Neuropsychology, 14,* 773–784.

Brandt, J., Folstein, S. E., and Folstein, M. F. (1988). Differential cognitive impairment in Alzheimer's disease and Huntington's disease. *Annals of Neurology, 23,* 555–561.

Brandt, J., Folstein, S. E., Wong, D. F., Links,

J., Dannals, R. F., McDonnell-Sill, A., Starkstein, S., Anders, P., Strauss, M. E., Tune, L. E., Wagner, H. N., Jr., and Folstein, M. F. (1990). D$_2$ receptors in Huntington's disease: Positron emission tomography findings and clinical correlates. *Journal of Neuropsychiatry and Clinical Neurosciences, 2,* 20–27.

Brandt, J., Quaid, K. A., Folstein, S. E., Garber, P., Maestri, N. E., Abbott, M. H., Slavney, P. R., Franz, M. L., Kasch, L., and Kazazian, H. H., Jr. (1989). Presymptomatic diagnosis of delayed-onset disease with linked DNA markers: The experience in Huntington's disease. *Journal of the American Medical Association, 261,* 3108–3114.

Brandt, J., Strauss, M. E., Larus, J., Jensen, B., Folstein, S. E., and Folstein, M. F. (1984). Clinical correlates of dementia and disability in Huntington's disease. *Journal of Clinical Neuropsychology, 6,* 401–412.

Brock, D.J.H., Mennie, M., Curtis, A., Millan, F. A., Barron, L., Raeburn, J. A., Dinwoodie, D., Holloway, S., Crosbie, A., Wright, A., and Pullen, I. (1989). Predictive testing for Huntington's disease with linked DNA markers. *Lancet, 2,* 463–466. [Published erratum appears in *Lancet, 2,* 636.]

Brouwers, P., Cox, C., Martin, A., Chase, T., and Fedio, P. (1984). Differential perceptual-spatial impairment in Huntington's and Alzheimer's dementias. *Archives of Neurology, 41,* 1073–1076.

Bryois, C. (1989). [The length of survival and cause of death in Huntington's chorea.] *Schweizer Archiv fur Neurologie und Psychiatrie, 140,* 101–115.

Burns, A., Folstein, S. E., Brandt, J., and Folstein, M. F. (1990). Clinical assessment of irritability, aggression, and apathy in Huntington's and Alzheimer's disease. *Journal of Nervous and Mental Disease, 178,* 20–26.

Butters, N. (1984). The clinical aspects of memory disorders: Contributions from experimental studies of amnesia and dementia. *Journal of Clinical Neuropsychology, 6,* 17–36.

Butters, N., and Albert, M. S. (1982). Processes underlying failures to recall remote events. In L. S. Cermak, ed., *Human Memory and Amnesia.* Hillsdale, NJ: Erlbaum, pp. 257–274.

Butters, N., Albert, M. S., Sax, D. S., Miliotis, P., Nagode, J., and Sterste, A. (1983). The effect of verbal mediators on pictorial memory in brain-damaged patients. *Neuropsychologia, 21,* 307–323.

Butters, N., Granholm, E., Salmon, D. P., Grant, I., and Wolfe, J. (1987). Episodic and semantic memory: A comparison of amnesic and demented patients. *Journal of Clinical and Experimental Neuropsychology, 9,* 479–497.

Butters, N., Heindel, W. C., and Salmon, D. P. (1990a). Dissociation of implicit memory in dementia: Neurological implications. *Bulletin of the Psychonomic Society, 28,* 359–366.

Butters, N., Salmon, D. P., Cullum, C. M., Cairns, P., Tröster, A., Jacobs, D., Moss, M., and Cermak, L. (1988). Differentiation of amnesic and demented patients with the Wechsler Memory Scale-Revised. *The Clinical Neuropsychologist, 2,* 133–148.

Butters, N., Salmon, D. P., and Heindel, W. C. (1990b). Processes underlying the memory impairments of demented patients. In E. Goldberg, ed., *Contemporary Neuropsychology and the Legacy of Luria.* Hillsdale, NJ: Lawrence Erlbaum, pp. 99–126.

Butters, N., Sax, D. S., Montgomery, K., and Tarlow, S. (1978). Comparison of the neuropsychological deficits associated with early and advanced Huntington's disease. *Archives of Neurology, 35,* 585–589.

Butters, N., Wolfe, J., Granholm, E., and Martone, M. (1986). An assessment of verbal recall, recognition and fluency abilities in patients with Huntington's disease. *Cortex, 22,* 11–32.

Butters, N., Wolfe, J., Martone, M., Granholm, E., and Cermak, L. S. (1985). Memory disorders associated with Huntington's disease: Verbal recall, verbal recognition, and procedural memory. *Neuropsychologia, 23,* 729–743.

Bylsma, F. W., Brandt, J., and Strauss, M. E. (1990). Aspects of procedural memory are differentially impaired in Huntington's disease. *Archives of Clinical Neuropsychology, 5,* 287–297.

Bylsma, F. W., Brandt, J., and Strauss, M. E. (1992). Personal and extrapersonal orientation in Huntington's disease patients and those at risk. *Cortex, 28,* 113–122.

Bylsma, F. W., Rebok, G., and Brandt, J. (1991). Long-term retention of implicit learning in Huntington's disease. *Neuropsychologia, 29,* 1213–1221.

Bylsma, F. W., Rothlind, J., Hall, M. H., Folstein, S. E., and Brandt, J. (1993). Assessment of adaptive functioning in Huntington's disease. *Movement Disorders, 8,* 183–190.

Caine, E. D., Bamford, K. A., Schiffer, R. B., Shoulson, I., and Levy, S. (1986). A controlled neuropsychological comparison of Huntington's disease and multiple sclerosis. *Archives of Neurology, 43,* 249–254.

Caine, E. D., Ebert, M. H., and Weingartner,

H. (1977). An outline for the analysis of dementia. The memory disorder of Huntington's disease. *Neurology, 27,* 1087–1092.

Caine, E. D., Hunt, R. D., Weingartner, H., and Ebert, M. H. (1978). Huntington's dementia. Clinical and neuropsychological features. *Archives of General Psychiatry, 35,* 378–384.

Caplan, L. R., Schmahmann, J. D., Kase, C. S., Feldman, E., Baquis, G., Greenberg, J. P., Gorelick, P. B., Helgason, C., and Hier, D. B. (1990). Caudate infarcts. *Archives of Neurology, 47,* 133–143.

Codori, A. M., and Brandt, J. (1994). Psychological costs and benefits of predictive testing for Huntington's disease. *American Journal of Medical Genetics (Neuropsychiatric Genetics), 54,* 174–184.

Cohen, N. J., and Squire, L. R. (1980). Preserved learning and retention of pattern-analyzing skill in amnesia: Dissociation of knowing how and knowing that. *Science, 210,* 207–210.

Conneally, P. M. (1984). Huntington's disease: Genetics and epidemiology. *American Journal of Human Genetics, 36,* 506–526.

Corkin, S. (1968). Acquisition of motor skill after bilateral medial temporal lobe excision. *Neuropsychologia, 6,* 255–265.

Coyle, J. T., and Schwarz, R. (1976). Lesion of striatal neurons with kainic acid provides a model for Huntington's chorea. *Nature, 263,* 244–246.

Cummings, J. L. (1990). *Subcortical Dementia.* New York: Oxford University Press.

Curie, J., MacArthur, C., Ramsden, B., Lynch, J., and Maruff, P. (1992). High-resolution eye movement recording in the early diagnosis of Huntington's disease. *Neuropsychiatry, Neuropsychology and Behavioral Neurology, 5,* 46–52.

de la Monte, S. M., Vonsattel, J.-P., and Richardson, E. P., Jr. (1988). Morphometric demonstration of atrophic changes in the cerebral cortex, white matter, and neostriatum in Huntington's disease. *Journal of Neuropathology and Experimental Neurology, 47,* 516–525.

Delis, D. C., Kramer, J. H., Kaplan, E., and Ober, B. A. (1987). *The California Verbal Learning Test.* San Antonio, TX: The Psychological Corporation.

Delis, D. C., Massman, P. J., Butters, N., Salmon, D. P., Cermak, L. S., and Kramer, J. H. (1991). Profiles of demented and amnesic patients on the California Verbal Learning Test: Implications for the assessment of memory disorders. *Psychological Assessment: A Journal of Consulting and Clinical Psychology, 3,* 19–26.

Dewhurst, K., Oliver, J. E., and McKnight, A. L. (1970). Socio-psychiatric consequences of Huntington's disease. *British Journal of Psychiatry, 116,* 255–258.

Diamond, R., White, R. F., Myers, R. H., Mastromauro, C., Koroshetz, W. J., Butters, N., Rothstein, D. M., Moss, M. B., and Vasterling, J. (1992). Evidence of presymptomatic cognitive decline in Huntington's disease. *Journal of Clinical and Experimental Neuropsychology, 14,* 961–975.

Dom, R., Malfroid, M., and Baro, F. (1976). Neuropathology of Huntington's chorea. Studies of the ventrobasal complex of the thalamus. *Neurology, 26,* 64–68.

Duyao, M. P., Ambrose, C. M., Myers, R. H., Novelletto, A., Persichetti, F., Frontali, M., Folstein, S., Ross, C., Franz, M., Abbott, M., Gray, J., Conneally, P., Young, A., Penney, J., Hollingsworth, Z., Shoulson, I., Lazzarini, A., Falek, A., Koroshetz, W., Sax, D., Bird, E., Vonsattel, J., Bonilla, E., Alvir, J., Bickham Conde, J., Cha, J.-H., Dure, L., Gomez, F., Ramos, M., Sanchez-Ramos, J., Snodgrass, S., de Young, M., Wexler, N., Moscowitz, C., Penchaszadeh, G., MacFarlane, H., Anderson, M., Jenkins, B., Srinidhi, J., Barnes, G., Gusella, J., and MacDonald, M. (1993). Trinucleotide repeat length instability and age of onset in Huntington's disease. *Nature Genetics, 4,* 387–392.

Farrer, L. A. (1986). Suicide and attempted suicide in Huntington disease: Implications for preclinical testing of persons at risk. *American Journal of Medical Genetics, 24,* 305–311.

Fedio, P., Cox, C. S., Neophytides, A., Canal-Frederick, G., and Chase, T. N. (1979). Neuropsychological profile of Huntington's disease. In T. N. Chase, N. S. Wexler, and A. Barbeau, eds., *Advances in Neurology, Vol. 23: Huntington's Disease.* New York: Raven Press, pp. 239–255.

Fisher, J. M., Kennedy, J. L., Caine, E. D., and Shoulson, I. (1983). Dementia in Huntington's disease: A cross-sectional analysis of intellectual decline. In R. Mayeux and W. G. Rosen, eds., *The Dementias.* New York: Raven Press, pp. 229–238.

Folstein, M. F., Folstein, S. E., and McHugh, P. R. (1975). 'Mini-Mental State': A practical method for grading the cognitive state of patients for the clinician. *Journal of Psychiatric Research, 12,* 189–198.

Folstein, S. E. (1989). *Huntington's Disease: A*

Disorder of Families. Baltimore: The Johns Hopkins University Press.

Folstein, S. E., Abbott, M. H., Chase, G. A., Jensen, B. A. and Folstein, M. F. (1983a). The association of affective disorder with Huntington's disease in a case series and in families. *Psychological Medicine, 13,* 537–542.

Folstein, S. E., Brandt, J., and Folstein, M. F. (1990). Huntington's disease. In J. L. Cummings, ed., *Subcortical Dementia*. New York: Oxford University Press, pp. 87–107.

Folstein, S. E., Chase, G. A., Wahl, W. E., McDonnell, A. M., and Folstein, M. F. (1987). Huntington disease in Maryland: Clinical aspects of racial variation. *American Journal of Human Genetics, 41,* 168–179.

Folstein, S. E., Franz, M. L., Jensen, B. A., Chase, G. A., and Folstein, M. F. (1983b). Conduct disorder and affective disorder among the offspring of patients with Huntington's disease. *Psychological Medicine, 13,* 45–52.

Folstein, S. E., Peyser, C., Starkstein, and Folstein, M. F. (1991). Subcortical triad of Huntington's disease: A model for a neuropathology of depression, dementia, and dyskinesia. In B. J. Carroll and J. E. Barrett, eds., *Psychopathology and the Brain*. New York: Raven Press, pp. 65–75.

Folstein, S. E., Phillips, J. A., 3d, Meyers, D. A., Case, G. A., Abbott, M. H., Franz, M. L., Waber, P. G., Kazazian, H. H., Jr., Conneally, P. M., Hobbs, W., Tanzi, K., Faryniarz, A., Gibbons, K., and Gusella, J. (1985). Huntington's disease: Two families with differing clinical features show linkage to the G8 probe. *Science, 229,* 776–779.

Forno, L. S., and Jose, C. (1973). Huntington's chorea: A pathological study. In A. Barbeau, T. N. Chase, and G. W. Paulson, eds., *Advances in Neurology, Vol. 1: Huntington's Chorea, 1872–1972*. New York: Raven Press, pp. 453–470.

Foster, N. L., Chase, T. N., Denaro, A., Hare, T. A., and Tamminga, C. A. (1983). THIP treatment of Huntington's disease. *Neurology, 33,* 637–639.

Fuld, P. A., Katzman, R., Davies, P., and Terry, R. D. (1982). Intrusions as a sign of Alzheimer dementia: Chemical and pathological verification. *Annals of Neurology, 11,* 155–159.

Girotti, F., Marano, R., Soliveri, P., Geminiani, G., and Scigliano, G. (1988). Relationship between motor and cognitive disorders in Huntington's disease. *Journal of Neurology, 235,* 454–457.

Gordon, W. P., and Illes, J. (1987). Neurolinguis-tic characteristics of language production in Huntington's disease: A preliminary report. *Brain and Language, 31,* 1–10.

Graf, P., Squire, L. R., and Mandler, G. (1984). The information that amnesic patients do not forget. *Journal of Experimental Psychology. Learning, Memory, and Cognition, 10,* 164–178.

Grafton, S. T., Mazziotta, J. C., Pahl, J. J., St. George-Hyslop, P., Haines, J. L., Gusella, J., Hoffman, J. M., Baxter, L. R., and Phelps, M. E. (1990). A comparison of neurological, metabolic, structural, and genetic evaluations in persons at risk for Huntington's disease. *Annals of Neurology, 28,* 614–621.

Grafton, S. T., Mazziotta, J. C., Pahl, J. J., St. George-Hyslop, P., Haines, J. L., Gusella, J., Hoffman, J. M., Baxter, L. R., and Phelps, M. E. (1992). Serial changes of cerebral glucose metabolism and caudate size in persons at risk for Huntington's disease. *Archives of Neurology, 49,* 1161–1167.

Granholm, E., and Butters, N. (1988). Associative encoding and retrieval in Alzheimer's and Huntington's disease. *Brain and Cognition, 7,* 335–347.

Gusella, J. F., Wexler, N. S., Conneally, P. M., Naylor, S. L., Anderson, M. A., Tanzi, R. E., Watkins, P. C., Ottina, K., Wallace, M. R., Sakaguchi, A. Y., Young, A. B., Shoulson, I., Bonilla, E., and Martin, J. B. (1983). A polymorphic DNA marker genetically linked to Huntington's disease. *Nature, 306,* 234–238.

Haines, J. L., Tanzi, R., Wexler, N. S., Harper, P., Folstein, S., Cassiman, J., Meyers, R., Young, A., Hayden, M., Falek, A., Tolosa, E., Crespi, S., Campanella, G., Holmgren, G., Anvret, M., Kanazawa, I., Gusella, J., and Conneally, M. (1986). No evidence of linkage heterogeneity between Huntington's disease and G8 (D4S10). *American Journal of Human Genetics, 39,* A156 (Abst.).

Hantraye, P., Riche, D., Maziere, M., and Isacson, O. (1990). A primate model of Huntington's disease: Behavioral and anatomical studies of unilateral excitotoxic lesions of the caudate-putamen in the baboon. *Experimental Neurology, 108,* 91–104.

Harper, P. S. (1991). *Huntington's Disease*. London: W. B. Saunders Co.

Hayden, M. R., Hewitt, J., Stoessl, A. J., Clark, C., Ammann, W., and Martin, W.R.W. (1987). The combined use of positron emission tomography and DNA polymorphisms for preclinical detection of Huntington's disease. *Neurology, 37,* 1441–1447.

Heathfield, K.W.G., and McKenzie, I. C. (1971). Huntington's chorea in Bedfordshire, England. *Guy's Hospital Report, 120,* 295–309.

Hedreen, J. C., Peyser, C. E., Folstein, S. E., and Ross, C. A. (1991). Neuronal loss in layers V and VI of the cerebral cortex in Huntington's disease. *Neuroscience Letters, 133,* 257–261.

Heindel, W. C., Butters, N., and Salmon, D. P. (1988). Impaired learning of a motor skill in patients with Huntington's disease. *Behavioral Neuroscience, 102,* 141–147.

Heindel, W. C., Salmon, D. P., and Butters, N. (1991). The biasing of weight judgments in Alzheimer's and Huntington's disease: A priming or programming phenomenon? *Journal of Clinical and Experimental Neuropsychology, 13,* 189–203.

Heindel, W. C., Salmon, D. P., Shults, C. W., Walicke, P. A., and Butters, N. (1989). Neuropsychological evidence for multiple implicit memory systems: A comparison of Alzheimer's, Huntington's, and Parkinson's disease patients. *Journal of Neuroscience, 9,* 582–587.

Hodges, J. R., Salmon, D. P., and Butters, N. (1990). Differential impairment of semantic and episodic memory in Alzheimer's and Huntington's diseases: A controlled prospective study. *Journal of Neurology, Neurosurgery and Psychiatry, 53,* 1089–1095.

Hodges, J. R., Salmon, D. P., and Butters, N. (1991). The nature of the naming deficit in Alzheimer's and Huntington's disease. *Brain, 114,* 1547–1558.

Huntington's Disease Collaborative Research Group. (1993). A novel gene containing a trinucleotide repeat that is expanded and unstable on Huntington's disease chromosomes. *Cell, 72,* 971–983.

Illes, J. (1989). Neurolinguistic features of spontaneous language production dissociate three forms of neurodegenerative disease: Alzheimer's, Huntington's, and Parkinson's. *Brain and Language, 37,* 628–642.

Jacobs, D., Salmon, D. P., Tröster, A. I., and Butters, N. (1990a). Intrusion errors in the figural memory of patients with Alzheimer's and Huntington's disease. *Archives of Clinical Neuropsychology, 5,* 49–57.

Jacobs, D., Tröster, A. I., Butters, N., Salmon, D. P., and Cermak, L. S. (1990b). Intrusion errors on the visual reproduction test of the Wechsler Memory Scale and the Wechsler Memory Scale–Revised: An analysis of demented and amnesic patients. *The Clinical Neuropsychologist, 4,* 177–191.

Jason, G. W., Pajurkova, E. M., Suchowersky, O., Hewitt, J., Hilbert, C., Reed, J., and Hayden, M. (1988). Presymptomatic neuropsychological impairment in Huntington's disease. *Archives of Neurology, 45,* 769–773.

Josiassen, R. C., Curry, L. M., and Mancall, E. L. (1983). Development of neuropsychological deficits in Huntington's disease. *Archives of Neurology, 40,* 791–796.

Kaplan, E., Goodglass, H., and Weintraub, S. (1978). *The Boston Naming Test.* Boston: E. Kaplan and H. Goodglass.

Klawans, H. L., Goetz, C. G., and Perlik, S. (1980). Presymptomatic and early detection in Huntington's disease. *Annals of Neurology, 8,* 343–347.

Knopman, D. S., and Nissen, M. J. (1987). Implicit learning in patients with probable Alzheimer's disease. *Neurology, 37,* 784–788.

Knopman, D. S., and Nissen, M. J. (1991). Procedural learning is impaired in Huntington's disease: Evidence from the serial reaction time task. *Neuropsychologia, 29,* 245–254.

Kopelman, M. D. (1989). Remote and autobiographical memory, temporal context memory and frontal atrophy in Korsakoff and Alzheimer patients. *Neuropsychologia, 27,* 437–460.

Kramer, J. H., Delis, D. C., Blusewicz, M. J., Brandt, J., Ober, B. A., and Strauss, M. (1988). Verbal memory errors in Alzheimer's and Huntington's dementias. *Developmental Neuropsychology, 4,* 1–15.

Kramer, J. H., Levin, B., Brandt, J., and Delis, D. C. (1989). Differentiation of Alzheimer's, Huntington's, and Parkinson's diseases on the basis of verbal learning characteristics. *Neuropsychology, 3,* 111–120.

Kuhl, D. E., Metter, E. J., Riege, W. H., and Markham, C. H. (1984). Patterns of cerebral glucose utilization in Parkinson's disease and Huntington's disease. *Annals of Neurology, 15*(Suppl.), S119–S125.

Kuhl, D. E., Phelps, M. E., Markham, C. H., Metter, E. J., Reige, W. H., and Winter, J. (1982). Cerebral metabolism and atrophy in Huntington's disease determined by ^{18}FDG and computed tomographic scan. *Annals of Neurology, 12,* 425–434.

Kuwert, T., Lange, H. W., Langen, K.-J., Herzog, H., Aulich, A., and Feinendegen, L. E. (1990). Cortical and subcortical glucose consumption measured by PET in patients with Huntington's disease. *Brain, 113,* 1405–1423.

Lam, R. W., Bloch, M., Jones, B., Marcus, A. M., Fox, S., Ammann, W., and Hayden, M. R. (1988). Psychiatric morbidity associated with early clinical diagnosis of Huntington disease in a predictive testing program. *Journal of Clinical Psychiatry, 49,* 444–447.

Lange, H. W. (1981). Quantitative changes of telencephalon, diencephalon, and mesencephalon in Huntington's chorea, postencephalitic, and idiopathic parkinsonism. *Verhandlungen der Anatomischen Gesellschaft, 75,* 923–925.

Lanto, A. B., Riege, W. H., Mazziotta, J. C., Pahl, J. J., and Phelps, M. E. (1990). Increased false alarms in a subset of persons at-risk for Huntington's disease. *Archives of Clinical Neuropsychology, 5,* 393–404.

Ludlow, C. L., Connor, N. P., and Bassich, C. J. (1987). Speech timing in Parkinson's and Huntington's disease. *Brain and Language, 32,* 195–214.

Lyle, O. C., and Gottesman, I. I. (1977). Premorbid psychometric indicators of the gene for Huntington's disease. *Journal of Clinical and Consulting Psychology, 45,* 1011–1022.

Lyle, O. C., and Gottesman, I. I. (1979). Subtle cognitive deficits as 15- to 20-year precursors of Huntington's disease. In T. N. Chase, N. S. Wexler, and A. Barbeau, eds., *Advances in Neurology, Vol. 23: Huntington's Disease.* New York: Raven Press, pp. 227–237.

Lyle, O. C., and Quast, W. (1976). The Bender Gestalt: Use of clinical judgment versus recall scores in prediction of Huntington's disease. *Journal of Consulting and Clinical Psychology, 44,* 229–232.

Martin, A., and Fedio, P. (1983). Word production and comprehension in Alzheimer's disease: The breakdown of semantic knowledge. *Brain and Language, 19,* 124–141.

Martin, W.R.W., Clark, C., Ammann, W., Stoessl, A. J., Shtybel, W., and Hayden, M. R. (1992). Cortical glucose metabolism in Huntington's disease. *Neurology, 42,* 223–229.

Martone, M., Butters, N., Payne, M., Becker, J. T., and Sax, D. S. (1984). Dissociations between skill learning and verbal recognition in amnesia and dementia. *Archives of Neurology, 41,* 965–970.

Massman, P. J., Delis, D. C., Butters, N., Levin, B. E., and Salmon, D. P. (1990). Are all subcortical dementias alike?: Verbal learning and memory in Parkinson's and Huntington's disease patients. *Journal of Clinical and Experimental Neuropsychology, 12,* 729–744.

Mattis, S. (1988). *Dementia Rating Scale* (manual). Odessa, FL: Psychological Assessment Resources.

Mayeux, R., Stern, Y., Herman, A., Greenbaum, L., and Fahn, S. (1986). Correlates of early disability in Huntington's disease. *Annals of Neurology, 20,* 727–731.

Mazziotta, J., Phelps, M. E., Pahl, J. J., Huang, S. C., Baxter, L. R., Reige, W. H., Hoffman, J. M., Kuhl, D. E., Lanto, A. B., Wapenski, J. A., and Markham, C. (1987). Reduced cerebral glucose metabolism in asymptomatic subjects at risk for Huntington's disease. *New England Journal of Medicine, 316,* 357–362.

McGeer, E. G., and McGeer, P. L. (1976). Duplication of biochemical changes of Huntington's chorea. In A. Barbeau and J. R. Brunette, eds., *Progress in Neuro-genetics.* Amsterdam: Excerpta Medica Foundation, pp. 645–650.

McHugh, P. R. (1989). The neuropsychiatry of basal ganglia disorders: A triadic syndrome and its explanation. *Neuropsychiatry, Neuropsychology, and Behavioral Neurology, 2,* 239–247.

McHugh, P. R., and Folstein, M. F. (1973). Subcortical dementia. Address to the American Academy of Neurology, Boston, MA.

McHugh, P., and Folstein, M. F. (1975). Psychiatric syndromes of Huntington's chorea: A clinical and phenomenologic study. In D. F. Benson and D. Blumer, eds., *Psychiatric Aspects of Neurologic Disease.* New York: Grune and Stratton, Inc., pp. 267–286.

Meissen, G. J., Meyers, R. H., Mastromauro, C. A., Koroshetz, W. J., Klinger, K. W., Farrer, L. A., Watkins, P. A., Gusella, J. F., Bird, E. D., and Martin, J. B. (1988). Predictive testing for Huntington's disease with use of a linked DNA marker. *New England Journal of Medicine, 318,* 535–542.

Mendez, M. F., Adams, N. L., and Lewandowski, K. S. (1989). Neurobehavioral changes associated with caudate lesions. *Neurology, 39,* 349–354.

Merritt, A. D., Conneally, P. M., Rahman, N. F., and Drew, A. L. (1969). Juvenile Huntington's chorea. In A. Barbeau and J. R. Brunette, eds., *Progress in Neuro-genetics, Vol. 1.* Amsterdam: Excerpta Medica Foundation, pp. 645–650.

Milner, B. (1962). Les troubles de la memoire accompagnant des lesions hippocampiques bilaterales. *Physiologie de l'Hippocampe.* Paris: Centre National de la Recherche Scientific, pp. 257–272.

Mindham, R.H.S., Steele, C., Folstein, M. F., and Lucas, J. (1985). A comparison of the frequency of major affective disorder in Huntington's disease. *Journal of Neurology, Neurosurgery and Psychiatry, 48,* 1172–1174.

Mohr, E., Brouwers, P., Claus, J. J., Mann,

U. M., Fedio, P., and Chase, T. N. (1991). Visuospatial cognition in Huntington's disease. *Movement Disorders, 6,* 127–132.

Money, J. (1976). *A Standardized Road Map Test of Directional Sense.* San Rafael, CA: Academic Therapy Publications.

Monsch, A. U., Bondi, M. W., Butters, N., Paulsen, J. S., Salmon, D. P., Brugger, P., and Swenson, M. R. (1994). A comparison of category and letter fluency in Alzheimer's and Huntington's Disease. *Neuropsychology, 8,* 25–30.

Morris, M. J., Tyler, A., Lazarou, L., Meredith, L., and Harper, P. S. (1989). Problems in genetic prediction for Huntington's disease. *Lancet, 2,* 601–603. [Published erratum in *Lancet, 2,* 756, 1989.]

Moses, J. A., Jr., Golden, C. J., Berger, P. A., and Wisniewski, A. M. (1981). Neuropsychological deficits in early, middle, and late stages of Huntington's disease as measured by the Luria-Nebraska Neuropsychological Battery. *International Journal of Neuroscience, 14,* 95–100.

Moss, M. B., Albert, M. S., Butters, N., and Payne, M. (1986). Differential patterns of memory loss among patients with Alzheimer's disease, Huntington's disease, and alcoholic Korsakoff's syndrome. *Archives of Neurology, 43,* 239–246.

Myers, R. H., Sax, D. S., Koroshetz, W. J., Mastromauro, C., Cupples, L. A., Kiely, D. K., Pettengill, F. K., and Bird, E. D. (1991). Factors associated with slow progression in Huntington's disease. *Archives of Neurology, 48,* 800–804.

Myers, R. H., Sax, D. S., Schoenfeld, M., Bird, E. D., Wolfe, P. A., Vonsattel, J. P., White, R. F., and Martin, J. B. (1985). Late onset of Huntington's disease. *Journal of Neurology, Neurosurgery and Psychiatry, 48,* 530–534.

Oscar-Berman, M., and Zola-Morgan, S. (1980). Comparative neuropsychology and Korsakoff's syndrome. I—Spatial and visual reversal learning. *Neuropsychologia, 18,* 499–512.

Oscar-Berman, M., Zola-Morgan, S. M., Öberg, R.G.E., and Bonner, R. T. (1982). Comparative neuropsychology and Korsakoff's syndrome. III—Delayed response, delayed alternation, and DRL performance. *Neuropsychologia, 20,* 187–202.

Paulsen, J. S., Butters, N., Salmon, D. P., Heindel, W. C., and Swenson, M. R. (1993). Prism adaptation in Alzheimer's and Huntington's disease. *Neuropsychology, 7,* 73–81.

Penney, J. B., Young, A. B., Shoulson, I.,

Starosta-Rubenstein, S., Snodgras, S. R., Sanchez-Ramos, J., Ramos-Arroyo, M., Gomez, F., Penchaszadeh, G., Alvir, J., Esteves, J., Dequiroz, I., Marsol, N., Moreno, H., Conneally, P. M., Bonilla, E., and Wexler, N. S. (1990). Huntington's disease in Venezuela: 7 years of follow-up on symptomatic and asymptomatic individuals. *Movement Disorders, 5,* 93–99.

Petejan, J. H., Jarcho, L. W., and Thurman, D. J. (1979). Motor unit control in Huntington's disease: A possible presymptomatic test. In T. N. Chase, N. S. Wexler, and A. Barbeau, eds., *Advances in Neurology, Vol. 23: Huntington's Disease.* New York: Raven Press, pp. 163–175.

Podoll, K., Caspary, P., Lange, H. W., and Noth, J. (1988). Language functions in Huntington's disease. *Brain, 111,* 1475–1503.

Potegal, M. (1971). A note on spatial-motor deficits in patients with Huntington's disease: A test of a hypothesis. *Neuropsychologia, 9,* 233–235.

Randolph, C. (1991). Implicit, explicit, and semantic memory functions in Alzheimer's disease and Huntington's disease. *Journal of Clinical and Experimental Neuropsychology, 13,* 479–494.

Randolph, C., Braun, A. R., Goldberg, T. E., and Chase, T. (1993). Semantic fluency in Alzheimer's, Parkinson's, and Huntington's disease: Dissociation of storage and retrieval failures. *Neuropsychology, 7,* 82–88.

Reid, I. C., Besson, J.A.O., Best, P. V., Sharp, P. F., Gemmell, H. G., and Smith, F. W. (1988). Imaging of cerebral blood flow markers in Huntington's disease using single photon emission computed tomography. *Journal of Neurology, Neurosurgery, and Psychiatry, 51,* 1264–1268.

Reynolds, G. P., Pearson, S. J., and Heathfield, K.W.G. (1990). Dementia in Huntington's disease is associated with neurochemical deficits in the caudate nucleus, not the cerebral cortex. *Neuroscience Letters, 113,* 95–100.

Rothlind, J., Brandt, J., Zee, D., Codori, A. M., and Folstein, S. E. (1993a). Unimpaired verbal memory and oculomotor control in asymptomatic adults with the genetic marker for Huntington's disease. *Archives of Neurology, 50,* 799–802. [Published erratum appears in *Archives of Neurology, 51,* 268.]

Rothlind, J. C., Bylsma, F. W., Peyser, C., Folstein, S. E., and Brandt, J. (1993b). Cognitive and motor correlates of everyday functioning in early Huntington's disease. *Journal of Nervous and Mental Disease, 181,* 194–199.

Saint-Cyr, J. A., Taylor, A. E., and Lang, A. E. (1988). Procedural learning and neostriatal dysfunction in man. *Brain, 111*, 941–959.

Salmon, D. P., Kwo-on-Yuen, P. F., Heindel, W. C., Butters, N., and Thal, L. J. (1989). Differentiation of Alzheimer's disease and Huntington's disease with the Dementia Rating Scale. *Archives of Neurology, 46*, 1204–1208.

Sanberg, P. R., and Coyle, J. T. (1984). Scientific approaches to Huntington's disease. *CRC Critical Reviews in Clinical Neurobiology, 1*, 1–44.

Sano, M. (1991). Basal ganglia diseases and depression. *Neuropsychiatry, Neuropsychology and Behavioral Neurology, 4*, 41–48.

Sax, D. S., O'Donnell, B., Butters, N., Menzer, L., Montgomery, K., and Kayne, H. L. (1983). Computed tomographic, neurologic, and neuropsychologic correlates of Huntington's disease. *International Journal of Neuroscience, 18*, 21–36.

Schacter, D. L. (1987). Implicit memory: Historical and current status. *Journal of Experimental Psychology. Learning, Memory and Cognition, 13*, 501–518.

Schretlen, D., and Bobholz, J. (1992). Standardization and initial validation of a brief test of executive attentional ability. *Journal of Clinical and Experimental Neuropsychology, 14*, 65 (Abst.).

Shelton, P. A., and Knopman, D. S. (1991). Ideomotor apraxia in Huntington's disease. *Archives of Neurology, 48*, 35–41.

Shoulson, I. (1990). Huntington's disease: Cognitive and psychiatric features. *Neuropsychiatry, Neuropsychology and Behavioral Neurology, 3*, 15–22.

Shoulson, I., and Fahn, S. (1979). Huntington's disease: Clinical care and evaluation. *Neurology, 29*, 1–3.

Shoulson, I., Goldblatt, D., Charlton, M., and Joynt, R. J. (1978). Huntington's disease: Treatment with muscimol, a GABA-mimetic drug. *Annals of Neurology, 4*, 279–284.

Shoulson, I., Odoroff, C., Oakes, D., Behr, J., Goldblatt, D., Caine, E., Kennedy, J., Miller, C., Bamford, K., Rubin, A., Plumb, S., and Kurlan, R. (1989). A controlled clinical trial of Baclofen as protective therapy in early Huntington's disease. *Annals of Neurology, 25*, 252–259.

Shoulson, I., Plassche, W., and Odoroff, C. (1982). Huntington disease: Caudate atrophy parallels functional impairment. *Neurology, 32*, A143 (Abst.).

Smith, S., Butters, N., White, R., Lyon, L.,

and Granholm, E. (1988). Priming semantic relations in patients with Huntington's disease. *Brain and Language, 33*, 27–40.

Sotrel, A., Paskevich, P. A., Kiely, D. K., Bird, E. D., Williams, R. S., and Myers, R. H. (1991). Morphometric analysis of the prefrontal cortex in Huntington's disease. *Neurology, 41*, 1117–1123.

Speedie, L. J., Brake, N., Folstein, S. E., Bowers, D., and Heilman, K. M. (1990). Comprehension of prosody in Huntington's disease. *Journal of Neurology, Neurosurgery, and Psychiatry, 53*, 607–610.

Starkstein, S. E., Brandt, J., Bylsma, F., Peyser, C., Folstein, M., and Folstein, S. E. (1992). Neuropsychological correlates of brain atrophy in Huntington's disease: A magnetic resonance imaging study. *Neuroradiology, 34*, 487–489.

Starkstein, S., Brandt, J., Folstein, S. E., Strauss, M. E., Berthier, M. L., Pearlson, G. D., Wong, D., McDonnell, A., and Folstein, M. (1988). Neuropsychological and neuroradiological correlates in Huntington's disease. *Journal of Neurology, Neurosurgery, and Psychiatry, 51*, 1259–1263.

Strauss, M. E., and Brandt, J. (1986). Attempt at preclinical identification of Huntington's disease using the WAIS. *Journal of Clinical and Experimental Neuropsychology, 8*, 210–218.

Strauss, M. E., and Brandt, J. (1990). Are there neuropsychological manifestations of the gene for Huntington's disease in asymptomatic, at-risk individuals? *Archives of Neurology, 47*, 905–908.

Tanahashi, N., Meyer, J. S., Ishikawa, Y., Kandula, P., Mortel, K. F., Rogers, R. L., Gandhi, S., and Walker, M. (1985). Cerebral blood flow and cognitive testing correlate in Huntington's disease. *Archives of Neurology, 42*, 1169–1175.

Tian, J. R., Zee, D. S., Lasker, A. G., and Folstein, S. E. (1991). Saccades in Huntington's disease: Predictive tracking and interaction between release of fixation and initiation of saccades. *Neurology, 41*, 875–881.

Tröster, A. I., Salmon, D. P., McCullough, D., and Butters, N. (1989). A comparison of the category fluency deficits associated with Alzheimer's and Huntington's disease. *Brain and Language, 37*, 500–513.

Vonsattel, J. P., Myers, R. H., Stevens, T. J., Ferrante, R. J., Bird, E. D., and Richardson, E. P., Jr. (1985). Neuropathological classification of Huntington's disease. *Journal of Neuropathology and Experimental Neurology, 44*, 559–577.

Wallesch, C. W., and Fehrenbach, R. A. (1988). On the neurolinguistic nature of language abnormalities in Huntington's disease. *Journal of Neurology, Neurosurgery and Psychiatry, 51,* 367–373.

Weinberger, D. R., Berman, K. F., Iadarola, M., Driesen, N., and Zec, R. F. (1988). Prefrontal cortical blood flow and cognitive function in Huntington's disease. *Journal of Neurology, Neurosurgery, and Psychiatry, 51,* 94–104.

Weingartner, H., Caine, E. D., and Ebert, M. H. (1979). Encoding processes, learning, and recall in Huntington's disease. In T. N. Chase, N. S. Wexler, and A. Barbeau, eds., *Advances in Neurology, Vol. 23: Huntington's Disease.* New York: Raven Press, pp. 215–226.

Wexler, N. S. (1979). Perceptual-motor, cognitive, and emotional characteristics of persons at-risk for Huntington's disease. In T. N. Chase, N. S. Wexler, and A. Barbeau, eds., *Advances in Neurology, Vol. 23: Huntington's Disease.* New York: Raven Press, pp. 257–271.

Wiggins, S., Whyte, P., Huggins, M., Adam, S., Theilmann, J., Bloch, M., Sheps, S. B., Schechter, M. T., and Hayden, M. R. (1992). The psychological consequences of predictive testing for Huntington's disease. Canadian Collaborative Study of Predictive Testing. *New England Journal of Medicine, 327,* 1401–1405.

Wilson, R. S., Como, P. G., Garron, D. C., Klawans, H. L., Barr, A., and Klawans, D. (1987). Memory failure in Huntington's disease. *Journal of Clinical and Experimental Neurology, 9,* 147–154.

Young, A. B., Greenamyre, J. T., Hollingsworth, Z., Albin, R., D'Amato, C., Shoulson, I., and Penney, J. B. (1988). NMDA receptor losses in putamen from patients with Huntington's disease. *Science, 241,* 981–983.

Young, A. B., Penney, J. B., Starosta-Rubenstein, S., Markel, D. S., Berent, S., Giordani, B., Ehrenkaufer, R., Jewett, D., and Hichwa, R. (1986). PET scan investigations of Huntington's disease: Cerebral metabolic correlates of neurological features and functional decline. *Annals of Neurology, 20,* 296–303.

Young, A. B., Penney, J. B., Starosta-Rubenstein, S., Markel, D., Berent, S., Rothley, J., Betley, A., and Hichwa, R. (1987). Normal caudate glucose metabolism in persons at risk for Huntington's disease. *Archives of Neurology, 44,* 254–257.

Yudofsky, S. C., Silver, J. M., Jackson, W., Endicott, J., and Williams, D. (1986). The overt aggression scale of the objective rating of verbal and physical aggression. *American Journal of Psychiatry, 143,* 35–39.

Zweig, R. M., Koven, S. J., Hedreen, J. C., Maestri, N. E., Kazazian, II. II., Jr., and Folstein, S. E. (1989). Linkage to the Huntington's disease locus in a family with unusual clinical and pathological features. *Annals of Neurology, 26,* 78–84.

15

The Effects of Cerebral Vascular Disease on Neuropsychological Functioning

GREGORY G. BROWN, ANNE DULL BAIRD, MARK W. SHATZ, and ROBERT A. BORNSTEIN

About one liter of blood—nearly one fifth of cardiac output—passes through the brain each minute. Blood supplies the brain with glucose and oxygen, while dispersing the heat and metabolic products of cerebral activity (Toole, 1990, pp. 28–29). The brain can tolerate only a brief cessation in the delivery of glucose and oxygen and the removal of metabolites before neural functioning is disrupted. Diseases that clog or rupture vessels, reduce the content of glucose and oxygen in the blood, or affect the autoregulation of blood flow can cause severe neurological and behavioral deficits.

Although comparison of stroke incidence rates for different countries is complicated by differences in the methods of diagnosing stroke, by differences in the method of population sampling and by age differences, the age-adjusted incidence rate of stroke in the Pacific Rim countries, especially Japan and Taiwan, appears to be 1.5 to 2 times the rate of North America and Europe (Katsuki et al., 1965; Matsumoto et al., 1973; Tanaka et al., 1981; Bamford et al., 1988; Ricci et al., 1989; Hu et al., 1992). Comparisons among countries that involve such large differences in culture and race do not permit the separation of environmental and biological factors that underlie incidence rates. However, the wide variation in stroke incidence reported for different Chinese cities suggests that environmental factors, such as variations in salt consumption, might contribute importantly to the incidence of stroke (Li et al., 1985).

Stroke is the third leading cause of death in the United States. Although the age-adjusted annual death rate from cerebrovascular disease has steadily declined in the United States, cerebrovascular disease still caused approximately 60 deaths per 100,000 people in 1988 (American Heart Association, 1992). The reduction in stroke mortality, especially since 1970, appears to be related to a lower incidence of stroke, at least in rural White populations, and to an increase in survival following stroke (Wolf et al., 1992). Although improved acute stroke care has probably contributed to improved survival, the more frequent diagnosis of mild stroke has also contributed to the higher survival rates (Wolf et al., 1992). With improved survival and the aging of the United States population, cerebrovascular disease has become a major cause of disability, causing economic loss, in addition to the cost of medical care and treatment (Kurtzke, 1980). Since neuropsychological measures are sensitive to the brain changes associated with stroke and have implications for adaptive behavior outside the laboratory, they provide a bridge between the physiological changes associated with stroke and its effects on quality of life. This chapter will review the consequences of cerebral vascular disease and its treatment as manifested on standardized neuropsychological tests. Because many studies of affective changes following stroke have not used standardized psychological tests, they will not be reviewed here. Instead, the reader is referred to the recent review by Starkstein et al. (1991).

Metabolic Effects of Complete Cerebral Ischemia

Stroke is the rapid onset of focal neurological deficit. It is usually caused by cerebrovascular disease, but other diseases such as neoplasm may present with a strokelike syndrome. Strokes may be the result of cerebral hemorrhage or cerebral ischemia. In the latter, blood flow to neural tissue is insufficient to maintain physiological function. Cerebral infarction occurs when ischemia is severe enough to produce nerve cell death (Mohr et al., 1980).

The effects of total cerebral ischemia on cellular metabolism occur rapidly. Within seconds after cessation of blood flow, glucose metabolism declines, until it is 15% of its normal level 30 seconds later. Slowing of the electroencephalogram may be observed as soon as 5 seconds after the onset of ischemia. Twenty to 25 seconds later it becomes isoelectric. The alterations in glucose metabolism, as well as the abrupt termination in venous removal of lactic acid and other metabolites, causes acidic pH levels in the brain. An excess of metabolites may dilate cerebral vessels and lead to a loss of autoregulation (Hødt-Rasmussen et al., 1967). The acidosis may alter the excitability of neural tissue (Reivich and Waltz, 1980), stimulate the swelling of glial cells, depress the synthesis of molecular energy when blood flow returns after ischemia, and, perhaps, potentiate the formation of free radical molecules that cause membrane damage (Siesjo, 1985). Levine and colleagues (1992) have proposed that the period of acidosis, which can be dynamically measured in humans by in vivo 31-phosphorus nuclear magnetic resonance spectroscopy, might define a therapeutic window during which acute therapies could improve the survival of brain tissue.

The ability of mitochondria to produce the high-energy phosphates necessary to fuel the activities of a nerve cell declines rapidly in the first minute of total ischemia (Reivich and Waltz, 1980). Since the distribution of potassium, sodium, and calcium across the cell membrane depends on active pumps that use high energy phosphates as fuel, these ionic channels collapse and the resting potential dissipates (Meyer et al., 1976). The influx of calcium into the cell may stimulate a cascade of events that disrupts cell structure, alters the function of receptors and ionic channels, blocks the production of molecular energy, and, possibly, fragments DNA (Siesjo, 1990).

Alteration and loss of presynaptic vesicles occurs 3 to 4 minutes into the ischemic period (Williams and Grossman, 1970). These alterations are accompanied by the release of the neurotransmitters dopamine, serotonin, and norepinephrine into the extracellular space and cerebrospinal fluid (Meyer et al., 1974). Disordered cholinergic transmission after acute stroke may add a neurogenic component to metabolic factors, causing a disruption of autoregulation (Ott et al., 1975).

Between the first and fourth hours after complete cerebral ischemia, the blood becomes stagnant, changes occur in the thin internal lining of the blood vessels, edema develops, and the regional collapse of autoregulation occurs. Although histologic changes continue to develop over the hours and days following ischemia, the type of change depends on the duration and severity of the ischemia, as well as chronicity (Garcia, in press). Acute changes (≤6 hours) involve shrinkage, scalloping, and swelling of neurons; delayed changes (6 to 48 hours) include the alteration of the genetic material in neurons; subacute changes (2 days to 2 weeks) involve an abundant reaction of inflammatory cells; and chronic changes (>2 weeks) consist of the liquefaction and cavitation of the infarcted tissue, with a surrounding zone of astrocyte proliferation (Garcia and Brown, 1992; Garcia, in press).

The Distribution of Cerebral Vessels and Their Collaterals

Two anatomical facts in great part determine the focus and severity of cerebral ischemia— the topography of the major arterial trees and their interconnectedness. Pairs of carotid and vertebral arteries bring blood to the brain. Figure 15-1 shows that the cerebral circulation divides into an anterior division, where the anterior and middle cerebral arteries form the rostral extension of the internal carotid artery, and a posterior division formed by the vertebral-basilar-posterior cerebral arterial network. Although the posterior communicating artery connects these two arterial divisions, little blood is exchanged in normals (Toole, 1990, p. 9).

Several important connections, in addition to the posterior communicating artery, exist among the major arteries of the brain. The two anterior cerebral arteries are connected by the anterior communicating artery (ACoA). Together the two pairs of anterior and posterior cerebral arteries, the ACoA, the posterior communicating artery, and the carotid arteries form a vascular network at the base of the brain called the circle of Willis (see Figs. 15-1 and 15-2). The major cerebral arteries are also joined at their ends by small vessels that pass through the lepto-

meninges. Further, the pericallosal branch of the anterior cerebral artery communicates with the posterior cerebral artery, as it bends around the splenium of the corpus callosum (Van der Drift and Kok, 1972). The external carotid artery has connections with the internal carotid artery, primarily through the ophthalmic artery (Osborn, 1980, pp. 78–85). This complex of connections is a network available to provide a second or collateral source of blood flow when a major artery becomes occluded. Individual variability in this pattern of collateral supply is an important factor in determining the pattern and severity of damage in stroke. Nilsson et al. (1979) have shown that patients with occlusion of an internal carotid artery and collateral flow through the circle of Willis have normal regional blood flow values in the hemisphere ipsilateral to the occlusion, whereas those with collateral flow through the ophthalmic or leptomeningeal arteries had flow values 40% to 50% below normal.

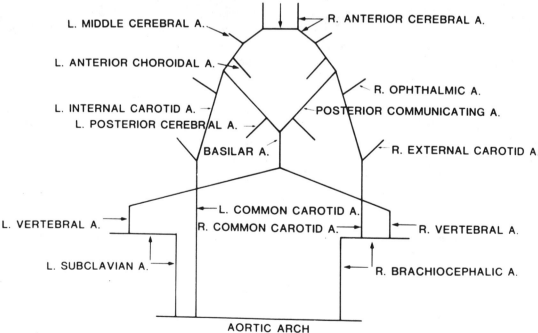

Figure 15-1. A schematic diagram of the major vessels supplying blood to the brain. The polygon shaped like a baseball field at the top of the diagram is the circle of Willis. (Reproduced with permission from Brown et al., 1986.)

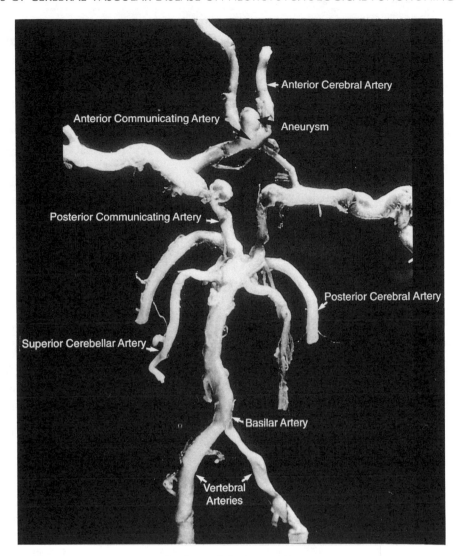

Figure 15-2. Arteries at the base of the brain. The anterior communicating artery and an ACoA aneurysm are indicated by black arrows. The arteries composing the circle of Willis are also seen (see text). (Adapted courtesy of Hirano, 1988, p. 29, Fig. 67.)

Neuropsychology of Cerebral Ischemia

The Behavioral Effects of Stroke in the Carotid Arterial System

Typically, strokes produce focal or multifocal neurobehavioral deficits. Because each carotid artery supplies blood to one cerebral hemisphere, lateralized deficits are common among stroke victims. In addition to producing focal or lateralized neuropsychological symptoms, stroke typically disrupts general behavioral functions that depend on the integrative activity of the entire brain (Hom, 1991).

MOTOR IMPAIRMENT. Reitan and Fitzhugh (1971) studied the effects of lateralized strokes on motor performance measured by Halstead's Finger Tapping Test, the Smedley Hand Dynamometer, and Halstead's Tactual Performance Test (TPT). These authors studied 15 triads of patients composed of one patient with a left hemisphere cerebrovascular lesion, one with a right hemisphere lesion, and one with diffuse cerebrovascular disease. The triads were matched on age, education, and duration of diagnosis. Diagnoses were made on the basis of a "complete neurological evaluation"; no patient was on any medication at the time of the study.

Reitan and Fitzhugh found that within-subject comparisons of left- and right-handed performance revealed a clearer picture of lateralized motor deficit than did between-group comparisons. As an example, patients with right hemisphere strokes did not differ from those with left hemispheric strokes on finger tapping or TPT performance with the right hand. However, when difference scores between the two hands were calculated, the left and right hemisphere stroke patients did differ on both measures of motor functioning.

Although the within-group data of Reitan and Fitzhugh clearly demonstrated lateralized motor effects, the absence of a normal control group coupled with a dominance of the right hand for grip strength and finger tapping makes it difficult to decide if one hemisphere has greater bilateral control over those motor functions. If one hemisphere does have bilateral motor control, then one might falsely infer bilateral cerebral involvement from the effects of a unilateral lesion. Evidence for left hemisphere control of motor behaviors that involve "manual skill requiring several hand movements" has been reported by several authors (Liepmann, 1913; Kimura and Archibald, 1974; Kimura, 1977).

To pursue this laterality issue further, Haaland and Delaney (1981) studied the motor performance of 26 patients with left hemisphere strokes and 17 with right hemisphere strokes. Both groups were evaluated on grip strength, finger tapping, grooved pegboard, maze coordination, vertical groove steadiness, and static steadiness about 2 years after their stroke. Haaland and Delaney's analysis showed that the left hemisphere does not exercise greater bilateral control over the types of motor tasks they studied. They did find that their motor tasks were unequal in their sensitivity to the ipsilateral effects of stroke. The hand ipsilateral to the stroke differed from the performance of controls only on the grooved pegboard, maze coordination, and steadiness tests, whereas the hand contralateral to the stroke was impaired relative to controls on grip strength, finger tapping, grooved pegboard, and maze coordination.

Finlayson and Reitan (1980) also found no convincing evidence that cerebrovascular lesions, traumatic brain injuries, or neoplasms of the left hemisphere produce greater ipsilateral deficit on grip strength and finger tapping than the same type of lesion in the right hemisphere. They argued that some of the evidence for greater left hemispheric control of ipsilateral motor performance is explained by right hand dominance for these tasks. Because right handers perform better on grip strength tests with the right hand, it is not surprising that the left hand of patients with left hemisphere lesions is relatively worse than the right hand following right hemisphere lesions. Depending on how the research design is developed, one might confuse this dominant hand effect for greater bilateral control by the left hemisphere. However, more recently Hom and Reitan (1982) controlled for dominant hand effects by comparing right and left hemispheric stroke patients on T scores standardized separately for the right and left hands. They concluded that the right hemisphere is "predominant" for ipsilateral functions that integrate perceptual and motor activity, such as TPT.

Investigators who have found greater left hemisphere control over the left hand than right hemisphere control over the right hand did not base their findings on tests of finger tapping or grip strength (Kimura and Archibald, 1974; Kimura, 1977). Instead, data from their stroke patients imply greater bilateral control of a series of skilled movements by the left hemisphere.

We may infer several generalizations about the motor performance of stroke patients from the studies in this section. In right handers, grip strength and finger tapping are selectively impaired on the hand contralateral to the hemisphere with the cerebrovascular lesion. Neither the right nor the left hemisphere predominates in the bilateral control of grip strength, finger flexion, or simple coordination. Tests that depend heavily on intact motor steadiness or coordination show greater ipsilateral effects than do finger tapping or grip strength. The left hemisphere may have greater bilateral control than the right over motor tests that involve a series of learned movements, especially when responding to verbal commands. However, the right hemisphere may have greater bilateral control over movements involving a spatial component.

SENSORY DEFICITS. Reitan and Fitzhugh (1971) also studied the lateralization of deficits in single and double simultaneous visual, auditory, and tactile stimulation, finger gnosis, and finger graphesthesia. When comparing left and right hemisphere lesion patients, only one right-sided sensory test produced a significant group difference, whereas seven left-sided sensory measures differed by group. Only the comparison between the right and left hands during double simultaneous stimulation of the two hands produced a clear crossover effect, suggesting a strong lateralizing sign. Overall, the patterns of between and within group comparisons suggested greater bilateral control of tactile processing by the right hemisphere, greater contralateral loss in visual functioning after right hemisphere lesions, and very little lateralization of simple auditory perception. Boll (1974) has shown that for a mixed group of lateralized trauma, stroke, and tumor patients, right hemisphere lesions are associated with a greater number of ipsilateral errors on tests of finger gnosis, finger graphesthesia, and tactile form recognition than for patients with left hemisphere lesions. He also reported a greater number of contralateral errors among right hemisphere lesion patients than left. More recently, Hom and Reitan (1982) have confirmed poorer ipsilateral performance on sensory-motor measures following right hemispheric lesions compared with left.

INTELLECTUAL FUNCTIONING. Reitan and Fitzhugh (1971) examined the effects of stroke on Wechsler-Bellevue I scores. Although patients with left hemispheric strokes scored worse on Verbal IQ than patients with right hemispheric strokes, there was no difference between the two groups on Performance IQ. Nonetheless, the within-group comparisons showed a more strongly lateralized pattern; left hemispheric stroke patients scored significantly worse on Verbal IQ than Performance IQ, whereas right hemispheric stroke patients scored significantly worse on Performance than Verbal IQ. The between and within-group findings together suggested that left hemispheric vascular lesions affect both Verbal and Performance IQs, although Verbal IQ is affected to a greater extent. In a similar study that included a healthy control group, Reitan (1970) clearly showed that left hemispheric stroke depresses both Verbal and Performance IQs, with Verbal IQ more severely depressed than Performance IQ. In that same study, he also found that right hemispheric stroke patients had significantly lower Verbal and Performance IQs than controls, although, not surprisingly, Performance IQ was more significantly impaired than Verbal IQ. Recently, Hom and Reitan (1990) replicated these findings using the Wechsler Adult Intelligence Scale. The one exception was that even though the Verbal IQ of the right hemisphere stroke patients was numerically smaller than the Verbal IQ of healthy controls, the difference was not significant.

In summary, lateralized stroke produces predictable differences in Verbal and Performance IQs that are best detected by within-subject comparisons. However, left hemispheric strokes appear to more consistently produce general impairment of intellectual functioning than does right hemispheric stroke. The question of what conditions must be met for strokes of the right hemisphere to disrupt intellectual functioning generally remains a lively issue. It is very likely to be unresolved until mediating factors such as intrahemispheric localization of the stroke, lesion size, and chronicity are accounted for in study designs.

GENERAL ADAPTIVE FUNCTIONING. Indices of general adaptive functioning studied in stroke fall into two classes. The first class is composed of indices, such as the Halstead Impairment Index and the Average Impairment Index, that sum over scores obtained from separate tests. These indices measure the additive effects of impairment of discrete functions. The second class of indices is comprised of scores from single tests, such as the Halstead Category Test and the Trail Making Test, that reflect the integrated, interactive behavior of the brain. Lateralized stroke lowers scores on both types of indices, regardless of the side of the lesion. In particular, Hom and Reitan (1990) have found that left and right hemispheric stroke produced similar levels of impairment on the Halstead Impairment Index, the Halstead Category Test, Trail Making Test–Part B, the Digit Symbol subtest from the WAIS, and the memory score from the Tactual Performance Test. These findings imply that lateralized stroke impairs general adaptive brain functions, such as abstraction and some measures of incidental memory and attention (Hom, 1991).

Transient Ischemia

Some patients with cerebrovascular disease will develop focal neurological deficit that reverses within 24 hours. Although the criterion of one day is commonly used to define these transient ischemic attacks (TIA) in clinical research and practice, most carotid artery TIAs are much briefer, typically lasting less than 10 minutes (Pessin et al., 1977). Nonetheless, the 24-hour criterion is uniformly used to identify patients in neuropsychological studies of TIA.

Although a few neuropsychological studies of TIA patients have been published, most neuropsychological data on TIA patients come from presurgical studies of individuals receiving carotid endarterectomies. Altogether we found 10 papers reporting neuropsychological findings on patients with TIAs of the anterior circulation (Duke et al., 1968; Goldstein et al., 1970; Horne and Royle, 1974; Haynes et al., 1976; Matarazzo et al., 1979; Delaney et al., 1980; Hemmingsen et al., 1982; Baird et al., 1984; Parker et al., 1986; Casey et al., 1989). Although we attempted to exclude all studies that included patients with fixed strokes, even minor ones, the remaining studies varied in their description of the methods used to rule out stroke. Consequently, some of the patients in the remaining studies might have had minor, fixed neurological deficits.

With this caveat in mind, we identified three neuropsychological tests, Finger Oscillation, Trail Making Test, and the Wechsler Adult Intelligence Scale (unrevised) that were given with sufficient frequency across these eleven groups to permit statistical analysis. To place scores from these tests on a common scale, we converted the values for Full Scale IQ (FSIQ), Total Time on Trails B, and Dominant Hand Finger Oscillation to T scores using the age and education norms provided by Heaton et al. (1991). The mean FSIQ, Trails B time, and Finger Tapping scores for each study were transformed into T scores and plotted in Figure 15-3. As can be seen, most T scores for the cognitive measures, FSIQ and Trails B time, fell below the normative mean T score of 50. By contrast, T scores for Finger Tapping, although more widely distributed than for the cognitive measures, tended to center around 50. Statistical testing confirmed these visual impressions; whereas the mean T score for FSIQ and for Trails B time fell significantly below 50 (mean FSIQ = 33.2, $t(8) = 2.92$, $p < .01$; mean Trails B time = 37.6, $t(9) = 2.94$, $p < .01$), mean Finger Tapping T score did not significantly differ from 50 (mean = 46.4, $t(9) = .87$, $p = .137$, all tests were one-tailed).

Our review suggests that TIA patients often have cognitive deficits that persist after their clinical symptoms subside. That TIA patients experience relatively little motor abnormality is not surprising since patients with persistent motor deficits on neurological exam should have been diagnosed as having stroke rather than TIA. That some of the studies reviewed above might not have adequately screened patients for stroke raises the question of whether the findings from our review might reflect small strokes occurring in a subgroup of patients. However, the results from a study by Delaney et al.

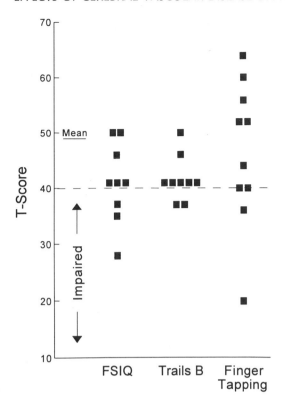

Figure 15-3. T scores adjusted for age and education using the Heaton et al. (1991) norms. Each data point is based on the mean of an entire sample.

(1980), who did carefully screen for stroke, support our general conclusions. They found TIA patients impaired on tests of concept formation, perceptual-motor integration, verbal fluency, and memory, but unimpaired on tests of simple motor or sensory functioning.

The studies reviewed above examined patients with TIAs of the anterior cerebral circulation. Several additional investigations provide information about the neuropsychological functioning of patients with vertebrobasilar ischemia (VBI). Ponsford et al. (1980) have reported on 10 patients with VBI; four of the 10 patients had symptoms on neurological examination and, perhaps, had infarction rather than transient ischemia. In five cases angiography was performed to confirm the diagnosis. Patients with vertebrobasilar ischemic disease performed worse than matched controls on some memory tests

(e.g., the Visual Reproduction and Associate Learning subtests from the Wechsler Memory Scale). No differences were found on tests of general orientation, prose recall (immediate or delayed), or Lhermitte and Signoret's (1972) tests of spatial and logical arrangement. Vertebrobasilar patients performed like control subjects on Benton's Facial Recognition Test and on the Block Design and Picture Completion subtests of the WAIS. Additionally, the authors found that the Wechsler Memory Quotient was lower than the WAIS Verbal IQ in nine of 10 patients. They concluded that patients with vertebrobasilar ischemic disease have a specific problem with memory functioning rather than a global dementia.

Research in our laboratory failed to confirm the consistent presence of memory deficit in patients with the symptoms and angiographic findings of vertebrobasilar ischemia (Baird et al., 1984). Five of 11 of our VBI patients had Wechsler Memory Quotients 10 or more points higher than their Full Scale IQ. Further, we could not distinguish patients with symptoms and angiographic findings associated with carotid disease from those with vertebrobasilar disease (Baird et al., 1984). Perez and associates also found nearly equal Full Scale IQs (mean, 97.15) and Wechsler Memory Quotients (mean, 96.81) in 16 VBI patients (Perez et al., 1975a,b). If most of the patients studied by Ponsford et al. (1980) had admitting complaints of memory loss, then they studied a more selective sample of VBI patients than did we or Perez et al. Given the variety of complaints with which VBI patients present (Futty et al., 1977) and the wide distribution of sites in the brain stem, cerebellum, midbrain, diencephalon, and cerebrum that may be involved, it is unlikely that any one symptom would be present in most patients with VBI, unless it was a necessary criterion for the diagnosis.

Neuropsychological Correlates of Cerebral Angiography and Blood Flow

Although the site of the stenosis or occlusion is apparently not related to specific neuropsychological deficits (Baird et al., 1984), summary ratings of the extent of stenosis of the major cerebral vessels is correlated with general indices of neuropsychological functioning, at least among individuals with TIAs or minor stroke (Baird et al., 1985). Moreover, because nearly all of the vessels rated in Baird's study were judged to be angiographically patent, the extent of patency was not useful in accounting for differences in the level of neuropsychological functioning. Consequently, Baird and colleagues (1985) concluded that ratings of patency were a poor substitute for a measure of cerebral blood flow. When cerebral blood flow has been measured, asymmetry of blood flow is highly correlated with neuropsychological signs of asymmetry among patients with lateralized stroke (Brown et al., 1991a). The site of depressed cerebral blood flow appears to more strongly predict neuropsychological impairment than angiographic measures of stenosis or occlusion.

The Neuropsychology of Hemorrhage

The neuropsychological literature discussed above primarily involved patients with ischemic stroke. This section focuses on patients with vascular anomalies that commonly produce hemorrhagic stroke. Such patients frequently present with a neurological deficit that gradually develops over five to 30 minutes and with some change in alertness (Kase et al., 1992). We will review the neuropsychological effects of cerebral hemorrhage associated with cerebral aneurysms and arteriovenous malformations. Although the literature on the effects of hypertension on neuropsychological functioning is reviewed below, so few studies have examined the neuropsychological effects of hypertensive hemorrhage that we will not attempt to review this topic.

Cerebral Aneurysms

An aneurysm is a thin-walled balloon-shaped dilatation of a vessel (see Fig. 15-2). Patients with aneurysms frequently present with hemorrhage; the rupture of an intracranial aneurysm may cause bleeding into brain parenchyma, the ventricular system, or subarachnoid spaces. Other aneurysms are found incidently on imaging studies of the head or on cerebral angiography when evaluating a patient for nonhemorrhagic neurologic disorders.

Aneurysms can disrupt cerebral functioning by rupturing, shedding emboli, producing mass effects, and causing hydrocephalus or spasm of the cerebral vessels (Mohr et al., 1992). The hemorrhage disrupts the normal supply of oxygen and glucose to brain tissue and disrupts removal of heat and byproducts from metabolic activities. Consequently, areas of infarction develop. The blood itself can be toxic to brain tissue, and this may be another source of neuronal dysfunction (Fein, 1975). Hemorrhage and the surgical removal of aneurysms can cause vasospasm. This constriction of cerebral vessels reduces cerebral blood flow and disrupts energy metabolism (Powers and Grubb, 1987). The cascade of metabolic effects caused by vasospasm can eventually lead to brain infarction.

In general, studies of the neuropsychological effects of hemorrhage due to aneurysmal rupture have examined three issues: the neuropsychological effects of surgical removal of aneurysms of the anterior communicating artery, the effects of aneurysm site on the pattern of neuropsychological deficit, and factors predicting outcome. Because most patients investigated in this literature were studied after hemorrhage and surgery, the effects of these two factors are difficult to separate. The interesting syndrome following surgical removal of ACoA aneurysms has recently been reviewed elsewhere (Brown et al., 1991b, DeLuca and Cicerone, 1991; DeLuca, 1992); therefore, we will not discuss it in this chapter.

Because the investigation of patients with ischemic stroke has provided neuropsychology with many of its principles of localization of functioning, the natural inclination is to assume that the site of cerebral hemorrhage has a powerful effect on the pattern of subsequent neuropsychological deficits. However, much of the evidence contradicts this assumption. Stabell (1991) reported that neither the site nor the side of a hemorrhage was associated with particular patterns of neuropsychological impairment in a large sample of patients with subarachnoid hemorrhage. Similarly, Richardson (1991) found that patients studied 6 weeks following aneurysmal subarachnoid hemorrhage displayed disrupted performance on a broad range of neuropsychological tests regardless of site. For example, Richardson (1991) found that patients with aneurysms of the left middle and left internal carotid arteries were no more impaired than patients with aneurysms on the right on measures of object naming latency, synonym vocabulary, fluent word generation, and verbal memory.

Nonetheless, some investigators have found that either the severity or the pattern of neuropsychological deficit was associated with the rupture or surgery of aneurysms at particular sites. For example, Bornstein et al. (1987) found that patients with ACoA aneurysms were over-represented among patients with poor neuropsychological functioning following subarachnoid hemorrhage. However, the impairment of aneurysmal patients who displayed poor performance was rather broad, encompassing the impairment of intelligence, concept formation and abstraction, attention, and memory. Contrary to the finding of wide-ranging deficits associated with ACoA aneurysms, DeLuca and colleagues have found that ACoA patients with Full Scale IQs in the middle of the normal range may, nonetheless, have impaired immediate and delayed recall (DeLuca and Cicerone, 1991; DeLuca, 1992). Turning to aneurysms at other sites, Barbarotto et al. (1989) concluded that patients with surgical removal of lateralized aneurysms of the middle and posterior communicating artery experience lateralized neuropsychological deficits. However, the authors qualified their conclusion by observing that in individual cases the extent of the neuropsychological deficit is broader than the pattern expected from the side of the aneurysm alone. Further, the data presented in the paper indicate that patients with surgical removal of left hemispheric aneurysms are often impaired on the same measures as those with right

hemispheric aneurysms. Additionally, the data analysis did not involve a direct comparison of the left and right hemispheric patients. Consequently, the paper by Barbarotto and colleagues does not strongly contradict Stabell's (1991) finding that side of hemorrhage does not predict the pattern of subsequent neuropsychological deficit.

Several issues should be considered when reviewing studies of localization of neuropsychological deficit associated with cerebral aneurysms. Studies differ about what aspect of the lesion is being lateralized or localized. For some studies, the site of the aneurysm, perhaps visualized on cerebral angiography, is the basis for the localization. In other studies, the site of the hemorrhage provides the localizing information. Because an aneurysmal hemorrhage is often larger than the aneurysm and because hemorrhages often change in size during the first 48 hours after a bleed, the location of the aneurysm as determined by cerebral angiography and the location of the hemorrhage as seen on computed tomography or magnetic resonance imaging are generally not coextensive. Too often, neuropathological factors associated with generalized neuropsychological dysfunction, such as generalized vasospasm, hydrocephalus, generalized edema, and intraventricular hemorrhage, are not separated from more focal factors, such as focal vasospasm, intracerebral hemorrhage, and infarction. The type of hemorrhage (subarachnoid, intraventricular, intracerebral) should be considered in studies of neuropsychological asymmetries following lateralized hemorrhage. Methods of pattern or profile analysis, such as those discussed when examining neuropsychological asymmetries following lateralized stroke, have not generally been used in the study of neuropsychological asymmetries following lateralized hemorrhage. Comparisons based on profiles can be more powerful than univariate analyses because patterns are defined within subjects and therefore can be useful in separating specific deficits from more general decline. Finally, the current literature suggests that future studies of lateralization or localization of functioning should not combine patients with hemorrhage and patients with ischemic stroke.

Recent studies of the recovery of neuropsychological functioning after cerebral hemorrhage generally find that patients who survive improve (Richardson, 1991; Stabell, 1991), although earlier studies were more pessimistic (Ljunggren et al., 1985; Sonesson et al., 1987). Like ischemic stroke, much of the improvement appears to occur within the first 6 months (Adams et al., 1976; Richardson, 1991). However, individual subjects can continue to improve for longer periods. There is little consensus about factors that predict the extent of neuropsychological deficit following aneurysmal hemorrhage or predict the extent of recovery. Richardson (1991) found that recent hemorrhage (6 weeks versus 6 months) and postsurgical vasospasm predicted poorer neuropsychological performance. Bornstein et al. (1987) found that increasing age, hemorrhage associated with ACoA aneurysms, and poor postsurgical neurological status predicted worse neuropsychological functioning. In Stabell's (1991) study, age, hypertension, neurological status at admission, hydrocephalus, postsurgical vasospasm producing delayed ischemic deterioration, intraventricular hemorrhage, and intracerebral hemorrhage were associated with neuropsychological outcome. Other researchers have also found that perioperative vasospasm and systemic hypertension are predictors of poor

functional recovery (Krayenbuhl et al., 1972; Adams et al., 1976). Building a theory capable of predicting recovery of functioning following aneurysmal hemorrhage remains a challenge to neuropsychological research. Perhaps, a useful scale could be developed from the factors identified in Stabell's study. A starting point might involve a scale that gave one point to each factor identified in Stabell's study. The equal weighting could be modified as more was learned about the relative importance of different prognostic factors.

Arteriovenous Malformations

An arteriovenous malformation (AVM) is a congenital entanglement of blood vessels that forms an abnormal connection between the arterial and venous circulation (Adams and Victor, 1985, p. 622). Arteriovenous malformations are fetal abnormalities arising about 3 weeks after conception, when primitive vessels divide into arteries and veins (Stein and Wolpert, 1980). An arrest at this early stage in the epigenesis of cerebral vessels produces a pipe-like connection or fistula, which replaces the capillary bed. As seen in Figure 15-4, blood is generally supplied to the nidus or core of an AVM by several feeding arteries and leaves the core through an enlarged draining vein. AVMs are relatively rare, with only 2000 new cases identified each year in the United States (Stein

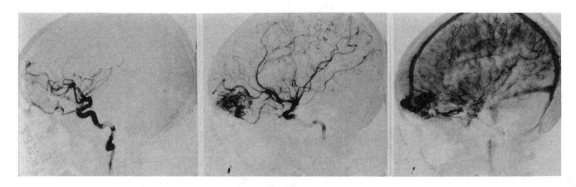

Figure 15-4. Cerebral angiogram of an arteriovenous malformation. (A) Early arterial phase: arrows point to two hypertrophied feeder-arteries. (B) Arterial phase: arrow points to the nidus of the arteriovenous malformation. (C) Venous phase: arrow points to large draining vein. (Reprinted with permission from Brown et al., 1991b.)

and Wolpert, 1980). However, many cases of asymptomatic AVMs go undetected. McCormick (1966), for example, found 24 (12.2%) symptomatic AVMs among the 196 AVMs identified during 4530 consecutive autopsies. Although the majority of AVMs that become symptomatic present with hemorrhage, AVMs make up only 2% to 9% of all hemorrhages (Perret and Nishioka, 1966; Perret, 1975; Gross et al., 1984) and about 1% of all strokes (Mohr et al., 1986). Hemorrhagic AVMs typically occur in the second through fifth decades. The rarity of cases occurring in the first decade probably reflects the slow development of the abnormality (Stein and Wolpert, 1980).

Presurgical impairment of cognitive functioning varies widely in patients with AVMs. The impairment can be manifested as a specific neurobehavioral syndrome or as a general disruption of adaptive functioning (Reitan and Wolfson, 1985). In early studies of patients coming to surgery, the frequency of cognitive impairment ranged from none (Constans and Assal, 1971) to 50% (Olivecrona and Reeves, 1948). Perhaps the most important limitation of these studies was that none used well-validated measures of neuropsychological functioning.

A study by Waltimo and Putkonen (1974) represented a turning point in the neuropsychological analysis of AVMs. They administered the Wechsler Adult Intelligence Scale (WAIS), the Benton Visual Retention Test (BVRT), Token Test, and tests of immediate and delayed memory to 40 patients with AVMs. In comparing patients with left- or right-sided AVMs, no differences were found on any of the cognitive measures. Additional analyses did not indicate any relationship between overall intellectual performance (i.e., Full Scale IQ) and size, laterality, or symptoms of the AVM. However, there was a trend toward an association between neurobehavioral impairment and previous hemorrhage.

In an additional analysis, patients were grouped on the basis of the uniformity of their cognitive performance. Those with obvious cognitive deficits and a large Verbal-Performance IQ difference were placed into one group ("high inequality"), and the remainder of patients were placed in a second group. "High inequality" was found to be associated to a greater extent with right-sided malformations. Waltimo and Putkonen concluded that AVMs do not produce the kind of specific cognitive changes typically seen with acute focal lesions involving equivalent areas of the brain.

Despite the findings of Waltimo and Putkonen, case studies and small group studies suggest that, in some cases, localization of an AVM by neuropsychological methods is possible (Close et al., 1977; Conley et al., 1980). Mahalick et al. (1991) also reported lateralized neuropsychological deficits in a moderately large group of patients with lateralized AVMs. Brown and colleagues (1989) compared the accuracy of neuropsychological measures in predicting the laterality of AVMs with their accuracy in predicting the laterality of ischemic stroke. Information from seven commonly used neuropsychological measures was analyzed using three techniques: discriminant function analysis (DFA), clinical judgment, and actuarial signs. Although neuropsychological findings were significantly related to the laterality of ischemic stroke for all three methods, only clinical judgments were significantly related to laterality of AVMs for the complete sample. However, when neuropsychological evidence of lateralized dysfunction was clearly evident, actuarial signs and clinical ratings were as accurate in classifying the laterality of AVMs as they were in classifying the laterality of ischemic stroke. The results of this study are consistent with the findings of Waltimo and Putkonen in suggesting that AVMs will not always produce the kind of cognitive effects that might be expected from knowledge of its location. Nonetheless, when neuropsychological signs of asymmetry are clearly present, the laterality of AVMs can be predicted as accurately as the laterality of thrombotic-embolic strokes. Neuropathological features of AVMs that might be responsible for their variable neuropsychological effects are discussed in Brown et al. (1989, 1991b). Because lateralized AVMs more variably produce lateralized neuropsychological dysfunction than lateralized ischemic stroke, patients with lateralized AVMs should not be grouped with patients with lateralized ischemic stroke in laterality studies of cerebrovascular disease.

Distinguishing the Effects of Stroke from the Effects of Other Brain Diseases

Stroke and Tumors

Distinguishing patients with rapidly growing tumors from stroke patients is a challenging clinical problem, because patients from each group often have lateralized findings and moderate to severe impairment of general neuropsychological functioning. Finkelstein's (1977) BRAIN program, a set of automated rules for interpreting the Halstead-Reitan Neuropsychological Test Battery, includes an algorithm for making this distinction. It reaches the diagnosis "cerebrovascular accident" if the patient has evidence of brain dysfunction, with lateralized deficits characterized either by a severe deficit in finger tapping or by a moderate finger tapping deficit coupled with disturbance in tactile functioning mediated by the cortex and lateralized to the same hand. The program relies on tests of finger gnosis, finger graphesthesia, and the single or double stimulation of face and hand as tactile-cortical tests. Finkelstein's program has other diagnostic rules for identifying vascular abnormalities with recent bleeding and diffuse cerebral atherosclerosis. He also has separate rules for detecting metastatic carcinoma and slowly growing tumors. In the original validation study, Finkelstein's program correctly diagnosed nine of 12 patients with cerebrovascular accidents and eight of 12 with fast growing tumors. For only three patients were these two diagnoses confused. Reitan and Wolfson (1994) have recently shown that although lateralized tumors and strokes produce the same degree of disturbance of language and constructional praxis, lateralized stroke produces more pronounced impairment of contralateral finger tapping.

Dementia of the Alzheimer Type and Multi-Infarct Dementia

As Hachinski (1990) has observed, there has been a recent resurgence of interest in vascular dementia. The increased interest followed the discovery that many patients with Alzheimer's disease and some elderly individuals without large vessel infarcts have a rarefication of the white matter, leukoaraiosis, that can be observed on computed tomography or magnetic resonance imaging of the head. Because initial studies found an association between leukoaraiosis on the one hand and subcortical ischemia or stroke risk factors on the other, some investigators argued that vascular disease contributed more to dementing conditions than previously thought. However, the association between leukoaraiosis and dementia was weakened when several studies found that leukoaraiosis could be observed on magnetic resonance images of individuals who had normal neuropsychological functioning (Hunt et al., 1989; Leys et al., 1990).

The neuropathological description of vascular dementia remains a matter of debate. Modern positron-emission computed tomography studies do support the argument of Hachinski et al. (1974) that vascular dementia is not the result of a chronic ischemia caused by atherosclerosis. However, the alternative view—that of the various types of tissue changes seen in cerebrovascular disease, only multiple completed infarctions producing a total volume of tissue softening exceeding 50 ml contribute to cognitive impairment in dementia—has recently been challenged (e.g., Hachinski, 1990). Critical areas of the brain have been identified, such as the left angular gyrus, the upper mesencephalon, and thalamus, where either single infarcts or small infarct volumes can produce a dementing syndrome (Benson and Cummings, 1982; Katz et al., 1987). Further, neuropathological studies of patients with vascular dementia have revealed a variety of brain changes in addition to complete infarction. These include laminar necrosis (neuronal death in selective layers of the cortex), granular cortical atrophy (multiple cortical scars), subcortical leukoencephalopathy ("pallor," "cavitation," or focal areas of "reactive" astrogliosis involving white matter), lacunar infarcts, and gliosis or incomplete ischemic necrosis (Garcia and Brown, 1992). In part, as a recognition of the potential multiple mechanisms by which vascular disease might cause dementia, the report of the NINDS-AIREN International Workshop on Vascular Dementia recommended that the term vascular dementia, abbreviated VaD, replace the term multi-infarct dementia as the generic term used to classify dementia caused by vascular disease (Roman et al., 1993).

Some of the neuropsychological research on VaD has attempted to separate VaD from Alzheimer's disease. For example, in two studies Perez and associates (1975b, 1976) found that patients with dementia of the Alzheimer's type (DAT) generally perform more poorly than patients with multi-infarct dementia (MID) on the WAIS Full Scale IQ or on WAIS subtests. DAT patients did score worse than MID patients on the Wechsler Memory Quotient and on all the subtests of the WMS, other than information and logical memory (Perez et al., 1975a).

Initial research on a WAIS profile discussed by Fuld (1984) indicated that it might be useful in distinguishing AD patients from VaD patients (Brinkman and Braun, 1984; Fuld, 1984). However, recent work has failed to replicate these earlier results (Gfeller and Rankin, 1991). The profile depends on the finding that the differential effects of scopolamine on WAIS subtests paralleled the differential effects of early AD on WAIS subtests (Drachman and Leavitt, 1974). A considerable literature exists about the use of this profile in the differential diagnosis of dementia (Fuld, 1986; Satz et al., 1990). The interested reader is encouraged to review these papers.

Much of the neuropsychological literature on the differential diagnosis of AD and VaD has been motivated by the idea that AD and VaD impair somewhat different abilities and therefore should display either a different

pattern of impairment or different kinds of errors. Further, patients with VaD are thought to show more variable performance. Benton (1988) has observed that tests of these hypotheses often have failed to take into account the considerable variability found in AD, have failed to consider the possibility that different patterns of performance might be associated with different levels of dementia severity, and have failed to use appropriate statistical methods for comparing group profiles, relying instead on multiple univariate tests. However, two recent studies have found that AD and VaD patients matched on overall level of dementia severity do show either different types of errors on some neuropsychological tasks or different patterns of performance across structured and unstructured tests (Mendez and Ashla-Mendez, 1991; Gainotti et al., 1992). Despite the methodological criticisms presented by Benton (1988), possible neuropsychological contributions to the differential diagnosis of AD and VaD remains an active area of research.

Stroke Risk Factors and Neuropsychological Correlates

A comprehensive understanding of the neuropsychological consequences of cerebrovascular disease requires consideration of the potential impact of systemic diseases or conditions that are associated with the occurrence of stroke. These include hypertension, diabetes mellitus, hyperlipidemia, cardiac disease, and age. In addition to their association with the occurrence of stroke, these risk factors have potential neuropsychological sequelae, and may also influence the natural recovery process. Furthermore, these factors could potentially influence the outcome of treatment for stroke. It is therefore worthwhile to include in this chapter a discussion of the neuropsychological correlates of various risk factors for cerebrovascular disease. Because a review of the effects of age on neuropsychological functioning would be lengthy, it will not be reviewed here. To some extent, risk factors may be associated with different forms of cerebrovascular disease, and in many cases the neurobehavioral correlates have not been investigated specifically in reference to stroke. The following sections will attempt to summarize current opinion regarding the neuropsychological effects of the principal stroke risk factors.

Hypertension

Hypertension is the strongest medical risk factor of stroke (Shekelle et al., 1974; Kannel et al., 1976; Salonen et al., 1982), and is the most extensively studied in regard to neuropsychological sequelae. This is a chronic disorder that affects approximately 25% of the adult population in the United States (Kaplan, 1983). The precise mechanism by which hypertension influences cognitive function is not known, but studies of cerebral blood flow have demonstrated diminished flow that is greatest in the frontal and temporal regions and is related to duration of illness (Rodriguez et al., 1987). Nonetheless, in elderly individuals without stroke the activation of whole brain blood flow appears unrelated to a composite index of stroke risk that includes hypertension (Ewing et al., 1989). Therefore, stroke risk factors do not appear to constrain the blood supply to the brain during the times of increased cognitive functioning, even though hypertension might be associated with an altered blood flow landscape.

The early studies (Enzer et al., 1942; Apter et al., 1951) indicate a long history to the recognition of neurobehavioral correlates of hypertension. An extensive review of this literature has recently been provided by Waldstein et al. (1991a). This report, in addition to a previous review (Bornstein and Kelly, 1991), indicate that there is considerable variability in the methodological sophistication of these studies in this area. However, there appear to be a sufficient number of reasonably well-controlled studies that permit some conclusions about the neuropsychological consequences of hypertension.

There appears to be some consensus that subtle neuropsychological impairment can be associated with hypertension, and may be present in the early stages of illness. Several studies have controlled for the effects of age and education, and some of these have also controlled for other potentially confounding medical conditions including other risk factors for stroke. One recent study (Waldstein et al., 1991b) also controlled for the potential effect of awareness of a chronic illness in addition to other potential confounding factors. The evidence for neuropsychological abnormality related to hypertension is strongest in the areas of attention, memory, and concept formation. Less consistent support has been found for relationships between hypertension and measures of visuospatial construction, mental flexibility, and response speed. There is no evidence of a substantial progression in neurobehavioral dysfunction associated with chronic hypertension. In general, the difference between group means tends to persist over time, even though in some cases treatment-related improvements may be demonstrated.

Most of the studies reviewed by Bornstein and Kelly (1991) and Waldstein et al. (1991a) were designed to examine the interactions of age and hypertension on neuropsychological function, or attempted to isolate the effects of hypertension by controlling for age and excluding patients with other potential cerebrovascular risk factors. A variety of statistical and experimental controls have been employed to permit a more careful study of the effects of hypertension, but these studies may not reflect the clinical reality that many patients have multiple stroke risk factors. A recent study (Desmond et al., 1993) employed logistic regression analyses that controlled for demographic factors, and adjusted for the effects of other stroke risk factors. In a large stroke-free sample of elderly subjects, there was no significant effect of hypertension on any area of cognitive performance. This is consistent with the effects of a large-scale epidemiological study (Farmer et al., 1987) that found a relationship between abnormalities in verbal memory and definite hypertension but no correlation with lesser degrees of illness. The conclusions reached by Desmond et al. (1993) and Farmer et al. (1987) are somewhat divergent from those that appear to be drawn from more narrowly focused studies of the effects of hypertension. This divergence may reflect the heterogeneity of hypertension as well as the numerous methodological issues that complicate the examination of the neurobehavioral consequences of hypertension (Waldstein et al., 1991a). As indicated in that review, there may be specific subgroups of hypertensives who are at increased risk for neuropsychological dysfunction. Although hypertension is the most carefully studied stroke risk factor in the neuropsychological literature, further investigations are necessary to clarify these relationships. Other studies will also be necessary to examine the potential effects of other stroke risk factors. The available evidence on the neurobehavioral consequences of diabetes mellitus and serum lipids are reviewed below.

Diabetes Mellitus

Diabetes is associated with increased risk of stroke, and several possible mechanisms for neurological dysfunction have been proposed (Bornstein and Kelly, 1991). Before 1980 there were very few studies, and most subsequent studies have been conducted with juvenile-onset diabetes. Holmes and her colleagues (1983, 1986; Holmes, 1990) found that hypoglycemic blood levels were associated with impaired performance on measures of verbal fluency, speed of recall, and decision-making speed. This neurobehavioral dysfunction appears to be related to severity of illness (Skenazy and Bigler, 1984) and the control of serum glucose levels (Holmes, 1986).

Meuter et al. (1980) examined neuropsychological performance in adult-onset diabetics and found that deficits on tests of reaction time, concentration, and memory were more common than in patients with juvenile onset. The recent report by Desmond et al. (1993) provides an evaluation of the effects of diabetes in the context of other demographic and stroke risk factors. In that sample of stroke-free elderly community volunteers, diabetes was related to deficits in abstract reasoning and visuospatial function after the effects of

demographic factors and other risk factors were adjusted. This is consistent with the study by Meuter et al. (1980) and suggests that neurobehavioral dysfunction may be associated with adult-onset diabetes. It is unclear whether these deficits are different from those observed in patients with juvenile onset, or what factors may be predictive of dysfunction. It may be that duration of illness or severity of glucose intolerance may be important factors.

Serum Lipids

Although serum cholesterol is an important predictor of cardiovascular disease, it appears to be a relatively weak predictor of stroke (Gordon et al., 1981). Nevertheless, the recognized atherogenic potential of elevated serum lipids, and the association with other forms of vascular disease suggest that the examination of potential neuropsychological correlates of hyperlipidemia may be worthwhile. In rare instances, extremely high levels of serum lipids may result in a form of dementia (Heilman and Fisher, 1974). Perlmuter et al. (1988) found that in non-insulin-dependent diabetics, elevated triglycerides were related to poorest performance in measures of attention and reaction time. Furthermore, lowering of serum cholesterol and triglyceride levels have been found to improve cognitive function (Reitan and Shipley, 1963; Rogers et al., 1989). There was an interaction with age in the study by Reitan and Shipley, although this is difficult to interpret because subjects were divided at the age of 40 years. The significance of the study by Rogers is also complicated by the fact that the patients in that study had cerebrovascular disease. Thus, these studies do not clearly permit an examination of the effects of serum lipids in elderly stroke-free subjects. Desmond et al. (1993), however, have provided data directly to this point. In that study, elevated cholesterol was associated with memory dysfunction. These few studies do not permit a firm conclusion that elevated cholesterol or triglyceride levels are associated with cognitive deficit. However, there is some suggestion that hyperlipidemia may be related to other deficits in elderly subjects at risk for stroke. Furthermore, the preliminary treatment data suggest that these abnormalities may be reversible to some degree. The study by Desmond et al. (1993) suggests that the effects of elevated cholesterol may be independent of other risk factors.

Summary: Stroke Risk Factors

The effects of stroke risk factors on neuropsychological performance have begun to provide some consistent evidence of an association with cognitive deficit. This relationship is most clearly demonstrated in relation to hypertension, although some preliminary evidence indicates adverse neuropsychological consequences of glucose intolerance and hyperlipidemia. The possibility that these risk factors may represent the basis for "silent" infarctions, and may also be the basis for cognitive deficit, clearly emphasizes the need for further examination of the consequences of these disorders. Furthermore, the preliminary data regarding treatment of these conditions, and concomitant beneficial effect on cognitive function deserves much further investigation. It is likely that within at least some of these risk factors there may be a considerable degree of heterogeneity, and the specific characteristics or factors associated with cognitive deficit require further clarification. Finally, there are complex methodological issues such as those identified by Waldstein et al. (1991a) in relation to hypertension, which will likely complicate the study of the neuropsychological effects of other stroke risk factors. The carefully designed studies by Waldstein et al. (1991b) and Desmond et al. (1993) herald the future, and suggest that considerable progress is likely to be achieved.

Treatment

Drug Therapies

Unfortunately, drug trials generally do not include neuropsychological assessments of patients. Instead, patients are assessed with neurological ratings scales and activities of daily living inventories. Although the size of large-scale drug trials is often used as a justification to exclude neuropsychological evaluations of patients, the greater sensitivity of neuropsychological methods to cognitive deficits in stroke would allow an effect to be detected with smaller sample sizes. A current trial funded by NINDS to examine the effects of the calcium channel blocker nimodipine on cognitive function and mood in vascular dementia does involve more thorough neuropsychological evaluations than most previous stroke studies. This study may provide evidence of the utility of neuropsychological assessment in drug studies that can be used to justify including neuropsychological assessment in drug studies of other types of cerebrovascular disease.

Cerebrovascular Surgeries

Patients with cerebrovascular occlusive disease undergo cerebral revascularization chiefly to reduce risk of a major thromboembolic stroke. In carotid endarterectomy (CE), the neurosurgeon cuts into the extracranial portion of the carotid artery and excises the atherosclerotic blockage. In the past, when arterial stenosis is intracranial or when atherosclerosis totally occludes the extracranial carotid, superficial temporal to middle cerebral artery (STA-MCA) bypass has been considered. In this procedure a branch of the middle cerebral artery is sewn to a scalp artery, the superficial temporal artery, in order to provide additional blood supply beyond the point of blockage.

In the last decade, large randomized clinical trials were accomplished for both CE and STA-MCA bypass. Stroke and mortality were the main dependent variables in both studies. Neither included neuropsychological or cerebral blood flow measures.

In the EC/IC (extracranial-intracranial) Bypass Study, which examined the STA-MCA procedures (EC/IC Bypass Study Group, 1985), 1377 patients underwent randomization to surgery or to medical treatment alone. Neither the surgical group as a whole nor subgroups based on angiographic findings showed reduced frequency of fatal and nonfatal strokes; patients with severe middle cerebral artery stenosis or symptoms persisting after complete carotid occlusion had significantly poorer outcomes than medically treated patients. In both medical and surgical treatment groups, patients with symptoms within 30 days of randomization had worse prognoses than those whose most recent symptoms were 30 to 90 days away. Whether or not the patient had a natural collateral arterial supply to the brain regions threatened by stenotic disease had no effect (Barnett et al., 1987). The randomized study included functional ratings at entry, 6 weeks later, and every 3 months thereafter (Haynes et al., 1987). Analyses of ratings from the modified Katz Activities of Daily Living Scale showed deterioration in surgically treated patients relative to medically treated patients 6 weeks and 4.5 months after entry into the study; functional status of the two treatment groups was equivalent thereafter. Reports of these findings provoked many criticisms about the generalizability of the results, especially in the light of the large number of patients not enrolled at some participating centers (Ausman and Diaz, 1986; Day et al., 1986; Sundt, 1987). However, criticism of the internal validity of the study was minimal.

Several randomized CE trials have been conducted or are under way. The North American Symptomatic Carotid Endarterectomy Trial examined surgical efficacy in patients with severe stenosis (70% to 99%) and in those with moderate stenosis (30% to 69%) (North American Symptomatic Carotid Endarterectomy Trial Collaborators, 1991). For study enlistment, patients were required to have experienced an ipsilateral TIA or nondisabling stroke within 120 days of enrollment. Recruitment of patients with severe stenosis was stopped early because interim analyses showed a clear surgical benefit over medical treatment alone in the 659 patients who already had undergone study. Patients who had undergone endarterectomy had a decreased risk of fatal and nonfatal ipsilateral stroke, the chief end point of the study, as well as diminished overall probability of

stroke or death. Results of this study for patients with moderate stenosis are not yet available. The results of other trials of surgery for asymptomatic patients are unclear; studies available to date do not come out unequivocally in favor of surgery (Barnett and Haines, 1993).

In addition to looking at stroke and death as end points of analysis, neurobehavioral scientists have been interested in surgical effects on adaptive functioning and life quality. Some have asked whether cerebral revascularization might improve rather than merely stabilize cognitive, perceptual, and motor functioning. Some studies have included measures of subjective well-being, general health, and real-world functioning. In recent years, it has become more obvious that the appropriate comparison is not between surgical treatment and untreated cerebrovascular occlusive disease. Rather the choice lies between aggressive medical treatment of stroke-related risk factors and medical treatment plus surgical intervention (Meyer et al., 1990).

NEUROBEHAVIORAL CAROTID ENDARTERECTOMY STUDIES. In addition to specifying medical treatment, sophisticated examination of effects of CE requires researchers to minimize and monitor gains likely due to natural recovery and practice effects. Use of a comparison group that undergoes assessment at the same intervals is probably the most powerful technique employed. Half of the studies utilized a comparison group of unoperated patients with cerebrovascular occlusive disease. In the case of the study by Meyer and his coworkers (1990), this comparison group was a true control group with randomized assignment. The next closest to a true match was Greiffenstein's (1988) group of patients whose carotid endarterectomies were delayed or cancelled. The other five cerebrovascular comparison groups are more mixed or approximate (Parker et al., 1986; de Leo et al., 1987; Baird et al., 1988; Casey et al., 1989; Sirkka et al., 1992). Tables 15-1 and 15-2 list major studies of the past decade. When the same center has produced multiple studies, the most recent or representa-

Table 15-1. Description of Carotid Endarterectomy (CE) Studies with Neuropsychological Data

Authors	No. of CEs	Preoperative Symptoms	Preoperative Angiography	Comparison Groups	Follow-up	Neuropsychological Measures	Conclusions
Sirkka et al. (1992)	44	8 stroke, 31 TIA, 5 symptomatic	More severe in operated group than comparison group	1. Healthy controls. 2. Medically treated patients with TIAs and stratus correlated with carotid disease. Hypertension and other risk factors were more severe in operated group.	No preop testing. Tested 8 yrs after surgery or 11 yrs after initiation of medical treatment.	Nine cognitive and memory tests. Global life quality measure based on interview.	1. No overall group differences in neuropsych. test performance or life quality. 2. Operated stroke patients described poorer life quality than stroke patients who had medical treatment only.
Mononen et al. (1990)	46	16 stroke, 30 TIA, 67% of strokes had occurred <6 mos. before CE	Significant internal carotid artery steneosis		1–3 days before CE. 2 wks and 2 mos. after CE.	Word Fluency, Stroop color, serial learning, digit span, facial recognition, visual memory, recognition of concrete pictures.	1. Before surgery, TIA and stroke groups did not differ on neuropsych. tests. 2. At both post-op testings, TIA patients showed more improvement on outcome measures than stroke patients. 3. Two mos. post-op, in TIA patients greatest gains were in tests corresponding to side of surgery.
Meyer et al. (1990)	8	All had diagnosis of multi-infarct dementia	In CE group, 3 patients had unilateral carotid stenosis, 2 had carotid occlusion on the other, and 3 had bilateral carotid stenosis	After candidacy for surgery for extracranial occlusive disease was determined, patients were randomly assigned to medical treatment only (N = 18) or to CE (N = 8) or STA-MCA bypass (N = 10). Groups were similar on age, sex, CT findings, and stroke risk factors.	Pre-op and every 3–9 months for average of 21 months	Cognitive Capacity Screening Examination, shown sensitive to fluctuations in multi-infarct dementia, concurrent rCBF	1. No group differences on the cognitive measure or rCBF. All groups showed preserved cognition and rCBF over time. 2. STA-MCA bypass group showed rCBF increases between 13 and 24 mos., but these gains did not continue. 3. All groups failed to show decline that might be expected over time if they received neither medical or surgical treatment.

Study	N	Symptoms	Carotid stenosis	Comparison/other groups	Testing times	Tests	Results
Casey et al. (1989)	24	TIAs	Significant atheroma ipsilateral to side of surgery	Patients with TIAs but no significant carotid stenosis on side of symptoms	Pre-op and 8 weeks post-op	8 cognitive, perceptual, and motor tests, including IQ and memory indices	1. Patients with right (R) (CE), left (L) (CE), and no surgery showed gains on IQ, memory, and left visual field scanning. 2. There are no group differences in changes at follow-up.
Baird et al. (1988)	14	TIAs, Reversible ischemic neurological deficit (RINDs), and strokes. Proportion of RINDs or strokes within 6 wks of baseline did not differ for combined surgical groups and cerebrovasc. comparison group.		1. 17 patients who were considered for surgery & underwent angiography. 2. 11 patients with spinal complaints only. 3. 16 STA MCA bypass, 10 vertebrobasilar revascularization patients, and 8 patients with multiple revascularization also were included in the study but were not directly compared with the CE group.	Pre-op and 6 weeks post-op	A mean impairment rating reflecting scores from 8 measures and a broad-band life quality measure.	1. Surgical and comparison groups showed gains at follow-up. 2. Gains at 6 months did not differ between the CE and unoperated cerebrovascular group on the impairment and life quality ratings nor between the CE and spinal complaints groups on the mean impairment rating.
Greiffenstein et al. (1988)	30	R CE group: 5 stroke, 8 TIA, 2 both. L CE group: 6 stroke, 7 TIA, 2 both. Delayed surgery group: 9 stroke (7 with TIAs also), 6 TIA only. All patients with TIA or stroke in last 6 mos.	4 R CE, 5 L CE, and 3 delayed CE patients had > 75% carotid stenosis	15 patients selected for CE but for whom surgery was delayed or cancelled	For R CE and L CE groups: 1 wk to 1 day pre-op; 2–3 mos. post-op. For unoperated group: 1 wk pre-op and 1 wk after cancellation of surgery	WAIS-R, Buschke Selective Reminding Test, Trails, Tapping, Digit Symbol Substitution. Scores from the last three measures were combined into a mental speed composite.	1. Overall all 3 groups improved at follow-up. 2. The right CE group showed bigger gains on the mental speed composite and the selective reminding test than the other 2 groups.
de Leo et al. (1987)	25	TIAs	All 25 patients had carotid stenosis, 17 had stenosis >75%	13 medically treated patients with carotid atherosclerosis	For CE patients: pre-op, 2 wks post-op, 8 mos. post-op. For un-	L hemisphere–related: Word Pairs, Story Recall, Word Flu-	1. At baseline testing, unoperated group was better than surgical group only on Word Fluency.

(continued)

Table 15-1. Description of Carotid Endarterectomy (CE) Studies with Neuropsychological Data *(Continued)*

Authors	No. of CEs	Preoperative Symptoms	Preoperative Angiography	Comparison Groups	Follow-up	Neuropsychological Measures	Conclusions
					operated patients: baseline and 8 mos. later	ency, Digit Span, Similarities. R hemisphere–related: Visual Retention Test, Street Completion Test, Block Design, Depression and Quality of Life ratings scales	2. No statistically significant changes were noted in the CE groups at 2 wks post-op. 3. At 8-month follow-up there were no statistically significant differences between operated and unoperated groups. 4. At 8-month follow-up, when R CE and L CE groups were evaluated separately, gains were noted only in Word Fluency and only for R CE patients. 5. At 8-month follow-up, self-rated depression decreased more for operated than unoperated patients; there were no group differences in life quality changes.
Hemmingsen et al. (1986)	31	1–50 TIAs; most recent TIA was between few days and several mos. of baseline testing	All had carotid stenosis; 4 had contralateral carotid occlusion	11 patients undergoing surgery for vascular disease affecting the legs. Cerebral angiography was not done in this group, but CT and rCBF showed that 7 had cerebral atrophy and 2 had hypodense CT lesions with associated areas of low blood flow.	1–2 wks pre-op; 3–5 mos. post-op	L hemisphere–related: Word Pairs, Story Recall R hemisphere–related: Visual gestalt General: Digit Span, Digit Symbol, Trails A and B	1. At baseline, no significant group differences. 2. R CE patients improved in 10/10 scores; L CE patients on 9/10 scores. Comparison group improved on 3 scores, worsened on 5, and was stable on 3. 3. Improvement tended to be greatest on test related to side of operation. 4. There was no correlation between regional blood flow change and change in neuropsycholog-

	N					
						ical test performance. Only 2 of 7 CE patients with low flow preoperatively showed improvement post-op.
Parker et al. (1986)	36	28% of operated group (CD-0) and 29% of unoperated group had history of stroke, 47% of operated group and 43% of unoperated group had fixed neurological deficit	19% of operated group and 14% of unoperated group had >75% left carotid stenosis; 25% of operated group and 21% of unoperated had >75% right carotid stenosis	1. 17 patients with symptomatic carotid artery disease. These patients either refused surgery or were not candidates for CE (CD-N). 2. 26 patients who underwent surgery not impinging on brain functions (GSC).	For carotid artery disease groups, baseline assessment was within 1 wk of angiogram. For general surgery group, baseline was within 1 wk before surgery. Follow-up assessments were 6 and 24 mos. later.	Extended Halstead-Reitan Battery and measures of life quality, mood state, and self-esteem	1. Mortality: 11%—CD-0; 6%—CD-N; 12%—GSC. 2. Mean TIAs in follow-up: 1.2—CD-0; 0.9—CD-N. 3. No Group X Trial interactions on Average Impairment and component tests, on Performance tests, on Full Scale IQ, on 6 WMS scores, on the Sickness Impact Profile scores, on the Profile of Mood States, and in the Tennessee Self-Concept Scale. A Group X Trial interaction was seen for the Verbal IQ whereby both carotid artery disease groups had lower Verbal IQs than the GSC group on baseline and 24-month testing. 4. Patients with severe bilateral or unilateral carotid stenosis did now show dramatic post-CE changes.
Bennion et al. (1985)	53	18 patients had evidence of ≥1 remote infarct	10 patients had >50% carotid stenosis but ≤75%; 33 patients had >75% stenosis; 10 patients had <50% stenosis with ulceration		Pre-op; 3–7 days post-op; 3 mos. post-op	Ravens, spatial orientation, Vocabulary, Arithmetic, Short-term memory, Finger Tapping	Improved test performance at first post-op testing was followed by a decrease to post-op levels 3 mos. after surgery. This pattern was more pronounced on patients with >50% stenosis and failed to reach significance in patients with ≤50% stenosis.

(continued)

Table 15-1. Description of Carotid Endarterectomy (CE) Studies with Neuropsychological Data (*Continued*)

Authors	No. of CEs	Preoperative Symptoms	Preoperative Angiography	Comparison Groups	Follow-up	Neuropsychological Measures	Conclusions
Cushman et al. (1984)	34	16 patients with TIAs; 18 patients with small, stable stroke; 21 patients had first ischemic episode within 6 mos. of surgery; 15 patients had ischemic episode within 1 wk of operation	14 patients had >75% internal carotid stenosis. Of these 14, 12 had carotid occlusion on one side and stenosis on other, 2 had severe bilateral stenosis		Within 3 days before surgery; 4 to 12 days post-op	Mean of ranks of difference scores for Buschke's Selective Reminding Test, Trail Making Test, Digit Symbol Substitution Test, Finger Tapping, Sensory-Perceptual Exam	1. Patients with >50% somatosensory evoked potential (SEP) amplitude reductions during surgery had less change or negative change on neuropsychological tests. 2. Patients with >75% carotid stenosis were more likely to have sizable amplitude reductions. 3. In general patients with history of stroke or with >75% stenosis ranked lower on behavioral change scores. 4. Patients with no pre-op history of stroke were more likely to have post-op ischemic attacks. 5. Degree of neuropsychological change did not correlate with time since first or most recent pre-op ischemic episode.
Diener et al. (1984)	23	15 patients with TIAs, 5 patients with minor strokes, 3 asymptomatic patients	11 had unilateral stenosis >50%; 12 had bilateral stenosis or occlusion combined with stenosis; 1 patient had intraoperative ischemia		1 week pre-op; 10 mos. post-op	Culture-fair intelligence test and digit symbol test. Visual retention, attention test, revision test, attention stress test, Vienna reaction timer, Freiburg Personality Inventory, two self-rating tests	In both unilateral and bilateral stenosis groups, intelligence scores increased, visual retention errors increased, and there was no change in attention and psychomotor speed tests

Study	N	Subjects	Follow-up	Measures	Results
Jacobs et al. (1983)	24	History of TIA or small, stable stroke; no patients with fixed neurological deficits. Low flow endangered brain (LFEB) group: 12 patients with ≥75% reduction in total cross-sectional area of carotid arteries. Hemodynamically insignificant group: 12 patients with <25% unilateral stenosis or small ulcerated lesion. Hemodynamically insignificant group selected to match on recency of precipitating event, no. of strokes, and total duration of symptomatic cerebrovascular disease	Pre-op, 1 wk, 1 mo., 3 mos., 6 mos. post. The last follow-up time was used in the analysis	Buschke's Selective Reminding Test, Trails Test, Digit Symbol Substitution Test, Sensory Perceptual Exam, Finger Tapping	1. All four Buschke measures improved after surgery in LFEB group, and there was a Group X Sessions interaction for two measures. 2. Trails B improved significantly in the LFEB group, and again there was a Group X Sessions interaction. 3. There were neither Group nor Sessions effects for other variables.
Fraser et al. (1983)	35	31 had TIA; 4 had completed stroke	Pre-op: 6 mos. and 18 mos. post-op	WAIS VIQ, WAIS PIQ, WMQ	1. 35 patients seen at 6-mo. follow-up show improvement on all three measures. 2. 15 patients seen so far at 18 mos. show return to baseline.

Table 15-2. Measures and Controls for Practice Effects and Natural History in Neuropsychological Studies of Carotid Endarterectomy

Author	Comparison Group with Cerebrovascular Disease	Comparison Group without Cerebrovascular Disease	Randomized Assignment to Surgical Treatment	Multiple Preoperative Neuropsychological Assessments	Multiple Postoperative Neuropsychological Assessments	Alternate Forms	Concurrent rCBF Measures	Analysis of Effects for Side of Surgery
				Technique				
Sirkka et al. (1992)	+	+	–	–	–	–	–	–
Mononen et al. (1990)	–	–	–	–	+	–	–	+
Meyer et al. (1990)	+	–	+	–	+	–	+	–
Casey et al. (1989)	+	–	–	–	–	+	–	+
Baird et al. (1988)	+	+	–	–	–	+	–	–
Greiffenstein et al. (1988)	+	–	–	–	–	+	–	+
de Leo et al. (1987)	+	–	–	–	+ (surgical group only)	+	–	+
Hemmingsen et al. (1986)	–	+	–	–	–	+	+	+
Parker et al. (1986)	+	+	–	–	+	–	–	–
Bennion et al. (1985)	–	–	–	–	+	+	–	+
Cushman et al. (1984)	–	–	–	–	–	+	–	–
Diener et al. (1984)	–	–	–	–	–	+	–	–
Jacobs et al. (1983)	–	–	–	–	+	+	–	–
Fraser et al. (1983)	–	–	–	–	+	–	–	–

tive one is cited. These results suggest that studies more frequently than not find stabilized performance after surgery rather than lasting improvement, regardless of whether follow-up included a group of patients with cerebrovascular disease but no cerebral revascularization.

To get a more detailed look at the effects of natural recovery and practice effects, half of the reports in the last decade included multiple postoperative assessments (Fraser et al., 1983; Jacobs et al., 1983; Bennion et al., 1985; Parker et al., 1986; de Leo et al., 1987; Meyer et al., 1990; Mononen et al., 1990). Of these studies, two reports, both without comparison groups of unoperated patients, found stable improvement in one subgroup of CE patients compared to another (Jacobs et al., 1983; Mononen et al., 1990) but did not necessarily report improvement in the collapsed group of CE patients. Studies by Fraser et al. (1983) and Bennion et al. (1985) found improvement at the first postoperative assessment with a return to the preoperative baseline at the later follow-up. The other studies yielded negative results. Although the variance in follow-up intervals makes it difficult to compare studies, in general, one can state that adding follow-up intervals tends to weaken rather than support the evidence for significant post-CE behavioral improvement.

No report included data from more than one preoperative assessment. Multiple baseline assessments could provide a purer assessment of changes related to practice effects or natural recovery.

The majority of studies used alternate forms as a method of minimizing practice effects. Inspection of Tables 15-1 and 15-2 suggests the absence of a relationship between the use of alternate forms and the positive or negative results of the study.

Correlating test scores with results of physiological measures such as regional cerebral blood flow (rCBF) (Meyer et al., 1990) and cortical evoked potentials (Cushman et al., 1984) is another way to sift out practice effects, measurement error, and Hawthorne effects. These measures apparently have not

been utilized thus far in studies showing postoperative gains in performance.

Six of 14 studies examined the question of changes related to the side of surgery (Bennion et al., 1985; Hemmingsen et al., 1986; de Leo et al., 1987; Greiffenstein et al., 1988; Casey et al., 1989; Mononen et al., 1990). This level of analysis not only may be more sensitive to any changes that have occurred but also is a way of extracting any gains due strictly to practice effects. Four of these studies found evidence of postoperative improvement at least in a subset of CE patients; only one of eight studies that did not look at side of operation noted gains following surgery. Therefore, this work indicates that future research should try to group patients or tests by side of surgery.

At least two studies have shown larger jumps in test performance in patients undergoing right CE than in individuals with left CE (de Leo et al., 1987; Greiffenstein et al., 1988). These changes were not necessarily on tests sensitive to right hemisphere dysfunction, but occurred on measures such as a word fluency test (de Leo et al., 1987) and a verbal memory test (Greiffenstein et al., 1988). One can only speculate that the basis for these findings might lie in the greater role of the right hemisphere in problem solving.

In trying to sort out effects of natural recovery, practice on tests, and revascularization, it is important to recognize the diversity of CE candidates in terms of severity and recency of their symptoms and with respect to pattern and degree of carotid stenosis. For instance, the work of Meyer and colleagues (1990) involves only patients with multi-infarct dementia, whereas the reports of Hemmingsen et al. (1986), de Leo et al. (1987), and Casey et al. (1989) include only TIA patients. Review of recent work suggests that favorable results in CE patients may tend to cluster in patients who had TIAs only before surgery, but the extant literature leaves open the possibility that postoperative gains may be due to natural recovery from small strokes. For example, Mononen et al. (1990) found that TIA patients showed more postoperative improvement than stroke patients, despite the fact that the two groups did not differ on baseline testing. The Hemmingsen et al. (1986) and de Leo et al. (1987) papers report at least small postoperative gains; these studies included only TIA patients. However, the Casey et al. (1989) study, the most rigorous in terms of excluding subjects with evidence of stroke by CT, symptom duration, or neurological exam results, found no postoperative benefit for TIA patients, which excluded not only stroke patients but also TIA patients with positive neurological exam or CT findings.

At least three studies support the notion that CE is more likely to produce neurobehavioral change, positive (Jacobs et al., 1983; Bennion et al., 1985) or negative (Cushman et al., 1984), when patients have high-grade carotid stenosis in both arteries or on the side corresponding to symptom attacks. Such results are, of course, in line with the results of randomized clinical trials, which quickly showed a surgical benefit for patients with carotid narrowing 70% or greater on the side consistent with symptoms (North American Symptomatic Carotid Endarterectomy Trial Collaborators, 1991). However, in the neuropsychology literature this result has not been clear-cut; Parker and colleagues' study (1986) found no marked postoperative changes in a subset of patients with unilateral or bilateral carotid stenosis greater than 75%.

NEUROBEHAVIORAL STA-MCA BYPASS STUDIES. In the past decade, fewer studies with fewer subjects have been conducted to study STA-MCA bypass than conducted to study CE (Drinkwater et al., 1984; Younkin et al., 1985; Nielsen et al., 1986; LaBlanc et al., 1987; Baird et al., 1988; Meyer et al., 1990). Compared to CE studies, more STA-MCA bypass candidates have had strokes. None of the recent studies restricts subjects to those with TIAs only. Only the Nielsen et al. (1986) study separated subjects or outcome measures by side of surgery. None of the recent group studies strongly supported a benefit from surgery. Drinkwater and colleagues' (1984) direct comparison of CE and STA-MCA bypass patients suggested greater postoperative changes in the CE group.

Very positive reports have come from case studies. These studies detail isolated instances of reversal of fixed severe behavioral and neurological deficits, including aphasia (Hart et al., 1985), hemiplegia (Macon and Rice, 1985), dementia (LeBlanc et al., 1987), and visual field cuts (Benzel and Mirfarkhraee, 1987). However, these studies permit no direct assessment of the role of practice effect and natural recovery in postoperative improvement.

STA-MCA bypass studies (Younkin et al., 1985; LeBlanc et al., 1987; Meyer et al., 1990) more frequently have included neurophysiological measures than CE reports. In all three studies it was found that increases in neuropsychological performance were not reliably accompanied by improved rCBF. In at least one study, this result was interpreted as evidence that improved test scores resulted from natural recovery rather than from revascularization (Younkin, 1985).

Just as the Fraser et al. (1983) and Bennion et al. (1985) CE reports describe initial postoperative cognitive increments with a subsequent return to baseline, Meyer et al. (1990) found that cognitive improvement in STA-MCA bypass patients was not maintained, and Younkin et al. (1985) noted that postsurgical increases in rCBF at 3 months were reversed to baseline at 9 months. Both CE and STA-MCA bypass studies suggest that homeostatic mechanisms, permanent effects of previous ischemic episodes, or other neuropathological conditions may tend to mitigate against lasting functional gains after revascularization. Stabilization of neurological status may be a more consistent benefit.

SUMMARY: CEREBROVASCULAR SURGERY. It is unfortunate that the larger randomized studies cited heretofore have not systematically included assessment of neurobehavioral status and regional cerebral blood flow or another neurophysiological measure of brain function. The absence of randomized, large-scale behavioral studies and the diversity of the studies that have been done prevent behavioral scientists from making more major contributions to the discussion of the utility of these procedures. One can state that whereas stabilization commonly has been achieved after CE and STA-MCA bypass, clear cognitive benefits of surgery over medical treatment have emerged only in a minority of studies conducted over the past decade.

In planning future behavioral studies of revascularization procedures, it seems important to focus on subgroups of patients according to symptom duration and angiographic lesions. Studies of patients with TIAs only before STA-MCA bypass might fill a particular gap. Similarly, research involving CE candidates with severe stenosis on the symptomatic side are likely to be especially fruitful. Researchers may be able to increase the sensitivity of their methods by subgrouping patients or measures according to side of surgery. Rigorous elucidation and administration of concurrent medical treatment of cerebrovascular disease also should lead to more confident conclusions. Future researchers can draw much from this long line of study.

Recovery and Rehabilitation

Recovery

At some point in sustained cerebral ischemia, sufficient damage is done to a nerve cell that it can no longer rebuild itself after the ischemic event and it dies. Jones and associates have shown that even when ischemia of one hemisphere is not complete, cell death and contralateral hemiparesis can occur after 3 hours of reduced blood flow (Jones et al., 1981). After infarction, the process of recovery becomes complex, involving a reduction of edema, restoration of normal neurotransmitter activity and metabolism, changes in regional cerebral blood flow, and the reorganization of brain systems. In their recent review of the literature, Meier and Strauman (1991) show that scores on neuropsychological tests given soon after stroke are correlated with subsequent recovery of cognitive and motor function. Further, Heaton and Pendleton (1981) reviewed studies that showed that psychological tests can predict some activities of daily living following stroke, such

as disposition from a rehabilitation program (home versus institutional placement) and rehabilitation gains in self-care, ambulation, dressing, and mobility.

Although such reviews indicate that neuropsychological findings obtained soon after stroke are related to outcome, current studies have failed to find a highly accurate set of predictors. Meier and Strauman (1991) urge the use of an individual differences model for predicting outcome that takes into account demographic factors, such as age and education, in addition to disease factors, such as lesion size and location. Further, neuropsychological models need to be integrated with pathophysiological data on brain changes occurring soon after stroke. We need to learn more about the reorganization of brain and behavior during the early poststroke period. Improvement in neuropsychological functioning during recovery needs to be systematically related to changes in regional cerebral blood flow, cerebral metabolism, neurotransmitter levels, structural damage, and edema. Does the adequacy of collateral flow predict better recovery of neuropsychological functioning? How much recovery might be associated with the return of neurotransmitters to normal levels in the blood and cerebrospinal fluid? Does the pattern of metabolic change during recovery provide any evidence that intact brain regions take over the function of infarcted brain regions? In answering these questions, neuropsychological data will often serve as criteria rather than predictors. Future research should also aim at developing metabolic-rCBF-behavioral profiles to identify those patients who do not recover.

Rehabilitation

In contrast to the extensive and specific literature on neuropsychological rehabilitation following closed head injury (CHI), little literature exists on neuropsychological rehabilitation following cerebrovascular disease (CVD). To a great extent this disparity reflects the differing prototypic patterns of behavior deficit following CVD and CHI. These differences in prototypic behavior deficit rest in turn on differences in prototypic patho-physiology; whereas CHI generally produces diffuse neuronal damage, CVD generally produces focal damage. Obviously, generalities such as this obscure data at the level of the individual patient, whose lesion might not be so easily classified as focal or diffuse. Nevertheless, these differences color attempts to develop systematic research and theory general enough to be applied to the neuropsychological rehabilitation of both CVD and CHI patients.

The most far-reaching and comprehensive approach to neuropsychological rehabilitation stems from the early work of Weinberg and colleagues (1979) on the amelioration of deficits in visuospatial function. This study set the stage for systematic efforts to address the problems of hemi-inattention commonly seen in patients with strokes of the right hemisphere. The early research of Weinberg and colleagues can be viewed as an application of well-established behavioral learning principles to the problem of remediation of deficits due to underlying neurologic disease.

The initial phases of treatment of visuospatial function use increased stimulus salience with the goal of rebuilding or retraining the habit strength of scanning into the neglected field. Once sufficient habit strength is established under conditions of high stimulus salience, some degree of generalization is found in naturalistic settings that inherently suffer from high levels of stimulus competition and reduced discriminative salience. Next, attempts are made to alter internal cognitive processes, such as scanning speed, which typically function at an automatic level. Again the procedures for pacing begin with externalizing to heighten salience followed by progressive fading of the external cues. Parenthetically, this technique for externalizing internal mental processes followed by rehearsal and reinternalization was adopted with great success for use in the amelioration of attentional deficits in closed head injury patients by Ben-Yishay and his colleagues (1979).

This general approach to the remediation of visuospatial deficits through a focus on improved scanning and attention has been widely adapted by other researchers. For example, Young et al. (1983) used a combination of scanning training and block design training to improve neuropsychological test performance in a group of patients with right hemispheric CVD. Pizzamiglio and colleagues (1992) used four separate procedures (scanning, reading, copying and figure description) with a group of patients with chronic right hemisphere brain damage (10 patients with stroke, three patients with postsurgical evacuation of hematoma). Each procedure was hypothesized to improve scanning. Within each training procedure the patient's performance was initially supported by high intensity cues such as flashing lights or verbal or tactile stimulation. As training progressed, the degree of external support provided was tapered down. In addition to improvement on laboratory measures, these patients were also shown to improve on a set of functional measures such as "serving tea," which may more realistically model common daily activities that may be disrupted by hemispatial inattention.

A somewhat different approach emphasizing the perceptual rather than attentional dimensions of hemispatial neglect in patients with right hemisphere brain injuries has been developed by Gianutsos and colleagues (see Gianutsos and Matheson [1987] for overview). Although this approach was not developed specifically for use with patients with cerebrovascular disease, it provides an important conceptual contrast to the rehabilitation training in the Weinberg et al. tradition. Gianutsos begins by moving the initial focus of rehabilitation backwards toward the beginning of the hierarchy of sensory and motor processes leading to vision. By doing so, deficits in fundamental processes such as acuity, binocular function, field of vision and oculomotor function are often discovered. When present, these deficits can contribute to the clinical picture, which might have been erroneously interpreted as a pure neglect. After careful analysis of the exact nature of the visual problem, the patient is confronted with exercises designed to heighten awareness of the underlying problem. Often this is accomplished through repetition of some of the diagnostic measures on which deficits were shown. Once the patient has come to the point of recognizing the parameters of the underlying deficit, attempts at retraining begin. The retraining relies primarily on repetition and practice with the goal of achieving some degree of central reorganization of the response. Finally, any residual deficits are approached by attempts to improve "self-management." In many respects, this final phase of treatment converges with the end stage of the Weinberg et al. approach. That is to say, the patient is taught to externalize and make overt what was typically an automatic process so that intact reasoning and problem solving skills or learned compensatory strategies can be brought into play.

These papers are a sampling of the studies in this literature. Additional reviews of the rehabilitation of cognitive function following stroke can be found in Bornstein and Brown (1991).

Summary

We began with the observation that neuropsychological evaluations could play a critical role relating the anatomical and physiological effects of cerebrovascular disease to the capacity for self-care and independent living. Few of the papers that we reviewed made such a direct connection. There is a considerable need to study the adjustment of patients with cerebrovascular disease in their homes, their neighborhoods, and their places of work. The number of studies predicting vocational adjustment, response to rehabilitation, and quality of life from neuropsychological data is embarrassingly small for an empirical science. Perhaps neuropsychologists have been so enchanted by the task of predicting brain dysfunction from behavioral variables that we have been distracted from the equally important task of predicting social and psychological competence at daily activities. We hope that future research will redress this imbalance.

References

Adams, C.B.T., Loach, A. B., and O'Laoire, S. (1976). Intracranial aneurysms: Analysis of results of microneurosurgery. *British Medical Journal, 2*, 607–609.

Adams, R. D., and Victor, M. (1985). *Principles of Neurology* (3rd ed.). New York: McGraw-Hill, Inc.

American Heart Association. (1992). *Heart and Stroke Facts.* Dallas, TX.

Apter, N. S., Halstead, W. C., and Heimburger, R. F. (1951). Impaired cerebral functions in essential hypertension. *American Journal of Psychiatry, 107*, 808–813.

Ausman, J. I., and Diaz, F. G. (1986). Critique of the extracranial-intracranial bypass study. *Surgical Neurology, 26*, 218–221.

Baird, A. D., Adams, K. M., Shatz, M. W., Ausman, J. I., Diaz, F. G., and Dujovny, M. (1988). Neurobehavioral and life quality changes after cerebral revascularization. *Journal of Consulting and Clinical Psychology, 56*, 148–151. [Published erratum appears in *Journal of Consulting and Clinical Psychology, 56*, 489, 1988.]

Baird, A. D., Adams, K. M., Shatz, M. W., Brown, G. G., Diaz, F. G., and Ausman, J. I. (1984). Can neuropsychological tests detect the sites of cerebrovascular stenoses and occlusions? *Neurosurgery, 14*, 416–423.

Baird, A. D., Boulos, R., Mehta, B., Adams, K. M., Shatz, M. W., Ausman, J. I., Diaz, F. G., and Dujovny, M. (1985). Cerebral angiography and neuropsychological measurement: The twain they meet. *Surgical Neurology, 23*, 641–650.

Bamford, J., Sandercock, P., Dennis, M., Warlow, C., Jones, L., McPherson, K., Vessey, M., Fowler, G., Molyneaux, A., Hughes, T., Burn, J., and Wade, D. (1988). A prospective study of acute cerebrovascular disease in the community: The Oxfordshire Community Stroke Project 1981–86. 1. Methodology, demography and incident cases of first-ever stroke. *Journal of Neurology, Neurosurgery and Psychiatry, 51*, 1373–1380.

Barbarotto, R., De Santis, A., Laiacona, M., Basso, A., Spagnoli, D., and Capitani, E. (1989). Neuropsychological follow-up of patients operated for aneurysms of the middle cerebral artery and posterior communicating artery. *Cortex, 25*, 275–288.

Barnett, H.J.M., and Haines, S. J. (1993). Carotid endarterectomy for asymptomatic carotid stenosis (Editorial). *New England Journal of Medicine, 328*, 276–279.

Barnett, H.J.M., Sackett, D., Taylor, D. W., Haynes, B., Peerless, S. J., Meissner, I., Hachinski, V., and Fox, A. (1987). Are the results of the extracranial-intracranial bypass trial generalizable? *New England Journal of Medicine, 316*, 820–824.

Bennion, R. S., Owens, M. L., and Wilson, S. E. (1985). The effect of unilateral carotid endarterectomy on neuropsychological test performance in 53 patients. *Journal of Cardiovascular Surgery, 26,* 21–26.

Benson, D. F., and Cummings, J. L. (1982). Angular gyrus syndrome simulating Alzheimer's disease. *Archives of Neurology, 39,* 616–620.

Benton, A. (1988). Differentiating Alzheimer's disease from other dementias. *Bulletin of Clinical Neuroscience, 53,* 35–40.

Ben-Yishay, Y., Rattok, J., and Diller, L. (1979). A clinical strategy for the systematic amelioration of attentional disturbances in severe head trauma patients. In Y. Ben-Yishay, ed., *Working Approach to Remediation of Cognitive Deficits in Brain Damaged Persons* (Rehabilitation Monograph No. 60). New York: New York University Medical Center, pp. 1–27.

Benzel, E. C., and Mirfarkhraee, M. (1987). Complete homonymous hemianopia: Reversal with arterial bypass. *Southern Medical Journal, 80,* 249–251.

Boll, T. J. (1974). Right and left hemisphere damage and tactile perception: Performance of the ipsilateral and contralateral sides of the body. *Neuropsychologia, 12,* 235–238.

Bornstein, R. A., and Brown, G. G. (1991). *Neurobehavioral Aspects of Cerebrovascular Disease.* New York: Oxford University Press.

Bornstein, R. A., and Kelly, M. P. (1991). Risk factors for stroke and neuropsychological performance. In R. A. Bornstein and G. G. Brown, eds., *Neurobehavioral Aspects of Cerebrovascular Disease.* New York: Oxford University Press, pp. 182–201.

Bornstein, R. A., Weir, B.K.A., Petruk, K. C., and Disney, L. B. (1987). Neuropsychological function in patients after subarachnoid hemorrhage. *Neurosurgery, 21,* 651–654.

Brinkman, S. D., and Braun, P. (1984). Classification of dementia patients by a WAIS profile related to central cholinergic deficiencies. *Journal of Clinical Neuropsychology, 6,* 393–400.

Brown, G. G., Baird, A. D., and Shatz, M. W. (1986). The effects of cerebrovascular disease and its treatment on higher cortical functioning. In I. Grant and K. M. Adams, ed., *Neuropsychological Assessment of Neuropsychiatric Disorders.* New York: Oxford University Press, pp. 384–414.

Brown, G. G., Ewing, J. R., Robertson, W. M., and Welch, K.M.A. (1991a). Cerebral blood flow and neuropsychological asymmetries in unilateral stroke. *Stroke, 22,* 1384–1388.

Brown, G. G., Spicer, K. B., and Malik, G. (1991b). Neurobehavioral correlates of arteriovenous malformations and cerebral aneurysms. In R. A. Bornstein and G. G. Brown, eds., *Neurobehavioral Aspects of Cerebrovascular Disease.* New York: Oxford University Press, pp. 202–223.

Brown, G. G., Spicer, K. B., Robertson, W. M., Baird, A. D., and Malik, G. (1989). Neuropsychological signs of lateralized arteriovenous malformations: Comparison with ischemic stroke. *The Clinical Neuropsychologist, 3,* 340–352.

Casey, J. E., Ferguson, G. G., Kimura, D., and Hachinski, V. C. (1989). Neuropsychological improvement versus practice effect following unilateral carotid endarterectomy in patients without stroke. *Journal of Clinical and Experimental Neuropsychology, 11,* 461–470.

Close, R. A., O'Keefe, A. M., and Buchheit, W. A. (1977). The determination of speech organization in a patient with an arteriovenous malformation. *Neurosurgery, 1,* 111–113.

Conley, F. K., Moses, J. A., Jr., and Helle, T. L. (1980). Deficits of higher cortical functioning in two patients with posterior parietal arteriovenous malformations. Use of the standardized Luria-Nebraska Neuropsychological Battery for pre- and postoperative assessment. *Neurosurgery, 7,* 230–237.

Constans, J. P., and Assal, G. (1971). Evolution de la symptomatologie neuropsychologique d'une série d'anevrismes arterio-veineux opérés. *Neurochiurgia, 14,* 201–216.

Cushman, L., Brinkman, S. D., Ganji, S., and Jacobs, L. A. (1984). Neuropsychological impairment after carotid endarterectomy correlates with intraoperative ischemia. *Cortex, 20,* 403–412.

Day, A. L., Rhoton, A. L., Jr., and Little, J. R. (1986). The extracranial-intracranial bypass study. *Surgical Neurology, 26,* 222–226.

Delaney, C., Wallace, J. D., and Egelko, S. (1980). Transient cerebral ischemic attacks and neuropsychological deficit. *Journal of Clinical Neuropsychology, 2,* 107–114.

de Leo, D., Serraiotto, L., Pellegrini, C., Magni, G., Franceschi, L., and Deriu, G. P. (1987). Outcome from carotid endarterectomy. Neuropsychological performances, depressive symptoms and quality of life: 8 month follow-up. *International Journal of Psychiatry in Medicine, 17,* 317–325.

DeLuca, J. (1992). Cognitive dysfunction after aneurysm of the anterior communicating artery. *Journal of Clinical and Experimental Neuropsychology, 14,* 924–934.

DeLuca, J., and Cicerone, K. D. (1991). Confabulation following aneurysm of the anterior communicating artery. *Cortex, 27,* 417–423.

Desmond, D. W., Tatemichi, T. K., Paik, M., and Stern, Y. (1993). Risk factors for cerebrovascular disease as correlates of cognitive function in a stroke-free cohort. *Archives of Neurology, 50,* 162–166.

Diener, H. C., Hamster, W., and Seboldt, H. (1984). Neuropsychological functions after carotid endarterectomy. *European Archives of Psychiatry and Neurological Sciences, 234,* 74–77.

Drachman, D. A., and Leavitt, J. (1974). Human memory and the cholinergic system: A relationship to aging? *Archives of Neurology, 30,* 113–121.

Drinkwater, J. E., Thompson, S. K., and Lumley, J.S.P. (1984). Cerebral function before and after extra-intracranial carotid bypass. *Journal of Neurology, Neurosurgery and Psychiatry, 47,* 1041–1043.

Duke, R., Bloor, B., Nugent, G. R., and Majzoub, H. (1968). Changes in performance on WAIS, Trail Making Test and Finger Tapping Test associated with carotid artery surgery. *Perceptual and Motor Skills, 26,* 399–404.

EC/IC Bypass Study Group. (1985). Failure of extracranial-intracranial arterial bypass to reduce the risk of ischemic stroke: Results of an international randomized trail. *New England Journal of Medicine, 313,* 1191–1200.

Enzer, N., Simonson, E., and Blankstein, S. S. (1942). Fatigue of patients with circulatory insufficiency, investigated by means of the fusion frequency of flicker. *Annals of Internal Medicine, 16,* 701–707.

Ewing, J. R., Brown, G. G., Gdowski, J. W., Simkins, R., Levine, S. R., and Welch, K.M.A. (1989). Stroke risk and age do not predict behavioral activation of brain blood flow. *Annals of Neurology, 25,* 571–576.

Farmer, M. E., White, L. R., Abbott, R. D., Kittner, S. J., Kaplan, E., Wolz, M. M., Brody, J. A., and Wolf, P. A. (1987). Blood pressure and cognitive performance. The Framingham Study. *American Journal of Epidemiology, 126,* 1103–1114.

Fein, J. M. (1975). Cerebral energy metabolism after subarachnoid hemorrhage. *Stroke, 6,* 1–8.

Finkelstein, J. W. (1977). BRAIN. A computer program for interpretation of the Halstead-Reitan Neuropsychological Battery (Doctoral Dissertation, Columbia University, 1976). *Dissertation Abstracts International, 37,* 5349B.

Finlayson, M.A.J., and Reitan, R. M. (1980).

Effect of lateralized lesions on ipsilateral and contralateral motor functioning. *Journal of Clinical Neuropsychology, 2,* 237–243.

Fraser, P., Lane, B., Knight, D. K., and Walker, M. G. (1983). Cognitive function after carotid endarterectomy. *British Journal of Surgery, 70,* 388 (Abst.).

Fuld, P. A. (1984). Test profile of cholinergic dysfunction and of Alzheimer-type dementia. *Journal of Clinical Neuropsychology, 6,* 380–392.

Fuld, P. A. (1986). Pathological and chemical validation of behavioral features of Alzheimer's disease. In L. W. Poon, ed., *Handbook for Clinical Memory Assessment of Older Adults.* Washington, D.C.: American Psychological Association, pp. 302–306.

Futty, D. E., Conneally, M., Dyken, M. L., Price, T. R., Haerer, A. F., Poskanzer, D. C., Swanson, P. D., Calanchini, P. R., and Gotshall, R. A. (1977). Cooperative study of hospital frequency and character of transient ischemic attacks. V. Symptom analysis. *Journal of the American Medical Association, 238,* 2386–2390.

Gainotti, G., Parlato, V., Monteleone, D., and Carlomagno, S. (1992). Neuropsychological markers of dementia on visual-spatial tasks: A comparison between Alzheimer's type and vascular forms of dementia. *Journal of Clinical and Experimental Neuropsychology, 14,* 239–252.

Garcia, J. (in press). Mechanisms of cell death in ischemia. In L. R. Caplan, ed., *Scientific Basis of Stroke and Its Treatment.* London: Springer-Verlag.

Garcia, J., and Brown, G. G. (1992). Vascular dementia: Neuropathologic alterations and metabolic brain changes. *Journal of the Neurological Sciences, 109,* 121–131.

Gfeller, J. D., and Rankin, E. J. (1991). The WAIS-R profile as a cognitive marker of Alzheimer's disease: A misguided venture? *Journal of Clinical and Experimental Neuropsychology, 13,* 629–636.

Gianutsos, R., and Matheson, P. (1987). The rehabilitation of visual perceptual disorders attributable to brain injury. In M. Meier, A. Benton, and L. Diller, eds., *Neuropsychological Rehabilitation.* New York: Guilford Press, pp. 202–241.

Goldstein, S. G., Kleinknecht, R. A., and Gallo, A. E., Jr. (1970). Neuropsychological changes associated with carotid endarterectomy. *Cortex, 6,* 308–322.

Gordon, T., Kannel, W. B., Castelli, W. P., and Dawber, T. R. (1981). Lipoproteins, cardiovascular disease, and death: The Framingham Study. *Archives of Internal Medicine, 141,* 1128–1131.

Greiffenstein, M. F., Brinkman, S., Jacobs, L., and Braun, P. (1988). Neuropsychological improvement following endarterectomy as a function of outcome measure and reconstructed vessel. *Cortex, 24,* 223–230.

Gross, C. R., Kase, C. S., Mohr, J. P., Cunningham, S. C., and Baker, W. E. (1984). Stroke in south Alabama: Incidence and diagnostic features—a population based study. *Stroke, 15,* 249–255.

Haaland, K. Y., and Delaney, H. D. (1981). Motor deficits after left or right hemisphere damage due to stroke or tumor. *Neuropsychologia, 19,* 17–27.

Hachinski, V. C. (1990). The decline and resurgence of vascular dementia. *Canadian Medical Association Journal, 142,* 107–111.

Hachinski, V. C., Lassen, N. A., and Marshall, J. (1974). Multi-infarct dementia. A cause of mental deterioration in the elderly. *Lancet, 2,* 207–210.

Hart, R. P., Rosner, M. J., and Muizelaar, P. (1985). Recovery from aphasia following extracranial-intracranial bypass surgery: Case report. *Journal of Clinical and Experimental Neuropsychology, 7,* 224–230.

Haynes, C. D., Gideon, D. A., King, G. D., and Dempsey, R. L. (1976). The improvement of cognition and personality after carotid endarterectomy. *Surgery, 80,* 699–704.

Haynes, R. B., Mukherjee, J., Sackett, D. L., Taylor, D. W., Barnett, H.J.M., and Peerless, S. J. (1987). Functional status changes following medical or surgical treatment for cerebral ischemia. Results of the extracranial-intracranial bypass study. *Journal of the American Medical Association, 257,* 2043–2046.

Heaton, R. K., Grant, I., and Matthews, C. G. (1991). *Comprehensive Norms for an Expanded Halstead-Reitan Battery: Demographic Corrections, Research Findings, and Clinical Applications.* Odessa, FL: Psychological Assessment Resources, Inc.

Heaton, R. K., and Pendleton, M. G. (1981). Use of neuropsychological tests to predict adult patients' everyday functioning. *Journal of Consulting and Clinical Psychology, 49,* 807–821.

Heilman, K., and Fisher, W. R. (1974). Hyperlipidemic dementia. *Archives of Neurology, 31,* 67–68.

Hemmingsen, R., Mejsholm, B., Boysen, G., and Engell, H. C. (1982). Intellectual function in patients with transient ischemic attacks (TIA) or minor stroke. Long-term improvement after carotid endarterectomy. *Acta Neurologica Scandinavica, 66,* 145–159.

Hemmingsen, R., Mejsholm, B., Vorstrup, S., Lester, J., Engell, H. C., and Boysen, G. (1986). Carotid surgery, cognitive function, and cerebral blood flow in patients with transient ischemic attacks. *Annals of Neurology, 20,* 13–19.

Hirano, A. (1988). *Color Atlas of Pathology of the Nervous System* (2nd ed.). New York: Igaku-Shoin Medical Publishers.

Hødt-Rasmussen, K., Skinhøj, E., Paulson, O., Ewald, J., Bjerrum, J. K., Fahrenkrug, A., and Lassen, N. A. (1967). Regional cerebral blood flow in acute apoplexy: The "luxury perfusion syndrome" of the brain. *Archives of Neurology, 17,* 271–281.

Holmes, C. S. (1986). Neuropsychological profiles in men with insulin-dependent diabetes. *Journal of Consulting and Clinical Psychology, 54,* 386–389.

Holmes, C. S. (1990). *Neuropsychological and Behavioral Aspects of Diabetes.* New York: Springer-Verlag.

Holmes, C. S., Hayford, J. T., Gonzalez, J. L., and Weydert, J. A. (1983). A survey of cognitive functioning at different glucose levels in diabetic persons. *Diabetes Care, 6,* 180–185.

Holmes, C. S., Koepke, K. M., and Thompson, R. G. (1986). Visual reaction time: Simple versus complex performance impairments during three blood glucose levels. *Psychoneuroendocrinology, 11,* 353–357.

Hom, J. (1991). Contributions of the Halstead-Reitan Battery in the neuropsychological investigation of stroke. In R. A. Bornstein and G. G. Brown, eds., *Neurobehavioral Aspects of Cerebrovascular Disease.* New York: Oxford University Press, pp. 165–181.

Hom, J., and Reitan, R. M. (1982). Effect of lateralized cerebral damage upon contralateral and ipsilateral sensorimotor performances. *Journal of Clinical Neuropsychology, 4,* 249–268.

Hom, J., and Reitan, R. M. (1990). Generalized cognitive function after stroke. *Journal of Clinical and Experimental Neuropsychology, 12,* 644–654.

Horne, D., and Royle, J. (1974). Cognitive changes after carotid endarterectomy. *Medical Journal of Australia, 1,* 316–317.

Hu, H.-H., Sheng, W.-Y., Chu, F.-L., Lan, C.-F., and Chiang, B. N. (1992). Incidence of stroke in Taiwan. *Stroke, 23,* 1237–1241.

Hunt, A. L., Orrison, W. W., Yeo, R. A., Haaland, K. Y., Rhyne, R. L., Garry, P. J., and Rosenberg, G. A. (1989). Clinical significance of MRI white matter lesions in the elderly. *Neurology*, 39, 1470–1474.

Jacobs, L. A., Ganji, S., Shirley, J. G., Morrell, R. M., and Brinkman, S. D. (1983). Cognitive improvement after extracranial reconstruction for the low flow-endangered brain. *Surgery*, 93, 683–687.

Jones, T. H., Morawetz, R. B., Crowell, R. M., Marcoux, F. W., FitzGibbon, S. J., DeGirolami, U., and Ojemann, R. G. (1981). Thresholds of focal cerebral ischemia in awake monkeys. *Journal of Neurosurgery*, 54, 773–782.

Kannel, W. B., Dawber, T. R., Sorlie, P., and Wolf, P. A. (1976). Components of blood pressure and risk of atherothrombotic brain infarction: The Framingham Study. *Stroke, 7*, 327–331.

Kaplan, N. M. (1983). Hypertension: Prevalence, risks, and effects of therapy. *Annals of Internal Medicine*, 98, 705–709.

Kase, C. S., Mohr, J. P., and Caplan, L. R. (1992). Intracerebral hemorrhage. In H. J. Barnett, J. P. Mohr, B. M. Stein, and F. M. Yatsu, eds., *Stroke Pathophysiology, Diagnosis and Management* (2nd ed.). New York: Churchill Livingstone, pp. 561–616.

Katsuki, S., Hirota, Y., Adazome, T., Takeya, S., Omae, T., and Takano, S. (1965). Epidemiological studies on cerebrovascular diseases in Hisayama, Kyushu Island, Japan: Part 1. With particular reference to cerebrovascular status. *Japanese Heart Journal*, 5, 12–36.

Katz, D. I., Alexander, M. P., and Mandell, A. M. (1987). Dementia following strokes in the mesencephalon and diencephalon. *Archives of Neurology*, 44, 1127–1133.

Kimura, D. (1977). Acquisition of a motor skill after left-hemisphere damage. *Brain, 100*, 527–542.

Kimura, D., and Archibald, Y. (1974). Motor functions of the left hemisphere. *Brain*, 97, 337–350.

Krayenbuhl, H. A., Yasargil, M. G., Flamm, E. S., and Tew, J. M., Jr. (1972). Microsurgical treatment of intracranial saccular aneurysms. *Journal of Neurosurgery*, 37, 678–686.

Kurtzke, J. F. (1980). Epidemiology of cerebrovascular disease. In *Cerebrovascular Survey Report*. Bethesda, MD: Office of Scientific and Health Reports, pp. 135–176.

LeBlanc, R., Tyler, J. L., Mohr, G., Meyer, E., Diksic, M., Yamamoto, L., Taylor, L., Gauthier, S., and Hakim, A. (1987). Hemodynamic and metabolic effects of cerebral revasculariza-tion. *Journal of Neurosurgery, 66*, 529–535. [Published erratum appears in *Journal of Neurosurgery, 67*, 474, 1987.]

Levine, S. R., Helpern, J. A., Welch, K.M.A., Van de Linde, A.M.Q., Sawaya, K. L., Brown, E. E., Ramadan, N. M., Deveshwar, R. K., and Ordidge, R. J. (1992). Human focal cerebral ischemia: Evaluation of brain pH and energy metabolism with P-31 NMR spectroscopy. *Radiology,. 185*, 537–544.

Leys, D., Soetaert, G., Petit, H., Fauquette, A., Pruvo, J.-P., and Steinling, M. (1990). Periventricular and white matter magnetic resonance imaging hyperintensities do not differ between Alzheimer's disease and normal aging. *Archives of Neurology*, 47, 524–527.

Lhermitte, F., and Signoret, J. L. (1972). Analyse neuropsychologique des syndrome amnesiques. *Revue Neurologique (Paris), 126*, 161–178.

Li, S. C., Schoenberg, B. S., Wang, C. C., Cheng, X. M., Bolis, C. L., and Wang, K. J. (1985). Cerebrovascular disease in the People's Republic of China: Epidemiologic and clinical features. *Neurology*, 35, 1708–1713.

Liepmann, H. (1913). Motor aphasia, anarthria, and apraxia. In *Transactions of the 17th International Congress of Medicine*, Sec. XI, Part II, pp. 97–106.

Ljunggren, B., Sonesson, B., Saveland, H., and Brandt, L. (1985). Cognitive impairment and adjustment in patients without neurological deficits after aneurysmal SAH and early operation. *Journal of Neurosurgery, 62*, 673–679.

Macon, J. B., and Rice, J. F. (1985). Reversal of fixed hemiplegia due to middle cerebral artery occlusion by delayed superficial temporal to middle cerebral artery bypass graft: Case report. In R. F. Spetzler, L. P. Carter, W. R. Selman, and N. A. Martin, eds., *Cerebral Revascularization for Stroke*. New York: Thieme-Stratton, pp. 470–474.

Mahalick, D. M., Ruff, R. M., and U, H. S. (1991). Neuropsychological sequelae of arteriovenous malformations. *Neurosurgery*, 29, 351–357.

Matarazzo, R. G., Matarazzo, J. D., Gallo, A. E., and Wiens, A. T. (1979). IQ and neuropsychological changes following carotid endarterectomy. *Journal of Clinical Neuropsychology*, 1, 97–116.

Matsumoto, N., Whisnant, J. P., Kurland, L. T., and Okazaki, H. (1973). Natural history of stroke in Rochester, MN, 1955 through 1969: An extension of a previous study, 1945 through 1954. *Stroke, 4*, 20–29.

McCormick, W. F. (1966). The pathology of vascular ('arteriovenous') malformations. *Journal of Neurosurgery, 24,* 807–816.

Meier, M. J., and Strauman, S. E. (1991). Neuropsychological recovery after cerebral infarction. In R. A. Bornstein and G. G. Brown, eds., *Neurobehavioral Aspects of Cerebrovascular Disease.* New York: Oxford University Press, pp. 271–296.

Mendez, M. F., and Ashla-Mendez, M. (1991). Differences between multi-infarct dementia and Alzheimer's disease on unstructured neuropsychological tasks. *Journal of Clinical and Experimental Neuropsychology, 13,* 923–932.

Meuter, F., Thomas, W., Gruneklee, D., Gries, F., and Lohmann, R. (1980). Psychometric evaluation of performance in diabetes mellitus. *Hormone and Metabolic Research, 9* (suppl.), 9–17.

Meyer, J. S., Deshmukh, U. D., and Welch, K.M.A. (1976). Experimental studies with the pathogenies of cerebral ischemia and infarction. In R.W.R. Russell, ed., *Cerebral Artery Disease.* New York: Churchill-Livingstone, pp. 57–84.

Meyer, J. S., Lotfi, J., Martinez, G., Caroselli, J. S., Mortel, K. F., and Thornby, J. I. (1990). Effects of medical and surgical treatment on cerebral perfusion and cognition in patients with chronic cerebral ischemia. *Surgical Neurology, 34,* 301–308.

Meyer, J. S., Welch, K.M.A., Okamoto, S., and Shimazu, K. (1974). Disordered neurotransmitter function: Demonstration by measurement of norepinephrine and 5-hydroxytryptamine in CSF of patients with recent cerebral infarction. *Brain, 97,* 654–664.

Mohr, J. P., Fisher, C. M., and Adams, R. D. (1980). Cerebrovascular disease. In K. J. Isselbach, R. D. Adams, E. Braunwald, R. G. Petersdorf, and J. D. Wilson, eds., *Harrison's Principles of Internal Medicine* (9th ed.). New York: McGraw-Hill, pp. 1911–1942.

Mohr, J. P., Kistler, J. P., and Fink, M. E. (1992). Intracranial aneurysms. In H. J. Barnett, J. P. Mohr, B. M. Stein, and F. M. Yatsu, eds., *Stroke Pathophysiology, Diagnosis, and Management* (2nd ed.). New York: Churchill-Livingstone, pp. 617–644.

Mohr, J. P., Tatemichi, T. K., Nichols, F. C., III., and Stein, B. M. (1986). Vascular malformations of the brain: Clinical considerations. In H. J. Barnett, J. P. Mohr, B. M. Stein, and F. M. Yatsu, eds., *Stroke Pathophysiology, Diagnosis, and Management* (vol. 2). New York: Churchill-Livingstone, pp. 679–719.

Mononen, H., Lepojarvi, M., and Kallanranta, T. (1990). Early neuropsychological outcome after carotid endarterectomy. *European Neurology, 30,* 328–333.

Nielsen, H., Hojer-Pedersen, E., Gulliksen, G., Haase, J., and Enevoldsen, E. (1986). Reversible ischemic neurological deficit and minor strokes before and after EC/IC bypass surgery: A neuropsychological study. *Acta Neurologica Scandinavica, 73,* 615–618.

Nilsson, B., Cronqvist, S., and Ingvar, D. H. (1979). Regional cerebral blood flow (rCBF) studies in patients to be considered for extracranial-intracranial bypass operations. In J. S. Meyer, H. Lechner, and M. Reivich, eds., *Cerebral Vascular Disease 2: Proceedings of the 9th International Salzburg Conference.* Amsterdam: Excerpta Medica, pp. 295–300.

North American Symptomatic Carotid Endarterectomy Trial Collaborators (1991). Beneficial effect of carotid endarterectomy in symptomatic patients with high-grade carotid stenosis. *New England Journal of Medicine, 325,* 445–453.

Olivecrona, H., and Reeves, J. (1948). Arteriovenous aneurysms of the brain: Their diagnosis and treatment. *Archives of Neurology and Psychiatry, 59,* 567–602.

Osborn, A. G. (1980). *An Introduction to Cerebral Angiography.* New York: Harper and Row.

Ott, E. O., Abraham, J., Meyer, J. S., Achari, A. N., Chee, A.N.C., and Mathew, N. T. (1975). Disordered cholinergic neurotransmission and dysautoregulation after acute cerebral infarction. *Stroke, 6,* 172–180.

Parker, J. C., Smarr, K. L., Granberg, B. W., Nichols, W. K., and Hewett, J. E. (1986). Neuropsychological parameters of carotid endarterectomy: A two-year prospective analysis. *Journal of Consulting and Clinical Psychology, 54,* 676–681.

Perez, F. I., Gay, J.R.A., Taylor, R. L., and Rivera, V. M. (1975a). Patterns of memory performance in the neurologically impaired aged. *Canadian Journal of Neurological Sciences, 2,* 347–355.

Perez, F. I., Rivera, V. M., Meyer, J. S., Gay, J.R.A., Taylor, R. L., and Mathew, N. T. (1975b). Analysis of intellectual and cognitive performance in patients with multi-infarct dementia, vertebrobasilar insufficiency with dementia and Alzheimer's disease. *Journal of Neurology, Neurosurgery and Psychiatry, 38,* 533–540.

Perez, F. I., Stump, D. A., Gay, J. R., and Hart, V. R. (1976). Intellectual performance in multi-infarct dementia and Alzheimer's disease: A replication study. *Canadian Journal of Neurological Sciences, 3,* 181–187.

Perlmuter, L. C., Nathan, D. M., Goldfinger, S. H., Russo, P. A., Yates, J., and Larkin, M. (1988). Triglyceride levels affect cognitive function in noninsulin-dependent diabetics. *Journal of Diabetic Complications, 2,* 210–213.

Perret, G. (1975). The epidemiology and clinical course of arteriovenous malformations. In H. W. Pia, J.R.W. Gleave, E. Grote, and J. Zierski, eds., *Cerebral Angiomas: Advances in Diagnosis and Therapy.* New York: Springer-Verlag, pp. 21–26.

Perret, G., and Nishioka, H. (1966). Report on the cooperative study of intracranial aneurysms and subarachnoid hemorrhage. Section VI. Arteriovenous malformations. An analysis of 545 cases of cranio-cerebral arteriovenous malformations and fistulae reported to the cooperative study. *Journal of Neurosurgery, 25,* 467–490.

Pessin, M. S., Duncan, G. W., Mohr, J. P., and Poskanzer, D. C. (1977). Clinical and angiographic features of carotid transient ischemic attacks. *New England Journal of Medicine, 296,* 358–362.

Pizzamiglio, L., Antonucci, G., Judica, A., Montenero, P., Razzano, C., and Zoccolotti, P. (1992). Cognitive rehabilitation of the hemineglect disorder in chronic patients with unilateral right brain damage. *Journal of Clinical and Experimental Neuropsychology, 14,* 901–923.

Ponsford, J. L., Donnan, G. A., and Walsh, K. W. (1980). Disorders of memory in vertebrobasilar disease. *Journal of Clinical Neuropsychology, 2,* 267–276.

Powers, W. J., and Grubb, R. L., Jr. (1987). Hemodynamic and metabolic relationships in cerebral ischemia and subarachnoid hemorrhage. In J. H. Wood, ed., *Cerebral Blood Flow: Physiologic and Clinical Aspects.* New York: McGraw-Hill, pp. 387–401.

Reitan, R. M. (1970). Presentation 15. In A. L. Benton, ed., *Behavioral Change in Cerebrovascular Disease.* New York: Harper and Row, pp. 155–165.

Reitan, R. M., and Fitzhugh, K. B. (1971). Behavioral deficits in groups with cerebral vascular lesions. *Journal of Consulting and Clinical Psychology, 37,* 215–223.

Reitan, R. M., and Shipley, R. E. (1963). The relationship of serum cholesterol changes to psychological abilities. *Journal of Gerontology, 18,* 350–357.

Reitan, R. M., and Wolfson, D. (1985). *The Halstead-Reitan Neuropsychological Test Battery.* Tucson, AZ: Neuropsychology Press.

Reitan, R. M., and Wolfson, D. (1994). Dissociation of motor impairment and higher-level brain deficits in strokes and cerebral neoplasms. *Clinical Neuropsychologist, 8,* 193–208.

Reivich, M., and Waltz, A. G. (1980). Circulatory and metabolic factors in cerebrovascular disease. In *Cerebrovascular Survey Report.* Bethesda, MD: Office of Scientific and Health Reports, pp. 55–134.

Ricci, S., Celani, M. G., Guercini, G., Rucireta, P., Vitali, R., La Rosa, F., Duca, E., Ferraguzzi, R., Paolotti, M., Seppoloni, D., Caputo, N., Chiurulla, C., Scaroni, R., and Signorini, E. (1989). First-year results of a community-based study of stroke incidence in Umbria, Italy. *Stroke, 20,* 853–857.

Richardson, J. T. (1991). Cognitive performance following rupture and repair of intracranial aneurysm. *Acta Neurologica Scandinavica, 83,* 110–122.

Rodriguez, G., Arvigo, F., Marenco, S., Nobili, F., Romano, P., Sandini, G., and Rosadini, G. (1987). Regional cerebral blood flow in essential hypertension: Data evaluation by a mapping system. *Stroke, 18,* 13–20.

Rogers, R. L., Meyer, J. S., McClintic, K., and Mortel, K. F. (1989). Reducing hypertriglyceridemia in elderly patients with cerebrovascular disease stabilizes or improves cognition and cerebral perfusion. *Angiology, 40,* 260–269.

Roman, G. C., Tatemichi, T. K., Erkinjuntti, T., Cummings, J. L., Masdeu, J. C., Garcia, J. H., Amaducci, L., Orgogozo, J.-M., Brun, A., Hofman, A., Moody, D. M., O'Brien, M. D., Yamaguchi, T., Grafman, J., Drayer, B. P., Bennett, D. A., Fisher, M., Ogata, J., Kokmen, E., Bermejo, F., Wolf, P. A., Gorelick, P. B., Bick, K. L., Pajeau, A. K., Bell, M. A., DeCarli, C., Culebras, A., Korczyn, A. D., Bogousslavsky, J., Hartmann, A., and Scheinberg, P. (1993). Vascular dementia: Diagnostic criteria for research studies. Report of the NINDS-AIREN International Workshop. *Neurology, 43,* 250–260.

Salonen, J. T., Puska, P., Tuomilehto, J., and Homan, K. (1982). Relation of blood pressure, serum lipids, and smoking to the risk of cerebral stroke—a longitudinal study in Eastern Finland. *Stroke, 13,* 327–333.

Satz, P., Hynd, G. W., D'Elia, L., Daniel, M. H., Van Gorp, W., and Connor, R. (1990). A WAIS-R marker for accelerated aging and dementia, Alzheimer's type? Base rates of the

Fuld formula in the WAIS-R standardization sample. *Journal of Clinical and Experimental Neuropsychology, 12,* 759–765.

Shekelle, R. B., Ostfeld, A. M., and Klawans, H. L., Jr. (1974). Hypertension and risk of stroke in an elderly population. *Stroke, 5,* 71–75.

Siesjo, B. K. (1985). Acid-base homeostasis in the brain: Physiology, chemistry, and neurochemical pathology. In K. Kogure, K.-A. Hossmann, B. K. Siesjo, and F. A. Welsh, eds., *Progress in Brain Research* (vol. 63). New York: Elsevier Press, pp. 121–154.

Siesjo, B. K. (1990). Calcium in the brain under physiological and pathological conditions. *European Neurology, 30* (Suppl. 2), 3–9, 39–41.

Sirkka, A., Salenius, J.-P., Portin, R., and Nummenmaa, T. (1992). Quality of life and cognitive performance after carotid endarterectomy during long-term follow-up. *Acta Neurologica Scandinavica, 85,* 58–62.

Skenazy, J. A., and Bigler, E. D. (1984). Neuropsychological findings in diabetes mellitus. *Journal of Clinical Psychology, 40,* 246–258.

Sonesson, B., Ljunggren, N. B., Saveland, H., and Brandt, L. (1987). Cognition and adjustment after late and early operation for ruptured aneurysm. *Neurosurgery, 21,* 279–287.

Stabell, K. E. (1991). *Neuropsychological Investigation of Patients with Surgically Treated Aneurysm Rupture at Different Cerebral Sites.* Oslo, Norway: Institute of Psychology, University of Oslo.

Starkstein, S. E., Bolla, K. I., and Robinson, R. G. (1991). Dementia syndrome of depression in patients with stroke. In R. A. Bornstein and G. G. Brown, eds., *Neurobehavioral Aspects of Cerebrovascular Disease.* New York: Oxford University Press, pp. 202–223.

Stein, B. M., and Wolpert, S. M. (1980). Arteriovenous malformations of the brain. I: Current concepts and treatment. *Archives of Neurology, 37,* 1–5.

Sundt, T. M., Jr. (1987). Was the international randomized trial of extracranial-intracranial arterial bypass representative of the population at risk? *New England Journal of Medicine, 316,* 814–816.

Tanaka, H., Ueda, Y., Date, C., Baba, T., Yamashita, H., Hayashi, M., Shoji, H., Owada, K., Baba, K.-I., Shibuya, M., Kon, T., and Detels, R. (1981). Incidence of stroke in Shibata, Japan: 1976–1978. *Stroke, 12,* 460–466.

Toole, J. F. (1990). *Cerebrovascular Disorders* (4th ed.). New York: Raven Press.

Van der Drift, J.H.A., and Kok, K. D. (1972). Steal mechanisms between the carotid and vertebrobasilar systems. In J. S. Meyer, M. Reivich, H. Lechner, and O. Eichhorn, eds., *Research on the Cerebral Circulation: Fifth International Salzburg Conference.* Springfield, IL: Charles C. Thomas, pp. 325–336.

Waldstein, S. R., Manuck, S. B., Ryan, C. M., and Muldoon, M. F. (1991a). Neuropsychological correlates of hypertension: Review and methodologic considerations. *Psychological Bulletin, 110,* 451–468.

Waldstein, S. R., Ryan, C. M., Manuck, S. B., Parkinson, D. K., and Bromet, E. J. (1991b). Learning and memory function in men with untreated blood pressure elevation. *Journal of Consulting and Clinical Psychology, 59,* 513–517.

Waltimo, O., and Putkonen, A.-R. (1974). Intellectual performance of patients with intracranial arteriovenous malformations. *Brain, 97,* 511–520.

Weinberg, J., Diller, L., Gordon, W. A., Gerstman, L. J., Lieberman, A., Lakin, P., Hodges, G., and Ezrachi, O. (1979). Training sensory awareness and spatial organization in people with right brain damage. *Archives of Physical Medicine and Rehabilitation, 60,* 491–496.

Williams, V., and Grossman, R. G. (1970). Ultrastructure of cortical synapses after failure of presynaptic activity in ischemia. *Anatomical Record, 166,* 131–141.

Wolf, P. A., Cobb, J. L., and D'Agostino, R. B. (1992). Epidemiology of stroke. In H.J.M. Barnett, B. M. Stein, J. P. Mohr, and F. M. Yatsu, eds., *Stroke Pathophysiology, Diagnosis, and Management* (2nd ed.). New York: Churchill-Livingstone, pp. 3–27.

Young, G. C., Collins, D., and Hren, M. (1983). Effect of pairing scanning training with block design training in the remediation of perceptual problems in left hemiplegics. *Journal of Clinical Neuropsychology, 5,* 201–212.

Younkin, D., Hungerbuhler, J. P., O'Connor, M., Goldberg, H., Burke, A., Kushner, M., Hurtig, H., Obrist, W., Gordon, J., Gur, R., and Reivich, M. (1985). Superficial temporal-middle cerebral artery anastomosis: Effects on vascular, neurologic, and neuropsychological functions. *Neurology, 35,* 462–469.

16 The Neuropsychological Correlates of Acute and Chronic Hypoxemia

SEAN B. ROURKE and KENNETH M. ADAMS

The adult human brain—though it accounts for only 2% of a person's total body weight—consumes approximately 20% to 25% of the total amount of oxygen inspired (Schneck, 1993). Whereas other organs and tissues in the human body can withstand deprivations of oxygen for extended periods of time, even subtle deviations in the oxygen supply to the brain can result in significant and enduring neurobehavioral sequelae. A complete deprivation of oxygen (i.e., anoxia) can occur following a cardiac arrest (Parkin et al., 1987; Bigler and Alfano, 1988; Schneck, 1993), cerebral vascular accident (Brown et al., 1986; Bornstein and Brown, 1991; Schneck, 1993), botched suicide by attempted hanging (Mosko et al., 1989; Medalia et al., 1991; Markowitsch, 1992), or toxic gas exposure (Bryer et al., 1988; Vieregge et al., 1989; Messier and Myers, 1991). If the anoxia continues for more than a few minutes, an anoxic/ischemic encephalopathy will likely ensue, frequently involving both neuropsychological impairments and neuroradiological abnormalities. Equally salient neurobehavioral effects may also occur, however, when the brain is supplied with a physiologically inadequate amount of oxygen (i.e., hypoxemia) over an extended period of time.

This chapter delineates the neuropsychological correlates of hypoxemia. We will present a summary of the studies that have focused specifically on the effects of acute hypoxemia on brain functioning (i.e., studies of persons at altitude or in decompression chambers), as well as those that have examined the neurobehavioral sequelae of chronic exposure to hypoxemia (i.e., in chronic obstructive pulmonary disease [COPD] and in patients with sleep-disordered breathing and sleep apnea syndrome). The treatment effects of supplemental oxygen and continuous positive airway pressure for patients with COPD and sleep apnea syndrome will also be presented. The chapter will conclude with a description of the clinical neuropsychological implications that pertain to the treatment of hypoxemic patients.

Mechanics of Respiration and Oxygenation: A Brief Summary for the Neuropsychologist

The cardiopulmonary system plays a critical role in maintaining the integrity of the central nervous system by providing it with a constant supply of oxygen and glucose, and by removing the by-products of metabolism. The exchange of gases occurs via diffusion across the alveolar-capillary membranes in the respiratory zone of the lungs. Efficient respiration and subsequent oxygenation of tissues requires a sufficient number of alveolar-capillary units for gas exchange to take place, enough hemoglobin to carry oxygen in the blood, an efficient ventilation-perfusion matching, and an adequate cardiac output (West, 1982).

Several indicators can be used to assess the efficiency of the cardiopulmonary system and, subsequently, the amount of oxygen available to tissues. There are two simple tests of lung function: the forced expiratory volume ($FEV_{1.0}$) and the forced vital capacity (FVC). $FEV_{1.0}$ is the volume of air (in liters) that can be forcibly exhaled in one second from full inspiration; FVC is the total volume of gas that can be exhaled after a full inspiration. The normal range for each of these measures depends on a person's age, sex, height, weight, and ethnic origin; the normal ratio of $FEV_{1.0}$ to FVC is approximately 80% (West, 1982). In obstructive lung diseases (e.g., COPD), both the $FEV_{1.0}$ and FVC are reduced, resulting in a ratio below 80%.

Blood gases provide information about the availability of oxygen and carbon dioxide in the blood (i.e., the partial pressure of oxygen [PaO_2] and carbon dioxide [$PaCO_2$] in arterial blood—both measured in millimeters of mercury [mm Hg]). In a normal healthy subject, the PaO_2 and $PaCO_2$ are approximately 95 mm Hg (range 85 to 100) and 40 mm Hg (range 37 to 43), respectively; the partial pressure of oxygen tends to decrease with advancing age, probably due to increasing ventilation-perfusion inequality, whereas the partial pressure of carbon dioxide does not change with age (West, 1982). An individual experiences hypoxemia when his or her PaO_2 value drops below the normal range, and hypercapnia when his or her $PaCO_2$ levels exceed the normal range. Both of these abnormal conditions can occur simultaneously in the same individual. The amount of oxygen carried in the blood is determined primarily by the saturation of hemoglobin with oxygen (SaO_2). A number of factors influence the oxygen-carrying capacity of hemoglobin: PaO_2, $PaCO_2$, temperature, pH, 2,3-diphosphoglycerate (DPG), and the oxygen dissociation curve (West, 1982).

There are four primary causes of hypoxemia or reduced PaO_2: hypoventilation, diffusion impairment, shunts, and ventilation-perfusion inequality (West, 1982, 1985). Hypoventilation occurs when there is a reduction in the amount of gas that is available to

the alveoli but no corresponding decrease in oxygen consumption. As a result, a person becomes hypoxemic and severely hypercapnic. A diffusion impairment results when there is a decrease in the amount of oxygen that diffuses into the pulmonary capillary blood. Shunts occur when some blood enters the arterial system without passing through ventilated portions of the lung. Finally, in ventilation-perfusion inequality, gas transfer becomes inefficient because there is a mismatch between ventilation and blood flow in various regions of the lung (West, 1982).

Neuropsychological Effects of Acute Exposure to Hypoxemia

Much of what we know about the effects of acute hypoxemia on brain functioning has come from studies of individuals and small groups at very high altitude or in compression chambers that simulate high altitude. Predictable neurological sequelae have been observed at increasing elevations above sea level (see Table 16-1).

High Altitude Studies

A number of investigators have demonstrated that exposure to high altitude, without supplemental oxygen, can be associated with neuropsychological deficits that are detectable following return to sea level. Impairments in basic sensory and perceptual (especially visual) functions have been noted, as well as deficits in attention, concentration, memory, abstraction and cognitive flexibility, word-finding, psychomotor ability, and on tests of simple motor skills (Ryn, 1971; Gibson et al., 1981; Townes et al., 1984; West, 1986; Petiet et al., 1988; Hornbein et al., 1989; Regard et al., 1989; Cavaletti et al., 1990). Although certain neuropsychological deficits may recover after descent from high altitude, residual deficits may persist after prolonged periods, particularly on tests of concentration (Regard et al., 1989), memory (Ryn, 1971; Hornbein et al., 1989; Regard et al., 1989; Cavaletti et al., 1990), visual confrontational naming (Petiet et al., 1988),

Table 16-1. Neuropsychological Changes at Altitude

Altitude (m)	PaO_2 (mm Hg)	$PaCO_2$ (mm Hg)	Possible Neuropsychological Changes/Signs
Sea level	95	38	Normal
1500	85	38	Impaired dark adaptation
3000–4500	60–45	36–34	Impaired concentration; impaired short-term memory; hyperventilation
4500–6000	45–35	34–30	Lethargy, euphoria, irritability, hallucinations, impaired critical judgment, muscular incoordination
Above 6000	<35	<30	Loss of consciousness

Source: Reproduced from Grant and Heaton (1985) with permission.

abstract reasoning and cognitive flexibility (Ryn, 1971; Petiet et al., 1988; Regard et al., 1989), and on tests of fine motor skills (Townes et al., 1984; West, 1986; Hornbein et al., 1989; Regard et al., 1989; Hornbein, 1992). Further evidence that high altitude causes brain damage is provided by studies demonstrating abnormal electroencephalographic recordings (Ryn, 1971; Forster et al., 1975; Fukushima et al., 1988) and brain morphology, using computed tomography (CT) (Fukushima et al., 1988) and magnetic resonance imaging (MRI) (Garrido et al., 1993) in persons exposed to extreme elevations. In the Garrido et al. (1993) study, of 26 elite high altitude climbers (mean age 35 years) that were given MRIs after their return to sea level (approximately 9 months after their exposure to altitude), 46% of the climbers had abnormal MRIs relative to an age- and sex-matched group of controls.

While the above studies suggest a reliable effect of hypoxemia on brain functioning, a few altitude studies have not shown any neuropsychological deficits in comparable groups of subjects tested after return to sea level (Clark et al., 1983; Jason et al., 1989), despite the use of a comprehensive neuropsychological test battery.

Several factors have likely contributed to the differential neuropsychological recovery observed in persons exposed to acute hypoxemia: (1) methodological differences across studies (e.g., highly educated subjects in a number of studies, differing severity and duration of hypoxemic exposures, subject vari-

ability in response to hypoxemic state, possibly due to subject variability in the hypoxic ventilatory response (Hornbein et al., 1989), inconsistency of neuropsychological instruments employed, and length of test intervals); (2) the effects of environmental conditions at altitude (e.g., extreme cold, injuries in falls, sleep deprivation, fatigue, etc.); and (3) repeated or prolonged exposure to hypoxemia at high altitudes, which may increase the risk of permanent neuropsychological impairment (Hornbein et al., 1989).

Decompression and Simulated Altitude Studies

Neuropsychological deficits like those detected at high altitude have also been observed in subjects tested in decompression or altitude chambers (Lewis and Baddeley, 1981; Vaernes et al., 1984; Logie and Baddeley, 1985; Hornbein et al., 1989), particularly impairments in memory (Biersner and Cameron, 1970; O'Reilly, 1974; Logue et al., 1986; Hornbein et al., 1989) and on tests of cognitive flexibility and perceptual and psychomotor efficiency (O'Reilly, 1974; Carter, 1979; Logue et al., 1986), which can reverse after return to normal surface pressure (Logue et al., 1986).

In summary, the results from both altitude and decompression/simulated altitude studies suggest that brief hypoxemia has the potential to compromise cerebral functioning. The amount of neuropsychological recovery from these effects also appears to be variable.

Neuropsychological Effects of Chronic Exposure to Hypoxemia: Chronic Obstructive Pulmonary Disease

The term chronic obstructive pulmonary disease has been in widespread use for several decades (Petty, 1985a). During this time, pulmonary clinicians have disagreed about the defining characteristics and pathological conditions of COPD. For the purpose of this chapter, we borrow from a definition provided by Petty, a leading pulmonary clinician:

COPD is an all inclusive and nonspecific term referring to the condition in patients who have chronic cough and expectoration and various degrees of exertional dyspnea with a significant and progressive reduction in expiratory airflow as measured by the forced expiratory volume in 1 second (FEV$_1$). This airflow abnormality *does not* (italics added) show major reversibility in response to pharmacological agents. Both inflammatory damage to airways and alveoli are present postmortem. Terms such as chronic obstructive airways disease (COAD), chronic obstructive lung disease (COLD), chronic airflow obstruction or chronic airways obstruction (CAO), chronic airflow limitation (CAL), etc., all mean the same thing. (Petty [1985], pp. 3–4.)

The primary clinical signs of COPD include chronic cough, chronic expectoration, shortness of breath during physical exertion and reduction in expiratory airflow as measured by spirometry. Expiratory airflow obstruction is the single most common feature in all of the disease processes that fall under the rubric of COPD (Cugell, 1988). Obstruction can occur at various stages along the tracheobronchial tree, depending on the etiology. A distinction is often made between those disease states that occur predominantly in upper portions of the tracheobronchial tree (e.g., laryngeal lesions, tumors, and tracheomalacia) versus those that occur in lower portions—below the larynx or the tracheal bifurcation (e.g., asthma, chronic bronchitis, emphysema, and bronchiolitis); other chronic airway diseases that cannot be localized as upper or lower in nature include cystic fibrosis and bronchiectasis (Cugell, 1988).

It is important to make a distinction between obstructive lung diseases that are reversible and those that are irreversible (Petty, 1990). According to Petty (1990), patients with acute and intermittent asthma (i.e., those who experience symptom-free periods reversible by medication or time), should not be classified as having COPD. In contrast, patients with emphysema and/or chronic bronchitis should be classified as having COPD because they experience chronic symptoms that, at best, can only be partially reversed in the early stages of the disease; in the later stages of COPD, there is an irreversible progressive deterioration of cardiopulmonary function.

The major subtypes of COPD—chronic bronchitis and emphysema—although representing somewhat distinct syndromes that often coexist concomitantly, can result in subnormal amounts of gas exchange in the lungs and decreased arterial oxygen tension. Clinically, the patient with chronic bronchitis, once referred to as the "blue bloater" because of his or her cyanotic and edematous appearance, is most often obese, experiences severe hypoxemia, has a long history of chronic cough with sputum production, heart enlargement, cor pulmonale (i.e., right ventricular enlargement and dysfunction), secondary polycythemia (i.e., increased number of erythrocytes and erythroblasts), low ventilatory response to blood gas challenges, chronic airway inflammation as judged postmortem, and early death (West, 1982; Petty, 1985a; Flenley, 1991). In contrast, the patient with emphysema (i.e., the "pink puffer"), while experiencing similar airflow obstruction, generally exhibits relatively preserved blood gases, hyperinflated lungs, a greater amount of dyspnea than cough, tissue destruction including loss of alveolar architecture and elastic recoil, small cardiac shadows on chest x-ray, low body weight, and few signs of cor pulmonale (West, 1982; Petty, 1985a; Flenley, 1991). Whereas emphysema and chronic bronchitis represent prototypic examples of physiologic extremes, in clinical practice, *both* airway inflammation and tissue destruction are commonly present in COPD patients (Petty, 1985a).

Chronic obstructive pulmonary disease is relatively common; the prevalence rate for the United States in 1980 was 4.75%. The incidence of COPD is increasing and is currently the fifth leading cause of death in the United States (Tockman et al., 1985). The etiology and the primary determinant of COPD mortality is clearly a function of cigarette smoking. However, in a small number of cases, occupational fumes and dust, bronchiectasis, cystic fibrosis, and a number of congenital disorders of defective airway defense also can cause significant damage to airways which can lead to subsequent chronic hypoxemia (Howard, 1990). Ventilation-perfusion mismatching is the most common cause of hypoxemia in COPD (West, 1982; Georgopoulos and Anthonisen, 1990; Flenley, 1991), although an element of alveolar hypoventilation may also be present in COPD patients during an acute exacerbation of chronic respiratory failure (Flenley, 1991). The cardiopulmonary symptoms of COPD develop insidiously over a period of approximately 30 years (Petty, 1988), and eventually lead to significant deleterious effects on the patient's psychosocial and neurocognitive functioning (Grant et al., 1987; Kaplan and Atkins, 1988; McSweeny and Labuhn [Chapter 23]).

Chronic obstructive pulmonary disease is not reversible and cannot be "cured." However, it can be managed using a combination of approaches. Make (1991) suggests that the primary goals of COPD management should be (1) reduction of airflow obstruction, (2) prevention or treatment of complications associated with the disease, and (3) improvement of quality of life. Bronchodilator medications are used to help keep airways open and antibiotics are used to treat or prevent infection (Make, 1991; Saroea, 1993). Pulmonary rehabilitation programs, which include patient and family education, breathing training, smoking cessation and systematic exercise, help the patient to learn how to cope with the effects of the disease as well

as how to maximize function (Petty, 1985b, 1988; Ries, 1990, 1991; Make 1991; Casaburi and Petty, 1993; Haas et al., 1994). Finally, supplemental oxygen use can be helpful in returning arterial oxygen levels and blood chemistry closer to normal (Petty, 1985c, 1988; Make, 1991; Niewoehner, 1994).

The physical effects of COPD and hypoxemia are well known and include decreased cardiac efficiency, decreased ability to engage in sustained physical activity, adverse changes in blood chemistry and chronic shortness of breath (Hodgkin, 1979). However, considering COPD as a condition that affects only the cardiopulmonary system does not capture the complete clinical picture, because chronic exposure to hypoxemia can also lead to compromised cerebral functioning. In the next major section, we will focus on the neuropsychological aspects of irreversible chronic lung disease processes that occur in the lower portions of the respiratory system, particularly chronic bronchitis and emphysema (i.e., COPD), because they are likely to represent the most common referrals for neuropsychological consultation from pulmonary medicine. Additionally, however, we also believe that COPD is a significant neuromedical risk factor that should be considered in the differential diagnosis of patients with long histories of smoking who present initially with neuropsychiatric or systemic illnesses for neuropsychological evaluation.

The preceding represents only a cursory overview of the pathophysiology, etiology, epidemiology, and treatment of COPD. Interested readers are strongly encouraged to consult other sources. Good introductions may be found in chapters by Cugell (1988) and Niewoehner (1994) or the position paper by Edelman et al. (1992); a more comprehensive treatment is available in the book by Petty (1985d).

Neuropsychological Aspects of COPD

Although cognitive difficulties associated with hypoxemia secondary to COPD were described as early as 1954 by Westlake and

Kaye, systematic neuropsychological investigations of hypoxemic COPD have appeared only relatively recently. In 1973, a group of Florida investigators performed the first systematic study that examined the neuropsychological sequelae of COPD, and the role that one month of supplemental oxygen may have on reversing any observed neuropsychological deficits (Krop et al., 1973). In this study, 10 hypoxemic COPD patients (with $PaO_2 < 55$ mm Hg) exhibited neuropsychological deficits, when tested breathing room air, on simple motor and (visual-spatial) perceptual-motor abilities, relative to a comparison group of 12 COPD patients with similar degrees of airway obstruction, but with less hypoxemia (i.e., $PaO_2 > 55$ mm Hg). Both groups had intelligence quotients and memory functioning within the normal range.

After one month of continuous oxygen therapy (prescribed 24 hrs/day), the treated group of 10 hypoxemic COPD patients with $PaO_2 < 55$ mm Hg (tested while receiving supplemental oxygen), exhibited significant improvements in neuropsychological functioning. Mean PaO_2 rose from 51 mm Hg to 75 mm Hg while patients were on supplemental oxygen, although no changes were observed in $PaCO_2$ or on spirometry values (FEV_1 or FVC). In the treated group, neuropsychological improvements were noted on the Wechsler Intelligence scales (WAIS or Wechsler-Bellevue Full Scale and Performance IQs), the Wechsler Memory Scale (WMS), the Finger Tapping Test, and the Bender Gestalt Test. In contrast, no improvements were observed in the untreated comparison group of COPD patients in neuropsychological functioning.

There were a number of methodological problems with this initial study (i.e., small sample size, neuropsychological testing performed at baseline while patients breathed room air and at follow-up while receiving oxygen, medical stabilization of patients prior to testing, and lack of an appropriate "control" group without COPD to evaluate practice effects); however, the results suggested that COPD patients with significant hypoxemia (i.e., $PaO_2 < 55$ mm Hg) experience neu-

ropsychological deficits, and that partial reversal of these deficits was possible with supplemental oxygen treatment.

Multicenter Clinical Trials: The Effects of Severity of Hypoxemia on Neuropsychological Performance in COPD Patients

Two large multicenter trials sponsored by the National Heart, Lung, and Blood Institute (NHLBI) have replicated and extended the Krop et al. (1973) findings (Nocturnal Oxygen Therapy Group, 1980; Intermittent Positive Pressure Breathing Group, 1983). The main purpose of the Nocturnal Oxygen Therapy (NOTT) Trial was to compare the effects of continuous (at least 20 hours per day) versus nocturnal (at least 12 hours at night) oxygen treatment in the management of COPD patients with moderate to severe levels of hypoxemia. The Intermittent Positive Pressure Breathing (IPPB) Trial was performed to evaluate the effectiveness of IPPB in mildly hypoxemic patients. Extensive medical and neuropsychological evaluations were performed in both multicenter studies, and an attempt was made to relate neuropsychological performance to pulmonary-medical predictors. Similar neuropsychological batteries were employed in both the NOTT (Grant et al., 1982) and the IPPB (Prigatano et al., 1983) studies with the goal of later combining them into one data bank. This combined data bank (Grant et al., 1987), which will be summarized below, provided the first comprehensive evaluation of the neuropsychological correlates of large groups of COPD patients that varied in severity of hypoxemia (the effects of oxygen supplementation on neuropsychological status to be presented later in the chapter). For the effects of hypoxemia on life-quality in COPD patients, see McSweeny and Labuhn (Chapter 23).

The combination of the NOTT and the IPPB allowed for stratification of 302 COPD patients into three levels of hypoxemia "severity": (1) mild ($PaO_2 > 59$ mm Hg; N = 86); (2) moderate (PaO_2 50 to 59 mm Hg; N = 155); and (3) severe ($PaO_2 < 50$ mm Hg; N = 61). Basic demographic and pulmonary characteristics of the three groups of COPD patients and the matched controls (N = 99) are presented in Table 16-2. This table contains useful patient information for the non-medical clinician that can be used to broadly estimate the medical "severity" of a COPD patient referred for a neuropsychological consultation. Overall, groups were not different on demographic characteristics, suggesting that groups were probably comparable in premorbid neuropsychological functioning (see Grant et al. [1987] for additional pulmonary-medical information).

Overall, there was a progressive worsening of neuropsychological functioning with increasing level of hypoxemic severity despite comparable age, education, and Verbal IQ scores. See Table 16-3 for a selected sample of neuropsychological test performance. An examination of the summary indices indicated that control subjects performed significantly better than all three hypoxemic groups on the Average Impairment Rating (AIR) (Russell et al., 1970). Moderate and severe hypoxemic groups, while not being statistically different from one another on the AIR, were significantly worse than the mild hypoxemic group. On both the Halstead Impairment Index (HII) and the Brain Age Quotient (BAQ), controls and mild hypoxemic COPD patients, and, moderate and severe hypoxemic patients, performed similarly.

In order to evaluate the neuropsychological performance of COPD patients and controls in a more comprehensive fashion, a factor analysis was performed to reduce the number of variables (i.e., 27) into a few relevant dimensions. A four-factor solution was obtained, which accounted for 58% of the variance (variables were retained if they had factor loadings greater than 0.5, and all four factors had eigenvalues greater than 1). Factor 1 was represented by tests of verbal intelligence (e.g., WAIS verbal subtests, Story Learning, and Aphasia Screening Exam errors). Factor 2, a perceptual learning and problem-solving factor, was composed of tests thought to be sensitive to the effects of brain dysfunction (e.g., Block Design, Picture Arrangement, and Object Assembly subtests from the WAIS, Category Test, Tactual Performance Test: total time per block, as well as memory, and location, and Figural Memory from the WMS). Factor 3 contained tests of alertness and psychomotor speed (e.g., Digit Vigilance, Speech Sounds Per-

Table 16-2. Basic Demographic and Pulmonary Characteristics of Combined NOTT/IPPB Patients and Controls: Means and Standard Deviations (SD)

	Group 1 Controls (N = 99)	Group 2 Mildly Hypoxemic COPD (N = 86)	Group 3 Moderately Hypoxemic COPD (N = 155)	Group 4 Severely Hypoxemic COPD (N = 61)
Age[a]	63.1 (10.3)	61.6 (7.5)	64.3 (8.2)	65.9 (8.3)
Education	10.2 (3.6)	9.7 (3.0)	9.8 (3.7)	9.4 (3.4)
Sex–Male	75 (76%)	76 (88%)	119 (77%)	48 (77%)
PaO_2 (mm Hg) (resting, room air)		67.8 (6.3)	54.4 (2.7)	44.4 (4.1)
$PaCO_2$ (mm Hg) (resting, room air)		34.9 (4.1)	42.1 (7.4)	45.8 (8.4)
FEV_1% predicted (prebronchodilator, best value)		38.0 (12.1)	29.3 (12.5)	30.9 (14.9)
FVC_1% predicted (prebronchodilator, best value)		68.2 (17.5)	53.2 (16.9)	54.3 (18.0)

Source: Reproduced from Grant and Heaton (1985) with permission.

[a]ANOVA ($p < .05$), group 4 significantly older than group 2 (Neuman Keuls).

Table 16-3. Neuropsychological Test Performance of Patients in Three Hypoxemic Groupings, and Nonpatient Controls: Means and Standard Deviations (SD)

Test	Group 1 Nonpatient Controls (N = 99)	Group 2 Mildly Hypoxemic COPD (N = 86)	Group 3 Moderately Hypoxemic COPD (N = 155)	Group 4 Severely Hypoxemic COPD (N = 61)	Group[a] Differences
Average Impairment Rating	1.69 (0.62)	1.81 (0.58)	2.13 (0.72)	2.38 (0.72)	_ 1 2 3 4
Halstead Impairment Index	0.59 (0.26)	0.65 (0.23)	0.73 (0.24)	0.77 (0.23)	1 2 3 4
Brain Age Quotient	91.2 (16.5)	89.1 (13.4)	79.9 (20.1)	76.6 (17.3)	1 2 3 4
WAIS Verbal IQ	107.2 (14.6)	104.8 (15.1)	102.7 (16.3)	101.6 (14.9)	1 2 3 4
WAIS Performance IQ	108.6 (11.8)	105.1 (10.5)	101.5 (13.8)	98.5 (13.5)	1 2 3 4
WAIS Full Scale IQ	108.3 (13.0)	105.4 (13.1)	102.5 (15.4)	100.5 (14.4)	1 2 3 4
Digit Symbol Scaled Score	7.4 (2.5)	6.3 (2.0)	5.7 (2.8)	5.1 (2.5)	_ 1 2 3 4
Trail Making Test–Part B (seconds)	122.0 (62)	124.0 (60)	156.0 (78)	183.0 (81)	1 2 3 4
Category Test (errors)	65.2 (26.4)	80.7 (22.6)	77.0 (27.2)	86.7 (27.8)	_ 1 2 3 4
Tactual Performance Test (mins/block)	0.83 (0.53)	0.92 (0.70)	1.48 (1.50)	2.17 (2.09)	1 2 3 4
WMS Story (Immediate Recall)	20.3 (6.1)	17.9 (6.5)	17.8 (6.5)	18.0 (7.0)	_ 1 2 3 4
WMS Story (% loss)	14.7 (18.6)	20.3 (19.7)	20.3 (20.5)	22.3 (22.4)	1 2 3 4
WMS Figures (Immediate Recall)	7.9 (3.1)	6.8 (3.3)	6.0 (3.1)	5.5 (4.2)	_ 1 2 3 4
WMS Figures (% loss)	15.0 (29.3)	13.5 (36.4)	19.4 (35.6)	35.9 (41.0)	1 2 3 4

Source: Reproduced from Grant and Heaton (1985) with permission.

Note: A complete listing of test results is provided in Grant et al. (1987).

[a] Groups underlined together are not significantly different from each other.

ception, Seashore Rhythm Test, Trail Making Test–Part B, Digit Symbol subtest from the WAIS, Sentence Writing Time, and Grooved Pegboard). Finally, Factor 4, which contained Finger Tapping and Hand Dynamometer, represented a simple motor skills factor.

Factor-analytically derived ability scores were calculated for the COPD patients and controls (see Fig. 16-1). The overall MANOVA was significant, indicating that neuropsychological test performance was affected by hypoxemia. Post-hoc univariate analyses revealed that COPD patients performed progressively worse with increasing severity of hypoxemia on three of the four factors; no differences were observed across groups on the verbal-intelligence factor. The perceptual learning and problem-solving factor appeared to be the most effective in separating the hypoxemic groups, with the moderately hypoxemic group performing intermediate to the mild and severe groups.

The tests that made up this factor have been previously shown to be the most sensitive to brain dysfunction (Reitan and Wolfson, 1993). Alertness and psychomotor speed were affected only by severe hypoxemia, whereas motor skills were affected by both moderate and severe hypoxemic levels.

These neuropsychological findings also have implications for quality of life. If we assume that different aspects of quality of life depend on different neurocognitive skills, it follows that certain areas of functioning will be more or less affected by different degrees of hypoxemia. This concept is discussed in more detail in Chapter 23 (McSweeny and Labuhn).

Prediction of Neuropsychological Status According to Hypoxemia Severity

As part of the combined NOTT/IPPB evaluation, an attempt was made to determine if it would be possible to predict which patients would be likely to manifest neuropsychological deficits (Grant et al., 1987); this information would be valuable to clinicians involved in the evaluation and treatment of COPD patients. The AIR was selected as an overall measure of brain functioning. To achieve optimal sensitivity and specificity, an AIR score of 2.10 was chosen, which classified 20.6% of older controls as impaired (the standard 1.55 cutoff for the AIR was not used because it classified roughly 50% of elderly controls as "brain damaged"); this 20.6% represented the "risk of impairment" related to age. This amount was then subtracted from the total percentage of COPD patients that were classified as impaired at each of the three severity levels of hypoxemia. With the age factor removed, the risk of neuropsychological impairment attributable to severity level of hypoxemia, was 6% in the mildly hypoxemic group, 24% in the moderately hypoxemic group, and 41% in the severely hypoxemic group (Grant et al., 1987).

Relationship of Neuropsychological Status to Medical-Pulmonary Variables

If severity of hypoxemia influences the neuropsychological status of COPD patients, one would also expect to find evidence that medical-pulmonary indicators are associated with neuropsychological test performance. To address this issue, Grant and his colleagues performed a series of multiple regressions with backward elimination to determine if any of the medical parameters could predict neuropsychological performance (AIR) beyond the contribution of age and education. Medical predictors known to be important in COPD (e.g., FEV_1, respiratory rate, exercise capacity as measured by bicycle ergometer, PaO_2, $PaCO_2$, pH, hemoglobin, and, systolic and diastolic pressure) were entered in an attempt to predict the AIR (Grant et al., 1987).

Overall, with all variables entered, the multiple R was equal to .65 ($R^2 = .42$); vari-

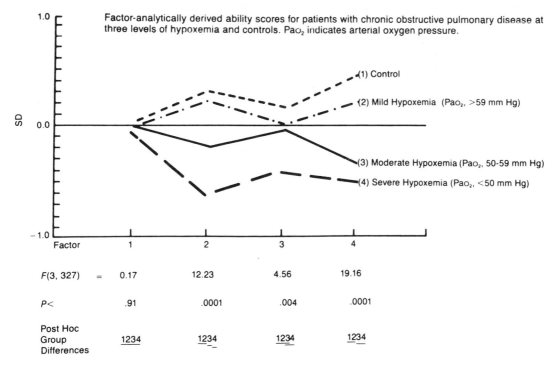

Factor-analytically derived ability scores for patients with chronic obstructive pulmonary disease at three levels of hypoxemia and controls. PaO_2 indicates arterial oxygen pressure.

Factor	1	2	3	4
$F(3, 327) =$	0.17	12.23	4.56	19.16
$P<$	.91	.0001	.004	.0001
Post Hoc Group Differences	1234	1234	1234	1234

Figure 16-1. Neuropsychological performance of COPD patients at three levels of hypoxemia severity and age-matched controls. (Reproduced from Grant et al. [1987] with permission.)

ables eliminated that were not significant at the .10 level resulted in a multiple R of .63 ($R^2 = .40$). Of those variables that remained in the equation, education and age accounted for 25% and 5% of the variance of AIR, respectively, while respiratory rate and PaO_2 each contributed 5% to the prediction (Grant et al., 1987). Further evidence for a relationship between medical-pulmonary parameters (PaO_2 and FEV_1) and neuropsychological status has been observed using multiple regression in a smaller sample (n = 66) of hypoxemic patients (mean PaO_2 and $PaCO_2$ of 67 and 41 mm Hg, respectively) (Fix et al., 1982).

While the effects of age and education on neuropsychological test performance have been well established (Heaton et al., 1986; Heaton et al., 1991; Heaton, 1992), the degree of hypoxemia, however, contributed only modestly to neuropsychological status, and pulmonary function tests had little or no predictive power. These findings suggest that the etiology of the neuropsychological deficits in COPD patients is attributable to additional factors other than the demographic and standard medical-pulmonary in-dicators examined in the study of Grant et al. (1987). Other possible factors that may be involved include desaturations during sleep (more on this point below), psychological response to chronic illness (e.g., increased depression, anxiety, somatization, withdrawal, etc.), concurrent illnesses (e.g., hypertension, cardiac insufficiency), increased susceptibility to diseases (e.g., pneumonia), increased fatigue, and sensory decrements (Grant et al., 1987; Rourke et al., 1993).

Neuropsychological Effects of Chronic Exposure to Hypoxemia: Sleep-Disordered Breathing and Sleep Apnea Syndrome

Sleep plays an important restorative and maintenance role in many physiological systems in man, but none perhaps more important than in the central nervous system. It is a complex cyclical rhythm of physiologically distinct stages involving light sleep (stages 1–2), slow-wave sleep (stages 3–4), and rapid eye movement (REM) sleep. Fluc-

tuations in levels of PaO_2 and $PaCO_2$ occur to varying degrees across sleep stages, but these have little functional significance in normal healthy adults; however, they do exert significant effects in patients with compromised respiratory systems, e.g., COPD (Berry and Block, 1988; Martin, 1990), or in persons with sleep-disordered breathing or the sleep apnea syndrome.

Sleep-Disordered Breathing and Sleep Apnea Syndrome in "Normal" Controls

Sleep-disordered breathing (SDB), which occurs predominantly during light (stages 1 and 2) and REM sleep (Berry and Block, 1988; Wiegand and Zwillich, 1994), is characterized by the presence of apneas (complete cessation in breathing), hypopneas (partial cessation of respiration), and oxygen desaturations occurring subsequent to hypopneic events (Berry and Block, 1988; Ancoli-Israel and Coy, 1994). The sleep apnea syndrome (SAS) is diagnosed when apneas last at least 10 seconds and occur more than 30 times over a period of 7 hours of sleep (Association of Sleep Disorders Centers and the Association for the Psychophysiological Study of Sleep, 1979). An apnea index (i.e., AI: number of apneas per hour of sleep) of 5 or higher (Guilleminault et al., 1978), or a respiratory disturbance index (i.e., RDI: number of apneas plus the number of hypopnea per hour of sleep) of 10 or higher (Romaker and Ancoli-Israel, 1987), have also been used to diagnose SAS, although diagnostic cutoffs for the AI and RDI have varied across studies.

The prevalence of SAS in middle-aged populations has been estimated to fall between 1% and 10% (Peter et al., 1985; Fleury, 1992; Jennum and Sjol, 1992; Young et al., 1993); rates in healthy elderly are substantially higher—24% to 75% (Ancoli-Israel, 1989; Fleury, 1992). The large variability in the prevalence of SAS in the elderly has been attributed to different AI and RDI cutoffs, small sample sizes, and nonrepresentative samples (Ancoli-Israel, 1989). In addition, a number of investigators have questioned the use of similar AI and RDI cutoffs for both middle-aged and elderly samples

(Berry et al., 1984; Ancoli-Israel, 1989; Ancoli-Israel et al., 1991b; Ancoli-Israel and Coy, 1994). Nevertheless, in a study of 427 randomly selected elderly people (age greater than 65 years, sample mean age = 72.5 (6.1) years) that avoided many prior methodological shortcomings, only 24% had an AI of 5 or greater while 62% had a RDI of 10 or greater (Ancoli-Israel et al., 1991b). With respect to sex differences in SAS, men have been found to exhibit more breathing abnormalities during sleep than women, including nocturnal oxygen desaturations and SAS (Block et al., 1979; Ancoli-Israel et al., 1987), although men and women may differ in the clinical features of SAS (Ambrogetti et al., 1991). Some authors have proposed that only postmenopausal women may suffer from SAS (Block et al., 1979); others have demonstrated that body mass index in women may be a major risk factor for the appearance of SAS (Guilleminault et al., 1988). Other risk factors for SAS, in addition to male gender and a high body mass index, include consumption of tobacco and alcohol (Jennum and Sjol, 1992, 1993) as well as other CNS depressant drugs.

There are a substantial number of clinical features associated with SDB and SAS (Romaker and Ancoli-Israel, 1987). These include loud snoring (Jennum and Sjol, 1992, 1993), major cardiovascular risk factors (Jennum et al., 1992) including hypertension (Kimoff et al., 1991; Klitzman and Miller, 1994) and cardiac arrhythmias (Kimoff et al., 1991; Klitzman and Miller, 1994); leg kicks (Ancoli-Israeli et al., 1985); confusion, enuresis, and impotence at nighttime (Romaker and Ancoli-Israel, 1987), and excessive daytime sleepiness (Lavie, 1983; Bolitschek et al., 1990; Kimoff et al., 1991); morning headache (Jennum et al., 1994); a significantly higher frequency of auto accidents (Findley et al., 1988, 1989b), particularly with severe apnea (Findley et al., 1989a); affective disturbances such as irritability, anxiety, and depression (Kales et al., 1985; Klonoff et al., 1987); cognitive complaints of concentration and memory problems, which show high correlations with mood; insomnia and hypersomnia (Jennum and Sjol, 1994); and neuropsycho-

logical impairments (Kales et al., 1985; Berry et al., 1986; Block et al., 1986; Findley et al., 1986; Greenberg et al., 1987; Bedard et al., 1991b; Froehling, 1991; Cheshire et al., 1992; Bedard et al., 1993; Borak et al., 1993).

When middle-aged patients with SAS show deficits on formal neuropsychological tests, these tend to occur in the areas of intellectual efficiency (Findley et al., 1986; Telakivi et al., 1988; Bedard et al., 1991b; Montplaisir et al., 1992), attention and concentration (Findley et al., 1986; Greenberg et al., 1987; Bedard et al., 1991b; Sloan, 1991; Bedard et al., 1993; Borak et al., 1993), memory (Kales et al., 1985; Findley et al., 1986; Bedard et al., 1991b, 1993; Borak et al., 1993; Naegele et al., 1995), perceptual-motor organization and efficiency (Findley et al., 1986; Greenberg et al., 1987; Walsleben et al., 1989; Bedard et al., 1991b, 1993; Borak et al., 1993), executive functioning (Bedard et al., 1991b, 1993; Naegele et al., 1995), and on tests of simple motor skills (Findley et al., 1986; Greenberg et al., 1987; Bedard et al., 1991b, 1993). As one might expect, a number of investigators have demonstrated significant relationships between neuropsychological deficits and measures of SDB (i.e., AI, RDI, and oxygen desaturations), in middle-aged subjects who snore heavily or in asymptomatic and symptomatic patients with SAS (Block et al., 1979; Yesavage et al., 1985; Berry et al., 1986; Block, 1986; Findley et al., 1986; Greenberg et al., 1987; Telakivi et al., 1988; Bliwise et al., 1989; Ancoli-Israel et al., 1991a; Cheshire et al., 1992; Borak et al., 1993); however, this has not always been the case (Berry et al., 1987; Hayward et al., 1992; Merrion, 1992; Telakivi et al., 1993; Phillips et al., 1994), and some have suggested that the neuropsychological deficits are related to sleep disruption or impaired alertness associated with sleep fragmentation (Sloan et al., 1989; Cammermeyer, 1991; Stone et al., 1994), premorbid functioning (Nichols, 1991) or neuromedical risk factors (Nichols et al., 1988).

Recently, there has been an attempt to determine the extent to which sleep disruption or sleep fragmentation and nocturnal hypoxemia contribute to the neurocognitive impairments observed in patients with SDB and SAS (Sloan et al., 1989; Bedard et al., 1991a,b; Cheshire et al., 1992; Montplaisir et al., 1992; Bedard et al., 1993; Naegele et al., 1995). On the one hand, a number of investigators have found that the neuropsychological deficits in SDB or SAS are more related to impaired alertness associated with sleep disruption, rather than to the number of oxygen desaturations (Sloan et al., 1989; Cammermeyer, 1991; Stone et al., 1994). In contrast, Findley and his colleagues found significant correlations between cognitive impairments and degree of hypoxemia during sleep and wakefulness, but not with sleep fragmentation (Findley et al., 1986). Still others have shown that both sleep disruption and extent of nocturnal hypoxemia are important determinants of neuropsychological performance (Bedard et al., 1991b; Cheshire et al., 1992; Montplaisir et al., 1992; Naegele et al., 1995). For example, Bedard and his colleagues demonstrated that deficits in attention and memory were more related to sleep disruption, whereas declines in general intellectual measures, executive-type tasks, and psychomotor performance were related to the severity of hypoxemia (Bedard et al., 1991b; Montplaisir et al., 1992; Naegele et al., 1995).

Sleep-Disordered Breathing and Sleep Apnea in COPD Patients

Individuals with SDB/SAS and cardiopulmonary disturbances—such as COPD—have increased morbidity and mortality risks, compared with COPD patients who do not experience suppressed cardiac output with subsequent reductions in cerebral oxygen transport and increased hypoxemia nocturnally (Grant et al., 1982).

The reported incidence of sleep-associated hypoxemia in patients with COPD varies considerably across studies. A review by Vos and colleagues reported that between 67% and 100% of COPD patients experience nocturnal hypoxemic episodes, whereas 71% to 100% of them have associated breathing disorders (Vos et al., 1991). The high prevalence of SDB and SAS has been largely attributed

to the inclusion of COPD patients with the "blue bloater" profile (Douglas et al., 1979; Berry and Block, 1988). Furthermore, COPD patients who experience nocturnal desaturations show evidence of more abnormal cardiopulmonary hemodynamics than COPD patients without such desaturations (Fletcher et al., 1989). One study reported that 43% of COPD patients with daytime awake PaO_2 of 60 to 70 mm Hg (excluding those with SAS) were nocturnal desaturators (Levi-Valensi et al., 1990). Similarly, signs of nocturnal REM-related oxyhemoglobin desaturation have been reported in 27% of COPD patients with a daytime $PaO_2 > 60$ mm Hg (Fletcher et al., 1987). Other researchers have recently noted that both daytime SaO_2 and hypercapnia are added risks factors for the development of nocturnal hypoxemia (Bradley et al., 1990).

Sleep-disordered breathing and sleep apnea syndrome thus appear to play a significant role in the everyday functioning of individuals without obvious lung disease, and represent an additional risk factor for COPD patients, particularly those patients who already experience significantly elevated hypoxemic levels (i.e., lower PaO_2). This added risk factor may also help to explain why daytime PaO_2 levels have correlated only modestly with neuropsychological status in COPD patients.

Supplemental Oxygen Therapy and Continuous Positive Airway Pressure: Treatment Options for Patients with Chronic Hypoxemia

Given the established association between chronic hypoxemia and neuropsychological performance in patients with sleep-disordered breathing, sleep apnea syndrome, or COPD, one might expect that the administration of supplemental oxygen would correct the hypoxemia and reverse or improve the observed neuropsychological deficits, as well as affect other clinical features that are normally present. In addition, continuous positive airway pressure (CPAP), a technique that maintains the upper airway open, and prevents collapse during sleep by providing pressure through a nasal mask from an air compressor, may also show similar benefits by reducing SDB and SAS during the night.

Oxygen Supplementation: Possible Benefits for Hypoxemic COPD Patients

The administration of supplemental oxygen therapy to hypoxemic COPD patients has been shown to improve neuropsychological functioning (Krop et al., 1973; Heaton et al., 1983), EEG parameters (Brezinova et al., 1979), exercise tolerance (Stein et al., 1982), sleep status (Calverley et al., 1982), survival (Nocturnal Oxygen Therapy Group, 1980; Report of the Medical Research Council Working Party, 1981; Heaton et al., 1983; Cooper et al., 1987; Shachor et al., 1989), and to reduce hemodynamic abnormalities (Timms et al., 1985) and pulmonary hypertension (Klein et al., 1986; Weitzenblum et al., 1989, 1992), although it has had little or no benefit on psychosocial functioning (Heaton et al., 1983; Lahdensuo et al., 1989). In patients with SDB and SAS, oxygen therapy has been shown to improve physiologic sleep parameters in some studies (Smith et al., 1984; Block et al., 1989), particularly oxygenation (Block et al., 1989), although this is not always the case (Block et al., 1987).

The effects of short-term oxygen therapy (i.e., several days to one month) showed some initial promise of improving cognitive functioning in a group of elderly men with organic brain syndrome (Jacobs et al., 1969, 1972), particularly with respect to memory functioning (Krop et al., 1977), and in a small group of COPD patients with hypoxemia (Krop et al., 1973). However, other investigators have been unable to replicate these results with similar elderly patient groups (Goldfarb et al., 1972; Thompson et al., 1976; Raskin et al., 1978), in patients with SDB or SAS (Block et al., 1989), or in COPD patients with moderately severe levels of hypoxemia (Wilson et al., 1985).

With respect to supplemental oxygen therapy on a longer term basis, the multicenter NOTT (1980) will be described below in detail because it represents the most compre-

hensive study to date that has examined the effects of long-term supplemental oxygen on the neuropsychological performance of COPD patients with hypoxemia (Heaton et al., 1983). Of the 150 COPD patients that were enrolled, 78 received continuous oxygen therapy (COT) (average 20.7 [SD = 3.7] hrs/day) while 72 received nocturnal oxygen therapy (NOT) (average 11.9 [SD = 2.1] hrs/ day). In addition, a subsample of 37 patients (20 COT and 17 NOT) were examined at 1 year.

After 6 months of oxygen supplementation, both the NOT and COT groups exhibited similar performance on the AIR, a summary measure of neuropsychological performance. An examination of the individual tests revealed that the COPD patients as a group improved significantly more than did nonpatient controls on only three tests: the Trail Making Test, the Finger Tapping Test, and the Hand Dynamometer (see Table 16-4). On the other neuropsychological tests, COPD patients generally improved at the 6-month evaluation; however, these changes were attributable to practice effects because controls also exhibited similar changes (Heaton et al., 1983).

A divergence occurred after 12 months of oxygen supplementation such that the COT group (N = 20) showed improved neuropsychological performance relative to the NOT group (N = 17). That is, those COPD patients who had been receiving COT performed significantly better on four of the five summary measures (i.e., WAIS Performance IQ, AIR, Brain Age Quotient, and the Halstead Impairment Index); the NOT and COT groups did not differ in Verbal IQ (see Fig. 16-2 for performance on AIR).

As part of the NOTT (1980), blind clinical ratings were also performed in order to better appreciate the neuropsychological changes that occurred at the individual level. The neuropsychological tests were organized into seven ability domains with one overall global rating. After 6 months of oxygen therapy, 42% of the COPD patients tested on room air were rated as "improved," relative to only 6% of the controls. As Table 16-5 illustrates, "improved" performances (i.e.,

Table 16-4. Changes in Neuropsychological Functioning with 6 Months of Oxygen Treatment (Patients) versus No Treatment: Means and Standard Deviations (SD)

	Normal Controls (N = 53)		Matched COPD Group (N = 55)	
	Baseline	6 months	Baseline	6 months
Summary Scores				
WAIS Verbal IQ	107.6 (15.1)	109.2 (15.1)	102.1 (15.3)	103.6 (13.6)
WAIS Performance IQ	108.1 (10.1)	111.7 (11.9)	98.2 (16.1)	102.5 (5.3)
Average Impairment Rating	1.72 (0.63)	1.59 (0.60)	2.20 (0.82)	2.04 (0.81)
Halstead Impairment Index	0.61 (0.25)	0.56 (0.29)	0.74 (0.24)	0.69 (0.28)
Brain Age Quotient	91.1 (16.7)	96.8 (18.1)	76.6 (22.5)	83.4 (23.5)
Halstead-Reitan Tests				
Category Test (errors)	63.8 (25.3)	54.1 (25.0)	79.6 (26.5)	70.7 (29.1)
Trails B (seconds)	118.0 (61.9)	119.5 (68.4)	160.5 (90.3)	138.0 (84.8)[a]
TPT (mins/block)	0.88 (0.62)	0.71 (0.39)	1.78 (1.85)	1.58 (1.54)
Memory (correct)	6.5 (2.0)	6.7 (1.9)	5.4 (2.0)	5.5 (2.0)
Location (correct)	2.3 (2.2)	2.8 (2.1)	1.6 (1.5)	1.5 (1.5)
Speech sounds perception (errors)	9.1 (8.3)	8.4 (6.3)	13.4 (10.8)	14.1 (15.1)
Seashore Rhythm (correct)	23.2 (3.8)	24.6 (3.5)	22.6 (4.7)	22.3 (5.9)
Tapping (avg. 2 hands)	44.2 (7.8)	44.1 (7.3)	40.3 (7.8)	43.1 (7.5)[a]
Sensory (errors)	9.1 (9.8)	6.4 (8.1)	14.7 (11.2)	14.4 (11.8)
Aphasia (errors)	6.8 (5.2)	6.4 (6.3)	8.9 (8.0)	8.1 (8.2)
Spatial relation (errors)	2.9 (1.6)	2.9 (1.5)	3.6 (2.3)	3.7 (2.1)
Added Neuropsychological Tests				
Grip strength (kg, 2 hands)	40.9 (12.5)	37.7 (11.7)	30.8 (11.0)	31.9 (11.9)[a]
Pegboard (avg. sec, 2 hands)	86.1 (23.4)	85.8 (21.9)	121.0 (59.7)	113.9 (55.5)
Verbal learning (imm. recall)	19.4 (6.2)	20.4 (5.9)	18.5 (7.1)	19.5 (7.7)
Verbal % loss (30-min delay)	19.8 (19.7)	16.3 (18.1)	22.6 (23.0)	16.8 (22.3)
Nonverbal learning (imm. recall)	7.9 (3.4)	8.5 (3.4)	5.4 (3.1)	6.2 (3.4)
Nonverbal % loss (30-min delay)	19.8 (25.5)	15.6 (25.3)	34.6 (35.5)	25.1 (26.6)

Source: Reproduced from Heaton (1988) with permission.

[a] COPD group shows significantly more improvement than untreated controls ($p < 0.01$).

which were virtually all in the clinical rating category of "a little better") were noted in verbal skills, abstraction and cognitive flexibility, and on tests of simple sensory and motor skills. Nevertheless, the authors cautioned that the improvements in neuropsychological performance were "relatively subtle," and that the changes "did not constitute a major reversal of neuropsychologic impairment in the patients with COPD" (Heaton et al., 1983).

A number of researchers have examined the metabolic effects of oxygen on energy-producing pathways in an attempt to explain possible mechanisms underlying the hypoxemia-induced neuropsychological deficits observed in COPD patients and the slight improvements observed with oxygen therapy. However, results from these studies have indicated that PaO_2 levels must be extremely low (i.e., during conditions of anoxia or ischemia), for alterations in energy producing pathways to be affected (Siesjo et al., 1974; Blass and Gibson, 1979). Because hypoxemic COPD patients generally do not experience PaO_2 levels low enough for energy-producing pathways to be affected (Blass and Gibson, 1979), researchers have turned to the role that oxygen plays in the biosynthesis and degradation of various neurotransmitters (Gibson and Duffy, 1981; Gibson et al., 1981; Broderick and Gibson, 1989) and have found that most pathways are sensitive to hypoxemic conditions. In particular, cholinergic pathways (e.g., those involving acetylcholine) have been shown to be sensi-

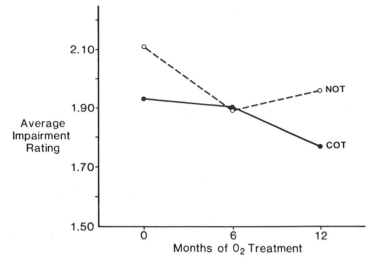

Figure 16-2. Mean Average Impairment Ratings for continuous oxygen treatment (solid line) and nocturnal oxygen treatment (dotted line) groups that completed neuropsychological evaluations at baseline and after 6 and 12 months of oxygen treatment. (Reproduced from Heaton et al. [1983] with permission.)

tive to hypoxemia. As a result, a decline of acetylcholine may be responsible for the observed declines in cognitive performance (Gibson and Duffy, 1981; Gibson et al., 1981; Bartus et al., 1982; Freeman and Gibson, 1988). However, given that trials with cholinergic drug treatment only partially reverse hypoxic-induced neuropsychologic deficits (Gibson et al., 1983; Freeman et al., 1986), other neurotransmitter systems may also be implicated (Freeman and Gibson, 1988; Broderick and Gibson, 1989).

Continuous Positive Airway Pressure (CPAP): Possible Benefits for Sleep-Disordered Breathing and Sleep Apnea Syndrome

The choice of treatments for SDB and SAS often depends on the severity of the symp-

Table 16-5. Percentages of Subjects Rated as Improved from Baseline to 6-Month Neuropsychological Evaluations

	Untreated Normal Subjects (N = 53)	Matched Subjects with COPD (N = 55)	Chi-Square
Simple motor	5.6	41.8	19.7[a]
Simple sensory	1.9	21.8	10.3[b]
Complex perceptual-motor	22.2	32.0	1.3
Attention	11.1	19.6	1.5
Memory	30.8	29.4	0.0
Abstraction/flexibility	11.3	34.0	7.8[a]
Verbal	7.6	25.5	6.2[c]
Global judgment	5.6	41.8	19.7[a]

Source: Reproduced from Heaton (1988) with permission.

[a] $p < 0.001$.

[b] $p < 0.01$.

[c] $p < 0.05$.

toms, the magnitude of the clinical complications, and the type of apnea—obstructive, central, or mixed (Klonoff et al., 1987). While CPAP is extremely effective in reducing or eliminating SDB, behavioral interventions including weight reduction, change in diet, exercise, decrease in alcohol consumption, sedatives and antihistamines (particularly in the evenings), changes in sleep position (Petty, 1985b; Kaplan and Atkins, 1988), and in some situations, the administration of tricyclic antidepressants, have proved to be useful in treating SDB (Kimoff et al., 1991). In more severe cases of SAS, however, surgical procedures such as tracheostomy, uvulopalapharyngoplasty (UPP), and tonsillectomy are often preferable.

Improvements in sleep architecture and reduction in daytime sleepiness have been noted with CPAP in patients with SDB and SAS (Lamphere et al., 1989; Bedard et al., 1993; Borak et al., 1993; Engleman et al., 1993). In addition, several studies have demonstrated that significant improvements in neuropsychological performance occur with CPAP (Bearpark et al., 1987; Derderian et al., 1988; Cammermeyer, 1991; Froehling, 1991; Scheltens et al., 1991; Walker, 1991; Bedard et al., 1993); however, a few studies have not shown improvements (Borak et al., 1993; Engleman et al., 1993). When neuropsychological deficits persist following CPAP, they tend to occur on tasks requiring planning and manual dexterity (Montplaisir et al., 1992; Bedard et al., 1993). Patients with SDB and SAS also exhibit deficits in event-related potentials, with partial improvement occurring after two nights (Walsleben et al., 1989) and 6 weeks of treatment with CPAP treatment (Rumbach et al., 1991). Finally, it is important to note that the discontinuation of CPAP for one night can result in the reversal of treatment gains (Kribbs et al., 1993).

Clinical Implications of the Neuropsychological Deficits Associated with Hypoxemia

The accumulation of evidence from studies of individuals at high altitude or with sleep-disordered breathing, sleep apnea syndrome, and chronic obstructive pulmonary disease strongly suggests that both acute and chronic exposures to hypoxemia can significantly impair neurobehavioral functioning. Although some neuropsychological deficits improve with supplemental oxygen therapy in persons with cardiopulmonary disorders, or with nasal continuous positive airway pressure in persons with sleep disorders, other deficits persist. These residual neuropsychological deficits that remain after treatment may indicate that permanent cerebral damage has been sustained, and indeed there is some postmortem evidence that suggests this is the case. Certainly, in COPD patients who by definition have a progressive deteriorating course, it is unlikely that oxygen therapy will be able to permanently arrest the neurobehavioral deficits that occur as a complication of severely compromised cardiopulmonary function. On the other hand, once sleep fragmentation and exposures to hypoxemia have been corrected using CPAP in persons with sleep-disordered breathing and sleep apnea syndrome, more complete neuropsychological recovery may occur after longer periods of CPAP than examined to date. The amount and extent of this recovery would also likely depend on a person's premorbid functioning (age and education experience), psychoactive substance abuse history, coexisting psychiatric disorders (e.g., mood disorders), and accumulated neuromedical risk factors (e.g., history of head injuries, hypertension, diabetes, etc.).

Our analysis also highlights the dearth of psychological data on treatments and outcome of patients with acute and chronic hypoxic exposure. The depression and despair that accompany the downward physical course of COPD have been noted (Sawyer et al., 1983), but the more subtle and individual reactions of individuals to focal neuropsychological deficits have been addressed, we believe, on an ad hoc basis.

In this respect, we feel that prospective studies must be done. For example, there is no systematic basis upon which pulmonary medicine physicians can determine how depression and/or subtle neuropsychological deficits might shape home and community care guidance for post-hypoxic patients. Research on pulmonary disease has encompassed psychological and neuropsychological methods to a greater extent than in other internal medicine domains, but more remains to be done to maximize the benefit from this research at the level of the individual case.

Finally, how might the neuropsychologic profile of persons with increasing severity of hypoxemia—whether from sleep-disordered breathing, sleep apnea syndrome, recent high altitude exposure, or COPD—affect their everyday functioning? Because of deficits in cognitive flexibility, problem solving, and abstraction, hypoxemic individuals may experience difficulty at work or in situations that demand flexibility of thought and logical analysis. In addition, they may also have problems in adhering to rehabilitation programs that are presented in a complex and ambiguous fashion. As a result, clinicians may experience better compliance and success rates if rehabilitation regimens are presented in a clear, straightforward, and supportive manner (Grant et al., 1982; Prigatano and Grant, 1988).

In contrast, persons with hypoxemia do exhibit some relative strengths. Specifically, verbal skills tend to be spared, and aspects of memory, especially retention, tend to be preserved. As a result, clinicians can expect that these individuals will generally be able to express themselves and communicate with others, and be able to remember simple instructions concerning their treatment regimen (Prigatano and Grant, 1988). It can also be beneficial for clinicians to explain to the patient's spouses and family members the nature and severity of the neuropsychological dysfunction that can be expected, as well as the compensatory and external support measures that can be taken to maximize the patient's everyday functioning (Grant et al., 1982). Finally, by evaluating each patient's adaptive strengths and weaknesses, individually tailored rehabilitation regimens can be formulated and implemented with the best chance for success (Greenberg, 1987).

Acknowledgment

The authors are grateful for suggestions by John McSweeny, Ph.D., and also for his willingness to permit several sentences, originally contained in Chapter 23, to be moved to this chapter in order to facilitate a coordinated presentation of material on the biomedical and epidemiological aspects of COPD. This work was supported by VA Merit Review Grant SA325 and the National Institute on Alcoholism and Alcohol Abuse Center Grant on Alcohol and Aging (AA7678).

References

Ambrogetti, A., Olson, L. G., and Saunders, N. A. (1991). Differences in the symptoms of men and women with obstructive sleep apnoea. *Australian and New Zealand Journal of Medicine, 21,* 863–866.

Ancoli-Israel, S. (1989). Epidemiology of sleep disorders. *Clinics in Geriatric Medicine, 5,* 347–362.

Ancoli-Israel, S., and Coy, T. (1994). Are breathing disturbances in elderly equivalent to sleep apnea syndrome? *Sleep, 17,* 77–83.

Ancoli-Israel, S., Klauber, M. R., Butters, N., Parker, L., and Kripke, D. F. (1991a). Dementia in institutionalized elderly: Relation to sleep apnea. *Journal of the American Geriatrics Society, 39,* 258–263.

Ancoli-Israel, S., Kripke, D. F., Klauber, M. R., Mason, W. J., Fell, R., and Kaplan, O. (1991b). Sleep-disordered breathing in community-dwelling elderly. *Sleep, 14,* 486–495.

Ancoli-Israel, S., Kripke, D. F., and Mason, W. (1987). Characteristics of obstructive and central sleep apnea in the elderly: An interim report. *Biological Psychiatry, 22,* 741–750.

Ancoli-Israel, S., Kripke, D. F., Mason, W., and Kaplan, O. J. (1985). Sleep apnea and periodic movements in an aging sample. *Journal of Gerontology, 40,* 419–425.

Association of Sleep Disorders Centers and the Association for the Psychophysiological Study of Sleep. (1979). Diagnostic classification of sleep and arousal disorders. *Sleep, 2,* 1–137.

Bartus, R. T., Dean, R. L., III, Beer, B., and Lippa, A. S. (1982). The cholinergic hypothesis of geriatric memory dysfunction. *Science, 217,* 408–417.

Bearpark, H., Grunstein, R., Touyz, S., Channon, L., and Sullivan, C. (1987). Cognitive and psychological dysfunction in sleep apnea before and after treatment with CPAP. *Sleep Research, 16,* 303.

Bedard, M. A., Montplaisir, J., Malo, J., Richer, F., and Rouleau, I. (1993). Persistent neuropsychological deficits and vigilance impairment in sleep apnea syndrome after treatment with continuous positive airways pressure (CPAP). *Journal of Clinical and Experimental Neuropsychology, 15,* 330–341.

Bedard, M. A., Montplaisir, J., Richer, F., and Malo, J. (1991a). Nocturnal hypoxemia as a determinant of vigilance impairment in sleep apnea syndrome. *Chest, 100,* 367–370.

Bedard, M. A., Montplaisir, J., Richer, F., Rouleau, I., and Malo, J. (1991b). Obstructive sleep apnea syndrome: Pathogenesis of neuropsychological deficits. *Journal of Clinical and Experimental Neuropsychology, 13,* 950–964.

Berry, D.T.R., and Block, A. J. (1988). Sleep-disordered breathing in patients with COPD. In A. J. McSweeny and I. Grant, eds., *Chronic Obstructive Pulmonary Disease: A Behavioral Perspective.* New York: Marcel Dekker, Inc., pp. 19–38.

Berry, D.T.R., Phillips, B. A., Cook, Y. R., Schmitt, F. A., Gilmore, R. L., Patel, R., Keener, T. M., and Tyre, E. (1987). Sleep-disordered breathing in healthy aged persons: Possible daytime sequelae. *Journal of Gerontology, 42,* 620–626.

Berry, D.T.R., Webb, W. B., and Block, A. J. (1984). Sleep apnea syndrome: A critical review of the apnea index as a diagnostic criterion. *Chest, 86,* 529–531.

Berry, D.T.R., Webb, W. B., Block, A. J., Bauer, R. M., and Switzer, D. A. (1986). Nocturnal hypoxia and neuropsychological variables. *Journal of Clinical and Experimental Neuropsychology, 8,* 229–238.

Biersner, R. J., and Cameron, B. J. (1970). Memory impairment during a deep helium dive. *Aerospace Medicine, 41,* 658–661.

Bigler, E. D., and Alfano, M. (1988). Anoxic encephalopathy: Neuroradiological and neuropsychological findings. *Archives of Clinical Neuropsychology, 3,* 383–396.

Blass, J. P., and Gibson, G. E. (1979). Consequences of mild, graded hypoxia. *Advances in Neurology, 26,* 229–250.

Bliwise, D. L., Ingham, R. H., Nino-Murcia, G., Pursley, A. M., and Dement, W. C. (1989). Five-year follow-up of sleep related respiratory disturbances and neuropsychological variables in elderly subjects. *Sleep Research, 18,* 202.

Block, A. J. (1986). Neuropsychological aspects of

long-term oxygen therapy. *European Journal of Respiratory Disease, 69,* 417–419.

Block, A. J., Berry, D., and Webb, W. (1986). Nocturnal hypoxemia and neuropsychological deficits in men who snore. *European Journal of Respiratory Disease, 69,* 405–408.

Block, A. J., Boysen, P. G., Wynne, J. W., and Hunt, L. A. (1979). Sleep apnea, hypopnea and oxygen desaturation in normal subjects: A strong male predominance. *The New England Journal of Medicine, 300,* 513–517.

Block, A. J., Hellard, D. W., and Cicale, M. J. (1987). Snoring, nocturnal hypoxemia, and the effect of oxygen inhalation. *Chest, 92,* 411–417.

Block, A. J., Hellard, D. W., and Switzer, D. A. (1989). Nocturnal oxygen therapy does not improve snorers' intelligence. *Chest, 95,* 274–278.

Bolitschek, J., Aigner, K., and Schindl, R. (1990). Sleep apnoea and the work site. *Pneumologie, 44,* 892–894.

Borak, J., Cieslicki, J., Szelenberger, W., Wilczak-Szadkowska, H., Koziej, M., and Zielinski, J. (1993). Psychopathological characteristics of the consequences of obstructive sleep apnea prior to and 3 months after CPAP. *Psychiatria Polska, 27,* 43–55.

Bornstein, R. A., and Brown, G. (1991). *Neurobehavioral Aspects of Cerebrovascular Disease.* New York: Oxford University Press.

Bradley, T. D., Mateika, J., Li, D., Avendamo, M., and Goldstein, R. S. (1990). Daytime hypercapnia in the development of nocturnal hypoxemia in COPD. *Chest, 97,* 308–312.

Brezinova, V., Calverley, P.M.A., Flenley, D. C., and Townsend, H.R.A. (1979). The effect of long-term oxygen therapy on the EEG in patients with chronic stable ventilatory failure. *Bulletin Europeen de Physiopathologie Respiratoire, 15,* 603–609.

Broderick, P. A., and Gibson, G. E. (1989). Dopamine and serotonin in rat striatum during in vivo hypoxic-hypoxia. *Metabolic Brain Disease, 4,* 143–153.

Brown, G. G., Baird, A. D., and Shatz, M. W. (1986). The effects of cerebrovascular disease and its treatment on higher cortical functioning. In I. Grant and K. M. Adams, eds., *Neuropsychological Aspects of Neuropsychiatric Disorders.* New York: Oxford University Press, pp. 384–414.

Bryer, J. B., Heck, E. T., and Reams, S. H. (1988). Neuropsychological sequelae of carbon monoxide toxicity at eleven-year follow-up. *The Clinical Neuropsychologist, 2,* 221–227.

Calverley, P.M.A., Brezinova, V., Douglas, N. J., Catterall, J. R., and Flenley, D. C. (1982). The effect of oxygenation on sleep quality in chronic bronchitis and emphysema. *American Review of Respiratory Diseases, 126,* 206–210.

Cammermeyer, M. (1991). Sleep fragmentation or oxygen desaturation as etiology of cognitive disability with obstructive sleep apnea. *Dissertation Abstracts International, 52,* 2498.

Carter, R. C. (1979). Mental abilities during a simulated dive to 427 meters underwater. *Journal of Applied Psychology, 64,* 449–454.

Casaburi, R., and Petty, T. L. (1993). *Principles and Practice of Pulmonary Rehabilitation.* Philadelphia: W. B. Saunders.

Cavaletti, G., Garavaglia, P., Arrigoni, G., and Tredici, G. (1990). Persistent memory impairment after high altitude climbing. *International Journal of Sports Medicine, 11,* 176–178.

Cheshire, K., Engleman, H., Deary, I., Shapiro, C., and Douglas, N. J. (1992). Factors impairing daytime performance in patients with sleep apnea/hypopnea syndrome. *Archives of Internal Medicine, 152,* 538–541.

Clark, C. F., Heaton, R. K., and Wiens, A. N. (1983). Neuropsychological functioning after prolonged high altitude exposure in mountaineering. *Aviation, Space, and Environmental Medicine, 54,* 202–207.

Cooper, C. B., Waterhouse, J., and Howard, P. (1987). Twelve year clinical study of patients with hypoxic cor pulmonale given long term domiciliary oxygen therapy. *Thorax, 42,* 105–110.

Cugell, D. W. (1988). COPD: A brief introduction for behavioral scientists. In A. J. McSweeny and I. Grant, eds., *Chronic Obstructive Pulmonary Disease: A Behavioral Perspective.* New York: Marcel Dekker, Inc., pp. 1–18.

Derderian, S. S., Bridenbaugh, R. H., and Rajagopal, K. R. (1988). Neuropsychologic symptoms in obstructive sleep apnea improve after treatment with nasal continuous positive airway pressure. *Chest, 94,* 1023–1027.

Douglas, N. J., Calverley, P.M.A., Leggett, R.J.E., Brash, H. M., Flenley, D. C., and Brezinova, V. (1979). Transient hypoxaemia during sleep in chronic bronchitis and emphysema. *The Lancet, 1,* 1–4.

Edelman, N. H., Kaplan, R. M., Buist, A. S., Cohen, A. B., Hoffman, L. A., Kleinheinz, M. E., Snider, G. L., and Speizer, F. E. (1992). Chronic obstructive pulmonary disease. Task Force on Research and Education for the Prevention and Control of Respiratory Diseases. *Chest, 102* (Suppl. 3), 243S–256S.

Engleman, H. M., Cheshire, K. E., Deary, I. J., and Douglas, N. J. (1993). Daytime sleepiness, cognitive performance and mood after continuous positive airway pressure for the sleep apnoea/hypopnoea syndrome. *Thorax, 48,* 911–914.

Findley, L. J., Barth, J. T., Powers, D. C., Wilhoit, S. C., Boyd, D. G., and Suratt, P. M. (1986). Cognitive impairment in patients with obstructive sleep apnea and associated hypoxemia. *Chest, 90,* 686–690.

Findley, L. J., Fabrizio, M., Thommi, G., and Suratt, P. M. (1989a). Severity of sleep apnea and automobile crashes. *The New England Journal of Medicine, 320,* 868–869.

Findley, L. J., Fabrizio, M. J., Knight, H., Norcross, B. B., Laforte, A. J., and Suratt, P. M. (1989b). Driving simulator performance in patients with sleep apnea. *American Review of Respiratory Diseases, 140,* 529–530.

Findley, L. J., Univerzagt, M. E., and Suratt, P. M. (1988). Automobile accidents involving patients with obstructive sleep apnea. *American Review of Respiratory Diseases, 138,* 337–340.

Fix, A. J., Golden, C. J., Daughton, D., Kass, I., and Bell, C. W. (1982). Neuropsychological deficits among patients with chronic obstructive pulmonary disease. *International Journal of Neuroscience, 16,* 99–105.

Flenley, D. C. (1991). Oxygen therapy in the treatment of COPD. In N. S. Cherniack, ed., *Chronic Obstructive Pulmonary Disease.* Philadelphia: W. B. Saunders, pp. 468–476.

Fletcher, E. C., Luckett, R. A., Miller, T., Costarangos, C., Kutka, N., and Fletcher, J. G. (1989). Pulmonary vascular hemodynamics in chronic lung disease patients with and without oxyhemoglobin desaturation during sleep. *Chest, 95,* 157–166.

Fletcher, E. C., Miller, J., Divine, G. W., Fletcher, J. G., and Miller, T. (1987). Nocturnal oxyhemoglobin desaturation in COPD patients with arterial oxygen tensions above 60 mm Hg. *Chest, 92,* 604–608.

Fleury, B. (1992). Sleep apnea syndrome in the elderly. *Sleep, 15,* S39–S41.

Forster, H. V., Soto, R. J., Dempsey, J. A., and Hosko, M. J. (1975). Effect of sojourn at 4,300 m altitude on electroencephalogram and visual evoked response. *Journal of Applied Physiology, 39,* 109–113.

Freeman, G. B., and Gibson, G. E. (1988). Dopamine, acetylcholine, and glutamate interactions

in aging: Behavioral and neurochemical correlates. *Annals New York Academy of Sciences,*
515, 191–201.

Freeman, G. B., Nielsen, P., and Gibson, G. E.
(1986). Behavioral and neurochemical correlates
of morphine and hypoxia interactions. *Pharmacology, Biochemistry and Behavior, 24,* 1687–
1693.

Froehling, B. (1991). Neuropsychological dysfunction in sleep apnea syndromes: Response to
nasal continuous positive airway pressure treatment. *Dissertation Abstracts International,*
52, 3336.

Fukushima, M., Kobayashi, T., Kubo, K., Yoshimura, K., and Shibamoto, T. (1988). A case of
high altitude pulmonary edema followed by
brain computerized tomography and electroencephalogram. *Aviation, Space, and Environmental Medicine, 59,* 1076–1079.

Garrido, E., Castello, A., Ventura, J. L., Capde-
vila, A., and Rodriguez, F. A. (1993). Cortical
atrophy and other brain magnetic resonance
imaging (MRI) changes after extremely high-
altitude climbs without oxygen. *International
Journal of Sports Medicine, 14,* 232–234.

Georgopoulos, D., and Anthonisen, N. R. (1990).
Continuous oxygen therapy for the chronically
hypoxemic patient. *Annual Review of Medicine,*
41, 223–230.

Gibson, G. E., and Duffy, T. E. (1981). Impaired
synthesis of acetylcholine by mild hypoxic hypoxia or nitrous oxide. *Journal of Neurochemistry, 36,* 28–33.

Gibson, G. E., Pelmas, C. J., and Peterson, C.
(1983). Cholinergic drugs and 4-aminopyridine
alter hypoxic-induced behavioral deficits. *Pharmacology, Biochemistry and Behavior, 18,*
909–916.

Gibson, G. E., Pulsinelli, W., Blass, J. P., and
Duffy, T. E. (1981). Brain dysfunction in mild
to moderate hypoxia. *The American Journal of
Medicine, 70,* 1247–1253.

Goldfarb, A. I., Hochstadt, N. J., Jacobson,
J. H., II, and Weinstein, E. A. (1972). Hyperbaric oxygen treatment of organic mental syndrome in aged persons. *Journal of Gerontology,*
27, 212–217.

Grant, I., and Heaton, R. K. (1985). Neuropsychiatric abnormalities in advanced COPD. In
T. L. Petty, ed., *Chronic Obstructive Pulmonary Disease.* New York: Marcel Dekker, Inc.,
pp. 355–373.

Grant, I., Heaton, R. K., McSweeny, A. J., Adams, K. M., and Timms, R. M. (1982). Neuropsychologic findings in hypoxemic chronic ob-

structive pulmonary disease. *Archives of
Internal Medicine, 142,* 1470–1476.

Grant, I., Prigatano, G. P., Heaton, R. K.,
McSweeny, A. J., Wright, E. C., and Adams,
K. M. (1987). Progressive neuropsychologic im-
pairment and hypoxemia. *Archives of General
Psychiatry, 44,* 999–1006.

Greenberg, G. D. (1987). Neuropsychological,
affective, and psychosocial aspects of sleep apnea syndromes. *Dissertation Abstracts International, 47,* 4649.

Greenberg, G. D., Watson, R. K., and Deptula,
D. (1987). Neuropsychological dysfunction in
sleep apnea. *Sleep, 10,* 254–262.

Guilleminault, C., Quera-Salva, M. A., Partinen,
M., and Jamieson, A. (1988). Women and the
obstructive sleep apnea syndrome. *Chest, 93,*
104–109.

Guilleminault, C., van den Hoed, J., and Mitler,
M. M. (1978). Clinical overview of the sleep
apnea syndromes. In C. Guilleminault and W.
Dement, eds., *Sleep Apnea Syndromes.* New
York: Alan R. Liss, pp. 1–12.

Haas, F., Axen, K., Salazar-Schicchi, J., and
Haas, A. (1994). Pulmonary rehabilitation. In
G. L. Baum and E. L. Wolinsky, eds., *Textbook
of Pulmonary Diseases* (5th ed., vol. 2). Philadelphia: W. B. Saunders, pp. 1215–1244.

Hayward, L., Mant, A., Eyland, A., Hewitt, H.,
Purcell, C., Turner, J., Goode, E., Le Count,
A., Pond, D., and Saunders, N. (1992). Sleep
disordered breathing and cognitive function in
a retirement village population. *Age and Ageing, 21,* 121–128.

Heaton, R. K. (1988). Psychological effects of
oxygen therapy for COPD. In A. J. McSweeny
and I. Grant, eds., *Chronic Obstructive Pulmonary Disease: A Behavioral Perspective.* New
York: Marcel Dekker, Inc., pp. 105–122.

Heaton, R. K. (1992). *Comprehensive Norms for
an Expanded Halstead-Reitan Battery: A Supplement for the Wechsler Adult Intelligence
Scale-Revised.* Odessa, FL: Psychological Assessment Resources.

Heaton, R. K., Grant, I., and Matthews, C. G.
(1986). Differences in neuropsychological test
performance associated with age, education,
and sex. In I. Grant and K. M. Adams, eds.,
*Neuropsychological Aspects of Neuropsychiat-
ric Disorders.* New York: Oxford University
Press, pp. 100–120.

Heaton, R. K., Grant, I., and Matthews, C. G.
(1991). *Comprehensive Norms for an Expanded
Halstead-Reitan Battery: Demographic Corrections, Research Findings, and Clinical Applica-*

tions. Odessa, FL: Psychological Assessment Resources.

Heaton, R. K., Grant, I., McSweeny, A. J., Adams, K. M., and Petty, T. L. (1983). Psychologic effects of continuous and nocturnal oxygen therapy in hypoxemic chronic obstructive pulmonary disease. *Archives of Internal Medicine, 143,* 1941–1947.

Hodgkin, J. (1979). *Chronic Obstructive Pulmonary Disease.* Park Ridge, IL: American College of Chest Physicians.

Hornbein, T. F. (1992). Long term effects of high altitude on brain function. *International Journal of Sports Medicine, 13,* S43–S45.

Hornbein, T. F., Townes, B. D., Schoene, R. B., Sutton, J. R., and Houston, C. S. (1989). The cost to the central nervous system of climbing to extremely high altitude. *The New England Journal of Medicine, 321,* 1714–1719.

Howard, P. (1990). Natural history of obstructive airways disease and hypoxia: Implications for therapy. *Lung, 168* (Suppl.), 743–750.

Intermittent Positive Pressure Breathing Group. (1983). Intermittent positive pressure breathing therapy of chronic obstructive pulmonary disease: A clinical trial. *Annals of Internal Medicine, 99,* 612–620.

Jacobs, E. A., Alvis, H. J., and Small, S. M. (1972). Hyperoxygenation: A central nervous system activator? *Journal of Geriatric Psychiatry, 5,* 107–121.

Jacobs, E. A., Winter, P. M., Alvis, H. J., and Small, S. M. (1969). Hyperoxygenation effect on cognitive functioning in the aged. *The New England Journal of Medicine, 281,* 753–757.

Jason, G. W., Pajurkova, E. M., and Lee, R. G. (1989). High-altitude mountaineering and brain function: Neuropsychological testing of members of a Mount Everest expedition. *Aviation, Space, and Environmental Medicine, 60,* 170–173.

Jennum, P., Hein, H. O., Suadicani, P., and Gyntelberg, F. (1992). Cardiovascular risk factors in snorers: A cross-sectional study of 3,323 men aged 54 to 74 years: The Copenhagen study. *Chest, 102,* 1371–1376.

Jennum, P., Hein, H. O., Suadicani, P., and Gyntelberg, F. (1994). Headache and cognitive dysfunctions in snorers: A cross-sectional study of 3323 men aged 54 to 74 years: the Copenhagen Male Study. *Archives of Neurology, 51,* 937–942.

Jennum, P., and Sjol, A. (1992). Epidemiology of snoring and obstructive sleep apnoea in a Danish population, age 30–60. *Journal of Sleep Research, 1,* 240–244.

Jennum, P., and Sjol, A. (1993). Snoring, sleep apnoea and cardiovascular risk factors: The MONICA II study. *International Journal of Epidemiology, 22,* 439–444.

Jennum, P., and Sjol, A. (1994). Self-assessed cognitive function in snorers and sleep apneics: An epidemiological study of 1,504 females and males aged 30–60 years: the Dan-MONICA II Study. *European Neurology, 34,* 204–208.

Kales, A., Caldwell, A. B., Cadieux, R. J., Vela-Bueno, A., Ruch, L. G., and Mayes, S. D. (1985). Severe obstructive sleep apnea—II: Associated psychopathology and psychosocial consequences. *Journal of Chronic Disorders, 38,* 427–434.

Kaplan, R. M., and Atkins, C. J. (1988). Behavioral interventions for patients with COPD. In A. J. McSweeny and I. Grant, eds., *Chronic Obstructive Pulmonary Disease: A Behavioral Perspective.* New York: Marcel Dekker, Inc., pp. 123–162.

Kimoff, R. J., Cosio, M. G., and McGregor, M. (1991). Clinical features and treatment of obstructive sleep apnea. *Canadian Medical Association Journal, 144,* 689–695.

Klein, G., Ruhle, K. H., and Matthys, H. (1986). Long-term oxygen therapy versus IPPB therapy in patients with COLD and respiratory insufficiency: Survival and pulmonary hemodynamics. *European Journal of Respiratory Disease, 146,* 409–415.

Klitzman, D., and Miller, A. (1994). Obstructive sleep apnea syndrome: Complications and sequelae. *The Mount Sinai Journal of Medicine, 61,* 113–121.

Klonoff, H., Fleetham, J., Tayor, R., and Clark, C. (1987). Treatment outcome of obstructive sleep apnea: Physiological and neuropsychological concomitants. *The Journal of Nervous and Mental Disease, 175,* 208–212.

Kribbs, N. B., Pack, A. I., Kline, L. R., Getsy, J. E., Schuett, J. S., Henry, J. N., Maislin, G., and Dinges, D. F. (1993). Effects of one night without nasal CPAP treatment on sleep and sleepiness in patients with obstructive sleep apnea. *American Review of Respiratory Disorders, 147,* 1162–1168.

Krop, H. D., Block, A. J., and Cohen, E. (1973). Neuropsychologic effects of continuous oxygen therapy in chronic obstructive pulmonary disease. *Chest, 64,* 317–322.

Krop, H. D., Block, A. J., Cohen, E., Croucher, R., and Shuster, J. (1977). Neuropsychological effects of continuous oxygen therapy in the aged. *Chest, 72,* 737–743.

Lahdensuo, A., Ojanen, M., Ahonen, A., Laitinen, J., Poppius, H., Salorinne, Y., Tammivaara, R., Tukiainen, P., Venho, K., and Vikka, V. (1989). Psychosocial effects of continuous oxygen therapy in hypoxaemic chronic obstructive pulmonary disease patients. *European Respiratory Journal, 2,* 977–980.

Lamphere, J., Roehrs, T., Wittig, R., Zorick, F., Conway, W. A., and Roth, T. (1989). Recovery of alertness after CPAP in apnea. *Chest, 96,* 1364–1367.

Lavie, P. (1983). Incidence of sleep apnea in a presumably healthy working population: A significant relationship with excessive daytime sleepiness. *Sleep, 6,* 312–318.

Levi-Valensi, P., Aubry, P., and Rida, Z. (1990). Nocturnal hypoxemia and long-term oxygen therapy in COPD patients with daytime PaO_2 60–70 mm Hg. *Lung, 168* (Suppl.), 770–775.

Lewis, V. J., and Baddeley, A. D. (1981). Cognitive performance, sleep quality and mood during deep oxyhelium diving. *Ergonomics, 24,* 773–793.

Logie, R. H., and Baddeley, A. D. (1985). Cognitive performance during simulated deep-sea diving. *Ergonomics, 28,* 731–746.

Logue, P. E., Schmitt, F. A., Rogers, H. E., and Strong, G. B. (1986). Cognitive and emotional changes during a simulated 686-m deep dive. *Undersea Biomedical Research, 13,* 225–235.

Make, B. (1991). COPD: Management and rehabilitation. *American Family Physician, 43,* 1315–1324.

Markowitsch, H. J. (1992). The neuropsychology of hanging: An historical perspective. *Journal of Neurology, Neurosurgery, and Psychiatry, 55,* 507–512.

Martin, R. J. (1990). The sleep-related worsening of lower airways obstruction: Understanding and intervention. *Medical Clinics of North America, 74,* 701–714.

Medalia, A. A., Merriam, A. E., and Ehrenreich, J. H. (1991). The neuropsychological sequelae of attempted hanging. *Journal of Neurology, Neurosurgery, and Psychiatry, 54,* 546–548.

Merrion, M. J. (1992). The relative influence of hypoxemia versus hypersomnolence on the behavioral morbidity of sleep apnea. *Dissertation Abstracts International, 53,* 569.

Messier, L. D., and Myers, R.A.M. (1991). A neuropsychological screening battery for emergency assessment of carbon-monoxide-poisoned patients. *Journal of Clinical Psychology, 47,* 675–684.

Montplaisir, J., Bedard, M. A., Richer, F., and Rouleau, I. (1992). Neurobehavioral manifestations in obstructive sleep apnea syndrome before and after treatment with continuous positive airway pressure. *Sleep, 15,* S17–S19.

Mosko, S., Zetin, M., Glen, S., Garber, D., DeAntonio, M., Sassin, J., McAnich, J., and Warren, S. (1989). Self-reported depressive symptomatology, mood ratings, and treatment outcome in sleep disorders patients. *Journal of Clinical Psychology, 45,* 51–60.

Naegele, B., Thouvard, V., Pepin, J. L., Levy, P., Bonnet, C., Perret, J. E., Pellat, J., and Feuerstein, C. (1995). Deficits of cognitive executive functions in patients with sleep apnea syndrome. *Sleep, 18,* 43–52.

Nichols, C. D. (1991). Determinants of neuropsychological deficits in obstructive sleep apnea syndrome. *Dissertation Abstracts International, 52,* 1074.

Nichols, C. D., Kapen, S., and Greiffenstein, M. F. (1988). Determinants of neuropsychological deficits in obstructive sleep apnea. *Sleep Research, 17,* 227.

Niewoehner, D. (1994). Clinical aspects of chronic obstructive pulmonary disease. In G. L. Baum and E. L. Wolinsky, eds., *Textbook of Pulmonary Diseases* (5th ed., vol. 2). Philadelphia: W. B. Saunders, pp. 995–1027.

Nocturnal Oxygen Therapy Group. (1980). Continuous or nocturnal oxygen therapy in hypoxemic chronic obstructive lung disease: A clinical trial. *Annals of Internal Medicine, 93,* 391–398.

O'Reilly, J. P. (1974). Performance decrements under hyperbaric He-O_2. *Undersea Biomedical Research, 1,* 353–361.

Parkin, A. J., Miller, J., and Vincent, R. (1987). Multiple neuropsychological deficits due to anoxic encephalopathy: A case study. *Cortex, 23,* 655–665.

Peter, J. H., Kohler, V., Mayer, J., Podszus, T., Penzel, T., and Von-Wichert, P. (1985). The prevalence of sleep apnea activity. *Sleep Research, 14,* 197.

Petiet, C. A., Townes, B. D., Brooks, R. J., and Kramer, J. H. (1988). Neurobehavioral and psychosocial functioning of women exposed to high altitude in mountaineering. *Perceptual and Motor Skills, 67,* 443–452.

Petty, T. L. (1985a). Definitions, clinical assessment, and risk factors. In T. L. Petty, ed., *Chronic Obstructive Pulmonary Disease* (2nd ed., rev./expanded). New York: Marcel Dekker, Inc., pp. 1–30.

Petty, T. L. (1985b). Pulmonary rehabilitation. In T. L. Petty, ed., *Chronic Obstructive Pulmo-*

nary Disease. New York: Marcel Dekker, pp. 339–354.

Petty, T. L. (1985c). Long-term outpatient oxygen therapy. In T. L. Petty, ed., *Chronic Obstructive Pulmonary Disease* (2nd ed., rev./expanded). New York: Marcel Dekker, Inc., pp. 375–388.

Petty, T. L. (1985d). *Chronic Obstructive Pulmonary Disease* (2nd ed., rev./expanded). New York: Marcel Dekker, Inc.

Petty, T. L. (1988). Medical management of COPD. In A. J. McSweeny and I. Grant, eds., *Chronic Obstructive Pulmonary Disease: A Behavioral Perspective.* New York: Marcel Dekker, Inc., pp. 87–103.

Petty, T. L. (1990). Definitions in chronic obstructive pulmonary disease. *Clinics in Chest Medicine, 11,* 363–373.

Phillips, B. A., Berry, D.T.R., Schmitt, F. A., Harbison, L., and Lipke-Molby, T. (1994). Sleep-disordered breathing in healthy aged persons: Two- and three-year follow-up. *Sleep, 17,* 411–415.

Prigatano, G. P., and Grant, I. (1988). Neuropsychological correlates of COPD. In A. J. McSweeny and I. Grant, eds., *Chronic Obstructive Pulmonary Disease: A Behavioral Perspective.* New York: Marcel Dekker, Inc., pp. 39–57.

Prigatano, G. P., Parsons, O., Wright, E., Levin, D. C., and Hawryluk, G. (1983). Neuropsychological test performance in mildly hypoxemic patients with chronic obstructive pulmonary disease. *Journal of Consulting and Clinical Psychology, 51,* 108–116.

Raskin, A., Gershon, S., Crook, T. H., Sathananthan, G., and Ferris, S. (1978). The effects of hyperbaric and normobaric oxygen on cognitive impairment in the elderly. *Archives of General Psychiatry, 35,* 50–56.

Regard, M., Oelz, O., Brugger, P., and Landis, T. (1989). Persistent cognitive impairment in climbers after repeated exposure to extreme altitude. *Neurology, 39,* 210–213.

Reitan, R. M., and Wolfson, D. (1993). *The Halstead-Reitan Neuropsychological Test Battery: Theory and Clinical Interpretation* (2nd ed.). Tucson: Neuropsychology Press.

Report of the Medical Research Council Working Party. (1981). Long term domiciliary oxygen therapy in chronic hypoxic cor pulmonale complicating chronic bronchitis and emphysema. *Lancet, 1,* 681–686.

Ries, A. L. (1990). Position paper of the American Association of Cardiovascular and Pulmonary Rehabilitation: Scientific basis of pulmonary rehabilitation. *Journal of Cardiopulmonary Rehabilitation, 10,* 418–441.

Ries, A. L. (1991). Pulmonary rehabilitation: Rationale, components, and results. *Journal of Cardiopulmonary Rehabilitation, 11,* 23–28.

Romaker, A. M., and Ancoli-Israel, S. (1987). The diagnosis of sleep-related breathing disorders. *Clinics in Chest Medicine, 8,* 105–117.

Rourke, S. B., Grant, I., and Heaton, R. K. (1993). Neurocognitive aspects of chronic obstructive pulmonary disease. In R. Casaburi and T. L. Petty, eds., *Principles and Practice of Pulmonary Rehabilitation.* Philadelphia: W. B. Saunders Company, pp. 79–91.

Rumbach, L., Krieger, J., and Kurtz, D. (1991). Auditory event-related potentials in obstructive sleep apnea: Effects of treatment with nasal continuous positive airway pressure. *Electroencephalography and Clinical Neurophysiology, 80,* 454–457.

Russell, E. W., Neuringer, C., and Goldstein, G. (1970). *Assessment of Brain Damage: A Neuropsychological Key Approach.* New York: Wiley and Sons, Inc.

Ryn, Z. (1971). Psychopathology in alpinism. *Acta Medica Polinska, 12,* 453–467.

Saroea, H. G. (1993). Chronic obstructive pulmonary disease: Major objectives of management. *Postgraduate Medicine, 94,* 113–116, 121–122.

Sawyer, J. D., Adams, K. M., Conway, W. L., Reeves, J., and Kvale, P. A. (1983). Suicide in cases of chronic obstructive pulmonary disease. *Journal of Psychiatric Treatment and Evaluation, 5,* 281–283.

Scheltens, P., Visscher, F., Van Keimpema, A.R.J., Lindeboom, J., Taphoorn, M.J.B., and Wolters, E. C. (1991). Sleep apnea syndrome presenting with cognitive impairment. *Neurology, 41,* 155–156.

Schneck, S. A. (1993). Clinical neurology. In R. J. Joynt, ed., *Cerebral Anoxia.* Hagerstown, MD: Harper and Row, pp. 1–25.

Shachor, Y., Liberman, D., Tamir, A., Schindler, D., Weiler, Z., and Bruderman, I. (1989). Long-term survival of patients with chronic obstructive pulmonary disease following mechanical ventilation. *Israel Journal of Medical Science, 25,* 617–619.

Siesjo, B. K., Johannson, H., Ljunggren, B., and Norberg, K. (1974). Brain dysfunction in cerebral hypoxia and ischemia. In F. Plum, ed., *Brain Dysfunction in Metabolic Disorders.* New York: Raven Press, pp. 75–112.

Sloan, K., Craft, S., and Walsh, J. K. (1989). Neuropsychological function in obstructive sleep apnea with and without hypoxemia. *Sleep Research, 18,* 304.

Sloan, K. A. (1991). Neuropsychological function in obstructive sleep apnea. *Dissertation Abstracts International, 51,* 4068.

Smith, P. L., Haponik, E. F., and Bleecker, E. R. (1984). The effects of oxygen in patients with sleep apnea. *American Review of Respiratory Diseases, 130,* 958–963.

Stein, D. A., Bradley, B. L., and Miller, W. C. (1982). Mechanisms of oxygen effects on exercise in patients with chronic obstructive pulmonary disease. *Chest, 81,* 6–10.

Stone, J., Morin, C. M., Hart, R. P., Remsberg, S., and Mercer, J. (1994). Neuropsychological functioning in older insomniacs with or without obstructive sleep apnea. *Psychology and Aging, 9,* 231–236.

Telakivi, T., Kajaste, S., Partinen, M., Brander, P., and Nyholm, A. (1993). Cognitive function in obstructive sleep apnea. *Sleep, 16,* S74–S75.

Telakivi, T., Kajaste, S., Partinen, M., Koskenvuo, M., Salmi, T., and Kaprio, J. (1988). Cognitive function in middle-aged snorers and controls: Role of excessive daytime somnolence and sleep-related hypoxic events. *Sleep, 11,* 454–462.

Thompson, L. W., Davis, G. C., Obrist, W. D., and Heyman, A. (1976). Effects of hyperbaric oxygen on behavioral and physiological measures in elderly demented patients. *Journal of Gerontology, 31,* 23–28.

Timms, R. M., Khaja, F. U., Williams, G. W., and the Nocturnal Oxygen Therapy Group. (1985). Hemodynamic response to oxygen therapy in chronic obstructive pulmonary disease. *Annals of Internal Medicine, 102,* 29–36.

Tockman, M. S., Khoury, M. J., and Cohen, B. H. (1985). The epidemiology of COPD. In T. L. Petty, ed., *Chronic Obstructive Pulmonary Disease* (2nd ed., rev./expanded). New York: Marcel Dekker, Inc., pp. 43–92.

Townes, B. D., Hornbein, T. F., Schoene, R. B., Sarnquist, F. H., and Grant, I. (1984). Human cerebral function at extreme altitude. In J. B. West and S. Lahiri, eds., *High Altitude and Man.* Bethesda, MD: American Physiological Society, pp. 31–36.

Vaernes, R. J., Owe, J. O., and Myking, O. (1984). Central nervous reactions to a 6.5-hour altitude exposure at 3048 meters. *Aviation, Space, and Environmental Medicine, 55,* 921–926.

Vieregge, P., Klostermann, W., Blumm, R. G., and Borgis, K. J. (1989). Carbon monoxide poisoning: Clinical, neurophysiological, and brain imaging observations in acute disease and follow-up. *Journal of Neurology, 236,* 478–481.

Vos, P.J.E., Folgering, H.T.M., and van Herwaarden, C.L.A. (1991). Prevalence of oxygen desaturations and associated breathing disorders during sleep in patients with chronic obstructive pulmonary disease. In J. H. Peter, T. Penzel, T. Podszus, and P. von Wichert, eds., *Sleep and Health Risk.* Berlin: Springer-Verlag, pp. 246–250.

Walker, C. P. (1991). Neuropsychological changes in obstructive sleep apnea syndrome patients following nasal CPAP treatment. *Dissertation Abstracts International, 52,* 1087.

Walsleben, J. A., Squires, N. K., and Rothenberger, V. L. (1989). Auditory event-related potentials and brain dysfunction in sleep apnea. *Electroencephalography and Clinical Neurophysiology, 74,* 297–311.

Weitzenblum, E., Apprill, M., and Oswald, M. (1992). Benefit from long-term O_2 therapy in chronic obstructive pulmonary disease patients. *Respiration, 59* (Suppl. 1), 14–17.

Weitzenblum, E., Oswald, M., Mirhom, R., Kessler, R., and Apprill, M. (1989). Evolution of pulmonary haemodynamics in COLD patients under long-term oxygen therapy. *European Respiratory Journal, 2* (Suppl. 7), 669s–673s.

West, J. B. (1982). *Pulmonary Pathophysiology: The Essentials* (2nd ed.). Baltimore: Williams and Wilkins.

West, J. B. (1985). *Respiratory Physiology: The Essentials* (3rd ed.). Baltimore: Williams and Wilkins.

West, J. B. (1986). Do climbs to extreme altitude cause brain damage? *The Lancet, 2,* 387–388.

Westlake, E. K., and Kaye, M. (1954). Raised intracranial pressure in emphysema. *British Journal of Medicine, 1,* 302–304.

Wiegand, L., and Zwillich, C. W. (1994). Obstructive sleep apnea. *Disease-a-Month, 40,* 197–252.

Wilson, D. K., Kaplan, R. M., Timms, R. M., and Dawson, A. (1985). Acute effects of oxygen treatment upon information processing in hypoxemic COPD patients. *Chest, 88,* 239–243.

Yesavage, J., Bliwise, D., Guilleminault, C., Carskadon, M., and Dement, W. (1985). Preliminary communication: Intellectual deficit and sleep-related respiratory disturbance in the elderly. *Sleep, 8,* 30–33.

Young, T., Palta, M., Dempsey, J., Skatrud, J., Weber, S., and Badr, S. (1993). The occurrence of sleep-disordered breathing among middle-aged adults. *The New England Journal of Medicine, 328,* 1230–1235.

17 Neuropsychological Findings in HIV Infection and AIDS

MARK D. KELLY, IGOR GRANT, ROBERT K. HEATON, THOMAS D. MARCOTTE, and the HNRC GROUP

Acquired immunodeficiency syndrome (AIDS), a clinical syndrome that results from the progressive destruction of cellular immune function, was first described in 1981. The primary etiology of AIDS is infection with type 1 human immunodeficiency virus (HIV-1). The hallmark of HIV-1 infection is the progressive depletion of CD4$^+$ helper T cells, which are extensively involved in coordinating the body's immune response (Nair and Schwartz, 1994). Moreover, HIV commonly invades the central nervous system and is causally linked to a variety of neurological and neuropathological disorders (McArthur, 1994; Wiley and Achim, 1994; Wiley et al., 1994). The most severe manifestation of HIV infection in the brain is HIV-1–associated dementia (HAD). This infrequent neurobehavioral disorder is characterized by moderate to severe cognitive and psychomotor slowing, impaired concentration and attention, memory disturbances, and often motor incoordination and weakness (Navia et al., 1986a,b; Price and Brew, 1988; Kaemingk and Kaszniak, 1989).

A more common neurobehavioral complication of HIV-1 infection is termed *mild neurocognitive disorder* (Grant and Martin, 1994; Grant and Atkinson, 1995; Grant et al., 1995) or minor cognitive/motor disorder (MCMD) (Working Group of the American Academy of Neurology AIDS Task Force, 1991). This condition is diagnosed when a person exhibits deficits in at least two behav-

ioral or ability domains based on comprehensive neuropsychological testing (e.g., attention, learning, verbal skills, psychomotor abilities, or memory) and the level of impairment is significant enough to have a noticeable impact on day-to-day functioning (e.g., work performance, activities of daily living). The neurocognitive impairment observed in MCMD is considerably less severe than that seen in HAD. This chapter will focus on these two disorders and will further describe the often subtle HIV-associated neuropsychological changes observed during the asymptomatic and early stages of this disease. The clinical significance of neuropsychological impairment in medically asymptomatic HIV-positive individuals will also be discussed.

Evolution of HIV Infection

The rate of progression of HIV infection from seroconversion to AIDS varies greatly, with an estimated average time of 10 years. In general terms, once an individual has been infected with HIV he or she usually has a prolonged period with minimal or no physical symptoms (asymptomatic). Following this variable period during which there is a progressive loss of CD4 lymphocytes and consequently a sustained deterioration of cell-mediated immunity, HIV-infected persons develop a variety of opportunistic infections, tumors, or neurological illnesses. The Centers for Disease Control (CDC) have defined three clinical levels of HIV infection: asymptomatic, minor symptoms, and AIDS-defining conditions (Categories A, B, and C, respectively) (CDC, 1992). In addition, these categories are each further divided into three strata based on CD4 lymphocyte counts (≥ 500, 200–499, and ≤ 200). Individuals who have CD4 counts less than 200 are defined as having AIDS. Hence, persons with AIDS are defined by their clinical condition (Category C diseases), or by CD4 counts of 200 or less (i.e., groups A3, B3, and C3), or both. Table 17-1 summarizes the 1993 CDC classification system. The reader is referred to McCutchan (1994) for a detailed discussion of the clinical course of HIV infection.

HIV-Associated Dementia

Central nervous system involvement and neurobehavioral abnormalities are often observed in advanced stages of HIV infection (Levy et al., 1985; Grant and Heaton, 1990; Hesselink et al., 1994). The most severe and debilitating neurological complication of AIDS is HIV-associated dementia. The annual incidence of HAD, however, is low, the disorder occurring in only 5% to 7% of symptomatic HIV-infected persons (McArthur et al., 1993; Maj et al., 1994). The overall prevalence of HIV-associated dementia is estimated at 5% to 15% in this population. The constellation of cognitive

deficits exhibited by patients with HAD is similar to that associated with "subcortical dementias" (Navia et al., 1986a,b; Navia, 1990). For example, HAD patients manifest psychomotor slowing, loss of concentration, impaired abstracting ability, and mild to moderate memory deficits (Janssen et al., 1988; Poutiainen et al., 1988; Perdices and Cooper, 1989). Similar cognitive symptoms have also been described in patients with Huntington's disease (HD) and Parkinson's disease (PD), which are both prototypical examples of subcortical dementia (McHugh and Folstein, 1975; Cummings, 1986, 1990).

The term "subcortical" has the neuropathological meaning of white matter and deep gray matter involvement within the brain. From a neuropsychological perspective, however, "subcortical" reflects disturbances in cognitive functions attributed to the integrity of the striatum and frontostriatal connections. Thus, neurological diseases that involve the frontal cortex or pathways to and from the frontal lobe and striatum present as "subcortical" from a neuropsychologist's point of view. The main clinical features in the neuropsychological concept of subcortical deficits include slowness of information processing, reduced fluency, impaired motor skills, and impaired free recall of recently learned information within the setting of good recognition recall (Butters et al., 1988; Folstein et al., 1990).

The classification of HAD as a form of

Table 17-1. CDC 1993 Classification System for HIV Infection

CD4+ cell count categories	Clinical Categories		
	A—Asymptomatic or lymphadenopathy	B—Symptomatic, but not A or C conditions	C—AIDS-indicator conditions
>500/mm³	A-1	B-1	**C-1**
200–499/mm³	A-2	B-2	**C-2**
<200/mm³	**A-3**	**B-3**	**C-3**

Bold entry means CDC 1992 AIDS-indicator conditions (A-3, B-3, C-1, C-2, C-3).

Category A includes acute HIV infection, asymptomatic infection, and progressive generalized lymphadenopathy.

Category B includes conditions associated with HIV infection, but which were *not* included in the CDC's 1987 case surveillance definition of conditions associated with *severe* immunodeficiency. Examples of "less severe" conditions include oropharyngeal candidiasis (thrush), persistent vulvovaginal candidiasis, severe cervical dysplasia or carcinoma, oral hairy leukoplakia, and recurrent herpes zoster involving more than one dermatome.

Category C conditions are those associated with severe immunodeficiency identified in the CDC's 1987 surveillance definitions for AIDS.

subcortical dementia is consistent with the distribution of neuropathological changes often found in other frontostriatal disorders such as Huntington's or Parkinson's disease (Sharer, 1992). Radiological and neuropathological studies demonstrate mild to moderate cerebral atrophy in patients with HAD, and reveal abnormalities in central white matter and in deep gray matter structures such as the basal ganglia and thalamus (Pumarola-Sune et al., 1987; Ekholm and Simon, 1988; Grant et al., 1988; Olsen et al., 1988). Primary histopathological findings from postmortem brains of HIV-infected persons consist of diffuse white matter pallor and a perivascular inflammatory reaction due to the infiltration of the parenchyma by macrophages and lymphocytes. In addition, reactive gliosis (proliferation of astroglia), white matter vacuolation, demyelination, and neuronal loss, especially in the basal ganglia, but also in the cortex, often occur in cases of HAD. The various neuropathological stages and classifications of HIV CNS disease are described in Budka et al. (1991).

HAD almost always occurs in the late stages of HIV infection, usually within the context of severe immunosuppression and other AIDS-defining illnesses, although in rare cases HAD can appear as the first or even the only AIDS-defining medical condition (Navia and Price, 1987; Janssen et al., 1992). HAD also carries a poor prognosis for long-term survival (median survival time = 6 months; Navia et al., 1986a,b; Day et al., 1992; McArthur et al., 1993).

Minor Cognitive/Motor Disorder

More common than frank dementia is the comparatively subtle cognitive impairment commonly referred to as mild neurocognitive disorder (Grant and Atkinson, 1995) or minor cognitive/motor disorder (MCMD) (Working Group of the American Academy of Neurology AIDS Task Force, 1991). In order to meet diagnostic criteria, patients must exhibit deficits in at least two neuropsychological domains and, although daily functioning is affected, such functional impairment is considerably less severe than that seen with HAD. Even these milder neuropsychological disorders are most commonly seen in HIV-positive individuals with more advanced disease (CDC B and C categories). However, there is also a subgroup of HIV-positive individuals in the relatively early stages of infection (CDC A) who experience MCMD despite the fact that their medical disease is not very far advanced (Heaton et al., 1994b). Multidisciplinary baseline data from a large HIV-positive cohort (n = 654) indicated that 12.5% of *all HIV-positive subjects* were diagnosed with MCMD (within each classification group: 5% of all CDC A's, 27% of all CDC B's, and 24% of all CDC C's were diagnosed with MCMD) (Heaton and Grant, 1995). Included in Tables 17-2 and 17-3 are the diagnostic criteria for both HAD and MCMD as proposed by the AAN working group and separately by Grant and Atkinson (1995). The Grant-Atkinson and AAN criteria are comparable in many respects; however, the former may be more suitable for research purposes because the neuropsychological criteria for MND are more precisely defined. Furthermore, the Grant-Atkinson criteria for MND require presence of a documented cognitive disturbance, whereas AAN criteria for MCMD could be met on the basis only of motor difficulties and incoordination (see Table 17-3B).

It is not known at present whether HAD and MCMD are related to each other. Perhaps these two disorders are separate entities that differ not only in severity of presentation and impacts on daily living, but also in clinical course and possibly even in pathogenesis. Available evidence at the present time suggests that milder HIV-associated neurobehavioral disorders may not typically progress to HAD (e.g., McKegney et al., 1990; Saykin et al., 1991; Selnes et al., 1992). It is possible that some of the late-stage severe cognitive decline reflects activation of viral copathogens in the brain, such as cytomegalovirus (CMV) (Ellis et al., 1995), which, independently or through an interaction with HIV, produce dementia and/or delirium. Therefore, pending the outcome of longer term

Table 17-2. HIV-1–Associated Cognitive Disorders Related to Dementia

As Defined by Grant and Atkinson	As Proposed by AAN Working Group
HIV-1–Associated Dementia (HAD)	*Probable[a] HIV-1–Associated Dementia Complex*
1. *Marked acquired impairment in cognitive functioning,* involving at least two ability domains (e.g., memory, attention); typically the impairment is in multiple domains, especially in learning of new information, slowed information processing, and defective attention/concentration. The cognitive impairment can be ascertained by history, mental status examination, or neuropsychological testing.	1. *Acquired abnormality in at least two of the following cognitive abilities* (present for at least 1 month): attention/concentration; speed of information processing; abstraction/reasoning; visuospatial skills; memory/learning; speech/language. *Cognitive dysfunction causes impairment in work or activities of daily living.*
2. The cognitive impairment produces *marked interference with day-to-day functioning* (work, home life, social activities).	2. *At least one of the following:* a. acquired abnormality in motor functioning b. decline in motivation or emotional control or change in social behavior
3. The marked cognitive impairment has been present for at least 1 month.	3. Absence of clouding of consciousness during a period long enough to establish presence of #1.
4. The pattern of cognitive impairment *does not meet criteria for delirium* (e.g., clouding of consciousness is not a prominent feature); or, if delirium is present, criteria for dementia need to have been met on a prior examination when delirium was not present.	4. Absence of another cause of the above cognitive, motor, or behavioral symptoms or signs (e.g., active CNS opportunistic infection or malignancy, psychiatric disorders, substance abuse).
5. There is *no evidence of another, preexisting etiology* that could explain the dementia, e.g., other CNS infection, CNS neoplasm, cerebrovascular disease, preexisting neurological disease, or severe substance abuse compatible with CNS disorder.	

Source: From Grant and Martin, 1994, p. 362.

[a]The designation *probable* is used when criteria are met, there is no other likely cause, and data are complete. The designation *possible* is used if another potential etiology is present whose contribution is unclear, or where dual diagnosis is possible, or when the evaluation is not complete.

longitudinal studies, the mild and severe cognitive disorders probably should be considered as separate conditions.

San Diego HIV Neurobehavioral Research Center (HNRC)

Because several readily available comprehensive reviews of the neuropsychology of HIV have been published recently (e.g., see Grant and Martin, 1994; Hinkin et al., 1995), we have chosen to focus much of this chapter on the newly emerging neuropsychological data from the largest series that has undertaken full longitudinal neurobehavioral assessment of HIV-infected persons—the San Diego HIV Neurobehavioral Research Cen-

ter (HNRC). In emphasizing some of these recent data, we attempt also to place these in the context of other recent research.

The HNRC is an NIMH-funded research center created in 1989 to examine the prevalence, etiology, pathogenesis, natural history, and features of neurobehavioral disorders associated with HIV infection. The research program is conducted by investigators from several departments of the School of Medicine of the University of California at San Diego, in collaboration with the Veterans Affairs Medical Center and the U.S. Naval Medical Center, San Diego. The HNRC's original research plan involved a comprehensive and multidisciplinary longitudinal assessment of 500 HIV antibody positive

Table 17-3. HIV-1–Associated Cognitive Disorders Related to Neurocognitive or Cognitive/Motor Disorder

As Defined by Grant and Atkinson	As Proposed by AAN Working Group
HIV-1–Associated Mild Neurocognitive Disorder (MND)	*Probable[a] HIV-1–Associated Minor Cognitive/Motor Disorder*

1. Acquired impairment in cognitive functioning, involving at least two ability domains, documented by performance of at least 1.0 standard deviations below age-education–appropriate norms on standardized neuropsychological tests. The neuropsychological assessment must survey at least the following abilities: verbal/language; attention/speeded processing; abstraction; memory (learning; recall); complex perceptual-motor performance; motor skills.	1. Acquired cognitive/motor/behavior abnormalities (must have both a and b):
	
	  a. At least two of the following symptoms present for at least one month verified by a reliable history:
	
	    i. impaired attention or concentration
	    ii. mental slowing
	    iii. impaired memory
	    iv. slowed movements
	    v. incoordination
	
	  b. Acquired cognitive/motor abnormality verified by clinical neurologic examination or neuropsychological testing.

2. The cognitive impairment produces at least mild interference in daily functioning (at least one of the following):
 	
  a. Self-report of reduced mental acuity, inefficiency in work, homemaking, or social functioning.
 	
  b. Observation by knowledgeable others that the individual has undergone at least mild decline in mental acuity with resultant inefficiency in work, homemaking, or social functioning.
	2. Cognitive/motor/behavioral abnormality causes mild impairment of work or activities of daily living (objectively verifiable or by report of key informant).

3. The cognitive impairment has been present at least one month.	3. Does not meet criteria for HIV-1–associated dementia complex or HIV-1–associated myelopathy.
4. Does not meet criteria for delirium or dementia.	4. Absence of another cause of the above cognitive/motor/behavioral abnormality (e.g., active CNS opportunistic infection or malignancy, psychiatric disorders, substance abuse).
5. There is no evidence of another preexisting cause for the MND.[b]	

Source: From Grant and Martin, 1994, pp. 362–363.

[a] The designation *probable* is used when criteria are met, there is no other likely cause, and data are complete. The designation *possible* is used if another potential etiology is present whose contribution is unclear, or where a dual diagnosis is possible, or when the evaluation is not complete.

[b] If the individual with suspected MND also satisfies criteria for a *major depressive episode* or *substance dependence*, the diagnosis of MND should be deferred to a subsequent examination conducted at a time when the major depression has remitted or at least 1 month has elapsed following termination of dependent-substance use.

(HIV+) and negative (HIV−) gay or bisexual adult men. Although the HNRC has continued to enroll and evaluate additional HIV+ minority men and women (particularly Latinas), the results below summarize the findings of the first 500 male subjects (77% White, 12% African-American, 9% Hispanic, and 2% other) studied longitudinally over a 5-year period. A detailed description of the "HNRC 500" and the comprehensive neuropsychological evaluation is reported in Heaton et al. (1995).

Consistent with the recommendations of the NIMH Workgroup on Neuropsychological Assessment in HIV Infection (Butters et al., 1990), the HNRC relied heavily on blind clinical ratings of comprehensive neuropsychological test data to identify and characterize impairment in individual HIV+ and HIV− subjects. The utility of blind clinical rating methods has been described in detail elsewhere (Heaton et al., 1994a). Briefly, to make a clinical rating the clinician is provided with demographic information, raw scores, and demographically corrected standard scores for each subject on all of the test measures in the neuropsychological battery, but is blinded to the subject's HIV status. The clinician then rates a subject's performance within each of eight major cognitive ability areas (verbal, abstraction, psychomotor, attention, learning, memory (forgetting), motor, and sensory), using the following nine-point scale: 1 = above average functioning; 2 = average; 3 = below average; 4 = borderline/atypical; 5 = definite mild impairment; 6 = mild to moderate impairment; 7 = moderate impairment; 8 = moderate to severe impairment; 9 = severe impairment. In addition to individual clinical ratings on the eight ability areas, a global clinical rating is made based on the same nine-point scale described above. A global rating of "impaired" (≥5) requires a minimum of "definite mild impairment" on at least two of the eight ability areas (i.e., a single, isolated ability deficit would not qualify for a global rating within the "impaired" range). In other words, even a severe deficit in just one ability area would fail to place a person in the globally impaired category.

Figure 17-1 shows the global clinical rating scores for all subjects in the HNRC 500 series. Two striking findings should be noted in this figure. The first is that 69% of CDC A, 56% of CDC B, and 45% of CDC C HIV+ individuals exhibited performance within the normal range on an 8-hour comprehensive neuropsychological examination. The second is the steadily progressive rate of neuropsychological impairment observed across CDC groups and the fact that the control group evidenced a base rate of 17%. Each succes-

sive stage of HIV disease category was associated with a higher rate of overall impairment (i.e., CDC A = 31%, CDC B = 44%, and CDC C = 56%). Moreover, neuropsychological impairment was not only more prevalent in the later stages of HIV infection, but when it occurred it was likely to be more severe and to affect more cognitive ability areas than in the medically asymptomatic stage. That is to say, when NP impairment was found in asymptomatic subjects (CDC A) it tended to be milder and to affect fewer ability areas (only two areas versus more than two) as compared to findings in the symptomatic group (CDC C), where a greater number of ability areas were affected, and with greater severity. In particular, the Group C HIV+ subjects had significantly higher rates of impairment in five out of eight cognitive ability areas which constitute the global clinical rating score. This latter finding is consistent with previous studies that have reliably found increased rates of neuropsychological impairment in persons diagnosed with AIDS (CDC C). In a review of 12 such studies that categorized individuals with regard to presence or absence of neuropsychological impairment, the median prevalence of impairment among subjects with AIDS diagnoses was 55% (Grant et al., 1987; Tross et al., 1988; Miller et al., 1990; Naber et al., 1990; Lunn et al., 1991; Skoraszewski et al., 1991; Wilkins et al., 1991; Grant et al., 1992a; McAllister et al., 1992; Riedel et al., 1992; Bornstein et al., 1993; Maj et al., 1994).

Figure 17-2 shows the frequency of deficits that were observed within each of the eight major ability areas for HIV+ subjects who were rated globally as being neuropsychologically impaired. What can be seen from this figure is that only two ability areas, learning of new information and attention/speed of information processing, are affected in greater than half of the HIV+ HNRC 500 subjects. In the other six cognitive domains less than 50% of HIV+ individuals evidenced impairment. One consequence of this finding is that individual group mean comparisons on tests (e.g., HIV+ subjects versus HIV− controls on WAIS-R Information or Block Design subtests) are not likely

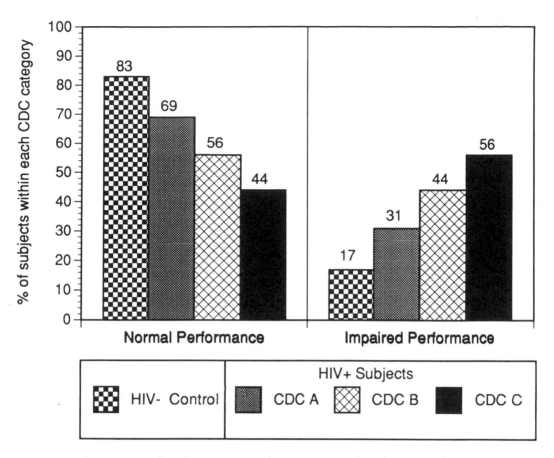

Figure 17-1. Clinical rating scores for HIV− controls and HIV+ subjects on a comprehensive neuropsychological test battery. Note: Impaired Performance required a clinical rating with a minimum of "definite mild impairment" on at least two of eight neuropsychological ability areas.

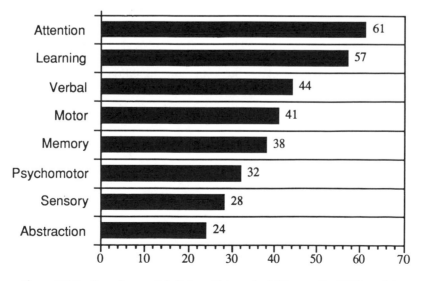

Figure 17-2. Prevalence of deficits within each ability area for HIV+ subjects rated as neuropsychologically impaired.

to detect true differences in the prevalence of neurocognitive deficits because on any given test the majority of subjects with "good" scores will negate the minority of "poor" scores from individuals who are impaired on that measure. Therefore, careful attention needs to be focused on patterns of deficits that may be present in only a minority of subjects and may be relatively subtle in nature.

Two additional methods were developed by the San Diego HNRC for classifying HIV + subjects and HIV − controls as being neuropsychologically impaired or unimpaired: Global Deficit Scores and Factor Analysis Scores (Heaton et al., 1995). Global Deficit Scores provide an objective summary score based on levels of impairment on a reduced subset of tests from the comprehensive battery (identified by logistic regression) that best discriminated controls from HIV + subjects who were rated as impaired by the clinician. The tests that made up the Global Deficit Score included Boston Naming Test, Thurstone Word Fluency Test, the Paced Auditory Serial Additional Test, Figure Memory Test (Learning and Memory components), Story Memory Test (Memory component), Finger Tapping (average of dominant and nondominant hand scores) and Grooved Pegboard (average of dominant and nondominant hand scores).

The second approach to identifying neuropsychological impairment was based upon Factor Analysis Scores. Subjects who had two or more factor scores in the impaired range (defined as at least one standard deviation below the HIV − control group) were classified as having global neuropsychological impairment. A comparison of the results between the clinical ratings, which are viewed as the "gold standard," and the other two statistical methods are shown in Table 17-4. All three methods show increased rates of neuropsychological impairment among HIV + groups compared to HIV − controls. In addition, there was a steady gradient of greater impairment across HIV + asymptomatic, mildly symptomatic, and symptomatic subjects, respectively. This finding was true regardless of whether identification was performed by clinical ratings, global deficit scores, or factor analytic summary scores.

Neuropsychological Results in the Asymptomatic Phase of HIV Infection

One of the major research questions addressed by the HNRC has been whether there is an increased risk of neuropsychological impairment in the early, asymptomatic, or minimally symptomatic stages of HIV infection. This has been an area of ongoing controversy and debate among HIV/AIDS researchers. For thoughtful reviews of the methodological and conceptual issues surrounding the study of cognitive change seen with HIV infection, the reader is referred to Grant and Heaton (1990), Van Gorp et al. (1993), and Bornstein (1994). Some research studies have found no impairment in the early stages of HIV infection (Goethe et al., 1989; Janssen et al., 1989; McArthur et al., 1989; Miller et al., 1990; Selnes et al., 1995), but others have clearly detected an increase in the likelihood of mild impairment in asymptomatic or mildly symptomatic HIV + persons (Grant et al., 1987; Wilkie et al.,

Table 17-4. Prevalence of Neuropsychological Impairment

Method	HIV − Controls (n = 111)	HIV + CDC A (n = 249)	HIV + CDC B (n = 86)	HIV + CDC C (n = 54)	χ^2	p
Clinical Ratings	17%	31%	44%	56%	30.8	< .001
Global Deficit Scores	15%	27%	37%	45%	20.3	< .001
Factor Scores	24%	36%	50%	55%	14.8	< .002

Note: In comparison to the Clinical Ratings, the Global Deficit Scores had a sensitivity of 69.1%, a specificity of 91.4%, and an overall agreement rate of 84.2%. The Factor Scores resulted in a classification agreement with the Clinical Ratings of 75.8%, with 70.4% sensitivity and 78.5% specificity.

1990; Stern et al., 1991; Bornstein et al., 1992; A. Martin et al., 1992; E. Martin et al., 1992, 1995). A recent literature review of 57 studies that compared the performance of HIV seropositive asymptomatic and seronegative controls reported remarkably inconsistent findings (White et al., 1995). Forty-seven percent of studies found no significant neuropsychological differences between the HIV-positive subjects and controls, 21% had inconclusive results, and 32% found significant group differences. Of the 30 studies that reported prevalence of neuropsychological deficits between subject groups, there was almost a threefold increase in the rate of neuropsychological impairment among asymptomatic HIV-positive (HIV+) groups than HIV-negative (HIV−) controls (median prevalence figures were 35% versus 12%, respectively). This aggregate finding is quite consistent with the results of Heaton et al. (1995) with a sample of 500 adult men (i.e., neuropsychological impairment was found in 31% of asymptomatic, CDC A HIV+ subjects and 17% of the HIV− controls). However, it should also be stressed that roughly 70% of asymptomatic HIV+ subjects were *not* impaired and that neuropsychological deficits may be subtle and variable across individuals.

White et al. (1995) also evaluated the relationship between various methodological features and study conclusions. The most important factor that determined study outcome was the length and comprehensiveness of the neuropsychological test battery. Compared to studies that used brief or intermediate screening batteries, those that employed comprehensive neuropsychological testing were almost three times more likely to find an increased rate of neuropsychological impairment in asymptomatic HIV+ subjects (groups differences evidenced in 22%, 24%, and 62% for small, medium, and large batteries, respectively). This finding suggests a necessity for a relatively comprehensive testing approach, particularly with subjects in the early stages of HIV infection. However, the administration of a large battery of neuropsychological tests may not be prag-

matic or feasible within the clinical setting. Therefore, selection and inclusion of measures particularly sensitive to subcortical abnormalities is recommended (e.g., speed of information processing, fluency, divided and sustained attention, working memory, and long-term memory) (Butters et al., 1990).

Suggested Test Battery for Assessment of HIV-Associated Cognitive Impairment

Careful selection of tests to adequately evaluate a person with HIV infection is of critical importance. A small test battery will likely be insufficiently sensitive to detect impairment in asymptomatic subjects, given that there may be only mild deficits across a range of ability areas. However, a large comprehensive battery may be costly and impractical. One solution is to develop a test battery that has sufficient specificity, sensitivity and breadth of cognitive domains assessed to detect subtle impairments. Listed in Table 17-5 is a recommended test battery from the HNRC Neuropsychology Core (Heaton and Grant, 1995). This battery of neuropsychological tests takes 4 hours to administer in the clinical setting by a trained psychometrist. The results allow a clinician to rate eight cognitive ability areas and derive a summary deficit score and level of impairment. Also listed in Table 17-5 are two "step down" protocols (1.5 hours and 45 minutes) for subjects who cannot complete the entire battery based on medical considerations (i.e., fatigue, significant immunosuppression, etc.).

In addition to traditional neuropsychological tests, the use of computerized measures to assess cognitive function in HIV+ individuals may also be advantageous to the clinician (Miller and Wilkie, 1994). Computerized assessment of reaction time and speed of information processing appear to be highly sensitive to subtle cognitive impairments (Perdices and Cooper, 1989; Wilkie et al., 1990). Moreover, certain reaction time tasks can separate out the effects of motor slowing that is observed in persons with HIV infec-

Table 17-5. Suggested Neuropsychological Test Battery[a]

(V)	Boston Naming Test[b,c]		(A)	WAIS-R Digit Span
(V)	Thurstone Word Fluency (written)[c]		(A)	WAIS-R Arithmetic
(V)	WAIS-R Vocabulary		(A)	Paced Auditory Serial Addition Test[b,c]
(V)	Letter and Category Fluency (oral)			
(E)	Category Test		(PM)	WAIS-R Block Design[c]
(E)	Trail Making Test[b,c]		(PM)	WAIS-R Digit Symbol
(L,M)	Story Memory Test[b,c]		(MO)	Grooved Pegboard[b,c]
(L,M)	California Verbal Learning Test		(MO)	Finger Tapping[c]
(L,M)	Figure Memory Test[c]			
			(S)	Sensory Perceptual Exam

Note: Clinical Rating Areas: V = verbal; E = executive function (abstraction/cognitive flexibility); PM = complex perceptual-motor skills; A = attention/speed of information processing; L = learning; M = memory; S = sensory-perceptual skills; MO = motor skills.

[a] Additional test measures may be added based on professional judgment and/or preference (e.g., computerized reaction time and speed of information-processing tasks).

[b] 45-minute step-down battery

[c] 1.5-hour step-down protocol

tion from changes in speed of decision making (A. Martin et al., 1993; E. Martin et al., 1992, 1995).

As mentioned previously, HIV infection of the brain appears to affect especially subcortical, frontostriatal pathways earlier in the course of disease. One standardized test that has been shown to differentiate memory deficits associated with cortical versus subcortical dementias is the California Verbal Learning Test (CVLT) (Delis et al., 1991; Massman et al., 1992). A recent study (Peavy et al., 1994) compared the performance of HIV+ and HIV− subjects on the CVLT and classified their performance as "normal," similar to Huntington's disease patients (HD), or similar to Alzheimer's disease patients (AD). Results from this study found that 39 of the 40 HIV− controls (98%) were classified as normal and one individual as HD. Of the 94 asymptomatic HIV+ subjects, 78 were classified as normal (83%), 15 as HD (16%), and one as AD (1%). Out of the 31 symptomatic HIV+ subjects, 20 were classified as normal (65%), 10 as HD (32%), and one as AD (3%). These findings are consistent with the view that of those HIV+ subjects who demonstrate memory deficits on the CVLT, their performance profile is similar qualitatively, though generally is less impaired, than that of HD patients (which is prototypical of subcortical dysfunction).

Features Associated With Neuropsychological Impairments

Neurological Examination and Brain Imaging

HIV-positive subjects from the "HNRC 500" study (Heaton et al., 1995) who were found to have neuropsychological impairment at their baseline visit were also significantly more likely to show evidence of central nervous system abnormalities on neurological examination and magnetic resonance imaging (MRI) scan of the brain. The prevalence of neurological symptoms (affective, cognitive, and sensorimotor) has been observed to progressively increase with advancing CDC stage of HIV infection (8% of HIV− controls, 24% of CDC A, 52% of CDC B, and 56% of CDC C HNRC subjects had three or more neurological symptoms on structured interview) (Mehta et al., 1996). Neurological signs were less likely to be elicited, but also increased with disease progression (e.g., proportions with three or more neurological signs were: HIV− = 0%; CDC A = 2%; CDC B = 8%; CDC C = 13%) (Mehta et al., 1996). Quantitative image analytic techniques that estimate the degree of brain volume loss revealed that medically symptomatic HIV+ HNRC subjects had significant increases in subcortical fluid volumes, reduced volume of cerebral white matter, and reduced cerebral gray matter volumes. HIV-positive subjects with neuropsychological impairment were also likely to evidence central brain atrophy on their MRI scans. These findings are consistent with previous reports of deep white matter and basal ganglia damage in HIV infection (Hesselink, et al., 1994; Martin, 1994).

Neuropathology

Persons dying with frank HIV dementia tend to have greater viral burden in the brain at autopsy than those who die free of dementia (Wiley and Achim, 1994). Little is known regarding the relationship of neuropsychological impairment (short of gross dementia) to neuropathological outcomes. Earlier, we presented preliminary data suggesting that a measure of HIV burden, but not nonspecific gliosis, related to antemortem neuropsychological performance (Grant et al., 1992b). Recent studies have demonstrated that synapto-dendritic damage may be a critical aspect of neuronal pathology in HIV infection (Wiley et al., 1991; Masliah et al., 1992, in press), That is to say, damage to the neocortex of HIV-infected patients includes vacuolization of dendrites, dystrophic alterations, loss of spines and disruption of the dendritic cytoskeleton of neurons. Interesting is the finding from HNRC pilot work of a relationship between preagonal neuropsychological impairment and decline in dendritic density seen at the time of neuropsychological examination. Masliah et al. (manuscript in preparation) have found significant correlations between neuropsychological global clinical ratings as well as ratings of abstraction ability obtained in the year preceding death and damage to the dendritic field at postmortem examination. If confirmed, this finding suggests that postsynaptic events might underlie the neurocognitive disorder observed in HIV-infected persons.

Medical and Immune Functioning

Although it is true that the rate of neurocognitive impairment is highest among those in the most advanced stage of HIV disease, specific indicators of disease progression (e.g., T4 count or serum $\beta2$ microglobulin) are poor predictors of impairment (Diehr and Grant, 1995; Heaton et al., 1995). There are three exceptions to this general statement. First, persons experiencing a significant T4 drop (i.e., below 400) in the first few years after seroconversion are more likely to undergo neuropsychological worsening than those whose T4 counts stay higher. Second, those with histories of syphilis, gonorrhea, and other venereal diseases tend to have higher rates of impairment than those without such histories (Wallace et al., submitted). Third, the presence of CMV complications (CMV retinitis) is associated with increased rates of neuropsychological impairment (McCutchan and Grant, 1995). In particular, the HNRC examined neuropsychological test performance of 16 HIV-infected patients with recently diagnosed CMV-retinitis (CMV-R) and 32 controls matched for age, education, CD4 cell counts, and disease stage. Based on blinded clinical ratings of global impairment (at least mild impairment in two or more ability domains), higher impairment rates in the CMV-R group (69%) compared to HIV+ "controls" (37%; $p = .04$) were found (Heaton and Grant, 1995).

Depression

In analyzing data from the full HNRC 500 series, neuropsychological impairment showed weak, but statistically significant, associations with emotional distress, although in this case causal links are particularly difficult to ascertain. For example, an association of neuropsychological impairment with depression could be due to stress caused by perception of neuropsychological disability; alternatively, depression might affect some neuropsychological test performances, or both depression and neuropsychological test performance may reflect underlying brain dysfunction, especially in the basal ganglia (Mapou et al., 1993). In order to determine whether the differing rates of neuropsychological impairment could be explained by mood factors, Heaton et al. (1995) examined impairment rates after excluding all subjects who had major depression (SCID-diagnosed) or who evidenced at least moderate mood disturbance on the Hamilton Rating Scale for Depression (≥ 15). This resulted in 62 subjects being excluded. Impairment rates remained essentially the same as with the total sample (HIV$-$, 17.7%; CDC A, 31.0%; CDC B, 37.5%; CDC C, 50.0%), with all HIV$+$ groups having significantly higher rates of impairment compared to HIV$-$ controls. The neurocognitive disturbances observed across successive stages of HIV infection therefore could not be explained by presence of mood disturbances. This finding is consistent with previous work that the presence of mood disturbance does not appear to confound interpretation of neuropsychological test results with HIV$+$ persons (Atkinson et al., 1988; Hinkin et al., 1992; Grant et al., 1993). There also were no significant differences between HIV$+$ and HIV$-$ groups on the POMS Tension/Anxiety Scale, and the rate of generalized anxiety disorder was in fact actually lower for HIV$+$ subjects compared to controls.

Antiretrovirals

Although zidovudine (AZT) is generally thought to produce some benefit in HIV-associated neurological complications (Portegies, 1994), this effect is not fully confirmed (see review in Schmitt et al., 1994; Grant et al., 1995). There are many possible explanations for these variable results, including development of AZT-resistant strains and inefficient penetration of AZT into the brain. With respect to the latter, levels of AZT reached within tissue compartments of the brain and cerebral ventricles have been reported to be about 10% to 25% of plasma values (Tartaglione et al., 1991). Decisions regarding treatment of HNRC subjects with antiretroviral medications were based entirely upon clinical considerations. To date, there is a nonsignificant trend ($p = .06$) for HIV$+$ subjects being treated with AZT to have a higher rate of neuropsychological impairment (41.6% versus 32.3%, AZT treated and nontreated, respectively) (Heaton and Grant, 1995). This is almost entirely due to the CDC B group, for which neuropsychological impairment rates for AZT treated and untreated subjects were 50% and 32.1%, respectively. Impairment rates were almost identical for treated and untreated subjects in CDC A and CDC C. There were also no significant relationships between rates of neuropsychological impairment and duration of AZT treatment. There were not enough persons receiving treatment with other antiretrovirals (e.g., ddI, ddC) to analyze their effects. In summary, the HNRC has not observed an association between amount or duration of AZT treatment and neuropsychological impairment.

Neuropsychological Impairment and Mortality

The HNRC has examined mortality rates in 499 HIV$+$ subjects who were diagnosed as having either normal performance ($n = 271$) or impaired performance but not meeting criteria for MCMD (called "deficits", $n = 164$), or who met criteria for MCMD (as defined earlier) ($n = 64$) based on a comprehensive neuropsychological test battery (Heaton and Grant, 1995). The "deficits" classification meant that subjects exhibited deficits in two or more ability areas, but everyday functioning was not disrupted. Univariate analyses revealed that diagnostic classification of MCMD at baseline evaluation was a stronger predictor of death (risk ratio [RR] $= 2.9$) than "deficits" alone (RR $= 1.3$). In order to control for degree of immunosuppression, baseline CD4 count was added to the statistical model. As can be seen in Table 17-6, the diagnosis of MCMD increases risk of death 2.4 times, even when adjusted for CD4. Also of importance, the presence of subtle cognitive deficits insufficient to reach full MCMD diagnosis ("neuropsychological impaired") still increases relative risk of mortality by 1.8. These findings indicate that the detection of neuropsychological impairment signals a change that has neurobiological significance, and they are consistent with previous reports of increased risk of death being associated with the presence of neuropsycho-

Table 17-6. Mortality Risk for HIV+ HNRC Subjects by Clinical Diagnosis

Diagnosis	Risk Ratio (RR)	95% CI	p
Normal neuropsychological performance	1.0	—	—
Impaired neuropsychological performance[a]	1.8	1.1, 2.9	.02
Minor cognitive motor disorder	2.4	1.4, 4.1	.002

Note: Risk of death was adjusted for baseline CD4 counts.

[a] Defined as deficits in two or more neuropsychological domains that do not appear to disrupt everyday functioning.

logical impairment (Mayeux et al., 1993; Grant et al., 1994).

Everyday Vocational Functioning and HIV-Associated Cognitive Impairment

Neuropsychological impairment, although subtle at times, appears to be associated with significant psychosocial morbidity. Heaton et al. (1994b) have recently completed an initial attempt to relate neuropsychological impairment to employment variables in 289 HIV+, nondemented HNRC subjects. The unemployment rate among neuropsychologically impaired subjects was significantly higher than it was for unimpaired HIV+ subjects (27% versus 10%, $p < .001$). Moreover, those neuropsychologically impaired HIV+ subjects who were employed were five times more likely than unimpaired subjects to report reduced ability to perform the jobs they had (30% versus 6%, $p < .001$). These associations between neuropsychological impairment and employment status and complaints could not be explained on the basis of concurrent medical symptoms or emotional distress. That is, if the analyses were restricted to subjects who had only mild NP impairment, the relationships between impairment and the employment variables remained significant. Thus, even mild neuropsychological impairment in some HIV+ subjects may interfere with vocational functioning, and therefore may be considered "clinically significant." However, it should be emphasized that HIV+ individuals are *not* generally un-

able or less able to function in a competitive workplace. Indeed, based on the data which were presented in Figure 17-1, most HIV-infected persons do not show neuropsychological impairment (particularly during the asymptomatic stage) and of those who do, only a subset report difficulties performing their jobs.

Longitudinal Findings

The HNRC has recently completed an analysis of annual follow-up evaluations from the longitudinal series. Blind clinical ratings of the test data reveal that overall significant worsening of neuropsychological functioning during a 1-year period after a baseline exam was quite rare for HIV− controls (<4%), but gradually increased with each CDC stage (i.e., a decline in neuropsychological functioning was seen in 16.5% of CDC A, 23.6% of CDC B, and 41.9% of CDC C subjects). An analysis of the findings for the subjects who completed their 2-year follow-up evaluations revealed that neuropsychological worsening at any time over a 2-year period was more likely to occur in HIV+ subjects than in HIV− subjects. Once again, within the HIV+ groups, CDC C subjects demonstrated the highest rate of neuropsychological worsening (75.0%), followed by the CDC B (54.3%), CDC A (29.0%), and HIV− (11.1%) subjects. In summary, there is evidence of decline in neuropsychological function in some persons at all stages of HIV-1 infection. There is some increased risk of such decline in the asymptomatic phase of disease and the incidence is higher in more advanced phases of illness (Heaton and Grant, 1995; Grant et al., 1992b; 1995).

Summary

As emphasized previously, HIV disease is both a neurobehavioral as well as an immune-medical disorder (Grant and Atkinson, 1990). This fact should be of great interest to neuropsychologists, because the most common form of morbidity in the long asymptomatic phase of HIV disease involves subtle neurocognitive disturbance. In the

United States it is estimated that one million persons are HIV-infected; the vast majority of these are asymptomatic carriers. If it is correct that almost a fifth of these individuals have neuropsychological impairments over and above those found in "at-risk" seronegative groups, then as many as 200,000 persons may be suffering from HIV-related neurocognitive decline in this country alone. Because self-report of memory problems, cognitive inefficiency, and so forth has only a modest association with actual test performance in these groups, neuropsychological testing is important both to rule *out* neurocognitive decline based on complaints that may actually be related to anxiety or depression, as well as to rule *in* the possibility that mild neurocognitive disorder is present, but silent.

From the preceding review it should be obvious that seropositive status cannot and should not be used as a surrogate marker for cognitive impairment. Furthermore, even when mild neuropsychological impairment is definitively established, this does not necessarily lead to disturbance in occupational or social functioning. Thus, neuropsychologists should be cautious not to overinterpret their positive findings to the possible social detriment of their patients. Having stated this caveat, we would emphasize, however, that the presence of neuropsychological impairment in seropositive persons is not necessarily benign. Unemployment is doubled in neuropsychologically impaired but medically asymptomatic seropositive individuals (Heaton et al., 1994b). Thus, the assessment of each case must proceed in a standardized, yet individualized manner, beginning with the gathering of a complete history, including history of previous neuromedical events (such as head injury) and substance abuse, and then proceed to neuropsychological assessment with tests proven to be sensitive to the effects of HIV on the central nervous system. An example of a battery of such tests, which have shown themselves to be useful in HNRC research, is presented in this chapter.

Given what we know at present about the likely neuropathogenesis of the cognitive disorders associated with HIV, there is rea-

son to be optimistic that such disorders may prove to be reversible with specific treatment. For example, it is possible that AZT, especially if administered in higher than usual doses (e.g., 1000 mg daily rather than the usual 500 mg daily) may have some beneficial effects on CNS functioning. Conceivably, newer antiretroviral agents such as Stavudine (D4T), which may penetrate even better into the central nervous system, might prove to be even more efficacious. At the same time, agents such as ddI and ddC, although effective against HIV, are unlikely to benefit CNS complications, because they do not penetrate well across the blood-brain barrier.

Newer, theoretically more interesting therapeutic agents are on the horizon. At the time of this writing, the National Institute of Mental Health was completing a multicenter trial of Peptide T, one of whose actions might be to displace gp120 (a viral envelope glycoprotein) from critical receptor sites on neural cells. It is also possible that if one of the mechanisms of synaptodendritic injury involves activation of NMDA receptors with resultant neuronal damage due to influx of calcium, then calcium channel blocking drugs or NMDA receptor antagonist drugs may have some value in the future. Additionally, if, as has been speculated, some of the synaptodendritic damage is mediated by abnormal release of cytokines (e.g., tumor necrosis factor–α; interleukin-6) (Masliah et al., in press), then it may be possible that substances that lessen release or antagonize actions of such cytokines may be of value. For example, some investigations are currently under way to examine the possible beneficial effects of agents with anti–TNF-α effects, such as pentoxifylline.

In summary, the spectrum of HIV disease challenges neuropsychologists to broaden their interests to include neurovirology and neuroimmunology. Insights gained thereby will extend well beyond the province of HIV disease toward an understanding of the mechanisms whereby neuroinflammatory processes—activated either by infectious agents or autoimmune processes—produce cognitive disturbance. Importantly, and in contrast to many other conditions with which neuropsychologists must deal (e.g., Alzheimer's disease, stroke, sequelae of head injury), neuropsychological assessment of patients with the neuroinflammatory disorders will be important in early detection of complications at a phase when these are still reversible. Thus, neuropsychologists should see themselves as having an opportunity to play a critical part in the neuromedical effort to diagnose, develop new treatments for, and monitor outcomes in, diseases such as HIV infection.

References

Atkinson, J. H., Grant, I., Kennedy, C. J., Richman, D. D., Spector, S. A., and McCutchan, J. A. (1988). Prevalence of psychiatric disorders among men infected with human immunodeficiency virus: A controlled study. *Archives of General Psychiatry, 45,* 859–864.

Bornstein, R. A. (1994). Methodological and conceptual issues in the study of cognitive change in HIV infection. In I. Grant and A. Martin, eds., *Neuropsychology of HIV Infection.* New York: Oxford University Press, pp. 146–160.

Bornstein, R. A., Nasrallah, H. A., Para, M. F., Whitacre, C. C., Rosenberger, P., and Fass, R. J. (1993). Neuropsychological performance in symptomatic and asymptomatic HIV infection. *AIDS, 7,* 519–524.

Bornstein, R. A., Nasrallah, H. A., Para, M. F., Whitacre, C. C., Rosenberger, P., Fass, R. J., and Rice, R., Jr. (1992). Neuropsychological performance in asymptomatic HIV infection. *Journal of Neuropsychiatry and Clinical Neurosciences, 4,* 386–394.

Budka, H., Wiley, C. A., Kleihues, P., Artigas, J., Asbury, A. K., Cho, E.-S., Cornblath, D. R., Dal Canto, M. C., DeGirolami, U., Dickson, D., Epstein, L. G., Esiri, M. M., Giangaspero, F., Gosztonyi, G., Gray, F., Griffin, J. W., Henin, D., Iwasaki, Y., Janssen, R. S., Johnson, R. T., Lantos, P. L., Lyman, W. D., McArthur, J. C., Nagashima, K., Peres, N., Petito, C. K., Price, R. W., Rhodes, R. H., Rosenblum, M., Said, G., Scaravilli, F., Sharer, L. R., and Vinters, H. V. (1991). HIV-associated disease of the nervous system: Review of nomenclature and proposal for neuropathology-based terminology. *Brain Pathology, 1,* 143–152.

Butters, N., Grant, I., Haxby, J., Judd, L. L., Martin, A., McClelland, J., Pequegnat, W.,

Schacter, D., and Stover, E. (1990). Assessment of AIDS-related cognitive changes: Recommendations of the NIMH Workshop on Neuropsychological Assessment Approaches. *Journal of Clinical and Experimental Neuropsychology, 12,* 963–978.

Butters, N., Salmon, D. P., Heindel, W., and Granholm, E. (1988). Episodic, semantic, and procedural memory: Some comparisons of Alzheimer and Huntington disease patients. In R. D. Terry, ed., *Aging and the Brain.* New York: Raven Press, pp. 63–87.

Centers for Disease Control. (1992). 1993 revised classification system for HIV infection and expanded surveillance case definition for AIDS among adolescents and adults. *Morbidity and Mortality Weekly Report, 41* (Suppl. 44–17), 1–19.

Cummings, J. L. (1986). Subcortical dementia. Neuropsychology, neuropsychiatry, and pathophysiology. *British Journal of Psychiatry, 149,* 682–697.

Cummings, J. L. (1990). *Subcortical Dementia.* New York: Oxford University Press.

Day, J. J., Grant, I., Atkinson, J. H., Brysk, L. T., McCutchan, J. A., Hesselink, J. R., Heaton, R. K., Weinrich, J. D., Spector, S. A., and Richman, D. D. (1992). Incidence of dementia in a two year follow-up of AIDS and ARC patients on an initial Phase II AZT placebo-controlled study: San Diego Cohort. *Journal of Neuropsychiatry and Clinical Neurosciences, 4,* 15–20.

Delis, D. C., Massman, P. J., Butters, N., Salmon, D. P., Cermak, L. S., and Kramer, J. H. (1991). Profiles of demented and amnesic patients on the California Verbal Learning Test: Implications for the assessment of memory disorders. *Psychological Assessment, 3,* 19–26.

Diehr, M., and Grant, I. (1995). Immune measures and change in neuropsychological status in non-AIDS HIV-1 infection. *Unpublished manuscript.* HNRC, San Diego, CA.

Ekholm, S., and Simon, J. H. (1988). Magnetic resonance imaging and the acquired immunodeficiency syndrome dementia complex. *Acta Radiologica, 29,* 227–230.

Ellis, R., Schrier, R., Wiley, C., McCutchan, J. A., Grant, I., and the HNRC Group (1995). Clinically unrecognized cytomegalovirus brain infection at autopsy is associated with neurocognitive impairment in AIDS. Abstract No. 288 (poster presentation) of the 2nd National Conference on Human Retrovirus and Related Infections, American Society for Microbiology, Washington, D.C.

Folstein, S. E., Brandt, J., and Folstein, M. (1990). Huntington's disease. In J. L. Cummings, ed., *Subcortical Dementia*. New York: Oxford University Press, pp. 87–107.

Goethe, K. E., Mitchell, J. E., Marshall, D. W., Brey, R. L., Cahill, W. T., Leger, G. D., Hoy, L. J., and Boswell, R. N. (1989). Neuropsychological and neurological function of human immunodeficiency virus seropositive asymptomatic individuals. *Archives of Neurology, 46,* 129–133.

Grant, I., and Atkinson, J. H. (1990). The evolution of neurobehavioral complications of HIV infection. *Psychological Medicine, 20,* 747–754.

Grant, I., and Atkinson, J. H. (1995). Psychobiology of HIV Infection. In H. I. Kaplan and B. J. Sadock, eds., *Comprehensive Textbook of Psychiatry/VI*. Baltimore: Williams and Wilkins, pp. 1644–1669.

Grant, I., Atkinson, J. H., Hesselink, J. R., Kennedy, C. J., Richman, D. D., Spector, S. A., and McCutchan, J. A. (1987). Evidence for early central nervous system involvement in the acquired immunodeficiency syndrome (AIDS) and other human immunodeficiency virus (HIV) infections. Studies with neuropsychologic testing and magnetic resonance imaging. *Annals of Internal Medicine, 107,* 828–836.

Grant, I., Atkinson, J. H., Hesselink, J. R., Kennedy, C. J., Richman, D. D., Spector, S. A., and McCutchan, J. A. (1988). Human immunodeficiency virus-associated neurobehavioral disorder. *Journal of the Royal College of Physicians of London, 22,* 149–157.

Grant, I., Caun, K., Kingsley, D.P.E., Winer, J., Trimble, M. R., and Pinching, A. J. (1992a). Neuropsychological and NMR abnormalities in HIV infection. The St. Mary's-Queen Square Study. *Neuropsychiatry, Neuropsychology, and Behavioral Neurology, 5,* 185–193.

Grant, I., and Heaton, R. K. (1990). Human immunodeficiency virus-1 (HIV-1) and the brain. *Journal of Consulting and Clinical Psychology, 58,* 22–30.

Grant, I., Heaton, R. K., Atkinson, J. H., Deutsch, R., Nelson, J., and McCutchan, J. A. (1994). Cognitive impairment predicts death in HIV+ men. Paper presented at the annual meeting of the American Psychiatric Association, Philadelphia, PA.

Grant, I., Heaton, R. K., Atkinson, J. H., and the HNRC Group (1995). Neurocognitive disorders in HIV-1 infection. In M.B.A. Oldstone and L. Vitkovic, eds., *Current Topics in Microbiology and Immunology, HIV and Dementia*. Heidelberg: Springer-Verlag, pp. 9–30.

Grant, I., Heaton, R. K., Atkinson, J. H., Wiley, C. A., Kirson, D., Velin, R. A., Chandler, J. L., McCutchan, J. A., and the HNRC Group. (1992b). HIV-1 associated neurocognitive disorder. *Clinical Neuropharmacology, 15* (Suppl. 1), 364A–365A.

Grant, I., and Martin, A. (1994). *Neuropsychology of HIV Infection*. New York: Oxford University Press.

Grant, I., Olshen, R. A., Atkinson, J. H., Heaton, R. K., Nelson, J., McCutchan, J. A., and Weinrich, J. D. (1993). Depressed mood does not explain neuropsychological deficits in HIV-infected persons. *Neuropsychology, 7,* 53–61.

Heaton, R. K., and Grant, I. (1995). Neurobehavioral Progress Report/Preliminary Studies. In I. Grant, ed., *HIV Neurobehavioral Research Center* (Research plan presented to the National Institute of Mental Health, Office on AIDS, May 1), San Diego, CA, pp. 321–330.

Heaton, R. K., Grant, I., Butters, N., White, D. A., Kirson, D., Atkinson, J. H., McCutchan, J. A., Taylor, M., Kelly, M. D., Ellis, R. J., Wolfson, T., Velin, R., Marcotte, T. D., Hesselink, J. R., Jernigan, T. L., Chandler, J., Wallace, M., Abramson, I., and the HNRC Group. (1995). The HNRC 500—Neuropsychology of HIV infection at different disease stages. *Journal of the International Neuropsychological Society, 1,* 231–251.

Heaton, R. K., Kirson, D., Velin, R. A., Grant, I., and the HNRC Group. (1994a). The utility of clinical ratings for detecting cognitive change in HIV infection. In I. Grant and A. Martin, eds., *Neuropsychology of HIV Infection*. New York: Oxford University Press, pp. 188–206.

Heaton, R. K., Velin, R. A., McCutchan, J. A., Gulevich, S., Atkinson, J. H., Wallace, M. R., Godfrey, H., Kirson, D., Grant, I., and the HNRC Group. (1994b). Neuropsychological impairment in HIV-infection: Implications for employment. *Psychosomatic Medicine, 56,* 8–17.

Hesselink, J. R., Jernigan, T. L., and Heindel, W. C. (1994). Structural brain imaging of HIV infection. In I. Grant and A. Martin, eds., *Neuropsychology of HIV Infection*. New York: Oxford University Press, pp. 108–129.

Hinkin, C. H., Van Gorp, W. G., and Satz, P. (1995). Neuropsychological and neuropsychiatric aspects of HIV infection in adults. In H. I. Kaplan and B. J. Sadock, eds., *Comprehensive Textbook of Psychiatry/VI*. Baltimore: Williams and Wilkins, pp. 1669–1680.

Hinkin, C. H., van Gorp, W. G., Satz, P., Weisman, J. D., Thommes, J., and Buckingham, S. (1992). Depressed mood and its relationship to neuropsychological test performance in HIV-1 seropositive individuals. *Journal of Clinical and Experimental Neuropsychology, 14,* 289–297.

Janssen, R. S., Nwanyanwu, O. C., Selik, R. M., and Stehr-Green, J. K. (1992). Epidemiology of human immunodeficiency virus encephalopathy in the United States. *Neurology, 42,* 1472–1476.

Janssen, R. S., Saykin, A. J., Cannon, L., Campbell, J., Pinsky, P. F., Hessol, N. A., O'Malley, P. M., Lifson, A. R., Doll, L. S., Rutherford, G. W., and Kaplan, J. E. (1989). Neurological and neuropsychological manifestations of HIV-1 infection: Association with AIDS-related complex but not asymptomatic HIV-1 infection. *Annals of Neurology, 26,* 592–600.

Janssen, R. S., Saykin, A. J., Kaplan, J. E., Spira, T. J., Pinsky, P. F., Sprehn, G. C., Hoffman, J. C., Mayer, W. B., Jr., and Schonberger, L. B. (1988). Neurological complications of human immunodeficiency virus infection in patients with lymphadenopathy syndrome. *Annals of Neurology, 23,* 49–55.

Kaemingk, K. L., and Kaszniak, A. W. (1989). Neuropsychological aspects of human immunodeficiency virus infection. *The Clinical Neuropsychologist, 3,* 309–326.

Levy, R. M., Bredesen, D. E., and Rosenblum, M. L. (1985). Neurological manifestations of the acquired immunodeficiency syndrome (AIDS): Experience at UCSF and review of the literature. *Journal of Neurosurgery, 62,* 475–495.

Lunn, S., Skydsbjerg, M., Schulsinger, H., Parnas, J., Pedersen, C., and Mathiesen, L. (1991). A preliminary report on the neuropsychologic sequelae of human immunodeficiency virus. *Archives of General Psychiatry, 48,* 139–142.

Maj, M., Satz, P., Janssen, R., Zaudig, M., Starace, F., D'Elia, L., Sughondhabirom, B., Mussa, M., Naber, D., Ndetei, D., Schulte, G., and Sartorius, N. (1994). WHO Neuropsychiatric AIDS Study, cross-sectional Phase II. Neuropsychological and neurological findings. *Archives of General Psychiatry, 51,* 51–61.

Mapou, R. L., Law, W. A., Martin, A., Kampen, D., Salazar, A. M., and Rundell, J. R. (1993). Neuropsychological performance, mood, and complaints of cognitive and motor difficulties in individuals infected with the human immunodeficiency virus. *Journal of Neuropsychiatry and Clinical Neurosciences, 5,* 86–93.

Martin, A. (1994). HIV, cognition, and the basal ganglia. In I. Grant and A. Martin, eds., *Neuropsychology of HIV Infection.* New York: Oxford University Press, pp. 234–259.

Martin, A., Heyes, M. P., Salazar, A. M., Kampen, D. L., Williams, J., Law, W. A., Coats, M. E., and Markey, S. P. (1992). Progressive slowing of reaction time and increasing cerebrospinal fluid concentrations of quinolinic acid in HIV-infected individuals. *Journal of Neuropsychiatry and Clinical Neurosciences, 4,* 270–279.

Martin, A., Heyes, M. P., Salazar, A. M., Law, W. A., and Williams, J. (1993). Impaired motor-skill learning, slowed reaction time, and elevated cerebrospinal fluid quinolinic acid in a subgroup of HIV-infected individuals. *Neuropsychology, 7,* 149–157.

Martin, E. M., Pitrak, D. L., Robertson, L. C., Novak, R., Mullane, K., and Pursell, K. (1995). Global-local analysis in HIV-1 infection. *Neuropsychology, 9,* 102–109.

Martin, E. M., Sorensen, D. J., Robertson, L. C., Edelstein, H. E., and Chirurgi, V. A. (1992). Spatial attention in HIV-1 infection: A preliminary report. *Journal of Neuropsychiatry and Clinical Neurosciences, 4,* 288–293.

Masliah, E., Achim, C. L., Ge, N., DeTeresa, R., Terry, R. D., and Wiley, C. A. (1992). Spectrum of human immunodeficiency virus-associated neocortical damage. *Annals of Neurology, 32,* 321–329.

Masliah, E., Ge, N., Achim, C. L., DeTeresa, R., and Wiley, C. A. (in press). Patterns of neurodegeneration in HIV encephalitis. *Journal of NeuroAIDS.*

Massman, P. J., Delis, D. C., Butters, N., Dupont, R. M., and Gillin, J. C. (1992). The subcortical dysfunction hypothesis of memory deficits in depression: Neuropsychological validation in a subgroup of patients. *Journal of Clinical and Experimental Neuropsychology, 14,* 687–706.

Mayeux, R., Stern, Y., Tang, M-X, Todak, G., Marder, K., Sano, M., Richards, M., Stein, Z., Ehrhardt, A. A., and Gorman, J. M. (1993). Mortality risks in gay men with human immunodeficiency virus infection and cognitive impairment. *Neurology, 43,* 176–182.

McAllister, R. H., Herns, M. V., Harrison, M.J.G., Newman, S. P., Connolly, S., Fowler, C. J., Fell, M., Durrance, P., Manji, H., Kendall, B. E., and Valentine, A. R. (1992). Neurological and neuropsychological performance in HIV seropositive men without symptoms. *Journal of Neurology, Neurosurgery, and Psychiatry, 55,* 143–148.

McArthur, J. C. (1994). Neurological and neuropathological manifestations of HIV infection. In I. Grant and A. Martin, eds., *Neuropsychology of HIV Infection.* New York: Oxford University Press, pp. 56–107.

McArthur, J. C., Hoover, D. R., Bacellar, H., Miller, E. N., Cohen, B. A., Becker, J. T., Graham, N.M.H., McArthur, J. H., Selnes, O. A., Jacobson, L. P., Visscher, B. R., Concha, M., and Saah, A. (1993). Dementia in AIDS patients: Incidence and risk factors. *Neurology, 43,* 2245–2253.

McArthur, J. C., Cohen, B. A., Selnes, O. A., Kumar, A. J., Cooper, K., McArthur, J. H., Soucy, G., Cornblath, D. R., Chmiel, J. S., Wang, M. C., Starkey, D. L., Ginzburg, H., Ostrow, D., Johnson, R. T., Phair, J. P., and Polk, B. F. (1989). Low prevalence of neurological and neuropsychological abnormalities in otherwise healthy HIV − 1-infected individuals: Results from the Multicenter AIDS Cohort Study. *Annals of Neurology, 26,* 601–611.

McCutchan, J. A. (1994). Virology, immunology, and clinical course of HIV infection. In I. Grant and A. Martin, eds., *Neuropsychology of HIV Infection.* New York: Oxford University Press, pp. 23–40.

McCutchan, J. A., and Grant, I. (1995). Preliminary studies of neuropsychological deficits associated with CMV-R. In I. Grant, ed., *HIV Neurobehavioral Research Center* (Research plan presented to the National Institute of Mental Health, Office on AIDS, May 1), San Diego, CA, pp. 647–649.

McHugh, P. R., and Folstein, M. F. (1975). Psychiatric syndromes of Huntington's chorea: A clinical and phenomenologic study. In D. F. Benson and D. Blumler, eds., *Psychiatric Aspects of Neurologic Disease.* New York: Grune and Stratton, Inc., pp. 267–286.

McKegney, F. P., O'Dowd, M. A., Feiner, C., Selwyn, P., Drucker, E., and Friedland, G. H. (1990). A prospective comparison of neuropsychologic function in HIV-seropositive and seronegative methadone-maintained patients. *AIDS, 4,* 565–569.

Mehta, P., Gulevich, S. J., Thal, L. J., Jin, H., Olichney, J. M., McCutchan, J. A., Heaton, R., Hurray, C. A., Kirson, D., Kaplanski, G., Nelson, J., Atkinson, J. H., Wallace, M., Grant, I., and the HNRC Group (1996). Neurological symptoms, not signs, are common in early HIV infection. *Journal of NeuroAIDS,1,*67–85.

Miller, E. N., Selnes, O. A., McArthur, J. C., Satz, P., Becker, J. T., Cohen, B. A., Sheridan, K., Machado, A. M., Van Gorp, W. G., and Visscher, B. (1990). Neuropsychological performance in HIV-1-infected homosexual men: The Multicenter AIDS Cohort Study (MACS). *Neurology, 40,* 197–203.

Miller, E. N., and Wilkie, F. L. (1994). Computerized testing to assess cognition in HIV-positive individuals. In I. Grant and A. Martin, eds., *Neuropsychology of HIV Infection.* New York: Oxford University Press, pp. 161–175.

Naber, D., Perro, C., Schick, U., Schmauss, M., Erfurth, A., Bove, D., Goebel, F. D., and Hippius, H. (1990). Psychiatric symptoms and neuropsychological deficits in HIV infection. In W. E. Bunney, Jr., H. Hippius, G. Laakmann, and M. Schmauss, eds., *Neuropsychopharmacology: Proceedings of the XVIth CINP Congress, Munich, Aug. 15–19, 1988.* Munich: Springer-Verlag, pp. 745–755.

Nair, M.P.N., and Schwartz, S. A. (1994). Immunopathogenesis of HIV infections: CNS-immune interactions. In I. Grant and A. Martin, eds., *Neuropsychology of HIV Infection.* New York: Oxford University Press, pp. 41–55.

Navia, B. A. (1990). The AIDS dementia complex. In J. L. Cummings, ed., *Subcortical Dementia.* New York: Oxford University Press, pp. 181–198.

Navia, B. A., Cho, E. S., Petito, C. K., and Price, R. W. (1986b). The AIDS dementia complex: II. Neuropathology. *Annals of Neurology, 19,* 525–535.

Navia, B. A., Jordan, B. D., and Price, R. W. (1986a). The AIDS dementia complex: I. Clinical features. *Annals of Neurology, 19,* 517–524.

Navia, B. A., and Price, R. W. (1987). The acquired immunodeficiency syndrome dementia complex as the presenting or sole manifestation of human immunodeficiency virus infection. *Archives of Neurology, 44,* 65–69.

Olsen, W. L., Longo, F. M., Mills, C. M., and Norman, D. (1988). White matter disease in AIDS: Findings at MR imaging. *Radiology, 169,* 445–448.

Peavy, G., Jacobs, D., Salmon, D. P., Butters, N., Delis, D. C., Taylor, M., Massman, P., Stout, J. C., Heindel, W. C., Kirson, D., Atkinson, J. H., Chandler, J. L., Grant, I., and the HNRC Group. (1994). Verbal memory performance of patients with human immunodeficiency virus infection: Evidence of subcortical dysfunction. *Journal of Clinical and Experimental Neuropsychology, 16,* 508–523.

Perdices, M., and Cooper, D. A. (1989). Simple and choice reaction time in patients with human immunodeficiency virus infection. *Annals of Neurology, 25,* 460–467.

Portegies, P. (1994). AIDS dementia complex: A review. *Journal of Acquired Immune Deficiency Syndromes, 7* (Suppl. 2), S38–48; discussion, S48–49.

Poutiainen, E., Iivanainen, M., Elovaara, I., Valle, S. L., and Lahdevirta, J. (1988). Cognitive changes as early signs of HIV infection. *Acta Neurologica Scandinavica, 78,* 49–52.

Price, R. W., and Brew, B. J. (1988). The AIDS dementia complex. *Journal of Infectious Diseases, 158,* 1079–1083.

Pumarola-Sune, T., Navia, B. A., Cordon-Cardo, C., Cho, E. S., and Price, R. W. (1987). HIV antigen in the brains of patients with the AIDS dementia complex. *Annals of Neurology, 21,* 490–496.

Riedel, R. R., Helmstaedter, C., Bulau, P., Durwen, H. F., Brackmann, H., Fimmers, R., Clarenbach, P., Miller, E. N., and Bottcher, M. (1992). Early signs of cognitive deficits among human immunodeficiency virus-positive hemophiliacs. *Acta Psychiatrica Scandinavica, 85,* 321–326.

Saykin, A. J., Janssen, R. S., Sprehn, G. C., Kaplan, J. E., Spira, T. J., and O'Connor, B. (1991). Longitudinal evaluation of neuropsychological function in homosexual men with HIV infection: 18-month follow-up. *Journal of Neuropsychiatry and Clinical Neurosciences, 3,* 286–298.

Schmitt, F. A., Dickson, L. R., and Brouwers, P. (1994). Neuropsychological response to antiretroviral therapy in HIV infection. In I. Grant and A. Martin, eds., *Neuropsychology of HIV Infection.* New York: Oxford University Press, pp. 276–294.

Selnes, O. A., Galai, N., Bacellar, H., Miller, E. N., Becker, J. T., Wesch, J., Van Gorp, W., and McArthur, J. C. (1995). Cognitive performance after progression to AIDS: A longitudinal study from the Multicenter AIDS Cohort Study. *Neurology, 45,* 267–275.

Selnes, O. A., McArthur, J. C., Royal, W., 3rd, Updike, M. L., Nance-Sproson, T., Concha, M., Gordon, B., Solomon, L., and Vlahov, D. (1992). HIV-1 infection and intravenous drug use: Longitudinal neuropsychological evaluation of asymptomatic subjects. *Neurology, 42,* 1924–1930.

Sharer, L. R. (1992). Pathology of HIV-1 infection of the central nervous system. A review. *Journal of Neuropathology and Experimental Neurology, 51,* 3–11.

Skoraszewski, M. J., Ball, J. D., and Mikulka, P. (1991). Neuropsychological functioning of HIV-infected males. *Journal of Clinical and Experimental Neuropsychology, 13,* 278–290.

Stern, Y., Marder, K., Bell, K., Chen, J., Dooneief, G., Goldstein, S., Mindry, D., Richards, M., Sano, M., Williams, J., Gorman, J., Ehr-

hardt, A., and Mayeux, R. (1991). Multidisciplinary baseline assessment of homosexual men with and without human immunodeficiency virus infection. III. Neurologic and neuropsychological findings. *Archives of General Psychiatry, 48,* 131–138.

Tartaglione, T. A., Collier, A. C., Coombs, R. W., Opheim, K. E., Cummings, D. K., Mackay, S. R., Benedetti, J., and Corey, L. (1991). Acquired immunodeficiency syndrome. Cerebrospinal fluid findings in patients before and during long-term oral zidovudine therapy. *Archives of Neurology, 48,* 695–699. [Published erratum appears in *Archives of Neurology, 48,* 1238, 1991.]

Tross, S., Price, R. W., Navia, B., Thaler, H. T., Gold, J., Hirsch, D. A., and Sidtis, J. J. (1988). Neuropsychological characterization of the AIDS dementia complex: A preliminary report. *AIDS, 2,* 81–88.

Van Gorp, W. G., Lamb, D. G., and Schmitt, F. A. (1993). Methodologic issues in neuropsychological research with HIV-spectrum disease. *Archives of Clinical Neuropsychology, 8,* 17–33.

Wallace, M. R., Heaton, R. K., McCutchan, J. A., Malone, J. L., Velin, R., Nelson, J., Miller, L. K., Weiss, P. J., Oldfield, E. C., and Grant, I. (Submitted). Neurocognitive impairment in HIV infection is correlated with sexually transmitted disease history. *Journal of Infectious Diseases.*

White, D. A., Heaton, R. K., Monsch, A. U., and the HNRC Group. (1995). Neuropsychological studies of asymptomatic human immunodeficiency virus-type 1 infected individuals. *Journal of the International Neuropsychological Society, 1,* 304–315.

Wiley, C. A., and Achim, C. L. (1994). Human immunodeficiency virus encephalitis is the pathological correlate of dementia in acquired immunodeficiency syndromes. *Annals of Neurology, 36,* 673–676.

Wiley, C. A., Masliah, E., and Achim, C. L. (1994). Measurement of CNS HIV burden and its association with neurologic damage. *Advances in Neuroimmunology, 4,* 319–325.

Wiley, C. A., Masliah, E., Morey, M., Lemere, C., DeTeresa, R., Grafe, M., Hansen, L., and Terry, R. (1991). Neocortical damage during HIV infection. *Annals of Neurology, 29,* 651–657.

Wilkie, F. L., Eisdorfer, C. E., Morgan, R., Loewenstein, D. A., and Szapocznik, J. (1990). Cognition in early human immunodeficiency virus infection. *Archives of Neurology, 4,* 433–440.

Wilkins, J. W., Robertson, K. R., Snyder, C. R., Robertson, W. K., van der Horst, C., and Hall, C. D. (1991). Implications of self-reported cognitive and motor dysfunction in HIV-positive patients. *American Journal of Psychiatry, 148*, 641–643.

Working Group of the American Academy of Neurology AIDS Task Force. (1991). Nomenclature and research case definitions for neurologic manifestations of human immunodeficiency virus–type 1 (HIV-1). *Neurology, 41*, 778–785.

18 The Neurobehavioral Correlates of Alcoholism

SEAN B. ROURKE and TOR LØBERG

In 1994, a survey sponsored by the National Institute on Alcohol Abuse and Alcoholism (NIAAA) revealed that 51.6% of adults surveyed were classified as current drinkers; 8.6% of adults, representing 15.2 million Americans, met DSM-IV criteria for alcohol abuse and/or dependence, with men being three times more likely to meet the criteria than women (Grant, 1994). These recent figures are comparable to those obtained in a 1988 survey sponsored by the NIAAA using DSM-III-R criteria (Grant et al., 1991). It is estimated that 10% of those who meet the criteria for Alcohol Dependence fulfill criteria for an "organic brain syndrome" (Horvath, 1973), and approximately 50% (range 31% to 85%) of the remaining alcoholics exhibit mild to moderate impairment on neuropsychological testing when abstinent for 3 to 4 weeks (Grant et al., 1984; Eckardt and Martin, 1986; Parsons, 1986a, Rourke and Grant, 1995).

The main goal of this chapter is to delineate the neurobehavioral correlates of alcoholism. We have divided the chapter into seven major sections. In the first, we briefly describe the diagnosis of alcoholism and related disorders, and the clinical course associated with the "typical" alcoholic. Next, we summarize the neurobehavioral findings associated with alcoholism, as well as the neuroimaging, electrophysiological, and neuropathological correlates. In this section, we focus primarily on chronic alcoholics who do not meet criteria for either an amnestic disorder and/or a dementia associated with alcoholism. A brief description of the models that have been proposed to explain the brain dysfunction associated with alcoholism is presented in the third section. A summary of the neurobehavioral and neuroimaging findings associated with the Wernicke-Korsakoff syndrome is presented in the next section. While there is no doubt that alcohol is a neurotoxic agent, we present a conceptual model in the fifth section to illustrate the multifactorial etiology of the neurobehavioral impairments that are detected in alcoholics. Next, we summarize the evidence for the recovery of brain structure and function, and identify some of the variables that may mediate this recovery. Finally, we will focus on clinical implications and the role of neuropsychological performance in the treatment outcome of alcoholics.

Diagnosis of Alcoholism and Clinical Course

Diagnosis of Alcohol Dependence and Alcohol-Related Disorders

Alcohol Dependence, or simply alcoholism, refers to a constellation of symptoms that develop in the context of a maladaptive pattern of alcohol consumption and continue despite adverse life consequences. In the most recent update (the fourth edition) of the

Diagnostic and Statistical Manual of Mental Disorders (DSM-IV) (American Psychiatric Association, 1994), Alcohol Dependence falls under Substance-Related Disorders, and more specifically, Substance Dependence. The diagnosis for Alcohol Dependence is reproduced below:

Alcohol Dependence

A maladaptive pattern of alcohol use, leading to clinically significant impairment or distress by *three* (or more) of the following, occurring at any time in the same 12-month period:

1. tolerance, as defined by either of the following:
   a. a need for markedly increased amounts of alcohol to achieve intoxication or desired effect
   b. markedly diminished effect with continued use of the same amount of alcohol
2. withdrawal, as manifested by either of the following:
   a. the characteristic alcohol withdrawal syndrome that occurs after cessation of (or reduction in) alcohol use that has been heavy and prolonged, and which has two (or more) of the following that develop within several hours to a few days: autonomic hyperactivity (e.g., sweating or pulse rate greater than 100), increased hand tremor, insomnia, nausea or vomiting, transient visual, tactile, or auditory hallucinations or illusions, psychomotor agitation, anxiety, or grand mal seizures.
   b. the same (or a closely related) substance is taken to relieve or avoid withdrawal symptoms
3. alcohol is often taken in larger amounts or over a longer period than was intended
4. there is a persistent desire or unsuccessful efforts to cut down or control alcohol use
5. a great deal of time is spent in activities necessary to obtain alcohol, use alcohol, or recover from its effects
6. important social, occupational, or recreational activities are given up or reduced because of substance use
7. the alcohol use is continued despite knowledge of having a persistent or recurrent physical or psychological problem that is likely to have been caused or exacerbated by alcohol (e.g., continued drinking despite recognition that an ulcer was made worse by alcohol consumption).

(DSM-IV: pp. 181, 198–199)

According to DSM-IV criteria, a person is diagnosed as having Alcohol Dependence if he or she has three or more of the above symptoms; in addition, the diagnosis specifies the conditions for physiological dependence, the presence of which is indicated by tolerance and/or withdrawal symptoms. Further course specifiers are used to reflect the amount of time that a person has been abstinent (i.e., Early versus Sustained Remission) and whether there have been any symptoms of dependence or abuse during this time (i.e., Partial versus Full Remission) (American Psychiatric Association, 1994). Alcohol Abuse is similar to Alcohol Dependence in some respects (i.e., both refer to a maladaptive use of alcohol that leads to clinically significant impairment or distress), but the former does not involve tolerance, withdrawal, or a pattern of compulsive use, as is the case with the latter diagnosis (American Psychiatric Association, 1994).

Severe cognitive disorders occur in approximately 10% of persons diagnosed with Alcohol Dependence (Horvath, 1973). The DSM-IV diagnostic criteria for these disorders are listed below. (See *Wernicke-Korsakoff Syndrome*, below, for a summary of the neurobehavioral and neuroimaging correlates of Alcohol-Induced Persisting Amnestic Disorder, and refer to Martin et al. [1986, 1989] for more information regarding Alcohol-Induced Persisting Dementia.)

Alcohol-Induced Persisting Amnestic Disorder

A. The development of memory impairment as manifested by impairment in the ability to learn new information or the inability to recall previously learned information.
B. The memory disturbance causes a significant impairment in social or occupational functioning and represents a significant decline from a previous level of functioning.
C. The memory disturbance does not occur exclusively during the course of a delirium or a dementia and persists beyond the usual duration of Alcohol Intoxication and Withdrawal.
D. There is evidence from the history, physical examination, or laboratory findings that the memory disturbance is etiologically related to the persisting effects of alcohol use.

(DSM-IV: p. 162)

Alcohol-Induced Persisting Dementia

A. The development of multiple cognitive deficits manifested by both
   1. memory impairment (impaired ability to learn new information or to recall previously learned information)
   2. one (or more) of the following cognitive disturbances:
      a. aphasia (language disturbance)
      b. apraxia (impaired ability to carry out motor activities despite intact motor function)
      c. agnosia (failure to recognize or identify objects despite intact sensory function)
      d. disturbance in executive functioning (i.e., planning, organizing, sequencing, abstracting)
B. The cognitive deficits in A1 and A2 each cause significant impairment in social or occupational functioning and represent a significant decline from a previous level of functioning.
C. The deficits do not occur exclusively during the course of a delirium and persist beyond the usual duration of Alcohol Intoxication or Withdrawal.
D. There is evidence from the history, physical examination, or laboratory findings that the deficits are etiologically related to the persisting effects of alcohol use.

(DSM-IV: p. 154)

Although most alcoholics do not meet criteria for either of these severe cognitive disorders listed above, many (i.e., approximately 50%) nevertheless demonstrate significant cognitive deficits that can have important effects on their treatment compliance and everyday functioning (see Fig. 18-1 below). According to the DSM-IV, patients with mild to moderate cognitive deficits who meet criteria for Alcohol Dependence, but who do not meet criteria for an Alcohol-Induced Amnestic or Dementia Disorder, are given an additional diagnosis of Alcohol-Related Disorder NOS (American Psychiatric Association, 1994); see the next section for the neurobehavioral and neuroimaging correlates of alcoholics who meet this latter criteria. Refer also to Figure 18-1 for an additional nosology to better characterize the neurocognitive status of alcoholics with extended periods of abstinence (Grant et al., 1987b).

The Use of Questionnaires and Biochemical Markers to Identify Alcoholism and Alcohol-Related Disorders

While the DSM-IV classification system represents one approach to diagnosing alcoholism and alcoholism-related disorders, several others are also available (e.g., the use of questionnaires and biochemical markers).

There are several clinical and research questionnaires that have been developed to identify persons with alcohol-related disorders. These include the ALCADD Test (Manson, 1949), the Michigan Alcoholism Screening Test (Selzer, 1971), the Iowa Scale of Preoccupation with Alcohol (Mulford and Miller, 1960), the Alcohol Use Inventory (Wanberg et al., 1977), the Severity of Alcohol Dependence Questionnaire (Stockwell et al., 1979), the Drinking Profile (Marlatt, 1976), the Lifetime Drinking History (Skinner, 1979), the Alcohol Research Center Intake Interview (Schuckit et al., 1988), the Semi-Structured Assessment for the Genetics of Alcoholism Interview (SSAGA) (Bucholz et al., 1994), and questionnaires constructed by Cahalan and his colleagues (Cahalan, 1978). Psychometrically, research studies have demonstrated that the Alcohol Use Inventory and Alcohol Research Center Intake Interview are well validated; the Michigan Alcoholism Screening Test, Lifetime Drinking History, and the SSAGA have good reliability (Skinner and Sheu, 1982; Bucholz et al., 1994); and the Drinking Profile and the progressive diagnostic schema for alcoholism from the New York State Research Institute on Alcoholism in Buffalo have good clinical utility (Marlatt, 1976; Brown and Lyons, 1981).

In addition to questionnaires designed specifically for alcohol use disorders, there are also a number of standardized psychiatric interview schedules that include subsections that address alcohol use disorders, as well as other psychiatric and medical illnesses. Four of these instruments have been recently reviewed (Grant and Towle, 1990): the Composite International Diagnostic Interview: Authorized Core Version 1.0 (CIDI-Core), developed by the WHO in 1990; the Sched-

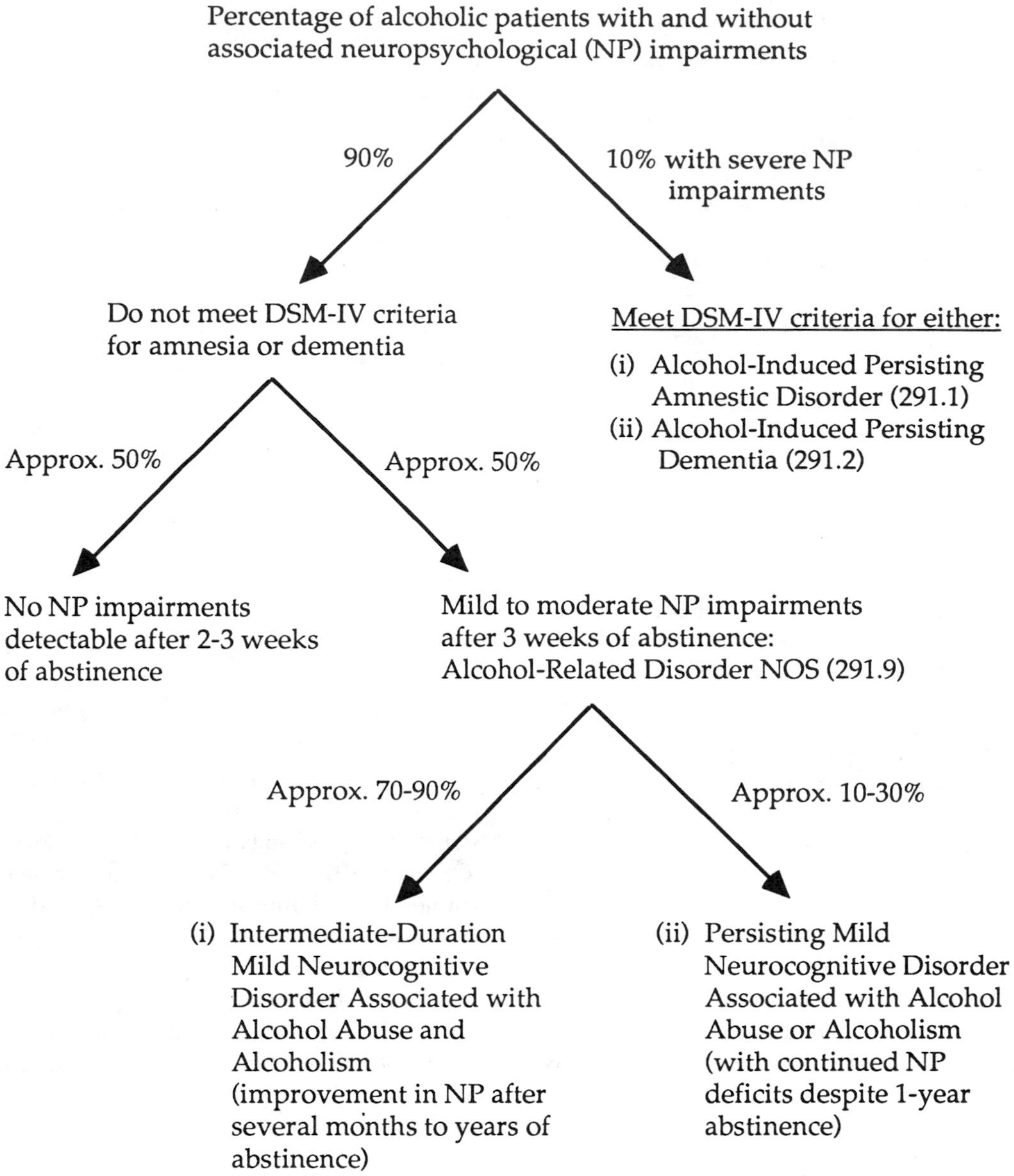

Percentage of alcoholic patients with and without
associated neuropsychological (NP) impairments

90%   10% with severe NP
                        impairments

Do not meet DSM-IV criteria   Meet DSM-IV criteria for either:
for amnesia or dementia
                                     (i) Alcohol-Induced Persisting
                                          Amnestic Disorder (291.1)
                                     (ii) Alcohol-Induced Persisting
Approx. 50%   Approx. 50%   Dementia (291.2)

No NP impairments   Mild to moderate NP impairments
detectable after 2-3 weeks after 3 weeks of abstinence:
of abstinence   Alcohol-Related Disorder NOS (291.9)

Approx. 70-90%   Approx. 10-30%

(i) Intermediate-Duration   (ii) Persisting Mild
     Mild Neurocognitive   Neurocognitive Disorder
     Disorder Associated with   Associated with Alcohol
     Alcohol Abuse and   Abuse or Alcoholism
     Alcoholism   (with continued NP
     (improvement in NP after   deficits despite 1-year
     several months to years of   abstinence)
     abstinence)

Figure 18-1. Prevalence of neuropsychological deficits associated with alcoholism.

ule for Clinical Assessment in Neuropsychiatry (SCAN), developed by the Medical Research Council Social Psychiatry Unit in
1989; the Structured Clinical Interview for
DSM-III-R (SCID) developed in 1988 by the
New York State Psychiatric Institute Biometrics Research Department; and the Alcohol
Use Disorders and Associated Disabilities
Interview Schedule (AUDADIS), developed
in 1989 by the NIAAA.

One limitation of using questionnaires to
detect alcoholism or alcohol-related disorders, however, is that this method usually
relies solely on the subjective report of the
patient or subject, although collateral confirmation is solicited in some cases. One approach to circumvent this problem is to rely
on biochemical markers available from a standard blood and serum draw. For example, it
has been well known for some time that

biochemical markers such as gamma-glutamyl transferase (GGT), aspartate amino-transferase (SGOT), alanine aminotransferase (SGPT), mean corpuscular volume (MCV), and lipoproteins become elevated with heavy alcohol consumption (Barboriak et al., 1980; Eckardt et al., 1981; Shaper et al., 1985; Whelan, 1992), or as the severity of alcohol dependence increases (Monteiro and Masur, 1987).

While the ability to detect whether or not someone has a problem with alcohol consumption by using a single laboratory test has obvious appeal, a number of investigators have reported that biochemical markers lack adequate sensitivity and specificity when used as separate indices of heavy drinking (Garvin et al., 1981; Vanclay et al., 1991; Rosman, 1992; Hoeksema and de Bock, 1993). Diagnostic accuracy does improve, however, when biochemical markers are used in combination (Barboriak et al., 1980; Eckardt et al., 1981; Papoz et al., 1981; Shaper et al., 1985; Halvorson et al., 1993), or when they are supplemented with alcohol screening questionnaires (Levine, 1990), or with information on the history of traumatic injuries (Skinner et al., 1985), although a few studies have demonstrated that questionnaires like the Michigan Alcohol Screening Test may be better at detecting alcoholism than biochemical markers like GGT (Bell and Steensland, 1987; Levine, 1990; Dobkin et al., 1991).

Recent studies using carbohydrate-deficient transferrin (CDT), a new biochemical marker for the detection of alcohol abuse (Rosman, 1992; Potter, 1994), suggest that CDT may have better sensitivity and specificity than other conventional markers and may not be as affected by liver disease as many of the other biochemical markers (Rosman, 1992). Furthermore, serum CDT, which has sensitivity comparable to that of GGT, has been shown to have better specificity (Bell et al., 1994).

There are a number of factors that are likely to contribute to the variable sensitivity and specificity of biochemical markers in detecting heavy drinking and/or alcoholism. For example, Skinner et al. (1985) have em-phasized that the frequency of drinking, the quantity of alcohol consumed per day, and the length of time a person has been abstinent are important factors to consider when evaluating biochemical markers; Irwin and his colleagues (1988) have stressed the importance of examining intrasubject variability (see below). Furthermore, despite the large number of studies demonstrating the efficacy of biochemical markers in "alcoholic" samples, several investigators have cautioned against the use of these markers to identify problem drinking or alcoholism in young persons (Nystrom et al., 1993), psychiatric patients (Latcham, 1986), medical patients seen in family practice (Hoeksema and de Bock, 1993), or community samples (Vanclay et al., 1991).

Many clinicians rely on standard laboratory cutoffs to determine whether a biochemical marker is the "abnormal" range; Irwin and his colleagues, however, have demonstrated that intrasubject variability in blood chemistry markers is more useful in detecting changes in drinking status (Irwin et al., 1988). Specifically, they obtained blood samples from 53 men with a diagnosis of primary alcoholism at discharge (i.e., after 4 weeks of abstinence), as well as at 3 months after discharge, in order to examine how changes in drinking status corresponded with changes in biochemical markers (Irwin et al., 1988). Face-to-face interviews were carried out in order to collect information on drinking status, and at least one resource person was contacted for confirmation of drinking status. Changes in blood chemistry values were calculated and then used to generate rules to reflect whether or not a subject had returned to drinking; a cross-validation was subsequently carried out with a second group of alcoholic men (n = 82) from the same alcohol treatment program. Based on the blood chemistry data, a parallel combination of a percent increase in GGT of $\geq$ 20%, in SGOT of $\geq$ 40% and in SGPT of $\geq$ 20% over discharge values obtained several months earlier was highly sensitive (i.e., 95% of the drinkers were correctly classified) and moderately specific (i.e., 80% of the abstainers were correctly classified) (Irwin et al., 1988);

those alcoholics who remained sober typically had values that either decreased or remained the same at follow-up. The rules that Irwin and his colleagues developed were also useful in classifying alcoholics when their biochemical values fell within the clinical laboratories' so-called "normal" range. Since the publication of this study, other investigators have reported similar results: biochemical markers may be more useful in assessing change in drinking status (Keso and Salaspuro, 1989), particularly decreases in alcohol consumption (Duckert et al., 1992) or abstinence (Keso and Salaspuro, 1989; Pol et al., 1990), than in detecting whether or not a person is "alcoholic."

For more information regarding the sensitivity and specificity of various biochemical markers for alcohol-related disorders, we refer the reader to the following recent reviews (Mihas and Tavassoli, 1992; Allen et al., 1994; Conigrave et al., 1995).

Clinical Course Associated with Alcoholism

Understanding the natural history of alcoholism has practical usefulness for both clinicians and researchers. For clinicians, it can help identify the time course associated with the emergence of various alcohol-related symptoms, and it can dictate when different treatment interventions should be implemented depending on the severity of the alcohol-related symptoms (Schuckit et al., 1993). For researchers in the field of neuropsychology, knowledge of the clinical course of alcoholism is important because of the neuromedical events and systemic illnesses that can often arise during the course of alcoholism (e.g., head injuries, blackouts, hypertension, diabetes, withdrawal seizures, hepatic dysfunction, chronic obstructive pulmonary disease); these can have separate and additive negative effects on the brain independent of the neurotoxic effects of alcohol (see *Multifactorial Etiology of Neuropsychological Deficits*, below).

A recent study by Schuckit and his colleagues (1993) provides useful information about the relative appearance of the various symptoms that occur with alcohol depen-

dence (Schuckit et al., 1993). In their study, 636 male inpatients with primary alcoholism and a mean age and education of 45.0 and 12.8 years, respectively, were administered a structured interview regarding the age at which 21 alcohol-related major life events first occurred; the information from the patients was also further corroborated with at least one resource person. Of the 21 alcohol-related life events, the alcoholics as a group experienced an average of 10.9 events. These alcohol-dependent men experienced several alcohol-related problems by their late twenties (e.g., 96% drank before noon, 74% had binges of drinking lasting for 12 hours straight). By their early thirties, there was evidence that alcohol had begun to interfere with functioning in multiple life areas (e.g., 91% were experiencing a withdrawal syndrome, 82% were having blackouts, 49% were involved in auto accidents, 76% were having morning shakes). By age 34, 86% reported that they had lost control of their drinking. More serious job- and social-related problems occurred in their late thirties (43% had been fired, 61% were divorced or separated). Finally, when alcoholic subjects reached their late thirties and early forties, there was evidence of severe long-term consequences related to alcohol use (i.e., between the ages of 40 and 42, 5% had withdrawal convulsions, 24% had been hospitalized, 37% endorsed that their physician had noted health problems, and 26% had hepatitis/pancreatitis) (Schuckit et al., 1993).

Schuckit and his colleagues further explored whether there were any subgroups within this sample that varied in the emergence of alcohol-related symptoms. Interestingly, the order of occurrence of these 21 symptoms of alcohol dependence was consistent across the sample when they were divided according to subjects' age of onset of Alcohol Dependence (≤ 30 years, > 30 years), or the presence of family history of Alcoholism, a secondary diagnosis of Drug Dependence or Depressive Disorder, or a primary diagnosis of Antisocial Personality Disorder (Schuckit et al., 1993).

The results from the above study suggest

that alcohol-related health consequences are extremely common in alcoholic men, especially when they have reached their late thirties and early forties. It is not until this point in time (i.e., after heavy drinking for 10 to 15 years), that most alcohol-dependent men will seek treatment for their alcohol-related medical problems. If neuropsychological deficits are also present when the alcoholic patient is recently detoxified (i.e., sober for 2 to 3 weeks), one needs to entertain the possibility that the etiology of these deficits is multifactorial. See *Multifactorial Etiology of Neuropsychological Deficits*, below, for a detailed review of the medical problems that arise during the course of alcoholism, or that occur as a consequence of heavy alcohol use (e.g., head injuries sustained during intoxication), which can contribute in both direct and indirect ways to neurobehavioral dysfunction.

Neurobehavioral and Neuroimaging Findings Associated with Alcoholism

While damage to or dysfunction of the functional and structural integrity of the human brain is most striking in the approximately 10% of alcoholic patients who meet criteria for either an Alcohol-Induced Amnestic or Alcohol-Induced Dementia Disorder (Horvath, 1973; American Psychiatric Association, 1994), many of the remaining 90% of alcoholics who do not meet criteria for either of these disorders nevertheless demonstrate clear evidence of brain damage and dysfunction after 2 to 3 weeks of detoxification. See *Wernicke-Korsakoff Syndrome*, below, for a summary of the neurobehavioral and neuroimaging correlates associated with Alcohol-Induced Amnestic Disorder.

The bulk of the neuropsychological studies of alcoholics to date has been performed on recently detoxified alcoholics. In general, the findings are consistent across different samples, and even across national comparisons. For the most part, the "typical" recently detoxified alcoholic studied has been a White male in his mid-forties who has completed a couple of years of college education, and who has a history of heavy alcohol consumption

for the past 10 to 20 years. Usually the assessment has taken place several weeks after admittance to a 28-day alcohol dependence treatment program; most often this has occurred in a Veterans Affairs Medical Center. Neuropsychological testing is generally delayed at least 2 to 3 weeks in order to avoid any acute withdrawal side effects from the cessation of alcohol (e.g., autonomic hyperactivity, tremulousness) and to avoid any possible psychoactive effects of medications administered during acute detoxification (e.g., benzodiazepines) that are given prophylactically to reduce the likelihood of severe withdrawal symptoms (e.g., seizures).

Does Alcohol Cause Brain Damage?

Rather consistent findings have emerged regarding the intellectual and neuropsychological ability patterns of recently detoxified alcoholics. Perhaps the most convincing evidence that chronic heavy alcohol use can lead to brain damage and dysfunction has come from comparisons of recently detoxified alcoholics with patients who have confirmed brain damage.

The first formal and systematic neuropsychological study of alcoholics occurred in 1960 when Reitan and his colleagues compared hospitalized alcoholics with brain-damaged patients and control subjects on the Halstead-Reitan Neuropsychological Test Battery (Fitzhugh et al., 1960). Results from this study indicated that alcoholics performed at levels similar to those of brain-damaged subjects on the Halstead measures and on the Trail Making Test, but more like controls on the Wechsler-Bellevue subtests. Furthermore, the alcoholics, when compared with the controls, exhibited worse performance on the Category Test, the Halstead Impairment Index, and the Tactual Performance Test total time. A subsequent study by these investigators, which included a larger number of subjects, revealed similar findings (Fitzhugh et al., 1965). Since these initial studies, other investigators have confirmed that recently detoxified alcoholics can perform at levels similar to those of brain-damaged patients on the Category Test

(Jones and Parsons, 1971) and the Halstead-Reitan Battery (Miller and Orr, 1980; Goldstein and Shelly, 1982). Furthermore, given the fact that the Halstead Impairment Index (a summary index of impaired performance on seven measures that are generally quite sensitive to the overall condition of the brain) was either significantly higher in alcoholics than nonalcoholic controls, or in the impaired range according to normative data, in 18 of 20 studies reviewed, confirms that alcoholism can cause brain damage and dysfunction (Parsons and Leber, 1981).

Intellectual Performance in Recently Detoxified Alcoholics

Despite clear evidence of brain damage and dysfunction on neuropsychological tests, recently detoxified alcoholics generally perform at levels comparable to those of nonalcoholic controls on Verbal and Full Scale IQ values, but often show lower Performance IQ values because of inferior performances on Block Design, Object Assembly, and Digit Symbol subtests from the Wechsler-Bellevue or Wechsler Adult Intelligence Scales (original or revised versions) (Kleinknecht and Goldstein, 1972; Miller and Orr, 1980; Parsons and Farr, 1981; Tarter and Van Thiel, 1985; Grant, 1987). In the review by Parsons and Leber (1981), the mean Verbal and Performance IQ values of alcoholics across 14 studies was 108.7 and 104.7, respectively; in eight of the studies where subtest scores were reported, Block Design, Object Assembly, and Digit Symbol subtest scores from the WAIS were significantly lower than those of controls in 100%, 89%, and 75% of the studies evaluated, respectively (Parsons and Leber, 1981).

Neuropsychological Deficits in Recently Detoxified Alcoholics

Although not all recently detoxified alcoholics show evidence of brain damage and dysfunction on formal neuropsychological testing, there is a "typical" neurocognitive profile that is generally observed in chronic detoxified alcoholics who are sober for 2 to 4 weeks. That is, alcoholics generally display intact verbal skills and have intelligence quotients within the normal range, but often show impairments on tests of novel problem solving and abstract reasoning, learning and memory, visual-spatial analysis, and complex perceptual-motor integration and on tests of simple motor skills.

Most of the research in the field of alcoholism has involved the study of alcoholic men, but both male and female alcoholics generally show similar patterns of neuropsychological deficits (Fabian et al., 1981; Silberstein and Parsons, 1981; Fabian and Parsons, 1983); women, however, often show deficits after shorter drinking histories than men (Fabian et al., 1981; Acker, 1985; Glenn and Parsons, 1990). On the other hand, some investigators have reported that alcoholic women may escape deficits on learning and memory tests (Sparadeo et al., 1983; Fabian et al., 1984) even when matched on years of alcoholic drinking (Sparadeo et al., 1983). Nevertheless, on balance, both male and female alcoholics, when compared with demographically matched nonalcoholic controls, generally perform less accurately on neuropsychological testing and take more time to complete these tests. They also show reduced neurocognitive efficiency on summary measures that consider both accuracy and time together (Glenn and Parsons, 1990, 1991a), as well as on tests that sample verbal skills, learning and memory, problem solving and abstracting, and perceptual-motor skills (Glenn and Parsons, 1992).

Next, we turn to a more detailed description of the neuropsychological ability patterns that have been generally associated with alcoholism, and refer the reader to a number of excellent reviews that have previously been published for additional information (Kleinknecht and Goldstein, 1972; Tarter, 1980; Chelune and Parker, 1981; Parsons and Farr, 1981; Goldman, 1983; Tarter and Van Thiel, 1985; Eckardt and Martin, 1986; Ryan and Butters, 1986; Grant, 1987; Parsons, 1987; Reed and Grant, 1990; Parsons and Nixon, 1993). It is worth noting that most studies to date of chronic alcoholics have utilized the Halstead-Reitan Neuropsychological Test Battery (HRB) (Parsons and Farr, 1981; Parsons and Leber, 1981; Grant, 1987; Parsons, 1987), often supplemented with the WAIS/WAIS-R and/or WMS/WMS-R, although evaluations of alcoholics have also been carried out using the Luria-Nebraska Neuropsychological Battery (Chmielewski and Golden, 1980; de Obaldia et al., 1981).

Attention and Concentration Skills

Mixed results have been obtained regarding whether alcoholics have deficits in attention and concentration (Miller and Orr, 1980). Tests of attention and concentration from the HRB (Speech Sounds Perception Test and Seashore Rhythm Test) were found to be impaired in 62% and 44% of the alcoholic samples reviewed (Parsons and Leber, 1981).

Abstraction, Problem Solving, and Executive Functioning

Alcoholics most frequently perform in the impaired range on neuropsychological tests that place demands on abstraction, reasoning and problem-solving skills, and cognitive flexibility. For example, alcoholics were impaired on the Category Test in 89% of the studies reviewed (i.e., 17 of 19), relative to controls or normative data that indicated impairment (Parsons and Leber, 1981). Alcoholics have the most difficulty on subtest 4 from the Category Test, a subtest requiring spatial discrimination (Jones and Parsons, 1972); in addition, length of drinking history in alcoholics has been shown to be positively associated with the number of errors on the Category Test (Jones and Parsons, 1971). Deficits have also been noted on other nonverbal reasoning and problem-solving tests—for example, the Raven's Progressive Matrices (Jones and Parsons, 1972) and the Levine Hypothesis Testing procedure (Turner and Parsons, 1988; Schaeffer et al., 1989)—as well as on verbal reasoning and problem-solving measures—for example the Conceptual Level Analogy Test (Yohman and Parsons, 1987; Turner and Parsons, 1988), the Word Finding Test (Reitan, 1972; Turner

and Parsons, 1988), and the Shipley Institute of Living Scale Abstracting Test (Silberstein and Parsons, 1981; Turner and Parsons, 1988).

Tests of cognitive flexibility (e.g., Part B of the Trail Making Test) revealed impairments in 80% of the studies reviewed (i.e., 12 of 15) (Parsons and Leber, 1981). Alcoholics have also been shown to be impaired on the Wisconsin Card Sorting Test (WCST). In general, they make more total errors and require more trials to reach the criterion level (Tarter and Parsons, 1971; Joyce and Robbins, 1991; Beatty et al., 1993), and tend to make elevated rates of perseverative responses and errors (Tarter and Parsons, 1971; Joyce and Robbins, 1991; Beatty et al., 1993). It has been suggested that this pattern of performance on the WCST reflects a deficit in the ability to sustain and persist with problem-solving tasks (Tarter and Parsons, 1971). When one examines the effects of age and length of drinking history on WCST performance, younger alcoholics tend to show less deficits (Cynn, 1992), whereas considerably more deficits are evident in older alcoholics and in those with more than 10 years of drinking (Tarter, 1973). Finally, Parsons and colleagues have also demonstrated that alcoholics have problem-solving deficits on ecologically valid measures of abstraction (e.g., on a Piagetian-type task [Nixon and Parsons, 1991]), and on an Adaptive Skills Battery (Patterson et al., 1988).

Visual-Spatial and Complex Perceptual-Motor Integration

Complex perceptual-motor deficits are common in alcoholics. One of the more common tests that assesses this cognitive domain is the Tactual Performance Test from the HRB, which has previously revealed impairments in 84% of the 19 studies reviewed by Parsons and Leber (1981). Deficits in visuoperceptual and visuospatial processing also occur, both on tests with a motor component (e.g., Visual Search [Glosser et al., 1977; Bertera and Parsons, 1978]) and those without (e.g., on the Embedded Figures Test [Donovan et al., 1976; Brandt et al., 1983]).

Learning and Memory

Initial evaluations of learning and memory performance using the Memory Quotient (MQ) from the Wechsler Memory Scale (WMS) revealed that alcoholics generally exhibit intact memory functioning and have comparable memory quotient relative to their IQ values (Butters et al., 1977; Parsons and Prigatano, 1977; Løberg, 1980a; Ryan and Butters, 1980a). However, although alcoholics without memory complaints were comparable to nonalcoholics on the MQ from the WMS, alcoholics were found to be impaired relative to controls when memory tests were made more difficult (Ryan and Butters, 1980a; Brandt et al., 1983). Later modifications to the original WMS (Russell, 1975), which resulted in separate learning, recall, and retention measures for verbal and visual information, revealed that some alcoholics do have mild deficits in learning and memory for both verbal and figural information (Hightower and Anderson, 1986; Nixon et al., 1987). In the study by Nixon and colleagues, using Russell's modification to the WMS (Russell, 1975), alcoholics were found to recall less verbal and figural information at immediate and delay conditions, with both verbal and figural learning being affected to the same degree (Nixon et al., 1987). When these investigators calculated savings or retention scores for both groups (i.e., taking into account the amount of information that had been acquired when evaluating recall scores), alcoholics were not found to differ from controls. What this pattern of performance on the revised WMS suggests is that alcoholics have deficits with acquisition and encoding, and possibly with retrieval, but not with retention of information once adjustments are made for the amount of information acquired (Nixon et al., 1987).

Similar findings have also been obtained using the WMS-R (Ryan and Lewis, 1988). That is, alcoholics differed from controls in level of performance on all five summary measures from the WMS-R, but not with respect to their pattern of performance. Although the authors of this study did not make

a distinction between learning ability and savings or retention of information, the differences between the alcoholics and controls on the Memory summary scores (i.e., Verbal, Visual, and General Memory) indicate that alcoholics have a generalized learning impairment, while the difference scores between General Memory and Delayed Memory for each group were virtually identical, thus suggesting similar savings or retention of information across both groups. We would like to stress that it is important to make a distinction between learning and savings or "memory," because if an alcoholic has both a learning *and* a retention problem, a separate neuropathological process may be present (e.g., Alcohol-Induced Persisting Dementia or Amnestic Disorder).

Over the years, there has been controversy in the literature regarding whether alcoholics perform differentially on verbal and visual learning and memory tasks. For example, several studies have indicated that alcoholics are impaired on visual learning (Leber et al., 1981; Fabian et al., 1984), but perform normally on verbal learning tests (Leber et al., 1981; Yohman and Parsons, 1985). More recent studies, however, have shown that alcoholics have deficits also on verbal learning tests. For example, alcoholics were found to have acquisition deficits on the Luria Memory word test, but comparable rates of retention (Sherer et al., 1992). Using the California Verbal Learning Test (CVLT), Kramer and colleagues demonstrated that alcoholics have deficits on immediate and free recall, reduced performance on recognition testing, and produce more intrusions and false-positive errors than expected (Kramer et al., 1989). Consistent with studies using the WMS and WMS-R, alcoholics exhibited comparable retention on the CVLT to that of controls, when adjustments were made for the amount of material acquired. A similar pattern of immediate and free recall and recognition performance has also been obtained using the Rey Auditory Verbal Learning Test (Tuck and Jackson, 1991).

A number of investigators have questioned the external validity of the learning and memory findings obtained in the laboratory with alcoholics, and have subsequently developed more ecologically valid learning and memory tests. For example, Becker and his colleagues compared both young and old alcoholics on an ecologically relevant task (i.e., learning to associate names with faces) (Becker et al., 1983b). They found that alcoholics made more errors and were not able to achieve the same criterion level as a demographically matched group of controls (Becker et al., 1983b). In contrast, their recognition performance for the faces and names, and their retention was similar to controls. Becker and his colleagues attributed the learning problem in alcoholics to a deficit in forming associations during encoding, rather than to a visuoperceptual deficit (Becker et al., 1983b). Learning impairments on this face-name test have also been replicated with a VA sample of alcoholics (Schaeffer and Parsons, 1987), as well as with a community sample of male and female alcoholics (Everett et al., 1988).

Simple Motor Skills

The evidence for simple motor deficits in alcoholics has been inconsistent. While one study showed that alcoholics have deficits on tests of fine-motor coordination, but not necessarily on a test of grip strength (Parsons et al., 1972), another study reported impairments in fine-motor coordination, grip strength, and motor speed (Tarter and Jones, 1971). Impairments in motor speed (Finger Tapping) have been reported in 29% of studies reviewed (i.e., four of 14 studies) (Parsons and Leber, 1981). Another study showed that alcoholics were 9.3% slower than age-matched controls on motor speed (York and Biederman, 1991). Because polyneuropathy occurs in 20% to 74% of alcoholics (Feuerlein, 1977; Franceschi et al., 1984; Neundorfer et al., 1984; Tuck and Jackson, 1991), it is possible that the variability in motor test performance in alcoholics may be the result of a combination of peripheral and/or central nerve dysfunction or deterioration.

Given the robust nature of the neuropsy-

chological deficits observed in alcoholics, we next turn to a summary of the neuroimaging, electrophysiological, and neuropathological correlates associated with alcoholism.

Neuroimaging Findings in Alcoholics

Neuroradiological techniques have evolved considerably over the past 40 years. Pneumoencephalographic studies provided the first evidence of ventricular dilatation in alcoholics, reflecting cortical and cerebellar atrophy (Haug, 1968; Brewer and Perrett, 1971). This technique, in which air is exchanged for cerebrospinal fluid (CSF), enabled investigators to examine the contrast between cerebral tissue and CSF-containing spaces. However, because of the associated morbidity and pain to subjects, this technique never achieved widespread use.

The advent of computed tomography (CT) quickly replaced pneumoencephalography. A number of CT reviews have appeared in recent years (Wilkinson, 1982; Carlen and Wilkinson, 1983; Bergman, 1987; Carlen and Wilkinson, 1987; Ron, 1987; Wilkinson, 1987). These reviews, from groups of investigators in various countries, provide extensive cross-validation of the neuroradiological abnormalities in heterogeneous groups of alcoholics. In general, increases of CSF in subarachnoid spaces and in the ventricular system (i.e., lateral and third ventricles) were interpreted to reflect cortical and subcortical atrophy, respectively. Increases in cortical CSF have generally been observed in alcoholics of all ages, whereas increased CSF in the ventricular system has predominantly been seen in older and nutritionally compromised alcoholics. Cortical atrophy tends to be more evident bilaterally in frontal and frontal-temporal-parietal areas of the brain, although reduced density only in the left hemisphere of alcoholics has been reported (Golden et al., 1981). In a review of 14 CT studies by Cala and colleagues, the rate of cerebral atrophy ranged from 4% to 100% (Cala and Mastaglia, 1981). The extremely large variability in the prevalence rate of atrophy reflects to a large degree the referral source of alcoholics tested; many of the earlier studies either did not screen for adverse neuromedical and neurological abnormalities, or had selected alcoholics patients for clinical suspicion of central nervous system damage (Bergman et al., 1980a; Carlen and Wilkinson, 1980; Ron, 1983).

In one of the largest studies of alcoholics using CT imaging, Bergman and colleagues (1980a) demonstrated that a group of 148 male alcoholic patients had significantly more evidence of cerebral atrophy, relative to a random sample of men (n = 200) not diagnosed with alcoholism. Cortical changes were evident across the entire age range in the alcoholics, whereas central changes accelerated with increasing age, particularly in those alcoholics with longer drinking histories (Bergman et al., 1980a).

Using a semiautomated method for estimating CSF volumes obtained from CT imaging (Zatz et al., 1982), Jernigan and her colleagues examined fluid volumes in various intracranial zones in 46 male chronic alcoholics (excluding those with liver disease) and compared them with 31 male normal volunteers (Jernigan et al., 1982). Correcting for cerebral changes that occur with normal aging (i.e., by using z-scores corrected for changes due to aging), these investigators found that alcoholics had significantly more CSF than the control group on all sulcal measures (i.e., sulcal score at low and high convexity sections, and at the level of the ventricles). Group differences, however, on the measure of ventricular CSF volume fell short of significance ($p < 0.06$). No significant correlations were observed between the number of years of alcoholic drinking and any CSF measurement. In a subsequent investigation, Pfefferbaum and his colleagues examined the vulnerability of various brain structures to age, level of alcohol consumption, and nutritional status (Pfefferbaum et al., 1988). They utilized a similar semiautomated technique to measure the percentage of fluid at the ventricles and cortical sluci, and found that male alcoholics as a group had more CSF than controls for both ventricular and sulcal CT measures. Interestingly, the ventricular enlargement was evident only

in older alcoholics, whereas increases in sulcal CSF were evident across the entire age range. Years of alcoholic drinking were correlated with both cortical and ventricular CT measures. In addition, the central ventricular measure, but not the cortical measures, was significantly associated with a measure of body weight, a body mass index, hematocrit, and mean corpuscular volume, suggesting that nutritional status may have been compromised in these alcoholics. These results support the theory that cerebral structures (cortical and subcortical) are differentially affected by the neurotoxic effects of alcohol. That is, alcohol appears to affect cortical structures, regardless of age, whereas subcortical structures appear to be more affected by nutritional status (i.e., acute thiamine deficiency) and/or age.

Most of the CT studies have been conducted with alcoholic men, but CT studies carried out in Sweden (Bergman, 1985, 1987), England (Jacobson, 1986a,b), and Germany (Mann et al., 1992) have indicated that women also demonstrate similar abnormal brain morphology, although the abnormalities tend to be evident after a much shorter drinking history and with a lower daily intake of alcohol, than they are with alcoholic men. Given recent reports that drinking patterns of women are changing, and are becoming much more like that of men, this trend could have serious medical and neuropsychological consequences (Mercer and Khavari, 1990).

Increases in CSF in chronic alcoholics have consistently been demonstrated on CT scanning using linear measurements, clinical ratings, and volumetric analyses. While inferences have been made regarding the meaning of these CSF changes, studies using magnetic resonance imaging (MRI) over the last several years have enabled researchers to address more directly whether cortical and subcortical CSF changes reflect volume reductions in cortical and/or subcortical tissues generally and, more specifically, in gray and/or white matter areas.

Jernigan and her colleagues examined 28 chronic alcoholics and 36 age- and sex-matched nonalcoholics with MRI and brain morphometric analyses (Jernigan et al., 1991a). The focus of their study was to (1) evaluate the relationship between CSF volume increases and gray matter losses, as well as the signal hyperintensities occurring in the white matter, and (2) correlate the cognitive losses observed in the alcoholics with various MR indices. The results from their study indicated that the increases in CSF (in cortical and ventricular areas) were associated with significant volume reductions in specific cerebral gray matter structures (both cortical and subcortical). Specifically, the chronic alcoholics demonstrated significant volume reductions in subcortical structures (e.g., caudate and diencephalon) as well as in cortical volumes (e.g., mesial temporal cortex, dorsolateral frontal cortex, and parieto-occipital cortex). In addition, the alcoholics had significantly more white matter signal hyperintensities than did the controls. With respect to the relationship between neuropsychological performance and MRI indices, there were substantially more significant correlations between cognitive measures and subcortical fluid volumes (i.e., six of 13) than with cortical fluid volumes (i.e., three of 13 were significant); gray and white matter volumes did not relate in any significant way to cognitive measures. Jernigan and her colleagues also noted that the reductions in cortical tissue in the superior frontal and parietal areas in alcoholics are consistent with neuropathological reports (see results from Harper's group listed below).

Research at the Palo Alto VA Medical Center and Stanford University (Pfefferbaum et al., 1992) has extended the findings reported by Jernigan and her group in San Diego. A similar semiautomated procedure with MRI was used, which allowed subcortical regions to be segmented into CSF and brain tissue, and cortical regions into CSF, gray matter and white matter. Forty-nine alcoholics were tested 3 to 4 weeks after their last drink and compared with 43 healthy controls. Adjusting for the effects of aging, the alcoholics had decreased parenchymal volume and increased CSF (alcoholics had 30% more CSF than controls); these included significant reductions in cortical and subcortical gray mat-

ter volume, as well as loss of white matter (Pfefferbaum et al., 1992). Other groups of investigators, using MRI, have also commented on changes in white matter of alcoholics (Chick et al., 1989; Gallucci et al., 1989). Most current research studies use MRI, rather than CT, when available; however, correlations between CT- and MRI-derived estimates of cortical and ventricular CSF volumes are highly correlated (>0.80), although MRI tends to produce larger sulcal volumes, whereas both CT and MRI appear to be equally sensitive to ventricular volumes (Pfefferbaum et al., 1993).

Relation of Neuroimaging and Neuropsychological Variables

Attempts to find associations between neuropsychological test performance and brain imaging correlates have generally been disappointing (Pfefferbaum et al., 1988; Jernigan et al., 1991a; Rourke et al., 1993). That is, while Pearson correlations between CT measures and neuropsychological performance with alcoholics were highly significant in most cases (i.e., 33 of 45 were significant), only two of 45 remained significant once age was partialled out (Bergman et al., 1980b). Bergman and colleagues also did not find any significant correlations between alcohol consumption or neuropsychological test performance with CT brain measures in a large random sample of men (n = 200) and women (n = 200) not diagnosed with alcoholism (Bergman et al., 1983).

Nevertheless, there are reports in the literature of associations between specific neuropsychological tests and CSF volumes, or structures adjacent to these fluid-filled areas. For example, in one study, CT scan measures of the third ventricle, but not the lateral ventricles, were associated with memory performance in male alcoholics (Acker et al., 1987); in another study, mean CT thalamic density was shown to be correlated with verbal and symbol digit paired-associated learning test performance (Gebhardt et al., 1984). Finally, Bergman and colleagues reported that learning and memory performance was related to central changes in 106 alcoholics, whereas performance on the Halstead Impairment Index was related to cortical changes (Bergman et al., 1980c).

Attempts at correlating CT scan findings with drinking history have yielded results that have been remarkably disappointing (Ron, 1983). According to Ron, correlations between indices of atrophy and drinking history are either insignificant or low order in most instances, and when they are significant, these correlations tend to be markedly reduced when appropriate age corrections are introduced.

Functional Neuroimaging: Cerebral Blood Flow and Metabolism in Alcoholics

Cerebral blood flow (CBF) is normally proportional to metabolic brain activity (except under severe pathological conditions such as significant cerebrovascular disease), and is therefore a sensitive measure of neuronal function. Blood flow imaging techniques— for example, xenon injection and inhalation, positron-emission tomography (PET), and single photon emitted computed tomography (SPECT)—have the advantage over computed tomography and magnetic resonance brain imaging, in that they provide a window through which the brain can be examined in a more functional and dynamic state. Studies of CBF in "normal" healthy volunteers have demonstrated an inverse relationship with age and cerebrovascular status (Shaw et al., 1984; Gur et al., 1987). A gender effect has also been observed, with men showing reduced CBF as compared with women (Mathew et al., 1986), although this effect disappears after the sixth decade of life (Shaw et al., 1984).

Most studies of chronic alcoholics without the Wernicke-Korsakoff syndrome have shown reductions and/or abnormalities, particularly in frontal and parietal areas, using both cerebral blood flow (Rogers et al., 1983; Ishikawa et al., 1986; Berglund et al., 1987; Hata et al., 1987; Dally et al., 1988; Melgaard et al., 1990; Mathew and Wilson, 1991; Erbas et al., 1992; Caspari et al., 1993; Nicolas et al., 1993) and brain metabolism techniques (Samson et al., 1986; Sachs et al.,

1987; Wik et al., 1988; Gilman et al., 1990; Volkow et al., 1992; Adams et al., 1993; Wang et al., 1993; Volkow et al., 1994), which tend to improve after several weeks of abstinence (Ishikawa et al., 1986; Berglund et al., 1987; Hata et al., 1987; Caspari et al., 1993; Volkow et al., 1994).

Electrophysiological Findings in Alcoholics

Neurophysiological aberrations (EEG and event-related potentials—ERPs) have frequently been observed in alcoholics. In general, differences on electrophysiological measures in alcoholics seem to depend on recency and intensity of alcohol use, family history loading for alcoholism, which particular component of the electrophysiological response is examined, and what tasks or stimuli are used to elicit the electrophysiological response.

Alcoholics have been shown to have increased latencies and longer transmission times on auditory brain stem potentials, suggesting possible demyelination (Begleiter et al., 1981). In one study, 41% of alcoholics had abnormal auditory brain stem responses, which were associated with the age of the subject, CT evidence of cerebral atrophy, and severity of neurological complications (Chu et al., 1982). In a subsequent follow-up study with alcoholics by Chu, the CT abnormalities (i.e., enlarged brain stem cistern or possible brain stem atrophy) were confirmed to be associated with abnormal auditory brain responses (Chu, 1985).

Alcoholics have also been shown to have reduced amplitudes of N100, N200, P300, and increased latency of P300 (Emmerson et al., 1987; Miyazato and Ogura, 1993; Kaseda et al., 1994). In a review by Oscar-Berman, P300 amplitude (i.e., a late positive waveform elicited during the discrimination of a stimulus) was found to be the most reliable finding (more reliable than the P300 latency) in abstinent alcoholics (Oscar-Berman, 1987).

Event-related potential measures are reliable over time. Similar test-retest correlations for visual and auditory ERP measures were observed in controls and alcoholics, with N1 and P3 amplitudes the most reliable

(Sinha et al., 1992). However, those alcoholics who relapse show differences on ERP measures when compared to those who remain abstinent (Parsons, 1994b). There may also be gender effects on ERPs, given that male alcoholics show abnormalities on ERP (N1, NdA, and P3 amplitudes) whereas females do not (Parsons et al., 1990b). There have been several attempts to correlate ERP and neuropsychological test findings. When significant correlations are found, they tend to occur between P300 amplitude and/or P300 latency and tests of perceptual-motor functioning (Patterson et al., 1989; Parsons et al., 1990b), and on tests of delayed figural memory (Patterson et al., 1989). The relationship between ERP and memory may not be as reliable; another group of investigators did not find significant correlations between ERP measures and MQ score from the WMS (Romani and Cosi, 1989).

Abnormal ERP findings, particularly reduced average P300 amplitudes, are more pronounced in alcoholics who are family history positive (FH+)—that is, have alcoholic first-degree relatives—relative to family history negative (FH−) alcoholics (Patterson et al., 1987; Whipple et al., 1988; Parsons et al., 1990b; Pfefferbaum et al., 1991). Because the reduced P300 in the FH+ alcoholics has been shown to be independent of lifetime alcohol consumption, several investigators have suggested that it may be a biological marker of risk for alcoholism (Begleiter et al., 1984; Pfefferbaum et al., 1991). As such, there is growing evidence that the P300 is genetically determined, and it may also be involved with the dopaminergic system, particularly the D_2 dopamine receptor gene (Noble et al., 1994).

Significant correlations between ERP and CT brain measures have also been established (Ogura and Miyazato, 1991). In one study, N100 was related to ventricular size thought to reflect subcortical structures, whereas the P300 was related to both cortical and subcortical structures in the alcoholics, as indicated by the width of the cortical sulci and the ventricular system (Kaseda et al., 1994). In addition, alcoholics with CT abnormalities (i.e., enlarged cortical sulci) show further reduced P300 relative to alcoholics without CT abnormalities (Begleiter et al., 1980).

Neuropathology in Alcoholism

Further evidence that alcoholism causes brain damage has come from autopsy studies (Courville, 1955; Torvik et al., 1982; Torvik, 1987; Harper and Kril, 1990). These studies indicate that alcoholics have reduced brain weights (Harper and Blumbergs, 1982; Torvik, 1987), as well as increased pericerebral spaces that reflect changes in the proportion of brain volume to intracranial volume (Harper and Kril, 1985; Harper et al., 1990).

Since the mid-1980s, Harper and his colleagues have carried out a number of morphometric and histological examinations of the brains of alcoholics. The first study in this series demonstrated that chronic alcoholics have significant reductions in white matter tissue in the cerebral hemispheres, as well as increased ventricular volume, but no significant differences in the mean volume of cortical gray matter, or in the volume of the basal ganglia (Harper et al., 1985). These morphometric differences were also most pronounced in those alcoholics with a history of cirrhosis or Wernicke's encephalopathy (Harper et al., 1988a). Three subsequent studies were carried out and focused on specific white and gray matter volumes. Specifically, Harper and his colleagues found a reduction in the size of the corpus callosum (Harper and Kril, 1988) and a selective loss in the number of neurons in the superior frontal cortex, but not in the motor cortex (Harper et al., 1987; Kril and Harper, 1989), or in the frontal cingulate and temporal cortices (Kril and Harper, 1989); the reductions in the superior frontal cortex occurred mainly in the terminal branches of the arbor (Harper and Corbett, 1990) and in neurons greater than 90 μ^2 (Harper and Kril, 1989). In addition to the selective loss of superior frontal neurons, a significant reduction in the mean neuronal surface area was also noted in the superior frontal as well as the motor and cingulate cortical areas (Kril and Harper, 1989). These latter data indicate that shrinkage of the neuronal cell body is quite wide-spread in a number of cortical areas, as compared to actual neuronal loss, and may provide the basis for the clinical improvements on neurobehavioral testing and on neuroimaging in alcoholics through rearborization once abstinence is achieved (Harper and Kril, 1990). This possibility seems tenable, especially given the results from animal studies showing dendritic alterations with chronic ethanol treatment (McMullen et al., 1984; Durand et al., 1989), as well as recovery in dendritic morphology with abstinence (McMullen et al., 1984) in the hippocampus (King et al., 1988), particularly in the terminal segments of this structure (Pentney et al., 1989; Pentney, 1991).

With respect to changes at the neuroreceptor level, a 40% reduction in the density of cholinergic muscarinic receptors was found in the frontal cortex of alcoholics, following a histological examination that compared the brains of 30 alcoholics to 49 age-matched controls who were nondemented (Freund and Ballinger, 1988). In a follow-up study, these investigators demonstrated similar reductions in the putamen (i.e., 40% of cholinergic muscarinic receptors), but not in receptor densities of benzodiazepine receptors (Freund and Ballinger, 1989). These investigators suggest that neuronal loss and/or the loss of respective receptors in the brains of alcoholics is not random, and that alcohol may affect certain receptors in specific brain areas (Freund and Ballinger, 1989). In a more recent study, muscarinic receptors were found to be reduced by 40% in temporal cortex, as well as in frontal and putamen areas, while benzodiazepine receptors decreased by 30% in the hippocampus, 30% in the frontal cortex, but not in the putamen or the temporal cortex (Freund and Ballinger, 1991).

In addition to cerebral gray matter changes with alcoholism, a number of investigators have shown that alcohol may also cause a disproportionate atrophy of white matter (de la Monte, 1988; Jensen and Pakkenberg, 1993). In one study, alcoholics had similar brain weights and subcortical nuclei size, when compared with a demographically matched control group, but had evidence of mild atrophy of the cerebral cortex, enlargement of the ventricular system, and moderate atrophy of white matter that corresponded well to amount of ventricular enlargement (de la Monte, 1988). Support for the differential effects on cerebral white matter with heavy exposure to alcohol is also supported by a recent neuropathological animal study (Hansen et al., 1991).

Proposed Theoretical Models to Explain the Effects of Alcoholism on Brain Functioning

Right Hemisphere Dysfunction Model

In 1972, Jones and Parsons suggested that the right hemisphere might be more vulnerable to long-term alcohol exposure than the left hemisphere (Jones and Parsons, 1972). This led to the right hemisphere dysfunction (RHD) model of alcoholism. In view of the gross structural similarity of the two hemispheres of the brain, this was a new as well as intriguing hypothesis. In support of the RHD model, in connection with heavy alcohol use, prominent difficulties have been observed with visuospatial integration, disproportionately worse Performance IQ than Verbal IQ, and impaired motor regulation of the left hand (Parsons et al., 1972), all findings that could implicate RHD. Subsequent studies by Parsons and colleagues, as well as by other investigators, have provided further support for the RHD model, as indicated by the pattern of performance on the Tactual Performance Test—reduced performance with the left hand by right-handed individuals (Fabian et al., 1981; Jenkins and Parsons, 1981), reduced performance on a visual search test (Chandler and Parsons, 1977), and worse performance on the Rey-Osterrieth Complex Figure Test relative to a verbal learning test performance (Miglioni et al., 1979). Several neuropsychological follow-up studies (Page and Schaub, 1977; Schau et al., 1980; Berglund et al., 1987) also provide support for the RHD model. Using experimental techniques to study brain lateralization, Kostandov et al. (1982)

found that using a paradigm to study differences in left and right visual field perception and lateral evoked potentials, both nonalcoholics given alcohol and abstinent alcoholics evidenced a slower processing rate in the right than in the left hemisphere (Kostandov et al., 1982). Consistent with this finding, male alcoholics have also been shown to exhibit a pattern of RHD on a dichotic listening task (Drake et al., 1990).

Despite the research supporting the RHD model, there are, however, a number of problems with this model. For example, tasks generally thought to be "right hemispheric" are not entirely specific to that brain region. Further, many of the "right hemisphere" tasks are inherently harder, or more novel than "left hemisphere" tasks. Thus, what we might be measuring is selective difficulty, which alcoholics experience on more demanding tests. In addition, recovery for such "right hemisphere" functions might also take more time. Sex differences may play a role; in a review of 14 studies in general neuropsychology, men with left and right-sided lesions showed the expected VIQ-PIQ differences, whereas women did not show such a pattern (Inglis and Lawson, 1981). Similarly, male alcoholics were found to exhibit the RHD pattern on dichotic listening, but not alcoholic women (Drake et al., 1990). Also, women show less impairment on visuospatial and tactile-spatial tests, which may suggest that less lateralization in brain organization occurs in women; if this were the case, one may also expect less dramatic lateralization differences (Silberstein and Parsons, 1979). Depressive symptomatology, which frequently occurs in alcoholics undergoing detoxification, has been shown to relate significantly to impaired Performance IQ in alcoholics (Løberg, 1980b). Because many "right hemisphere" tests are timed, depression-related lack of motivation and psychomotor retardation might contribute to poor performance, although there is no strong evidence to support this mechanism.

Several additional studies are inconsistent with the RHD model. Prigatano (1980) reported that men tested before disulfiram treatment had higher Performance than Verbal IQ values (Prigatano, 1980). Also, although alcoholics had lower Performance relative to Verbal IQ values, there were no differences in left or right hand performance on the Tactual Performance Test, the Finger Tapping Test, or on Finger Agnosia or Finger-Tip Writing tests (Barron and Russell, 1992). Furthermore, in one study, motor speed was found to be slower in the dominant as compared to the nondominant hand, and significantly more static tremor was found in the right than the left hand (Løberg, 1980a). Adams and his colleagues found practically the same level on Performance and Verbal IQ's at initial testing for both recently detoxified and long-term abstinent male alcoholics (Grant et al., 1979a), and a quantitatively higher Performance IQ than Verbal IQ for both groups 1 year later (Adams et al., 1980). The latter, may, of course, be due to the effect of practice on timed performance tests. O'Leary and colleagues found Performance IQ and Verbal IQ to be equal in field-independent alcoholics (O'Leary et al., 1977a). Fitzhugh and colleagues found quantitatively higher Performance than Verbal IQ in both studies of alcoholic male subjects (Fitzhugh et al., 1960, 1965). While alcoholics frequently perform poorly on the WAIS Block Design subtest, they do not resemble RHD patients in their pattern of performance (Akshoomoff et al., 1989). Using a dichotic listening paradigm, Ellis (1990) found that both hemispheres were affected by alcoholism and aging. Finally, an extensive review of the RHD model by Ellis and Oscar-Berman (1989) found similar patterns of functional laterality with alcoholism.

Frontal Lobe Dysfunction Model

Another hypothesis that has been proposed to explain the neuropsychological deficits observed in alcoholics is the frontal lobe dysfunction model (Parsons and Leber, 1981) and the fronto-limbic-diencephalic dysfunction model (Tarter, 1973, 1975). If this axis is extended to include frontoparietal regions, the brain stem, and the vermis of the cerebellum, it is certainly compatible with structural and functional evidence of alcohol-related findings in intermediate and long-term alcoholism. Yet it is distinct from the hypothesis of lateralized and also diffuse damage. Tarter's hypothesis does reconcile pneumoencephalographic, CT, and pathological findings, which generally show symmetrical lesions, although there is one study that reported less density in the left hemisphere using CT densitometry (Golden et al., 1981). However, given the known variability of densitometric measurements, and the fact that these findings have not been replicated, the findings of Golden et al. remain tenuous.

Nevertheless, the lack of CT support for brain asymmetry in alcoholism need not reflect the RHD model, because functional asymmetry is possible despite symmetric CT findings (and, conversely, patients are sometimes functionally intact despite clear CT abnormalities; see Lewin, 1980). Tarter suggests that the commonly observed deficits of alcoholics in categorizing or abstraction (in the absence of other severe impairment) is very consistent with selective frontal lobe dysfunction. The finding of Berglund and others that frontal regional blood flow was most clearly related to Block Design performance may also imply that of the different brain systems relevant for such a task, the frontal lobes play a significant part at least in the early abstinence phase in alcoholics.

Diffuse or Generalized Dysfunction Model

Two studies carried out by Goldstein and Shelly provide support for the diffuse or generalized dysfunction model associated with alcoholism. Using the neuropsychological key approach, alcoholics have been shown to have a diffuse pattern of deficits (Goldstein and Shelly, 1980). In a subsequent evaluation by Goldstein, right-handed alcoholics were compared with right-handed brain-damaged patients who had well-documented left hemisphere damage, right hemisphere damage, frontal or frontal-temporal lesions, parietal, occipital, or parieto-occipital lesions, and diffuse brain damage not associated with alcoholism (Goldstein and Shelly, 1982). Alcohol-

ics with an Average Impairment Rating greater than 1.55 were included and compared to the brain-damaged patients; all recently detoxified alcoholics performed in the brain-damage range on the AIR. Two discriminant function analyses were carried out, one including both sensory-motor and cognitive tests, and the other including only the cognitive tests. Alcoholics were often classified as similar to patients with diffuse brain damage of nonalcoholic etiology, when compared with brain-damaged subjects with anterior, posterior, and diffuse pathology. When alcoholics were compared with left, right, and diffuse brain-damaged patients, using both cognitive and sensory-motor measures, alcoholics were more similar to the diffuse brain-damaged group. Eliminating the sensory-motor measures led to a slight indication of right hemisphere dysfunction, but this was not dramatic (Goldstein and Shelly, 1982).

Premature Aging Model

There are two variants of the premature aging model: the accelerated aging hypothesis and the increased vulnerability hypothesis. In the accelerated aging version, both young and old alcoholics perform at inferior levels on neuropsychological tests relative to their age-matched controls (Noonberg et al., 1985). With respect to the increased vulnerability hypothesis, alcoholics and controls perform similarly then later diverge, with the alcoholics showing increasing deficits with age relative to the controls. Much of the support for the premature aging hypothesis has come from studies showing similarities between young alcoholics and old nonalcoholic controls. For example, although alcoholics and controls as a group performed similarly on the Shipley Vocabulary, and the Comprehension and Similarities subtests from the WAIS, the young alcoholics performed significantly worse than both the young and old controls on the Brain Age Quotient (BAQ), with the latter groups performing similarly. When the individual tests from the BAQ were examined (not corrected for age), the overall pattern on the individual subtests from the BAQ was similar across groups, with the young alcoholics performing intermediate to the young and old controls (Hochla and Parsons, 1982); length of alcoholism history or duration of abstinence was not related to performance in the alcoholics on the BAQ. Although there are a number of other studies that have supported the premature aging model (Blusewicz et al., 1977a,b; Parsons and Leber, 1981; Hochla and Parsons, 1982), more recent studies do not (Ryan and Butters, 1984; Burger et al., 1987; Kramer et al., 1989).

Grant and associates (1984) found that whereas both recently abstinent alcoholic status and age (i.e., growing older) were related to a decline in learning and problem solving, aging but not alcoholism was associated with reduction in psychomotor speed and attention (Grant et al., 1984). Furthermore, there were no alcohol by age interactions. These data cast some doubt on the premature aging mechanism, and suggest that aging and alcoholism have independent effects on the brain, a finding that was supported in a more recent study that found both quantitative and qualitative differences in verbal learning performance between alcoholics and controls using the California Verbal Learning Test (Kramer et al., 1989).

Wernicke-Korsakoff Syndrome/ Alcohol-Induced Persisting Amnestic Disorder

Neurobehavioral Findings

The Wernicke-Korsakoff Syndrome (WKS), also referred to as Alcohol-Induced Persisting Amnestic Disorder in DSM-IV, has been well researched over the past several decades and is described in more detail in several recent reviews (Butters and Salmon, 1986; Martin et al., 1986; Butters and Granholm, 1987; Salmon and Butters, 1987; Martin et al., 1989; Jacobson et al., 1990; Salmon et al., 1993).

The Wernicke part of the syndrome involves the presentation of a clinical triad of symptoms, which include global confusion or delirium, abnormal eye movements (e.g.,

ophthalmoplegia, nystagmus), and gait ataxia. Confabulation, if present, occurs predominantly in the early stages of the WKS. It is now well established that this clinical triad arises because of a severe thiamine deficiency, and if not properly treated, death may ensue after several weeks. However, with aggressive treatment, involving large doses of thiamine supplementation, the delirium clears, and the ophthalmoplegia and ataxia improve dramatically, although other features such as peripheral neuropathy and amnesia usually persist. These residual symptoms have come to be referred to as the alcoholic Korsakoff syndrome. The residual memory deficits consist of a severe anterograde amnesia (with increased sensitivity to interference) and a temporally graded retrograde amnesia, which are over and above the cognitive deficits (e.g., visuoperceptual, perceptual-motor, abstracting, and problem-solving impairments) that frequently are present secondary to a long history of severe alcohol use (Butters and Salmon, 1986).

It is important to note that while the alcoholic Korsakoff syndrome is the expected sequel to Wernicke's encephalopathy, a recent study indicated that of 44 patients diagnosed with Alcohol Amnestic Disorder (DSM-III-R), 33 of the cases had no obvious neurological symptoms of Wernicke's disease (Blansjaar and Van Dijk, 1992). In another study, of 70 cases of Wernicke's encephalopathy that were identified at autopsy (i.e., in 0.8% of all 8,735 autopsies and 12.5% of all examined alcoholics), 22 were characterized as active, whereas 48 were inactive (chronic); in addition, one third of the cases with inactive encephalopathy resembled a pure Korsakoff psychosis, while the remaining cases exhibited a pattern of a global dementia ("alcoholic dementia") (Torvik et al., 1982). These two studies illustrate that WKS may be more heterogeneous than previously thought (see Bowden [1990] for an excellent review of this area of controversy).

One of the hallmark features of WKS is the dramatic difference between the patients' IQ (Wechsler, 1955, 1981), which is often relatively comparable to that of non-WKS alcoholics and controls, and their severely impaired MQ from the Wechsler Memory Scale (WMS) (Wechsler and Stone, 1945). It is not uncommon for this difference to be 20 to 30 points (e.g., IQ = 100, MQ = 70–80) (Butters and Cermak, 1980). In addition, however, because WKS subjects have normal attention and concentration, the revised WMS, which has indices that do not confound attention/concentration with memory, may actually better reflect the severity of their memory performance; this is indicated by a study by Butters and colleagues that demonstrated that WKS subjects have WMS-R General and Memory indices of 65 and 57, respectively (Butters et al., 1988). Patients with KS also show evidence of frontal lobe dysfunction. That is, patients with frontal lobe lesions, but who are not amnesic, perform similarly to patients with WKS on the WCST, as well as on the initiation and perseveration subtests from the Dementia Rating Scale (Janowsky et al., 1989). This frontal lobe dysfunction may also contribute to impairments in other neuropsychological areas. Finally, the impairments in planning and executive functioning appear to be independent of other impairments in memory and visuoperceptive ability (Joyce and Robbins, 1991).

Wernicke-Korsakoff Syndrome/Alcohol-Induced Persisting Amnestic Disorder: Neuroimaging and Neuropathology Findings

The neuropathology of WKS is also well established. Specifically, the thiamine deficiency is thought to cause hemorrhagic lesions in the brain stem, cell loss in the periaqueductal and periventricular gray matter, and midline diencephalic nuclei, particularly the dorsomedial nucleus of the thalamus and the mammillary bodies. In addition, cell loss in the area of the nucleus basalis, which includes the medial septal nucleus, the nucleus of the diagonal band of Broca, and the nucleus basalis Maynert neurons in the substantia inominata, may also occur (Arendt et al., 1983). Recent research has provided data to suggest that there may a genetic predisposition (i.e., an abnormality in the enzyme transketolase) to the development of WKS (Blass and Gibson, 1977), particularly since not all malnourished alcoholics develop WKS.

The majority of WKS cases have occurred in persons with lengthy and heavy alcohol consumption histories, although a number of case studies have emphasized that Korsakoff's syndrome (KS) can develop without any history of alcohol abuse or dependence. For example, Cole and colleagues (1992) presented evidence that KS can develop following a left (dominant) thalamic infarction. Vighetto and colleagues (1991) reported on a 37-year-old man with multiple sclerosis with disseminated white matter lesions especially in both medial temporal lobes, who initially presented with an acute amnestic syndrome consistent with KS. Parkin et al. (1991) reported that the retrograde and anterograde memory deficits of a woman with anorexia nervosa (after intravenous feeding and intestinal surgery) was similar to the memory disorder found in WKS (Parkin et al., 1991, 1993). Other investigators have also found similar findings with other anorexia nervosa patients (Beatty et al., 1989; Becker et al., 1990). The WKS cases that develop secondary to anorexia nervosa (i.e., with severe thiamine deficiency), as well as with thalamic infarcts, and not in the context of serious alcohol consumption, underscore the importance of thalamic structures in the neuropathology of the disorder.

A Comparison of Nonamnesic and Amnesic (Wernicke-Korsakoff) Alcoholics

A few studies have addressed the neuroimaging and neuropathology similarities and differences between nonamnesic (i.e., non-Korsakoff) alcoholics and amnesics (i.e., alcoholics with Korsakoff syndrome). In 1988, Shimamura and colleagues used a quantitative method to compare tissue densities on CT imaging in six areas (thalamus, head of the caudate, putamen, anterior white matter, posterior white matter, and centrum semiovale) and fluid volumes in seven areas (total

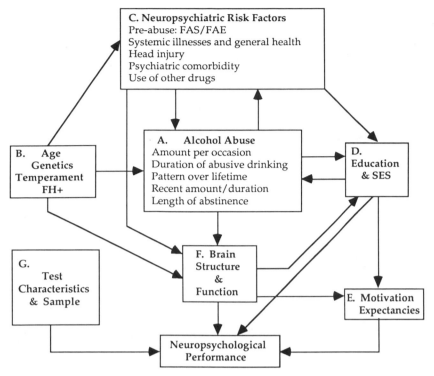

Figure 18-2. Variables to consider in any causal model of alcohol-associated neuropsychological deficit. (Modified from Grant [1987], p. 320.)

ventricular space, third ventricle, interventricular region, frontal sulci, peri-sylvian region, medial cerebellum, and vertex) in a small group of patients with Korsakoff syndrome, age-matched alcoholic subjects, and age-matched healthy control subjects (Shimamura et al., 1988). Results from their study revealed that the Korsakoff patients had greater bilateral decreases in the region of the thalamus, as well as increased fluid volumes in the area of the third ventricle, as compared with the non-Korsakoff alcoholics. The lower densities observed in the thalamus of the Korsakoff patients, along with greater fluid volume in the frontal sulci, were correlated with performance on memory tests. Alcoholic and Korsakoff subjects, however, demonstrated similar enlargement of frontal and peri-sylvian sulci (Shimamura et al., 1988). Similar findings have been reported by another group of investigators who found that many Korsakoff patients show evidence of cerebral damage, particularly frontal

shrinkage, in addition to diencephalic lesions; both non-Korsakoff and Korsakoff alcoholics exhibit similar cortical atrophy, as indicated by similar sulcal and sylvian fissure widths (Jacobson and Lishman, 1990).

Jernigan and colleagues have recently replicated their CT findings with Korsakoff and non-Korsakoff alcoholics using MRI (Jernigan et al., 1991b). That is, although both alcoholic groups showed significant increases in CSF in both subarachnoid spaces and the ventricular system as compared to controls, the Korsakoff subjects also showed increased fluid volume in the ventricles relative to the nonamnesic alcoholics. With respect to gray matter volumes, post-hoc analyses revealed that both alcoholic groups showed losses of gray matter in diencephalic structures, as well as in the parietal and superior frontal cortices; however, the Korsakoff alcoholics also experienced additional tissue loss in the anterior diencephalon (which included septal nuclei and anterior hypothalamic gray matter) and in the mesial temporal and orbito-frontal cortical areas. These results have been supported by a recent neuropathological examination of Korsakoff patients; 38 of 43 cases experienced atrophy in the dorsomedial nucleus of the thalamus and all evidenced mamillary body atrophy (Victor et al., 1989).

Although the results from Shimamura et al. (1988) and Jernigan et al. (1991b) provide evidence to support the notion of two distinct and separable neuropathological processes associated with alcoholism, there continues to be a debate whether this distinction can be made clinically (Bowden, 1990). In addition, the neuropathological results presented above, and a recent MRI study showing similar cortical and subcortical lesions in alcoholic Korsakoff patients and chronic alcoholics without cognitive deficits (Blansjaar et al., 1992), further emphasize the heterogeneity of WKS.

The Multifactorial Etiology of Neuropsychological Deficits in Nonamnesic Alcoholics

While there is no doubt that alcohol is a neurotoxic agent, the amount of variance in neuropsychological test performance that is explained by alcohol consumption variables is low, at least in human studies. One reason for this low association is that heavy alcohol consumption can also lead indirectly to neurocognitive dysfunction by compromising other systems of the human body (e.g., heart, liver, endocrine system) (Rubin, 1989). Because approximately 50% of recently detoxified alcoholics (range 31% to 85%) show evidence of neuropsychological dysfunction when sober for 3 to 4 weeks, the search for the determinants of this dysfunction, over and above the contribution of alcohol neurotoxicity, has tremendous clinical implications. Several investigators have discussed the possible multifactorial etiology for the neuropsychological deficits observed in alcoholics (Tarter and Alterman, 1984; Adams and Grant, 1986; Tarter and Edwards, 1986; Grant, 1987). Grant (1987) has created an excellent model that accounts for a num-

ber of variables that could directly or indirectly contribute to the neuropsychological deficits in recently detoxified alcoholics. We present this model below with slight modifications (see Fig. 18-2), and proceed to delineate the potential determinants, grouped into seven subsections, that should be considered when interpreting neuropsychological deficits in alcoholics, whether in the research or clinical setting.

We begin by presenting a summary of the studies that have examined the relationship between alcohol consumption variables and neuropsychological test performance. We then proceed to describe the contributions of age and genetics, neuropsychiatric risk factors—premorbid and concurrent, the influence of education, motivation and expectancies, and test characteristics and sample, on the neuropsychological test performance in recently detoxified alcoholics. We devote a significant portion of the chapter to a summary of these determinants because we feel that in order to fully explain the variability in the prevalence of deficits observed in alcoholics, it is important to consider multiple etiologies, in addition to the neurotoxic effects of alcohol. A more complete understanding of these determinants may also help shed some light on the variability in brain recovery in alcoholics that has been reported in the literature, as well as point to more promising avenues for the treatment of neurocognitive impairments.

Drinking Indices and Neuropsychological Performance

There are two main approaches to the issue of predicting neuropsychological performance from drinking history. One approach has been to compare neuropsychological performance of groups with different levels of alcohol consumption (e.g., social drinkers, problem drinkers, and alcoholics). Such studies can be said to be exploring the "continuity" notion: that there is putative progressive neuropsychological decline with amount of drinking, detectable even at the social drinking level. On the other hand, some investigators have utilized the correlational approach of analyzing the relationship between drinking dimensions (e.g., years of excessive drinking, amount consumed at drinking occasion) and neuropsychological measures specifically in abusive drinkers.

In support of the continuity notion of impairment originally proposed by Ryback (1971), Parker and Noble (1977) have investigated cognitive functioning in social drinkers. They found that good performance on tests of abstraction and adaptive abilities were negatively associated with the amount of alcohol per drinking occasion in male social drinkers. These results were subsequently replicated in their laboratory with male college students and social drinkers (Parker et al., 1980, 1983; Parker and Noble, 1980), as well as replicated by another group of investigators (Mac Vane et al., 1982). Parsons and Fabian (1982), as well as Parker's group (Parker, 1982), have provided valuable comments on the previous studies of social drinkers (Parker and Noble, 1977, 1980; Jones and Jones, 1980; Parker et al., 1980).

The findings of Parker and colleagues could be summarized as follows: the abstracting score from the Shipley Institute of Living Scale was found to be negatively associated with the amount of alcohol per drinking occasion in male social drinkers and college students, whereas lifetime consumption and current frequency of drinking was not (Parker and Noble, 1977, 1980; Parker et al., 1980, 1983). A later study by this same group of investigators showed that psychological distress could not account for the differences (Parker et al., 1991). Another group of investigators reported similar findings with social drinking; increased alcohol consumption per occasion and total lifetime consumption was associated with worse neuropsychological performance in college students (Hannon et al., 1983, 1985, 1987), although replication of Parker's studies have not always been consistent (Parsons and Fabian, 1982).

In contrast, a number of reports and reviews have been unable to document social drinking effects on neuropsychological test performance. In a review of the literature on the effects of "social drinking" on neuropsychological test performance, Hill argued that there is no compelling evidence that moderate intake of alcohol results in permanent alteration in the structural integrity of the brain (Hill and Ryan, 1985). In another review by Bowden, he reiterated the same opinion and proposed that previous associations between social drinking and neuropsychological test performance did not properly account for innate ability, demographics, and variations in drinking behavior (Bowden, 1987); similar conclusions have also been reached in Grant's (1987) review. In a prospective study of the development of alcohol and other drug use behaviors in adolescents and young adults (Rutgers Health and Human Development Project), there was little direct relation between cognitive performance and "social" drinking in a young sample (Bates and Tracy, 1990). Although most of the research with social drinking has been carried out with men, there does not appear to any relationship between social drinking and neurocognitive performance in women (Carey and Maisto, 1987), even with mild to moderate social drinking (Waugh et al., 1989). Finally, according to an extensive review of the literature by Parsons (1986b), there does not appear to be any consistent evidence to suggest that social drinking causes neuropsychological impairment.

Correlational studies relating length of excessive drinking to neuropsychological impairment in *alcoholics* have also generally been disappointing (i.e., correlations are usually in the 0.20 to 0.30 range). One possibility for the attenuated correlations may be inaccuracy of self-report of drinking (Fuller et al., 1988). Nevertheless, when relationships are found, they are most often in the expected direction: the greater the intake or length of drinking, the worse the neuropsychological test performance (Parsons, 1989). The maximum quantity frequency (MQF) of alcohol consumption over the past 6 months has often been demonstrated to be the best predictor of neuropsychological impairment (Schaeffer and Parsons, 1986), although some studies have shown that longer alcohol consumption leads to more neuropsychological deficits (Jones and Parsons, 1971; Tarter,

1973). Some investigators (e.g., Eckardt and colleagues [1978]), have argued for the use of nonlinear regression models (i.e., curvilinear) to explain the relationship between cognitive measures in alcoholics and various consumption scores. However, Adams and his colleagues have been unable to replicate Eckardt's results using analagous quadratic equations, and they have suggested that linear models may be more parsimonious (Adams and Grant, 1984).

Finally, Parsons and Stevens (1986) reported that in 57% of the studies they reviewed (i.e., 16 of 28), one or more significant correlations were observed between duration of alcohol abuse and neuropsychological test performance; however, in 12 of the 28 studies (or 43%), there was no relationship. Furthermore, Parsons and Stevens did not find that demographics (i.e., age, education, and sex) or length of abstinence (i.e., difference of less than 10 days or greater than 10 days of abstinence) influenced these results. In contrast to their review of the human studies, their review of the animal literature did provide convincing evidence that performance deficits and neuroanatomical changes occur in detoxified animals that are fed alcohol whose nutrition is comparable to control animals. Parsons and Stevens further reported that the animal studies suggest a duration threshold effect for impairment. That is, impairments are not detected up until a certain point, but after a consumption threshold has been reached, there is a negative inverse relation between amount of alcohol and performance. They also suggest that impairments may increase with age but reach an asymptote, after which no further increase in consumption is associated with a further decrease in performance (Parsons and Stevens, 1986).

The Influence of Age on Neuropsychological Test Performance

There continues to be controversy about when neuropsychological deficits first can be detected, and which variables seem to mediate this emergence. Some investigators have suggested that neuropsychological impair-

ments are not detectable in alcoholics until they reach their mid to late forties (Jones and Parsons, 1971; Klisz and Parsons, 1977; Grant et al., 1979a; Adams et al., 1980; Eckardt et al., 1995), whereas other investigators have reported neuropsychological deficits regardless of age (Eckardt et al., 1980b; Ryan and Butters, 1980b; Brandt et al., 1983). Furthermore, age of onset of heavy alcohol use may also influence neuropsychological test performance, with those beginning at an early age showing more deficits (Portnoff, 1982). Also, we believe that age and drinking patterns may interact, such that older alcoholics who continue to drink at levels comparable to those of their younger years may suffer more brain damage, particularly in those older alcoholics who have already begun to show neuropsychological deficits. Clearly, further research is needed to clarify the independent role of age, as well as its interaction with other medical disorders, on the emergence of neuropsychological deficits in alcoholics.

THE ROLE OF GENETICS. One may assume that there is probably not one gene for alcohol dependence or alcohol abuse as defined by diagnostic manuals. However, it seems probable that certain subtypes of alcoholism (e.g., essential, primary, or Type II) (Cloninger, 1987) are more influenced by heredity than other types. Probably different features of alcoholism or drinking behavior are differentially dependent on genetic characteristics. Couzigou and colleagues (1993) point to some areas of investigation that have provided interesting results in animal models (i.e., voluntary ethanol consumption, and sensitivity to ethanol and ethanol withdrawal). These investigators suggest that reinforcement, learned behavioral disorder, blocking reinforcement, alcohol resistance, relapse and binge intoxication predisposition, and satiety represent phenomena of importance in alcoholism that can be examined using animal models.

Extensive research in the genetics laboratory have relied on biological markers, including the P300 event-related potential (see below for more information on the electrophysiological determinants), the A1 allele of the D2 dopamine receptor, monoamine oxidase activity in platelets, and adenylate cyclase activity. Couzigou et al. (1993) have provided a recent review of the findings. They warn that potential genetic mechanisms probably are complex. That is, alcoholism is a clinically heterogeneous disorder with variable age of onset. It may also not be caused by any one single gene, but may develop from the additive effects of multiple genes (polygenetic inheritance); in addition, single mutations at different genetic loci may also result in clinically indistinguishable disease states (genetic heterogeneity). Other important determinants include the fact that not every individual who inherits the genes is likely to develop the disorder (reduced penetrance); the disorder may reflect a complex interaction between alleles at several loci (epistatic effects), and a substantial number of individuals without a disease genotype may manifest alcoholism resulting from nongenetic causes (phenocopies).

Couzigou's comments notwithstanding, investigators have been able to show that there is a genetic component to alcoholism by using a number of methodological approaches (i.e., by comparing twins; children with a biological parent who is alcoholic, but who are adopted and brought up in nonalcoholic families; children of alcoholics; and alcoholics with a positive family history for alcoholism) (Schuckit, 1987; Anthenelli and Schuckit, 1990; Schuckit, 1994). Given the evidence for a genetic component in alcoholism, there has been an interest over the past several years in determining whether there are premorbid neuropsychiatric risk factors that may lead to neuropsychological deficits prior to the beginning of heavy alcohol use, and whether having these risk factors explains some of the variance in neuropsychological test performance in adult alcoholics. We next turn to an examination of these potential premorbid neuropsychiatric risk factors.

TEMPERAMENT AND CHILDHOOD BEHAVIOR SYMPTOMS. Tarter has in several contexts discussed the role of "activity level" as a risk factor for alcoholism, and more recently he

has reintroduced the concept of temperament, which may be operationalized into dimensions of activity level, emotionality, and sociability (Tarter, 1988). Currently, Tarter and his colleagues are conducting a large-scale longitudinal project in Pittsburgh, where he is collecting extensive psychological and neurophysiological information on children at risk (also including videotape analyses of family interactions). Prospective studies such as this should provide important answers to the alcoholism etiology questions. Tarter has also commented in a number of reviews on the high prevalence of juvenile attention deficit disorder among alcoholics, particularly among essential or primary alcoholics.

Løberg has proposed that there may be a quite direct and causal connection between behavioral hyperactivity and substance abuse (due to low CNS activation levels) (Løberg, 1989), although other investigators have found that hyperreactivity, rather than hyperactivity, may be important. For example, Peterson and colleagues found a highly significant relationship between cognitive impairment, cardiovascular hyperreactivity, and susceptibility to the reactivity-dampening effects of alcohol in nonalcoholic sons of male alcoholics (Peterson et al., 1992). Given these results, it may be that both hyperactivity (low CNS activation) and hyperreactivity (high CNS activation) play a role in vulnerability to excessive alcohol use, and perhaps they lead to different mechanisms for developing alcohol and other substance abuse problems. We feel that more research in this area is worth pursuing to test the hypothesis that in hyperactivity (low CNS activation), the felt benefits from alcohol could be its (pseudo-)stimulant initial effects, while in hyperreactivity (high CNS activation), it could be the anxiolytic or soothing effect. If this hypothesis is correct, this may translate into quite different treatment implications and types of interventions.

PREMORBID NEUROPSYCHOLOGICAL DEFICITS. The search to determine whether neuropsychological deficits exist prior to the beginning of heavy alcohol use has proceeded along two lines. One approach has been to study individuals at high risk for the development of alcoholism (i.e., children of alcoholics [COA])—mostly sons of male alcoholics), and to compare them to demographically matched individuals without a family history of alcoholism on intellectual and neuropsychological tests, as well as on electrophysiological measures of brain functioning. This approach has been driven largely by the fact that alcoholics who also have a positive family history for alcoholism demonstrate more neuropsychological deficits in some studies than those without alcoholic family members (see below). A second approach has been to administer questionnaires that retrospectively assess childhood behavioral disturbances in adult alcoholics, and to determine if these symptoms and disturbances relate to residual neuropsychological test performance as adults. Ultimately, both approaches have tremendous clinical implications in that they may help to identify individuals who are at risk for a more severe course of alcoholism or for more neurobehavioral impairments, as well as target them for primary prevention and/or intervention (Bates and Pandina, 1992).

Regarding the intellectual or academic deficits in COA, some studies have not revealed any deficits (Johnson and Rolf, 1988; Bates and Pandina, 1992; Ozkaragoz and Noble, 1995); other studies have shown that COA, relative to children without alcoholic family members, have lower verbal ability and academic achievement (Tarter et al., 1984; Drejer et al., 1985; Parsons, 1989; Sher et al., 1991), and more psychiatric distress and alcohol/drug problems (Sher et al., 1991).

With regard to the neuropsychological deficits in COA, some studies have found deficits (Tarter et al., 1984, 1989a; Ozkaragoz and Noble, 1995), while others have not (Schuckit et al., 1987; Workman-Daniels and Hesselbrock, 1987; Bates and Pandina, 1992). In those studies that have found deficits, the pattern of results do not suggest generalized effects (Tarter et al., 1989a), but rather specific deficits on tests measuring verbal skills and language processing (Tarter

et al., 1984, 1989b; Parsons, 1989), visual scanning and attention, planning ability (Tarter et al., 1984, 1989a,b; Ozkaragoz and Noble, 1995), perceptual-motor performance and abstraction (Tarter et al., 1984; Parsons, 1989; Peterson and Pihl, 1990), and memory (Tarter et al., 1984; Parsons, 1989; Ozkaragoz and Noble, 1995). The fact that adult male COA have deficits in visual-spatial learning that resemble the deficits found in children may suggest that certain deficits may be premorbid (Garland et al., 1993).

While there continues to be controversy regarding the neuropsychological deficits in COA, one possible explanation for the mixture of findings is the failure to consider comorbid psychopathology (Gillen and Hesselbrock, 1992). For example, Gillen and Hesselbrock have shown that neuropsychological deficits in the areas of higher level motor control and verbal concept formation occur in alcoholics with antisocial personality disorder (ASPD); however, there was no ASPD and family history interaction. In contrast, another group of investigators demonstrated that young adult COA exhibited more childhood attentional and social problems, but not elevated rates of cognitive problems, drug use, or mental health problems (Alterman et al., 1989b). Alterman and colleagues have suggested that it may be important to consider both drinking and familial alcoholism risk status when performing comparisons on neuropsychological tests (Alterman et al., 1986), although they were unable to find a relationship between heavy drinking and familial risk with neuropsychological performance in college men in one of their subsequent studies (Alterman and Hall, 1989).

Hesselbrock and colleagues (1985b) have reported that Attention Deficit Disorder/hyperactivity and conduct disorder prior to age 12 predicted onset of drinking. However, they were unable to detect any neuropsychological performance differences in young adults who were characterized as being at high or low risk, and there was also no difference between these subjects when the data were broken down according to frequency of intoxication, or when a second cohort similar in age was compared on neuropsychological tests, based on whether neither parent, one parent, or both parents were alcoholics (Hesselbrock et al., 1985b). What these results may suggest is that a higher prevalence of childhood problem behaviors may be related to the development of a variety of psychiatric problems, in addition to alcoholism.

In a recent review of the literature on the neuropsychological differences in individuals who are at high risk for the development of alcoholism, including studies of alcoholics with a positive family history (FH +) Hesselbrock and his colleagues proposed that the evidence in support of neuropsychological differences between low- and high-risk individuals is not strong and that variations in the literature are likely the result of differences in study design and methodology, and in how family history of alcoholism is characterized (Hesselbrock et al., 1991). According to Hesselbrock et al., the strongest differences and deficits in children of alcoholics, as well as in FH + alcoholics, occur on tests of verbal ability and abstracting/conceptual reasoning skills. Hesselbrock proposed that a number of additional factors may explain the equivocal results that have been obtained (e.g., drinking of mother, parental psychiatric comorbidity, conduct disorder).

A number of years ago, Tarter and his colleagues developed a 50-item questionnaire that assessed childhood "minimal brain dysfunction" (MBD) symptoms (Tarter et al., 1977). This MBD inventory has been shown to capture four factors: hyperactivity-impulsivity, attentional-socialization problems, antisocial behavior, and learning disability (Alterman and Gerstley, 1986; Alterman and McLellan, 1986). In a series of studies using this inventory, Tarter and his colleagues found that primary alcoholics reported more childhood MBD symptoms than less severe drinkers (secondary alcoholics), psychiatric patients, and controls (Tarter et al., 1977); in addition, he found that alcoholics characterized as essential and reactive differed in their retrospective accounts of symptoms of hyperactivity and MBD, with the former having twice as many symptoms as the latter (Tarter, 1982). This finding has

also been replicated (i.e., essential alcoholics scored higher on the BDI, the Neuropsychological Impairment Scale, and had a tendency to report more symptoms on the MBD questionnaire) (Braggio et al., 1991). In another study, alcoholics who scored high on the MBD inventory were found to report more psychopathology on the MMPI, differed in alcoholism use patterns and consequences, had worse emotional and psychosocial functioning, and were more likely to use other drugs (Alterman et al., 1985b). The results obtained using the MBD questionnaire are generally consistent with previous findings that those alcoholics with a positive family history for alcoholism begin drinking at an earlier age and have increased prevalence of childhood history of learning problems, hyperactivity, conduct disorder, and an adult history of antisocial behavior (Goodwin, 1983). In sum, these results suggest that primary or essential alcoholics, and possibly those with a family history for alcoholism, are more at risk for antecedent neuropsychiatric deficits.

ELECTROPHYSIOLOGICAL FINDINGS IN CHILDREN OF ALCOHOLICS. In parallel with the neurocognitive studies of COA, investigators have attempted to determine whether there are electrophysiological abnormalities in COA that may predispose one to develop alcoholism.

Comparisons of EEG activity between individuals at low and high risk for alcoholism have produced mixed results. For example, there were no differences on four measures of EEG activity in a study that compared male COA to those without positive FH for alcoholism, suggesting that EEG does not effectively discriminate between individuals at high and low risk for alcoholism prior to alcohol administration (Cohen et al., 1991). However, EEGs of young male COA do show different EEG wave patterns than those without a positive FH risk when given an alcohol challenge (Ehlers and Schuckit, 1990, 1991).

Far more electrophysiological studies have been carried out examining various wave forms from event-related potentials (ERP) in individuals at low versus high risk for alcoholism. Many investigators have reported electrophysiological abnormalities, particularly differences in P300, in adolescent males with FH + (Begleiter et al., 1984; Whipple et al., 1988; O'Connor and Tasman, 1990; Porjesz and Begleiter, 1990, 1991, 1993) as well as in boys whose fathers are characterized as Type 2 alcoholics (Begleiter et al., 1987). There are, however, some investigators who have not been able to find any FH effect of alcoholism in latency or amplitude of P300, although in some of their studies latency increased and amplitude decreased with increase in reported amount of alcohol consumption (Polich and Bloom, 1986, 1988; Polich et al., 1988a,b).

Some investigators have suggested that P300 may provide a phenotypic marker for alcoholism (Begleiter and Porjesz, 1990; Porjesz and Begleiter, 1993), which may also predict later substance (including alcohol) abuse in young boys (Berman et al., 1993). However, Polich and colleagues (1994) have argued that the P300 may not be specific to alcoholism, because it is often abnormal in a number of other neuropsychiatric patient groups. In their recent meta-analysis of the P300 findings in COA, they calculated that the most reliable finding with COA is the reduction in P300 amplitude using the most difficult visual tasks, and that the variability obtained in past studies can be explained by a number of moderator variables (e.g., age of the individual, source of recruitment, stimulus material used to elicit the ERP (task difficulty and modality), and the strength of family history for alcoholism) (Polich et al., 1994).

THE INFLUENCE OF FAMILY HISTORY OF ALCOHOLISM ON NEUROPSYCHOLOGICAL DIFFERENCES IN ALCOHOLICS. In trying to explain the neuropsychological deficits in alcoholics, investigators have compared alcoholics with positive and negative family histories for alcoholism (FH + and FH −, respectively). In one study, male alcoholics with family histories of alcoholism were found to have an earlier onset of alcoholism, report more symptoms of childhood conduct disorder, tended to have higher level of depressive symptoms, and performed worse on the Shipley Abstraction Test, relative to male alcoholics without such histories (Schaeffer et al., 1988). An earlier study also suggested that alcoholics' deficits in abstracting/problem solving, and possibly learning and memory, may antedate alcohol use in FH + individuals, and that the lack of interaction between FH and alcohol/control status suggested alcoholism and FH have additive effects on neuropsychological test performance (Schaeffer et al., 1984). In a review of the FH studies carried out in the Oklahoma laboratory, neuropsychological deficits were found to be more prominent in male alcoholics with an alcoholic father and/or in those with a history of childhood behavioral disorders, although Cloninger's Type 1 and Type 2 classification (i.e., consideration of the course of alcoholism, psychiatric comorbidity, and personality traits) may have contributed to the variability across studies (Parsons, 1989; Parsons and Nixon, 1993). In contrast to studies demonstrating FH effects, a number of investigators have been unable to find differences between FH + and FH − alcoholics using various classification schemes that classified alcoholics according to strength of FH (Alterman et al., 1987; Reed et al., 1987).

The Influence of Pre-Abuse Neuropsychiatric Risk Factors

FETAL ALCOHOL SYNDROME AND FETAL ALCOHOL EFFECTS. Alcohol and other drugs consumed during pregnancy can have a variety of neurological effects on the developing fetus (Chiriboga, 1993). Some investigators have suggested that maternal alcohol abuse during the second and third trimesters results in greater consequences on growth and neurobehavioral development than alcohol consumed during the first trimester (Aronson and Olegard, 1987). However, another study demonstrated that alcohol causes damage to the CNS throughout the entire pregnancy (Coles et al., 1985). Mental retardation and microcephaly are commonly observed in fetal alcohol syndrome (FAS), although a partial syndrome, fetal alcohol effects (FAE), can result in neurobehavioral sequelae that are evident at birth or that manifest later in development (Smith and Eckardt, 1991).

In the developing fetus, exposure to alcohol can cause morphological abnormalities, intellectual and cognitive impairments, and lead to behavioral disturbances. For example, frequent heavy drinking during pregnancy significantly predicted a decrease in head size at 18 months, although the average daily volume was a better predictor of growth deficits than frequent heavy drinking (Day et al., 1991a). In addition, children exposed to alcohol before birth have been shown to be smaller in weight, height, and head circumference at 3 years (Day et al., 1991b). Reduced corpus callosum, basal ganglia, and thalamic structures have also been noted using MRI in FAS children that have IQs in the mentally retarded range (Mattson et al., 1992).

There is continued controversy regarding the critical threshold of drinking that leads to fetal effects. Recently it has been suggested that the threshold may be around 30 to 40 g/day (well above the level defined as moderate drinking), though the authors of the study state that current evidence is insufficient (Plant et al., 1993). Several other investigators argue against the use of a cutoff as the critical determinant, and point to the increasing probability of damage with increasing amounts of alcohol. Russell et al. examined growth, dysmorphology, and cognitive development in 6-year-old children exposed to alcohol prenatally (Russell et al., 1991). Even after excluding children born to mothers who drank over seven drinks a day, and children with probable/possible FAE, Russell and colleagues found significant effects of maternal drinking on cognitive functions (and head circumference).

Decrements in intellectual performance have been reported with prenatal alcohol exposure (Conry, 1990; Nanson and Hiscock, 1990; Streissguth et al., 1990; Smith and Eckardt, 1991; Mattson et al., 1992; Caruso and ten Bensel, 1993), in infants born to mothers with more than one indication of problem drinking (Russell et al., 1991), and

in children raised by an alcoholic father (Ervin et al., 1984). Consumption of two or more drinks per day on average was associated with a 7-point decrement in IQ in 482 7-year-old children (Streissguth et al., 1990). In addition, the effect of prenatal alcohol exposure was exacerbated if parental education was low and with increased number of children in the home; learning problems were associated with binge drinking (i.e., with more than five drinks per occasion) (Streissguth et al., 1990). A follow-up of these children (n = 462) at age 14 revealed that the number of drinks per occasion was the strongest alcohol predictor, and alcohol exposure prenatally was associated with attention and memory deficits in a dose-dependent fashion (Streissguth et al., 1994). Neuropsychological impairments are also common (Streissguth et al., 1989; Conry, 1990; Smith and Eckardt, 1991; Mattson et al., 1992; Streissguth et al., 1994), and some evidence suggests that prenatal alcohol exposure may lead to a nonverbal learning disability profile (Streissguth et al., 1989; Don and Rourke, 1995).

The Influence of Concurrent Neuromedical Risk Factors in Alcoholics

THE EFFECTS OF HEPATIC DYSFUNCTION ON NEUROPSYCHOLOGICAL TEST PERFORMANCE. It is well established that hepatic dysfunction and disease can result in neuropsychological dysfunction (Tarter et al., 1987). For example, biochemical measures of hepatic dysfunction have been shown to correlate with neuropsychological dysfunction in alcoholics with cirrhosis (Tarter et al., 1986b), particularly on tests of memory performance (Arria et al., 1991a). Psychomotor, visuopractic, and abstracting abilities can recover following liver transplantation; memory deficits, however, may persist (Arria et al., 1991b). The fact that alcoholics and nonalcoholics with cirrhosis display similar neuropsychological deficits (Tarter et al., 1986a, 1988) suggests that alcohol is not the only etiological mechanism for brain dysfunction in alcoholics.

Although less than one third of alcoholics

or heavy drinkers develop serious alcohol-related liver damage (Grant et al., 1988), elevated levels of liver enzymes in noncirrhotic alcoholics have been shown to be significantly related to a number of neuropsychological measures, particularly those that assess visuoperceptual and visuoconceptual abilities.

A study by Irwin and colleagues illustrates the effects of liver enzymes on neuropsychological test performance (Irwin et al., 1989). Blood and serum were collected from 132 primary alcoholic men 24 to 48 hours after admission, but approximately a mean of 7 days after their last drink. Based on blood and serum values, alcoholics were divided into three groups according to their plasma levels of GGT at admission. There were 69 men with normal GGT values (<40 IU/L), 41 men with moderately elevated GGT levels ($40 \leq GGT \leq 100$ IU/L), and 22 with extremely elevated GGT levels (>100 IU/L). There were no differences in age, education, and WAIS-R Vocabulary scores, suggesting that groups were comparable on premorbid neuropsychological functioning. When the three groups were compared on a brief battery of neuropsychological tests, which included the Trail Making Test (Parts A and B), WAIS-R Digit Symbol, and Visual Search, significant differences emerged as GGT level increased. When multiple regressions were performed to examine the influence of various parameters (i.e., GGT, liver injury tests, demographics, alcohol consumption, and depressive symptoms as measured by the Hamilton Depression Rating Scale) on neuropsychological test performance, it was found that over and above the expected influence of age and education, GGT contributed a significant amount of variance to Trails B and Visual Search. In addition, even when other liver function tests were included in the analyses, GGT continued to explain Visual Search, Digit Symbol, and Trails B performance, suggesting that level of GGT in alcoholics is associated with neuropsychological deficits in the areas of visuoperceptual and visuoconceptual functions (Irwin et al., 1989).

In a later study by Irwin and his colleagues (Schafer et al., 1991), liver function tests and depression at admission were found to be related to neuropsychological dysfunction in alcoholics, but not at discharge several weeks later. In a study by another group of investigators, liver enzyme levels, when collected from alcoholics at hospital admission, were shown to have continued effects on neuropsychological test performance at least 21 days later, particularly on tests of visuoperceptual and conceptual abilities (Richardson et al., 1991).

THE IMPACT OF HEAD INJURY ON NEUROPSYCHOLOGICAL TEST PERFORMANCE. Head injuries are extremely common in alcoholics and they represent a significant risk factor for neuropsychological impairment independent of the neurotoxic effects of alcohol. Traumatic head injuries appear to be two to four times more prevalent in alcoholics than in the general population (Hillbom and Holm, 1986). Excessive alcohol consumption has been shown to lead to increased susceptibility to head injuries in both alcoholic and control groups (Hillbom and Holm, 1986), as well as worse head injury outcome (Ruff et al., 1990). In fact, heavy alcohol use and head injury severity may lead to independent or interactive effects on neuropsychological performance and outcome (Solomon and Malloy, 1992; Dikmen et al., 1993). For example, one study showed a significant interaction between head injury severity (i.e., length of post-traumatic amnesia) and alcohol use, with increasing memory deficits occurring with increasing alcohol use (Brooks et al., 1989). Family history for alcoholism may also be a significant risk factor, because alcoholics with positive family risk have been shown to have elevated rates of closed head injuries (60% in FH+ versus 35% in FH−) (Alterman and Tarter, 1985).

One group of investigators have found that a history of head injuries independently predicted neuropsychological deficits, particularly on a factor of verbal skills and on a factor that reflected nonverbal learning and problem solving (Grant et al., 1984). In another study, alcoholics with head injuries performed significantly worse than alcoholics without head injuries on the Halstead Impairment Index, the Finger Tapping Test (dominant hand) and on the Location score from the Tactual Performance Test (Hillbom and Holm, 1986). In contrast to those studies finding an effect of mild head injuries on neuropsychological test performance in alcoholics, one group of investigators did not find that alcoholics with head injuries differed on neuropsychological tests, as compared to alcoholics without head injuries, when loss of consciousness was for less than 60 minutes (Alterman et al., 1985a). Finally, there is one study showing that severity of head injury did not influence memory performance on the WMS-R (Ryan and Lewis, 1988).

HORMONAL DISRUPTION. Alcoholics shortly after detoxification show abnormalities in the activation of the hypothalamic-pituitary-gonadal (HPG) axis, which may help to explain some of the signs and symptoms of acute and subacute withdrawal (Adinoff et al., 1991). However, disruptions in the HPG may only be an influence in the short term, because normalization of hormonal function may occur with longer abstinence (i.e., alcoholics sober for 1 year have been shown to demonstrate normal neuropsychological, neuroradiological and neuroendocrine functioning) (Marchesi et al., 1992, 1994).

There has been an attempt to examine how dysfunction in the HPG axis may relate to neuropsychological deficits in recently detoxified alcoholics. Specifically, a study by Errico and colleagues examined whether visuospatial impairment in alcoholics was related to dysfunction in the HPG axis. Controls showed the expected relationship between visual-spatial performance and testosterone and FSH; however, none of the correlations between the hormones and the neuropsychological test results were significant in the alcoholics who performed worse on those measures. These authors concluded that alcoholism disrupts the relationship between HPG axis and neuropsychological test performance (Errico et al., 1992). A subsequent study showed that alcoholics also have an attenuated cortical response (Errico et al., 1993). In regard to cyclic hormonal variations being a possible artifact in interpretation, it

should also be mentioned that no differences in neuropsychological test performance have been found in menstruating versus nonmenstruating women (Fabian et al., 1980)

NUTRITION. A few studies in the early 1980s examined how nutrition may impact neuropsychological test performance in alcoholics. These studies provided evidence that folic acid level was related to deficits on a number of neuropsychological tests in recently detoxified alcoholics (Albert et al., 1982, 1983). The authors of these studies suggested that nutrition effects may be important only early in the detoxification process, whereas the more longstanding neuropsychological deficits that are detected may be related to the neurotoxic effects of alcohol. In a more recent study, alcoholics who had lower serum levels of thiamine scored lower on intellectual and visual-spatial tasks relative to controls. There were a few significant correlations between thiamine level and neuropsychological test performance; however, regression analyses revealed that duration of alcohol intake and educational level were the major contributors to neuropsychological test performance (Molina et al., 1994).

PSYCHOPHYSIOLOGICAL ACTIVITY. Braggio and colleagues (1991) have provided some evidence to suggest that electromyogram, skin conductance level, and systolic blood pressure may be mediators of neuropsychological test performance in alcoholics (Braggio and Pishkin, 1991, 1992). Also, alcoholics have significantly lower natural killer cell activity compared with control subjects (Irwin et al., 1990), which could also result in increased susceptibility to a number of medical diseases, with subsequent neuropsychological implications.

POSSIBLE EFFECTS OF HYPOXEMIA. It is estimated that between 83% and 94% of alcoholics smoke cigarettes (Ayers et al., 1976; DiFranza and Guerrera, 1990). It is well established that chronic obstructive pulmonary disease (COPD) can cause significant neuropsychological impairment with increasing severity of hypoxemia (Grant et al.,

1987a; see also Rourke and Adams, Chapter 16). Although most neuropsychological studies of alcoholics generally exclude those with obvious lung disease or COPD, it is possible that mild levels of hypoxemia in those who are in the early stages of COPD may contribute to neuropsychological deficits independent of alcohol. In addition, because chronic alcohol consumption can also lead to increasing nighttime hypoxemia and sleep apnea, particularly in older men, additional deficits may be observed in alcoholics with such conditions (Vitiello et al., 1987).

SLEEP DISTURBANCES. Notwithstanding possible nighttime hypoxemia in alcoholics, there are a number of sleep abnormalities that persist for extended periods of time after detoxification that may also contribute to daytime impairments. For example, young primary alcoholics have been shown to have sleep patterns typical of older controls (Gillin et al., 1990b); in addition, length of abstinence, drinks per drinking day in past 3 months, and maximum number of withdrawal symptoms ever experienced by the patient were related to sleep abnormalities (Gillin et al., 1990b). Furthermore, alcoholics (both primary and those with a secondary depression) have significantly longer sleep latency and less sleep efficiency, less total sleep time, and delta sleep than controls; primary alcoholics with secondary depression have shorter REM latency and less non-REM sleep than alcoholics without secondary depression (Gillin et al., 1990a). Finally, there is also some evidence that decreases in slow wave sleep in alcoholics may be related to increased atrophy of the cerebral cortex (Ishibashi et al., 1987).

BLACKOUTS, SEIZURES, AND EFFECTS OF RE-PEATED WITHDRAWAL FROM ALCOHOL. There are a number of consequences that result from heavy drinking (e.g., blackouts, seizures, and repeated withdrawals) that could indirectly influence brain functioning. For example, of 135 alcoholics seeking help for an alcohol/drug problem, 86% reported having experienced alcohol-related blackouts (Campbell and Hodgins, 1993); these black-

outs were found to be related to the severity of alcohol problems (i.e., those with blackouts started drinking at a younger age, drank larger amounts, had greater dependence, were more likely to have delirium tremens, shakes, and family history of alcoholism). Approximately 14% to 21% of hospitalized alcoholics report having had seizures, typically of the grand mal variety (Feuerlein, 1977; Neundorfer et al., 1984; Tuck and Jackson, 1991). Although a small study showed that alcoholics who presented to the hospital experiencing withdrawal seizures (n = 12) were not different from those without (n = 22) on intellectual or neuropsychological measures, African-American alcoholics were more likely than White alcoholics in this study to experience seizures (Tarter et al., 1983). In another study, African-American alcoholics with seizure histories performed worse on intellectual and neuropsychological tests compared to African-American alcoholics without such histories; there were no differences among White alcoholics (Goldstein et al., 1983). Regarding alcohol withdrawals, male and female alcoholics have been shown to perform worse on memory testing when repeated withdrawals occurred in the past year (Glenn et al., 1988). Finally, alcoholics who also use depressants and opiates may have more neuropsychological impairments than those who consume only alcohol (Grant et al., 1977, 1978, 1979b; Carlin et al., 1978; Carlin, 1986; see also Carlin and O'Malley, Chapter 19).

THE INFLUENCE OF PSYCHIATRIC COMOR-BIDITY ON NEUROPSYCHOLOGICAL TEST PER-FORMANCE IN ALCOHOLICS. Are the psychiatric disorders (personality disorders, mood and anxiety/phobic disorders) "pre-alcoholic"? Do they contribute to alcohol misuse, or are they caused by alcohol abuse and dependence? For instance, depression may well be understood as a consequence of the alcoholic career (i.e., as a psychological response to failure to honor obligations because of lack of commitment to obligations related to family or work, to legal or economic problems, etc.) leading to remorse and guilt. Biochemically, because of the CNS depressant effect of alcohol, anxiety might be explained in a similar vein, and the phobias may be understood as an effective classical conditioning to strong stimuli (e.g., crowds, social settings) when in the withdrawal state with an autonomic nervous system in a state of arousal akin to that of anxiety or fright.

Although some investigators have shown that alcoholics with Antisocial Personality Disorder (ASPD) perform worse on neuropsychological testing (Gorenstein, 1982; Hesselbrock et al., 1985a; Malloy et al., 1989, 1990), this has not always been the case (Hoffman et al., 1987; Sutker and Allain, 1987). One possible reason for these discrepant findings may be that some ASPD substance abusers may have histories of "minimal brain dysfunction," Attention Deficit Disorder (ADD), and/or developmental disorders (Tarter and Edwards, 1986) before they begin substance use. Another reason may be that certain deviant behaviors (e.g., drinking-related arrests) may be common to both antisocial personality and alcoholism, and these may carry with them higher neuromedical risks leading to specific neuropsychological deficits (Gorenstein, 1987). That is, alcoholics with ASPD may have a higher prevalence of neuropsychological deficits because they begin drinking earlier and suffer more alcohol-related problems, including more blackouts, more frequent sleep disturbances, and engage in more polydrug use (particularly barbiturates, opiates, marijuana), than those alcoholics without ASPD (Malloy et al., 1990). Finally, violent, recently detoxified alcoholics have been shown to have more severe neuropsychological impairments (e.g., on abstraction and mental coordination) and more deviant personality profiles on the MMPI, compared with nonviolent alcoholics (Løberg, 1981).

To circumvent the problem of discrete classification associated with the diagnosis of ASPD, Glenn and her colleagues carried out a study to examine how "subclinical" levels of antisocial behaviors influenced neuropsychological impairment in adult alcoholics (i.e., they included subjects who did not meet criteria for ASPD, but nevertheless had

a number of symptoms that were characteristic of this disorder); in this study, they also investigated how childhood behavioral disorder symptoms and affective symptomatology affected neuropsychological performance (Glenn et al., 1993). While there was quite a bit of overlap in variance across the three psychiatric symptoms sampled, all three areas were negatively related to neuropsychological test performance; of the three factors, the childhood behavior symptoms proved to be the most consistent predictor of neuropsychological performance for both male and female alcoholics and controls. These factors could not, however, fully account for the neuropsychological deficits, because the deficits remained after covariate analyses were carried out to eliminate the former influences (Glenn et al., 1993). What may be occurring is that alcoholics inherit certain temperament traits that increase their vulnerability to a variety of negative outcomes including antisocial personality and alcoholism (Parsons and Nixon, 1993).

Personality characteristics using the MMPI are also quite consistent in several studies of recently detoxified alcoholics, with elevations on the Depression and Psychopathic Deviate scales (Løberg, 1981), the highest scale being determined by sample characteristics and admittance criteria. There is a robust cross-national consistency in these findings, even when cluster-derived personality subtypes of alcoholics are considered (Løberg and Miller, 1986). Personality disturbances, based on the MMPI, show many significant correlations with drinking variables, but few with neuropsychological test variables; however, alcoholics with severe neuropsychological impairment often show quite pathological personality profiles (Løberg, 1981; Løberg and Miller, 1986). There is some indication that depression may be related to Performance IQ and Trails B; however, few significant correlations are observed between neuropsychological test measures and MMPI clinical scales, suggesting that the Halstead-Reitan Battery is sufficiently robust not to be much influenced by mild to moderate psychopathology.

Goldstein and Shelly used the MMPI to

classify alcoholics as normal, depressed, or psychotic and then compared them on intellectual and neuropsychological measures (Goldstein et al., 1985). There were no differences in intellectual or neuropsychological performance in alcoholics who were classified as "normal" and "depressed" using the MMPI; however, alcoholics classified as "psychotic" were more impaired with regard to conceptual and visual-spatial skills; 80% of the "psychotic" alcoholics were classified as impaired using an AIR of 1.55, whereas only 50% of the other groups were similarly classified; "psychotic" alcoholics also had lower verbal skills (Goldstein et al., 1985). There are, however, some apparently discrepant findings and infrequent relations between neuropsychological test performances and personality when correlations are performed (Løberg and Miller, 1986). For example, it may be that certain personality profile types may be associated with elevated levels of neuropsychological impairments, which are not obvious when simple correlations are made between neuropsychological test measures and individual clinical scales from the MMPI (Løberg, 1981, Goldstein et al., 1985).

Psychiatric symptomatology, particularly depressive and anxiety symptoms, are extremely common during heavy drinking and during detoxification in alcoholics. In one study, 82% of alcoholics (350 of 428 patients) presented to treatment with depressive symptomatology (Angelini et al., 1990). Depressive symptomatology may be explained both biochemically, since alcohol is a CNS depressant, and psychologically, due to remorse and guilt over actions not taken, obligations not fulfilled, and actions performed that should not have been undertaken while drinking. As to the prevalence of personality disorders, 78% of alcoholics admitted to an addiction treatment unit (n = 178) had at least one personality disorder, with the average being 1.8 per patient (DeJong et al., 1993).

Brown and her colleagues at the San Diego VA Medical Center have documented that significant changes in depressive (Brown and Schuckit, 1988; Brown et al., 1995) and anxiety (Brown et al., 1991) symptoms occur in primary alcoholics during detoxification. For example, whereas 42% of alcoholic men had clinically significant levels of depression within 48 hours of admission into an inpatient unit (i.e., with Hamilton Depression Rating Scores of ≥ 20), only 6% had elevated levels at discharge 4 weeks later. This level of depressive symptomatology at discharge corresponds well with previous reports that alcohol-dependent men do not have elevated rates for major depressive disorder independent of alcohol-induced mood syndromes (Schuckit et al., 1994). With regard to anxiety, 98% of men (n = 171) reported at least one symptom of anxiety during drinking or withdrawal, but only 4% fulfilled criteria for generalized anxiety disorder with protracted abstinence (i.e., > 3 months) (Schuckit et al., 1990). In another report by these investigators, 40% of primary alcoholic men reported significantly elevated levels of state anxiety at admission, which had returned to within the normal range by the second week of treatment, and further reductions were evident with continued abstinence (Brown et al., 1991). For information on how to clinically separate affective and anxiety disorders from the substance-induced effects of alcohol and drugs, we refer the interested reader to the study of Anthenelli and Schuckit (1993).

In a study that examined the diagnostic accuracy of various instruments to detect depression in recently detoxified alcoholics (i.e., in 250 patients who were admitted to an inpatient treatment facility), 62%, 54%, and 27% of them were classified as "depressed" according to the MMPI Depression scale (≥ 70), the Beck Depression Inventory (BDI ≥ 13), and the DSM-III Diagnostic Interview Schedule (DIS) (Hesselbrock et al., 1983). Using the DIS as the criterion, the sensitivity of the MMPI and BDI to identify current "depression" was 71% and 88%, respectively, and the specificity was 52% and 57%, respectively. Only 18% were consistently classified as "depressed" by all three measures; 26% were classified as nondepressed using the three measures (Hesselbrock et al., 1983). Although there are some methodological problems inherent in this study (e.g., timing of the three interviews relative to days abstinent—the MMPI was administered the day of admission, the BDI on the second day, and the DIS within a week), these results suggest that when using the MMPI and the BDI, one may frequently be assessing dysphoric mood associated with detoxification from alcohol use rather than detecting a major depressive episode.

A number of investigators have also carried out studies to examine how subclinical levels of depressive and anxiety symptoms influence neuropsychological test performance. For example, Sinha and colleagues demonstrated that scores on the Beck Depression Inventory correlated with an overall measure of neuropsychological impairment in both FH+ and FH− alcoholics. Scores on the Hamilton Depression Rating Scale were also shown to be related to Trails B and WAIS Digit Symbol when alcoholics were on average 12 days sober (Schafer et al., 1991). At the 3-month follow-up, estimates of drinking following discharge and severity of depressive symptoms were significantly related to neuropsychological test performance. However, in another study, severity of depressive symptoms (using the Beck Depression Inventory) was not associated with cognitive impairment 7 to 14 days after admission or at 6 months (Clark et al., 1984).

It seems accurate to conclude that depression and anxiety are frequent consequences of heavy drinking, but ASPD seems to predate alcohol abuse. Only in more extreme alcohol-related personality and neuropsychological disorders do there appear to be consistent relationships between neuropsychological and psychiatric status. Some subgroups, however, notably violent alcoholics and alcoholics who have suffered prior head injuries, may be exceptions to this general trend.

Education Influences

Certain intellectual and neuropsychological abilities are affected by level of formal education (Heaton et al., 1991; Heaton, 1992; see also Heaton et al., Chapter 7). To illustrate this relationship in alcoholics, when 14 samples of alcoholics were ranked according to their level of education and their performance on the Halstead Impairment Index, alcoholics with lower education were more often impaired (Grant et al., 1984). In addition, there may be an interaction between drinking and education, because heavy drinkers with low education generally show more neuropsychological deficits (Williams and Skinner, 1990).

A number of investigators have examined the relationship between premorbid functioning (using in most cases the Vocabulary subtest from the WAIS/WAIS-R) and neuropsychological deficits observed in alcoholics. Some have suggested that neuropsychological deficits in alcoholics may be explained by premorbid differences, because a number of studies have found that the level of neuropsychological deficits parallels Vocabulary level (Draper and Manning, 1982; Cutting, 1988; Emmerson et al., 1988). Lower Vocabulary scores in alcoholics may also be a surrogate indicating past learning problems in school. Along these lines, 40% of alcohol-dependent male adults were found to have had special education, remedial services, or repeated grade failure (concurrent with a familial history of alcoholism and current indices of learning disability) (Rhodes and Jasinski, 1990). The authors from this study also suggested that having a history of childhood learning disorders may be related to the development of alcoholism (i.e., a compromised central nervous system may make one less resistant to familial or social risk factors for the development of unhealthy drinking practices). Residual learning problems may also explain some of the neuropsychological impairment found among detoxified alcoholics (Løberg, 1989; Rhodes and Jasinski, 1990).

The Influence of Motivation and Expectancies on Neuropsychological Test Performance in Alcoholics

Parsons and his group have carried out a number of studies to determine whether motivation or expectancies about one's performance may explain the neuropsychological differences that are often observed between alcoholics and controls. In one of their first studies, his laboratory showed that both alcoholics and controls do show a trend to improve their performance on a face-name learning task when monetary incentives were made contingent on their performance; however, though alcoholics did show deficits on this task, the authors did not find an interaction between group membership and incentive (Schaeffer and Parsons, 1988). A similar paradigm, used to evaluate motivational effects on problem-solving ability in alcoholics, also showed no interaction between incentive and group performance (Schaeffer et al., 1989). In both of the preceding studies, depressive symptoms, as measured by the Beck Depression Inventory, could not account for these differences. Because alcoholics rate themselves as being more impaired cognitively (Shelton and Parsons, 1987; Errico et al., 1990), their reduced expectancies may in some way affect their performance on neuropsychological tests. A study by Sander et al. (1989) addressed this issue and found that alcoholics do have reduced expectancies about their performance, which also correlate with their actual neuropsychological performance; however, neuropsychological differences persist when one statistically removes the variance associated with pretest expectancies (Sander et al., 1989). Finally, both alcoholics and controls respond similarly to experimental manipulations that enhance personal involvement or reduce negative affect, further suggesting that motivation differences do not explain neuropsychological deficits in alcoholics (Nixon et al., 1992).

A number of self-report instruments have been developed to assess cognitive complaints (Heaton and Pendleton, 1981; Chelune et al., 1986; Shelton and Parsons, 1987; O'Donnell et al., 1993). The Neuropsychological Impairment Scale (NIS) (O'Donnell et al., 1993) and the Patient's Assessment of Own Functioning Inventory (PAOF) (Heaton and Pendleton, 1981; Chelune et al., 1986) have been used to assess cognitive symptoms in recovering alcoholics (Shelton and Parsons, 1987; Errico et al., 1990; O'Donnell et al., 1994). There are a number of problems, however, with using these instruments to detect cerebral dysfunction in alcoholics (Shelton and Parsons, 1987), as well as with other psychiatric patients (Chelune et al., 1986), because they tend to be significantly related to drinking intensity (Shelton and Parsons, 1987; Ryan and Lewis, 1988), level of depression, and anxiety (Shelton and Parsons, 1987; Errico et al., 1990), and/or personality disturbances on the MMPI (Chelune et al., 1986), rather than to actual neuropsychological test performance.

Test Characteristics and Sample

A recent study by Parsons and his group revealed that community alcoholics performed intermediate to VA alcoholics and controls on a number of neuropsychological measures suggesting that referral source is an important determinant of whether deficits will be present (Tivis et al., 1993). Furthermore, alcoholics who declined participation in a research study on the effects of alcohol on brain functioning performed worse on the Shipley Abstraction Test, suggesting that alcoholics who are enrolled may not be as impaired as those that decline (Nixon et al., 1988). More research is also needed to evaluate the sensitivity and specificity of measures to detect impairment in alcoholics, particularly because there is considerable overlap in distributions even on the most discriminating measures that separate alcoholics and controls (Parsons, 1994a).

Neurobehavioral Recovery and Neuroimaging Reversibility in Alcoholics

Neurobehavioral Recovery

The extent to which CNS abnormalities persist in alcoholics, or recover with increasing length of stable abstinence, is an area of continuing debate. Certainly, if one were to focus only on the data from recently detoxified alcoholics tested weeks to several months after their last drink, one might erroneously conclude that alcohol causes chronic and permanent CNS damage. However, studies that have examined alcoholics after longer periods of abstinence have been able to show that neurobehavioral recovery continues for several months, and perhaps years, after a person stops drinking. A nosology that takes into account this time course, as well as the differential rate of neurobehavioral recovery, has been previously described (Grant et al., 1987b) (see Fig. 18-1).

Since the first systematic neuropsychological investigation of alcoholics (Fitzhugh et al., 1960), a significant number of studies have focused on the neuropsychological recovery of alcoholics, particularly with respect to the effects that increasing length of abstinence, resumption of drinking, and age at testing may have on the amount of recovery.

Of the studies that have examined alcoholics after short periods of abstinence (i.e., weeks to several months), some have shown improvements in neuropsychological functioning (Smith and Layden, 1972; Farmer, 1973; Bean and Karasievich, 1975; Cermak and Ryback, 1976; Sharp et al., 1977; Ayers et al., 1978; Ellenberg et al., 1980; Guthrie and Elliott, 1980; Hester et al., 1980; Kish et al., 1980; Leber et al., 1981; Gechter, 1987; McIntyre, 1987; Muuronen et al., 1989), particularly with "experience-dependent" stimulation or training (Goldman et al., 1983, 1985; Forsberg and Goldman, 1985, 1987; Goldman and Goldman, 1988; Stringer and Goldman, 1988; Roehrich and Goldman, 1993); others, however, have shown little neuropsychological recovery with short periods of abstinence (Page and Linden, 1974; Clarke and Haughton, 1975; Page and Schaub, 1977; Eckardt et al., 1979, 1980b; Ryan and Butters, 1980b; Claiborn and Greene, 1981; de Obaldia et al., 1981; Brandt et al., 1983; Unkenstein and Bowden, 1991).

There are also conflicting reports on the extent of neuropsychological recovery in alcoholics who have maintained longer periods of abstinence (i.e., many months to several years). Some investigators have shown that long-term abstinence can be associated with normal or improved neuropsychological functioning (Long and McLachlan, 1974; McLachlan and Levinson, 1974; Templer et

al., 1975; Berglund et al., 1977; O'Leary et al., 1977b; Grant et al., 1979a; Adams et al., 1980; Chaney et al., 1980; Schau et al., 1980; Fabian and Parsons, 1983; Grant et al., 1984, 1987b; Gardner et al., 1989; Marchesi et al., 1992; Reed et al., 1992); others, however, have been unable to demonstrate much change with long-term abstinence (Eckardt et al., 1980a; Ryan et al., 1980; Brandt et al., 1983; Yohman et al., 1985; Parsons et al., 1990a).

With respect to resumption of drinking, a number of longitudinal studies have examined the effects of interim drinking on neuropsychological recovery. Those alcoholics who maintained continuous abstinence, or demonstrated "improved drinking habits" over a follow-up period, showed more neuropsychological recovery and less deficits at follow-up, relative to alcoholics who resumed drinking at moderate or severe levels (McLachlan and Levinson, 1974; Berglund et al., 1977; Gregson and Taylor, 1977; Adams et al., 1980; Eckardt et al., 1980a; Guthrie and Elliott, 1980; Abbott and Gregson, 1981; Fabian and Parsons, 1983; Yohman et al., 1985; Grant et al., 1987b; Muuronen et al., 1989; Parsons et al., 1990a); however, there are two reports that have not found an effect of level of interim drinking on neuropsychological performance (O'Leary et al., 1977b; Schau et al., 1980).

The effect of aging on neuropsychological test performance is well established (Reitan and Wolfson, 1985; Heaton et al., 1991). The similarity in neuropsychological test performance between elderly normal controls and alcoholics has led a number of investigators to propose that alcoholism leads to premature aging (Fitzhugh et al., 1965; Blusewicz et al., 1977a,b). In one variant of this hypothesis (i.e., "accelerated aging") (Ryan and Butters, 1980b; Hochla and Parsons, 1982; Noonberg et al., 1985), alcoholics of all ages show neuropsychological deficits similar to nonalcoholics 10 to 15 years their senior. In a second variant, the "increased vulnerability" (Jones and Parsons, 1971; Klisz and Parsons, 1977; Bertera and Parsons, 1978) hypothesis, only older alcoholics show deficits; younger alcoholics perform at levels comparable to those of similarly age-matched nonalcoholics. Other investigators, however, have proposed that alcohol and aging may result in separate effects or "independent decrements" on neuropsychological performance (Ryan and Butters, 1980b; Becker et al., 1983a; Grant et al., 1984; Kramer et al., 1989). Not all of the above studies matched young and old alcoholics on length of alcoholic drinking. Some studies have noted that increased length of drinking history was related to worse neuropsychological performance in alcoholics (Jones, 1971; Tarter and Parsons, 1971; Klisz and Parsons, 1977; Goldman et al., 1983; DeFranco et al., 1985; Bolter and Hannon, 1986); however, others have shown that similar deficits exist regardless of age or length of drinking history (Ryan and Butters, 1980b; Noonberg et al., 1985).

At least four methodological shortcomings likely contribute to the discrepant findings in the literature regarding the rate and amount of neuropsychological recovery in alcoholics. First, many of the longitudinal studies, particularly those in the 1970s and early 1980s, did not include age- and education-matched control groups to correct for demographic differences and the effects of practice (Smith and Layden, 1972; Farmer, 1973; Long and McLachlan, 1974; McLachlan and Levinson, 1974; Page and Linden, 1974; Bean and Karasievich, 1975; Cermak and Ryback, 1976; Berglund et al., 1977; Page and Schaub, 1977; Ayers et al., 1978; Guthrie and Elliott, 1980; Hester et al., 1980; Kish et al., 1980; Gechter, 1987; Muuronen et al., 1989; Unkenstein and Bowden, 1991).

Second, many studies have not screened and/or controlled for adverse neuromedical confounds or risk factors that predate, coexist with, or occur as a consequence of heavy alcohol consumption (Tarter and Edwards, 1986). These risk factors or confounds likely contribute or lead to neuropsychological impairments over and above the neurotoxic effects of alcohol. Along these lines, investigators have shown that alcoholics with "minimal brain dysfunction" symptoms (Tarter, 1982; de Obaldia and Parsons, 1984), head injuries (Grant et al., 1984; Alterman

and Tarter, 1985; Adams and Grant, 1986; Hillbom and Holm, 1986; Solomon and Malloy, 1992), or liver dysfunction/pathology (Acker et al., 1982; Tarter et al., 1986b, 1988; Irwin et al., 1989; Arria et al., 1991a; Schafer et al., 1991) perform worse on neuropsychological testing. The extent to which these symptoms, events, and conditions influence the rate and amount of neuropsychological recovery when subjects are followed over time has yet to be addressed.

Third, psychometric evaluations were often conducted during the first 2 weeks of abstinence before acute withdrawal effects and detoxification were complete (Smith and Layden, 1972; Farmer, 1973; Long and McLachlan, 1974; Page and Linden, 1974; Bean and Karasievich, 1975; Clarke and Haughton, 1975; Cermak and Ryback, 1976; O'Leary et al., 1977b; Page and Schaub, 1977; Sharp et al., 1977; Ayers et al., 1978; Eckardt et al., 1979, 1980b; Chaney et al., 1980; Ellenberg et al., 1980; Guthrie and Elliott, 1980; Hester et al., 1980; Kish et al., 1980; Schau et al., 1980; Claiborn and Greene, 1981; McIntyre, 1987; Muuronen et al., 1989).

Fourth, failure to use a number of tests to adequately represent a single neuropsychological ability area, or to sample a wide range of neuropsychological abilities, has most likely led to an inaccurate estimation of neuropsychological deficits. This is particularly salient when performance on one test is used to infer performance on a neuropsychological ability, or when the task difficulty/complexity is manipulated. Relative to all of the studies carried out on the neuropsychological recovery of alcoholics, only a selected number of cross-sectional (de Obaldia et al., 1981; Grant et al., 1984; Adams and Grant, 1986; Reed et al., 1992) and longitudinal studies (Long and McLachlan, 1974; Page and Linden, 1974; Page and Schaub, 1977; Eckardt et al., 1979, 1980a,b; Adams et al., 1980; Chaney et al., 1980; Schau et al., 1980; Claiborn and Greene, 1981; Fabian and Parsons, 1983; Yohman et al., 1985; Grant et al., 1987b; McIntyre, 1987; Parsons et al., 1990a) have included a comprehensive sampling of neuropsychological abilities.

Neuroimaging Evidence for Reversibility in Structural Brain Abnormalities

If there is evidence of neurobehavioral recovery in alcoholics, one would also expect to see evidence at the structural and functional level for brain recovery. In fact, several investigators have provided evidence to suggest that brain morphology can improve with stable and increasing length of abstinence.

In 1978, Carlen and his colleagues demonstrated a measurable decrease in the degree of cerebral atrophy using CT, as well as some functional improvement, in four of eight chronic alcoholics who had maintained their abstinence over the interim. These results represented the first report of reversible cerebral "atrophy" in recently abstinent chronic alcoholics using CT scanning. Since this time, there have been a number of CT as well as MRI reports that have documented reductions in cortical and central CSF volumes with extended periods of abstinence or in alcoholics who improve their drinking habits (Artmann et al., 1981; Ron et al., 1982; Carlen and Wilkinson, 1983; Ron, 1983; Carlen et al., 1984; Jacobson, 1986a; Carlen and Wilkinson, 1987; Muuronen et al., 1989; Mann et al., 1993; Rourke et al., 1993; Marchesi et al., 1994; Shear et al., 1994; Drake et al., 1995).

Whereas most of these studies have been with male alcoholics, a cross-sectional comparison of CT parameters in 26 recently detoxified female alcoholics (abstinent a mean of 33 days) and eight long-term female abstinent alcoholics (abstinent a mean of 3.3 years) recruited from local AA chapters indicated that female AA members were more comparable to nonalcoholic female controls; in addition, there was some indication that cerebral changes were evident after briefer periods of abstinence than with male AA members (Jacobson, 1986a). Thus, although female alcoholics may experience cerebral structural abnormalities similar to those obtained in male alcoholics that tend to appear after shorter and less intense drinking careers, they may also tend to recover more quickly than their male counterparts.

More recently, using MRI, significant decreases in total CSF, ventricular and subarachnoid volumes have been observed in nine chronic alcoholics after 5 weeks of alcohol abstinence (Mann et al., 1989). In another MRI study (Zipursky et al., 1989), ventricular volume from 10 alcoholics were compared to 10 age-matched controls. Alcoholics had significantly larger ventricles at the time of their first MRI scan (scan within 2 weeks of alcohol withdrawal; mean 7.3 days); however 19 to 28 days later (mean 22.6 days), the difference between alcoholics and controls was no longer significant. Whether these fluid changes represent changes in hydration is still being debated (Harper et al., 1988b; Schroth et al., 1988; Smith et al., 1988; Mander et al., 1989). Two recent MRI reports have demonstrated that decreases in CSF were associated with increases in tissue volumes, particularly white matter, in alcoholics who maintained stable abstinence over 3 months (Shear et al., 1994) and 1 year (Drake et al., 1995). Longitudinal MRI follow-up of larger groups of chronic alcoholics who are able to maintain their abstinence will likely help to delineate the permanence of cerebral structural abnormalities in alcoholics.

Clinical Implications and Treatment Outcome

Even though the mild to moderate neuropsychological deficits that are often detected in alcoholics after 2 to 4 weeks of detoxification are not severe enough to warrant a diagnosis of either an Alcohol-Induced Persisting Dementia or an Alcohol-Induced Amnestic Disorder (American Psychiatric Association, 1994), these deficits can, however, have significant effects on the treatment compliance, after-care success, employment, and everyday functioning of recovering alcoholics (Gregson and Taylor, 1977; O'Leary et al., 1979; Eckardt et al., 1980a; Guthrie and Elliott, 1980; Abbott and Gregson, 1981; Donovan et al., 1984, 1985, 1986; Leber et al., 1985; McCrady and Smith, 1986; Alterman et al., 1989a; Trivedi and Raghavan, 1989; Goldman, 1990; Parsons et al., 1990a; Glenn and Parsons, 1991b).

One limitation in many inpatient alcohol and drug treatment programs is that it is difficult and time consuming to make accommodations for individual patients who might have quite different neuropsychological abilities and deficits. For example, some younger healthy alcoholic patients may be relatively normal from a neurocognitive perspective, and may be more ready to pay attention, assimilate new information (e.g., relapse prevention material), and be able to reason, problem-solve, and use their intact abstracting skills to see how a number of factors have contributed to the development of their disease, and how they might make life changes to help maintain their abstinence and to develop more adaptable behaviors. In contrast, many older alcoholics who have a number of medical complications and neuromedical risk factors may have many neuropsychological deficits that place significant limitations on their ability to utilize the standard treatment modalities for alcoholism. In a recent study, elderly alcoholics were found to experience more severe withdrawal symptoms (i.e., more cognitive impairment, disorientation and confusion, increased daytime sleepiness, weakness, cardiac disease and high blood pressure) than younger alcoholics, despite similar recent drinking history and educational experience (Brower et al., 1994). Overall, these results suggest that treatment for alcoholism may take longer in elderly patients, and interventions should target the medical comorbidity (Brower et al., 1994) as well as develop ways to circumvent the neuropsychological deficits that are often prevalent in elderly alcoholics.

A number of investigators have explored how neuropsychological test performance during inpatient treatment may predict treatment success and compliance, later relapse, and everyday functioning. Some have demonstrated that neuropsychological performance is associated or predictive of time in residence (Fals-Stewart and Schafer, 1992), relapse (Gregson and Taylor, 1977), therapists' ratings of improvement during therapy (Parsons, 1983) as well as prognosis (Leber et al., 1985), length of abstinence, treatment compliance and aftercare success, and later employment (O'Leary et al., 1979; Walker et al., 1983; Donovan et al., 1984, 1985, 1986). In one study, alcoholics who remained sober through one year were better educated and had higher memory scores at baseline than those alcoholics who relapsed (George et al., 1992). However, in contrast, there are a number of reports in which neuropsychological test performance is not related to treatment outcome (Eckardt et al., 1988; Prange, 1988; Macciocchi et al., 1989; Alterman et al., 1990).

Glenn and Parsons recently examined how a number of variables collected at baseline (i.e., depressive symptoms, neuropsychological test performance, psychosocial maladjustment, previous treatment, and childhood ADD symptoms) predict resumption of drinking in alcoholics 14 months later (Parsons et al., 1990a; Glenn and Parsons, 1991b). They found that alcoholics who later resumed drinking performed significantly worse at baseline on all five factors that explained 27% of the variance. Overall, 75% of the sample was correctly classified, and depressive symptoms at baseline were discovered to be the most predictive of relapse. When they excluded neuropsychological test performance from the model, the classification rate was slightly reduced to 72.5% (Glenn and Parsons, 1991b). These results provide further support that neuropsychological test performance by itself does not significantly predict later relapse or treatment success. We believe that further studies are needed to determine how neuropsychological test performance may be more of a mediator or intervening variable in a model that also incorporates measures of social support, affective symptomatology, and measures of everyday functioning when trying to predict treatment compliance, success, and everyday functioning.

Finally, we believe that the benefits of cognitive stimulation and remediation during treatment, an area that Goldman and his colleagues have been developing over the past several years (Forsberg and Goldman, 1987; Roehrich and Goldman, 1993), has considerable promise. In Roehrich and Goldman's most recent study, alcoholics who received ecologically relevant or neuropsychological remediation during inpatient treatment showed more cognitive improvements over the course of their treatment, decreased affective symptomatology, a decline in their self-reported cognitive complaints, and were able to learn more information on relapse prevention (Roehrich and Goldman, 1993).

References

Abbott, M. W., and Gregson, R.A.M. (1981). Cognitive dysfunction in the prediction of relapse in alcoholics. *Journal of Studies on Alcohol, 42*, 230–243.

Acker, C. (1985). Performance of female alcoholics on neuropsychological testing. *Alcohol and Alcoholism, 20*, 379–386.

Acker, C., Jacobson, R. R., and Lishman, W. A. (1987). Memory and ventricular size in alcoholics. *Psychological Medicine, 17*, 343–348.

Acker, W., Aps, E. J., Majumdar, S. K., Shaw, G. K., and Thomson, A. D. (1982). The relationship between brain and liver damage in chronic alcoholic patients. *Journal of Neurology, Neurosurgery and Psychiatry, 45*, 984–987.

Adams, K. M., Gilman, S., Koeppe, R. A., Kluin, K. J., Brunberg, J. A., Dede, D., Berent, S., and Kroll, P. D. (1993). Neuropsychological deficits are correlated with frontal hypometabolism in positron emission tomography studies of older alcoholic patients. *Alcoholism: Clinical and Experimental Research, 17*, 205–210.

Adams, K. M., and Grant, I. (1984). Failure of nonlinear models of drinking history variables to predict neuropsychological performance in alcoholics. *American Journal of Psychiatry, 141*, 663–667.

Adams, K. M., and Grant, I. (1986). Influence of premorbid risk factors on neuropsychological performance in alcoholics. *Journal of Clinical and Experimental Neuropsychology, 8*, 362–370.

Adams, K. M., Grant, I., and Reed, R. (1980). Neuropsychology in alcoholic men in their late thirties: One-year follow-up. *American Journal of Psychiatry, 137*, 928–931.

Adinoff, B., Risher-Flowers, D., De Jong, J., Ravitz, B., Bone, G. H., Nutt, D. J., Roehrich, L., Martin, P. R., and Linnoila, M. (1991). Disturbances of hypothalamic-pituitary-adrenal axis functioning during ethanol withdrawal in six men. *American Journal of Psychiatry, 148*, 1023–1025.

Akshoomoff, N. A., Delis, D. C., and Kiefner, M. G. (1989). Block constructions of chronic alcoholic and unilateral brain-damaged patients: A test of the right hemisphere vulnerability hypothesis of alcoholism. *Archives of Clinical Neuropsychology, 4*, 275–281.

Albert, M., Butters, N., Rogers, S., Pressman, J., and Geller, A. (1982). A preliminary report: Nutritional levels and cognitive performance in chronic alcohol abusers. *Drug and Alcohol Dependence, 9*, 131–142.

Albert, M., Butters, N., Rogers, S., Pressman, J., and Geller, A. (1983). Nutritional links between cognitive performance and alcohol misuse. *Digest of Alcoholism Theory and Application, 2*, 44–47.

Allen, J. P., Litten, R. Z., Anton, R. F., and Cross, G. M. (1994). Carbohydrate-deficient transferrin as a measure of immoderate drinking: Remaining issues. *Alcoholism: Clinical and Experimental Research, 18*, 799–812.

Alterman, A. I., Bridges, K. R., and Tarter, R. E. (1986). The influence of both drinking and familial risk statuses on cognitive functioning of social drinkers. *Alcoholism: Clinical and Experimental Research, 10*, 448–451.

Alterman, A. I., and Gerstley, L. J. (1986). Predictive validity of four factors derived from an 'Hyperactivity/MBD' questionnaire. *Drug and Alcohol Dependence, 18*, 259–271.

Alterman, A. I., Gerstley, L. J., Goldstein, G., and Tarter, R. E. (1987). Comparisons of the cognitive functioning of familial and nonfamilial alcoholics. *Journal of Studies on Alcohol, 48*, 425–429.

Alterman, A. I., Goldstein, G., Shelly, C., Bober, B., and Tarter, R. E. (1985a). The impact of mild head injury on neuropsychological capacity in chronic alcoholics. *International Journal of Neuroscience, 28*, 155–162.

Alterman, A. I., and Hall, J. G. (1989). Effects of social drinking and familial alcoholism risk on cognitive functioning: Null findings. *Alcoholism: Clinical and Experimental Research, 13*, 799–803.

Alterman, A. I., Holahan, J. M., Baughman, T. G., and Michels, S. (1989a). Predictors of alcoholics' acquisition of treatment-related knowledge. *Journal of Substance Abuse Treatment, 6*, 49–53.

Alterman, A. I., Kushner, H., and Holahan, J. M. (1990). Cognitive functioning and treatment outcome in alcoholics. *Journal of Nervous and Mental Disease, 178,* 494–499.

Alterman, A. I., and McLellan, A. T. (1986). A factor-analytic study of Tarter's "Hyperactivity-MBD" questionnaire. *Addictive Behaviors, 11,* 287–294.

Alterman, A. I., Searles, J. S., and Hall, J. G. (1989b). Failure to find differences in drinking behavior as a function of familial risk for alcoholism: A replication. *Journal of Abnormal Psychology, 98,* 50–53.

Alterman, A. I., and Tarter, R. E. (1985). Relationship between familial alcoholism and head injury. *Journal of Studies on Alcohol, 46,* 256–258.

Alterman, A. I., Tarter, R. E., Baughman, T. G., Bober, B. A., and Fabian, S. A. (1985b). Differentiation of alcoholics high and low in childhood hyperactivity. *Drug and Alcohol Dependence, 15,* 111–121.

American Psychiatric Association. (1987). *Diagnostic and Statistical Manual of Mental Disorders* (3rd ed., rev.). Washington, D.C.: American Psychiatric Association.

American Psychiatric Association. (1994). *Diagnostic and Statistical Manual of Mental Disorders* (4th ed.). Washington, D.C.: American Psychiatric Association.

Angelini, G., Bogetto, F., Borio, R., Meluzzi, A., Mucci, P., Patria, D., Ricciardi, G., and Torta, R. (1990). Clinico-nosographic remarks on the relationship between depression and alcoholism in a population of 450 hospitalized alcoholics. *Minerva Psichiatrica, 31,* 41–45.

Anthenelli, R. M., and Schuckit, M. A. (1990). Genetic studies of alcoholism. *International Journal of the Addictions, 25,* 81–94.

Anthenelli, R. M., and Schuckit, M. A. (1993). Affective and anxiety disorders and alcohol and drug dependence: Diagnosis and treatment. *Journal of Addictive Diseases, 12,* 73–87.

Arendt, T., Bigl, V., Arendt, A., and Tennstedt, A. (1983). Loss of neurons in the nucleus basilis of Meynert in Alzheimer's disease, paralysis agitans and Korsakoff's disease. *Acta Neuropathologica, 61,* 101–108.

Aronson, M., and Olegard, R. (1987). Children of alcoholic mothers. *Pediatrician, 14,* 57–61.

Arria, A. M., Tarter, R. E., Kabene, M. A., Laird, S. B., Moss, H., and Van Thiel, D. H. (1991a). The role of cirrhosis in memory functioning of alcoholics. *Alcoholism: Clinical and Experimental Research, 15,* 932–937.

Arria, A. M., Tarter, R. E., Starzl, T. E., and Van Thiel, D. H. (1991b). Improvement in cognitive functioning of alcoholics following orthotopic liver transplantation. *Alcoholism: Clinical and Experimental Research, 15,* 956–962.

Artmann, H., Gall, M. V., Hacker, H., and Herrlich, J. (1981). Reversible enlargement of cerebral spinal fluid spaces in chronic alcoholics. *American Journal of Neuroradiology, 2,* 23–27.

Ayers, J., Ruff, C. F., and Templer, D. I. (1976). Alcoholism, cigarette smoking, coffee drinking and extraversion. *Journal of Studies on Alcohol, 37,* 983–985.

Ayers, J. L., Templer, D. I., Ruff, C. F., and Barthlow, V. L. (1978). Trail making test improvement in abstinent alcoholics. *Journal of Studies on Alcohol, 39,* 1627–1629.

Barboriak, J. J., Jacobson, G. R., Cushman, P., Herrington, R. E., Lipo, R. F., Daley, M. E., and Anderson, A. J. (1980). Chronic alcohol abuse and high density lipoprotein cholesterol. *Alcoholism: Clinical and Experimental Research, 4,* 346–349.

Barron, J. H., and Russell, E. W. (1992). Fluidity theory and neuropsychological impairment in alcoholism. *Archives of Clinical Neuropsychology, 7,* 175–188.

Bates, M. E., and Pandina, R. J. (1992). Familial alcoholism and premorbid cognitive deficit: A failure to replicate subtype differences. *Journal of Studies on Alcohol, 53,* 320–327.

Bates, M. E., and Tracy, J. I. (1990). Cognitive functioning in young "social drinkers": Is there impairment to detect? *Journal of Abnormal Psychology, 99,* 242–249.

Bean, K. L., and Karasievich, G. O. (1975). Psychological test results at three stages of inpatient alcoholism treatment. *Journal of Studies on Alcohol, 36,* 838–852.

Beatty, W. W., Bailly, R. C., and Fisher, L. (1989). Korsakoff-like amnesic syndrome in a patient with anorexia and vomiting. *International Journal of Clinical Neuropsychology, 11,* 55–65.

Beatty, W. W., Katzung, V. M., Nixon, S. J., and Moreland, V. J. (1993). Problem-solving deficits in alcoholics: Evidence from the California Card Sorting Test. *Journal of Studies on Alcohol, 54,* 687–692.

Becker, J. T., Butters, N., Hermann, A., and D'Angelo, N. (1983a). A comparison of the effects of long-term alcohol abuse and aging on the performance of verbal and nonverbal divided attention tasks. *Alcoholism: Clinical and Experimental Research, 7,* 213–219.

Becker, J. T., Butters, N., Hermann, A., and D'Angelo, N. (1983b). Learning to associate names and faces: Impaired acquisition on an ecologically relevant memory task by male alcoholics. *Journal of Nervous and Mental Disease, 171,* 617–623.

Becker, J. T., Furman, J. M., Panisset, M., and Smith, C. (1990). Characteristics of the memory loss of a patient with Wernicke-Korsakoff's syndrome without alcoholism. *Neuropsychologia, 28,* 171–179.

Begleiter, H., and Porjesz, B. (1990). Neuroelectric processes in individuals at risk for alcoholism. *Alcohol and Alcoholism, 25,* 251–256.

Begleiter, H., Porjesz, B., Bihari, B., and Kissin, B. (1984). Event-related brain potentials in boys at risk for alcoholism. *Science, 225,* 1493–1496.

Begleiter, H., Porjesz, B., and Chou, C. L. (1981). Auditory brainstem potentials in chronic alcoholics. *Science, 211,* 1064–1066.

Begleiter, H., Porjesz, B., Rawlings, R., and Eckardt, M. (1987). Auditory recovery function and P3 in boys at high risk for alcoholism. *Alcohol, 4,* 315–321.

Begleiter, H., Porjesz, B., and Tenner, M. (1980). Neuroradiological and neurophysiological evidence of brain deficits in chronic alcoholics. *Acta Psychiatrica Scandinavica, 62,* 3–13.

Bell, H., and Steensland, H. (1987). Serum activity of gamma-glutamyltranspeptidase (GGT) in relation to estimated alcohol consumption and questionnaires in alcohol dependence syndrome. *British Journal of Addiction, 82,* 1021–1026.

Bell, H., Tallaksen, C.M.E., Try, K., and Haug, E. (1994). Carbohydrate-deficient transferrin and other markers of high alcohol consumption: A study of 502 patients admitted consecutively to a medical department. *Alcoholism: Clinical and Experimental Research, 18,* 1103–1108.

Berglund, M., Hagstadius, S., Risberg, J., Johanson, T. M., Bliding, A., and Mubrin, Z. (1987). Normalization of regional cerebral blood flow in alcoholics during the first 7 weeks of abstinence. *Acta Psychiatrica Scandinavica, 75,* 202–208.

Berglund, M., Leijonquist, H., and Horlen, M. (1977). Prognostic significance and reversibility of cerebral dysfunction in alcoholics. *Journal of Studies on Alcohol, 38,* 1761–1770.

Bergman, H. (1985). Cognitive deficits and morphological cerebral changes in a random sample of social drinkers. *Recent Developments in Alcoholism, 3,* 265–276.

Bergman, H. (1987). Brain dysfunction related to alcoholism: Some results from the KARTAD Project. In O. A. Parsons, N. Butters, and P. E.

Nathan, eds., *Neuropsychology of Alcoholism: Implications for Diagnosis and Treatment.* New York: Guilford Press, pp. 21–44.

Bergman, H., Axelsson, G., Idestrom, C. M., Borg, S., Hindmarsh, T., Makower, J., and Mutzell, S. (1983). Alcohol consumption, neuropsychological status and computer-tomographic findings in a random sample of men and women from the general population. *Pharmacology, Biochemistry, and Behavior, 18,* 501–505.

Bergman, H., Borg, S., Hindmarsh, T., Idestrom, C. M., and Mutzell, S. (1980a). Computed tomography of the brain and neuropsychological assessment of male alcoholic patients and a random sample from the general male population. *Acta Psychiatrica Scandinavica, 286* (Suppl.), 77–88.

Bergman, H., Borg, S., Hindmarsh, T., Idestrom, C. M., and Mutzell, S. (1980b). Computed tomography of the brain, clinical examination and neuropsychological assessment of a random sample of men from the general population. *Acta Psychiatrica Scandinavica, 286* (Suppl.), 47–56.

Bergman, H., Borg, S., Hindmarsh, T., Idestrom, C. M., and Mutzell, S. (1980c). Computed-tomography of the brain and neuropsychological assessment of alcoholic patients. *Advances in Experimental Medicine and Biology, 126,* 771–786.

Berman, S. M., Whipple, S. C., Fitch, R. J., and Noble, E. P. (1993). P3 in young boys as a predictor of adolescent substance use. *Alcohol, 10,* 69–76.

Bertera, J. H., and Parsons, O. A. (1978). Impaired visual search in alcoholics. *Alcoholism: Clinical and Experimental Research, 2,* 9–14.

Blansjaar, B. A., and van Dijk, J. G. (1992). Korsakoff minus Wernicke syndrome. *Alcohol and Alcoholism, 27,* 435–437.

Blansjaar, B. A., Vielvoye, G. J., van Dijk, J. G., and Rijnders, R. J. (1992). Similar brain lesions in alcoholics and Korsakoff patients: MRI, psychometric and clinical findings. *Clinical Neurology and Neurosurgery, 94,* 197–203.

Blass, J. P., and Gibson, G. E. (1977). Abnormality of a thiamine-requiring enzyme in patients with Wernicke-Korsakoff syndrome. *New England Journal of Medicine, 297,* 1367–1370.

Blusewicz, M. J., Dustman, R. E., Schenkenberg, T., and Beck, E. C. (1977a). Neuropsychological correlates of chronic alcoholism and aging. *Journal of Nervous and Mental Disease, 165,* 348–355.

Blusewicz, M. J., Schenkenberg, T., Dustman, R. E., and Beck, E. C. (1977b). WAIS performance in young normal, young alcoholic, and elderly normal groups: An evaluation of organicity and mental aging indices. *Journal of Clinical Psychology, 33,* 1149–1153.

Bolter, J. F., and Hannon, R. (1986). Lateralized cerebral dysfunction in early and late stage alcoholics. *Journal of Studies on Alcohol, 47,* 213–218.

Bowden, S. C. (1987). Brain impairment in social drinkers? No cause for concern. *Alcoholism: Clinical and Experimental Research, 11,* 407–410.

Bowden, S. C. (1990). Separating cognitive impairment in neurologically asymptomatic alcoholism from Wernicke-Korsakoff syndrome: Is the neuropsychological distinction justified? *Psychological Bulletin, 107,* 355–366.

Braggio, J. T., and Pishkin, V. (1991). Psychophysiological activity as a mediator of neuropsychological test performance in alcoholics. *Perceptual and Motor Skills, 72,* 593–594.

Braggio, J. T., and Pishkin, V. (1992). Systolic blood pressure and neuropsychological test performance of alcoholics. *Alcoholism: Clinical and Experimental Research, 16,* 726–733.

Braggio, J. T., Pishkin, V., Parsons, O. A., Fishkin, S. M., and Tassey, J. R. (1991). Differences between essential and reactive alcoholics on tests of neuropsychological functioning and affect. *Psychological Reports, 69,* 1131–1136.

Brandt, J., Butters, N., Ryan, C., and Bayog, R. (1983). Cognitive loss and recovery in longterm alcohol abusers. *Archives of General Psychiatry, 40,* 435–442.

Brewer, C., and Perrett, L. (1971). Brain damage due to alcohol consumption: An airencephalographic, psychometric and electroencephalographic study. *British Journal of Addiction, 66,* 170–182.

Brooks, N., Symington, C., Beattie, A., Campsie, L., Bryden, J., and McKinlay, W. (1989). Alcohol and other predictors of cognitive recovery after severe head injury. *Brain Injury, 3,* 235–246.

Brower, K. J., Mudd, S., Blow, F. C., Young, J. P., and Hill, E. M. (1994). Severity and treatment of alcohol withdrawal in elderly versus younger patients. *Alcoholism: Clinical and Experimental Research, 18,* 196–201.

Brown, J., and Lyons, J. P. (1981). A progressive diagnostic schema for alcoholism with evidence for clinical efficacy. *Alcoholism: Clinical and Experimental Research, 5,* 17–25.

Brown, S. A., Inaba, R. K., Gillin, J. C.,

Schuckit, M. A., Stewart, M. A., and Irwin, M. R. (1995). Alcoholism and affective disorder: Clinical course of depressive symptoms. *American Journal of Psychiatry, 152,* 45–52.

Brown, S. A., Irwin, M., and Schuckit, M. A. (1991). Changes in anxiety among abstinent male alcoholics. *Journal of Studies on Alcohol, 52,* 55–61.

Brown, S. A., and Schuckit, M. A. (1988). Changes in depression among abstinent alcoholics. *Journal of Studies on Alcohol, 49,* 412–417.

Bucholz, K. K., Cadoret, R., Cloninger, C. R., Dinwiddie, S. H., Hesselbrock, V. M., Nurnberger, J. I., Jr., Reich, T., Schmidt, I., and Schuckit, M. A. (1994). A new, semistructured psychiatric interview for use in genetic linkage studies: A report on the reliability of the SSAGA. *Journal of Studies on Alcohol, 55,* 149–158.

Burger, M. C., Botwinick, J., and Storandt, M. (1987). Aging, alcoholism, and performance on the Luria-Nebraska Neuropsychological Battery. *Journal of Gerontology, 42,* 69–72.

Butters, N., and Cermak, L. S. (1980). *Alcoholic Korsakoff's Syndrome: An Information Processing Approach to Amnesia.* New York: Academic Press.

Butters, N., Cermak, L. S., Montgomery, K., and Adinolfi, A. (1977). Some comparisons of the memory and visuoperceptive deficits of chronic alcoholics and patients with Korsakoff's disease. *Alcoholism: Clinical and Experimental Research, 1,* 73–80.

Butters, N., and Granholm, E. (1987). The continuity hypothesis: Some conclusions and their implications for the etiology and neuropathology of alcoholic Korsakoff's syndrome. In O. A. Parsons, N. Butters, and P. E. Nathan, eds., *Neuropsychology of Alcoholism: Implications for Diagnosis and Treatment.* New York: Guilford Press, pp. 176–206.

Butters, N., and Salmon, D. P. (1986). Etiology and neuropathology of alcoholic Korsakoff's syndrome: New findings and speculations. In I. Grant, ed., *Neuropsychiatric Correlates of Alcoholism.* Washington, D.C.: American Psychiatric Press, pp. 61–108.

Butters, N., Salmon, D. P., Cullum, C. M., Cairns, P., Tröster, A. I., Jacobs, D., Moss, M., and Cermak, L. S. (1988). Differentiation of amnesic and demented patients with the Wechsler Memory Scale-Revised. *The Clinical Neuropsychologist, 2,* 133–148.

Cahalan, D. (1978). Subcultural differences in drinking behavior in U.S. national surveys and selected European studies. In P. E. Nathan,

G. A. Marlatt, and T. Løberg, eds., *Alcoholism: New Directions in Behavioral Research and Treatment*. New York: Plenum Press, pp. 235–253.

Cala, L. A., and Mastaglia, F. L. (1981). Computerized tomography in chronic alcoholics. *Alcoholism: Clinical and Experimental Research, 5,* 283–294.

Campbell, W. G., and Hodgins, D. C. (1993). Alcohol-related blackouts in a medical practice. *American Journal of Drug and Alcohol Abuse, 19,* 369–376.

Carey, K. B., and Maisto, S. A. (1987). Effect of a change in drinking pattern on the cognitive function of female social drinkers. *Journal of Studies on Alcohol, 48,* 236–242.

Carlen, P. L., and Wilkinson, D. A. (1980). Alcoholic brain damage and reversible deficits. *Acta Psychiatrica Scandinavica, 286* (Suppl.), 103–118.

Carlen, P. L., and Wilkinson, D. A. (1983). Assessment of neurological dysfunction and recovery in alcoholics: CT scanning and other techniques. *Substance and Alcohol Actions/Misuse, 4,* 191–197.

Carlen, P. L., and Wilkinson, D. A. (1987). Reversibility of alcohol-related brain damage: Clinical and experimental observations. *Acta Medica Scandinavica, 717* (Suppl.), 19–26.

Carlen, P. L., Wilkinson, D. A., Wortzman, G., and Holgate, R. (1984). Partially reversible cerebral atrophy and functional improvement in recently abstinent alcoholics. *Le Journal Canadien des Sciences Neurologiques, 11,* 441–446.

Carlin, A. S. (1986). Neuropsychological consequences of drug abuse. In I. Grant and K. M. Adams, eds., *Neuropsychological Assessment of Neuropsychiatric Disorders*. New York: Oxford University Press, pp. 478–497.

Carlin, A. S., Stauss, F. F., Adams, K. M., and Grant, I. (1978). The prediction of neuropsychological impairment in polydrug abusers. *Addictive Behaviors, 3,* 5–12.

Caruso, K., and ten Bensel, R. (1993). Fetal alcohol syndrome and fetal alcohol effects: The University of Minnesota experience. *Minnesota Medicine, 76,* 25–29.

Caspari, D., Trabert, W., Heinz, G., Lion, N., Henkes, H., and Huber, G. (1993). The pattern of regional cerebral blood flow during alcohol withdrawal: A single photon emission tomography study with 99mTc-HMPAO. *Acta Psychiatrica Scandinavica, 87,* 414–417.

Cermak, L. S., and Ryback, R. S. (1976). Recovery of verbal short-term memory in alcoholics. *Journal of Studies on Alcohol, 37,* 46–52.

Chandler, B. C., and Parsons, O. A. (1977). Altered hemispheric functioning under alcohol. *Journal of Studies on Alcohol, 38,* 381–391.

Chaney, E. F., O'Leary, M. R., Fehrenbach, P. A., and Donovan, D. (1980). Cognitive deficit in middle-aged alcoholics. *Drug and Alcohol Dependence, 6,* 219–226.

Chelune, G. J., Heaton, R. K., and Lehman, R.A.W. (1986). Neuropsychological and personality correlates of patients' complaints of disability. In G. Goldstein and R. E. Tarter, eds., *Advances in Clinical Neuropsychology* (vol. 3). New York: Plenum Press, pp. 95–126.

Chelune, G. J., and Parker, J. B. (1981). Neuropsychological deficits associated with chronic alcohol abuse. *Clinical Psychology Review, 1,* 181–195.

Chick, J. D., Smith, M. A., Engleman, H. M., Kean, D. M., Mander, A. J., Douglas, R.H.B., and Best, J.J.K. (1989). Magnetic resonance imaging of the brain in alcoholics: Cerebral atrophy, lifetime alcohol consumption, and cognitive deficits. *Alcoholism: Clinical and Experimental Research, 13,* 512–518.

Chiriboga, C. A. (1993). Fetal effects. *Neurologic Clinics, 11,* 707–728.

Chmielewski, C., and Golden, C. J. (1980). Alcoholism and brain damage: An investigation using the Luria-Nebraska Neuropsychological Battery. *International Journal of Neuroscience, 10,* 99–105.

Chu, N. S. (1985). Computed tomographic correlates of auditory brainstem responses in alcoholics. *Journal of Neurology, Neurosurgery and Psychiatry, 48,* 348–353.

Chu, N. S., Squires, K. C., and Starr, A. (1982). Auditory brain stem responses in chronic alcoholic patients. *Electroencephalography and Clinical Neurophysiology, 54,* 418–425.

Claiborn, J. M., and Greene, R. L. (1981). Neuropsychological changes in recovering men alcoholics. *Journal of Studies on Alcohol, 42,* 757–765.

Clark, D. C., Pisani, V. D., Aagesen, C. A., Sellers, D., and Fawcett, J. (1984). Primary affective disorder, drug abuse, and neuropsychological impairment in sober alcoholics. *Alcoholism: Clinical and Experimental Research, 8,* 399–404.

Clarke, J., and Haughton, H. (1975). A study of intellectual impairment and recovery rates in heavy drinkers in Ireland. *British Journal of Psychiatry, 126,* 178–184.

Cloninger, C. R. (1987). Neurogenetic adaptive mechanisms in alcoholism. *Science, 236,* 410–416.

Cohen, H. L., Porjesz, B., and Begleiter, H. (1991). EEG characteristics in males at risk for alcoholism. *Alcoholism: Clinical and Experimental Research, 15,* 858–861.

Cole, M., Winkelman, M. D., Morris, J. C., Simon, J. E., and Boyd, T. A. (1992). Thalamic amnesia: Korsakoff syndrome due to left thalamic infarction. *Journal of Neurological Sciences, 110,* 62–67.

Coles, C. D., Smith, I., Fernhoff, P. M., and Falek, A. (1985). Neonatal neurobehavioral characteristics as correlates of maternal alcohol use during gestation. *Alcoholism: Clinical and Experimental Research, 9,* 454–460.

Conigrave, K. M., Saunders, J. B., and Whitfield, J. B. (1995). Diagnostic tests for alcohol consumption. *Alcohol and Alcoholism, 30,* 13–26.

Conry, J. (1990). Neuropsychological deficits in fetal alcohol syndrome and fetal alcohol effects. *Alcoholism: Clinical and Experimental Research, 14,* 650–655.

Courville, C. B. (1955). *Effects of Alcohol on the Nervous System of Man.* Los Angeles: San Lucas Press.

Couzigou, P., Begleiter, H., Kiiranmaa, K., and Agarwal, D. P. (1993). Genetics and alcohol. In P. M. Verscuren, ed., *Health Issues Related to Alcohol Consumption.* New York: ILSI Press, pp. 281–329.

Cutting, J. C. (1988). Alcohol cognitive impairment and aging: Still an uncertain relationship. *British Journal of Addiction, 83,* 995–997.

Cynn, V. E. (1992). Persistence and problem-solving skills in young male alcoholics. *Journal of Studies on Alcohol, 53,* 57–62.

Dally, S., Luft, A., Ponsin, J. C., Girre, C., Mamo, H., and Fournier, E. (1988). Abnormal pattern of cerebral blood flow distribution in young alcohol addicts. *British Journal of Addiction, 83,* 105–109.

Day, N. L., Goldschmidt, L., Robles, N., Richardson, G., Cornelius, M., Taylor, P., Geva, D., and Stoffer, D. (1991a). Prenatal alcohol exposure and offspring growth at 18 months of age: The predictive validity of two measures of drinking. *Alcoholism: Clinical and Experimental Research, 15,* 914–918.

Day, N. L., Robles, N., Richardson, G., Geva, D., Taylor, P., Scher, M., Stoffer, D., Cornelius, M., and Goldschmidt, L. (1991b). The effects of prenatal alcohol use on the growth of children at three years of age. *Alcoholism: Clinical and Experimental Research, 15,* 67–71.

de la Monte, S. M. (1988). Disproportionate atrophy of cerebral white matter in chronic alcoholics. *Archives of Neurology, 45,* 990–992.

de Obaldia, R., Leber, W. R., and Parsons, O. A. (1981). Assessment of neuropsychological functions in chronic alcoholics using a standardized version of Luria's Neuropsychological Technique. *International Journal of Neuroscience, 14,* 85–93.

De Obaldia, R., and Parsons, O. A. (1984). Relationship of neuropsychological performance to primary alcoholism and self-reported symptoms of childhood minimal brain dysfunction. *Journal of Studies on Alcohol, 45,* 386–392.

DeFranco, C., Tarbox, A. R., and McLaughlin, E. J. (1985). Cognitive deficits as a function of years of alcohol abuse. *American Journal of Drug and Alcohol Abuse, 11,* 279–293.

DeJong, C. A., van den Brink, W., Harteveld, F. M., and van der Wielen, E. G. (1993). Personality disorders in alcoholics and drug addicts. *Comprehensive Psychiatry, 34,* 87–94.

DiFranza, J. R., and Guerrera, M. P. (1990). Alcoholism and smoking. *Journal of Studies on Alcohol, 51,* 130–135.

Dikmen, S. S., Donovan, D. M. Løberg T., Machamer, J. E., and Temkin, N. R. (1993). Alcohol use and its effects on neuropsychological outcome in head injury. *Neuropsychology, 7,* 296–305.

Dobkin, P., Dongier, M., Cooper, D., and Hill, J.-M. (1991). Screening for alcoholism in a psychiatric hospital. *Canadian Journal of Psychiatry, 36,* 39–45.

Don, A., and Rourke, B. P. (1995). Syndrome of nonverbal learning disabilities: Neurodevelopmental manifestations. In B. P. Rourke, ed., *Fetal Alcohol Syndrome,* Chapter 14. New York: Guilford Press, pp. 372–406.

Donovan, D. M., Kivlahan, D. R., and Walker, R. D. (1984). Clinical limitations of neuropsychological testing in predicting treatment outcome among alcoholics. *Alcoholism: Clinical and Experimental Research, 8,* 470–475.

Donovan, D. M., Kivlahan, D. R., and Walker, R. D. (1986). Alcoholic subtypes based on multiple assessment domains: Validation against treatment outcome. *Recent Developments in Alcoholism, 4,* 207–222.

Donovan, D. M., Kivlahan, D. R., Walker, R. D., and Umlauf, R. (1985). Derivation and validation of neuropsychological clusters among men alcoholics. *Journal of Studies on Alcohol, 46,* 205–211.

Donovan, D. M., Queisser, H. R., and O'Leary, M. R. (1976). Group embedded figures test performance as a predictor of cognitive impairment among alcoholics. *International Journal of the Addictions, 11,* 725–739.

Drake, A. I., Hannay, H. J., and Gam, J. (1990). Effects of chronic alcoholism on hemispheric functioning: An examination of gender differences for cognitive and dichotic listening tasks. *Journal of Clinical and Experimental Neuropsychology, 12,* 781–797.

Drake, A. I., Jernigan, T. L., Butters, N., Shear, P. K., and Archibald, S. L. (1995). Volumetric changes on magnetic resonance imaging in chronic alcoholics: A one year follow-up. *Journal of the International Neuropsychological Society, 1,* 393–394 (Abst.).

Draper, R. J., and Manning, A. (1982). Vocabulary deficit and abstraction impairment in hospitalized alcoholics. *Psychological Medicine, 12,* 341–347.

Drejer, K., Theilgaard, A., Teasdale, T. W., Schulsinger, F., and Goodwin, D. W. (1985). A prospective study of young men at high risk for alcoholism: Neuropsychological assessment. *Alcoholism: Clinical and Experimental Research, 9,* 498–502.

Duckert, F., Johnsen, J., Amundsen, A., Stromme, J., and Morland, J. (1992). Covariation between biological markers and self-reported alcohol consumption: A two-year study of the relationship between changes in consumption and changes in the biological markers gamma-glutamyl transpeptidase (GGT) and average volume per erythrocyte (MCV) among problem drinkers. *Alcohol and Alcoholism, 27,* 545–555.

Durand, D., Saint-Cyr, J. A., Gurevich, N., and Carlen, P. L. (1989). Ethanol-induced dendritic alterations in hippocampal granule cells. *Brain Research, 477,* 373–377.

Eckardt, M. J., and Martin, P. R. (1986). Clinical assessment of cognition in alcoholism. *Alcoholism: Clinical and Experimental Research, 10,* 123–127.

Eckardt, M. J., Parker, E. S., Noble, E. P., Feldman, D. J., and Gottschalk, L. A. (1978). Relationship between neuropsychological performance and alcohol consumption in alcoholics. *Biological Psychiatry, 13,* 551–565.

Eckardt, M. J., Parker, E. S., Noble, E. P., Pautler, C. P., and Gottschalk, L. A. (1979). Changes in neuropsychological performance during treatment for alcoholism. *Biological Psychiatry, 14,* 943–954.

Eckardt, M. J., Parker, E. S., Pautler, C. P., Noble, E. P., and Gottschalk, L. A. (1980a). Neuropsychological consequences of posttreatment drinking behavior in male alcoholics. *Psychiatry Research, 2,* 135–147.

Eckardt, M. J., Rawlings, R. R., Graubard, B. I.,

Faden, V., Martin, P. R., and Gottschalk, L. A. (1988). Neuropsychological performance and treatment outcome in male alcoholics. *Alcoholism: Clinical and Experimental Research, 12,* 88–93.

Eckardt, M. J., Ryback, R. S., and Pautler, C. P. (1980b). Neuropsychological deficits in alcoholic men in their mid thirties. *American Journal of Psychiatry, 137,* 932–936.

Eckardt, M. J., Ryback, R. S., Rawlings, R. R., and Graubard, B. I. (1981). Biochemical diagnosis of alcoholism: A test of the discriminating capabilities of gamma-glutamyl transpeptidase and mean corpuscular volume. *Journal of the American Medical Association, 246,* 2707–2710.

Eckardt, M. J., Stapleton, J. M., Rawlings, R. R., Davis, E. Z., and Grodin, D. M. (1995). Neuropsychological functioning in detoxified alcoholics between 18 and 35 years of age. *American Journal of Psychiatry, 152,* 53–59.

Ehlers, C. L., and Schuckit, M. A. (1990). EEG fast frequency activity in the sons of alcoholics. *Biological Psychiatry, 27,* 631–641.

Ehlers, C. L., and Schuckit, M. A. (1991). Evaluation of EEG alpha activity in sons of alcoholics. *Neuropsychopharmacology, 4,* 199–205.

Ellenberg, L., Rosenbaum, G., Goldman, M. S., and Whitman, R. D. (1980). Recoverability of psychological functioning following alcohol abuse: Lateralization effects. *Journal of Consulting and Clinical Psychology, 48,* 503–510.

Ellis, R. J. (1990). Dichotic asymmetries in aging and alcoholic subjects. *Alcoholism: Clinical and Experimental Research, 14,* 863–871.

Ellis, R. J., and Oscar-Berman, M. (1989). Alcoholism, aging, and functional cerebral asymmetries. *Psychological Bulletin, 106,* 128–147.

Emmerson, R. Y., Dustman, R. E., Heil, J., and Shearer, D. E. (1988). Neuropsychological performance of young nondrinkers, social drinkers, and long- and short-term sober alcoholics. *Alcoholism: Clinical and Experimental Research, 12,* 625–629.

Emmerson, R. Y., Dustman, R. E., Shearer, D. E., and Chamberlin, H. M. (1987). EEG, visually evoked and event related potentials in young abstinent alcoholics. *Alcohol, 4,* 241–248.

Erbas, B., Bekdik, C., Erbengi, G., Enunlu, T., Aytac, S., Kumbasar, H., and Dogan, Y. (1992). Regional cerebral blood flow changes in chronic alcoholism using Tc-99m HMPAO SPECT: Comparison with CT parameters. *Clinical Nuclear Medicine, 17,* 123–127.

Errico, A. L., Nixon, S. J., Parsons, O. A., and Tassey, J. (1990). Screening for neuropsychological impairment in alcoholics. *Psychological Assessment, 2*, 45–50.

Errico, A. L., Parsons, O. A., King, A. C., and Lovallo, W. R. (1993). Attenuated cortisol response to biobehavioral stressors in sober alcoholics. *Journal of Studies on Alcohol, 54*, 393–398.

Errico, A. L., Parsons, O. A., Kling, O. R., and King, A. C. (1992). Investigation of the role of sex hormones in alcoholics' visuospatial deficits. *Neuropsychologia, 30*, 417–426.

Ervin, C. S., Little, R. E., Streissguth, A. P., and Beck, D. E. (1984). Alcoholic fathering and its relation to child's intellectual development: A pilot investigation. *Alcoholism: Clinical and Experimental Research, 8*, 362–365.

Everett, M., Schaeffer, K. W., and Parsons, O. A. (1988). Learning impairment in male and female alcoholics. *Archives of Clinical Neuropsychology, 3*, 203–211.

Fabian, M. S., Hochla, N. A., Silberstein, J. A., and Parsons, O. A. (1980). Menstrual status and neuropsychological functioning. *Biological Psychology Bulletin, 6*, 37–45.

Fabian, M. S., Jenkins, R. L., and Parsons, O. A. (1981). Gender, alcoholism, and neuropsychological functioning. *Journal of Consulting and Clinical Psychology, 49*, 138–140.

Fabian, M. S., and Parsons, O. A. (1983). Differential improvement of cognitive functions in recovering alcoholic women. *Journal of Abnormal Psychology, 92*, 87–95.

Fabian, M. S., Parsons, O. A., and Sheldon, M. D. (1984). Effects of gender and alcoholism on verbal and visual-spatial learning. *Journal of Nervous and Mental Disease, 172*, 16–20.

Fals-Stewart, W., and Schafer, J. (1992). The relationship between length of stay in drug-free therapeutic communities and neurocognitive functioning. *Journal of Clinical Psychology, 48*, 539–543.

Farmer, R. H. (1973). Functional changes during early weeks of abstinence, measured by the Bender-Gestalt. *Quarterly Journal of Studies on Alcohol, 34*, 786–796.

Feuerlein, W. (1977). Neuropsychiatric disorders of alcoholism. *Nutrition and Metabolism, 21*, 163–174.

Fitzhugh, L. C., Fitzhugh, K. B., and Reitan, R. M. (1960). Adaptive abilities and intellectual functioning in hospitalized alcoholics. *Quarterly Journal of Studies on Alcohol, 21*, 414–423.

Fitzhugh, L. C., Fitzhugh, K. B., and Reitan, R. M. (1965). Adaptive abilities and intellectual functioning of hospitalized alcoholics: Further

considerations. *Quarterly Journal of Studies on Alcohol, 26*, 402–411.

Forsberg, L. K., and Goldman, M. S. (1985). Experience-dependent recovery of visuospatial functioning in older alcoholic persons. *Journal of Abnormal Psychology, 94*, 519–529.

Forsberg, L. K., and Goldman, M. S. (1987). Experience-dependent recovery of cognitive deficits in alcoholics: Extended transfer of training. *Journal of Abnormal Psychology, 96*, 345–353.

Franceschi, M., Truci, G., Comi, G., Lozza, L., Marchettini, P., Galardi, G., and Smirne, S. (1984). Cognitive deficits and their relationship to other neurological complications in chronic alcoholic patients. *Journal of Neurology, Neurosurgery and Psychiatry, 47*, 1134–1137.

Freund, G., and Ballinger, W. E., Jr. (1988). Loss of cholinergic muscarinic receptors in the frontal cortex of alcohol abusers. *Alcoholism: Clinical and Experimental Research, 12*, 630–638.

Freund, G., and Ballinger, W. E., Jr. (1989). Neuroreceptor changes in the putamen of alcohol abusers. *Alcoholism: Clinical and Experimental Research, 13*, 213–218.

Freund, G., and Ballinger, W. E. (1991). Loss of synaptic receptors can precede morphologic changes induced by alcoholism. *Alcohol and Alcoholism, 1* (Suppl.), 385–391.

Fuller, R. K., Lee, K. K., and Gordis, E. (1988). Validity of self-report in alcoholism research: Results of a Veterans Administration Cooperative Study. *Alcoholism: Clinical and Experimental Research, 12*, 201–205.

Gallucci, M., Amicarelli, I., Rossi, A., Stratta, P., Masciocchi, C., Zobel, B. B., Casacchia, M., and Passariello, R. (1989). MR imaging of white matter lesions in uncomplicated chronic alcoholism. *Journal of Computer Assisted Tomography, 13*, 395–398.

Gardner, M. K., Clark, E., Bowman, M. A., and Miller, P. J. (1989). Analogical reasoning abilities of recovering alcoholics. *Alcoholism: Clinical and Experimental Research, 13*, 508–511.

Garland, M. A., Parsons, O. A., and Nixon, S. J. (1993). Visual-spatial learning in nonalcoholic young adults with and those without a family history of alcoholism. *Journal of Studies on Alcohol, 54*, 219–224.

Garvin, R. B., Foy, D. W., and Alford, G. S. (1981). A critical examination of gamma-glutamyl transpeptidase as a biochemical marker for alcohol abuse. *Addictive Behaviors, 6*, 377–383.

Gebhardt, C. A., Naeser, M. A., and Butters, N. (1984). Computerized measures of CT scans of alcoholics: Thalamic region related to memory. *Alcohol, 1,* 133–140.

Gechter, G. L. (1987). Changes in neuropsychological functions among detoxifying and recovering alcoholics as measured by the Luria Nebraska Neuropsychological Battery. *Dissertation Abstracts International, 48,* 262–B.

George, D. T., Lindquist, T., Rawlings, R. R., Eckardt, M. J., Moss, H., Mathis, C., Martin, P. R., and Linnoila, M. (1992). Pharmacologic maintenance of abstinence in patients with alcoholism: No efficacy of 5-hydroxytryptophan or levodopa. *Clinical Pharmacology Therapy, 52,* 553–560.

Gillen, R., and Hesselbrock, V. (1992). Cognitive functioning, ASP, and family history of alcoholism in young men at risk for alcoholism. *Alcoholism: Clinical and Experimental Research, 16,* 206–214.

Gillin, J. C., Smith, T. L., Irwin, M., Kripke, D. F., Brown, S., and Schuckit, M. (1990a). Short REM latency in primary alcoholic patients with secondary depression. *American Journal of Psychiatry, 147,* 106–109.

Gillin, J. C., Smith, T. L., Irwin, M., Kripke, D. F., and Schuckit, M. (1990b). EEG sleep studies in "pure" primary alcoholism during subacute withdrawal: Relationships to normal controls, age, and other clinical variables. *Biological Psychiatry, 27,* 477–488.

Gilman, S., Adams, K., Koeppe, R. A., Berent, S., Kluin, K. J., Modell, J. G., Kroll, P., and Brunberg, J. A. (1990). Cerebellar and frontal hypometabolism in alcoholic cerebellar degeneration studied with positron emission tomography. *Annals of Neurology, 28,* 775–785.

Glenn, S. W., Errico, A. L., Parsons, O. A., King, A. C., and Nixon, S. J. (1993). The role of antisocial, affective, and childhood behavioral characteristics in alcoholics' neuropsychological performance. *Alcoholism: Clinical and Experimental Research, 17,* 162–169.

Glenn, S. W., and Parsons, O. A. (1990). The role of time in neuropsychological performance: Investigation and application in an alcoholic population. *The Clinical Neuropsychologist, 4,* 344–354.

Glenn, S. W., and Parsons, O. A. (1991a). Impaired efficiency in female alcoholics' neuropsychological performance. *Journal of Clinical and Experimental Neuropsychology, 13,* 895–908.

Glenn, S. W., and Parsons, O. A. (1991b). Prediction of resumption of drinking in posttreatment alcoholics. *International Journal of the Addictions, 26,* 237–254.

Glenn, S. W., and Parsons, O. A. (1992). Neuropsychological efficiency measures in male and female alcoholics. *Journal of Studies on Alcohol, 53,* 546–552.

Glenn, S. W., Parsons, O. A., Sinha, R., and Stevens, L. (1988). The effects of repeated withdrawals from alcohol on the memory of male and female alcoholics. *Alcohol and Alcoholism, 23,* 337–342.

Glosser, G., Butters, N., and Kaplan, E. (1977). Visuoperceptual processes in brain damaged patients on the digit symbol substitution test. *International Journal of Neuroscience, 7,* 59–66.

Golden, C. J., Graber, B., Blose, I., Berg, R., Coffman, J., and Bloch, S. (1981). Difference in brain densities between chronic alcoholic and normal control patients. *Science, 211,* 508–510.

Goldman, M. S. (1983). Cognitive impairment in chronic alcoholics: Some cause for optimism. *American Psychologist, 38,* 1045–1054.

Goldman, M. S. (1990). Experience-dependent neuropsychological recovery and the treatment of chronic alcoholism. *Neuropsychology Review, 1,* 75–101.

Goldman, M. S., Klisz, D. K., and Williams, D. L. (1985). Experience-dependent recovery of cognitive functioning in young alcoholics. *Addictive Behaviors, 10,* 169–176.

Goldman, M. S., Williams, D. L., and Klisz, D. K. (1983). Recoverability of psychological functioning following alcohol abuse: Prolonged visual-spatial dysfunction in older alcoholics. *Journal of Consulting and Clinical Psychology, 51,* 370–378.

Goldman, R. S., and Goldman, M. S. (1988). Experience-dependent cognitive recovery in alcoholics: A task component strategy. *Journal of Studies on Alcohol, 49,* 142–148.

Goldstein, G., and Shelly, C. (1980). Neuropsychological investigation of brain lesion localization in alcoholism. *Advances in Experimental Medicine and Biology, 126,* 731–743.

Goldstein, G., and Shelly, C. (1982). A multivariate neuropsychological approach to brain lesion localization in alcoholism. *Addictive Behaviors, 7,* 165–175.

Goldstein, G., Shelly, C., Mascia, G. V., and Tarter, R. E. (1985). Relationships between neuropsychological and psychopathological dimensions in male alcoholics. *Addictive Behaviors, 10,* 365–372.

Goldstein, G., Tarter, R. E., Shelly, C., Alterman, A. I., and Petrarulo, E. (1983). Withdrawal seizures in black and white alcoholic patients: Intellectual and neuropsychological sequelae. *Drug and Alcohol Dependence, 12,* 349–354.

Goodwin, D. W. (1983). Familial alcoholism: A separate entity? *Substance and Alcohol Actions/Misuse, 4,* 129–136.

Gorenstein, E. E. (1982). Frontal lobe functions in psychopaths. *Journal of Abnormal Psychology, 91,* 368–379.

Gorenstein, E. E. (1987). Cognitive-perceptual deficit in an alcoholism spectrum disorder. *Journal of Studies on Alcohol, 48,* 310–318.

Grant, B. F., and Towle, L. H. (1990). Standardized diagnostic interviews for alcohol research. *Alcohol Health and Research World, 14,* 340–348.

Grant, B. F. (1994). Alcohol consumption, alcohol abuse and alcohol dependence: The United States as an example. *Addiction, 89,* 1357–1365.

Grant, B. F., Dufour, M. C., and Harford, T. C. (1988). Epidemiology of alcoholic liver disease. *Seminars in Liver Disease, 8,* 12–25.

Grant, B. F., Harford, T. C., Chou, P., Pickering, R., Dawson, D. A., Stinson, F. S., and Noble, J. (1991). Prevalence of DSM-III-R alcohol abuse and dependence. *Alcohol Health and Research World, 15,* 91–96.

Grant, I. (1987). Alcohol and the brain: Neuropsychological correlates. *Journal of Consulting and Clinical Psychology, 55,* 310–324.

Grant, I., Adams, K. M., Carlin, A. S., and Rennick, P. M. (1977). Neuropsychological deficit in polydrug users: A preliminary report of the findings of the collaborative neuropsychological study of polydrug users. *Drug and Alcohol Dependence, 2,* 91–108.

Grant, I., Adams, K. M., Carlin, A. S., Rennick, P. M., Judd, L. L., and Schooff, K. (1978). The collaborative neuropsychological study of polydrug users. *Archives of General Psychiatry, 35,* 1063–1074.

Grant, I., Adams, K., and Reed, R. (1979a). Normal neuropsychological abilities of alcoholic men in their late thirties. *American Journal of Psychiatry, 136,* 1263–1269.

Grant, I., Adams, K. M., and Reed, R. (1984). Aging, abstinence, and medical risk factors in the prediction of neuropsychologic deficit among long-term alcoholics. *Archives of General Psychiatry, 41,* 710–718.

Grant, I., Prigatano, G. P., Heaton, R. K., McSweeny, A. J., Wright, E. C., and Adams, K. M. (1987a). Progressive neuropsychologic impairment and hypoxemia. *Archives of General Psychiatry, 44,* 999–1006.

Grant, I., Reed, R., and Adams, K. M. (1987b). Diagnosis of intermediate-duration and subacute organic mental disorders in abstinent alcoholics. *Journal of Clinical Psychiatry, 48,* 319–323.

Grant, I., Reed, R., Adams, K., and Carlin, A. (1979b). Neuropsychological function in young alcoholics and polydrug abusers. *Journal of Clinical Neuropsychology, 1,* 39–47.

Gregson, R. A., and Taylor, G. M. (1977). Prediction of relapse in men alcoholics. *Journal of Studies on Alcohol, 38,* 1749–1760.

Gur, R. C., Gur, R. E., Obrist, W. D., Skolnick, B. E., and Reivich, M. (1987). Age and regional cerebral blood flow at rest and during cognitive activity. *Archives of General Psychiatry, 44,* 617–621.

Guthrie, A., and Elliott, W. A. (1980). The nature and reversibility of cerebral impairment in alcoholism: Treatment implications. *Journal of Studies on Alcohol, 41,* 147–155.

Halvorson, M. R., Campbell, J. L., Sprague, G., Slater, K., Noffsinger, J. K., and Peterson, C. M. (1993). Comparative evaluation of the clinical utility of three markers of ethanol intake: The effect of gender. *Alcoholism: Clinical and Experimental Research, 17,* 225–229.

Hannon, R., Butler, C. P., Day, C. L., Khan, S. A., Quitoriano, L. A., Butler, A. M., and Meredith, L. A. (1985). Alcohol use and cognitive functioning in men and women college students. *Recent Developments in Alcoholism, 3,* 241–252.

Hannon, R., Butler, C. P., Day, C. L., Khan, S. A., Quitoriano, L. A., Butler, A. M., and Meredith, L. A. (1987). Social drinking and cognitive functioning in college students: A replication and reversibility study. *Journal of Studies on Alcohol, 48,* 502–506.

Hannon, R., Day, C. L., Butler, A. M., Larson, A. J., and Casey, M. (1983). Alcohol consumption and cognitive functioning in college students. *Journal of Studies on Alcohol, 44,* 283–298.

Hansen, L. A., Natelson, B. H., Lemere, C., Niemann, W., De Teresa, R., Regan, T. J., Masliah, E., and Terry, R. D. (1991). Alcohol-induced brain changes in dogs. *Archives of Neurology, 48,* 939–942.

Harper, C., and Corbett, D. (1990). Changes in the basal dendrites of cortical pyramidal cells from alcoholic patients: A quantitative Golgi study. *Journal of Neurology, Neurosurgery and Psychiatry, 53,* 856–861.

Harper, C. G., and Blumbergs, P. C. (1982). Brain weights in alcoholics. *Journal of Neurology, Neurosurgery and Psychiatry, 45,* 838–840.

Harper, C., and Kril, J. (1985). Brain atrophy in chronic alcoholic patients: A quantitative pathological study. *Journal of Neurology, Neurosurgery and Psychiatry, 48,* 211–217.

Harper, C. G., and Kril, J. J. (1988). Corpus callosal thickness in alcoholics. *British Journal of Addiction, 83,* 577–580.

Harper, C. G., and Kril, J. (1989). Patterns of neuronal loss in the cerebral cortex in chronic alcoholic patients. *Journal of the Neurological Sciences, 92,* 81–89.

Harper, C., and Kril, J. J. (1990). Neuropathology of alcoholism. *Alcohol and Alcoholism, 25,* 207–216.

Harper, C., Kril, J., and Daly, J. (1987). Are we drinking our neurones away? *British Medical Journal (Clinical Research Edition), 294,* 534–536.

Harper, C., Kril, J., and Daly, J. (1988a). Does a "moderate" alcohol intake damage the brain? *Journal of Neurology, Neurosurgery and Psychiatry, 51,* 909–913.

Harper, C. G., Kril, J. J., and Daly, J. M. (1988b). Brain shrinkage in alcoholics is not caused by changes in hydration: A pathological study. *Journal of Neurology, Neurosurgery and Psychiatry, 51,* 124–127.

Harper, C. G., Kril, J. J., and Holloway, R. L. (1985). Brain shrinkage in chronic alcoholics: A pathological study. *British Medical Journal, 290,* 501–504.

Harper, C. G., Smith, N. A., and Kril, J. J. (1990). The effects of alcohol on the female brain: A neuropathological study. *Alcohol and Alcoholism, 25,* 445–448.

Hata, T., Meyer, J. S., Tanahashi, N., Ishikawa, Y., Imai, A., Shinohara, T., Velez, M., Fann, W. E., Kandula, P., and Sakai, F. (1987). Three-dimensional mapping of local cerebral perfusion in alcoholic encephalopathy with and without Wernicke-Korsakoff syndrome. *Journal of Cerebral Blood Flow and Metabolism, 7,* 35–44.

Haug, J. O. (1968). Pneumoencephalographic evidence of brain damage in chronic alcoholics: A preliminary report. *Acta Psychiatrica Scandinavica, 203,* 135–143.

Heaton, R. K. (1992). *Comprehensive Norms for an Expanded Halstead-Reitan Battery: A Supplement for the Wechsler Adult Intelligence Scale-Revised.* Odessa, Florida: Psychological Assessment Resources.

Heaton, R. K., Grant, I., and Matthews, C. G. (1991). *Comprehensive Norms for an Expanded Halstead-Reitan Battery: Demographic Corrections, Research Findings, and Clinical Applications.* Odessa, Florida: Psychological Assessment Resources.

Heaton, R. K., and Pendleton, M. G. (1981). Use of neuropsychological tests to predict adult patients' everyday functioning. *Journal of Consulting and Clinical Psychology, 49,* 807–821.

Hesselbrock, M. N., Hesselbrock, V. M., Tennen, H., Meyer, R. E., and Workman, K. L. (1983). Methodological considerations in the assessment of depression in alcoholics. *Journal of Consulting and Clinical Psychology, 51,* 399–405.

Hesselbrock, M. N., Weidenman, M. A., and Reed, H. B. (1985a). Effect of age, sex, drinking history and antisocial personality on neuropsychology of alcoholics. *Journal of Studies on Alcohol, 46,* 313–320.

Hesselbrock, V., Bauer, L. O., Hesselbrock, M. N., and Gillen, R. (1991). Neuropsychological factors in individuals at high risk for alcoholism. *Recent Developments in Alcoholism, 9,* 21–40.

Hesselbrock, V. M., Stabenau, J. R., and Hesselbrock, M. N. (1985b). Minimal brain dysfunction and neuropsychological test performance in offspring of alcoholics. *Recent Developments in Alcoholism, 3,* 65–82.

Hester, R. K., Smith, J. W., and Jackson, T. R. (1980). Recovery of cognitive skills in alcoholics. *Journal of Studies on Alcohol, 41,* 363–367.

Hightower, M. G., and Anderson, R. P. (1986). Memory evaluation of alcoholics with Russell's revised Wechsler Memory Scale. *Journal of Clinical Psychology, 42,* 1000–1005.

Hill, S. Y., and Ryan, C. (1985). Brain damage in social drinkers? Reasons for caution. *Recent Developments in Alcoholism, 3,* 277–288.

Hillbom, M., and Holm, L. (1986). Contribution of traumatic head injury to neuropsychological deficits in alcoholics. *Journal of Neurology, Neurosurgery and Psychiatry, 49,* 1348–1353.

Hochla, N.A.N., and Parsons, O. A. (1982). Premature aging in female alcoholics: A neuropsychological study. *Journal of Nervous and Mental Disease, 170,* 241–245.

Hoeksema, H. L., and de Bock, G. H. (1993). The value of laboratory tests for the screening and recognition of alcohol abuse in primary care patients. *Journal of Family Practice, 37,* 268–276.

Hoffman, J. J., Hall, R. W., and Bartsch, T. W.

(1987). On the relative importance of "psychopathic" personality and alcoholism on neuropsychological measures of frontal lobe dysfunction. *Journal of Abnormal Psychology, 96,* 158–160.

Horvath, T. B. (1973). Clinical spectrum and epidemiological features of alcoholic dementia. In J. G. Rankin, ed., *Alcohol, Drugs and Brain Damage.* Toronto, Ontario: Addiction Research Foundation, pp. 1–16.

Inglis, J., and Lawson, J. S. (1981). Sex differences in the effects of unilateral brain damage on intelligence. *Science, 212,* 693–695.

Irwin, M., Baird, S., Smith, T. L., and Schuckit, M. (1988). Use of laboratory tests to monitor heavy drinking by alcoholic men discharged from a treatment program. *American Journal of Psychiatry, 145,* 595–599.

Irwin, M., Caldwell, C., Smith, T. L., Brown, S., Schuckit, M. A., and Gillin, J. C. (1990). Major depressive disorder, alcoholism, and reduced natural killer cell cytotoxicity: Role of severity of depressive symptoms and alcohol consumption. *Archives of General Psychiatry, 47,* 713–719.

Irwin, M., Smith, T. L., Butters, N., Brown, S., Baird, S., Grant, I., and Schuckit, M. A. (1989). Graded neuropsychological impairment and elevated gamma-glutamyl transferase in chronic alcoholic men. *Alcoholism: Clinical and Experimental Research, 13,* 99–103.

Ishibashi, M., Nakazawa, Y., Yokoyama, T., Koga, Y., Miyahara, Y., Hayashida, N., and Ohse, K. (1987). Cerebral atrophy and slow wave sleep of abstinent chronic alcoholics. *Drug and Alcohol Dependence, 19,* 325–332.

Ishikawa, Y., Meyer, J. S., Tanahashi, N., Hata, T., Velez, M., Fann, W. E., Kandula, P., Motel, K. F., and Rogers, R. L. (1986). Abstinence improves cerebral perfusion and brain volume in alcoholic neurotoxicity without Wernicke-Korsakoff syndrome. *Journal of Cerebral Blood Flow and Metabolism, 6,* 86–94.

Jacobson, R. (1986a). The contributions of sex and drinking history to the CT brain scan changes in alcoholics. *Psychological Medicine, 16,* 547–559.

Jacobson, R. (1986b). Female alcoholics: A controlled CT brain scan and clinical study. *British Journal of Addiction, 81,* 661–669.

Jacobson, R. R., Acker, C. F., and Lishman, W. A. (1990). Patterns of neuropsychological deficit in alcoholic Korsakoff's syndrome. *Psychological Medicine, 20,* 321–334.

Jacobson, R. R., and Lishman, W. A. (1990). Cortical and diencephalic lesions in Korsakoff's

syndrome: A clinical and CT scan study. *Psychological Medicine, 20,* 63–75.

Janowsky, J. S., Shimamura, A. P., Kritchevsky, M., and Squire, L. R. (1989). Cognitive impairment following frontal lobe damage and its relevance to human amnesia. *Behavioral Neuroscience, 103,* 548–560.

Jenkins, R. L., and Parsons, O. A. (1981). Neuropsychological effect of chronic alcoholism on tactual-spatial performance and memory in males. *Alcoholism: Clinical and Experimental Research, 5,* 26–33.

Jensen, G. B., and Pakkenberg, B. (1993). Do alcoholics drink their neurons away? *Lancet, 342,* 1201–1204.

Jernigan, T. L., Butters, N., DiTraglia, G., Schafer, K., Smith, T., Irwin, M., Grant, I., Schuckit, M., and Cermak, L. S. (1991a). Reduced cerebral grey matter observed in alcoholics using magnetic resonance imaging. *Alcoholism: Clinical and Experimental Research, 15,* 418–427.

Jernigan, T. L., Schafer, K., Butters, N., and Cermak, L. S. (1991b). Magnetic resonance imaging of alcoholic Korsakoff patients. *Neuropsychopharmacology, 4,* 175–186.

Jernigan, T. L., Zatz, L. M., Ahumada, A. J., Jr., Pfefferbaum, A., Tinklenberg, J. R., and Moses, J. A., Jr. (1982). CT measures of cerebrospinal fluid volume in alcoholics and normal volunteers. *Psychiatry Research, 7,* 9–17.

Johnson, J. L., and Rolf, J. E. (1988). Cognitive functioning in children from alcoholic and nonalcoholic families. *British Journal of Addiction, 83,* 849–857.

Jones, B. M. (1971). Verbal and spatial intelligence in short and long term alcoholics. *Journal of Nervous and Mental Disease, 15,* 292–297.

Jones, B., and Parsons, O. A. (1971). Impaired abstracting ability in chronic alcoholics. *Archives of General Psychiatry, 24,* 71–75.

Jones, B., and Parsons, O. A. (1972). Specific vs generalized deficits of abstracting ability in chronic alcoholics. *Archives of General Psychiatry, 26,* 380–384.

Jones, M. K., and Jones, B. M. (1980). The relationship of age and drinking history to the effects of alcohol on memory in women. *Journal of Studies on Alcohol, 41,* 179–186.

Joyce, E. M., and Robbins, T. W. (1991). Frontal lobe function in Korsakoff and non-Korsakoff alcoholics: Planning and spatial working memory. *Neuropsychologia, 29,* 709–723.

Kaseda, Y., Miyazato, Y., Ogura, C., Nakamoto, H., Uema, T., Yamamoto, K., and Ohta, I.

(1994). Correlation between event-related potentials and MR measurements in chronic alcoholic patients. *The Japanese Journal of Psychiatry and Neurology, 48,* 23–32.

Keso, L., and Salaspuro, M. (1989). Laboratory markers as compared to drinking measures before and after inpatient treatment for alcoholism. *Alcoholism: Clinical and Experimental Research, 13,* 449–452.

King, M. A., Hunter, B. E., and Walker, D. W. (1988). Alterations and recovery of dendritic spine density in rat hippocampus following long-term ethanol ingestion. *Brain Research, 459,* 381–385.

Kish, G. B., Hagen, J. M., Woody, M. M., and Harvey, H. L. (1980). Alcoholics' recovery from cerebral impairment as a function of duration of abstinence. *Journal of Clinical Psychology, 36,* 584–589.

Kleinknecht, R. A., and Goldstein, S. G. (1972). Neuropsychological deficits associated with alcoholism: A review and discussion. *Quarterly Journal of Studies on Alcohol, 33,* 999–1019.

Klisz, D. K., and Parsons, O. A. (1977). Hypothesis testing in younger and older alcoholics. *Journal of Studies on Alcohol, 38,* 1718–1729.

Kostandov, E. A., Arsumanov, Y. L., Genkina, O. A., Restchikova, T. N., and Shostakovich, G. S. (1982). The effects of alcohol on hemispheric functional asymmetry. *Journal of Studies on Alcohol, 43,* 411–426.

Kramer, J. H., Blusewicz, M. J., and Preston, K. A. (1989). The premature aging hypothesis: Old before its time? *Journal of Consulting and Clinical Psychology, 57,* 257–262.

Kril, J. J., and Harper, C. G. (1989). Neuronal counts from four cortical regions of alcoholic brains. *Acta Neuropathologica, 79,* 200–204.

Latcham, R. W. (1986). Gamma glutamyl transpeptidase and mean corpuscular volume: Their usefulness in the assessment of in-patient alcoholics. *British Journal of Psychiatry, 149,* 353–356.

Leber, W. R., Jenkins, R. L., and Parsons, O. A. (1981). Recovery of visual-spatial learning and memory in chronic alcoholics. *Journal of Clinical Psychology, 37,* 192–197.

Leber, W. R., Parsons, O. A., and Nichols, N. (1985). Neuropsychological test results are related to ratings of men alcoholics' therapeutic progress: A replicated study. *Journal of Studies on Alcohol, 46,* 116–121.

Levine, J. (1990). The relative value of consultation, questionnaires and laboratory investigation in the identification of excessive alcohol consumption. *Alcohol and Alcoholism, 25,* 539–553.

Lewin, R. (1980). Is your brain really necessary? *Science, 210,* 1232–1234.

Løberg, T. (1980a). Alcohol misuse and neuropsychological deficits in men. *Journal of Studies on Alcohol, 41,* 119–128.

Løberg, T. (1980b). Neuropsychological deficits in alcoholics: Lack of personality (MMPI) correlates. *Advances in Experimental Medicine and Biology, 126,* 797–808.

Løberg, T. (1981). MMPI-based personality subtypes of alcoholics: Relationships to drinking history, psychometrics and neuropsychological deficits. *Journal of Studies on Alcohol, 42,* 766–782.

Løberg, T. (1989). The role of neuropsychology in secondary prevention. In T. Løberg, W. R. Miller, P. E. Nathan, and G. A. Marlatt, eds., *Addictive Behaviors: Prevention and Early Intervention.* Amsterdam, The Netherlands: Swets and Zeitlinger, pp. 69–86.

Løberg, T., and Miller, W. R. (1986). Personality, cognitive, and neuropsychological correlates of harmful alcohol consumption: A cross-national comparison of clinical samples. *Annals of the New York Academy of Sciences, 472,* 75–97.

Long, J. A., and McLachlan, J.F.C. (1974). Abstract reasoning and perceptual-motor efficiency in alcoholics: Impairment and reversibility. *Quarterly Journal of Studies on Alcohol, 35,* 1220–1229.

Macciocchi, S. N., Ranseen, J. D., and Schmitt, F. A. (1989). The relationship between neuropsychological impairment in alcoholics and treatment outcome at one year. *Archives of Clinical Neuropsychology, 4,* 365–370.

MacVane, J., Butters, N., Montgomery, K., and Farber, J. (1982). Cognitive functioning in men social drinkers: A replication study. *Journal of Studies on Alcohol, 43,* 81–95.

Malloy, P., Noel, N., Longabaugh, R., and Beattie, M. (1990). Determinants of neuropsychological impairment in antisocial substance abusers. *Addictive Behaviors, 15,* 431–438.

Malloy, P., Noel, N., Rogers, S., Longabaugh, R., and Beattie, M. (1989). Risk factors for neuropsychological impairment in alcoholics: Antisocial personality, age, years of drinking and gender. *Journal of Studies on Alcohol, 50,* 422–426.

Mander, A. J., Young, A., Chick, J. D., and Best, J. J. (1989). The relationship of cerebral atrophy and T1 in alcoholics: An MRI study. *Drug and Alcohol Dependence, 24,* 57–59.

Mann, K., Batra, A., Gunthner, A., and Schroth, G. (1992). Do women develop alcoholic brain damage more readily than men? *Alcoholism: Clinical and Experimental Research, 16,* 1052–1056.

Mann, K., Mundle, G., Langle, G., and Petersen, D. (1993). The reversibility of alcoholic brain damage is not due to rehydration: A CT study. *Addiction, 88,* 649–653.

Mann, K., Opitz, H., Petersen, D., Schroth, G., and Heimann, H. (1989). Intracranial CSF volumetry in alcoholics: studies with MRI and CT. *Psychiatry Research, 29,* 277–279.

Manson, M. P. (1949). *The ALCADD Test.* Beverly Hills: Western Psychological Service.

Marchesi, C., De Risio, C., Campanini, G., Maggini, C., Piazza, P., Grassi, M., Chiodera, P., and Coiro, V. (1992). TRH test in alcoholics: Relationship of the endocrine results with neuroradiological and neuropsychological findings. *Alcohol and Alcoholism, 27,* 531–537.

Marchesi, C., De Risio, C., Campanini, G., Piazza, P., Grassi, M., Chiodera, P., Vescovi, P. P., and Coiro, V. (1994). Cerebral atrophy and plasma cortisol levels in alcoholics after short or a long period of abstinence. *Progress in Neuro-Psychopharmacology and Biological Psychiatry, 18,* 519–535.

Marlatt, G. A. (1976). The Drinking Profile: A questionnaire for the behavioral assessment of alcoholism. In E. J. Mash and L. G. Terdal, eds., *Behavioral Therapy Assessment: Design and Evaluation.* New York: Springer, pp. 121–137.

Martin, P. R., Adinoff, B., Weingartner, H., Mukherjee, A. B., and Eckardt, M. J. (1986). Alcoholic organic brain disease: Nosology and pathophysiologic mechanisms. *Progress in Neuro-Psychopharmacology and Biological Psychiatry, 10,* 147–164.

Martin, P. R., Eckardt, M. J., and Linnoila, M. (1989). Treatment of chronic organic mental disorders associated with alcoholism. *Recent Developments in Alcoholism, 7,* 329–350.

Mathew, R. J., and Wilson, W. H. (1991). Substance abuse and cerebral blood flow. *American Journal of Psychiatry, 148,* 292–305.

Mathew, R. J., Wilson, W. H. and Tant, S. R. (1986). Determinants of resting regional cerebral blood flow in normal subjects. *Biological Psychiatry, 21,* 907–914.

Mattson, S. N., Riley, E. P., Jernigan, T. L., Ehlers, C. L., Delis, D. C., Jones, K. L., Stern, C., Johnson, K. A., Hesselink, J. R., and Bellugi, U. (1992). Fetal alcohol syndrome: A case report of neuropsychological, MRI and EEG assessment of two children. *Alcoholism: Clinical and Experimental Research, 16,* 1001–1003.

McCrady, B. S., and Smith, D. E. (1986). Implications of cognitive impairment for the treatment of alcoholism. *Alcoholism: Clinical and Experimental Research, 10,* 145–149.

McIntyre, B. M. (1987). Functional neuropsychological impairment and recovery in alcoholics. *Dissertation Abstracts International, 47,* 4658–B.

McLachlan, J.F.C., and Levinson, T. (1974). Improvement in WAIS block design performance as a function of recovery from alcoholism. *Journal of Clinical Psychology, 30,* 65–66.

McMullen, P. A., Saint-Cyr, J. A., and Carlen, P. L. (1984). Morphological alterations in rat CA1 hippocampal pyramidal cell dendrites resulting from chronic ethanol consumption and withdrawal. *The Journal of Comparative Neurology, 225,* 111–118.

Melgaard, B., Henriksen, L., Ahlgren, P., Danielsen, U. T., Sørensen, H., and Paulson, O. B. (1990). Regional cerebral blood flow in chronic alcoholics measured by single photon emission computerized tomography. *Acta Neurologica Scandinavica, 82,* 87–93.

Mercer, P. W., and Khavari, K. A. (1990). Are women drinking more like men? An empirical examination of the convergence hypothesis. *Alcoholism: Clinical and Experimental Research, 14,* 461–466.

Miglioni, M., Buchtel, H. A., Campanini, T., and De Risio, C. (1979). Cerebral hemispheric lateralization of cognitive deficits due to alcoholism. *Journal of Nervous and Mental Disease, 167,* 212–217.

Mihas, A. A., and Tavassoli, M. (1992). Laboratory markers of ethanol intake and abuse: A critical appraisal. *The American Journal of the Medical Sciences, 303,* 415–428.

Miller, W. R., and Orr, J. (1980). Nature and sequence of neuropsychological deficits in alcoholics. *Journal of Studies on Alcohol, 41,* 325–337.

Miyazato, Y., and Ogura, C. (1993). Abnormalities in event-related potentials: N100, N200 and P300 topography in alcoholics. *The Japanese Journal of Psychiatry and Neurology, 47,* 853–862.

Molina, J. A., Bermejo, F., del Ser, T., Jimenez-Jimenez, F. J., Herranz, A., Fernandez-Calle, P., Ortuno, B., Villanueva, C., and Sainz, M. J. (1994). Alcoholic cognitive deterioration and nutritional deficiencies. *Acta Neurologica Scandinavica, 89,* 384–390.

Monteiro, M. G., and Masur, J. (1987). Correlation between biological state markers of alcohol abuse and severity of alcohol dependence syndrome. *Alcohol, 4,* 135–137.

Mulford, H. A., and Miller, D. E. (1960). Drinking in Iowa: Preoccupation with alcohol and definitions of alcohol, heavy drinking and trouble due to drinking. *Quarterly Journal of Studies on Alcohol, 21,* 279–291.

Muuronen, A., Bergman, H., Hindmarsh, T., and Telakivi, T. (1989). Influence of improved drinking habits on brain atrophy and cognitive performance in alcoholic patients: A 5-year follow-up study. *Alcoholism: Clinical and Experimental Research, 13,* 137–141.

Nanson, J. L., and Hiscock, M. (1990). Attention deficits in children exposed to alcohol prenatally. *Alcoholism: Clinical and Experimental Research, 14,* 656–661.

Neundorfer, B., Claus, D., and Burkowski, H. (1984). Neurological complications of chronic alcoholism. *Wiener Klinische Wochenschrift, 96,* 576–580.

Nicolas, J. M., Catafau, A. M., Estruch, R., Lomena, F. J., Salamero, M., Herranz, R., Monforte, R., Cardenal, C., and Urbano-Marquez, A. (1993). Regional cerebral blood flow-SPECT in chronic alcoholism: Relation to neuropsychological testing. *Journal of Nuclear Medicine, 34,* 1452–1459.

Nixon, S. J., Errico, A. L., Parsons, O. A., Leber, W. R., and Kelley, C. J. (1992). The role of instructional set on alcoholic performance. *Alcoholism: Clinical and Experimental Research, 16,* 949–954.

Nixon, S. J., Kujawski, A., Parsons, O. A., and Yohman, J. R. (1987). Semantic (verbal) and figural memory impairment in alcoholics. *Journal of Clinical and Experimental Neuropsychology, 9,* 311–322.

Nixon, S. J., and Parsons, O. A. (1991). Alcohol-related efficiency deficits using an ecologically valid test. *Alcoholism: Clinical and Experimental Research, 15,* 601–606.

Nixon, S. J., Parsons, O. A., Schaeffer, K. W., and Hale, R. L. (1988). Subject selection biases in alcoholic samples: Effects on cognitive performance. *Journal of Clinical Psychology, 44,* 831–836.

Noble, E. P., Berman, S. M., Ozkaragoz, T. Z., and Ritchie, T. (1994). Prolonged P300 latency in children with the D2 dopamine receptor A1 allele. *American Journal of Human Genetics, 54,* 658–668.

Noonberg, A., Goldstein, G., and Page, H. A. (1985). Premature aging in male alcoholics: "Accelerated aging" or "increased vulnerability"? *Alcoholism: Clinical and Experimental Research, 9,* 334–338.

Nystrom, M., Perasalo, J., Pikkarainen, J., and Salaspuro, M. (1993). Conventional laboratory tests as indicators of heavy drinking in young university students. *Scandinavia Journal of Primary Health Care, 11,* 44–49.

O'Connor, S., and Tasman, A. (1990). The application of electrophysiology to research in alcoholism. *Journal of Neuropsychiatry and Clinical Neuroscience, 2,* 149–158.

O'Donnell, W. E., De Soto, C. B., and De Soto, J. L. (1993). Validity and reliability of the revised neuropsychological impairment scale (NIS). *Journal of Clinical Psychology, 49,* 372–382.

O'Donnell, W. E., De Soto, C. B., and De Soto, J. L. (1994). Neuropsychological symptoms in a cross-sectional sample of abstinent alcoholics. *Psychological Reports, 75,* 1475–1484.

O'Leary, M. R., Donovan, D. M., and Chaney, E. F. (1977a). The relationship of perceptual field orientation to measures of cognitive functioning and current adaptive abilities in alcoholics and nonalcoholics. *Journal of Nervous and Mental Disease, 165,* 275–282.

O'Leary, M. R., Donovan, D. M., Chaney, E. F., and Walker, R. D. (1979). Cognitive impairment and treatment outcome with alcoholics: Preliminary findings. *Journal of Clinical Psychiatry, 40,* 397–398.

O'Leary, M. R., Radford, L. M., Chaney, E. F., and Schau, E. J. (1977b). Assessment of cognitive recovery in alcoholics by use of the trail-making test. *Journal of Clinical Psychology, 33,* 579–582.

Ogura, C., and Miyazato, Y. (1991). Cognitive dysfunctions of alcohol dependence using event related potentials. *Japanese Journal of Alcohol and Drug Dependence, 26,* 331–340.

Oscar-Berman, M. (1987). Alcohol-related ERP changes in cognition. *Alcohol, 4,* 289–292.

Ozkaragoz, T. Z., and Noble, E. P. (1995). Neuropsychological differences between sons of active alcoholic and non-alcoholic fathers. *Alcohol and Alcoholism, 30,* 115–123.

Page, R. D., and Linden, J. D. (1974). "Reversible" organic brain syndrome in alcoholics: A psychometric evaluation. *Quarterly Journal of Studies on Alcohol, 35,* 98–107.

Page, R. D., and Schaub, L. H. (1977). Intellectual functioning in alcoholics during six months' abstinence. *Journal of Studies on Alcohol, 38,* 1240–1246.

Papoz, L., Warnet, J. M., Pequignot, G., Eschwege, E., Claude, J. R., and Schwartz, D. (1981). Alcohol consumption in a healthy population: Relationship to gamma-glutamyl transferase activity and mean corpuscular volume. *Journal of the American Medical Association, 245,* 1748–1751.

Parker, D. A., Parker, E. S., Brody, J. A., and Schoenberg, R. (1983). Alcohol use and cognitive loss among employed men and women. *American Journal of Public Health, 73,* 521–526.

Parker, E. S. (1982). Comments on "cognitive functioning in men social drinkers; A replication study." *Journal of Studies on Alcohol, 43,* 170–177.

Parker, E. S., Birnbaum, I. M., Boyd, R. A., and Noble, E. P. (1980). Neuropsychologic decrements as a function of alcohol intake in male students. *Alcoholism: Clinical and Experimental Research, 4,* 330–334.

Parker, E. S., and Noble, E. P. (1977). Alcohol consumption and cognitive functioning in social drinkers. *Journal of Studies on Alcohol, 38,* 1224–1232.

Parker, E. S., and Noble, E. P. (1980). Alcohol and the aging process in social drinkers. *Journal of Studies on Alcohol, 41,* 170–178.

Parker, E. S., Parker, D. A., and Harford T. C. (1991). Specifying the relationship between alcohol use and cognitive loss: The effects of frequency of consumption and psychological distress. *Journal of Studies on Alcohol, 52,* 366–373.

Parkin, A. J., Blunden, J., Rees, J. E., and Hunkin, N. M. (1991). Wernicke-Korsakoff syndrome of nonalcoholic origin. *Brain and Cognition, 15,* 69–82.

Parkin, A. J., Dunn, J. C., Lee, C., O'Hara, P. F., and Nussbaum, L. (1993). Neuropsychological sequelae of Wernicke's encephalopathy in a 20-year-old woman: Selective impairment of a frontal memory system. *Brain and Cognition, 21,* 1–19.

Parsons, O. A. (1983). Cognitive dysfunction and recovery in alcoholics. *Substance and Alcohol Actions/Misuse, 4,* 175–190.

Parsons, O. A. (1986a). Alcoholics' neuropsychological impairment: Current findings and conclusions. *Annals of Behavioral Medicine, 8,* 13–19.

Parsons, O. A. (1986b). Cognitive functioning in sober social drinkers: A review and critique. *Journal of Studies on Alcohol, 47,* 101–114.

Parsons, O. A. (1987). Intellectual impairment in alcoholics: Persistent issues. *Acta Medica Scandinavica, 717* (Suppl.), 33–46.

Parsons, O. A. (1989). Impairment in sober alcoholics' cognitive functioning: The search for determinants. In T. Løberg, W. R. Miller, P. E. Nathan, and G. A. Marlatt, eds., *Addictive Behaviors: Prevention and Early Intervention.* Amsterdam, The Netherlands: Swets and Zeitlinger, pp. 101–116.

Parsons, O. A. (1994a). Determinants of cognitive deficits in alcoholics: The search continues. *The Clinical Neuropsychologist, 8,* 39–58.

Parsons, O. A. (1994b). Neuropsychological measures and event-related potentials in alcoholics: Interrelationships, long-term reliabilities, and prediction of resumption of drinking. *Journal of Clinical Psychology, 50,* 37–46.

Parsons, O. A., and Fabian, M. S. (1982). Comments on "Cognitive functioning in men social drinkers: A replication study." *Journal of Studies on Alcohol, 43,* 178–182.

Parsons, O. A., and Farr, S. P. (1981). The neuropsychology of alcohol and drug use. In S. B. Filskov and T. S. Boll, eds., *Handbook of Clinical Neuropsychology.* New York: Wiley Press, pp. 320–365.

Parsons, O. A., and Leber, W. R. (1981). The relationship between cognitive dysfunction and brain damage in alcoholics: Causal, interactive, or epiphenomenal? *Alcoholism: Clinical and Experimental Research, 5,* 326–343.

Parsons, O. A., and Nixon, S. J. (1993). Neurobehavioral sequelae of alcoholism. *Neurologic Clinics, 11,* 205–218.

Parsons, O. A., and Prigatano, G. P. (1977). Memory functioning in alcoholics. In I. M. Birnbaum and E. S. Parker, eds., *Alcohol and Human Memory.* Hillsdale, NJ: Lawrence Erlbaum, pp. 185–194.

Parsons, O. A., Schaeffer, K. W., and Glenn, S. W. (1990a). Does neuropsychological test performance predict resumption of drinking in posttreatment alcoholics? *Addictive Behaviors, 15,* 297–307.

Parsons, O. A., Sinha, R., and Williams, H. L. (1990b). Relationships between neuropsychological test performance and event-related potentials in alcoholic and nonalcoholic samples. *Alcoholism: Clinical and Experimental Research, 14,* 746–755.

Parsons, O. A., and Stevens, L. (1986). Previous alcohol intake and residual cognitive deficits in detoxified alcoholics and animals. *Alcohol and Alcoholism, 21,* 137–157.

Parsons, O. A., Tarter, R. E., and Edelberg, R. (1972). Altered motor control in chronic alcoholics. *Journal of Abnormal Psychology, 80,* 308–314.

Patterson, B. W., Parsons, O. A., Schaeffer, K. W., and Errico, A. L. (1988). Interpersonal problem solving in alcoholics. *Journal of Nervous and Mental Disease, 176,* 707–713.

Patterson, B. W., Sinha, R., Williams, H. L., Parsons, O. A., Smith, L. T., and Schaeffer, K. W. (1989). The relationship between neuropsychological and late component evoked potential measures in chronic alcoholics. *International Journal of Neuroscience, 49,* 319–327.

Patterson, B. W., Williams, H. L., McLean, G. A., Smith, L. T., and Schaeffer, K. W. (1987). Alcoholism and family history of alcoholism: Effects on visual and auditory event-related potentials. *Alcohol, 4,* 265–274.

Pentney, R. J. (1991). Remodeling of neuronal dendritic networks with aging and alcohol. *Alcohol and Alcoholism, 1* (Suppl.), 393–397.

Pentney, R. J., Quackenbush, L. J., and O'Neill, M. (1989). Length changes in dendritic networks of cerebellar purkinje cells of old rats after chronic ethanol treatment. *Alcoholism: Clinical and Experimental Research, 13,* 413–419.

Peterson, J. B., Finn, P. R., and Pihl, R. O. (1992). Cognitive dysfunction and the inherited predisposition to alcoholism. *Journal of Studies on Alcohol, 53,* 154–160.

Peterson, J. B., and Pihl, R. O. (1990). Information processing, neuropsychological function, and the inherited predisposition to alcoholism. *Neuropsychology Review, 1,* 343–369.

Pfefferbaum, A., Ford, J. M., White, P. M., and Mathalon, D. (1991). Event-related potentials in alcoholic men: P3 amplitude reflects family history but not alcohol consumption. *Alcoholism: Clinical and Experimental Research, 15,* 839–850.

Pfefferbaum, A., Lim, K. O., Zipursky, R. B., Mathalon, D. H., Rosenbloom, M. J., Lane, B., Ha, C. N., and Sullivan, E. V. (1992). Brain gray and white matter volume loss accelerates with aging in chronic alcoholics: A quantitative MRI study. *Alcoholism: Clinical and Experimental Research, 16,* 1078–1089.

Pfefferbaum, A., Rosenbloom, M., Crusan, K., and Jernigan, T. L. (1988). Brain CT changes in alcoholics: Effects of age and alcohol consumption. *Alcoholism: Clinical and Experimental Research, 12,* 81–87.

Pfefferbaum, A., Sullivan, E. V., Rosenbloom, M. J., Shear, P. K., Mathalon, D. H., and Lim, K. O. (1993). Increase in brain cerebrospinal fluid volume is greater in older than in younger alcoholic patients: A replication study and CT/MRI comparison. *Psychiatry Research: Neuroimaging, 50,* 257–274.

Plant, M., Sullivan, F. M., Guerri, C., and Abel, E. L. (1993). Alcohol and pregnancy. In P. M. Verscuren, ed., *Health Issues Related to Alcohol Consumption.* New York: ILSI Press, pp. 245–262.

Pol, S., Poynard, T., Bedossa, P., Naveau, S., Aubert, A., and Chaput, J. C. (1990). Diagnostic value of serum gamma-glutamyl-transferase activity and mean corpuscular volume in alcoholic patients with or without cirrhosis. *Alcoholism: Clinical and Experimental Research, 14,* 250–254.

Polich, J., and Bloom, F. E. (1986). P300 and alcohol consumption in normals and individuals at risk for alcoholism: A preliminary report. *Progress in Neuro-Psychopharmacology and Biological Psychiatry, 10,* 201–210.

Polich, J., and Bloom, F. E. (1988). Event-related brain potentials in individuals at high and low risk for developing alcoholism: Failure to replicate. *Alcoholism: Clinical and Experimental Research, 12,* 368–373.

Polich, J., Burns, T., and Bloom, F. E. (1988a). P300 and the risk for alcoholism: Family history, task difficulty, and gender. *Alcoholism: Clinical and Experimental Research, 12,* 248–254.

Polich, J., Haier, R. J., Buchsbaum, M., and Bloom, F. E. (1988b). Assessment of young men at risk for alcoholism with P300 from a visual discrimination task. *Journal of Studies on Alcohol, 49,* 186–190.

Polich, J., Pollock, V. E., and Bloom, F. E. (1994). Meta-analysis of P300 amplitude from males at risk for alcoholism. *Psychological Bulletin, 115,* 55–73.

Porjesz, B., and Begleiter, H. (1990). Event-related potentials in individuals at risk for alcoholism. *Alcohol, 7,* 465–469.

Porjesz, B., and Begleiter, H. (1991). Neurophysiological factors in individuals at risk for alcoholism. *Recent Developments in Alcoholism, 9,* 53–67.

Porjesz, B., and Begleiter, H. (1993). Neurophysiological factors associated with alcoholism. In W. A. Hunt and S. J. Nixon, eds., *Alcohol-Induced Brain Damage.* Rockville, MD: National Institute on Alcohol Abuse and Alcoholism, pp. 89–120.

Portnoff, L. A. (1982). Halstead-Reitan impairment in chronic alcoholics as a function of age of drinking onset. *Clinical Neuropsychology, 4,* 115–119.

Potter, B. J. (1994). Carbohydrate-deficient transferrin and the detection of alcohol abuse: A horse of a different color? *Alcoholism: Clinical and Experimental Research, 18,* 774–777.

Prange, M. E. (1988). Relapsed versus non-relapsed alcohol abusers: Coping skills, stressful life events and neuropsychological functioning. *Dissertation Abstracts International, 49,* 549–B.

Prigatano, G. P. (1980). Neuropsychological functioning of recidivist alcoholics treated with disulfiram: A follow-up report. *International Journal of the Addictions, 15,* 287–294.

Reed, R. J., and Grant, I. (1990). The long-term neurobehavioral consequences of substance abuse: Conceptual and methodological challenges for future research. *NIDA Research Monograph, 101,* 10–56.

Reed, R., Grant, I., and Adams, K. M. (1987). Family history of alcoholism does not predict neuropsychological performance in alcoholics. *Alcoholism: Clinical and Experimental Research, 11,* 340–344.

Reed, R. J., Grant, I., and Rourke, S. B. (1992). Long-term abstinent alcoholics have normal memory. *Alcoholism: Clinical and Experimental Research, 16,* 677–683.

Reitan, R. M. (1972). Verbal problem-solving as related to cerebral damage. *Perceptual and Motor Skills, 34,* 515–524.

Reitan, R. M., and Wolfson, D. (1985). *The Halstead-Reitan Neuropsychological Test Battery.* Tucson, AZ: Neuropsychology Press.

Rhodes, S. S., and Jasinski, D. R. (1990). Learning disabilities in alcohol-dependent adults: A preliminary study. *Journal of Learning Disabilities, 23,* 551–556.

Richardson, E. D., Malloy, P. F., Longabaugh, R., Williams, J., Noel, N., and Beattie, M. C. (1991). Liver function tests and neuropsychologic impairment in substance abusers. *Addictive Behaviors, 16,* 51–55.

Roehrich, L., and Goldman, M. S. (1993). Experience-dependent neuropsychological recovery and the treatment of alcoholism. *Journal of Consulting and Clinical Psychology, 61,* 812–821.

Rogers, R. L., Meyer, J. S., Shaw, T. G., and Mortel, K. F. (1983). Reductions in regional cerebral blood flow associated with chronic consumption of alcohol. *Journal of the American Geriatrics Society, 31,* 540–543.

Romani, A., and Cosi, V. (1989). Event-related potentials in chronic alcoholics during withdrawal and abstinence. *Neurophysiology Clinics, 19,* 373–384.

Ron, M. A. (1983). The alcoholic brain: CT scan and psychological findings. *Psychological Medicine Monograph, 3,* 1–33.

Ron, M. A. (1987). The brain of alcoholics: An overview. In O. A. Parsons, N. Butters, and P. E. Nathan, eds., *Neuropsychology of Alcoholism: Implications for Diagnosis and Treatment.* New York: Guilford Press, pp. 11–20.

Ron, M. A., Acker, W., Shaw, G. K., and Lishman, W. A. (1982). Computerized tomography of the brain in chronic alcoholism: A survey and follow-up study. *Brain, 105,* 497–514.

Rosman, A. S. (1992). Utility and evaluation of biochemical markers of alcohol consumption. *Journal of Substance Abuse, 4,* 277–297.

Rourke, S. B., Grant, I., Jernigan, T. L., and Reed, R. J. (1993). Negative computed tomography findings in male long-term abstinent alcoholics. *The Clinical Neuropsychologist, 7,* 343.

Rourke, S. B., and Grant, I. (1995). Neuropsychological deficits in male alcoholics: Part II. Using clinical ratings to delineate the effects of interim drinking and length of abstinence on the prevalence of deficits. *Journal of the International Neuropsychological Society, 1,* 327.

Rubin, E. (1989). How alcohol damages the body. *Alcohol Health and Research World, 13,* 322–327.

Ruff, R. M., Marshall, L. F., Klauber, M. R., Blunt, B. A., Grant, I., Foulkes, M. A., Eisenberg, H., Jane, J., and Marmarou, A. (1990). Alcohol abuse and neurological outcome of the severely head injured. *Journal of Head Trauma Rehabilitation, 5,* 21–31.

Russell, E. W. (1975). A multiple scoring method for the assessment of complex memory functions. *Journal of Consulting and Clinical Psychology, 43,* 800–809.

Russell, M., Czarnecki, D. M., Cowan, R., McPherson, E., and Mudar, P. J. (1991). Measures of maternal alcohol use as predictors of development in early childhood. *Alcoholism: Clinical and Experimental Research, 15,* 991–1000.

Ryan, C., and Butters, N. (1980a). Further evidence for a continuum-of-impairment encompassing male alcoholic Korsakoff patients and chronic alcoholic men. *Alcoholism: Clinical and Experimental Research, 4,* 190–198.

Ryan, C., and Butters, N. (1980b). Learning and memory impairments in young and old alcoholics: Evidence for the premature-aging hypothesis. *Alcoholism: Clinical and Experimental Research, 4,* 288–293.

Ryan, C., and Butters, N. (1984). Alcohol consumption and premature aging: A critical review. *Recent Developments in Alcoholism, 2,* 223–250.

Ryan, C., and Butters, N. (1986). The neuropsychology of alcoholism. In D. Wedding, A. Horton, and J. Webster, eds., *The Neuropsychology Handbook.* New York: Springer-Publishing Co., pp. 376–409.

Ryan, C., Butters, N., DiDario, B., and Adinolfi, A. (1980). The relationship between abstinence and recovery of function in male alcoholics. *Journal of Clinical Neuropsychology, 2,* 125–134.

Ryan, J. J., and Lewis, C. V. (1988). Comparison of normal controls and recently detoxified alcoholics on the Wechsler Memory Scale-Revised. *The Clinical Neuropsychologist, 2,* 173–180.

Ryback, R. S. (1971). The continuum and specificity of the effects of alcohol on memory: A review. *Quarterly Journal of Studies on Alcohol, 32,* 955–1016.

Sachs, H., Russell, J.A.G., Christman, D. R., and Cook, B. (1987). Alteration of regional cerebral glucose metabolic rate in non-Korsakoff chronic alcoholism. *Archives of Neurology, 44,* 1242–1251.

Salmon, D. P., and Butters, N. (1987). The etiology and neuropathology of alcoholic Korsakoff's syndrome: Some evidence for the role of the basal forebrain. *Recent Developments in Alcoholism, 5,* 27–58.

Salmon, D. P., Butters, N., and Heindel, W. C. (1993). Alcoholic dementia and related disorders. In R. W. Parks, R. F. Zec, and R. S. Wilson, eds., *Neuropsychology of Alzheimer's Disease and Other Dementias.* New York: Oxford University Press, pp. 186–209.

Samson, Y., Baron, J. C., Feline, A., Bories, J., and Crouzel, C. (1986). Local cerebral glucose utilization in chronic alcoholics: A positron tomographic study. *Journal of Neurology, Neurosurgery and Psychiatry, 49,* 1165–1170.

Sander, A. M., Nixon, S. J., and Parsons, O. A. (1989). Pretest expectancies and cognitive impairment in alcoholics. *Journal of Consulting and Clinical Psychology, 57,* 705–709.

Schaeffer, K. W., and Parsons, O. A. (1986). Drinking practices and neuropsychological test performance in sober male alcoholics and social drinkers. *Alcohol, 3,* 175–179.

Schaeffer, K. W., and Parsons, O. A. (1987). Learning impairment in alcoholics using an ecologically relevant test. *Journal of Nervous and Mental Disease, 175,* 213–218.

Schaeffer, K. W., and Parsons, O. A. (1988).

Learning and memory test performance in alcoholics as a function of monetary incentive. *International Journal of Neuroscience, 38,* 311–319.

Schaeffer, K. W., Parsons, O. A., and Errico, A. L. (1988). Abstracting deficits and childhood conduct disorder as a function of familial alcoholism. *Alcoholism: Clinical and Experimental Research, 12,* 617–618.

Schaeffer, K. W., Parsons, O. A., and Errico, A. L. (1989). Performance deficits on tests of problem solving in alcoholics: Cognitive or motivational impairment? *Journal of Substance Abuse, 1,* 381–392.

Schaeffer, K. W., Parsons, O. A., and Yohman, J. R. (1984). Neuropsychological differences between male familial and nonfamilial alcoholics and nonalcoholics. *Alcoholism: Clinical and Experimental Research, 8,* 347–351.

Schafer, K., Butters, N., Smith, T., Irwin, M., Brown, S., Hanger, P., Grant, I., and Schuckit, M. (1991). Cognitive performance of alcoholics: A longitudinal evaluation of the role of drinking history, depression, liver function, nutrition, and family history. *Alcoholism: Clinical and Experimental Research, 15,* 653–660.

Schau, E. J., O'Leary, M. R., and Chaney, E. F. (1980). Reversibility of cognitive deficit in alcoholics. *Journal of Studies on Alcohol, 41,* 733–740.

Schroth, G., Naegele, T., Klose, U., Mann, K., and Petersen, D. (1988). Reversible brain shrinkage in abstinent alcoholics, measured by MRI. *Neuroradiology, 30,* 385–389.

Schuckit, M. A. (1987). Biological vulnerability to alcoholism. *Journal of Consulting and Clinical Psychology, 55,* 301–309.

Schuckit, M. A. (1994). A clinical model of genetic influences in alcohol dependence. *Journal of Studies on Alcohol, 55,* 5–17.

Schuckit, M. A., Butters, N., Lyn, L., and Irwin, M. (1987). Neuropsychologic deficits and the risk for alcoholism. *Neuropsychopharmacology, 1,* 45–53.

Schuckit, M. A., Irwin, M., and Brown, S. A. (1990). The history of anxiety symptoms among 171 primary alcoholics. *Journal of Studies on Alcohol, 51,* 34–41.

Schuckit, M. A., Irwin, M., Howard, T., and Smith, T. (1988). A structured diagnostic interview for identification of primary alcoholism: A preliminary evaluation. *Journal of Studies on Alcohol, 49,* 93–99.

Schuckit, M. A., Irwin, M., and Smith, T. L. (1994). One-year incidence rate of major depression and other psychiatric disorders in 239 alcoholic men. *Addiction, 89,* 441–445.

Schuckit, M. A., Smith, T. L., Anthenelli, R., and Irwin, M. (1993). Clinical course of alcoholism in 636 male inpatients. *American Journal of Psychiatry, 150,* 786–792.

Selzer, M. L. (1971). The Michigan Alcoholism Screening Test: The quest for a new diagnostic instrument. *American Journal of Psychiatry, 127,* 1653–1658.

Shaper, A. G., Pocock, S. J., Ashby, D., Walker, M., and Whitehead, T. P. (1985). Biochemical and haematological response to alcohol intake. *Annals of Clinical Biochemistry, 22,* 50–61.

Sharp, J. R., Rosenbaum, G., Goldman, M. S., and Whitman, R. D. (1977). Recoverability of psychological functioning following alcohol abuse: Acquisition of meaningful synonyms. *Journal of Consulting and Clinical Psychology, 45,* 1023–1028.

Shaw, T. G., Mortel, K. F., Meyer, J. S., Rogers, R. L., Hardenberg, J., and Cutaia, M. M. (1984). Cerebral blood flow changes in benign aging and cerebrovascular disease. *Neurology, 34,* 855–862.

Shear, P. K., Jernigan, T. L., and Butters, N. (1994). Volumetric magnetic resonance imaging quantification of longitudinal brain changes in abstinent alcoholics. *Alcoholism: Clinical and Experimental Research, 18,* 172–176.

Shelton, M. D., and Parsons, O. A. (1987). Alcoholics' self-assessment of their neuropsychological functioning in everyday life. *Journal of Clinical Psychology, 43,* 395–403.

Sher, K. J., Walitzer, K. S., Wood, P. K., and Brent, E. E. (1991). Characteristics of children of alcoholics: Putative risk factors, substance use and abuse, and psychopathology. *Journal of Abnormal Psychology, 100,* 427–448.

Sherer, M., Nixon, S. J., Parsons, O. A., and Adams, R. L. (1992). Performance of alcoholic and brain-damaged subjects on the Luria Memory Word Test. *Archives of Clinical Neuropsychology, 7,* 499–504.

Shimamura, A. P., Jernigan, T. L., and Squire, L. R. (1988). Korsakoff's syndrome: Radiological (CT) findings and neuropsychological correlates. *Journal of Neuroscience, 8,* 4400–4410.

Silberstein, J. A., and Parsons, O. A. (1979). Neuropsychological impairment in female alcoholics. In M. Galanter, ed., *Currents in Alcoholism.* New York: Grune and Stratton, pp. 481–495.

Silberstein, J. A., and Parsons, O. A. (1981). Neuropsychological impairment in female alco-

holics: Replication and extension. *Journal of Abnormal Psychology, 90,* 179–182.

Sinha, R., Bernardy, N., and Parsons, O. A. (1992). Long-term test-retest reliability of event-related potentials in normals and alcoholics. *Biological Psychiatry, 32,* 992–1003.

Skinner, H. A. (1979). *Lifetime Drinking History* (Unpublished manual). Addiction Research Foundation.

Skinner, H. A., Holt, S., Schuller, R., Roy, J., and Israel, Y. (1985). Identification of alcohol abuse: Trauma and laboratory indicators. In N. C. Chang and H. M. Chao, eds., *Early Identification of Alcohol Abuse.* Washington, D.C.: NIAAA, pp. 285–301.

Skinner, H. A., and Sheu, W. J. (1982). Reliability of alcohol use indices: The lifetime drinking history and the MAST. *Journal of Studies on Alcohol, 43,* 1157–1170.

Smith, J. W., and Layden, T. A. (1972). Changes in psychological performance and blood chemistry in alcoholics during and after hospital treatment. *Quarterly Journal of Studies on Alcohol, 33,* 379–394.

Smith, K. J., and Eckardt, M. J. (1991). The effects of prenatal alcohol on the central nervous system. *Recent Developments in Alcoholism, 9,* 151–164.

Smith, M. A., Chick, J. D., Engleman, H. M., Kean, D. M., Mander, A. J., Douglas, R. H., and Best, J. J. (1988). Brain hydration during alcohol withdrawal in alcoholics measured by magnetic resonance imaging. *Drug and Alcohol Dependence, 21,* 25–28.

Solomon, D. A., and Malloy, P. F. (1992). Alcohol, head injury, and neuropsychological function. *Neuropsychology Review, 3,* 249–280.

Sparadeo, F. R., Zwick, W., and Butters, N. (1983). Cognitive functioning of alcoholic females: An exploratory study. *Drug and Alcohol Dependence, 12,* 143–150.

Stockwell, T., Hodgson, R., Edwards, G., Taylor, C., and Rankin, H. (1979). The development of a questionnaire to measure severity of alcohol dependence. *British Journal of Addiction, 74,* 79–87.

Streissguth, A. P., Barr, H. M., and Sampson, P. D. (1990). Moderate prenatal alcohol exposure: Effects on child IQ and learning problems at age 7½ years. *Alcoholism: Clinical and Experimental Research, 14,* 662–669.

Streissguth, A. P., Bookstein, F. L., Sampson, P. D., and Barr, H. M. (1989). Neurobehavioral effects of prenatal alcohol: Part III. PLS analyses of neuropsychologic tests. *Neurotoxicology and Teratology, 11,* 493–507.

Streissguth, A. P., Sampson, P. D., Olson, H. C., Bookstein, F. L., Barr, H. M., Scott, M., Feldman, J., and Mirsky, A. F. (1994). Maternal drinking during pregnancy: Attention and short-term memory in 14-year-old off-spring—A longitudinal prospective study. *Alcoholism: Clinical and Experimental Research, 18,* 202–218.

Stringer, A. Y., and Goldman, M. S. (1988). Experience-dependent recovery of block design performance in male alcoholics: Strategy training versus unstructured practice. *Journal of Studies on Alcohol, 49,* 406–411.

Sutker, P. B., and Allain, A. N. (1987). Cognitive abstraction, shifting, and control: Clinical sample comparisons of psychopaths and nonpsychopaths. *Journal of Abnormal Psychology, 96,* 73–75.

Tarter, R. E. (1973). An analysis of cognitive deficits in chronic alcoholics. *Journal of Nervous and Mental Disease, 157,* 138–147.

Tarter, R. E. (1975). Brain damage associated with chronic alcoholism. *Diseases of the Nervous System, 36,* 185–187.

Tarter, R. E. (1980). Brain damage in chronic alcoholics: A review of the psychological evidence. In D. Richter, ed., *Addiction and Brain Damage.* Baltimore: University Park Press, pp. 267–297.

Tarter, R. E. (1982). Psychosocial history, minimal brain dysfunction and differential drinking patterns of male alcoholics. *Journal of Clinical Psychology, 38,* 867–873.

Tarter, R. E. (1988). Are there inherited behavioral traits that predispose to substance abuse? *Journal of Consulting and Clinical Psychology, 56,* 189–196.

Tarter, R. E., and Alterman, A. I. (1984). Neuropsychological deficits in alcoholics: Etiological considerations. *Journal of Studies on Alcohol, 45,* 1–9.

Tarter, R. E., and Edwards, K. L. (1986). Multifactorial etiology of neuropsychological impairment in alcoholics. *Alcoholism: Clinical and Experimental Research, 10,* 128–135.

Tarter, R. E., Goldstein, G., Alterman, A., Petrarulo, E. W., and Elmore, S. (1983). Alcoholic seizures: Intellectual and neuropsychological sequelae. *Journal of Nervous and Mental Disease, 171,* 123–125.

Tarter, R. E., Hays, A. L., Sandford, S. S., and Van Thiel, D. H. (1986a). Cerebral morphological abnormalities associated with non-alcoholic cirrhosis. *Lancet, 2,* 893–895.

Tarter, R. E., Hegedus, A. M., Goldstein, G., Shelly, C., and Alterman, A. I. (1984). Adolescent sons of alcoholics: Neuropsychological and personality characteristics. *Alcoholism: Clinical and Experimental Research, 8,* 216–222.

Tarter, R. E., Hegedus, A. M., Van Thiel, D. H., Edwards, N., and Schade, R. R. (1987). Neurobehavioral correlates of cholestatic and hepatocellular disease: Differentiation according to disease specific characteristics and severity of the identified cerebral dysfunction. *International Journal of Neuroscience, 32,* 901–910.

Tarter, R. E., Hegedus, A. M., Van Thiel, D. H., Gavaler, J. S., and Schade, R. R. (1986b). Hepatic dysfunction and neuropsychological test performance in alcoholics with cirrhosis. *Journal of Studies on Alcohol, 47,* 74–77.

Tarter, R. E., Jacob, T., and Bremer, D. A. (1989a). Cognitive status of sons of alcoholic men. *Alcoholism: Clinical and Experimental Research, 13,* 232–235.

Tarter, R. E., Jacob, T., and Bremer, D. L. (1989b). Specific cognitive impairment in sons of early onset alcoholics. *Alcoholism: Clinical and Experimental Research, 13,* 786–789.

Tarter, R. E., and Jones, B. M. (1971). Motor impairment in chronic alcoholics. *Diseases of the Nervous System, 32,* 632–636.

Tarter, R. E., McBride, H., Buonpane, N., and Schneider, D. U. (1977). Differentiation of alcoholics: Childhood history of minimal brain dysfunction, family history, and drinking pattern. *Archives of General Psychiatry, 34,* 761–768.

Tarter, R. E., and Parsons, O. A. (1971). Conceptual shifting in chronic alcoholics. *Journal of Abnormal Psychology, 77,* 71–75.

Tarter, R. E., and Van Thiel, D. H. (1985). *Alcohol and the Brain: Chronic Effects.* New York: Plenum Press.

Tarter, R. E., Van Thiel, D. H., Arria, A. M., Carra, J., and Moss, H. (1988). Impact of cirrhosis on the neuropsychological test performance of alcoholics. *Alcoholism: Clinical and Experimental Research, 12,* 619–621.

Templer, D. I., Ruff, C. F., and Simpson, K. (1975). Trail making test performance of alcoholics abstinent at least a year. *International Journal of the Addictions, 10,* 609–612.

Tivis, L. J., Parsons, O. A., Glenn, S. W., and Nixon, S. J. (1993). Differences in cognitive impairment between VA and community treatment center alcoholics. *Psychology of Addictive Behaviors, 7,* 43–51.

Torvik, A. (1987). Brain lesions in alcoholics: Neuropathological observations. *Acta Medica Scandinavica, 717* (Suppl.), 47–54.

Torvik, A., Lindboe, C. F., and Rogde, S. (1982). Brain lesions in alcoholics: A neuropathological study with clinical correlations. *Journal of the Neurological Sciences, 56,* 233–248.

Trivedi, S., and Raghavan, R. (1989). Cognitive functioning of alcoholics and its relationship with prognosis. *Drug and Alcohol Dependence, 23,* 41–44.

Tuck, R. R., and Jackson, M. (1991). Social, neurological and cognitive disorders in alcoholics. *Medical Journal of Australia, 155,* 225–229.

Turner, J., and Parsons, O. A. (1988). Verbal and nonverbal abstracting: Problem-solving abilities and familial alcoholism in female alcoholics. *Journal of Studies on Alcohol, 49,* 281–287.

Unkenstein, A. E., and Bowden, S. C. (1991). Predicting the course of neuropsychological status in recently abstinent alcoholics: A pilot study. *The Clinical Neuropsychologist, 5,* 24–32.

Vanclay, F., Raphael, B., Dunne, M., Whitfield, J., Lewin, T., and Singh, B. (1991). A community screening test for high alcohol consumption using biochemical and haematological measures. *Alcohol and Alcoholism, 26,* 337–346.

Victor, M., Adams, R. D., and Collins, G. H. (1989). *The Wernicke-Korsakoff Syndrome.* Philadelphia: F. A. Davis Company.

Vighetto, A., Charles, N., Salzmann, M., Confavreux, C., and Aimard, G. (1991). Korsakoff's syndrome as the initial presentation of multiple sclerosis. *Journal of Neurology, 238,* 351–354.

Vitiello, M. V., Prinz, P. N., Personius, J. P., Nuccio, M. A., Ries, R. K., and Koerker, R. M. (1987). History of chronic alcohol abuse is associated with increased nighttime hypoxemia in older men. *Alcoholism: Clinical and Experimental Research, 11,* 368–371.

Volkow, N. D., Hitzemann, R., Wang, G. J., Fowler, J. S., Burr, G., Pascani, K., Dewey, S. L., and Wolf, A. P. (1992). Decreased brain metabolism in neurologically intact healthy alcoholics. *American Journal of Psychiatry, 149,* 1016–1022.

Volkow, N. D., Wang, G. J., Hitzemann, R., Fowler, J. S., Overall, J. E., Burr, G., and Wolf, A. P. (1994). Recovery of brain glucose metabolism in detoxified alcoholics. *American Journal of Psychiatry, 151,* 178–183.

Walker, R. D., Donovan, D. M., Kivlahan, D. R., and O'Leary, M. R. (1983). Length of stay, neuropsychological performance, and aftercare: Influences on alcohol treatment outcome. *Journal of Consulting and Clinical Psychology, 51,* 900–911.

Wanberg, K. W., Horn, J. L., and Foster, F. M. (1977). A differential assessment model for alcoholism: The scales of the Alcohol Use Inventory. *Journal of Studies on Alcohol, 38,* 512–543.

Wang, G. J., Volkow, N. D., Roque, C. T., Cestaro, V. L., Hitzemann, R. J., Cantos, E. L., Levy, A. V., and Dhawan, A. P. (1993). Functional importance of ventricular enlargement and cortical atrophy in healthy subjects and alcoholics as assessed with PET, MR imaging, and neuropsychologic testing. *Radiology, 186,* 59–65.

Waugh, M., Jackson, M., Fox, G. A., Hawke, S. H., and Tuck, R. R. (1989). Effect of social drinking on neuropsychological performance. *British Journal of Addiction, 84,* 659–667.

Wechsler, D. (1955). *Manual for the Wechsler Adult Intelligence Scale.* New York: The Psychological Corporation.

Wechsler, D. (1981). *Wechsler Adult Intelligence Scale-Revised Manual.* New York: The Psychological Corporation.

Wechsler, D., and Stone, C. P. (1945). *Wechsler Memory Scale Manual.* New York: The Psychological Corporation.

Whelan, G. (1992). Biological markers of alcoholism. *Australian and New Zealand Journal of Medicine, 22,* 209–213.

Whipple, S. C., Parker, E. S., and Noble, E. P. (1988). An atypical neurocognitive profile in alcoholic fathers and their sons. *Journal of Studies on Alcohol, 49,* 240–244.

Wik, G., Borg, S., Sjogren, I., Wiesel, F. A., Blomqvist, G., Borg, J., Greitz, T., Nyback, H., Sedvall, G., Stone-Elander, S., and Widen, L. (1988). PET determination of regional cerebral glucose metabolism in alcohol-dependent men and healthy controls using ^{11}C-glucose. *Acta Psychiatrica Scandinavica, 78,* 234–241.

Wilkinson, D. A. (1982). Examination of alcoholics by computed tomographic (CT) scans: A critical review. *Alcoholism: Clinical and Experimental Research, 6,* 31–45.

Wilkinson, D. A. (1987). Discussion: CT scan and neuropsychological assessments of alcoholism. In O. A. Parsons, N. Butters, and P. E. Nathan, eds., *Neuropsychology of Alcoholism: Implications for Diagnosis and Treatment.* New York: Guilford Press, pp. 76–102.

Williams, C. M., and Skinner, A. E. (1990). The cognitive effects of alcohol abuse: A controlled study. *British Journal of Addiction, 85,* 911–917.

Windle, M., and Blane, H. T. (1989). Cognitive

ability and drinking behavior in a national sample of young adults. *Alcoholism: Clinical and Experimental Research, 13,* 43–48.

Workman-Daniels, K. L., and Hesselbrock, V. M. (1987). Childhood problem behavior and neuropsychological functioning in persons at risk for alcoholism. *Journal of Studies on Alcohol, 48,* 187–193.

Yohman, J. R., and Parsons, O. A. (1985). Intact verbal paired-associate learning in alcoholics. *Journal of Clinical Psychology, 41,* 844–851.

Yohman, J. R., and Parsons, O. A. (1987). Verbal reasoning deficits in alcoholics. *The Journal of Nervous and Mental Disease, 175,* 219–223.

Yohman, J. R., Parsons, O. A., and Leber, W. R. (1985). Lack of recovery in male alcoholics' neuropsychological performance one year after treatment. *Alcoholism: Clinical and Experimental Research, 9,* 114–117.

York, J. L., and Biederman, I. (1991). Hand movement speed and accuracy in detoxified alcoholics. *Alcoholism: Clinical and Experimental Research, 15,* 982–990.

Zatz, L. M., Jernigan, T. L., and Ahumada, A. J., Jr. (1982). Changes on computed cranial tomography with aging: Intracranial fluid volume. *American Journal of Neuroradiology, 3,* 1–11.

Zipursky, R. B., Lim, K. O., and Pfefferbaum, A. (1989). MRI study of brain changes with short-term abstinence from alcohol. *Alcoholism: Clinical and Experimental Research, 13,* 664–666.

19 Neuropsychological Consequences of Drug Abuse

ALBERT S. CARLIN and STEPHANIE O'MALLEY

Neuropsychological consequences of drug abuse continue to be of considerable importance in neuropsychiatric populations. Many patients consume licit or illicit psychoactive substances in prescribed or uncontrolled ways. This chapter reviews the evidence of various relationships between drug consumption and behavior, with particular reference to the long-term neurobehavioral impact of drug abuse.

It is commonly assumed that the abuse of most psychoactive substances results in neuropsychological deficit. Whether this attitude reflects a sense of moral retribution or the belief that repeated trips across the blood-brain barrier must exact their toll is an open question. Certainly, most psychoactive drugs affect neuropsychological functioning acutely. The acute effects can be studied in a straightforward way by administering the drug under study in known dosage to subjects and then comparing either pre-post or drug-placebo performance.

The long-term consequences of chronic drug use are more difficult to assess. The problem arises not only in the assessment of neuropsychological status, but in assigning any observed deficit to the appropriate cause. As will be seen, investigations of drug consequences are frequently cross-sectional; subjects have established drug-abuse careers so that it is difficult to differentiate premorbid impairment from drug-induced impairment. The accurate determination of past psychoactive drug use with regard to chronicity and frequency is vital, but also difficult. Exposure to adulterants, the prevalence of multiple drug use, and the impact of route of administration all contribute to the uncertainties of attributing any observed impairment to the drug(s) under consideration. In addition, the neuropsychological status of drug users may be influenced by their medical or developmental history, independently or through interactions with drug use.

Neuropsychological consequences, as the term is used in this chapter, are relatively enduring deficits in behavior that presumably reflect changes in brain function. Actual structural changes may or may not be observed; data from brain imaging, electrophysiology, or neuropathology will be referred to where relevant.

The chapter will focus on studies employing relatively systematic, objective behavioral assessments thought to reflect cortical integrity. For the most part, animal research will be omitted since the results are difficult to extrapolate to humans because of between-species differences in brain and behavior and in drug dose, pattern of use, and route of administration. For example, animal studies frequently involve much larger doses than humans self-administer; furthermore, it is unclear that dose per kilogram or square meter is a valid translation from humans to animals of different species and size.

The entire gamut of psychoactive drugs has not received equal attention from those investigating neuropsychological consequences. Drug classes that were developed and marketed with therapeutic intent have been much less thoroughly studied than illicit and recreational drugs. Thus, LSD, marijuana, and solvents have been the target of neuropsychological studies far more often than opiates, sedative hypnotics, and minor tranquilizers. More recently, cocaine has been the focus of such investigations.

The following review has been organized by drug class only for convenience of exposition, with full awareness that much drug abuse is, in fact, polydrug use. Often it is extremely difficult to classify people according to meaningful drug categories because heavy marijuana users may also drink heavily, opiate users may also use marijuana and cocaine, cocaine users typically abuse alcohol, and so on. With this caveat in mind, what are some of the neuropsychological findings related to drug abuse?

LSD, PCP, and Other Hallucinogenic Drugs

LSD (Lysergic Acid Diethylamide)

The long-term neuropsychological consequences of LSD use have been studied by several investigators. McGlothlin and colleagues (1969) examined a group of individuals who had initially received LSD as an adjunct to psychotherapy. Many of them continued using LSD in a nonmedical setting, resulting in a median of 75 LSD exposures (range, 20 to 1,100). Other drug use was minimal in this somewhat older (mean age, 40), relatively well-educated group. Subjects were excluded who showed evidence of severe psychopathology before exposure to LSD or who had extensive drug abuse histories or preexisting neurological pathology. Because the LSD-using subjects were initially psychotherapy patients, they were compared with other psychotherapy patients who had not been exposed to LSD or other hallucinogens. Both groups were given a selection of subtests of the Halstead-Reitan Battery. In addition, the Shipley-Hartford, Porteus Maze, Witkin's Embedded Figures, Guilford's Associational Fluency Test, Minnesota Perceptuo-Diagnostic Test, and a map-reading task were administered. A clinical interview was also carried out. The LSD group performed significantly worse on only one test, Category. However, no correlation was found between number of LSD ingestions and performance on this task. One of the two tests that did correlate with the number of LSD ingestions revealed better performance with greater use (Rhythm) while the other showed worse performance with greater use (Map Reading). The authors concluded that there was a possible association between LSD use and minimal brain dysfunction, but acknowledged the difficulty of establishing a causal relationship.

Illicit LSD users were studied by Cohen and Edwards (1969) with the complete Halstead-Reitan Battery as well as the Raven Progressive Matrices and the same test of spatial orientation (map reading) used by McGlothlin et al. (1969). These authors found that the LSD users differed from a comparison sample matched for age and education on Trails A and map following. On both tests, the LSD users scored worse than did the controls. Among the LSD users, a correlation was found between number of experiences and worse performance on Trails A and the Raven test. The authors concluded that although no generalized neuropsychological deficit is associated with LSD use, visual spatial orientation was impaired. The authors also provided the caveat that subject selection variables might have biased their results, because obviously impaired persons had been excluded as unable to complete the testing. Unfortunately, they provided no information about numbers of subjects excluded. It should also be noted that the drug users in this study had significant experience with a number of drugs other than LSD.

Wright and Hogan (1972) attempted to replicate the findings of Cohen and Edwards (1969) using similar subjects, although their LSD users had a lower exposure to LSD (median of 20 exposures versus 50). Wright and Hogan also added the WAIS and the aphasia screening test to the battery used by Cohen and Edwards. They found that the LSD users performed better on the Information subtest of the WAIS and worse on the Comprehension subtest. No significant differences were found on other test scores nor on the Impairment Index. Aphasia screening scores were compared to a subgroup of college students, and although both groups evidenced a low rate of errors, they did not differ statistically. The authors concluded that they failed to replicate the findings of even mild impairment in LSD users. It is, of course, possible that the group studied by Wright and Hogan was not sufficiently exposed to LSD for impairment to emerge.

Evidence of deleterious consequences of LSD use is provided by Acord (1972), who also had the most liberal definition of LSD abuse. His subjects were 40 inpatients and outpatients selected from the psychiatric services of a large military hospital who had used LSD at least once. He reported that their mean scores on the Category Test and the time, memory, and localization portions of the Tactual Performance Test (TPT) exceeded the usual cutoffs for impairment. Although striking, these results are difficult to interpret because there was no control group and because of the possibility that psychopathology or other factors inherent to being a psychiatric patient could affect neuropsychological performance. The importance of eliminating the contribution of uncontrolled variables is especially important in the light of the liberal inclusion criteria.

As a follow-up to this investigation, Acord and Barker (1973) compared 15 persons who had used hallucinogenic drugs at least once with 15 persons who denied use of drugs except for marijuana. In addition, all subjects were free of intracranial pathology, medically prescribed psychoactive drugs, and psychopathology beyond character disorder or behavior disorder. Subjects were inpatients, outpatients, and staff of a large military hospital. Subjects were essentially similar in age, education, and Navy General Classification test scores. All subjects received the Category Test, Trails B, and TPT location (it is assumed that these subjects were adminis-

tered the entire TPT, but only the location scores are reported). Hallucinogenic users scored significantly worse on Category and TPT location. The scores of the experimental group approached or exceeded cutoff scores proposed by Halstead (1947) and Reitan (1955). The authors did not indicate the proportion of subjects who were patients or nonpatients in each group and also did not specify the extent of other drug involvement. Thus, it is not possible to determine whether the findings are related to hallucinogenic drug use, patient status, use of other drugs, or other selection factors. The rather liberal inclusion criterion, which lacks face validity, suggests that the last-mentioned possibility must be entertained seriously.

Aside from problems in sample selection and inadequate consideration of obvious sources of neuropsychological variance, the studies above, and many to be reviewed below, relied wholly on univariate statistical comparisons to examine their hypotheses. Failure to employ multivariate statistical approaches, or at least to correct for use of multiple t or F tests by strategies such as the Bonferroni inequality method (Grove and Andreasen, 1982) open the findings to the criticism that they might be capitalizing on chance factors. At the same time exclusive reliance on measures of central tendency (avoiding clinical scoring and inference) assumes a uniformity of area of impairment that may not exist. Some users of the drugs in question may experience primarily spatial deficits, while others may demonstrate verbal impairment. Combining these subjects might well obscure their impairment through averaging of scores.

PCP (Phencyclidine)

A study of phencyclidine (PCP) abusers by Carlin et al. (1979) provides a useful model of how possible contaminating variables can be isolated (if not controlled for) and how the more powerful reliance on clinical inference can be used to study the possible deleterious consequences of hallucinogenic drug abuse. The complete Halstead-Reitan Battery was administered to 12 chronic PCP abusers, 12 polydrug abusers who did not consume PCP, and 12 normal controls who engaged in minimal drug use. A drug use history for the past 10 years preceding the study was conducted, as was a review of medical neurological history. The drug use data were presented in milligrams of substance or occasions of use per week based on a 10-year average. They revealed that both drug-using groups used equivalent amounts of heroin and stimulants; the polydrug group consumed more depressants and opiates than did the PCP group who consumed more PCP and hallucinogens.

Neuropsychological performance was rated on a six-point scale ranging from above average performance to severely impaired. The ratings were carried out by a clinician who was provided the protocols of all 36 subjects and who had no information regarding group membership. Both drug-using groups contained significantly more persons judged to be impaired, than did non–drug-using controls. Mean subtest score differences and appropriate statistical tests were also presented in this publication, but because of small sample size and variability, the differences were less dramatic. Medical-neurologic risk was independent of neuropsychological status, as was recent drug consumption as reflected by positive urine tests. Because of the now common pattern of multiple drug abuse, only indirect evidence of the impact of PCP could be provided; but the fact that the PCP users consumed substantially less sedative hypnotics (the class that previous research has associated with neuropsychological [NP] impairment) at least suggested that abuse of substances other than PCP or hallucinogens did not explain the PCP users' impairment.

A more recent study by Cosgrove and Newell (1991) compared chronic PCP-using polydrug abusers with polydrug abusers who used no PCP. The PCP users in this study reduced or stopped their PCP use and were tested just after reducing their drug use and again 4 weeks later. Because of a large number of measures (12) and few subjects (15 per group) the authors could not use multivariate statistics. They instead computed an impairment ratio. They found that the PCP users improved somewhat on a number of measures while the non–PCP-using polydrug abusers did somewhat worse. Once again, small sample sizes and multiple measures render the results difficult to interpret.

MDMA (3,4-methylenedioxy-methamphetamine)

Extasy, or MDMA (3,4-methylenedioxy-methamphetamine), is a "designer drug" that has achieved notoriety, first as a benign source of enhancement of personal insight, and then as another potentially damaging substance. The consequences of chronic use of MDMA were investigated by Krystal et al. (1992). A small sample of nine young adults was examined using the WAIS-R, portions of the Wechsler Memory Scale, the Boston Naming Test, Trail Making Test, Tactual Performance Test, Finger Oscillation Test, Lafayette Pegboard Test, Grip Strength, Beck Depression Inventory, and the Hamilton Depression Scale. The selection of instruments was in part dictated by the authors' hypothesis that MDMA use would be associated with destruction of central serotonin (5-HT) terminals and lowered levels of 5-HT in the brain. Many of the subjects had exposure to a wide variety of hallucinogenic substances and seven of the nine had previously established psychiatric diagnoses. Subjects' performances were rated for impairment based on deviation from national norms. The results are difficult to interpret because of the absence of any comparison groups, but many of the subjects did have scores that fell into the impaired range. Although the use of other drugs and the presence of psychiatric history makes it difficult to establish a direct relationship between MDMA use and neuropsychological impairment, this investigation is of interest because of its attempt to test specific hypotheses about specific induced deficits.

Taken as an aggregate, the studies described above suggest that LSD has little enduring impact on higher level cognitive functioning. The studies of Acord, and Acord and Barker are contaminated by mixing patients with "normals" and by an inclusion criterion so liberal it renders their results almost meaningless. It is also apparent from the results of Carlin et al. (1979) that the impact of the class of drugs, hallucinogens, cannot be meaningfully considered. It is possible that some classes of hallucinogens might be implicated in the emergence of neuropsychological deficit while others might not be. It is also possible the impairment associated with LSD use requires greater exposure than experienced by subjects studied by Cohen and Edwards (1969), McGlothlin et al. (1969), and Wright and Hogan (1972), while the greater use of both LSD and PCP of subjects studied by Carlin et al. (1979) was sufficient to reveal a subtle relationship. It seems fair to conclude that if there are deleterious consequences of LSD, they are subtle, easily obscured by dose differences, and have a low prevalence among users.

Marijuana

The neuropsychology of marijuana use has also been studied extensively. Culver and King (1974) examined the neuropsychological performance of three groups of Dartmouth undergraduates from the 1971 and 1972 classes. The three groups were marijuana users, marijuana plus LSD users, and nonusers of drugs. The Halstead-Reitan Battery was administered. The data were analyzed separately for each year and then combined into a larger sample. Although sample sizes were relatively small, the cross-validation offered by this study is of great interest. On each occasion of retesting, new significant differences appeared, and previously observed differences disappeared or reappeared among the groups and classes of different years. Consistent differences were found only for the Trail Making Test: the marijuana group performed significantly better than the LSD group. The marijuana group also drank more alcohol than the controls; the LSD group also used more marijuana and drank more than the marijuana group. The analysis was repeated with statistical control for amount of alcohol consumed with identical NP results.

The pattern of greater exposure to any one

drug being related to more exposure to a greater variety of drugs was also reported by Rochford et al. (1977), who studied drug use among medical students. They found that marijuana smokers were a subset of those who used alcohol. Those who used hallucinogens, stimulants and opiates were a subset of the marijuana abusers. These authors also found that there were no differences between the marijuana smokers and the non drug-using medical students on TPT, Trails A and B, the Hutt Adaptation of the Bender-Gestalt, and the Minnesota Perceptuo-Diagnostic Test. This study replicates that of Grant et al. (1973), which used the complete Halstead-Reitan Battery, and found only one statistically significant difference, which the authors attributed to chance.

Carlin and Trupin (1977) studied persons who smoked daily for an average of 5 years and compared them to a group who were matched for age, education, and intelligence. Their marijuana subjects, in contrast to those of Culver and King (1974), did worse on Trails B. Schwartz (1991) found significant memory impairment among 10 marijuana users whose use pattern met criteria for cannabis dependence. The impairment was most striking on initial evaluation with some improvement on retest 6 weeks later. Even then marijuana users still demonstrated worsened memory than did control subjects. These findings may be the result of assessing subjects while intoxicated—hence their improvement. Or, more ominously, the emergence of this level of impairment may reflect increasing potency of marijuana now available.

The lack of consistent findings from these empirical studies failed to support the clinical reports of Kolansky and Moore (1971, 1972) who observed organic-like impairment among a group of adolescent psychiatric patients who were heavy consumers of marijuana. It may be that Grant et al. (1973), Culver and King (1974), Carlin and Trupin (1977), and Rochford et al. (1977) studied biased samples of brighter and less impaired users. By focusing on college students the empirical studies might have been sampling from a population unlikely to contain many impaired persons. The empirically studied persons might have been the survivors, whereas Kolansky and Moore (1971, 1972) reported on the casualties. If one were to assume that impairment emerges with heavier daily use and longer exposure, it may be that the pattern of marijuana smoking by most users in most Western countries may not be intense enough, nor extend over a long enough period, for measurable consequences to emerge.

A number of foreign cultures exist within which marijuana use has a longer tradition. Chronic cannabis users were studied in Egypt (Souief, 1975), Jamaica (Rubin and Comitas, 1975), and Costa Rica (Satz et al., 1976). The Jamaican study is in many ways the more relevant as an investigation of persons who are functioning and who are also very long term and very heavy users. This society has a tradition of cannabis use within which many view the drug as curative, benign, or even as a work enhancer. Rubin and Comitas (1975) reported no significant differences between users and nonusers on an extensive battery of NP tests. Unfortunately, cross-cultural differences and attempts to cope with these confounded the interpretation of these results. The Information, Vocabulary, and Picture Arrangement subtests of the WAIS were not used due to the subjects' unfamiliarity with the required knowledge and skills, and the authors acknowledged the questionable relevance of other subtests, but included them in an effort to have some metric of comparison for users and nonusers. Their report suggested that the child's version of the TPT was used, as was the child's version of the Category Test. Thus, the lack of significance on many tests of the WAIS may be a function of a floor effect; that is, the absence of difference may reflect inapplicability of test items so that groups had little room to differ. Similarly, and perhaps of greater importance, use of the children's version of two of the most sensitive tests of higher level cognitive functioning (Category, TPT), might have created an artificial ceiling that obscured any drug effects. Satz et al. (1976) carried out a more extensive evaluation with greater sensitivity

to cross-cultural issues in their Costa Rica study. Pretesting was carried out to assure cultural compatibility of the Williams Memory Scale, Wechsler Memory Scale, Facial Recognition Memory Test, Benton Visual Retention Test, the IPAT Culture Fair Test and a short form of the Spanish version of the WAIS. Appropriate multivariate statistics failed to demonstrate differences between users, occasional users, and nonusers.

Page et al. (1988), in a follow-up of the Satz et al. study, located many of the original subjects and retested them 4 years later. Additional measures of memory (selective reminding, Rey-Osterreith Complex Figure, Rey-Davis), and of sustained attention and concentration were added to the instruments Satz et al. had used. These authors found that the marijuana users were slower and had greater difficulty with self paced measures that required sustained attention than did nonusers. These findings suggest that more sensitive measures may be required to detect the negative consequences of marijuana use.

Overall, the majority of controlled studies have failed to relate marijuana use to neuropsychological dysfunction. In the light of clinical reports such as those of Kolansky and Moore (1971, 1972), caution should be exercised in dismissing the drug as harmless. It is possible that the deficit is more subtle than can be detected by many commonly used instruments or that the studies of users who were not patients systematically excluded impaired persons through biased sampling. It is also possible that users who have been studied have not smoked enough marijuana long enough to produce measurable impairment. Changes in potency and in patterns of use may increase the possibility of discovering impairment among chronic users.

Solvents

In contrast to the preceding drugs of abuse, whose long-term deleterious consequences have not been established, the adverse effects of exposure to solvents are clear and obvious. Many of the initial published reports are case histories documenting peripheral neuropathy and cerebellar dysfunction (Grabski, 1961; Knox and Nelson, 1966; Kelly, 1975; Malm and Lying-Tunell, 1980; Lewis et al., 1981).

Turning to neuropsychological studies, we have the report of Dodds and Santostefano (1964), who compared teenage glue sniffers and nonsniffers on a variety of cognitive measures, including the Benton Visual Retention Test, and found no significant differences. Tsushima and Towne (1977) compared paint sniffers with nonsniffers matched for age, education, and socioeconomic status on a number of tests that are subparts of the Halstead-Reitan Battery (Tapping, Rhythm, Trails A and B) and on the coding subtest of the WISC, the Stroop Color-Word test, the Graham Kendall Memory for Designs, and the Peabody Picture Vocabulary Test. They found marked differences on 13 of 15 measures, the sniffers performing significantly worse. The sniffers differed on vocabulary-estimated IQ and thus it is possible that lower IQ functioning might account for both the glue sniffing and lower performance on other tests. There was a significant association between length of abuse history and impairment. However, the nature of the relationship is puzzling; it is nonlinear, with relatively uniform performance until history of use exceeds 11 years, at which time a marked decrement appears. Either a threshold phenomenon exists or the results reflect a peculiar cohort difference.

A more clear-cut finding is provided by Berry et al. (1977), who examined glue sniffers and compared their performance on the Halstead-Reitan Battery with that of siblings and peers. They found significant differences (glue sniffers scoring worse) for verbal and full scale IQ, TPT time and memory, and impairment in sensory perceptual and motor functioning. The glue sniffers also had a higher Impairment Index and Average Impairment Rating. It is of interest that other measures of higher level functioning showed little or no differences.

Several reports have described the effects of accidental acute exposure to solvents in the workplace or of chronic low level industrial exposure. Among New York City sewage treatment workers exposed to a variety of solvents including benzene and toluene, both subjective complaints and objective findings of impairment (Block Design, Embedded Figures, Digit Symbol, Grooved Pegboard, Benton Visual Retention Test) were greater among those with longer exposure (Kraut et al., 1988). Three wharf workers exposed to toluene diisocynate were found to have progressive deficits—their performance worsened over time from exposure (Singer and Scott, 1987). Longer term but lower level exposure to toluene among nonpatients was not associated with lowered neuropsychological functioning nor with neuroradiological changes (Juntunen et al., 1985). Interestingly, among these subjects greater exposure to toluene was associated with heavy drinking.

One difficulty in research with solvents is that the concoctions that people inhale tend to contain a large variety of aldehydes, ketones, and aromatic compounds, each of which might have a different spectrum of neurotoxicity. So far, the weight of evidence from case reports suggests that toluene can cause cerebral and cerebellar atrophy, with lesser peripheral effects; some of the aldehydes and ketones (e.g., methylbutylketone), on the other hand, produce marked neuropathy but uncertain cerebral effects. The properties of many other aromatic compounds are largely unknown.

Opiates

In the light of the number of years opiates have been widely available and widely abused, the relative paucity of research on their neuropsychological consequences is surprising. Two earlier studies (Brown and Partington, 1942; Pfeffer and Ruble, 1946) failed to find any impairment that could be associated with opiate use. These two studies are more of historic than substantive interest at this time because their methodology is not comparable to the more recent studies that use more refined measures of neuropsychological functioning.

Korin (1974) compared 27 Vietnam-era

veterans who abused heroin with 17 who abused nonopiate drugs on a battery of tests that included the Bender-Gestalt. He found that heroin abusers performed worse on the Bender-Gestalt, but pointing out that personality traits are also likely to be reflected by the Bender-Gestalt, he refrained from interpreting the results as suggesting neuropsychological impairment in the heroin abusers. Although the latter study differentiated between detoxified and currently using subjects, it did not provide any estimates of chronicity or frequency of use.

A more elaborate study of neuropsychological assessment of Vietnam-era veteran heroin abusers was carried out by Fields and Fullerton (1974), who relied on the Halstead-Reitan Battery. A group of heroin abusers, addicted from 1 to 10 years (mean length of addiction, 4.9 years), was compared with a group of brain-damaged subjects and a group of mixed non–drug-abusing, non–brain-injured patients, all of whom were matched for education, age, and sex. They found that the heroin-addicted sample tended to perform somewhat better than the control group and that both performed significantly better than the brain-damaged comparison group. They concluded that their sample of heroin addicts failed to evidence deleterious consequences of heroin addiction. Although they administered the Halstead-Reitan Battery, which is readily amenable to clinical ratings and classification, Fields and Fullerton (1974) relied strictly on comparisons of group central tendencies for various tests. As discussed previously, such a strategy runs the risk of failing to identify drug effects that express themselves in different ways in different subjects.

The complexities inherent in sample selection and interpretation of neuropsychological data are illustrated by two publications by the same group of authors that provide differing conclusions. Rounsaville et al. (1981) compared opiate addicts with epileptics, using an impairment rating based on the sum of the number of tests on which each subject's score was one standard deviation from the mean in the direction of impairment on those tasks making up the Lafayette Clinic

Neuropsychological Assessment Battery (Adams et al., 1975). These scores allowed the authors to classify subjects as demonstrating no impairment, mild impairment, and moderate to severe impairment. The two groups did not differ on either impairment rating or on mean individual test scores. It was concluded that opiate abusers manifested neuropsychological impairment. In a later paper, using the same opiate-abusing sample and the same epileptic comparison group, but with the addition of a non–opiate-abusing comparison group of low socioeconomic status workers, Rounsaville et al. (1982) arrived at the opposite conclusion. Their data were unchanged, but their finding that the worker group was as impaired as both the opiate abusers and the epilepsy comparison group caused them to reevaluate the meaning of their findings.

Several possible conclusions can be drawn from these two papers. Either the epilepsy group was not neuropsychologically impaired and hence neither were the opiate subjects; or the worker group was impaired, as were the two original groups. It is also possible that the groups differed in some important way. For example, in both papers the addicts were described as predominantly White while no ethnic or racial descriptor was provided for the comparison groups. Could cultural differences beyond those of education and socioeconomic class have accounted for the differences? The freedom to choose among these alternative explanations indicates no conclusions can be drawn from these studies.

Hill et al. (1979) compared heroin abusers, alcohol abusers, and controls on brain computed tomographic (CT) and neuropsychological testing. Acquiring both a physical measure and a behavioral measure of cortical integrity provides a unique opportunity to explore the relationships among these measures. Overall, they found that alcoholics were most impaired compared to controls, with opiate addicts most often falling between these two groups on selected subtests of the Halstead-Reitan Battery (TPT, Tapping and Category), the Raven Progressive matrices, the Shipley-Hartford and the Peabody Picture Vocabulary Test. These authors found that length of opiate abuse career was associated with greater impairment. They also found that remission in opiate abusers was complexly related to impairment; those in remission performed somewhat better on Category and somewhat worse on TPT than current users. A small but significant correlation ($r = 0.27$) was found between CT-measured ventricle/brain ratio and errors on Category and TPT total time. Interestingly, the investigators also found that opiate abusers had somewhat smaller ventricles and narrower sulci than controls (alcoholics had enlargement of both). The authors speculated that this might be the result of an allergic phenomenon that results in chronic swelling of brain tissue. The relatively weak relationship between CT scan and neuropsychological test findings is disappointing, but consistent with data emerging from comparisons of CT and NP measures in alcoholics (for discussions of this issue, see Ron, 1983; Grant, 1987; and Chapter 18, this volume).

Strang and Gurling (1989) were able to study seven older heroin addicts who were being maintained on heroin in Great Britain. This sample, although small, allowed some mitigation of problems with adulterants. However, all their subjects had also extensively used alcohol or other drugs in the past—some quite recently. As with Hill et al. (1979) some CT scans indicated a degree of morphological changes and some neuropsychological data indicated the presence of impairment, but these were not necessarily found in the same subjects. No relationship was found between estimated lifetime use and impairment.

Hendler et al. (1980) compared chronic pain patients who received only narcotics with those receiving only benzodiazepines using the WAIS, Wechsler Memory Scale, and Bender-Gestalt tests, as well as on EEG measures. The subjects in this study were not "addicts" and no data were provided on length of use other than a history of drug use for 1 month prior to admission. They found chronic pain patients treated with narcotics to be less impaired than those treated with benzodiazepines. In this report it is difficult to sort out acute effects from long-term consequences.

Although the relative paucity of neuropsychological research on the long-term consequences of opiate addiction dictates caution in arriving at a conclusion, it appears that abuse of these drugs is not associated with easily detectable impairment. The opiates will be considered again later in this chapter in the discussion of polydrug research.

Sedative-Hypnotics

Despite the widespread use of barbiturates and other sedative-hypnotics, including diazepam and other anxiolytics, relatively little research has been carried out on the neuropsychological consequences of long-term use of these substances. Isbell et al. (1950) and Kornetsky (1951) studied the effects of short-term chronic administration of pentobarbital in five prison inmates using the Bender-Gestalt Test, Koh's Block Test, and projective measures. They found impairment during intoxication and withdrawal, but none after 60 days of abstinence. Hill and Belleville (1953) and Wikler et al. (1955) employed similar techniques and found deficits associated with acute effects, but no long-term effects. These studies all examined relatively short-term use of these substances in persons whose cumulative lifetime use of barbiturates was actually quite low.

Bergman and colleagues (1980) studied 55 patients who were exclusive abusers of sedative and hypnotic drugs, most of whom had abused these substances for 5 years or less, but some of whom had used them for more than 10 years. Following withdrawal, they were tested using an intelligence battery developed in Sweden, the Trail Making Test, and the Memory for Designs. This patient group was matched with a non–drug-using sample on the basis of age, education, sex, and level of employment. Comparisons were carried out on both separate test scores and on judgments of impairment that were performed by psychologists blind to group membership.

The investigators found that the drug-abusing sample was significantly more impaired as measured both by clinical judgments based on test protocols and on group comparison of test scores. Performance on tests that were believed to be resistant to intellectual impairment did not differ. The authors concluded that the observed impairment in exclusive abusers of sedative hypnotic drugs was the result of the use of these substances. They did not report a relationship between cumulative consumption and impairment nor did they address premorbid status. A number of observations of differences in leisure activities, living situation, and employment stability could have been either a function of drug-induced impairment, premorbid differences or sequelae of functional disorders, such as depression. By examining a group of abusers of a single class of substance, this study has taken an important step toward elucidating the longer term effects of the sedative-hypnotic drugs. A follow-up study carried out 5 years later on 30 of the same subjects found only slight improvement. Computed tomography scans of these subjects revealed dilated ventricles, but not the widened sulci seen in alcoholics.

Long-term benzodiazepine users who could not be considered drug abusers and who used few other psychoactive drugs except for antidepressants provided a relatively pure group for study by Golombok et al. (1988). A computed index of lifetime consumption of benzodiazepine correlated modestly with a variety of measures of neuropsychological functioning. Higher lifetime consumption was associated with lowered performance on tasks thought to assess posterior cortical function. These results held, even when state anxiety was statistically controlled. No consistent relationship was found between use of antidepressants and neuropsychological deficit.

The studies of users of exclusive categories of drugs, such as that of Golombok et al. (1988), provide evidence of possible long-term deleterious consequences of chronic use of barbiturates and benzodiazepines. Replications of these findings will be needed to confirm this conclusion and elucidate the nature of the relationship.

Stimulants

The amphetamines and cocaine, including the crack form, are stimulants that have similar effects but vary in their rate of onset and duration of action. Cocaine and crack are currently the most widely abused stimulant drugs although the amphetamines are once again becoming popular and available. Concerns about potential adverse effects of central stimulants on neurocognitive functioning were first raised by a series of case reports of arteritis (Citron et al., 1962; Rumbaugh and Fang, 1980), vasculitis (Bostwick, 1981), and intracranial hemorrhage (Cahill et al., 1981). More recently, studies using SPECT and PET scans have found evidence of reductions in cortical perfusion (Holman et al., 1991), cerebellar blood flow (Volkow et al., 1988), and glucose utilization in the basal ganglia (Volkow, 1991). In addition, animal studies suggested neurotoxic actions of amphetamine in animals (Ellinwood and Cohen, 1971).

Studies of neuropsychological functioning of stimulant abusers have been relatively limited although efforts in this area have increased in recent years. With regard to amphetamine abuse, only two studies have been conducted using primary amphetamine abusers. In the first study, Rylander (1969) reported that 28% of 50 Swedish amphetamine addicts were impaired on the Benton Test of Memory for Designs. In the second study, Trites et al. (1974) compared the performance of 50 amphetamine abusers on the Halstead-Reitan Battery to test norms and cutoff scores; they found subnormal performance on the Tactual Performance Test and the Trails B.

More recently, several controlled studies of the neuropsychological functioning of cocaine abusers have been reported. O'Malley et al. (1992) compared the performance of 20 recently abstinent primary cocaine abusers with 20 age- and education-matched controls on the WAIS-R, the Halstead Category Test, the Finger Oscillation test, and the Neuropsychological Screening Battery (NSB). The average pattern of cocaine use was over 400 grams of cocaine taken over approximately 4 years. The cocaine abusers performed more poorly than controls on the arithmetic subtest of the WAIS-R, the Symbol Digit Modalities test, a measure of verbal memory, the Category test and the summary score of the NSB. Fifty percent of the cocaine abusers scored in the impairment range on the NSB summary score, in contrast to 15% of the controls. Briefer periods of abstinence were associated with poorer performance on a number of the measures that discriminated cocaine abusers from normal controls.

In a second study, O'Malley et al. (1989; as described in O'Malley and Gawin, 1990) compared 25 primary cocaine abusers to 25 age-, education-, sex-, and race-matched normal controls using the extended Halstead-Reitan Battery. For data analyses, the neuropsychological tests were classified according to eight ability areas and multivariate analyses were then used to compare the cocaine abusers and controls on each of these ability areas and on a group of summary measures (i.e., Verbal IQ, Performance IQ, and the Average Impairment Rating). The cocaine abusers did not differ on measures of verbal skills, attention, abstraction and cognitive flexibility, learning or incidental memory, or simple sensory abilities. Cocaine abusers performed more poorly, however, on complex psychomotor skills, memory tests, and simple motor skills. When individual tests were examined, the cocaine abusers were found to perform more poorly on spatial relations, grooved pegboard, grip strength, Trails A, spatial relations, and nonverbal memory. None of the individual summary scores discriminated between the two groups. The cocaine abusers' scores were in the normal range on all tests except grip strength and spatial relations. Because these subjects had been abstinent four months on average, the data suggest that cocaine-related disruptions in complex psychomotor and simple motor functioning may persist for extended periods after the achievement of initial abstinence.

Two other studies provide evidence for verbal memory deficits in cocaine abusers. Manschreck et al. (1990) contrasted the performance of 33 Bahamian cocaine freebase users who had been abstinent 59 days on average with the performance of 21 age-, education-, and gender-matched Bahamian controls. The two groups were comparable on the Mini-Mental State Exam, the Shipley Hartford, and measures of speech, semantic processing, contextual memory, and motor synchrony. Cocaine abusers, however, performed more poorly on a signal-detection memory test that provides an index of verbal memory. In the second study, 16 schizophrenics who abused cocaine were compared with 35 schizophrenics without a history of cocaine use (Sevy et al., 1990). Cocaine abusers were also more likely to report cannabis and opiate use, but the percentage of patients who reported alcohol use did not differ between the two groups (although data are not reported on the amount of alcohol used). Subjects were tested 3 weeks after admission to an inpatient unit as part of a larger study of positive and negative syndromes in chronic schizophrenia. The two groups were comparable on demographics, variables related to the severity of their psychiatric illness, and measures of intelligence. The cocaine abusers, however, did more poorly on tests of conceptual encoding and verbal memory.

Research on cocaine-related neuropsychological deficits has typically used cross-sectional designs, thereby limiting the conclusions that can be drawn about the potential contribution of drug versus premorbid characteristics to observed deficits and about whether these deficits are transient or permanent. Bauer and his colleagues, however, have conducted a series of studies in which cocaine-dependent subjects were tested after 1, 3, and 12 weeks of verified abstinence and compared to non–drug-dependent controls studied after comparable intervals. The number of cocaine abusers studied varied from between 11 and 16 and the number of non–drug-dependent controls ranged from 15 to 16 across the various studies. Cocaine abusers were found to perform more poorly than controls on a number of measures across the

12 weeks. Using visual and auditory discrimination tasks similar to the Reitan-Klove Sensory Perceptual Examination, cocaine-dependent patients were found to respond more slowly than controls across all three sessions, suggesting a persistent subclinical impairment of psychomotor performance (Roberts and Bauer, 1993). Slow reaction times consistent with motor dysfunction were also found for cocaine abusers in a second experiment requiring subjects to respond to auditory tones (Bauer, 1994). In addition, evidence of a mild, stable resting hand tremor was found for the cocaine-dependent subjects that also persisted across 12 weeks of abstinence (Bauer, 1993b). Cocaine-dependent subjects, however, were similar to controls on body sway and action tremor.

An unexpected finding of the research on cognitive correlates of cocaine use is that cocaine abusers performed better than controls on isolated tests: oral fluency (O'Malley et al., 1992); the SPAN of Attention Test from the Cognitive Diagnostic Battery (Sevy et al., 1990), a maze-tracing task (Manschreck et al., 1990), the Speech Sounds Perception Test (O'Malley et al., 1989), and a measure of visual tracking accuracy (Bauer, 1993a). Although these differences may be due to chance or to premorbid characteristics of individuals who are drawn to cocaine, future studies should consider the possibility that chronic cocaine administration may result in hypersensitivity of specific neurophysiological systems.

General Observations on Investigations Attempting to Study Effects of Single-Drug Classes

With some exceptions, many of the studies reported above were carried out on multiple-drug abusers. The authors chose to focus on a drug of interest or notoriety and either ignored use of other drugs or minimized their potential contaminating effects.

A major difficulty in studying neuropsychological consequences among polydrug abusers is the inability to assign any observed consequences to any particular drug or combination of drugs. For example, Bruhn and Maage (1975) studied four groups of Danish prisoners who varied in drug use from none to heavy use of several substances. They formed the groups based on interviews that explored the varieties of substances abused and the intensity of use. Based on a statistical analysis of WAIS and the Halstead-Reitan Test Battery, they found no differences among the four groups. The groups were formed based on frequency of use prior to incarceration; but in a correlated fashion, those who used drugs more frequently used a greater variety as well. As a result, the groups varied simultaneously in both frequency and extent of use.

Another methodological difficulty has to do with selection of relevant controls. Are conclusions best drawn from comparing the performance of drug abusers to a normal nonpatient, non–drug-using group? No doubt many drug abusers are suffering from serious psychopathology as well as the consequences of drug use and, therefore, it is not clear whether observed differences should be ascribed to psychopathology (e.g., mood disorder, thought disorder) or drug use. Depending on the characteristics of the drug-abusing sample, a comparison group of psychiatric patients might well be included in neuropsychological studies of drug abusers.

Although composition of the drug-abuse group itself seems straightforward, questions can be raised about the definitions of abuse and whether or not the groups studied are in fact sufficiently homogeneous. For example, Acord (1972), and Acord and Barker (1973) defined a group of psychedelic abusers as persons who used the substance under consideration one or more times, a strategy that allows a larger study group, but one of doubtful validity. Even if history of use and measures of chronicity and frequency are taken into account, it is difficult to determine appropriate cutoff points to define group membership. Is an experimental user one who used a substance one, five, or ten times? Experimental, moderate, and heavy use are arbitrary distinctions, and one investigator's moderate user may be another's heavy user.

Because studies of the consequences of

drug abuse examine subjects after they have already been exposed to drugs, it is difficult to ascribe differences to the drugs consumed and not to preexisting factors that might have produced impairment or increased vulnerability to drug effects. Examples of potential confounds include history of childhood illness, learning disabilities, brain trauma, or other neurological illness. To some extent one can account for these potentially contaminating events by excluding subjects who have such histories. Beyond the inherent limitations of historical data, excluding such subjects can influence the sampling procedures in an unknown fashion and lessen the validity and generalizability of the findings.

The difficulties faced by Rounsaville et al. (1981, 1982) in concluding whether or not their heroin addicts were neuropsychologically impaired were not only a function of what constitute appropriate comparison groups, but also problems in defining what is impairment. Reitan and Davison (1974) have described the four methods of inference required to assess neuropsychological functioning and have cautioned that studies that rely only on analysis of central tendency are likely to overlook impairment by averaging away differences among subjects who might have very different patterns of disability. Relying on the addition of a clinical rating of impairment can obviate this problem and allow for a more powerful analysis. Using all available methods of inference, each protocol is judged by a clinician as to whether or not it represents impaired functioning, the nature of the impairment, and its severity. Heaton et al. (1981) showed that two suitably trained clinicians could achieve high reliability in clinical ratings of Halstead-Reitan Battery results; furthermore, the clinicians were more accurate in identifying impairment than existing actuarial methods.

The Collaborative Neuropsychological Study of Polydrug Users (CNSP) attempted to address many of the problems described above. The results of the CNSP have been described in detail in a number of publications (Grant et al., 1977; Carlin et al., 1978; Grant et al., 1978a,b,c; Carlin et al., 1980). The CNSP compared the Halstead-Reitan

performance of polydrug abusers with that of groups of psychiatric patients and nonpatient non–drug-users. Utilizing a 2×3 design in which group membership and neuropsychological status served as independent variables, drug use, which was determined by querying 10-year history of frequency of use for seven categories of drugs (alcohol, marijuana, sedatives, stimulants, hallucinogens, opiates, and antipsychotics) served as the dependent variables in a multivariate analysis of variance (MANOVA). Drug use was found to be associated with impairment.

Associated significant univariate effects were found for two substances: opiates and sedatives. Follow-up evaluations carried out 3 months later found substantially similar results with only mild improvement in the polydrug sample. It was found that polydrug abusers reported more illness events than did psychiatric patients, who in turn reported more events than did nonpatients. A medical history questionnaire score accounted for 20% of the variance in the Halstead Impairment Index. When the six medical history items that might possibly predict neuropsychological impairment and predated drug use were examined, it was found that only one (learning disability) was associated with sedative and opiate use; a history of learning disability showed a weak inverse relationship with amount of sedative use. It appeared that health events occurring prior to or independent of drug use could be associated with impairment, independent of or in interaction with drug abuse.

The hypothesis that premorbid status and other factors interact to affect the relationship between drug use and impairment was examined via further analysis of the data provided by the CNSP. Carlin et al. (1978) found that measures of drug use motivation and life style predicted impairment better than did drug use history alone. "Straight," self-medicating drug abusers were far more likely to be impaired than streetwise, social recreational users. Further analysis of these data revealed a complex relationship between drug use, "streetwise" status, and neuropsychological impairment (Carlin et al., 1980). Their findings suggest that there is group of polydrug abusers whose health history contributes to their neuropsychological impairment either independently of drug use or through increasing their vulnerability to neurotoxic effects of drugs at lower levels of exposure.

What can be concluded from the CNSP findings? The foremost finding is that the relationship between consumption of psychoactive drugs of abuse and neuropsychological impairment is complex and precludes a simple answer to whether drug abuse is related to brain damage. It would appear that the answer must state that some impaired polydrug abusers have "done themselves in" through extensive use of opiates, alcohol, and perhaps sedative-hypnotics. Another group either were impaired prior to drug use or were more vulnerable to the neurotoxic effects of drug abuse as the result of health events preceding or independent of drug use.

Summary

Many of the studies in the literature date from the 1970s, when concern about drug abuse became more prominent. Except for a number of studies that reflect current concern about cocaine and a spate of clinical reports and studies of the effects of accidental exposure to solvents, the relatively straightforward paradigm of determining if drug abuse causes brain damage is not being actively pursued. This probably is a reflection of a growing awareness of the complexity of the issue. Even for as notorious a neurotoxin as alcohol, it has been difficult to establish anything resembling a dose-response relationship between consumption and deficit. Binge use versus chronic maintenance, premorbid vulnerability, preexisting socioeducational differences can exacerbate deficit or even protect the subject from deficit (Grant, 1987; Reed and Grant, 1990). For drugs other than alcohol the complexities grow. Dose becomes less definable; purity, adulterants, route of administration all further compound the problem.

With few exceptions, the majority of studies have been hampered by small sample sizes. Small to moderate sample sizes and small to moderate effect sizes can be expected to increase the rate of nonreplication. Large samples and efforts to create more homogeneous subgroups of subject types will be required to clarify neuropsychological consequences of drugs of abuse and increase the meaningfulness of answers.

Meta-analysis may also have some value for summarizing the data from extant studies. This methodology attempts to estimate effect size in order to cumulate research findings across studies (Hunter et al., 1982). Superior to "vote counting" in which studies supporting or failing to support a relationship are tallied, this method might allow a reconciliation of the studies implicating or failing to implicate psychoactive substances in neuropsychological impairment. Adequacy of control groups, entry criteria, health factors and other possible contaminating variables, extensiveness and intensity of drug use, and other relevant variables can be coded and entered into the analysis. Appropriate computations could determine effect size. That is, an overall determination can be made of the extent of the relationship between consumption of a substance and measures of impairment that is relatively independent of traditional statistical significance. This determination is of particular importance if the impact of the drug on neuropsychological integrity is modest, as is likely for most substances. A modest or even small effect size does not suggest that the health implications are trivial. The example of cigarette smoking demonstrates that a modest effect size can translate into a major public health problem.

In the face of methodological difficulties facing research on the neuropsychological consequences of drug abuse, it is not surprising that definitive statements that are empirically supported are difficult to come by. Most of the studies have been cross-sectional in nature. An alternative strategy is to study the neuropsychological functioning across time for substance abusers who achieve abstinence in order to better understand the time course of observed difficulties. Another approach, but one unlikely to be carried out due to the relatively high cost, is a longitudinal study in which several cohorts at risk for drug misuse are followed over time.

Future research based on specific hypotheses about the nature or location of deficit would bring fresh interest to the area. For example, theoretical speculation that the consequences of cocaine use grow from depletion of dopamine in specific sites should result in specific studies of the consequences of chronic cocaine administration in man and animals. Krystal et al. (1992) attempted this approach in their investigation of MDMA. The results of initial studies examining a range of ability areas can be used to develop studies focused on specific abilities that appear to be affected by a drug. In the case of cocaine abuse, for example, further inquiry into the nature and time course of memory, cognitive-motor, and motor skills seems warranted.

Whether or not the research literature currently provides definitive answers about the impact of drug abuse on cognitive functioning, information about any significant drug abuse history and pattern must be seen as vital in neuropsychiatric settings. The knowledge that a particular patient has a history of multiple substance abuse would potentially figure prominently in the construction of any model of behavioral deficit. In closing, we might offer that research on the neuropsychological effects of drug abuse may well advance into relevant health domains where other sources of impairment (e.g., cerebrovascular disease) may coexist with the likelihood of drug-modulated cerebral deficit.

References

Acord, L. D. (1972). Hallucinogenic drugs and brain damage. *Military Medicine, 137,* 18–19.

Acord, L. D., and Barker, D. D. (1973). Hallucinogenic drugs and cerebral deficit. *Journal of Nervous and Mental Disease, 156,* 281–283.

Adams, K. M., Rennick, P., Schooff, K., and Keegan, J. (1975). Neuropsychological measurement of drug effects: Polydrug research. *Journal of Psychedelic Drugs, 7,* 151–160.

Bauer, L. O. (1993a). Eye movements in recovering substance abusers: A prospective study. *Addictive Behaviors, 18,* 465–472.

Bauer, L. O. (1993b). Motoric signs of CNS dysfunction associated with alcohol and cocaine withdrawal. *Psychiatry Research, 47,* 69–77.

Bauer, L. O. (1994). Vigilance in recovering cocaine dependent and alcohol dependent patients: A prospective study. *Addictive Behaviors, 19,* 599–607.

Bergman, H., Borg, S., and Holm, L. (1980). Neuropsychological impairment and exclusive abuse of sedatives or hypnotics. *American Journal of Psychiatry, 137,* 215–217.

Berry, G. J., Heaton, R. K., and Kirby, M. W. (1977). Neuropsychological deficits of chronic inhalant abusers. In B. Rumac and A. Temple, eds., *Management of the Poisoned Patient.* Princeton: Science Press, pp. 9–31.

Bostwick, D. G. (1981). Amphetamine induced cerebral vasculitis. *Human Pathology, 12,* 1031–1033.

Brown, R. R., and Partington, J. E. (1942). A psychometric comparison of narcotic addicts with hospital attendants. *Journal of General Psychology, 27,* 71–79.

Bruhn, P., and Maage, N. (1975). Intellectual and neuropsychological functions in young men with heavy and long-term patterns of drug abuse. *American Journal of Psychiatry, 132,* 397–401.

Cahill, D. W., Knipp, H., and Mosser, J. (1981). Intracranial hemorrhage with amphetamine abuser (letter). *Neurology, 31,* 1058–1059.

Carlin, A. S., Grant, I., Adams, K. M., and Reed, R. (1979). Is phencyclidine (PCP) abuse associated with organic brain impairment? *American Journal of Drug and Alcohol Abuse, 6,* 273–281.

Carlin, A. S., Stauss, F. F., Adams, K. M., and Grant, I. (1978). The prediction of neuropsychological impairment in polydrug abusers. *Addictive Behaviors, 3,* 5–12.

Carlin, A. S., Stauss, F. F., Grant, I., and Adams, K. M. (1980). Drug abuse style, drug use type, and neuropsychological deficit in polydrug users. *Addictive Behaviors, 5,* 229–234.

Carlin, A. S., and Trupin, E. (1977). The effects of long-term chronic cannabis use on neuropsychological functioning. *International Journal of the Addictions, 12,* 617–624.

Citron, B. P., Halpern, M., McCarron, M., Lundberg, G. D., McCormick, R., Pincus, I. J., Tatter, D., and Haverback, B. J. (1962). Necrotizing angitis associated with drug abuse. *Journal of Nervous and Mental Disease, 134,* 162–168.

Cohen, S., and Edwards, A. E. (1969). LSD and organic brain impairment. *Drug Dependence, 2,* 1–4.

Cosgrove, J., and Newell, T. G. (1991). Recovery of neuropsychological functions during reduction in use of phencyclidine. *Journal of Clinical Psychology, 47,* 159–169.

Culver, C. M., and King, F. W. (1974). Neuropsychological assessment of undergraduate marihuana and LSD users. *Archives of General Psychiatry, 31,* 707–711.

Dodds, J., and Santostefano, S. (1964). A comparison of the cognitive functioning of glue-sniffers and nonsniffers. *Journal of Pediatrics, 64,* 565–570.

Ellinwood, E. H., and Cohen, S. (1971). Amphetamine abuse. *Science, 171,* 420–421.

Fields, F.R.J., and Fullerton, J. R. (1974). The influence of heroin addiction on neuropsychological functioning. *Veterans Administration Newsletter for Research in Mental Health and Behavioral Sciences, 16,* 20–25. Washington, D.C., Department of Medicine and Surgery, Veterans Administration.

Golombok, S., Moodley, P., and Lader, M. (1988). Cognitive impairment in long-term benzodiazepine users. *Psychological Medicine, 18,* 365–374.

Grabski, D. A. (1961). Toluene sniffing producing cerebellar degeneration. *American Journal of Psychiatry, 118,* 461–462.

Grant, I. (1987). Alcohol and the brain: Neuropsychological correlates. *Journal of Consulting and Clinical Psychology, 55,* 310–324.

Grant, I., Rochford, J., Fleming, T., and Stunkard, A. J. (1973). A neuropsychological assessment of the effects of moderate marihuana use. *Journal of Nervous and Mental Disease, 156,* 278–280.

Grant, I., Adams, K. M., Carlin, A. S., and Rennick, P. M. (1977). Neuropsychological deficit in polydrug users. A preliminary report of the findings of the collaborative neuropsychological study of polydrug users. *Drug and Alcohol Dependence, 2,* 91–108.

Grant, I., Adams, K. M., Carlin, A. S., Rennick, P. M., Judd, L. L., Schooff, K., and Reed, R. (1978a). Organic impairment in polydrug abusers: Risk factors. *American Journal of Psychiatry, 135,* 178–184.

Grant, I., Adams, K. M., Carlin, A. S, Rennick, P. M., Judd, L. L., and Schooff, K. (1978b). The collaborative neuropsychological study of polydrug abusers. *Archives of General Psychiatry, 35,* 1063–1073.

Grant, I., Adams, K. M., Carlin, A. S, Rennick, P. M., Judd, L. L., Schooff, K., and Reed, R. (1978c). The neuropsychological effects of polydrug abuse. In D. R. Wesson, A. S. Carlin, K. M. Adams, G. Beschner, eds., *Polydrug Abuse: The Results of a National Collaborative Study.* San Francisco: Academic Press, pp. 223–261.

Grove, W. M., and Andreasen, N. C. (1982). Simultaneous tests of many hypotheses in exploratory research. *Journal of Nervous and Mental Disease, 170,* 3–8.

Halstead, W. C. (1947). *Brain and Intelligence.* Chicago: University of Chicago Press.

Heaton, R. K., Grant, I., Anthony, W. Z., and Lehman, R. A. (1981). A comparison of clinical and automated interpretation of the Halstead-Reitan Battery. *Journal of Clinical Neuropsychology, 3,* 121–141.

Hendler, N., Cimini, C., Ma, T., and Long, D. (1980). A comparison of cognitive impairment due to benzodiazepines and to narcotics. *American Journal of Psychiatry, 137,* 828–830.

Hill, H. E., and Belleville, R. E. (1953). Effects of chronic barbiturate intoxication on motivation and muscular coordination. *Archives of Neurology and Psychiatry, 70,* 180–188.

Hill, S. Y., Reyes, R. B., Mikhael, M., and Ayre, F. (1979). A comparison of alcoholics and heroin abusers: Computerized transaxial tomography and neuropsychological functioning. *Currents in Alcoholism, 5,* 187–205.

Holman, B. L., Carvalho, P. A., Mendelson, J., Teoh, S. K., Nardin, R., Hallgring, E., Hebben, N., and Johnson, K. A. (1991). Brain perfusion is abnormal in cocaine-dependent polydrug users: A study using technetium-99m-HMPAO and SPECT. *The Journal of Nuclear Medicine, 32,* 1206–1210.

Hunter, J. E., Schmidt, F. L., and Jackson, G. B. (1982). *Meta-analysis: Cumulating Research Findings Across Studies.* Beverly Hills: Sage Publications.

Isbell, H., Altschul, S., Kornetsky, C. H., Elseman, A. J., Flanery, H. G., and Fraser, H. F. (1950). Chronic barbiturate intoxication: An experimental study. *Archives of Neurology and Psychiatry, 68,* 1–28.

Juntunen, J., Matikainen, E., Antti-Poika, M., Suoranta, H., and Valle, M. (1985). Nervous system effects of long-term occupational exposure to toluene. *Acta Neurologica Scandinavica, 72,* 512–517.

Kelly, T. (1975). Prolonged cerebellar dysfunction associated with paint sniffing. *Pediatrics, 56,* 605–606.

Knox, J., and Nelson, J. (1966). Permanent encephalopathy from toluene inhalation. *New England Journal of Medicine, 275,* 1494–1496.

Kolansky, H., and Moore, W. T. (1971). Effects of marihuana on adolescents and young adults. *Journal of the American Medical Association, 216,* 486–492.

Kolansky, H., and Moore, W. T. (1972). Toxic effects of chronic marihuana use. *Journal of the American Medical Association, 222,* 35–41.

Korin, H. (1974). Comparison of psychometric measures in psychiatric patients using heroin and other drugs. *Journal of Abnormal Psychology, 83,* 208–212.

Kornetsky, C. H. (1951). Psychological effects of chronic barbiturate intoxication. *Archives of Neurology and Psychiatry, 65,* 557–567.

Kraut, A., Lilis, R., Marcus, M., Valciukas, J. A., Wolff, M. S., and Landrigan, P. J. (1988). Neurotoxic effects of solvent exposure on sewage treatment workers. *Archives of Environmental Health, 43,* 263–268.

Krystal, J. H., Price, L. H., Opsahl, C., Ricaurte, G. A., and Heninger, G. R. (1992). Chronic 3,4-methylenedioxymethamphetamine (MDMA) use: Effects on mood and neuropsychological function. *American Journal of Drug and Alcohol Abuse, 18,* 331–341.

Lewis, J. D., Moritz, D., and Mellis, L. (1981). Long-term toluene abuse. *American Journal of Psychiatry, 138,* 368–370.

Malm, G., and Lying-Tunell, U. (1980). Cerebellar dysfunction related to toluene sniffing. *Acta Neurologica Scandinavica, 62,* 188–190.

Manschreck, T. C., Schneyer, M. L., Weisstein, C. C., Laughery, J., Rosenthal, J., Celada, T., and Berner, J. (1990). Free base cocaine and memory. *Comprehensive Psychiatry, 31,* 369–375.

McGlothlin, W. H., Arnold, D. O., and Freedman, D. X. (1969). Organicity measures following repeated LSD ingestion. *Archives of General Psychiatry, 21,* 704–709.

O'Malley, S., Adamse, M., Heaton, R. K., and Gawin, F. H. (1992). Neuropsychological impairment in chronic cocaine abusers. *American Journal of Drug and Alcohol Abuse, 18,* 131–144.

O'Malley, S. S., and Gawin, F. H. (1990). Abstinence symptomology and neuropsychological impairment in chronic cocaine abusers. *National Institute on Drug Abuse Research Monograph, 101,* 179–190.

O'Malley, S. S., Gawin, F. H., Heaton, R. K., and Kleber, H. D. (1989). Cognitive deficits associated with cocaine abuse. Paper presented at the Annual Meeting of the American Psychiatric Association, San Francisco, CA, May, 1989.

Page, J. B., Fletcher, J. M., and True, W. R. (1988). Psychosociocultural perspectives on chronic cannabis use: The Costa Rican follow-up. *Journal of Psychoactive Drugs, 20,* 57–65.

Pfeffer, A. Z., and Ruble, D. C. (1946). Chronic psychosis and addiction to morphine. *Archives of Neurology and Psychiatry, 56,* 665–672.

Reitan, R. M. (1955). Investigation of the validity of Halstead's measure of biological intelligence. *Archives of Neurology and Psychiatry, 73,* 28–35.

Reitan, R. M., and Davison, L. A. (1974). *Clinical Neuropsychology: Current Status and Applications.* Washington, D.C.: V. H. Winston and Sons.

Reed, R. J., and Grant, I. (1990). The long-term neurobehavioral consequences of substance abuse: Conceptual and methodological challenges for future research. *National Institute on Drug Abuse Research Monograph, 101,* 10–56.

Roberts, L. A., and Bauer, L. O. (1993). Reaction time during cocaine versus alcohol withdrawal: Longitudinal measures of visual and auditory suppression. *Psychiatry Research, 46,* 229–237.

Rochford, J., Grant, I., and LaVigne, G. (1977). Medical students and drugs. Further neuropsychological and use pattern considerations. *International Journal of the Addictions, 12,* 1057–1065.

Ron, M. A. (1983). The alcoholic brain: CT scan and psychological findings. *Psychological Medicine (Monograph Suppl.), 3,* 1–33.

Rounsaville, B. J., Jones, C., Novelly, R. A., and Kleber, H. D. (1982). Neuropsychological functioning in opiate addicts. *Journal of Nervous and Mental Disease, 170,* 209–216.

Rounsaville, B. J., Novelly, R. A., Kleber, H. D., and Jones, C. (1981). Neuropsychological impairment in opiate addicts: Risk factors. *Annals of the New York Academy of Science, 362,* 79–80.

Rubin, J., and Comitas, L. (1975). *Ganja in Jamaica: A Medical and Anthropological Study of Chronic Marihuana Use.* The Hague: Mouton.

Rumbaugh, C. L., and Fang, H.C.H. (1980). The effects of drug abuse on the brain. *Medical Times, 108,* 37s–52s.

Rylander, G. (1969). Clinical and medico-criminological aspects of addiction to central stimulating drugs. In F. Sjoqvist and M. Tottie, eds., *Abuse of Central Stimulants.* Stockholm: Almqvist and Wiksell, pp. 251–274.

Satz, P., Fletcher, J. M., and Sutker, L. S. (1976). Neuropsychologic, intellectual and personality correlates of chronic marijuana use in native Costa Ricans. *Annals of the New York Academy of Science, 282,* 266–306.

Schwartz, R. H. (1991). Heavy marijuana use and recent memory impairment. *Psychiatric Annals, 21,* 80–82.

Sevy, S., Kay, S. R., Opler, L. A., and van Praag, H. M. (1990). Significance of cocaine history in schizophrenia. *The Journal of Nervous and Mental Disease, 178,* 642–648.

Singer, R., and Scott, N. E. (1987). Progression of neuropsychological deficits following toluene diisocyanate exposure. *Archives of Clinical Neuropsychology, 2,* 135–144.

Souief, M. I. (1975). Chronic cannabis users: Further analysis of objective test results. *Bulletin on Narcotics, 4,* 1–26.

Strang, J., and Gurling, H. (1989). Computerized tomography and neuropsychological assessment in long-term high-dose heroin addicts. *British Journal of Addiction, 84,* 1011–1019.

Trites, R. L., Suh, M., Offord, D., Nieman, G., and Preston, D. (1974). Neuropsychologic and psychosocial antecedents and chronic effects of prolonged use of solvents and methamphet-amines. Paper presented at the meeting of the International Psychiatric Research Society, Ottawa, Canada.

Tsushima, W. T., and Towne, W. S. (1977). Effects of paint sniffing on neuropsychological test performance. *Journal of Abnormal Psychology, 86,* 402–407.

Volkow, N. D., Fowler, J. S., Wolf, A. P., Hitzemann, R., Dewey, S., Bendriem, B., Alpert, R., and Hoff, A. (1991). Changes in brain glucose metabolism in cocaine dependence and withdrawal. *American Journal of Psychiatry, 148,* 621–626.

Volkow, N. D., Mullani, N., Gould, K. L., Adler, S., and Krajewski, K. (1988). Cerebral blood flow in chronic cocaine users: A study with positron emission tomography. *British Journal of Psychiatry, 152,* 641–648.

Wikler, A., Fraser, H. F., Isbell, H., and Pescor, F. T. (1955). Electroencephalograms during cycles of addiction to barbiturates in man. *Electroencephalography and Clinical Neurophysiology, 7,* 1–13.

Wright, M., and Hogan, T. P. (1972). Repeated LSD ingestion and performance on neuropsychological tests. *Journal of Nervous and Mental Disease, 154,* 432–438.

20 Neuropsychological Aspects of Schizophrenia

ROBERT S. GOLDMAN, BRADLEY N. AXELROD,
and STEPHEN F. TAYLOR

Schizophrenia is a chronic psychiatric disorder characterized by disruption in affective, cognitive, and social domains that results in generally poor ability to maintain adaptive functioning in the community. This disorder usually manifests itself between the ages of 18 and 25. It has a lifetime prevalence ranging from 0.5% to 1.0% of the population (American Psychiatric Association, 1994), with no apparent gender discrepancy. The current diagnostic formulation of schizophrenia emphasizes a core set of symptoms. Individuals with schizophrenia have abnormalities in perception, usually in the form of auditory hallucinations. Delusional ideation often characterizes the disturbed thought content in these individuals, while abnormalities in form of thought are seen in such symptoms as loosening of associations, tangential speech, thought blocking, and neologistic speech. Additional characteristics can include flattened or inappropriate affect, lack of motivation, poor social interaction, as well as idiosyncratic mannerisms and behaviors.

The fact that the symptoms described above are not present in all schizophrenic patients is one sense in which schizophrenia is a heterogeneous disorder. To better characterize the most commonly observed clusters of symptoms, nosological efforts have sought to group patients into subtypes. Such distinctions as paranoid-nonparanoid and process-reactive have attempted to differentiate the disorder in terms of illness course,

treatment effectiveness, longer-term outcome and neuropsychological status (Nicholson and Neufeld, 1993). More recently, the distinction between "positive" symptoms (e.g., delusions, hallucinations, loosening of associations) and "negative" symptoms (e.g., poor motivation, asociality, affective blunting, thought blocking, diminished speech content) has received increased attention. While positive symptoms improve with neuroleptic treatment, negative symptoms are less responsive to traditional pharmacotherapy and have been associated with structural anatomic changes, poor outcome, and the presence of persistent neuropsychological deficits (Addington et al., 1991; Breier et al., 1991; Williamson et al., 1991; Goldman et al., 1993). Formal diagnostic criteria for schizophrenia have traditionally emphasized positive symptoms, as seen in the *Diagnostic and Statistical Manual* of the American Psychiatric Association (American Psychiatric Association, 1987). The recent revision of this manual (DSM-IV, American Psychiatric Association, 1994) more fully incorporates the presence of negative symptoms into the diagnostic criteria for schizophrenia.

The etiology of schizophrenia remains unclear. Various causes have been proposed, including immunologic/viral factors (Kirch, 1993) and embryogenetic disruption in neuroanatomical development (Breslin and Weinberger, 1990). Some support for genetic factors in schizophrenia has come from concordance rates approaching 50% for monozygotic twins in European and American studies (Onstad et al., 1991; Kendler and Diehl, 1993). The less than perfect concordance suggests the influence of additional nongenetic factors in the etiology of schizophrenia. With respect to treatment, neuroleptic medication has been somewhat successful in ameliorating many of the psychotic symptoms commonly observed (Kane and Marder, 1993), but deficiencies in long-term social and vocational outcome persist despite symptom reduction (Jaeger and Douglas, 1992). Because antipsychotic medications appear to act by blocking dopaminergic receptor activity, neurobiological research has focused on disruptions in the dopaminergic system as a possible etiologic component of schizophrenia (Crow, 1980).

Regarding the neuropsychology of schizophrenia, the notion of deterioration in cognitive and behavioral functions was implicit in the initial conceptualization of the disorder. Kraepelin (1919) labeled this disorder "dementia praecox" defining it as an irreversible, deteriorative condition. With respect to the term, "dementia," modern clinical neuropsychology is concerned with describing and understanding the nature of the neurobehavioral dysfunction in schizophrenia. The direct examination of neuropsychological functions in schizophrenia follows from several continuing lines of research. The role of disrupted attention began with systematic, experimental investigations of reaction time parameters in differentiating schizophrenics from nonpsychiatric individuals (Shakow, 1963). Simultaneously, clinicians were also aware that schizophrenic patients performed abnormally on measures of general intellectual functioning (Heaton and Crowley, 1981). In fact, performance on most measures of neuropsychological functioning showed schizophrenics to perform at a level similar to patients with known neurological damage. The repeated finding of abnormal mentation in schizophrenia led Heaton (1980) to conclude that schizophrenics perform in this manner because they are indeed "brain-damaged." Until the present time, neuropsychologists were frequently requested to dichotomize schizophrenia as having either a "functional" or "organic" etiology. Considering schizophrenia as a psychiatric disorder with neuropsychological correlates more accurately characterizes the illness and transcends the outmoded functional/organic dichotomy. Current approaches to studying brain-behavior relationships in schizophrenia seek to better understand the various neurobehavioral systems that may be affected by this disorder.

In this chapter we present the neuropsychological aspects of schizophrenia, focusing on attention, executive function, and memory. We will also consider the relationship of medications and clinical symptoms to neuropsychological functions in schizophrenia. We begin with a consideration of methodological factors as they apply to clinical neuropsychological investigations of schizophrenia.

Methodological Considerations

Diagnostic Heterogeneity

The heterogeneous clinical appearance of schizophenia may reflect that it is an inherently heterogeneous disorder, with varied causes and/or pathophysiological mechanisms (Heinrichs, 1993). Many diagnoses in medicine have some physiologic marker that establishes the presence of pathology and reflects the mechanism of the illness. Typically, one or more diagnostic markers, including symptom presentation, clinical course, and laboratory tests, will establish a diagnosis. In contrast, psychiatric diagnoses rest solely on a set of behavioral symptoms derived from self-report and clinical observation. Difficulties with self-report are particularly problematic in schizophrenia, where psychosis hinders the ability of patients to describe their symptoms. Since we have only an inadequate understanding of the mechanisms of psychiatric illness at present, diagnostic nosologies for psychiatric disorders are often based on evolving, consensual agreement. Systematic clinical ratings such as the Structured Clinical Interview for DSM-III-R (SCID; American Psychiatric Association, 1990) and the Schedule for the Assessment of Schizophrenia and Depression (SADS; Spitzer and Endicott, 1973) have been developed to better standardize the diagnosis of schizophrenia. Because studies of the neuropsychological aspects of any disorder depend on the accuracy of the diagnosis, the use of standard diagnostic criteria in the past 20 years has improved the opportunities for meaningful findings in schizophrenia.

Nonetheless, when samples of schizophrenic patients are well characterized with respect to diagnosis, and matched on standard demographic factors (age, level of education, sex, socioeconomic status), the degree of neuropsychological impairment still remains variable among these otherwise homogeneous patients (Shallice et al., 1991). Subject characteristics specific to schizophrenia may contribute to the heterogeneous neuropsychological picture. These potentially confounding factors include age of onset, length and number of hospitalizations, and medication status, which may not be equivalent among individuals.

Two ways of resolving the heterogeneity of the illness have been used in neuropsychological studies of schizophrenia. The first method attempts to explain the nature of heterogeneity in schizophrenia by prospectively examining the relationship of subject characteristics to cognitive performance. For example, Crawford and colleagues (1992) compared intellectual test performance among groups of community-dwelling and long-term hospitalized schizophrenic patients to determine the effects of chronicity of the illness on intellectual functioning. They found that patients with longer-term hospitalization performed significantly worse than community-dwelling patients. A more common methodological solution is to consider illness-specific factors as "confounds." As with all experimental confounds the goal is to control for these factors by matching subject groups on these variables. If schizophrenia is an inherently heterogeneous disorder, however, then matching to increase homogeneity may artificially remove information

about the range of neuropsychological dysfunction.

Estimating Premorbid Functioning

In order to consider pathological changes in mentation, it is vital to have an accurate premorbid referent of intellectual status. School records provide a cognitive picture of the individual prior to the onset of illness. However, these data may be confounded by subtle developmental abnormalities (Erlenmeyer-Kimling et al., 1993) that could yield suboptimal academic performance. Another method for establishing premorbid intellectual functioning is to use the intellectual status of the patient's family (Saykin et al., 1991). This approach offers the advantage of measuring intellectual potential independent of the deleterious consequences of the schizophrenic disorder. However, this method may overestimate actual premorbid cognitive status, because the schizophrenic individual may not have obtained the potential suggested by the familial intellectual climate.

The most commonly used psychometric methods of estimating premorbid function include regression based algorithms employing demographic information (Wilson et al., 1978; Barona et al., 1984) and cognitive measures that estimate premorbid intellectual functioning (e.g., Vocabulary from the WAIS-R; National Adult Reading Test [NART; Nelson and Willison, 1991; Crawford et al., 1992; O'Carroll et al., 1992]; Wide Range Achievement Test-Revised Reading [WRAT-R; Jastak and Jastak, 1984]). The regression-based estimation formulas, which rely on education and current occupation, may underestimate intellectual functioning because individuals with schizophrenia usually do not achieve optimal educational and occupational status, as the result of illness onset in late adolescence. The use of a vocabulary measure may be confounded by illness acuity and the presence of severe thought disorder in some patients, at the time of assessment. Among the test-based premorbid indices, reading fluency measures

(NART, WRAT-R) may offer a more accurate prediction because these measures are less sensitive to thought disorder, illness severity, and occupational attainment.

Relevant Comparison Groups

Schizophrenics are deficient relative to normal controls on most measures of cognition in almost every study attempting this comparison (e.g., Braff et al., 1991). Before considering deficits in a variety of functional domains as specific concomitants of schizophrenia, comparisons with other psychiatric disorders are necessary (Goldsamt et al., 1993). For example, memory impairment, attentional abnormalities, and executive dysfunction have also been observed in mood disorders (Harvey et al., 1986; Sackeim and Steif, 1988; Sackeim et al., 1992). The cognitive deficits observed in other psychiatric disorders serve to illustrate that neuropsychological impairment is not the exclusive domain of schizophrenia. Therefore, inclusion of psychiatric patient groups is necessary to differentiate the secondary effects of hospitalization, level of psychopathology, and medication from the primary effects of schizophrenia on mentation.

Matched Tasks

Measuring test performance of individuals with schizophrenics has given rise to an enduring controversy over whether specific or generalized deficits account for the abnormal performance. Investigators often ask questions of the form: "Is ability X (e.g., recall of word lists) *differentially* impaired in comparison to ability Y (e.g., language comprehension)?" A finding of greater impairment in an ability such as word recall, when one can demonstrate relatively less impaired language comprehension, would be taken as implicating word recall processes in the pathophysiology of the illness. Chapman and Chapman (1973, 1989) argue from a psychometric point of view that one must first match the discriminative power of this task with the task from which one is claiming to differenti-

ate it before a differential deficit is demonstrated. If these tests are not first matched with respect to variance and reliability, then no discrimination can be made across the cognitive domains which the tasks are purported to measure. In other words, if the variances of the above two tasks are heterogeneous, such that word recall has a normal distribution while the language comprehension task is positively skewed (low ceiling), then attempting to make comparisons across these tasks may lead to the erroneous conclusion that a differential deficit exists in word recall. This conclusion would be an artifact of the different psychometric properties of these tasks. To match tests on discriminative power, one needs to test normal subjects of a wide range of abilities and use test items that yield the same error rate for the less accurate subjects on both tests. Recently, Braff and colleagues (1991) addressed the comparability of task performance by using normative data as the benchmark by which to compare their patient sample. This method effectively matched task variances relative to the normal population, one of the psychometric properties discussed by Chapman and Chapman (1973).

Neuropsychological Findings

While it is accepted that general neuropsychological impairment is associated with schizophrenia, studies have examined the integrity of specific neuropsychological functions in the disorder. Using this approach, a number of functional domains have been implicated as centrally relevant to the neuropsychology of schizophrenia. Specifically, attention, executive function, and memory have received the greatest consideration. The following sections will discuss the major findings in each of these neuropsychological domains.

Attention

Since the initial descriptions of schizophrenia by Kraepelin (1919) and Bleuler (1911/1950), deficits in attention, what William James called "a taking possession by the mind" (James, 1890) have figured prominently in the disorder. The concept of attention is familiar enough and schizophrenic patients are disturbed enough in mental faculties, that impaired attention in schizophrenia bears a strong face validity. A large literature on the topic of attention in experimental psychology, as well as in neuropsychology, attests to the popularity of this concept in schizophrenia research. However, the prevalence of the term has engendered a wide variety of uses, many quite imprecise and variable, even in experimental settings. Furthermore, even with the most restrictive and well-defined usage, the process of attention requires highly integrated, widely distributed central nervous system (CNS) functioning and is thus susceptible to a multitude of local and generalized impairments of the CNS.

THE CONCEPT OF ATTENTION. The development of cognitive psychology and information processing approaches has led to considerable refinement and component dissection of the process of attention, potentially offering researchers the ability to identify specific processing deficits in schizophrenia. At a general level, attention involves selective processing of stimuli that occurs with a specific intensity or capacity (Kahneman, 1973; Mesulam, 1985). Using specific experimental paradigms, information processing operations have been characterized as preprocessing, sensory storage, stimulus switching, alerting/orienting, response selection, channel capacity, and vigilance (Posner and Boies, 1971; Sanders, 1980). Earlier theories of attention tended to emphasize a processing "bottleneck," or filtering based on simple physical characteristics, (e.g., location or color), which occurred in the early stages of processing (Broadbent, 1958). Subsequent theorists posited a filter occurring later in the processing flow, after stimulus characteristics (e.g., form or semantic content) had been identified (Deutsch and Deutsch, 1963; Norman, 1968). However, recent developments emphasize a limited-capacity processing pool

that is flexibly allocated at various stages of processing, with later stages requiring more resources (Kahneman, 1973). Congruent with this notion is the distinction between *automatic processes*—high capacity, fast, parallel, difficult to modify and occurring without awareness—and *controlled processes*—effortful, slow, limited capacity, serial, and subject to interference (Shiffrin and Schneider, 1977; Posner, 1978).

Investigators have specified in more precise ways what aspects of attention are dysfunctional in schizophrenia using the above theoretical constructs. We will discuss a few examples to illustrate how some paradigms examining attention can serve as potential vulnerability markers of the disorder, or begin to integrate behavior with neurophysiological investigation.

VULNERABILITY INDICATORS. Studies of attention in schizophrenia have made significant use of the notion of "vulnerability indicators" (Zubin and Spring, 1977). These indicators are abnormalities that are present in schizophrenic patients both during and between periods of acute psychosis. They are also present in the family members of schizophrenic patients, but are not present in healthy controls or nonschizophrenic psychiatric patients. Abnormal function that persists, even when the patient is not experiencing florid symptoms, is thought more likely to reflect "trait" processes. This contrasts with dysfunction caused by the disruptive "state" of active psychosis. Furthermore, the presence of a dysfunction in genetically related individuals suggests familial transmission of the trait. However, further studies (e.g., twin studies) must be performed to distinguish a common genetic inheritance from a common family environment.

The continuous performance task (CPT) has been proposed as a vulnerability indicator (Nuechterlein and Dawson, 1984). The CPT taps the process of "vigilance" or "maintenance" of attention over time. This task requires the subject to monitor a continuous presentation of "noise" stimuli for a specific target (e.g., an A followed by an X) in a string of letters presented visually or auditorily. The CPT has lent itself to the application of "signal detection" methodology, which derives from a subject's error rates (errors of commission and errors of omission), independent measures of perceptual sensitivity, and response threshold. Patients in the active phase of their illness show clear performance decrements in their ability to identify the target (Orzack and Kornetsky, 1966; Asarnow and MacCrimmon, 1978). Other investigators have found persistent deficits in patients who are symptom-free and out of a psychotic episode, suggesting that this task may tap a trait deficit in the illness (Wohlberg and Kornetsky, 1973; Asarnow and MacCrimmon, 1978; Nuechterlein, et al., 1986). Patients with schizophrenia also demonstrate less perceptual sensitivity to targets in the CPT (Cornblatt et al., 1989) relative to patients with affective disorders. Children at high risk (Nuechterlein, 1983) and family members (Wood and Cook, 1979) also demonstrate diminished perceptual sensitivity when investigators have used a sensitive, degraded-stimulus version of the task, which is designed to put a significant processing load on performance. An interesting comparison between high-risk children and children with attentional deficit disorder (ADD) revealed that the high-risk children had lowered perceptual sensitivity, whereas the children with ADD had a lowered response criterion (Nuechterlein, 1983).

Other tasks have also been proposed as sensitive indices of processing deficits in schizophrenic patients and their genetically and phenomenologically related groups. One of the most well-studied disturbances related to attention has been eye-movement abnormalities. Many schizophrenic patients and some first-degree relatives exhibit irregular visual tracking in tasks that normally engage smooth pursuit mechanisms (Holzman, 1987). The appearance of this trait in families suggests that the abnormality could serve as a phenotypic marker of genetic vulnerability (Grove et al., 1992). For an extensive discussion of the use of vulnerability indicators in the study of attention, the reader is referred

to an influential review by Nuechterlein and Dawson (1984).

REACTION TIME. Early studies of attention in schizophrenia were dominated by measurements and theories derived from reaction time paradigms. Schizophrenic patients are consistently slower than normal subjects when asked to lift their index finger in response to a signal (imperative stimulus), and they cannot utilize a preparatory signal to speed reaction time in the same way as normal subjects (Shakow, 1963). Specifically, whereas normal controls respond faster for regular preparatory intervals than for irregular intervals, up to 25 seconds in length, schizophrenic patients do not benefit from this regularity for intervals longer than 3 seconds. "Crossover" refers to the point at which the reaction time for the irregular preparatory interval is faster than the regular interval. The "crossover effect" refers to the finding that patients with schizophrenia have a significantly earlier crossover than do non-patient controls. Shakow (1963) interpreted the early crossover as a failure to "maintain segmental set" (i.e., maintain a selective focus on stimuli). In a different, but related, paradigm, schizophrenics show a differential slowing to imperative stimuli that switch modalities (Sutton and Zubin, 1965). This latter finding led Zubin (1975) to suggest that schizophrenia impairs attentional switching, not selective attention.

While these interpretations have introduced important psychological constructs to the study of psychiatric pathophysiology, no single theory has been able to account for all of the experimental findings. With current data, no definitive conclusion can be made about whether single or multiple "lesions" exist or where in the stream of information processing they might occur. In spite of the sophisticated and well-replicated work done in the area of reaction time in the 1960s and 1970s, these paradigms have been largely neglected in recent years. For an excellent overview of reaction time literature, the reader is referred to reviews by Nuechterlein (1977) and Rist and Cohen (1991).

EARLY, AUTOMATIC STIMULUS PROCESSING. Both the CPT and RT paradigms likely depend on the integrity of widely distributed CNS networks, thus making them vulnerable to many possible local and systemic disturbances. An alternative approach has been to examine processing that occurs at very early stages in the CNS, sometimes referred to as "pre-attentive" or "automatic." In backward-masking paradigms, a target stimulus (typically a letter) is presented for just enough time to enable recognition. After an interval of 20 to 500 msec, a masking stimulus is presented and the subject must report the identity of the target stimulus. With the backward-presented mask, patients with schizophrenia exhibit a greater decrement in detection accuracy than do normal subjects (Posner and Presti, 1987). Because this processing impairment occurs with depressed and bipolar patients during symptomatic episodes, Saccuzo and Braff (1981) assessed masking performance eight times over the course of hospitalization for groups of good- and poor-prognosis schizophrenics, as well as nonpsychotic psychiatric controls. They found that masking deficits nearly remitted for the good-prognosis schizophrenics and the affectively disturbed patients, but persisted for the poor-prognosis schizophrenics. Furthermore, normal individuals given methylphenidate (a dopamine agonist) exhibit this same susceptibility to the masking stimulus (Braff and Huey, 1988), suggesting the role of dopaminergic hyperactivity in this phenomenon.

One interpretation of the backward-masking findings has been that patients with schizophrenia or schizophrenia spectrum disorders have slowed processing of information in the early stages of perception (Braff and Saccuzzo, 1985). Other investigators have suggested that the abnormalities lie in visual systems. Breitmeyer (1984) interpreted visual masking effects on the basis of two classes of hypothesized visual channels. "Sustained" channels are more sensitive to stimuli with high spatial frequency and low temporal frequency, and with longer response latencies and firing duration. "Transient" channels are more sensitive to low spatial and high temporal frequency, with short response latency and firing duration. This theory suggests that hyperactive transient channel activity from the masking stimulus could interfere with the target stimulus identification (see Schuck and Lee, 1989, for a discussion). Although the physiology of this processing deficit has yet to be confirmed, this task paradigm offers a substantially refined and mechanistically testable definition of one aspect of attentional dysfunction.

The acoustic startle, or pre-pulse inhibition (PPI), paradigm uses an automatically occurring response and bolsters the theory that schizophrenic patients have a faulty filter in the early stages of stimulus processing. This is known as the "sensory gating" hypothesis (McGhie and Chapman, 1961; Venables, 1964; Braff and Geyer, 1990). In the PPI experiments, a warning tone precedes, by 0 to 2000 msec, a very loud acoustic stimulus that causes an eye blink. In normal individuals, the warning tone attenuates or inhibits the eye blink when it occurs 60 to 120 msec prior to the startle stimulus. Individuals with schizophrenia show a failure to inhibit their eye blink in comparison to normals (Braff et al., 1978). This finding is interpreted to mean that a breakdown occurs in the normal physiological processes that use the warning signal to "gate" the incoming startle-stimulus. This paradigm has found considerable utility as an animal model. An analogous paradigm in the rat suggests involvement of dopaminergic systems in this response, with attenuated PPI seen after infusion of dopamine agonists, an effect blocked by dopamine antagonists (Swerdlow et al., 1990). While correspondence between animal and human systems can never be exact, an animal model such as this enables significant manipulation of experimental variables not possible in humans and provides a means of screening for new pharmacological agents to treat schizophrenia.

Executive Function

The concept of executive functioning includes such abilities as maintenance and shifting of cognitive sets, hypothesis testing, and goal-directed problem solving. These seemingly varied abilities all involve executive control of behavior. From a neurological perspective, these functions are thought to be mediated and coordinated largely by the frontal system and its interconnections with other brain regions (Milner, 1963, 1964; Fuster, 1980). Neuropsychologists have employed a number of tasks to purportedly evaluate executive functions. These typically include measures of fluency generation (Verbal: Controlled Oral Word Association Test; Visual: Design Fluency Test), sorting (e.g., Object Sorting Test), and hypothesis testing (e.g., Halstead Category Test; Tower of Hanoi; Wisconsin Card Sorting Test) measures. Studies using patients with focal neurological impairment in the frontal lobes have found deficient performance on most of these tasks relative to normal controls (e.g., Milner, 1963, 1964).

WISCONSIN CARD SORTING TEST. The Wisconsin Card Sorting Test (WCST) has received the greatest amount of attention in the study of executive functioning in schizophrenia (Van der Does and Van den Bosch, 1992). The WCST requires the subject to sort a deck of 128 cards on the basis of the color, shape, or number of figures on each card. The only feedback provided by the examiner is whether each response is correct or incorrect. The "correct" principle changes surreptitiously during the course of the task. Commonly reported scores include categories achieved and perseveration. Perseveration on this task refers to the failure to change one's response based on the feedback from the examiner and to adhere instead to an incorrect principle (for a more thorough description of the WCST refer to Heaton and colleagues, 1993).

The first published study of patients with schizophrenia using the WCST (Fey, 1951) observed that schizophrenic patients performed significantly worse on the task than a sample of normal controls. Since the 1980s, a flurry of studies using the WCST to examine executive functioning in schizophrenia has emerged. Most studies revealed that patients with schizophrenia generate more persevera-

tion and fewer categories relative to normal controls (Robinson et al., 1980; Williamson et al., 1989; Morrison-Stewart et al., 1992). Franke and colleagues (1992) evaluated WCST performance in schizophrenic patients, healthy siblings, and samples of normal controls. They found that the healthy siblings of patients with schizophrenia generated greater perseveration than did the normal controls. In contrast, using pairs of monozygotic twins discordant for schizophrenia, Goldberg and colleagues (1990b) demonstrated affected (schizophrenic) co-twins to generate significantly fewer categories. Unaffected co-twins performed within normal limits relative to a sample of nonpsychiatric twins. This methodology offers promise in more specifically detecting the neuropsychological deficits that are part of schizophrenia against the background of premorbid and environmental factors.

NEUROIMAGING. Through the use of neuroimaging techniques such as positron-emission tomography (PET) and single photon emission computed tomography (SPECT), investigators have found reduced regional cerebral blood flow and reduced glucose metabolism in the frontal regions of schizophrenic patients (Buchsbaum et al., 1982; Wolkin et al., 1985; Volkow et al., 1986; Gur et al., 1989; Sagawa et al., 1990). To elucidate the neuroanatomical substrate of deficient WCST performance, PET activation techniques have simultaneously measured regional cerebral blood flow while patients performed the WCST. A series of pioneering activation studies conducted at the National Institute of Mental Health (NIMH) by Weinberger and colleagues found reduced blood flow in the dorsolateral prefrontal cortex of patients with schizophrenia while they performed the WCST (Berman et al., 1986; Weinberger et al., 1986, 1988; Goldberg et al., 1987). The findings were specific to the WCST and to the frontal regions. Reduced activation was not observed in any other cortical area, nor did attentional control tasks demonstrate frontal lobe involvement. Studying monozygotic twins, Berman et al. (1992) found consistent hypofrontality in the schizophrenic proband during WCST performance, whereas the unaffected co-twins did not demonstrate hypofrontality relative to normal controls.

On the basis of these activation studies it may be tempting to conclude that impaired WCST performance is specific to schizophrenia. However, findings from behavioral studies that have used the WCST demonstrate a relative lack of diagnostic specificity. Most studies that have compared nonschizophrenic psychiatric patients (e.g., mood disorder, bipolar disorder) to schizophrenics were unable to differentiate the patient groups from each other (Heinrichs, 1990; Morice, 1990; Axelrod et al., 1994). Some of our recent work contradicts these (our own) findings in that schizophrenic patients performed significantly worse on the WCST relative to mood-disordered patients (Goldman et al., 1992). The differences in these findings may reflect the heterogeneity of samples of schizophrenics in terms of neuropsychological performance (Seidman, 1990; Shallice et al., 1991). Furthermore, the poor performance of the other psychiatric patient groups may be mediated by factors other than specific deficits in the anterior portion of the brain. That other brain regions may be involved in WCST performance was exemplified by Goldberg et al. (1990a), who found that the WCST scores of patients with Huntington's disease were comparable to those of schizophrenic patients. Although the groups did not differ with regard to their performance levels, regional cerebral blood flow data of these groups revealed lowered blood flow in the frontal lobes and greater blood flow in the parietal regions for the schizophrenic patients. In contrast, the Huntington's disease patients demonstrated the opposite blood flow pattern. Because accurate WCST performance requires intact attention and working memory (Bellini et al., 1991), often deficient in patients with mood disorder (Sweet et al., 1992), disruption in these functions may also result in deficient WCST test scores. To achieve a better understanding of the extent to which the WCST represents a behavioral marker of frontal lobe function in schizophrenia, researchers will need to acquire a more complete understanding of the functional neuroanatomy of the WCST, both in normal controls and in multiple diagnostic groups.

WISCONSIN CARD SORTING TEST TRAINING STUDIES. Another methodological approach to determining the degree of impairment in frontal lobe functioning in schizophrenia stems from attempts to behaviorally improve performance on the WCST. The premise underlying this approach assumes that the density of impairment in a particular neuropsychological function can be indexed through measuring the extent of performance change following external cueing. Goldberg and colleagues (1987) at the NIMH first attempted to characterize the malleability of impaired executive functioning in chronic, nonleukotomized schizophrenics. Following standard administration of the WCST, they provided progressively more extensive cueing strategies. They found that performance improved when schizophrenics were provided with card-by-card instruction. The effect, however, was limited only to the card-by-card instruction condition; the performance of schizophrenics quickly deteriorated when cueing was discontinued. Furthermore, patient performance remained deficient following a 2-week retest interval. On the basis of these findings, Goldberg et al. (1987) concluded that schizophrenics maintain dense impairment in executive function.

Subsequent studies addressed the potential role of motivational factors in the lack of performance facilitation documented by the Goldberg et al. (1987) study. Some studies utilizing instructional cueing in the context of motivational enhancement (monetary reinforcement) found that schizophrenics improved their performance with the use of cueing strategies; monetary incentive alone was not sufficient to normalize performance (Bellack et al., 1990; Green et al., 1992). Summerfelt and colleagues (1991) also found monetary incentives to enhance WCST performance, but they did not examine the potential contribution of cueing strategies. Goldman et al. (1992) found that schizophrenics were able to benefit from minimal cueing alone provided at the outset of the task, and at three other intervals during task performance. An examination of the individual learning curves of the cohort revealed that perseveration emerged early in the task and remained relatively invariant. The findings suggested that while schizophrenics can maintain a cognitive strategy, the deficit lies in their inability to generate an appropriate cognitive set. Goldman et al. (1992) found that the optimal time for schizophrenics to incorporate a cognitive set is at the beginning of a task such as the WCST, before faulty self-generated cognitive strategies are established.

The bulk of cueing studies to date suggests there is some plasticity in executive function in schizophrenia. In terms of explanatory cognitive mechanisms, it is possible that external cueing may help to circumvent deficiencies in the self-monitoring abilities of schizophrenics. Deficiencies in self-monitoring, and in the ability of schizophrenics to profit from past regularities in behavior, are at the core of a number of theories attempting to link the psychological deficit in schizophrenia with deficiencies in the frontal lobe and its interconnections with temporolimbic functions (Stuss et al., 1983; Levin, 1984; Hemsley, 1987; Frith and Done, 1988; Gray et al., 1991; Gold et al., 1992a). In this vein, perseveration, distractibility, and difficulty formulating a cognitive set can be seen as elements of the schizophrenic's deficiencies in regulating cognition. Cueing may then serve to provide an organizational structure or schema, to replace faulty cognitive set generation. However, it is also possible that cueing may reduce task novelty, reduce difficulty level of a neuropsychological task, improve motivational aspects, and otherwise intervene to change other nonspecific dimensions of a task. Further training studies are needed to probe parametrically the extent of the density of impairment in executive function and other cognitive deficits in schizophrenia.

Memory

A number of studies have implicated impaired memory functioning in schizophrenia. The relevance of examining memory function is predicated on the often observed findings of temporal lobe abnormalities in schizophrenia that have been revealed through studies of neuropathology, structural neuroimaging, and functional neuroimaging. Postmortem studies of temporal-limbic structures in schizophrenic patients have reported reduced tissue volume in the temporal lobe region, amygdala, and hippocampal structures, relative to normal controls (Bogerts et al., 1985; Brown et al., 1986; Crow, 1990). There also appears to be greater volume loss in the left temporal lobe in comparison to the right temporal lobe in patients with schizophrenia (Crow, 1990). In vivo structural imaging (MRI) studies corroborate the structural abnormalities of reduced volume in the temporal region, including the hippocampus, amygdala, and parahippocampal gyrus (Suddath et al., 1989, 1990). Lower metabolic rates have also been revealed by PET in the left temporal lobe region in schizophrenics (Buchsbaum, 1990; Tamminga et al., 1992), again possibly suggesting lateralization of dysfunction to the left hemisphere.

The traditional neuropsychological assessment of memory function typically includes measures of immediate, recent, and delayed recall of verbal and visual-spatial material. Recognition memory for information from these domains is also usually assessed. Recall memory requires individuals to generate previously encoded information without the assistance of cueing, while recognition memory capitalizes on the comparative ease of identifying correct responses from a list that contains distracter items. The primary issues that have been investigated with respect to neuropsychological studies of memory functioning in schizophrenia include the verbal/visual dichotomy, as well as the dissociation between recall and recognition memory.

With regard to the comparison of memory of verbal versus visual material, most studies have failed to find differences between these modalities despite the suggestion of greater left hemisphere neuroanatomical abnormality in schizophrenia. Calev et al. (1987), in a well-controlled study that matched verbal and visual stimuli by difficulty level, found schizophrenic patients to be equally impaired for both types of stimuli relative to a nonschizophrenic comparison group. Saykin and colleagues (1991) used clinical measures to assess the integrity of semantic memory, verbal learning, and visual memory processes, among other cognitive functions. Specifically, they used the visual reproduction subtest from the Wechsler Memory Scale as the measure of visual memory. Their measures of verbal learning included the California Verbal Learning Test and the Paired Associate Learning Subtest from the Wechsler Memory Scale. Finally, semantic memory was assessed by use of the Logical Memory Test from the Wechsler Memory Scale. Saykin and colleagues, in a sample of inpatients with schizophrenia, found that all three of these memory domains fell close to three standard deviations below the mean relative to a nonpsychiatric population. Performance on the different types of memory tasks did not differ from each other. Similarly, Gold and colleagues (1992a) found that performance in different types of memory functions, including recall, rate of learning, and recognition, were impaired relative to normal controls. While Calev (1984a) also found recognition memory performance of schizophrenics to be impaired relative to control subjects, he reported that among schizophrenics, recognition memory was significantly superior to recall memory.

An emerging finding from recent investigations of memory functioning in schizophrenia is the notion that memory may be relatively more impaired than other neuropsychological functions. Tamlyn et al. (1992) found all aspects of memory functioning to be disproportionately impaired relative to patients' level of intelligence. Memory functioning was unrelated to motivation, attention, and chronicity of illness. Gold and colleagues (1992b) compared the performance of 45 medication-stabilized schizophrenic patients on the Wechsler Memory Scale–Revised (WMS-R; Wechsler, 1987) with general intellectual and WRAT-R reading performance. They found that indices of verbal memory, visual memory, and delayed memory all fell significantly lower than current intellectual functioning, which itself was below predicted premorbid intellectual status. Saykin et al. (1991) as well as Braff and

his colleagues (1991) found general neuropsychological dysfunction in samples of medication-free and medication-stabilized samples of schizophrenic patients. Furthermore, both studies found greater impairment in memory functions (e.g., verbal learning and memory, visual memory) relative to their generally depressed cognitive status. Interestingly, these two studies found memory functioning to be significantly more impaired than measures of executive functioning, including the WCST.

While it appears that memory function may be more selectively impaired relative to other neuropsychological functions in schizophrenia, it is important to note that memory deficits are also frequently observed in mood disorders (Frith et al., 1983; Sackeim et al., 1992). Few studies to date have explicitly contrasted memory functioning in schizophrenia relative to other psychiatric groups. A number of studies that have examined memory in both schizophrenic and mood-disordered populations found the patient groups not to differ from each other (Harvey et al., 1986; Hoff et al., 1990; Tompkins et al., 1995); a recent study, however, found schizophrenics to generally perform worse on memory tasks even when controlling for general intellectual differences (Goldberg et al., 1993a). However, detailed analyses of multiple memory functions need to be systematically conducted across these patient populations. For example, it is possible that depressed patients may demonstrate a relationship between depth of mood disorder and severity of memory function (Goldberg et al., 1993a), while the relationship of illness acuity to severity of memory impairment is unclear in schizophrenia.

Other Neuropsychological Functions

Most neuropsychological research in schizophrenia has focused on attention, executive function, and memory. We have therefore detailed the findings in these three major areas. Although research exists relating to visual-spatial processing and motor abilities, the number of studies have been limited and will not be extensively discussed.

Briefly, the findings in the area of visual-spatial problem solving have suggested lesser impairment in constructional ability against the background of generally impaired neuropsychological functions (Kolb and Whishaw, 1983; Braff et al., 1991; Saykin et al., 1991; Tompkins et al., 1995). As task complexity increases and the need for integration with other neuropsychological functions occurs, schizophrenics can be expected to demonstrate relatively greater levels of spatial impairment (Levin et al., 1989).

Similarly, motor abilities decrease as the complexity of the task increases. For example, Braff et al. (1991) found simple motor speed in a sample of patients with schizophrenia to be comparable to normal controls, whereas performance on a measure of manual dexterity and perceptual integration was significantly more impaired. Of course, the findings of all studies related to motor functioning must be viewed relative to the occurrence of medication-induced movement disorders, such as transient extrapyramidal symptoms and tardive dyskinesia (TD). In the case of TD, the association of the disorder itself with greater neuropsychological dysfunction relative to matched non-TD patients with schizophrenia has been supported in some studies (e.g., Sorokin et al., 1988; Brown et al., 1992) and refuted by others (e.g., Gold et al., 1991).

Medication and Neuropsychological Functioning

Neuroleptic medications are the primary psychopharmacological treatment of schizophrenia because they decrease the psychotic symptoms of paranoia, hallucinations, and thought disorder. Anticholinergic medications are used to treat the extrapyramidal side effects (e.g., akathisia, parkinsonian symptoms) of neuroleptics. Because neuroleptic and anticholinergic medications have potential impact on cognition, studies have specifically addressed these medication effects. However, research examining the possible influence of medications on cognitive functioning have demonstrated a number of methodological flaws, best described by

Spohn and Strauss (1989). The major limitation includes the inability of examining the direct, causal effect of medication on cognition, since cognitive performance can be confounded by general clinical change. An additional drawback is the difficulty of attributing neuropsychological change specifically to medication status in a design that compares medicated to unmedicated patients. In such studies, factors other than medication, such as illness acuity, may effect performance. Finally, the possibility of medication "carryover" in a study that evaluates patients first on and then off medication may also confound changes in neuropsychological test performance.

A number of recent review articles have synthesized the results of medication studies (Medalia et al., 1988; Spohn and Strauss, 1989; Cassens et al., 1990; King, 1990). Although many of the studies reviewed by these authors are limited by the methodological issues described above, there appears to be a convergence regarding medication effects on cognition. Neuroleptic medication is generally associated with decreased motor abilities in the acute (i.e., 1 to 3 months) phase of treatment, with minimal impact on other cognitive functions. Some measures of sustained attention have improved with acute neuroleptic treatment. Longer term neuroleptic treatment (>8 weeks) does not appear to have deleterious effects on cognitive test performance. However, the potential interaction of aging and chronic neuroleptic medication usage with cognition has yet to be evaluated.

Anticholinergic medications are also used in the treatment of schizophrenia, to control movement side effects from neuroleptic medications. Anticholinergics have been experimentally shown to disrupt memory function in normal controls (Drachman, 1977). In schizophrenics, relatively low doses of anticholinergic medications have been associated with relative deficits in free recall memory tasks, but have not been shown to be associated with recognition memory (Tune et al., 1982; Calev, 1984b; Perlick et al., 1986).

Few studies have addressed the cognitive

efficacy of a new class of antipsychotic agents known as atypical neuroleptics. Classen and Laux (1988) compared the cognitive performance of patients treated with clozapine (atypical neuroleptic, haldol or flupenthixol) over seven days. Sensorimotor functioning was unchanged, but a trend toward improved executive functioning was observed in the clozapine-treated patients. Goldberg et al. (1993b) found no positive cognitive efficacy in 13 patients over one year, despite significant symptom reduction. This study, however, was characterized by small sample size (n = 13) and marked variability in clozapine treatment regimens. Hagger et al. (1993) demonstrated significant improvement in measures of executive function and memory with clozapine monotherapy (6 weeks), which coincided with symptom improvement. Further cognitive improvement was demonstrated after 6 months of clozapine treatment.

The above studies were open trials. A double-blind study found limited beneficial cognitive effects of clozapine relative to Haldol after 10 weeks of treatment (Buchanan et al., 1994a). This improvement was seen relative to worsening of cognitive efficiency with Haldol (10 to 30 mg). Continued improvement in executive functions with clozapine treatment was seen over longer intervals (one year). Improved cognition was associated with enhanced quality of life but was orthogonal to positive and negative symptom reduction.

Symptoms and Cognition

POSITIVE AND NEGATIVE SYMPTOMS. Due to the heterogeneity of the schizophrenic syndrome, some researchers have proposed subsets of symptoms that point to subtypes of the disorder (cf. Nicholson and Neufeld, 1993). Crow (1980) proposed a distinction between type I and type II schizophrenia, with the former being largely composed of positive symptoms (Strauss et al., 1974). Positive symptoms include hallucinations, delusions, loosening of associations, and suspiciousness. Crow offered that type II schizophenia is primarily composed of negative symptoms

(Strauss et al., 1974), which include anergia, avolition, apathy, and asociality. Type I schizophrenia was thought to be mediated by hyperactivity in the dopaminergic system, whereas type II schizophrenia was considered to be associated with underlying structural impairment.

The distinction between positive and negative symptoms has served as a useful dichotomy for studying behavioral and pathophysiological aspects of schizophrenia. As stated earlier, negative symptoms are associated with poor medication response, and long-term treatment outcome (Breier et al., 1991; Goldman et al., 1993). Negative symptoms have also been shown to be related to enlarged ventricles by some researchers (Andreasen et al., 1982), yet contradictory findings have been reported (Keilp et al, 1988; Andreasen et al., 1990). Associations between negative symptom severity and aspects of neuropsychological functioning have found negative symptoms to be more associated with hypofrontality on cognitive and neuroradiological measures (Liddle, 1987; Liddle and Morris, 1991; Wolkin et al., 1992). Other studies have reported an association between negative symptom severity and decreased performance on tasks of visual-motor, visual-spatial, and attentional skills (Green and Walker, 1985, 1986; Nuechterlein et al., 1986; Walker and Lewine, 1988). While there is hope that the presence of negative symptoms connotate specific neuropsychological abnormalities, the majority of research in this area suggests that negative symptoms are related to generalized neuropsychological dysfunction (Andreasen et al., 1990; Addington et al., 1991). One problem with this area of research may stem from conceptualizing negative symptoms on a continuum, present to varying degrees in different patients. Carpenter et al. (1988) have suggested a categorical approach that distinguishes between potentially transient negative symptoms and a more enduring negative symptom subtype, termed the "deficit syndrome." Deficit syndrome patients have been shown to demonstrate greater neurological soft signs and more severe neuropsychological impairment relative to patients with less enduring negative symptoms (Wagman et al., 1987; Buchanan et al., 1990, 1994b).

In contrast to negative symptoms, positive symptoms are typically not associated with global cognitive dysfunction (Addington et al., 1991; Perlick et al., 1992; Goldman et al., 1993). Positive symptoms have been further subdivided into two distinct clusters: delusions/hallucinations and thought disorder (Bilder et al., 1985; Liddle and Morris, 1991). The presence of delusions and hallucinations are not significantly related to cognitive performance (e.g., Bilder et al., 1985; Liddle and Morris, 1991). On the other hand, thought disorder impacts on the aspects of neuropsychological functioning most associated with disrupted attention (Walker and Harvey, 1986; Harvey and Pedley, 1989).

LANGUAGE DYSFUNCTION. There is an extensive corpus of research that explicitly examines the relationship between thought disorder and language dysfunction, since disrupted thought process is often revealed in the speech of schizophrenic patients. From a psycholinguistic perspective, schizophrenics do not manifest a stable deficit in linguistic "competence," which is defined as the knowledge of syntactic and semantic rules. Rather, schizophrenics demonstrate impaired language "performance" (Schwartz, 1982), manifested in dysfunctional pragmatic aspects of speech. That is, schizophrenic speech can be marked by the failure to take into account the listener's point of reference (Cohen, 1976; Frith and Allen, 1988) as well as the tendency of schizophrenic patients to demonstrate inappropriate pausing and gesturing during expressive speech. On a theoretical level, the deficits in thought process and language in schizophrenia may be the result of a more general impairment in information processing. To this effect, it has been suggested that the expressive speech abnormalities of schizophrenics may reflect deficits in the filtering aspects of attentional processing (Schwartz, 1982). Alternatively, Frith (1992) has suggested that linguistic deficits, specifically the failure to incorporate

the framework of the listener, reflect impairment in self-monitoring and metarepresentation, which he attributes to an underlying frontotemporal dysfunction.

COGNITION AND ILLNESS ONSET. Recently, a number of investigations have attempted to delineate the relationship between neuropsychological parameters and the course of clinical symptoms. The major question in this area of research is whether first-episode schizophrenics demonstrate deficient cognition with the onset of clinical symptoms. Comparisons between chronic schizophrenic patients and patients with their first episode of schizophrenic symptoms yields information about the relationship between symptom onset and cognition. Hoff and colleagues (1992) found comparable neuropsychological deficiencies in first-episode patients relative to patients with chronic schizophrenia. Specifically, they reported deficits in attention, memory, executive functioning, and intellect occurring with the onset of psychotic symptoms. The implication of this study is that neuropsychological impairment may be present relatively early in the schizophrenic disorder, a finding supported by others (Bilder et al., 1992). In fact, high risk methodologies have demonstrated subtle cognitive abnormalities in individuals even before the onset of clinical symptoms (Erlenmeyer-Kimling et al., 1993). Studies that have examined the effect of duration of illness have suggested that the neuropsychological impairment in this disorder remains static rather than progressive (Heaton and Drexler, 1987; Goldberg et al., 1993c; Heaton et al., 1994).

Summary

It is clear from the present discussion that a number of widespread deficits in higher cortical function are associated with schizophrenia. Neuropsychological deficits appear to be primary consequences of the neurobiological aspects associated with schizophrenia. They are unlikely to represent epiphenomena of medication usage, because deficits are present at the time of the first psychotic break, if not before. Impairments have ranged from relatively elemental processes, such as reaction time, to more complex cognitive phenomena, as in the area of executive function. If the goal of neuropsychological approaches is to localize a unitary "lesion" through examination of brain-behavior relationships, then schizophrenia has proved to be a disappointment from this perspective. The accumulating findings suggest that schizophrenia is a disorder marked by disruption in the complex interrelationship between neuropsychological domains. There appears to be an emerging consensus that suggests that deficits in focal systems may give rise to multiple impairment in interrelated neural systems (Hemsley, 1987; Frith and Done, 1988; Levin et al., 1989; Gray et al., 1991). Specifically, the consistency and severity of deficits in memory, attentional processing, and executive function have argued for the primacy of frontotemporal dysfunction in contributing to the cognitive and clinical features of schizophrenia.

This notion will likely be further bolstered with research in the realm of cognitive neuroscience, such as the notion of "working memory" (cf. Baddeley, 1986). Working memory represents an elaboration of the notion of "short-term" memory (Tamlyn et al., 1992) and refers to the active maintenance and processing of information in the context of performing goal-oriented cognitive operations. It is thought to be a process that bridges executive functions with memory. As such, working memory has been neuroanatomically linked to the integrity of frontal-temporal connections and will likely provide insight into the disruption of integrated cognitive systems in schizophrenia (cf. Goldman-Rakic, 1991; Fleming et al., 1994). Further support for a neuroanatomic basis in more anterior brain regions has come from the functional neuroimaging work that has attempted to integrate neuroanatomy with cognition. Technologies that enable good regional identification of functional neuroanatomy, such as positron-emission tomography and functional magnetic resonance imaging, will no doubt play an increasingly important role (e.g., Buchsbaum et al., 1982; see review by Cleghorn et al., 1991) in the search for an underlying neuroanatomic basis of this disease.

References

Addington, J., Addington, D., and Maticka-Tyndale, E. (1991). Cognitive functioning and positive and negative symptoms in schizophrenia. *Schizophrenia Research*, 5, 123–134.

American Psychiatric Association. (1987). *Diagnostic and Statistical Manual of Mental Disorders* (3rd ed., rev.). Washington, D.C.: American Psychiatric Association.

American Psychiatric Association. (1990). *Structured Clinical Interview for DSM-III-R*. Washington, D.C.: American Psychiatric Association.

American Psychiatric Association. (1994). *Diagnostic and Statistical Manual of Mental Disorders* (4th ed.). Washington, D.C.: American Psychiatric Association.

Andreasen, N. C., Olsen, S. A., Dennert, J. W., and Smith, M. R. (1982). Ventricular enlargement in schizophrenia: Relationship to positive and negative symptoms. *American Journal of Psychiatry, 139,* 297–302.

Andreasen, N. C., Flaum, M., Swayze, V. W., II, Tyrrell, G., and Arndt, S. (1990). Positive and negative symptoms in schizophrenia: A critical reappraisal. *Archives of General Psychiatry, 47,* 615–621.

Asarnow, R. F., and MacCrimmon, D. J. (1978). Residual performance deficit in clinically remitted schizophrenics: a marker of schizophrenia? *Journal of Abnormal Psychology, 87,* 597–608.

Axelrod, B. N., Goldman, R. S., Tompkins, L. M., and Jiron, C. C. (1994). Differential patterns of performance on the Wisconsin Card Sorting Test in schizophrenia, mood disorder, and traumatic brain injury. *Neuropsychiatry, Neuropsychology, and Behavioral Neurology, 7,* 20–24.

Baddeley, A. (1986). *Working Memory*. New York: Oxford University Press.

Barona, A., Reynolds, C. R., and Chastain, R. (1984). A demographically based index of premorbid intelligence for the WAIS-R. *Journal of Consulting and Clinical Psychology, 52,* 885–887.

Bellack, A. S., Mueser, K. T., Morrison, R. L., Tierney, A., and Podell, K. (1990). Remediation of cognitive deficits in schizophrenia. *American Journal of Psychiatry, 147,* 1650–1655.

Bellini, L., Abbruzzese, M., Gambini, O., Rossi, A., Stratta, P., and Scarone, S. (1991). Frontal and callosal neuropsychological performances in schizophrenia. Further evidence of possible attention and mnesic dysfunctions. *Schizophrenia Research, 5,* 115–121.

Berman, K. F., Torrey, E. F., Daniel, D. G., and Weinberger, D. R. (1992). Regional cerebral blood flow in monozygotic twins discordant and concordant for schizophrenia. *Archives of General Psychiatry, 49,* 927–934.

Berman, K. F., Zec, R. F., and Weinberger, D. R. (1986). Physiologic dysfunction of dorsolateral prefrontal cortex in schizophrenia. II. Role of neuroleptic treatment, attention, and mental effort. *Archives of General Psychiatry, 43,* 126–135.

Bilder, R. M., Lipschutz-Broch, L., Reiter, G., Geisler, S. H., Mayerhoff, D. I., and Lieberman, J. A. (1992). Intellectual deficits in first-episode schizophrenia: Evidence for progressive deterioration. *Schizophrenia Bulletin, 18,* 437–448.

Bilder, R. M., Mukherjee, S., Rieder, R. O., and Pandurangi, A. K. (1985). Symptomatic and neuropsychological components of defect states. *Schizophrenia Bulletin, 11,* 409–419.

Bleuler, E. (1911/1950). *Dementia Praecox or the Group of Schizophrenias* (translated by J. Zinkin). New York: International Universities Press.

Bogerts, B., Meertz, E., and Schonfeldt-Bausch, R. (1985). Basal ganglia and limbic system pathology in schizophrenia: A morphometric study of brain volume and shrinkage. *Archives of General Psychiatry, 42,* 784–791.

Braff, D. L., and Geyer, M. A. (1990). Sensorimotor gating and schizophrenia. Human and animal model studies. *Archives of General Psychiatry, 47,* 181–188.

Braff, D., Heaton, R. K., Kuck, J., Cullum, M., Moranville, J., Grant, I., and Zisook, S. (1991). The generalized pattern of neuropsychological deficits in outpatients with chronic schizophrenia with heterogeneous Wisconsin Card Sorting Test results. *Archives of General Psychiatry, 48,* 891–898.

Braff, D. L., and Huey, L. (1988). Methylphenidate-induced information processing dysfunction in nonschizophrenic patients. *Archives of General Psychiatry, 45,* 827–832.

Braff, D. L., and Saccuzzo, D. P. (1985). The time course of information-processing deficits in schizophrenia. *American Journal of Psychiatry, 142,* 170–174.

Braff, D., Stone, C., Callaway, E., Geyer, M., Glick, I., and Bali, L. (1978). Prestimulus effects on human startle reflex in normals and schizophrenics. *Psychophysiology, 15,* 339–343.

Breier, A., Schreiber, J. L., Dyer, J., and Pickar, D. (1991). National Institute of Mental Health longitudinal study of chronic schizophrenia. Prognosis and predictors of outcome. *Archives of General Psychiatry, 48,* 239–246. [Published erratum appears in *Archives of General Psychiatry, 48,* 642.]

Breitmeyer, B. (1984). *Visual Masking: An Integrative Approach.* New York: Oxford University Press.

Breslin, N. A., and Weinberger, D. R. (1990). Schizophrenia and the normal functional development of the prefrontal cortex. *Development and Psychopathology, 2,* 409–424.

Broadbent, D. E. (1958). *Perception and Communication.* London: Pergamon Press, Ltd.

Brown, K. W., White, T., and Palmer, D. (1992). Movement disorders and psychological tests of frontal lobe function in schizophrenic patients. *Psychological Medicine, 22,* 69–77.

Brown, R., Colter, N., Corsellis, J. A., Crow, T. J., Frith, C. D., Jagoe, R., Johnstone, E. C., and Marsh, L. (1986). Postmortem evidence of structural brain changes in schizophrenia. Differences in brain weight, temporal horn area, and parahippocampal gyrus compared with affective disorder. *Archives of General Psychiatry, 43,* 36–42.

Buchanan, R. W., Holstein, C., and Breier, A. (1994a). The comparative efficacy and long-term effect of clozapine treatment on neuropsychological test performance. *Biological Psychiatry, 36,* 717–725.

Buchanan, R. W., Kirkpatrick, B., Heinrichs, D. W., and Carpenter, W. T., Jr. (1990). Clinical correlates of the deficit syndrome of schizophrenia. *American Journal of Psychiatry, 147,* 290–294.

Buchanan, R. W., Strauss, M. E., Kirkpatrick, B., Holstein, C., Breier, A., and Carpenter, W. T. (1994b). Neuropsychological impairments in deficit versus nondeficit forms of schizophrenia. *Archives of General Psychiatry, 51,* 804–811.

Buchsbaum, M. S. (1990). The frontal lobes, basal ganglia, and temporal lobes as sites for schizophrenia. *Schizophrenia Bulletin, 16,* 379–389.

Buchsbaum, M. S., Haier, R. J., Potkin, S. G., Nuechterlein, K., Bracha, H. S., Katz, M., Lohr, J., Wu, J., Lottenberg, S., Jerabek, P. A., Trenary, M., Tafalla, R., Reynolds, C., and Bunney, W. E. (1992). Frontostriatal disorder of cerebral metabolism in never-medicated schizophrenics. *Archives of General Psychiatry, 49,* 935–942.

Buchsbaum, M. S., Ingvar, D. H., Kessler, T., Water, R. N., Cappelletti, J., van Kammen, D. P., King, A. C., Johnson, J. L., Manning, R. G., Flynn, R. W., Mann, L. S., Bunney, W. E., and Sokoloff, L. (1982). Cerebral glucography with positron tomography: Use in normal subjects and in patients with schizophrenia. *Archives of General Psychiatry, 39,* 251–259.

Calev, A. (1984a). Recall and recognition in chronic nondemented schizophrenics: Use of matched tasks. *Journal of Abnormal Psychology, 93,* 172–177.

Calev, A. (1984b). Recall and recognition in mildly disturbed schizophrenics: The use of matched tasks. *Psychological Medicine, 14,* 425–429.

Calev, A., Korin, Y, Kugelmass, S, and Lerer, B. (1987). Performance of chronic schizophrenics on matched word and design recall tasks. *Biological Psychiatry, 22,* 699–709.

Carpenter, W. T., Jr., Heinrichs, D. W., and Wagman, A.M.I. (1988). Deficit and nondeficit forms of schizophrenia: The concept. *American Journal of Psychiatry, 145,* 578–583.

Cassens, G., Inglis, A. K., Appelbaum, P. S., and Gutheil, T. G. (1990). Neuroleptics: Effects on neuropsychological function in chronic schizophrenic patients. *Schizophrenia Bulletin, 16,* 477–499.

Chapman, L. J., and Chapman, J. P. (1973). *Disordered Thought in Schizophrenia.* New York: Appleton-Century-Crofts.

Chapman, L. J., and Chapman, J. P. (1989). Strategies for resolving the heterogeneity of schizophrenics and their relatives using cognitive measures. *Journal of Abnormal Psychology, 98,* 357–366.

Classen, W., and Laux, G. (1988). Sensorimotor and cognitive performance of schizophrenic inpatients treated with haloperidol, flupenthixol, or clozapine. *Pharmacopsychiatry, 21,* 295–297.

Cleghorn, J. M., Zipursky, R. B., and List, S. J. (1991). Structural and functional brain imaging in schizophrenia. *Journal of Psychiatry and Neuroscience, 16,* 53–74.

Cohen B. D. (1976). Referent communication in schizophrenia: The perseverative-chaining model. *Annals of the New York Academy of Sciences, 270,* 124–140.

Cornblatt, B. A., Lenzenweger, M. F., and Erlenmeyer-Kimling, L. (1989). The continuous performance test, identical pairs version: II. Contrasting attentional profiles in schizophrenic and depressed patients. *Psychiatry Research, 29,* 65–85.

Crawford, J. R., Besson, J.A.O., Bremner, M.,

Ebmeier, K. P., Cochrane, R.H.B., and Kirkwood, K. (1992). Estimation of premorbid intelligence in schizophrenia. *British Journal of Psychiatry, 161,* 69–74.

Crow, T. J. (1980). Molecular pathology of schizophrenia: More than one disease process? *British Medical Journal, 280,* 66–68.

Crow, T. J. (1990). Temporal lobe asymmetries as the key to the etiology of schizophrenia. *Schizophrenia Bulletin, 16,* 433–443.

Deutsch, J. A., and Deutsch, D. (1963). Attention: Some theoretical considerations. *Psychology Review, 70,* 80–90.

Drachman, D. A. (1977). Memory and cognitive function in man: Does the cholinergic system have specific role? *Neurology, 27,* 783–790.

Erlenmeyer-Kimling, L., Cornblatt, B. A., Rock, D., Roberts, S., Bell, M., and West, A. (1993). The New York High-Risk Project: Anhedonia, attentional deviance, and psychopathology. *Schizophrenia Bulletin, 19,* 141–153.

Fey, E. (1951). The performance of young schizophrenics and young normals on the Wisconsin Card Sorting Test. *Journal of Consulting Psychology, 15,* 311–319.

Fleming, K., Goldberg, T. E., and Gold, J. M. (1994). Applying working memory constructs to schizophrenic cognitive impairment. In A. S. David and J. C. Cutting, eds., *The Neuropsychology of Schizophrenia. Brain Damage, Behaviour and Cognition Series.* Hove, England: Lawrence Erlbaum Associates, pp. 197–213.

Franke, P., Maier, W., Hain, C., and Klingler, T. (1992). Wisconsin Card Sorting Test: An indicator of vulnerability to schizophrenia? *Schizophrenia Research, 6,* 243–249.

Frith, C. D. (1992). *The Cognitive Neuropsychology of Schizophrenia.* Hove, England: Lawrence Erlbaum Associates.

Frith, C. D., and Allen, H. A. (1988). Language disorders in schizophrenia and their implications for neuropsychology. In P. Bebbington and P. McGuffin, eds., *Schizophrenia: The Major Issues.* Oxford: Heinemann Professional Publishers, pp. 172–186.

Frith, C. D., and Done, D. J. (1988). Towards a neuropsychology of schizophrenia. *British Journal of Psychiatry, 153,* 437–443.

Frith, C. D., Stevens, M., Johnstone, E. C., Deakin, J. F., Lawler, P., and Crow, T. J. (1983). Effects of ECT and depression on various aspects of memory. *British Journal of Psychiatry, 142,* 610–617.

Fuster, J. M. (1980). *The Prefrontal Cortex.* New York: Raven Press.

Gold, J. M., Egan, M. F., Kirch, D. G., Goldberg, T. E., Daniel, D. G., Bigelow, L. B., and Wyatt, R. J. (1991). Tardive dyskinesia: Neuropsychological, computerized tomographic, and psychiatric symptom findings. *Biological Psychiatry, 30,* 587–599.

Gold, J. M., Randolph, C., Carpenter, C. J., Goldberg, T. E., and Weinberger, D. R. (1992a). Forms of memory failure in schizophrenia. *Journal of Abnormal Psychology, 101,* 487–494.

Gold, J. M., Randolph, C., Carpenter, C. J., Goldberg, T. E., and Weinberger, D. R. (1992b). The performance of patients with schizophrenia on the Wechsler Memory Scale-Revised. *The Clinical Neuropsychologist, 6,* 367–373.

Goldberg, T. E., Berman, K. F., Mohr, E., and Weinberger, D. R. (1990a). Regional cerebral blood flow and cognitive function in Huntington's disease and schizophrenia. A comparison of patients matched for performance on a prefrontal type task. *Archives of Neurology, 47,* 418–422.

Goldberg, T. E., Gold, J. M., Greenberg, R., Griffin, S., Schulz, S. C., Pickar, D., Kleinman, J. F., and Weinberger, D. R. (1993a). Contrasts between patients with affective disorders and patients with schizophrenia. *Americal Journal of Psychiatry, 150,* 1355–1362.

Goldberg, T. E., Greenberg, R. D., Griffin, S. J., Gold, J. M., Kleinman, J. E., Pickar, D., Schulz, S. C., and Weinberger, D. R. (1993b). The effect of clozapine on cognition and psychiatric symptoms in patients with schizophrenia. *British Journal of Psychiatry, 162,* 43–48.

Goldberg, T. E., Hyde, T. M., Kleinman, J. E., and Weinberger, D. R. (1993c). Course of schizophrenia: Neuropsychological evidence for a static encephalopathy. *Schizophrenia Bulletin, 19,* 797–804.

Goldberg, T. E., Ragland, J. D., Torrey, E. F., Gold, J. M., Bigelow, L. B., and Weinberger, D. R. (1990b). Neuropsychological assessment of monozygotic twins discordant for schizophrenia. *Archives of General Psychiatry, 47,* 1066–1072.

Goldberg, T. E., Weinberger, D. R., Berman, K. F., Pliskin, N. H., and Podd, M. H. (1987). Further evidence for dementia of the prefrontal type in schizophrenia? A controlled study of teaching the Wisconsin Card Sorting Test. *Archives of General Psychiatry, 44,* 1008–1014.

Goldman, R. S., Axelrod, B. N., Tandon, R., Ribeiro, S.C.M., Craig, K., and Berent, S. (1993). Neuropsychological prediction of treatment efficacy and one-year outcome in schizophrenia. *Psychopathology, 26,* 122–126.

Goldman, R. S., Axelrod, B. N., and Tompkins, L. M. (1992). Effect of instructional cues on schizophrenic patients' performance on the Wisconsin Card Sorting Test. *American Journal of Psychiatry, 149,* 1718–1722.

Goldman-Rakic, P. S. (1991). Prefrontal cortical dysfunction in schizophrenia: The relevance of working memory. In B. Carroll, ed., *Psychopathology and the Brain.* New York: Raven Press, pp. 1–23.

Goldsamt, L. A., Barros, J., Schwartz, B. J., Weinstein, C., and Iqbal, N. (1993). Neuropsychological correlates of schizophrenia. *Psychiatric Annals, 23,* 151–157.

Gray, J. A., Feldon, J., Rawlins, J.N.P., Hemsley, D. R., and Smith, A. D. (1991). The neuropsychology of schizophrenia. *Behavioral and Brain Sciences, 14,* 1–84.

Green, M. F., Satz, P., Ganzell, S., and Vaclav, J. F. (1992). Wisconsin Card Sorting Test performance in schizophrenia: Remediation of a stubborn deficit. *American Journal of Psychiatry, 149,* 62–67.

Green, M., and Walker, E. (1985). Neuropsychological performance and positive and negative symptoms in schizophrenia. *Journal of Abnormal Psychology, 94,* 460–469.

Green, M., and Walker, E. (1986). Symptom correlates of vulnerability to backward masking in schizophrenia. *American Journal of Psychiatry, 143,* 181–186.

Grove, W. M., Clementz, B. A., Iacono, W. G., and Katsanis, J. (1992). Smooth pursuit ocular motor dysfunction in schizophrenia: Evidence for a major gene. *American Journal of Psychiatry, 149,* 1362–1368.

Gur, R. E., Resnick, S. M., and Gur, R. C. (1989). Laterality and frontality of cerebral blood flow and metabolism in schizophrenia: Relationship to symptom specificity. *Psychiatry Research, 27,* 325–334.

Hagger C., Buckley, P., Kenny J. T., Friedman, L., Ubogy, D., and Meltzer, H. Y. (1993). Improvement in cognitive functions and psychiatric symptoms in treatment-refractory schizophrenic patients receiving clozapine. *Biological Psychiatry, 34,* 702–712.

Harvey, P. D., Earle-Boyer, E. A., Wielgus, M. S., and Levinson, J. C. (1986). Encoding, memory, and thought disorder in schizophrenia and mania. *Schizophrenia Bulletin, 12,* 252–261.

Harvey, P. D., and Pedley, M. (1989). Auditory and visual distractibility in schizophrenia: Clinical and medication status correlations. *Schizophrenia Research, 2,* 295–300.

Heaton R. K. (1980). *The Wisconsin Card Sorting Test Manual.* Odessa, FL: Psychological Assessment Resources, Inc.

Heaton, R. K., Chelune, G. J., Talley, J. L., Kay, G. G., and Curtiss, G. (1993). *The Wisconsin Card Sorting Test Manual-Revised and Expanded.* Odessa, FL: Psychological Assessment Resources, Inc.

Heaton, R. K., and Crowley, T. J. (1981). Effects of psychiatric disorders and somatic treatments on neuropsychological test results. In S. B. Filskov and T. J. Boll, eds., *Handbook of Clinical Neuropsychology.* New York: John Wiley, pp. 481–525.

Heaton, R. K., and Drexler, M. (1987). Clinical neuropsychological findings in schizophrenia and aging. In N. E. Miller and G. D. Cohen, eds., *Schizophrenia and Aging.* New York: Guilford Press, pp. 145–161.

Heaton R. K., Paulsen J. S., McAdams, L. A., Kuck, J., Zisook, S., Braff, D., Harris, J., and Jeste, D. (1994). Neuropsychological deficits in schizophrenics: Relationship to age, chronicity, and dementia. *Archives of General Psychiatry, 51,* 469–476.

Heinrichs, R. W. (1990). Variables associated with Wisconsin Card Sorting Test performance in neuropsychiatric patients referred for assessment. *Neuropsychiatry, Neuropsychology, and Behavioral Neurology, 3,* 107–112.

Heinrichs, R. W. (1993). Schizophrenia and the brain: Conditions for a neuropsychology of madness. *American Psychologist, 48,* 221–223.

Hemsley, D. R. (1987). An experimental psychological model for schizophrenia. In H. Hafner, W. F. Gattaz, and W. Janzavik, eds., *Search for the Causes of Schizophrenia.* Berlin/Heidelberg: Springer Verlag, pp. 179–188.

Hoff, A. L., Riordan, H., O'Donnell, D. W., Morris, L., and DeLisi, L. E. (1992). Neuropsychological functioning of first-episode schizophreniform patients. *American Journal of Psychiatry, 149,* 898–903.

Hoff, A. L., Shukla, S., Aronson, T., Cook, B., Ollo, C., Baruch, S., Jandorf, L., and Schwartz, J. (1990). Failure to differentiate bipolar disorder from schizophrenia on measures of neuropsychological function. *Schizophrenia Research 3,* 253–260.

Holzman, P. S. (1987). Recent studies in the psychophysiology of schizophrenia. *Schizophrenia Bulletin, 13,* 49–75.

Jaeger, J., and Douglas, E. (1992). Neuropsychiatric rehabilitation for persistent mental illness. *Psychiatric Quarterly, 63,* 71–94.

James, W. (1890). *The Principles of Psychology.* New York: Henry Holt.

Jastak, J. F., and Jastak, S. (1984). *The Wide Range Achievement Test-Revised.* Wilmington, DE: Jastak Associates, Inc.

Kahneman, D. (1973). *Attention and Effort.* Englewood Cliffs, NJ: Prentice-Hall, Inc.

Kane, J. M., and Marder, S. R. (1993). Psychopharmacologic treatment of schizophrenia. *Schizophrenia Bulletin, 19,* 287–302.

Keilp, J. G., Sweeny, J. A., Jacobsen, P., Solomon, C., St. Louis, L., Deck, M., Frances, A., and Mann, J. J. (1988). Cognitive impairment in schizophrenia: Specific relations to ventricular size and negative symptomatology. *Biological Psychiatry, 24,* 47–55.

Kendler, K. S., and Diehl, S. R. (1993). The genetics of schizophrenia: A current, genetic-epidemiologic perspective. *Schizophrenia Bulletin, 19,* 261–285.

King, D. J. (1990). The effect of neuroleptics on cognitive and psychomotor function. *British Journal of Psychiatry, 157,* 799–811.

Kirch, D. G. (1993). Infection and autoimmunity as etiologic factors in schizophrenia: A review and reappraisal. *Schizophrenia Bulletin, 19,* 355–370.

Kolb, B., and Whishaw, I. Q. (1983). Performance of schizophrenic patients on tests sensitive to left or right frontal, temporal or parietal function in neurological patients. *Journal of Nervous and Mental Disease, 171,* 435–443.

Kraepelin, E. (1919/1971). *Dementia Praecox and Paraphrenia* (translated by R. M. Barclay) (G. M. Robertson, ed.). Huntington, NY: R. E. Krieger Publishing Company, Inc., pp. 282–329.

Levin, S. (1984). Frontal lobe dysfunctions in schizophrenia. II. Impairments of psychological and brain functions. *Journal of Psychiatric Research, 18,* 57–72.

Levin, S., Yurgelun-Todd, D., and Craft, S. (1989). Contributions of clinical neuropsychology to the study of schizophrenia. *Journal of Abnormal Psychology, 98,* 341–356.

Liddle, P. F. (1987). Schizophrenic syndromes, cognitive performance and neurological dysfunction. *Psychological Medicine, 17,* 49–57.

Liddle, P. F., and Morris, D. L. (1991). Schizophrenic syndromes and frontal lobe performance. *British Journal of Psychiatry, 158,* 340–345.

McGhie, A., and Chapman, J. (1961). Disorders

of attention and perception in early schizophrenia. *British Journal of Medical Psychology, 34*, 103–116.

Medalia, A., Gold, J., and Merriam, A. (1988). The effects of neuroleptics on neuropsychological test results of schizophrenics. *Archives of Clinical Neuropsychology, 3*, 249–271.

Mesulam, M. M. (1985). Attention, confusional states and neglect. In M. M. Mesulam, ed., *Principles of Behavioral Neurology*. Philadelphia: F. A. Davis, pp. 125–168.

Milner, B. (1963). Effects of different brain lesions on card sorting. *Archives of Neurology, 9*, 90–100.

Milner, B. (1964). Some effects of frontal lobectomy in man. In J. M. Warren and K. Akert, eds., *The Frontal Granular Cortex and Behavior*. New York: McGraw Hill, pp. 313–334.

Morice, R. (1990). Cognitive inflexibility and prefrontal dysfunction in schizophrenia and mania. *British Journal of Psychiatry, 157*, 50–54.

Morrison-Stewart, S. L., Williamson, P. C., Corning, W. C., Kutcher, S. P., Snow, W. G., and Merskey, H. (1992). Frontal and non-frontal lobe neuropsychological test performance and clinical symptomatology in schizophrenia. *Psychological Medicine, 22*, 353–359.

Nelson, H. E., and Willison, J. R. (1991). The revised National Adult Reading Test–test manual. Windsor: NFER-Nelson.

Nicholson, I. R., and Neufeld, R.W.J. (1993). Classification of the schizophrenias according to symptomatology: A two-factor model. *Journal of Abnormal Psychology, 102*, 259–270.

Norman, D. A. (1968). Toward a theory of memory and attention. *Psychology Review, 75*, 522–536.

Nuechterlein, K. H. (1977). Reaction time and attention in schizophrenia: A critical evaluation of the data and theories. *Schizophrenia Bulletin, 3*, 373–428.

Nuechterlein, K. H. (1983). Signal detection in vigilance tasks and behavioral attributes among offspring of schizophrenic mothers and among hyperactive children. *Journal of Abnormal Psychology, 92*, 4–28.

Nuechterlein, K. H., and Dawson, M. E. (1984). Information processing and attentional functioning in the developmental course of schizophrenic disorders. *Schizophrenia Bulletin, 10*, 160–203.

Nuechterlein, K. H., Edell, W. S., Norris, M., and Dawson, M. E. (1986). Attentional vulnerability indicators, thought disorder, and negative symptoms. *Schizophrenia Bulletin, 12*, 408–426.

O'Carroll, R., Walker, M., Dunan, J., Murray, C., Blackwood, D., Ebmeier, K. P., and Goodwin, G. M. (1992). Selecting controls for schizophrenia research studies: The use of the National Adult Reading Test (NART) is a measure of premorbid ability. *Schizophrenia Research, 8*, 137–141.

Onstad, S, Skre, I., Torgersen, S., and Kringlen, E. (1991). Twin concordance for DSM-III-R schizophrenia. *Acta Psychiatrica Scandinavica, 83*, 395–401.

Orzack, M. H., and Kornetsky, C. (1966). Attention dysfunction in chronic schizophrenia. *Archives of General Psychiatry, 14*, 323–326.

Perlick, D., Mattis, S., Stastny, P., and Silverstein, B. (1992). Negative symptoms are related to both frontal and nonfrontal neuropsychological measures in chronic schizophrenia. *Archives of General Psychiatry, 49*, 245–246.

Perlick, D., Stastny, P., Katz, I., Mayer, M., and Mattis, S. (1986). Memory deficits and anticholinergic levels in chronic schizophrenia. *American Journal of Psychiatry, 143*, 230–232.

Posner, M. I. (1978). *Chronometric Explorations of Mind*. Hillsdale, NJ: Lawrence Erlbaum Associates.

Posner, M. I., and Boies, S. J. (1971). Components of attention. *Psychology Review, 78*, 391–408.

Posner, M. I., and Presti, D. (1987). Selective attention and cognitive control. *Trends in Neurosciences, 10*, 12–17.

Rist, F., and Cohen, R. (1991). Sequential effects in the reaction times of schizophrenics: Crossover and modality shift effects. In S. R. Steinhauer, J. H. Gruzelier, and J. Zubin, eds., *Handbook of Schizophrenia: Neuropsychology, Psychophysiology and Information Processing* (vol. 5). Amsterdam: Elsevier Science Publishers, pp. 241–271.

Robinson, A. L., Heaton, R. K., Lehman, R.A.W, and Stilson, D. W. (1980). The utility of the Wisconsin Card Sorting Test in detecting and localizing frontal lobe lesions. *Journal of Consulting and Clinical Psychology, 48*, 605–614.

Saccuzzo, D. P., and Braff, D. L. (1981). Early information processing deficit in schizophrenia. New findings using schizophrenic subgroups and manic control subjects. *Archives of General Psychiatry, 38*, 175–179.

Sackeim, H. A., Freeman, J., McElkiney, M., Coleman, E., Prudic, J., and Devanand, D. P. (1992). Effects of major depression on estimates of intelligence. *Journal of Clinical and Experimental Neuropsychology, 14*, 268–288.

Sackeim, H. A., and Steif, B. L. (1988). The neuropsychology of depression and mania. In A. Georgotas and R. Cancro, eds., *Depression and Mania*. New York: Elsevier, pp. 265–289.

Sagawa, K., Kawakatsu, S., Shibuya, I., Oiji, A., Morinobu, S., Komatani, A., Yazaki, M., and Totsuka, S. (1990). Correlation of regional cerebral blood flow with performance on neuropsychological tests in schizophrenic patients. *Schizophrenia Research, 3*, 241–246.

Sanders, A. F. (1980). Stage analysis of reaction processes. In E. Stelmach and J. Requin, eds., *Tutorials in Motor Behavior*. Amsterdam: North-Holland, pp. 331–354.

Saykin, A. J., Gur, R. C., Gur, R. E., Mozley, P. D., Mozley, L. H., Resnick, S. M., Kester, D. B., and Stafiniak, P. (1991). Neuropsychological function in schizophrenia. Selective impairment in memory and learning. *Archives of General Psychiatry, 48*, 618–624.

Schuck, J. R., and Lee, R. G. (1989). Backward masking, information processing and schizophrenia. *Schizophrenia Bulletin, 15*, 491–500.

Schwartz, S. (1982). Is there a schizophrenic language? *Behavioral and Brain Sciences, 5*, 579–626.

Seidman, L. J. (1990). The neuropsychology of schizophrenia: A neurodevelopmental and case study approach. *Journal of Neuropsychiatry and Clinical Neurosciences, 2*, 301–312.

Shakow, D. (1963). Psychological deficit in schizophrenia. *Behavioral Science, 8*, 275–305.

Shallice, T., Burgess, P. W., and Frith, C. D. (1991). Can the neuropsychological case-study approach be applied to schizophrenia? *Psychological Medicine, 21*, 661–673.

Shiffrin, R. M., and Schneider, W. (1977). Controlled and automatic human information processing: II. Perceptual learning, automatic attending, and a general theory. *Psychology Review, 84*, 127–190.

Sorokin, J. E., Giordani, B., Mohs, R. C., Losonczy, M. F., Davidson, M., Siever, L. J., Ryan, T. A., and Davis, K. L. (1988). Memory impairment in schizophrenic patients with tardive dyskinesia. *Biological Psychiatry, 23*, 129–135.

Spitzer, R. L., and Endicott, J. (1973). *Schedule for Affective Disorders and Schizophrenia (SADS)*. New York: Biometrics Research Branch, New York State Department of Mental Hygiene.

Spohn, H. E., and Strauss, M. E. (1989). Relation of neuroleptic and anticholinergic medication to cognitive functions in schizophrenia. *Journal of Abnormal Psychology, 98*, 367–380.

Strauss, J. S., Carpenter, W. T., Jr., and Bartko, J. J. (1974). The diagnosis and understanding of schizophrenia. Part III. Speculations on the processes that underlie schizophrenic symptoms and signs. *Schizophrenia Bulletin, 11*, 61–69.

Stuss, D. T., Benson, D. F., Kaplan, E. F., Weir, W. S., Naeser, M. A., Lieberman, I., and Ferrill, D. (1983). The involvement of orbitofrontal cerebrum in cognitive tasks. *Neuropsychologia, 21*, 235–248.

Suddath, R. L., Casanova, M. F., Goldberg, T. E., Daniel, D. G., Kelsoe, J. R., Jr., and Weinberger, D. R. (1989). Temporal lobe pathology in schizophrenia: A quantitative magnetic resonance imaging study. *American Journal of Psychiatry, 146*, 464–472.

Suddath, R. L., Christison, G. W., Torrey, E. F., Casanova, M. F., and Weinberger, D. R. (1990). Anatomical abnormalities in the brains of monozygotic twins discordant for schizophrenia. *New England Journal of Medicine, 322*, 789–794. [Published erratum appears in the *New England Journal of Medicine, 322*, 1616.]

Summerfelt, A. T., Alphs, L. D., Wagman, A.M.I., Funderburk, F. R., Hierholzer, R. M., and Strauss, M. E. (1991). Reduction of perseverative errors in patients with schizophrenia using monetary feedback. *Journal of Abnormal Psychology, 100*, 613–616.

Sutton, S., and Zubin, J. (1965). Effect of sequence on reaction time in schizophrenia. In A. T. Welford and J. E. Birren, eds., *Behavior, Aging and the Nervous System*. Springfield, IL: Charles C. Thomas, pp. 562–597.

Sweet, J. J., Newman, P, and Bell, B. (1992). Significance of depression in clinical neuropsychological assessment. *Clinical Psychology Review, 12*, 21–45.

Swerdlow, N. R., Braff, D. L., Masten, V. L., and Geyer, M. A. (1990). Schizophrenic-like sensorimotor gating abnormalities in rats following dopamine infusion into the nucleus accumbens. *Psychopharmacology, 101*, 414–420.

Tamlyn, D., McKenna, P. J., Mortimer, A. M, Lund, C. E., Hammond, S., and Baddeley, A. D. (1992). Memory impairment in schizophrenia: Its extent, affiliations and neuropsychological character. *Psychological Medicine, 22*, 101–115.

Tamminga, C. A., Thaker, G. K., Buchanan, R., Kirkpatrick, B., Alphs, L. D., Chase, T. N., and Carpenter, W. T. (1992). Limbic system abnormalities identified in schizophrenia using positron emission tomography with fluorodeoxyglucose and neocortical alterations with deficit syndrome. *Archives of General Psychiatry, 49,* 522–530.

Tompkins, L. M., Goldman, R. S., and Axelrod, B. N. (1995). Modifiability of neuropsychological dysfunction in schizophrenia. *Biological Psychiatry, 38,* 105–111.

Tune, L. E., Strauss, M. E., Lew, M. F., Breitlinger, E., and Coyle, J. T. (1982). Serum levels of anticholinergic drugs and impaired recent memory in chronic schizophrenic patients. *American Journal of Psychiatry, 139,* 1460–1462.

Van der Does, A. W., and Van den Bosch, R. J. (1992). What determines Wisconsin Card Sorting performance in schizophrenia? *Clinical Psychology Review, 12,* 567–583.

Venables, P. H. (1964). Input dysfunction in schizophrenia. In B. A. Maher, ed., *Progress in Experimental Personality Research* (vol. 1). New York: Academic Press, pp. 1–42.

Volkow, N. D., Brodie, J. D., Wolf, A. P., Angrist, B., Russell, J., and Cancro, R. (1986). Brain metabolism in patients with schizophrenia before and after acute neuroleptic administration. *Journal of Neurology, Neurosurgery, and Psychiatry, 49,* 1199–1202.

Wagman, A.M.I., Heinrichs, D. W., and Carpenter, W. T., Jr. (1987). Deficit and nondeficit forms of schizophrenia: Neuropsychological evaluation. *Psychiatry Research, 33,* 319–330.

Walker, E., and Harvey, P. D. (1986). Positive and negative symptoms in schizophrenia: Attentional performance correlates. *Psychopathology, 19,* 294–302.

Walker, E., and Lewine, R. J. (1988). The positive/negative symptom distinction in schizophrenia. Validity and etiological relevance. *Schizophrenia Research, 1,* 315–328.

Wechsler, D. (1987). *Wechsler Memory Scale–Revised.* New York: Psychological Corporation.

Weinberger, D. R., Berman, K. F., and Zec, R. F. (1986). Physiologic dysfunction of dorsolateral prefrontal cortex in schizophrenia. I. Regional cerebral blood flow evidence. *Archives of General Psychiatry, 43,* 114–124.

Weinberger, D. R., Berman, K. F., and Illowsky, B. P. (1988). Physiologic dysfunction of dorsolateral prefrontal cortex in schizophrenia. III. A new cohort and evidence for a monoaminergic mechanism. *Archives of General Psychiatry, 45,* 609–615.

Williamson, P. C., Kutcher, S. P., Cooper, P. W., Snow, W. G., Szalai, J. P., Kaye, H., Morrison, S. L., Willinsky, R. A., and Mamelak, M. (1989). Psychological, topographic EEG, and CT scan correlates of frontal lobe function in schizophrenia. *Psychiatry Research, 29,* 137–149.

Williamson, P., Pelz, D., Merskey, H., Morrison, S., and Conlon, P. (1991). Correlation of negative symptoms in schizophrenia with frontal lobe parameters on magnetic resonance imaging. *British Journal of Psychiatry, 159,* 130–134.

Wilson, R. S., Rosenbaum, G., Brown, G. G., Rourke, D., Whitman, D., and Grisell, J. (1978). An index of premorbid intelligence. *Journal of Consulting and Clinical Psychology, 46,* 1554–1555.

Wohlberg, G. W., and Kornetsky, C. (1973). Sustained attention in remitted schizophrenics. *Archives of General Psychiatry, 28,* 533–537.

Wolkin, A., Jaeger, J., Brodie, J. D., Wolf, A. P., Fowler, J., Rotrosen, J., Gomez-Mont, F., and Cancro, R. (1985). Persistence of cerebral metabolic abnormalities in chronic schizophrenia as determined by positron emission tomography. *American Journal of Psychiatry, 142,* 564–571.

Wolkin, A., Sanfilipo, A., Wolf, A. P., Angrist, B., Brodie, J. D., and Rotrosen, J. (1992). Negative symptoms and hypofrontality in chronic schizophrenia. *Archives of General Psychiatry, 49,* 959–965.

Wood, R. L., and Cook, M. (1979). Attentional deficit in the siblings of schizophrenics. *Psychological Medicine, 9,* 465–467.

Zubin, J. (1975). Problem of attention in schizophrenia. In M. L. Kietzman, S. Sutton, and J. Zubin, eds., *Experimental Approaches to Psychopathology.* New York: Academic Press, pp. 139–166.

Zubin, J., and Spring, B. (1977). Vulnerability—A new view of schizophrenia. *Journal of Abnormal Psychology, 86,* 103–126.

III Psychosocial Consequences of Neuropsychological Impairment

21 Mild Traumatic Brain Injury: Beyond Cognitive Assessment

STEVEN H. PUTNAM, SCOTT R. MILLIS, and KENNETH M. ADAMS

The assessment of patients who have sustained traumatic brain injury (TBI) represents the largest single expenditure of time for clinical neuropsychologists as a professional group (Putnam and DeLuca, 1990). Referral sources are diverse but typically include neurologists, physiatrists, psychiatrists, attorneys, insurance claims adjusters, case managers and others seeking information regarding the functional capabilities of the patient having sustained TBI. It has been suggested that the burgeoning interest in TBI may be responsible for the increased growth in professional neuropsychology in recent years (Putnam et al., 1994). Unquestionably TBI has been a primary impetus in bringing neuropsychology to the public's attention and into the courtroom. Indeed, assessment of the TBI patient represents a very significant challenge to the credibility of the profession at large. However, Matthews (1990) has voiced concerns about what he characterizes as the "malignant bloom nourished by the head injury industry" which, he predicts, "will end badly" (p. 33). Nonetheless, few would dispute the fact that understanding TBI is an essential requirement in contemporary neuropsychological practice.

This chapter will address milder spectrum TBI, emphasizing the assessment and understanding of these complex cases. It will cover definitional issues, the expected course of recovery, the varied influences that may pro- tract the symptom picture, and the assessment of malingering. We will focus on the psychosocial, psychophysiological, and motivational factors that may provide a useful conceptual framework for understanding mild TBI patients with chronic somatic and functional complaints. The chapter expands on earlier writings by the first two authors (Putnam and Millis, 1994).

Mild Traumatic Brain Injury

Definitional Issues

In a frequently cited but often criticized study, Rimel et al. (1981) defined mild TBI as cranial trauma producing an initial loss of consciousness limited to 20 minutes or less, a Glasgow Coma Scale (GCS) score between 13 and 15, and hospitalization of less than 48 hours. While these criteria gained general acceptance, the use of the GCS with mild TBI has been criticized because of its lack of sensitivity in discriminating milder spectrum brain injury (Jennett, 1989). Furthermore, the point in time after the injury during which to administer the GCS has not been uniformly agreed upon.

More recently, the Mild Traumatic Brain Injury Committee of the Head Injury Interdisciplinary Special Interest Group of the American Congress of Rehabilitation Medicine (ACRM) set forth a more detailed series of definitional criteria that, in effect, deems virtually any force to the head, with or without actual contact or external trauma, as being sufficient to produce mild TBI (Mild Traumatic Brain Injury Committee, 1993). The upper limits of these criteria require that the period of unconsciousness not exceed 30 minutes, posttraumatic amnesia (PTA) not exceed 24 hours, and the composite GCS after 30 minutes be between 13 and 15. The accuracy of retrospectively determined PTA has been questioned because of the interference of intervening events and the reports of others, and the uncertain criteria used to define it and its termination point (Gronwall and Wrightson, 1980; Goldstein and Levin, 1995). For instance, Gronwall and Wrightson (1980) found that one quarter of their patients with mild TBI made changes in their original estimation of PTA when interviewed again after several months. Regarding GCS, a score of 15 reflects no deficits in eye movement, motor skills, or verbalization but could still be present in a patient diagnosed with mild TBI. These consensus statements developed by the MTBIC will likely be welcomed by advocacy groups and many in the legal profession. However, widespread acceptance of an essential effect without a cause by clinical scientists is a matter of uncertainty at present. While these particular criteria raise many questions, universally accepted and applied definitional criteria, when possible, are an essential first step in determining accurate incidence rates for mild TBI.

Outcome From Mild TBI

Most individuals who have sustained mild TBI recover without extensive investment of treatment resources or significant complications. According to Gronwall and Wrightson (1974), patients who suffer concussion consistently show a slowing of information-processing immediately after injury. However, these authors assert that, "The rate almost always returns to normal when the patient is retested about 35 days after injury." They further conclude, "though there will always be some patients who will need to perpetuate their symptoms, almost all should recover from minor head injury with no disability" (p. 609).

Gentilini and coworkers (1985) compared 50 mild TBI patients with 50 matched controls who were tested at one month post-injury. A multivariate analysis performed for six neuropsychological tests—three memory measures, two attentional tests, and a test of intelligence—yielded no significant differences between the patients and the controls.

Rutherford et al. (1979) found that 85% of patients with mild TBI reported full recovery after 1 year. After 2 years, 94% of patients reported full recovery in a study conducted by Wrightson and Gronwall (1981). A three-center study conducted by a team of investigators (Levin et al., 1987b) found that a single uncomplicated mild TBI, while producing pervasive neurobehavioral impairments lasting for several days after the injury, was *not* associated with differences in enduring impairment of neuropsychological test performances when compared to demographically matched local controls. In discussing the findings from this study in a later paper, Ruff et al. (1989) note, "An important finding of these interviews was the lack of correspondence between the patients' subjective complaints, which remained virtually unchanged at one month, and the significant gains that they showed on the neuropsychological tests" (p. 186). Ruff et al. (1989) reasoned, "The patient's inaccurate assessments of their posttraumatic symptoms may be due to a variety of factors, such as premorbid personality characteristics, varying neuropathological substrates of injury, and primary and secondary psychological reactions to the trauma" (p. 186), and emphasized the role of post-assessment consultation regarding the patient's neuropsychological performances.

Dikmen and colleagues have been among the most prolific of recent investigators demonstrating resolution of acute, time-limited effects associated with mild TBI. Dikmen et al. (1986) included 20 patients who had sustained mild TBI and matched controls who were tested at 1 month and 1 year after the injury. At 3 months the only differences were found on a rhythm discrimination test and the 4-hour delayed recall trial on the Selective Reminding Test. By 1 year there were no significant differences between the patients and controls on any measures. Also of interest is the fact that at 1 year 10% of the mild TBI patients reported being unemployed. While this may seem high, it was the same rate of unemployment reported by the control group at the 1-month examination. This underscores the importance of having base rate data available and applying a case-control methodology.

Examining neuropsychological outcomes at 1 year after injury, Dikmen et al. (1995) reported no differences across the Halstead-Reitan Neuropsychological Test Battery between trauma controls and a TBI group that were able to follow commands within 1 hour. Although this group, as a whole, likely represented TBI of mild to moderate severity, there was complete resolution of deficits in attention, memory, problem solving, speed of information processing, motor skills, and general intellectual functions. This study and others from the Traumatic Coma Data Bank (Levin et al., 1987b) and the Traumatic Brain Injury Model Systems of Care (Kreutzer et al., 1993) (which are focused on more severe levels of TBI), describe *typical* patterns and levels of neuropsychological impairment associated with different degrees of TBI severity at different time intervals. This information can provide general reference points that are useful in evaluating the individual case.

The Postconcussion Syndrome and Persisting Symptom Picture

While persisting symptomatology is uncommon after mild TBI, there is a subset of patients who report disabling cognitive and emotional difficulties for years after injury. This has been loosely referred to as the postconcussion syndrome or PCS. "Postconcussional Disorder" has been proposed as a new research diagnosis category for the *Diagnostic and Statistical Manual of Mental Disorders,* fourth edition (DSM-IV) (American Psychiatric Association, 1994). DSM-IV de-

fines Postconcussional Disorder as "an acquired impairment in cognitive functioning, accompanied by specific neurobehavioral symptoms, that occurs as a consequence of closed head injury of sufficient severity to produce a significant cerebral concussion. The manifestations of concussion include loss of consciousness, posttraumatic amnesia, and less commonly, posttraumatic onset of seizures" (p. 704). Brown et al. (1994) have proposed more detailed criteria for the diagnosis of postconcussional disorder.

While neurophysiological processes may account for symptoms occurring shortly after mild TBI, other nonorganic factors may influence and even maintain the behavior of the patient reporting protracted and disabling symptoms. The particular nature of these polysymptomatic complaints in individual cases may be variable, but data derived from group studies reflect a certain degree of uniformity (Alves et al., 1986; Binder, 1986; Levin et al., 1987b; McMordie, 1988; Dikmen et al., 1989; Rutherford, 1989). To date, a number of factors have been identified that contribute to this polysymptomatic presentation, but no widely accepted model has been developed that accounts for both the emergence and the maintenance of these symptoms. Although neuropathological and neurophysiological substrates involving diffuse axonal injury, rotational acceleration/deceleration forces, reduced cerebral blood flow, cavitation dynamics, and diffuse cerebral shearing have become increasingly popular mechanistic or hypothetical explanations, many questions about each of these etiologies remain unanswered at present. However, the pseudomedical sound of their recitation makes their allure irresistible to those intending to ground PCS in a firm physiological context. As noted by Bohnen and Jolles (1992), "The aspecific and subjective nature of PCS causes researchers methodological difficulties when they try to quantify or conceptualize these complaints, and this has led to an ensueing controversy about the psychogenetic versus physiogenetic origin of the complaints" (p. 684). Similarly, Benton (1989), in reviewing

the history and epidemiology of the postconcussion syndrome concluded, "The concept
that it is a congeries of symptoms and complaints that has multiple determinants—
physical, psychological, and social—is now
generally accepted" (p. 6).

While PCS is frequently employed for categorizing these symptoms, as a diagnostic
construct it seems to obscure, if not ignore,
the role of individual differences in developmental history, character formation, and the
unique perceptual, behavioral and psychophysiological thresholds and responses exhibited by individual patients (Adams and
Putnam, 1991), as well as the importance of
population symptom base rates (Lees-Haley
and Brown, 1993). Insufficient attention has
been given to the contribution of these nonorganic factors in mild TBI, particularly in
the relatively rare cases with protracted
symptomatology. How both personality and
situational influences operate in symptom
production and persistence need careful consideration (MacKenzie et al., 1987). Until
recently, the role of patient *perception* in
symptom formation and maintenance has also
been incompletely addressed.

Methodological Considerations

The literature includes reports of patients
demonstrating rapid recovery of symptoms
after mild TBI (Dikmen et al., 1989; Alves
et al., 1993) as well as complicated and protracted recovery (Leininger et al., 1990).
However, to date no population-based studies are available that address recovery following mild TBI. Generalization based on the
available literature is limited by sampling
problems (Levin et al., 1987a; Dikmen et
al., 1992; Reitan and Wolfson, 1993). The
failure to distinguish between prospective
versus retrospective research, or, nonse-
lected consecutive versus selective samples,
represents a major methodological limitation
in much of the currently available literature.
Regarding the latter methodology, inclusion
into the study is often based on the poor
outcome demonstrated by the patients (e.g.,
Leininger et al., 1990) rather than the brain
injury per se (Dikmen et al., 1992). If one

investigates mild TBI by considering only
patients who come to a hospital or clinic
in association with ongoing difficulties, it is
probable that the sample will exhibit more
impairment than the general mild TBI population, which includes individuals who sustained an injury but have no continuing complaints. Similarly, failure of investigators to
consider litigation as a sample characteristic
continues to be a shortcoming. As noted
by Lees-Haley (1992), "litigation is a special
context that appears to have different base
rates and different evaluation requirements
than traditional therapeutic or clinical environments" (p. 387). Clearly, the source of
a study's patients and the conditions that
influence who is included in the sample significantly influences the extent to which the
results can be generalized beyond the study
sample.

Both the Alves et al. (1993) and Dikmen
et al. (1989) samples of uncomplicated mild
TBI patients included a very small number
who continued to report postconcussion-like
symptoms after 1 year or more. Alves et
al. (1993) characterized the continuation of
"persistent, multiple symptom constellations
consistent with clinical descriptions of post-
concussive syndrome" in their large sample
as "extremely rare" (p. 55). In discussing
their particular findings, Dikmen et al. (1989)
note, "These are the cases difficult for clinicians to understand and treat, and not the
majority of minor head injury patients who
may show acute, time limited effects" (p.
237). Fenton et al. (1993) found among a
sample of patients having sustained mild TBI
that those who demonstrated persisting
symptoms reported a significantly higher
number of adverse life events occurring in
the year preceding the injury vis-à-vis those
whose symptoms had resolved. These authors concluded, "The emergence and persistence of the postconcussional syndrome
are associated with social adversity before
the accident" (p. 493).

The lower prevalence of persistent PCS in
more severe cases of TBI may be associated
with the presence of "unambiguous neurological deficits . . . patients and their families
have a long interval to come to terms with

disability and the rate of recovery" (p. 68) (Alexander, 1992). Interestingly, it is the ambiguous and uncertain nature of many symptoms reported by mild TBI patients that may be a principal reason for the attention directed to them and thus, in an indirect fashion, contribute to their persistence.

Base Rate Considerations

Functional somatic complaints are commonly reported in nonpatient samples. Kellner and Sheffield (1973) reported that approximately 90% of healthy individuals reported experiencing various somatic symptoms during a 1-week period. These investigators surveyed two samples of normal individuals and actually found somatic complaints to be more prevalent than emotional complaints. The most commonly reported symptoms for normal subjects were headaches (49%), tiredness (47%), muscle pains and aches (42%), and irritability (34%). The authors suggested that these findings could help account for reported side effects associated with expectancy from medication use. They extrapolated that "frequently reported placebo side effects may be largely due to the suggestive effect of the placebo" (p. 104) and emphasized the importance of base rate data in the interpretation of such symptomatic reports. Escobar et al. (1987a) found that over 4% of community-residing normal subjects have *multiple* chronic functional somatic symptoms. In a Los Angeles community study, Escobar et al. (1987b) estimated that over 4% of the general population met the criteria for somatization; later they estimated this figure to be as high as 18% to 20% in Puerto Rico (Escobar et al., 1989). Swartz et al. (1990) have more recently suggested that 11.6% of the general population could have a somatization syndrome.

The base rate issue is particularly well illustrated by a recent study that reported that 52% of a sample of asymptomatic patients had various lumbar spine abnormalities and that only 36% demonstrated a *normal* disk at all levels (Jensen et al., 1994). The authors concluded, "The discovery of a bulge or protrusion on an MRI scan in a patient with low back pain may frequently be coincidental . . . Abnormalities of the lumbar spine by MRI examination can be meaningless if considered in isolation" (p. 72).

The issue of what is normal or pathological can be addressed empirically by considering the endorsement frequencies of nonclinical samples to statements regarding health and other matters. It is particularly illuminating to examine the percentage of normal subjects in the MMPI-2 standardization sample endorsing certain items possibly suggestive of deficient physical and emotional health (Butcher et al., 1989). Certain items illustrate particularly well the extent to which functional complaints seem to be typically reported by normal adults. For instance, in response to the item "I feel tired a good deal of the time," 34% and 25% of the females and males, respectively, positively endorsed the item. The item "I have few or no pains" was endorsed in the negative direction by almost 20% of the sample and the item "I forget where I leave things" was endorsed affirmatively by 37% to 40% of the standardization sample. Twenty-six percent of the female sample responded "false" to the item "I have very few headaches." Interestingly, in response to a number of MMPI-2 items, females produced higher endorsement rates than the males, a finding consistent with other reports (Pennebaker, 1982). Both Rutherford (1989) and Alves et al. (1993) found female gender to be associated with higher rates of symptom reporting in the post-acute phase following mild TBI.

Individual Thresholds and Symptom Perception

Symptom reporting often does not represent a one-to-one correspondence with physiological injury, but rather, represents the *perception* of the individual, a perception that may or may not always be corroborated objectively. This is demonstrated in the MMPI item endorsements of male TBI patients regarding memory and concentration problems. Little relationship was found between the item endorsements reflecting impaired memory and actual measurement of memory functioning in formal testing (Gass et al., 1990). Along the same line, older adults are inclined to overestimate their memory problems due to the *expectation* that memory decline was typically associated with normal aging (Cavanaugh, 1987). Depression has also been reported to be associated with the tendency to overestimate memory inefficiency (Williams et al., 1987). Watts (1995) has observed that "Depressed patients frequently attribute their cognitive problems to a permanent loss of mental powers, and this causes them additional distress" (p. 295), which further interferes with memory efficiency. Depressed medical patients have been reported to demonstrate deficiencies on measures involving psychomotor speed, problem solving, and recognition memory (Cole and Zarit, 1984).

Certain symptoms appear to be the normal experience even in individuals known to be in generally good health. Presumably, such individuals are not alarmed by the bodily sensations they experience (in the absence of a salient injury event), nor do they define such sensations as uniquely pathological or malignant. Rather, it could be inferred that this "physiological and psychological noise associated with everyday living" (Lees-Haley et al., 1993) is attributed to nonillness influences such as fatigue, stress, diet, normal aging, or perhaps simply not assigned any particular health significance.

An interesting psychometric parallel to this consideration of normality versus abnormality involves how subtest variability is interpreted on the Wechsler Adult Intelligence Scale–Revised (WAIS-R) (Wechsler, 1981). The narrow assumptions regarding normality employed by some practitioners suggests that performance should be relatively uniform and that subtest profile dispersion is pathognomonic. However, such a notion has received little support from empirical studies with the WAIS-R that indicate that ability variation, as defined by the performance of the WAIS-R standardization sample, is often considerable (Kaufman, 1990; Matarazzo, 1990; Putnam et al., 1992). Such a consider-

ation again underscores the importance of establishing the base rate of occurrence for behaviors in the general population for meaningful application to clinical samples.

Several studies have begun to do this with emphasis on TBI outcome. Gouvier et al. (1988) attempted to establish the base rate of occurrence of commonly identified postconcussional symptoms and found that symptoms such as visual problems, fatigue, and impatience were reported at a similar rate of frequency in a group of head-injured and non–head-injured subjects. McLean et al. (1983) found that non–head-injured controls did not differ from patients who were 1 month post-TBI in reporting such symptoms as headaches, dizziness, irritability, temper loss, sonophobia, photophobia, anxiety, and insomnia.

Lees-Haley and Brown (1993) studied the base rate of symptoms on a self-report checklist among a group of personal injury litigants whose claims did not involve central nervous system (CNS) injury or illness. In fact, patients were excluded from the study sample if they reported a history of head injury or other CNS conditions. A control group of family practice outpatients presenting a broad range of health complaints was also asked to complete the symptom checklist. Interestingly, Lees-Haley and Brown (1993) found that a number of symptoms often reported as part of the postconcussion syndrome were reported by the personal injury litigants at a much *higher* rate than the outpatient sample. Most notably, 92% reported sleeping problems, 89% depression, 88% headaches, 78% concentration problems, 77% irritability, and 53% memory problems. In contrast to this, the control subjects reported these symptoms at a significantly lower rate (e.g., memory problems 20%). While this study did not investigate the magnitude or intensity of complaints in these samples, the results affirm the fact that postconcussional symptoms occur frequently in the general population. Furthermore, the base rates of occurrence in non-CNS conditions are sufficiently high such that these symptoms would seem to have little or no diagnostic specificity relative to mild TBI or PCS. This would be especially true in the individual case examination conducted by the neuropsychologist. Lees-Haley et al. (1993) have urged caution "in using self-reports of complaints with high base rates in the uninjured population as indicia of psychological impairment" (p. 26).

With respect to the issue of memory complaints, it is of interest to note that Richardson and Snape (1984) reported that orthopedic trauma controls who had *not* sustained head injury, demonstrated impaired performances on free recall memory tasks. Richardson and Snape (1984) interpreted these findings as suggesting that state anxiety associated with traumatic injury may lead to an impairment of cognitive function by reducing the capacity of working memory. These findings are consistent with other investigations (Watts, 1995).

In spite of the fact that somatic and functional symptoms are part of normal human experience, certain individuals seem more disposed to attach meaning and significance to such symptoms. The role of expectancy in the etiology of somatic complaints after mild TBI has recently been discussed by Mittenburg et al. (1992). These investigators found that patients having sustained mild TBI consistently underestimated the normal prevalence of various somatic symptoms in their retrospective accounts when compared with the base rate established by normal controls. Mittenburg et al. (1992) suggested that "patients may reattribute benign emotional, physiological and memory symptoms to their head injury" (p. 203). On an a priori basis this tendency would appear to be even further accentuated in cases involving potential financial gain such as personal injury litigation or permanent disability. They proposed a model in which an initial activation of typical symptom expectancies occurs at the time of the head injury event which concomitantly induces autonomic/emotional arousal, followed by a *selective* or searching attention to one's internal state based on expectancy of change. This is followed by attentional bias and arousal augmenting symptom perception, which then elicits additional autonomic and emotional responses with a reinforcement of expectations. Mittenburg et al. (1992) argue that such circular reinforcement of expectations, may, in fact, account for the continuation of these symptoms in the absence of measurable neuropsychological impairment. Of course, individuals can be taught implicitly to interpret commonly occurring premorbid sensations as manifestations of brain damage following an injury event.

One possible conclusion derived from the Lees-Haley and Brown (1993) and Mittenburg et al. (1992) investigations is that while PCS-type symptoms are common even in the absence of CNS injury, the retrospective self-analysis performed by mild TBI patients often underestimates or dismisses the existence of preinjury symptoms. The salience and recency of the injury event may contribute to patients' attributing these symptoms predominantly to the TBI.

Expectancy: Positive and Negative Effects

A similar model of expectation and attribution has been helpful in understanding and treating chronic pain. Both experimental and clinical evidence suggests that self-directed selective attention enhances an individual's awareness of bodily sensations (Pennebaker and Skelton, 1978). Understandable attention to one's body, motivated by fear of further injury, may produce a selective perception of even normal physiological activity. Mechanic (1972) has similarly emphasized the role of patient perception and attribution in the formulation of pain complaints. Indeed, a person who has experienced physical trauma or disease is likely to become more aware of bodily sensations and may experience increased fear of further injury or disease. Bodily sensations that are out of the ordinary are detected and appraised in terms of prior experience and anticipation. This is based on the Schacter and Singer (1962) model of emotions, which emphasizes that "cognitive factors appear to be indispensable elements in any formulation of emotion" (p.

398). Schacter and Singer (1962) posit that emotion involves a process of initial physiological arousal and a subsequent attempt to define it in a manner that has meaning to the person at the time of occurrence. When individuals lack a clear explanation of what they are experiencing, psychosocial and contextual influences assume increased influence in the attribution process that unfolds. Once developed, an inaccurate attribution is often maintained because subsequent perceptions are selectively interpreted within the expectancy that has become established. This model highlights the susceptibility of the perceptions of some patients to the well-intentioned interpretations (misattributions) offered by providers and support groups regarding the "expected" course of symptoms. This may contribute to the increase in pervasive and at times disabling symptoms months after an injury event, subsequent to patients' being told by an authority figure they have a head injury and certain symptoms will, in fact, occur. As found in chronic pain samples, patients may continue to give credibility to their own perceptions of ill-health despite continual reassurances offered later that they are actually in good health (Pilowsky, 1967).

Symptom reporting can have the potential to develop into a self-perpetuating and self-validating cognitive scheme that becomes increasingly refractory to intervention while producing a disabled lifestyle in which the patient can avoid performance demands in a socially acceptable manner. It is clear, however, that this is an exception in the modal mild TBI clinical course. Each sensation that is interpreted as pain elicits a fear of worse pain to come, leading to increased concern with protecting oneself from further pain and injury. This may lead to increasing attention to one's bodily sensations and the use of more protective behaviors, loss of strength and flexibility, deconditioning, and the continuing reaction to pain with further avoidance, guarding, tension, and lassitude.

Some individuals seem to perceive a wide range of sensations in pain terms, perhaps most notably affective distress (Pennebaker, 1982). For these individuals, the experience of a mild TBI provides another opportunity for this cycle of somatic dysfunction to develop and flourish.

Psychosocial Contributions to the Persistence of Symptoms

Many symptoms are vague and subjective and thus open to diverse interpretations. Psychosocial factors implicated in the persistence of functional symptoms are likely multiple—social-interactional, characterological, and cultural. Regarding the interactional factors, Ford (1983) characterizes somatization as a form of social and emotional communication. Illness behavior serves to regulate and control important aspects of interpersonal relationships. For instance, children learn at an early age that stomachaches are often a means of avoiding what they perceive as unpleasant experiences such as going to school or separation from parents. It has been found that children in aversive school and family environments report more health problems than children in nonaversive settings (Pennebaker, 1982). This is not to imply secondary gain is always explanatory; increased stress levels have been associated with hormonal and autonomic changes that may increase one's susceptibility to illness (Selye, 1976; Rosenzweig and Lieman, 1982). Some have suggested that somatic complaints may even function as a depressive equivalent in families where illness models are present and the family has learned not to define distress in appropriate psychological terms. Furthermore, there is some evidence to support the contention that the learning of attitudes toward illness, and probably of certain physiological responses, may occur early in a child's development (Kellner, 1991). Children who are implicitly reinforced for playing the sick role appear to be more disposed to adopting such a role later in life (Whitehead et al., 1981).

Even within a short time following the injury event, somatic symptoms may be occurring for reasons that are quite different from when they were first produced. Rather than being entirely respondent to a sensory stimulus or tissue damage per se, they may be partially or completely under the control of psychosocial reinforcers. For instance, litigation or perceived financial incentive requiring the demonstration of disability could reinforce continued illness behavior (Butcher and Harlow, 1987). Rutherford (1989) suggested that litigation may have been associated with increased symptom reporting after mild TBI, particularly beyond the acute phase of recovery. Inadequate reinforcement of well behaviors may further maintain the patient's symptom course.

Examining the role of psychological trauma response to an injury event holds promise for better understanding the postconcussion syndrome. As emphasized by Everstine and Everstine (1993), "Anyone can be traumatized, from the most well-adjusted to the most troubled. For a clinician, it is the person's *mode* of responding that is the salient factor" (p. 7). Common trauma symptoms such as hypervigilance may be the psyche's response to avoid further injury.

Personality Considerations

Characterological and personality variables have been proposed as influencing symptom reporting following mild TBI (Adams and Putnam, 1991). Individuals differ in how they respond to symptoms acutely and the emotional significance ascribed to an injury or traumatic event (Kay et al., 1992). In this regard Costa and McCrae (1985) have stressed that "Physicians and medical researchers should consider the feasibility of consulting personality and other psychological data in making diagnoses, recognizing that there are individual differences in reporting styles even among psychiatrically normal patients" (p. 26).

Dicker (1992) has reasoned that the personality factors that increase a patient's risk of sustaining a mild TBI may also complicate recovery and subsequent adaptation following injury. Unfortunately, individual differences in personality may not be properly considered unless the patient presents with a behavioral disturbance or is highly symptomatic. The probative value of personality variables in evaluating and treating patients may be poorly appreciated by neuropsychol-

ogists. Adams (1989) believes the role of personality and emotional variables has been deemphasized in contemporary clinical neuropsychological assessment and facetiously proffers the historical perspective that even "the famous cases of aphasias, alexias, apraxias, aphemia without aphonia and a-*this*-ias without a-*that*-ias did not occur in people without premorbid personalities, developmental histories, defense mechanisms, hopes, fears, or inner emotional life!"

Watson and Pennebaker (1989) have argued that neuroticism represents a stable but pervasive dimension of personality that is highly associated with increased symptom reporting. The work of McCrae and Costa (1982) and Costa and McCrae (1985) has resulted in similar conclusions suggesting that neuroticism is reliably related to self-reported health status. Watson and Pennebaker (1989) have offered a thoughtful perspective on the relationship between neuroticism and the expression of physical symptomatology. First, such individuals are more sensitive to pain and respond more strongly to sensations of pain and discomfort. That is, they tend to report increased somatic problems in the absence of increased physical dysfunction. Second, they tend to be hypervigilant and may be more likely to notice and attend to *normal* body sensations and minor discomforts. In other words, their tendency may be to overinterpret common autonomic correlates of increased anxiety. A number of investigators have supported these well-established conclusions that patients who overreport somatic complaints demonstrate high levels of neuroticism (Barsky and Klerman, 1983; Quill, 1985; Pilowsky et al., 1987).

The disruptive emotional state of individuals demonstrating high neuroticism may facilitate the manifestation of physiological changes that are perceived as confirming evidence of their "illness." Consistent with this formulation, Middelboe et al. (1992), in a prospective study of 51 TBI patients, found that symptomatic patients produced a negativistic personality pattern with passive-aggressive traits, compared with nonsymptomatic patients, as measured by the Millon

Behavioral Health Inventory. Similarly, earlier studies have reported an association between PCS and neuroticism (Gruvstad et al., 1958; Mellergard, 1967; Keshavan et al., 1981), although failure to identify such a relationship has been reported as well (Modlin, 1967). In general, it appears that individuals high in neuroticism are more ruminative, apprehensive, and negativistic, characteristics that are associated with a biased style of perceiving one's health, but not with actual health status (Costa and McCrae, 1985).

Some persistent bodily complaints may be a reflection of an abnormally low sensory threshold (Pennebaker, 1982). Caldwell and Chase (1977) have noted that "fear arousal and anger arousal both lower the threshold of pain. Fear arousal reduces the pain threshold more than anger, so that increasing fear would especially intensify the experience of pain" (p. 143). Similarly, several studies have reported that anxiety actually lowers reported pain thresholds (Bronzo and Powers, 1967; Mersky, 1980) and may even amplify one's perception of pain (Barsky and Klerman, 1983). Generalized anxiety and somatic anxiety have been associated with nonspecific complaints such as fatigue, headache, dizziness, and a multitude of bodily discomforts (Taylor, 1953; Schwartz et al., 1978). Of course elevated anxiety is a very commonly reported sequela of mild TBI and PCS (Levin et al., 1987b; Rutherford, 1989; Gronwall et al., 1990) as well as traumatic events more generally (Everstine and Everstine, 1993).

Cultural Influences and Symptom Perception

Regarding cultural factors, it is well established that response to the perception of a loss of health occurs within an articulated cultural context wherein the individual, his or her family, the community, and health care providers respond in socially patterned ways. With respect to the latter, Shorter (1992) has presented a historical review that suggests that while somatization has always existed, its manifestations and treatment have changed to reflect the prevailing culture and health care milieu. Morris (1991) describes various shared cultural expectancies throughout history regarding the personal meaningfulness ascribed to painful experience. He offers that the process of interpreting pain occurs at the level of both the general culture as well as the subculture of the sufferer, and maintains that "When we fall into pain, we also fall into a net of already constructed meanings" (p. 19).

For instance, the subculture of the professional athlete may impose a different set of expectancies regarding recovery from an injury (e.g., concussion) than what is observed among certain other groups. National or ethnic groups may have their own particular empathic or stigmatizing modes of regard for injury victims.

Much of the work of Pennebaker and colleagues (1977) has emphasized how beliefs about one's body affect perceptions of physiological activity and that the perception of symptoms often originates from popularly held views in addition to physiological factors. Pennebaker and Epstein (1983) state, "To a large extent, beliefs about disease and symptoms derive from other individuals after the disorder has been diagnosed . . . disease knowledge—which is based in part on information from the medical establishment—is embellished by the patient within the context of his or her conceptions of the world" (p. 471). Humans are, of course, active perceivers of their environments and employ whatever information is available to understand bodily sensations and emotional experiences. As already stated, the accuracy of such perceptions is by no means assured and is susceptible to a variety of influences.

The work of Kuhn (1970) and Watson (1967) has emphasized how current paradigms of thought subtly shape perceptions in determining not only what is deemed important to attend to but how to interpret what is attended to. On a more individual level, it would be presumptuous to believe that individuals in the twentieth century are impervious to such cultural influences in the interpretation of bodily sensations. In addition to physician influence, situational cues provided by media and well-intentioned support groups may assist in symptom identification and passage into "patienthood" for certain individuals. Lees-Haley et al. (1993) have argued provocatively that this process can be understood in terms of the "Barnum effect," in which people ". . . will accept any reasonable sounding interpretation delivered by an authority figure as long as it seems somewhat tailored to them personally" (p. 22). Parsons (1966) has eloquently discussed the "sick role" and the legitimization of such a role being conferred by a health care professional. Once entry into patienthood becomes officially sanctioned, the patient is relieved of usual demands and the "sick role" takes precedence over all other social roles and expectations. Unfortunately, once this role becomes a part of the patient's self-identity and persona, it would seem that the relinquishing of this role may produce ambivalent feelings or even overt resistance in some individuals.

Peri-injury Considerations in Symptom Maintenance

Exploring important psychological events proximal to the injury is imperative, as is assessing the psychological trauma (Van Der Kolk, 1987) associated with the actual injury event. In other words, the sense of terror or of being unexpectedly victimized and the emotional sequelae are easily overlooked by providers attending to the more salient aspects of a patient's injuries. The role of recent significant losses, alterations in relationships, suppression of anger, alcohol and substance use, financial stresses, and the *symbolic* significance of the accident can greatly influence how the patient responds to the injury event. The critical role of disclosure and expression of feelings in response to traumatic events in psychosomatic processes and health has been eloquently reported on in a recent series of papers (Pennebaker and Beall, 1986; Pennebaker and Susman, 1988; Pennebaker et al., 1988) and merits careful consideration in cases involving personal injury and trauma. It is not a far reach from the immediate emotional impact to the presumed genesis of post-traumatic stress disorder.

There is some evidence to suggest that a higher frequency of learning disabilities and poor school attainments exists in mild TBI samples than in the general population (Dicker, 1992). Thus, the recognition of pre-existing cognitive deficits is critical so that treatment plans are realistic and specifically tailored to the patient. If premorbid learning disabilities are mistakenly diagnosed as residual to TBI, interventions that are addressed toward remediating these pseudo-TBI deficits will, of course, often be of limited efficacy. Furthermore, iatrogenic exacerbation may result as a consequence of the individual's remaining in the patient role for an extended period with little demonstration of benefit.

Another important consideration involves the assessment of comorbid medical and psychological factors in this group of patients. The importance of reviewing and integrating past medical, psychological, educational, and employment records with current examination data may illuminate one's examination findings in conceptualizing the individual case (Matarazzo, 1990). What is necessary is the challenging task of discriminating between several clinical presentations; those patients who may be deliberately producing false symptoms, those with unforeseen medical illnesses or complications associated with or antecedent to mild TBI, and those who have been socialized into a disabled lifestyle. Another important distinction involves malingering versus psychogenic or somatoform pain disorder (Everstine and Everstine, 1993) and the demoralization often associated with the latter.

Provider Response to the Patient in Influencing Recovery

The acceptance of patient reports regarding subjective complaints and the uncritically held conclusion that these invariably confirm the occurrence of a mild TBI needs to be tempered with appreciation for the impact providers have on the recently injured patient trying to understand and respond to his or her symptoms. The introduction of mild TBI educational materials such as videotapes and brochures, or the assignment to groups, is intended by providers to have a salutary effect. However, in some cases not involving bona fide symptoms such efforts can serve as the cognitive "label" in the Schacter and Singer (1962) model (and thus, identification as "patient") in response to the individual's physiological arousal. Perhaps the patient would have best been served by assurance that brain-behavior integrity was not compromised or that deficits will resolve.

An opposing position could be presented that suggests that when the patient's aroused state produces "evaluative needs," that is, the need for understanding of feelings, and when patients are not provided with an adequate explanation for their symptoms, they may become increasingly self-vigilant, which may in turn result in symptom magnification and maintenance. Cicerone (1991) contends that "Providing the patient with realistic explanations may prevent them from seeking alternative explanations for their neurologic symptoms or overreacting emotionally" (p. 35). Of course the critical issue is one of epistemology, definitive diagnosis, and what response will ultimately be best suited to the individual patient; that is, establishing the relationship of the patient's symptoms to the presumed mild TBI. For certain patients such "safe" exhortations may inaugurate the patient on the path of "patienthood" and facilitate a protracted role of disability. Those rare patients inclined to attribute more to the effects of an accident than what the facts support, or who may be curiously eager to embrace the patient role, could be particularly poorly served by such explanations.

Contemporary Issues in the Assessment of Malingering

Assessment of Exaggerated Impairment

Some clinicians doubt that patients can actually feign impairment, and they publicly worry that there is a current obsession with malingering that is akin to a witch-hunt. At the other extreme are clinicians who seem to "find" a malingerer behind every deficient test performance. As thorny as the issue may be, exaggerated impairment needs to be considered in the differential diagnosis of the mild TBI case because there are often power-

ful financial and social incentives that reward dysfunctional behavior. Poor effort will be encountered in neuropsychological examinations as surely as schoolchildren will feign stomachaches to avoid a dreaded examination. Carroll et al. (1995) found that 35% to 42% of medical costs in 1993 claimed by individuals in auto accidents were related to staged or nonexistent accidents, nonexistent injuries, or the inflation of claims for actual injuries. The failure to detect feigned impairment can lead to inappropriate treatment of patients, iatrogenic development of dysfunctional behavior, and misuse of limited healthcare resources.

The detection of feigned or exaggerated impairment is not accomplished with a single test but involves multiple methods and sources of information: (1) understanding the relationship between severity of injury and typical courses of cognitive and psychosocial outcome; (2) ruling out other medical conditions that may depress neuropsychological status; (3) identifying test performance patterns associated with incomplete effort or feigned impairment; and (4) understanding the role of psychosocial factors in the mild TBI case, as discussed earlier (Millis and Putnam, 1996).

Objectively establishing the initial severity of the injury is crucial in the neuropsychological assessment of the head injury case because there is a ". . . significant dose-response relationship between length of coma and level of cognitive impairment" (Dikmen et al., 1995, p. 83). As noted earlier in studies of consecutive mild TBI cases, neuropsychological deficits were apparent within a week after injury, but resolution of these deficits tended to occur within 1 to 3 months (Dikmen et al., 1986; Levin et al., 1987b).

The issue of exaggerated or feigned impairment then needs to be raised in the instance of the mild TBI case when the patient generates excessively poor neuropsychological test scores: ". . . significant neuropsychological impairment due to a mild TBI is as unlikely as is escaping an impairment in the case of a very severe head injury" (Dikmen et al., 1995, p. 87). Rather than relying on patient self-report of injury severity, the clinician is advised to obtain hospital emergency service and admission records to obtain measures of severity such as the Glasgow Coma Scale (Teasdale and Jennett, 1974), Time to Follow Commands (Dikmen et al., 1995), and the Galveston Orientation and Amnesia Test (Levin et al., 1979). In addition, neuropsychological outcome data from Dikmen et al. (1994, 1995), Kreutzer et al. (1993), and Levin et al. (1987b) provide information about typical neuropsychological impairment patterns after TBI. A discrepancy between a given patient's panel of test scores and expected outcome based on such group studies does not necessarily establish the presence of feigned impairment. However, it should alert the clinician to consider additional diagnostic possibilities.

Medical Conditions and Neuropsychological Status

The diagnosis of TBI exerts a seductive pull to attribute to the TBI everything that is wrong with the patient (Dikmen and Levin, 1993). In addition to evaluating patient effort and motivation, other medical conditions need to be ruled out as contributors to disability or poor neuropsychological test performance. The diagnostic possibilities in head injury cases are not limited simply to TBI versus malingering. Endocrine, hepatic, renal, pulmonary, cerebrovascular, and substance abuse disorders have been associated with neuropsychological impairment (Tarter et al., 1988). Premorbid substance abuse and learning disability deserve special attention because of their particularly high prevalence in head injury samples (Dicker, 1992; Dikmen and Levin, 1993).

Neuropsychological Tests in the Detection of Feigned Impairment

The development of psychometric methods to detect incomplete effort or impairment has been challenging, to be sure. Establishing a genuine malingering criterion group against which tests can be validated is difficult because, of course, bona fide malingerers in the world are generally reticent to present themselves to scientists for study. Most investigators have used either analogue designs in which normal subjects were coached to malinger or clinical samples in which optimal effort is suspect because of pending litigation, excessively poor test performance, and/ or below chance performance on symptom validity testing. Although both methods have limitations, they are yielding a converging pattern of findings, as will be discussed in the following section. In addition, there is accumulating evidence that neuropsychological test patterns associated with traumatic brain injury can be differentiated from those related to poor or incomplete effort.

FORCED-CHOICE MEASURES. The forced-choice format, also known as symptom validity testing, has been used to develop new procedures to detect incomplete effort (Pankratz et al., 1975). Conventional neuropsychological tests with a forced-choice format have also been used in this regard. Typically, a word or five-digit number is presented followed by a two-choice recognition task with the original stimulus item along with a distractor. Even if individuals were not presented the target items to remember, they would still obtain scores of about 50% correct simply on the basis of chance. Thus, as test scores decline below chance, it is increasingly likely that the individual is deliberately choosing wrong answers. Of the forced-choice measures, the Hiscock Forced-Choice Procedure (FCP; Hiscock and Hiscock, 1989) and the Portland Digit Recognition Test (Binder and Willis, 1991) have received the greatest attention in the empirical literature.

In the Hiscock FCP, the individual reads a five-digit number followed by a delay interval of 5, 10, or 15 seconds. Two five-digit numbers are then presented on a card, one of which was the number presented prior to the interval, and the individual is asked to identify the target. There are three blocks of 24 trials. Guilmette et al. (1993) reported that the mean group scores for patients with brain dysfunction (n = 20) and psychiatric inpatients (n = 20) were 96% and 98% correct, respectively. The nonpatient simulators (n = 20) instructed to feign impairment attained a significantly lower correct mean of 60%; 34% had scores that were significantly below chance. A cutoff score of 90% correct resulted in accurately classifying 90% of the simulators and patients with brain dysfunction. In a clinical study by Prigatano and Amin (1993), the mean correct score on the FCP was 74% for a group of six "suspected malingerers" and 99.5% for the brain-injured patient group. Similar findings were reported by Martin et al. (1993) using a computerized version of the FCP in differentiating brain-injured patients and normal control subjects from coached simulators. More recently, an abbreviated, 36-item version of the Hiscock FCP has been developed (Guilmette et al., 1994) with similar rates of sensitivity and specificity as the 72-item version. Pritchard and Moses (1992) have extended the Hiscock paradigm with a computer program that uses a dichotomous forced-choice procedure to test audition and vision along with memory.

The Portland Digit Recognition Test (PDRT: Binder and Willis, 1991) is similar to the FCP but uses longer delay intervals between stimulus presentation and response (5, 15, and 30 seconds) and has an interference task of counting backwards during the delay. Binder (1993b) found that mild TBI claimants seeking compensation (n = 47) achieved a group mean of 66% correct on the PDRT while a nonlitigating mixed neurologic disorder patient group (n = 34) obtained 84% correct. In an earlier study, a nonpatient group instructed to malinger (n = 13) got 53% correct with 15% scoring below chance (Binder and Willis, 1991). Cutoff scores for the PDRT have been based on the lowest scores obtained by nonlitigating patients with documented brain dysfunction. Further developments have included an abbreviated form of the PDRT (Binder, 1993a) and a computerized version of the PDRT with the addition of response latency as a measure to improve detection of poor effort (Rose et al., 1995).

Conventional neuropsychological measures with a forced-choice format also have shown promise in differentiating patients with brain dysfunction from analogue simulators and clinical malingerers. Litigating mild TBI claimants (n = 10) attained mean correct scores of 58% on the Words subtest and 56% on the Faces subtest of the Recognition Memory Test (RMT: Warrington, 1984) in contrast to 78% and 70% correct by a group of moderate and severe traumatic brain injury rehabilitation inpatients (n = 20) (Millis, 1992). A discriminant function with both RMT subtests correctly classified 76% of the subjects (Millis, 1992) and was cross-validated on a new sample of subjects with an overall correct classification rate of 83% (n = 86) (Millis and Putnam, 1994). In an analogue study, Iverson and Franzen (1994) reported that students and prison inmates instructed to malinger obtained group means of about 50% correct on both RMT subtests. Cutoff scores were derived for both subtests that accurately classified over 89% of the malingerers and patients with moderate and severe head injuries. Other conventional measures with a forced-choice format that show promise in detecting poor effort are the Seashore Rhythm Test and Speech-Sounds Perception Test (Heaton et al., 1978; Goebel, 1983; Trueblood and Schmidt, 1993). Iverson et al. (1994) developed a brief, forced-choice recognition memory task similar to the RMT, the 21-Item Test, which was effective in discriminating experimental malingerers from a mixed neurologic disorder group.

In summary, the use of forced-choice measures or symptom validity testing in the assessment of patient effort and motivation is strongly recommended. Although below chance performance is convincing evidence of poor effort, these measures do have limitations. The majority of malingerers tend not to perform below chance. In surveying analogue studies in which subjects were instructed to malinger, Hiscock et al. (1994) found that 0 to 34% of the subjects showed below-chance performance. The criterion of below-chance performance to diagnose malingering may be too stringent. A second problem with some forced-choice measures is that the intent of the test can be quite transparent to the malingerer. In response to these limitations, investigators have derived cutoff scores that have acceptable diagnostic efficiency but that are above chance level. A second response has been to use a multivariate approach that is not limited to forced-choice procedures in attempting to differentiate malingerers from patients with brain dysfunction.

MULTIVARIATE METHODS. In one of the earliest investigations that examined patterns of performance on the Halstead-Reitan Neuropsychological Test Battery (HRNTB), Heaton et al. (1978) compared 16 head-injured patients with 16 control subjects instructed to feign neuropsychological impairment. Their discriminant analysis correctly classified 100% of the subjects, but there were more predictor variables than subjects. Despite the methodological shortcomings, this study was influential in providing a particular focus for future research.

Mittenberg et al. (1993a) derived a discriminant function that included eight Wechsler Memory Scale–Revised subtests to differentiate 39 head-injured outpatients from 39 age-matched normal subjects instructed to feign head injury symptoms. Of the subjects, 91% were correctly classified and jackknife cross-validation achieved 87% accuracy. In this same study, the difference score between the Attention-Concentration Index (ACI) and General Memory Index (GMI) was also effective in differentiating the groups. Mittenberg et al. (1993a) found that the simulators' ACI scores tended to be lower than their GMI scores, whereas the head-injured patient group showed the inverse. Andrikopoulos (1995) replicated these ACI-GMI findings with a small group of mildly injured patients who were presumably not giving optimal effort. Bernard et al. (1993) also derived a discriminant function composed of WMS-R subtests that correctly classified 85% of the analogue simulators and 83% of head-injured patients. Cross-validation of the discriminant function on a new sample correctly classified 79% of the simulators and 80% of the patients.

A variety of other conventional neuropsy-chological tests have been used to detect exaggerated impairment. The Wechsler Adult Intelligence Scale–Revised has been used to derive a discriminant function composed of seven subtests that accurately classified 79% of head-injured patients (n = 67) and normal subjects instructed to malinger (n = 67) (Mittenberg et al., 1993b). In the same study, the Vocabulary–Digit Span difference in scale scores correctly classified 71% of the cases in a separate discriminant analysis. Millis et al. (1995) found that a linear composite of three variables from the California Verbal Learning Test (Delis et al., 1987) discriminated patients with moderate and severe brain injuries from litigating mild TBI claimants who scored below chance on a forced-choice measure with an overall hit rate of 91%. Jackknife cross-validation also yielded an overall hit rate of 91%. Iverson and Franzen (1994) reported that a discriminant function containing the WAIS-R Digit Span, Knox Cube Test, and both subtests from the Recognition Memory Test separated a group of experimental malingerers from a combined group of nonpatient control subject and brain-injured patients with an overall 98% correct classification rate and 100% correct on cross-validation.

In summary, the multivariate approach to detecting feigned impairment is likely to be as useful as symptom validity testing. However, many of the discriminant functions need to be cross-validated on new samples. Discriminant analysis uses a mathematical maximization procedure, and shrinkage in predictive power with new samples should be anticipated (Stevens, 1992). Of course, clinicians also need to be aware that the base rate prevalence of malingering in a sample will greatly affect the diagnostic accuracy of any test.

SENSORY-PERCEPTUAL TESTS. The sensory-perceptual examination from the Halstead-Reitan Neuropsychological Test Battery (Reitan and Wolfson, 1993) also shows promise in detecting poor effort. Both analogue simulators and clinical malingerers tend to make more errors on several sensory-perceptual tasks than do brain-injured patients, including Tactile Finger Recognition, Tests for Perception of Bilateral Sensory Stimulation, and Finger-tip Number Writing Perception (Heaton et al., 1978; Binder and Willis, 1991; Trueblood and Schmidt, 1993; Youngjohn et al., 1995). Additional research is needed, however, to determine optimal interpretive strategies and cutoff scores with these procedures.

REY'S TESTS. Rey's Dot Counting and 15-Item Test (Lezak, 1995) have been among the earliest and most popular tests used to detect poor effort in the neuropsychological examination. Overall, empirical support for Rey's test has been mixed, to say the least (e.g., Schretlen et al., 1991; Lee et al., 1992; Greiffenstein et al., 1994; Guilmette et al., 1994; Hiscock et al., 1994; Millis and Kler, 1995). These tests may be sensitive to more blatant forms of malingering, but symptom validity testing and the multivariate models described earlier are diagnostically superior to Rey's tests.

MINNESOTA MULTIPHASIC PERSONALITY INVENTORIES. The MMPI and MMPI-2 are commonly used in neuropsychological examinations (Jarvis and Barth, 1994). These instruments may be especially helpful in characterizing psychosocial and personality factors necessary in understanding neuropsychological test performance as well as overall psychological functioning. Investigations of consecutively admitted mild TBI patients have found that patients often report emotional distress soon after the injury, but tend to exhibit a decrease in symptoms at 12 and 18 months after injury, as measured by the MMPI (Dikmen et al., 1986). Dikmen et al. (1992) have commented that studies reporting elevated MMPI profiles among mild TBI patients 3 to 5 years after injury typically have been based on nonrepresentative samples of mild TBI patients. Thus, elevated MMPI or MMPI-2 profiles in the mild TBI case may alert the clinician to factors other than brain dysfunction that may be influencing patient presentation, such as premorbid psychosocial difficulties, reaction to other injuries sustained, malingering, or response to the litigation process (Dikmen et al., 1992). It is not clear, however, whether individuals who malinger neuropsychological deficits will elevate the traditional MMPI-2 validity scales in the same manner as individuals who exaggerate psychopathology. The nonpatient simulators instructed to malinger cognitive deficits in the studies by Heaton et al. (1978) and Lamb et al. (1994) did produce elevations on the F scale but the mean T scores were below 90.

The Fake Bad Scale (FBS: Lees-Haley et al., 1991) has shown some promise in the assessment of malingering in mild TBI. This scale was found to be significantly higher in a sample of mild TBI patients with persisting symptoms whose WAIS-R FSIQ scores were significantly lower in proximal retesting than a comparable group of patients whose FSIQ scores remained stable or improved (Putnam et al., 1995). Millis et al. (1995a) reported that the FBS differentiated patients with moderate and severe brain injuries (n = 20) from litigating mild TBI claimants who scored below chance on a forced-choice memory test (n = 20). A cutoff score was derived that accurately classified 90% of the patients with moderate and severe brain injuries and 95% of the litigating subjects. These findings are promising but additional work with the FBS is needed. For now, it appears that malingering in the neuropsychological examination is not necessarily accompanied by extreme elevations on F or Fb.

In summary, significantly below chance performance on symptom validity testing is persuasive evidence of exaggerated impairment. But this level of performance is likely to be a rare event in actual clinical practice. Analysis of injury severity information and comprehensive neuropsychological test data are necessary to determine whether a given patient profile is consistent with exaggerated impairment. Just as specific neuropsychological test patterns have been associated with various central nervous system disorders, it is reasonable to expect that feigned impairment has its own patterns of performance. Some of these patterns have been discerned, but much work remains.

Summary

This chapter has focused mainly on the assessment of TBI patients with persisting polysymptomatic complaints and of motivation in these patients. We have attempted to apply literature outside the mainstream of clinical neuropsychology to these complex cases in which symptoms appear disproportionate to the injury itself. We understand that these cases are, for the most part, exceptional, and do not represent the clinical course observed in most patients who have sustained an uncomplicated mild TBI. In a sense we have attempted to look beyond the rather simplistic notion of PCS to consider other factors that may be of probative value in conceptualizing these cases for clinical purposes. Of course, accurate understanding of etiology must precede appropriate intervention, when it is necessary. The premature acceptance of patient reports of disability and polysymptomatology as being directly associated with a mild uncomplicated TBI can be a disservice to the patient. What is needed is a careful consideration of a number of variables that we have attempted to identify in this chapter. To reflexively conclude that because a patient involved in a auto accident or fall reports a host of diagnostically nonspecific symptoms such as headaches, memory difficulties, or fatigue, these must be attributable to the injury is not responsible practice and represents confirmatory bias that retards further investigation and understanding. This may well be the eventual conclusion the examiner arrives at; however, it must be preceded by careful consideration of what is the reasonably expected course of recovery, the base rates of reported symptoms, individual personality variables, potential psychosocial forces impinging on the patient, and the representativeness of the effort delivered by the patient during examination. Of course, these influences can also be operative in cases in which neuropsychological symptoms are bona fide or organically based.

References

Adams, K. M. (1989). The role of emotional factors in neuropsychological assessment. Paper presented at the Northwest Neuropsychological Society Meeting, Seattle, WA.

Adams, K. M., and Putnam, S. H. (1991). What's minor about mild TBI? *Journal of Clinical and Experimental Neuropsychology, 13,* 350–356.

Alexander, M. P. (1992). Neuropsychiatric correlates of persistent postconcussive syndrome. *Journal of Head Trauma Rehabilitation, 7,* 60–69.

Alves, W. M., Colohan, A. R., O'Leary, T. L., Rimel, R. W., and Jane, J. A. (1986). Understanding posttraumatic symptoms after minor head injury. *Journal of Head Trauma Rehabilitation, 1,* 1–12.

Alves, W., Macciocchi, S. N., and Barth, J. T. (1993). Postconcussive symptoms after uncomplicated mild TBI. *Journal of Head Trauma Rehabilitation, 8,* 48–59.

American Psychiatric Association (APA). (1994). *Diagnostic and Statistical Manual of Mental Disorders* (4th ed.). Washington, D.C.: American Psychiatric Association Press.

Andrikopoulos, J. (1995). Disproportionate attention deficit in malingering. *Journal of the International Neuropsychological Society, 1,* 376 (abst.).

Barsky, A. J., and Klerman, G. L. (1983). Overview: Hypochondriasis, bodily complaints, and somatic styles. *American Journal of Psychiatry, 140,* 273–283.

Benton, A. L. (1989). Historical notes on the postconcussional syndrome. In H. S. Levin, H. M. Eisenberg, and A. L. Benton, eds., *Mild Head Injury.* New York: Oxford University Press, pp. 3–7.

Bernard, L. C., McGrath, M. J., and Houston, W. (1993). Discriminating between simulated malingering and closed head injury on the Wechsler Memory Scale-Revised. *Archives of Clinical Neuropsychology, 8,* 539–551.

Binder, L. M. (1986). Persisting symptoms after mild TBI: A review of the postconcussive syndrome. *Journal of Clinical and Experimental Neuropsychology, 8,* 323–346.

Binder, L. M. (1993a). An abbreviated form of the Portland Digit Recognition Test. *The Clinical Neuropsychologist, 7,* 104–107.

Binder, L. M. (1993b). Assessment of malingering after mild head trauma with the Portland Digit Recognition Test. *Journal of Clinical and Experimental Neuropsychology, 15,* 170–182.

Binder, L. M., and Willis, S. C. (1991). Assessment of motivation after financially compensable minor head injury. *Psychological Assessment, 3,* 175–181.

Bohnen, N., and Jolles, J. (1992). Neurobehavioral aspects of postconcussive symptoms after mild head injury. *Journal of Nervous and Mental Disease, 180,* 683–692.

Bronzo, A., Jr., and Powers, G. (1967). Relationship of anxiety with pain threshold. *Journal of Psychology, 66,* 181–183.

Brown, S. J., Fann, J. R., and Grant, I. (1994). Postconcussional disorder: Time to acknowledge a common source of neurobehavioral morbidity. *Journal of Neuropsychiatry and Clinical Neurosciences, 6,* 15–22.

Butcher, J. N., Dahlstrom, W. G., Graham, J. R., Tellegen, A., and Kaemmer, B. (1989). *Minnesota Multiphasic Personality Inventory-2: Manual for Administration and Scoring.* Minneapolis: University of Minnesota Press.

Butcher, J. N., and Harlow, T. (1987). Personality assessment in personal injury cases. In I. B. Weiner and A. K. Hess, eds., *Handbook of Forensic Psychology.* New York: John Wiley and Sons, pp. 128–154.

Caldwell, A. B., and Chase, C. (1977). Diagnosis and treatment of personality factors in chronic low back pain. *Clinical Orthopedics and Related Research, 129,* 141–149.

Carroll, S., Abrahamse, A., and Vaiana, M. (1995). *The Costs of Excess Medical Claims for Automobile Personal Injuries.* Santa Monica, CA: Rand Corporation.

Cavanaugh, J. C. (1987). Age differences in adults' self-reports of memory ability: It depends on how and what you ask. *International Journal of Aging and Human Development, 24,* 271–275.

Cicerone, K. D. (1991). Psychotherapy after mild traumatic brain injury: Relation to the nature and severity of subjective complaints. *Journal of Head Trauma Rehabilitation, 6,* 30–43.

Cole, K. D., and Zarit, S. H. (1984). Psychological deficits in depressed medical patients. *Journal of Nervous and Mental Disease, 172,* 150–155.

Costa, P. T., and McCrae, R. R. (1985). Hypochondriasis, neuroticism, and aging: When are somatic complaints unfounded? *American Psychologist, 40,* 19–28.

Delis, D. C., Kramer, J. H., Kaplan, E., and Ober, B. A. (1987). *California Verbal Learning Test: Adult Version.* San Antonio, TX: The Psychological Corporation.

Dicker, B. G. (1992). Profile of those at risk for minor head injury. *Journal of Head Trauma Rehabilitation, 7,* 83–91.

Dikmen, S. S., and Levin, H. S. (1993). Methodological issues in the study of mild head injury. *Journal of Head Trauma Rehabilitation, 8,* 30–37.

Dikmen, S. S., Machamer, J. E., Winn, H. R., and Temkin, N. R. (1995). Neuropsychological outcome at one-year post head injury. *Neuropsychology, 9,* 80–90.

Dikmen, S. S., McLean, A., and Temkin, N. (1986). Neuropsychological and psychosocial consequences of minor head injury. *Journal of Neurology, Neurosurgery and Psychiatry, 49,* 1227–1232.

Dikmen, S. S., Reitan, R. M., Temkin, N. R., and Machamer, J. E. (1992). Minor and severe head injury emotional sequelae. *Brain Injury, 6,* 477–478.

Dikmen, S. S., Temkin, N. R., and Armsden, G. (1989). Neuropsychological recovery: Relationship to psychosocial functioning and postconcussional complaints. In H. S. Levin, H. M. Eisenberg, and A. L. Benton, eds., *Mild Head Injury.* New York: Oxford University Press, pp. 229–241.

Dikmen, S. S., Temkin, N. R., Machamer, J. E., Holubkov, A. L., Fraser, R. T., and Winn, R. (1994). Employment following traumatic head injuries. *Archives of Neurology, 51,* 177–186.

Escobar, J. I., Burnam, M. A., Karno, M., Forsythe, A., and Golding, J. M. (1987a). Somatization in the community. *Archives of General Psychiatry, 44,* 713–718.

Escobar, J. I., Golding, J. M., Hough, R. L., Karno, M., Burnam, M. A., and Wells, K. B. (1987b). Somatization in the community: Relationship to disability and use of services. *American Journal of Public Health, 77,* 837–840.

Escobar, J. I., Rubio-Stipec, M., Canino, G., and Karno, M. (1989). Somatic symptom index (SSI): A new and abridged somatization construct. Prevalence and epidemiological correlates in two large community samples. *Journal of Nervous and Mental Disease, 177,* 140–146.

Everstine, D. S., and Everstine, L. (1993). *The Trauma Response: Treatment for Emotional Injury.* New York: W. W. Norton.

Fenton, G., McClelland, R., Montgomery, A., MacFlynn, G., and Rutherford, W. (1993). The postconcussional syndrome: Social antecedents and psychological sequelae. *British Journal of Psychiatry, 162,* 493–497.

Ford, C. V. (1983). *The Somatizing Disorders: Illness as a Way of Life.* New York: Elsevier Biomedical.

Gass, C. S., Russell, E. W., and Hamilton, R. A. (1990). Accuracy of MMPI-based inferences regarding memory and concentration in closed-head-trauma patients. *Psychological Assessment, 2,* 175–178.

Gentilini, M., Nichelli, P., Schoenhuber, R., Bortolotti, P., Tonelli, L., Falasca, A., and Merli,

G. A. (1985). Neuropsychological evaluation of mild head injury. *Journal of Neurology, Neurosurgery and Psychiatry, 48,* 137–140.

Goebel, R. A. (1983). Detection of faking on the Halstead-Reitan Neuropsychological Test Battery. *Journal of Clinical Psychology, 39,* 731–742.

Goldstein, F. C., and Levin, H. S. (1995). Post-traumatic and anterograde amnesia following closed head injury. In A. D. Baddeley, B. A. Wilson, and F. N. Watts, eds., *Handbook of Memory Disorders.* New York: Oxford University Press, pp. 187–210.

Gouvier, W. D., Uddo-Crane, M., and Brown, L. M. (1988). Base rates of post-concussional symptoms. *Archives of Clinical Neuropsychology, 3,* 273–278.

Greiffenstein, M. F., Baker, W. J., and Gola, T. (1994). Validation of malingered amnesia measures with a large clinical sample. *Psychological Assessment, 6,* 218–224.

Gronwall, D., and Wrightson, P. (1974). Delayed recovery of intellectual function after minor head injury. *Lancet, 2,* 605–609.

Gronwall, D., and Wrightson, P. (1980). Duration of post-traumatic amnesia after mild head injury. *Journal of Clinical Neuropsychology, 2,* 51–60.

Gronwall, D., Wrightson, P., and Waddell, P. (1990). *Head Injury: The Facts: A Guide for Families and Care-givers.* London: Oxford University Press.

Gruvstad, M., Kebbon, L., and Gruvstad, S. (1958). Social and psychiatric aspects of pre-trauma personality and posttraumatic insufficiency reactions in traumatic head injuries. *Acta Societatis Medicorum Uppsaliensis, 63,* 101–113.

Guilmette, T. J., Hart, K. J., and Giuliano, A. J. (1993). Malingering detection: The use of a forced-choice method in identifying organic versus simulated memory impairment. *The Clinical Neuropsychologist, 7,* 59–69.

Guilmette, T. J., Hart, K. J., Giuliano, A. J., and Leininger, B. E. (1994). Detecting simulated memory impairment: Comparison of the Rey Fifteen-Item Test and the Hiscock Forced-Choice Procedure. *The Clinical Neuropsychologist, 8,* 283–294.

Heaton, R. K., Smith, H. H., Lehman, R.A.W., and Vogt, A. T. (1978). Prospects for faking believable deficits on neuropsychological testing. *Journal of Consulting and Clinical Psychology, 46,* 892–900.

Hiscock, C. K., Branham, J. D., and Hiscock, M. (1994). Detection of feigned cognitive impair-

ment: The two-alternative forced-choice method compared with selected conventional tests. *Journal of Psychopathology and Behavioral Assessment, 16,* 95–110.

Hiscock, M., and Hiscock, C. K. (1989). Refining the forced-choice method for the detection of malingering. *Journal of Clinical and Experimental Neuropsychology, 11,* 967–974.

Iverson, G. L., and Franzen, M. D. (1994). The Recognition Memory Test, Digit Span, and Knox Cube Test as markers of malingered memory impairment. *Assessment, 1,* 323–334.

Iverson, G. L., Franzen, M. D., and McCracken, L. M. (1994). Application of a forced-choice memory procedure designed to detect experimental malingering. *Archives of Clinical Neuropsychology, 9,* 437–450.

Jarvis, P. E., and Barth, J. Y. (1994). *The Halstead-Reitan Neuropsychological Test Battery: A Guide to Interpretation and Clinical Applications.* Odessa, FL: Psychological Assessment Resources.

Jennett, B. (1989). Some international comparisons. In H. S. Levin, H. M. Eisenberg, and A. L. Benton, eds., *Mild Head Injury.* New York: Oxford University Press, pp. 22–34.

Jensen, M. C., Brant-Zawadzki, M. N., Obuchowski, N., Modic, M. T., Malkasian, D., and Ross, J. S. (1994). Magnetic resonance imaging of the lumbar spine in people without back pain. *New England Journal of Medicine, 331,* 69–73.

Kaufman, A. S. (1990). *Assessing Adolescent and Adult Intelligence.* Needham Heights, MA: Allyn and Bacon, Inc.

Kay, T., Newman, B., Cavallo, M., Ezrachi, O., and Resnick, P. (1992). Toward a neuropsychological model of functional disability after mild traumatic brain injury. *Neuropsychology, 6,* 371–384.

Kellner, R. (1991). *Psychosomatic Syndromes and Somatic Symptoms.* Washington, D.C.: American Psychiatric Association Press.

Kellner, R., and Sheffield, B. F. (1973). The one-week prevalence of symptoms in neurotic patients and normals. *American Journal of Psychiatry, 130,* 102–105.

Keshavan, M. S., Channabasavanna, S. M., and Reddy, G. N. (1981). Post-traumatic psychiatric disturbances: Patterns and predictors of outcome. *British Journal of Psychiatry, 138,* 157–160.

Kreutzer, J. S., Gordon, W. A., Rosenthal, M., and Marwitz, J. (1993). Neuropsychological characteristics of patients with brain injury: Preliminary findings from a multicenter investigation. *Journal of Head Trauma Rehabilitation*, 8, 47–59.

Kuhn, T. S. (1970). *The Structure of Scientific Revolutions* (2nd ed.). Chicago: University of Chicago Press.

Lamb, D. G., Berry, D.T.R., Wetter, M. W., and Baer, R. A. (1994). Effects of two types of information on malingering of closed head injury on the MMPI-2: An analog investigation. *Psychological Assessment*, 6, 8–13.

Lee, G. P., Loring, D. W., and Martin, R. C. (1992). Rey's 15-Item Visual Memory Test for the detection of malingering: Normative observations on patients with neurological disorders. *Psychological Assessment*, 4, 43–46.

Lees-Haley, P. R. (1992). Neuropsychological complaint base rates of personal injury claimants. *Forensic Reports*, 5, 385–391.

Lees-Haley, P. R., and Brown, R. S. (1993). Neuropsychological complaint base rates of 170 personal injury claimants. *Archives of Clinical Neuropsychology*, 8, 203–209.

Lees-Haley, P. R., English, L. T., and Glenn, W. J. (1991). A Fake Bad scale on the MMPI-2 for personal injury claimants. *Psychological Reports*, 68, 203–210.

Lees-Haley, P. R., Williams, C. W., and Brown, R. S. (1993). The Barnum effect and personal injury litigation. *American Journal of Forensic Psychology*, 11, 21–28.

Leininger, B. E., Gramling, S. E., Farrell, A. D., Kreutzer, J. S., and Peck, E. A. (1990). Neuropsychological deficits in symptomatic minor head injury patients after concussion and mild concussion. *Journal of Neurology, Neurosurgery and Psychiatry*, 53, 293–296.

Levin, H. S., Gary, H. E., Jr., High, W. M., Jr., Mattis, S., Ruff, R. M., Eisenberg, H. M., Marshall, L. F., and Tabaddor, K. (1987a). Minor head injury and the postconcussional syndrome: Methodological issues in outcome studies. In H. S. Levin, J. Grafman, and H. M. Eisenberg, eds., *Neurobehavioral Recovery from Head Injury*. New York: Oxford University Press, pp. 262–275.

Levin, H. S., Mattis, S., Ruff, R. M., Eisenberg, H. M., Marshall, L. F., Tabaddor, K., High, W. M., Jr., and Frankowski, R. F. (1987b). Neurobehavioral outcome following minor head injury: A three center study. *Journal of Neurosurgery*, 66, 234–243.

Levin, H. S., O'Donnell, V. M., and Grossman, R. G. (1979). The Galveston Orientation and Amnesia Test: A practical scale to assess cognition after head injury. *Journal of Nervous and Mental Diseases*, 167, 675–684.

Lezak, M. D. (1995). *Neuropsychological Assessment* (3rd ed.). New York, NY: Oxford University Press.

MacKenzie, E. J., Shapiro, S., Smith, R. T., Siegel, J. H., Moody, M., and Pitt, A. (1987). Factors influencing return to work following hospitalization for traumatic injury. *American Journal of Public Health*, 77, 329–334.

Martin, R. C., Bolter, J. F., Todd, M. E., Gouvier, W. D., and Niccolls, R. (1993). Effects of sophistication and motivation on the detection of malingered memory performance using a computerized forced-choice task. *Journal of Clinical and Experimental Neuropsychology*, 15, 867–880.

Matarazzo, J. D. (1990). Psychological assessment versus psychological testing: Validation from Binet to the school, clinic, and courtroom. *American Psychologist*, 45, 999–1017.

Matthews, C. (1990). They asked for a speech. *The Clinical Neuropsychologist*, 4, 327–336.

McCrae, R. R., and Costa, P. T. (1982). Self-concept and the stability of personality: Cross-sectional comparisons of self-reports and ratings. *Journal of Personality and Social Psychology*, 43, 1282–1292.

McLean, A. L., Temkin, N. R., Dikmen, S., and Wyler, A. R. (1983). The behavioral sequelae of head injury. *Journal of Clinical Neuropsychology*, 5, 361–376.

McMordie, W. R. (1988). Twenty-year follow-up of the prevailing opinion on the posttraumatic or postconcussional syndrome. *The Clinical Neuropsychologist*, 2, 198–212.

Mechanic, D. (1972). Social psychologic factors affecting the presentation of bodily complaints. *New England Journal of Medicine*, 286, 1132–1139.

Mellergard, M. (1967). Postconcussional complaints. Copenhagen: Munksgaard, Unpublished thesis, 165 pp.

Merskey, H. (1980). Pain and personality. In R. Sternbach, ed., *The Psychology of Pain*. New York: Raven Press, pp. 111–127.

Middelboe, T., Birket-Smith, M., Andersen, H. S., and Friis, M. L. (1992). Personality traits in patients with postconcussional sequelae. *Journal of Personality Disorders*, 6, 246–255.

Mild Traumatic Brain Injury Committee of the Head Injury Interdisciplinary Special Interest Group of the American Congress of Rehabilitation Medicine. (1993). Definition of mild traumatic brain injury. *Journal of Head Trauma Rehabilitation*, 8, 86–87.

Millis, S. R. (1992). The Recognition Memory Test in the detection of malingered and exaggerated memory deficits. *The Clinical Neuropsychologist, 6,* 406–414.

Millis, S. R., and Kler, S. (1995). Limitations of the Rey Fifteen-Item Test in the detection of malingering. *The Clinical Neuropsychologist, 9,* 241–244.

Millis, S. R., and Putnam, S. H. (1994). The Recognition Memory Test in the assessment of memory impairment after financially compensable mild head injury: A replication. *Perceptual and Motor Skills, 79,* 384–386.

Millis, S. R., and Putnam, S. H. (1996). Detection of malingering in postconcussive syndrome. In M. Rizzo and D. Tranel, eds., *Head Injury and Postconcussive Syndrome* (Ch. 25). New York: Churchill Livingstone, pp. 481–498.

Millis, S. R., Putnam, S. H., and Adams, K. M. (1995a). Neuropsychological malingering and the MMPI-2: Old and new indicators. Paper presented at the 30th Annual Symposium on Recent Developments in the USE of the MMPI-2, St. Petersburg Beach, FL.

Millis, S. R., Putnam, S. H., Adams, K. M., and Ricker, J. H. (1995b). The California Verbal Learning Test in the detection of incomplete effort in neuropsychological evaluation. *Psychological Assessment, 7,* 463–471.

Mittenberg, W., Azrin, R., Millsaps, C., and Heilbronner, R. (1993a). Identification of malingered head injury on the Wechsler Memory Scale–Revised. *Psychological Assessment, 5,* 34–40.

Mittenberg, W., DiGiulio, D. V., Perrin, S., and Bass, A. E. (1992). Symptoms following mild head injury: Expectation as etiology. *Journal of Neurology, Neurosurgery and Psychiatry, 55,* 200–204.

Mittenberg, W., Zielinski, R. E., Fichera, S. M., Heilbronner, R., and Youngjohn, J. R. (1993b). Identification of malingered head injury on the Wechsler Adult Intelligence Scale-Revised. Poster presentation at the meeting of the National Academy of Neuropsychology, Phoenix, AZ.

Modlin, H. C. (1967). The postaccident anxiety syndrome: Psychosocial aspects. *American Journal of Psychiatry, 123,* 1008–1012.

Morris, D. B. (1991). *The Culture of Pain.* Berkeley: University of California Press.

Pankratz, L., Fausti, S. A., and Peed, S. (1975). A forced-choice technique to evaluate deafness in the hysterical or malingering patient. *Journal of Consulting and Clinical Psychology, 43,* 421–422.

Parsons, T. (1966). Illness and the role of the physician: A sociological perspective. In W. R.

Scott and E. H. Volkart, eds., *Medical Care: Readings in the Sociology of Medical Institutions.* New York: John Wiley and Sons, pp. 271–280.

Pennebaker, J. W. (1982). *The Psychology of Physical Symptoms.* New York: Springer-Verlag.

Pennebaker, J. W., and Beall, S. K. (1986). Confronting a traumatic event: Toward an understanding of inhibition and disease. *Journal of Abnormal Psychology, 95,* 274–281.

Pennebaker, J. W., Burnam, M. A., Schaeffer, M. A., and Harper, D. C. (1977). Lack of control as a determinant of perceived physical symptoms. *Journal of Personality and Social Psychology, 35,* 167–174.

Pennebaker, J. W., and Epstein, D. (1983). Implicit psychophysiology: Effects of common beliefs and idiosyncratic physiological responses on symptom reporting. *Journal of Personality, 51,* 468–496.

Pennebaker, J. W., Kiecolt-Glaser, J. K., and Glaser, R. (1988). Disclosure of traumas and immune function: Health implications for psychotherapy. *Journal of Consulting and Clinical Psychology, 56,* 239–245.

Pennebaker, J. W., and Skelton, J. A. (1978). Psychological parameters of physical symptoms. *Personality and Social Psychology Bulletin, 4,* 524–530.

Pennebaker, J. W., and Susman, J. R. (1988). Disclosure of traumas and psychosomatic processes. Special issue: Stress and coping in relation to health and disease. *Social Science and Medicine, 26,* 327–332.

Pilowsky, I. (1967). Dimensions of hypochondriasis. *British Journal of Psychiatry, 113,* 89–93.

Pilowsky, I., Smith, Q. P., and Katsikitis, M. (1987). Illness behaviour and general practice utilisation: A prospective study. *Journal of Psychosomatic Research, 31,* 177–183.

Prigatano, G. P., and Amin, K. (1993). Digit Memory Test: Unequivocal cerebral dysfunction and suspected malingering. *Journal of Clinical and Experimental Neuropsychology, 15,* 537–546.

Pritchard, D., and Moses, J. (1992). Tests of neuropsychological malingering. *Forensic Reports, 5,* 287–290.

Putnam, S. H., Adams, K. M., and Schneider, A. M. (1992). One-day test-retest reliability of neuropsychological tests in a personal injury case. *Psychological Assessment, 4,* 312–316.

Putnam, S. H., and DeLuca, J. W. (1990). The *TCN* professional practice survey: Part I: General practices of neuropsychologists in primary employment and private practice settings. *The Clinical Neuropsychologist, 4*, 199–243.

Putnam, S. H., DeLuca, J. W., and Anderson, C. (1994). The second *TCN* salary survey: A survey of neuropsychologists, Part 2. *The Clinical Neuropsychologist, 8*, 245–282.

Putnam, S. H., Kurtz, J. E., Millis, S. R., and Adams, K. M. (1995). MMPI-2 correlates of unexpected cognitive deterioration in traumatic brain injury. Paper presented at the 103rd Annual Convention of the American Psychological Association, New York.

Putnam, S. H., and Millis, S. R. (1994). Psychosocial factors in the development and maintenance of chronic somatic and functional symptoms following mild traumatic brain injury. *Advances in Medical Psychotherapy, 7*, 1–22.

Quill, T. E. (1985). Somatization disorder: One of medicine's blind spots. *Journal of the American Medical Association, 254*, 3075–3079.

Reitan, R. M., and Wolfson, D. (1993). *The Halstead-Reitan Neuropsychological Test Battery: Theory and Clinical Interpretation* (2nd ed.). Tucson: Neuropsychology Press.

Richardson, J.T.E., and Snape, W. (1984). The effects of closed head injury upon human memory: An experimental analysis. *Cognitive Neuropsychology, 1*, 217–231.

Rimel, R. W., Giordani, B., Barth, J. T., Boll, T. J., and Jane, J. A. (1981). Disability caused by minor head injury. *Neurosurgery, 9*, 221–228.

Rose, F. E., Hall, S., and Szalda-Petree, A. D. (1995). Portland Digit Recognition Test-Computerized: Measuring response latency improves the detection of malingering. *The Clinical Neuropsychologist, 9*, 124–134.

Rosenzweig, M. R., and Leiman, A. L. (1982). *Physiological Psychology*. Lexington, MA: D. C. Heath and Company.

Ruff, R. M., Levin, H. S., Mattis, S., High, W. M., Jr., Marshall, L. F., Eisenberg, H. M., and Tabaddor, K. (1989). Recovery of memory after mild head injury: A three-center study. In H. S. Levin, H. M. Eisenberg, and A. L. Benton, eds., *Mild Head Injury*. New York: Oxford University Press, pp. 176–188.

Rutherford, W. H. (1989). Postconcussion symptoms: Relationship to acute neurological indices, individual differences, and circumstances of injury. In H. S. Levin, H. M. Eisenberg, and A. L. Benton, eds., *Mild Head Injury*. New York: Oxford University Press, pp. 217–228.

Rutherford, W. H., Merrett, J. D., and McDonald, J. R. (1979). Symptoms at one year follow-ing concussion from minor head injuries. *Injury, 10*, 225–230.

Schachter, S., and Singer, J. E. (1962). Cognitive, social, and physiological determinants of emotional state. *Psychological Review, 69*, 379–399.

Schretlen, D., Brandt, J., Krafft, L., and Van Gorp, W. (1991). Some caveats in using the Rey 15-Item Memory Test to detect malingered amnesia. *Psychological Assessment, 3*, 667–672.

Schwartz, G. E., Davidson, R. J., and Goleman, D. J. (1978). Patterning of cognitive and somatic processes in the self-regulation of anxiety: Effects of meditation versus exercise. *Psychosomatic Medicine, 40*, 321–328.

Selye, H. (1976). *The Stress of Life*. New York: McGraw-Hill.

Shorter, E. (1992). *From Paralysis to Fatigue: A History of Psychosomatic Illness in the Modern Era*. New York: Free Press.

Stevens, J. (1992). *Applied Multivariate Statistics for the Social Sciences* (2nd ed.). Hillsdale, NJ: Lawrence Erlbaum Associates.

Swartz, M., Landerman, R., George, L., Blazer, D., and Escobar, J. (1990). Somatization disorder. In L. N. Robins and D. Regier, eds., *Psychiatric Disorders in America*. New York: Free Press, pp. 200–257.

Tarter, R. C., Van Thiel, D. H., and Edwards, K. L. (1988). *Medical Neuropsychology: The Impact of Disease on Behavior*. New York: Plenum Press.

Taylor, J. A. (1953). A personality scale of manifest anxiety. *Journal of Abnormal and Social Psychology, 48*, 285–290.

Teasdale, G., and Jennett, B. (1974). Assessment of coma and impaired consciousness: A practical scale. *Lancet, 2*, 81–84.

Trueblood, W., and Schmidt, M. (1993). Malingering and other validity considerations in the neuropsychological evaluation of mild head injury. *Journal of Clinical and Experimental Neuropsychology, 15*, 578–590.

Van Der Kolk, B. (1987). *Psychological Trauma*. Washington, D.C.: American Psychiatric Association Press.

Warrington, E. K. (1984). *Recognition Memory Test. Manual*. Berkshire, England: NFER-Nelson.

Watson, D., and Pennebaker, J. W. (1989). Health complaints, stress, and distress: Exploring the central role of negative affectivity. *Psychological Review, 96*, 234–254.

Watson, R. I. (1967). Psychology: A prescriptive science. *American Psychologist, 22*, 435–443.

Watts, F. N. (1995). Depression and anxiety. In

A. D. Baddeley, B. A. Wilson, and F. N. Watts, eds., *Handbook of Memory Disorders.* New York: John Wiley and Sons, pp. 293–317.

Wechsler, D. (1981). *Wechsler Adult Intelligence Scale-Revised. Manual.* New York: The Psychological Corporation.

Whitehead, W. E., Winget, C., Fedoravicius, A. S., Wooley, S., and Blackwell, B. (1981). Learned illness behavior in patients with irritable bowel syndrome and peptic ulcer. *Digestive Diseases and Sciences, 27,* 202–208.

Williams, J. M., Little, M. M., Scates, S., and Blockman, N. (1987). Memory complaints and abilities among depressed older adults. *Journal of Consulting and Clinical Psychology, 55,* 595–598.

Youngjohn, J. R., Burrows, L., and Erdal, K. (1995). Brain damage or compensation neurosis? The controversial post-concussion syndrome. *The Clinical Neuropsychologist, 9,* 112–123.

Wrightson, P., and Gronwall, D. (1981). Time off work and symptoms after minor head injury. *Injury, 12,* 445–454.

22 Life Quality Outcome in Head Injury

SUREYYA DIKMEN, JOAN MACHAMER, TAMMY SAVOIE,
and NANCY TEMKIN

Traumatic head injuries represent an important health problem: they occur with high frequency; the population affected is, for the most part, previously healthy young people; and they are associated with high mortality and morbidity. Estimates of incidence vary because of how a head injury is defined, the method of case ascertainment used, and the specification of the population at risk. The best estimates are those based on hospitalized cases involving a head injury. The overall estimate of incidence based on seven U.S. studies is about 200/100,000 per year. This rate applied to the United States population of 1993 of 258 million results in about 516,000 cases of new brain injuries per year. This figure includes persons admitted for treatment as well as those who died before reaching a hospital. Approximately 77,000 of these brain injury victims die each year before reaching a hospital (Kraus, 1987; Universal Almanac, 1995). The incidence rate of all head injuries has to be several-folds higher because this figure does not include persons treated in emergency rooms as outpatients or those receiving no medical care. Using the Glasgow Coma Scale (Teasdale and Jennett, 1974) (the most commonly and widely used single index of severity measuring depth of coma), and some additional severity criteria, Gennarelli et al. (1994) reported that among hospitalized patients, approximately 25% of brain injury cases are severe and 9% are

moderately severe; 66% of patients are mildly injured.

The population affected by head injury is primarily young men. Men outnumber women with a ratio of 2 or 3 to 1. The most frequent age range is between 15 and 24 years old, with secondary elevations in childhood and older age. Moving vehicle accidents account for approximately 50% of the cases. Other causes include falls, assaults, and sporting accidents (Kraus, 1987). Although head injury can happen to anyone, there is an overrepresentation in the head-injured population of high risk takers and those with previous complicating circumstances (e.g., heavy alcohol and drug use, lower socioeconomic status, previous head injuries).

Numerous neuropsychological impairments occur as a consequence of traumatic head injuries. These impairments have received considerable clinical and research attention over the past 15 years. The type and severity of these impairments depend on the severity and particulars of the injury. A severe head injury has the potential to impair all major areas of neuropsychological functioning, including various aspects of cognition (e.g., attention, memory, reasoning), emotions (e.g., emotional lability, irritability), and physical abilities (e.g., hemiparesis, disturbance of balance). In contrast, mild head injuries may have selective, or no, long-term neuropsychological consequences (Dikmen et al., 1995a). These primary impairments caused by the trauma to the brain may recover entirely with time or recover partly with persistent residuals (Dikmen et al., 1983). These primary deficits, in turn, may hinder or prevent head-injured persons from functioning effectively in everyday life and fulfilling their primary psychosocial role activities (e.g., work, independent living).

The purpose of this chapter is to review what is currently known about disruptions in psychosocial role or everyday life activities reported in head-injured patients. The chapter has four sections discussing disruption in different psychosocial role activities—global outcome, functional independence and independent living, social integration and leisure activities, and employment—and a conclusion. This is not an exhaustive review of the literature but rather a selective one, both in terms of areas of functioning covered and studies within sections. We will review the evidence for morbidity seen in head-injured patients and risk factors contributing to the morbidity in these many areas of outcome. We also identify some of the gaps that exist in our current knowledge regarding psychosocial morbidity. We do not cover primary impairments in cognitive, emotional, or physical functioning. For a comprehensive review of these impairments, especially the cognitive ones, please refer to Dikmen et al. (1995a), Levin (1992), Levin et al. (1982, 1987), and Brooks (1984).

Global Outcome

The best available information about morbidity pertains to global outcome following severe head injury. This is the result of the standard methods of classifying severity of head injury and outcome proposed by the Glasgow group (Teasdale and Jennett, 1974; Jennett and Bond, 1975)—and their success in enlisting the cooperation of others to use these classifications in multicenter studies. Three large multicenter studies have been carried out over the past 15 years to examine outcome and factors influencing outcome in severely head-injured patients (the International Coma Data Bank, the pilot phase of the National Coma Data Bank [the first two summarized in Eisenberg and Weiner, 1987], and the Full Phase National Coma Data Bank Studies [Foulkes et al., 1991; Marshall et al., 1991; Vollmer et al., 1991]). According to the Glasgow definition, a severe head injury was designated by a Glasgow Coma Scale (GCS) score of 8 or lower at 6 hours or more following the injury. More recently, a severe head injury refers to a GCS of 8 or lower after resuscitation. The GCS is an index of depth of coma at a point in time and is based on responsiveness in eye opening and in verbal and motor modalities. A score of 3 indicates no responsiveness, even to pain, in all three modalities; a score of 15 implies full orientation (Teasdale and Jennett, 1974).

The Glasgow Outcome Scale (GOS) was developed in 1975 by Jennett and Bond to provide broad groupings describing the social capability of persons with brain damage, taking into account both neurological and mental deficits. The five categories of this scale are death, persistent vegetative state, severe disability, moderate disability, and good recovery. The differentiation among severe and moderate disability and good recovery is made on the basis of the patient's dependence on others for self-care activities and on the patient's ability to participate in normal social life, rather than on particular cognitive, neurological, or behavioral difficulties.

To briefly summarize the findings: Although there is some variability between studies, especially in the upper end of the GOS categories (good recovery and moderate disability), the available information, based on a large number of severe head injury cases, indicates that approximately 44% of such patients die, 3% are in a vegetative state, 10% are in the severe disability, 16% in the moderate disability, and 26% in the good recovery categories at about 6 months after the injury. Strong predictors of outcome at the time of hospital discharge include the intracranial diagnosis (e.g., based on computed tomography [CT] scan information including the presence and size of mass lesions, midline shift, and swelling), GCS score, and pupillary reactivity (Marshall et al., 1991). For example, a higher percentage of those with nonevacuated mass lesions or brain stem injuries died; the majority of those with no visible pathology fell into good and moderate disability outcome categories. Swelling (defined as compressed or absent cisterns) or midline shift greater than 5 mm seen on the CT scan was associated with the vegetative state. Head-injured patients with both pupils fixed and unreactive after resuscitation had poor outcome—74% had died or were vegetative at last contact—whereas less than 10% of those with reactive pupils throughout the hospital stay fell into these outcome categories.

Global outcome information is sparse for consecutive series representative of a broad spectrum of head injury severity. Our results, based on GOS at 1 year after the injury for consecutively hospitalized patients, indicated that approximately 70% fell in the good, 16% in the moderate, and 8% in the severe or vegetative categories and 6% of patients had died after 1 month of injury. These figures are based on 231 of 242 consecutively hospitalized adults who had survived to 1 month and who were seen at 1 year (Dikmen et al., 1988—Final Report). The overall outcome for the consecutive series is obviously more optimistic because deaths in the first month were excluded and a large fraction of patients in consecutive series are mildly injured as defined by the GCS at first assessment in the emergency room (13–15 = mild; 9–12 = moderate; 3–8 = severe). One hundred and fifty-two (66%) of the head injury cases were mild, 26 (11%) were moderate, and 53 (23%) were severe.

Global outcome obviously is related to severity of the head injury. Figure 22-1 shows the relationships of various indices of head injury severity and risk factors to GOS at 1 year. This sample consists of 466 cases from three longitudinal studies representing a broad spectrum of head injury severity described in detail elsewhere (Dikmen et al., 1995b). These were patients who were hospitalized and had survived to 1 month. As illustrated in this figure, more severe head injuries, as defined by these various indices,

are related to decreasing proportions of good outcome and increasing levels of disability as defined by the GOS. More specifically, individuals with longer time to following commands (i.e., time from injury to consistently following commands as defined by the motor component of the GCS), deeper coma as defined by the GCS, neurosurgical intervention (e.g., evacuation of subdural or intracerebral hematoma or debridement of contusion), and one or two nonreactive pupils and those with injury-related complications have greater disabilities, as represented by the GOS, than those who do not. The figure also shows that a higher proportion of younger individuals achieved good outcome as compared with older individuals, with noticeable decrease in good outcome after age 50. It is important to point out that the severity indices were examined one at a time without regard for other indices that were present. Therefore, cases with specific indices implying less severe injuries may have other indices suggesting a more severe head injury. For example, patients who experienced less than 1 hour of coma or had GCS scores of 13 to 15 may include cases of significant head injury (e.g., hematoma) and therefore poor outcomes. This, as well as other system injuries (e.g., orthopedic, soft tissue), may explain the fraction of cases with poor outcomes in the milder injury categories. Additionally, when comparing our results for patients who had GCS scores of 3 to 8 with those of the Coma Data Bank, the reader should note that the percentage of those in the Coma Data Bank is based on the total sample of severely head-injured patients whereas ours is based on all patients hospitalized and surviving for at least 1 month.

According to the Glasgow group, recovery from severe head injury occurs early, with only a few patients improving on the GOS ratings after about 6 months post-injury. Results from the International Coma Data Bank of over 500 survivors suggested that about two thirds of those categorized in the good recovery or moderate disability groups at 1 year had reached that category by 3 months and 90% of them had done so by 6 months (Jennett and Teasdale, 1981). A longer follow-up was conducted by Jennett et al.

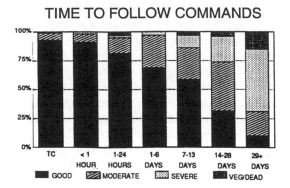

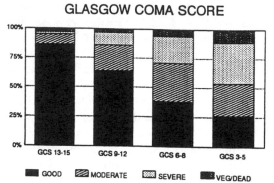

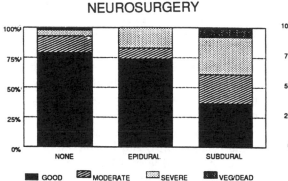

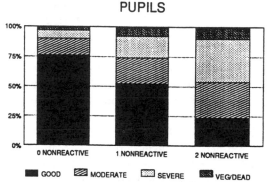

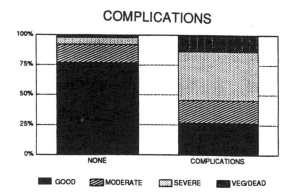

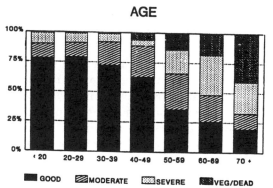

Figure 22-1. The relationship between various head injury severity indices and GOS. The subdural category includes neurosurgical intervention for subdural hematoma, intracerebral hematoma, or debridement of contusion. (Reproduced from Dikmen et al. [1995b] with permission.)

(1981) on 150 head-injured patients from Glasgow. They found that 10% of the subjects who were in the severe or moderate disability categories at 6 months after the injury had improved by at least one category to the moderate or good outcome categories by 1 year. Only 5% of a subset of patients followed up for at least 18 months continued to improve enough to reach another category after 1 year. Jennett and Teasdale (1981) note that although the majority of subjects reached their final GOS category soon after the injury, many continued to recover and show improvement in functioning without a big enough improvement to make a change in GOS category.

Although the GOS is essentially an index of reliance on outside support, some work has gone into delineating the nature of impairments and disabilities represented at its different levels. Clinical observations and the limited research done in this area strongly indicate that the major contributors to the disabilities are cognitive and emotional impairments rather than physical ones. In the 150 head-injured patients seen at least 1 year after the injury by Jennett et al. (1981), the cognitive and emotional components of the impairment were worse than the neurophysical (i.e., hemiparesis, dysphasia, cranial nerve deficits, epilepsy, ataxia) in over half the cases across good, moderate, and severe outcome categories. Levin et al. (1979) found that the level of cognitive impairment varied as a function of level of the GOS. Patients in the moderate and severe disability categories showed greater intellectual impairment than those in the good recovery group (e.g., good recovery median Verbal IQ [VIQ] = 94, Performance IQ [PIQ] = 100; moderate disability median VIQ = 90, PIQ = 88, severe disability median VIQ = 66, PIQ = 60) and also had difficulties with memory. Clifton et al. (1993) found that neuropsychological measures of motor functioning were closely related to GOS at 6 months after the injury. Levin et al. (1979) also found a relationship between behavioral disturbance and the GOS. In particular, they found that behavioral disturbances were common for those in the moderate and severe disability categories and were predominantly characterized by thinking disturbance (e.g., conceptual disorganization) and withdrawal-retardation (emotional withdrawal, motor retardation, blunted affect).

The kinds of psychosocial disabilities experienced within each of the GOS categories have been examined in depth by Tate et al. (1989). They interviewed 87 severely head-injured patients out of 100 consecutive patients who had attended an inpatient rehabilitation program. The interviews occurred on average 6 years after the injury. The areas investigated were vocational and avocational pursuits, functional independence, and social contact including the ability to form and maintain significant relationships. Outcome in these areas was combined to determine an overall assessment of social reintegration. Good reintegration was defined as being employed (full or part time), able to form and maintain significant interpersonal relationships, and able to function independently. For specifics of scoring and different levels of reintegration, please refer to Table 22-1 and to Tate et al. (1989).

Table 22-1 shows various psychosocial disabilities by GOS category for the 87 cases. The results indicate that although almost all of those in the good recovery GOS category were functioning independently in self-care activities and mobility, about half of the subjects were having major difficulties in areas of higher level functioning such as work, forming and maintaining significant interpersonal relationships, and having adequate social contacts and leisure interests.

Those with severe disability rate poorly in almost every aspect of psychosocial functioning. No subject with severe disability was able to live independently, and 94% were fully dependent on others, requiring custodial care. No one was working, and leisure interests were generally nonexistent; almost all the subjects were either socially isolated or had substantially limited social contacts (see Table 22-1). Those with moderate disability seem to be substantially limited, occupying an intermediate position between the good recovery and severe disability groups.

Summary

Considerable information exists on global outcome in severe head injury using the GOS. Outcomes associated with severe head injury are grim. Based on the Coma Data Bank, approximately 45% of patients die early and half of those surviving sustain sufficiently severe impairments to make them totally or significantly dependent on others. Even the good recovery category of the

Table 22-1. Specific Aspects of Psychosocial Reintegration for Good Recovery (GR), Moderate Disability (MD), and Severe Disability (SD)

	GR (n = 45)	MD (n = 26)	SD (n = 16)
Vocational/Avocational [a]			
Level 1	25	1	0
Level 2	15	11	1
Level 3	5	14	15
Significant Relationships [b]			
Level 1	25	3	0
Level 2	20	20	3
Level 3	0	3	13
Functional Independence [c]			
Level 1	42	4	0
Level 2	3	21	1
Level 3	0	1	15
Social Contacts			
Adequate	23	9	1
Limited	9	6	3
Socially isolated	13	11	12
Overall Social Reintegration			
Good	20	1	0
Subtantially limited	25	12	0
Poor	0	13	16

Adapted from Tate et al. (1989) with permission.

[a] Level 1 = employed full-time or part-time or had been post-injury
Level 2 = unemployed but has worked sporadically; sheltered workshop or avocational program
Level 3 = no work or avocational pursuit

[b] Level 1 = able to form and maintain significant interpersonal relationships
Level 2 = major difficulties with significant interpersonal relationships
Level 3 = unable to form significant relationships

[c] Level 1 = functions independently
Level 2 = requires support services and/or supported accommodation
Level 3 = fully dependent, needs custodial care

GOS, which includes approximately 50% of the surviving patients, does not assure close to pre-injury levels of functioning, as the results of Tate et al. (1989) amply document. Regardless of outcome category, cognitive and emotional—rather than neurophysical—impairments appear to be a major source of disability and reliance on others.

It is important to point out that persons with severe head injuries constitute approximately 25% of all those admitted to a hospital with head injury who survive (Gennarelli et al., 1994). The outcomes for the less severe cases are more optimistic, as seen in Figure 22-1 (e.g., GCS 13–15, time to follow commands <1 hour). As noted earlier, however, the GOS lacks detail and is not sufficiently sensitive to pick up more subtle disabilities that are likely to be associated with less severe injuries. Thus, while these results should not be interpreted to imply no difficulties in the "good recovery" group where most of the patients fall, they could be interpreted to mean that major disabilities requiring assistance from others are much less likely in less severely injured cases.

The GOS has been criticized from several perspectives: for its global nature (too few categories of outcome, especially at the high end); insensitivity to the degree of difficulties experienced by the less severely injured; insensitivity to recovery; poor operational definition of the categories, especially moderate disability and good recovery; confusion about how to classify patients if the impairments are due to other system injuries as opposed to central nervous system damage; and the mixing of impairments and disabilities. However, the GOS was meant to be a simple measure of an extremely important aspect of outcome—survival and degree of dependence on others. It was designed to provide a gross measure of functioning that might be predictable from data available soon after the injury. This in turn could help physicians and family in early management decisions about the severely injured patients. The GOS was not intended as a sensitive measure of functioning in head-injured patients, especially for those with mild or moderate head injuries. For the purpose it was intended, it has functioned well and its wide use has improved communication between researchers and clinicians. We now discuss specific disabilities.

Functional Independence and Independent Living

Impairments in functional independence represent the most severe forms of specific disabilities, and are clearly relevant to those with severe head injury. Indeed, most of the research conducted in this area has been done on subjects with severe head injuries. Recently, a few studies have examined functional independence in a series of head-injured patients representing a range of head injury severity. In this section, we will review findings relevant to a person's independence in self-care (i.e., eating, dressing, hygiene), ambulation (i.e., walking, running), mobility (i.e., ability to travel or get from one place to another), and living situation.

Self-Care

In a group of 102 adult patients consecutively admitted to a hospital for their head injury and surviving to 1 month, we found significant difficulties in self-care at 1 month but not at 1 year (McLean et al., 1993). This group included patients with a broad spectrum of head injury severity; about two thirds of the group had sustained milder injuries (i.e., GCS 13–15). At 1 month after the injury, 38% of the total group did not perform self-care activities or performed them with limitations, but by 1 year after the injury only 3% continued to be dependent in this area. Early limitations observed at 1 month appeared to be the result of the effects of the head injury as well as the impact of other system injuries sustained in the same accident. Self-care activities were examined in a more severely injured subgroup (n = 31) of the larger sample at 1, 12, and 24 months after the injury (Dikmen et al., 1993). This subgroup sustained moderate to severe head injuries, with Glasgow Coma Scale scores of 8 or less within 24 hours of the injury and/or post-traumatic amnesia of 2 weeks or more and/or time to follow commands greater than one day. At 1 month after the injury, 26% of the group were not performing any self-care activities and 42% were limited in self-care tasks. Similar to findings in the larger group, however, by 1 year after the injury, 90% of the sample were able to perform self-care without limitations and this percentage increased to 97% 2 years after the injury.

As the severity of the head injury increases, the probability of long-term difficul-ties in self-care activities also increases. For example, Thomsen (1984) followed very severely head-injured patients who had at least 1 month of post-traumatic amnesia (PTA). At 30 months after the injury, 24 out of 40 (60%) of the patients were dependent in self-care. Nine patients needed help washing, dressing, and eating. The remaining 15 could not be left alone. At the second evaluation, 10 to 15 years after the injury, 12 of the patients (30%) still had problems with self-care. Jacobs (1988) surveyed 142 families of severely head-injured patients. The families were chosen from 1700 families whose family member had sustained a severe head injury 1 to 6 years earlier and had received treatment in one of five inpatient rehabilitation programs in Los Angeles. No head injury severity information was provided. His results indicate that approximately 20% of these head-injured persons were dependent in basic self-care skills such as eating, dressing, toileting, grooming, and bathing. Although Jacobs presented no figures, and his results are based on an interview with the family member identified as the primary caregiver, he noted that most of the limitations in basic self-care skills were related to physical problems (e.g., poor balance requiring assistance in the shower). Thirty-seven percent of the patients had difficulties in higher-order self-care skills such as caring for health, personal safety, and purchasing or selecting appropriate clothing. He noted that these higher-order difficulties were related to cognitive deficits (e.g., failure to remember to keep a doctor's appointment).

Ambulation and Mobility

There are few figures available on ambulation and mobility. In our sample of 102 adult consecutive case patients representing a broad spectrum of head injury severity described earlier (McLean et al., 1993), 46% of this group were limited in ambulation (i.e., walking) and 56% were limited in their ability to get from one place to another (i.e., mobility/travel) 1 month after the injury. At 1 year, 28% had limitations in ambulation (i.e., walking, running) and 11% were not able to travel freely. In a subgroup of the sample representing the more severely injured that was followed for 2 years after the injury, limitations in ambulation were reported by approximately 40% at 1 year and 33% at 2 years. Mobility was limited in 25% of the cases at 1 year and 10% at 2 years (Dikmen et al., 1993). Jacobs (1988) reported that 1 to 6 years after the injury, 46% of his severely head-injured sample had problems with walking for long periods of time. Estimates of limitations in ambulation reported by these studies are higher than expected but explainable as they reflect predominantly poor stamina and inability to run or play sports, rather than basic walking. In terms of mobility, or ability to travel, the contribution of physical limitations appear to be negligible. More important are the higher level cognitive problems that seem to restrict travel. Jacobs (1988) found that although 94% of the head-injured subjects were driving before the injury, only 37% were able to do so after the injury, often because of difficulties in following directions or problems with getting lost.

Living Situation

Change in living situation as a function of head injury occurs due to the impaired ability of the individual to live independently. However, determination of deviations from age-appropriate living situations is complicated because this outcome is strongly influenced by the social support available. Living situation was examined in a representative, hospitalized series of 314 head-injured patients who lived independently before the injury and who represented a range of head injury severity (Dikmen et al., 1995b). Living situations considered to be independent included living alone, living with a spouse or significant other, or living with a roommate and/or friends. It is important to add that this index simply reflects living situation and not deficits in independent living skills. Table 22-2 presents living situation as a function of head injury severity. At one year after the injury, head-injured patients were significantly more likely to be living in dependent living situations than their healthy friends or comparison subjects who sustained trauma to body parts other than the head. One year after the injury, 76% of the head-injured patients returned to independent living, 15% lived with parents, and the others lived in more structured settings such as group homes or nursing homes. Living situation was significantly related to the severity of the head injury as measured by time to follow commands (TFC). As TFC increased, the percentage of patients living independently decreased. For example, while 89% of patients with TFC of 1 day or less lived independently at 1 year, this percentage de-

Table 22-2. Living Situation (%) at One Year for Individuals Independent Pre-Injury

| | FC (N = 54) | TC[a] (N = 95) | HI (N = 314) | TFC (Time to Follow Commands) | | | | | | r .49[a] |
				<1 hr (N = 117)	1–24 hr (N = 70)	25h–6d (N = 40)	7–13d[a] (N = 30)	14–28d[a] (N = 26)	≥29d[a] (N = 31)	
Independent	94	93	76	89	89	74	49	55	23	
Parents	6	5	15	11	6	18	30	32	31	
Group home	0	0	1	0	0	2	7	5	2	
Institution	0	0	6	0	1	2	13	8	44	
Other	0	2	1	0	4	4	0	0	0	

Source: Reproduced from Dikmen et al. (1995b) with permission.

FC refers to the friend control group, TC to the trauma control group, and HI to the head-injured group.

Percentages in the trauma controls (TC) column indicate the results of the comparison between trauma controls and the head-injured group as a whole.

Percentages in the TFC columns indicate the results of the comparisons between each TFC group and the trauma control group.

The correlation (r) in the last column reflects the relationship between level of severity (TFC) and outcome (see text).

[a]$p < .001$.

creased to 49% in the 7- to 13-day TFC group and 23% in the 29-day or greater TFC group. The majority of patients who were not living independently were living with parents at 1 year except for those with severe injuries (i.e., TFC ≥29 days); these, besides living with parents (31%), lived in group homes (2%) or nursing homes (44%). This reflects the greater need for support represented by the severely injured.

Other studies have reported living situation changes in more selective groups of patients, typically those with more severe head injuries and those seen in rehabilitation settings. Jacobs (1988), in his severely injured rehabilitation series, reported a decrease in age-appropriate living accommodations and an increase in living situations implying greater dependence on others. He reported a decrease in the percentage of head-injured subjects living with friends (22% before injury versus 9% after injury) or a spouse (31% before versus 22% after), and an increase in the percentage living with parents (35% before versus 48% after) or living in professionally supervised facilities (2% before versus 12% after) 1 to 6 years after the injury. Over time, with advancing age of parents and/or their loss, the head-injured person is oftentimes found to live alone. For instance, in Thomsen's (1984) series 60% of the patients were living with their parents at 2.5 years, a figure that dropped to 22% at 10 to 15 years. In contrast, the percent living alone increased from 8% to 48% over the same time period. The welfare of their head-injured child represents a significant concern for aging parents.

Limitations in higher level independent living skills such as responsibility for household business, money management, and child care occur. Based on reports of significant others, Jacobs (1988) found that 1 to 6 years after the injury 10% of his severely head-injured patients required assistance to accomplish these types of tasks and 39% needed the total support of someone else, although they were functionally independent in these areas before the injury. There are limited data on the cause of this disability, but head injury severity and associated cog-

nitive problems are likely candidates. For example, in our consecutive series (Dikmen et al., 1988), patients who had limitations in home management skills at 1 year after the injury had longer coma and poorer cognitive skills (e.g., median FSIQ = 105 among nonimpaired and FSIQ = 81 in those with impaired home management skills).

Summary

Problems in functional independence most often occur in the acute stages of head injury and in the more severely injured. Other system injuries sustained in the same accident significantly contribute to the limitations in the earlier stages after the injury in both mild and severe head injury cases. Even though subtle difficulties due to other system injuries continue (Dikmen et al., 1995b), significant long-term persistent limitations in self-care and mobility occur primarily in the very severely injured and are relatively rarer than other impairments in psychosocial role activities, to be described later. Difficulties in activities involving ambulation that are more demanding, such as running or playing sports, are more common than difficulties with basic walking. Head injuries are associated with loss of independence in living and this increases with increasing levels of head-injury severity. Among the less severely injured, the patient may move back to the parents' home; among the most severely injured, an increasing proportion of individuals require institutional support. The evidence indicates that the higher level skills required for independent living (i.e., homemaking, child care, money management, etc.) continue to be long-term problems for many more head-injured patients—more so than problems in functional independence. Tate et al. (1989) reported a similar finding in their evaluation of psychosocial functioning in severe head injury subjects classified on the GOS; many of those in the good recovery category had major difficulties in higher level psychosocial functional areas in spite of being independent in self-care and mobility. There are limited data pertaining to the cause of these disabilities. However, physical impairments are likely explanations for disabilities in basic self-care and ambulation; cognitive and emotional/behavioral impairments are likely to account for disabilities in higher level independent living skills.

Social Integration and Leisure Activities

Problems in social relationships are common clinical observations among head-injured patients. As the results by Tate et al. (1989) indicate, they are fairly common even among severely head-injured patients with good recovery according to the GOS and who are functionally independent.

Interpersonal Relationships and Social Activities

Social integration difficulties following head injury have been investigated by examining the interpersonal relationships and social activities of the head-injured patient and by assessing the subjective and objective burden on the patient's family. Social integration was examined by the Social Interaction subscale of the Sickness Impact Profile (SIP) (Bergner et al., 1976) in a series of prospective studies based on patients with a broad spectrum of head injury severity (McLean et al., 1984, 1993; Dikmen et al., 1993, 1995b). Compared to noninjured friends and those with injuries to body parts other than the head, persons with head injuries reported greater alterations in social interactions at 1 year after the injury. The difficulties in this area as measured by the SIP involve increased isolation as reflected in decreased number of friends, decreased length of visits with friends, decreased involvement in social group activities or outings, problems in establishing and maintaining meaningful relationships and increased irritability in interpersonal relationships. The relationship between social interaction problems and head injury severity, however, was poor. It is important to note that patients with severe head injuries with associated severe cognitive problems could not take the SIP, a self-report measure. This, together with lack of

awareness, may have led to lower morbidity estimates in the more severely injured and thus a poorer relationship between severity and outcome.

Brooks (1991) recently reviewed a significant amount of European work on social integration problems of head-injured patients and objective and subjective burden on the family. Most of this work is based on severely injured patients living at home, with the information gathered from relatives of the injured. The informant was a significant other because of concerns about the lack of awareness and ability of the patient to accurately assess social integration difficulties. While questions about the validity of reports of severely injured persons are unavoidable, it is important to point out that other sources of information represent different aspects of the problem and are subject to their own biases. For example, the relative's assessment of the patient is related to the relative's personality and to the stress the relative is experiencing (McKinlay and Brooks, 1984). Thus, different sources of information supplement, but do not replace, each other in portraying different aspects of morbidity.

The nature of the problems reported in these more severe cases is similar to the findings among patients with a broad spectrum of head injury severity examined with the SIP and reported earlier. Problems in the areas of interpersonal relationships and social activities after head injury are evidenced by a decrease in the number of close friends or acquaintances (Oddy et al., 1978b; Weddell et al., 1980), and less frequent outings or visits with others (Oddy and Humphrey, 1980; Weddell et al., 1980). For example, Weddell et al. (1980) found that in their sample of 44 severely head-injured subjects at 2 years after the injury, 21 had no friends they saw as often as once a week and six had no friends at all. These difficulties are related to the severity of the head injury and associated cognitive difficulties (Oddy et al., 1978b; Oddy and Humphrey, 1980). Those with more severe injuries, as indicated by post-traumatic amnesia of more than 1 week, were slower to recover in many areas of social life as compared with those with shorter post-traumatic amnesia (Oddy and Humphrey, 1980). At 6 months after the injury, only the more severely head-injured patients had significantly fewer friends and visited less often with friends as compared to before the injury (Oddy et al., 1978b). By 1 year after the injury, the number of friends held by the severely injured was no longer different from before the injury but the number of visits with others was still significantly less than before (Oddy and Humphrey, 1980).

Personality change in the patient has been identified as a contributing factor in social integration difficulties following the head injury. Hpay (1971) reported that personality characteristics like aggressiveness, increased irritability, or apathy were the main reasons for social pattern changes found in 21% of her severely injured sample. Weddell et al. (1980) found that those with personality change had significantly less contact with pre-injury friends than those without personality change, but there was no difference in the absolute number of friends held by the two groups at 2 years after the injury. The head-injured patients who had personality changes replaced old friendships with superficial relationships after the injury. They became friendly with people they met at the pub, or friends of their parents, or older people who may have been more tolerant of them. The investigators note that those with personality change were also significantly more likely to have memory and other cognitive impairments, be more dependent on their family, have fewer interests, be more frequently bored, and were less likely to have returned to work. Oddy and Humphrey (1980) did not find a relationship between social contact and adverse personality change. The authors note this is different from the findings of other studies, and attribute it to the relatively mild nature of the personality changes found in their sample.

Burden Experienced by Relatives

The other major area of investigation of social integration difficulties following head injury is the burden experienced by the family. Burden has been measured both objectively (i.e., financial aspects) as well as subjectively in terms of the stress or family friction attributed to the head injury. The financial burden of the family is related to the occupational and financial status of the head-injured patient before the injury and to the resources available to the family after the injury. Financial contributions were examined in a group of 330 head-injured patients representing a range of head injury severity who were workers before the injury (Dikmen et al., 1995b). In the year before the injury, 48% of the group were financially independent, 42% received financial assistance from family and/or friends, 5% received contributions from social subsidy systems (e.g. welfare, social security) and 5% from a combination of family/friends and social subsidy systems. The degree of financial independence before the injury probably reflects the demographic characteristics of the sample—many were young, with sporadic work histories. In the year after the injury only 20% were independent financially, with contributions coming from family/friends only (30%), a combination of family/friends and social subsidy systems (32%), or social subsidy systems only (19%). Income earned in the year after the injury decreased significantly as the length of coma increased, although specific information about the relationship between the severity of the head injury and the financial burden on the family was not examined. Other information about the financial impact on the family comes from anecdotal accounts of severe head injury cases rather than systematic research investigations of this topic. Jacobs (1988) interviewed families of severely head-injured patients who had been inpatients in a rehabilitation program. They found that most of the families of the patients they studied had financial problems due to the head injury. These problems were the result of the cost of medical and/or rehabilitation services needed, the adequacy of insurance coverage for these services, and the family's financial status before the injury. All or most of the family's financial resources were used to pay bills associated with the injury in 28% of the cases, and an additional 34% of the families reported mild to moderate financial drain. A number of family members had to give up a job or full-time schooling to take care of the head-injured patient.

Subjective burden on the family of the head-injured patient has been assessed by the amount of friction in the family (Oddy et al., 1978b; Oddy and Humphrey, 1980; Weddell et al., 1980), through depression and anxiety inventories (Oddy et al., 1978a; Livingston et al., 1985), and by subjective burden rated by the relative (McKinlay et al., 1981; Livingston et al., 1985; Brooks et al., 1986, 1987). In general, every study has found positive evidence of subjective burden experienced by family members, regardless of the way it is evaluated. For example, Oddy et al. (1978a) concluded that 25% of the relatives were experiencing significant stress as measured by the Wakefield Depression Scale and the relative's own report. In addition, approximately 25% of the relatives reported being ill since the patient's head injury, with most of the health problems occurring in the emotional area (i.e., received tranquilizers or antidepressants) or in physical problems exacerbated by stress (i.e., migraines, asthma, duodenal ulcer).

Research has consistently found that the subjective burden experienced by the family member is strongly related to the relative's report of adverse behavioral or personality changes in the head-injured patient (Oddy et al., 1978a; McKinlay et al., 1981; Brooks et al., 1986, 1987). McKinlay et al. (1981) found a significant relationship between the post-injury changes in the patient's emotional stability (i.e., temper, irritability, mood swings, depression, etc.), subjective symptoms (i.e., fatigue, poor concentration, headaches, etc.), disturbed behavior (violent and inappropriate social behavior), and the stress experienced by the relatives.

Other factors have not been as clearly related to the subjective burden reported by the family. Some research has indicated that severity of the head injury is significantly related to subjective burden (McKinlay et al., 1981; Brooks et al., 1986) but others have found no relationship (Oddy et al., 1978a). Brooks et al. (1987) found no relationship between the subjective burden experienced by relatives and the severity of the head

injury when PTA lasted 14 days or fewer. However, when PTA was greater than 14 days, the chance of high burden on the relative increased although this was not statistically significant. In addition, no relationship has been found between stress experienced by the relative and either length of hospital stay or degree of physical disability (Oddy et al., 1978a).

Early observations suggested that the stress experienced by the family was better handled by a parent than by the spouse of a severely head-injured patient (Panting and Merry, 1972; Thomsen, 1974). However, more recent findings contradict that. Comparisons between the stress experienced by wives and mothers after the patient's injury found no significant differences (Livingston et al., 1985; Brooks et al., 1987). The perceived burden in both groups was high (Livingston et al., 1985). Often, the concerns of the spouse are different from the concerns of the parent. Rosenbaum and Najenson (1976) reported that wives of severely head-injured men experience many changes in family life, and they find these changes disturbing. With the change of roles, they are faced with a greater responsibility in the care of children and management of household duties, less leisure time, and a restricted social life. They find their husband's disability to be a social handicap and they report that they have been deserted by old friends. Parents report concerns for the future of their dependent children. Weddell et al. (1980) found that many of the parents of disabled sons or daughters were at or beyond retirement age and were having difficulty handling the demands of the situation. Thomsen (1992) recommended that parents find alternative living situations for the dependent family member within a few years after the injury, especially in cases where the son or daughter has a severe behavioral disturbance. Finding long-term care for the dependent child and dealing with long-term financial issues were major preoccupations and concerns for many (Jacobs, 1988).

Several investigators have attempted to examine how perceived burden changes over time after the injury, with conflicting results. All agree that ratings of subjective burden reveal considerable stress in the first year after a severe injury (McKinlay et al., 1981; Livingston et al., 1985), and there is some evidence the relative's burden gets worse over time. Brooks et al. (1986) found that the stress experienced by the family member increased significantly from 1 to 5 years after the injury. Relatives reported more negative and distressing changes in the patient, including an increased incidence of violent behavior toward family members. Many relatives felt the patient could not be left alone. The reason why the subjective burden experienced by the relative gets worse over time may be that there is a genuine change in the patient; or it may be the result of a decreased tolerance for the behavior among family members; or the relative may be increasingly sensitive to the problem, such that it is no longer denied. An additional possibility is that the process of requesting relatives to repeatedly describe patient behavior and judge its relationship to the head injury many years after the occurrence of the injury may directly or indirectly contribute to the attribution (Brooks et al., 1986). These latter interpretations are consistent with the findings of a later cross-sectional study by Brooks et al. (1987) comparing subjective burden levels in relatives assessed one time, 2 to 7 years after the injury. They found consistently high levels of burden regardless of when the relative was evaluated, with no evidence of more burden in those assessed later after the injury as compared with those assessed earlier.

Not all aspects of subjective burden get worse over time. Oddy and Humphrey (1980) found that patients with adverse personality changes had increased family friction at 1 year after the injury if there was a sibling at home. However, by 2 years after the injury, they found no evidence of more friction in the head-injured patient's family than that found in comparison group families. They concluded that family relationships had settled down late after the injury.

Leisure and Recreation

Another aspect of social life affected by head injury is decreased participation in leisure and recreation activities (Oddy and Humphrey, 1980; Oddy et al., 1978b; Weddell et al., 1980). Although this area is an important one, it has not been studied as extensively as other areas of social integration. Significant disruption in leisure activities early and late after injury as examined with the SIP has been reported in patients with a broad spectrum of head injury severity (Dikmen et al., 1995b). As compared with their friends, head-injured patients report more health-related disruption in this area. Part of the disruption appears to be related to other system injuries sustained in the same accident. For example, patients with injuries to other parts of their body but not to the head showed disruption similar to that of patients with less severe head injuries. The type of difficulties reported by patients include cutting down on the number of and time involvement in hobbies, especially those requiring active physical participation, and replacing usual activities by inactive pastimes. Participation in fewer activities at 6, 12, and 24 months after the injury seems to be related to longer post-traumatic amnesia (Oddy et al., 1978b; Oddy and Humphrey, 1980). Oddy et al. (1978b) found a relationship between physical disability and participation in these activities at 6 months after the injury but at 12 and 24 months, physical injury no longer appeared to be a factor (Oddy and Humphrey, 1980). We reported similar results in a group of patients with mild head injury (Dikmen et al., 1986). Note that although many patients participate less frequently in leisure and recreation activities after the injury, this may not be a source of dissatisfaction for many of them. Oddy and Humphrey (1980) reported that patients did not appear to be motivated to perform leisure activities and were satisfied with a more restricted lifestyle. It is important to note that poor motivation and restricted lifestyle themselves are considered to be limitations following severe head injury.

Summary

Traumatic head injury may lead to loss of social network, both in quality and quantity, and impose subjective (e.g., stress) and objective (e.g., financial) hardships on the family. While objective burden is related to the cost of medical and rehabilitation treatment and loss of the patient's income and possibly the income of an additional family member, the reasons for the loss of friendships and for the subjective burden on the family is less clear. Head injury losses that make the injured person a different individual and that lead to role changes in the family are likely to be some of the causes. Subjective burden has been related to changes in behavior and personality of the head-injured person. It is not clear whether other impairments are less important or whether they have just not received as much research attention. Additional debatable questions include whether family stress increases over time and the reasons for it, and whether the stresses felt by wives are greater than those of parents or merely different.

Much of the information available is based on relatives' report because of concerns about the validity of patients' reports. However, the relative's assessment of the patient is related to the relative's personality and the stress the relative is experiencing. The available literature cannot separate the contribution of intrinsic personality of the relative versus relative's stress caused by the patient's behavior to the assessment made by the relative about the patient. An additional serious limitation of the literature is the lack of sufficient attention paid to leisure and pastime activities. Leisure activities become even more important when the patient is unable to work. Based on limited literature, but ample clinical observations, there is a decrease in leisure activities as the result of physical limitations precluding sports and cognitive and personality changes precluding demanding hobbies and outings with others.

Vocational Outcome

Much of the research on vocational outcome of head-injured survivors has focused on determining the percentage of patients who return to work, when they return after the injury, and what factors are related to the success or failure of returning to work. Factors that have been identified as important include indices of the severity of the injury (e.g., head injury severity, the severity of other system injuries, and associated neuropsychological or behavioral problems as a result of the injury) and premorbid variables such as demographic information (e.g., age, education) and prior work history (e.g., job stability, occupation, income). Other factors thought to be important relate to post-injury circumstances of the individual (e.g., social and financial support, rehabilitation services) or the employment environment (e.g., economic climate, employer's attitudes, geographic region). Only a few of these factors have received meaningful research efforts. Vocational outcome will be reviewed first by examining what is known about the effects of each major factor studied on rate of return to work and second by focusing on the difficulties faced by those who do go back to work.

Severity of Injury

NEUROLOGICAL SEVERITY OF BRAIN INJURY. Head injury severity has been evaluated in relation to vocational outcome by neurological indices such as coma length, coma depth, or length of post-traumatic amnesia and by injury-related neuropsychological or behavioral difficulties. Also included in this section is the severity of injuries to body parts other than the head.

The severity of the head injury is probably one of the most important predictors of return to work. Individuals with severe head injuries return to work more slowly or in some cases do not return to work at all, as compared to those with less severe head injuries. This is evidenced clearly in a study using a consecutive series of patients, representing a range of severity (see Table 22-3). Because this study will be referenced heavily in this section, it will be useful to give some details of the methodology. Dikmen et al. (1994) followed 366 head-injured workers for 2 years after the injury to determine the period of post-injury unemployment. Subjects who went back to work were considered as returned, regardless of length of employment. This study included subjects for whom some aspects of employment were reported by Dacey et al. (1991), Fraser et al. (1988), and McLean et al. (1993). The subjects in the study were hospitalized, consecutive admissions to Level 1 Trauma Center and represented a range of head injury severity. Workers were patients who described work as their primary role activity (in contrast to student or homemaker) although they may not have been employed at the time of injury. Severity of the head injury was evaluated by coma length, operationally defined as time to follow commands (TFC), and by coma depth assessed by Glasgow Coma Scale score (GCS) in the emergency room. Time taken to return to work was evaluated with survival methodology. Both TFC and GCS were significantly and systematically related to whether or not patients returned to work and when as seen in Table 22-3. At one month after the injury, the overall return to work rate was low but varied as a function of head injury severity. For example, 29% of the cases with TFC of 5 hours or less had returned to work; no one with TFC of 1 week or greater had gone back by 1 month. Many returned to work between 1 and 6 months after the injury, with substantial increases occurring in this time period for those with TFC of less than 2 weeks. The proportion of patients who returned by 6 months continued to vary as a function of head injury severity, a pattern true for all time frames (e.g., 65% returned in the TFC ≤5 hour group, 30% returned in TFC 7- to 13-day group, 2% returned in the TFC ≥29 day group at 6 months after the injury). By 1 year after the injury, the majority of head-injured patients who were less severely injured had returned to work and the percent return showed little change between 1 and 2 years after injury for these individuals. For example, 82% of the TFC less than or equal to 5 hour group had gone back to work by 1 year and 84% had returned by 2 years. Note that although these return-to-work rates may indicate high morbidity in the less severely injured, changes in employment are not unusual in this age group. A comparison group of workers who sustained trauma to the body but not to the head showed only slightly higher return to work rates at one year after

the injury as compared with those who had less severe head injuries. In contrast, return to work continued to improve between 1 and 2 years in those with more severe head injuries represented by TFC of more than 7 days. However, those with the most severe head injuries with TFC of 29 days or more showed very little improvement in return-to-work rate and only 8% had gone back by 2 years after the injury. Return-to-work rates as a function of the GCS are also provided in Table 22-3 with similar pattern of results to those of TFC.

MacKenzie et al. (1987) reported similar results examining the employment rate of 266 patients 1 year after traumatic injury. Inclusion in the study was based on any traumatic injury requiring hospitalization, not just head injury, and patients were classified on the basis of their most severe injury using the Abbreviated Injury Scale (Petrucelli et al., 1981). Subjects who sustained their most severe injury to the head were divided into groups on the basis of their AIS head score. There was a strong relationship between the severity of the head injury as reflected by the AIS head score and return to work rate at 6 and 12 months after the injury.

A number of studies have focused on return to work in well-defined mild head injury cases and have provided useful information about some factors that seem to influence outcome. Studies of nonhospitalized mild head injury patients generally report better return to work rates than do studies of patients with mild head injuries that require hospitalization. This may be due to greater head injury severity associated with hospitalization as well as the effect of other system injuries sustained in the same accident, which tends to hinder return to work, especially earlier in the recovery process. For example, Dikmen et al. (1986) evaluated the effect of other system injuries on return to major activity in a small group of hospitalized mild head injury cases. One of eight patients with isolated head injury had not resumed major activity at 1 month after the injury in contrast to nine out of eleven patients that had head and other system injuries. In contrast, Wrightson and Gronwall (1981) found that 82% of the nonhospitalized employed men studied who suffered a mild head injury and who sustained no other injuries that would interfere with work had returned to work within 1 week of the injury. All of them had returned within 1 month. Minderhoud et al. (1980) reported on rates of resumption of major prior activities (work or school) for 532 patients who received the diagnosis of concussion and were seen as outpatients following an accident. About 90% of the head-injured patients under the age of 60 had returned to their major activity in less than 3 months.

NEUROPSYCHOLOGICAL IMPAIRMENTS. The mechanisms responsible for unemployment have been investigated by a few studies. Impairments in cognitive functioning and/or behavioral difficulties at least in part reflect the severity of the head injury and are related to failure to return to work. For example, Dikmen et al. (1994) reported that neuropsychological status at 1 month after the injury was significantly related to whether or not a head-injured patient returned to work and when. They examined return to work rates using several indices of neuropsychological status at 1 month after the injury; the Halstead Impairment Index, time taken in seconds to write one's name using the dominant and nondominant hands, and testability (i.e., whether the subject was neurologically intact enough to allow testing). All of the neuropsychological indices significantly differentiated the groups on time to return to work with the lower functioning groups showing lower rates of return (see Table 22-3). The level of performance on neuropsychological measures reflect a combination of head injury severity and premorbid functioning, two factors important in return to work. Note the systematic relationship between the Halstead Impairment Index at 1 month after the injury and percent return to work. For example, 96% of those with 1-month Impairment Index scores of 0 to .2 had returned to work by 1 year after the injury whereas only 35% of the group with the highest Impairment index scores (.8 or worse) had returned by 1 year. The excellent return to work rate

in the best functioning group probably reflects a combination of mild head injury severity and good premorbid functioning. Fraser et al. (1988) reported that employed patients at 1 year demonstrated better neuropsychological functioning at 1 and 12 months after the injury and that the differences in neuropsychological functioning of the employed versus unemployed were more marked than neurological indices of severity. Schwab et al. (1993) also examined the relationship between cognitive functioning and concurrent employment status in 520 Vietnam veterans with penetrating head wounds 15 years after the injury. Variables that were significantly related to unemployment included verbal memory loss, visual perceptual memory deficit, post-traumatic epilepsy, visual field loss, paresis, psychological problems, and violent behavior.

OTHER SYSTEM INJURIES. The severity of other system injuries affects return to work early after the injury. Dikmen et al. (1994) examined the effect of injuries to the body sustained in the same accident as the head injury using the Abbreviated Injury Scale (AIS) score (Petrucelli et al., 1981) for upper and lower extremities and bony pelvis (e.g., contusions, dislocation, sprains, fractures, crush injuries). The Abbreviated Injury Scale evaluates the severity of the injury to different body regions on a scale from 0 (no injury) to 6 (maximum injury). The other variable examined in relation to return to work was a modified Injury Severity Score (ISS) (Baker et al., 1974), which combines the three most severely injured body regions on the AIS, excluding the head region (see Table 22-3). At one month after the injury, the effect of other system injuries showed systematic differences in return to work rates, with a higher percentage of head-injured patients with mild other system injuries (i.e., ISS ≤ 5) returning than those with more severe other system injuries. No one with severe injuries to the body (i.e., ISS ≥ 21) had returned by 1 month. By 6 months after the injury, the differences in percent return to work between patients with mild and moderate other system injuries had disappeared but the re-

Table 22-3. Cumulative Percent of Head-Injured Subjects Who Returned to Work[a]

	(n)	1 Month	6 Months	12 Months	24 Months
Demographics					
Age[b]					
≤20	(50)	14	51	72	77
21–30	(176)	15	50	65	69
31–40	(84)	23	55	72	78
41–50	(29)	24	62	70	73
≥51	(25)	5	32	36	46
Education[c]					
<HS	(64)	10	32	45	46
HS	(182)	12	52	70	76
AA/Voc-Tech Certificate	(74)	22	52	63	71
≥BA/BS	(44)	45	69	86	87
Gender					
Male	(282)	14	51	66	71
Female	(82)	28	45	65	70
Race					
White	(323)	15	51	66	72
Non-white	(41)	29	46	62	62
Marital Status					
Single	(246)	16	48	64	68
Married	(118)	23	58	71	76
Pre-Injury Information					
Stable[d]					
Yes	(207)	23	63	76	80
No	(157)	10	35	53	60
Earnings[c]					
<3000	(48)	14	22	50	56
3000–9999	(94)	18	55	72	79
10,000–19,999	(104)	18	49	64	68
20,000–29,999	(53)	20	56	65	72
≥30,000	(36)	22	76	80	83
Preexisting Condition[b]					
Yes	(130)	16	45	62	65
No	(234)	18	55	69	76
Neurological Severity					
GCS[d]					
≤8	(93)	0	13	26	37
9–12	(56)	4	44	56	64
13–15	(213)	25	63	80	83

turn to work rate for those with more severe other system injuries continued to be low and this pattern continued even at 2 years after the injury. A similar effect over the 2-year period after the injury occurred in the group with severe extremity and bony pelvis injuries (i.e., ≥3). It is important to note, however, that the low return to work rate in patients with severe other system injuries is probably also strongly affected by the severity of the head injury itself because those with severe other system injuries also tend to have severe head injuries (Dacey et al., 1991).

Premorbid Factors

Pre-injury factors such as demographic information, work history, and personality characteristics are considered to be important aspects of return to work. Dikmen et al. (1994) investigated the relationship of several of these factors to employment using the sample previously described.

Table 22-3. *(Continued)*

	(n)	1 Month	6 Months	12 Months	24 Months
TFC[d]					
≤5 hrs.	(177)	29	65	82	84
6–24 hrs.	(43)	4	55	67	70
25 hrs–6 days	(47)	2	45	67	72
7–13 days	(30)	0	30	46	69
14–28 days	(26)	0	9	21	38
≥29 days	(40)	0	2	6	8
Other System Injury Severity					
ISS[c]					
≤5	(150)	26	55	66	72
6–20	(100)	13	53	70	74
≥21	(33)	0	15	32	39
AIS Extremities[c]					
0	(147)	22	55	67	74
1–2	(72)	22	61	70	75
≥3	(64)	6	29	49	52
Neuropsychological Status—1 Month					
Untestable—CNS[d]					
Yes	(53)	0	0	6	16
No	(279)	20	59	77	81
Impairment Index[d]					
≤.2	(79)	38	89	96	96
.3–.4	(72)	20	57	74	75
.5–.7	(53)	10	42	66	73
.8–1.0 (or untestable)	(100)	5	22	35	46
Name Writing D[d]					
≤.50	(109)	34	72	87	88
.51–1.00	(118)	16	59	77	82
≥1.01 (or untestable)	(82)	1	9	19	27
Name Writing ND[d]					
≤1.30	(93)	34	75	88	90
1.31–2.00	(102)	19	62	84	91
≥2.01 (or untestable)	(114)	5	21	31	40

Source: Reproduced from Dikmen et al. (1994) with permission.

[a] HS indicates high school; AA/voc-tech, Associate of Arts or completion of a vocational/technical course; GCS, Glasgow Coma Scale; TFC, time to follow commands; ISS, Injury Severity Score (excluding the head); AIS, Abbreviated Injury Scale; and CNS, central nervous system.

[b] $p < .05$.

[c] $p < .01$.

[d] $p < .0001$.

Demographic characteristics that were significantly related to time to return to work included the age and educational level of the head-injured patient. Head-injured subjects over the age of 50 had lower return to work rates than younger head-injured subjects and it took a longer period of time to return for those who did go back (see Table 22-3). It is not clear why age is important to vocational outcome. Bruckner and Randle (1972) suggest that older patients are less likely to return to work because they are not as adaptable as younger people, and employers are less likely to take back employees with a limited working life. Other possibilities involve greater head injury–related morbidity associated with older age (Goldstein and Levin, 1995; Ross et al., 1995), which may make an older person less competitively employable, and better retirement options available to the older worker. Educational level was also significantly related to rate of return to work (see Table 22-3). Head-injured patients with bachelor's or higher degrees had the highest return to work rates, followed by high school graduates. Those who failed to complete high school were less likely than the others to return to work. Better pre-injury functioning, evidenced by superior intelligence, higher education, and professional training, may aid return to work because of the greater range of skills available (Humphrey and Oddy, 1980).

Rate of return to work is better if relatively more "stable" workers are considered (see Table 22-3). Dikmen et al. (1994) compared return to work rates in stable and sporadic pre-injury workers. Stable was defined as employed at the time of the injury in a job held at least 6 months. The results demonstrated that a higher percentage of stable workers returned to work than sporadic workers. For example, at 6 months after the injury 63% of the stable workers had returned whereas only 35% of the sporadic workers had gone back to work. This difference held at 2 years after the injury, with 80% of the stable workers back to work versus a 60% return rate in the sporadic pre-injury workers.

A different aspect of premorbid functioning has been evaluated by assessing the effect of preexisting conditions (e.g., previous head injury, chronic alcohol abuse) on return to work. It was expected that those with potential adjustment problems before the injury would be further handicapped following the head injury (Humphrey and Oddy, 1980). Dikmen et al. (1994) found a small but significant difference ($p < .05$) on return to work between those with and without preexisting conditions. Pre-injury characteristics are difficult to evaluate because of the variability in the severity of preexisting conditions and associated morbidity (ranging from none to significant), and/or the possibility that the preexisting conditions were resolved prior to the injury and were no longer of immediate relevance.

The best work on the effect of pre-injury functioning on post-injury return to work has been conducted on large samples of veterans from the Korean War (Dresser et al., 1973) and the Vietnam War (Schwab et al., 1993). Dresser et al. (1973) assessed the role of pre-injury cognitive functioning on employment after head injury sustained in the Korean War in 864 veterans. Most of the injuries sustained were penetrating head injuries. They examined the relationship between work status 15 years after the injury and mental status determined before the injury with the Armed Forces Qualification Test (AFQT). They also compared work status as a function of the severity of the injury. They found that the factors that predicted work status were the quality of the pre-injury brain as measured by the army test and the characteristics of the brain damage. Eighty-two percent of those with the best pre-injury scores on the AFQT were employed while 68% of those with the lowest scores on the test were employed. A combination of pre-injury mental status and depth of lesion showed that 52% of those with the lowest test scores and the greatest lesion depth were employed whereas 94% with the best army test scores and no dura penetration were employed. This study nicely illustrates that employment after the injury has much to do with the severity of injury as well as the pre-injury brain that is injured. Schwab et al. (1993) also found that pre-injury test scores on the AFQT were predictive of work status 15 years after the injury in Vietnam veterans. Not unexpectedly, they reported that post-injury intelligence measured by the AFQT 15 years after the injury had a better relationship to work status than the pre-injury assessment. Post-injury intelligence reflects a combination of pre-injury functioning and various aspects of the head injury. Post-injury intelligence combined with brain volume loss did best of all.

Post-injury Factors

Social support after the injury has been identified as a significant factor in a good prognosis for vocational outcome (Gilchrist and Wilkinson, 1979). However, relatively little research has been done in this area for head-injured subjects. The importance of social support in the general outcome of patients with various disabilities is well known. Lehmann et al. (1975) documented that the support available to stroke patients was more important than the severity of their impairments in determining whether or not they lived in the community rather than an institution. MacKenzie et al. (1987) found that social support, defined as the presence of at least one confidant, was one of the factors besides severity with the greatest independent contribution to return to work in their sample of pre-injury workers who had sustained trauma. Their results indicated that the odds of working full-time at 12 months were about twice as great if the patient had one or more confidants.

Multivariate Approach

Very few multivariate studies have been conducted on employment outcome. Dikmen et al. (1994) incorporated demographic information, head and other system injury severity indices, and 1-month post-injury neuropsychological functioning into a multivariate model and found the ability to predict outcome was significantly strengthened. The effect of certain powerful single predictors such as evidence of severe head injury was mitigated or exacerbated in the multivariate model to provide different predictions of outcome than what would have been estimated from the single predictor alone. Schwab et al. (1993) considered a number of disabilities assessed concurrently with work status at 15 years after the injury in Vietnam War veterans. They found that problems in cognitive functioning, neurological deficits, psychological problems and social functioning (i.e., violent behavior) related to work status in an additive fashion, so that the percent of head-injured veterans working showed a steady decrease as the number of disabilities increased.

Vocational Outcome of Returned Workers

The effect of the head injury on the type of job returned to and the head injury–related problems experienced at work have received relatively little study, compared to the amount of effort devoted to whether or not a patient returns at all. Most of the studies that have examined whether the head-injured subject returns to the same job or to another one have found that many of the returned workers go back to a lower level job than their pre-injury one (Bruckner and Randle, 1972; Gilchrist and Wilkinson, 1979; Weddell et al., 1980; van Zomeren and van den Burg, 1985). For example, Weddell et al. (1980) reported that those who were able to return to work 2 years after a severe head injury often had to find a new job. Although a few of these patients were able to find a different job with the same company, many of them had to look elsewhere and had tried a series of jobs. Some of them required assistance at work. In the Oddy and Humphrey (1980) study described earlier, no one who returned to work had been downgraded or had to take a less demanding job. However, they did report subtle changes on the part of some of the employers in terms of their lowered expectations of the employee. Humphrey and Oddy (1980) point out that return to the same job is no guarantee that the person is functioning at the same level on the job.

The effects of head injury on work performance has been reported in cases of mild head injury (Wrightson and Gronwall, 1981) and in the more severely head-injured (Oddy and Humphrey, 1980). Wrightson and Gronwall (1981) found that 60% of the mild head-injured subjects reported symptoms when they first returned to work, and 46% of them said they were not able to do their work as well as before the injury. Twenty percent continued to have symptoms at 90 days after the injury. Oddy and Humphrey (1980), working with more severe cases, found that 24% of the returned workers rated their ability to work at 2 years after the injury as poorer than before the injury.

Summary

Head-injured patients are at increased risk for experiencing problems in returning to

work. Those who do go back experience varying periods of unemployment and experience
difficulties in performing their jobs. However, as the above review indicates, many
factors influence outcome including those related to the person injured (e.g., pre-injury
cognitive competency, pre-injury work history, age, education), those related to the
injuries sustained in the same accident and
their severity (e.g., head injury, other system injuries), and post-injury circumstances
(e.g., social support). The available information clearly indicates that head injury severity is a very important factor and that this
factor most likely derives its importance from
associated neuropsychological and behavioral
impairments that decrease the probability
of competitive employment. Both pre-injury
and post-injury factors (e.g., employer attitude, social support, rehabilitation) may
compound or mitigate the effects of head
injury on employment. Relatively little information is available concerning the effect of
the head injury on job level, job performance, job stability, and other vocational
aspects of those who do return to work,
including the impact of rehabilitation on
outcome.

Chapter Summary

The literature reviewed indicates that head
injuries are associated with disabilities involving resumption of major psychosocial
role activities: in resumption of gainful employment, leisure activities, social integration, and even functional independence. Relatively speaking, impairments in higher level
activities such as work and social integration
are more frequent than impairments in basic
activities of functional independence. Success in resuming psychosocial role activities,
however, is determined by multiple factors.
It obviously matters how successful the individual was in performing those roles prior to
the injury. Injuries sustained in the same
accident, both to the head and to other systems, do matter. What also matter are the
circumstances of the individual after the injury (e.g., social support available). While all
those major sets of factors and their interac-

tions are probably important, the one set for
which most information exists is that pertaining to the head injury and its severity.
The studies that cover a spectrum of head
injury severity clearly demonstrate the
effect.

Head injury severity causes psychosocial
disabilities due to the associated cognitive,
emotional, and physical impairments. Although the literature documenting the neuropsychological mechanisms responsible for
these disabilities is relatively limited, both
clinical observations and the available published information indicate that in the long
term, the cognitive and emotional impairments have a much more limiting influence
than physical impairments. This applies
more to higher order psychosocial activities
than basic activities (e.g., work versus self-
care). Furthermore, although all losses or
changes probably influence the success with
which one resumes previous role activities,
emotional/behavioral changes (e.g., irritability, inappropriate behavior) may be relatively
more important for social integration than for
functional independence or work. Conversely, cognitive losses may be relatively
more important for gainful employment.
Data on differential impact of impairments
on these various outcomes are sparse,
however.

Clinical observations and research over the
past 15 years have increased our understanding of the nature of difficulties experienced
by some head-injured patients. However,
significant gaps exist in our knowledge about
outcome. More adequate information exists
for global outcome as measured by the Glasgow Outcome Scale, return to work, and
living situation. Less information exists for
specific functional independence skills and
for more complex psychosocial activities such
as social interactions, leisure and recreation,
performance on the job, and deficits in
higher level independent living skills. Other
than studies on employment, the majority of
the reports on psychosocial outcomes are
based on severely injured cases. Although
results based on severe cases reflect the difficulties likely to be experienced by the more
severely injured, they say little about the

nature or magnitude of the difficulties of the vast majority of cases who are less severely injured. A common mistake is to generalize the findings based on the more severe injuries to the less severe, and thus to overestimate morbidity due to head injury in general and for those with less severe injuries in particular. While this has drawn welcome attention to the neglected difficulties of head-injured patients, it is important to try to achieve more accurate and realistic estimates of morbidity.

Admittedly, attempting to identify head injury–related disabilities in the less severely injured is a much more challenging task, especially when the disabilities investigated are high order, complex functions such as work and social relationships. The effects of a severe head injury are likely to be marked, overriding the impact of all other factors and detectable by any means of comparison (Dikmen and Temkin, 1987). When the injury is less severe, there are ample opportunities for a poor outcome to be affected by or be the result of factors other than the head injury. The need for increasing rigor in methodology becomes even more important as the head injury severity decreases and the behavioral outcome of interest becomes more complex. While less severe head injuries represent a challenge, they also provide opportunities to investigate non-injury factors that may exacerbate (e.g., lack of social and emotional support) or mitigate (e.g., good coping skills) the effects of injury. Furthermore, despite the difficulties posed to investigations, mild head injury is important because of the large number of cases involved and the magnitude of the associated personal and financial costs.

Finally, most research on outcome following head injury has focused on primary impairments (e.g., neuropsychological test scores). However, if one is interested in the impact of trauma on the individual's ability to function in everyday life or fulfill his or her psychosocial role responsibilities, then one has to move beyond identification of primary impairments due to trauma. Impairments in cognition, emotional functioning and physical abilities may or may not be either felt or deemed relevant, depending on their magnitude on the one hand, and expectancies from the injured individual of his psychosocial role activities on the other hand. Alternatively, the psychosocial disabilities may be disproportionate to the magnitude of impairment. Examination of the relationship between impairments and disabilities and factors related to the individual or environment that exacerbate or mitigate the impact of impairment on disability has the potential of improving our understanding of mechanisms of disability and also increasing the alternatives for preventing or reducing disability.

Acknowledgment

This manuscript was supported by Grant HS06497 from the Agency for Health Care Policy and Research, Grant No. G00 800076 from the National Institute of Disability and Rehabilitation Research, and Grant No. NS 19643 from the National Institutes of Health.

References

Baker, S. P., O'Neill, B., Haddon, W., Jr., and Long, W. B. (1974). The Injury Severity Score: A method for describing patients with multiple injuries and evaluating emergency care. *Journal of Trauma, 14,* 187–196.

Bergner, M., Bobbitt, R. A., Pollard, W. E., Martin, D. P., and Gilson, B. S. (1976). The Sickness Impact Profile: Validation of a health status measure. *Medical Care, 14,* 57–67.

Brooks, D. N. (1991). The head-injured family. *Journal of Clinical and Experimental Neuropsychology, 13,* 155–188.

Brooks, N. (Ed.) (1984). *Closed Head Injury: Psychological, Social and Family Consequences.* Oxford: Oxford University Press.

Brooks, N., Campsie, L., Symington, C., Beattie, A., and McKinlay, W. (1986). The five year outcome of severe blunt head injury: A relative's view. *Journal of Neurology, Neurosurgery and Psychiatry, 49,* 764–770.

Brooks, N., Campsie, L., Symington, C., Beattie, A., and McKinlay, W. (1987). The effects of severe head injury on patient and relative within seven years of injury. *Journal of Head Trauma Rehabilitation, 2,* 1–13.

Bruckner, F. E., and Randle, A.P.H. (1972). Return to work after severe head injuries. *Rheu-*

matology and Physical Medicine, 11, 344–348.

Clifton, G. L., Kreutzer, J. S., Choi, S. C., Devany, C. W., Eisenberg, H. M., Foulkes, M. A., Jane, J. A., Marmarou, A., and Marshall, L. F. (1993). Relationship between Glasgow Outcome Scale and neuropsychological measures after brain injury. *Neurosurgery, 33*, 34–38.

Dacey, R., Dikmen, S., Temkin, N., McLean, A., Armsden, G., and Winn, H. R. (1991). Relative effects of brain and non-brain injuries on neuropsychological and psychosocial outcome. *Journal of Trauma, 31*, 217–222.

Dikmen, S., Machamer, J., and Temkin, N. (1993). Psychosocial outcome in patients with moderate to severe head injury: 2-year follow-up. *Brain Injury, 7*, 113–124.

Dikmen, S. S., Machamer, J. E., Winn, H. R., and Temkin, N. R. (1995a). Neuropsychological outcome at 1-year post head injury. *Neuropsychology, 9*, 80–90.

Dikmen, S., McLean, A., and Temkin, N. (1986). Neuropsychological and psychosocial consequences of minor head injury. *Journal of Neurology, Neurosurgery and Psychiatry, 49*, 1227–1232.

Dikmen, S., Reitan, R. M., and Temkin, N. R. (1983). Neuropsychological recovery in head injury. *Archives of Neurology, 40*, 333–338.

Dikmen, S. S., Ross, B. L., Machamer, J. E., and Temkin, N. R. (1995b). One year psychosocial outcome in head injury. *Journal of the International Neuropsychological Society, 1*, 67–77.

Dikmen, S., and Temkin, N. (1987). Problems and prospects in the determination of head injury effects and recovery in behavioral research. In H. S. Levin, H. M. Eisenberg, and J. Grafman, eds., *Neurobehavioral Recovery from Head Injury.* New York: Oxford University Press, pp. 73–88.

Dikmen, S. S., Temkin, N. R., Machamer, J. E., Holubkov, A. L., Fraser, R. T., and Winn, H. R. (1994). Employment following traumatic head injuries. *Archives of Neurology, 51*, 177–186.

Dikmen, S., Temkin, N., McLean, A., and Dacey, R. (1988). *Patient Characteristics and Head Injury Outcome.* (Final Report, RO1-HS05304). Seattle: University of Washington, Department of Rehabilitation Medicine.

Dresser, A. C., Meirowsky, A. M., Weiss, G. H., McNeel, M. L., Simon, G. A., and Caveness, W. F. (1973). Gainful employment following head injury. Prognostic factors. *Archives of Neurology, 29*, 111–116.

Eisenberg, H. M., and Weiner, R. L. (1987). Input variables: How information from the acute injury can be used to characterize groups of patients for studies of outcome. In H. S. Levin, J. Grafman, and H. M. Eisenberg, eds., *Neurobehavioral Recovery from Head Injury.* New York: Oxford University Press, pp. 13–29.

Foulkes, M. A., Eisenberg, H. M., Jane, J. A., Marmarou, A., Marshall, L. F., and the Traumatic Coma Data Bank Research Group. (1991). The Traumatic Coma Data Bank: Design, methods, and baseline characteristics. *Journal of Neurosurgery, 75* (Suppl.), S8–S13.

Fraser, R., Dikmen, S., McLean, A., Miller, B., and Temkin, N. (1988). Employability of head injury survivors: First year post-injury. *Rehabilitation Counseling Bulletin, 31*, 276–288.

Gennarelli, T. A., Champion, H. R., Copes, W. S., and Sacco, W. J. (1994). Comparison of mortality, morbidity, and severity of 59,713 head-injured patients with 114,447 patients with extracranial injuries. *Journal of Trauma, 37*, 962–968.

Gilchrist, E., and Wilkinson, M. (1979). Some factors determining prognosis in young people with severe head injuries. *Archives of Neurology, 36*, 355–359.

Goldstein, F. C., and Levin, H. S. (1995). Neurobehavioral outcome of traumatic brain injury in older adults: Initial findings. *Journal of Head Trauma Rehabilitation, 10*, 57–73.

Hpay, H. (1971). Psychosocial effects of severe head injury. In Scottish Home and Health Department (Great Britain), eds., *Proceedings of an International Symposium on Head Injuries.* Edinburgh: Churchill Livingstone, pp. 110–121.

Humphrey, M., and Oddy, M. (1980). Return to work after head injury: A review of post-war studies. *Injury, 12*, 107–114.

Jacobs, H. E. (1988). The Los Angeles Head Injury Survey: Procedures and initial findings. *Archives of Physical Medicine and Rehabilitation, 69*, 425–431.

Jennett, B., and Bond, M. (1975). Assessment of outcome after severe brain damage. *Lancet, 1*, 480–484.

Jennett, B., Snoek, J., Bond, M. R., and Brooks, N. (1981). Disability after severe head injury: Observations on the use of the Glasgow Outcome Scale. *Journal of Neurology, Neurosurgery and Psychiatry, 44*, 285–293.

Jennett, B., and Teasdale, G. (1981). *Management of Head Injuries. Contemporary Neurology Series 20.* Philadelphia: F. A. Davis Company.

Kraus, J. F. (1987). Epidemiology of head injury. In P. R. Cooper, ed., *Head Injury*. Baltimore: Williams and Wilkins, pp. 1–19.

Lehmann, J. F., DeLateur, B. J., Fowler, R. S., Jr., Warren, C. G., Arnhold, R., Schertzer, G., Hurka, R., Whitmore, J. J., Masock, A. J., and Chambers, K. H. (1975). Stroke rehabilitation: Outcome and prediction. *Archives of Physical Medicine and Rehabilitation, 56,* 383–389.

Levin, H. S. (1992). Neurobehavioral recovery. *Journal of Neurotrauma, 9* (Suppl. 1), S359–S373.

Levin, H. S., Benton, A. L., and Grossman, R. G. (1982). *Neurobehavioral Consequences of Closed Head Injury.* New York: Oxford University Press.

Levin, H. S., Grafman, J., and Eisenberg, H. M. (1987). *Neurobehavioral Recovery from Head Injury.* New York: Oxford University Press.

Levin, H. S., Grossman, R. G., Rose, J. E., and Teasdale, G. (1979). Long-term neuropsychological outcome of closed head injury. *Journal of Neurosurgery, 50,* 412–422.

Livingston, M. G., Brooks, D. N., and Bond, M. R. (1985). Patient outcome in the year following severe head injury and relatives' psychiatric and social functioning. *Journal of Neurology, Neurosurgery and Psychiatry, 48,* 876–881.

MacKenzie, E. J., Shapiro, S., Smith, R. T., Siegel, J. H., Moody, M., and Pitt, A. (1987). Factors influencing return to work following hospitalization for traumatic injury. *American Journal of Public Health, 77,* 329–334.

Marshall, L. F., Gautille, T., Klauber, M. R., Eisenberg, H. M., Jane, J. A., Luerssen, T. G., Marmarou, A., and Foulkes, M. A. (1991). The outcome of severe closed head injury. *Journal of Neurosurgery, 75* (Suppl.), S28–S36.

McKinlay, W. W., and Brooks, D. N. (1984). Methodological problems in assessing psychosocial recovery following severe head injury. *Journal of Clinical Neuropsychology, 6,* 87–99.

McKinlay, W. W., Brooks, D. N., Bond, M. R., Martinage, D. P., and Marshall, M. M. (1981). The short-term outcome of severe blunt head injury as reported by relatives of the injured persons. *Journal of Neurology, Neurosurgery and Psychiatry, 44,* 527–533.

McLean, A. Jr., Dikmen, S. S., and Temkin, N. R. (1993). Psychosocial recovery after head injury. *Archives of Physical Medicine and Rehabilitation, 74,* 1041–1046.

McLean, A., Jr., Dikmen, S., Temkin, N., Wyler, A. R., and Gale, J. L. (1984). Psychosocial functioning at 1 month after head injury. *Neurosurgery, 14,* 393–399.

Minderhoud, J. M., Boelens, M.E.M., Huizenga, J., and Saan, R. J. (1980). Treatment of minor head injuries. *Clinical Neurology and Neurosurgery, 82,* 127–140.

Oddy, M., and Humphrey M. (1980). Social recovery during the year following severe head injury. *Journal of Neurology, Neurosurgery and Psychiatry, 43,* 798–802.

Oddy, M., Humphrey, M., and Uttley, D. (1978a). Stresses upon the relatives of the head-injured patients. *British Journal of Psychiatry, 133,* 507–513.

Oddy, M., Humphrey, M., and Uttley, D. (1978b). Subjective impairment and social recovery after closed head injury. *Journal of Neurology, Neurosurgery and Psychiatry, 41,* 611–616.

Panting, A., and Merry, P. H. (1972). The long term rehabilitation of severe head injuries with particular reference to the need for social and medical support for the patient's family. *Rehabilitation, 38,* 33–37.

Petrucelli, E., States, J. D., and Hames, L. N. (1981). The Abbreviated Injury Scale: Evolution, usage and future adaptability. *Accident Analysis and Prevention, 13,* 29–35.

Rosenbaum, M., and Najenson, T. (1976). Changes in life patterns and symptoms of low mood as reported by wives of severely brain-injured soldiers. *Journal of Consulting and Clinical Psychology, 44,* 881–888.

Ross, B. L., Dikmen, S. S., and Temkin, N. R. (1995) The relationship between age and psychosocial outcome following traumatic head injury. Paper presented at the meeting of the International Neuropsychological Society, Seattle, WA.

Schwab, K., Grafman, J., Salazar, A. M., and Kraft, J. (1993). Residual impairments and work status 15 years after penetrating head injury: Report from the Vietnam Head Injury Study. *Neurology, 43,* 95–103.

Tate, R. L., Lulham, J. M., Broe, G. A., Strettles, B., and Pfaff, A. (1989). Psychosocial outcome for survivors of severe blunt head injury: The results from a consecutive series of 100 patients. *Journal of Neurology, Neurosurgery and Psychiatry, 52,* 1128–1134.

Teasdale, G., and Jennett, B. (1974). Assessment of coma and impaired consciousness. A practical scale. *Lancet, 2,* 81–84.

Thomsen, I. V. (1974). The patient with severe

head injury and his family. A follow-up study of 50 patients. *Scandinavian Journal of Rehabilitation Medicine, 6,* 180–183.

Thomsen, I. V. (1984). Late outcome of very severe blunt head trauma: A 10–15 year second follow-up. *Journal of Neurology, Neurosurgery and Psychiatry, 47,* 260–268.

Thomsen, I. V. (1992). Late psychosocial outcome in severe traumatic brain injury: Preliminary results of a third follow-up study after 20 years. *Scandinavian Journal of Rehabilitation Medicine Supplement, 26,* 142–152.

Universal Almanac. (1995). Kansas City, MO: Andrews and McMeel.

van Zomeren, A. H., and van den Burg, W. (1985). Residual complaints of patients two years after severe head injury. *Journal of Neurology, Neurosurgery and Psychiatry, 48,* 21–28.

Vollmer, D. G., Torner, J. C., Jane, J. A., Sadovnic, B., Charlebois, D., Eisenberg, H. M., Foulkes, M. A., Marmarou, A. and Marshall, L. F. (1991). Age and outcome following traumatic coma: Why do older patients fare worse? *Journal of Neurosurgery, 75* (Suppl.), S37–S49.

Weddell R., Oddy, M., and Jenkins, D. (1980). Social adjustment after rehabilitation: A two year follow-up of patients with severe head injury. *Psychological Medicine, 10,* 257–263.

Wrightson, P., and Gronwall, D. (1981). Time off work and symptoms after minor head injury. *Injury, 12,* 445–454.

23 The Relationship of Neuropsychological Functioning to Health-Related Quality of Life in Systemic Medical Disease: The Example of Chronic Obstructive Pulmonary Disease

A. JOHN MCSWEENY and KAREN T. LABUHN

The term "quality of life" has enjoyed colloquial use in several human service and health-related fields for some time, yet its use as a scientific concept is relatively recent. There has been a recent upsurge of interest in quality of life, and psychosocial factors in general, in the biomedical fields. A major conceptual impetus to the scientific application of psychosocial concepts in health care was provided by George Engel's (1980) paper on the biopsychosocial model of medicine. Using a systems theory framework, Engel argued that the inclusion of psychosocial information in the formulation of medical concepts, research, and patient care serves to make medicine a more scientific enterprise, when compared to more narrow biomedical models or to nonscientific "holistic" models.

The terms "quality of life" and, more specifically, "health-related quality of life" (Kaplan and Bush, 1982) are related to the psychosocial aspects of Engel's model of medicine (cf. Kaplan, 1990). Although formal studies of behavioral outcomes in medical research date back to the 1960s and earlier (Kaplan, 1990), articles on quality of life in the biomedical fields were quite rare fifteen years ago. Today, quality of life studies are common in the medical literature and several books now review the area in general as well as in reference to specific populations and subject areas (e.g., Wenger et al., 1984; Walker and Rosser, 1988; Spilker, 1990a, 1995; Tupper and Cicerone, 1990).

Neuropsychology has gone through a similar pattern of maturation in its development. Rourke (1982) has provided a brief history of clinical neuropsychology in which he notes that during its early phase the major focus in research was on discovering psychological correlates of localized brain lesions. This research interest had immediate clinical application in the form of neurodiagnosis and was easily comprehended and accepted by colleagues in neurology and neurosurgery. Thus, early lesion location research provided the evidence that clinical neuropsychology was a legitimate professional and scientific enterprise. The second phase of neuropsychology, according to Rourke, involved attempts to better understand the nature of the neuropsychological tasks used in research and clinical practice: neuropsychology's "cognitive" phase. Rourke believes that neuropsychology is now entering a "dynamic" phase that includes the study of brain development and environmental demands in addition to the more traditional interests of neuropsychology. As such, we have seen neuropsychology moving into a variety of new fields relevant to everyday life functioning. In child-oriented research, the major emphasis has been on developing a neuropsychology of learning and learning disabilities. In studies of adults, more emphasis has been placed on investigating the neuropsychological correlates of social role functioning, activities of daily living, emotionals, and related activities—quality of life. This shift of emphasis has been reinforced by the declining practical need for the use of neuropsychology in locating discrete lesions, given improved neuroradiologic techniques (although the diagnosis of diffuse processes such as the dementias remains important) and the concomitant increase in demand for neuropsychological services in rehabilitation settings.

Neuropsychologists are now being asked to go beyond discussing the brain when reporting their findings. Consumers of neuropsychological data want to know what the implications of the data are for the patient's life. Given that this is the case, it makes perfect sense for neuropsychologists to consider quality of life and related psychosocial concepts in their research and practice.

Traditionally, the central nervous system has been *the* organ system of interest to neuropsychologists. Accordingly, neuropsychological research has focused on various forms of primary neuropathology. Recently, the "nets" of neuropsychology have been cast more widely to include studies of systemic diseases that have secondary effects on CNS function. The term "medical neuropsychology" has been coined to characterize these studies. Chronic obstructive pulmonary disease (COPD) represents one of the more intensively studied systemic conditions in medical neuropsychology. In this chapter we use the example of COPD to illustrate strategies of investigating the impact of neuropsychological impairment, linked to a medical disorder, on health-related function and life quality. (For an introduction and overview of COPD, see Rourke and Adams, Chapter 16.)

The Concept of Quality of Life: Definition and Discussion

One result of the intensified interest in psychosocial issues in medicine is the development of the concept of quality of life or "life quality." As might be expected with any relatively new concept, several definitions have been offered. A review of alternative definitions of life quality reveals some com-

monalities but some variations as well, particularly in terms of comprehensiveness, specificity, and theoretical relevance. Some investigators have attempted to follow the dictum of the architect Ludwig Mies Van der Rohe that "Less is More," preferring brevity to complexity. Calman (1984), for example, defined quality of life as "the gap between the patient's expectations and achievements." Similarly, many researchers have utilized a single variable of human functioning, such as employment, general happiness, or sexual functioning, as an indicator of life quality in an ad hoc fashion (Levine and Croog, 1984). In contrast, other investigators have agreed with Dolly Parton that "More is more." Schipper et al. (1990) provide a multidimensional definition that involves five domains: (1) physical functioning, (2) occupational functioning, (3) psychological functioning, (4) social interaction, and (5) somatic sensation. Similarly, Wenger et al. (1984) have provided a very detailed definition of life quality that incorporates three basic dimensions (functional capacity, perceptions, and symptoms) and nine subdimensions (daily routine, social functioning, intellectual functioning, emotional functioning, economic status, health status, well-being or life satisfaction, and symptoms related to the disease under study as well as other diseases). Wenger et al. also provide a detailed rationale for the inclusion of each life-quality criterion.

Another issue in quality of life research is the perspective from which it is defined. Pearlman and Jonsen (1985) note that quality of life can be viewed from the vantage point of the patient, of an "onlooker of another's life situation" (i.e., a relative or physician), or society in general. Williams (1989a) has provided a similar analysis underlining the importance of viewing quality of life from all three viewpoints. The perspective issue is often reduced to a debate over the relative value of "subjective" versus "objective" viewpoints on quality of life, with the usual conclusion that both viewpoints should be considered, although the latter viewpoint is more amenable to scientific study.

McCullough (1984) argues that the perspective issue is quite complex and reflects a more general value issue. He notes that the use of objective measures by clinicians and researchers stems from a "beneficence model" of health care, which assumes that health professionals know "what promotes or protects the best interests of patients." This is a "remarkable claim" according to McCullough. The beneficence model can be contrasted with the "autonomy model," which depends on patients to provide knowledge about what is in their best interests. McCullough concludes that the beneficence and autonomy models have the same final goal: "seeking the greater balance of good over harm for the patient." However, the two models differ in terms of who should decide how to define what *good* or *harm* is, how the goal should be reached (i.e., what treatments should be used), and how the outcome should be measured.

McCullough's work on alternative models of health care and life quality should sensitize those of us who work with patients to the concept that the patient's viewpoint of what constitutes a good quality of life is at least as valid as what a researcher or clinician might suggest. Pearlman and Jonsen's discussion points out that the patient's "significant others," and even society in general may hold additional viewpoints on an appropriate definition of quality of life. From a practical standpoint, researchers and clinicians should try to incorporate these different perspectives in their definitions of quality of life. This is particularly important when the definition of quality of life has potential impact on the treatment of patients.

The preceding discussion points to some of the complexities in the concept of quality of life. More extensive discussions of the concept may be obtained in chapters by Fries and Spitz (1990), Schipper et al. (1990), and Spilker (1990b), which are all in the book edited by Spilker (1990a). The reader is also referred to a more recent book by Spilker (1996) as well as a discussion of the concept of quality of life that is specific to COPD in a paper by Curtis et al. (1994).

Methodological Issues in Health-Related Quality of Life Research

Several recent reviews have discussed the difficulties inherent in the measurement of quality of life (Guyatt et al., 1987c; Williams, 1989a,b; McSweeny, 1990; McSweeny and Labuhn, 1990). In particular, the validity and range of measurement devices represent particularly serious methodological problems in the quality of life research conducted before 1980 (McSweeny et al., 1982). Often authors failed to specify their assessment procedures other than in vague terms such as "psychiatric interview" or "nursing interview."

As Guyatt et al. (1987c) have noted, those studies that used formal psychometric procedures often depended on measures of physical or emotional functioning designed for the general or psychiatric populations. The instrument of choice in many of the early studies was the Minnesota Multiphasic Personality Inventory (MMPI; Dahlstrom et al., 1972). The MMPI has a long history of use in medical research and is the instrument that many medical researchers turn to first when investigating the psychosocial aspects of a medical problem. Unfortunately, this "old favorite" of medical psychologists is inadequate as a single instrument of quality of life. The MMPI is concerned with symptoms of personality and emotional disturbance, which makes it appropriate and useful for psychiatric diagnosis but not appropriate for the goals and hypotheses of most quality of life studies when used in isolation. Other aspects of life quality, including social adjustment, daily activities, and recreational activities, are not addressed by the MMPI or by the studies that used it as a single quality of life measure. In addition, the original clinical scales of the MMPI are heterogeneous in their content, and several, particularly that of depression (scale 2), include a variety of physical symptoms.

Thus, the meaning of a high score on any scale is not always clear without additional analysis. This is especially relevant when one considers the frequent finding of depression in COPD from MMPI-based studies. Toshima et al. (1992a) also note the Center for Epidemiologic Studies Depression Scale (CES-D; Radloff, 1977), which has been used in several studies of COPD, contains items that concern somatic symptoms that are common in chronic diseases. Thus, the CES-D also may not provide an accurate assessment of level of depression in persons with COPD.

Fortunately, the situation in regard to the adequacy of quality of life measurement has improved. The past 15 years have seen significant advancements in the development of the construct of quality of life as well as the instruments designed to measure the construct. Most authors now recommend that several aspects of life quality should be assessed in any study of the concept given its multidimensional nature. In addition, assessment from multiple perspectives—those of the patient, the caregivers, and relatives—are suggested (e.g., Williams, 1989a). Single-perspective, unidimensional, single-instrument evaluations of quality of life are now recognized as inadequate and are becoming rarer.

Psychometricians interested in medical research recently have developed several instruments designed specifically to measure quality of life or similar concepts. This has made it easier for neuropsychologists and life-quality researchers to conduct investigations and clinical work in the area. These instruments vary in their content, comprehensiveness, and established psychometric characteristics, but several show considerable promise. These "general" measures of quality of life—The Sickness Impact Profile (SIP: Bergner et al., 1981; Bergner, 1984), The Quality of Well Being Scale (QWB: Bush, 1984; Kaplan and Anderson, 1990), The McMaster Health Index Questionnaire (MHIQ: Chambers, 1984, 1988), The Nottingham Health Profile (NHP: Hunt et al., 1981; Hunt, 1984), and The Medical Outcomes Study Short Form 36 (MOS–SF-36: Stewart and Ware, 1992; Ware and Sherbourne, 1992)—are reviewed in some detail elsewhere (McSweeny, 1990; McSweeny and Creer, 1995). The basic characteristics of the instruments are offered in Table 23-1.

There is some debate as to the advantages and disadvantages of general versus disease-specific health-related quality of life measures. General measures permit comparisons among populations with different conditions and in general have a longer track record. In addition, they are more likely to detect unexpected effects in studies of any specific disease. Disease-specific measures, on the other hand, can be designed to include items that are particular to the condition being studied, as well as to omit items that are not particular to the condition. This permits brevity and maximizes the probability that the instrument will be sensitive to the effects of treatment. These issues are also discussed in Curtis et al. (1994) and McSweeny and Creer (1995). All things considered, the trend toward the use of disease-specific measures is clear, particularly in studies of cancer (Barofsky and Sugarbaker, 1990) and HIV infection (Wu and Rubin, 1992).

A few COPD-specific quality of life measures are now available. The best known and most completely described is the Chronic Respiratory Disease Questionnaire (CRDQ) developed by Guyatt and his colleagues (Guyatt et al., 1987b) and reviewed by Kaplan et al. (1993). The CRDQ contains 20 questions and covers four dimensions of functioning: dyspnea (shortness of breath), fatigue, emotional function and mastery or "a feeling of control over the disease" (Guyatt et al., 1987b). The CRDQ is administered to the patient by a trained interviewer and requires approximately 20 minutes to complete. In the initial evaluation, Guyatt and his colleagues found that the instrument was reliable and sensitive to the effects of bronchodilator or steroid treatment as well as a rehabilitation program. In addition, changes in the CRDQ were moderately but significantly related to changes in pulmonary function variables, exercise capability, and clinician or self improvement ratings. Subsequent studies (Guyatt et al., 1989; Jaeschke et al., 1989; Cottrell et al., 1992; Elliott et al., 1992; Goldstein et al., 1992; Martin, 1994; Wijkstra et al., 1994) have produced similar evidence for the reliability and validity of the CDRQ.

Table 23-1. Examples of Current Health-related Quality of Life Instruments

Instrument	Dimensions Examined	Length	Administration
Sickness Impact Profile (SIP)	Physical: ambulation, mobility, body care	136 items	Self or interviewer (30 minutes)
	Psychosocial: social interactions, communications, alertness, emotional behavior		
	Other: sleep/rest, eating, work, home management, recreational pastimes		
Quality of Well-being Scale (QWB)	Measures actual performance and preference: self-care, mobility, institutionalization, social activities, reports of symptoms and problems (including mental)	50 items[a]	Interviewer (15 minutes)
McMaster Health Index Questionnaire (MHIQ)	Physical: mobility, self-care, communication, and global physical functioning	59 items	Self-administered (20 minutes)
	Social: general well-being, work/social role performance, social support and participation and global social function		
	Emotional: self-esteem, findings about personal relationships and the future, critical life events, and global emotional functioning		
Medical Outcomes Study Short Form 36 (MOS–SF-36)	Physical functioning, role limitations due to physical problems, social functioning, bodily pain, general mental health, role limitations due to emotional problems, vitality, general health perceptions	36 items	Self-administered (10 minutes)
Nottingham Health Profile (NHP)	Six domains of experience: pain, physical mobility, sleep, emotional reactions, energy, social isolation	45 items	Self-administered (10 minutes)
	Seven domains of daily life: employment, household work, relationships, pesonal life, sex, hobbies, vacations		
Chronic Respiratory Disease Questionnaire (CRDQ)	Dyspnea, fatigue, emotional function, mastery	20 items	Interviewer (20 minutes)

[a]Although there are 50 major questions in the QWB, the incorporation of multiple items for multiple days results in total coverage extending to several hundred responses.

The St. George's Respiratory Questionnaire (SGRQ; Jones et al., 1991) is a 76-item questionnaire that measures three dimensions: (1) symptoms (associated with pulmonary disease), (2) activities (which are likely to be limited by dyspnea), and (3) impacts (social and psychological functioning). Studies conducted by Jones and his colleagues indicate that the test correlates to a respectable degree with the SIP and QWB and appears to be more sensitive than either of the other two instruments to changes in the level of disease severity, especially in cases of mild to moderately severe respiratory disease. In addition, they report significant correlations with specific symptoms of COPD, including dyspnea, exercise capability, and emotional status (Jones et al., 1994).

Other COPD-specific instruments, which are less well documented than the CRDQ and SGRQ, include a longer questionnaire by Guyatt and his colleagues (Guyatt et al., 1987c) and a Dutch questionnaire by Maillé et al. (1994), as well as questionnaires by Hanson (1982), Kinsman et al. (1983), Dardes et al. (1990), Moody et al. (1990,1991), and Cox et al. (1991).

Additional reviews of quality of life measurement are offered in several chapters in the book edited by Spilker (1990a, 1996) as well as in Wenger et al. (1984), Kaplan (1985), Bergner and Rothman (1987), Walker and Rosser (1988), Williams (1989a), Kaplan et al. (1993), Curtis et al. (1994), Jones et al. (1994), and McSweeny and Creer (1995).

Study Design Issues

McSweeny et al. (1982) noted several methodological problems with life quality research in addition to problems with measurement. First, many of the studies were restricted by sample size and representativeness. All of the studies prior to 1980 had sample sizes of less than 50. This fact limited the statistical conclusion validity and external validity (Cook and Campbell, 1979) of the studies. In less technical terms, conclusions drawn from these studies may not be considered to be reliable and cannot be generalized to other patients and settings.

A second methodological issue was noted by McSweeny et al. (1982) in all but one of the reports they reviewed: the lack of comparison groups matched in terms of age, sex, social position, and other factors that must be assessed separately from the effects of the disease to ensure internal validity (Cook and Campbell, 1979). Related to this is the fact that patients with various chronic diseases have very similar psychosocial pro-

files. Casseleth et al. (1984), for example, studied 758 patients from six different diagnostic groups (arthritis, diabetes, cancer, renal disease, dermatological disorders, and depression) using the Mental Health Index, a multiscale instrument concerned with different aspects of psychological distress and well-being (Veit and Ware, 1983). Casseleth et al. found no significant differences among the five groups of patients with a diagnosis of a chronic physical disease, which, in turn, did show some significant differences from the depressed group. Their findings raised the question of just how unique are the psychosocial consequences of COPD, at least when compared with other chronic diseases. Although more recent studies of life quality and COPD have employed control groups matched for the sociodemographic variables mentioned previously, they have not included a control group of patients with other chronic diseases (McSweeny and Labuhn, 1990). Thus, the uniqueness of the psychosocial aspects of COPD remains an open question.

A final problem noted by McSweeny et al. concerned data analysis. Most of the studies in their review contained no formal data analysis or only simple statistics, once again limiting the statistical conclusion validity of the studies. Fortunately, more recent studies have included appropriate methods of statistical data analysis.

Review of Life Quality in COPD

Emotional Disturbance

DEPRESSION. By far the most commonly reported emotional consequence associated with COPD is depression. Depressive symptoms, including pessimism, self-dislike, and feelings of sadness, have been reported in virtually every study of the psychological aspects of COPD as well as in reviews of the literature (Kent, 1977; Dudley et al., 1980; Greenberg et al., 1985; Light et al., 1985; Sandhu, 1986; McSweeny, 1988; Williams, 1989b; McSweeny and Labuhn, 1990; Kaplan et al., 1993; Curtis et al., 1994).

Although initial findings came from studies

in North America, highly similar results have emerged from more recent studies in the United Kingdom (Jones et al, 1989; Williams and Bury, 1989a,b) and Italy (Dardes et al., 1990). In some cases, the consistency across studies reflects the fact that the MMPI was used as the measure of depression and, as noted earlier, the MMPI depression scale contains several items concerned with somatic symptoms. However, depression has been noted to be the predominant emotional difficulty in studies that have used instruments other than the MMPI, including those that have utilized the perspective of a relative (McSweeny et al., 1982; Prigatano et al., 1984, Guyatt et al., 1987c; Jones et al., 1989; Williams and Bury, 1989a,b; Moody et al., 1990, 1991; Toshima et al., 1990, 1992a,b; Cox et al., 1991; Niederman et al., 1991; Eakin et al., 1992).

Depression appears to be a relatively common problem among COPD patients. Agle and Baum (1977) reported "significant" depression in 74% of their patients, whereas Light et al. (1985) and McSweeny et al. (1982) both reported that 42% of their patients were primarily depressed. McSweeny et al. noted that an additional 7% had symptoms of depression combined with other psychiatric symptoms. Toshima et al. (1992a) and Yellowlees (1987) reported lower rates of depression in COPD: 29% and 16%, respectively. The differences between the studies might reflect differences in patient samples and measurement methods, but the basic finding that COPD patients are a high risk for depression is consistent.

Undoubtedly depression is common in many chronic diseases. Friedman and Booth-Kewly (1987) performed a meta-analysis of 101 studies concerned with the psychological aspects of various chronic diseases and found that depression was the most commonly reported psychological symptom. However, in their recent review Kaplan et al. (1993) note that COPD patients are more likely to experience depression than patients with most other chronic diseases.

Opinions vary as to the causes of depression in COPD. Most writers have focused on the psychosocial consequences of COPD such as the loss of pleasurable activities, economic hardship, and difficulties in coping (Barstow, 1974; Dudley et al., 1980; Post and Collins, 1981; Williams, 1989b; Williams and Bury, 1989a). Others have suggested that physiological factors, including the hypoxygenation of the limbic system and related brain mechanisms, might also be relevant factors (Katz, 1980; McSweeny et al., 1982). Labuhn (1984) tested the relative importance of a variety of psychosocial, medical, and physiological factors in the development of depression in a group of 303 COPD patients, using multivariate casual-modeling methods known as path analysis. The results of this study suggest that although physiological factors did play an important role in the development of depression, the depression that COPD patients experience is largely a reaction to their situation. This study is described in more detail later.

More recently, Toshima et al. (1992a) found that level of depression in COPD patients was significantly correlated with measures of functional status, including activities of daily living, exercise endurance, perceptions of self-efficacy, and social support. In contrast, correlations between depression and physiologic measures, such as blood gases, were not generally significant. Toshima et al. also interpreted their data as supporting the functional or situational explanation of depression in COPD.

OTHER EMOTIONAL DISTURBANCES. A variety of other emotional disturbances have been reported in addition to depression. These include anxiety, irritability, hysterical disorders, somatic preoccupation, dependency, and aggressive behavior (Burns and Howell, 1969; Agle et al., 1973; Agle and Baum, 1977; Dudley et al, 1980; McSweeny et al., 1982; Kinsman et al., 1983; Prigatano et al., 1984; Greenberg et al., 1985; Gift et al., 1986; Sandhu, 1986; Guyatt et al., 1987c; Yellowlees et al., 1987; Williams and Bury, 1989a,b; Hodgkin, 1990; Karajgi et al., 1990; Toshima et al., 1990; Jones et al., 1994).

The findings of anxiety and somatic preoccupation appear to be fairly reliable across studies. Anxiety, in particular, is observed in almost all studies of COPD, irrespective of whether the MMPI is employed. It is not difficult to imagine that anxiety and concern about one's bodily condition would be a common occurrence in COPD. As was the case with depression, the rates of anxiety disorders do vary considerably from study to study. Agle and Baum (1977), for example, reported disabling anxiety in 96% of their patients; Yellowlees et al. (1987) reported that 34% of their patients suffered from excessive anxiety. At the lower end of the spectrum, Karajgi et al. (1990) reported that 16% of their COPD patients had an anxiety disorder, whereas Light et al. (1985) reported a rate of only 2%. McSweeny et al. (1982) reported somatic preoccupation in 8.7% of their patients in contrast to 0% in the demographically matched control group.

The findings of hysterical disorders, suspiciousness, and aggressive behavior have been less reliable. Although some of the earlier studies reported hysterical tendencies (e.g., Burns and Howell, 1969), later studies have not consistently confirmed these results. McSweeny et al. (1982) found that 2.7% of their COPD patients exhibited primarily hysterical symptoms compared with 1.5% of the older healthy individuals. In addition, the MMPI hysteria scale, which is often used as the criterion of hysterical complaints, contains a high number of somatic symptoms.

McSweeny et al. (1982) also failed to find unusual degrees of suspiciousness or anger, although relatives of the patients did report a moderately high degree of oppositional behavior. The lack of overt hostility is consistent with the clinical picture of the "emotional straitjacket" described by Dudley et al. (1973). On the basis of Dudley's (1969) classic studies of the psychophysiology of breathing, Dudley et al. (1973) suggested that the COPD patient learns to avoid the expression of strong emotions, including anger, to prevent the excessive oxygen uptake that occurs in conjunction with physiological arousal. This relationship between dyspnea and emotional status was also observed by Burns and Howell (1969), who found that "disproportionately breathless"

COPD patients had higher rates of emotional distress than the remaining COPD patients. In addition, the dyspnea improved with the resolution of emotional disturbance.

Social Role Functioning and Activities of Daily Living

GENERAL ACTIVITIES. The performance of basic social roles and activities of daily living (ADL) is often used as a standard for the impact of a disease entity on quality of life. Although early studies of COPD and quality of life concentrated on emotional functioning, several recent studies in North America, the United Kingdom and Europe have described the impact of COPD on social role functioning and ADL in some detail.

A relatively early study was conducted by Barstow (1974). She reported that "major changes" were evident in the "style of living" manifested by the COPD patients in her study. These included alterations in bathing, grooming, dressing, eating, sleeping, and mobility. She noticed, for example, that "the mode of dress was altered in favor of less restrictive clothing that was easily slipped on and off." Food intake was decreased by many of the patients because an overdistended stomach would interfere with diaphragmatic breathing. Sleep/rest difficulties received particular attention in Barstow's report. Disruptions of sleep because of cough, dyspnea, or restlessness were common. In addition, Barstow reported some sleep changes that were apparently related to endogenous depression.

The availability of the SIP in the late 1970s led to a series of studies on the effects of chronic illness with that instrument. Four such studies had been completed in the past decade. The first, conducted by McSweeny et al. (1982), revealed a broad range of disturbances in sleep and rest and activities of daily living. In all categories of the SIP except one, COPD patients reported a much higher percentage of impairment than did control subjects. The only category not affected differentially was employment, presumably because the COPD and control groups both contained many elderly retired persons. The areas of functioning found most severely affected were home management and sleep/rest. Eating and communication, on the other hand, seemed to be only moderately affected by the disease (Fig. 23-1). Additional results from the Katz Adjustment Scale–Form R (KAS-R; Katz and Lyerly, 1963), which represented the viewpoint of relatives, indicated that relatives regarded the patient's social role functioning as deficient; they expected less of the patients but still felt dissatisfied with the patients' performance of socially expected activities.

Prigatano et al. (1984) also utilized the SIP and KAS-R with COPD patients who had mild hypoxemia. Their findings were quite similar to those obtained by McSweeny et al. with severely hypoxemic patients, although, as might be expected, the degree of impairment was proportionately less. One interesting exception was that Prigatano et al. did find significant differences in employment status between COPD patients and controls. This appears to be because the control subjects in the study of Prigatano et al. were much more likely to be employed than those in that of McSweeny et al. (1982). This, in turn, is the result of a greater proportion of persons younger than 65 among the patients and controls in the Prigatano et al. study. In summary, employment status is more likely to be a significant issue for younger patients than for older patients and may be affected even in those who have small reductions in the availability of oxygenated blood.

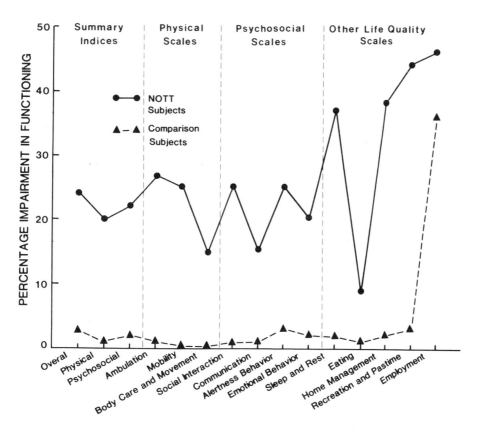

Figure 23-1. Mean Sickness Impact Profiles for patients with chronic obstructive pulmonary disease (COPD) and control subjects. Patients with COPD are significantly ($p < 0.001$) more impaired on all scales except employment using paired t tests (n = 66). NOTT = nocturnal oxygen therapy trial. (From McSweeny et al., 1982. Copyright, American Medical Association. Reprinted with permission.)

A third U.S. study with the SIP was conducted by Bergner et al. (1988) with three groups of COPD outpatients receiving home or office care. These patients, accordingly, were less ill than those in the McSweeny et al. study and, as was the case with the Prigatano et al. study, they were less impaired, although the overall level of impairment was still much higher than expected relative to norms.

Williams and Bury (1989a,b) studied 92 outpatients with COPD who, on average, were similar in severity of airways impairment and socioeconomic status to the patients in the study by Prigatano et al. (1984). Williams and Bury utilized a version of the SIP modified for use by British patients. Despite the differences in wording and the location of study (England versus the United States), the results were virtually identical to those of Prigatano et al. and differed from those of McSweeny et al. only in terms of degree of impairment.

A second British team, Jones et al. (1989), studied 160 outpatients who were slightly less impaired overall than the samples of Williams and Bury and Prigatano et al. in terms of lung function. Unlike Williams and Bury, Jones et al. used the standard SIP. The overall level of impairment was considerably lower than in the previous studies although for the most part the pattern of impairment was similar. Interestingly, employment was not greatly impaired in the Jones et al. study and it is worth noting that the patients were closer in age to those in the McSweeny et al. sample, which tends to confirm the point made earlier about the relationship of age to the significance of employment. Another interesting finding from Jones et al. was a correlation between quality of life as measured by the SIP and walking distance that was significantly higher than the correlation between spirometric (lung function) indices and walking distance.

Most recently, studies of COPD using the SIP have been conducted in Holland (Schrier et al., 1990) and Sweden (Ström et al., 1990). The Dutch study is particularly interesting because patients at a relatively early stage of the disease were included. As might be expected, the SIP profile for these patients are much more similar to those for normal elderly than the profiles from most of the other studies with the SIP. Still, significant differences between the patients and normal elderly were found for the three summary indices (Overall, Physical, and Psychosocial) as well as for the specific indices of Communication, Emotional Behavior, Sleep/Rest, Eating, Home Management, and Employment. Consistent with other studies, the authors found little relationship between SIP scores and lung function parameters.

Not all recent studies of COPD and quality of life have employed the SIP, of course. Other studies have employed the NHP (Alonso et al., 1992; Dompeling et al. 1992; van Schayck et al., 1992), the CRDQ (Guyatt et al., 1987b, 1989; Jaeschke et al., 1989; Cottrell et al., 1992; Elliott et al., 1992; Goldstein et al., 1992; Martin, 1994), the QWB (Kaplan et al., 1984; Anderson et al., 1989; Toshima et al., 1990; Eakin et al., 1992), the SGRQ (Jones et al., 1994), or alternative methods of assessing general life functioning (Kinsman et al., 1983; Guyatt et al., 1987c; Dardes et al., 1990; Moody et al., 1990, 1991; Cox et al., 1991; Maillé et al., 1994) and have produced comparable results. A questionnaire survey of 130 COPD patients by Hanson (1982) deserves some particular attention. Her survey included 40 questions about 11 areas, including several aspects of social role functioning and activities of daily living such as employment, self-care, home/personal business, marriage, care of grandchildren, and dependency on others. Hanson's results were consistent with those from the SIP-based studies in that she found a general negative effect of COPD across the different categories in her survey. One interesting aspect of her study is that her questionnaire was bipolar; that is, it allowed respondents to indicate a positive impact of COPD on different life areas as well as a negative impact. In fact, a few individuals did indicate a positive effect, ranging from 28% for care of grandchildren to 40% for marriage. One might be tempted to conclude that there is some benefit to adversity, but the meaning of her results are unclear given the lack of a comparison sample.

The samples in the studies described above were predominantly male. This is related to the fact that until recently, smoking was a predominantly male activity. Sexton and Monro (1988) have provided a specific investigation of female COPD patients. Seventy-two women with diagnosed COPD and 40 demographically similar women who had no chronic illness were compared on their perceived health status, problems of daily living, amount of subjective stress, and life satisfaction. In comparison with their healthy controls, the female COPD patients were found to have lower perceived health status, more subjective stress, and less life satisfaction. They also reported more problems in daily living. Major problems included shortness of breath and fatigue, loneliness and depression, and restricted household and social activities.

SEXUAL FUNCTIONING. One topic not assessed in detail in most of the previously described studies was that of sexual functioning. Other investigators, however, have paid more attention to this important aspect of life quality. In one of the earlier studies on the topic, Kass et al. (1972) reported that 19% of their male COPD patients were impotent. More recent studies have suggested even higher rates of sexual dysfunction among men. Fletcher and Martin (1982), for example, reported that 30% of their COPD patients were impotent and that an additional 5% had ceased intercourse because of dyspnea. Frequency of intercourse for the remaining 65% of their patients fell to 16% of predisease levels.

Sexton and Munro's (1985) study of the impact of COPD on the spouse's life also provides evidence of sexual dysfunction associated with the disease. These investigators compared the subjective experiences of 45 wives of male COPD patients with those of 30 age-matched women whose husbands had no chronic illness. The COPD wives reported significantly fewer marital relations than did the comparison wives. Fifty-four percent of the COPD wives no longer engaged in sexual relations. Forty-eight percent of these wives, versus 15% of the controls stated that they had no desire for sexual relations. The wives of the COPD patients also gave significantly lower ratings on their own health status, and this may account for their lack of sexual interest. Health differences between these two groups of age-matched wives could also be due to stressors related to living with a COPD patient, however. The COPD wives reported many difficulties with sleeping as the result of their husbands' breathing problems. They also had taken on many extra responsibilities and had given up many of their own social activities because of their husbands' illnesses.

Only limited data exist concerning sexual functioning in female COPD patients, although it is probably safe to assume that the factors that affect sexual functioning in men affect sexual functioning in women as well. One self-report study concerning sexual functioning in a mixed sex (62% men, 38% women) sample that does exist is the previously described one by Hanson (1982). She found that among the 11 life areas assessed in her study, sexual functioning was the area most consistently rated as being negatively affected by COPD. Thus, Hanson's results are consistent with the more objective findings from Fletcher and Martin (1982) and Kass et al. (1972) and also suggest that COPD presents problems for sexual functioning for women as well as for men. Unfortunately, Hanson did not report results separately for men and women, and we are still left in some doubt. Clearly, the sexual functioning of female COPD patients is a neglected area and in need of further research.

One controversy in the area of sexuality and COPD concerns whether the problems that are observed are largely secondary to a past history of marital and sexual difficulties or to the relatively immediate physical effects of the disease. Kass et al. (1972) reported on a sample of 90 men and 10 women and concluded that the sexual problems associated with COPD patients were *not* primarily due to the effects of the disease. Rather, such problems were the results of lifelong patterns of behavior. The presence of a wife who was angered by the level of support required by her husband was also mentioned as a common problem in the maintenance of good sexual functioning. The authors provided five case histories (all were of men) to illustrate their conclusions.

In contrast to the report of Kass et al. are the more recent findings of Fletcher and Martin (1982). Fletcher and Martin carefully assessed erectile dysfunction in relation to cardiopulmonary, hormonal, and neurovascular dysfunction. They concluded that

Data from this study suggest that sexual dysfunction and erectile impotence can accompany COPD in the absence of other known causes of sexual problems. Furthermore, sexual dysfunction tended to be worse in those subjects with more severe pulmonary function impairment as assessed by pulmonary function tests, blood gases, and exercise tests [p. 420].

Fletcher and Martin did note that several of their subjects who were impotent as ascertained by nocturnal penile tumescence had high T scores on some MMPI scales, but only one of their 20 subjects had clearly psychogenic impotence. In the remainder COPD was responsible for both sexual dysfunction and emotional disturbance independently, or at least some of the psychological distress was secondary to sexual failure brought on by the COPD.

In summary, COPD has a documented negative effect on sexual functioning in men and probably in women as well. Although psychosocial factors play an important role in sexual functioning, the sexual dysfunction associated with COPD is closely linked with cardiopulmonary dysfunction and hypoxemia. Additional discussion of sexuality and respiratory disease is available in chapters by McSweeny et al. (in press) and Selecky (1993).

HOBBIES AND RECREATIONAL ACTIVITIES. The effect of COPD on activities that bring enjoyment to one's life has been the object of several recent studies. McSweeny et al.

(1982) noted that their patients with COPD reported severe restrictions in recreation and other leisure time activities. The SIP results suggested a reduction of 40% to 50% in pleasurable activities, which is certainly an important aspect of life quality. Indeed, the category of Recreation and Pastimes showed the greatest level of impairment relative to the other categories on the SIP when compared with results in the control group. The results from the KAS-R indicated the relatives also recognized decrements in the free-time activities of the patients.

The studies by Prigatano et al. (1984), Bergner et al. (1988), Jones et al. (1989), Williams and Bury (1989a,b), Schrier et al. (1990), and Ström et al. (1990) produced results quite similar to those of McSweeny et al., with the exception that the effects were less severe. A reduction of 15% to 40% in pleasurable activities was seen in the mildly hypoxemic patients on the SIP. This was, again, the most impaired category on this test in three of the studies (Prigatano et al, 1984; Jones et al., 1989; Ström et al., 1990) and the second most impaired category in a fourth (Williams and Bury, 1989a,b). In addition KAS-R-results from Prigatano et al. indicated that the relatives were aware of the problem.

That there is a significant loss of pleasurable activities in COPD is relevant to theories of depression that suggest that the loss of reinforcers is a major contributory factor in the development of depression (Costello, 1972). Therefore, it is possible that helping COPD patients to maintain old hobbies and develop new ones might ameliorate the negative impact of COPD on emotional status.

Factors Affecting Life Quality in COPD

Demographic Factors

The studies described previously have indicated considerable variability in the quality of life of patients with COPD. Accordingly, factors that might modify the impact of COPD on quality of life have been a topic of interest to researchers.

McSweeny et al. (1982), Prigatano et al.

(1984), Guyatt et al. (1987c), and Williams and Bury (1989a,b) examined quality of life in relation to several demographic variables. Age was found to significantly contribute, in a negative fashion, to quality of life in the McSweeny et al. and Williams and Bury samples but not in the Prigatano et al. group. Guyatt et al. found that older patients reported fewer emotional problems than younger patients. While this finding is not consistent with the other studies of COPD it does agree with the results of a study involving patients with several other chronic diseases (Casseleth et al., 1984). The reasons for the discrepant findings concerning the relationship of age to quality of life remain unclear.

McSweeny et al., Prigatano et al., and Williams and Bury (1989a) have also reported significant effects for socioeconomic status and education on quality of life in COPD patients. Generally, better educated and more affluent patients fared better than those with less education and more limited resources.

Economic security has been found to be related to life satisfaction in several other studies. In a study of 163 COPD patients and their spouses, Young (1982) found that patients' monetary savings and health insurance, as well as their personal resources (positive illness perceptions, knowledge of the illness, regimen compliance, and religion) predicted better adaptation. The female COPD patients in Sexton and Munro's (1988) study identified financial concerns as one of their major problems. Similarly, the COPD wives in Sexton and Munro's (1985) earlier study had greater life satisfaction if they were satisfied with the amount of money that was available.

Physiologic Factors

Physiological factors related to the COPD disease process account for some of the limitations in life quality. There is ample evidence that respiratory functioning itself has a significant impact on patients' functioning. When bronchodilators are prescribed for symptomatic relief of breathing problems,

temporary improvements in patients' functional capacity and emotional states often are seen (Guyatt et al, 1987a). Oxygen treatment also may result in improved functioning for some, though not all patients (Petty, 1981; Heaton et al., 1983; Heaton, 1988).

Several investigators have examined the relation of exercise capability, pulmonary function variables and other measures of the efficiency of the cardiopulmonary system in relation to quality of life (McSweeny et al., 1982; Prigatano et al., 1984; Jones et al., 1989; Williams and Bury, 1989a,b; Schrier et al., 1990; Niederman et al., 1991; Toshima et al., 1992b; Wijkstra et al., 1994). The relationship between traditional spirometric variables or blood gases and quality of life has been found to be statistically significant in most of the studies but quite weak and probably of limited clinical significance. Although some contradictory data exist (Light et al., 1985; Wijkstra et al., 1994), the relationship between exercise capability and quality of life, on the other hand, appears to be quite robust. This would suggest that the ability to engage in physical activity is an important determinant in one's quality of life. Data from an evaluation of a rehabilitation program by Toshima and her colleagues (Toshima et al., 1992a) also support the relationship between exercise capability and depression. Those patients who improved in emotional status also improved in terms of treadmill performance.

Psychological and Behavioral Factors

PSYCHOLOGICAL ASSETS AND SOCIAL SUPPORT RESOURCES. A number of investigators have studied COPD patients' psychosocial assets and social support resources in relating to quality of life. Sandhu (1986) defines psychosocial assets as "those individual characteristics and social supports that allow coping with or modifying one's environment." After reviewing the chronic illness literature, he concluded that psychosocial assets seem to "play a major, perhaps central, role in the patient's ability to cope adaptively." Sandhu noted that high assets correlate with positive outcome in medical treatment, whereas low assets typically are associated with a variety of poor outcomes, including increased morbidity and mortality.

Investigations among asthma and COPD patients indicate that patients who have stronger psychosocial assets require less medication and adapt to life changes more readily (De Araujo et al., 1973), respond more positively to group therapy (Pattison et al., 1971), are less likely to be depressed (Toshima et al., 1992b) and have less dyspnea, better regimen compliance, and longer survival time (Dudley et al., 1980). It is important to recognize that the concept of psychosocial assets includes psychological characteristics of the patient, such as emotional stability and coping style, as well as the amount of support the person receives from external sources. Thus, while COPD patients' psychosocial assets do predict outcomes that are relevant to quality of life, it is unclear how much of the impact is related to the patients' internal psychological resources and how much is related to external social supports.

Recently, investigators have used more precise measures of external support. They also have attempted to study social support in relation to other factors that influence quality of life. Jensen (1983) studied the impact of social support and various risk factors in COPD patients' symptom management. He found that social support and life stress predicted the number of hospitalizations better than did the patient's demographic characteristics, the severity of the illness, or previous hospitalizations. Labuhn (1984) found that married COPD patients had better exercise tolerance than did single, widowed, or divorced patients, even controlling for age, disease severity, and neuropsychological functioning. Marriage did not have a significant influence on patients' depressed mood states, but it indirectly contributed to patients' physical and psychosocial functioning through its impact on their exercise capacity.

Two additional studies provide evidence concerning personal social supports and COPD patients' quality of life. Barstow (1974) conducted home interviews with COPD patients to assess their problems and coping strategies. The patients in this study identified the presence of a supportive spouse as the most important factor for successful coping. Sexton and Munro (1988) had similar findings in their study of female COPD patients. Ninety-five percent of the married patients identified their husbands as important sources of support. The husbands provided instrumental support by helping out with various household activities, treatments, and other things needed. About half of the COPD women talked their problems over with their husbands. They also turned to friends, relatives, and children for emotional support.

In the study by Young (1982), the availability of community resources was not directly related to patients' self-adaptation, but it did have a significant impact on the adaptation of the patients' spouses. Only 20% of Young's COPD patients reported that they received assistance from persons other than their spouses, children, and parents, and this may account for the greater importance of community support for the spouses. About two thirds of the COPD spouses in Sexton and Munro's (1985) study said that they relied on their sons and daughters for help. Forty-six percent of these wives identified the physician as an important source of support. Thirty-seven percent also relied on friends and 34% relied on neighbors.

Findings from the above studies have suggested that most COPD patients rely heavily on their immediate families for support, while family members may rely on each other as well as professional and community resources. It is important to consider the implications of these findings for patients who live alone as well as the quality of life of COPD patients' families. Additional investigations are needed to examine COPD family's social support needs in more detail, and to evaluate the effectiveness of interventions directed toward mobilizing supports.

Kaplan and his colleagues (Kaplan et al., 1993) review data from other studies of social support and chronic disease that provide additional evidence for the importance this variable in understanding the variability in the effects of COPD on quality of life.

COPING STRATEGIES. The specific coping strategies that COPD patients use to deal with the illness also affect their quality of life. Both cognitive and behavioral coping strategies are important. Fagerhaugh (1975) discusses "routing" as a basic behavioral strategy that COPD patients can use to conserve energy while carrying out their daily activities. Routing includes planning the number and types of activities that are needed, making judgments about when to delete, postpone, or condense activities, and anticipating obstacles and planning solutions. Halcomb (1984) emphasizes the changes in lifestyle that are necessary in order for COPD patients to improve their physical and mental well-being. Patients need guidance in learning how to mobilize support resources and deal with family and marital problems, as well as how to prevent and manage disease symptoms. Effective intervention should give the patient a sense of control over the environment. Stollenwerk (1985) also suggests that COPD patients' spiritual resources be assessed for their potential as a coping resource. In a study of self-care practices among COPD patients, she found that patients' values and spiritual beliefs affected their decisions regarding self-care, as well as their attitudes and emotional stability. Stollenwerk encourages professionals to become better aware of patients' values in order to assist individual patients to achieve their own goals.

SELF-EFFICACY AND MASTERY. Kaplan and his colleagues (Kaplan et al., 1993) have suggested that the concept of self-efficacy, originally described by Bandura (1977), is important in understanding a patient's ability to cope adequately with the effects of COPD and to benefit from pulmonary rehabilitation programs. In addition, Toshima et al. (1990) reported that a rehabilitation program improved self-efficacy expectations for walking more effectively than a simple education program with COPD patients. In a more recent study by Toshima et al. (1992b), self-efficacy for walking was not improved by rehabilitation nor was it related to QWB scores or depression as measured by the CES-D, although it was related to exercise capability.

Moody et al. (1991) assessed the personality variable of Mastery, as described by Guyatt et al. (1987b), in a sample of 45 COPD patients and reported a significant correlation with general quality of life as measured by a scale developed by Spitzer et al. (1981). Given the similarity of the concepts of Mastery and Self-Efficacy, the finding from Moody and her colleagues would appear to support the hypotheses of Kaplan and his colleagues. However, the importance of self-efficacy in the quality of life of COPD patients requires additional verification.

Treatment and Rehabilitation

The findings concerning the effects of treatment and rehabilitation on quality of life in COPD is mixed. Several controlled and uncontrolled studies have reported improvements in quality of life as a response to pulmonary rehabilitation (Atkins et al., 1984; Guyatt et al., 1987a; Kaplan and Atkins, 1988; Goldstein et al., 1992; Make et al., 1992; Emery et al., 1994; Manzetti et al., 1994; Petty, 1994) or oxygen therapy (Dardes et al., 1990). Other studies either have provided negative results or have been inconclusive (Heaton et al., 1983; Toshima et al., 1990; Elliott et al., 1992). In summary, rehabilitation and oxygen treatment appear to have a positive effect on quality of life in most cases, and further research is necessary to determine what aspects of rehabilitation and treatment are most likely to produce benefits in terms of quality of life.

The Relationship of Neuropsychological Functioning to Quality of Life in COPD

A preceding chapter (Rourke and Adams, Chapter 16) has detailed the neuropsychological findings in COPD. An obvious question is whether neuropsychological functioning is related to quality of life and, if so, is information about neuropsychological functioning useful in predicting quality of life?

Relatively simple analyses of the relationship between neuropsychological functioning and quality of life were made by McSweeny et al. (1982) and Prigatano et al. (1984) utilizing Pearson correlation coefficients and multiple regression analyses. McSweeny et al. found moderate (.34 to .45) but significant ($P<.01$) correlations between neuropsychological functioning as measured by the Average Impairment Rating of Russell et al. (1970) and Quality of Life as measured by the Sickness Impact Profile Total Score. Similarly, the clinician rating of neuropsychological impairment was found to make a significant contribution to a multiple regression analysis also incorporating measures of age, socioeconomic status, and severity of COPD as predictors and SIP Total Score as the dependent variable. The overall equation was also significant and accounted for 25% of the variance in quality of life. The results of this analysis led McSweeny et al. to suggest the heuristic model shown in Figure 23-2, which relates COPD, neuropsychological function-

ing, and other variables affecting quality of life.

Prigatano et al. (1984) also found a significant relationship between neuropsychological functioning and quality of life using the same summary indices as McSweeny et al. However, the relationship was less robust ($r=.25$, $p<.05$) and neuropsychological functioning did not contribute significantly to a multiple regression analysis predicting life quality. On the other hand Prigatano et al. did find more robust relationships between SIP Total and measures of emotional status including the Profile of Mood States (POMS; McNair et al., 1981) and the Depression and Psychasthenia scales of the MMPI.

McSweeny et al. (1985) took advantage of the availability of the combined data set described above in the discussion of the neuropsychological studies of Grant et al. (1987) to study the interrelationships between neuropsychological functioning and quality of life. More specifically, they intended to answer three basic questions. First, do neuropsychological measures predict life functioning in (a) impaired persons, and (b) normal

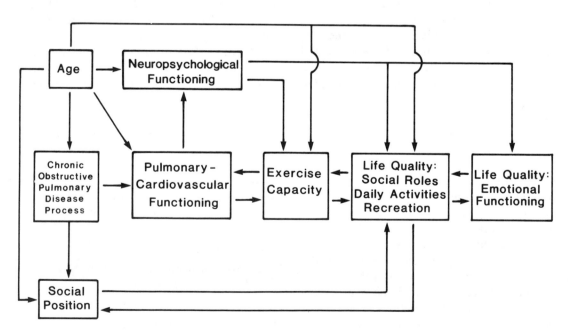

Figure 23-2. Heuristic model for interrelation of COPD and other variables affecting life quality. (From McSweeny et al., 1982. Copyright, American Medical Association. Reprinted with permission.)

subjects? Secondly, which neuropsychological measures predict which aspects of life functioning? Finally, do neuropsychological measures provide any predictive utility beyond easily available demographic data such as age and education? Analyses using simple correlations, canonical correlations, and multiple regression techniques revealed that neuropsychological measures can be used to predict quality of life. Neuropsychological status was more consistently related to activities of daily living and performance of basic social roles than to emotional functioning. Complex, multifunctional neuropsychological tasks, such as the Trail Making Test–Part B (Reitan and Wolfson, 1985), were found to be the best overall predictors of life functioning. On the other hand, more specific neuropsychological tests served as better predictors of specific life functions. The Aphasia Screening Examination (Reitan and Wolfson, 1985) served as the best predictor of communication skills, for example. Table 23-2 displays the results of the canonical correlation analysis that illustrate these findings. The

analysis relates several neuropsychological measures to the 12 dimensions of the SIP. Both canonical correlations produced were significant. The first correlation demonstrates the relationship between psychomotor tests and a variety of daily living and social-role activities; the second correlation demonstrates the relationship between basic language skills and the ability to communicate.

Stepwise multiple regression analyses, in which age and education were entered before neuropsychological variables, were used to examine the relative utility of neuropsychological tests in predicting various aspects of life quality. The results of these analyses, which are summarized in Table 23-3, indicate that variance contributed by the neuropsychological tests to the life quality indices was often significant and separate from the variance accounted for by age and education.

In summary, the study of McSweeny et al. (1985) provided empirical verification of the utility of neuropsychological measures for making predictions about life functioning,

Table 23-2. Coefficients of Canonical Variates for Correlations of Neuropsychological (NP) and Sickness Impact Profile (SIP) Variables

NP Variable	NP Coefficient	SIP Variable	SIP Coefficient	NP Variable	NP Coefficient	SIP Variable	SIP Coefficient
Trails-B	.45	Mobility	.44	Aphasia	.69	Commun	.97
Grip	−.43	Bodycare	.39	PIQ	.37	Recreat	−.43
Pegs	.35	Homecare	.38	Grip	.36	Bodycare	−.43
Sens/Per	.29	Social	−.38	TPT Time	−.34	Emotion	.36
PIQ	.27	Alertness	.22	VIQ	−.31	Mobility	.30
Log Mem	−.21	Work	.20	Speech	.28	Work	.19
Aphasia	.20	Eating	.18	Spatial	.26	Alert	−.14
Spatial	−.17	Commun	.16	Category	.20	Ambulat	−.14
Category	.16	Recreat	−.15	Trails-B	−.20	Sleep	−.13
Fig Mem	−.10	Ambulat	−.12	Log Mem	.16	Homecare	.05
TPT Time	−.10	Sleep	−.09	Pegs	.15	Social	−.04
Taps	.05	Emotion	.04	Taps	−.13	Eating	.01
Rhythm	.03			Sens/Per	−.13		
Speech	−.02			Fig Mem	.03		
VIQ	−.01			Rhythm	.01		

Abbreviations: Trails-B = Trail Making Test–Part B; Grip = Hand Dynamometer summed over hands; Pegs = Grooved Pegboard; Sens/Per = Sensory/Perceptual Examinations; PIQ = WAIS Performance IQ; Log Mem = Wechsler Logical Memory, percent retained; Aphasia = Reitan-Klove Aphasia Screening Test; Spatial = Russell-Neuringer Spatial Relations Score; Category = Halstead Category Test; Fig Mem = Wechsler Figural Memory, percent retained; TPT Time = Tactual Performance Test–Total Time; Taps = Finger Tapping Test summed over both hands; Rhythm = Seashore Rhythm Test; Speech = Speech-Sounds Perception Test; VIQ = Wechsler Verbal IQ; Social = Social Interaction; Commun = Communication; Recreat = Recreation; Ambulat = Ambulation; Emotion = Emotional Functioning.

Table 23-3. Multiple Regression Analyses Relating Neuropsychological Variables to Life Quality Variables in Patients

Life Quality Scores	NP Variables Entered (in order)	Multiple R	Increase in Multiple R	P
SIP Total	Pegs	.53	.19	<.001
	Grip			
	Trails-B			
Physical	Grip	.59	.22	<.001
	Pegs			
	Sens-Percept			
Psychosocial	Trails-B	.38	.14	<.001
Sleep	Trails-B	.26	.12	<.01
	Aphasia			
Emotion	VIQ	.29	.12	<.01
Body Care & Movement	Grip	.57	.21	<.001
	Trails-B			
	Sens-Percept			
Home Management	Grip	.45	.14	<.001
	Pegs			
Mobility	Pegs	.54	.19	<.001
Sociability	Grip	.32	.08	<.01
	Pegs			
Ambulation	Grip	.46	.16	<.001
	Sens-Percept			
Alertness	Grip	.43	.27	<.001
	Trails-B			
	Pegs			
Communication	Aphasia	.49	.21	<.001
	Pegs			
Recreation	TPT Time	.24	.06	<.02
Work	Speech	.29	.05	<.01
Eating	Trails-B	.40	.26	<.001
	Sens-Percept			
	Log Memory %			
KAS-R	Trails-B	.22	.18	<.05
Social Obstrep				
Acute Psychot	Taps	.26	.19	<.01
	Fig Memory %			
Withdrawn	Trails-B	.19	.18	N.S
Depression				
Social Roles	TPT	.44	.27	<.001
	Trails-B			
	Grip			
	Log Memory %			
Hobbies & Recreation	Trails-B	.42	.38	<.001
	Grip			
	Category			
	Rhythm			
	Aphasia			

Abbreviations: Pegs = Grooved Pegboard; Grip = Hand Dynamometer, summed across hands; Trails-B = Trail Making Test–Part B; Sens-Percept = Sensory Perceptual Examination; Aphasia = Reitan-Klove Aphasia Screening Test; VIQ = WAIS Verbal IQ; TPT Time = Tactual Performance Test, total time; Speech = Speech-Sounds Perception Test; Log Memory % = Wechsler Logical Memory, percent retained; Social Obstrep = Social Obstreperousness; Acute Psychot = Acute Psychoticism; Fig Memory % = Wechsler Figural Memory %, percent retained; Category = Halstead Category Test; Rhythm = Seashore Rhythm Test.

and in consequence, their potential utility in planning remedial programs.

Labuhn (1984) sought to investigate the interrelationships between life quality and other aspects of functioning in more detail. Specifically, she attempted to develop and test a multivariate model for explaining depression in COPD using path analysis (Asher, 1976). The model represented an attempt to integrate the various biological, psychological, and sociological explanations of depressed mood as applied to COPD patients. The path model (Fig. 23-3) included five sociodemographic variables and five clinical or disease-related variables. According to the model, one variable—perceived illness dysfunction (self-reported physical and psychosocial deficits as measured by the SIP)—has a direct impact on mood, with more dysfunctional patients having higher levels of depressed mood (POMS depression/dejection). Five variables—smoking, age, education, exercise tolerance, and arterial oxygen saturation—indirectly influence depressed

mood through their effects on other variables in the model. Three variables—neuropsychological impairment (Average Impairment Rating), occupational status, and marital status—were hypothesized to have both direct and indirect effects on depressed mood.

Ordinary least-squares, multiple-regression procedures were used to test the hypothesized linkages in the model. The resulting standardized β-coefficients are shown in Figure 23-3 and are listed in Table 23-4. Table 23-4 also offers a summary of the direct, indirect, and total effects of each predictor variable to depressed mood.

Perceived illness dysfunction as measured by the SIP, which reflects the patient's ability to carry out physical and psychosocial activities, clearly makes the largest contribution to emotional disturbance in the form of depression. Neuropsychological impairment also contributes heavily to depressed mood by affecting exercise tolerance, physical functioning, and psychosocial functioning. Neuropsychological impairment also serves as an

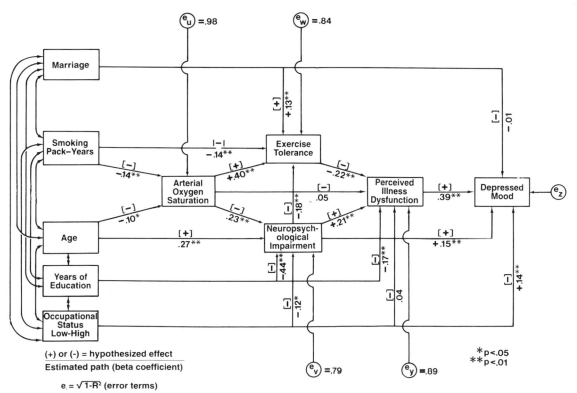

Figure 23-3. Path model for depressed mood in chronic obstructive pulmonary disease. (From Labuhn, 1984.)

Table 23-4. Direct, Indirect, and Total Effects of Predictors on the NOTT and IPPB Patients' Depressed Mood Scores

Predictor Variable	Direct Effect	Indirect Effect	Total Effect
Perceived illness dysfunction	+0.39	0.0000	+0.3900
Neuropsychological impairment	+0.15	+0.0973	+0.2473
Exercise tolerance	0.00	−0.0858	−0.0858
Arterial oxygen saturation	0.00	−0.1007	−0.1007
Occupational status (low-high)	+0.14	−0.0453	+0.0947
Education (low-high)	0.00	−0.0751	−0.0751
Age	0.00	+0.0834	+0.0834
Smoking pack-years	0.00	+0.0274	+0.0274
Marriage	−0.01	−0.0112	−0.0212

Source: Adapted from Labuhn (1984).

important intervening variable between depressed mood, oxygen saturation, education, and age.

Additional analyses by Labuhn revealed that the relative order of the predictor variables changes as the disease of COPD becomes more advanced. Psychosocial factors were relatively more important in the early stages of the disease; physiological and neuropsychological factors gained in importance during the later stages. However, emotional status was never a simple function of disease severity. A wide range of adjustment was seen at all stages of the disease.

Summary

This chapter has discussed the complexity of the effects of hypoxemia caused by chronic lung disease on cognition, emotion, experience, and behavior, as well as the interaction between these areas of functioning. It is clear that the neuropsychological research described has provided physicians with a more complete description and understanding of one of the diseases they must treat and manage. Likewise, neuropsychologists and other behavioral and neuroscientists may observe how their endeavors can have a scientific and practical impact on other fields. This research provides evidence of the utility of neuropsychological approaches, not only in understanding medical disorders, but also in rehabilitation and psychological intervention. If neuropsychological measures can be used to predict the ability of patients to carry out everyday life roles, they may also be employed to identify potential difficulties and potential assets when developing a psychological intervention or rehabilitation plan. Rourke et al. (1983) have provided a model of how this might be done with children, and it would appear to apply equally well to adults. In any case, the potential for useful information to emerge from neuropsychological and quality of life studies of medical disorders appears high. Perhaps the best evidence of this potential is the timely appearance of this volume.

Acknowledgment

The authors would like to thank Robert M. Kaplan, Barry J. Make, and Valery Walker for providing bibliographic resources for the preparation of this chapter.

References

Agle, D. P., and Baum, G. L. (1977). Psychological aspects of chronic obstructive pulmonary disease. *Medical Clinics of North America, 61,* 749–758.

Agle, D. P., Baum, G. L., Chester, E. H., and Wendt, M. (1973). Multidiscipline treatment of chronic pulmonary insufficiency. 1. Psychologic aspects of rehabilitation. *Psychosomatic Medicine, 35,* 41–49.

Alonso, J., Antó, J. M., González, M., Fiz, J. A., Izquierdo, J., and Morera, J. (1992). Measurement of general health status of non-oxygen-dependent chronic obstructive pulmonary disease patients. *Medical Care, 30* (Suppl. 5), MS125–MS135.

Anderson, J. P., Kaplan, R. M., Berry, C. C., Bush, J. W., and Rumbaut, R. G. (1989). Interday reliability of function assessment for a health-status measure: The Quality of Well Being Scale. *Medical Care, 27,* 1076–1083.

Asher, H. B. (1976). *Causal Modeling.* Beverly Hills: Sage Publishers.

Atkins, C. J., Kaplan, R. M., Timms, R. M., Reinsch, S., and Lofback, K. (1984). Behavioral exercise programs in the management of chronic obstructive pulmonary disease. *Journal of Consulting and Clinical Psychology, 52,* 591–603.

Barofsky, I., and Sugarbaker, P. H. (1990). Cancer. In B. Spilker, ed., *Quality of Life Assessments in Clinical Trials.* New York: Raven Press, pp. 419–440.

Bandura, A. (1977). Self-efficacy: Toward a unifying theory of behavioral change. *Psychological Review, 84,* 191–215.

Barstow, R. E. (1974). Coping with emphysema. *Nursing Clinics of North America, 9,* 137–145.

Bergner, M. (1984). The Sickness Impact Profile (SIP). In N. K. Wenger, M. E. Mattson, C. D. Furberg, and J. Elinson, eds., *Assessment of Quality of Life in Clinical Trials of Cardiovascular Therapies.* New York: Le Jacq Publishers, pp. 152–159.

Bergner, M., Bobbit, R. A., Carter, W. B., and Gilson, B. S. (1981). The Sickness Impact Profile: Development and final revision of a health status measure. *Medical Care, 19,* 787–805.

Bergner, M., Hudson, L. D., Conrad, D. A., Patmont, C. M., McDonald, G. J., Perrin, E. B., and Gilson, B. S. (1988). The cost and efficacy of home care for patients with chronic lung disease. *Medical Care, 26,* 566–579.

Bergner, M., and Rothman, M. L. (1987). Health status measures: An overview and guide for selection. *Annual Review of Public Health, 8,* 191–210.

Burns, B. H., and Howell, J.B.L. (1969). Disproportionately severe breathlessness in chronic bronchitis. *Quarterly Journal of Medicine, 38,* 277–294.

Bush, J. W. (1984). General Health Policy Model/ Quality of Well Being (QWB) Scale. In N. K. Wenger, M. E. Mattson, C. D. Furberg, and J. Elinson, eds., *Assessment of Quality of Life in Clinical Trials of Cardiovascular Therapies.* New York: Le Jacq Publishers, pp. 189–199.

Calman, K. C. (1984). Quality of life in cancer patients—an hypothesis. *Journal of Medical Ethics, 10,* 124–127.

Casseleth, B. R., Lusk, E. J., Strouse, T. B., Miller, D. S., Brown, L. L., Cross, P. A., and Tenaglia, A. N. (1984). Psychosocial status in chronic illness: A comparative analysis of six diagnostic groups. *New England Journal of Medicine, 311,* 506–511.

Chambers, L. W. (1984). The McMaster Health Index Questionnaire. In N. K. Wenger, M. E. Mattson, C. D. Furberg, and J. Elinson, eds. *Assessment of Quality of Life in Clinical Trials of Cardiovascular Therapies.* New York: Le Jacq Publishers, pp. 160–164.

Chambers, L. W. (1988). The McMaster Health Index Questionnaire: An update. In S. R. Walker and R. M. Rosser, eds., *Quality of Life: Assessment and Applications.* London: Ciba Foundation, pp. 113–311.

Cook, T. D., and Campbell, D. T. (1979). *Quasi-Experimentation: Design and Analysis Issues for Field Settings.* Chicago: Rand-McNally.

Costello, C. G. (1972). Depression: Loss of reinforcers or loss of reinforcer effectiveness? *Behavior Therapy, 2,* 240–247.

Cottrell, J. J., Paul, C., and Ferson, S. (1992). Quality of life measures in COPD patients: How do they compare? *American Review of Respiratory Disease, 145* (Suppl), A767.

Cox, N.J.M., Hendriks, J.C.M., Dijkhuizen, R., Binkhorst, R. A., and van Herwaarden, L. A. (1991). Usefulness of a medicopsychological questionnaire for lung patients. *International Journal of Rehabilitation Research, 14,* 267–272.

Curtis, J. R., Deyo, R. A., and Hudson, L. D. (1994). Pulmonary rehabilitation in chronic respiratory insufficiency. 7. Health-related quality of life among patients with chronic obstructive pulmonary disease. *Thorax, 49,* 162–170.

Dahlstrom, W. G., Welsh, G. S., and Dahlstrom, L. E. (1972). *An MMPI Handbook* (Rev. Ed.). Minneapolis: University of Minnesota.

Dardes, N., Chiappini, M. G., Moscatelli, B., Re, M. A., Pellicciotti, L., Benedetti, G., and Vulterini, S. (1990). Quality of life of COPD patients treated by long-term oxygen. *Lung, 168* (Suppl.), 789–793.

De Araujo, G., Van Arsdel, P. P., Jr., Holmes, T. H., and Dudley, D. L. (1973). Life change, coping ability and chronic intrinsic asthma. *Journal of Psychosomatic Research, 17,* 359–363.

Dompeling, E., van Grunsven, P. M., Molema, J., Verbeek, A.L.M., van Schayck, C. P., and van Weel, C. (1992). Early detection of patients with fast progressive asthma or chronic bronchitis in general practice. *Scandinavian Journal of Primary Health Care, 10,* 143–150.

Dudley, D. L. (1969). *Psychophysiology of Respiration in Health and Disease.* New York: Appleton-Century-Crofts.

Dudley, D. L., Glaser, E. M., Jorgenson, B. N., and Logan, D. L. (1980). Psychosocial concomitants to rehabilitation in chronic obstructive pulmonary disease, part I: Psychosocial and psychological considerations. *Chest*, 77, 413–420.

Dudley, D. L., Wermuth, C., and Hague, W. (1973). Psychosocial aspects of care in the chronic obstructive pulmonary disease patient. *Heart and Lung*, 2, 389–393.

Eakin, E. G., Sassi-Dambron, D., Kaplan, R. M., and Ries, A. L. (1992). Clinical trial of rehabilitation in chronic obstructive pulmonary disease. *Journal of Cardiopulmonary Rehabilitation*, 12, 105–110.'

Elliott, M. W., Simonds, A. K., Caroll, M. P., Wedzicha, J. A., and Branthwaite, M. A. (1992). Domiciliary nocturnal nasal intermittent positive pressure ventilation in hypercapnic respiratory failure due to chronic obstructive lung disease: Effects on sleep and quality of life. *Thorax*, 47, 342–348.

Emery, C. F., Hauck, E. R., MacIntyre, N. R., and Leatherman, N. E. (1994). Psychological functioning among middle-aged and older adult pulmonary patients in exercise rehabilitation. *Physical and Occupational Therapy in Geriatrics*, 12, 13–26.

Engel, G. L. (1980). The clinical application of the biopsychosocial model. *American Journal of Psychiatry*, 137, 535–544.

Fagerhaugh, S. (1975). Getting around with emphysema. In A. L. Strauss and B. G. Glaser, eds., *Chronic Illness and Quality of Life*. St. Louis: Mosby Press, pp. 99–107.

Fletcher, E. C., and Martin, R. J. (1982). Sexual dysfunction and erectile impotence in chronic obstructive pulmonary disease. *Chest*, 81, 413–421.

Fries, J. F., and Spitz, P. W. (1990). The hierarchy of patient outcomes. In B. Spilker, ed., *Quality of Life Assessments in Clinical Trials*. New York: Raven Press, pp. 25–36.

Friedman, H. S., and Booth-Kewley, S. (1987). The "disease-prone personality". A meta-analytic view of the construct. *American Psychologist*, 42, 539–555.

Gift, A. G., Plaut, S. M., and Jacox, A. (1986). Psychologic and physiologic factors related to dyspnea in subjects with chronic obstructive pulmonary disease. *Heart and Lung*, 15, 595–601.

Goldstein, R. S., Gort, E. H., Brown, D. L., Stubbing, D., Guyatt, G. H., and Avendano, M. A. (1992). A controlled trial of pulmonary rehabilitation. *American Review of Respiratory Disease*, 145 (Suppl), A767 (Abst.).

Grant, I., Prigatano, G. P., Heaton, R. K., McSweeny, A. J., Wright, E. C., and Adams, K. M. (1987). Progressive neuropsychological impairment in relation to hypoxemia in chronic obstructive pulmonary disease. *Archives of General Psychiatry*, 44, 999–1006.

Greenberg, G. D., Ryan, J. J., and Bourlier, P. F. (1985). Psychological and neuropsychological aspects of COPD. *Psychosomatics*, 26, 29–33.

Guyatt, G. H., Berman, L. B., and Townsend, M. (1987a). Long-term outcome after respiratory rehabilitation. *Canadian Medical Association Journal*, 137, 1089–1095.

Guyatt, G. H., Berman, L. B., Townsend, M., Pugsley, S. O., and Chambers, L. W. (1987b). A measure of quality of life for clinical trials in chronic lung disease. *Thorax*, 42, 773–778.

Guyatt, G. H., Townsend, M., Berman, L. B., and Pugsley, S. O. (1987c). Quality of life in patients with chronic airflow limitation. *British Journal of Diseases of the Chest*, 81, 45–54.

Guyatt, G. H., Townsend, M., Keller, J. L., and Singer, J. (1989). Should study subjects see their previous responses? Data from a randomized control trial. *Journal of Clinical Epidemiology*, 42, 913–920.

Halcomb, R. (1984). Promoting self-help in pulmonary patient education. *Respiratory Therapy*, 14, 49–54.

Hanson, E. I. (1982). Effects of chronic lung disease on life in general and sexuality: Perceptions of adult patients. *Heart and Lung*, 11, 435–441.

Heaton, R. K. (1988). Psychological effects of oxygen therapy for COPD. In A. J. McSweeny and I. Grant, eds., *Chronic Obstructive Pulmonary Disease: A Behavioral Perspective*. New York: Marcel Dekker, Inc., pp. 105–121.

Heaton, R. K., Grant, I., McSweeny, A. J., Adams, K. M., Petty, T. L., and the NOTT Study Group. (1983). Psychological effects of continuous and nocturnal oxygen therapy in hypoxemic chronic obstructive pulmonary disease. *Archives of Internal Medicine*, 143, 1941–1947.

Hodgkin, J. E. (1990). Prognosis in chronic obstructive pulmonary disease. *Clinics in Chest Medicine*, 11, 555–569.

Hunt, S. M. (1984). The Nottingham Health Profile. In N. K. Wenger, M. E. Mattson, C. D. Furberg, and J. Elinson, eds., *Assessment of Quality of Life in Clinical Trials of Cardiovascular Therapies*. New York: Le Jacq Publishers, pp. 165–169.

Hunt, S. M., McKenna, S. P., McEwen, J., Williams, J., and Papp, E. (1981). The Nottingham Health Profile: Subjective health status and medical consultations. *Social Science and Medicine, Part A, Medical Sociology, 15A*, 221–229.

Jaeschke, R., Singer, J., and Guyatt, G. H. (1989). Measurement of health status: Ascertaining the minimal clinically important difference. *Controlled Clinical Trials, 10*, 407–415.

Jensen, P. S. (1983). Risk, protective factors, and supportive interventions in chronic airway obstruction. *Archives of General Psychiatry, 40*, 1203–1207.

Jones, P. W., Baveystock, C. M., and Littlejohns, P. (1989). Relationships between general health measured with the Sickness Impact Profile and respiratory symptoms, physiological measures, and mood in patients with chronic airflow limitation. *American Review of Respiratory Disease, 140*, 1538–1543.

Jones, P. W., Quirk, F. H., and Baveystock, C. M. (1991). The St. George's Respiratory Questionnaire. *Respiratory Medicine, 85* (Suppl. B), 25–31, 33–37.

Jones, P. W., Quirk, F. H., and Baveystock, C. M. (1994). Why quality of life measures should be used in the treatment of patients with respiratory illness. *Monaldi Archives for Chest Disease, 49*, 79–82.

Kaplan, R. M. (1985). Quality of life assessment. In P. Karoly, ed., *Measurement Strategies in Health Psychology*. New York: Wiley-Interscience, pp. 115–146.

Kaplan, R. M. (1990). Behavior as the central outcome in health care. *American Psychologist, 45*, 1211–1220.

Kaplan, R. M., and Anderson, J. P. (1990). The General Health Policy Model: An integrated approach. In B. Spilker, ed., *Quality of Life Assessments in Clinical Trials*. New York: Raven Press, pp. 131–152.

Kaplan, R. M., and Atkins, C. J. (1988). Behavioral interventions for patients with COPD. In A. J. McSweeny and I. Grant, eds., *Chronic Obstructive Pulmonary Disease: A Behavioral Perspective*. New York: Marcel Dekker, Inc., pp. 123–162.

Kaplan, R. M., Atkins, C. J., and Timms, R. M. (1984). Validity of a quality of well-being scale as an outcome measure in chronic obstructive pulmonary disease. *Journal of Chronic Diseases, 37*, 85–95.

Kaplan, R. M., and Bush, J. W. (1982). Health-related quality of life measurement for evalua-tion research and policy analysis. *Health Psychology, 1*, 621–680.

Kaplan, R. M., Eakin, E. G., and Ries, A. L. (1993). Psychosocial issues in the rehabilitation of patients with chronic obstructive pulmonary disease. In R. Casaburi and T. L. Petty, eds., *Principles and Practice of Pulmonary Rehabilitation*. Philadelphia: W. B. Saunders, pp. 351–365.

Karajgi, B., Rifkin, A., Doddi, S., and Kolli, R. (1990). The prevalence of anxiety disorders in patients with chronic obstructive pulmonary disease. *American Journal of Psychiatry, 147*, 200–201.

Kass, I., Updegraff, K., and Muffly, R. B. (1972). Sex in chronic obstructive pulmonary disease. *Medical Aspects of Human Sexuality, 6*, 33–42.

Katz, I. R. (1980). Is there a hypoxic affective syndrome? *Psychosomatics, 23*, 846–853.

Katz, M. M., and Lyerly, S. B. (1963). Methods of measuring adjustment and behavior in the community: Rationale, description, discriminative validity and scale development. *Psychological Reports, 13*, 503–535.

Kent, D. L. (1977). Psychosocial implications of pulmonary disease. *Clinical Notes on Respiratory Diseases, 16*, 3–11.

Kinsman, R. A., Yaroush, R. A., Fernandez, E., Dirks, J. F., Schocket, M., and Fukuhara, J. (1983). Symptoms and experiences in chronic bronchitis and emphysema. *Chest, 83*, 755–761.

Labuhn, K. T. (1984). An analysis of self-reported depressed mood in chronic obstructive pulmonary disease. (Doctoral Dissertation, University of Michigan, 1984) *Dissertation Abstracts International, 45*, 524B.

Levine, S., and Croog, S. H. (1984). What constitutes quality of life: A conceptualization of the dimensions of life quality in healthy populations and patients with cardiovascular disease. In N. K. Wenger, M. E. Mattson, C. D. Furberg, and J. Elinson, eds., *Assessment of Quality of Life in Clinical Trials of Cardiovascular Therapies*. New York: LeJacq Publishers, pp. 46–58.

Light, R. W., Merrill, E. J., Despars, J. A., Gordon, G. H. and Mutalipassi, L. R. (1985). Prevalence of depression and anxiety in patients with COPD. Relationship to functional capacity. *Chest, 87*, 35–38.

Maillé, A. R., Kaptein, A. A., Konig, C.M.J., and Zwinderman, A. H. (1994). Developing a quality-of-life questionnaire for patients with respiratory illness. *Monaldi Archives for Chest Disease, 49*, 76–78.

Make, B., Glenn, K., Iklé, D., Bucher, B., Tuteur, D., Mason, U., Wamboldt, F., and Bethel, R. (1992). Pulmonary rehabilitation improves the quality of life of patients with chronic obstructive pulmonary disease (COPD). *American Review of Respiratory Disease, 145* (Suppl), A767 (Abst.).

Manzetti, J. D., Hoffman, L. A., Sereika, S. M., Sciurba, F. C., and Griffith, B. P. (1994). Exercise, education, and quality of life in lung transplant candidates. *Journal of Heart and Lung Transplantation, 13,* 297–305.

Martin, L. L. (1994). Validity and reliability of a quality-of-life instrument: The chronic respiratory disease questionnaire. *Clinical Nursing Research, 3,* 146–156.

McCullough, L. B. (1984). The concept of quality of life: A philosophical analysis. In N. K. Wenger, M. E. Mattson, C. D. Furberg, and J. Elinson, eds., *Assessment of Quality of Life in Clinical Trials of Cardiovascular Therapies.* New York: LeJacq Publishers, pp. 25–36.

McNair, D. M., Lorr, M., and Droppleman, L. F. (1981). *Manual for the Profile of Mood States.* San Diego: Educational and Industrial Testing Service.

McSweeny, A. J. (1988). Quality of life in relation to COPD. In A. J. McSweeny and I. Grant, eds., *Chronic Obstructive Pulmonary Disease: A Behavioral Perspective.* New York: Marcel Dekker, Inc., pp. 55–89.

McSweeny, A. J. (1990). Quality of life assessment in neuropsychology. In D. E. Tupper and K. D. Cicerone, eds., *The Neuropsychology of Everyday Life.* Amsterdam: Kluwer, pp. 185–217.

McSweeny, A. J., and Creer, T. L. (1995). Health-related quality-of-life assessment in medical care. *Disease-A-Month, 16,* 1–71.

McSweeny, A. J., Czajkowski, S., and Labuhn, K. T. (in press). Psychosocial factors in rehabilitation with chronic respiratory disease patients. In A. P. Fishman, ed., *Pulmonary Rehabilitation.* New York: Marcel Dekker, Inc.

McSweeny, A. J., Grant, I., Heaton, R. K., Adams, K. M., and Timms, R. M. (1982). Life quality of patients with chronic obstructive pulmonary disease. *Archives of Internal Medicine, 142,* 473–478.

McSweeny, A. J., Grant, I., Heaton, R. K., Prigatano, G. P., and Adams, K. M. (1985). Relationship of neuropsychological status to everyday functioning in healthy and chronically ill persons. *Journal of Clinical and Experimental Neuropsychology, 7,* 281–291.

McSweeny, A. J., and Labuhn, K. T. (1990). Chronic obstructive pulmonary disease. In B.

Spilker, ed., *Quality of Life Assessments in Clinical Trials.* New York: Raven Press, pp. 391–418.

Moody, L., McCormick, K., and Williams, A. (1990). Disease and symptom severity, functional status, and quality of life in chronic bronchitis and emphysema. *Journal of Behavioral Medicine, 13,* 297–306.

Moody, L., McCormick, K., and Williams, A. R. (1991). Psychophysiologic correlates of quality of life in chronic bronchitis and emphysema. *Western Journal of Nursing Research, 13,* 336–352.

Niederman, M. S., Clemente, P. H., Fein, A. M., Feinsilver, S. H., Robinson, D. A., Ilowite, J. S., and Bernstein, M. G. (1991). Benefits of a multidisciplinary pulmonary rehabilitation program. Improvements are independent of lung function. *Chest, 99,* 798–804.

Pattison, E. M., Rhodes, R. J., and Dudley, D. L. (1971). Response to group treatment in patients with severe chronic lung disease. *International Journal of Group Psychotherapy, 21,* 214–225.

Pearlman, R. A., and Jonsen, A. (1985). The use of quality-of-life considerations in medical decision making. *Journal of the American Geriatrics Society, 33,* 344–352.

Petty, T. L. (1981). Home oxygen in advanced chronic obstructive pulmonary disease. *Medical Clinics of North America, 65,* 615–627.

Petty, T. L. (1994). Pulmonary rehabilitation of early COPD: COPD as a systemic disease. *Chest, 105,* 1636–1637.

Post, L., and Collins, C. (1981–82). The poorly coping COPD patient: a psychotherapeutic perspective. *Journal of Psychiatry and Medicine, 11,* 173–182.

Prigatano, G. P., Wright, E. C., and Levin, D. (1984). Quality of life and its predictors in patients with mild hypoxemia and chronic obstructive pulmonary disease. *Archives of Internal Medicine, 144,* 1613–1619.

Radloff, L. S. (1977). The CES-D Scale: A self-report depression scale for research in the general population. *Applied Psychological Measurement, 1,* 385–401.

Reitan, R. M., and Wolfson, D. (1985). *The Halstead-Reitan Neuropsychological Test Battery: Theory and Clinical Interpretation.* Tucson: Neuropsychology Press.

Rourke, B. P. (1982). Central processing deficiencies in children: Towards a developmental neuropsychological model. *Journal of Clinical Neuropsychology, 4,* 1–18.

Rourke, B. P., Bakker, D. J., Fisk, J. L., and

Strang, J. D. (1983). *Child Neuropsychology: An Introduction to Theory, Research, and Clinical Practice.* New York: Guilford.

Russell, E. W., Neuringer, C., and Goldstein, G. (1970). *Assessment of Brain Damage: A Neuropsychological Key Approach.* New York: Wiley Interscience.

Sandhu, H. S. (1986). Psychosocial issues in chronic obstructive pulmonary disease. *Clinics in Chest Medicine, 7,* 629–642.

Schipper, H., Clinch, J., and Powell, V. (1990). Definitions and conceptual issues. In B. Spilker, ed., *Quality of Life Assessments in Clinical Trials.* New York: Raven Press, pp. 11–24.

Schrier, A. C., Dekker, F. W., Kaptein, A. A., and Dikjman, J. H. (1990). Quality of life in elderly patients with chronic nonspecific lung disease seen in family practice. *Chest, 98,* 894–899.

Selecky, P. A. (1993). Sexuality and the patient with lung disease. In R. Casaburi and T. L. Petty, eds., *Principles and Practice of Pulmonary Rehabilitation.* Philadelphia: W. B. Saunders, pp. 382–391.

Sexton, D. L., and Monro, B. H. (1985). Impact of a husband's chronic illness (COPD) on the spouse's life. *Research in Nursing and Health, 8,* 83–90.

Sexton, D. L., and Monro, B. H. (1988). Living with a chronic illness. The experience of women with chronic obstructive pulmonary disease (COPD). *Western Journal of Nursing Research, 10,* 26–44.

Spilker, B. (1990a). *Quality of Life Assessments in Clinical Trials.* New York: Raven Press.

Spilker, B. (1990b). Introduction. In B. Spilker, ed., *Quality of Life Assessments in Clinical Trials.* New York: Raven Press, pp. 3–10.

Spilker, B. (1996). *Quality of Life Assessment and Pharmacoeconomics in Clinical Trials* (2nd ed.). New York: Raven Press.

Spitzer, W. O., Dobson, A. J., Hall, J., Chesterman, E., Levi, J., Shepherd, R., Battista, R. N., and Catchlove, B. R. (1981). Measuring the quality of life of cancer patients: A concise QL-index for use by physicians. *Journal of Chronic Diseases, 34,* 585–597.

Stewart, A. L., and Ware, J. E. (1992). *Measuring Functioning and Well-being: The Medical Outcomes Study Approach.* Durham, NC: Duke University Press.

Stollenwerk, R. (1985). An emphysema client: Self care. *Home Healthcare Nurse, 3,* 36–40.

Ström, K., Boe, J., Herala, M., Boman, G., and Gustavii, A. (1990). Assessment of two oxygen treatment alternatives in the home. *International Journal of Technology Assessment in Health Care, 6,* 489–497.

Toshima, M. T., Blumberg, E., Ries, A. L., and Kaplan, R. M. (1992a). Does rehabilitation reduce depression in patients with chronic obstructive pulmonary disease? *Journal of Cardiopulmonary Rehabilitation, 12,* 261–269.

Toshima, M. T., Kaplan, R. M., and Ries, A. L. (1990). Experimental evaluation of rehabilitation in chronic obstructive pulmonary disease: Short-term effects on exercise endurance and health status. *Health Psychology, 9,* 237–252.

Toshima, M. T., Kaplan, R. M., and Ries, A. L. (1992b). Self-efficacy expectations in chronic obstructive pulmonary disease rehabilitation. In R. Schwarzer, ed., *Self-efficacy: Thought Control of Action.* Washington, D.C.: Hemisphere Publishing Corp., pp. 325–354.

Tupper, D. E., and Cicerone, K. D. (1990). *The Neuropsychology of Everyday Life.* Amsterdam: Kluwer.

van Schayck, C. P., Rutten-van Mölken, M.P.M.H., van Doorslaer, E.K.A., Folgering, H., and van Weel, C. (1992). Two-year bronchodilator treatment in patients with mild airflow obstruction. Contradictory effects on lung function and quality of life. *Chest, 102,* 1384–1391.

Veit, C. T., and Ware, J. E. (1983). The structure of psychological distress and well-being in general populations. *Journal of Consulting and Clinical Psychology, 51,* 730–742.

Walker, S. R., and Rosser, R. M. (1988). *Quality of Life: Assessment and Applications.* London: Ciba Foundation.

Ware, J. E., and Sherbourne, C. D. (1992). The MOS 36-item short-form health survey (SF-36): I. Conceptual framework and item selection. *Medical Care, 30,* 473–483.

Wenger, N. K., Mattson, M. E., Furberg, C. D., and J. Elinson. (1984). *Assessment of Quality of Life in Clinical Trials of Cardiovascular Therapies.* New York: Le Jacq Publishers.

Wijkstra, P. J., TenVergert, E. M., Van Altena, R., Otten, V., Postma, D. S., Kraan, J., and Koëter, G. H. (1994). Reliability and validity of the chronic respiratory questionnaire (CRQ). *Thorax, 49,* 465–467.

Williams, S. J. (1989a). Assessing the consequences of chronic respiratory disease: A critical review. *International Disability Studies, 11,* 161–166.

Williams, S. J. (1989b). Chronic respiratory illness and disability: A critical review of the psychosocial literature. *Social Science and Medicine, 28,* 791–803.

Williams, S. J., and Bury, M. R. (1989a). 'Breathtaking': The consequences of chronic respiratory disorder. *International Disability Studies, 11,* 114–120.

Williams, S. J., and Bury, M. R. (1989b). Impairment, disability and handicap in chronic respiratory illness. *Social Science and Medicine, 29,* 609–616.

Wu, A. W., and Rubin, H. R. (1992). Measuring health status and quality of life in HIV and AIDS. *Psychology and Health, 6,* 251–264.

Yellowlees, P. M. (1987). The treatment of psychiatric disorders in patients with chronic airways obstruction. *Medical Journal of Australia, 147,* 349–352.

Yellowlees, P. M., Alpers, J. H., Bowden, J. J., Bryant, G. D., and Ruffin, R. E. (1987). Psychiatric morbidity in patients with chronic airflow obstruction. *Medical Journal of Australia, 146,* 305–307.

Young, R. F. (1982). Marital adaptation and response in chronic illness: The case of COPD. (Doctoral Dissertation, Wayne State University, 1981.) *Dissertation Abstracts International 42,* 4947A.

AUTHOR INDEX

TEST INDEX

SUBJECT INDEX

Abstraction abilities, 13–14, 35
in alcoholics, 431
Acalculia, 48, 53
ACoA aneurysms, 351–352
Acoustic startle paradigm, 510
Activities of daily living (ADL), 584
Age, aging, 23
aging-related heterogeneity, 212
depression, cognition, and, 212
Halstead-Reitan studies, 29–31
and head injury recovery, 554,
569
and intelligence, 45–46
and memory, 51
and neuropsychological test
performance, 75–76, 143–
144, 171–172
and "normality" or normative
data, 172
the very elderly, 153–159, 172
Age-Associated Memory
Impairment (AAMI), 110, 112
Agnosia, 48, 141
AIDS, neuropsychological findings,
403–422. See also HIV
infection
Alcohol Dependence. See
Alcoholism, alcohol abuse
Alcoholic dementia, 441
Alcoholic Korsakoff syndrome, 185–
186, 252–253, 322, 441
Alcohol-induced persisting amnestic
disorder, 441–444. See also
Wernicke-Korsakoff syndrome
brain damage, 429
DSM-IV criteria for, 424
Alcohol-induced persisting
dementia
brain damage, 429
DSM-IV criteria for, 425
Alcoholism, alcohol abuse, 423–
485. See also Wernicke-
Korsakoff syndrome
abstraction, problem solving, 431
accelerated aging model, 459
age and test performance, 446–
450
alcohol-induced persisting
amnestic disorder, 424, 441–
444

alcohol-induced persisting
dementia, 425, 429
and Antisocial Personality
Disorder, 448, 455
attention and concentration skills,
431
and Attention Deficit Disorder,
448, 455
biochemical markers for, 425–428
and brain dmage, 429–430, 437
cerebral blood flow and
metabolism, 436
children of alcoholics (COA),
studies of, 448–450
clinical course of, 428–429
clinical implications, treatment
outcome, 461–463
complex perceptual-motor
deficits, 431
concurrent neuromedical risk
factors, 451–457
continuity notion of impairment,
445
and CSF volume, 433–435
and depression, 456–457
diagnosis of dependence and
alcohol-related disorders,
423–425
diffuse or generalized dysfunction
model, 440
drinking indices, 444–446
DSM-IV criteria for, 424
education influences, 457
electrophysiological findings,
436–437
etiology, multifactorial, 444–458
executive functioning, 431
family history studies, 448–450
fetal alcohol syndrome, fetal
alcohol effects, 450–451
frontal lobe dysfunction model,
439–440
gender difference, 423, 434, 439
genetics, role of, 446–447
head injury, 452–453
heavy drinking, effects of, 454
hepatic dysfunction, 451–452
hormonal disruption, after
detoxification, 453
hypoxemia, effects of, 453

increased vulnerability
hypothesis, 459
and Korsakoff's syndrome, 235
medical consequences, 428
memory and learning, 432–433,
452
motivation, expectancies, and test
performance, 457–458
motor deficits, 433
neurobehavioral findings, 429–
433
neurobehavioral recovery, 458–
460
neuroimaging findings, 433–436
neuroimaging reversibility, 461
neuropathology, from autopsies,
437–438
neuropsychological deficits and
detoxification, 430–431
neuropsychological vs.
neuroimaging variables, 435–
436
nutrition and test performance,
453
and "organic brain syndromes,"
423
among pilots, 108
premature aging model, 440–441,
459
premorbid risk factors, 447–450
psychiatric comorbidity, 454–457
psychophysiological activity, 453
questionnaires used to identify,
425–426
right hemisphere dysfunction
model, 438–439
sleep disturbances, 454
social consequences, 428
test characteristics and sample,
458
visual-spatial integration, 431
withdrawal, effects of, 454
Alzheimer's disease (AD), 94, 103,
110–111, 155, 164, 244–245
Alzheimer's Disease and Related
Disorders Association, 168
Assessment Battery for, 105
autopsy verification of, 168, 174
cognitive markers for incipient
AD, 175